Second Canadian Edition

A Child's World

INFANCY THROUGH ADOLESCENCE

Diane E. Papalia

Sally Wendkos Olds

Ruth Duskin Feldman

Richard Kruk
University of Manitoba

McGraw-Hill
Ryerson

Toronto Montréal Boston Burr Ridge, IL Dubuque, IA Madison, WI New York San Francisco St. Louis Bangkok Bogotá Caracas Kuala Lumpur Lisbon London Madrid Mexico City Milan New Delhi Santiago Seoul Singapore Sydney Taipei

A Child's World: Infancy Through Adolescence
Second Canadian Edition

Statistics Canada information is used with the permission of Statistics Canada. Users are forbidden to copy this material and/or redisseminate the data, in an original or modified form, for commercial purposes, without the expressed permission of Statistic Canada. Information on the availability of the wide range of data from Statistics Canada can be obtained from Statistics Canada's Regional Offices, its World Wide Web site at http://www.statcan.ca and its toll-free access number 1-800-263-1136

ISBN-13: 978-0-07-078100-9
ISBN-10: 0-07-078100-1

1 2 3 4 5 6 7 8 9 10 QPD 0 9 8

Printed and bound in the United States of America

Care has been taken to trace ownership of copyright material contained in this text; however, the publisher will welcome any information that enables them to rectify any reference or credit for subsequent editions.

Editorial Director: Joanna Cotton
Publisher: Nicole Lukach
Senior Developmental Editor: Suzanne Simpson Millar
Editorial Associate: Marina Seguin
Supervising Editor: Elizabeth Priest
Copy Editor: Erin Moore
Senior Production Coordinator: Jennifer Hall
Cover and Interior Design: Liz Harasymczuk
Cover Image: © Ellen B. Senisi/The Image Works
Page Layout: Aptara, Inc.
Printer: Quebecor Printing Dubuque

Library and Archives Canada Cataloguing in Publication

A child's world: infancy through adolescence / Diane E. Papalia ... [et al.]. — 2nd Canadian ed.

Includes bibliographical references and index.
ISBN 978-0-07-078100-9

1. Child development—Textbooks. 2. Child psychology—Textbooks. 3. Adolescence—Textbooks. I. Papalia, Diane E.

HQ767.9.C4438 2008   305.231   C2008-900789-1

To our parents,
Madeline and Edward Papalia,
Leah and Samuel Wendkos,
Boris and Rita Duskin,
and Walerian and Zofia Kruk
for their unfailing love, nurturance, and
confidence in us, and for their abiding conviction
that childhood is a wondrous time of life.

And to our children,
Anna Victoria,
Nancy, Jennifer, and Dorri,
Steven, Laurie, and Heidi,
Ian Benjamin Austin,
and our grandchildren,
Stefan, Maika, Anna, Lisa, and Nina,
Daniel, Emmett, Rita, Carol, Eve, and Isaac,
who have helped us revisit childhood
and see its wonders and challenges
with new eyes.

About the Authors

As a professor, **Diane E. Papalia** taught thousands of undergraduates at the University of Wisconsin–Madison. She received her bachelor's degree, majoring in psychology, from Vassar College and both her master's degree in child development and family relations and her Ph.D. in life-span developmental psychology from West Virginia University. She has published numerous articles in such professional journals as *Human Development, International Journal of Aging and Human Development, Sex Roles, Journal of Experimental Child Psychology, and Journal of Gerontology.* Most of these papers have dealt with her major research focus, cognitive development from childhood through old age. She is especially interested in intelligence in old age and factors that contribute to the maintenance of intellectual functioning in late adulthood. She is a Fellow in the Gerontological Society of America. She is the coauthor of *A Child's World,* now in its ninth edition, with Sally Wendkos Olds and Ruth Duskin Feldman; of *Adult Development and Aging,* now in its second edition, with Harvey L. Sterns, Ruth Duskin Feldman, and Cameron J. Camp; of *Psychology* with Sally Wendkos Olds; and of *Child Development: A Topical Approach* with Dana Gross and Ruth Duskin Feldman.

Sally Wendkos Olds is an award-winning professional writer who has written more than 200 articles in leading magazines and is the author or coauthor of seven books addressed to general readers, in addition to the three textbooks she has coauthored with Dr. Papalia. Her newest book, *A Balcony in Nepal: Glimpses of a Himalayan Village,* describes her encounters with the people and way of life in a remote hill village in eastern Nepal. The updated and expanded third edition of her classic book *The Complete Book of Breastfeeding* was published in 1999. She is also the author of *The Working Parents' Survival Guide* and *The Eternal Garden: Seasons of Our Sexuality* and the coauthor of *Raising a Hyperactive Child* (winner of the Family Service Association of America National Media Award) and *Helping Your Child Find Values to Live By.* She has spoken widely on the topics of her books and articles to both professional and lay audiences, in person and on television and radio. She received her bachelor's degree from the University of Pennsylvania, where she majored in English literature and minored in psychology. She was elected to Phi Beta Kappa and was graduated summa cum laude.

About the Authors

Ruth Duskin Feldman is an award-winning writer and educator. With Diane E. Papalia and Sally Wendkos Olds, she coauthored the fourth, seventh, eighth, ninth, and tenth editions of *Human Development* and the eighth, ninth, and tenth editions of *A Child's World.* She also is coauthor of *Adult Development and Aging* and of *Child Development: A Topical Approach.* A former teacher, she has developed educational materials for all levels from elementary school through college and has prepared ancillaries to accompany the Papalia-Olds books. She is author or coauthor of four books addressed to general readers, including *Whatever Happened to the Quiz Kids? Perils and Profits of Growing Up Gifted,* republished in 2000 as an Authors Guild Back-in-Print edition of iUniverse. She has written for numerous newspapers and magazines and has lectured extensively and made national and local media appearances throughout the United States on education and gifted children. She received her bachelor's degree from Northwestern University, where she was graduated with highest distinction and was elected to Phi Beta Kappa.

Richard Kruk has taught undergraduate and graduate students at universities and colleges, in Quebec, Ontario, Manitoba, and Saskatchewan, and is currently a member of the faculty at the Department of Psychology of the University of Manitoba, teaching school psychology. He received his bachelor's degree, specializing in psychology, from the University of Toronto, and both his master's degree and Ph.D. from the Ontario Institute for Studies in Education of the University of Toronto, where he focused on reading difficulty, perceptual development, and applied linguistics. He continued his research training in an SSHRC-sponsored post-doctoral fellowship in Australia, examining the relationships between perceptual development and cognitive skills related to reading difficulty. He has published articles in such professional journals as *Cognitive Neuropsychology, Journal of Learning Disabilities, Ophthalmic and Physiological Optics,* and *Human Factors,* written book chapters on reading processes, and co-edited, with Dale Willows and Evelyn Corcos, *Visual Processes in Reading and Reading Disabilities,* published by Lawrence Erlbaum Associates. Most of his published work has dealt with his major research focus: perceptual and neurological factors related to reading skill development and to difficulties children face in learning to read.

Brief Contents

Contents

Preface

In writing the Second Canadian Edition of *A Child's World,* I was astounded by the rich and diverse new discoveries made by researchers and others in Canada to our understanding of children and youth. The title of this book, *A Child's World,* reflects a vision of studying child development as an exciting journey of exploration into the special world of children. Through the vibrant illustrations and real-life examples, the co-authors and I seek to make the world of children come alive. By studying this book, students will gain a perspective on child development, and see how the world looks from the standpoint of the child. This book contributes to how students understand the unique experiences of child development in the Canadian context, and from the point of view of those who work with children. It was a delightful challenge to show how Canadian perspectives have changed since the First Canadian Edition was written, reflecting a wealth of high-quality research.

Aims of the Second Canadian Edition

The key aims of this Second Canadian Edition have been to update and re-frame the entire book—in its design, content, and pedagogical features—and substantially streamline the text. As always, the co-authors and I seek to emphasize the continuity of development and its contrasts across cultures, to highlight interrelationships among the physical, cognitive, and psychosocial domains, and to integrate theoretical, research-related, and practical concerns.

Truly Canadian content

The specifically Canadian goals are to emphasize research, issues, and values that are uniquely ours, and to highlight excellent research and policy in Canada which has improved our understanding of children and promoted healthy development.

> Among the many examples of Canadian content include the important contribution of our universal health care policy to the healthy growth and well-being of children across the country, made-in-Canada initiatives and policies for public health and social justice, including reproductive health technology laws, the legalization of gay marriage, and the growing body of knowledge about the world of children in Canada being generated by the National Longitudinal Survey of Children and Youth.

Diversity—A Reflection of Our Nation

This text reflects the diversity of Canada, and is written to be relevant to Canadian students and instructors, with current research and information reflecting the realities of our population, and with special attention to the fact that Canada stands out in the world as a distinct society, with two official languages and a multitude of cultures. *A Child's World* is based on our values: We celebrate our diversity as a population and welcome the differences in views, attitudes, and ideas that exist among us. Each chapter has been reconceived to showcase Canadian developmental contexts and values, with a seamless and organic incorporation of national and international research. The fact that hundreds of new Canadian references have been added to the list of Canadian contributions that appeared in the previous edition is a wonderful reflection of the excellent contributions that we have made to how we understand the world of the developing child.

Some examples of new information highlighting the diversity of Canada's population include sections on the health and educational needs of Aboriginal children, research on continued positive growth experienced by children who are new immigrants to Canada, as indicated by a growing proportion of immigrant children who successfully complete post-secondary education.

The Second Canadian Edition at a Glance

Organization

This book takes a *chronological* approach, describing all aspects of development during each period of childhood. With this approach, students gain a sense of the multifaceted sweep of child development. The chapters fall into six parts:

- Part 1 summarizes the history, basic concepts, theories and research tools in the field of child development.
- Part 2 describes the beginnings of life, including the influences of heredity and environment, pregnancy and prenatal development, birth, and the newborn baby.
- Parts 3 through 6 are divided into three chapters each, covering physical, cognitive, and psychosocial development during infancy and toddlerhood, early childhood, middle childhood, and adolescence.

In this edition, we have carefully assessed and improved the organization of material within and among chapters. See "Content Changes" on page xv for a list of detailed changes.

Pedagogical Features

The Learning System

Our comprehensive Learning System is a coordinated set of elements that work together to foster active learning.

Guideposts for study. This list of questions at the beginning of each chapter highlights the key concepts to learn. Each Guidepost appears again to introduce the related text section.

Checkpoints. These questions placed in the margins throughout each chapter help students assess how well they grasp the concepts in the preceding text sections.

What's Your View? These critical thinking questions, placed in the margins throughout each chapter and in the boxed features, encourage students to examine their thoughts about the information presented in the text.

Summary and Key Terms. At the end of each chapter, these resources, organized under the Guideposts, help students review the chapter and check their learning.

For more description and illustration of the Learning System, see the Visual Walk-Through on page xxii.

Focus Vignettes

Focus Vignettes introduce each chapter by highlighting a famous or remarkable person in the stage of development covered by the chapter. Frequent chapter references to the opening focus vignettes encourage students to apply the chapter's concepts to the life of the person profiled.

Boxed Features

Four types of boxes enhance our text by highlighting topics related to the main text:

The Research World: Provide an in-depth examination of research topics briefly mentioned in the text.

The Everyday World: Deal with a variety of practical applications of research.

Around the World: Offer windows on child development in societies other than our own (in addition to the cultural coverage already in the chapters).

The Social World: Discuss social issues or problems that have an impact on child development.

For further description and illustration of the boxed features, see the Visual Walk-Through on page xxiv.

Content Changes

Following is a chapter-by-chapter list of the most important new and heavily revised material in the Second Canadian Edition.

Chapter 1: Studying a Child's World

- Updated Social World Box: The Residential School Experience of Aboriginal Children
- Section on developmental process—change and stability moved to first section for emphasis
- Updated highlights of Canadian immigration and family patterns
- Expanded discussions of race/ethnicity and critical/sensitive periods
- Expanded box on critical period in language development
- Recent highlights from the Canadian National Longitudinal Survey of Children and Youth (NLSCY)
- Section on "An Emerging Consensus" moved to end of chapter to serve as summary

Chapter 2: A Child's World: How We Discover It

- New Research World Box on the adaptive value of immaturity
- New section on evolutionary/sociobiological theory
- New table on developmental considerations in ethics of research
- Revised figure illustrating Bronfenbrenner's theory
- Revised treatment of Vygotsky, now under cognitive perspective
- Expanded introduction to cognitive neuroscience, now under research methods
- New section on collaborative research methods
- Major new section on research ethics
- Description of the Tri-Council Policy Statement on ethics in research involving diverse populations

Chapter 3: Forming a New Life: Conception, Heredity, and Environment

- Updated Canadian birth statistics
- Recent Canadian government policies on assisted reproductive technologies, and genetic testing
- New box on multiple births
- Expanded Research World box on genetic testing
- New figures on hereditary composition of the zygote, and gene-environment interaction
- Revised discussion of assisted reproductive technology

- New treatment of epigenesis
- Revised discussions of genome imprinting, influences on intelligence, and schizophrenia

Chapter 4: Pregnancy and Prenatal Development

- New table on early signs of pregnancy
- New figure on fertilization/implantation and embryonic development
- New Everyday World box on mourning a miscarriage or stillbirth
- New table on prenatal assessment techniques
- New figures on trends in prenatally acquired AIDS, and miscarriage rates as a function of maternal age
- Updated Social World box on fetal welfare and mothers' rights with Canadian perspectives
- Current Canadian research and policy initiatives on prenatal and postnatal health
- Updated sections on prenatal influences, especially maternal nutrition, maternal age, and environmental hazards
- New major section on monitoring prenatal development and preconception care

Chapter 5: Birth and the Newborn Baby

- Revised discussion of labour and childbirth stages, with new discussion of episiotomy and new section on electronic fetal monitoring
- Current policies and statistics in Canadian childbirth practices
- Recent Canadian statistics on high-risk birth events including perinatal conditions and low birth weight
- New figure on proportion of preterm and postmature infants in Canada
- Revised information on neonatal appearance, administration of APGAR scale, and low birth weight
- New table on neonatal skin conditions
- New table of international prevalence of low birth weight by regions
- New section on states of arousal and activity levels in newborns
- New sections on parents' roles, including cross-cultural comparisons of infant care
- New discussion of evolution and parent-child bonding

Chapter 6: Physical Development and Health During the First Three Years

- Current recommendations on early feeding from Canadian sources
- New figures of human nervous system and fetal nervous system development
- New Research World box on autism "epidemic" and table on signs of autism
- Expanded discussion of Thelen's dynamic systems theory of infant motor development
- Revised figure on trends in infant mortality
- New table on recommendations to prevent Sudden Infant Death Syndrome (SIDS)
- Revised information on breastfeeding, brain development (including studies of Romanian orphans), infant mortality, and SIDS in Canada
- New Social World box on shaken baby syndrome

Chapter 7: Cognitive Development During the First Three Years

- Updated information on the use of U.S.-based intelligence tests in Canada
- New table on the HOME inventory for infants and toddlers
- New Everyday World box on too much television watching by infants and toddlers, with a new figure on amount of time spent on media activities by young children
- New discussion of A, not-B error from perspective of developmental systems theory
- New discussion of plausibility of precocious infant abilities from evolutionary perspective

- New discussion of evolution of language
- Reorganized material on Piagetian tasks and information processing
- Revised language milestones table

Chapter 8: Psychosocial Development During the First Three Years

- New Everyday World box on how postpartum depression affects early development
- New Around the World box on struggles with toddlers
- Expanded sections on empathy and measuring temperament
- New section on gender differences in baby boys and girls
- Revised discussion of parental employment and effects of early child care in Canada

Chapter 9: Physical Development and Health in Early Childhood

- New Around the World box on surviving the first five years of life
- New figures on comparative child mortality, and major causes of death
- Current Canadian statistics on children's diets, malnutrition, and food-bank use
- Major new section on sleep patterns and problems
- New information on exposure to pesticides and air pollution
- Revised discussions of obesity (overweight), enuresis, and lead exposure
- Revised discussion of race/ethnicity, socioeconomic status, and health in Canadian children

Chapter 10: Cognitive Development in Early Childhood

- New Research World box on private speech
- Age-of-entry to kindergarten effects
- Revised discussion of numerical abilities and influences on memory development
- New table on key elements of number sense in children
- Revised section on literacy and social interaction
- Revised section on the child in kindergarten

Chapter 11: Psychosocial Development in Early Childhood

- New information on cultural influences on emotional regulation
- Expanded section on self-esteem
- New section on evolutionary perspective on gender development
- Updated Research World box on the case against corporal punishment
- New Research World box on whether play has an evolutionary basis
- New major section on special behavioural concerns
- Revised discussions of gender differences in sibling relations
- Expanded discussion of only child

Chapter 12: Physical Development and Health in Middle Childhood

- New section on brain development in middle childhood
- New figure on reduction of grey matter density in the cerebral cortex
- New Everyday World box on how Barbie dolls affect body image
- Revised discussions of growth hormone therapy, overweight, stuttering, and asthma
- New table on a strategy to stop the overweight epidemic

Chapter 13: Cognitive Development in Middle Childhood

- New discussion of genetic, neurological, and racial/cultural influences on intelligence
- Revised information on executive function, attention, and working memory
- Revised Everyday World box on math wars with latest recommendations for teaching math
- New discussion of gender and achievement

- New figure on percentage of children using computers at home
- New section on Julian Stanley's research on the profoundly gifted
- New section on educational needs of Aboriginal children and children learning English as an additional language
- Expanded and updated information on learning disabilities

Chapter 14: Psychosocial Development in Middle Childhood

- New discussion of gender differences in peer group relations
- New Everyday World box on talking to children about terrorism and war
- New table on children's reactions to trauma
- New discussion of evolutionary perspective on gender differences in aggression
- Revised discussion of effects of family structures

Chapter 15: Physical Development and Health in Adolescence

- New section on the adolescent brain
- Revised figures on the prevalence of high-risk behaviours in Canadian adolescents
- Expanded secion on adolescence as a social construction
- New Around the World box on the globalization of adolescence
- New sections on health problems, health-related behaviours, and depression
- Revised discussion of nutrition, eating disorders, and drug use

Chapter 16: Cognitive Development in Adolescence

- New section on changes in information processing during adolescence
- Expanded section on Gilligan's theory of moral development
- New section on pro-social behaviour and volunteer activity
- New figure on the percentage of school drop-outs by age and income
- New section on student motivation and school achievement, from an international perspective
- Revised discussion of gender and school achievement, dropping out of high school, and working outside of school

Chapter 17: Psychosocial Development in Adolescence

- Updated Social World box on youth violence
- New figure on trends in teenage birth rates
- New table on the Psychological Control Scale
- New table on items used to assess perceived areas of parental versus adolescent authority
- New sections on cliques and crowds
- Revised discussions of ethnic factors in identity formation, sexual orientation, sexual attitudes and behaviour, and teen pregnancy and childbearing
- Section on sexually transmitted diseases moved from Chapter 15 for better integration with other material on sexuality
- Revised sections on adolescents and parents and sibling relationships
- Revised discussion of romantic relationships
- Expanded section on genetic and neurological factors in delinquency
- New table on effective measures to discourage delinquency
- New section on emerging adulthood

Supplements

A Child's World, Second Canadian Edition, is accompanied by a complete learning and teaching package keyed into the learning system. Each component of this package has been thoroughly revised and expanded to include important new course material. Please contact your McGraw-Hill Ryerson *i*Learning Sales Specialist for more information.

For the Instructor

Online Learning Centre (OLC)

Instructor's resources are available for download on the Instructor's Centre of the Online Learning Centre, at www.mcgrawhill.ca/olc/papalia. These include:
- Instructor's Manual
- Computerized Test Bank
- PowerPoint Presentations

Instructor CD-ROM (ICD)

Resources available on the Instructor's CD-ROM include:
- Instructor's Manual
- Computerized Test Bank
- PowerPoint Presentations
- Printable Test Bank in Rich Text Format

Instructor's Manual

The Instructor's Manual, fully adapted for a Canadian audience, provides a variety of tools for both seasoned instructors and those new to the child development course. Available on the OLC and the ICD.

Computerized Test Bank

This comprehensive test bank has been fully revised for the Second Canadian Edition and includes a wide range of multiple-choice, fill-in-the-blank, critical thinking, and essay questions from which instructors can create their test material. Organized by chapter, the questions are designed to test factual, applied, and conceptual understanding. This can also be printed out for a paper-based test bank. Available on the OLC and the ICD.

PowerPoint Presentations

These presentations cover the key points of each chapter. They can be used as is, or you can modify them to meet your specific needs. Available on the OLC and the ICD.

McGraw-Hill's Visual Asset Database

McGraw-Hill's Visual Assets Database for Lifespan Development (www.mhhe.com/vad) is an online database of videos for use in the developmental psychology classroom, created specifically for instructors. You can customize classroom presentations by downloading the videos to your computer and showing them on their own, or by inserting them into your course cartridge or PowerPoint presentations. Contact your *i*Learning Sales Specialist for more information.

For the Student

Online Learning Centre

Available at **www.mcgrawhill.ca/olc/papalia,** the Online Learning Centre provides a range of resources to help you succeed in your studies, organized by chapter. Each chapter's content will include videos of child development experts and teens discussing important issues. Also included will be quiz material to allow you to study (and check your answers) as you progress through each chapter, including fill-in-the-blank questions, multiple-choice questions, true/false questions, and short-answer quizzes.

Additional Resources

LifeMap CD-ROM: The LifeMap CD gives students an opportunity to expand and test their understanding of course material. In addition to a multiple-choice quiz with feedback for each chapter, the CD includes videos of children engaged in activities described in the text; interviews with children, teens, and parents; and comments from experts on various child development topics. Each video is accompanied by an overview, study questions, and Web links to encourage further exploration of the topic. The LifeMap CD also features an interactive timeline outlining the stages of human development from conception to adolescence.

Annual Editions: Child Growth and Development: This Fifteenth Edition of Annual Editions, Child Growth and Development, provides convenient, inexpensive access to current articles selected from the best of the public press. Organizational features include: an annotated listing of selected World Wide Web sites; an annotated table of contents; a topic guide; a general introduction; brief overviews for each section; a topical index; and an instructor's resource guide with testing materials.

Taking Sides: Clashing Views in Childhood and Society: Taking Sides: Clashing Views in Childhood and Society presents current controversial issues in a debate-style format designed to stimulate student interest and develop critical thinking skills. Each issue is thoughtfully framed with an issue summary, an issue introduction, and a postscript. An instructor's manual with testing material is available for each volume.

Understanding Children: An Interview and Observation Guide for Educators: This hands-on guide for interviewing and observing children in educational settings is a supplement for child development courses taken by elementary and middle school education majors. It includes a rationale for interviewing and observing children as a way to understand their behaviour, learning, and development and makes connections to the work of major developmental theorists and educational researchers. It provides practical tips for incorporating observations and interviews of children into teachers' busy schedules and discusses the analysis of observational data and its uses for guiding educational practices (e.g., instruction, cooperative grouping, and parent conferences).

Acknowledgements

I am grateful to the many friends and colleagues who, through their work and interest, helped me clarify my thinking about child development from Canadian perspectives. I am especially grateful for the valuable help given by those who reviewed the first Canadian Edition of *A Child's World* and the manuscript drafts of this second edition, whose evaluations and suggestions helped greatly in the preparation of this new edition. These reviewers, who are affiliated with both two-year and four-year institutions, are as follows.

Anna Baas-Anderson, Sheridan College Institute of Technology and Advanced Learning
Gordon Beckett, Sheridan College Institute of Technology and Advanced Learning
Patricia Corson, Ryerson University
Nukte Edguer, Brandon University
Georgina King, Seneca College
Mary Knight, Durham College
David Lockwood, Humber College Institute of Technology and Advanced Learning
Nicki Monahan, George Brown College
Ron Niemi, University of Manitoba
Susan Numerow, Langara College
Linda Pipe, Loyalist College
Marilyn Quinn, Niagara College
Vidya Rampersad, Humber College Institute of Technology and Advanced Learning
Allison Soave, Niagara College
Colleen Thomas, George Brown College
Leland Woodson, Kwantlen University College
Sandra Yorke, Durham College

I also appreciate the strong support from the staff of McGraw-Hill Ryerson. Karen Ritcey, sponsoring editor, had the insight and forethought to recognize the need for a second edition, and began the process of starting this project. Nicole Lukach, Publisher, Elizabeth Priest, Supervising Editor, and Kelly Dickson, Editorial Services Manager, played excellent supporting roles in ensuring that this new edition was produced flawlessly. Erin Moore, copy editor, did painstaking and excellent work of checking the final versions of the text. For any writer, development editors have a huge impact on the success and quality of the final product. Jennifer DiDomenico and Suzanne Simpson Millar were my key supports at McGraw-Hill Ryerson in developing the content of the second edition, and in providing me with unfailing support, patience and guidance as I worked through the changes in the text. Their wisdom and good judgment have made a great impact on the quality of this book.

I also thank the authors of the Eleventh Edition of *A Child's World* in the U.S., Diane Papalia, Sally Wendkos Olds, and Ruth Duskin Feldman for providing a wonderful source of current information that was included to supplement the revisions to the Canadian edition.

Thanks also go to my colleagues and friends at the University of Manitoba Department of Psychology. My many discussions and debates with them about issues in Canadian developmental psychology, the need for current information to be available in excellent-quality texts on child development, and the spirit of collegiality that pervades the Department, inspired me once again in the writing of this edition. I also had the great fortune of working with a graduate student, Shannon Rioch, who helped in finding current Canadian research and information that were significant in ensuring the quality of the updates to the material in the book. As always, the support of my partner, Brenda Austin-Smith, who gave me strength in working through the revisions, and to Ian, now in early childhood after toddlerhood when the first edition was completed, who inspired my work and added to my growing sense of wonder.

As always, I look forward to hearing comments from readers of this Second Canadian Edition. Questions, observations, and insights from you are the key sources of recommendations and guides that will keep future Canadian editions of *A Child's World* current, informative, and useful to future generations of Canadians dedicated to working with and studying children.

Visual Walk-Through

Learning System for

A comprehensive, unified **Learning System** helps students focus the conceptual framework for each chapter, and is carried across There are four parts to the Learning System:

Checkpoints

These detailed marginal questions, at the end of chapter sections, enable students to test their understanding of what they have read. Students should be encouraged to pause and review any section for which they cannot answer one or more checkpoints.

> **Checkpoint** ✔
>
> *Can you . . .*
> ✔ Identify nutritional and sleep needs of school-age children and tell why it is important to meet them?

Guideposts for Study

Similar to learning objectives, these questions are posed at the beginning of each chapter to capture interest and motivate students to look for answers as they read. Broad enough to form a coherent outline of chapter content, these questions are also specific enough to invite careful study. Each Guidepost is then repeated in the margin at the beginning of the applicable section, and in the Chapter Summaries.

Guideposts for Study

1. How do school-age children's bodies and brains grow and develop?

2. What are the nutritional and sleep needs of middle childhood?

3. What gains in motor skills typically occur at this age, and what kinds of physical play do boys and girls engage in?

4. What are the principal health, fitness, and safety concerns in middle childhood?

Guidepost 1

How do school-age children's bodies and brains grow and develop?

Aspects of Physical Development

If we were to walk by a typical elementary school just after the 3 o'clock bell, we would see a virtual explosion of children of all shapes and sizes. Tall ones, short ones, husky ones, and skinny ones would be bursting out of the school doors into the open air. We would see that school-age children look very different from children a few years younger.

A Child's World

their reading, as well as review and retain what they learn. It forms with supplements.

What's Your View?

These periodic margin questions challenge students to interpret, apply, or critically evaluate information presented in the text.

> **What's your view** ?
>
> • If obesity tends to run in families, either because of heredity or lifestyle, how can parents who have not been able to control their own weight help their children?

Chapter Summaries

The Chapter Summaries are organized by the major topics in each chapter, with Guideposts appearing under the appropriate topics. Each Guidepost is followed by a series of brief statements restating the most important points that fall under it, thus creating a self-testing, question-answer format. Students should be encouraged to try to answer each Guidepost question before reading the summary material that follows. Key terms are listed for review under relevant summary topics, in the order in which they first appear, and are cross-referenced to pages where they are defined.

Summary and Key Terms

Aspects of Physical Development

Guidepost 1 How do school-age children's bodies annd brains grow and develop?

- Physical development is less rapid in middle childhood than in earlier years. Wide differences in height and weight exist.

- Children with retarded growth due to growth-hormone deficiency may be given synthetic growth hormone. Although the hormone is sometimes prescribed for short children who do *not* have hormone deficiency, extreme caution is advised in such cases.

- The permanent teeth arrive in middle childhood. Dental health has improved, in part because of the use of sealants on chewing surfaces.

- Many children engage in organized, competitive sports.

- A sound physical education program should aim at skill development for all children and should emphasize enjoyment and lifelong fitness rather than competition.

rough-and-tumble play (326)

Health and Safety

Guidepost 4 What are the principal health, fitness, and safety concerns in middle childhood?

- Middle childhood is a relatively healthy period; most children are immunized against major illnesses, and the death rate is the lowest in the lifespan. However, many children, especially

Boxed Features

The Second Canadian Edition includes four different types of feature boxes. Each box contains a critical thinking What's Your View? question.

For a detailed list of new and revised boxes in the second edition, see Content Changes, on page xv.

The Research World

These boxes report on exciting new developments or current controversies in the field of child development.

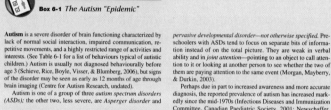

The Research World

Box 6-1 *The Autism "Epidemic"*

Autism is a severe disorder of brain functioning characterized by lack of normal social interaction, impaired communication, repetitive movements, and a highly restricted range of activities and interests. (See Table 6-1 for a list of behaviours typical of autistic children.) Autism is usually not diagnosed behaviourally before age 3 (Schieve, Rice, Boyle, Visser, & Blumberg, 2006), but signs of the disorder may be seen as early as 12 months of age through brain imaging (Centre for Autism Research, undated).

Autism is one of a group of three *autism spectrum disorders (ASDs);* the other two, less severe, are *Asperger disorder* and

pervasive developmental disorder—not otherwise specified. Preschoolers with ASDs tend to focus on separate bits of information instead of on the total picture. They are weak in verbal ability and in *joint attention*—pointing to an object to call attention to it or looking at another person to see whether the two of them are paying attention to the same event (Morgan, Mayberry, & Durkin, 2003).

Perhaps due in part to increased awareness and more accurate diagnosis, the reported prevalence of autism has increased markedly since the mid-1970s (Infectious Diseases and Immunization Committee, Canadian Paediatric Society, 2001; Newschaffer, Falb, & Gurney, 2005). According to parental reports, at least 300,000 children—approximately 5.6 in 1,000 U.S. children ages 4 through 17—have been diagnosed with autism, 4 out of 5 of them boys (Schieve et al., 2006). A U.S. study in 2002 found that 1 in 150 eight-year-olds has autism or one of the related disorders (Autism and Developmental Disabilities Monitoring

Table 6-1	Possible Signs of Autism

Children with autism may show the following characteristics in varying combinations and degrees of severity:

Inappropriate laughing or giggling

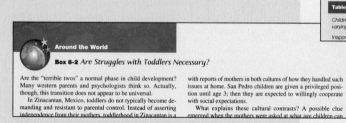

Around the World

Box 8-2 *Are Struggles with Toddlers Necessary?*

Are the "terrible twos" a normal phase in child development? Many western parents and psychologists think so. Actually, though, this transition does not appear to be universal.

In Zinacantan, Mexico, toddlers do not typically become demanding and resistant to parental control. Instead of asserting independence from their mothers, toddlerhood in Zinacantan is a

with reports of mothers in both cultures of how they handled such issues at home. San Pedro children are given a privileged position until age 3; then they are expected to willingly cooperate with social expectations.

What explains these cultural contrasts? A possible clue emerged when the mothers were asked at what age children can

Around the World

This feature offers windows on child development in societies other than our own (in addition to the multicultural coverage in the text itself). Topics include cross-cultural comparisons of fatherhood, struggles with toddlers, healthcare, and popularity.

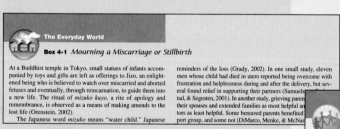

The Everyday World

Box 4-1 *Mourning a Miscarriage or Stillbirth*

At a Buddhist temple in Tokyo, small statues of infants accompanied by toys and gifts are left as offerings to Jizo, an enlightened being who is believed to watch over miscarried and aborted fetuses and eventually, through reincarnation, to guide them into a new life. The ritual of *mizuko kuyo,* a rite of apology and remembrance, is observed as a means of making amends to the lost life (Orenstein, 2002).

The Japanese word *mizuko* means "water child." Japanese

reminders of the loss (Grady, 2002). In one small study, eleven men whose child had died in utero reported being overcome with frustration and helplessness during and after the delivery, but several found relief in supporting their partners (Samuelsson, Rådestad, & Segesten, 2001). In another study, grieving parents found their spouses and extended families as most helpful and professionals as least helpful. Some bereaved parents benefited from a support group, and some not (DiMarco, Menke, & McNamara,

The Everyday World

These boxes highlight practical applications of research findings. Subjects include imaginary companions, mourning a miscarriage or stillbirth, effects of television and postpartum depression, among others.

The Social World

Box 17-2 *An Epidemic of Youth Violence*

On April 20, 1999, 18-year-old Eric Harris and 17-year-old Dylan Klebold entered Columbine High School in Littleton, Colorado, wearing black trench coats and carrying a rifle, a semi-automatic pistol, two sawed-off shotguns, and more than 30 homemade bombs. Laughing and taunting, they began spraying bullets at fellow students, killing 12 classmates and one

brain, particularly the prefrontal cortex, which is critical to judgment and impulse suppression (refer back to Chapter 15). Another answer is availability of guns in a culture that "romanticizes gunplay" (Weinberger, 2001, p. 2).

Youth violence is strongly related to the presence of gangs at school (NCES, 2003; "Youth Violence," 2001). The brutal mur-

The Social World

These are in-depth views of topics pertaining to different stages of development. Topics include the experience of First Nations children in residential schools, fetal welfare and mothers' rights, as well as youth violence, among others.

Second Canadian Edition

A Child's World

INFANCY THROUGH ADOLESCENCE

CHAPTER ONE

Studying A Child's World

There is nothing permanent except change.

—Heraclitus, fragment (sixth century B.C.E)

Focus *Victor, the Wild Boy of Aveyron**

Victor

On January 8, 1800, a naked boy, his face and neck heavily scarred, appeared on the outskirts of the village of Saint-Sernin in the sparsely populated province of Aveyron in south central France. The boy, who was only four and a half feet tall but looked about 12 years old, had been spotted several times during the previous two and a half years, climbing trees, running on all fours, drinking from streams, and foraging for acorns and roots.

When the dark-eyed boy came to Saint-Sernin, he neither spoke nor responded to speech. Like an animal accustomed to living in the wild, he spurned prepared foods and tore off the clothing people tried to put on him. It seemed clear that he had either lost his parents or been abandoned by them, but how long ago this had occurred was impossible to tell.

The boy appeared during a time of intellectual and social ferment, when a new, scientific outlook was beginning to replace mystical speculation. Philosophers debated questions about the nature of human beings—questions that would become central to the study of child development. Are the qualities, behaviour, and ideas that define what it means to be human inborn or acquired, or both? How important is social contact during the formative years? Can its lack be overcome? A study of a child who had grown up in isolation might provide evidence of the relative impact of "nature" (inborn characteristics) and "nurture" (upbringing, schooling, and other societal influences).

After initial observation, the boy, who came to be called Victor, was sent to a school for deaf-mutes in Paris. There, he was turned over to Jean-Marc-Gaspard Itard, an ambitious 26-year-old practitioner of the emerging science of "mental medicine," or psychiatry. Itard believed that Victor's development had been limited by isolation and that he simply needed to be taught the skills that children in civilized society normally acquire.

Itard took Victor into his home and, during the next five years, gradually "tamed" him. Itard first awakened his pupil's ability to discriminate sensory experience through hot baths and dry rubs. He then moved on to painstaking, step-by-step training of emotional responses and instruction in moral and social behaviour, language, and thought.

But the education of Victor (which was dramatized in Francois Truffaut's film *The Wild Child*) was not an unqualified success. The boy did make remarkable progress: He learned the names of many objects and could read and write simple sentences; he could express desires, obey commands, and exchange ideas. He showed affection, especially for Itard's housekeeper, Madame Guérin, as well as such emotions as pride, shame, remorse, and the desire to please. However, aside from uttering some vowel and consonant sounds, he never learned to speak. Furthermore, he remained totally focused on his own wants and needs and never seemed to lose his yearning "for the freedom of the open country and his indifference to most of the pleasures of social life" (Lane, 1976, p. 160). When the study ended, Victor—no longer able to fend for himself, as he had done in the wild—went to live with Madame Guérin until his death in his early forties in 1828.

● ● ●

Why did Victor fail to fulfill Itard's hopes for him? The boy may have been a victim of brain damage, autism (a brain disorder involving lack of social responsiveness), or severe early maltreatment. Itard's instructional methods, advanced as they were, may have been inadequate. Itard himself came to believe that the effects of long isolation could not be fully overcome, and that Victor may have been too old, especially for language learning.

Although Victor's story does not yield definitive answers to the questions Itard set out to explore, it is important because it was one of the first systematic attempts to study child development. Since Victor's time, we have learned much about how children develop, but developmental scientists are still investigating such fundamental questions as the relative importance of nature and nurture and how they work together. Victor's story dramatizes the challenges and complexities of the scientific study of child development—the study on which you are about to embark.

In this chapter, we describe how the field of child development has itself developed as scientists have learned more about infants, children, and adolescents. We present the goals and basic concepts of the field today. We identify aspects of development and show how they interrelate. We summarize major developments during each period of a child's life. We look at influences on development and the contexts in which it occurs.

After you have read and studied this chapter, you should be able to answer each of the Guidepost questions that appear at the top of the next page. Look for them again in the margins, where they point to important concepts throughout the chapter. To check your understanding of these Guideposts, review the end-of-chapter summary. Checkpoints located at periodic spots throughout the chapter will help you verify your understanding of what you have read.

*Sources of information about Victor were Frith (1989) and Lane (1976).

1. What is child development, and how has its study evolved?

2. What aspects and periods of development do developmental scientists study?

3. What kinds of influences make one child different from another?

4. What are six fundamental points about child development on which consensus has emerged?

The Study of Child Development: Then and Now

Guidepost 1

What is child development, and how has its study evolved?

child development Scientific study of processes of change and stability from conception through adolescence

quantitative change Change in number or amount, such as in height, weight, or size of vocabulary

qualitative change Change in kind, structure, or organization, such as the change from nonverbal to verbal communication

The field of **child development** is the scientific study of processes of change and stability in human children. Developmental scientists—people engaged in the professional study of child development—look at ways in which children change from conception through adolescence, as well as at characteristics that remain fairly stable.

Developmental scientists study two kinds of change: *quantitative* and *qualitative*. **Quantitative change** is a change in number or amount, such as in height, weight, size of vocabulary, or frequency of communication. Quantitative changes are largely *continuous* throughout childhood. **Qualitative change** is a change in kind, structure, or organization. Qualitative change is *discontinuous:* It is marked by the emergence of new phenomena that cannot be anticipated easily on the basis of earlier functioning. One example is the change from a nonverbal child to one who understands words and can use them to communicate.

Along with changes such as these, most people show an underlying *stability,* or constancy, in aspects of personality and behaviour. For example, about 10 to 15 percent of children are consistently shy, and another 10 to 15 percent are very bold. Although various influences can modify these traits, they tend to persist to a moderate degree, especially in children at one extreme or the other (see Chapter 3).

Which of a child's characteristics are most likely to endure? Which are likely to change, and why? These are among the questions that developmental scientists seek to answer.

Early Approaches

The formal *scientific* study of child development is relatively new. Looking back, we can see dramatic changes in the ways of investigating the world of childhood.

Forerunners of the scientific study of child development were *baby biographies,* journals kept to record the early development of a single child. One early journal, published in 1787 in Germany, contained Dietrich Tiedemann's (1897/1787) observations of his infant son's sensory, motor, language, and cognitive development. Typical of the speculative nature of such observations was Tiedemann's conclusion, after watching the infant suck more continuously on a cloth tied around something sweet than on a nurse's finger, that sucking appeared to be "not instinctive, but acquired" (Murchison & Langer, 1927, p. 206).

It was Charles Darwin, originator of the theory of evolution, who first emphasized the *developmental* nature of infant behaviour. In 1877, in the belief that human beings could be better understood by studying their origins—both as a species and as individuals—Darwin published an abstract of his notes on his son's sensory, cognitive, and emotional development during the first 12 months (Keegan & Gruber, 1985; see Focus vignette at the beginning of Chapter 7). Darwin's journal gave "baby biographies" scientific respectability; about 30 more were published during the next three decades (Dennis, 1936).

Developmental Psychology Becomes a Science

By the end of the nineteenth century, several important trends were preparing the way for the scientific study of child development. Scientists had unlocked the mystery of conception and (as in the case of Victor) were arguing about the relative importance of "nature" and "nurture" (inborn characteristics and external influences). The discovery of germs and immunization made it possible for many more children to survive infancy. Because of an abundance of cheap labour, children were less needed as workers. Laws protecting them from long workdays let them spend more time in school, and parents and teachers became more concerned with identifying and meeting children's developmental needs. The new science of psychology taught that people could understand themselves by learning what had influenced them as children.

Still, this new discipline had far to go. Adolescence was not considered a separate period of development until the early twentieth century, when G. Stanley Hall, a pioneer in child study, published a popular (though unscientific) book called *Adolescence* (1904/1916). Hall was truly one of the early applied developmental psychologists, promoting child study, parent education, and child welfare, and influencing how professionals work with children (Brooks-Gunn & Duncan-Johnson, 2006).

In Canada, early research in child development began with James Baldwin and his students, including Frederick Tracy, in the late 1800s, who focused on mental development in childhood. With the emerging interest in "mental hygiene" in the 1920s and '30s, institutes of child study were established in Montreal and Toronto, directed by Katharine Banham and William Blatz (Wright, 2002). Since that time, Canadian researchers across the country have made significant contributions to our understanding of child development (Wright, 1999). Figure 1-1 presents summaries, in historical order, of the ideas and contributions of Darwin, Hall, and other early pioneers in the study of child development.

Almost from the start, developmental science has been interdisciplinary (Parke, 2004). Today students of child development draw collaboratively from a wide range of disciplines, including psychology, psychiatry, sociology, anthropology, biology, genetics (the study of inherited characteristics), family science (the interdisciplinary study of family relations), education, history, and medicine. This book includes findings from research in all these fields.

Studying the Lifespan

Lifespan studies in Canada and the United States grew out of programs designed to follow children through to adulthood. William E. Blatz, founder of St. George's School for Child Study at the University of Toronto, Department of Psychology in the 1920s, carried out a longitudinal project at Regal Road Public School in Toronto studying behavioural difficulties and adjustment of 1,400 children from the school years through adolescence and into adulthood (Raymond, 1991; Wright 2002). Blatz was also instrumental in developing the laboratory school for the Dionne Quintuplets, the first known set of identical quintuplets, in the 1930s; however, the ethics of the quintuplets' lack of privacy and freedom to withdraw have been questioned (Prochner & Doyon, 1997).

Today the study of child development is part of the broader study of *human development,* which covers the entire lifespan from conception to death. Although growth and development are most obvious in childhood, they occur throughout life. Indeed, such aspects of adult development as the timing of parenthood, maternal employment, and marital satisfaction have an impact on the way children develop.

New Frontiers

Although children have been the focus of scientific study for more than one hundred years, this exploration is an ever-evolving endeavour. The questions that developmentalists seek to

What's your view ?

• What reasons do you have for studying child development?

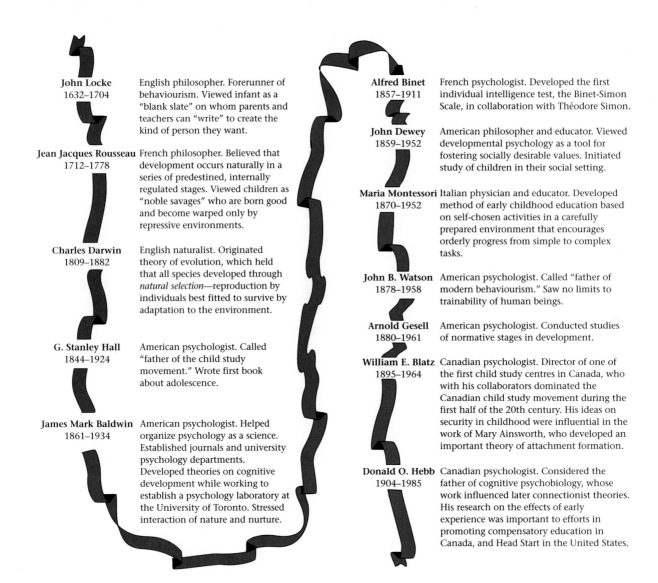

Figure 1-1

Some pioneers in the study of a child's world: A timeline

Checkpoint ✓

Can you . . .

✔ Distinguish between quantitative and qualitative development and give an example of each?

✔ Trace highlights in the evolution of the study of child development?

✔ Name some pioneers in that study and summarize their most important contributions?

✔ Give examples of practical applications of research on child development?

answer, the methods they use, and the explanations they propose are more sophisticated than they were even 25 years ago. These shifts reflect progress in understanding, as new investigations build on or challenge those that went before. They also reflect the changing cultural and technological context. Sensitive instruments that measure eye movements are turning up intriguing connections between infant visual attentiveness and childhood intelligence. Cameras, video recorders, and computers allow investigators to scan infants' facial expressions for early signs of emotions and to analyze how mothers and babies communicate. Advances in brain imaging make it possible to probe the mysteries of temperament and to pinpoint the sources of logical thought.

The traditional distinction between *basic research*, the kind undertaken purely in a spirit of intellectual inquiry, and *applied research*, which addresses a practical problem, is becoming less meaningful. Increasingly, research findings have direct application to child rearing, education, health, and social policy. For example, research into preschool children's understanding of death can enable adults to help a child deal with bereavement; research on children's memory can help determine the weight to be given children's courtroom testimony; and research on factors that increase the risks of low birth weight, antisocial behaviour, and teenage suicide can suggest ways to prevent these ills.

The Study of Child Development: Basic Concepts

Guidepost 2

What aspects and periods of development do developmental scientists study?

The processes of change and stability that developmental scientists study occur in all three aspects, or domains, of the self and throughout all five periods of childhood and adolescence.

Domains of Development

For purposes of study, developmental scientists separate the three domains: *physical development, cognitive development,* and *psychosocial development.* Actually, though, these domains of development are interrelated.

Growth of the body and brain, sensory capacities, motor skills, and health are part of **physical development** and may influence other aspects of development. For example, a child with frequent ear infections may develop language more slowly than a child without this problem. During puberty, dramatic physiological and hormonal changes affect the developing sense of self.

Change and stability in mental abilities, such as learning, memory, language, thinking, moral reasoning, and creativity constitute **cognitive development.** They are closely related to physical and emotional growth. The ability to speak depends on the physical development of the mouth and brain. A child who has difficulty with words may evoke negative reactions in others, influencing the child's popularity and sense of self-worth.

Change and stability in personality, emotional life, and social relationships together constitute **psychosocial development,** and this can affect cognitive and physical functioning. Anxiety about taking a test can impair performance. Social support can help children cope with the potentially negative effects of stress on physical and mental health. Conversely, physical and cognitive capacities affect psychosocial development by contributing to self-esteem and social acceptance.

Although we will be looking separately at physical, cognitive, and psychosocial development, a child is more than a bundle of isolated parts. Development is a unified process. Throughout the text, we will highlight links among the three domains of development.

physical development Growth of body and brain, including patterns of change in sensory capacities, motor skills, and health

cognitive development Pattern of change in mental abilities, such as learning, attention, memory, language, thinking, reasoning, and creativity

psychosocial development Pattern of change in emotions, personality, and social relationships

Periods of Development

There is no single, objectively definable moment when a child becomes an adolescent, or an adolescent becomes an adult. Thus, the concept of periods of development is an arbitrary one adopted for purposes of social discourse. We call such a concept a **social construction:** an idea about the nature of reality accepted by members of a particular society at a particular time on the basis of shared subjective perceptions or assumptions.

Indeed, the concept of childhood itself can be viewed as a social construction. Some evidence indicates that children in earlier times were regarded and treated much like small adults. However, this suggestion has been disputed (Ariès, 1962; Elkind, 1986; Pollock, 1983). Archaeological finds from ancient Greece show that children played with clay dolls and "dice" made of bones of sheep and goats. Pottery and tombstones depict children sitting on high chairs and riding goat-pulled carts (Mulrine, 2004).

In industrial societies, as we have mentioned, the concept of adolescence as a period of development is quite recent. Until the early twentieth century, young people were considered children until they left school (often well before age 13), married or got a job, and entered the adult world. By the 1920s, with the establishment of comprehensive high schools to meet the needs of a growing economy and with more families able to support extended formal education for their children, the teenage years had become a distinct period of development (Keller, 1999). In some preindustrial societies, the concept of adolescence still does not exist. The Chippewa, for example, have only two periods of childhood: from birth until the child walks, and from walking to puberty. What we call adolescence is, for them, part of adulthood (Broude, 1995), as was true in societies before industrialization.

social construction Concept about the nature of reality, based on societally shared perceptions or assumptions

Checkpoint

Can you . . .

✔ Identify three domains of development and give examples of how they are interrelated?

✔ Name five periods of child development (as defined in this book) and list several key issues or events of each period?

In this book, we follow a sequence of five periods generally accepted in North American and European industrial societies. After describing the crucial changes that occur in the first period, before birth, we trace all three aspects of development through infancy and toddlerhood, early childhood, middle childhood, and adolescence (see Table 1-1). Again, these age divisions are approximate and somewhat arbitrary.

Table 1-1	Typical Major Developments in Five Periods of Child Development		
Age Period	**Physical Developments**	**Cognitive Developments**	**Psychosocial Developments**
Prenatal Period (conception to birth)	Conception occurs The genetic endowment interacts with environmental influences from the start. Basic body structures and organs form. Brain growth spurt begins. Physical growth is the most rapid in the lifespan. Vulnerability to environmental influences is great.	Abilities to learn and remember and to respond to sensory stimuli are developing.	
Infancy and Toddlerhood (birth to age 3)	All senses and body systems operate at birth to varying degrees. The brain grows in complexity and is highly sensitive to environmental influence. Physical growth and development of motor skills are rapid.	Abilities to learn and remember are present, even in early weeks. Use of symbols and ability to solve problems develop by end of second year. Comprehension and use of language develop rapidly.	Attachments to parents and others form. Self-awareness develops. Shift from dependence to autonomy occurs. Interest in other children increases.
Early Childhood (3 to 6 years)	Growth is steady; appearance becomes more slender and proportions more adultlike. Appetite diminishes, and sleep problems are common. Handedness appears; fine and gross motor skills and strength improve.	Thinking is somewhat egocentric, but understanding of other people's perspectives grows. Cognitive immaturity leads to some illogical ideas about the world. Memory and language improve. Intelligence becomes more predictable.	Self-concept and understanding of emotions become more complex; self-esteem is global. Independence, initiative, self-control, and self-care increase. Gender identity develops. Play becomes more imaginative, more elaborate, and more social. Altruism, aggression, and fearfulness are common. Family is still focus of social life, but other children become more important. Attending preschool is common.
Middle Childhood (6 to 11 years)	Growth slows. Strength and athletic skills improve. Respiratory illnesses are common, but health is generally better than at any other time in lifespan.	Egocentrism diminishes. Children begin to think logically but concretely. Memory and language skills increase. Cognitive gains permit children to benefit from formal schooling. Some children show special educational needs and strengths.	Self-concept becomes more complex, affecting self-esteem. Coregulation reflects gradual shift in control from parents to child. Peers assume central importance.
Adolescence (11 to about 20 years)	Physical growth and other changes are rapid and profound. Reproductive maturity occurs. Major health risks arise from behavioural issues, such as eating disorders and drug abuse.	Ability to think abstractly and use scientific reasoning develops. Immature thinking persists in some attitudes and behaviours. Education focuses on preparation for university or vocation.	Search for identity, including sexual identity, becomes central. Relationships with parents are generally good. Peer groups help develop and test self-concept but also may exert an anti-social influence.

Although individual differences exist in the way children deal with the characteristic events and issues of each period, developmental scientists suggest that certain basic needs must be met and certain tasks mastered for normal development to occur. Infants, for example, are dependent on adults for food, clothing, and shelter as well as for human contact and affection. They form attachments to parents and caregivers, who also become attached to them. With the development of speech and self-locomotion, toddlers become more self-reliant; they need to assert their autonomy but also need parents to set limits on their behaviour. During early childhood, children develop more self-control and more interest in other children. During middle childhood, control over behaviour gradually shifts from parent to child, and the peer group becomes increasingly important. A main task of adolescence is the search for identity—personal, sexual, and occupational. As adolescents become physically mature, they deal with conflicting needs and emotions as they prepare to leave the parental nest.

What's your view ?

- Can you think of a reason why various societies divide the periods of development differently?

Influences on Development

Guidepost 3

What kinds of influences make one child different from another?

Students of development are interested in processes of development that affect every normal child, but they also want to know about **individual differences,** both in influences on development and in its outcome. Children differ in sex, height, weight, and body build; in constitutional factors such as health and energy level; in intelligence; and in personality characteristics and emotional reactions. The contexts of their lives and lifestyles differ, too: the homes, communities, and societies they live in, the relationships they have, the kinds of schools they go to (or whether they go to a formal school at all), and how they spend their free time.

individual differences
Differences among children in characteristics, influences, or developmental outcomes

Heredity, Environment, and Maturation

Some influences on development originate primarily with **heredity,** inborn traits or characteristics inherited from the biological parents. Other influences come largely from the inner and outer **environment,** the world outside the self beginning in the womb, and the learning that comes from experience—including *socialization,* a child's induction into the value system of the culture. Which of these factors—heredity or environment—has more impact on development? This issue (dramatized by our Focus on Victor) once aroused intense debate. Theorists differed in the relative importance they gave to *nature* (heredity) and *nurture* (environmental influences both before and after birth).

heredity Inborn influences or traits inherited from biological parents

environment Totality of nonhereditary, or experiential, influences on development

Today, scientists in the field of behavioural genetics have found ways to measure more precisely the roles of heredity and environment in the development of specific traits within a population. When we look at a particular child, however, research with regard to almost all characteristics points to a blend of inheritance and experience. Thus, even though intelligence is strongly affected by heredity, environmental factors such as parental stimulation, education, and peer influence also influence it. Although there still is considerable dispute about the relative importance of nature and nurture, contemporary theorists and researchers are more interested in finding ways to explain how they work together.

Many typical changes of infancy and early childhood, such as the emergence of the abilities to walk and talk, are tied to **maturation** of the body and brain—the unfolding of a universal, natural sequence of physical changes and behaviour patterns, including readiness to master new abilities such as walking and talking. These maturational processes, which are seen most clearly in the early years, act in concert with the influences of heredity and environment. As children grow into adolescents and then into adults, individual differences in innate characteristics (heredity) and life experience (environment) play an increasing role as children adapt to the internal and external conditions in which they find themselves.

maturation Unfolding of a natural sequence of physical and behavioural changes, including readiness to master new abilities

Even in maturational processes that all children undergo, rates and timing of development vary. Throughout this book, we talk about average ages for the occurrence of certain events, such as the first word, the first step, the first menstruation or "wet dream," and the development of logical thought. But these ages are *merely* averages. Only when deviation from the average is extreme should we consider development exceptionally advanced or delayed.

In trying to understand child development, then, we need to look at the *inherited* characteristics that are unique to each child. We also need to consider the many *environmental,* or experiential, factors that affect children, especially such major contexts as family, neighbourhood, socio-economic status, ethnicity, and culture. We need to consider how heredity and environment interact; this will be discussed in Chapter 3. We need to understand which developments are primarily maturational and which are more subject to individual differences. We need to look at influences that affect many or most people at a certain age or a certain time in history and also at those that affect only certain individuals. Finally, we need to look at how timing can accentuate the impact of certain influences.

Contexts of Development

Human beings are social beings. Right from the start, they develop within a social and historical context. For an infant, the immediate context is normally the family; and the family in turn is subject to the wider and ever-changing influences of neighbourhood, community, and society.

Family

nuclear family Kinship and household unit made up of parents and their natural or adopted children

The **nuclear family** is a two-generational kinship, economic, and household unit consisting of two parents and their natural or adopted children (Hareven, 1986). Today most families are urban; they have fewer children, and both parents work outside the home. Children spend much of their time in school or child care. Children of divorced parents live with one or the other parent or move back and forth between them. Households often include a stepparent and stepsiblings or a parent's live-in partner. There are increasing numbers of single and childless adults, unmarried parents, and gay and lesbian households (Hernandez, 1997, 2004; Teachman, Tedrow, & Crowder, 2000; Lipman, Offord, Dooley & Boyle, 2002).

extended family Kinship network of parents, children, and other relatives, sometimes living together in an extended-family household

In many societies, such as those of Asia and Latin America, the **extended family**—a multi-generational kinship network of grandparents, aunts, uncles, cousins, and more distant relatives—is the traditional family form. Many or most people live in *extended-family households,* where they have daily contact with kin. However, that pattern is now eroding in developing countries, due to industrialization and migration to urban centres (N. M. Brown, 1990; Gorman, 1993).

In Canada, it is not uncommon for extended families to be spread through all regions of the country, with family members moving for work or education. However, among many Canadian ethnic groups, particularly Aboriginal Canadians—including First Nations, Inuit, and Metis—the extended family is an integral part of children's experiences (Ward, 1998). Grandparents traditionally assumed a major role in raising children in Aboriginal communities, and despite the practices of the mainstream culture that undermined this strength of Aboriginal families (see Box 1-1), the traditional roles are beginning to return (Parler, 2001).

Recent immigrant families from Asia, Africa, the Caribbean, and Europe also involve the extended family in child rearing (Baker, 2001; Ochieng, 2003). Close extended family ties provide strong support systems, and extended-family households are common. Social roles tend to be flexible: Across many countries, adult immigrants often share breadwinning, and children are given responsibility for younger brothers and sisters (Harrison, Wilson, Pine, Chan, & Buriel, 1990; Levitt, Guacci-Franco, & Levitt, 1993; Walsh, Shulman, Bar-On, & Tsur, 2006). Often these households are headed by women (Stewart, Neufeld, Harrison, Spitzer, Hughes, & Makwrimba, 2006).

The role of the community in bringing up children is also significant among religious-based settlements, such as Mennonites in Manitoba and Ontario, and Hutterites in Alberta, who live apart from mainstream Canadian society (Ingoldsby & Smith, 2005; Dreidger, 2000; Peter, 1983).

Socio-economic Status and Neighbourhood

socio-economic status (SES) Combination of economic and social factors describing an individual or family, including income, education, and occupation

Socio-economic status (SES) combines several related factors, including income, education, and occupation. Throughout this book, we describe many studies that relate SES to developmental processes (such as differences in mothers' verbal interaction with their children) and to developmental outcomes and other **risk factors** (such as health and family

risk factors Conditions that increase the likelihood of a negative developmental outcome

Box 1-1 *The Residential School Experience of Aboriginal Children*

The importance of looking at the life course in its social and historical context is exemplified by the experience of Aboriginal youth in Canada from the 1920s to the 1970s. Before that time, Aboriginal communities gave children the freedom to explore their environment and to develop independence, without the use of corporal punishment (Johnson & Cremo, 1995). Aboriginal languages and traditional spirituality and customs flourished. The established European majority saw the typical child-rearing practice of Aboriginal communities as permissive and neglectful. Drawing upon public opinion and an emphasis on assimilation to the majority culture, the federal government in the 1920s followed a policy of removing Aboriginal children from their families and placing them in government-sponsored residential schools (Sinclair, Phillips, & Bala, 1991) typically run by church missionaries (Miller, 1996). The era of residential schools, which ended in the 1970s, exacted a huge toll in human suffering of members of Aboriginal communities. The residential school authorities did not permit the children to use their home languages, and as a consequence of their experiences the children lost touch with their cultures and traditional ways (Grant, 1996). In some cases, evidence of physical, psychological, and sexual abuse along with human rights violations emerged. The impact of this experience on the cohort of Aboriginal youth from the early 1920s to the 1970s involved feelings of inferiority, apathy, unwillingness to work, confusion over values, and anti-religious attitudes (Grant, 1996). Today, the effects of the residential school era are beginning to be addressed. Part of this process involves recognizing the practice as a form of cultural genocide (Miller, 1996), and emphasizing healing, and renewing of language and cultural traditions for future generations of Aboriginal people by promoting distinct Aboriginal people's educational programs. Government initiatives in response to demands for justice and responsibility by Aboriginal organizations and people, like a Statement of Reconciliation, apologizing to the people who experienced abuse, an Aboribinal Healing Foundation for community-based healing projects, and a truth and reconciliation process as a form of restorative justice, are beginning to address past and present cultural loss. Aboriginal groups are emerging as a political force changing the social and cultural landscape through the Assembly of First Nations, Aboriginal educational institutions, and popular cultural outlets like the Aboriginal People's Television Network.

As the history of the residential school cohort of Aboriginal youth has emerged, their life experiences—as documented by interviews with former students and school and government officials, archival data, and photographs—give researchers a window into the processes of development and their links with socio-historical change. The longer-term effects of the residential school era are being documented particularly with children of survivors, and changes in the roles of elders and Aboriginal education.

Aboriginal children during residential school internment. The experience of growing up in a Church-run residential school shows how a government policy can affect children's current and future development.

What's your view

Can you think of a major cultural event within your lifetime that shaped the lives of families and children? How would you go about studying such effects?

Check it out

For more information on this topic, go to **www.mcgrawhill.ca/olc/papalia.**

environment; see Table 1-2). It is generally not SES itself that affects these outcomes, but factors associated with SES, such as the kinds of homes and neighbourhoods children live in and the quality of nutrition, supervision, schooling, and other opportunities available to them. The National Longitudinal Survey of Children and Youth (NLSCY), begun in 1994, is tracking 35,000 children from all regions of Canada every two years from birth. Results from this survey have already shown that although coming from a disadvantaged neighbourhood is related to emotional and behaviour problems in childhood, the most powerful factor that predicts future behaviour problems is family socio-economic status (Boyle & Lipman, 1998; Willms, 2002; Yange, Leventhal, Brooks-Gunn & Earls, 2005). Poor children with emotional or behavioural problems suffer in their cognitive potential and school performance even more (Evans, 2004). The harm done by poverty may be indirect, through its impact on parents' emotional state, parenting practices, and on the home environment. The challenges of poverty can strain relationships and drain time and energy from parenting. (In Chapter 14 we'll look more closely at indirect effects of poverty.) In addition, living

Table 1-2	Higher Risk for Low-income Children
Outcome	**Low-income Children's Higher Risk Relative to More Affluent Children**
Mental Health	
Emotional Problems	1.3 times more likely
Behavioural Problems	1.3 times more likely
Family Environment	
Single Parent	5.5 times more likely
Ineffective Parenting	1.04 times more likely
Parental Depression	1.8 times more likely
Family Dysfunction	1.3 times more likely

Source: Adapted from Beiser, Hou, Hyman, & Tousignant, 2002, p. 222.

in more affluent and cohesive neighbourhoods is associated with higher levels of school readiness, and school performance (Boyle, Georgiades, Racine & Mustard, 2007; Brooks-Gunn, Britto, & Brady, 1998; Brooks-Gunn & Duncan, 1997; Duncan & Brooks-Gunn, 1997; Kohen, Hertzman, & Brooks-Gunn, 1998; McLoyd, 1998). However, children in more affluent families also may be at risk. Under pressure to achieve and often left on their own by busy parents, these children have high rates of substance abuse, anxiety, and depression (Luthar & Latendresse, 2005).

Often, children from low SES families that move to high SES neighbourhods show fewer behavioural and family problems, and less delinquency than those whose families stay in low SES neighbourhoods. However, older youth, between ages 16 and 18 years, who experience such neighbourhood transition, are more likely to show increased behavioural and family problems. This kind of pattern shows that the benefits of a neighbourhood change can sometimes be limited to specific periods of childhood (Fauth, Leventhal, & Brooks-Gunn, 2005).

SES limits a family's choice of where to live. Researchers have begun to study how the composition of a neighbourhood affects the way children turn out. So far, the most powerful factors seem to be average neighbourhood *income* and *human capital*—the presence of educated, employed adults who can build the community's economic base and provide models of what a child can hope to achieve (Brooks-Gunn et al., 1997; Leventhal & Brooks-Gunn, 2000; Leventhal & Brooks-Gunn, 2003). Threats to children's well-being multiply if several risk factors—conditions that increase the likelihood of a negative outcome—coexist (Willms, 2002). Living in a poor neighbourhood with large numbers of people who are unemployed and on welfare makes it less likely that effective social support will be available (Black & Krishnakumar, 1998; Willms, 2002). As well, living in persistent poverty is associated with larger risk of negative outcomes. Wide disparities in wealth are connected with the health of the population. With more inequity in income, population health tends to fare poorly in general. People with the lowest incomes typically have the poorest health outcomes, but this has an impact beyond the poorest members of a population (Leventhal & Brooks-Gunn, 2003). About one in eight Canadian children aged 12 years or younger experience a severe period of poverty (four or more consecutive years of family income below the poverty line) (Canadian Council on Social Development, 2001). Still, the resilience of such people as Supreme Court Justice Rosalie Abella, former Ontario Lieutenant-Governor Lincoln Alexander, the first black Member of Parliament, and Prime Ministers Jean Chretien and Brian Mulroney, who rose from humble backgrounds to high achievement, show that positive development can occur despite serious risk factors (Kim-Cohen, Moffitt, Caspi, & Taylor, 2004).

Culture and Ethnicity

Culture refers to a society's or group's total way of life, including customs, traditions, beliefs, values, language, and physical products, from tools to artworks—all the learned behaviour passed on from parents to children. Culture is constantly changing, often through

culture A society's or group's total way of life, including customs, traditions, beliefs, values, language, and physical products—all learned behaviour passed on from parents to children

contact with other cultures. After immigrant groups live in Canada for more than a generation, some of their parenting practices shift from a pattern typically used in the country of origin to one more commonly used by parents in mainstream Canadian families.

An **ethnic group** consists of people united by ancestry, race, religion, language, and/or national origins, which contribute to a sense of shared identity and shared attitudes, beliefs, and values. Most ethnic groups trace their roots to a country of origin, where they or their forebears had a common culture that continues to influence their way of life.

Canada has always been a nation of immigrants and ethnic groups. In 2002 alone, 229,121 new immigrants came to Canada, with Ontario attracting the largest number of immigrants, over 50 percent. This was followed by Quebec and British Columbia, each attracting about 15 percent of the total immigrant population (Canadian Council on Social Development, 2007). The two founding groups, English and French, live alongside a third group of more recent immigrants who consist of many distinct ethnic groups—who come from all regions of the world. About 28 percent of the Canadian population identifies itself as having origins other than British, French, or Canadian, with visible minorities constituting over 11 percent of the population (Health Canada, 1999). The majority of current immigrants arriving in Canada are from Asia and Africa. Between 2002 and 2004 most immigrants were from Asia, despite a slight decline in recent years, from 62 percent in 2001 and 2002 to 57 percent in 2004. The number of Africans arriving in Canada as permanent residents has almost doubled since 1998, from 14,500 to 27,600 in 2004 (Statistics Canada, 2007). There is also diversity within ethnic groups. Québécois, Franco-Ontarians, Franco-Manitobans, and Acadians—all French Canadians—have different histories and cultures and socio-economic status. Similarly, African-Canadian descendants of immigrants from the United States differ from those of Caribbean ancestry. Asian-Canadians, too, come from a variety of countries with distinct cultures and linguistic groups. Aboriginal peoples constitute the original inhabitants of Canada and are made up of many linguistic and ethnic groups: First Nations, Inuit, and Metis populations represent a diverse group of about one million people in Canada. With 11 language groups and 58 dialects across 596 bands, living in 2,284 reserves, and in small and large urban centres, there is a large amount of cultural and linguistic diversity along with differences in values both between and within Aboriginal communities (Kirmayer, Brass, & Tait, 2000).

In large, multi-ethnic societies such as Canada, immigrant or minority groups *acculturate,* or adapt, to the majority culture by learning the language and customs needed to get along in the dominant culture while trying to preserve some of their own cultural practices and values (Johnson et al., 2003). (Acculturation is not the same as cultural *assimilation,* in which the minority simply adopts the ways of the majority.) Children often grow up in neighbourhoods with other members of their own ethnic group, reinforcing shared cultural patterns. These cultural patterns may influence the composition of the household, its economic and social resources, the way its members act toward one another, the foods they eat, the games children play, the way they learn, and how well they do in school. Immigrant children generally enjoy good health, exeriencing less frequent hospitalization than their non-immigrant counterparts, particularly for those living in low-SES circumstances (Flynn, McNeil, Maloff, Mutasingwa et al., 2006; Guttmann, Dick, & To, 2004; Wen et al., 1996), and this might be partly due to effective parenting practices by immigrant parents (Beiser, Hou, Hyman, & Tousignant, 2002). However, the effects of chronic poverty are universal.

According to the National Longitudinal Survey of Children and Youth (NLSCY), children of immigrant families do at least as well as, and in some cases better than, Canadian-born children in reading, writing, and mathematics achievement, particularly for parents whose first language is either English or French. Some children of immigrant parents do worse than children whose parents were born in Canada. However, as they gain years of experience in the school system, these children typically catch up or exceed their Canadian-born counterparts (Warswick, 2001).

The term *race,* historically and popularly viewed as an identifiable biological category, is now considered to be a social construct. There is no clear scientific consensus on its definition, and it is impossible to measure reliably (American Academy of Pediatrics Committee on Pediatric Research, 2000; Bonham, Warshauer-Baker, & Collins, 2005;

ethnic group Group united by ancestry, race, religion, language, and/or national origins, which contribute to a sense of shared identity

Helms, Jernigan, & Mascher, 2005; Lin & Kelsey, 2000; Smedley & Smedley, 2005; Sternberg, 2005). Human genetic variation occurs along a broad continuum, and 90 percent of such variation occurs *within* rather than among socially defined races (Bonham et al., 2005; Ossorio & Duster, 2005). Nevertheless, race as a social category remains a factor in research because it makes a difference in "how individuals are treated, where they live, their employment opportunities, the quality of their health care, and whether [they] can fully participate" in their society (Smedley & Smedley, 2005, p. 23).

Categories of culture, race, and ethnicity are fluid (Bonham et al., 2005; Sternberg, 2005), "continuously shaped and redefined by social and political forces" (Fisher et al., 2002, p. 1026). Geographic dispersion and intermarriage together with adaptation to varying local conditions have produced a great heterogeneity of physical and cultural characteristics within populations (Smedley & Smedley, 2005; Sternberg, 2005). Thus, a person such as the golf champion Tiger Woods, who has a black father and an Asian-American mother, may fall into more than one racial/ethnic category and may identify more strongly with one or another at different times (Hitlin, Brown, & Elder, 2006; Lin & Kelsey, 2000). A term such as *black* or *Hispanic* can be an **ethnic gloss**—an overgeneralization that obscures or blurs such variations (Parke, 2004; Trimble & Dickson, 2005).

ethnic gloss Overgeneralization about an ethnic or cultural group that blurs or obscures variations within the group or overlaps with other such groups

The Historical Context

At one time developmental scientists paid little attention to the historical context—the time in which children grow up. Then, as the early longitudinal studies of childhood extended into the adult years, investigators began to focus on how particular experiences, tied to time and place, affect the course of children's lives. The Regal Road study sample would have lived through the Great Depression and reached adulthood during the Second World War. What did it mean to be a child in these periods? To be an adolescent? To become an adult? The answers differ in important ways (Modell, 1989).

Children of European settlers at Confederation often worked from an early age, and networks of kinship with neighbours gave a secure social base where few social institutions existed (Parr, 1982). Children were often institutionalized until the family could use them as labour, or until a widowed father remarried. As Canada developed as an industrial nation in the late 1800s and early 1900s, a new perspective on child care emerged aiming to protect children's health, ensure access to quality education, and place victims of abuse and neglect into individual homes rather than large institutions (Sutherland, 2000). In Canada today, in a more culturally diverse country, children are brought up in ways that are substantially changed from those of past generations because of ideas, customs, and practices that evolved over the past 50 years (Sutherland, 2000). The perspective has progressed from children being regarded as family property during Canada's colonial period, to being viewed as dependent on the protection of the state during the first half of the twentieth century, to being recognized as having inherent rights after the Second World War, particularly with the 1982 Canadian Charter of Rights and Freedoms (Howe, 1995).

Today, as we'll discuss in the next section, the historical context is part of the study of development.

Checkpoint

Can you . . .

✔ Explain why individual differences tend to increase with age?

✔ Give examples of the influences of family and neighbourhood composition, socio-economic status, culture, ethnicity, and historical context?

Normative and Non-normative Influences

To understand similarities and differences in development, we must look at influences that impinge on many or most people and at those that touch only certain individuals.

A **normative** event is experienced in a similar way by most people in a group. *Normative age-graded influences* are highly similar for people in a particular age group. They include biological events (such as puberty) and social events (such as entry into formal education). The timing of biological events is fixed, within a normal range. (Children don't experience puberty at age 3.) The timing of social events is more flexible and varies in different times and places, within maturational limits. Children in North American and European industrial societies generally begin formal education around age 5 or 6; but in some developing countries, schooling begins much later, if at all.

normative Characteristic of an event that occurs in a similar way for most people in a group

Normative history-graded influences are common to a particular **cohort:** a group of people who share a similar experience, in this case growing up at the same time in the same place, such as living in Canada during the Great Depression. Depending on when and where they live, entire generations of children may feel the impact of wars, famines, or nuclear explosions. In North American and European countries, medical advances, as well as improvements in nutrition and sanitation, have dramatically reduced infant and child mortality. As children grow up, they are likely to be influenced by computers, digital television, the Internet, and other technological developments. Social changes, such as the increase in numbers of employed mothers, have greatly altered family life.

A **historical generation** is not the same as an *age cohort:* a group of people born at about the same time. A historical generation may contain more than one cohort, but not all cohorts are part of historical generations unless they experience major, shaping historical events at a formative point in their lives (Rogler, 2002).

Non-normative influences are unusual events that have a major impact on individual lives and may cause stress because they are unexpected. They are either typical events that happen at an atypical time of life (such as marriage in the early teens, or the death of a parent when a child is young) or atypical events (such as having a birth defect or being in an automobile crash). They can also, of course, be happy events (such as winning a scholarship). Young people may help create their own non-normative life events—say, by driving after drinking or by applying for a scholarship—and thus participate actively in their own development.

Timing of Influences: Critical or Sensitive Periods

In a well-known study, Konrad Lorenz (1957), an Austrian zoologist, waddled, honked, and flapped his arms—and got newborn ducklings to follow him as they would the mother duck. Lorenz showed that newly hatched ducklings will instinctively follow the first moving object they see, whether or not it is a member of their own species. This phenomenon is called **imprinting,** and Lorenz believed that it is automatic and irreversible. Usually, this instinctive bond is with the mother; but if the natural course of events is disturbed, other attachments, like the one to Lorenz—or none at all—can form. Imprinting, said Lorenz, is the result of a *predisposition toward learning:* the readiness of an organism's nervous system to acquire certain information during a brief *critical period* in early life.

A **critical period** is a specific time when a given event, or its absence, has a specific impact on development. If a necessary event does not occur during a critical period of maturation, normal development will not occur; and the resulting abnormal patterns may be irreversible (Knudsen, 1999; Kuhl, Conboy, Padden, Nelson, & Pruitt, 2005). However, the length of a critical period is not absolutely fixed; if ducklings' rearing conditions are varied to slow their growth, the usual critical period for imprinting can be extended, and imprinting itself may even be reversed (Bruer, 2001).

Do human beings experience critical periods? One example occurs during gestation. If a woman receives X-rays, takes certain drugs, or contracts certain diseases at certain times during pregnancy, the fetus may show specific ill effects, depending on the nature of the "shock" and on its timing. Critical periods also occur early in childhood. A child deprived of certain kinds of experience during a critical period is likely to show permanent stunting of physical development. For example, if a muscle problem interfering with the ability to focus both eyes on the same object is not corrected early in life, the brain mechanisms necessary for binocular depth perception probably will not develop (Bushnell & Boudreau, 1993).

The concept of critical periods is controversial. Because many aspects of development, even in the physical domain, have been found to show **plasticity,** or modifiability of performance, it may be more useful to think about **sensitive periods,** when a child's development is especially responsive to certain kinds of experiences, but later experience continues to influence development (Bruer, 2001; Knudson, 1999; Kuhl et al., 2005). Box 1-2 discusses how the concepts of critical and sensitive periods apply to language development.

cohort Group of people who share a similar experience, such as growing up at the same time and in the same place

historical generation A group of people strongly influenced by a major historical event during their formative period

non-normative Characteristic of an unusual event that happens to a particular person, or a typical event that happens at an unusual time of life

What's your view

- Can you think of a historical event that has moulded your own life? If so, in what ways?

imprinting Instinctive form of learning in which, during a critical period in early development, a young animal forms an attachment to the first moving object it sees, usually the mother

critical period Specific time when a given event, or its absence, has the greatest impact on development

plasticity Modifiability, or "moulding," of the brain through experience

sensitive periods Times in development when a person is particularly open to certain kinds of experiences

Checkpoint

Can you . . .

✔ Give examples of normative age-graded, normative history-graded, and non-normative influences? (Include some normative history-graded influences that affected different generations.)

✔ Explain the concept of "critical" periods and give examples?

Box 1-2 *Is There a Critical Period for Language Acquisition?*

In 1970, a 13½-year-old girl named Genie (not her real name) was discovered in a suburb of Los Angeles (Curtiss, 1977; Fromkin, Krashen, Curtiss, Rigler, & Rigler, 1974; Pines, 1981; Rymer, 1993). The victim of an abusive father, she had been confined for nearly 12 years to a small room in her parents' home, tied to a potty chair and cut off from normal human contact. She weighed only 59 pounds, could not straighten her arms or legs, could not chew, had no bladder or bowel control, and did not speak. She recognized only her own name and the word *sorry.*

Only three years before, Eric Lenneberg (1967, 1969) had proposed that there is a critical period for language acquisition, beginning in early infancy and ending around puberty. Lenneberg argued that it would be difficult, if not impossible, for a child who had not yet acquired language to do so after that age.

The discovery of Genie offered the opportunity for a test of Lenneberg's hypothesis. Could Genie be taught to speak, or was it too late? The U.S. National Institutes of Mental Health (NIMH) funded a study, and a series of researchers took over Genie's care and gave her intensive testing and language training.

Genie's progress during the next few years (before the NIMH withdrew funding and her mother regained custody) both challenges and supports the idea of a critical period for language acquisition. Genie did learn some simple words and could string them together into primitive, but rule-governed, sentences. She also learned the fundamentals of sign language. But she never used language normally, and "her speech remained, for the most part, like a somewhat garbled telegram" (Pines, 1981, p. 29). When her mother became unable to manage Genie's challenging behaviour, welfare offices placed Genie into a series of poorly supervised foster homes, where she regressed into total silence.

What explains Genie's initial progress and her inability to sustain it? The fact that she was just beginning to show signs of puberty at age 13½ may indicate that she was still in the critical period, though near its end. The fact that she apparently had learned a few words before being locked up at the age of 20 months may mean that her language-learning mechanisms may have been triggered early in the critical period, allowing later learning to occur. On the other hand, the fact that she was so abused and neglected may have retarded her so much—emotionally, socially, and cognitively—that, like Victor, she cannot be considered a true test of the critical period (Curtiss, 1977).

Case studies like those of Genie and Victor dramatize the difficulty of acquiring language after the early years of life, but they do not permit conclusive judgments because there are too many complicating factors. Because of the brain's plasticity, some researchers consider the prepubertal years a *sensitive*

rather than *critical* period for learning language (Newport, Bavelier, & Neville, 2001; Schumann, 1997). Researchers seeking study participants who lack early exposure to language, but whose environment and development are otherwise normal, have therefore turned to deaf persons for whom American Sign Language (ASL) is the primary language. In one cross-sectional study, the older a person had been when first exposed to ASL, the more likely that person was to sign ungrammatically and inconsistently (Newport, 1991).

Other research has focused on a shorter critical period early in life. Sometime between 6 and 12 months, babies normally begin to "specialize" in perceiving the sounds of their native language and lose the ability to perceive sounds of other languages. In one study (Kuhl, Conboy, Padden, Nelson, & Pruitt, 2005; see Chapter 7), infants who, at 7 months, had already developed this specialized phonetic perception showed more advanced language abilities two years later than did 7-month-olds who were better able to discriminate *non*-native sounds. This research, these investigators suggest, may point to a critical period for phonetic perception: if infants do not begin to focus exclusively on the sounds of their native language during that period, their language development is slowed. This may explain why learning a second language in adulthood is not as easy as in early childhood (Newport, 1991).

If a critical period for language learning exists, what explains it? Do the brain's mechanisms for acquiring language decay as the brain matures? That would seem strange, since other cognitive abilities improve. An alternative hypothesis is that this very increase in cognitive sophistication interferes with an adolescent's or adult's ability to learn a language. Young children acquire language in small chunks that can be readily digested. Older learners, when they first begin learning a language, tend to absorb a great deal at once and then may have trouble analyzing and interpreting it (Newport, 1991).

What's your view?

Do you see any ethical problems in the studies of Genie and Victor? Is the knowledge gained from such studies worth any possible damage to the individuals involved? (Keep this question, and your answer, in mind when you read the section on ethics of research in Chapter 2.)

Check it out

For more information on this topic, go to **www.mcgrawhill.ca/olc/papalia.**

Guidepost 4

What are six fundamental points about child development on which consensus has emerged?

An Emerging Consensus

As the study of children has matured, a consensus has emerged on several fundamental points.

1. *All domains of development are interrelated.* Although developmental scientists often look separately at various *domains,* or aspects, of development, each affects the others. For example, increasing physical mobility helps a baby learn about the world. The hormonal and physical changes of puberty affect emotional development.

2. *Normal development includes a wide range of individual differences.* Each child, from the start, is unlike anyone else in the world. One is outgoing, another shy. One is agile, another awkward. How do those differences, and a multitude of others, come about? Some of the influences on individual development are inborn; others come from experience, or, most often, from a combination of the two. Family characteristics, the effects of gender, social class, and ethnicity, and the presence or absence of physical, mental, or emotional disability all affect the way a child develops.

3. *Children help shape their own development and influence others' responses to them.* Right from the start, through the responses they evoke in others, infants mould their environment and then respond to the environment they have helped create. Influence is *bi-directional:* When babies babble and coo, adults tend to talk to them, and babies then "talk" more.

4. *Historical and cultural contexts strongly influence development.* Each child develops within a specific environment, bounded by time and place. A child born in Canada today is likely to have experiences very different from those of a child born in colonial Canada, and also from a child born in Morocco or Greenland.

5. *Early experience is important, but children can be remarkably resilient.* A traumatic incident or a severely deprived childhood may well have grave emotional consequences, but the life histories of countless people show that often the effects of risks to healthy development, such as growing up in low-income families, can be overcome, particularly in the presence of protective factors such as a supportive family environment.

6. *Development in childhood is connected to development throughout the rest of life.* At one time, it was believed that growth and development end, as this book does, with adolescence. Today most developmental scientists agree that development goes on throughout life. As long as people live, they have the potential to change.

Checkpoint ✔

Can you . . .

✔ Summarize six fundamental points of agreement that have emerged from the study of child development?

Summary and Key Terms

The Study of Child Development: Then and Now

Guidepost 1 What is child development, and how has its study evolved?

- Child development as a field of scientific study focuses on processes of change and stability from conception through adolescence.
- The scientific study of child development began toward the end of the nineteenth century. Adolescence was not considered a separate phase of development until the early twentieth century. The field of child development is now part of the study of the entire life span, or human development.
- Ways of studying child development are still evolving, making use of advanced technologies.
- The distinction between basic and applied research has become less meaningful.

**child development (4)   quantitative change (4)
qualitative change (4)**

The Study of Child Development: Basic Concepts

Guidepost 2 What aspects and periods of development do developmental scientists study?

- Developmental scientists study developmental change, both quantitative and qualitative, as well as stability of personality and behaviour.
- The three major domains, or aspects, of development that developmental scientists study are physical, cognitive, and psychosocial. Each affects the others.
- The concept of periods of development is a social construction. In this book, child development is divided into five periods: the prenatal period, infancy and toddlerhood, early childhood, middle childhood, and adolescence. In each period, children have characteristic developmental needs and tasks.

**physical development (7)   cognitive development (7)
psychosocial development (7)   social construction (7)**

Influences on Development

Guidepost 3 What kinds of influences make one child different from another?

- Influences on development come from both heredity and environment. Many typical changes during childhood are related to maturation. Individual differences increase with age.

- In some societies, the nuclear family predominates; in others, the extended family.

- Socioeconomic status (SES) affects developmental processes and outcomes through the quality of home and neighbourhood environments and of nutrition, medical care, supervision, and schooling. The most powerful neighbourhood influences seem to be neighbourhood income and human capital. Multiple risk factors increase the likelihood of poor outcomes.

- Other important environmental influences stem from culture, ethnicity, and historical context. In large, multi-ethnic societies, immigrant groups often acculturate to the majority culture while preserving aspects of their own.

- Influences may be normative (age graded or history graded) or non-normative.

- There is strong evidence of critical or sensitive periods for certain types of early development.

**individual differences (9)   heredity (9)   environment (9)
maturation (9)   nuclear family (10)   extended family (10)
socio-economic status (SES) (10)   risk factors (10)   culture (12)
ethnic group (13)   ethnic gloss (14)   normative (14)
cohort (15)   historical generation (15)   non-normative (15)
imprinting (15)   critical period (15)   plasticity (15)
sensitive periods (15)**

An Emerging Consensus

Guidepost 4 What are six fundamental points about child development on which consensus has emerged?

- Consensus has emerged on several important points. These include (1) the interrelationship of domains of development, (2) the existence of a wide range of individual differences, (3) the bi-directionality of influence, (4) the importance of history and culture, (5) children's potential for resilience, and (6) continuity of development throughout life.

CHAPTER TWO

2

A Child's World:
How We Discover It

There is one thing even more vital to science than intelligent methods; and that is, the sincere desire to find out the truth, whatever it may be.

—Charles Sanders Peirce, Collected Papers, vol. 5, 1934

Focus *Margaret Mead, Pioneer in Cross-cultural Research*

Margaret Mead

Margaret Mead (1901–1978) was a world-famous American anthropologist. In the 1920s, at a time when it was rare for a woman to expose herself to the rigours of field work with remote, preliterate peoples, Mead spent nine months on the South Pacific island of Samoa, studying girls' adjustment to adolescence. Her best-selling first book, *Coming of Age in Samoa* (1928), challenged accepted views about the inevitability of adolescent rebellion.

An itinerant childhood built around her parents' academic pursuits prepared Mead for a life of roving research. In New Jersey, her mother, who was working on her doctoral thesis in sociology, took Margaret along on interviews with recent Italian immigrants—the child's first exposure to fieldwork. Her father, a professor at the University of Pennsylvania's Wharton business school, taught her respect for facts and "the importance of thinking clearly" (Mead, 1972, p. 40). He stressed the link between theory and application—as Margaret did when, years later, she applied her theories of child rearing to her daughter. Margaret's grandmother, a former schoolteacher, sent her out in the woods to collect and analyze mint specimens. "I was not well drilled in geography or spelling," Mead wrote in her memoir *Blackberry Winter* (1972, p. 47). "But I learned to observe the world around me and to note what I saw."

Margaret took copious notes on the development of her younger brother and two younger sisters. Her curiosity about why one child in a family behaved so differently from another led to her later interest in temperamental variations within a culture.

How cultures define male and female roles was another research focus. Margaret saw her mother and her grandmother as educated women who had managed to have husbands, children, and professional careers; and she expected to do the same. She was dismayed when, at the outset of her career, the distinguished anthropologist Edward Sapir told her she "would do better to stay at home and have children than to go off to the South Seas to study adolescent girls" (Mead, 1972, p. 11).

Margaret's choice of anthropology as a career was consistent with her homebred respect for the value of all human beings and their cultures. Recalling her father's insistence that the only thing worth doing is to add to the store of knowledge, she saw an urgent need to document once-isolated cultures now "vanishing before the onslaught of modern civilization" (Mead, 1972, p. 137).

"I went to Samoa—as, later, I went to the other societies on which I have worked—to find out more about human beings, human beings like ourselves in everything except their culture," she wrote. "Through the accidents of history, these cultures had developed so differently from ours that knowledge of them could shed a kind of light upon us, upon our potentialities and our limitations" (Mead, 1972, p. 293). The ongoing quest to illuminate those "potentialities and limitations" is the business of theorists and researchers in human development.

• • •

Margaret Mead's life was all of a piece. The young girl who filled notebooks with observations about her siblings became the scientist who travelled to distant lands and studied cultures very different from her own.

Mead's story underlines several important points about the study of child development. First, the study of children is not dry, abstract, or esoteric. It deals with the substance of real life.

Second, a cross-cultural perspective can reveal which patterns of behaviour, if any, are universal and which are not. Most studies of child development have been done in North American and European societies, using white, middle-class participants. Today developmental scientists are increasingly conscious of the need to expand the research base, as Mead and her colleagues sought to do.

Third, theory and research are two sides of the same coin. As Mead reflected on her own experiences and observed the behaviour of others, she formed tentative explanations, or theories, to be tested by additional research. Because theory and research are so closely interrelated, we introduce in this chapter an overview both of major theories of human development and of research methods used to study it.

In the first part of this chapter, we present major issues and theoretical perspectives that underlie much research in child development. In the remainder of the chapter, we look at how researchers gather and assess information, so that you will be better able to judge whether their conclusions rest on solid ground.

After you have read and studied this chapter, you should be able to answer each of the Guidepost questions that appear at the top of the next page. Look for them again in the margins, where they point to important concepts throughout the chapter. To check your understanding of these Guideposts, review the end-of-chapter summary. Checkpoints located throughout the chapter will help you verify your understanding of what you have read.

Guideposts for Study

1. What purposes do theories serve, and what are two basic issues on which developmental theorists differ?

2. What are five theoretical perspectives on child development, and what are some theories representative of each?

3. How do developmental scientists study children, and what are the advantages and disadvantages of each research method?

4. What ethical problems may arise in research on children?

Guidepost 1

What purposes do theories serve, and what are two basic issues on which developmental theorists differ?

theory Coherent set of logically related concepts that seeks to organize, explain, and predict data

hypotheses Possible explanations for phenomena, used to predict the outcome of research

mechanistic model Model that views development as a passive, predictable response to stimuli

Basic Theoretical Issues

Developmental scientists have come up with many theories about how children develop. A **theory** is a set of logically related concepts or statements, which seeks to describe and explain development and to predict what kinds of behaviour might occur under certain conditions. Theories organize data, the information gathered by research, and are a rich source of **hypotheses**—tentative explanations or predictions that can be tested by further research.

Theories change to incorporate new findings. Sometimes research supports a hypothesis and the theory on which it was based. At other times, as with Mead's findings challenging the inevitability of adolescent rebellion, scientists must modify their theories to account for unexpected data. Research findings often suggest additional questions and hypotheses to be examined and provide direction for dealing with practical issues.

The way theorists explain development depends in part on the way they view two basic issues: (1) whether children are active or passive in their own development; and (2) whether development is continuous or occurs in stages. A third issue, concerning how development is influenced by heredity and environment, was introduced in Chapter 1 and will be discussed more fully in Chapter 3.

Issue 1: Are Children Active or Passive in Their Development?

Are children active or passive in their own development? This controversy goes back to the eighteenth century. The English philosopher John Locke held that a young child is a tabula rasa—a "blank slate"—on which society "writes." In contrast, the French philosopher Jean Jacques Rousseau believed that children are born "noble savages" who develop according to their own positive natural tendencies unless corrupted by society. We now know that both views are too simplistic. Children have their own internal drives and needs that influence development; but children also are social animals, who cannot develop optimally in isolation.

The debate over Locke's and Rousseau's philosophies led to two contrasting models, or images, of development: mechanistic and organismic. Locke's view was the forerunner of the **mechanistic model** of development. In this model, people are like machines that react to environmental input (Pepper, 1942, 1961). Fill a car with gas, turn the ignition key, press the accelerator, and the vehicle will move. In the mechanistic view, human behaviour is much the same. If we know enough about how the human "machine" is put together and about the internal and external forces impinging on it, we can predict what the person will do. Mechanistic research seeks to identify and isolate the factors that make people behave as they do. For example, to explain why some college students drink too much alcohol, a mechanistic theorist might look for environmental influences, such as advertising and whether the person's friends drink to excess.

Rousseau was the precursor of the **organismic model** of development. This model sees people as active, growing organisms that set their own development in motion (Pepper, 1942, 1961). They initiate events; they do not just react. The impetus for change is internal. Environmental influences do not cause development, though they can speed or slow it. Because human behaviour is an organic whole, it cannot be predicted by breaking it down into simple responses to environmental stimulation. An organismic theorist, in studying why some adolescents drink too much, would be likely to look at what kinds of situations they choose to participate in and with whom. Do they choose friends who like to party or who are more studious?

Issue 2: Is Development Continuous, or Does It Occur in Stages?

The mechanistic and organismic models also differ on the second issue: Is development continuous, or does it occur in stages?

Mechanistic theorists see development as continuous, like walking or crawling up a ramp (see Figure 2-1), underlying processes, enabling prediction of later behaviours from earlier ones. These theorists focus on quantitative change: for example, changes in the frequency with which a response is made, rather than changes in the type of response.

Organismic theorists emphasize qualitative change. They see development as occurring in a series of distinct stages, like stair steps. At each stage, people cope with different kinds of problems and develop different kinds of abilities. Each stage builds on the previous one and prepares the way for the next.

A Shifting Balance

As the study of human development has evolved, the mechanistic and organismic models have shifted in influence and support (Parke, Ornstein, Rieser, & Zahn-Waxler, 1994). Most of the early theoretical pioneers, including Sigmund Freud, Erik Erikson, and Jean Piaget, favoured organismic or stage approaches. The mechanistic view gained support during the 1960s with the popularity of learning theories derived from the work of John B. Watson. (We discuss all these theorists in the next section.)

Today much theory and research attention is focused on the biological and evolutionary bases of behaviour. Instead of looking for broad stages, developmental scientists seek to discover what specific types of behaviour show continuity or lack of continuity and what processes are involved in each. Instead of debating active versus passive development, they often find that influences are *bi-directional:* people change their world even as it changes

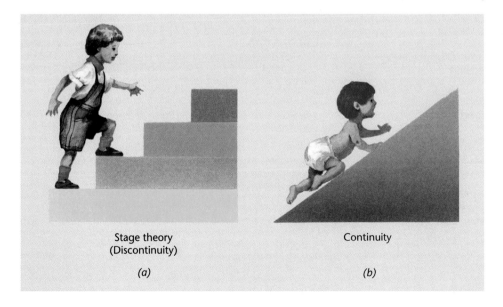

Stage theory
(Discontinuity)

(a)

Continuity

(b)

Figure 2-1

A major difference among developmental theories is *(a)* whether development occurs in distinct stages, as Piaget, Freud, and Erikson maintained or *(b)* whether it proceeds continuously, as learning theorists and information-processing theorists propose

Checkpoint ✓

Can you . . .

✔ State two basic issues regarding the nature of child development?

✔ Contrast the mechanistic and organismic models of development?

Guidepost 2

What are five theoretical perspectives on child development, and what are some theories representative of each?

psychoanalytic perspective
View of development as shaped by unconscious forces

them. A baby girl born with a cheerful disposition is likely to get positive reactions from adults, which strengthen her trust that her smiles will be rewarded and motivate her to smile more. As children grow older, their natural tendencies lead them to choose or initiate activities, such as studying a musical instrument, that further develop those tendencies.

Theoretical Perspectives

Despite the growing consensus on the basic issues just discussed, many investigators view development from differing theoretical perspectives. Theories generally fall within these broad perspectives, each of which emphasizes different kinds of developmental processes. These perspectives influence the questions researchers ask, the methods they use, and the ways they interpret data. Therefore, to evaluate and interpret research, it is important to recognize the theoretical perspective on which it is based.

Five major perspectives (summarized in Table 2-1) underlie much influential theory and research on child development: (1) *psychoanalytic* (which focuses on unconscious emotions and drives); (2) *learning* (which studies observable behaviour); (3) *cognitive* (which analyzes thought processes); (4) *contextual* (which emphasizes the impact of the historical, social, and cultural context) and (5) *evolutionary/sociobiological* (which considers evolutionary and biological underpinnings of behaviour).

Perspective 1: Psychoanalytic

The **psychoanalytic perspective** views development as shaped by unconscious forces that motivate human behaviour. Sigmund Freud (1856–1939), a Viennese physician, developed psychoanalysis, a therapeutic approach aimed at giving patients insight into unconscious emotional conflicts. Other theorists and practitioners, including Erik H. Erikson, have expanded and modified the psychoanalytic perspective.

Sigmund Freud: Psychosexual Development

Freud (1953, 1964a, 1964b) believed that people are born with biological drives that must be redirected to make it possible to live in society. By asking his patients questions designed

Table 2-1	Five Perspectives on Human Development	

Perspective	Important Theories	Basic Beliefs
Psychoanalytic	Freud's psychosexual theory	Behaviour is controlled by powerful unconscious urges.
	Erikson's psychosocial theory	Personality is influenced by society and develops through a series of crises.
Learning	Behaviourism, or traditional learning theory (Pavlov, Skinner, Watson)	People are responders; the environment controls behaviour.
	Social-learning (social-cognitive) theory (Bandura)	Children learn in a social context by observing and imitating models; person is an active contributor to learning.
Cognitive	Piaget's cognitive-stage theory	Qualitative changes in thought occur between infancy and adolescence. Person is active initiator of development.
	Information-processing theory	Human beings are processors of symbols.
Contextual	Bronfenbrenner's bioecological theory	Development occurs through interaction between a developing person and five surrounding, interlocking contextual systems of influences, from microsystem to chronosystem.
	Vygotsky's socio-cultural theory	Socio-cultural context is central to development.
Evolutionary/ Sociobiological	Bowlby's and Ainsworth's attachment theory	Human beings have the adaptive mechanisms to survive; critical or sensitive periods are stressed; biological and evolutionary bases for behaviour and predisposition toward learning are important.

to summon up long-buried memories, Freud concluded that the sources of emotional disturbances lay in repressed traumatic experiences of early childhood.

Freud proposed three hypothetical parts of the personality—the *id*, the *ego*, and the *superego*—that develop early in life. Newborns are governed by the *id*, the seat of unconscious instinctual drives; it seeks immediate gratification under the *pleasure principle*. When gratification is delayed, as when infants have to wait to be fed, they begin to see themselves as separate from the outside world. The *superego*, which develops at about age 5 or 6, contains the conscience; it incorporates socially approved "shoulds" and "should nots" into the child's own value system. The superego is highly demanding; if its demands are not met, a child may feel guilty and anxious. The *ego*, the conscious self, develops gradually during the first year or so and operates under the *reality principle*. The ego's aim is to find reasonably realistic ways to gratify the *id* that are also acceptable to the *superego*.

Freud proposed that personality forms through unconscious conflicts between the inborn urges of the id and the requirements of civilized life. These conflicts occur in an unvarying sequence of five maturationally based stages of **psychosexual development** (see Table 2-2), in which pleasure shifts from one body zone to another—from the mouth to the anus and then to the genitals. At each stage, the behaviour that is the chief source of gratification (or frustration) changes—from feeding to elimination and eventually to sexual activity.

Freud considered the first three stages—those of the first five or six years of life—crucial for personality development. He suggested that if children receive too little or too much gratification in any of these stages, they are at risk of *fixation*—an arrest in development that can show up in adult personality. Babies whose needs are not met during the *oral stage*, when feeding is the main source of pleasure, may become nail-biters or develop "bitingly" critical personalities. A person who, as a toddler, had too-strict toilet training may be fixated at the *anal stage*. Such a person may be obsessively clean, rigidly tied to schedules and routines, or defiantly messy.

According to Freud, a key event in psychosexual development occurs in the *phallic stage* of early childhood, which focuses on the genitals. Children discover the physical differences between males and females. Boys develop sexual desire for their mothers and have aggressive urges toward their fathers, whom they both fear and regard as rivals. (Freud called this development the *Oedipus complex*.) Girls, according to Freud, experience *penis envy*, the repressed wish to possess a penis and the power it stands for.

The Viennese physician Sigmund Freud developed an influential but controversial theory of childhood emotional development.

psychosexual development In Freudian theory, an unvarying sequence of stages of personality development during infancy, childhood, and adolescence, in which gratification shifts from the mouth to the anus and then to the genitals

Table 2-1 *(continued)*

Technique Used	Stage-Oriented	Causal Emphasis	Active or Passive Individual
Clinical observation	Yes	Innate factors modified by experience	Passive
Clinical observation	Yes	Interaction of innate and experiential factors	Active
Rigorous scientific (experimental) procedures	No	Experience	Passive
Rigorous scientific (experimental) procedures	No	Experienced modified by innate factors	Active and passive
Flexible interviews; meticulous observation	Yes	Interaction of innate and experiential factors	Active
Laboratory research; technological monitoring of physiologic responses	No	Interaction of innate and experiential factors	Active and passive
Naturalistic and laboratory observation	No	Interaction of innate and experiential factors	Active or passive (theorists vary)
Naturalistic observation and analysis	No	Interaction of innate and experiential factors	Active
Cross-cultural research; observation of child interacting with more competent person	No	Experience	Active

Table 2-2	Developmental Stages According to Various Theories		
Psychosexual Stages (Freud)	**Psychosocial Stages (Erikson)**	**Cognitive Stages (Piaget)**
Oral (birth to 12–18 months). Baby's chief source of pleasure involves mouth-oriented activities (sucking and feeding).	*Basic trust versus mistrust (birth to 12–18 months)*. Baby develops sense of whether world is a good and safe place. Virtue: hope.	*Sensorimotor (birth to 2 years)*. Infant gradually becomes able to organize activities in relation to the environment through sensory and motor activity.
Anal (12–18 months to 3 years). Child derives sensual gratification from withholding and expelling feces. Zone of gratification is anal region, and toilet training is important activity.	*Autonomy versus shame and doubt (12–18 months to 3 years)*. Child develops a balance of independence and self-sufficiency over shame and doubt. Virtue: will.	*Pre-operational (2 to 7 years)*. Child develops a representational system and uses symbols to represent people, places, and events. Language and imaginative play are important manifestations of this stage. Thinking is still not logical.
Phallic (3 to 6 years). Child becomes attached to parent of the other sex and later identifies with same-sex parent. Superego develops. Zone of gratification shifts to genital region.	*Initiative versus guilt (3 to 6 years)*. Child develops initiative when trying out new activities and is not overwhelmed by guilt. Virtue: purpose.	
Latency (6 years to puberty). Time of relative calm between more turbulent stages.	*Industry versus inferiority (6 years to puberty)*. Child must learn skills of the culture or face feelings of incompetence. Virtue: skill.	*Concrete operations (7 to 11 years)*. Child can solve problems logically if they are focused on the here and now, but cannot think abstractly.
Genital (puberty through adulthood). Re-emergence of sexual impulses of phallic stage, channelled into mature adult sexuality.	*Identity versus identity confusion (puberty to young adulthood)*. Adolescent must determine own sense of self ("Who am I?") or experience confusion about roles. Virtue: fidelity.	*Formal operations (11 years through adulthood)*. Person can think abstractly, deal with hypothetical situations, and think about possibilities.
	Intimacy versus isolation (young adulthood). Person seeks to make commitments to others; if unsuccessful, may suffer from isolation and self-absorption. Virtue: love.	
	Generativity versus stagnation (middle adulthood). Mature adult is concerned with establishing and guiding the next generation or else feels personal impoverishment. Virtue: care.	
	Integrity versus despair (late adulthood). Elderly person achieves acceptance of own life, allowing acceptance of death, or else despairs over inability to relive life. Virtue: wisdom.	

Note: All ages are approximate.

Children eventually resolve their anxiety over these feelings by identifying with the same-sex parent and move into the *latency stage* of middle childhood, a period of relative emotional calm and intellectual and social exploration. They redirect their sexual energies into other pursuits, such as schoolwork, skill-building, relationships, and hobbies.

The *genital stage,* the final one, lasts throughout adulthood. The sexual urges repressed during latency now resurface to flow in socially approved channels, which Freud defined as heterosexual relations with persons outside the family of origin.

Freud's theory made historic contributions and inspired a whole generation of followers, some of whom took psychoanalytic theory in new directions. Some of Freud's ideas, such as his notions of the Oedipus crisis and penis envy, now are widely considered obsolete. Others, such as the concepts of the id and superego, cannot be empirically tested. Although Freud opened our eyes to the importance of early sexual urges, many psychoanalysts today reject his narrow emphasis on sexual and aggressive drives to the exclusion of other motives. Nevertheless, several of his central themes have "stood the test of time" (Westen, 1998, p. 334). Freud made us aware of the importance of unconscious thoughts, feelings, and motivations; the role of childhood experiences in forming personality; the ambivalence of emotional responses, especially responses to parents; the role of mental representations of the self and others in the establishment of intimate relationships; and the path of normal development from an immature, dependent state to a mature, interdependent one. In all these ways, Freud left an indelible mark on psychoanalysis and developmental psychology (Westen, 1998).

We need to remember that Freud's theory grew out of his place in history and in society. Freud based his theories about normal development, not on a population of average children, but on a clientele of upper-middle-class adults, mostly women, in therapy. His concentration on the influences of sexual urges and early experience did not take into account other, and later, influences on personality—including the influences of society and culture, which many heirs to the Freudian tradition, such as Erik Erikson, stress.

Erik Erikson: Psychosocial Development

Erik Erikson (1902–1994), a German-born psychoanalyst who originally was part of Freud's circle in Vienna, modified and extended Freudian theory by emphasizing the influence of society on the developing personality. Whereas Freud maintained that early childhood experiences permanently shape personality, Erikson contended that ego development is lifelong.

Erikson's (1950, 1982; Erikson, Erikson, & Kivnick, 1986) theory of **psychosocial development** covers eight stages across the lifespan (refer to Table 2-2), which we will discuss in the appropriate chapters. Each stage involves what Erikson originally called a "crisis" in personality—a major psychosocial theme that is particularly important at that time but will remain an issue to some degree throughout the rest of life. These issues, which emerge according to a maturational timetable, must be satisfactorily resolved for healthy ego development. Erikson later dropped the term "crisis" and referred instead to conflicting or competing tendencies.

Each stage requires the balancing of a positive trait and a corresponding negative one. Although the positive quality should predominate, some degree of the negative is needed as well. The critical theme of infancy, for example, is *basic trust versus basic mistrust*. People need to trust the world and the people in it, but they also need to learn some mistrust to protect themselves from danger. The successful outcome of each stage is the development of a particular "virtue" or strength—in this first stage, the "virtue" of *hope*.

Erikson's theory is important because of its emphasis on social and cultural influences and on development beyond adolescence. He is perhaps most widely known for his concept of the *identity crisis*, which has entered public parlance and has generated considerable research (see Chapter 17).

Perspective 2: Learning

The **learning perspective** maintains that development results from *learning*, a long-lasting change in behaviour based on experience, or adaptation to the environment. Learning theorists are concerned with finding out the objective laws that govern changes in observable behaviour. They see development as continuous (not in stages) and emphasize quantitative change.

Learning theorists have helped to make the study of human development more scientific. Their terms are defined precisely, and their theories can be tested in the laboratory. Two important learning theories are behaviourism and social learning theory.

Learning Theory 1: Behaviourism

Behaviourism is a mechanistic theory, which describes observed behaviour as a predictable response to experience. Although biology sets limits on what people do, behaviourists view the environment as much more influential. They hold that human beings at all ages learn about the world the same way other organisms do: by reacting to conditions, or aspects of their environment, that they find pleasing, painful, or threatening. Behavioural research focuses on *associative learning*, in which a mental link is formed between two events. Two kinds of associative learning are *classical conditioning* and *operant conditioning*.

Classical Conditioning The Russian physiologist Ivan Pavlov (1849–1936) devised experiments in which dogs learned to salivate at the sound of a bell that rang at feeding time.

The psychoanalyst Erik H. Erikson departed from Freudian theory in emphasizing societal, rather than chiefly biological, influences on personality.

psychosocial development In Erikson's eight-stage theory, the socially and culturally influenced process of development of the ego, or self

Checkpoint ✔

Can you . . .

✔ Identify the chief focus of the psychoanalytic perspective?

✔ Name Freud's five stages of development and three parts of the personality?

✔ Tell two ways in which Erikson's theory differs from Freud's, and list its eight stages?

learning perspective View of development that holds that changes in behaviour result from experience, or adaptation to the environment

behaviourism Learning theory that emphasizes the predictable role of environment in causing observable behaviour

classical conditioning Learning based on associating a stimulus that does not ordinarily elicit a particular response with another stimulus that ordinarily does elicit the response

What's your view

- In an experiment with classical conditioning, what standards would you suggest to safeguard participants' rights?

operant conditioning Learning based on reinforcement or punishment

reinforcement In operant conditioning, a stimulus that encourages repetition of a desired behaviour

punishment In operant conditioning, a stimulus that discourages repetition of a behaviour

The American psychologist B. F. Skinner formulated the principles of operant conditioning.

These experiments were the foundation for **classical conditioning,** in which a response (salivation) to a stimulus (the bell) is evoked after repeated association with a stimulus that normally elicits it (food).

The American behaviourist John B. Watson (1878–1958) applied stimulus–response theories to children, claiming that he could mould any infant in any way he chose. In one of the earliest and most famous demonstrations of classical conditioning in human beings (Watson & Rayner, 1920), he taught an 11-month-old baby known as "Little Albert" to fear furry white objects.

In this study, Albert was exposed to a loud noise just as he was about to stroke a furry white rat. The noise frightened him, and he began to cry. After repeated pairings of the rat with the loud noise, Albert whimpered with fear whenever he saw the rat. Although such research would be considered unethical today, the study did show that a baby could be conditioned to fear things he had not been afraid of before.

Critics of such methods sometimes associate conditioning with thought control and manipulation. Actually, as we will discuss in Chapter 7, classical conditioning is a natural form of learning that occurs even without intervention. By learning what events go together, children can anticipate what is going to happen, and this knowledge makes their world a more orderly, predictable place.

Operant Conditioning Baby Terrell lies peacefully in his crib. When he happens to smile, his mother goes over to the crib and plays with him. Later his father does the same thing. As this sequence is repeated, Terrell learns that his behaviour (smiling) can produce a desirable consequence (loving attention from a parent); and so he smiles again to attract his parents' attention. An originally accidental behaviour (smiling) has become a conditioned response.

This kind of learning is called **operant conditioning** because the individual learns from the consequences of "operating" on the environment. Unlike classical conditioning, operant conditioning involves voluntary behaviour, such as Terrell's smiling.

The American psychologist B. F. Skinner (1904–1990), who formulated the principles of operant conditioning, worked primarily with rats and pigeons, but Skinner (1938) maintained that the same principles apply to human beings. He found that an organism will tend to repeat a response that has been reinforced by desirable consequences and will suppress a response that has been punished. Thus, **reinforcement** is the process by which a behaviour is strengthened, increasing the likelihood that the behaviour will be repeated. In Terrell's case, his parents' attention reinforces his smiling. **Punishment** is the process by which a behaviour is weakened, *decreasing* the likelihood of repetition. If Terrell's parents frowned when he smiled, he would be less likely to smile again. Whether a consequence is reinforcing or punishing depends on the person. What is reinforcing for one person may be punishing for another. For example, for a child who likes being alone, being sent to his or her room could be reinforcing rather than punishing.

Reinforcement can be either positive or negative. Positive reinforcement consists of giving a reward, such as food, gold stars, money, or praise—or playing with a baby. Negative reinforcement consists of taking away something the individual does not like (known as an aversive event), such as a loud noise. Negative reinforcement is sometimes confused with punishment. However, they are different. Punishment suppresses a behaviour by bringing on an aversive event (such as spanking a child or giving an electric shock to an animal), or by removing a positive event (such as watching television). When an older baby signals a wet diaper, the removal of the diaper may encourage the child to signal again the next time a diaper is wet.

Reinforcement is most effective when it immediately follows a behaviour. If a response is no longer reinforced, it will eventually be *extinguished,* that is, return to its original (baseline) level. If, after a while, no one reacts to Terrell when he smiles, he may not stop smiling but will do so far less than if his smiling still brought reinforcement.

Behaviour modification, or behaviour therapy, is a form of operant conditioning used to eliminate undesirable behaviour or to instill positive behaviour. Behaviour modification is particularly effective among children with special needs, such as youngsters with mental or emotional disabilities. However, Skinnerian psychology is limited in application because it does not adequately address individual differences and cultural and social influences.

Learning Theory 2: Social Learning (Social Cognitive) Theory

Social learning theory maintains that children learn social behaviours by observing and imitating models. The Canadian-born psychologist Albert Bandura (b. 1925) developed many of the principles of social learning theory, also known as *social cognitive theory,* which today is more influential than behaviourism.

Whereas behaviourists see the environment, acting upon the child, as the chief impetus for development, Bandura (1977, 1989; Bandura & Walters, 1963) suggests that the impetus for development is bi-directional. Bandura called this concept **reciprocal determinism**—the child acts on the world as the world acts on the child.

Classic social learning theory maintains that people learn appropriate social behaviour chiefly by observing and imitating models, that is, by watching other people. This process is called *modelling* or **observational learning.** People initiate or advance their own learning by choosing models to imitate, say, a parent or a popular sports hero. According to this theory, imitation of models is the most important element in how children learn a language, deal with aggression, develop a moral sense, and learn gender-appropriate behaviours. However, observational learning can occur even if the child does not imitate the observed behaviour.

The specific behaviour people imitate depends on what they perceive as valued in their culture. If all the teachers in Carlos' school are women, he probably will not copy their behaviour, which he may consider "unmanly." However, if he meets a male teacher he likes, he may change his mind about the value of teachers as models.

Bandura's (1989) newest version of social learning theory is called *social cognitive theory.* The evolution from one name to the other reflects Bandura's increasing emphasis on cognitive processes as central to development. Cognitive processes are at work as people observe models, learn "chunks" of behaviour, and mentally put the chunks together into complex new behaviour patterns. Rita, for example, imitates the toes-out walk of her dance teacher but models her dance steps after those of Carmen, a slightly more advanced student. Even so, she develops her own style of dancing by putting her observations together into a new pattern.

Through feedback on their behaviour, children gradually form standards for judging their own actions and become more selective in choosing models who exemplify those standards. They also begin to develop a sense of **self-efficacy,** confidence in their ability to succeed.

Perspective 3: Cognitive

The **cognitive perspective** focuses on thought processes and the behaviour that reflects those processes. This perspective encompasses both organismic and mechanistically influenced theories. It includes Piaget's **cognitive-stage theory** and Vygotsky's socio-cultural theory of cognitive development. It also includes the information-processing approach and neo-Piagetian theories, which combine elements of information-processing and Piagetian theory.

Jean Piaget's Cognitive-Stage Theory

Our understanding of how children think owes a great deal to the work of the Swiss theoretician Jean Piaget (1896-1980). Piaget's cognitive-stage theory was the forerunner of today's "cognitive revolution" with its emphasis on mental processes. Piaget, a biologist and philosopher by training, viewed development organismically, as the product of children's efforts to understand and act on their world.

As a young man studying in Paris, Piaget set out to standardize the tests Alfred Binet had developed to assess the intelligence of French schoolchildren. Piaget became intrigued by the children's wrong answers, finding in them clues to their thought processes. Piaget's *clinical method* combined observation with flexible questioning. To find out how children think, Piaget followed up their answers with more questions, and he designed tasks to test his tentative conclusions. In this way he discovered that a typical 4-year-old believes that pennies or flowers are more numerous when arranged in a line than when heaped or piled up. From his observations of his own and other children, Piaget created a comprehensive theory of cognitive development.

social learning theory Theory that behaviours are learned by observing and imitating models; also called *social cognitive theory*

reciprocal determinism Bandura's concept that behaviour is determined bi-directionally, by the child and the environment acting on each other

Checkpoint ✔

Can you . . .

✔ Identify the chief concerns, strengths, and weaknesses of the learning perspective?

✔ Tell how classical conditioning and operant conditioning differ?

✔ Distinguish among positive reinforcement, negative reinforcement, and punishment?

✔ Compare behaviourism and social learning (social cognitive) theory?

observational learning Learning through watching the behaviour of others

self-efficacy Sense of one's own capability to master challenges and achieve goals

cognitive perspective View that thought processes are central to development

cognitive-stage theory Piaget's theory that children's cognitive development advances in a series of four stages involving qualitatively distinct types of mental operations

According to social learning theory, children learn by imitating the behaviour of adult models—such as this grandfather mowing the lawn.

The Swiss psychologist Jean Piaget studied children's cognitive development by observing and talking with his own youngsters and others.

organization Piaget's term for integration of knowledge into systems

schemes Piaget's term for organized patterns of behaviour used in different situations

adaptation Piaget's term for adjustment to new information about the environment

assimilation Piaget's term for incorporation of new information into an existing cognitive structure

accommodation Piaget's term for changes in a cognitive structure to include new information

equilibration Piaget's term for the tendency to seek a stable balance among cognitive elements

Piaget suggested that cognitive development begins with an inborn ability to adapt to the environment. By rooting for a nipple, feeling a pebble, or exploring the boundaries of a room, young children develop a more accurate picture of their surroundings and greater competence in dealing with them.

Piaget described cognitive development as occurring in four qualitatively different stages (listed in Table 2-2 and discussed in detail in later chapters), which represent universal patterns of development. At each stage a child's mind develops a new way of operating. From infancy through adolescence, mental operations evolve from learning based on simple sensory and motor activity to logical, abstract thought. This cognitive growth occurs through three interrelated processes: *organization, adaptation,* and *equilibration.*

Organization is the tendency to create increasingly complex cognitive structures: systems of knowledge or ways of thinking that incorporate more and more accurate images of reality. These structures, called **schemes,** are organized patterns of behaviour that a person uses to think about and act in a situation. Take sucking, for example. As children acquire more information, their schemes become more and more complex. An infant has a simple scheme for sucking, but soon develops varied schemes for how to suck at the breast, a bottle, or a thumb.

Adaptation is Piaget's term for how children handle new information in light of what they already know. Adaptation involves two steps: (1) **assimilation,** taking in new information and incorporating it into existing cognitive structures, and (2) **accommodation,** modifying one's cognitive structures to include the new information.

Equilibration—a constant striving for a stable balance, or equilibrium—dictates a shift from assimilation to accommodation. When children cannot handle new experiences within their existing cognitive structures, they experience an uncomfortable state of disequilibrium. By organizing new mental patterns that integrate the new experience, they restore equilibrium. Take sucking, again. A breast- or bottle-fed baby who begins to suck on the spout of a "sippy" cup is showing assimilation—using an old scheme to deal with a new situation. When the infant discovers that sipping from a cup requires different tongue and mouth movements from those used to suck on a breast or bottle, she accommodates by modifying the old scheme. She has adapted her original sucking scheme to deal with a new experience: the cup. Thus, assimilation and accommodation work together to produce equilibrium. Throughout life, the quest for equilibrium is the driving force behind cognitive growth.

Piaget's observations have yielded much information and some surprising insights. Who, for example, would have thought that most children younger than 7 do not realize that a ball of clay that has been rolled into a "worm" before their eyes still contains the same amount of clay? Or that an infant might think that a person who has moved out of sight no longer exists? Piaget has shown us that children's minds are not miniature adult minds. Knowing how children think makes it easier for parents and teachers to understand them and teach them.

Yet Piaget seems to have seriously underestimated the abilities of infants and young children. Some contemporary psychologists question his distinct stages, pointing instead to evidence that cognitive development is more gradual and continuous. Furthermore, as we will see, later research has challenged Piaget's idea that thinking develops in a single, universal progression leading to formal thought. Instead, children's cognitive processes seem closely tied to specific content (what they are thinking *about*) as well as to the context of a problem and the kinds of information and thought a culture considers important (Case & Okamoto, 1996).

Lev Vygotsky's Socio-cultural Theory

The Russian psychologist Lev Semenovich Vygotsky (1896–1934) focused on the social and cultural processes that guide children's cognitive development. Vygotsky's (1978)

socio-cultural theory, like Piaget's theory, stresses children's active engagement with their environment; but, whereas Piaget described the solo mind taking in and interpreting information about the world, Vygotsky saw cognitive growth as a *collaborative* process. Children, said Vygotsky, learn through social interaction. They acquire cognitive skills as part of their induction into a way of life. Shared activities help children internalize their society's modes of thinking and behaving and make those folkways their own. As we discuss in Chapter 10, Vygotsky placed special emphasis on *language*—not merely as an expression of knowledge and thought but as an essential *means* to learning and thinking about the world.

According to Vygotsky, adults or more advanced peers must help direct and organize a child's learning before the child can master and internalize it. This guidance is most effective in helping children cross the **zone of proximal development (ZPD),** the gap between what they are already able to do and what they are not quite ready to accomplish by themselves. (*Proximal* means "nearby.") Children in the ZPD for a particular task can almost, but not quite, perform the task on their own. With the right kind of guidance, however, they can do it successfully. Responsibility for directing and monitoring learning gradually shifts to the child—much as, when an adult teaches a child to float, the adult first supports the child in the water and then lets go gradually as the child's body relaxes into a horizontal position.

Some followers of Vygotsky (Wood, 1980; Wood, Bruner, & Ross, 1976) have applied the metaphor of scaffolds—the temporary platforms on which construction workers stand—to this way of teaching. **Scaffolding** is the temporary support that parents, teachers, or others give a child in doing a task until the child can do it alone.

Vygotsky's theory has important implications for education and for cognitive testing. Tests that focus on a child's potential for learning provide a valuable alternative to standard intelligence tests that assess what the child has already learned; and many children may benefit from the sort of expert guidance Vygotsky prescribes.

The Information-Processing Approach

The **information-processing approach** attempts to explain cognitive development by analyzing the mental processes involved in perceiving and handling information. The information-processing approach is not a single theory but a framework that underlies a wide range of theories and research.

Some information-processing theorists compare the brain to a computer. Sensory impressions go in; behaviour comes out. But what happens in between? How does the brain use sensory perceptions, say, of an unfamiliar face to recognize that face again?

Information-processing researchers *infer* what goes on between a stimulus and a response. For example, they may ask a person to recall a list of words and then observe any difference in performance if the person repeats the list over and over before being asked to recall the words. Through such studies, some researchers have developed *computational models* or flow charts that analyze the specific steps children go through in gathering, storing, retrieving, and using information.

Despite the use of the "passive" computer model, information-processing theorists, like Piaget, see people as actively thinking about their world. Unlike Piaget, these theorists generally do *not* propose stages of development. Instead, they view development as continuous. They note age-related increases in the speed, complexity, and efficiency of mental processing and in the amount and variety of material that can be stored in memory. Brain imaging research, discussed later in this chapter, supports important aspects of information-processing models, such as the existence of separate physical structures to handle conscious and unconscious memory (Schacter, 1999; Yingling, 2001).

The information-processing approach has practical applications. It enables researchers to estimate an infant's later intelligence from the efficiency of his or her sensory perception and processing. It enables parents and teachers to help children learn by making them more aware of their own mental processes and of strategies to enhance them. Psychologists use information-processing models to test, diagnose, and treat learning problems (R. M. Thomas, 1996; Williams, 2001).

According to the Russian psychologist Lev Semenovich Vygotsky, children learn through social interaction.

socio-cultural theory Vygotsky's theory of how contextual factors affect children's development

zone of proximal development (ZPD) Vygotsky's term for the difference between what a child can do alone and with help

scaffolding Temporary support to help a child master a task

information-processing approach Approach to the study of cognitive development by observing and analyzing the mental processes involved in perceiving and handling information

Checkpoint

Can you . . .

✔ Contrast Piaget's assumptions and methods with those of classical learning theory?

✔ List three interrelated principles that bring about cognitive growth, according to Piaget, and give an example of each?

✔ Explain how Vygotsky's theory differs from Piaget's?

✔ Tell how Vygotsky's theory applies to educational teaching and testing?

contextual perspective View of development that sees the individual as inseparable from the social context

bioecological theory Bronfenbrenner's approach to understanding processes and contexts of development

microsystem Bronfenbrenner's term for a setting in which a child interacts with others every day, face to face

mesosystem Bronfenbrenner's term for linkages of two or more microsystems

exosystem Bronfenbrenner's term for linkages between two or more settings, one of which does not contain the child

Neo-Piagetian Theories

Since the 1980s, some developmental psychologists have sought to integrate elements of Piaget's theory with the information-processing approach. Instead of describing a single, general system of increasingly logical mental operations, these neo-Piagetian theorists focus on *specific* concepts, strategies, and skills. They suggest that children develop cognitively by becoming more efficient at processing information. Because of its emphasis on efficiency of processing, the neo-Piagetian approach helps account for individual differences in cognitive ability and for uneven development in various domains (Case, 1985, 1992).

Perspective 4: Contextual

From the **contextual perspective.** development can be understood only in its social context. Contextualists see the individual, not as a separate entity interacting with the environment, but as an inseparable part of it. Vygotsky's socio-cultural theory, which we discussed as part of the cognitive perspective, can also be classified as contextual.

Urie Bronfenbrenner's Bioecological Theory

The American psychologist Urie Bronfenbrenner's (1979, 1986, 1994; Bronfenbrenner & Morris, 1998) **bioecological theory** describes the range of interacting influences that affect a developing child. Every biological organism develops within ecological systems that support or stifle its growth. Just as we need to understand the ecology of the ocean or the forest if we wish to understand the development of a fish or a tree, we need to understand the ecology of the human environment if we wish to understand how children develop.

According to Bronfenbrenner, development occurs through regular, active, two-way interactions between a developing child and the immediate, everyday environment—processes that are affected by more remote contexts of which the child may not even be aware. To understand these processes, we must study the multiple contexts in which they occur. These contexts begin with the home, classroom, and neighbourhood; connect outward to societal institutions, such as educational and transportation systems; and finally encompass cultural and historical patterns that affect the family, the school, and virtually everything else in a person's life. By highlighting the interrelated contexts of, and influences on, development, Bronfenbrenner's theory helps us understand the complex processes that underlie such diverse phenomena as academic achievement and anti-social behaviour.

Bronfenbrenner identified five interlocking contextual systems, from the most intimate to the broadest: the *microsystem, mesosystem, exosystem, macrosystem,* and *chronosystem.* The first four systems are like hollow cylinders that fit inside one another, encasing the developing person. The fifth, the chronosystem, adds the dimension of time. Figure 2-2 shows what we would see if we sliced the nested cylinders across the middle. Keep in mind that the boundaries between the systems are fluid; although we separate the various levels of influence for purposes of illustration, in reality they continually interact.

The **microsystem** is a pattern of activities, roles, and personal, face-to-face relationships within a setting, such as the home, school, workplace, or neighbourhood, in which a person functions on a firsthand, day-to-day basis. Bidirectional influences flow back and forth. How, for example, does a new baby affect the parents' lives? How do their feelings and attitudes affect the baby? It is through the microsystem that more distant influences from the outer circles reach the developing child.

The **mesosystem** is the interaction of two or more microsystems that contain the developing child. It may include linkages between home and school (such as parent–teacher conferences) or between the family and the peer group. Attention to mesosystems can alert us to differences in the ways the same person acts in different settings. For example, a child who can satisfactorily complete a school assignment at home may become tongue-tied when asked a question about the assignment in class.

The **exosystem,** like a mesosystem, consists of linkages between two or more settings. However, in an exosystem, unlike a mesosystem, at least one of these settings—such as parents' workplaces and parents' social networks—does not contain the developing child

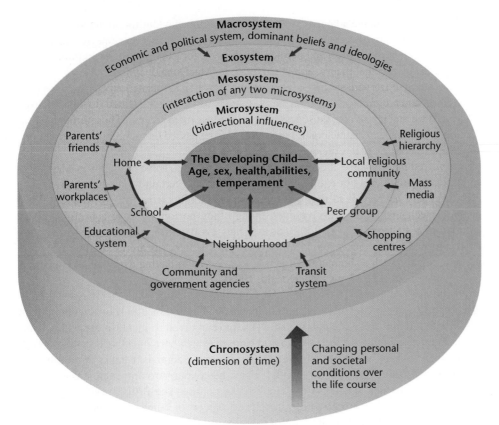

Figure 2-2

Bronfenbrenner's bioecological theory. Concentric circles show five levels of environmental influence, from the most intimate environment (innermost circle) to the broadest—all within the dimension of time. The circles form a set of nested influences, like egg-shaped containers that fit inside one another, encasing the developing person. The figure shows what we would see if we sliced the nested "containers" across the middle and looked inside. Keep in mind that the boundaries are fluid, and the containers are interconnected.

Source: Adapted from Cole & Cole, 1989

and thus affects the child only indirectly. A woman whose employer encourages breast-feeding by providing pumping and milk-storage facilities may be more likely to continue nursing her baby.

The **macrosystem** consists of overall cultural patterns, like those Margaret Mead studied: dominant values, beliefs, customs, and economic and social systems of a culture or subculture, which filter down in countless ways to individuals' daily lives. For example, whether a child grows up in a nuclear or extended-family household is strongly influenced by a culture's macrosystem.

The **chronosystem** adds the dimension of time: the degree of stability or change in a child's world. This can include changes in family composition, place of residence, or parents' employment, as well as larger events such as wars, economic cycles, and waves of migration. Changes in family patterns (such as the increase in numbers of working mothers in industrial societies and the decline of the extended-family household in developing countries) are chronosystem factors.

According to Bronfenbrenner, a person is not merely an outcome of development, but also a shaper of it. People affect their own development through their biological and psychological characteristics, talents and skills, disabilities, and temperament.

A major contribution of the contextual perspective has been its emphasis on the social component in development. Research attention has shifted from the individual to larger, interactional units—parent and child, sibling and sibling, the entire family, the neighbourhood, and broader societal institutions. The contextual perspective also reminds us that the development of children in one culture or one group within a culture (such as white, middle-class Canadians) may not be an appropriate norm for children in other societies or cultural groups.

Perspective 5: Evolutionary/Sociobiological

The **evolutionary/sociobiological perspective** proposed by E. O. Wilson (1975) focuses on evolutionary and biological bases of behaviour. Influenced by Darwin's theory of evolution, it draws on findings of anthropology, ecology, genetics, ethology, and evolutionary

macrosystem Bronfenbrenner's term for overall cultural patterns

chronosystem Bronfenbrenner's term for effects of time on other developmental systems

Checkpoint ✔

Can you . . .

✔ State the chief assumptions of the contextual perspective?

✔ Name and differentiate Bronfenbrenner's five systems of contextual influence?

evolutionary/sociobiological perspective View of human development that focuses on evolutionary and biological bases of social behaviour

psychology to explain the adaptive, or survival, value of behaviour for an individual or species. The evolutionary/sociobiological approach is not necessarily a separate theoretical perspective; it both borrows from and predicts findings of, for example, social learning theory, cognitive-developmental theory, and contextualism (MacDonald, 1988, 1998).

According to Darwin, species have developed through the related processes of *survival of the fittest* and *natural selection*. Species with traits better adapted (fitted) to their environments survive and reproduce; those less adapted (or less fitted) do not. Thus, through reproduction, more adaptive characteristics are *selected* to be passed on to future generations, and less adaptive characteristics die out.

"Evolved mechanisms" are behaviours that developed to solve problems in adapting to an earlier environment. For example, sudden aversion to certain foods during pregnancy may originally have evolved to protect the vulnerable fetus from toxic substances. Such evolved mechanisms may survive even though they no longer serve a useful purpose (Bjorklund & Pellegrini, 2000, 2002), or they may evolve further in response to changing environmental conditions. Although most evolved mechanisms are tailored to a specific problem, others, such as human intelligence, are viewed as having evolved to help people face a wide range of problems (MacDonald, 1998).

Ethology is the study of the distinctive adaptive behaviours of animal species. Ethologists suggest that, for each species, certain innate behaviours, such as squirrels' burying of nuts in the fall and spiders' spinning of webs, have evolved to increase the odds of survival. Another example, studied by Konrad Lorenz, is newborn ducklings' instinct to follow their mother (refer back to Chapter 1). By observing animals, usually in their natural surroundings, ethologists seek to identify which behaviours are universal and which are specific to a particular species or are modified by culture. The British psychologist John Bowlby (1969) applied ethological principles to aspects of human development. For example, he viewed infants' attachment to a caregiver as a mechanism that evolved to protect them from predators.

Evolutionary psychology applies Darwinian principles to individual behaviour. According to this theory, people unconsciously strive not only for personal survival, but also to perpetuate their genetic legacy. They do so by seeking to maximize their chances of having offspring who will inherit their characteristics and survive to reproduce. However, an evolutionary perspective does *not* necessarily reduce human behaviour entirely to the effects of genes seeking to reproduce themselves. It also places great weight on the environment to which a person must adapt. A *developmental systems approach* views human development as the outcome of a dynamic process of bi-directional interaction between person and environment (Bjorklund & Pellegrini, 2000; Lickliter & Honeycutt, 2003; Nelson, 2005; see Chapter 3).

Evolutionary *developmental* psychologists apply evolutionary principles to child development. They study such topics as parenting strategies, gender differences in play, and peer relations, and they identify behaviours that are adaptive at different ages (see Box 2-1).

How Theory and Research Work Together

No one theory of human development is universally accepted, and no single theoretical perspective explains all facets of development. Lacking a widely accepted "grand" theory (such as those of Freud and Piaget), the trend today is toward smaller, more limited "mini-theories" aimed at explaining specific phenomena, such as how poverty influences family relations.

As we mentioned at the beginning of this chapter, theories of child development often grow out of, and are tested by, research. Although most researchers are eclectic, drawing from a variety of theoretical perspectives, research questions and methods often reflect a researcher's particular orientation. For example, in trying to understand how a child develops a sense of right and wrong, a behaviourist would examine what kinds of behaviour the parents have punished or praised. A social learning theorist would focus on imitation of moral examples, possibly in stories or in movies. An information-processing researcher might do a task analysis to identify the steps a child goes through in determining the range of moral options available and deciding which to pursue.

ethology Study of distinctive adaptive behaviours of species of animals that have evolved to increase survival of the species

evolutionary psychology Application of Darwinian principles of natural selection and survival of the fittest to individual behaviour

Checkpoint

Can you . . .

✔ Identify the chief focus of the evolutionary/sociobiological perspective, and explain how Darwin's theory of evolution underlies this perspective?

✔ Tell what kinds of topics ethologists and evolutionary psychologists study?

What's your view

• Which theoretical perspective would be most useful for (a) a parent trying to get a child to say "please," (b) a teacher interested in stimulating critical thinking, (c) a researcher studying siblings' imitation of one another?

Box 2-1 *The Adaptive Value of Immaturity*

In comparison with other animals and even with other primates, human beings take a long time to grow up. Chimpanzees reach reproductive maturity in about eight years, rhesus monkeys in about four years, and lemurs in only two years or so. Human beings, by contrast, do not reach full growth and physical maturity until the early teenage years and, at least in modern industrialized societies, typically reach cognitive and psychosocial maturity even later. During much of that time, they remain largely dependent on their parents or other caregivers.

From the point of view of evolutionary theory, this prolonged period of immaturity may be essential to survival and well-being. Human beings are social animals, and a long, protective childhood may serve as essential preparation for the social problem-solving skills needed in adulthood. Human communities and cultures are highly complex, and there is much to learn in order to "know the ropes." Thus, childhood may be an evolved mechanism that allows for the development of social competency.

Human intelligence, too, may be an evolved characteristic. The fossil record indicates that during the past 4 million years, the human brain has tripled in volume. At the same time, its period of development has nearly doubled. The human brain, despite its rapid prenatal growth, is much less fully developed at birth than the brains of other primates; if the fetus's brain attained full human size before birth, its head would be too big to go through the birth canal. Instead, the human brain continues to grow in size and complexity throughout childhood, eventually far surpassing the brains of our simian cousins in the capacities for language and thought. The human brain's slower development gives it greater flexibility, or *plasticity,* as not all connections are "hard wired" at an early age. One theorist has called this plasticity "the human species's greatest adaptive advantage" (Bjorklund, 1997, p. 157).

The extended period of immaturity and dependency during infancy and childhood allows children to spend much of their time in play; and, as Piaget maintained, it is largely through play that cognitive development occurs. Play also enables children to develop motor skills and experiment with social roles. It is a vehicle for creative imagination and intellectual curiosity, the hallmarks of the human spirit.

Some aspects of immaturity serve immediate adaptive purposes. For example, some primitive reflexes, such as rooting for the nipple, which are protective for newborns, disappear when no longer needed. Research on animals suggests that the immaturity of early sensory and motor functioning may protect infants from overstimulation. By limiting the amount of information they have to deal with, it may help them focus on experiences essential to survival, such as feeding and attachment to the mother. Later, as mentioned in Box 1-2 in Chapter 1, infants' limited memory capacity may simplify the processing of linguistic sounds and facilitate early language learning.

Limitations on the way young children think also may have adaptive value. For example, young children are unrealistic in assessing their own abilities, believing they can do more than they actually can. This immature self-judgment, by reducing fear of failure, may encourage children to try new things.

All in all, evolutionary theory and research suggest that immaturity is not necessarily equivalent to deficiency and that some attributes of infancy and childhood have persisted because they are appropriate to the tasks of a particular time of life.

What's your view

Can you think of additional examples of the adaptive value of immaturity? Can you think of ways in which immaturity may *not* be adaptive?

Check it out

For more information on this topic, go to **www.brazelton-institute.com/** for the Brazelton Institute at Harvard Medical School. Follow the link *The Brazelton Scale: What Is It?* to learn about the scale. The scale shows how much such immature creatures as human newborns can do in responding to the world. This Web site also offers a preview of the discussion of the Brazelton Scale in Chapter 5. See also **www.mcgrawhill.ca/olc/papalia.**

Source: Bjorklund, 1997; Bjorklund & Pellegrini, 2000, 2002; Flinn & Ward, 2005.

Research Methods

Researchers in child development work within two methodological traditions: *quantitative* and *qualitative.* **Quantitative research** deals with objectively measurable data. Quantitative researchers may study, for example, how much fear or anxiety children feel before surgery, as measured by standardized tests, physiological changes, or statistical analysis. **Qualitative research** involves the interpretation of nonnumerical data, such as the nature or quality of participants' subjective experiences, feelings, or beliefs. Qualitative researchers may study how children describe their emotions before surgery (Morse & Field, 1995).

Quantitative research is based on the **scientific method,** which characterizes most scientific inquiry. Its usual steps are:

- *Identifying a problem* to be studied, often on the basis of a theory or of previous research

quantitative research Research that deals with objectively measurable data

qualitative research Research that involves the interpretation of nonnumerical data, such as subjective experiences, feelings, or beliefs

scientific method System of established principles and processes of scientific inquiry

Guidepost 3

How do developmental scientists study children, and what are the advantages and disadvantages of each research method?

sample Group of participants chosen to represent the entire population under study

random selection Achieving representativeness by allowing each person in a population an equal and independent chance of being chosen.

- *Formulating hypotheses* to be tested by research
- *Collecting data*
- *Analyzing the data* to determine whether or not they support the hypothesis
- *Disseminating findings* so that other observers can check, learn from, analyze, repeat, and build on the results

Qualitative research is more open-ended. Instead of generating hypotheses from previous research, qualitative researchers often gather and examine data to see what hypotheses or theories may emerge. Qualitative research can be a rich source of insights into attitudes and behaviour.

Although most developmental scientists have been trained in quantitative methods, the need for qualitative research is increasingly recognized. The selection of quantitative or qualitative methods depends on a number of factors: the topic for study, how much is already known about it, the researcher's theoretical orientation, and the setting. Quantitative research is often done in controlled laboratory settings. Qualitative research is usually conducted in everyday settings. Each of these two distinct methodologies can provide rich information about child development.

Sampling

To be sure that the results of research are true generally, and not just for specific participants, quantitative researchers need to control who gets into the study. Because studying an entire *population* (a group to whom the findings may apply) is usually too costly and time-consuming, investigators select a **sample,** a smaller group within the population. The sample should adequately represent the population under study that is, it should show relevant characteristics in the same proportions as in the entire population. Otherwise the results cannot properly be generalized, or applied to the population as a whole. To judge how generalizable the findings are likely to be, researchers carefully compare the characteristics of the people in the sample with those of the population as a whole.

Often researchers seek to achieve representativeness through **random selection,** in which each person in a population has an equal and independent chance of being chosen. If we wanted to study the effects of an educational program, one way to select a random sample would be to put all the names of participating children into a large bowl, stir it, and then draw out a certain number of names. A random sample, especially a large one, is likely to represent the population well. Unfortunately, a random sample of a large population is often difficult to obtain. Instead, many studies use samples selected for convenience or accessibility (for example, children born in a particular hospital or attending a particular day care centre). The findings of such studies may not apply to the population as a whole.

In qualitative research, samples tend to be small and need not be random. Participants in this kind of research may be chosen for their ability to communicate the nature of their experience, such as how it feels to go through a particular type of surgery.

Forms of Data Collection

Common ways of gathering data (see Table 2-3) include self-reports (verbal reports by study participants), tests and other behavioural measures, and observation. Depending in part on time and financial constraints, researchers may use one or more of these data collection techniques in any research design. Qualitative research tends to depend heavily on interviews and on observation in natural settings, whereas quantitative research makes use of more structured methods. Currently there is a trend toward increased use of self-reports and observation in combination with more objective measures.

Self-Reports: Diaries, Interviews, Questionnaires

The simplest form of self-report is a diary or log. Adolescents may be asked, for example, to record what they eat each day, or the times when they feel depressed. In studying young children, parental self-reports—diaries, journals, interviews, or questionnaires—are commonly used, often together with other methods, such as videotaping or recording. Parents

Table 2-3	Characteristics of Major Methods of Data Collection		
Type	**Main Characteristics**	**Advantages**	**Disadvantages**
Self-report: diary, interview, or questionnaire	Participants are asked about some aspect of their lives; questioning may be highly structured or more flexible.	Can provide firsthand information about a person's life, attitudes, or opinions.	Participants may not remember information accurately or may distort responses in a socially desirable way; how question is asked or by whom may affect answer.
Behavioural and performance measures	Participants are tested on abilities, skills, knowledge, competencies, or physical responses.	Provides objectively measurable information; avoids subjective distortions.	Cannot measure attitudes or other non-behavioural phenomena; results may be affected by extraneous factors.
Naturalistic observation	People are observed in their normal setting, with no attempt to manipulate behaviour.	Provides good description of behaviour; does not subject people to unnatural settings that may distort behaviour.	Lack of control; observer bias.
Laboratory observation	Participants are observed in the laboratory, with no attempt to manipulate behaviour.	Provides good descriptions; greater control than naturalistic observation, since all participants are observed under same conditions.	Observer bias; controlled situation can be artificial.

may be videotaped playing with their babies and then may be shown the tapes and asked to explain why they reacted as they did.

In a face-to-face or telephone interview, researchers ask questions about attitudes, opinions, or behaviour. Interviews may cover such topics as parent–child relationships, sexual activities, and occupational goals. In a structured interview, each participant is asked the same set of questions. An open-ended interview is more flexible; as in Piaget's clinical method, the interviewer can vary the topics and order of questions and can ask follow-up questions based on the responses. To reach more people and protect their privacy, researchers sometimes distribute a printed questionnaire, which participants fill out and return.

By questioning a large number of people, investigators get a broad picture—at least of what the respondents say they believe or do or did. However, people willing to participate in interviews or fill out questionnaires tend to be an unrepresentative sample. Furthermore, heavy reliance on self-reports may be unwise, since people may not have thought about what they feel and think, or they honestly may not know. Some people forget when and how events actually took place, and others consciously or unconsciously distort their replies to fit what is considered socially desirable.

How a question is asked, and by whom, as well as what type of instrument that is used can affect the answer or how the answer is interpreted by the researcher. When questioned about risky or socially disapproved behaviour, such as sexual habits and drug use, respondents may be more candid in responding to a computerized survey than to a paper-and-pencil one (Turner et al., 1998).

Behavioural and Performance Measures

For many kinds of research, investigators use more objective measures of behaviour or performance instead of, or in addition to, self-reports or observation. Tests and other behavioural and neuropsychological measures, including mechanical and electronic devices, may be used to assess abilities, skills, knowledge, competencies, or physiological responses, such as heart rate and brain activity. Although these measures are less subjective than self-reports or personal observation, such factors as fatigue and self-confidence can affect results.

Some written tests, such as intelligence tests, compare performance with that of other test-takers. Such tests can be meaningful and useful only if they are both *valid* (that is, the tests measure the abilities they claim to measure) and *reliable* (that is, the results are reasonably consistent from one time to another). (The validity of intelligence tests is in question, as we discuss in Chapter 13.) To avoid bias, tests must be *standardized*, that is, given and scored by the same methods and criteria for all test-takers.

When measuring a characteristic such as intelligence, it is important to define exactly what is to be measured in a way that other researchers will understand and can comment about the results. For this purpose, research scientists use **operational definitions**—definitions stated solely in terms of the operations or procedures used to produce or measure a phenomenon. Intelligence, for example, can be defined as the ability to achieve a certain score on a test covering logical relationships, memory, and vocabulary recognition. Some people may not agree with this definition, but no one can claim that it is not clear.

For most of the history of psychology, theorists and researchers studied cognitive processes apart from the physical structures of the brain in which these processes occur. Now, sophisticated imaging instruments, such as magnetic resonance imaging (MRI) (see Figure 2-3), magneto-encephalography (MEG) and positron emission tomography (PET), make it possible to see the brain in action. The new field of **cognitive neuroscience** is linking our understanding of cognitive functioning with what happens in the brain (Gazzaniga, 2000; Humphreys, 2002; Posner & DiGirolamo, 2000). *Developmental cognitive neuroscience* focuses on how cognitive growth occurs as the brain interacts with the environment (Johnson, 1999, 2001) and why some children do not develop normally (Posner & DiGirolamo, 2000). This new branch of science may shed light on whether intelligence is general or specialized, what influences readiness for formal learning (Byrnes & Fox, 1998), and why common memory failures occur (Schacter, 1999).

Social cognitive neuroscience is an emerging interdisciplinary field that bridges brain, mind, and behaviour, bringing together data from cognitive neuroscience, social psychology, and the information-processing approach. Social cognitive neuroscientists use brain imaging and studies of people with brain injuries to figure out how neural pathways control such behavioural processes as memory and attention, which in turn influence attitudes and emotions, and to identify the brain systems involved in schizophrenia, anxiety, phobias, and learning disorders (Azar, 2002a; Ochsner & Lieberman, 2001).

Naturalistic and Laboratory Observation

Observation can take two forms: **naturalistic observation** and **laboratory observation.** In naturalistic observation, researchers look at children in real-life settings. The researchers do

---

operational definitions Definitions stated in terms of operations or procedures used to produce or measure a phenomenon

cognitive neuroscience Study of links between neural processes and cognitive abilities

naturalistic observation Research method in which behaviour is studied in natural settings without intervention or manipulation

laboratory observation Research method in which all participants are observed in the same situation, under controlled conditions

Figure 2-3

An image of the brain, produced by magnetic resonance imaging (MRI). A large cylindrical magnet creates a magnetic field around the head. Sensors record magnetic signals from various brain structures, such as nerve tissue, blood vessels, fluid, and bone, each of which has different magnetic properties and thus appears differently in the image. MRI can show a three-dimensional image in great anatomical detail. Functional MRI records changes in brain activity by measuring the amount of blood that travels to specific regions of the brain.

Source: Blakemore & Choudbury, 2006.

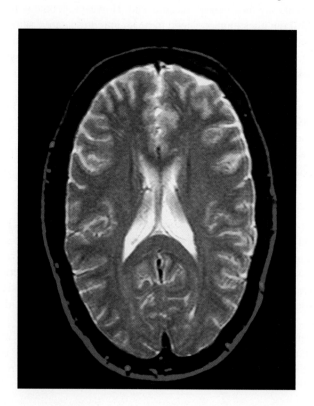

not try to alter behaviour or the environment; they simply record what they see. In laboratory observation, researchers observe and record behaviour in a controlled situation, such as a laboratory. By observing all participants under the same conditions, investigators can more clearly identify any differences in behaviour not attributable to the environment.

Both kinds of observation can provide valuable descriptions of behaviour, but they have limitations. For one, they do not explain why children behave as they do, though they may suggest interpretations. Then, too, an observer's presence can alter behaviour. When children know they are being watched, they may act differently. Finally, there is a risk of observer bias: the researcher's tendency to interpret data to fit expectations, or to emphasize some aspects and minimize others.

During the 1960s, laboratory observation was most commonly used so as to achieve more rigorous control. Now such technological devices as portable videotape recorders and computers, which increase objectivity and enable researchers to analyze moment-by-moment changes in facial expressions or other behaviour (Gottman & Notarius, 2000). Such methods make naturalistic observation more accurate and objective than it otherwise would be.

Basic Research Designs

A research design is a plan for conducting a scientific investigation: what questions are to be answered, how participants are to be selected, how data are to be collected and interpreted, and how valid conclusions can be drawn. Four of the basic designs used in developmental research are case studies, ethnographic studies, correlational studies, and experiments. Each design has advantages and drawbacks, and each is appropriate for certain kinds of research problems (see Table 2-4).

Case Studies

A **case study** is a study of a single case or individual, such as Victor (discussed in the Focus of Chapter 1). A number of theories, notably Freud's, have grown out of clinical case studies, which include careful observation and interpretation of what patients say and do. Case studies also may use behavioural or neuropsychological measures and biographical, autobiographical, or documentary materials.

Case studies offer useful, in-depth information. They can explore sources of behaviour and can test treatments. They also can suggest a need for other research. Another important advantage is flexibility: the researcher is free to explore avenues of inquiry that arise during

case study Study covering a single case or life

Checkpoint ✔

Can you . . .

✔ Explain the purpose of random selection and tell how it can be achieved?

✔ Compare the advantages and disadvantages of various forms of data collection?

✔ Explain how brain research contributes to the understanding of cognitive processes and social behaviours and attitudes?

Table 2-4	Basic Research Designs		
Type	**Main Characteristics**	**Advantages**	**Disadvantages**
Case study	Study of single individual in depth.	Flexibility; provides detailed picture of one person's behaviour and development; can generate hypotheses.	May not generalize to others; conclusions not directly testable; cannot establish cause and effect.
Ethnographic study	In-depth study of a culture or subculture.	Can help overcome culturally based biases in theory and research; can test universality of developmental phenomena.	Subject to observer bias.
Correlational study	Attempt to find positive or negative relationship between variables.	Allows prediction of one variable on basis of another; can suggest hypotheses about causal relationships.	Cannot establish cause and effect.
Experiment	Controlled procedure in which an experimenter controls the independent variable to determine its effect on the dependent variable; may be conducted in the laboratory or field.	Establishes cause-and-effect relationships; highly controlled procedure that can be repeated by another investigator. Degree of control is greatest in the laboratory experiment.	Findings, especially when derived from laboratory experiments, may not generalize to situations outside the laboratory.

the course of the study. However, case studies have shortcomings. From studying Victor, for instance, we learn much about the development of a single child, but not how the information applies to children in general. Furthermore, case studies cannot explain behaviour with certainty, because there is no way to test their conclusions. Even though it seems reasonable that Victor's severely deprived environment caused or contributed to his language deficiency, it is impossible to know whether he would have developed normally with a normal upbringing.

Ethnographic Studies

ethnographic study In-depth study of a culture, which uses a combination of methods including participant observation

participant observation Research method in which the observer lives with the people or participates in the activity being observed

An **ethnographic study** seeks to describe the pattern of relationships, customs, beliefs, technology, arts, and traditions that make up a society's way of life. Ethnographic research can be qualitative, quantitative, or both. It uses a combination of methods, including participant observation. **Participant observation** is a form of naturalistic observation in which researchers live or participate in the societies or groups they observe, as Margaret Mead (1928, 1930, 1935) did, often for long periods of time.

Because of ethnographers' involvement in the events or societies they are observing, their findings are especially open to observer bias. On the positive side, ethnographic research can help overcome cultural biases in theory and research (see Box 2-2). Ethnography demonstrates the error of assuming that principles developed from research in western cultures are universally applicable.

Correlational Studies

correlational study Research design intended to discover whether a statistical relationship between variables exists

A **correlational study** is an attempt to find a *correlation,* or statistical relationship, between *variables,* phenomena that change or vary among people or can be varied for purposes of research. Correlations are expressed in terms of direction (positive or negative) and magnitude (degree). Two variables that are related *positively* increase or decrease together. A positive, or direct, correlation between televised violence and aggressiveness would exist if children who watch more violent television tend to fight more than children who watch less violent television. Two variables have a *negative,* or inverse, correlation if, as one increases, the other decreases. Studies show a negative correlation between amount of schooling and the risk of developing dementia (mental deterioration) due to Alzheimer's disease in old age. In other words, the less education, the more dementia (Katzman, 1993).

Correlations are reported as numbers ranging from -1.0 (a perfect negative relationship) to $+1.0$ (a perfect positive relationship). Perfect correlations are rare. The closer a correlation comes to -1.0 or $+1.0$, the stronger the relationship, either positive or negative. A correlation of zero means that the variables have no relationship (see Figure 2-4).

Correlations enable us to predict one variable on the basis of another. On the basis of a positive correlation between watching televised violence and aggression, we can predict that children who watch violent shows are more likely to get into fights than children who do *not* watch such shows. The greater the magnitude of the correlation between two variables, the greater the ability to predict one from the other.

Although strong correlations may suggest possible causes, these are merely hypotheses that need to be examined very critically. We cannot be sure from a positive correlation between televised violence and aggressiveness that watching televised violence causes aggressive play; we can conclude only that the two variables are related. It is possible that the causation goes the other way: aggressive play may lead children to watch more violent programs. Or a third variable—perhaps an inborn predisposition toward aggressiveness, or living in a more violent environment—may cause a child both to watch violent programs and to act aggressively. Similarly, we cannot be sure that schooling protects

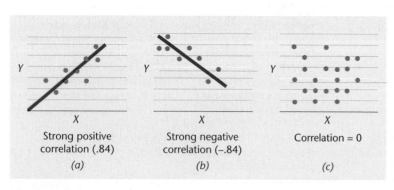

Figure 2-4

Correlational studies may find positive or negative correlations or no correlation. In a positive, or direct, correlation (a), data plotted on a graph cluster around a line showing that one variable (X) increases as the other variable (Y) increases. In a negative, or inverse, correlation (b), one variable (X) increases as the other variable (Y) decreases. No correlation, or a zero correlation (c), exists when increases and decreases in two variables show no consistent relationship (that is, data plotted on a graph show no pattern).

Box 2-2 *Purposes of Cross-cultural Research*

When David, an American child, was asked to identify the missing detail in a picture of a face with no mouth, he said, "The mouth." But Ari, an Asian immigrant child of the same age in Israel, said that the *body* was missing. Since art in his culture does not present a head as a complete picture, he thought the absence of a body was more important than the omission of "a mere detail like the mouth" (Anastasi, 1988, p. 360).

By looking at children from different cultural groups, researchers can learn in what ways development is universal (and thus intrinsic to the human condition) and in what ways it is culturally determined. For example, children everywhere learn to speak in the same sequence, advancing from cooing and babbling to single words and then to simple combinations of words. The words vary from culture to culture, but around the world toddlers put them together to form sentences similar in structure. Such findings suggest that the capacity for learning language is universal and inborn.

On the other hand, culture can exert a surprisingly large influence on early motor development. African babies, whose parents often prop them in a sitting position and bounce them on their feet, tend to sit and walk earlier than U.S. babies (Rogoff & Morelli, 1989).

The society in which children grow up influences the skills they learn and the kinds of friendships they form. However, even though Canadian culture in general is more independent than Chinese cultures, Canadian individuals are as connected to their close friends as are Chinese individuals (Benjamin, Schneider, Greenman, & Hum, 2001; Li, 2002).

One important reason to conduct research among different cultural groups is to recognize biases in traditional North American and European theories and research that often go unquestioned until they are shown to be a product of cultural influences. For example, it has been assumed that because Chinese cultures are collectivistic shyness-sensitivity is positively correlated with peer acceptance in school settings for Chinese children (Chen, He, De Oliveira, Lo Coco, Zappulla, Kaspar, Schneider, Alvarez Valdivia, Tse, & DeSouza, 2004). However, more recent results show that shyness-sensitivity is not significantly related to peer relationships in Chinese culture (Chen et al., 2004).

Since so much research in child development has focused on industrialized societies, many people have defined typical development in these societies as the norm, or standard of behaviour. Measuring against this "norm" leads to narrow—and often,

wrong—ideas about development. Pushed to its extreme, this belief can cause the development of children in other ethnic and cultural groups to be seen as deviant (Rogoff & Morelli, 1989).

Barriers exist to our understanding of cultural differences, particularly those involving minority subcultures. As with David and Ari in our opening example, a question or task may have different conceptual meanings for different cultural groups. Sometimes the barriers are linguistic. In a study of children's understanding of kinship relations among the Zinacanta people of Chiapas, Mexico (Greenfield & Childs, 1978), instead of asking "How many brothers do you have?" the researchers—knowing that the Zinacantas have separate terms for older and younger siblings—asked, "What is the name of your older brother?" Using the same question across cultures might have obscured, rather than revealed, cultural differences and similarities (Parke, 2004).

There may also be communication problems between tester and testees, especially when they have different first languages and cultural backgrounds (Van de Vijver, 2002; Van de Vijver & Tanzer, 2004). According to Reynolds et al. (1999), most psychologists in North America are white and speak only standard English, so they are unable to communicate accurately with cross-cultural children, to the extent of being intimidating and insensitive to ethnic pronunciation of words on an assessment.

In this book we discuss several influential theories developed from research in societies that do not hold up when tested on people from other cultures—theories about gender roles, abstract thinking, moral reasoning, and other aspects of human development. Throughout this book, we consistently look at children in cultures and subcultures other than the dominant English and French in Canada to show how closely development is tied to society and culture and to add to our understanding of normal development in many settings.

What's your view

Can you think of a situation in which you made an incorrect assumption about a person because you were unfamiliar with her or his cultural background?

Check it out

For more information on this topic, go to **www.mcgrawhill.ca/olc/papalia**.

---

against dementia; it may be that another variable, such as socio-economic status, might explain both lower levels of schooling and higher levels of dementia. The only way to show with certainty that one variable causes another is through a controlled experiment—something that, in studying human beings, is not always possible for practical or ethical reasons.

Experiments

An **experiment** is a controlled procedure in which the experimenter manipulates variables to learn how one affects another. Scientific experiments must be conducted and reported in such a way that another experimenter can *replicate* them, that is, repeat them in exactly the same way with different participants to verify the results and conclusions. Figure 2-5 shows how an experiment might be designed.

experiment Rigorously controlled, replicable procedure in which the researcher manipulates variables to assess the effect of one on the other

Figure 2-5

Design for an experiment. This experiment takes a random sample from the larger population being studied, randomly assigns participants to either the experimental (*E*) or control (*C*) group, and exposes the experimental group to a treatment that is not given to the control group. By comparing the two groups after the experimental group has received the treatment, the researcher can conclude that any difference between them is due to the experimental treatment.

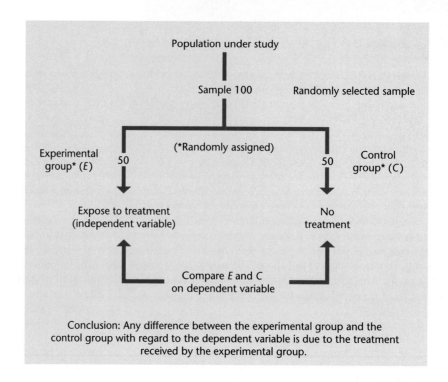

Population under study

Sample 100   Randomly selected sample

(*Randomly assigned)

Experimental group* (*E*)   50   50   Control group* (*C*)

Expose to treatment (independent variable)   No treatment

Compare *E* and *C* on dependent variable

Conclusion: Any difference between the experimental group and the control group with regard to the dependent variable is due to the treatment received by the experimental group.

experimental group In an experiment, the group receiving the treatment under study

control group In an experiment, a group of people similar to the people in the experimental group who do not receive the treatment whose effects are to be measured

Groups and Variables A common way to conduct an experiment is to divide the participants into two kinds of groups. An **experimental group** is composed of people who are to be exposed to the experimental manipulation or *treatment*—the phenomenon the researcher wants to study. Afterward, the effect of the treatment will be measured one or more times to find out what changes, if any, it caused. A **control group** is composed of people who are similar to the experimental group but do not receive the treatment, or receive a different treatment. An experiment may include one or more of each type of group. Or, if the experimenter wants to compare the effects of different treatments (say, of two methods of teaching), the overall sample may be divided into *treatment groups,* each of which receives one of the treatments under study. To ensure objectivity, some experiments, particularly in medical research, use *double-blind* procedures, in which neither participants nor experimenters know who is receiving the treatment and who is instead receiving an inert placebo.

One team of researchers (Whitehurst et al., 1988) wanted to find out what effect dialogic reading, a special method of reading picture books to very young children, might have on their language and vocabulary skills. The researchers compared two groups of middle-class children ages 21 to 35 months. In the experimental group, the parents adopted the new read-aloud method (the treatment), which consisted of encouraging children's active participation and giving frequent, age-based feedback. In the control group, parents simply read aloud as they usually did. After 1 month, the children in the experimental group were 8.5 months ahead of the control group in level of speech and 6 months ahead in vocabulary; 9 months later, the experimental group was still 6 months ahead of the controls. It is fair to conclude, then, that this read-aloud method improved the children's language and vocabulary skills.

In this experiment, the type of reading approach was the independent variable, and the children's language skills were the dependent variable. An **independent variable** is something over which the experimenter has direct control. A **dependent variable** is something that may or may not change as a result of changes in the independent variable; in other words, it depends on the independent variable. In an experiment, a researcher manipulates the independent variable to see how changes in it will affect the dependent variable.

independent variable In an experiment, the condition over which the experimenter has direct control

dependent variable In an experiment, the condition that may or may not change as a result of changes in the independent variable

Random Assignment If an experiment finds a significant difference in the performance of the experimental and control groups, how do we know that the cause was the independent variable, in other words that the conclusion is valid? For example, in the read-aloud experiment, how can we be sure that the reading method and not some other factor (such as intelligence) caused the difference in language development of the two groups? The best way to control for effects of such extraneous factors is **random assignment:** assigning the participants to groups in such a way that each person has an equal chance of being placed in any group. (Random assignment is different from random selection, which determines who gets into the full sample.)

If assignment is random and the sample is large enough, differences in such factors as age, sex, race, IQ, and socio-economic status will be evenly distributed so that the groups initially are as alike as possible in every respect except for the variable to be tested. Otherwise, unintended differences between the groups might confound, or contaminate, the results, and any conclusions drawn from the experiment would have to be viewed with great suspicion. To control for confounds, the experimenter must make sure that everything except the independent variable is held constant during the course of the experiment. For example, in the read-aloud study, parents of the experimental and control groups must spend the same amount of time reading to their children. When participants in an experiment are randomly assigned to treatment groups, and conditions other than the independent variable are carefully controlled, the experimenter can be reasonably confident that a causal relationship has (or has not) been established—that any differences between the reading skills of the two groups are due to the reading method and not some other factor.

Of course, with respect to some variables we might want to study, such as age, gender, and race/ethnicity, random assignment is not possible. We cannot assign Terry to be 5 years old and Brett to be 10, or one to be a boy and the other a girl, or one to be African and the other Asian. When studying such a variable—for example, whether boys or girls are stronger in certain abilities—researchers can strengthen the validity of their conclusions by randomly selecting participants and by trying to make sure that they are statistically equivalent in other ways that might make a difference in the study.

Because race (as discussed in Chapter 1) has no widely agreed meaning, some researchers argue that racial categories should not be used as independent variables in psychological research, for example, on intergroup variations in intelligence. Instead, researchers can substitute meaningful underlying variables that are often masked by racial categories, such as socio-economic status and test-taking skills (Helms, Jernigan, & Mascher, 2005).

Laboratory, Field, and Natural Experiments The control necessary for establishing cause and effect is most easily achieved in *laboratory experiments*. In a laboratory experiment the participants are brought to a special place where they experience conditions manipulated by the experimenter. The experimenter records the participants' reactions to these conditions, perhaps comparing them with their own or other participants' behaviour under different conditions.

random assignment Assignment of participants in an experiment to groups in such a way that each person has an equal chance of being placed in any group

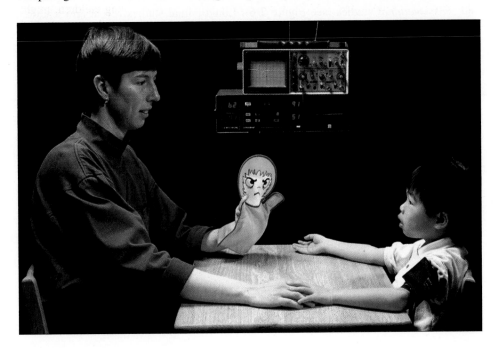

Experiments use strictly controlled procedures that manipulate variables to determine how one affects another. To study emotional resiliency, this research project monitors the heart rate and blood pressure of young children as they explain their feelings in response to a hand puppet's happy or angry face.

However, not all experiments can be readily done in the laboratory. A field experiment is a controlled study conducted in a setting that is part of everyday life, such as a child's home or school. The experiment in which parents tried out a new way of reading aloud was a field experiment.

Laboratory and field experiments differ in two important respects. One is the *degree of control* exerted by the experimenter; the other is the degree to which findings can be *generalized* beyond the study situation. Laboratory experiments can be more rigidly controlled and are thus easier to replicate; however, the results may be less generalizable to real life. Because of the artificiality of the situation, participants may not act as they normally would. Thus, if children who watch violent television shows in the laboratory become more aggressive in that setting, we cannot be sure that children who watch a lot of violent shows at home hit their younger brothers or sisters more often than children who watch fewer such shows.

When, for practical or ethical reasons, it is impossible to conduct a true experiment, a natural experiment may provide a way of studying certain events. A natural experiment compares people who have been accidentally "assigned" to separate groups by circumstances of life—one group of children who were exposed, say, to famine or HIV or superior education, and another group who were not. A natural experiment, despite its name, is actually a correlational study, because controlled manipulation of variables and random assignment to treatment groups are not possible.

One natural experiment dealt with what happened when a casino opened on an Aboriginal reservation in North Carolina, boosting the income of tribal members (Costello, Compton, Keeler, & Angold, 2003). The study found a decline in behavioural disorders among children in these families as compared with children in the same area whose families did not receive increased income. However, being correlational, the study could not prove that the increased income *caused* improvements in mental health.

Controlled experiments have important advantages over other research designs: the ability to establish cause-and-effect relationships and to permit replication. However, such experiments can be too artificial and too narrowly focused. In recent decades, therefore, many researchers have concentrated less on laboratory experimentation or have supplemented it with a wider array of methods.

Developmental Research Designs

The two most common research strategies used to study child development are *longitudinal* and *cross-sectional* studies (see Figure 2-6). Longitudinal studies reveal how children change or stay the same as they grow older; cross-sectional studies show similarities and differences among age groups. Because each of these designs has drawbacks, researchers also have devised *sequential* designs. To directly observe change, *microgenetic* studies can be used.

Checkpoint ✔

Can you . . .

✔ Compare the uses and drawbacks of case studies, ethnographic studies, correlational studies, and experiments?

✔ Explain why only a controlled experiment can establish causal relationships?

✔ Distinguish among laboratory, field, and natural experiments, and tell what kinds of research seem most suitable to each setting?

Figure 2-6

Common developmental designs. In this *cross-sectional* study, 2-, 4-, 6-, and 8-year-olds were tested in 2006 to obtain data about age differences. In the *longitudinal* study, participants were measured in 2006, when they were 2 years old; follow-up testing is done when the children are 4, 6, and 8 to measure age-related changes. (*Note:* Dots indicate times of measurement.)

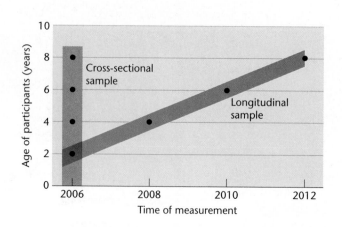

Longitudinal, Cross-Sectional, and Sequential Studies

In a **longitudinal study,** researchers study the same child or children more than once, sometimes years apart. They may measure a single characteristic, such as vocabulary size, height, or aggressiveness, or they may look at several aspects of development to find relationships among them. The National Longitudinal Survey of Children and Youth, designed to assess behavioural and emotional development from birth to young adulthood, measures Canadian children on a variety of characteristics every two years. The study has shown that a child's family socio-economic status (SES) has a large influence on later school achievement (Ryan & Adams, 1998). Over and above individual SES, though, the study also found that average classroom SES influences student achievement: when high SES children are clustered in a classroom, academic achievement improves on average, whereas classrooms with low average SES tend to do worse academically even after taking into account individual children's SES (Frempong & Willms, 2002). SES accounts for much of the variability in vulnerability to behaviour problems in children in lone-parent families (Ross, Roberts, & Scott, 1998; Lippman, Offord, Dooley, & Boyle, 2002), but that the presence of protective factors like having close affectionate relationships or authoritative parenting can reduce the likelihood that a child will develop difficult behaviours (Jenkins & Keating, 1999; Miller, Jenkins, & Keating, 2002).

In a **cross-sectional study**, children of different ages are assessed at one time. In one cross-sectional study, researchers asked 3-, 4-, 6-, and 7-year-olds about what a pensive-looking woman was doing, or about the state of someone's mind. These researchers found a striking increase with age in children's awareness of thinking as a mental activity (J. H. Flavell, Green, & Flavell, 1995). These findings strongly suggest that as children become older, their understanding of mental processes improves. However, we cannot draw such a conclusion with certainty. We don't know whether the 7-year-olds' awareness of mental activity when they were 3 years old was the same as that of the current 3-year-olds in the study. The only way to see whether change occurs with age is to conduct a longitudinal study of a particular person or group.

Both longitudinal and cross-sectional designs have strengths and weaknesses (see Table 2-5). Longitudinal research, by repeatedly studying the same people, can track individual patterns of continuity and change. It avoids confounding developmental effects with effects of cohort membership (the differing experiences of children born, for example, before and after the advent of the Internet). However, a longitudinal study done on one cohort may not apply to another. (The results of a study of children born in the 1920s may not apply to children born in the 1990s.) Furthermore, longitudinal studies generally are more time-consuming and expensive than cross-sectional studies; it is hard to keep track of a large group of participants over the years, to keep records, and to keep the study going despite turnover in research personnel. Then there is the problem of attrition: participants may die, move away, or drop out. Another likely difficulty is bias in the sample: People who volunteer for such studies, and especially those who stay with them, tend to be above

longitudinal study Study design to assess changes in a sample over time

cross-sectional study Study design in which people of different ages are assessed on one occasion

Table 2-5	Longitudinal, Cross-sectional, and Sequential Research: Pros and Cons		
Type of Study	**Procedure**	**Advantages**	**Disadvantages**
Longitudinal	Data are collected on same person or persons over a period of time	Can show age-related change or continuity; avoids confounding age with cohort effects	Time-consuming, expensive; problems of attrition, bias in sample, and effects of repeated testing; results may be valid only for cohort tested or sample studied
Cross-sectional	Data are collected on people of different ages at the same time	Can show similarities and differences among age groups; speedy, economical; no problem of attrition or repeated testing	Cannot establish age effects; masks individual differences; can be confounded by cohort effects
Sequential	Data are collected on successive cross-sectional or longitudinal samples	Can avoid drawbacks of both cross-sectional and longitudinal designs	Requires large amount of time and effort and the analysis of very complex data

average in intelligence and socio-economic status. Also, results can be affected by repeated testing: Participants may do better in later tests because of familiarity with test materials and procedures.

Advantages of cross-sectional research include speed and economy; data can be gathered fairly quickly from large numbers of people. A drawback of cross-sectional studies is that they may overlook individual differences by focusing on group averages. Their major disadvantage, however, is that the results may be affected by cohort differences—the differing experiences of children born at different times, for example, before and after the advent of the Internet. Cross-sectional studies are sometimes interpreted as yielding information about developmental changes, but such information is often misleading. Thus, although cross-sectional studies still dominate the field—no doubt because they are so much easier to do—the proportion of research devoted to longitudinal studies, especially short-term ones, is increasing.

The **sequential study**—a sequence of cross-sectional and/or longitudinal studies—is a complex strategy designed to overcome the drawbacks of longitudinal and cross-sectional research shown in Table 2-5. Researchers may assess a cross-sectional sample on two or more occasions in sequence to find out how members of each age cohort have changed. This procedure permits researchers to separate age-related changes from cohort effects. Another sequential design consists of a sequence of longitudinal studies, running concurrently but starting one after another. This design enables researchers to compare individual differences in the course of developmental change. A combination of cross-sectional and longitudinal sequences (as shown in Figure 2-7) can provide a more complete picture of development than would be possible with longitudinal or cross-sectional research alone.

The major drawbacks of sequential studies relate to time, effort, and complexity. Sequential designs require large numbers of participants and the collection and analysis of huge amounts of data over a period of years. Interpreting their findings and conclusions can demand a high degree of sophistication.

Microgenetic Studies

Because change usually happens slowly, developmental scientists rarely can observe it directly in everyday life. But what if the process could be compressed into a very short time? A **microgenetic study** does just that. Over a short time span, participants are repeatedly exposed to a stimulus for change or opportunity for learning, over a short time, enabling researchers to see and analyze the processes by which change occurs. Vygotsky used such "microgenesis experiments" to see how much children's performance could be improved over a brief interval.

In an experiment examining number conservation, measuring children's abilities to identify which of two rows of buttons contained the greater amount, 5-year-old children who had not yet mastered number conservation were given four training sessions in one of three different conditions: receiving feedback on performance, feedback with request

sequential study Study design that combines cross-sectional and longitudinal techniques

microgenetic study Study design that allows researchers to directly observe change by repeated testing over a short time

Checkpoint ✔

Can you . . .

✔ List advantages and disadvantages of longitudinal, cross-sectional, and sequential research?

✔ Explain how microgenetic studies are done and what kinds of data they can reveal?

✔ Discuss the advantages and disadvantages of collaborative research?

Figure 2-7

A sequential design. Two successive cross-sectional groups of 2-, 4-, 6-, and 8-year-olds were tested in 2006 and 2008. Also, a longitudinal study of children first measured in 2006, when they were 2 years old, will be followed by a similar longitudinal study of children who were 2 years old in 2008.

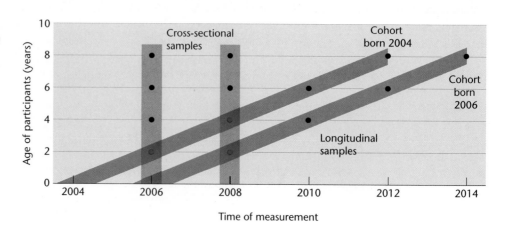

to explain their reasoning, or feedback with request to explain the experimenter's reasoning (Siegler, 1995). Each training session involved 12 trials, during which it was possible to track the progress children made in learning. Children who were asked to explain the experimenter's reasoning did better than the other two groups. The method allowed Siegler to identify the kinds of reasoning that children were using, and to track what children who successfully learned had realized about the task; namely, that the length of the row did not predict the number of buttons in the row, and that the manner in which the row length and number of buttons were manipulated did predict the number of buttons.

Collaborative Research

Throughout much of the history of the field of child development, investigators have worked individually or in small groups at a single laboratory or site. Many important advances have come from such research, but the current trend is to broaden the research base.

Researchers use various means to share and pool data. One is the archiving of data sets for use by other researchers. Another is *meta-analysis,* a statistical analysis of the findings of multiple studies. A third and increasingly common approach is collaborative research by multiple researchers at multiple sites, sometimes with government or foundation funding. This collaborative model can trace development within a population on a very broad scale. It makes possible larger, more representative samples; makes it easier to carry out longitudinal studies that might otherwise be hampered by researcher attrition and burnout; and permits a blending of theoretical perspectives (Parke, 2004).

An example of collaborative research is the National Institute of Child Health and Human Development (NICHD) Study of Early Child Care, discussed in Chapter 8. Another example is the planned National Children's Study (2004), a prospective study of influences on children's health. This 21-year multi-sited study, under auspices of the U.S. Department of Health and Human Services and other government agencies, will begin with couples of childbearing age who are not yet expecting a child and then follow the children they bear, from conception to adulthood.

A difficulty with the collaborative model is the need for group consensus on all aspects of the research, from the initial design to the writing of the report. Achieving consensus can be cumbersome and may require difficult compromises. The more flexible single-investigator or single-site model may be better suited to experimental work and to the development of novel methods and approaches.

Ethics of Research

Guidepost 4

What ethical problems may arise in research on children?

Should research that might harm its participants ever be undertaken? How can we balance the possible benefits against the risk of mental, emotional, or physical injury to individuals?

In resolving such ethical dilemmas, researchers are supposed to be guided by three principles: (1) beneficence: the obligation to maximize potential benefits to participants and minimize possible harm; (2) respect for participants' autonomy and protection of those who are unable to exercise their own judgment; and (3) justice: inclusion of diverse groups while being sensitive to any special impact the research situation may have on them. In evaluating risks and benefits, researchers should be sensitive to cultural issues and values (Fisher et al., 2002). They should also consider children's developmental needs (Thompson, 1990), as well as rights of participants. These rights include informed consent and avoidance of deception, protection from harm and loss of dignity, and guarantees of privacy and confidentiality. Participants must also have the right to decline or withdraw at any time, and investigators must be responsible for correcting any undesirable effects. Three Canadian government research funding bodies—SSHRC, NSERC, and CIHR—have

Checkpoint ✔

Can you . . .

✔ Name three principles that govern inclusion of participants in research?

✔ Name five rights of research participants?

✔ Give examples of how the developmental needs of children, and of children from diverse populations should be accommodated in research?

developed a recent policy on ethical conduct for research involving humans, called the Tri-Council Policy Statement: Ethical Conduct for Research Involving Humans (Adair, 2001; NSERC, 2000), which has been adopted by universities across Canada. The policy is based on principles of ethics that include, in addition to those listed above, protection of vulnerable persons. Information about this policy is available online at **www.nserc.ca.**

Even research that seems to involve minimal risk may be too risky for a particular child at a particular level of development. An important need is to develop standards for age-appropriate treatment of children in research. One ethicist (Thompson, 1990) has suggested research-based guidelines (see Table 2-6), which you may wish to review after you have read the relevant chapters in this book. For example, infants' and very young children's ability to cope with the stress of the research situation may hinge on the presence of a parent or trusted caregiver, a familiar setting and procedure, and familiar objects.

Let's look more closely at a few specific ethical considerations that can present problems.

Right to Informed Consent

Informed consent exists when participants voluntarily agree to be in a study, are competent to give consent, are aware of the risks as well as the potential benefits, and are not being exploited. The National Commission for the Protection of Human Subjects of Biomedical and Behavioural Research (1978) recommends that children age 7 or over be asked to give their own consent to take part in research and that children's objections should be overruled only if the research promises direct benefit to the child.

However, some ethicists argue that young children cannot give meaningful, voluntary *consent* because they cannot fully understand what is involved. They can merely *assent,* that is, agree to participate. Young children are less capable than adults of understanding what they are getting into and of making an informed decision on whether or not to participate. The usual procedure, therefore, when children under 18 are involved, is to ask the parents or legal guardians and sometimes school personnel to give consent.

The Assent Requirement

In addition to parental permission, investigators must obtain assent, agreement to participate, from children participating in a research project when an ethics review board has determined, on the basis of the ages, maturity, and psychological state of the children involved, that child participants are capable of providing assent. Thus, the child's refusal to participate is binding (Dexema, 2006).

Avoidance of Deception

Can informed consent exist if participants are deceived about the nature or purpose of a study or about the procedures to which they will be subjected? Suppose that children are

Table 2-6	Developmental Considerations in Children's Participation in Research	
Younger children are especially vulnerable to:		*Older children are especially vulnerable to:*
Stressful or unfamiliar situations		Apparent approval or disapproval by the researcher
Absence of parent or caregiver		Sense of failure, threats to self-esteem
Situations arousing inappropriate shame, guilt, or embarrassment		Expressed or implied comparisons with others
Coercion, deception, and unreasonable demands		Implied racial, ethnic, or socio-economic biases
		Threats to privacy

Source: Based on Thompson, 1990.

told they are trying out a new game when they are actually being tested on their reactions to success or failure? Experiments like this have added to our knowledge but at the cost of the participants' right to know what they were getting involved in.

Ethical guidelines call for withholding information *only* when it is essential to the study; and then investigators should avoid methods that could cause pain, anxiety, or harm. Participants should be debriefed afterward to let them know the true nature of the study and why deception was necessary and to make sure they have not suffered as a result.

Right to Self-esteem

Some studies have a built-in "failure factor." Researchers give harder and harder tasks until the participant is unable to do them. Might this inevitable failure affect a participant's self-worth? Similarly, when researchers publish findings that middle-class children are academically superior to poor children, unintentional harm may be done to some participants' self-esteem. Even if such studies may lead to beneficial interventions for poor children, they also may affect teachers' expectations and students' performance.

Right to Privacy and Confidentiality

Not all ethical issues have clear answers; some hinge on researchers' judgment and scruples. In this grey area are issues having to do with privacy and with protecting the confidentiality of personal information that participants may reveal in interviews or questionnaires.

What if, during the course of research, an investigator suspects that a child may have a learning disability or some other treatable condition? Is the researcher obliged to share such information with the parents or guardians or to recommend services that may help, when sharing the information might contaminate the research findings? Such a decision should not be made lightly; sharing information of uncertain validity might create damaging misconceptions about a child. On the other hand, researchers need to know and inform participants of their legal responsibility to report abuse or neglect or any other illegal activity of which they become aware.

Research with Diverse Populations

Developmental researchers in Canada often work with children who are new immigrants, or members of minority populations. In designing their studies, researchers must be sensitive to the appropriateness of the instruments they use to ensure that results are free of bias, and also that the dignity of participants is protected, over and above the protections in place for majority population individuals.

In Canada Aboriginal populations have distinctive perspectives that stem from their cultures and histories. The Tri-Council Policy Statement recognizes that Aboriginal Peoples' customs and interests must be protected. Thus, researchers are expected to be sensitive to the reasons why some Aboriginal participants might feel apprehensive in taking part in research or responding to researchers. In conducting research with Aboriginal children, researchers are expected to conduct their work in respectful ways to protect against the possibility that the research inadvertently promotes inaccurate or insensitive outcomes contributing to the stigmatization of Aboriginal communities. Treating Aboriginal groups simply as sources of data, or if data were used inappropriately, or if invalid measures were used, then negative repercussions for the well-being of the community could be an unexpected and harmful consequence (Government of Canada, n.d.).

Summary and Key Terms

Basic Theoretical Issues

Guidepost 1 What purposes do theories serve, and what are two basic theoretical issues on which developmental theorists differ?

- A theory is used to explain data and generate hypotheses that can be tested by research.
- Developmental theories differ on three basic issues: the relative importance of heredity and environment, the active or passive character of development, and the existence of stages of development.
- Some theorists subscribe to a mechanistic model of development; others to an organismic model.

  theory (22)   hypotheses (22)
  mechanistic model (22)   organismic model (23)

Theoretical Perspectives

Guidepost 2 What are five theoretical perspectives on child development, and what are some theories representative of each?

- The psychoanalytic perspective sees development as motivated by unconscious emotional drives or conflicts. Leading examples are Freud's and Erikson's theories.
- The learning perspective views development as a result of learning based on experience. Leading examples are Watson's and Skinner's behaviourism and Bandura's social learning theory.
- The cognitive perspective is concerned with thought processes. Leading examples are Piaget's cognitive-stage theory, Vygotsky's socio-cultural theory, the information-processing approach, and neo-Piagetian theories.
- The contextual perspective focuses on interaction between the individual and the social context. A leading example is Bronfenbrenner's bioecological theory.
- The evolutionary/sociobiological perspective, represented by E. O. Wilson, is based in part on Darwin's theory of evolution and describes adaptive behaviours that promote survival. A leading example is Bowlby's attachment theory.

  psychoanalytic perspective (24)
  psychosexual development (25)
  psychosocial development (27)   learning perspective (27)
  behaviourism (27)   classical conditioning (28)
  operant conditioning (28)   reinforcement (28)
  punishment (28)   social learning theory (29)
  reciprocal determinism (29)   observational learning (29)
  self-efficacy (29)   cognitive perspective (29)
  cognitive-stage theory (29)   organization (30)
  schemes (30)   adaptation (30)   assimilation (30)
  accommodation (30)   equilibration (30)

socio-cultural theory (31)   zone of proximal development (ZPD) (31)   scaffolding (31)
information-processing approach (31)
contextual perspective (32)   bioecological theory (32)
microsystem (32)   mesosystem (32)   exosystem (32)
macrosystem (33)   chronosystem (33)
evolutionary/sociobiological perspective (33)
ethology (34)   evolutionary psychology (34)

Research Methods

Guidepost 3 How do developmental scientists study children, and what are the advantages and disadvantages of each research method?

- Research can be quantitative, qualitative, or both.
- To arrive at sound conclusions, quantitative researchers use the scientific method.
- Random selection of a research sample can ensure generalizability.
- Three forms of data collection are self-reports, observation, and behavioural or performance measures.
- Two basic qualitative designs used in developmental research are the case study and ethnographic study. Cross-cultural research can indicate whether certain aspects of development are universal or culturally influenced.
- Two quantitative designs are the correlational study and experiment. Only experiments can firmly establish causal relationships.
- Experiments must be rigorously controlled so as to be valid and replicable. Random assignment of participants can ensure validity.
- Laboratory experiments are easiest to control and replicate, but findings of field experiments may be more generalizable. Natural experiments may be useful in situations in which true experiments would be impractical or unethical.
- The two most common designs used to study age-related development are longitudinal and cross-sectional. Cross-sectional studies compare age groups; longitudinal studies describe continuity or change in the same participants. The sequential study is intended to overcome the weaknesses of the other two designs. A microgenetic study enables direct observation of change over a short period of time.

  quantitative research (35)   qualitative research (35)
  scientific method (35)   sample (36)   random selection (36)
  operational definitions (38)   cognitive neuroscience (38)
  naturalistic observation (38)   laboratory observation (38)
  case study (39)   ethnographic study (40)
  participant observation (40)   correlational study (40)
  experiment (41)   experimental group (42)
  control group (42)   independent variable (42)
  dependent variable (42)   random assignment (43)
  longitudinal study (45)   cross-sectional study (45)
  sequential study (46)   microgenetic study (46)

Ethics of Research

Guidepost 4 What ethical problems may arise in research on children?

- Researchers seek to resolve ethical issues on the basis of principles of beneficence, respect, and justice.

- Ethical issues in research on child development involve the rights of participants to informed consent, avoidance of deception, protection from harm and loss of dignity or self-esteem, and guarantees of privacy and confidentiality.

- Children's developmental needs and cultural differences should be considered in designing research.

CHAPTER THREE

Forming a New Life: Conception, Heredity, and Environment

*Of the cell, the wondrous seed
Becoming plant and animal and mind
Unerringly forever after its kind . . .*

—William Ellery Leonard, *Two Lives*, 1923

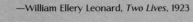

Focus *Louise Brown, the First "Test-tube Baby"**

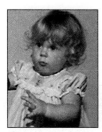

Louise Brown

The writer Aldous Huxley foresaw it in 1932: human life created in the laboratory. As Huxley described it in *Brave New World,* the feat would be accomplished by immersing female ova (egg cells), which had been incubated in test tubes, in a dish of free-swimming male sperm. Huxley envisioned his "brave new world" as 600 years off; yet it took only 46 years before a birth through *in vitro fertilization,* or fertilization outside the mother's body, became a reality.

Louise Brown, the world's first documented "test-tube baby," was born July 25, 1978, at a four-story red brick hospital in the old textile mill town of Oldham in northwest England. She had been conceived, not in a test tube, but by placing a ripe ovum from her 30-year-old mother, Lesley Brown, in a shallow glass dish with fluid containing sperm from her 38-year-old father, John Brown. After 2 days, during which the resulting single-celled organism multiplied to eight cells, the embryo had been implanted in Lesley's womb.

Until this precedent-shattering event, Lesley and her husband, a truck driver for the British Railway Network, were—by their own description—an ordinary couple who lived in a low-rent row house in Bristol. Although they were raising John's 17-year-old daughter from a previous marriage, they desperately wanted to have a baby together. After 7 years of failure to conceive, they turned to the then-experimental in vitro method. The fulfillment of the Browns' wish was the culmination of more than a decade of painstaking preparatory research by Patrick Steptoe, a gynecologist, and Robert Edwards, a physiologist at Cambridge University. The outcome was far more than a single baby. Steptoe's and Edwards's work gave birth to a new branch of medicine: *assisted reproductive technology.*

Questions were in the air as Lesley and John Brown awaited the birth of what was to be called, in banner headlines, the "Miracle Baby" and "Baby of the Century." Despite strenuous efforts by the couple and their doctors to keep the birth secret, the news leaked out, and was reported around the world.

The story launched a debate about the moral implications of tampering with nature—and, down the road, the possibility of mass baby farms and reproductive engineering, which could alter or custom design the "products" of reproduction. More immediately, what about the risks to mother and baby? What if the baby were born grossly deformed? Could any baby conceived in a laboratory dish have a normal life?

Lesley was checked and monitored more frequently than most expectant mothers are, and, as a precaution, spent the last three months of her pregnancy in the hospital. The birth took place about two weeks before the due date, by Caesarean delivery, because Lesley had developed toxemia (blood poisoning) and the fetus did not seem to be gaining weight. The delivery went smoothly without further complications.

The blond, blue-eyed, 2600 g baby was, from all accounts, a beautiful, normal infant, who emerged crying lustily. "There's no difference between her and any other little girl," her father maintained. "We just helped nature a bit" ("Louise Brown," p. 82).

Despite her highly publicized start, Louise Brown has led an unassuming life. On her 25th birthday, about 1,000 of the more than 3 million children worldwide now estimated to have been born through in vitro fertilization (Reaney, 2006; ICMART, 2006) gathered to celebrate the occasion. Brown, engaged to a bank security officer whom she has since married, said she had no immediate plans to start a family and just wanted to be treated as a "normal person." Her younger sister Natalie, also a "test-tube baby," had two children, both conceived normally (Daley, 2003). In January 2007, Brown herself, at 28, gave birth to a normally conceived son (Associated Press, 2007).

• • •

What made Louise Brown the person she is? Like any other child, she began with a hereditary endowment from her mother and father. For example, she has her father's stocky build, wide forehead, and chubby cheeks and her mother's tilted nose and curved mouth—as well as her mother's sudden temper. Louise also has been affected by a host of environmental influences, from that famous laboratory dish to the tremendous public interest in her story. As a preschooler, she was mentally precocious, mischievous, and (by her parents' admission) "spoiled." As a teenager, like many of her classmates, she liked to swim and ride horses, wore two gold studs in each ear, watched music videos, and had a crush on the actor Tom Cruise.

Most children do not become famous, especially at birth; but every child is the product of a unique combination of hereditary and environmental influences set in motion by the parents' decision to form a new life. We begin this chapter by describing how a life is conceived, either through normal reproduction or through alternative technologies, some of them developed since Louise Brown's birth. We examine the mechanisms and patterns of heredity—the inherited factors that affect development, we look at how heredity and environment work together and how their effects on development can be studied.

After you have read and studied this chapter, you should be able to answer each of the Guidepost questions that appear at the top of the next page. Look for them again in the margins, where they point to important concepts throughout the chapter. To check your understanding of these Guideposts, review the end-of-chapter summary. Checkpoints located throughout the chapter will help you verify your understanding of what you have read.

*Sources of information about Louise Brown were Barthel (1982); Faltermayer et al. (1996); Lawson (1993); "Louise Brown" (1984); "Louise Brown" (1994); "Test-tube Baby" (1978); "The First Test-tube Baby" (1978); and Van Dyck (1995).

Guideposts for Study

1. How does conception normally occur, and how have beliefs about conception changed?

2. What causes infertility, and what are alternative ways of becoming parents?

3. What genetic mechanisms determine sex, physical appearance, and other characteristics?

4. How are birth defects and disorders transmitted?

5. How do scientists study the relative influences of heredity and environment, and how do heredity and environment work together?

6. What roles do heredity and environment play in physical health, intelligence, and personality?

Guidepost 1

How does conception normally occur, and how have beliefs about conception changed?

Becoming Parents: How Conception Occurs

The timing, and circumstances of parenthood can have vast consequences for a child. Whether a birth was planned or accidental, whether the pregnancy was welcomed or unwanted, whether it came about through normal or extraordinary means, whether the parents were married or unmarried, and how old the parents were when a child was conceived or adopted are all factors in the *microsystem* identified in Bronfenbrenner's bioecological approach (refer back to Chapter 2). Whether the culture encourages large or small families, whether it values one sex over the other, and how much it supports families with children are macrosystem issues likely to influence that child's development.

We'll be bringing up such contextual issues throughout this book. For now, let's look at the act of conception and then at options for couples unable to conceive normally.

Changing Ideas about Conception*

Most adults, and even most children in industrialized countries have a reasonably accurate idea of where babies come from. Yet only a generation or two ago, many parents told their children that a stork had brought them. The folk belief that children came from wells, springs, or rocks was common in north and central Europe as late as the beginning of the twentieth century. Conception was believed to be influenced by cosmic forces. A baby conceived under a new moon would be a boy; during the moon's last quarter, a girl (Gélis, 1991).

Theories about conception go back to ancient times. The Greek physician Hippocrates, known as the father of European medicine, held that a fetus results from the joining of male and female seeds. The philosopher Aristotle had a contrary view: that "the woman functions only as a receptacle, the child being formed exclusively by means of the sperm" (Fontanel & d'Harcourt, 1997, p. 10). According to Aristotle, the production of male babies was in the natural order of things; a female came about only if development was disturbed.

Between the seventeenth and nineteenth centuries, a debate raged between two schools of biological thought. Harking back to Aristotle, the *animalculists* (so named because the male sperm were then called *animalcules*) claimed that fully formed "little people" were contained in the heads of sperm, ready to grow when deposited in the nurturing environment of the womb. The *ovists,* inspired by the work of the English physician William Harvey, held an opposite but equally incorrect view: that a female's ovaries contained tiny, already formed humans whose growth was activated by the male's sperm. Finally, in the late eighteenth century, the German-born anatomist Kaspar Friedrich Wolff demonstrated that embryos are not preformed in either parent and that both contribute equally to the formation of a new being.

*Unless otherwise referenced, this discussion is based on Eccles, 1982, and Fontanel & d'Harcourt, 1997.

How Fertilization Takes Place

Fertilization, or conception, is the process by which sperm and ovum—the male and female *gametes,* or sex cells—combine to create a single cell called a **zygote,** which then duplicates itself again and again by cell division to become a baby. But conception is not as simple as it sounds. Several independent events need to coincide to conceive a child. And, as we will discuss in the next chapter, not all conceptions end in birth.

At birth, a girl is believed to have about 2 million immature ova in her two ovaries, each ovum in its own small sac, or *follicle.* According to research in mice, new ova continue to develop during adulthood from stem cells in the ovary, and this may be true of adult women as well (Johnson, Canning, Kaneko, Pru, & Tilly, 2004). In a sexually mature woman, *ovulation*—rupture of a mature follicle in either ovary and expulsion of its ovum— occurs about once every 28 days until menopause. The ovum is swept along through the fallopian tube by tiny hair cells, called *cilia,* toward the uterus, or womb.

Sperm are produced in the testicles (testes), or reproductive glands, of a mature male at a rate of several hundred million a day and are ejaculated in the semen at sexual climax (see Figure 3-1). They enter the vagina and try to swim through the *cervix* (the opening of the uterus) and into the Fallopian tubes, but only a tiny fraction make it that far.

Fertilization normally occurs while the ovum is passing through the Fallopian tube. Contrary to previous guidelines, this six-day "fertile window" may occur any time between the 6th and 21st days of the menstrual cycle and can be highly unpredictable, even in women whose menstrual periods are regular (Wilcox, Dunson, & Baird, 2000). If fertilization does not occur, the sperm are absorbed by the woman's white blood cells, and the ovum passes through the uterus and exits through the vagina.

fertilization Union of sperm and ovum fuse to produce a zygote; also called *conception*

zygote One-celled organism resulting from fertilization

> ## Checkpoint ✔
>
> Can you . . .
>
> ✔ Compare historic and scientific views of conception?
>
> ✔ Explain how and when fertilization normally takes place?

Infertility

About 7 percent of Canadian couples experience infertility—the inability to conceive a baby after 12 months of trying (Centers for Disease Control & Prevention, 2005a; Wright, Chang, Jeng, & Macaluso, 2006)—during their reproductive years (Norris, 2001). Women's fertility begins to decline in the late 20s, with substantial decreases during the 30s. Men's fertility is less affected by age but declines significantly by the late 30s (Dunson, Colombo, & Baird, 2002).

> ## Guidepost 2
>
> What causes infertility, and what are alternative ways of becoming parents?

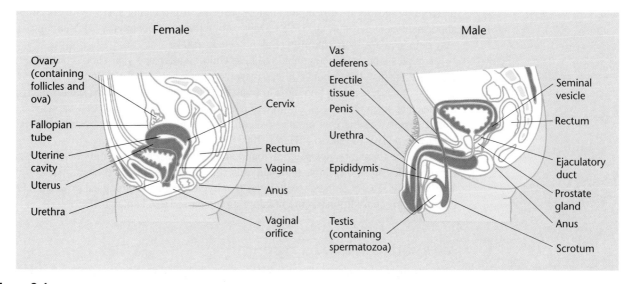

Figure 3-1
Human reproductive systems

Causes of Infertility

infertility Inability to conceive after 12 months of trying

Infertility is far from a new concern. To enhance fertility, doctors in ancient times advised men to eat fennel, and women to drink the saliva of lambs and wear necklaces of earthworms. After intercourse, the woman was supposed to lie flat with her legs crossed and "avoid becoming angry" (Fontanel & d'Harcourt, 1997, p. 10). By the late Middle Ages, the list of foods recommended to spur conception had expanded to include leeks, carrots, asparagus, and several kinds of nuts; by the Renaissance, squabs, sparrows, cockscombs and testicles, bull's genitals, truffles, mint, parsley, rice cooked in cow's milk, and various spices. In the early seventeenth century, Louise Bourgeois, midwife to Marie de Médicis, the queen of France, advocated bathing the vagina with camomile, mallow, marjoram, and catnip boiled in white wine.

Today we know that the most common cause of infertility in men is production of too few sperm. Although only one sperm is needed to fertilize an ovum, a sperm count lower than 60 to 200 million per ejaculation makes conception unlikely. Sometimes an ejaculatory duct is blocked, preventing the exit of sperm; or sperm may be unable to "swim" well enough to reach the cervix. Some cases of male infertility seem to have a genetic basis (King, 1996; Phillips, 1998; Galan, De Felici, Buch, Riero, Segura, Royo, Cruz, Real, & Ruiz, 2006; Phillips, 1998; Reijo, Alagappan, Patrizio, & Page, 1996).

In a woman, the cause of infertility may be the failure to produce ova or to produce normal ova; mucus in the cervix may prevent sperm from penetrating it; or a disease of the uterine lining may prevent implantation of the fertilized ovum. A major cause of declining fertility in women after age 30 is deterioration in the quality of their ova (Van Noord-Zaadstra et al., 1991). However, the most common female cause is the problem Lesley Brown had: blockage of the Fallopian tubes, preventing ova from reaching the uterus. In about half of these cases, the tubes are blocked by scar tissue from sexually transmitted diseases (King, 1996). (Table 3-1 lists major causes and treatments of male and female infertility.)

Infertility burdens a marriage emotionally. Partners may become frustrated and angry with themselves and each other and may feel empty, worthless, and depressed (Abbey, Andrews, & Halman, 1992; Jones & Toner, 1993). However, only when infertility leads to permanent, involuntary childlessness is it associated with long-term psychological distress (McQuillan, Greil, White, & Jacob, 2003).

Treatments for Infertility

Sometimes hormone treatment, drug therapy, or surgery may correct the problem. However, fertility drugs increase the likelihood of multiple, high-risk births (see Box 3-1). Also, men undergoing fertility treatment are at increased risk of producing sperm with chromosomal abnormalities (Levron et al., 1998). Daily supplements of coenzyme Q10, an antioxidant, may help increase sperm motility (Balercia et al., 2004).

Couples who have been unable to bear children after one year should not necessarily rush into fertility treatments. Unless there is a known cause for failure to conceive, the chances of success after 18 months to two years are high (Dunson, 2002). However, pregnancies that occur after a year or more of trying—even without treatment—need to be monitored closely, as there is greater risk of preterm births, low birth-weight babies, and Caesarean deliveries (Basso & Baird, 2003).

Because human beings seldom abandon their fondest hopes simply because they run into obstacles, it is no surprise that many infertile adults who want children, like Lesley and John Brown, eagerly embrace techniques that bypass ordinary biological processes. Others choose the more traditional route of adoption (discussed in Chapter 14).

Alternative Ways to Parenthood

Since the birth of Louise Brown in 1978, more than 3 million children worldwide have been conceived through *assisted reproduction technology (ART)* (Reaney, 2006; ICMART, 2006). Technology now enables many people to have children.

Table 3-1   Common Causes of Infertility in Men and Women

Condition	Explanations	Treatments
MALE CAUSES		
Abnormal sperm production or function	Abnormal shape or motility of sperm Low or no sperm production Undescended testicles Varicose veins in the scrotum Testosterone deficiency Klinefelter's syndrome Sexually transmitted diseases.	Fertility drugs Surgery to repair varicose veins or other obstructions Artificial insemination with donor sperm Injecting sperm directly into ovum.
Impaired delivery of sperm into vagina	*Sexual problems,* including erectile dysfunction, premature ejaculation, and painful intercourse *Physical problems,* including failure to produce semen, blockage of ejaculatory ducts, other structural defects, and antibodies that weaken or disable sperm	*Sexual problems* can be treated with medication or behavioural therapy. *Physical problems* may require surgery. Assisted reproduction techniques may include in vitro fertilization, electrical stimulation of ejaculation, or surgical retrieval of sperm (if blockage is present).
Age	Gradual decline in fertility, commonly in men older than 35.	
General health and lifestyle issues	Emotional stress, malnutrition, obesity, alcohol and drugs, tobacco smoking, cancer treatments, severe injury, surgery, and other medical conditions may impair sperm production.	Correct health and lifestyle problems if possible.
Environmental exposure	Overexposure to heat (in saunas or hot tubs), toxins, and certain chemicals, such as pesticides, lead, and chemical solvents.	Avoid unhealthy exposures.
FEMALE CAUSES		
Fallopian tube damage or blockage	*Most frequent cause:* inflammation of the fallopian tube due to chlamydia, a sexually transmitted disease; tubal damage with scarring may result in an ectopic pregnancy, in which the fertilized egg is unable to pass through the Fallopian tube and implant in the uterus. *Other causes:* benign uterine fibroid tumors and pelvic adhesions (bands of scar tissue) formed after pelvic infections, appendicitis, or pelvic or abdominal surgery.	Laparoscopic surgery to repair or open Fallopian tubes; in vitro fertilization.
Endometriosis	Uterine tissue implanted outside the uterus can lead to scarring and inflammation, which may prevent transfer of ovum to Fallopian tube and cause pelvic pain. Ovarian cysts.	Ovulation therapy (medication to stimulate ovulation) or in vitro fertilization.
Ovulation disorders	Any condition that prevents the release of a mature ovum from the ovary. Specific causes include hormonal deficiencies, injury to hypothalamus or pituitary gland, pituitary tumors; excessive exercise, and eating disorders.	Fertility drugs.
Polycystic ovary syndrome	Increase in production of the hormone androgen can prevent production of mature ovum. Common symptoms are absent or infrequent menstruation; dark or thick hair on chin, upper lip, or abdomen; acne; and oily skin.	Fertility drugs, particularly clomiphene.
Early menopause	Ovarian failure before age 35 may be associated with autoimmune disease, hypothyroidism (too little thyroid hormone), radiation or chemotherapy for cancer treatment, or tobacco smoking.	In vitro fertilization with donated ova.

Source: Based on Mayo Clinic (2005).

Artificial insemination—injection of sperm into a woman's vagina, cervix, or uterus—can be done when a man has a low sperm count. Sperm from several ejaculations can be combined for one injection. Thus, with help, a couple can produce their own biological offspring. If the man is infertile, a couple may choose artificial insemination by a donor (AID). If the woman has no explicable cause of infertility, the chances of success can be

Box 3-1 *What Causes Multiple Births?*

Laurie and her husband Steve had four children, ages 4 to 10. All had been singleton births. So when an ultrasound early in Laurie's fifth pregnancy at age 40 revealed that she was carrying twins, she and Steve were surprised. They learned that Laurie exemplified one of the main risk factors for multiple births: advanced maternal age.

Multiple births may occur in two ways. Most commonly, the mother's body releases two ova within a short time (or sometimes, perhaps, a single unfertilized ovum splits) and then both are fertilized. The resulting babies are dizygotic (two-egg) twins, commonly called fraternal twins. The second way is for a single fertilized ovum to split into two. The babies that result from this cell division are monozygotic (one-egg) twins, commonly called identical twins. Triplets, quadruplets, and other multiple births can result from either of these processes or a combination of both.

Monozygotic twins have the same hereditary makeup and are the same sex, but—in part because of differences in prenatal as well as postnatal experience—they differ in some respects. They may not be identical in temperament (disposition, or style of approaching and reacting to situations). In some physical characteristics, such as hair whorls, dental patterns, and handedness, they may be mirror images of each other; one may be left-handed and the other right-handed. Furthermore, differences between monozygotic twins tend to magnify as twins grow older, especially if they live apart. These differences may result from chemical modifications in a person's genome shortly after conception or may be due to later experiences or environmental factors, such as exposure to smoke or other pollutants (Fraga et al., 2005).

Dizygotic twins, who are created from different sperm cells and usually from different ova, are no more alike in hereditary makeup than any other siblings and may be the same sex or different sexes. Dizygotic twins tend to run in families (though not in Laurie's) and so may have a genetic basis, whereas monozygotic twins usually occur purely by chance (Martin & Montgomery, 2002; National Center for Health Statistics (NCHS), 1999). A tendency toward twinning seems to be inherited from a woman's mother; thus, when dizygotic twins "skip generations," it is normally because a mother of dizygotic twins has only sons to whom she cannot pass on the tendency (NCHS, 1999). The chance of having twins is also affected by diet; vegan women are only one-fifth as likely to have twins as women who include dairy products in their diet (Steinman, 2006).

The rate of monozygotic twins (about 4 per 1,000 live births) is constant at all times and places, but the rate of dizygotic twins, the more common type, varies (Martin & Montgomery, 2002; NCHS, 1999). For example, West African and African American women are more likely to have dizygotic twins than Caucasian women, who, in turn, are more likely to have them than Chinese or Japanese women (Martin & Montgomery, 2002).

The incidence of multiple births in Canada has grown rapidly. Between 1974 and 1990, live twin births increased by 35 percent, and the incidence of triplet and higher-order births increased by 250 percent (Millar, Wadhera, & Nimrod, 1992; Society of Obstetricians and Gynecologists of Canada, 2007). In 1997, 126 sets of triplets were born in Canada, a sharp increase from the 49 sets born in 1980 (Society of Obstetricians and Gynecologists of Canada, 2007). The rise in multiple births is due in part to a trend toward delayed childbearing, since such births are more common among older women (Life Site News, 2004). A more important factor in the multiple birth rate is the increased use of fertility drugs, which spur ovulation, and of ART technologies such as in vitro fertilization, which tend to be used more by older women (Hoyert et al., 2006; Martin et al., 2005). In Canada, about 17 percent of all multiple births result from fertility drugs; however, the rate is 60 percent for triplets, and 90 and 99 percent for quadruplets and quintuplets respectively (Multiple Births Canada, 2007).

The explosion of multiple births, especially triplets and higher-order multiples, is of concern because such births are associated with increased risks: pregnancy complications, premature delivery, low-birth-weight infants, and disability or death of the infant (Bernier & Gregoire, 2004; Hoyert et al., 2006; Jain, Missmer, & Hornstein, 2004; Martin et al., 2003; Martin, Hamilton et al., 2005; Multiple Births Canada, 2000; Wright, Schieve, Reynolds, & Jeng, 2003). Furthermore, triplets may be at higher risk for cognitive delays during the first two years. In a comparative study of 23 sets each of triplets, twins, and singleton infants, the triplets scored lowest on tests of mental development at 6, 12, and 24 months. This finding appeared to be related to the difficulty of giving sensitive mothering to three infants at the same time (Feldman & Eidelman, 2005). Perhaps because of such concerns, the proportion of artificial procedures involving three or more embryos declined between 1997 and 2001, and the birth rate for triplets and higher multiples, which had quadrupled since 1980, has since taken a slight downturn (Martin, Hamilton et al., 2006).

What's your view ?

Would you want to have twins or higher multiples? If you are a twin or higher multiple, how did that experience affect you?

Check it out !

For more information on multiple pregnancy and about raising twins, triplets, and higher multiples, go to **www.mcgrawhill.ca/olc/papalia.**

Pregnancies resulting in triplets or even higher multiples are increasingly common, in part because of the trend toward delayed motherhood and the use of fertility drugs and assisted reproduction techniques.

greatly increased by stimulating her ovaries to produce excess ova and injecting semen directly in the uterus (Guzick et al., 1999).

The most commonly used ART, and the one Lesley Brown used, is in vitro fertilization (IVF), fertilization outside the mother's body. First, fertility drugs are given to increase production of ova. Then a mature ovum is surgically removed, fertilized in a laboratory dish, and implanted in the mother's uterus. Usually 50,000 to 100,000 sperm are used to increase the chances of fertilization, and several embryos are transferred to the uterus to increase the chances of pregnancy. As we have mentioned, this procedure also increases the likelihood of multiple, usually premature, births—twins, triplets, or higher multiples (Wright et al., 2006).

A newer technique, *in vitro maturation (IVM)* is performed earlier in the monthly cycle, when as many as 30 to 50 egg follicles are developing. Normally, only one of these will mature. Harvesting a large number of follicles before ovulation is complete and then allowing them to mature in the laboratory can make hormone injections unnecessary and diminish the likelihood of multiple births (Duenwald, 2003).

IVF also can address severe male infertility. A single sperm can be injected into the ovum—a technique called *intracytoplasmic sperm injection (ICSI)*. This procedure is now used in the majority of IVF cycles (Van Voorhis, 2007).

Although success rates have improved since 1978 (Duenwald, 2003), ART is not always successful. According to current estimates, about 76 percent of attempts are successful (Collins & Vaan Steirteghem, 2004), but much fewer than this end in live births (Wright et al., 2003)—about 24 percent in Canada (Gunby, Daya, & IVF Directors Group of the Canadian Fertility and Andrology Society, 2006). For one thing, the likelihood of success with IVF using a woman's own ova drops precipitously with maternal age as the quality of ova declines: among Canadian women, 29 percent of attempts result in live births for women under 35 years, and the rate drops to 9 percent for women 38 to 40 years of age (Shanner & Nisker, 2001). A woman who is producing poor-quality ova or who has had her ovaries removed may try *ovum transfer*. In this procedure, an ovum, or *donor egg*— provided, usually anonymously, by a fertile young woman—is fertilized in the laboratory and implanted in the prospective mother's uterus. IVF using donor eggs tends to be highly successful (Van Voorhis, 2007). In *blastocyst transfer*, the fertilized ovum is kept in the culture until it grows to the blastocyst stage; but this method has been linked to an increase in identical twin births (Duenwald, 2003). Alternatively, the ovum can be fertilized in the donor's body by artificial insemination, and the embryo retrieved and inserted into the recipient's uterus. Two other techniques with higher success rates are gamete intrafallopian transfer (GIFT) and zygote intrafallopian transfer (ZIFT), in which the egg and sperm or the fertilized egg are inserted in the Fallopian tube (Schieve et al., 2002; Society for Assisted Reproductive Technology, 1993, 2002).

How do children conceived by artificial means turn out? Most of them do fine (Van Voorhis, 2007). A study of Iowa births between 1989 and 2002 did find a slightly increased risk of major birth defects associated with IVF (Van Voorhis et al., 2005). On the other hand, among 36,062 singleton pregnancies studied at Stamford Hospital in Connecticut, 1776 of them conceived through ovulation induction or IVF, use of these technologies was associated with increased risk of adverse outcomes, including fetal loss, but *not* of chromosomal or structural abnormalities (Shevell et al., 2005).

In a longitudinal study of 1,523 British, Belgian, Danish, Swedish, and Greek infants, there were no major differences in physical development, health, and other aspects of development at age 5 between those born through IVF or ICSI and those conceived normally. The groups also did not differ in behavioural problems or temperamental difficulties. However, children born through ICSI did have a higher rate of congenital urological and kidney abnormalities (Barnes et al., 2003; Sutcliffe, Loft, Wennerholm, Tarlatzis, & Bonduelle, 2003). Longitudinal studies of children conceived by IVF or by donor insemination found little or no difference in socio-emotional development at age 12 between these children and naturally conceived or adopted children (Golombok, MacCallum, & Goodman, 2001; Golombok, MacCallum, Goodman, & Rutter, 2002).

In surrogate motherhood, a fertile woman is impregnated by the prospective father, usually by artificial insemination. She carries the baby to term and gives the child to the

monozygotic (one-egg) twins Twins resulting from the division of a single zygote after fertilization; also called *identical twins*

dizygotic (two-egg) twins Twins conceived by the union of two different ova (or a single ovum that has split) with two different sperm cells; also called *fraternal twins*

Checkpoint

Can you . . .

✔ Identify several causes and treatments of male and female infertility?

✔ Describe four means of assisted reproduction, and mention several issues they raise?

✔ Distinguish between monozygotic and dizygotic twins, and tell how each comes about?

Guidepost 3

What genetic mechanisms determine sex, physical appearance, and other characteristics?

deoxyribonucleic acid (DNA)
Chemical that carries inherited instructions for the formation and function of body cells

genetic code Sequence of base pairs within DNA, which determine inherited characteristics

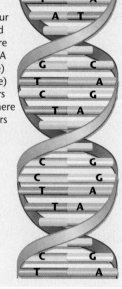

DNA is the genetic material in all living cells. It consists of four chemical units, called bases. These bases are the letters of the DNA alphabet. A (adenine) pairs with T (thymine) and C (cytosine) pairs with G (guanine). There are 3 billion base pairs in human DNA.

Letters of the DNA alphabet

T = Thymine
A = Adenine
G = Guanine
C = Cytosine

Figure 3-2

DNA: The genetic code

Source: Ritter, 1999.

father and his mate. Surrogate motherhood is strictly regulated in Canada. In 2004 the Canadian government passed the Canadian Assisted Human Reproductive Act, placing strict conditions on the practice, including a ban on payment to the surrogate mother (Department of Justice Canada, 2004). This act was developed in response to recommendations by the Royal Commission on New Reproductive Technologies (1993), which identified the need for legislation on reproductive and genetic technologies, not only for surrogacy but also sex selection, buying and selling of ova and sperm, human embryo cloning, and the use of human stem cells for research (Bernier & Gregoire, 2004).

How do parents of children born through surrogate mothers fare? A study of 42 families with infants born through surrogacy found that these parents adjusted better to their first year of parenthood than parents in control groups who had conceived children naturally or through egg donation (Golombok, Murray, Jadva, MacCallum, & Lycett, 2004).

Mechanisms of Heredity

The science of genetics is the study of heredity—the inborn factors, inherited from the biological parents, that affect development. When ovum and sperm unite—whether by normal fertilization or by assisted reproduction, as with Louise Brown—they endow the baby-to-be with a genetic makeup that influences a wide range of characteristics from colour of eyes and hair to health, intellect, and personality.

The Genetic Code

The basis of heredity is a chemical called **deoxyribonucleic acid (DNA).** The double-helix structure of DNA resembles a long, spiralling ladder whose steps are made of pairs of chemical units called *bases* (see Figure 3-2). The bases—adenine (A), thymine (T), cytosine (C), and guanine (G)—are the "letters" of the **genetic code,** which cellular machinery "reads."

Chromosomes are coils of DNA that consist of smaller segments called **genes,** the functional units of heredity. Each gene is located in a definite position on its chromosome and contains thousands of base pairs. The sequence of bases in a gene tells a cell how to make the proteins that enable it to carry out specific functions. The complete sequence of genes in the human body constitutes the **human genome.**

Every cell in the normal human body except the sex cells (sperm and ova) has 23 pairs of chromosomes—46 in all. Through a type of cell division called *meiosis,* which the sex cells undergo when they are developing, each sex cell ends up with only 23 chromosomes—one from each pair. Thus, when sperm and ovum fuse at conception, they produce a zygote with 46 chromosomes, 23 from the father and 23 from the mother.

Three-quarters of the genes every child receives are identical to those received by every other child; they are called *monomorphic genes.* The other one-quarter of a child's genes are *polymorphic genes,* which define each person as an individual. Since many of these come in several variations, and since meiotic division is random, it is virtually impossible for any two children (other than monozygotic twins) to receive exactly the same combination of genes.

At conception, then, the single-celled zygote has all the biological information needed to guide its development into a human baby. This happens through *mitosis,* a process by which the cells divide in half over and over again. When a cell divides, the DNA spirals replicate themselves, so that each newly formed cell has the same DNA structure as all the others. Thus, each cell division creates a duplicate of the original cell, with the same hereditary information. When development is normal, each cell (except the gametes) continues to have 46 chromosomes identical to those in the original zygote. As the cells divide and the child grows and develops, the cells differentiate, specializing in a variety of complex bodily functions.

Genes spring into action when conditions call for the information they can provide. Genetic action that triggers growth of body and brain is often regulated by hormonal levels—both in the mother and in the developing baby, which are affected by such environmental conditions as nutrition and stress. Thus, from the start, heredity and environment are interrelated (Brown, 1999).

What Determines Sex?

In many villages in Nepal, it is common for a man whose wife has borne no male babies to take a second wife. In some societies, a woman's failure to produce sons is justification for divorce. The irony in these customs is that it is the father's sperm that determines a child's sex.

At the moment of conception, the 23 chromosomes from the sperm and the 23 from the mother's ovum form 23 pairs. Twenty-two pairs are **autosomes,** chromosomes that are not related to sexual expression. The twenty-third pair are **sex chromosomes**—one from the father and one from the mother—which govern the baby's sex.

Sex chromosomes are either *X chromosomes* or *Y chromosomes.* The sex chromosome of every ovum is an X chromosome, but the sperm may contain either an X or a Y chromosome. The Y chromosome contains the gene for maleness, called the SRY gene. When an ovum (X) is fertilized by an X-carrying sperm, the zygote formed is XX, a female. When an ovum (X) is fertilized by a Y-carrying sperm, the resulting zygote is XY, a male (see Figure 3-3).

Initially, the embryo's rudimentary reproductive system is identical in males and females. About 6 to 8 weeks after conception, male embryos normally start producing the male hormone testosterone. Exposure to steady, high levels of testosterone results in the development of a male body with male sexual organs. However, the process is not automatic. Research with mice has found that hormones must first signal the SRY gene, which then triggers cell differentiation and formation of the testes. Without this signalling, a genetically male mouse will develop female genitals instead of male ones (Hughes, 2004; Meeks, Weiss, & Jameson, 2003; Nef et al., 2003). It is likely that a similar mechanism occurs in human males. Conversely, the development of the female reproductive system depends on a signalling molecule called *Wnt-4,* a variant form of which can "masculinize" a genetically female fetus (Biason-Lauber, Konrad, Navratil, & Schoenle, 2004; Hughes, 2004; Vainio, Heikkiia, Kispert, Chin, & McMahon, 1999).

Further complications arise from the fact that women have two X chromosomes, whereas men have only one. For many years researchers believed that the "duplicate" genes on one of a woman's two X chromosomes are inactivated, or "turned off." Recently, however, researchers sequencing the X chromosome discovered that only 75 percent of the genes on the extra X chromosome are inactive. About 15 percent remain active, and 10 percent are active in some women but not in others (Carrel & Willard, 2005). This variability in gene activity could help explain gender differences both in normal traits and in disorders linked to the X chromosome (discussed later in this chapter). The extra X chromosome also may help explain why women are generally healthier and more long-lived than men: Harmful changes in a gene on one X chromosome may be offset by a "backup copy" on the other X chromosome (Migeon, 2006).

Patterns of Genetic Transmission

During the 1860s, Gregor Mendel, an Austrian monk, laid the foundation for our understanding of patterns of inheritance. He crossbred pea plants that produced only yellow seeds with pea plants that produced only green seeds. The resulting hybrid plants produced only yellow seeds, meaning, he said, that yellow was *dominant* over green. Yet when he bred the yellow-seeded hybrids with each other, only 75 percent of their offspring had yellow seeds, and the other 25 percent had green seeds. This showed, Mendel said, that a hereditary characteristic (in this case, the colour green) can be *recessive,* that is, carried by an organism that does not express, or show, it.

chromosomes Coils of DNA that carry the genes

genes Small segments of DNA located in specific positions on particular chromosomes

human genome Complete sequence or mapping of genes in the human body and their locations

autosomes The 22 pairs of chromosomes not related to sexual expression

sex chromosomes Pair of chromosomes that determines sex: XX in the normal female, XY in the normal male

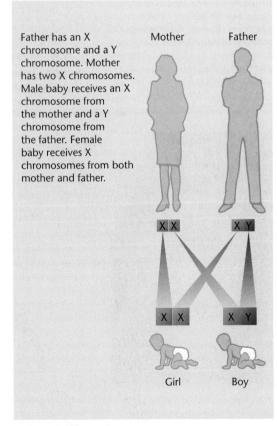

Father has an X chromosome and a Y chromosome. Mother has two X chromosomes. Male baby receives an X chromosome from the mother and a Y chromosome from the father. Female baby receives X chromosomes from both mother and father.

Figure 3-3

Determination of sex. Since all babies receive an X chromosome from the mother, sex is determined by whether an X or Y chromosome is received from the father.

Mendel also tried breeding for two traits at once. Crossing pea plants that produced round yellow seeds with plants that produced wrinkled green seeds, he found that colour and shape were independent of each other. Mendel thus showed that hereditary traits are transmitted separately.

Today we know that the genetic picture in humans is far more complex than Mendel imagined. Most human traits fall along a continuous spectrum (for example, from light skin to dark). It is hard to find a single normal trait that people inherit through simple dominant transmission other than the ability to curl the tongue lengthwise.

Dominant and Recessive Inheritance

Can you curl your tongue? If so, you inherited this ability through dominant inheritance. If your parents can curl their tongues but you cannot, recessive inheritance occurred. How do these two types of inheritance work?

Genes that can produce alternative expressions of a characteristic (such as ability or inability to curl the tongue) are called **alleles.** Every person receives a pair of alleles for a given characteristic, one from each biological parent. When both alleles are the same, the person is **homozygous** for the characteristic; when they are different, the person is **heterozygous.** In **dominant inheritance,** when a person is heterozygous for a particular trait, the dominant allele governs. In other words, when an offspring receives contradictory alleles for a trait, only one of them, the dominant one, will be expressed. **Recessive inheritance,** the expression of a recessive trait, occurs only when a person receives the recessive allele from both parents.

If you inherited one allele for tongue-curling ability from each parent (see Figure 3-4), you are homozygous for tongue curling and can curl your tongue. If, say, your mother passed on an allele for the ability and your father passed on an allele lacking it, you are heterozygous. Since the ability is dominant (D) and its lack is recessive (d), you, again, can curl your tongue. But if you received the recessive allele from both parents, you would not be a tongue-curler.

Most traits result from **polygenic inheritance,** the interaction of several genes. Whereas more than 1,000 rare genes individually determine abnormal traits, no known single gene by itself significantly accounts for individual differences in any complex normal behaviour. Instead, such behaviours are likely to be influenced by many genes with small but sometimes

alleles Two or more alternative forms of a gene that can occupy the same position on paired chromosomes and affect the same trait

homozygous Possessing two identical alleles for a trait

heterozygous Possessing differing alleles for a trait

dominant inheritance Pattern of inheritance in which, when a child receives contradictory alleles, only the dominant one is expressed

recessive inheritance Pattern of inheritance in which a child receives identical recessive alleles, resulting in expression of a nondominant trait

polygenic inheritance Pattern of inheritance in which multiple genes at different sites on chromosomes affect a complex trait

The ability to curl the tongue lengthwise, as this girl is doing, is unusual in that it is inherited through simple dominant transmission. Most normal traits are influenced by multiple genes, often in combination with environmental factors.

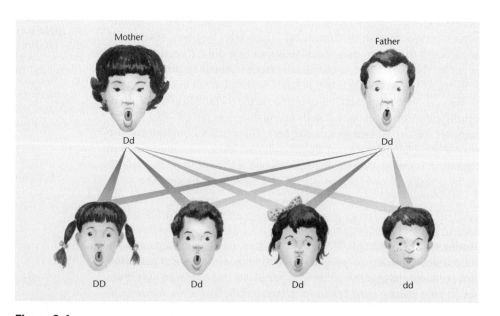

Figure 3-4

Dominant and recessive inheritance. Because of dominant inheritance, the same observable phenotype (in this case, the ability to curl the tongue lengthwise) can result from two different genotypes (DD and Dd). A phenotype expressing a recessive characteristic (such as inability to curl the tongue) must have a homozygous genotype (dd).

identifiable effects. Furthermore, there may be an average of 12 different versions, or variants, of each gene, each with varying influences (Stephens et al., 2001). Researchers in *molecular genetics* have begun to identify specific genes that contribute to particular behavioural traits (Plomin, 2001). So far, at least seven genes have been tentatively associated with intelligence and other cognitive abilities (Posthuma & de Gues, 2006).

Traits may be affected by **mutations:** permanent alterations in genetic material. A study comparing genomes of four racial/ethnic groups found that the lighter skin colour of Caucasians and Asians resulted from slight mutations—a change of just one letter of DNA code out of the 3.1 billion letters in the human genome—tens of thousands of years ago (Lamason et al., 2005).

Multifactorial transmission, a combination of genetic and environmental factors, plays a role in the expression of most traits. For example, children with attention-deficit hyperactivity disorder are more likely to show early anti-social behaviour if they were of low birth weight and have a variant of a gene called COMT (Thapar et al., 2005).

Genotypes and Phenotypes

If you can curl your tongue, that ability is part of your **phenotype,** the array of observable characteristics through which your **genotype,** or underlying genetic makeup, is expressed. Except for monozygotic twins, no two people have the same genotype. The phenotype is the product of the genotype and any relevant environmental influences. The difference between genotype and phenotype helps explain why a **clone** (a genetic copy of an individual) or even an identical twin can never be an exact duplicate of another person.

As Figure 3-4 shows, the same phenotypical characteristic may arise from different genotypes: either a homozygous combination of two dominant alleles or a heterozygous combination of one dominant allele and one recessive allele. If you are heterozygous for tongue curling and you and a mate who is also heterozygous for the trait have four children, the statistical probability is that one child will be homozygous for the ability, one will be homozygous lacking it, and the other two will be heterozygous. Thus, three of your children will likely have phenotypes that include tongue curling (they will be able to curl their tongues), but this ability will arise from two different genotypical patterns (homozygous and heterozygous).

Tongue curling has a strong genetic base; but for most traits, experience modifies the expression of the genotype. Let's say that Steven has inherited musical talent. If he takes music lessons and practises regularly, he may delight his family with his performances. If his family likes and encourages classical music, he may play Bach preludes; if the other children on his block influence him to prefer popular music, he may eventually form a rock group. However, if from early childhood he is not encouraged and not motivated to play music, and if he has no access to a musical instrument or to music lessons, his genotype for musical ability may not be expressed (or may be expressed to a lesser extent) in his phenotype. Some physical characteristics (including height and weight) and most psychological characteristics (such as intelligence and personality traits, as well as musical ability) are products of multifactorial transmission.

Genetic and Chromosomal Abnormalities

One of John and Lesley Brown's chief worries before Louise's birth—whether or not she would be a "normal" baby—is shared by every prospective biological parent. Babies born with serious birth defects are at high risk of dying at or shortly after birth or during infancy or childhood (Skjaerven, Wilcox, & Lie, 1999). Birth disorders are fairly rare, affecting only about 3 percent of live births (Waknine, 2006); the most prevalent defects are cleft lip or cleft palate, followed by Down syndrome. Other serious malformations involve the eye or the circulatory, orofacial, gastronomical, or musculoskeletal systems (CDC, 2006b). Birth disorders accounted for 27 percent of infant deaths in Canada in 1997 (CICH, 2000). Most of the serious malformations involve the circulatory or central nervous systems (see Table 3-2).

Checkpoint ✔

Can you . . .

✔ Explain why no two people, other than monozygotic twins, have the same genetic heritage?

✔ Explain why it is the sperm that determines a baby's sex?

✔ Tell how dominant inheritance and recessive inheritance work, and why most normal traits are not the products of simple dominant or recessive transmission?

mutations Permanent alterations in genes or chromosomes that may produce harmful characteristics

multifactorial transmission Combination of genetic and environmental factors to produce certain complex traits

phenotype Observable characteristics of a person

genotype Genetic makeup of a person, containing both expressed and unexpressed characteristics

clone *(verb)* To make a genetic copy of an individual; *(noun)* a genetic copy of an individual

Guidepost 4

How are birth defects and disorders transmitted?

Table 3-2   Some Birth Defects

Condition	Characteristics of Condition	Who Is at Risk	What Can Be Done
Alpha1 antitrypsin deficiency	Enzyme deficiency that can lead to cirrhosis of the liver in early infancy and emphysema and degenerative lung disease in middle age.	1 in 1,000 births to people of European descent	No treatment
Alpha thalassemia	Severe anemia that reduces ability of the blood to carry oxygen; nearly all affected infants are stillborn or die soon after birth.	Primarily families of Malaysian, African, and Southeast Asian descent	Frequent blood transfusions
Beta thalassemia (Cooley's anemia)	Severe anemia resulting in weakness, fatigue, and frequent illness; usually fatal in adolescence or young adulthood.	Primarily families of Mediterranean descent	Frequent blood transfusions
Cystic fibrosis	Body makes too much mucus, which collects in the lung and digestive tract; children do not grow normally and usually do not live beyond age 30; the most common inherited *lethal* defect among people of European descent.	1 in 2,000 births to people of European descent	Daily physical therapy to loosen mucus; antibiotics for lung infections; enzymes to improve digestion; gene therapy (in experimental stage)
Duchenne's muscular dystrophy	Fatal disease usually found in males, marked by muscle weakness; minor mental retardation not uncommon; respiratory failure and death usually occur in young adulthood.	1 in 3,000 to 5,000 male births	No treatment
Hemophilia	Excessive bleeding, usually affecting males rather than females; in its most severe form, can lead to crippling arthritis in adulthood.	1 in 10,000 families with a history of hemophilia	Frequent transfusions of blood with clotting factors
Neural-tube defects: Anencephaly	Absence of brain tissues; infants are stillborn or die soon after birth.	1 in 1,000	No treatment
Spina bifida	Incompletely closed spinal canal, resulting in muscle weakness or paralysis and loss of bladder and bowel control; often accompanied by hydrocephalus, an accumulation of spinal fluid in the brain, which can lead to mental retardation.	1 in 1,000	Surgery to close spinal canal may prevent further injury; shunt placed in brain drains excess fluid and prevents mental retardation
Phenylketonuria (PKU)	Metabolic disorder resulting in mental retardation.	1 in 10,000 to 25,000 births	Special diet begun in first few weeks of life can offset mental retardation
Polycystic kidney disease	*Infantile form:* enlarged kidneys, leading to respiratory problems and congestive heart failure. *Adult form:* kidney pain, kidney stones, and hypertension resulting in chronic kidney failure.	1 in 1,000	Kidney transplants
Sickle-cell anemia	Deformed, fragile red blood cells that can clog the blood vessels, depriving the body of oxygen; symptoms include severe pain, stunted growth, frequent infections, leg ulcers, gallstones, susceptibility to pneumonia, and stroke.	1 in 500 people of African descent	Painkillers, transfusions for anemia, and to prevent stroke, antibiotics for infections
Tay-Sachs disease	Degenerative disease of the brain and nerve cells, resulting in death before age 5.	1 in 3,000 people of eastern European Jewish descent, rarer in other groups	No treatment

Source: Adapted from AAP Committee on Genetics, 1996; Tisdale, 1988, pp. 68–69.

It is in genetic defects and diseases that we see most clearly the operation of dominant and recessive transmission in humans, and also of a variation, sex-linked inheritance. Some defects are due to abnormalities in genes or chromosomes, which may result from mutations: permanent alterations in genetic material that may produce harmful characteristics. Mutations can occur spontaneously or can be induced by environmental hazards, such as radiation.

Many disorders arise when an inherited predisposition interacts with an environmental factor, either before or after birth. Spina bifida (incomplete closure of the vertebral canal) and cleft palate (a fissure in the roof of the mouth) probably result from multifactorial transmission (Botto, Moore, Khoury, & Erickson, 1999). Attention deficit hyperactivity disorder is one of a number of behavioural disorders thought to be transmitted multifactorially.

Not all genetic or chromosomal abnormalities show up at birth. Symptoms of Tay-Sachs disease (a fatal degenerative disease of the central nervous system that at one time occurred mostly among Jews of eastern European ancestry) and sickle-cell anemia (a blood disorder most common among people of African descent) may not appear until at least 6 months of age; cystic fibrosis (a condition, especially common in children of northern European descent, in which excess mucus accumulates in the lungs and digestive tract), not until age 4; and glaucoma (a disease in which fluid pressure builds up in the eye) and Huntington's disease (a progressive degeneration of the nervous system) usually not until middle age.

Dominant or Recessive Inheritance of Defects

Most of the time, normal genes are dominant over those carrying abnormal traits, but sometimes the gene for an abnormal trait is dominant. When one parent has a dominant abnormal gene and one recessive normal gene and the other parent has two recessive normal genes, each of their children has a 50:50 chance of inheriting the abnormal gene. Among the 1,800 disorders known to be transmitted by dominant inheritance are achondroplasia (a type of dwarfism) and Huntington's disease.

Recessive defects are expressed only if a child receives the same recessive gene from each biological parent. Some defects transmitted recessively, such as Tay-Sachs disease and sickle-cell anemia, are more common among certain ethnic groups, which, through inbreeding (marriage and reproduction within the group) have passed down recessive characteristics (see Table 3-3).

Table 3-3	Chances of Genetic Disorders for Various Ethnic Groups	
If You Are	The Chance Is About	That
African descent	1 in 12	You are a carrier of sickle-cell anemia.
	7 in 10	You will have milk intolerance as an adult.
African descent male	1 in 10	You have a hereditary predisposition to develop hemolytic anemia after taking sulfa or other drugs.
African descent female	1 in 50	You have a hereditary predisposition to develop hemolytic anemia after taking sulfa or other drugs.
European descent	1 in 25	You are a carrier of cystic fibrosis.
	1 in 80	You are a carrier of phenylketonuria (PKU).
Jewish (Ashkenazic) descent	1 in 100	You are a carrier of familial dysautonomia.
Italian descent Greek descent	1 in 10	You are a carrier of beta thalassemia.
Armenian or Jewish (Sephardic) descent	1 in 45	You are a carrier of familial Mediterranean fever.
Afrikaner (Northern-European-descended South African) descent	1 in 330	You have porphyria.
Asian descent	almost 100%	You will have milk intolerance as an adult.

Source: Adapted from Milunsky, 1992, p. 122.

Defects transmitted by recessive inheritance are more likely to be lethal at an early age than those transmitted by dominant inheritance. If a dominantly transmitted defect killed before the age of reproduction, it could not be passed on to the next generation and therefore would soon disappear. A recessive defect can be transmitted by carriers who do not have the disorder and thus may live to reproduce.

Some traits are only partly dominant or partly recessive. In **incomplete dominance** a trait is not fully expressed. For example, people with only one sickle-cell allele and one normal allele do not have sickle-cell anemia but do show some manifestations of the condition, such as shortness of breath at high altitudes.

Sex-linked Inheritance of Defects

In **sex-linked inheritance** (see Figure 3-5) certain recessive disorders linked to genes on the sex chromosomes show up differently in male and female children. Red-green colour-blindness is one of these sex-linked conditions. Another is hemophilia, a disorder in which blood does not clot when it should.

Sex-linked recessive traits are carried on one of the X chromosomes of an unaffected mother. The mother is a *carrier;* she does not have the disorder but can pass on the gene to her children. Sex-linked disorders almost always appear only in male children; in females, a normal dominant gene on the X chromosome from the father overrides the defective gene on the X chromosome from the mother. Boys are more vulnerable to these disorders because there is no opposite dominant gene on the shorter Y chromosome from the father to override a defect on the X chromosome from the mother.

Occasionally, a female does inherit a sex-linked condition. For example, if her father is a hemophiliac and her mother happens to be a carrier for the disorder, the daughter has a 50 percent chance of receiving the abnormal X chromosome from each parent and having the disease.

incomplete dominance Pattern of inheritance in which a child receives two different alleles, resulting in partial expression of a trait

sex-linked inheritance Pattern of inheritance in which certain characteristics carried on the X chromosome inherited from the mother are transmitted differently to her male and female offspring

Genome Imprinting

Genome, or genetic, imprinting is the differential expression of certain genetic traits, depending on whether the trait has been inherited from the mother or the father. In imprinted gene pairs, genetic information inherited from the parent of one sex is activated, but genetic information from the other parent is not. Imprinted genes play an important role in regulating fetal growth and development. When a normal pattern of imprinting is disrupted, abnormal fetal growth or congenital growth disorders may result (Hitchins & Moore, 2002).

Scientists have studied genome imprinting in mice by artificially manipulating their genetic makeup. Mice with two maternal copies of a gene in the region of chromosome 11 and a disabled paternal gene are born 70 percent smaller than their normal littermates, whereas mice with two paternal copies and a disabled maternal gene are about 30 percent larger than normal (Cattanach & Kirk, 1985).

What explains these differences? One widely accepted hypothesis, proposed by the evolutionary biologist David Haig (1993; Haig & Westoby, 1989), is that a pregnant woman unconsciously seeks to "ration" her nutritive resources between herself and her

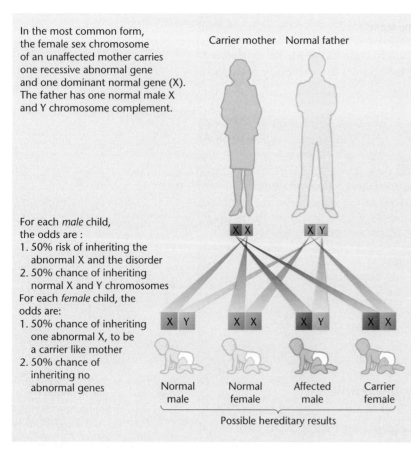

In the most common form, the female sex chromosome of an unaffected mother carries one recessive abnormal gene and one dominant normal gene (X). The father has one normal male X and Y chromosome complement.

Carrier mother   Normal father

For each *male* child, the odds are :
1. 50% risk of inheriting the abnormal X and the disorder
2. 50% chance of inheriting normal X and Y chromosomes
For each *female* child, the odds are:
1. 50% chance of inheriting one abnormal X, to be a carrier like mother
2. 50% chance of inheriting no abnormal genes

Normal male   Normal female   Affected male   Carrier female

Possible hereditary results

Figure 3-5
Sex-linked inheritance of a birth defect.

fetus, ensuring her own ability to survive and have future children. Fathers, on the other hand, are concerned (from an evolutionary point of view) only with their own offspring, not with any other children the mother may have. Thus imprinted genes that limit fetal growth may be a mother's defence against extra demands on her, while imprinted genes from the father may serve as a check so that growth is not abnormally slowed. The fact that imprinting occurs only in mammals and that most imprinted genes are expressed in the mother's placenta, the seat of fetal nourishment, supports this theory (Tilghman, 1999).

Chromosomal Abnormalities

Chromosomal abnormalities typically occur because of errors in cell division, which result in an extra or missing chromosome. Some of these errors happen in the sex cells during meiosis. For example, Klinefelter syndrome is caused by an extra sex chromosome (shown by the pattern XXY). Turner syndrome results from a missing sex chromosome (XO). The likelihoood of errors in meiosis may increase in women age 35 or older. (University of Virginia Health System, 2004). Characteristics of the most common sex chromosome disorders are shown in Table 3-4.

Other chromosomal abnormalities occur in the autosomes during cell division. **Down syndrome,** the most common of these, is responsible for about 40 percent of all cases of moderate-to-severe mental retardation (Pennington, Moon, Edgin, Stedron, & Nadel, 2003). The condition is also called *trisomy-21,* because it is usually caused by an extra 21st chromosome or the translocation of part of the 21st chromosome onto another chromosome. The most obvious physical characteristic associated with the disorder is a downward-sloping skin fold at the inner corners of the eyes.

About 1 in every 800 Canadian babies born alive has Down syndrome (Heath Canada, 2002). The risk is greatest with older parents and teenagers, although in general more children with Down syndrome are born to younger women, given that younger women give birth to more children than older women. When the mother is under age 35, the disorder is more likely to be hereditary. The extra chromosome seems to come from the mother's ovum in 95 percent of cases (Antonarakis & Down Syndrome Collaborative Group, 1991); the other 5 percent of cases seem to be related to the father.

The brains of children with Down syndrome appear normal at birth but shrink in volume by young adulthood, particularly in the hippocampal area, resulting in cognitive dysfunction (Pennington et al., 2003). The prognosis for these children is brighter than was once thought. As adults, many live in small group homes and support themselves; they tend to do well in structured job situations. More than 70 percent of people with Down

Checkpoint ✓

Can you . . .

✔ Compare the operation of dominant inheritance, recessive inheritance, sex-linked inheritance, and genome imprinting in transmission of birth defects?

Down syndrome Chromosomal disorder characterized by moderate-to-severe mental retardation

Table 3-4	Sex Chromosome Abnormalities		
Pattern/Name	**Characteristic***	**Incidence**	**Treatment**
XYY	Male; tall stature; tendency to low IQ, especially verbal.	1 in 1,000 male births	No special treatment
XXX (triple X)	Female, normal appearance, menstrual irregularities, learning disorders, mental retardation.	1 in 1,000 female births	Special education
XXY (Kleinfelter)	Male, sterility, underdeveloped secondary sex characteristics, small testes, learning disorders.	1 in 1,000 male births	Hormone therapy, special education
XO (Turner)	Female, short stature, webbed neck, impaired spatial abilities, no menstruation, infertility, underdeveloped sex organs, incomplete development of secondary sex characteristics.	1 in 1,500 to 2,500 female births	Hormone therapy, special education
Fragile X	Minor-to-severe mental retardation; symptoms, which are more severe in males, include delayed speech and motor development, speech impairments, and hyperactivity; the most common *inherited* form of mental retardation.	1 in 1,200 male births; 1 in 2,000 female births	Educational and behavioural therapies when needed

*Not every affected person has every characteristic.

syndrome live into their 60s, but they are at elevated risk of dying early from various causes, including leukemia, cancer, Alzheimer's disease, and cardiovascular disease (Hayes & Batshaw, 1993; Hill et al., 2003; Schupf, Kapell, Nightingale, Rodriguez, Tycko, Mayeux, 1998).

Genetic Counselling and Testing

Genetic counselling can help prospective parents assess their risk of bearing children with genetic or chromosomal defects. People who have already had a child with a genetic defect, who have a family history of hereditary illness, who suffer from conditions known or suspected to be inherited, or who come from ethnic groups at higher-than-average risk of passing on genes for certain diseases can get information about their likelihood of producing affected children.

A genetic counsellor may be a pediatrician, an obstetrician, a family doctor, a nurse, or a genetic specialist. She or he takes a family history and gives the prospective parents and any biological children physical examinations. Laboratory investigations of blood, skin, urine, or fingerprints may be performed. Chromosomes from body tissues may be analyzed and photographed, and the photographs enlarged and arranged according to size and structure on a chart called a *karyotype*. This chart can show chromosomal abnormalities and can indicate whether a person who appears normal might transmit genetic defects to a child (see Figure 3–6). The counsellor tries to help clients understand the mathematical risk of a particular condition, explains its implications, and presents information about alternative courses of action.

Geneticists have made great contributions to avoidance of birth defects. For example, since so many Jewish couples have been tested for Tay-Sachs genes, far fewer Jewish babies have been born with the disease (Kolata, 2003); in fact, it is now far more likely to affect non-Jewish babies (Kaback et al., 1993). Similarly, screening and counselling of women of childbearing age from Mediterranean countries, where beta thalassemia (refer back to Table 3-2) is common, has brought a decline in births of affected babies and greater knowledge of the risks of being a carrier (Cao, Saba, Galanello, & Rosatelli, 1997).

Today, researchers are rapidly identifying genes that contribute to many serious diseases and disorders, as well as those that influence normal traits. Their work is likely to lead to widespread **genetic testing** to reveal genetic profiles—a prospect that involves dangers as well as benefits (see Box 3-2).

---

genetic counselling Clinical service that advises couples of their probable risk of having children with hereditary defects

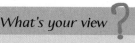

What's your view

- Should genetic counselling be compulsory before marriage?

Checkpoint

Can you . . .

✔ Tell three ways in which chromosomal disorders occur?

✔ Explain the purposes of genetic counselling?

genetic testing Procedure for ascertaining genetic makeup to identify predispositions to herditary diseases or disorders

---

Figure 3-6

A karyotype is a photograph that shows the chromosomes when they are separated and aligned for cell division. We know that this is a karyotype of a person with Down syndrome, because there are three chromosomes instead of the usual two on chromosome 21. Since pair 23 consists of two X's, we know that this is the karyotype of a female.

Source: Babu & Hirschhorn, 1992; March of Dimes, 1987.

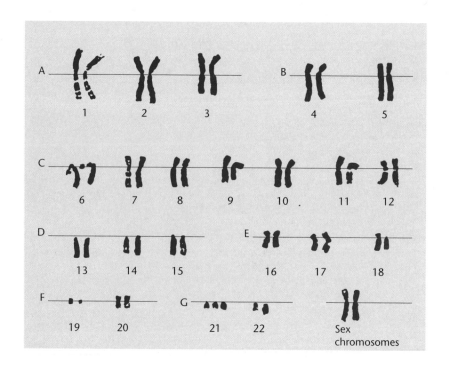

Box 3-2 *Genetic Testing, Genetic Engineering, and Medical Genetics*

The complete sequence of genes in the human body constitutes the *human genome.* Scientists have now finished mapping the human genome, which is estimated to contain between 20,000 and 25,000 genes (International Human Genome Sequencing Consortium, 2004). Among the interesting findings are that all but 300 human genes have counterparts in mice (Wade, 2001), and the genomes of humans and chimpanzees are nearly 99 percent alike (Clark et al., 2003). Indeed, chimps and humans of the same sex are no more different genetically than are men and women (Rozen et al., 2003).

The mapping of the human genome has greatly advanced our ability to identify which genes influence specific traits or behaviours and the developmental unfolding of these traits (Parke, 2004). A new field of science, *genomics,* the study of the functions and interactions of the various genes, will have untold implications for *medical genetics,* the application of genetic information to therapeutic purposes (McKusick, 2001; Patenaude, Guttmacher, & Collins, 2002). As efforts shift from finding genes to understanding how they affect behaviour, scientists will be able to identify genes that cause, trigger, or increase susceptibility to particular disorders so as to screen at-risk population groups (Khoury, McCabe, & McCabe, 2003).

The genetic information gained from such research could increase our ability to predict, prevent, control, treat, and cure disease—even to pinpoint specific drug treatments to specific individuals. Already, genetic screening of newborns is saving lives and preventing mental retardation by permitting identification and treatment of infants with such disorders as sickle-cell anemia and phenylketonuria (PKU) (Holtzman, Murphy, Watson, & Barr, 1997; Khoury et al., 2003). Genetic screening for breast cancer probably would identify 88 percent of all high-risk persons, significantly more than are currently identified (Pharaoh et al., 2002). Genetic information can help people decide whether to have children and with whom, and it can help people with family histories of a disease to know the worst that is likely to happen (Post, 1994; Wiggins et al., 1992).

Gene therapy (repairing genes, or replacing abnormal genes with normal ones), once a bright hope, appears to have dimmed for the time being. In 2000, French researchers reversed severe combined immunodeficiency, a serious immune disease, in ten babies from 1 to 11 months old by taking bone marrow cells from the babies, genetically altering the cells, and then injecting them into the babies. One year later, the patients remained healthy (Cavazanna-Calvo et al., 2000). But three of the children have since developed leukemia, and one of the three has died. In 1999 another death occurred in a gene therapy experiment at the University of Pennsylvania (Harris, 2005).

Genetic testing itself involves such ethical and political issues as privacy and fair use of genetic information (Clayton, 2003; Jeffords & Daschle, 2001; Patenaude et al., 2002). Although medical data are supposed to be confidential, it is almost impossible to keep genetic information private. Some courts have ruled that blood relatives have a legitimate claim to information about a patient's genetic health risks that may affect them, even though such disclosures violate confidentiality (Clayton, 2003). In Canada, it is recommended that people undergoing genetic testing be made aware of its consequences and limitations. The consequences include the potential for discrimination, negative impact on the family, and potential loss of some types of support services

such as life insurance, especially for those likely to have genetically based late-onset diseases (Jamieson, 2001).

A major concern is *genetic determinism:* the misconception that a person with a gene for a disease is bound to get the disease. All genetic testing can tell us is the *likelihood* that a person will get a disease. Most diseases involve a complex combination of genes or depend in part on lifestyle or other environmental factors (Clayton, 2003; Plomin & Rutter, 1998; Rutter, 2002). Job and insurance discrimination on the basis of genetic information has occurred—even though tests may be imprecise and unreliable and people deemed at risk of a disease may never develop it (Clayton, 2003; Khoury et al., 2003; Lapham, Kozma, & Weiss, 1996). This could lead, according to a policy report issued to the Canadian government, to a new socially stigmatized group of the "not-yet-ill" (Jamieson, 2001, p. 2).

The psychological impact of test results is another concern (Patenaude et al., 2002). Predictions are imperfect; a false positive result may cause needless anxiety, and a false negative result may lull a person into complacency. And what if a genetic condition is incurable? Is there any point in knowing you have the gene for a potentially debilitating condition if you cannot do anything about it? A panel of experts has recommended against genetic testing for diseases for which there is no known cure (Institute of Medicine [IOM], 1993).

Additional concerns involve the testing of children. Should a child be tested to benefit a sibling or someone else? How will a child be affected by learning that he or she is likely to develop a disease 20, 30, or 50 years later? The American Academy of Pediatrics Committee on Bioethics (2001) recommends against genetic testing of children for conditions that cannot be treated in childhood.

Particularly chilling is the prospect that genetic testing could be misused to justify sterilization of people with "undesirable" genes or abortion of a normal fetus with the "wrong" genetic makeup (Harmon, 2005; Plomin & Rutter, 1998). Gene therapy has the potential for similar abuse. Should it be used to make a short child taller or a chubby child thinner? To improve an unborn baby's appearance or intelligence? The path from therapeutic correction of defects to genetic engineering for cosmetic or functional purposes may well be a slippery slope (Anderson, 1998), leading to a society in which some parents could afford to provide the "best" genes for their children and others could not (Rifkin, 1998). Some advocates for persons with disabilities fear that reducing the number of children born with a defect such as Down syndrome would divert research attention and research dollars to treatment for those who already have the condition (Harmon, 2005).

Within the next 15 years, genetic testing "will almost certainly revolutionize the practice of medicine" (Anderson, 1998, p. 30). It is not yet clear whether the benefits will outweigh the risks.

What's your view

Would you want to know that you had a gene predisposing you to lung cancer? To Alzheimer's disease? Would you want your child to be tested for these genes?

Check it out

For more information on this topic, go to **www.mcgrawhill.ca/olc/papalia,** and **www.ornl.gov/hgmis/resource/medicine.html.**

Guidepost 5

How do scientists study the relative influences of heredity and environment, and how do heredity and environment work together?

Monozygotic twins separated at birth are sought after by researchers who want to study the impact of genes on personality. These twins, adopted by different families and not reunited until age 31, both became firefighters. Was this a coincidence, or did it reflect the influence of heredity?

behavioural genetics
Quantitative study of relative hereditary and environmental influences

heritability Statistical estimate of contribution of heredity to individual differences in a specific trait within a given population

Nature and Nurture: Influences of Heredity and Environment

How do nature and nurture influence development? That question was a major issue among early psychologists and the general public (refer back to Chapters 1 and 2). Today it has become clear that, while certain rare physical disorders are virtually 100 percent inherited, phenotypes for most complex normal traits, such as those having to do with health, intelligence, and personality, are subject to a complex array of hereditary and environmental forces. Let's see how scientists study and explain the influences of heredity and environment and how these two forces work together.

Studying the Relative Influences of Heredity and Environment

One approach to the study of heredity and environment is quantitative: it seeks to measure how much heredity and environment influence particular traits. This is the traditional goal of the science of **behavioural genetics.**

Measuring Heritability

Heritability is a statistical estimate of how great a contribution heredity makes toward individual differences in a specific trait at a certain time *within a given population.* Heritability does *not* refer to the relative influence of heredity and environment in a particular individual; those influences may be virtually impossible to separate. Nor does heritability tell us how traits develop. It merely indicates the statistical extent to which genes contribute to a trait.

Heritability is expressed as a proportion ranging from 0.0 to 1.0; the higher the number, the greater the heritability of a trait, with 1.0 meaning that genes are 100 percent responsible for variances in the trait within the population. Since heritability cannot be measured directly, researchers in behavioural genetics rely chiefly on three types of correlational research: family, adoption, and twin studies.

These studies are based on the assumption that immediate family members are more genetically similar than more distant relatives, monozygotic twins are more genetically similar than dizygotic twins, and adopted children are genetically more like their biological families than their adoptive families. Thus, if heredity is an important influence on a particular trait, siblings should be more alike than cousins with regard to that trait, monozygotic twins should be more alike than dizygotic twins, and adopted children should be more like their biological parents than their adoptive parents. By the same token, if a shared environment exerts an important influence on a trait, persons who live together should be more similar than persons who do not live together.

Family studies go beyond noting similarities in traits among family members, as we did for Louise Brown and her mother and father. Researchers measure the degree to which biological relatives share certain traits and whether the closeness of the familial relationship is associated with the degree of similarity. If the correlation is strong, the researchers infer a genetic influence. However, family studies cannot rule out environmental influences on a trait. A family study alone cannot tell us whether obese children of obese parents inherited the tendency or whether they are fat because their diet is like that of their parents. For that reason, researchers do adoption studies, which can separate the effects of heredity from those of a shared environment.

Adoption studies look at similarities between adopted children and their adoptive families and also between adopted children and their biological families. When adopted children are more like their biological parents and siblings in a particular trait (say, obesity), we see the influence of heredity. When they resemble their adoptive families more, we see the influence of environment.

Studies of twins compare pairs of monozygotic twins and same-sex dizygotic twins. (Same-sex twins are used so as to avoid any confounding effects of gender.) Monozygotic twins are twice as genetically similar, on average, as dizygotic twins, who are no more genetically similar than other same-sex siblings. When monozygotic twins are more **concordant** (that is, have a statistically greater tendency to show the same trait) than dizygotic twins, we see the likely effects of heredity. Concordance rates, which may range from zero to 100 percent, tell what percentage of pairs of twins in a sample are concordant, or similar.

When monozygotic twins show higher concordance for a trait than do dizygotic twins, the likelihood of a genetic factor can be studied further through adoption studies. Studies of monozygotic twins separated in infancy and reared apart have found strong resemblances between the twins. Such findings support a hereditary basis for many normal and abnormal characteristics (McGuffin et al., 2001).

Critics of behavioural genetics claim that its assumptions and methods tend to maximize the importance of hereditary effects and minimize environmental ones. Furthermore, there are great variations in the findings, depending on the source of the data. For example, twin studies generally come up with higher heritability estimates than adoption studies do. This wide variability, critics say, "means that no firm conclusions can be drawn about the relative strength of these influences on development" (Collins, Maccoby, Steinberg, Hetherington, & Bornstein, 2000, p. 221).

Behavioural geneticists recognize that the effects of genetic influences, especially on behavioural traits, are rarely inevitable. Even in a trait strongly influenced by heredity, the environment can have substantial impact (Rutter, 2002), as much as 50 percent. In fact, environmental interventions sometimes can overcome genetically "determined" conditions. For example, a special diet begun soon after birth often can prevent mental retardation in children with the genetic disease phenylketonuria (PKU) (Plomin & DeFries, 1999; refer back to Table 3-2).

Effects of the Prenatal Environment

Two additional types of twin studies—*co-twin control* and *chorion control* studies—allow researchers to look at the nature and timing of non-genetic influences in the womb (Phelps, Davis, & Schartz, 1997). *Co-twin control studies* compare the prenatal (or postnatal) development and experiences of one monozygotic twin with those of the other, who serves as a one-person "control group." *Chorion control studies* focus on prenatal influences by comparing two types of monozygotic twins: (1) *monochorionic* twins, who developed within the same fluid-filled sac and thus had a similar prenatal environment, and (2) *dichorionic* twins, who grew within separate sacs, as about one-third of monozygotic twins, like all dizygotic twins, do.

Monochorionic twins normally share blood and have similar hormonal levels, which affect brain development. They also share exposure to any infectious agents that come from the mother's body. Because dichorionic twins are attached to different parts of the uterine wall, one twin may be better nourished than the other and better protected against infection. Twin studies that do not take account of these factors may either underestimate or overestimate genetic influences. Monochorionic twins tend to be more concordant than dichorionic twins in IQ, certain personality patterns, and cholesterol levels.

Checkpoint

Can you . . .

✔ State the basic assumption underlying studies of behavioural genetics and how it applies to family studies, twin studies, and adoption studies?

✔ Cite criticisms of the behavioural genetics approach?

✔ Identify two types of twin studies that focus on environmental influences in the womb?

How Heredity and Environment Work Together

Today many developmental scientists have come to regard a solely quantitative approach to the study of heredity and environment as simplistic. They see these two forces as fundamentally intertwined. Instead of looking at genes and experience as operating independently on an organism, scientists influenced by contemporary evolutionary and developmental theory see both as part of a complex *developmental system* (Gottlieb, 1991; Lickliter & Honeycutt, 2003). From conception on, a combination of constitutional (biological and psychological), social, economic, and cultural factors help shape development. The more advantageous these circumstances and the experiences to which they give rise, the greater is the likelihood of optimum development.

Let's consider several ways in which inheritance and experience work together.

Reaction Range and Canalization

Many characteristics vary, within limits, under varying hereditary or environmental conditions. The concepts of *reaction range* and *canalization* can help us visualize how this happens.

Body size, for example, depends largely on biological processes, which are genetically regulated. Even so, a range of sizes is possible, depending on environmental opportunities and constraints and a person's own behaviour. In societies in which nutrition has dramatically improved, an entire generation has grown up to tower over the generation before. The better-fed children share their parents' genes but have responded to a healthier world. Once a society's average diet becomes adequate for more than one generation, however, children tend to grow to heights similar to their parents'. Ultimately, height has genetic limits: we don't see people who are only a foot tall, or any who are 10 feet tall.

Heredity can influence whether a **reaction range** is wide or narrow. For example, a child born with a defect producing mild retardation is more able to respond to a favourable environment than a child born with more severe limitations. A child of normal native intelligence is likely to have a higher IQ if raised in an enriched home and school environment than if raised in a more restrictive environment; but a child with more native ability will probably have a much wider reaction range (see Figure 3-7).

The metaphor of **canalization** illustrates how heredity restricts the range of development for some traits. After a heavy storm, the rainwater that has fallen on a pavement has to go somewhere. If the street has potholes, the water will fill them. If deep canals have been dug along the edges of the street, the water will flow into the canals instead. Some human characteristics, such as eye colour, are so strongly programmed by the genes that they are said to be highly canalized: there is little opportunity for variance in their expression.

Certain behaviours also develop along genetically "dug" channels; it takes an extreme change in environment to alter their course. Behaviours that depend largely on

---

reaction range Potential variability, depending on environmental conditions, in the expression of a hereditary trait

canalization Limitation on variance of expression of certain inherited characteristics

---

Figure 3-7

Intelligence and reaction range. Children with different genotypes for intelligence will show varying reaction ranges when exposed to a restricted (blue portion of bar) or enriched (entire bar) environment.

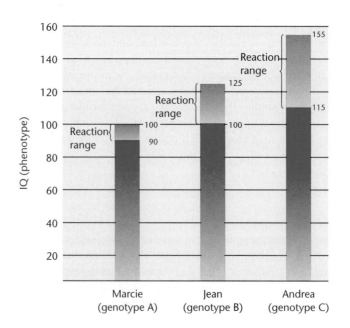

maturation seem to appear when a child is ready. Normal babies follow a typical sequence of motor development: crawling, walking, and running, in that order, at certain approximate ages. Still, this development is not completely canalized; experience can affect its pace and timing.

Cognition and personality are more subject to variations in experience: the kinds of families children grow up in, the schools they attend, and the people they encounter. Consider language. Before children can talk, they must reach a certain level of neurological and muscular maturation. No 6-month-old could speak this sentence, no matter how enriched the infant's home life might be. Yet environment does play a large part in language development. If parents encourage babies' first sounds by talking back to them, children are likely to start to speak earlier than if their early vocalizing is ignored.

Recently scientists have begun to recognize that a usual or typical experience, too, can dig canals, or channels for development (Gottlieb, 1991). For example, infants who hear only the sounds peculiar to their native language soon lose the ability to perceive sounds characteristic of other languages (see Chapter 7). Throughout this book you will find many examples of how socio-economic status, neighbourhood conditions, and educational opportunity can powerfully shape developmental outcomes, from the pace and complexity of language development to the likelihood of early sexual activity and anti-social behaviour.

Genotype–Environment Interaction

Genotype–environment interaction usually refers to the effects of similar environmental conditions on genetically different individuals. To take a familiar example, many people are exposed to pollen and dust, but people with a genetic predisposition are more likely to develop allergic reactions. Some researchers point out that interactions can work the other way as well: Genetically similar children often develop differently, depending on their home environment (Collins et al., 2000). As we discuss in Chapter 8, a child born with a "difficult" temperament may develop adjustment problems in one family and thrive in another, depending largely on parental handling. Thus it may take the interaction of hereditary and environmental factors, not just one or the other, to produce certain conditions.

genotype–environment interaction The portion of phenotypic variation that results from the reactions of genetically different individuals to similar environmental conditions

Genotype–Environment Correlation

The environment often reflects or reinforces genetic differences. That is, certain genetic and environmental influences tend to act in the same direction. This is called **genotype–environment correlation,** or *genotype–environment covariance,* and it works in three ways to strengthen the phenotypic expression of a genotypic tendency (Bergeman & Plomin, 1989; Scarr, 1992; Scarr & McCartney, 1983):

genotype–environment correlation Tendency of certain genetic and environmental influences to reinforce each other; may be passive, reactive (evocative), or active; also called *genotype–environment covariance*

- *Passive correlations:* Parents, who provide the genes that predispose a child toward a trait, also tend to provide an environment that encourages the development of that trait. For example, a musical parent is likely to create a home environment in which music is heard regularly, to give a child music lessons, and to take the child to musical events. If the child inherited the parent's musical talent, the child's musicality will reflect a combination of genetic and environmental influences. This type of correlation is called *passive* because the child does not control it; it is most applicable to young children, whose parents, the source of their genetic legacy, also have a great deal of control over their early experiences.
- *Reactive, or evocative, correlations:* Children with differing genetic makeups evoke different responses from adults. Parents who are *not* musically inclined may make a special effort to provide musical experiences to a child who shows interest and ability in music. This response, in turn, strengthens the child's genetic inclination toward music.

- *Active correlations:* As children get older and have more freedom to choose their own activities and environments, they actively select or create experiences consistent with their genetic tendencies. A child with a talent for music will probably seek out musical friends, take music classes, and go to concerts if such opportunities are available. A shy child is likely to spend more time in solitary pursuits than an outgoing youngster. This tendency to seek out environments compatible with one's genotype is called **niche-picking;** it helps explain why identical twins reared apart tend to be quite similar.

niche-picking Tendency of a person, especially after early childhood, to seek out environments compatible with his or her genotype

What Makes Siblings So Different?

Although two children in the same family may bear a striking physical resemblance, siblings can differ greatly in intellect and especially in personality (Plomin, 1989). One reason may be genetic differences, which lead children to need different kinds of stimulation or to respond differently to a similar home environment. For example, one child may be more affected by family discord than another (Rutter, 2002). In addition, studies in behavioural genetics suggest that many of the experiences that strongly affect development differ for different children in a family (McGuffin et al., 2001; Plomin & Daniels, 1987; Plomin & DeFries, 1999).

These **non-shared environmental effects** result from the unique environment in which each child in a family grows up. What factors contribute to this non-shared environment? One is family composition—the differences between boys' and girls' experiences, or between those of firstborns and laterborns. Another is the way parents and siblings treat each child. Certain events, such as illnesses and accidents, and experiences outside the home (for example, with teachers and peers) affect one child and not another. Behavioural geneticists conclude that, while heredity accounts for most of the similarity between siblings, the non-shared environment accounts for most of the difference. Indeed, a great deal of research across the lifespan suggests that most of the variability in behavioural traits in the population as a whole is environmental, but of the non-shared type (McClearn et al., 1997; Plomin, 1996; Plomin & Daniels, 1987; Plomin & DeFries, 1999; Plomin, Owen, & McGuffin, 1994). However, methodological challenges and additional empirical evidence point to the more moderate conclusion that non-shared environmental effects do not greatly outweigh shared ones; rather, there seems to be a balance between the two (Rutter, 2002).

Genotype–environment correlations may play an important role in the non-shared environment. Children's genetic differences may lead parents and siblings to react to them differently and treat them differently; and genes may influence how children perceive and respond to that treatment, and what its outcome will be. Children also mould their own environments by the choices they make—what they do and with whom—and their genetic makeup influences these choices. In other words, "genes drive experience" (Scarr & McCartney, 1983, p. 425). A child who has inherited artistic talent may spend a great deal of time creating "masterpieces" in solitude, while a sibling who is athletically inclined spends more time playing ball with others. Thus, not only will the children's abilities (in, say, painting or soccer) develop differently, but their social lives will be different as well. These differences tend to be accentuated as children grow older and have more experiences outside the family (Bergeman & Plomin, 1989; Bouchard, 1994; Plomin, 1990, 1996; Plomin et al., 1994; Scarr, 1992; Scarr & McCartney, 1983).

The old nature–nurture puzzle is far from resolved; we know now that the problem is far more complex than previously thought. A variety of research designs can continue to augment and refine our understanding of the forces affecting development.

non-shared environmental effects The unique environment in which each child grows up, consisting of distinctive influences or influences that affect one child differently from another

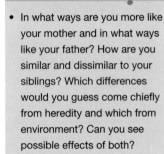

What's your view

- In what ways are you more like your mother and in what ways like your father? How are you similar and dissimilar to your siblings? Which differences would you guess come chiefly from heredity and which from environment? Can you see possible effects of both?

Epigenesis: Environmental Influence on Gene Expression

At one time, most scientists believed that the genes a child inherits were firmly established during fetal development, though their effects on behavioiur could be modified by experience. Now, mounting evidence suggests that gene expression iteslf is controlled by a third component, a mechanism that controls the functioning of genes without affecting their DNA structure. This phenomenon is called **epigenesis.** Furthermore, far from being fixed once and for all, epigenetic activity is affected by a continuing bi-directional interplay with non-genetic influences (Gottlieb, 2007; Rutter, 2007).

Epigenesis (meaning "on the genes"), or the epigenetic framework, refers to chemical molecules attached to a gene, which alter the way a cell "reads" the gene's DNA. The epigenetic framework can be visualized as a "code written in pencil in the margins around the DNA" (Gosden & Feinberg, 2007, p. 731). Because every cell in the body inherits the same DNA sequence, the function of these epigenetic markers is to differentiate different types of body cells. They do so by "switching" particular genes on or off during embryonic formation. Sometimes errors arise in the process, which may lead to birth defects or disease (Gosden & Feinberg, 2007).

Epigenetic markers may contribute to such common ailments as cancer, diabetes, and heart disease. Epigenesis may also explain why one monozygotic twin is susceptible to a disease such as schizophrenia whereas the other twin is not, and why some twins get the same disease but at different ages (Fraga et al., 2005; Wong, Gottesman, & Petronia, 2005).

Epigenetic changes can occur throughout life in response to environmental factors such as nutrition and stress (Rakyan & Beck, 2006). In one twin study, blood analysis showed epigenetic differences in 35 percent of the sample, and these differences were associated with age and lifestyle (Fraga et al., 2005).

Epigenetic modifications, especially those that occur early in life, may even be heritable. Studies of human sperm cells found age-related epigenetic variations capable of being passed on to future generations (Rakyan & Beck, 2006).

epigenesis Mechanism that turns genes on or off and determines functions of body cells

Checkpoint ✔

Can you . . .

✔ Explain and give at least one example of reaction range, canalization, genotype–environment interaction, and genotype–environment correlation?

✔ List three kinds of influences that contribute to non-shared environmental effects?

✔ Cite criticisms of behavioural genetics research"?

✔ Explain how epigenesis works?

Some Characteristics Influenced by Heredity and Environment

 Guidepost 6

What roles do heredity and environment play in physical health, intelligence, and personality?

Keeping in mind the complexity of unravelling the influences of heredity and environment, let's look at what is known about their roles in producing certain characteristics.

Physical and Physiological Traits

Not only do monozygotic twins generally look alike; they are also more concordant than dizygotic twins in their risk for such medical disorders as hypertension (high blood pressure), heart disease, stroke, rheumatoid arthritis, peptic ulcers, and epilepsy (Brass, Isaacsohn, Merikangas, & Robinette, 1992; Plomin et al., 1994). Lifespan, too, seems to be influenced by genes (Sorensen, Nielsen, Andersen, & Teasdale, 1988).

Obesity, sometimes called simply *overweight,* is a multifactorial condition. It is defined in childhood as having a body mass index, or BMI (comparison of weight to height), at or above the 95th percentile for age and sex. Twin studies, adoption studies, and other research suggest that 40 to 70 percent of the risk is genetic. A longitudinal study of risk factors for heart disease, begun in 1973 in the Bogalusa, Louisiana, area, has linked specific genes and their chromosomal locations to body mass measurements taken over several decades (Chen et al., 2004). One key gene, *GAD2* on chromosome 10, normally controls appetite; but an abnormal version of this gene can stimulate hunger and overeating (Boutin et al., 2003).

In Canada, childhood obesity and low levels of activity have been identified as important issues; the proportion of obese children has increased in the last generation—from 5 percent to approximately 15 percent among 7- to 13-year-olds, between 1981 and 1997 (Thompson, Campagna, Rehman, Murphy, Rasmussen, & Ness, 2005), and over one-third of Canadian children from 2 to 11 years are either overweight or obese (Statistics Canada, 2003). The prevalence of overweight is linked to lower activity levels, as well as family income. Children from lower income families are more likely to be overweight than children from higher income families (Statistics Canada, 2003), possibly because of the quality of food available to low income families, as well as the higher stress levels in poorer families

obesity Extreme overweight in relation to age, sex, height, and body type; sometimes defined as having a body mass index (weight-for-height) at or above the 85th or 95th percentile of growth curves for children of the same age and sex

that could be linked to increases in appetites and overeating (Phipps, Burton, Osberg, & Lethbridge, 2006).

The kind and amount of food eaten in a particular home or in a particular social or ethnic group and the amount of exercise that is encouraged can increase or decrease the likelihood that a person will become overweight. The rapid rise in the prevalence of obesity in western countries seems to result from the interaction of a genetic predisposition with inadequate exercise (Leibel, 1997). Obesity is discussed further in Chapters 9, 12, and 15.

Intelligence and School Achievement

Although no genes for intelligence have been conclusively identified (Sternberg et al., 2005), heredity exerts a strong influence on general intelligence (as measured by intelligence tests) and, to a lesser extent, on specific abilities such as memory, verbal ability, and spatial ability (McClearn et al., 1997; Petrill et al., 2004; Plomin et al., 1994; Plomin & DeFries, 1999; Plomin & Spinath, 2004). Experience counts, too; as Figure 3-7 shows, an enriched or impoverished environment can substantially affect the development and expression of innate ability (Neisser et al., 1996).

Evidence of the role of heredity in intelligence comes from adoption and twin studies. Adopted children's IQs are consistently closer to the IQs of their biological mothers than to those of their adoptive parents and siblings, and monozygotic twins are more alike in intelligence than dizygotic twins. This pattern is also true of performance on elementary school achievement tests and on National Merit Scholarship examinations given to high school students in the United States. The studies yield a consistent estimate of heritability of about 50 percent for spatial abilities, meaning that genetic differences explain about half of the observed variation among members of a population. A close correlation between verbal and spatial abilities suggests a genetic link among the components of intelligence (Petrill et al., 2004; Plomin & DeFries, 1999). Indeed, it is likely that the same genes that affect one cognitive ability also affect other cognitive abilities (Plomin & Spinath, 2004). Furthermore, the genetic influence, which is primarily responsible for stability in cognitive performance, increases with age. The shared family environment seems to have a strong influence on young children but a diminishing influence on adolescents and adults, who are more apt to find their own niche by actively selecting environments compatible with their hereditary abilities and related interests. The *non*-shared environment, in contrast, is influential throughout life and is primarily responsible for changes in cognitive performance (Bouchard, 2004; Petrill et al., 2004; Plomin & Spinath, 2004).

Personality

temperament Characteristic disposition, or style of approaching and reacting to situations

Scientists have identified genes directly linked with specific personality traits, such as neuroticism, which may contribute to depression and anxiety (Lesch et al., 1996). Heritability of personality traits appears to be between 40 and 50 percent, and there is little evidence of shared environmental influence (Bouchard, 2004).

Temperament, a person's characteristic style of approaching and reacting to situations, appears to be largely inborn and is often consistent over the years, though it may respond to special experiences or parental handling (A. Thomas & Chess, 1984; A. Thomas, Chess, & Birch, 1968). Siblings—both twins and nontwins—tend to be similar in temperament (Saudino, Wertz, Gagne, & Chawla, 2004). An observational study of 100 pairs of 7-year-old siblings (half of them adoptive siblings and half siblings by birth) found significant genetic influences on activity, sociability, and emotionality (Schmitz, Saudino, Plomin, Fulker, & DeFries, 1996).

Religiousness is subject to both genetic and environmental influences, according to a study of 169 monozygotic and 104 dizygotic twin pairs from Minnesota. Parenting and family life have the strongest influence in childhood, but genetic influences become more predominant from adolescence on (Koenig, McGue, Krueger, & Bouchard, 2005).

Psychopathology

There is evidence for a strong hereditary influence on **schizophrenia** and autism, among other disorders. Both tend to run in families and to show greater concordance between monozygotic twins than between dizygotic twins. However, heredity alone does not produce such disorders; an inherited tendency can be triggered by environmental factors. For example, children with a short form of the serotonin transporter gene 5-HTTLPR are vulnerable to depression if they have cold, unsupportive families but not if they have supportive, nurturing ones (Taylor et al., 2006). (Autism is discussed in Box 6-1 in Chapter 6 and depression in Chapters 14 and 15.)

Schizophrenia is now widely considered a neurological disorder (Gray & Thompson, 2004). Characterized by loss of contact with reality and by such symptoms as hallucinations and delusions, it has multifactorial causes (Berry, Jobanputra, & Pal, 2003; Tuulio-Henriksson et al., 2002; Vaswani & Kapur, 2001). The risk of schizophrenia is 10 times as great among siblings and offspring of schizophrenics as among the general population; and twin and adoption studies suggest that this increased risk comes from shared genes, not shared environments. The estimated genetic contribution is as high as 80 to 85 percent (McGuffin, Owen, & Farmer, 1995; Picker, 2005).

No single gene appears to be responsible (Picker, 2005). Research has identified several gene variants that increase susceptibility to schizophrenia (Cannon et al., 2005; Egan et al., 2004; Xu et al., 2005). A postmortem examination suggests that the disorder may originate in a lack of a chemical called *reelin*, which helps position nerve cells in the developing brain (Impagnatiello et al., 1998).

Because not all monozygotic twins are concordant for the illness, its cause cannot be purely genetic. Co-twin studies suggest that a prenatal viral infection, carried in the blood shared by monochorionic twins, may play a part (Phelps et al., 1997). In a study of the incidence of schizophrenia among all persons born in Denmark between 1935 and 1978, people born in urban areas were more likely to be schizophrenic than those born in rural areas, perhaps because of greater likelihood of birth complications and of exposure to infections during pregnancy and childhood (Mortenson et al., 1999). Schizophrenia may stem from a series of neurological insults in fetal life (Picker, 2005; Rapoport, Addington, Frangou, & Psych, 2005), such as exposure to influenza in the first trimester of pregnancy (Brown, Begg, et al., 2004) and to maternal rubella and respiratory infections in the second and third trimesters. Infants born in urban areas or in late winter or early spring appear to be at increased risk, as are those whose mothers experienced obstetric complications or who were poor or severely deprived as a result of war or famine (Picker, 2005). A link between fetal malnutrition and schizophrenia has been demonstrated in studies in the Netherlands (Susser & Lin, 1992), Finland (Wahlbeck, Forsen, Osmond, Barker, & Eriksson, 2001), and China (St. Clair et al., 2005).

Advanced paternal age is a risk factor for schizophrenia. In large population-based studies in Jerusalem and Denmark, the risk of the disorder was greatly increased when the father was 50 years old or more (Byrne, Agerbo, Ewald, Eaton, & Mortenson, 2003; Malaspina et al., 2001). A study of 700,000 Swedish births estimated that 15.5 percent of schizophrenia cases involved a father who was over 30 at the time of the birth (Sipos et al., 2004).

In this chapter we have looked at some ways in which heredity and environment act to make children what they are. A child's first environment is the world within the uterus, which we discuss in Chapter 4.

schizophrenia Mental disorder marked by loss of contact with reality; symptoms include hallucinations and delusions

Checkpoint ✓

Can you . . .

✔ Assess the evidence for genetic and environmental influences on obesity, intelligence, and temperament?

Summary and Key Terms

Becoming Parents: How Conception Occurs

Guidepost 1 How does conception normally occur, and how have beliefs about conception changed?

- Early beliefs about conception reflected incorrect beliefs about nature and about male and female anatomy.

- Fertilization, the union of an ovum and a sperm, results in the formation of a one-celled zygote, which then duplicates itself by cell division.

fertilization (55)   zygote (55)

Infertility

Guidepost 2 What causes infertility, and what are alternative ways of becoming parents?

- The most common cause of infertility in men is a low sperm count; the most common cause in women is blockage of the Fallopian tubes.

- Assisted reproduction by in vitro fertilization or other means may involve ethical and practical issues.

- Multiple births can occur either by the fertilization of more than one ovum (or one ovum that has split) or by the splitting of one fertilized ovum.

infertility (56)

Mechanisms of Heredity

Guidepost 3 What genetic mechanisms determine sex, physical appearance, and other characteristics?

- The basic functional units of heredity are the genes, which are made of deoxyribonucleic acid (DNA). DNA carries the biochemical instructions, or genetic code, that governs bodily functions and determines inherited characteristics. Each gene seems to be located by function in a definite position on a particular chromosome. The complete sequence of genes in the human body is the human genome.

- Dizygotic (fraternal) twins have different genetic makeups and may be of different sexes; monozygotic (identical) twins have the same genetic makeup but may differ in some respects.

- At conception, each normal human being receives 23 chromosomes from the mother and 23 from the father. These form 23 pairs of chromosomes—22 pairs of autosomes and 1 pair of sex chromosomes. A child who receives an X chromosome from each parent will be a female. If the child receives a Y chromosome from the father, a male will be conceived.

- The simplest patterns of genetic transmission are dominant and recessive inheritance. When a pair of alleles are the same, a person is homozygous for the trait; when they are different, the person is heterozygous.

- Most normal human characteristics are the result of polygenic inheritance or multifactorial transmission, or sometimes of mutations. Except in the case of monozygotic twins, each child inherits a unique genotype, but the phenotype may not express the underlying genotype.

  monozygotic (one-egg) twins (59)
  dizygotic (two-egg) twins (59)
  deoxyribonucleic acid (DNA) (60)   genetic code (60)
  chromosomes (61)   genes (61)   human genome (61)
  autosomes (61)   sex chromosomes (61)   alleles (62)
  homozygous (62)   heterozygous (62)
  dominant inheritance (62)   recessive inheritance (62)
  polygenic inheritance (62)   mutations (63)
  multifactorial transmission (63)   phenotype (63)
  genotype (63)   clone (63)

Genetic and Chromosomal Abnormalities

Guidepost 4 How are birth defects and disorders transmitted?

- Birth defects and diseases may result from simple dominant, recessive, or sex-linked inheritance, from mutations; from genome imprinting; or from chromosomal anomalies.

- Genetic counselling can provide information about the mathematical odds of bearing children with certain defects. Genetic testing involves risks as well as benefits.

  incomplete dominance (66)   sex-linked inheritance (66)
  Down syndrome (67)   genetic counselling (68)
  genetic testing (68)

Nature and Nurture: Influences of Heredity and Environment

Guidepost 5 How do scientists study the relative influences of heredity and environment, and how do heredity and environment work together?

- Research in behavioural genetics is based on the assumption that the relative influences of heredity and environment can be measured statistically. If heredity is an important influence on a trait, genetically closer persons will be more similar in that trait. Family studies, adoption studies, and studies of twins enable researchers to measure the heritability of specific traits.

- Critics claim that traditional behavioural genetics is too simplistic. Instead, they study complex developmental systems, reflecting a confluence of constitutional, economic, social, and biological influences.

- The concepts of reaction range, canalization, genotype–environment interaction, genotype–environment correlation (or covariance), and niche-picking describe ways in which heredity and environment work together.
- Siblings tend to be more different than alike in intelligence and personality. Many experiences that strongly affect development are different for each sibling.

  behavioural genetics (70)   heritability (70)
  concordant (71)   reaction range (72)
  canalization (72)   genotype–environment interaction (73)
  genotype–environment correlation (73)   niche-picking (74)
  non-shared environmental effects (74)   epigenesis (75)

Some Characteristics Influenced by Heredity and Environment

Guidepost 6   What roles do heredity and environment play in physical health, intelligence, and personality?

- Health, obesity, longevity, intelligence, and temperament are influenced by both heredity and environment, and their relative influences may vary across the lifespan.
- Schizophrenia is a psychopathological disorder influenced by both heredity and environment.

  obesity (75)   temperament (76)   schizophrenia (77)

CHAPTER FOUR

4

Pregnancy and Prenatal Development

*If I could have watched you grow
as a magical mother might,
if I could have seen through my magical transparent belly,
there would have been such ripening within . . .*

—Anne Sexton, 1966

Focus *Karen Lutke and Fetal Alcohol Syndrome*

Fetal alcohol syndrome (FAS) and fetal alcohol effects (FAS/E) are clusters of abnormalities shown by children whose mothers drank during pregnancy, and are leading causes of mental retardation. But in the late 1970s, when Jan Lutke adopted the first of her eight adopted children diagnosed with FAS/E, the facts about FAS were not widely publicized or scientifically investigated, though the syndrome had been observed for centuries.

The child, a girl named Karen, was diagnosed at age 3 with FAS. She was removed from her birth mother soon after she was born and was placed in a succession of family and foster-care homes for the first 3 years of her life. Her disruptive behaviour and hyperactivity made it difficult for caregivers to cope, and she was ultimately placed in a resource facility before being adopted by Lutke.

Seventeen years later, as Lutke relates in *Works in Progress: The Meaning of Success for Individuals with FAS/E* (Lutke, 2000), Karen is typical of young Canadian adults with FAS. She is a self-assured young woman, who works as a dog-groomer, and she gives public talks on FAS. Despite her successes, she has had to overcome the challenges of a lower-than-average IQ, immature social and emotional functioning, and susceptibility to perseveration, repeating stereotyped behaviour. Throughout her life, in particular during her adolescence, a key factor in her successful development was unobtrusive supervision by peer mentors, older unaffected siblings, adult friends, and social services staff. This supervision worked to protect her from poor decisions that could have led to dangerous situations. With an emphasis on her strengths, Karen has acquired skills needed for active and independent living, while at the same time developing techniques for overcoming the challenges of potentially difficult behaviour, particularly that associated with perseveration.

Fetal alcohol syndrome had been identified during the 1970s, while Karen was growing up. Once alcohol enters a fetus' blood-stream, it remains there in high concentrations for long periods of time, causing brain damage and harming other body organs. There is no cure. As one medical expert wrote, "for the fetus the hangover may last a lifetime" (Enloe, 1980, p. 15).

● ● ●

For students of child development, the story of Karen Lutke is a hopeful note on the successes that are possible with a supportive home environment, but also a reminder of the responsibility prospective biological parents have for the crucial development that occurs before birth. The uterus is the developing child's first environment, and its impact on the child is immense. In addition to what the mother does and what happens to her, there are other environmental influences, from those that affect the father's sperm to the technological, social, and cultural environment, which may affect the kind of prenatal care a woman gets.

In this chapter we begin by looking at the experience of pregnancy and how prospective parents prepare for a birth. We trace how the fertilized ovum becomes an embryo and then a fetus, already with a personality of its own. Then we discuss environmental factors that can affect the developing person-to-be, describe techniques for determining whether development is proceeding normally, and explain the importance of prenatal care.

After you have read and studied this chapter, you should be able to answer each of the Guidepost questions that appear at the top of the next page. Look for them again in the margins, where they point to important concepts throughout the chapter. To check your understanding of these Guideposts, review the end-of-chapter summary. Checkpoints located at periodic spots throughout the chapter will help you verify your understanding of what you have read.

1. What are the three stages of prenatal development, and what happens during each stage?

2. What environmental influences can affect prenatal development?

3. What techniques can assess a fetus' health and well-being, and what is the importance of prenatal and preconception care?

Guidepost 1

What are the three stages of prenatal development, and what happens during each stage?

Prenatal Development: Three Stages

If you had been born in China, you would probably celebrate your birthday on your estimated date of conception rather than your date of birth. This Chinese custom recognizes the importance of *gestation,* the approximately 9-month (or 266-day) period of development between conception and birth. Scientists, too, date *gestational age* from conception. *Gestational age* is usually dated from the first day of an expectant mother's last menstrual cycle. The normal range of gestation is between 38 and 42 weeks.

For many women, the first clear (but not necessarily reliable) sign of pregnancy is a missed menstrual period. But even before that first missed period, a pregnant woman's body undergoes subtle but noticeable changes. Table 4-1 lists early signs and symptoms of pregnancy. Although these signs are not unique to pregnancy, a woman who experiences one or more of them may wish to take a home pregnancy test or to seek medical confirmation that she is pregnant.

Table 4-1	Early Signs and Symptoms of Pregnancy
Physical Change	**Causes and Timing**
Tender, swollen breasts	Increased production of the female hormones estrogen and progesterone stimulates breast growth to prepare for producing milk (most noticeable in a first pregnancy).
Fatigue; need to take extra naps	Woman's heart is pumping harder and faster to produce extra blood to carry nutrients to the unborn baby. Stepped-up production of hormones takes extra effort. Progesterone depresses central nerous system and may cause sleepiness. Concerns about pregnancy may sap energy.
Slight bleeding or cramping	"Implantation bleeding" may occur about 10 to 14 days after fertilization when fertilized ovum attaches to lining of uterus. Many women also have cramps (similar to menstrual cramps) as the uterus begins to enlarge.
Nausea with or without vomiting	Rising levels of estrogen produced by placenta and fetus cause stomach to empty more slowly. Also, heightened sense of smell may trigger nausea in response to certain odours, such as coffee, meat, dairy products, or spicy foods. "Morning sickness" may begin as early as 2 weeks after conception, but usually around 4 to 8 weeks, and may occur at any time of day.
Food cravings	Hormonal changes may change food preferences, especially during first trimester, when hormones have greatest impact.
Frequent urination	Enlarging uterus during first trimester exerts pressure on the bladder.
Frequent, mild headaches	Increased blood circulation caused by hormonal changes may bring these on.
Constipation	Increase in progesterone may slow digestion, so food passes more slowly through intestinal tract.
Mood swings	Flood of hormones early in pregnancy can produce emotional highs and lows.
Faintness and dizziness	Lightheaded feeling may be triggered by blood vessel dilation and low blood pressure; also may be triggered by low blood sugar.
Raised basal body temperature	Basal body temperature (taken first thing in the morning) normally rises soon after ovulation each month and then drops during menstruation. With the absence of menstruation due to pregnancy, the typical drop in temperature does not occur.

Source: Mayo Clinic, 2005.

Prenatal development takes place in three stages: *germinal, embryonic,* and *fetal.* (Table 4-2 gives a month-by-month description.) During these three stages of gestation, the original single-celled zygote grows into an *embryo* and then a *fetus.* What turns a single-celled zygote into a creature with a specific shape and pattern? Research suggests that an identifiable group of genes is responsible for this transformation in vertebrates, presumably including human beings. These genes produce molecules called *morphogens,* which are switched on after fertilization and begin sculpting arms, hands, fingers, vertebrae, ribs, a brain, and other body parts (Echeland et al., 1993; Kraus, Concordet, & Ingham, 1993; Riddle, Johnson, Laufer, & Tabin, 1993).

Both before and after birth, development proceeds according to two fundamental principles. Growth and motor development occur from top down and from the centre of the body outward.

The **cephalocaudal principle** (from Latin, meaning "head to tail") dictates that development proceeds from the head to the lower part of the trunk. An embryo's head, brain, and eyes develop earliest and are disproportionately large until the other parts catch up. At 2 months of gestation, the embryo's head is half the length of the body. By the time of birth, the head is only one-fourth the length of the body but is still disproportionately large. According to the **proximodistal principle** (from Latin, "near to far"), development proceeds from parts near the centre of the body to outer ones. The embryo's head and trunk develop before the limbs, and the arms and legs before the fingers and toes.

Germinal Stage (Fertilization to 2 Weeks)

During the **germinal stage,** from fertilization to about 2 weeks of gestational age, the zygote divides, becomes more complex, and is implanted in the wall of the uterus (see Figure 4-1).

Within 36 hours after fertilization, the zygote enters a period of rapid cell division and duplication, or *mitosis* (refer back to Chapter 3). Seventy-two hours after fertilization, it has divided into 16 to 32 cells; a day later it has 64 cells. This division continues until the original single cell has developed into the 800 billion or more specialized cells that make up the human body.

While the fertilized ovum is dividing, it is also making its way down the Fallopian tube to the uterus, a journey of 3 or 4 days. Its form changes into a fluid-filled sphere, a *blastocyst,* which floats freely in the uterus for a day or two and then begins to implant itself in the uterine wall. The blastocyst actively participates in the implanting process through a complex system of hormonally regulated signalling (Norwitz, Schust, & Fisher, 2001).

Only about 10 to 20 percent of fertilized ova complete the task of implantation and continue to develop. For implantation to be successful, a protein called L-selectin, secreted for only a short time during a woman's monthly cycle, must interlock with carbohydrate molecules on the surface of the uterus, stopping the blastocyst's free-floating motion (Genbacev et al., 2003).

Before implantation, as cell differentiation begins, some cells around the edge of the blastocyst cluster on one side to form the *embryonic disk,* a thickened cell mass from which the embryo begins to develop. This mass is already differentiating into two layers. The upper layer, the *ectoderm,* will become the outer layer of skin, the nails, hair, teeth, sensory organs, and the nervous system, including the brain and spinal cord. The lower layer, the *endoderm,* will become the digestive system, liver, pancreas, salivary glands, and respiratory system. Later a middle layer, the *mesoderm,* will develop and differentiate into the inner layer of skin, muscles, skeleton, and excretory and circulatory systems.

Other parts of the blastocyst begin to develop into organs that will nurture and protect the unborn child (see Figure 4-2): the *placenta,* the *umbilical cord,* and the *amniotic sac* with its outer layers, the *amnion,* and *chorion.* The *placenta,* which has several important functions, will be connected to the embryo by the *umbilical cord.* Through this cord the placenta delivers oxygen and nourishment to the developing baby and removes its body wastes. Nutrients from the mother pass from her blood to the embryonic blood vessels, which are then carried, via the umbilical cord, to the embryo. In turn, embryonic blood vessels in the umbilical cord carry embryonic wastes to the placenta where they can be

cephalocaudal principle Principle that development proceeds in a head-to-tail direction; that is, upper parts of the body develop before lower parts

proximodistal principle Principle that development proceeds from within to without; that is, parts of the body near the centre develop before the extremities

germinal stage First 2 weeks of prenatal development, characterized by rapid cell division, increasing complexity and differentiation, and implantation in the wall of the uterus

Table 4-2	Prenatal Development

Month	Description

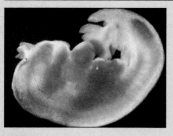

1 month

During the first month, growth is more rapid than at any other time during prenatal or postnatal life: The embryo reaches a size 10,000 times greater than the zygote. By the end of the first month, it measures about 1.5 cm in length. Blood flows through its veins and arteries, which are very small. It has a minuscule heart, beating 65 times a minute. It already has the beginnings of a brain, kidneys, liver, and digestive tract. The umbilical cord, its lifeline to the mother, is working. By looking very closely through a microscope, it is possible to see the swellings on the head that will eventually become eyes, ears, mouth, and nose. Its sex cannot yet be determined.

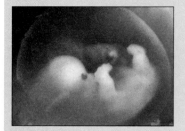

2 months

By the end of the second month, the organism is less than 2.5 cm long and weighs only 2.2g. Its head is half its total body length. Facial parts are clearly developed, with tongue and teeth buds. The arms have hands, fingers, and thumbs, and the legs have knees, ankles, and toes. It has a thin covering of skin and can make handprints and footprints. Bone cells appear at about 8 weeks. Brain impulses coordinate the function of the organ system. Sex organs are developing; the heartbeat is steady. The stomach produces digestive juices; the liver, blood cells. The kidneys remove uric acid from the blood. The skin is now sensitive enough to react to tactile stimulation. If an aborted 8-week-old fetus is stroked, it reacts by flexing its trunk, extending its head, and moving back its arms.

3 months

By the end of the third month, the fetus weighs about 30 g, and measures about 7.5 cm in length. It has fingernails, toenails, eyelids (still closed), vocal cords, lips, and a prominent nose. Its head is still large—about one-third its total length—and its forehead is high. Sex can easily be determined. The organ systems are functioning, and so the fetus may now breathe, swallow amniotic fluid into the lungs and expel it, and occasionally urinate. Its ribs and vertebrae have turned into cartilage. The fetus can now make a variety of specialized responses: It can move its legs, feet, thumbs, and head; its mouth can open and close and swallow. If its eyelids are touched, it squints; if its palm is touched, it makes a partial fist; if its lip is touched, it will suck; and if the sole of the foot is stroked, the toes will fan out. These reflexes will be present at birth but most will be less easily elicited during the first months of life because brain development will permit voluntary control.

4 months

The body is catching up to the head, which is now only one-fourth the total body length, the same proportion it will be at birth. The fetus now measures 20 to 25 cm and weighs about 175 g. The umbilical cord is as long as the fetus and will continue to grow with it. The placenta is now fully developed. The mother may be able to feel the fetus kicking, a movement known as quickening, which some societies and religious groups consider the beginning of human life. The reflex activities that appeared in the third month are now brisker because of increased muscular development.

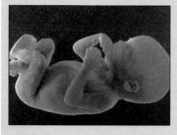

5 months

The fetus, now weighing about 350 to 450 g and measuring about 30 cm, begins to show signs of an individual personality. It has definite sleep–wake patterns, has a favourite position in the uterus (called its lie), and becomes more active—kicking, stretching, squirming, and even hiccupping. By putting an ear to the mother's abdomen, it is possible to hear the fetal heartbeat. The sweat and sebaceous glands are functioning. The respiratory system is not yet adequate to sustain life outside the womb; a baby born at this time does not usually survive. Coarse hair has begun to grow for eyebrows and eyelashes, fine hair is on the head, and a woolly hair called lanugo covers the body.

Table 4-2 Prenatal Development (*Continued*)

Month	Description
 6 months	The rate of fetal growth has slowed down a little—by the end of the sixth month, the fetus is about 35 cm long and weighs 575 g. It has fat pads under the skin; the eyes are complete, opening, closing, and looking in all directions. It can hear, and it can make a fist with a strong grip. A fetus born during the sixth month still has only a slight chance of survival, because the breathing apparatus has not matured. However, some fetuses of this age do survive outside the womb.
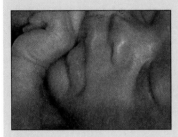 7 months	By the end of the seventh month, the fetus, about 40 cm long and weighing 1.5 to 2.5 kg, now has fully developed reflex patterns. It cries, breathes, swallows, and may suck its thumb. The lanugo may disappear at about this time, or it may remain until shortly after birth. Head hair may continue to grow. The chances that a fetus weighing at least 1.5 kg will survive are fairly good, provided it receives intensive medical attention. It will probably need to be kept in an incubator until a weight of 2.5 kg is attained.
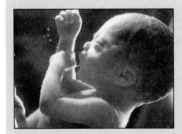 8 months	The 8-month-old fetus is 45 to 50 cm long and weighs between 2 and 3 kg. Its living quarters are becoming cramped, and so its movements are curtailed. During this month and the next, a layer of fat is developing over the fetus's entire body, which will enable it to adjust to varying temperatures outside the womb.
 9 months–newborn	About a week before birth, the fetus stops growing, having reached an average weight of about 3.5 kg and a length of about 50 cm, with boys tending to be a little longer and heavier than girls. Fat pads continue to form, the organ systems are operating more efficiently, the heart rate increases, and more wastes are expelled through the umbilical cord. The reddish colour of the skin is fading. At birth, the fetus will have been in the womb for about 266 days, although gestational age is usually estimated at 280 days, since most doctors date the pregnancy from the mother's last menstrual period.

Note: Even in these early stages, individuals differ. The figures and descriptions given here represent averages.

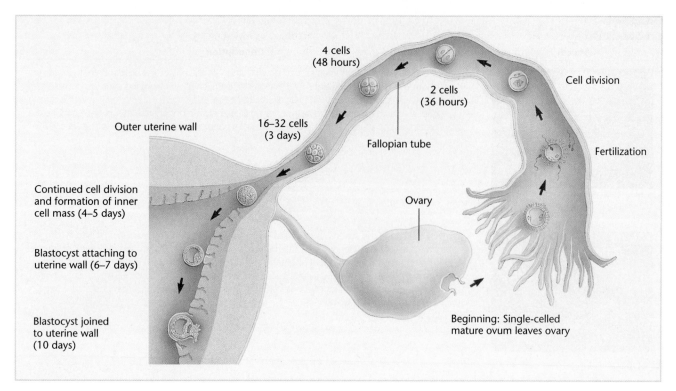

Figure 4-1

Early development of a human embryo. This simplified diagram shows the progress of the ovum as it leaves the ovary, is fertilized in the Fallopian tube, and then divides while travelling to the lining of the uterus. Now a blastocyst, it is implanted in the uterus, where it will grow larger and more complex until it is ready to be born.

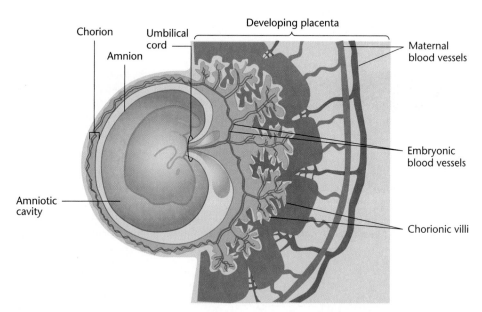

Figure 4-2

The developing embryo. After implantation in the uterine wall, the embryo is enclosed and cushioned by the fluid-filled *amniotic cavity,* or amniotic sac. The surrounding membrane, the *amnion,* gradually expands to enlarge the cavity in which the growing embryo (and later the fetus) floats. Through the *umbilical cord,* the embryo receives nourishment and oxygen from the mother and eliminates wastes. This is accomplished through a complex system of exchange of blood between the maternal and embryonic circulatory systems. This exchange takes place across the *placenta,* without direct contact between the two blood systems. The exchange occurs through the action of tiny hairlike projections from the outer membrane, the *chorion,* which diffuse and exchange the blood.

eliminated by maternal blood vessels. The mother's and embryo's circulatory systems are not directly linked; instead, this exchange occurs by diffusion across the blood vessel walls. The placenta also helps to combat internal infection and gives the unborn child immunity to various diseases. It produces the hormones that support pregnancy, prepares the mother's breasts for lactation, and eventually stimulates the uterine contractions that will expel the baby from the mother's body. The *amniotic sac* is a fluid-filled membrane that encases the developing baby, protecting it and giving it room to move. The *trophoblast*, the outer cell layer of the blastocyst (which becomes part of the placenta), produces tiny threadlike structures that penetrate the lining of the uterine wall and enable the developing organism to cling there until it is fully implanted in the uterine lining.

Embryonic Stage (2 to 8 Weeks)

During the **embryonic stage,** the second stage of gestation, from about 2 to 8 weeks, the organs and major body systems—respiratory, digestive, and nervous—develop rapidly. This is a critical period, when the embryo is most vulnerable to destructive influences in the prenatal environment (see Figure 4-3). An organ system or structure that is still developing at the time of exposure to a destructive or harmful element is most likely to be affected. Defects that occur later in pregnancy are likely to be less serious. (In Chapter 6, we discuss brain growth and development, which begins during the embryonic stage and continues after birth and beyond.)

The most severely defective embryos seldom survive beyond the first *trimester,* or 3-month period, of pregnancy. A **spontaneous abortion,** commonly called a *miscarriage,* is the expulsion from the uterus of an embryo or fetus that is unable to survive outside the womb. As many as 1 in 4 recognized pregnancies end in miscarriage, and the actual figure may be as high as 1 in 2 because many spontaneous abortions take place before the woman realizes she is pregnant. About 3 out of 4 miscarriages occur during the first trimester (Neville, undated). Most miscarriages result from abnormal pregnancies; about 50 to 70 percent involve chromosomal abnormalities. "Losing" an unborn baby can be extremely painful, as we discuss in Box 4-1.

Males are more likely than females to be spontaneously aborted or *stillborn* (dead at birth). Thus, although about 125 males are conceived for every 100 females—a fact that has been attributed to the greater mobility of sperm carrying the smaller Y chromosome—only 105 boys are born for every 100 girls (Grech, Vassalo-Aglus, & Savona-Ventura, 2003). Males' greater vulnerability continues after birth: More of them die early in life (Statistics Canada, 1997; 2002), and at every age they are more susceptible to many disorders. Furthermore, the proportion of male births appears to be falling in Canada, the United States, and several European countries, while the incidence of birth defects among males is rising (Davis, Gottlieb, & Stampnitzky, 1998; Grech et al., 2003).

embryonic stage Second stage of gestation (2 to 8 weeks), characterized by rapid growth and development of major body systems and organs

spontaneous abortion Natural expulsion from the uterus of an embryo or fetus that cannot survive outside the womb; also called miscarriage

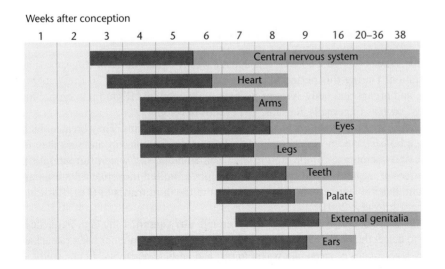

Figure 4-3

When birth defects occur. Body parts and systems are most vulnerable to damage when they are developing most rapidly (dark areas), generally within the first trimester of pregnancy.

Note: Intervals of time are not all equal.

Source: J. E. Brody, 1995; data from March of Dimes

Box 4-1 *Mourning a Miscarriage or Stillbirth*

At a Buddhist temple in Tokyo, small statues of infants accompanied by toys and gifts are left as offerings to Jizo, an enlightened being who is believed to watch over miscarried and aborted fetuses and eventually, through reincarnation, to guide them into a new life. The ritual of *mizuko kuyo,* a rite of apology and remembrance, is observed as a means of making amends to the lost life (Orenstein, 2002).

The Japanese word *mizuko* means "water child." Japanese Buddhists believe that life flows into an organism gradually, like water, and a mizuko is somewhere on the continuum between life and death (Orenstein, 2002). In English, by contrast, there is no word for a miscarried, aborted, or stillborn fetus, nor any ritual of mourning. Families, friends, and health professionals tend to avoid talking about such losses, which may seem insignificant compared with the loss of a living child (Van, 2001). Or people make unhelpful comments such as, "It was better this way" or "This happens all the time." Grief can be more wrenching without social support, and "the silence our society cases over the topic makes it hard for women and families to get the information and help they need" (Grady, 2002, p. 1).

How do prospective parents cope with the loss of a child they never knew? Because each person's or couple's experience of loss is unique, it is hard to generalize (Van, 2001). A woman may feel a sense of inadequacy or failure. Often there is anger (at herself or others for not being able to prevent the miscarriage or stillbirth, or at her partner for not being supportive enough), guilt (if the woman had mixed feelings about becoming a mother, or if she thinks the loss of the baby may have resulted from something she did), or anxiety ("Will I be able to have another child?"). Children in the family may blame themselves, especially if they had some negative feelings about the expected birth. The parents may mourn not only for what is now lost but for what the lost child might have become. Feelings of pain and grief may recur, often on the expected due date or on the anniversary of the loss (Neville, undated).

Differences in the ways men and women grieve may be a source of tension and divisiveness in a couple's relationship (Caelli, Downie, & Letendre, 2002). The man may have been less focused on the pregnancy, and his body does not give him physical reminders of the loss (Grady, 2002). In one small study, eleven men whose child had died in utero reported being overcome with frustration and helplessness during and after the delivery, but several found relief in supporting their partners (Samuelsson, Radestad, & Segesten, 2001). In another study, grieving parents perceived their spouses and extended families as most helpful and their doctors as least helpful. Some bereaved parents benefited from a support group, and some not (DiMarco, Menke, & McNamara, 2001). Couples who have gone through pregnancy loss may need extra-compassionate care during a later pregnancy (Caelli et al., 2002).

Grief counselors suggest that adjustment to a pregnancy loss may be eased if the parents are allowed to see the remains—something that is often not possible. Other suggestions are (Brin, 2004; Grady, 2002; Neville, undated):

- Set aside time to talk about the loss.
- Create and hold a memorial ceremony or ritual; online resources may help.
- Name the miscarried or stillborn baby.
- Plant a tree or flowering bush in the lost baby's name.
- Write poetry or keep a journal.
- Put items such as an ultrasound photo in a memory box.
- Create a special certificate.
- Seek private counselling or a support group.

What's your view?

- Have you ever had a spontaneous abortion (miscarriage) or stillbirth, or do you know anyone who has? If so, how did you or your acquaintance cope with the loss? How did others react to it?
- Do you think recognition of such losses through ceremonies or rituals would be helpful?

Check it out!

For more information on this topic, go to **www.mcgrawhill.ca/olc/papalia,** and **www.nationalshareoffice.com** for information on miscarriage support groups and items for creating appropriate rituals.

Fetal Stage (8 Weeks to Birth)

fetal stage Final stage of gestation (from 8 weeks to birth), characterized by increased detail of body parts and greatly enlarged body size

The appearance of the first bone cells at about 8 weeks signals the **fetal stage,** the final stage of gestation. During this period, the fetus grows rapidly to about 20 times its previous length, and organs and body systems become more complex. Right up to birth, "finishing touches" such as fingernails, toenails, and eyelids develop.

Fetuses are not passive passengers in their mothers' wombs. They breathe, kick, turn, flex their bodies, do somersaults, squint, swallow, make fists, hiccup, and suck their thumbs. The flexible membranes of the uterine walls and amniotic sac, which surround the protective buffer of amniotic fluid, permit and stimulate limited movement. Fetuses also can feel pain, but it is unlikely that they do so before the third trimester (Lee, Ralston, Drey, Partridge, & Rosen, 2005).

ultrasound Prenatal medical procedure using high-frequency sound waves to detect the outline of a fetus and its movements, in order to determine whether a pregnancy is progressing normally

Scientists can observe fetal movement through **ultrasound,** using high-frequency sound waves to detect the outline of the fetus. Other instruments can monitor heart rate, changes in activity level, states of sleep and wakefulness, and cardiac reactivity. In one study, fetuses

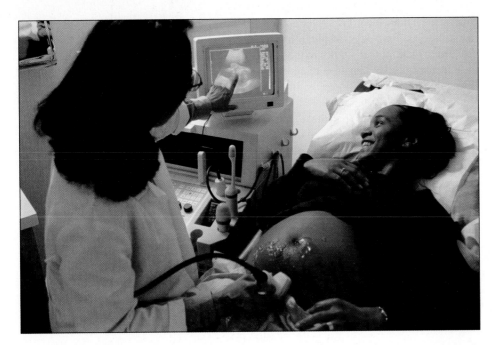

The most effective way to prevent birth complications is early prenatal care, which may include ultrasound checkups, such as this woman is having, to follow the fetus' development. Ultrasound is a diagnostic tool that presents an immediate image of the fetus in the womb.

monitored from 20 weeks of gestation until term had decreasing but more variable heart rates—possibly in response to the increasing stress of the mother's pregnancy—and greater cardiac response to stimulation. They also showed less, but more vigorous, activity—perhaps a result of the increasing difficulty of movement for a growing fetus in a constricted environment, as well as of maturation of the nervous system. A significant "jump" in all these aspects of fetal development seems to occur between 28 and 32 weeks; it may help explain why infants born prematurely at this time are more likely to survive and flourish than those born earlier (DiPietro et al., 1996). This "jump" occurred among fetuses in two contrasting cultures, Baltimore, U.S., and Lima, Peru—suggesting that this aspect of fetal neurological development is universal (DiPietro et al., 2004).

The movements and activity level of fetuses show marked individual differences, and their heart rates vary in regularity and speed. There also are differences between males and females. Male fetuses, regardless of size, are more active and tend to move more vigorously than female fetuses throughout gestation. Thus infant boys' tendency to be more active than girls may be at least partly inborn (DiPietro et al., 1996).

Beginning at about week 12 of gestation, the fetus swallows and inhales some of the amniotic fluid in which it floats. The amniotic fluid contains substances that cross the placenta from the mother's bloodstream and enter the fetus's own bloodstream. Taking in these substances may stimulate the budding senses of taste and smell and may contribute to the development of organs needed for breathing and digestion (Mennella & Beauchamp, 1996a; Ronca & Alberts, 1995; Smotherman & Robinson, 1995, 1996). Mature taste cells appear at about 14 weeks of gestation. The olfactory system, which controls the sense of smell, is also well developed before birth (Bartoshuk & Beauchamp, 1994; Mennella & Beauchamp, 1996a).

Fetuses respond to the mother's voice and heartbeat and the vibrations of her body, suggesting that they can hear and feel. Hungry infants, no matter on which side they are held, turn toward the breast in the direction from which they hear the mother's voice (Noirot & Algeria, 1983, cited in Rovee-Collier, 1996). Thus familiarity with the mother's voice may have an evolutionary survival function: to help newborns locate the source of food. Responses to sound and vibration seem to begin at 26 weeks of gestation, rise, and then reach a plateau at about 32 weeks (Kisilevsky, Muir, & Low, 1992).

Fetuses seem to learn and remember. In one experiment, 3-day-old infants sucked more on a nipple that activated a recording of a story their mother had frequently read aloud during the last 6 weeks of pregnancy than they did on nipples that activated recordings of two other stories. Apparently, the infants recognized the pattern of sound they had heard in the womb. A control group, whose mothers had not recited a story before birth, responded

Checkpoint

Can you . . .

✔ Identify two principles that govern physical development and give examples of their application during the prenatal period?

✔ Describe how a zygote becomes an embryo?

✔ Explain why defects and miscarriages are most likely to occur during the embryonic stage?

✔ Describe findings about fetal activity, sensory development, and memory?

equally to all three recordings (DeCasper & Spence, 1986). Similar experiments have found that newborns 2 to 4 days old prefer musical and speech sequences heard before birth. They also prefer their mother's voice to those of other women, female voices to male voices, and their mother's native language to another language (DeCasper & Fifer, 1980; DeCasper & Spence, 1986; Moon, Cooper, & Fifer, 1993; Fifer & Moon, 1995; Lecanuet, Granier-Deferre, & Busnel, 1995).

How do we know that these preferences develop before rather than after birth? Newborns were given the choice of sucking to turn on a recording of the mother's voice or a "filtered" version of her voice as it might sound in the womb. The newborns sucked more often to turn on the filtered version, suggesting that fetuses develop a preference for the kinds of sounds they hear before birth (Fifer & Moon, 1995; Moon & Fifer, 1990). In another study when 60 fetuses heard a female voice reading, their heart rate increased if the voice was their mother's and decreased if it belonged to a stranger (Kisilevsky et al., 2003).

Prenatal Development: Environmental Influences

Guidepost 2

What environmental influences can affect prenatal development?

teratogenic Capable of causing birth defects

Maternal Factors

Because the prenatal environment is the mother's body, virtually everything that affects her well-being, from her diet to her moods, may alter her unborn child's environment and influence its growth (see Box 4-2). However, not all environmental hazards are equally risky for all fetuses. Some factors that are **teratogenic** (birth defect-producing) in some cases have little or no effect in others. The timing of exposure (refer back to Figure 4-3), the dose, duration, and interaction with other teratogenic factors may make a difference. Sometimes vulnerability may depend on a gene either in the fetus or in the mother. For example, fetuses with a particular variant of a growth gene, called *transforming growth factor alpha,* have six times more risk than other fetuses of developing a cleft palate if the mother smokes while pregnant (Hwang et al., 1995).

Technology that permits a woman to view images of her fetus early in her pregnancy may help motivate her to engage in nurturing behaviours, such as eating properly and abstaining from alcohol and drugs (Salisbury, Law, LaGasse, & Lester, 2003).

Nutrition and Maternal Weight

Women need to eat more than usual when pregnant: typically, 300 to 500 more calories a day, including extra protein. Pregnant women who gain between 10 and 20 kg are less likely to miscarry or to bear babies who are stillborn or whose weight at birth is dangerously low (Abrams & Parker, 1990; Ventura, Martin, Curtin, & Mathews, 1999). However, desirable weight gain depends on individual factors, such as height and weight before pregnancy (Martin, Hamilton, et al., 2005).

Malnutrition during fetal growth may have long-range effects. In rural Gambia, in western Africa, people born during the "hungry" season, when foods from the previous harvest are badly depleted, are 10 times more likely to die in early adulthood than people born during other parts of the year (Moore et al., 1997). Psychiatric examinations of Dutch military recruits whose mothers had been exposed to wartime famine during pregnancy suggest that severe prenatal nutritional deficiencies in the first or second trimesters affect the developing brain, increasing the risk of antisocial personality disorders at age 18 (Neugebauer, Hoek, & Susser, 1999). In rural areas of northern England and Wales, rising stroke rates among middle-aged adults were associated with poverty and poor nutrition 50 years earlier, when those adults were born (Barker & Lackland, 2003). Children whose mothers had low Vitamin D levels late in pregnancy had low bone mineral content at age 9, potentially increasing their risk of osteoporosis in later life (Javaid et al., 2006). And, as reported in Chapter 3, a Finnish study found a link between fetal undernutrition and schizophrenia (Wahlbeck et al., 2001).

The Social World

Box 4-2 *Fetal Welfare versus Mothers' Rights*

A Winnipeg woman is apprehended by Child and Family Services for inhaling solvents while pregnant. A court orders her to enter a treatment program after finding her mentally incompetent, despite contrary evidence in a psychiatric report. A year later, the decision is overturned by the Manitoba Court of Appeal, and by the Supreme Court of Canada, arguing that there is no legal basis to order addicted pregnant women to seek treatment to protect the developing fetus (Kuxhaus, 1997).

In this case, the issue is the conflict between protection of a fetus and a woman's right to privacy or to make her own decisions about her body. It is tempting to require a pregnant woman to adopt practices that will ensure her baby's health, or to stop or punish her if she doesn't. But what about her personal freedom? Can civil rights be abrogated for the protection of the unborn?

The argument about the right to choose abortion, which rests on similar grounds, is far from settled. But the example just given deals with a different aspect of the problem. What can or should society do about a woman who does *not* choose abortion, but instead goes on carrying the baby while engaging in behaviour destructive to it, or refuses tests or treatments that medical providers consider essential to its welfare?

Should a woman be forced to submit to intrusive procedures that pose a risk to her, such as a surgical delivery or intrauterine transfusions, when doctors say such procedures are essential to the delivery of a healthy baby? Should a woman from a fundamentalist sect that rejects modern medical care be taken into custody until she gives birth? Such measures have been invoked and have been defended as protecting the rights of the unborn. But women's rights advocates claim that they reflect a view of women as mere vehicles for carrying offspring, and not as persons in their own right (Greenhouse, 2000b).

Medical professionals warn that such measures also may have important practical drawbacks. Legal coercion could jeopardize the doctor–patient relationship. Coercion could also open the door to go further into pregnant women's lives—demanding prenatal screening and fetal surgery or restricting their diet, work, and athletic and sexual activity (Kolder, Gallagher, & Parsons, 1987). For these reasons, the overwhelming attitude of medical, legal, and social critics is that the state should intervene only in circumstances in which there is a high risk of serious disease or a high degree of accuracy in the test for a defect, strong evidence that the proposed treatment will be effective,

danger that deferring treatment until after birth will cause serious damage, minimal risk to the mother and modest interference with her privacy, and persistent but unsuccessful efforts to educate her and obtain her informed consent.

Does a woman have the right to knowingly ingest a substance, such as alcohol or another drug, that can permanently damage her unborn child? Some advocates for fetal rights think it should be against the law for pregnant women to smoke or use alcohol, even though these activities are legal for other adults. Other experts argue that incarceration for substance abuse is unworkable and self-defeating. They say that expectant mothers who have a drinking or drug problem need education and treatment, not prosecution (Boyd, 2004; Drug Policy Alliance, 2004; Marwick, 1997, 1998). If failure to follow medical advice can bring forced surgery, confinement, or criminal charges, some women may avoid doctors altogether and thus deprive their fetuses of needed prenatal care (Nelson & Marshall, 1998).

There has been no successful prosecution of a Canadian woman for abusing dangerous substances while pregnant. An alternative, and likely more effective, way to help ensure that pregnant women avoid ingesting harmful substances is public education (Ruttman, Field, Lundquist, Callahan, & Jackson, 2000). As an example, across Canada provincial liquor boards and commissions now employ advertising campaigns to alert pregnant women to the dangers of alcohol consumption during pregnancy.

What's your view

Does society's interest in protecting an unborn child justify coercive measures against pregnant women who ingest harmful substances or refuse medically indicated treatment? Should pregnant women who refuse to stop drinking or get treatment be incarcerated until they give birth? Should mothers who repeatedly give birth to children with FAS be sterilized? Should liquor companies be held liable if adequate warnings are not on their products? Would your answers be the same regarding smoking or use of cocaine or other potentially harmful substances?

Check it out

For more information on this topic, go to **www.mcgrawhill.ca/ olc/papalia.**

Malnourished women who take dietary supplements while pregnant tend to have bigger, healthier, more active, and more visually alert infants (J. L. Brown, 1987; Vuori et al., 1979); and women with low zinc levels who take daily zinc supplements are less likely to have babies with low birth weight and small head circumference (Goldenberg et al., 1995). In a large-scale randomized study of low-income households in 347 Mexican communities, women who took nutrient-fortified dietary supplements while pregnant or lactating tended to have infants who grew more rapidly and were less likely to be anemic (Rivera, Sotres-Alvarez, Habicht, Shamah, & Villalpando, 2004). However, certain vitamins (including A, B$_6$, C, D, and K) can be harmful in excessive amounts. Iodine deficiency, unless corrected before the third trimester of pregnancy, can cause cretinism, which may involve severe neurological abnormalities or thyroid problems (Cao et al., 1994; Hetzel, 1994).

Only recently have we learned of the critical importance of folic acid, or folate (a B vitamin) in a pregnant woman's diet. For some time, scientists have known that China has the highest incidence in the world of babies born with the neural-tube defects anencephaly and spina bifida (refer back to Table 3-2), but it was not until the 1980s that researchers linked that fact with the timing of the babies' conception. Traditionally, Chinese couples marry in January or February and try to conceive as soon as possible. That means pregnancies often begin in the winter, when rural women have little access to fresh fruits and vegetables, important sources of folic acid.

After medical detective work established the lack of folic acid as a cause of neural-tube defects, China embarked on a massive program to give folic acid supplements to prospective mothers, which resulted in a large reduction in the prevalence of these defects (Berry et al., 1999). In Canada, women of childbearing age are now urged to include this vitamin in their diets by eating plenty of fresh fruits and vegetables, or taking vitamin supplements, even before becoming pregnant, since damage from folic acid deficiency can occur during the early weeks of gestation (Society of Obstetricians and Gynaecologists of Canada [SOGC], 1993). However, folic acid supplementation alone may not always reduce the incidence of open neural tube deficits: in Nova Scotia, reduced incidence occurred only after the start of a province-wide initiative to fortify all grain products with folic acid (Persad, Van den Hof, Dube & Zimmer, 2002). In general, if all women took 5 milligrams of folic acid each day before pregnancy and during the first trimester, an estimated 85 percent of neural-tube defects could be prevented (Wald, 2004). Canadian initiatives designed to promote healthy prenatal development, like the Healthy Babies, Healthy Children program in Ontario, and the Building Better Babies Pregnancy Outreach Program, operated by the Tillicum Haus Native Friendship Centre in British Columbia, provide education and material support like food and vitamin supplements to pregnant women.

Fish appears to be "brain food" for a fetus. In one study, the more fish a mother had eaten during the second trimester of pregnancy, the better her 6-month-old infant performed on a test of visual memory. However, eating fish with high mercury levels tended to depress infants' scores (Oken et al., 2005). In other studies, newborns whose mothers' blood contained high levels of docosahexaenoic acid (DHA), an omega-3 fatty acid found in certain fish, such as Atlantic salmon and tuna, showed more mature sleep patterns (a sign of advanced brain development) than infants whose mothers' blood had lower levels of DHA (Cheruku, Montgomery-Downs, Farkas, Thoman, & Lammi-Keefe, 2002), and also were more attentive at 12 and 18 months (Colombo et al., 2004).

Obese women also risk having children with neural-tube defects. Women who, before pregnancy, weigh more than 80 kg or have an elevated body mass index (weight compared with height) are more likely to produce babies with such defects, regardless of folate intake.

Obesity also increases the risk of other complications of pregnancy, including miscarriage, stillbirth, and *neonatal death* (death during the first month of life) (Cnattingius, Bergstrom, Lipworth, & Kramer, 1998; Goldenberg & Tamura, 1996; G. M. Shaw, Velie, & Schaffer, 1996; Werler, Louik, Shapiro, & Mitchell, 1996). Either overweight or underweight can be risky: Among women having their first babies, those who were overweight before pregnancy had the most risk of stillbirth or of losing their babies during the first week of life. On the other hand, underweight women are more likely to have dangerously small babies (Cnattingius et al., 1998).

Physical Activity

Moderate exercise does not seem to endanger the fetuses of healthy women (Committee on Obstetric Practice, 2002. Riemann & Kanstrup Hansen, 2000). Regular exercise prevents constipation and improves respiration, circulation, muscle tone, and skin elasticity, all of which contribute to a more comfortable pregnancy and an easier, safer delivery.

Employment during pregnancy generally entails no special hazards. However, strenuous working conditions, occupational fatigue, and long working hours may be associated with a greater risk of premature birth (Luke et al., 1995).

The Society of Obstetricians and Gynaecologists of Canada (2000) recommends that women in low-risk pregnancies be guided by their own abilities and stamina. The safest

Checkpoint ✔

Can you . . .

✔ Summarize recommendations concerning an expectant mother's diet and physical activity?

course seems to be for pregnant women to exercise moderately, not pushing themselves and not raising their heart rate above 150, and, as with any exercise, tapering off at the end of each session rather than stopping abruptly.

Drug Intake

Practically everything an expectant mother takes in makes its way to the uterus. Drugs may cross the placenta, just as oxygen, carbon dioxide, and water do. Vulnerability is greatest in the first few months of gestation, when development is most rapid. Some problems resulting from prenatal exposure to drugs can be treated if the presence of a drug can be detected early.

What are the effects of the use of specific drugs during pregnancy? Let's look first at medical drugs; then at alcohol, nicotine, and caffeine; and finally at some illegal drugs: marijuana, opiates, and cocaine.

Medical Drugs It was once thought that the placenta protected the fetus against drugs the mother took during pregnancy—until the early 1960s, when a tranquilizer called *thalidomide* was banned after it was found to have caused stunted or missing limbs, severe facial deformities, and defective organs in some 12,000 babies worldwide, with about 120 survivors living in Canada today. The thalidomide disaster sensitized medical professionals and the public to the potential dangers of taking drugs while pregnant. Today, nearly 30 drugs have been found to be teratogenic in clinically recommended doses (Koren, Pastuszak, & Ito, 1998). Among them are the antibiotic tetracycline; certain barbiturates, opiates, and other central nervous system depressants; several hormones, including diethylstilbestrol (DES) and androgens; certain anti-cancer drugs, such as methotrexate; Accutane, a drug often prescribed for severe acne; and Aspirin and other nonsteroidal anti-inflammatory drugs, which should be avoided during the third trimester. Angiotensin-converting enzyme (ACE) inhibitors and nonsteroidal anti-inflammatory drugs (NSAIDs), such as naproxen and ibuprofen, have been linked to birth defects when taken anytime from the first trimester on (Ofori, Oraichi, Blais, Rey, & Berard, 2006; Cooper et al., 2006). Methamphetamine use during pregnancy is associated with restricted fetal growth as well as increased risk of premature delivery and other complications (Smith et al., 2006).

Effects may be far-reaching and long-lasting. In one study, Danish men in their thirties whose mothers had taken phenobarbital during pregnancy (especially during the last trimester) had significantly lower verbal intelligence scores than a control group. Coming from a lower socio-economic background or having been the product of an unwanted pregnancy tended to magnify the negative outcome, showing an interaction of environmental factors before and after birth (Reinisch, Sanders, Mortensen, Psych, & Rubin, 1995).

The effects of taking a drug during pregnancy do not always show up immediately. In the late 1940s and early 1950s, the synthetic hormone diethylstilbestrol (DES) was widely prescribed (ineffectually, as it turned out) to prevent miscarriage. Not until years later, when the daughters of women who had taken DES during pregnancy reached puberty, did about 1 in 1,000 develop a rare form of vaginal or cervical cancer (Giusti, Iwamoto, & Hatch, 1995; Swan, 2000; Treffers, Hanselaar, Helmerhorst, Koster, & van Leeuwen, 2001). Now in midlife, DES women have nearly twice the risk of breast cancer as women who were not exposed to DES in utero (Palmer et al., 2006). DES sons have had malformations in the genital tract (Treffers et al., 2001; Wilcox, Baird, Weinberg, Hornsby, & Herbst, 1995).

Infants whose mothers took antidepressants such as Prozac during pregnancy tend to show signs of disrupted neurobehavioural activity (Zeskind & Stephens, 2004). These infants also have an increased risk of severe respiratory failure (Chambers et al., 2006). Using prescription medication while breastfeeding is a cause for concern, given that medications could pass into breast milk, affecting the nursing child. The Motherisk program at Toronto's Hospital for Sick Children reports that most prescription drugs do not pose a risk to the breastfed infant; the major exceptions being medications for cancer therapy and anticonvulsants (Moretti, Lee, & Ito, 2000). Drugs of abuse, like alcohol, cocaine, and amphetamines, should be avoided as they have been found to pass through to breast milk. Pregnant women should not take over-the-counter drugs without consulting a doctor (Koren et al., 1998);

about 1 in 4 Canadian women reports using medication during pregnancy (Human Resources Development Canada, 1996).

fetal alcohol syndrome (FAS)
Combination of mental, motor, and developmental abnormalities affecting the offspring of some women who drink heavily during pregnancy

What's your view

• Thousands of adults now alive suffered gross abnormalities because, during the 1950s, their mothers took the tranquilizer thalidomide during pregnancy. As a result, the use of thalidomide was banned in Canada and some other countries. Now thalidomide has been found to be effective in treating or controlling many illnesses, from mouth ulcers to brain cancer. Should its use for these purposes be permitted even though there is a risk that pregnant women might take it? If so, what safeguards should be required?

Alcohol Like Karen Lutke, about 1 infant in 750 suffers from **fetal alcohol syndrome (FAS),** a combination of slow prenatal and postnatal growth, facial and bodily malformations, and disorders of the central nervous system. Over 100 FAS affected infants are born in Canada each year (Willms, 2002). FAS and other, less severe, alcohol-related conditions are estimated to occur in nearly 1 in every 100 births (Sokol, Delaney-Black, & Nordstrom, 2003). FAS is the third leading cause of mental retardation in Canada (Connor & Mcintyre, 2002) and is a risk factor for development of drinking problems and alcohol disorders in young adulthood (Alati et al., 2006; Baer, Sampson, Barr, Connor, & Streissguth, 2003). Problems related to the central nervous system in infancy, can include poor sucking response, brain-wave abnormalities, and sleep disturbances (Carter et al., 2005; Sokol et al., 2003); and, throughout childhood, slow information processing, poor social judgment, short attention span, restlessness, irritability, hyperactivity, learning disabilities, retarded growth, memory deficits, motor impairments, and aggressiveness (Connor & Mcintyre, 2002; Sood et al., 2001). Prebirth exposure to alcohol seems to affect a portion of the *corpus callosum,* which coordinates signals between the two hemispheres of the brain. In macaques (and, presumably, in humans as well) the affected portion, toward the front of the head, is involved in initiating voluntary movement and other higher-order processing (Miller, Astley, & Clarren, 1999).

For every child with FAS, as many as 10 others may be born with *fetal alcohol effects.* This less severe condition can include mental retardation, retardation of intrauterine growth, and minor congenital abnormalities.

Even moderate drinking may harm a fetus, and the more the mother drinks, the greater the effect. About 18 percent of Canadian mothers consumed some alcohol during pregnancy (Connor & Mcintyre, 2002). Furthermore, more than half of women of childbearing age who do not use birth control (and therefore could become pregnant) report alcohol use (Tsai & Floyd, 2004). According to research with rats, even a single drinking binge of 4 hours or more can do tremendous damage to the developing brain (Ikonomidou et al., 2000). Moderate or heavy drinking during pregnancy seems to alter the character of a newborn's cry, an index of neurobehavioural status. (So does moderate smoking during pregnancy.) Disturbed neurological and behavioural functioning may, in turn, affect early social interaction with the mother, which is vital to emotional development (Nugent, Lester, Greene, Wieczorek-Deering, & O'Mahony, 1996). Heavy drinkers who continue to drink after becoming pregnant are likely to have babies with reduced skull and brain growth as compared with babies of nondrinking women or expectant mothers who stop drinking (Handmaker et al., 2006).

Some FAS problems recede after birth; but others, such as retardation, behavioural and learning problems, and hyperactivity, tend to persist. Unfortunately, enriching these children's education or general environment does not seem to enhance their cognitive development (Kerns, Don, Mateer, & Streissguth, 1997; Spohr, Willms, & Steinhausen, 1993; Streissguth et al., 1991; Strömland & Hellström, 1996). Because there is no known safe level of drinking during pregnancy, it is best to avoid alcohol from the time a woman begins *thinking* about becoming pregnant until she stops breast-feeding (AAP Committee on Substance Abuse and Committee on Children with Disabilities, 1993; Sokol et al., 2003).

Nicotine About a quarter of Canadian women report smoking during pregnancy (Human Resources Development Canada, 1996), with 84 percent of smokers continuing throughout pregnancy, and 90 percent doing so during the first trimester (CICH, 2000; Willms, 2002). Tobacco use by pregnant women early in pregnancy can cause miscarriage, neonatal death, low birth weight, and need for intensive care for infants (DiFranza & Lew, 1995; Connor & Mcintyre, 2002). Women who smoke during pregnancy are more than one and a half times as likely as nonsmokers to bear low–birth weight babies (weighing less than 2500 grams at birth). Even light smoking (fewer than five cigarettes a day) is associated with a greater risk of low birth weight (Martin, Hamilton, et al., 2005; Shankaran et al., 2004; Hoyert, Mathews, Menacker, Strobino, & Guyer, 2006). Indeed, maternal smoking has

A woman who drinks and smokes while pregnant is taking grave risks with her future child's health.

been identified as the single most important factor in low birth weight in developed countries (DiFranza, Aligne, & Weitzman, 2004).

Tobacco use during pregnancy also brings increased risks of miscarriage, growth retardation, stillbirth, small head circumference, sudden infant death, colic in early infancy, hyperkinetic disorder (excessive movement), and long-term respiratory, neurological, cognitive, and behavioural problems (American Academy of Pediatrics Committee on Substance Abuse, 2001; DiFranza et al., 2004; Hoyert, Mathews, et al., 2006; Linnet et al., 2005; Martin, Hamilton, et al., 2006; Shankaran et al., 2004; Smith et al., 2006; Sondergaard, Henriksen, Obel, & Wisborg, 2001; Shah, Sullivan, & Carter, 2006; Connor & Mcintyre, 2002).

In a controlled study, newborns whose mothers had smoked during pregnancy (but had not used drugs and had taken no more than three alcoholic drinks per month) showed more evidence of neurological toxicity (such as overexcitability and stress) than infants of non-smoking mothers (Law et al., 2003). The effects of prenatal exposure to secondhand smoke on cognitive development tend to be worse when the child also experiences socio-economic hardships, such as substandard housing, malnutrition, and inadequate clothing during the first two years of life (Rauh et al., 2004).

Women who smoke during pregnancy also tend to smoke after giving birth, and each type of exposure seems to have independent effects (DiFranza et al., 2004). One study separated the effects of prenatal and postnatal exposure by examining 500 newborns about 48 hours after birth, while they were still in the hospital's nonsmoking maternity ward and thus had not been exposed to smoking outside the womb. Newborns whose mothers had smoked during pregnancy were shorter and lighter and had poorer respiratory functioning than babies of nonsmoking mothers (Stick, Burton, Gurrin, Sly, & LeSouëf, 1996).

Smoking during pregnancy seems to have some of the same effects on children when they reach school age as drinking during pregnancy: poor attention span, hyperactivity, anxiety, learning and behaviour problems, perceptual-motor and linguistic problems, poor IQ scores, low grade placement, and neurological problems (Landesman-Dwyer & Emanuel, 1979; Milberger, Biederman, Faraone, Chen, & Jones, 1996; Naeye & Peters, 1984; D. Olds, Henderson, & Tatelbaum, 1994a, 1994b; Streissguth et al., 1984; Wakschlag et al., 1997; Weitzman, Gortmaker, & Sobol, 1992; Willms, 2002; Wright et al., 1983). An 18-year Ottawa study found both short-term and long-term effects: lowered birth weight, nicotine withdrawal tremors in the first days after birth, delays in learning to use language sounds leading to delayed speech development, impulsiveness and hyperactivity, and a slightly lower IQ (Fried, James, & Watkinson, 2001; Fried & Watkinson, 2001; Connor & Mcintyre, 2002). These effects were lessened if mothers reduced or stopped smoking during pregnancy. A more recent concern involves maternal and infant exposure to environmental tobacco smoke (ETS), or second-hand smoke. About 13 percent of pregnant non-smokers in Canada report living with a partner who smokes (Health Canada, 1999). ETS exposure appears to have the same effects on prenatal and postnatal development as does smoking by pregnant women (Cornelius & Day, 2000), and in addition increases the risk of sudden infant death syndrome (SIDS) and inner ear infection in infancy (Helgason & Lund, 2001).

Caffeine Can the caffeine a pregnant woman swallows in coffee, tea, cola, or chocolate cause trouble for her fetus? For the most part, the answer is no (Leviton & Cowan, 2002). It does seem clear that caffeine is not a teratogen for human babies (Christian & Brent, 2001; Hinds, West, Knight, & Harland, 1996). A controlled study of 1,205 new mothers and their babies showed no effect of reported caffeine use on low birth weight, premature birth, or retarded fetal growth (Santos, Victora, Huttly, & Carvalhal, 1998). On the other hand, four or more cups of coffee a day may dramatically increase the risk of sudden death in infancy (Bech, Nohr, Vaeth, Henriksen, & Olsen, 2005; Ford et al., 1998).

In some research, caffeine consumption has been associated with spontaneous abortion (Dlugosz et al., 1996; Infante-Rivard, Fernández, Gauthier, David, & Rivard, 1993), with risk of first-trimester spontaneous abortion increasing with amount of caffeine consumed (Cnattingius, Signorello et al., 2000). Other studies suggest that moderate caffeine use—five cups a day or less—does not increase the risk of miscarriage (Klebanoff, Levine, DerSimonian, Clemens, & Wilkins, 1999; Mills et al., 1993). Studies of a possible link between caffeine consumption and spontaneous abortion have had mixed results (Cnattingius et al., 2000; Dlugosz et al., 1996; Infante-Rivard, Fernández, Gauthier, David, & Rivard, 1993; Klebanoff, Levine, DerSimonian, Clemens, & Wilkins, 1999; Mills et al., 1993; Signorello et al., 2001).

Marijuana and Cocaine Although findings about marijuana use by pregnant women are mixed (Dreher, Nugent, & Hudgins, 1994; Lester & Dreher, 1989), some evidence suggests that heavy use can lead to birth defects and increased risk of attention disorders and learning problems later in life (Fried, Watkinson, & Willan, 1984; March of Dimes Birth Defects Foundation, 2004). A Canadian study found temporary neurological disturbances, such as tremors and startles, as well as higher rates of low birth weight in the infants of marijuana smokers (Fried, Watkinson, & Willan, 1984). An analysis of blood samples from the umbilical cords of 34 newborns found a greater prevalence of cancer-causing mutations in the infants of mothers who smoked marijuana. These women did not use tobacco, cocaine, or opiates, suggesting that marijuana use alone can increase cancer risk (Ammenheuser, Berenson, Babiak, Singleton, & Whorton, 1998). In two longitudinal studies, prenatal use of marijuana was associated with impaired attention, impulsivity, and difficulty in use of visual and perceptual skills after age 3, suggesting that the drug may affect functioning of the brain's frontal lobe (Fried, 2002; Fried & Smith, 2001). In a study of pregnant mice, marijuana use at the time of conception or early in pregnancy tended to prevent implantation in the uterus (Wang et al., 2006).

Cocaine use during pregnancy has been associated with spontaneous abortion, delayed growth, premature labour, low birth weight, small head size, birth defects, and impaired neurological development (Bunikowski et al., 1998; Chiriboga, Brust, Bateman, & Hauser, 1999; Macmillan et al., 2001; March of Dimes Birth Defects Foundation, 2004a; Scher, Richardson, & Day, 2000; Shankaran et al., 2004). In some studies, cocaine-exposed newborns show acute withdrawal symptoms and sleep disturbances (O'Brien & Jeffery, 2002; Wagner, Katikaneni, Cox, & Ryan, 1998). So great has been the concern about "crack babies" that some authorities have taken criminal action against expectant mothers suspected of using cocaine (see Box 4-2).

More recent studies found no specific connection between prenatal cocaine exposure and physical, motor, cognitive, emotional, or behavioural deficits that could not also be attributed to other risk factors, such as low birth weight, exposure to tobacco, alcohol, marijuana or a poor home environment (Frank, Augustyn, Knight, Pell, & Zuckerman, 2001; Messinger et al., 2004; Singer et al., 2004).

HIV/AIDS

Acquired immune deficiency syndrome (AIDS) is a disease caused by the human immunodeficiency virus (HIV), which undermines functioning of the immune system. If an expectant mother has the virus in her blood, perinatal transmission may occur: the virus may cross over to the fetus' bloodstream through the placenta during pregnancy, labour, or delivery or, after birth, through breast milk.

The biggest risk factor for perinatal HIV transmission is a mother who is unaware she has HIV. New pediatric AIDS cases have declined steadily in the United States since 1992 due to routine testing and treatment of pregnant women and newborn babies and to advances in the prevention, detection, and treatment of HIV infection in infants. This decline accelerated in 1994 with the introduction of continuous pre- and postnatal administration of the drug zidovudine, commonly known as AZT as well as other antiviral drugs. As a result, the estimated rate of perinatal HIV infection is now less than 2 percent. In 2004, an estimated 48 perinatally acquired cases of AIDS were reported, down 95 percent from 1992. However, as with adults, HIV-AIDS tends to be underreported in children. The risk of transmission also can be reduced by choosing Caesarean delivery, especially when a woman has not received antiretroviral therapy, and by promotion of alternatives to breastfeeding (CDC, 2006a).

Other Maternal Illnesses

Prospective parents should try to prevent all infections—common colds, flu, urinary tract and vaginal infections, as well as sexually transmitted diseases. If the mother does contract an infection, she should have it treated promptly. Pregnant women also should be screened for thyroid deficiency, which can affect their children's future cognitive performance (Haddow et al., 1999).

Rubella (German measles), if contracted by a woman before her 11th week of pregnancy, is almost certain to cause deafness and heart defects in her baby. Chances of catching rubella during pregnancy have been greatly reduced in Canada since the late 1960s, when a vaccine was developed that is now routinely administered to infants and children (CICH, 2000). However, rubella is still a serious problem in non-industialized countries where inoculations are not routine (Plotkin, Katz, & Cordero, 1999).

Offspring of mothers with diabetes are two to five times more likely to develop birth defects, especially of the heart and of the spinal cord (neural tube defects), than offspring of other women. Research on mice suggests why: high blood glucose levels, typical in diabetics, deprive an embryo of oxygen, with resultant cell damage, during the first eight weeks of pregnancy, when its organs are forming. Women with diabetes need to be sure their blood glucose levels are under control before becoming pregnant (Li, Chase, Jung, Smith, & Loeken, 2005). Use of multivitamin supplements during the three months before conception and the first three months of pregnancy can help reduce the risk of diabetes-associated birth defects (Correa, Botto, Lin, Mulinare, & Erickson, 2003).

An infection called toxoplasmosis, caused by a parasite harboured in the bodies of cattle, sheep, and pigs and in the intestinal tracts of cats, typically produces either no symptoms or symptoms like those of the common cold. In a pregnant woman, however, especially in the second and third trimesters of pregnancy, it can cause fetal brain damage, severely impaired eyesight or blindness, seizures, or miscarriage, stillbirth, or death of the baby. Although as many as 9 out of 10 of these babies may appear normal at birth, more than half of them have later problems, including eye infections, hearing loss, and learning disabilities. Treatment with two antiparasitic drugs, pyrimethamine and sulfadiazine, during the first year of life can reduce brain and eye damage (McLeod et al., 2006).

To avoid infection, expectant mothers should not eat raw or very rare meat, should wash hands and all work surfaces after touching raw meat, should peel or thoroughly wash raw fruits and vegetables, and should not dig in a garden where cat feces are buried. Women who have a cat should have it checked for the disease, should not feed it raw meat, and, if possible, should have someone else empty the litter box (March of Dimes, 2002) or should do it often, wearing gloves (Kravetz & Federman, 2002).

Maternal Stress

Some tension and worry during pregnancy are normal and do not necessarily increase risks of birth complications, such as low birth weight, according to an analysis of many studies (Littleton, Breitkopf, & Berenson, 2006). Moderate maternal stress may even spur organization of the developing brain. In a series of studies, 2-year-olds whose mothers had shown moderate anxiety midway through pregnancy scored higher on measures of motor and mental development (DiPietro, 2004; DiPietro, Novak, Costigan, Atella, & Reusing, 2006).

On the other hand, unusual maternal stress during pregnancy may negatively impact the offspring (Dingfelder, 2004; Huizink, Mulder, & Buitelaar, 2004). In one study, women whose partners or children died or were hospitalized for cancer or heart attacks were at elevated risk of giving birth to children with malformations, such as cleft lip, cleft palate, and heart malformations (Hansen, Lou, & Olsen, 2000). As reported in Chapter 6, major stress during the 24th to 28th weeks of pregnancy may produce autism by deforming the developing brain (Beversdorf et al., 2001).

A mother's self-reported anxiety during pregnancy has been associated with 8-month-olds' inattentiveness during a developmental assessment (Huizink, Robles de Medina, Mulder, Visser, & Buitelaar, 2002) and preschoolers' negative emotionality or behavioural disorders in early childhood (Martin, Noyes, Wisenbaker, & Huttunen, 2000; O'Connor, Heron, Golding, Beveridge, & Glover, 2002). Other studies found links between expectant mothers' perceptions of stress and their fetuses' activity levels (DiPietro, Hilton, Hawkins, Costigan, & Pressman, 2002).

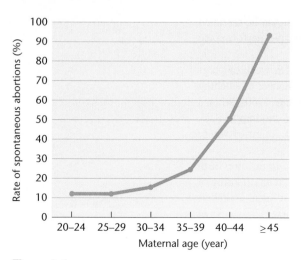

Figure 4-4

Miscarriage rates as a function of maternal age.

Source: Heffner, 2004, p. 1927; adapted from Menken et al. (1986), and Anderson, Wohlfahrt, Christens, Olsen, & Melbye (2000).

Maternal Age

On December 30, 2006, in Barcelona, Spain, a 67-year old woman became the oldest woman on record to give birth. The woman (whose name was not released) had become pregnant after in vitro fertilization. She gave birth to twins by Caesarean section. Women today typically start having children later in life than was true 15 or 20 years ago, often because they spend their early adult years getting advanced education and establishing careers (Canadian Institute of Child Health [CICH], 2000; Mathews & Ventura, 1997; Ventura et al., 1999). About a third of all Canadian babies are born to women over the age of 30 (Canadian Institute of Child Health, 2000).

How does delayed childbearing affect the risks to mother and baby? Pregnant women who are older are more likely to suffer complications due to diabetes, high blood pressure, or severe bleeding. Most risks to the infant's health are not much greater than for babies born to younger mothers. Still, after age 35 there is more chance of miscarriage or stillbirth (see Figure 4.4), and more likelihood of premature delivery, retarded fetal growth, other birth-related complications, or birth defects, such as Down syndrome (refer back to Chapter 3). In fact, the risk of miscarriage reaches 90 percent for women age 45 or older (Heffner, 2004). However, due to widespread screening for fetal defects among older expectant mothers, fewer babies with prenatally identified defects are born nowadays (Berkowitz, Skovron, Lapinski, & Berkowitz, 1990; P. Brown, 1993; Cunningham & Leveno, 1995).

Women age 40 and over are at increased risk of needing operative deliveries (Caesarean or by forceps or vacuum extraction—see Chapter 5). Risks of all birth complications are increased, and the infants are more likely to be born prematurely and underweight (Gilbert, Nesbitt, & Danielsen, 1999). Women who give birth after age 50 are two to three times more likely than younger women to have babies who are very small, born prematurely, or stillborn (Salihu, Shumpert, Slay, Kirby, & Alexander, 2003). Not all of these risks apply to women who become pregnant by in vitro fertilization, using ova donated by younger women. In those pregnancies, which are generally screened and monitored closely, the risks of both miscarriage and chromosomal abnormalities are consistent with the age of the donor (Heffner, 2004).

Adolescents also tend to have premature or underweight babies—perhaps because a young girl's still-growing body consumes vital nutrients the fetus needs (Fraser, Brockert, & Ward, 1995). These newborns are at heightened risk of death in the first month, disabilities, or health problems. If teenage mothers are unwed, they are likely to suffer great financial hardship and may drop out of school, narrowing their future vocational choices. And, try as they may to do their best at mothering, their lack of parenting skills may put their babies at a disadvantage (AAP Committee on Adolescence, 1999; Alan Guttmacher Institute, 1999a; Children's Defense Fund, 1998; Dahinten & Willms, 2002). Risks of teenage pregnancy are discussed further in Chapter 17.

Outside Environmental Hazards

Air pollution, chemicals, radiation, extremes of heat and humidity, and other hazards of modern life can affect prenatal development. Pregnant women who regularly breathe air that contains high levels of fine combustion-related particles are more likely to bear infants who are premature or undersized (Parker, Woodruff, Basu, & Schoendorf, 2005) or have chromosomal abnormalities (Bocskay et al., 2005). Exposure to high concentrations of disinfection byproducts is associated with low birth weight and slowed fetal growth (Hinckley, Bachand, & Reif, 2005). Women who work with chemicals used in manufacturing semiconductor chips have about twice the rate of miscarriage as other female workers (Markoff, 1992), and women exposed to DDT tend to have more preterm births (Longnecker, Klebanoff, Zhou, & Brock, 2001). Two common insecticides, chlorpyrifos and diazinon, apparently cause stunting of prenatal growth (Whyatt et al., 2004). Research in the United Kingdom found a 33-percent increase in risk of nongenetic birth defects among families living within 3 kilometres of hazardous waste sites (Vrijheld et al., 2002).

Fetal exposure to low levels of environmental toxins, such as lead, mercury, and dioxin, as well as nicotine and ethanol, may help explain the sharp rise in asthma, allergies, and autoimmune disorders such as lupus in recent years (Dietert, 2005). Childhood cancers, including leukemia, have been linked to pregnant mothers' drinking chemically contaminated ground water (Boyles, 2002) and use of home pesticides (Menegaux et al., 2006). Infants exposed prenatally even to low levels of lead, especially during the third trimester, tend to show IQ deficits at ages 6 to 10 (Schnaas et al., 2006).

Women who have routine dental X-rays during pregnancy triple their risk of having full-term, low–birth weight babies (Hujoel, Bollen, Noonan, & del Aguila, 2004). In utero exposure to radiation has been linked to greater risk of mental retardation, small head size, chromosomal malformations, Down syndrome, seizures, and poor performance on IQ tests and in school (Yamazaki & Schull, 1990).

Paternal Factors

A man's exposure to lead, marijuana or tobacco smoke, large amounts of alcohol or radiation, DES, certain pesticides, or high ozone levels may result in abnormal or poor quality sperm (Sokol et al., 2006; Swan et al., 2003). Offspring of male workers at a British nuclear processing plant were found to have an elevated risk of being born dead (Parker, Pearce, Dickinson, Aitkin, & Craft, 1999). Also, babies whose fathers had diagnostic X-rays within the year prior to conception tend to have low birth weight and slowed fetal growth (Shea, Little, & the ALSPAC Study Team, 1997). And fathers whose diet is low in vitamin C are more likely to have children with birth defects and certain types of cancer (Fraga et al., 1991). A study of 2,000 farm couples showed that preconception exposure to herbicides by fathers resulted in an increased risk of early miscarriage (Arbuckle, Savitz, Mery, & Curtis, 1999). Pesticide residues have been found in samples of semen of farmers, which could account for the increased risk of early miscarriage (Arbuckle, Schrader, Cole, Hall, Bancej, Turner, & Claman, 1999).

A man's use of cocaine can cause birth defects in his children. The cocaine seems to attach itself to his sperm, and this cocaine-bearing sperm then enters the ovum at conception. Other toxins, such as lead and mercury, may "hitchhike" onto sperm in the same way (Yazigi, Odem, & Polakoski, 1991).

Older fathers may be a significant source of birth defects due to damaged or deteriorated sperm. Advanced age of the father also may be a factor in a disproportionate number of cases of schizophrenia (Byrne et al., 2003; Malaspina et al., 2001) and of autism and related disorders (Reichenberg et al., 2006). In 2004 about 10 percent of fathers of new babies were ages 35 to 55 and over (Martin, Hamilton et al., 2006).

Men who smoke have an increased likelihood of transmitting genetic abnormalities (AAP Committee on Substance Abuse, 2001). A pregnant woman's exposure to the father's secondhand smoke has been linked with low birth weight, infant respiratory infections, sudden infant death, and cancer in childhood and adulthood (Ji et al., 1997; D. H. Rubin, Krasilnikoff, Leventhal, Weile, & Berget, 1986; Sandler, Everson, Wilcox, & Browder, 1985; Wakefield, Reid, Roberts, Mullins, & Gillies, 1998). In a study of 214 nonsmoking mothers in New York City, exposure to *both* paternal smoking and urban air pollution resulted in a 7-percent reduction in birth weight and a 3-percent reduction in head circumference (Perera, Rauh, et al., 2004).

Monitoring and Promoting Prenatal Development

Not long ago, almost the only decision parents had to make about their babies before birth was the decision to conceive; most of what happened in the intervening months was beyond their control. Now we have an array of tools to assess an unborn baby's progress and well-being (see Table 4-3), and even to intervene to correct some abnormal conditions.

Progress is being made in the use of noninvasive procedures, such as ultrasound and blood tests, to detect chromosomal abnormalities. Contrary to earlier findings, amniocentesis

Checkpoint ✓

Can you . . .

✔ Describe the short-term and long-term effects on the developing fetus of a mother's use of medical and recreational drugs during pregnancy?

✔ Summarize the risks of maternal illnesses and stress, delayed childbearing, and exposure to chemicals and radiation?

What's your view ?

• Since cocaine, marijuana, tobacco, and other substances can produce genetic abnormalities in a man's sperm, should fertile men be forced to abstain from them? How could such a prohibition be enforced?

Checkpoint ✓

Can you . . .

✔ Identify at least three ways in which environmentally caused defects can be influenced by the father?

Guidepost 3

What techniques can assess a fetus' health and well-being, and what is the importance of prenatal and preconception care?

Table 4-3	Prenatal Assessment Techniques
Assessment Technique	**Procedure**
Ultrasound	A picture of the uterus, fetus, and placenta is created by sound waves. Used to check fetal growth, gestational age, multiple pregnancies, uterine abnormalities, structural abnormalities in the fetus, viability of the fetus, and to guide other procedures like amniocentesis.
Amniocentesis	A sample of amniotic fluid, containing fetal cells, is withdrawn and analyzed for genetic or multifactorial defects, and all recognizable chromosomal disorders. Recommended for parents who may be carriers of genetic diseases.
Chorionic villus sampling	Samples of tissue from the ends of villi (hairlike projections of the chorion—the membrane surrounding the fetus), are made up of fetal cells. These are tested for birth defects and disorders.
Embryoscopy	Insertion of a tiny viewing scope into a pregnant woman's abdomen; provides a clear look at embryos as young as 6 weeks, and can be useful for early diagnosis and treatment of embryonic and fetal abnormalities.
Preimplantation genetic diagnosis	Identification of some genetic defects in embryos of four to eight cells, which were conceived by in vitro fertilization and have not yet been implanted in the mother's uterus. Defective embryos are not implanted.
Umbilical cord sampling	Taking samples of a fetus's blood from the umbilical cord under the guidance of ultrasound, to check for infection, anemia, heart failure, and certain metabolic disorders and imunodeficiencies.
Maternal blood tests	Blood sample taken from the mother between the 16th and 18th weeks of pregnancy is tested for the amount of alpha fetoprotein (AFP) it contains. High levels of AFP indicate presence of defects in the brain or spinal cord, such as anencephaly, or spina bifida. Can also predict cases of Down syndrome.

Sources: Canadian Early and Mid-Trimester Amniocentesis Trial [CEMAT] Group, 1998; D'Alton & DeCherney, 1993; Haddow et al., 1992; Kurjak, Kupesic, Matijevic, Kos, & Marton, 1999; Quintero, Abuhamad, Hobbins, & Mahoney, 1993; Ventura, Martin, Curtin, & Mathews, 1998.

and chorionic villus sampling, which can be used earlier in pregnancy, carry only a slightly higher miscarriage risk (Caughey, Hopkins, & Norton, 2006; Eddleman et al., 2006). Screening is most effective when begun during the first trimester (Simpson, 2005). In one study, a combination of three noninvasive tests conducted at 11 weeks of gestation predicted the presence of Down syndrome with 87 percent accuracy. When the 11-week tests were followed by further noninvasive testing early in the second trimester, accuracy reached 96 percent (Malone et al., 2005).

Screening for treatable defects and diseases is only one reason for the importance of prenatal care. Early, high-quality prenatal care, which includes educational, social, and nutritional services, can help prevent maternal and infant death and other complications of birth. It can provide first-time mothers with information about pregnancy, childbirth, and infant care. Poor women who get prenatal care benefit by being put in touch with other needed services, and they are more likely to get medical care for their infants after birth (Shiono & Behrman, 1995).

Disparities in Prenatal Care

In Canada prenatal care is widespread, but despite universal health insurance, socioeconomic status affects the quality of prenatal care provided to pregnant women (Canadian Perinatal Surveillance System, 2000; Willms, 2002). As an indicator of different effectiveness of prenatal care, low-income groups experience over 150 percent the infant mortality rate of higher-income groups. However, with a general decline in infant mortality in Canada, the disparity in infant mortality rates between income groups, regions in Canada, and males and females is decreasing (Dzakpasu, Joseph, Kramer, & Allen, 2000; see Figure 4-5).

Even as usage of prenatal care has increased, rates of low birth weight and premature birth have worsened (Kogan et al., 1998; Ventura et al., 1999). Why?

One answer is the increasing number of multiple births, which require especially close prenatal attention. Twin pregnancies often end, for precautionary reasons, in early births, either induced or by Caesarean delivery. Intensive prenatal care may allow early detection of problems requiring immediate delivery, as, for example, when one or both fetuses are not thriving. This may explain why a Canadian study of twin births between 1986 and 1997 found parallel upward trends in use of prenatal care and rates of preterm birth—along with a decline in mortality of twin infants (Joseph, Marcoux, Ohlsson, Liu, Allen, Kramer, & Wen, 2001).

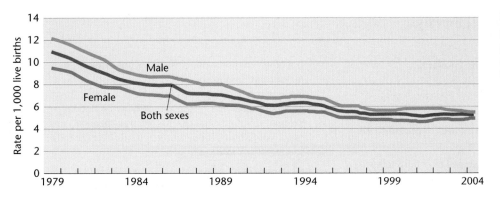

Figure 4-5

Infant mortality rates in Canada.

Source: Statistics Canada, 2006. *Deaths 2004*. Catalogue no. 84F0211XIE. Ottawa, ON: Minister of Industry.

Another possible explanation for these parallel trends is that the benefits of prenatal care are not evenly distributed, particularly in northern and remote communities. Merely increasing the quantity of prenatal care does not address the *content* of care (Misra & Guyer, 1998). Most prenatal care programs in Canada focus on screening for major complications and are not designed to attack the causes of low birth weight. A U.S. national panel has recommended that prenatal care be restructured to provide more visits early in the pregnancy and fewer in the last trimester. In fact, care should begin *before* pregnancy. Prepregnancy counselling could make more women aware, for example, of the importance of getting enough folic acid in their diet and making sure that they are immune to rubella. In addition, care needs to be made more accessible to poor and minority women (Shiono & Behrman, 1995).

The Need for Preconception Care

A more fundamental answer to disparities in prenatal care is that even early prenatal care is insufficient; care should begin *before* pregnancy to identify preventable risks. The Centers for Disease Control and Prevention (2006c) has issued comprehensive, research-based guidelines for *preconception care* for all women of childbearing age. Such care should include:

- *Physical examinations* and the taking of medical and family histories.
- *Vaccinations* for rubella and hepatitis B.
- *Risk screening* for genetic disorders and infectious diseases such as STDs.
- *Counselling* women to avoid smoking and alcohol, maintain a healthy body weight, and take folic acid supplements.

Interventions should be provided where risks are indicated and also between pregnancies for women who have had poor pregnancy outcomes in the past.

The CDC (2006c) urges all adults to create a reproductive life plan so as to focus attention on reproductive health, avoid unintended pregnancies, and improve pregnancy outcomes.

Good prenatal and preconception care can give every child the best possible chance for entering the world in good condition to meet the challenges of life outside the uterus—challenges we discuss in the next three chapters.

Checkpoint

Can you . . .

✔ Describe seven techniques for identifying defects or disorders prenatally?

✔ Tell why early, high-quality prenatal care is important, how it could be improved, and why preconception care is important?

✔ Discuss possible reasons for disparities in utilization of prenatal care?

What's your view

- Can you suggest ways to induce more pregnant women to seek early prenatal or preconception care?

Summary and Key Terms

Prenatal Development: Three Stages

Guidepost 1 What are the three stages of prenatal development, and what happens during each stage?

- Prenatal development occurs in three stages of gestation: the germinal, embryonic, and fetal stages.

- Growth and development both before and after birth follow the cephalocaudal principle (head to tail) and the proximodistal principle (centre outward).

- About one-third of all conceptions end in spontaneous abortion, usually in the first trimester of pregnancy.

- As fetuses grow, they move less, but more vigorously. Swallowing amniotic fluid, which contains substances from the mother's body, stimulates taste and smell. Fetuses seem able to hear, exercise sensory discrimination, learn, and remember.

**cephalocaudal principle (83)   proximodistal principle (83)
germinal stage (83)   embryonic stage (87)   spontaneous
abortion (87)   fetal stage (88)   ultrasound (88)**

Prenatal Development: Environmental Influences

Guidepost 2 What environmental influences can affect prenatal development?

- The developing organism can be greatly affected by its prenatal environment. The likelihood of a birth defect may depend on the timing and intensity of an environmental event and its interaction with genetic factors.

- Important environmental influences involving the mother include nutrition, physical activity, smoking, intake of alcohol or other drugs, transmission of maternal illnesses or infections, maternal age, incompatibility of blood type, and external environmental hazards, such as chemicals and radiation. External influences may also affect the father's sperm.

**teratogenic (90)   fetal alcohol syndrome (FAS) (94)
acquired immune deficiency syndrome (AIDS) (96)**

Monitoring and Promoting Prenatal Development

Guidepost 3 What techniques can assess a fetus' health and well-being, and what is the importance of prenatal and preconception care?

- Ultrasound, amniocentesis, chorionic villus sampling, embryoscopy, preimplantation genetic diagnosis, umbilical cord sampling, and maternal blood tests can be used to determine whether an unborn baby is developing normally. Some abnormal conditions can be corrected through fetal therapy.

- Early, high-quality prenatal care is essential for healthy development. It can lead to detection of defects and disorders and, especially if begun early and targeted to the needs of at-risk women, may help reduce maternal and infant death, low birth weight, and other birth complications.

- Differences in prenatal care may be a factor in disparities in low birth weight and perinatal death.

- Preconception care for every woman of childbearing age would reduce unintended pregnancies and increase the chances of good pregnancy outcomes.

5 CHAPTER FIVE

Birth and the Newborn Baby

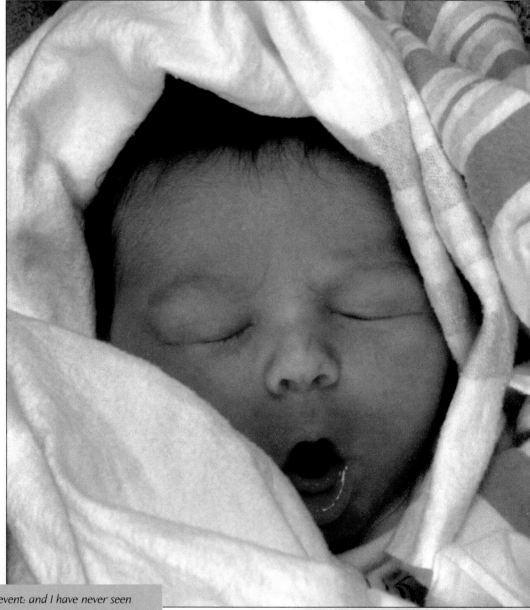

A newborn baby is an extraordinary event; and I have never seen two babies who looked exactly alike. Here is the breathing miracle who could not live an instant without you, with a skull more fragile than an egg, a miracle of eyes, legs, toenails, and lungs.

—James Baldwin, *No Name in the Street*, 1972

Focus *The Birth of Elvis Presley**

Elvis Presly

Elvis Presley (1935–1977) was born in a 30- by 15-foot cottage in East Tupelo, Mississippi. Today, the modest birthplace of the now-legendary "king" of rock music is painted sparkling white, the walls are papered with primroses, and dainty curtains hang at the windows—among the many homey touches added for the benefit of tourists. But, like many of the popular myths about Elvis' early life, this "cute little doll house" (Goldman, 1981, p. 60) bears only slight resemblance to the reality: a bare board shack with no indoor plumbing or electricity, set in a dirt-poor hamlet that wasn't much more than "a wide spot in the road" (Clayton & Heard, 1994, p. 8).

During the Great Depression, Elvis' near-illiterate father, Vernon Presley, sometimes did odd jobs for a farmer named Orville Bean, who owned much of the town. Elvis' mother, Gladys, was vivacious and high-spirited, as talkative as Vernon was taciturn. She, like Vernon, came from a family of sharecroppers and migrant workers. She had moved to East Tupelo to be close to the garment factory where she worked.

Gladys first noticed handsome Vernon on the street and then, soon after, met him in church. They eloped on June 17, 1933. Vernon was 17 and Gladys, 21. They borrowed the three dollars for the marriage licence.

At first the young couple lived with friends and family. When Gladys became pregnant, Vernon borrowed $180 from his employer, Bean, to buy lumber and nails and, with the help of his father and older brother, built a two-room cabin next to his parents' house on Old Saltillo Road. Bean, who owned the land, was to hold title to the house until the loan was paid off.

Vernon and Gladys moved into their new home in December 1934, about a month before she gave birth. Her pregnancy was a difficult one; her legs swelled, and she finally quit her job at the garment factory, where she had to stand on her feet all day pushing a heavy steam iron.

When Vernon got up for work in the wee hours of January 8, a bitterly cold morning, Gladys was hemorrhaging. The midwife told Vernon to get the doctor, Will Hunt. (His $15 fee was paid by welfare.) At about 4 o'clock in the morning, Dr. Hunt delivered a stillborn baby boy, Jesse Garon. The second twin, Elvis Aron, was born about 35 minutes later. Gladys—extremely weak and losing blood—was taken to the hospital charity ward with baby Elvis. They stayed there for more than 3 weeks.

Baby Jesse remained an important part of the family's life. Gladys frequently talked to Elvis about his brother. "When one twin died, the one that lived got the strength of both," she would say (Guralnick, 1994, p. 13). Elvis took his mother's words to heart. Throughout his life, his twin's imagined voice and presence were constantly with him.

As for Elvis' birthplace, he lived there only until the age of 3. Vernon, who sold a pig to Bean for $4, was accused of altering the cheque to $40. He was sent to prison, and when the payment on the house loan came due, Bean evicted Gladys and her son, who had to move in with family members. In later years, Elvis would drive back to East Tupelo (now Tupelo's suburban Presley Heights). He would sit in his car in the dark, looking at the cottage on what is now called Elvis Presley Drive and "thinking about the course his life had taken" (Marling, 1996, p. 20).

• • •

Elvis Presley is just one of many well-known people born at home. At one time, medical care during pregnancy was rare, and the prevalence of birth complications, stillbirth, and maternal mortality was higher than it is today. A rising standard of living, together with medical advances, has eased childbirth and reduced its risks. Today, the overwhelming majority of births in Canada (but a smaller proportion in some European countries) occur in hospitals. However, there is a small but growing movement back to home birth, as is still the custom in many less industrialized countries.

In this chapter, we describe how babies come into the world: the stages, methods, joys, and complications of birth. We describe how newborn infants look and how their body systems work. We discuss ways to assess their health, and how birth complications can affect development. We also consider how the birth of a baby affects the people most vital to the infant's well-being: the parents.

After you have read and studied this chapter, you should be able to answer each of the Guidepost questions that appear at the top of the next page. Look for them again in the margins, where they point to important concepts throughout the chapter. To check your understanding of these Guideposts, review the end-of-chapter summary. Checkpoints located throughout the chapter will help you verify your understanding of what you have read.

*Sources of information about Elvis Presley's birth were Clayton & Heard (1994); Dundy (1985); Goldman (1981); Guralnick (1994); and Marling (1996).

Guideposts for Study

1. How do customs surrounding birth reflect culture, and how has childbirth changed in developed countries?

2. How does labour begin, what happens during each of the three stages of childbirth, and what alternative methods of delivery are available?

3. How do newborn infants adjust to life outside the womb, and how can we tell whether a new baby is healthy and is developing normally?

4. What complications of childbirth can endanger newborn babies, and what are the long-term prospects for infants with complicated births?

5. How do parents bond with and care for their baby?

Guidepost 1

How do customs surrounding birth reflect culture, and how has childbirth changed in developed countries?

Childbirth and Culture: How Birthing Has Changed*

Customs surrounding childbirth reflect the beliefs, values, and resources of a culture. In many pre-contact Aboriginal communities, childbirth was assisted by a midwife, who administered traditional herbs and medicines, and whose role included transmitting values from one generation to the next (Carroll & Benoit, 2001). Among the Carrier people in B.C., the reproductive role was a source of social status, and women who raised families successfully were influential in their communities, with the wisdom of elderly women recognized in the esteem in which grandmothers were held (Carroll et al., 2001).

Before the twentieth century, childbirth in Europe, and in Canada, followed a familiar pattern, much as in some developing countries today (see Box 5-1). Birth was a female social ritual. The woman, surrounded by female relatives and neighbours, sat up in her own bed, modestly draped in a sheet; if she wished, she might stand, walk around, or squat over a birth stool. Chinks in the walls, doors, and windows were stuffed with cloth to keep out chills and evil spirits. The prospective father was nowhere to be seen; he may have been out gathering firewood. Not until the fifteenth century, was a doctor present, and then only for wealthy women if complications arose.

The midwife who presided over the event had no formal training; she offered "advice, massages, potions, irrigations, and talismans." Salves made of fat of viper, gall of eel, powdered hoof of donkey, tongue of chameleon, or skin of snake or hare might be rubbed on the prospective mother's abdomen to ease her pain or hasten her labour; but "the cries of the mother during labour were considered to be as natural as those of the baby at birth" (Fontanel & d'Harcourt, 1997, p. 28).

After the baby emerged, the midwife cut and tied the umbilical cord and cleaned and examined the newborn, testing the reflexes and joints. The other women helped the new mother wash and dress, made her bed with clean sheets, and served her food to rebuild her strength. Within a few hours or days, a peasant mother would be back at work in the fields; a more affluent or noble woman could "lie in" and rest for several weeks.

Reducing the Risks of Childbirth

Childbirth in those times was "a struggle with death" (Fontanel & d'Harcourt, 1997, p. 34) for both mother and baby. In seventeenth- and eighteenth-century France, a woman had a 1 in 10 chance of dying while, or shortly after, giving birth. Thousands of babies were stillborn, and 1 out of 4 who were born alive died during its first year.

The development of the science of obstetrics early in the nineteenth century professionalized childbirth, especially in urban settings. Even though most deliveries still

*This discussion is based largely on Eccles, 1982; Fontanel & d'Harcourt, 1997; Gelis, 1991; and Scholten, 1985.

Box 5-1 *Having a Baby in the Himalayas*

Between 1993 and 1995, Sally Olds, one of the authors of this book, made four visits to Badel, a remote hill village in the small Asian country of Nepal, where she stayed with local families. The following account (Olds, 2002) from her journal describes a visit that she, the friend she travelled with, and their guide, Buddi, made to the village midwife.

Sabut Maya Mathani Rai has been helping childbearing mothers for almost 50 of her 75 years. Only three days ago she attended the birth of a baby girl.

When Sabut Maya attends a woman about to give birth, she says, "First I feel on the outside of the woman's belly. I look to see where is the head and the other organs. I help the mother push down when her time comes."

She does not use forceps. "I don't have any instruments," she says. "I just use my hands. If the baby is upside down, I turn it from the outside."

Nepali hill women usually give birth right after, or in the middle of, working in house or fields. The delivery may occur inside or outside of the house, depending on when the woman goes into labour. Women usually give birth on their knees. This kneeling position allows the mother to use her strong thigh and abdominal muscles to push the baby out. If the mother has other children, they usually watch, no matter how small they are. But the husbands don't want to watch and the women don't want them there.

Most women are not attended by a midwife; they handle the delivery and dispose of the placenta and umbilical cord themselves. Buddi's mother once gave birth on the path as she was walking back from working in the fields, and then asked for her husband's knife to cut the cord.

"If the baby is not coming fast, I use special medicine," the midwife says. "I put grasses on the mother's body and I massage her with oil from a special plant. I don't give the mother any herbs or anything like that to eat or drink, only hot water or tea."

In a complicated birth—if, say, the baby is not emerging or the mother gets sick—the midwife calls the *shaman* (spiritual healer). Inevitably, some babies and some mothers die. In most cases, however, all goes well, and most deliveries are easy and quick.

How is the newborn cared for? "After the baby is born I wash the baby," says the midwife. "I leave this much of the cord on the baby [indicating about half an inch] and I tie it up with very good cotton. Then I wrap a piece of cotton cloth around the baby's tummy. This stays on for a few days until the cord falls off." Sometimes a small piece of the umbilical cord is saved and inserted into a metal bead that will be given to the child to wear on a string around the neck, to ward off evil spirits. A family member flings the placenta high up on a tree near the house to dry out; eventually it is thrown away.

A midwife in Kathmandu, Nepal, oils a newborn baby.

No one but the mother—not even the father—is allowed to hold the baby at first. This may help to protect both mother and baby from infection and disease when they are most vulnerable. Then, at 3 days of age for a girl or 7 days for a boy (girls are thought to mature earlier), a purification rite and naming ceremony takes place.

My friend and I tell how in our culture women lie on their backs, a position unknown in most traditional societies, and how the doctor sometimes breaks the woman's water. We also describe how a doctor sometimes puts on surgical gloves and reaches inside the woman to turn a baby in a breech or other position. "We don't have gloves and we don't have instruments," the midwife repeats. "We don't do any of those things. I'm just a helper." Sabut Maya really is a combination of midwife and doula (described in this chapter)—a kind of helper now seen with growing frequency in delivery rooms of Europe and North America. It seems ironic that it has taken the industrialized world so long to rediscover some of the wisdom that "primitive" societies have known for centuries.

What's your view

What aspects of traditional ways of delivering babies might enhance childbearing practices without giving up medical techniques that save lives? Could advanced medical techniques be introduced into traditional societies without invalidating practices that seem to serve women in those societies well?

Check it out

For more information on this topic, go to **www.mcgrawhill.ca/olc/papalia**.

occurred at home and women were on hand to help and offer emotional support, a (male) physician was usually in charge, with surgical instruments ready in case of trouble. Midwives were now given training, and obstetrics manuals were widely disseminated.

After the turn of the twentieth century, maternity hospitals, where conditions were antiseptic and medical management was easier, became the birth setting of choice for those who could afford them (though not for many country women, like Gladys Presley), and anaesthesia for pain relief became standard practice. In 1926, the first year national statistics were taken, 18 percent of Canadian deliveries took place in hospitals; by 1960 the rate was 95 percent, and by 1983 the rate was over 99 percent (Leacy, 1983). A growing number are now attended by registered midwives or certified nurse-midwives (AOM, n.d.; CAM, 2006; Martin, Hamilton et al., 2006).

The dramatic reductions in risks surrounding pregnancy and childbirth, particularly during the past 50 years, are largely due to the availability of antibiotics, blood transfusions, safe anaesthesia, improved hygiene, and drugs for inducing labour when necessary. In addition, improvements in prenatal assessment and care make it far more likely that a baby will be born healthy.

Still, childbirth is not risk free for women or babies. Obese women, those with difficult medical histories, those who have had previous Caesarean deliveries, and those who have had several children are at elevated risk of hemorrhage and other dangerous complications (Chazotte, quoted in Bernstein, 2003).

Contemporary Settings for Childbirth

The medicalization of childbirth has had its costs. "To many, a hospital birth has become a surgical act in which the woman is hooked up to a monitor and stretched out on a table under glaring lights and the stares of two or three strangers, her feet in stirrups" (Fontanel & d'Harcourt, 1997, p. 57). Today some women in industrialized countries are opting for the emotionally satisfying experience of home birth, usually attended by a registered midwife, and with the resources of medical science close at hand in case of need. About a third of Canadian women indicate preferences for birthing centres rather than hospitals, while 80 percent indicate a willingness to be cared for by a nurse or midwife after birth (Wen et al., 1999); however, attitudes towards home birth are mixed (Tyson, 1991).

Hospitals, too, are finding ways to "humanize" childbirth; in Canada hospitals are adopting a family-centred approach, emphasizing the importance of a warm, comforting, one-room quiet home-like environment for labour, birth, and recovery together with family members (Health Canada, 2000), which is being met with overwhelming acceptance (Janssen, Klein, Harrri, Soolsma, & Seymour, 2000). This family-centred approach emphasizes education and preparation for childbirth and encourages birthing mothers and their families to be more active in deciding how birthing takes place, and in encouraging family members to be present during labour and birth (Roudebush, Kaufman, Johnson, Araham, & Clayton, 2006).

In Canada, about 99 percent of babies are born in hospitals; 96 percent are attended by physicians and 4 percent by midwives. Most midwives are graduates of four-year university or college programs in midwifery, or registered nurses with special training in midwifery; some have been trained by apprenticeship. A midwife may or may not work under a doctor's direction. In Canada from the 1990s to the present, midwives attained legal status in Quebec, Ontario, Manitoba, Alberta, British Columbia, and the NWT, and midwives are gaining recognition as regulated health providers in other provinces and territories. The trend is moving towards provincially funded independent certified midwives working in all settings—a significant shift from earlier decades in which midwives had no legal status in Canada (Benoit & Carroll, 2005). In traditional Aboriginal practices, the midwife plays a prominent role.

In many provinces in Canada, such as British Columbia, Aboriginal midwifery, which incorporates traditional and contemporary Aboriginal practices, is slowly becoming recognized and supported by mainstream health authorities (Carroll et al., 2001; Revised Statutes of British Columbia, 1996). New training programs for Aboriginal midwifery have been established, which combine traditional and mainstream approaches. Most Aboriginal midwives work in birthing clinics located in northern regions, and they use a combination of traditional and contemporary techniques and tools (Benoit & Carroll, 2005).

In many traditional cultures, childbearing women are attended by a *doula* (a word derived from Ancient Greek for the most important female servant). Today, a doula can furnish emotional support and, unlike a doctor, can stay at a woman's bedside throughout labour. In Canada, doulas (who often take special training) attend only 1 percent of births; they are, however, gaining wider acceptance (Gilbert, 1998).

Checkpoint ✔

Can you . . .

✔ Identify at least three ways in which childbirth has changed in developed countries?

✔ Give reasons for the reduction in risks of pregnancy and childbirth?

✔ Weigh the comparative advantages of various settings and attendants for childbirth?

The Birth Process

Labour is an apt term. Chiefly because of the size of the fetal head, birth is hard work for both mother and baby—but work that yields a rich reward. From an evolutionary perspective, the advantage of an enlarged head that can contain a brain capable of advanced thought outweighs the difficulty of passing through the birth canal (Bjorklund & Pellegrini, 2000).

Parturition—the process of uterine, cervical, and other changes that brings on labour, or normal vaginal childbirth—typically begins about 2 weeks before delivery, when the balance between progesterone and estrogen shifts. During most of gestation, progesterone keeps the uterine muscles relaxed and the cervix firm. During parturition, sharply rising estrogen levels stimulate the uterus to contract and the cervix to become more flexible. The timing of parturition seems to be determined by the rate at which the placenta produces a protein called *corticotropin-releasing hormone (CRH),* which also promotes maturation of the fetal lungs to ready them for life outside the womb. The rate of CRH production as early as the fifth month of pregnancy may predict whether a baby will be born early, "on time," or late (Smith, 1999; Smith, 2007).

The uterine contractions that expel the fetus begin—typically, 266 days after conception—as mild tightenings of the uterus. A woman may have felt "false" contractions (known as *Braxton-Hicks contractions*) during the final months of pregnancy, or even as early as the second trimester, when the muscles of the uterus would tighten for 30 to 60 seconds or as long as two minutes. These "false" contractions may help tone the uterine muscles and promote the flow of blood to the placenta. In comparison with Braxton-Hicks contractions, which are relatively mild and irregular and then subside, "real" labour contractions are more frequent, rhythmic, and painful, and they increase in frequency and intensity.

parturition Process of uterine, cervical, and other changes, usually lasting about 2 weeks, preceding childbirth

How does labour begin, what happens during each of the three stages of childbirth, and what alternative methods of delivery are available?

Stages of Childbirth

Labour takes place in three overlapping stages (see Figure 5-1). The *first stage,* dialation of the cervix is the longest, typically lasting 12 to 14 hours for a woman having her first child. In later births the first stage tends to be shorter. During this stage, regular and increasingly frequent uterine contractions—15 to 20 minutes apart at first—cause the cervix to shorten and dilate, or widen, in preparation for delivery. Toward the end of the first stage, contractions occur every 2 to 5 minutes. This stage lasts until the cervix is fully open (10 centimetres) so the baby can descend into the birth canal.

The *second stage, descent and emergence of the baby,* typically lasts up to an hour or two. It starts when the baby's head begins to move through the cervix into the vaginal canal, and it ends when the baby emerges completely from the mother's body. If this stage lasts longer than 2 hours, signalling that the baby needs more help, a doctor may grasp the baby's head with forceps or, more often, use vacuum extraction with a suction cup to pull

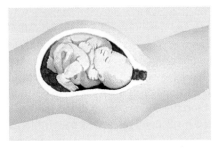

(a) First stage

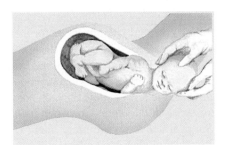

(b) Second stage

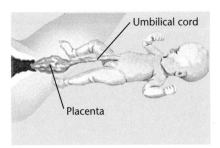

(c) Third stage

Figure 5-1

The first three stages of childbirth. *(a)* During the first stage of labour, a series of stronger and stronger contractions dilates the cervix, the opening to the mother's womb. *(b)* During the second stage, the baby's head moves down the birth canal and emerges from the vagina. *(c)* During the brief third stage, the placenta and umbilical cord are expelled from the womb. Then the cord is cut.

Source: Adapted from Lagercrantz & Slotkin, 1986.

it out of the mother's body (Curtin & Park, 1999). At the end of this stage, the baby is born; but it is still attached to the placenta in the mother's body by the umbilical cord, which must be cut and clamped.

The *third stage, expulsion of the placenta,* lasts between 10 minutes and one hour. During this stage the placenta and the remainder of the umbilical cord are expelled from the mother.

At one time, an *episiotomy,* a surgical cut between the vagina and anus, was made just before delivery to enlarge the vaginal opening, speed delivery, and prevent the vagina from tearing. The assumption was that a "clean" incision would heal better than a spontaneous tear. However, many studies have disproved this theory, and experts now agree that episiotomy should *not* be done routinely. It is recommended only under special circumstances, such as a very large baby, a forceps birth, or indications of trouble with the baby's heartrate.

Electronic Fetal Monitoring

Electronic fetal monitoring is often used to track the fetus' heartbeat during labour and delivery and to indicate how the fetal heart is responding to the stress of uterine contractions. Monitoring can detect any serious problems and alert the attending physician or midwife that a fetus needs help. Sometimes electronic fetal monitoring is used late in pregnancy if there are signs that the fetus may be at risk.

Electronic fetal monitoring can be done *externally,* by placing a monitor on the mother's abdomen and securing it with elastic belts, or *internally,* by inserting a wire into the cervix and resting it on the baby's head. The internal method is more accurate but can be used only when the cervix is already open, and it carries a risk of infection. Monitoring can be done remotely by *telometry,* sending information about the fetal heart rate and the woman's contractions to a monitor at another location, such as the nurses' station.

Electronic fetal monitoring can provide valuable information in high-risk deliveries, including those in which the fetus is very small, is premature, is in a breech position (feet or buttocks down), or seems to be in distress, or in which labour is induced through administration of drugs. Yet monitoring has drawbacks when used routinely in low-risk pregnancies. It is costly; it restricts the mother's movements during labour; and, most important, it has an extremely high "false positive" rate, suggesting that fetuses are in trouble when they are not. Such warnings may prompt doctors to deliver by the riskier Caesarean method (described in the next section) rather than vaginally (Nelson, Dambrosia, Ting, & Grether, 1996).

Vaginal versus Caesarean Delivery

The usual method of childbirth, described above, is vaginal delivery. **Caesarean delivery** is a surgical procedure to remove the baby from the uterus through an incision in the mother. In 2005–2006, 26 percent of Canadian births occurred this way, as compared with only 5 percent in the late 1960s (Canadian Institute for Health Information [CIHI], 2007; Canadian Perinatal Surveillance System, 2000; Guyer et al., 1999). This increase in Caesarean birth rates has prompted the development of strategies to reduce the rate, as a way of controlling potential complications for the mother and newborn, as well as for future pregnancies (Betran, Merialdi, Lauer, Bing-Shun, Thomas, Van Look, & Wagner, 2007).

The operation is commonly performed when labour progresses too slowly, when the fetus seems to be in trouble, or when the mother is bleeding vaginally. Often a Caesarean is needed when the fetus is in the breech position (feet first) or in the transverse position (lying crosswise in the uterus), or when its head is too big to pass through the mother's pelvis. Surgical deliveries are more likely when the birth involves a first baby, a large baby, or an older mother or a mother who has had a previous Caesarean. Thus the increase in Caesarean rates since 1970 is in part a reflection of a proportional increase in first births, a rise in average birth weight, and a trend toward later childbirth (Guyer et al., 1999; Martin et al., 2003; Martin, Hamilton, et al., 2005). Other suggested explanations include increased use of electronic fetal monitoring, physicians' fear of malpractice litigation, and the desire to avoid a difficult labour (Martin et al., 2003; Martin, Hamilton, et al., 2005; Sachs, Kobelin, Castro, & Frigoletto, 1999).

Caesarean birthrates in Canada are among the highest in the world, but rising rates in European countries during the past decade have narrowed the gap (Notzon, 1990; Sachs et al., 1999). In Europe, the average rate of Caesarean deliveries is 19 percent (Bertrand et al., 2007). Despite efforts to decrease the rate of Caesarean birth, it has increased in developing countries over the last decade (Bertrand et al., 2007). However, the percentage of vaginal births after a previous Caesarean has remained stable (Canadian Perinatal Surveillance System, 2000).

There is growing belief that the Caesarean delivery is unnecessary or harmful in many cases (Curtin & Park, 1999). About 4 percent of Caesareans result in serious complications, such as bleeding and infections (Nelson et al., 1996; Silver et al., 2006). For the baby, there may be an important risk in bypassing the struggle to be born, which apparently stimulates the production of stress hormones that may aid in the adjustment to life outside the womb (Lagercrantz & Slotkin, 1986).

Caesarean deliveries carry risks of serious maternal complications, such as bleeding, infections, and bowel injury (Nelson, Dambrosia, Ting, & Grether, 1996; Silver et al., 2006). They also (as we will discuss in a subsequent section) deprive the baby of important benefits of normal birth. However, despite these disadvantages of Caesarean birth, a vaginal delivery for a woman who has had an earlier Caesarean delivery should be attempted only with caution. A comparison of 17,898 U.S. women who attempted vaginal births after a previous Caesarean with 15,801 U.S. women who elected a repeat Caesarean found greater (though still low) risks of uterine rupture and brain damage associated with vaginal birth after Caesarean (Landon et al., 2004). The same result was found in a previous study conducted in Nova Scotia (McMahon, Luther, Bowes, & Olshan, 1996). And, among 313,238 Scottish women giving birth after previous Caesareans, the risk of the infant's dying during delivery was about 11 times higher in vaginal deliveries than in planned repeat Caesareans (Smith, Pell, Cameron, & Dobbie, 2002). Perhaps these considerations figure in the 8-percent increase since 1994 in Caesarean births after previous Caesarean delivery (Canadian Perinatal Surveillance System, 2000). For pregnancies complicated by factors like unusual fetal position or large head size, a Caesarean delivery can be life saving (Armson, 2007) Today, if a woman has had a Caesarean delivery, chances are more than 80 percent that any subsequent deliveries will be by Caesarean (CIHI, 2007; Martin, Hamilton et al., 2006).

Medicated versus Nonmedicated Delivery

In the mid-nineteenth century, Queen Victoria became the first woman in history to be put to sleep during delivery, that of her eighth child. Sedation with ether or chloroform became common practice as more births took place in hospitals (Fontanel & d'Harcourt, 1997).

During the twentieth century, several alternative methods of **natural, or prepared, childbirth** were developed. These methods minimize or eliminate the use of drugs that may pose risks for babies and enable both parents to participate fully in a natural, empowering experience. In 1914 Dr. Grantly Dick-Read, an English gynecologist, suggested that pain in childbirth was caused mostly by fear of the unknown and the resulting muscular tension. His "Childbirth without Fear" method educates expectant mothers about the physiology of reproduction and trains them in physical fitness and in breathing and relaxation during labour and delivery.

The Lamaze method, introduced by the French obstetrician Fernand Lamaze in the late 1950s, teaches expectant mothers to work actively with their bodies through controlled breathing. The woman is trained to pant or breathe rapidly "in sync" with the increasing intensity of her contractions and to concentrate on other sensations to ease the perception of pain. She learns to relax her muscles as a conditioned response to the voice of her "coach" (usually the prospective father, other family member, or a friend), who attends classes with her, takes part in the delivery, and helps with the exercises. Other methods use mental imagery, massage, gentle pushing, and deep breathing. One technique, introduced by the French physician Michael Odent, is submersion of the labouring mother in a soothing pool of water. Perhaps most extreme is the Bradley Method, which disavows all obstetrical procedures and other medical interventions.

natural, or prepared, childbirth
Methods of childbirth that use instruction, breathing exercises, and social support to induce controlled physical responses to uterine contractions and reduce fear and pain

What's your view ❓

- If you or your partner were expecting a baby, and the pregnancy seemed to be going smoothly, would you prefer (a) medicated or non-medicated delivery, (b) hospital, birth centre, or home birth, and (c) attendance by a physician or midwife? Give reasons. If you are a man, would you choose to be present at the birth? If you are a woman, would you want your partner present?

Checkpoint ✔

Can you . . .

✔ Describe the three stages of vaginal childbirth?

✔ Discuss the uses and disadvantages of Caesarean births and explain the purpose of electronic fetal monitoring and the dangers of its routine use?

✔ Compare medicated delivery, and natural or prepared childbirth?

✔ Weigh the comparative advantages of various types of settings and attendants for childbirth?

✔ Compare the functions of a midwife and a doula?

Guidepost 3

How do newborn infants adjust to life outside the womb, and how can we tell whether a new baby is healthy and is developing normally?

neonatal period First 4 weeks of life, a time of transition from intrauterine dependency to independent existence

Improvements in medicated delivery during the past two decades have led more mothers to choose pain relief, sometimes along with natural methods. General anesthesia, which renders the woman completely unconscious and greatly increases the risks to mother and baby, is rarely used, even in Caesarean births (Eltzschig et al., 2003). A woman may be given local (vaginal) anesthesia, also called a *pedunal block,* if she wants and needs it, usually during the second stage of labour or when forceps are used. Or she can receive an *analgesic* (painkiller), which reduces the perception of pain by depressing the activity of the central nervous system. However, analgesics may slow labour, cause maternal complications, and make the baby less alert after birth. Approximately 60 percent of women in labour have regional (*epidural or spinal*) injections (Eltzschig et al., 2003). Regional anesthesia, which is injected into a space in the spinal cord between the vertebrae in the lumbar (lower) region, blocks the nerve pathways that would carry the sensation of pain to the brain. Epidurals given early can shorten labour with no added risk of needing Caesarean delivery (Wong et al., 2005).

Regional injections have become increasingly common as physicians have found effective ways to relieve pain with smaller doses of medication (Hawkins, 1999). "Walking epidurals" enable a woman to feel sensations, move her legs, and fully participate in the birth. In a recent analysis of 10 studies involving 2,369 births in Europe, the United States, and Canada, women who had regional injections (epidurals) enjoyed more effective pain relief—but longer labour—than women who had narcotic injections, and their babies tended to arrive in healthier condition (Halpern, Leighton, Ohlsson, Barrett, & Rice, 1998).

Any of these newer forms of anesthesia allow a woman to remain alert and active and participate in all the decisions during the process of birth; being conscious also allows her to enjoy holding her newborn immediately afterwards. However, these drugs pass through the placenta to enter the fetal blood supply and tissues and thus may pose some danger to the baby.

Pain relief should not be the only consideration in a decision about whether a woman should have anesthesia. More important to her satisfaction with the childbirth experience may be her involvement in decision making, her relationship with the professionals caring for her, and her expectations about labour. Social and cultural attitudes and customs also may play a part (Eltzschig et al., 2003). A woman and her doctor should discuss the various options early in pregnancy, but her choices may change once labour is under way.

Childbearing women are sometimes attended by a *doula,* an experienced mentor, coach, and helper who can furnish emotional support and information and can stay at a woman's bedside throughout labour. Unlike a midwife, a doula does not participate in the delivery but supports the mother throughout the process (see Box 5-1). In 11 randomized, controlled studies, women attended by doulas had shorter labour, less anesthesia, and fewer forceps and Caesarean deliveries than mothers who had not had doulas (Klaus & Kennell, 1997). In Canada, doulas (who often take special training) attend only 1 percent of births; they are, however, gaining wider acceptance (Gilbert, 1998).

The Newborn Baby

Birth is stressful for babies. The struggle to be born apparently stimulates the infant's body to produce huge amounts of two stress hormones, adrenaline and noradrenaline. The surge of these hormones at birth clears the lungs of excess fluid to permit breathing, mobilizes stored fuel to nourish cells, and sends blood to the heart and brain. Also, by making the baby more alert and ready to interact with another person, these hormones may promote bonding with the mother. This, as we have mentioned, is an important advantage of vaginal birth. Caesarean deliveries bypass the experience of labour, which may help a baby adjust to life outside the womb (Lagercrantz & Slotkin, 1986).

The first 4 weeks of life, the **neonatal period,** is a time of transition from the uterus, where a fetus is supported entirely by the mother, to an independent existence. What are the physical characteristics of newborn babies, and how are they equipped for this crucial transition?

Size and Appearance

An average newborn, or **neonate,** in Canada is about 50 cm long and weighs about 3.5 kg. At birth, 92 percent of full-term babies weigh between 2.5 and 5 kg and are between 45 and 55 cm long. Boys tend to be slightly longer and heavier than girls, and a firstborn child is likely to weigh less at birth than laterborns. In their first few days, neonates lose as much as 10 percent of their body weight, primarily because of a loss of fluids. They begin to gain weight again at about the fifth day and are generally back to birth weight by the 10th to the 14th day.

New babies have distinctive features, including a large head (a quarter of the body length) various skin conditions (which are temporary—see Table 5-1), birthmarks (which are permanent), and a receding chin (which makes it easier to nurse). At first, a neonate's head may be long and misshapen because of the "moulding" that eased its passage through the mother's pelvis. This temporary shaping was possible because an infant's skull bones are not yet fused; they will not be completely joined for 18 months. The places on the head where the bones have not yet grown together—the soft spots, or **fontanels**—are covered by a tough membrane; they will close over within the first month of life. Since the cartilage in the baby's nose also is malleable, the trip through the birth canal may leave the nose looking misshapen for a few days.

Many newborns have a pinkish cast; their skin is so thin that it barely covers the capillaries through which blood flows. However, a baby's skin colour can vary greatly, depending on the baby's age, racial or ethnic origin, health status, temperature, the environment, and whether the baby is crying. During the first few days, some neonates are very hairy because some of the **lanugo,** a fuzzy prenatal hair, has not yet fallen off. All new babies (except those born post-term, after 41 weeks of gestation) are covered with **vernix caseosa** ("cheesy varnish"), an oily protection against infection that is absorbed into the skin after birth.

neonate Newborn baby, up to 4 weeks old

fontanels Soft spots on head of young infant

lanugo Fuzzy prenatal body hair, which drops off within a few days after birth

vernix caseosa Oily substance on a neonate's skin that protects against infection

Table 5-1	Neonatal Skin Conditions		
Condition	**Description**	**Cause**	**Duration**
Blue colouring	Bluish colour on hands and feet*	Immature blood circulation	Normal colour should appear within several days
Milia	Tiny, white, hard, pimple-like spots on nose, chin, or forehead	Immature oil glands	Disappear on their own
Stork bites (or salmon patches)	Small pink or red patches on baby's eyelids, between the eyes, on upper lip, or back of neck, most visible during crying	Concentration of immature blood vessels	Most soon fade and disappear
Mongolian spots	Blue or purple splotches on lower back and buttocks	Concentration of pigmented cells; tends to occur in dark-skinned babies	Usually disappears within first 4 years
Erythema toxicum	Red rash similar to flea bites, usually on chest and back	Cause unknown; appears in half of all babies, but most commonly in premature infants	Usually disappears in a few days
Acne neonatorum (baby acne)	Pimples on cheeks and forehead	Maternal hormones; about one-fifth of neonates develop this condition in first month	Disappears in a few months.
Strawberry hemangioma (strawberry mark)	Bright or dark red, raised or swollen, bumpy area, usually on head	Concentration of tiny, immature blood vessels; often develop within first two months; most common in premature babies and in girls	Often grow in size for several months and then fade gradually, disappearing by 9 years
Port wine stain	Flat pink, red, or purple birthmark, usually on head or neck but may cover large areas of body	Concentration of dilated capillaries (tiny, immature blood vessels)	Do *not* disappear; may become darker and bleed as child grows older; may be treated by laser surgery.

*Bluish colouring on other parts of body is abnormal.

"Witch's milk," a secretion that sometimes leaks from the swollen breasts of newborn boys and girls around the third day of life, was believed during the Middle Ages to have special healing powers. Like the whitish or blood-tinged vaginal discharge of some newborn girls, this fluid emission results from high levels of the hormone estrogen, which is secreted by the placenta just before birth, and goes away within a few days or weeks. A newborn, especially if premature, also may have swollen genitals.

Body Systems

The newborn's need to survive puts a host of new demands on the body systems. Before birth, blood circulation, breathing, nourishment, elimination of waste, and temperature regulation were accomplished through the mother's body. After birth, babies must do all of this themselves (see Table 5-2). Most of this transition occurs during the first 4 to 6 hours after delivery (Ferber & Makhoul, 2004).

The fetus and mother have separate circulatory systems and separate heartbeats; the fetus' blood is cleansed through the umbilical cord, which carries "used" blood to the placenta and returns a fresh supply (refer back to Figure 4-2 in Chapter 4). After birth, the baby's circulatory system must operate on its own. A neonate's heartbeat is fast and irregular, and blood pressure does not stabilize until about the 10th day of life.

The fetus gets oxygen through the umbilical cord, which also carries away carbon dioxide. A newborn needs much more oxygen than before and must now get it alone. Most babies start to breathe as soon as they are exposed to air. If breathing has not begun within about 5 minutes, the baby may suffer permanent brain injury caused by **anoxia,** lack of oxygen or *hypoxia,* a reduced oxygen supply. Because infants' lungs have only one-tenth as many air sacs as adults' do, infants (especially those born prematurely) are susceptible to respiratory problems. Anoxia or hypoxia may occur during delivery (though rarely so) as a result of repeated compression of the placenta and umbilical cord with each contraction. This form of *birth trauma* can leave permanent brain damage, causing mental retardation, behaviour problems, or even death.

In the uterus, the fetus relies on the umbilical cord to bring food from the mother and to carry fetal body wastes away. At birth, babies have a strong sucking reflex to take in milk, and their own gastrointestinal secretions to digest it. During the first few days infants excrete **meconium,** a stringy, greenish-black waste matter formed in the fetal intestinal tract. When the bowels and bladder are full, the sphincter muscles open automatically; a baby will not be able to control these muscles for many months.

Three or four days after birth, about half of all babies (and a larger proportion of babies born prematurely) develop **neonatal jaundice:** their skin and eyeballs look yellow. This kind of jaundice is caused by the immaturity of the liver. Usually it is not serious, does not need treatment, and has no long-term effects. However, because healthy Canadian newborns usually go home from the hospital within 48 hours or less (Liu et al., 2002), jaundice may go unnoticed and may lead to complications (AAP Committee on Quality Improvement, 2002).

anoxia Lack of oxygen, which may cause brain damage

meconium Fetal waste matter, excreted during the first few days after birth

neonatal jaundice Condition, in many newborn babies, caused by immaturity of liver and evidenced by yellowish appearance; can cause brain damage if not treated promptly

Table 5-2	A Comparison of Prenatal and Postnatal Life	
Characteristic	**Prenatal Life**	**Postnatal Life**
Environment	Amniotic fluid	Air
Temperature	Relatively constant	Fluctuates with atmosphere
Stimulation	Minimal	All senses stimulated
Nutrition	Dependent on mother's blood	Dependent on external food and functioning of digestive system
Oxygen supply	Passed from maternal bloodstream through the placenta	Passed from neonate's lungs to pulmonary blood vessels
Metabolic elimination	Passed into maternal bloodstream through the placenta	Discharged by skin, kidneys, lungs, and gastrointestinal tract

Source: Timiras, 1972, p. 174.

More severe jaundice is treated by putting the baby under fluorescent lights and sometimes by exchange transfusion of the baby's blood. Severe jaundice that is not monitored and treated promptly may result in brain damage.

The layers of fat that develop during the last two months of fetal life enable healthy full-term infants to keep their body temperature constant after birth despite changes in air temperature. Newborn babies also maintain body temperature by increasing their activity when air temperature drops.

Medical and Behavioural Assessment

Although the great majority of births result in normal, healthy babies, some do not. The first few minutes, days, and weeks after birth are crucial for development. It is important to know as soon as possible whether a baby has any problem that needs special care.

The Apgar Scale

One minute after delivery, and then again 5 minutes after birth, most babies are assessed using the **Apgar scale** (see Table 5-3). Its name, after its developer, Virginia Apgar (1953), helps us remember its five subtests: *a*ppearance (colour), *p*ulse (heart rate), *g*rimace (reflex irritability), *a*ctivity (muscle tone), and *r*espiration (breathing). The newborn is rated 0, 1, or 2 on each measure, for a maximum score of 10. A 5-minute score of 7 to 10 indicates that the baby is in good to excellent condition (Ventura et al., 1998). A score between 5 and 7 at one minute may mean the baby needs help to establish breathing; nurses may dry the baby vigorously with a towel while oxygen is held under the nose, and the test should be repeated every 5 minutes up to 20 minutes (American Academy of Pediatrics [AAP] Committee on Fetus and Newborn & American College of Obstetricians and Gynecologists [ACOG] Committee on Obstetric Practice, 2006).

A score below 5 (unlikely except in a small percentage of premature newborns or those delivered by emergency Caesarean) means the baby needs immediate lifesaving treatment. If resuscitation is successful, bringing the baby's score to 5 or more, no long-term damage is likely to result (AAP Committee on Fetus and Newborn and American College of Obstetricians and Gynecologists [ACOG] Committee on Obstetric Practice, 1996; 2006; Society of Obstetricians and Gynaecologists of Canada [SOGC], 1998; 1996a).

An infant's score may be affected by the amount of medication the mother received; or neurological or cardiorespiratory conditions may interfere with one or more vital signs. Premature infants (those born before 37 weeks of gestation) may score low because of physiological immaturity. Scores of 0 to 3 at 10, 15, and 20 minutes after birth are increasingly associated with cerebral palsy (muscular impairment due to brain damage before or during birth) or other future neurological problems; such conditions may

Checkpoint ✔

Can you . . .

✔ Describe the normal size and appearance of a newborn and name several temporary skin conditions and other changes that occur within the first few days?

✔ Compare four fetal and neonatal body systems?

✔ Identify two dangerous conditions that can appear soon after birth?

Apgar scale Standard measurement of a newborn's condition; it assesses *a*ppearance, *p*ulse, *g*rimace, *a*ctivity, and *r*espiration

Table 5-3	Apgar Scale		
Sign*	**0**	**1**	**2**
Appearance (colour)	Blue, pale	Body pink, extremities blue	Entirely pink
Pulse (heart rate)	Absent	Slow (below 100)	Rapid (over 100)
Grimace (reflex irritability)	No response	Grimace	Coughing, sneezing, crying
Activity (muscle tone)	Limp	Weak, inactive	Strong, active
Respiration (breathing)	Absent	Irregular, slow	Good, crying

*Each sign is rated in terms of absence or presence from 0 to 2; highest overall score is 10.

Source: Adapted from V. Apgar, 1953.

or may not be caused by oxygen deprivation (ACOG, 1996; SOGC, 1998; 1996). Low Apgar scores are also more likely with repeated Caesarean deliveries (Burt, Vaughan, & Daling, 1988).

In general, Apgar scores at 5 minutes reliably predict survival during the first month of life (Casey, McIntire, & Leveno, 2001). However, a low Apgar score alone does not necessarily indicate anoxia or predict neonatal death. Prematurity, low birth weight, trauma, infection, birth defects, medication given to the mother, and other conditions may affect the results (AAP Committee on Fetus and Newborn and ACOG Committee on Obstetric Practice, 1996, 2006).

Assessing Neurological Status: The Brazelton Scale

The **Brazelton Neonatal Behavioural Assessment Scale (NBAS)** is used to assess neonates' responsiveness to their physical and social environment, to identify problems in neurological functioning, and to predict future development. The test is named for its designer, T. Berry Brazelton (1973, 1984; Brazelton & Nugent, 1995). It assesses *motor organization* as shown by such behaviours as activity level and the ability to bring a hand to the mouth; *reflexes; state changes,* such as irritability, excitability, and ability to quiet down after being upset; *attention and interactive capacities,* as shown by general alertness and response to visual and auditory stimuli; and indications of *central nervous system instability,* such as tremors and changes in skin colour. The NBAS takes about 30 minutes, and scores are based on a baby's best performance. A newer version, the Newborn Behavioural Observations system (NBO) (Nugent, Keefer, O'Brien, Johnson, & Blanchard, 2005) was developed specifically for clinicians caring for newborns in hospital, clinic, or home settings.

Neonatal Screening for Medical Conditions

Children who inherit the enzyme disorder phenylketonuria, or PKU (refer back to Table 3-2 in Chapter 3), will become mentally retarded unless they are fed a special diet beginning in the first 3 to 6 weeks of life (National Institutes of Health [NIH] Consensus Development Panel, 2001). Screening tests that can be administered soon after birth can often discover such correctable defects. In one study, newborns identified by screening were less likely to be retarded or to need hospitalization than those identified by clinical diagnosis. One drawback is that the tests can generate false-positive results, which suggest that a problem exists when it does not, and may trigger anxiety and costly, unnecessary treatment (Waisbren et al., 2003).

Routine screening of all newborn babies for such rare conditions as PKU (1 case in 10,000 to 25,000 births), congenital hypothyroidism (1 in 3,600 to 5,000), galactosemia (1 in 60,000 to 80,000), and other, even rarer disorders is expensive. Yet the cost of testing thousands of newborns to detect one case of a rare disease may be less than the cost of caring for one mentally retarded person for a lifetime. All provinces require routine screening for PKU and congenital hypothyroidism; provinces vary on requirements for other screening tests (Society of Obstetricians and Gynaecologists of Canada, 1996b).

Now, the advent of tandem mass spectrometry, in which a single blood specimen can be screened for 20 or more disorders, has prompted many developed countries to expand their mandatory screening programs (Howell, 2006). The American College of Medical Genetics (ACOG) recommends that screening be extended to 29 treatable conditions as well as 25 related but secondary conditions (USDHHS, Maternal and Child Health Bureau, 2005), and further expansion may follow (Howell, 2006). Critics warn against expanding screening too rapidly without adequate research support, including cost-benefit data (Botkin et al., 2006). Advocates argue that, although problems remain to be worked out in the operation of these programs, it is wrong to let children who might have been helped by screening suffer or even die in the meantime. Canada lags behind the rest of the developed world in infant screening practices. There is a wide disparity in the number of conditions screened for (ranging from 3 to 28, depending on province or territory), which has raised calls for more consistency and wider scope in infant screening practices across the country (Hanley, 2005).

States of Arousal and Activity Levels

Babies have an internal "clock" that regulates their daily cycles of eating, sleeping, and elimination and perhaps even their moods. These periodic cycles of wakefulness, sleep, and activity, which govern an infant's **state of arousal,** or degree of alertness (see Table 5-4), seem to be inborn and highly individual. Changes in state are coordinated by multiple areas of the brain and are accompanied by changes in the functioning of virtually all body systems (Ingersoll & Thoman, 1999).

Most newborns spend about 75 percent of their time—up to 18 hours a day—asleep but awaken every three to four hours, day and night, for feeding (Ferber & Makhoul, 2004; Hoban, 2004). Newborns' sleep alternates between quiet (regular) and active (irregular) sleep. Active sleep appears rhythmically in cycles of about one hour and accounts for up to 50 percent of a newborn's total sleep time. It is probably the equivalent of rapid eye movement (REM) sleep, which in adults is associated with dreaming. The amount of REM sleep declines to less than 30 percent of daily sleep time by age 3 and continues to decrease steadily throughout life (Hoban, 2004).

Beginning in the first month, nighttime sleep periods gradually lengthen and total sleep time diminishes as babies grow more wakeful in the daytime. Some infants begin to sleep through the night as early as 3 months of age. By six months, an infant typically sleeps for 6 hours straight at night, but brief nighttime waking is normal even during late infancy and toddlerhood. A 2-year-old typically sleeps about 13 hours a day, including a single nap, usually in the afternoon (Hoban, 2004).

Cultural variations in feeding practices may affect sleep patterns. Many Canadian parents time the evening feeding so as to encourage nighttime sleep. Mothers in rural Kenya allow their babies to nurse as they please, and their 4-month-olds continue to sleep only 4 hours at a stretch (Broude, 1995).

Some parents and caregivers spend a great deal of time and energy trying to change babies' states—mostly by soothing a fussy infant to sleep. Although crying is usually more distressing than serious, it is particularly important to quiet low–birth weight babies, because quiet babies maintain their weight better. Steady stimulation is the time-proven way to soothe crying babies: by rocking or walking them, wrapping them snuggly, or letting them hear rhythmic sounds (see Box 5-2).

state of arousal An infant's physiological and behavioural status at a given moment in the periodic daily cycle of wakefulness, sleep, and activity

Checkpoint ✔

Can you . . .

✔ Discuss patterns of sleep, arousal, and activity and variations in newborns' states?

✔ Tell how sleep patterns change, and how cultural practices can affect these patterns?

Table 5-4	States of Arousal in Infancy			
State	**Eyes**	**Breathing**	**Movements**	**Responsiveness**
Regular sleep	Closed; no eye movement	Regular and slow	None, except for sudden, generalized startles	Cannot be aroused by mild stimuli
Irregular sleep	Closed; occasional rapid eye movements	Irregular	Muscles twitch, but no major movements	Sounds or light bring smiles or grimaces in sleep
Drowsiness	Open or closed	Irregular	Somewhat active	May smile, startle, suck, or have erections in response to stimuli
Alert inactivity	Open	Even	Quiet; may move head, limbs, and trunk while looking around	An interesting environment (with people or things to watch) may initiate or maintain this state.
Waking activity and crying	Open	Irregular	Much activity	External stimuli (such as hunger, cold, pain, being restrained, or being put down) bring about more activity, perhaps starting with soft whimpering and gentle movements and turning into a rhythmic crescendo of crying or kicking, or perhaps beginning and enduring as uncoordinated thrashing and spasmodic screeching.

Source: Adapted from information in Prechtl & Beintema, 1964; P. H. Wolff, 1966.

Guidepost 4

What complications of childbirth can endanger newborn babies, and what are the long-term prospects for infants with complicated births?

preterm (premature) infants Infants born before completing the 37th week of gestation

small-for-gestational age infants Infants whose birth weight is less than that of 90 percent of babies of the same gestational age, as a result of slow fetal growth

low birth weight Weight of less than 2,500 g at birth because of prematurity or being small for date

perinatal Period from 28 weeks' gestation to 7 days after birth

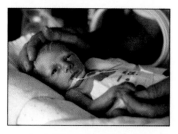

The antiseptic, temperature-controlled crib, or isolette, in which this premature baby lies has holes through which the infant can be examined, touched, and massaged. Frequent human contact helps low–birth weight infants thrive.

Complications of Childbirth—
and Their Aftermath

"It must be a boy," say some mothers whose labour and delivery prove long and difficult. This old adage seems to bear some truth: boys' deliveries are somewhat more likely to involve complications than girls', in part because boy babies tend to be larger. In two large Irish and Dutch studies, male babies took longer to emerge and were more likely to suffer fetal distress, to require forceps or Caesarean delivery, and to have low Apgar scores than female babies (Bekedam, Engelsbel Mol, Buitendijk, & van der Pal-de Bruin, 2002; Eogan, Geary, O'Connell, & Keane, 2003).

Most babies are born healthy, but some remain in the womb too briefly or too long or are born very small—complications that can impair their chances of survival and well-being. Others are born dead or die soon after birth. Let's look at some of these potential complications of birth and at ways to increase the chances of favourable outcomes.

Prematurity and Low Birth Weight

Low–birth weight babies may be either *preterm* or *small-for-gestational age,* or both (see Figure 5-2 for proportions of preterm, term, and postmature births in Canada). About 2 out of 3 babies with low birth weight are **preterm (premature) infants,** born before completing the 37th week of gestation (Martin, Hamilton, Sutton et al., 2005). (Preterm babies born close to term may be of normal birth weight and may have few or mild health problems.) The increase in preterm births may in part reflect the rise in multiple births from the use of new reproductive technology, in Caesarean deliveries, induced labour, and births to older women, ages 35 and up (Kramer et al., 1998). **Small-for-gestational age infants,** who may or may not be preterm, weigh less than 90 percent of all babies of the same gestational age. Their small size is generally the result of inadequate prenatal nutrition, which slows fetal growth. Much of the increased prevalence of low birth weight is attributed to the rise in multiple births.

In 2005–2006, about one in 16, or 6.1 percent of babies born in Canada had **low birth weight**—they weighed less than 2,500 g at birth (CIHI, 2007). Very-low–birth weight babies, who weigh less than 1,500 g, accounted for 1.1 percent of births in 1998. Low birth weight, which has been trending downward slightly since the late 1980s (Canadian Perinatal Health Report, 2000; Canadian Institute of Child Health [CICH], 2000), contributes to **perinatal** illnesses, the leading cause of infant death in Canada. The next leading cause of death in Canadian infants is birth defects (CICH, 2000). Preventing and treating low birth weight can increase the number of babies who survive the first year of life.

How Many Babies Are Preterm, and Why?

The causes of preterm birth are not fully understood, but this trend may in part reflect the rise in multiple births and induced and Caesarean deliveries (Martin, Hamilton et al., 2006).

Figure 5-2

Preterm and postmature infants as proportions of all live singleton births, Canada, 2003. Proportions of preterm births increase in cases of multiple births (57% of twins, and 98% of higher-order multiples).

Source: Fiore, 2003; Health Canada, 2004; Joseph, Huang, Liu, Ananth, Allen, Sauve, & Kramer, 2007.

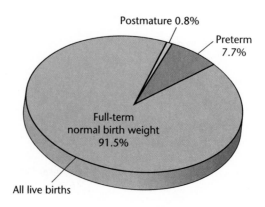

Postmature 0.8%

Preterm 7.7%

Full-term normal birth weight 91.5%

All live births

Preterm birth accounts for nearly half of all neurological birth defects, such as cerebral palsy, and more than two-thirds of infant deaths. More than 70 percent of preterm births are late preterm, delivered between 34 and 36 weeks' gestation; these babies tend to weigh more and to be at lower risk than those born earlier in gestation (Martin, Hamilton, et al., 2006).

Such measures as enhanced prenatal care, nutritional interventions, home monitoring of uterine activity, and administration of drugs, bed rest, and hydration for women who go into labour early have failed to stem the tide of premature births (Goldenberg & Rouse, 1998; Lockwood, 2002). One promising treatment is a form of the hormone progesterone called *hydroxyprogesterone caproate,* or *17P.* In a two-and-a-half-year trial at 13 major medical research centres in the United States, giving 17P to women who had borne premature babies reduced repeat preterm births by as much as one-third (Meis et al., 2003).

How Many Babies are Low Birth Weight, and Why? As mentioned above, very-low–birth weight babies accounted for 1.1 percent of births in Canada. Very-low–birth weight babies are nearly 100 times more likely to die during their first year of life than babies of normal birth weight, and moderately low–birth weight babies (between 1,500 and 2,499 grams at birth) are more than five times more likely to die. Much of the increase in low birth weight since the mid-1980s, like the rise in premature births, is likely due to increased use of induced and Caesarean deliveries, delayed childbearing, fertility drugs, and multiple births; but low birth weight also is increasing among single births (Martin, Hamilton, et al., 2006; CIHI, 2007).

Overall, 15.5 percent of all births, or more than 20 million infants worldwide—more than 95 percent of them in developing countries—have low birth weight (see Table 5-5). (The true extent of low birth weight may be much higher because as many as 3 out of 4 newborns in the developing world are not weighed.) Low birth weight in developing regions stems primarily from the mother's poor health and nutrition (United Nations Children's Fund and World Health Organization, 2004).

Who Is Likely to Have a Low–Birth Weight Baby?

Factors increasing the likelihood that a woman will have an underweight baby include: (1) *demographic and socio-economic factors,* such as being under age 17 or over 40, poor, unmarried, or undereducated (Willms, 2002); (2) *medical factors predating the pregnancy,* such as having no prior children or more than four, being short or thin, having had previous low–birth weight infants or multiple miscarriages, having had low birth weight herself, or having genital or urinary abnormalities or chronic hypertension; (3) *prenatal behavioural and environmental factors,* such as poor nutrition, inadequate prenatal care, smoking, use of alcohol or other drugs, or exposure to stress, abuse, high altitude, or toxic substances; (Connor & McIntyre, 2002); and (4) *medical conditions associated with the pregnancy,* such as vaginal bleeding, infections, high or low blood pressure, anemia, too little weight gain, and having last given birth less than 6 months or 10 or more years before conception (Arias, MacDorman, Strobino, & Guyer, 2003; S. S. Brown, 1985; Chomitz, Cheung, & Lieberman, 1995; Conde-Agudelo, Rosas-Bermúdez, Kafury-Goeta, 2006; Murphy, Schei, Myhr, & Du Mont, 2001; Nathanielsz, 1995; Shiono & Behrman, 1995; Wegman, 1992; Zhu, Rolfs, Nangle, & Horan, 1999). The safest interval between pregnancies is 18 to 23 months (Zhu et al., 1999). Depression during pregnancy is another risk factor; screening for depression is a critical part of prenatal care (Yonkers, quoted in Bernstein, 2003; Sommers & Willms, 2002).

Many of these factors are interrelated, and socio-economic status cuts across many of them. Teenagers' higher risk of having low–birth weight babies may stem more from malnutrition and inadequate prenatal care than from age, since teenagers who become pregnant are likely to be poor. Federal and provincial programs are designed to prevent low birth weight by providing prenatal care and nutrition for pregnant women who are in risk groups such as low socio-economic status (CICH, 2000; Dahinten & Willms, 2002). At least one-fifth of all low birth weights are attributed to smoking. Even before they become pregnant, women can reduce their chances of having a low–birth weight baby by eating well, not smoking or using drugs, drinking little or no alcohol, and getting good medical care (Chomitz et al., 1995; Shiono & Behrman, 1995; Willms, 2002).

Table 5-5	Percentage and Number of Low–Birth Weight Infants by United Nations Regions, 2000*	

	% Low–Birth Weight Infants
WORLD	**15.5**
More developed	7.0
Less developed	16.5
Least developed countries	18.6
AFRICA	**14.3**
Eastern Africa	13.5
Middle Africa	12.3
Northern Africa	15.3
Southern Africa	14.6
Western Africa	15.4
ASIA**	**18.3**
Eastern Asia**	5.9
South-central Asia	27.1
South-eastern Asia	11.6
Western Asia	15.4
EUROPE	**6.4**
Eastern Europe	6.4
Northern Europe	6.5
Southern Europe	5.9
Western Europe	6.7
LATIN AMERICA AND CARIBBEAN	**10.0**
Caribbean	13.7
Central America	10.1
South America	9.6
NORTHERN AMERICA	**7.7**
OCEANIA**	**10.5**
Australia/New Zealand	6.5
Melanesia	10.8
Micronesia	12.7
Polynesia	3.8

*The latest available estimates by country and territory, on which these global and regional estimates are calculated, may refer to an earlier or a more recent year than 2000 (*see Table 3*). However, considering that low birth weight rates are changing only slowly, the latest rates available have been taken to also refer to the year 2000 for the calculation of these global and regional estimates.

**Australia, Japan and New Zealand have been excluded from the regional estimates, but are included in the total for developed countries.

Source: United Nations Children's Fund & World Health Organization (2004).

Although Canada is more successful than most countries in *saving* low–birth weight babies, the rate of such births to Canadian women is higher than in many European nations, but not as high as in the United States or the United Kingdom (CICH, 2000; UNICEF, 1996). One of the factors thought to contribute to the incidence of low–birth weight children is the dramatic increase in multiple births in Canada, associated with the use of new reproductive technologies like fertility drugs and in vitro fertilization. In 1976 the multiple birth rate in Canada was 936 per 100,000 births; by 1996, the number climbed to 2,469. About half of multiple births are preterm compared to 6 percent of single births (CICH, 2000). Low– and very-low–birth weights occur about nine times more often for multiple rather than single births (Multiple Births Canada, 2005).

Definitions for low and high birth weight might be inappropriate for some ethnic groups in Canada. A study of first-year growth rates of Canadian children of Chinese descent indicated that although their length growth was similar to the national average, their weight was below average, despite diets consistent with Canadian Paediatric Society guidelines (Sit, Yeung, He, & Anderson, 2001). On the other hand, the birth weights of Aboriginal Canadian infants are higher than the national average, which might reflect a genetic predisposition to having heavier babies (CICH, 2000).

Immediate Treatment and Outcomes

The most pressing fear for very small babies is that they will die in infancy. Because their immune systems are not fully developed, they are especially vulnerable to infection, which has been linked to slowed growth and developmental delays (Stoll et al., 2004). Their nervous systems may not be mature enough for them to perform functions basic to survival, such as sucking, and they may need to be fed intravenously (through the veins). Feeding them mothers' milk can help prevent infection (AAP Section on Breastfeeding, 2005; Furman, Taylor, Minich, & Hack, 2003). Because they do not have enough fat to insulate them and to generate heat, it is hard for them to stay warm. Low Apgar scores in preterm newborns are a strong indication of heightened risk and of the need for intensive care (Weinberger et al., 2000).

A low–birth weight baby is placed in an *incubator* (an antiseptic, temperature-controlled crib) and fed through tubes. To counteract the sensory impoverishment of life in an incubator, hospital workers and parents are encouraged to give these small babies special handling. Gentle massage seems to foster growth, weight gain, motor activity, alertness, and behavioural organization, as assessed by the Brazelton NBAS (T. M. Field, 1986, 1998b; T. Field, Hernandez-Reif, & Freedman, 2004; Schanberg & Field, 1987). A combination of massage and lullabies can shorten the hospital stay (T. Field, Hernandez-Reif, & Freedman, 2004; Standley, 1998).

Premature infants tend to show uneven state development. Compared with full-term infants the same age, they are more alert and wakeful and have longer stretches of quiet sleep and more REMs in active sleep. On the other hand, their sleep can be more fragmented, with more transitions between sleeping and waking (Ingersoll & Thoman, 1999). Kangaroo care, a method of skin-to-skin contact in which a newborn is laid face down between the mother's breasts after birth and carried there as many hours a day as possible, can help preemies—and full-term infants—make the adjustment from fetal life to the jumble of sensory stimuli in the outside world. This soothing maternal contact seems to reduce stress on the central nervous system and help with self-regulation of sleep and activity, even with only one hour of contact (Ferber & Makhoul, 2004).

Respiratory distress syndrome, also called *hyaline membrane disease,* is common in preterm babies who lack an adequate amount of *surfactant,* an essential lung-coating substance that keeps air sacs from collapsing. These babies may breathe irregularly or stop breathing altogether. Since 1994, administering surfactant to high-risk preterm newborns has dramatically increased survival rates (Corbet et al., 1995; Goldenberg & Rouse, 1998; Horbar et al., 1993; Martin, Hamilton et al., 2005; Msall, 2004; Stoelhorst et al., 2005) as well as neurological and developmental status at 18 to 22 months (Vohr, Wright, Poole, & McDonald for the NICHD Neonatal Research Network Follow-up Study, 2005). Since 2000 the percentage of very-low–birth weight infants who survived unimpaired has increased further (Wilson-Costello et al., 2007).

Long-term Outcomes

Even if low–birth weight babies survive the dangerous early days, there is concern for their future. For example, both preterm and small-for-gestational-age infants may be at increased risk of adult-onset diabetes (Hofman et al., 2004; Sperling, 2004). Small-for-gestational-age infants appear to be at increased risk of cardiovascular disease (Sperling, 2004).

In longitudinal studies of extremely low–birth weight infants (about 500 to 1,000 grams at birth) and those born before 26 weeks of gestation, the survivors tend to be smaller than full-term children and more likely to have neurological, sensory, cognitive, educational, and behavioural problems (Anderson, Doyle, and the Victorian Infant Collaborative

Study Group, 2003; Marlow, Wolke, Bracewell, & Samara for the EPICure Study Group, 2005; Mikkola et al., 2005; Saigal, Stoskopf, Streiner, & Burrows, 2001). Among a cohort of extremely low–birth weight infants born in Finland in 1996–1997, only 26 percent showed normal development at age 5 (Mikkola et al., 2005).

The less low–birth weight children weigh at birth, the lower their IQs and achievement test scores tend to be and the more likely they are to require special education or to repeat a grade (Saigal, Hoult, Streiner, Stoskopf, & Rosenbaum, 2000). Cognitive deficits, especially in memory and processing speed, have been noted among very-low–birth weight babies by 5 or 6 months of age (about 1,000 to 1,500 grams at birth), continuing through childhood (Rose & Feldman, 2000; Rose, Feldman, & Jankowski, 2002) and tend to persist into adulthood (Fearon et al., 2004; Greene, 2002; Hack et al., 2002; Hardy, Kuh, Langenberg, & Wadsworth, 2003). Very-low–birth weight children and adolescents also tend to have more behavioural and mental health problems than those born at normal weight (Hack et al., 2004).

On the other hand, in a longitudinal study of 296 infants who weighed, on average, just over 1,000 grams at birth and were considered borderline retarded, most showed cognitive improvement in early childhood and intelligence in the normal range by age 8. Children in two-parent families, those whose mothers were highly educated, those who had not suffered significant brain damage, and those who did not need special help did best (Ment et al., 2003). And, in a prospective longitudinal study of 166 extremely low–birth weight babies born in 1977 to 1982 in Ontario, a significant majority overcame earlier difficulties to become functioning young adults, finishing high school, working, and living independently and many of them pursuing postsecondary education. The children were predominantly white and from two-parent families, about half of them of high SES. Children with disabilities had been integrated into regular schools and provided with classroom assistants (Saigal et al., 2006). Birth weight alone, then, does not necessarily determine the outcome. Environmental factors make a difference, as we discuss in a subsequent section.

Canadian research on long-term effects found that a large percentage of extremely low–birth weight (ELBW) children experience developmental coordination disorder (DCD) by middle childhood (51 percent of their sample, compared to up to 9 percent of the normal birth weight population) (Holsti, Grunau, & Whitfield, 2002). These children experienced impaired motor coordination, lower academic achievement, particularly mathematics, and lower intelligence scores on measures involving motor coordination, compared with ELBW children who did not develop DCD. ELBW children also tend to score lower-than-normal birth weight chidren on language measures (Grunau, Kearney, & Whitfield, 1990). Grunau and colleagues also examined long-term effects of ELBW on pain perception in childhood. They found that ELBW children's parents, when asked to rate their child's pain sensitivity at 18 months, reported lower pain sensitivity than did parents of normal birth weight children. They found that the child's temperament affected rated pain sensitivity only in full birth weight children, and that parental style did not affect the ratings of pain sensitivity (Grunau, Whitfield, & Petrie, 1994).

Postmaturity

Close to 1 percent of pregnant women have not gone into labour 2 weeks after the due date, or 42 weeks after the last menstrual period (Joseph et al., 2007). At that point, a baby is considered **postmature.** Postmature babies tend to be long and thin, because they have kept growing in the womb but have had an insufficient blood supply toward the end of gestation. Possibly because the placenta has aged and become less efficient, it may provide less oxygen. The baby's greater size also complicates labour: The mother has to deliver a baby the size of a normal 1-month-old.

Because postmature fetuses are at risk of brain damage or even death, doctors sometimes induce labour or perform Caesarean deliveries. The increasing use of induction and Caesarean delivery probably explains a decline in post-term births in recent years (Martin, Hamilton et al., 2006).

What's your view ?

• In view of the long-term outlook for babies of very low birth weight and the expense involved in helping them survive, how much of society's resources should be put into rescuing these babies?

postmature Referring to a fetus not yet born as of 2 weeks after the due date or 42 weeks after the mother's last menstrual period

Stillbirth

A stillbirth is a tragic union of opposites—birth and death. Sometimes fetal death is diagnosed prenatally; in other cases, as with Elvis Presley's twin brother, the baby's death is discovered during labour or delivery.

Stillbirth, the death of a fetus at or after the 20th week of gestation, accounts for more than half of perinatal deaths (deaths that occur during or within 24 hours after childbirth) in developing countries. Boys are more likely to be stillborn than girls (Bekedam, Engelsbel, Mol, Buitendijk, & van der Pal-de Bruin, 2002; Eogan, Geary, O'Connell, & Keane, 2003). Although the cause of stillbirth is not clearly understood, many stillborn infants are small for their gestational age, indicating malnourishment in the womb (Surkan et al., 2004).

Women over age 35 are more likely than other women to experience stillbirth, and stillbirth rates for this age group have increased, as have rates among women under age 20 (Ananth, Liu, Kinzler, & Kramer, 2005; Heffner, 2004). Also, the risk increases as the pregnancy enters postmaturity (Kirkham & Grzybowski, 2005).

The number of third-trimester stillbirths in Canada has been substantially reduced during the past two decades. This improvement may be due to electronic fetal monitoring, ultrasound, and other measures to identify fetuses at risk for pre-eclampsia (a toxic condition) or restricted growth. Fetuses believed to have these problems can then be delivered prematurely (Goldenberg & Rouse, 1998).

stillbirth The death of a fetus at or after the 20th week of gestation

Checkpoint ✔

Can you . . .

✔ Discuss the risk factors, treatment, and outcomes for low–birth weight babies?

✔ Explain the risks attending postmaturity?

✔ State risk factors for stillbirth, and explain why stillbirth rates have decreased?

Can a Supportive Environment Overcome Effects of Birth Complications?

A child's prospects for overcoming the early disadvantage of low birth weight depend on several interacting factors. One is the family's socio-economic circumstances (Aylward, Pfeiffer, Wright, & Verhulst, 1989; McGauhey, Starfield, Alexander, & Ensminget, 1991; Ross, Lipper, & Auld, 1991; Willms, 2002). Another is the quality of the early environment.

The Infant Health and Development Program

The Infant Health and Development Program (IHDP) (1990) followed the cognitive development of 985 preterm, low–birth weight babies—most of them from poor and disadvantaged families in which the mother had no more than a high school education—in eight parts of the United States from birth to age 3 (Brooks-Gunn, 2003). One-third of the heavier (but still low–birth weight) babies and one-third of the lighter ones were randomly assigned to "intervention" groups. Their parents received home visits, counselling, information about children's health and development, and instruction in children's games and activities; at 1 year, these babies entered an educational day care/preschool program.

When the program stopped, the 3-year-olds in both the lower– and higher–birth weight intervention groups were doing better on cognitive and social measures, were much less likely to show mental retardation, and had fewer behavioural problems than the groups that had received only follow-up (Brooks-Gunn, Klebanov, Liaw, & Spiker, 1993). By age 5, the children in the lower–birth weight intervention group no longer held a cognitive edge over the comparison group. Furthermore, having been in the intervention program made no difference in health or behaviour (Brooks-Gunn et al., 1994). By age 8, the cognitive superiority of children in the higher–birth weight intervention group over their counterparts in the follow-up group had dwindled to 4 IQ points; and all four groups had substantially below-average IQs and vocabulary scores (McCarton et al., 1997; McCormick, McCarton, Brooks-Gunn, Belt, & Gross, 1998).

Still, the intervention did seem to yield some long-term benefits. At age 18, among the 636 youths who remained in the study, those in the heavier intervention group scored modestly higher in math achievement, and those in the lighter intervention group in reading, than their respective control groups—if they had experienced the preschool program. Still, both groups performed well below age norms (McCormick et al., 2006).

Thanks to their own resilience, fully a third of the at-risk children studied by Emmy Werner and her colleagues developed into self-confident, successful adults.

Perhaps for such an intervention to have more lasting effects, it needs to continue beyond age 3 (Blair, 2002).

Closer studies of the full IHDP sample underline the importance of what goes on in the home. Children whose mothers reported having experienced stressful events—illnesses, deaths of friends or family members, moves, or changes in schooling or work—during the last 6 months of the child's first year showed less cognitive benefit from the intervention at age 3 (Klebanov, Brooks-Gunn, & McCormick, 2001). Children who got little parental attention and care were more likely to be undersized and to do poorly on cognitive tests than children from more favourable home environments (Kelleher et al., 1993; McCormick et al., 1998). Those whose cognitive performance stayed high had mothers who themselves scored well on cognitive tests and were responsive and stimulating. Babies with more than one risk factor (such as poor neonatal health plus a less educated or less responsive mother) fared worst (Liaw & Brooks-Gunn, 1993).

The Kauai Study

A longer-term study shows how a favourable environment can counteract effects of low birth weight, birth injuries, and other birth complications. For more than 4 decades, Emmy E. Werner (1987, 1995) and a research team of pediatricians, psychologists, public health workers, and social workers have followed 698 children born in 1955 on the Hawaiian island of Kauai—from the prenatal period through birth, and then into young adulthood. The researchers interviewed the mothers; recorded their personal, family, and reproductive histories; monitored the course of their pregnancies; and interviewed them again when the children were 1, 2, and 10 years old. They also observed the children interacting with their parents at home and gave them aptitude, achievement, and personality tests in elementary and high school. The children's teachers reported on their progress and their behaviour. The young people themselves were interviewed at ages 18 and 30.

Among the children who had suffered problems at or before birth, physical and psychological development was seriously impaired *only* when they grew up in persistently poor environmental circumstances. From toddlerhood on, unless the early damage was so serious as to require institutionalization, those children who had a stable and enriching environment did well (E. E. Werner, 1985, 1987). In fact, they had fewer language, perceptual, emotional, and school problems than children who had *not* experienced unusual stress at birth but who had received little intellectual stimulation or emotional support at home (E. E. Werner, 1989; E. E. Werner et al., 1968). The children who had been exposed to *both* birth-related problems and later stressful experiences showed the worst health problems and the most retarded development (E. E. Werner, 1987).

Given a supportive environment, then, many children can overcome a poor start in life. Even more remarkable is the resilience of children who escape damage despite *multiple* sources of stress. Even when birth complications were combined with such environmental risks as chronic poverty, family discord, divorce, or parents who were mentally ill, many children came through relatively unscathed. Of the 276 children who at age 2 had been identified as having four or more risk factors, two-thirds developed serious learning or behaviour problems by the age of 10 or, by age 18, had become pregnant, gotten in trouble with the law, or become emotionally troubled. Yet by age 30, one-third of these highly at-risk children had managed to become "competent, confident, and caring adults" (E. E. Werner, 1995, p. 82). Of those who experience multiple risks, most do well behaviourally, socially, and in terms of their health outcomes (Willms, 2002).

protective factors Influences that reduce the impact of early stress and tend to predict positive outcomes

Protective factors, which tended to reduce the impact of early stress, fell into three categories: (1) individual attributes that may be largely genetic, such as energy, sociability, and intelligence; (2) affectionate ties with at least one supportive family member; and (3) rewards at school, work, or place of worship that provide a sense of meaning and control over one's life (E. E. Werner, 1987). While the home environment seemed to have the most marked effect in childhood, in adulthood the individuals' own qualities made a greater difference (E. E. Werner, 1995). The positive effects of healthy parenting and family functioning, with responsive parents and the presence of opportunities to learn, can be much more influential to development than the negative effects of low SES (Willms, 2002).

These studies underline the need to look at child development in context. They show how biological and environmental influences interact, making resiliency possible even in babies born with serious complications. (Characteristics of resilient children are further discussed in Chapter 14.)

Newborns and Parents

Birth is a major transition, not only for the baby, but for the parents as well. The mother's body systems have undergone massive physical change. For both mother and father, especially with a first birth, the newcomer in their lives brings insistent demands that challenge their ability to cope and force adjustments in their relationship. Meanwhile, parents (and, perhaps, siblings) are getting acquainted with this newcomer—developing emotional bonds and becoming familiar with the infant's patterns of sleeping, waking, feeding, and activity.

Childbirth and Bonding

How and when does the **caregiver–infant bond**—the close, caring connection between caregiver and newborn—develop? Some researchers studying this topic have followed the ethological approach (introduced in Chapter 2), which considers behaviour in human beings, as in animals, to be biologically determined and emphasizes critical, or sensitive, periods for development of certain behaviours.

As we mentioned in Chapter 1, Konrad Lorenz (1957) demonstrated that newly hatched ducklings will follow the first moving object they see, usually the mother—a phenomenon called **imprinting.** However, research has concluded that, unlike the animals Lorenz studied, a critical period for bonding does *not* exist in human beings (Chess & Thomas, 1982; Klaus & Kennell, 1982; M. E. Lamb, 1983). This finding can relieve the worry and guilt sometimes felt by adoptive parents and those who have to be separated from their infants after birth.

Fathers, like mothers, form close bonds with their babies. The babies contribute simply by doing the things normal babies do: opening their eyes, grasping their fathers' fingers, or moving in their fathers' arms. Fathers who are present at the birth of a child often see the event as a "peak emotional experience" (May & Perrin, 1985), but a man can become emotionally committed to his newborn whether or not he attended the birth (Palkovitz, 1985).

From an evolutionary perspective, parental bonding may be a mechanism to ensure that the parents invest the tremendous energy and resources needed to enable a helpless infant to survive and reproduce. Evolutionary developmental psychologists point out that child rearing involves a balancing act between the needs of the parents and those of the offspring (Bjorklund & Pellegrini, 2000). Bonding helps ensure that the benefits to the parents are worth the cost. See Box 5-2.

What do Newborns Need from their Mothers?

A series of pioneering experiments with monkeys by Harry Harlow and his colleagues established that more than feeding is involved in the mother–infant bond. In these experiments, rhesus monkeys were separated from their mothers 6 to 12 hours after birth and raised in a laboratory. The infant monkeys were put into cages with one of two kinds of surrogate "mothers": a plain cylindrical wire-mesh form or a form covered with terry cloth. Some monkeys were fed from bottles connected to the wire "mothers"; others were "nursed" by the warm, cuddly cloth ones. When the monkeys were allowed to spend time with either kind of "mother," they all spent more time clinging to the cloth surrogates, even if they were being fed only by the wire ones. In an unfamiliar room, the babies "raised" by cloth surrogates showed more natural interest in exploring than those "raised" by wire surrogates, even when the appropriate "mothers" were there.

Checkpoint ✔

Can you . . .

✔ Discuss the effectiveness of the home environment and of intervention programs in overcoming effects of low birthweight and other birth complications?

✔ Name three protective factors identified by the Kauai study?

Guidepost 5

How do parents bond with and care for their baby?

caregiver–infant bond The feeling of close, caring connection between the caregiver and his or her newborn

imprinting Instinctive form of learning in which, during a critical period in early development, a young animal forms an attachment to the first moving object it sees, usually the mother

In a series of classic experiments, Harry Harlow and Margaret Harlow showed that food is not the most important way to a baby's heart. When infant rhesus monkeys could choose whether to go to a wire surrogate "mother" or a warm, soft terry-cloth "mother," they spent more time clinging to the cloth mother, even if they were being fed by bottles connected to the wire mother.

Box 5-2 *Comforting a Crying Baby*

All babies cry. It is their only way to let us know they are hungry, uncomfortable, lonely, or unhappy. And since few sounds are as distressing as a baby's cry, parents or other caregivers usually rush to feed or pick up a crying infant. As babies quiet down and fall asleep or gaze about in alert contentment, they may show that their problem has been solved. At other times, the caregiver cannot figure out what the baby wants. The baby keeps crying. It is worth trying to find ways to help: Babies whose cries bring relief seem to become more self-confident, seeing that they can affect their own lives.

In Chapter 7 we discuss several kinds of crying and what the crying may mean. Unusual, persistent crying patterns may be early signs of trouble. For healthy babies who just seem unhappy, the following may help (Eiger & Olds, 1999).

- Hold the baby, perhaps laying the baby on his or her stomach on your chest, to feel your heartbeat and breathing. Or sit with the baby in a comfortable rocking chair.
- Put the baby in a carrier next to your chest and walk around.
- If you are upset, ask someone else to hold the baby; infants sometimes sense and respond to their caregivers' moods.
- Pat or rub the baby's back, in case a bubble of air is causing discomfort.
- Wrap the baby snuggly in a small blanket; some infants feel more secure when firmly swaddled from neck to toes, with arms held close to the sides.
- Make the baby warmer or cooler; put on or take off clothing or change the room temperature.
- Give the baby a massage or a warm bath.
- Sing or talk to the baby. Or provide a continuous or rhythmic sound, such as music from the radio, a simulated heartbeat, or background noise from a whirring fan, vacuum cleaner, or other appliance.
- Take the baby out for a ride in a stroller or car seat—at any hour of the day or night. In bad weather, some parents walk around in an enclosed mall; the distraction helps them as well as the baby.
- If someone other than a parent is taking care of the baby, it sometimes helps if the caregiver puts on a robe or a sweater that the mother or father has recently worn so the baby can sense the familiar smell.
- Pick up on the baby's signals.

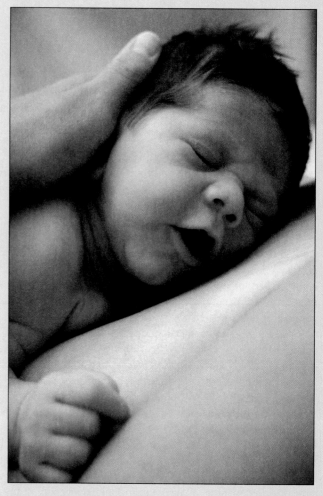

This crying baby may quiet when held stomach down on his mother's chest.

What's your view ?

Have you ever tried to soothe a crying baby? What techniques seemed to work best?

Check it out !

For more information on this topic, go to **www.mcgrawhill.ca/olc/papalia.**

Apparently, the monkeys also remembered the cloth surrogates better. After a year's separation, the "cloth-raised" monkeys eagerly ran to embrace the terry-cloth forms, whereas the "wire-raised" monkeys showed no interest in the wire forms (Harlow & Zimmerman, 1959). None of the monkeys in either group grew up normally, however (Harlow & Harlow, 1962), and none were able to nurture their own offspring (Suomi & Harlow, 1972).

In another study, baby rats whose mothers licked them frequently turned out to be less anxious and fearful and produced lower levels of stress hormones than rats who had been licked less. The researchers found that maternal licking activated a gene that relieves stress (Caldji, Diorio, & Meaney, 2003).

It is hardly surprising that a dummy mother would not provide the same kinds of stimulation and opportunities for positive development as a live mother and that a mother's physical demonstrativeness would soothe her baby's stress. These experiments show that feeding is not the most important thing babies get from their mothers. Mothering includes the comfort of close bodily contact and, at least in monkeys, the satisfaction of an innate need to cling.

Human infants also have needs that must be satisfied if they are to grow up normally. It is the task of parents to try to meet those needs.

The Father's Role

The fathering role is a social construction, having different meanings in different cultures. The role may be taken or shared by someone other than the biological father: the mother's brother, as in Botswana (where young mothers remain with their own childhood family until their partners are in their forties), or a grandfather, as in Vietnam (Engle & Breaux, 1998; Richardson, 1995; Townsend, 1997). In some societies, fathers are more involved in their young children's lives—economically, emotionally, and in time spent—than in other cultures. In many parts of the world, what it means to be a father has changed—and is changing (Engle & Breaux, 1998).

Among the Huhot people of Inner Mongolia, a province of China, fathers traditionally are responsible for economic support and discipline and mothers for nurturing (Jankowiak, 1992). Fathers are stern and aloof, and their children respect and fear them. Men almost never hold infants. Fathers interact more with toddlers but perform child care duties only if the mother is absent. However, urbanization and maternal employment are changing these attitudes. Fathers—especially college-educated ones—now seek more intimate relationships with children, especially sons. China's official one-child policy has accentuated this change, leading both parents to be more deeply involved with their only child (Engle & Breaux, 1998; see Chapter 11).

Among the Aka people of central Africa, in contrast with the Huhot, fathers are as nurturant and emotionally supportive as mothers. In fact, "Aka fathers provide more direct infant care than fathers in any other known society" (Hewlett, 1992, p. 169).

In Canada and some other countries, fathers' involvement in caregiving and play has greatly increased since 1970 as more mothers have begun to work outside the home and concepts of fathering have changed (Cabrera et al., 2000; Casper, 1997; Pleck, 1997). A father's frequent and positive involvement with his child, from infancy on, is directly related to the child's well-being and physical, cognitive, and social development (Cabrera et al., 2000; Kelley, Smith, Green, Berndt, & Rogers, 1998; Shannon, Tamis-LeMonda, London, & Cabrera, 2002).

Concepts of fathering have changed in recent decades. This father, comforting his son, will play an important part in the child's development.

What's your view

• "Despite the increasingly active role many of today's fathers play in child raising, a mother will always be more important to babies and young children than a father." Do you agree or disagree?

• How do you think your relationship with your father might have been different if you had grown up among the Huhot people of Inner Mongolia? Among the Aka people?

Infant Care: A Cross-Cultural View

Infant care practices and patterns of interaction with infants vary greatly around the world, depending on environmental conditions and the culture's view of infants' nature and needs. In Bali, infants are believed to be ancestors or gods brought to life in human form and thus must be treated with utmost dignity and respect. The Beng people of West Africa think that young babies can understand all languages, whereas people in the Micronesian atoll of Ifaluk believe that babies cannot understand language at all, and therefore adults do not speak to them (DeLoache & Gottlieb, 2000).

In some societies, as Margaret Mead found in the South Seas, infants have multiple caregivers. Among the Efe people of central Africa, for example, infants typically receive care from five or more people in a given hour and are routinely breastfed by other women besides the mother (Tronick, Morelli, & Ivey, 1992). Among the Gusii people in western Kenya, where infant mortality is high, parents are more likely than

Checkpoint ✔

Can you . . .

✔ Summarize research on bonding between parents and newborns?

✔ Compare the roles of mothers and fathers in meeting newborn's needs?

✔ Give examples of cultural differences in care and treatment of newborns?

those in industrial societies to keep their infants close to them, respond quickly when they cry, and feed them on demand (LeVine, 1974, 1989, 1994). The same is true of Aka foragers in central Africa, who move around frequently in small, tightly knit groups marked by extensive sharing, cooperation, and concern about danger. However, Ngandu farmers in the same region, who tend to live farther apart and to stay in one place for long periods of time, are more likely to leave their infants alone and to let them fuss or cry, smile, vocalize, or play (Hewlett, Lamb, Shannon, Leyendecker, & Schölmerich, 1998).

We need to remember, then, that patterns of parent–infant interaction we take for granted may be culture based.

The birth of a baby, as momentous an achievement as it is, marks the launching of a challenging but rewarding journey—the journey through a child's world. In Part 3, we will examine our rapidly growing understanding of the physical, cognitive, and psychosocial developments of infancy and toddlerhood.

Summary and Key Terms

Childbirth and Culture: How Birthing Has Changed

Guidepost 1 How do customs surrounding birth reflect culture, and how has childbirth changed in developed countries?

- In Europe, Canada, and the United States, childbirth before the twentieth century took place in a manner much like that in some developing countries today. Birth was a female ritual, which occurred at home and was attended by a midwife. Pain relief was minimal, and risks for mother and baby were high.

- The development of the science of obstetrics professionalized childbirth. Births took place in hospitals, attended by physicians. Medical advances dramatically improved safety.

- Today delivery at home or in birth centres attended by midwives can be a relatively safe alternative to physician-attended hospital delivery for women with normal, low-risk pregnancies.

The Birth Process

Guidepost 2 How does labour begin, what happens during each of the three stages of childbirth, and what alternative methods of delivery are available?

- Labour normally begins after a preparatory period of parturition.

- Birth normally occurs after a preparatory period of parturition and consists of three stages: (1) dilation of the cervix; (2) descent and emergence of the baby; (3) expulsion of the umbilical cord and the placenta.

- Electronic fetal monitoring is widely used during labour and delivery. It is intended to detect signs of fetal distress, especially in high-risk births.

- The rate of Caesarean births in Canada is at a record high.

- Natural or prepared childbirth can minimize the need for pain-killing drugs and maximize parents' active involvement.

- Modern epidurals can give effective pain relief with smaller doses of medication than in the past.

- The presence of a doula can provide physical benefits as well as emotional support.

  parturition (109) **electronic fetal monitoring (110)**
  Caesarean delivery (110) **natural, or prepared, childbirth (111)**

The Newborn Baby

Guidepost 3 How do newborn infants adjust to life outside the womb, and how can we tell whether a new baby is healthy and is developing normally?

- The neonatal period is a time of transition from intrauterine to extrauterine life. During the first few days, the neonate loses weight and then regains it; the lanugo (prenatal hair) falls off and the protective coating of vernix caseosa dries up. The fontanels (soft spots) in the skull close within the first 18 months.

- At birth, the circulatory, respiratory, gastrointestinal, and temperature regulation systems become independent of the mother's. If a newborn cannot start breathing within about 5 minutes, brain injury may occur.

- Newborns have a strong sucking reflex and secrete meconium from the intestinal tract. They are commonly subject to neonatal jaundice, due to immaturity of the liver.

- At 1 minute and 5 minutes after birth, a neonate's Apgar score can indicate how well he or she is adjusting to extrauterine life. The Brazelton Neonatal Behavioural Assessment Scale can assess responses to the environment and predict future development.

- Neonatal screening is done for certain rare conditions, such as PKU and congenital hypothyroidism. A newborn's state of arousal is governed by periodic cycles of wakefulness, sleep, and activity, which seem to be inborn.

- Sleep takes up the major but a diminishing amount of a neonate's time.

- Individual differences in newborns' activity levels show stability and may be early indicators of temperament.

- Parents' responsiveness to babies' states and self-initiated activity levels is an important bidirectional influence on development.

  **neonatal period (112)   neonate (113)   fontanels (113)
  lanugo (113)   vernix caseosa (113)   anoxia (114)
  meconium (114)   neonatal jaundice (114)   Apgar scale (115)
  Brazelton Neonatal Behavioural Assessment Scale (NBAS) (116)
  state of arousal (117)**

Complications of Childbirth— and Their Aftermath

Guidepost 4 What complications of childbirth can endanger newborn babies, and what are the long-term prospects for infants with complicated births?

- Complications of childbirth include postmature birth, prematurity, low birth weight, and stillbirth.
- Postmature births have decreased with the increase in induced and Caesarean deliveries.
- A small minority of infants suffer lasting effects of birth trauma.
- Low–birth weight babies may be either preterm (premature) or small-for-gestational age. Low birth weight is a major factor in infant mortality and can cause long-term physical and cognitive problems. Very low–birth weight babies have a less promising prognosis than those who weigh more.

- A supportive postnatal environment and other protective factors can often improve the outcome for babies suffering from birth complications.
- Stillbirth has been substantially reduced in Canada but still accounts for half of perinatal deaths in the developing world.

  **preterm (premature) infants (118)   small-for-gestational age infants (118)   low birth weight (118)   perinatal (118)
  postmature (122)   stillbirth (123)   protective factors (124)**

Newborns and Parents

Guidepost 5 How do parents bond with and care for their baby?

- Researchers following the ethological approach have suggested that there is a critical period for the formation of the mother–infant bond, much like imprinting in some animals. However, research has not confirmed this hypothesis. Fathers typically bond with their babies whether or not they are present at the birth.
- Infants have strong needs for maternal closeness and warmth as well as physical care.
- Fatherhood is a social construction. Fathering roles differ in various cultures.
- Child raising practices and caregiving roles vary around the world.

  caregiver–infant bond (125)   imprinting (125)

CHAPTER SIX

Physical Development and Health During the First Three Years

There he lay upon his back
The yearling creature, warm and moist with life
To the bottom of his dimples.—to the ends
Of the lovely tumbled curls about his face.

—Elizabeth Barrett Browning, *Aurora Leigh*, 1857

Focus *Helen Keller and the World of the Senses**

Helen Keller

"What we have once enjoyed we can never lose," the author Helen Keller (1880–1968) once wrote. "A sunset, a mountain bathed in moonlight, the ocean in calm and in storm— we see these, love their beauty, hold the vision to our hearts. All that we love deeply becomes a part of us" (Keller, 1929, p. 2).

This quotation is especially remarkable— and especially poignant—in view of the fact that Helen Keller never saw a sunset, or a mountain, or moonlight, or an ocean, or anything else after the age of 19 months. It was then that she contracted a mysterious fever, which left her deaf and with inexorably ebbing sight.

Before her illness, Helen had been a normal, healthy baby— lively, friendly, and affectionate. Now she became expressionless and unresponsive. At 1 year, she had begun to walk; now she clung to her mother's skirts or sat in her lap. She had also begun to talk; one of her first words was *water*. After her illness, she continued to say "wah-wah," but not much else.

Her distraught parents first took her to a mineral spa and then to medical specialists, but there was no hope for a cure. At a time when physical and cognitive development normally enter a major growth spurt, the sensory gateways to the exploration of Helen's world had slammed shut—but not entirely. Deprived of two senses, she leaned more heavily on the other three, especially smell and touch. She later explained that she could tell a doctor from a carpenter by the odours of ether or wood that came from them. She used her ever-active fingertips to trace the "delicate tremble of a butterfly's wings . . . , the soft petals of violets . . . , the clear, firm outline of face and limb, the smooth arch of a horse's neck and the velvety touch of his nose" (Keller, 1920, pp. 6–7). Memories of the daylight world she had once inhabited helped her make sense of the unrelieved night in which she now found herself.

Helen realized that she was not like other people, but at first she had no clear sense of who or what she was. "I lived in a world that was a no-world. . . . I did not know that I knew [anything], or that I lived or acted or desired" (1920, p. 113). Sometimes, when family members were talking to each other, she would stand between them and touch their lips, and then frantically move her own—but nothing happened. Her frustration found its outlet in violent, inconsolable tantrums; she would kick and scream until she was exhausted.

Out of pity, her parents indulged her whims. Finally, more in desperation than in hope, they engaged a teacher for her: a young woman named Anne Sullivan, who herself had limited vision and who had been trained in a school for the blind. Arriving at the Keller home, Sullivan found 6-year-old Helen to be "wild, wilful, and destructive" (Lash, 1980, p. 348). Once, after figuring out how to use a key, Helen locked her mother in the pantry. Another time, frustrated by her teacher's attempts to spell the word *doll* into her palm, she hurled her new doll to the floor, smashing it to bits.

Yet, that same day, the little girl made her first linguistic breakthrough. As she and her teacher walked in the garden, they stopped to get a drink at the pump. Sullivan placed Helen's hand under the spout, at the same time spelling "w-a-t-e-r" over and over into her other hand. "I stood still," Keller later wrote, "my whole attention fixed upon the motions of her fingers. Suddenly I felt a misty consciousness as of something forgotten—a thrill of returning thought; and somehow the mystery of language was revealed to me. I knew then that 'w-a-t-e-r' meant the wonderful cool something that was flowing over my hand. That living word awakened my soul, gave it light, hope, joy, set it free!" (Keller, 1905, p. 35).

• • •

The story of how Anne Sullivan tamed this unruly child and brought her into the light of language and thought is a familiar and inspiring one. One lesson we can draw from the story of Helen Keller's early development is the central importance of the senses—the windows to a baby's world—and their connection with all other aspects of development. Had Helen Keller not lost her vision and hearing, or had she been born without one or the other, or both, her physical, cognitive, and psychosocial development undoubtedly would have been quite different.

In this chapter, we show how sensory perception goes hand in hand with an infant's growing motor skills and shapes the astoundingly rapid development of the brain. We describe typical growth patterns of body and brain, and we see how a nourishing environment can stimulate both. We see how infants, who spend most of their time sleeping and eating, become busy, active toddlers and how parents and other caregivers can foster healthy growth and development. We discuss threats to infant life and health and how to ward them off.

After you have read and studied this chapter, you should be able to answer each of the Guidepost questions that appear at the top of the next page. Look for them again in the margins, where they point to important concepts throughout the chapter. To check your understanding of these Guideposts, review the end-of-chapter summary. Checkpoints located throughout the chapter will help you verify your understanding of what you have read.

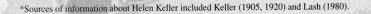

*Sources of information about Helen Keller included Keller (1905, 1920) and Lash (1980).

Guideposts for Study

1. How do babies grow, and how and what should babies be fed?

2. How does the brain develop, and how do environmental factors affect its early growth?

3. How do the senses develop during infancy?

4. What are some early milestones in motor development, and what are some influences on it?

5. How can we enhance babies' chances of survival and health?

Growth and Nutrition

Patterns of Growth

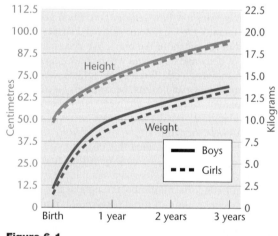

Guidepost 1

How do babies grow, and how and what should babies be fed?

Children grow faster during the first 3 years, especially during the first few months, than they ever will again (see Figure 6-1). At 5 months, the average baby boy's birth weight has doubled to 7 kg, and, by 1 year, has nearly tripled to 10 kg. This rapid growth rate tapers off during the second and third years; a boy typically gains about 2 kg by his second birthday and 1.5 kg by his third, when he tips the scales at about 14 kg. A boy's height typically increases by 25 cm during the first year (making the typical 1-year-old boy about 75 cm tall), by almost 13 cm during the second year (so that the average 2-year-old boy is approaching 90 cm tall); and by a little more than 8 cm during the third year to top 95 cm. Girls follow a parallel pattern but are slightly smaller; at 3, the average girl weighs 500 g less and is 1 cm shorter than the average boy (Kuczmarski et al., 2000).

Teething usually begins around 3 or 4 months, when infants begin grabbing almost everything in sight to put into their mouths; but the first tooth may not actually arrive until sometime between 5 and 9 months of age, or even later. By the first birthday, babies generally have 6 to 8 teeth; by age 2½, they have a mouthful of 20.

As a baby grows, body shape and proportions change too; a 3-year-old is typically slender compared with a chubby, potbellied 1-year-old. Physical growth and development follow the maturational principles introduced in Chapter 3: the cephalocaudal principle and proximodistal principle. According to the cephalocaudal principle, growth occurs from top down. Because the brain grows so rapidly before birth, a newborn baby's head is disproportionately large. By 1 year, the brain is 70 percent of its adult weight, but the rest of the body is only about 10 to 20 percent of adult weight. The head becomes proportionately smaller as the child grows in height and the lower parts of the body develop (see Figure 6-2). As we'll see later in this chapter, sensory and motor development proceed according to the same principle: infants learn to use the upper parts of the body before the lower parts. They see objects before they can control their trunk, and they learn to do many things with their hands long before they can crawl or walk. According to the proximodistal principle (inner to outer), growth and motor development proceed from the centre of the body outward. In the womb, the head and trunk develop before the arms and legs, then the hands and feet, and then the fingers and toes. During infancy and early childhood, the limbs continue to grow faster than the hands and feet. Similarly, babies first develop the ability to use their upper arms and upper legs (which are closest to the centre of the body), then the forearms and forelegs, then hands and feet, and finally, fingers and toes.

Figure 6-1

Growth in height and weight during infancy and toddlerhood. Babies grow most rapidly in both height and weight during the first few months of life, then taper off somewhat by age 3. Baby boys are slightly larger, on average, than baby girls. *Note:* Curves shown are for the 50th percentiles for each sex.

Source: Kuczmarski et al., 2000

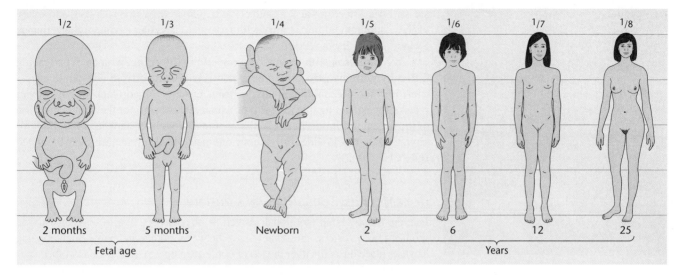

| 1/2 | 1/3 | 1/4 | 1/5 | 1/6 | 1/7 | 1/8 |

| 2 months | 5 months | Newborn | 2 | 6 | 12 | 25 |

Fetal age   Years

Figure 6-2

Changes in proportions of the human body during growth. The most striking change is that the head becomes smaller relative to the rest of the body. The fractions indicate head size as a proportion of total body length at several ages. More subtle is the stability of the trunk proportions (from neck to crotch). The increasing leg proportion is almost exactly the reverse of the decreasing head proportion.

Influences on Growth

The genes an infant inherits have a strong influence on whether the child will be tall or short, thin or stocky, or somewhere in between. This genetic influence interacts with such environmental influences as nutrition and living conditions, which also affect general health and well-being. For example, Japanese children in the United States, for example, are taller and weigh more than children the same age in Japan, probably because of dietary differences (Broude, 1995).

Well-fed, well-cared-for children grow taller and heavier than less nourished and nurtured children. They also mature sexually and attain maximum height earlier, and their teeth erupt sooner. Today, children in many industrialized countries are growing taller and maturing sexually at an earlier age than a century ago (see Chapter 15), probably because of better nutrition, improved sanitation, and the decrease in child labour. Better medical care, especially immunization and antibiotics, also plays a part; heart disease, kidney disease, and some infectious illnesses can have grave effects on growth. Children who are ill for a long time may never achieve their genetically programmed stature because they may never make up for the loss of growth time while they were sick. Malnutrition, even apart from the effects of such related factors as low birth weight and illness, can interfere with normal cognitive growth (Rose, 1994).

Nourishment

From the beginnings of human history, babies were breast fed. Babies fed nonhuman milk were likely to fall ill and die. Following the discovery of germs in 1878, mothers were warned to avoid the "poisonous bottle" at all costs (Fontanel & d'Harcourt, 1997, p. 121).

Beginning in the first decade of the twentieth century, with the advent of dependable refrigeration, pasteurization, and sterilization, manufacturers began to develop formulas to modify and enrich cow's milk for infant consumption and to improve the design of bottles. Bottle-feeding became safe, nutritious, and popular.

During the next half-century, formula feeding became the norm in Canada and some other industrialized countries despite medical recommendations for breastfeeding. By 1971, only 25 percent of Canadian mothers even tried to nurse. Since then, recognition of the benefits of breast milk has brought about a reversal of this trend, so that today about 77 percent of new mothers in Canada breastfeed. However, only about 35 percent

*Unless otherwise referenced, the historical material in this section is based on Eccles (1982) and Fontanel & d'Harcourt (1997).

Breast milk can be called the "ultimate health food" because it offers so many benefits to babies—physical, cognitive, and emotional.

are still breastfeeding at 3 months (Palda, Guise & Wathen, 2004), and many of these supplement breast milk with formula (Canadian Perinatal Surveillance System, 2000; Ryan, 2000).

In comparison with the national rate of breastfeeding, women experiencing difficulty with breastfeeding, younger women, women from non-white ancestries, low socio-economic status, or from Eastern Canada tend to have lower rates of breastfeeding, the majority of whom cite concern for the baby's nutrition as the reason to formula-feed (Williams, Innis, Vogel, & Stephen, 1999; Zadoroznyj, 2007). Worldwide, only about one-half of all infants are ever breastfed (UNICEF, 2002).

Breastfeeding: Benefits and Cautions

Feeding a baby is an emotional as well as physical act. Warm contact with the mother's body fosters emotional linkage between mother and baby. Such bonding can take place through either breast- or bottle-feeding and through many other caregiving activities, most of which can be performed by fathers as well as mothers.

Breast milk is almost always the best food for newborns and is recommended for at least the first 12 months. The only acceptable alternative is an iron-fortified formula based on either cow's milk or soy protein and containing supplemental vitamins and minerals. The World Health Organization and Canadian Task Force on Preventative Health Care and other Canadian health authorities (Canadian Paediatric Society, Dieticians of Canada and Health Canada, 1998; Palda et al., 2004) recommend that babies be exclusively breastfed for six months. If direct breastfeeding is not possible, as with premature infants, the baby should receive expressed human milk—milk squeezed from the mother's, or another mother's, breast. Breastfeeding should begin immediately after birth and should continue for *at least* the first year. Infants weaned during the first year should receive iron-fortified formula. At one year, babies can switch to cow's milk.

Breast milk is more digestible and more nutritious than formula and is less likely to produce allergic reactions (Canadian Paediatric Society, Dietitians of Canada and Health Canada, 1998; Eiger & Olds, 1999). Human milk is a complete source of nutrients for at least the first 6 months; during this time breastfed babies normally do not need any other food other than a vitamin D supplement (Canadian Paediatric Society, Dietitians of Canada and Health Canada, 1998; Walker, Conn, Davies, & Moore, 2005).

The health advantages of breastfeeding are striking (AAP Section on Breastfeeding, 2005). Among the illnesses prevented or minimized by breastfeeding are diarrhea, respiratory infections, otitis media (an infection of the middle ear), and staphylococcal, bacterial, and urinary tract infections (AAP Section on Breastfeeding, 2005; Black, Morris, & Bryce, 2003; Canadian Paediatric Society, Dietitians of Canada and Health Canada, 1998). Breastfeeding may reduce the risk of postneonatal death (death that occurs between 28 days and one year) (Chen & Rogan, 2004).

Breastfeeding seems to have benefits for visual acuity (Makrides, Neumann, Simmer, Pater, & Gibson, 1995), neurological development (Lanting, Fidler, Huisman, Touwen, & Boersma, 1994), and long-term cardiovascular health (Owen, Whincup, Odoki, Gilg, & Cook, 2002), including cholesterol levels (Singhal, Cole, Fewtrell, & Lucas, 2004). It may help prevent obesity, diabetes lymphoma, leukemia, and Hodgkin disease (AAP Section on Breastfeeding, 2005; Owen, Martin, Whincup, Smith, & Cook, 2005; Stuebe, Rich-Edwards, Willett, Manson, & Michels, 2005). Babies who breastfeed are less likely to be overfed, as they actively regulate their own intake (American Heart Association et al., 2006). Studies also have shown slight benefits for cognitive development (AAP Section on Breastfeeding, 2005; Canadian Paediatric Society, Dietitians of Canada and Health Canada, 1998; Horwood & Fergusson, 1998; Jacobson, Chiodo, & Jacobson, 1999), even into young adulthood (Mortensen, Michaelson, Sanders, & Reinisch, 2002).

Breastfeeding also benefits the mother. Nursing mothers typically have less postpartum bleeding, quicker physical recovery, and an earlier return to their previous weight.

After menopause, they have less risk of breast cancer and ovarian cancer and possible less risk of osteoporosis and hip fractures (AAP Section on Breastfeeding, 2005).

Fortified breast milk or formula designed for premature infants is recommended as the preferred food for premature infants (Nutrition Committee, Canadian Paediatric Society, 1995) and for low–birth weight infants (Arslanoglu, Moro & Ziegler, 2006).

The Baby-Friendly Health Initiative (BFHI) was introduced in 1991 as a national campaign to encourage breastfeeding, including providing support and information on breastfeeding practices, in maternity hospitals across Canada (Martens, Phillips, Cheang, Rosolowich, & Breastfeeding Promotion Steering Committee of Manitoba, 2000). Adopting BFHI practices appears to reduce the likelihood of early weaning (Martens et al., 2000), but there is still a long way to go before this becomes standard practice in Canada (Walker et al., 2005).

Nursing mothers need to be as careful as pregnant women about what they take into their bodies. They should avoid the use of alcohol. Breastfeeding is inadvisable for a mother infected with the AIDS virus, which can be transmitted through her milk—but only if the mother has access to a safe alternative feeding method. Likewise, breastfeeding is discouraged if the mother has another infectious illness; if she has untreated active tuberculosis; or if she is taking any drug that would not be safe for the baby (AAP Section on Breastfeeding, 2005; Canadian Paediatric Society, Dietitians of Canada and Health Canada, 1998; Eiger & Olds, 1999; Miotti et al., 1999; Nduati et al., 2000; WHO/UNICEF Constitution on HIV Transmission and Breastfeeding, 1992).

Nutritional Concerns

Iron-deficiency anemia is the world's most common nutritional disorder, affecting as many as one fourth of all 6- to 24-month-old babies in Canada, particularly among First Nations and Inuit infants and children (Zlotkin, 2003). Infants with iron-deficiency anemia do more poorly on cognitive tests than other infants. They also tend to be less independent, joyful, attentive, and playful, and more wary, hesitant, and easily tired (Lozoff et al., 1998), and are more likely to repeat a grade, require special services in school, and experience lower achievement in schools as children or adolescents (Zlotkin, 2003). Adding iron supplements to the diet as early as 4 to 6 months, particularly for premature infants or for infants with low birth weight can prevent the development of anemia (Zlotkin, 2003).

Because infants fed plain cow's milk in the early months of life may suffer from iron deficiency, the Canadian Paediatric Society (Canadian Paediatric Society, Dietitians of Canada and Health Canada, 1998) recommends that babies receive breast milk or, alternatively, iron-fortified formula for at least the first year (Arslanoglu, 2006).

Iron-enriched solid foods—usually beginning with single-grain cereals—should be gradually introduced during the second half of the first year as a precaution against allergic reactions (Canadian Paediatric Society, Dietitians of Canada and Health Canada, 1998). At this time, too, fruit juice may be introduced (AAP Section on Breastfeeding, 2005). A study based on mothers' reports of toddlers' diets (Skinner, Carruth, Moran, Houck, & Coletta, 1999) did not support earlier findings that large amounts of fruit juice interfere with growth (M. M. Smith & Lifshitz, 1994).

At 1 year, babies can switch from breast (or bottle) to cow's milk if they are getting a balanced diet of supplementary solid foods that provide one third of their caloric intake (Canadian Paediatric Society, Dietitians of Canada and Health Canada, 1998). To promote proper growth, the milk should be homogenized whole milk fortified with vitamin D, not skim milk or reduced-fat (1 or 2 percent) milk (Canadian Paediatric Society, Dietitians of Canada and Health Canada, 1998).

In many low-income communities around the world, malnutrition in early life is widespread—and often fatal. Malnutrition is implicated in more than half of deaths of children globally, and many children are irreversibly damaged by age 2 (World Bank, 2006). Undernourished children who survive their first five years are at high risk for stunted growth and poor health and functioning throughout life. In a longitudinal study of a large-scale government-sponsored nutritional program in 347 poor rural communities of Mexico, infants who received fortified nutrition supplements—along with nutrition

What's your view

- "Every mother who is physically able should breastfeed." Do you agree or disagree? Give reasons.

education, health care, and financial assistance for the family—showed better growth and lower rates of anemia than a control group of infants not yet assigned to the program (Rivera, Sotres-Alvarez, Habicht, Shamah, & Villalpando, 2004). (Malnutrition is further discussed in Chapter 9.)

Overweight has increased in infancy as in all age groups in Canada. Two factors seem to most strongly influence the chances that an obese child will become an obese adult: whether or not the child has an obese parent and the age of the child. Before 3 years of age, parental obesity is a stronger predictor of a child's obesity as an adult than is the child's own weight. Having one obese parent increases the odds of obesity in adulthood by 3 to 1, and if both parents are obese, the odds increase to more than 10 to 1 (AAP Committee on Nutrition, 2003). Among 70 children followed from 3 months to 6 years of age, little difference in weight and body composition appeared by age 2 between children with overweight mothers and children with lean mothers. However, by age 4, those with overweight mothers tended to weigh more, and by age 6, also had more body fat than those with lean mothers (Berkowitz, Stallings, Maislin, & Stunkard, 2005). Thus, a 1- or 2-year-old who has an obese parent—or especially two obese parents—may be a candidate for preventive efforts.

Another concern is a potential buildup of cholesterol, a waxy substance found in human and animal tissue. High levels of one type of cholesterol (LDL, or "bad" cholesterol) can dangerously narrow blood vessels, leading to heart disease. This condition is called atherosclerosis. Since atherosclerosis begins in childhood, so should heart disease prevention. In a controlled longitudinal study in Finland, a low-saturated fat, low-cholesterol diet beginning in the eighth month of infancy resulted in significant reductions in fat and cholesterol intake by age 5, with no effect on growth or neurological development (Rask-Nissilä et al., 2000).

All in all, the best ways parents can avoid obesity and cardiac problems in themselves and in their children is to adopt a more active lifestyle for the entire family—and for mothers to breastfeed their babies.

The Brain and Reflex Behaviour

What makes newborns respond to a nipple? What tells them to start the sucking movements that allow them to control their intake of fluids? These are functions of the **central nervous system**—the brain and spinal cord (a bundle of nerves running through the backbone)—and of a growing peripheral network of nerves extending to every part of the body. Through this network, sensory messages travel to the brain, and motor commands travel back.

Building the Brain

The growth of the brain both before birth and during the childhood years is fundamental to future physical, cognitive, and emotional development. Through various brain-imaging tools, researchers are gaining a clearer picture of how that growth occurs (Toga, Thompson, & Sowell, 2006). For example, from positron emission tomography (PET) scans showing patterns of glucose metabolism, which are indicators of changes in functional activity, we have learned that the brain's maturation takes much longer than was previously thought (Chugani, 1998).

The brain at birth weighs only about 25 percent of its eventual adult weight of 1.5 kg (Toga et al., 2006). It reaches nearly 90 percent of that weight by age 3. By age 6, it is almost adult size; but growth and functional development of specific parts of the brain continue into adulthood. Increases in brain weight and volume can be measured before birth by ultrasound and after birth by the circumference of the baby's head. These measurements provide a check on whether the brain is growing normally.

The brain's growth during the first 3 years is not smooth and steady; it occurs in fits and starts. **Brain growth spurts,** periods of rapid growth and development, coincide with

*Unless otherwise referenced, the discussion in this section is largely based on Gabbard (1996).

Checkpoint

Can you . . .

✔ Summarize typical patterns of growth during the first 3 years?

✔ Mention several factors that affect growth? Discuss two principles that affect growth?

✔ Summarize pediatric recommendations on early feeding and the introduction of cow's milk, solid foods, and fruit juices?

✔ Cite factors that contribute to obesity and cardiac problems in later life?

Guidepost 2

How does the brain develop, and how do environmental factors affect its early growth?

central nervous system Brain and spinal cord

brain growth spurts Periods of rapid brain growth and development

changes in cognitive behaviour (Fischer & Rose, 1994, 1995; Segalowitz, 1995). Different parts of the brain grow more rapidly at different times, and brain growth depends very much on the child's early experiences. Some events are called experience-expectant, such as language exposure, which give the brain signals to begin growing, and others are experience-dependent, like the specific language a child first learns, which help to shape the way the brain is growing (Segalowitz, 1995).

Major Parts of the Brain

Beginning about two weeks after conception, the brain gradually develops from a long hollow tube into a spherical mass of cells (Society for Neuroscience, 2005; see Figure 6-3). By birth, the growth spurt of the spinal cord and *brain stem* (the part of the brain responsible for such basic bodily functions as breathing, heart rate, body temperature, and the sleep–wake cycle) has almost run its course. The cerebellum (the part of the brain that maintains balance and motor coordination) grows fastest during the first year of life (Casaer, 1993).

The cerebrum, the largest part of the brain, is divided into right and left halves, or hemispheres, each with specialized functions. This specialization of the hemispheres is called **lateralization.** The left hemisphere is mainly concerned with language and logical thinking, the right hemisphere with visual and spatial functions such as map reading and drawing. The two hemispheres are joined by a tough band of tissue called the corpus callosum, which allows them to share information and coordinate commands. The corpus callosum grows dramatically during childhood, reaching adult size by about age 10.

Each cerebral hemisphere has four lobes, or sections: the occipital, parietal, temporal, and frontal lobes, which control different functions (see Figure 6-4) and develop at different

lateralization Tendency of each of the brain's hemispheres to have specialized functions

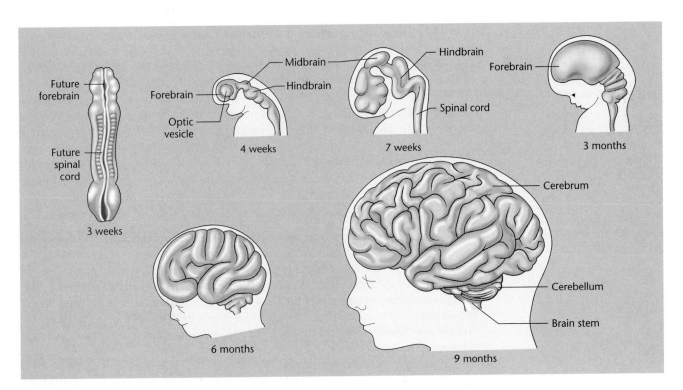

Figure 6-3

Brain development during gestation. Fetal nervous system development begins at about 3 weeks with the closing of the neural tube (left), from which will develop the brain and spinal cord. By 4 weeks, major regions of the brain appear in primitive form: the forebrain, midbrain, hindbrain, and optic vesicle, from which the eye develops. As the brain grows, the front part expands greatly to form the cerebrum, the large, convoluted upper mass which will be the seat of conscious brain activity. The brain stem, an extension of the spinal cord, is almost fully developed at birth, but the cerebellum (above the brain stem) grows most rapidly during the first year of life.

Source: Society for Neuroscience, 2005.

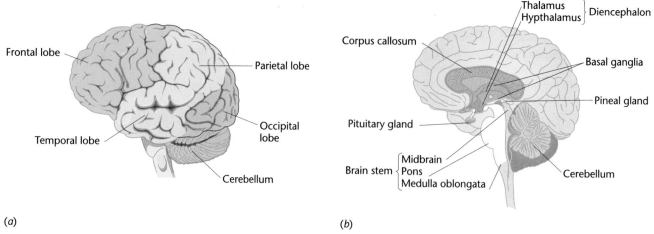

Figure 6-4

Parts of the brain, side view. The brain consists of three main parts: the brain stem, the cerebellum, and, above those, the large cerebrum. The brain stem, an extension of the spinal cord, is one of the regions of the brain most completely developed at birth. It controls such basic bodily functions as breathing, circulation, and reflexes. The cerebellum, at birth, begins to control balance and muscle tone; later it coordinates sensory and motor activity. The cerebrum constitutes almost 70 percent of the weight of the nervous system and handles thought, memory, language, and emotion. It is divided into two halves, or hemispheres, each of which has four sections, or lobes (right to left): (a) The occipital lobe processes visual information. (b) The temporal lobe helps with hearing and language. (c) The parietal lobe allows an infant to receive touch sensations and spatial information, which facilitates eye–hand coordination. (d) The frontal lobe develops gradually during the first year, permitting such higher-level functions as speech and reasoning. The cerebral cortex, the outer surface of the cerebrum, consists of grey matter; it is the seat of thought processes and mental activity. Parts of the cerebral cortex—the sensorimotor cortex and cingulate cortex—as well as several structures deep within the cerebrum, the thalamus, hippocampus, and basal ganglia, all of which control basic movements and functions, are largely developed at birth.

rates. The regions of the cerebral cortex (the outer surface of the cerebrum) that govern vision and hearing are mature by 6 months of age, but the areas of the frontal lobe responsible for making mental associations, remembering, and producing deliberate motor responses remain immature for several years (Gilmore et al., 2007).

The brain growth spurt that begins at about the third trimester of gestation and continues until at least the fourth year of life is important to the development of neurological functioning. Smiling, babbling, crawling, walking, and talking—all the major sensory, motor, and cognitive milestones of infancy and toddlerhood—reflect the rapid development of the brain, particularly the cerebral cortex. (Box 6-1 discusses autism, a disorder related to abnormal brain growth.)

Brain Cells

neurons Nerve cells

The brain is composed of **neurons** and *glial cells*. Neurons, or nerve cells, send and receive information. *Glial cells* support and protect the neurons.

Beginning in the second month of gestation, an estimated 250,000 immature neurons are produced every minute through cell division (mitosis). At birth, most of the more than 100 billion neurons in a mature brain are already formed but are not yet fully developed. The number of neurons increases most rapidly between the 25th week of gestation and the first few months after birth. This cell proliferation is accompanied by a dramatic growth in cell size.

Originally the neurons are simply cell bodies with a nucleus, or centre, composed of deoxyribonucleic acid (DNA), which contains the cell's genetic programming. As the brain grows, these rudimentary cells migrate to various parts of it (Bystron, Rakic, Molnar, & Blakemore, 2006). There they sprout axons and dendrites—narrow, branching extensions. Axons send signals to other neurons, and dendrites receive incoming messages from them, through synapses, the nervous system's communication links. The synapses are tiny gaps, which are bridged with the help of chemicals called neurotransmitters. Eventually a particular neuron may have anywhere from 5,000 to 100,000 synaptic connections to and from the body's sensory receptors, its muscles, and other neurons within the central nervous system.

The multiplication of dendrites and synaptic connections, especially during the last 2½ months of gestation and the first 6 months to 2 years of life (see Figure 6-5), accounts for much of the brain's growth in weight and permits the emergence of new perceptual, cognitive, and motor abilities. Most of the neurons in the cortex, which is responsible for complex, high-level functioning, are in place by 20 weeks of gestation, and its structure becomes fairly well defined during the next 12 weeks. Only after birth, however, do the cells begin to form connections that allow communication to take place.

As the neurons multiply, migrate to their assigned locations, and develop connections, they undergo the complementary processes of integration and differentiation. Through **integration,** the neurons that control various groups of muscles coordinate their activities. Through **differentiation,** each neuron takes on a specific, specialized structure and function.

Only about half the neurons originally produced survive and function in adulthood (Society for Neuroscience, 2005). At first the brain produces more neurons and synapses than it needs. Those that are not used or do not function well die out. This process of **cell death,** or pruning of excess cells and synapses, begins during the prenatal period and

integration Process by which neurons coordinate the activities of muscle groups

differentiation Process by which neurons acquire specialized structure and function

cell death Elimination of excess brain cells to achieve more efficient functioning

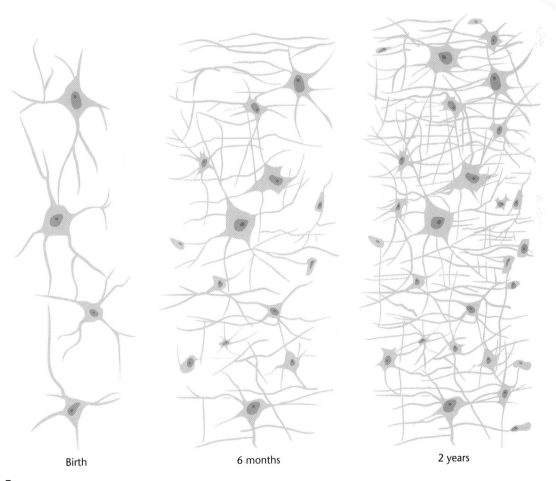

Birth   6 months   2 years

Figure 6-5

Growth of neural connections during first 2 years of life. The rapid increase in the brain's density and weight is due largely to the formation of dendrites, extension of nerve cell bodies, and the synapses that link them. This mushrooming communications network sprouts in response to environmental stimulation and makes possible impressive growth in every domain of development.

Source: Conel, 1959.

Autism is a severe disorder of brain functioning characterized by lack of normal social interaction, impaired communication, repetitive movements, and a highly restricted range of activities and interests. (See Table 6-1 for a list of behaviours typical of autistic children.) Autism is usually not diagnosed behaviourally before age 3 (Schieve, Rice, Boyle, Visser, & Blumberg, 2006), but signs of the disorder may be seen as early as 12 months of age through brain imaging (Centre for Autism Research, undated).

Autism is one of a group of three *autism spectrum disorders (ASDs);* the other two, less severe, are *Asperger disorder* and *pervasive developmental disorder—not otherwise specified.* Preschoolers with ASDs tend to focus on separate bits of information instead of on the total picture. They are weak in verbal ability and in *joint attention*—pointing to an object to call attention to it or looking at another person to see whether the two of them are paying attention to the same event (Morgan, Mayberry, & Durkin, 2003).

Perhaps due in part to increased awareness and more accurate diagnosis, the reported prevalence of autism has increased markedly since the mid-1970s (Infectious Diseases and Immunization Committee, Canadian Paediatric Society, 2001; Newschaffer, Falb, & Gurney, 2005). According to parental reports, at least 300,000 children—approximately 5.6 in 1,000 U.S. children ages 4 through 17—have been diagnosed with autism, 4 out of 5 of them boys (Schieve et al., 2006). A U.S. study in 2002 found that 1 in 150 eight-year-olds has autism or one of the related disorders (Autism and Developmental Disabilities Monitoring Network Surveillance Year 2002 Principal Investigators, 2007).

Some parents blame the preservative thimerosal, which contains a form of mercury and was widely used before the development of thimerosal-free vaccines. The prevalence of the disorder did decline after the U.S. Public Health Service recommended that thimerosal be removed from these vaccines as a precaution (Geier & Geier, 2006). However, the Centers for Disease Control and Prevention (2004), on the basis of multiple studies, concludes that no convincing evidence supports a causal connection between vaccines and autism.

Autism seems to involve a lack of coordination between different regions of the brain needed for complex tasks (Just, Cherkassky, Keller, Kana, & Minshew, 2007; Williams, Goldstein, & Minshew, 2006). In a brain imaging study, adults with autism used different parts of the brain than did adults without autism in trying to comprehend a sentence. The group with autism showed less activation in the front of the brain, which is involved in higher-level thinking, than in the rear section, which is involved

Table 6-1	Possible Signs of Autism

Children with autism may show the following characteristics in varying combinations and degrees of severity:

Inappropriate laughing or giggling

Lack of fear of danger

Apparent insensitivity to pain

Rejection of cuddling

Sustained unusual or repetitive play

Uneven physical or verbal skills

Avoidance of eye contact

Preferring to be alone

Difficulty expressing needs except through gestures

Inappropriate attachment to objects

Insistence on sameness

Echoing words or phrases

Inappropriate response to sound

Spinning objects or self

Difficulty interacting with others

Source: Autism Society of America (undated).

autism Pervasive developmental disorder of the brain, characterized by lack of normal social interaction, impaired communication and imagination, and repetitive, obsessive behaviours

continues after birth (see Figure 6-6), helping to create an efficient nervous system. The number of synapses seems to peak at about age 2, and their elimination continues well into adolescence. Even as some neurons die out, new research suggests, others may continue to form during adult life (Eriksson et al., 1998; Gould, Reeves, Graziano, & Gross, 1999). Meanwhile, connections among cortical cells continue to strengthen and to become more reliable and precise, enabling more flexible and more advanced motor and cognitive functioning (Society for Neuroscience, 2005).

Myelination

myelination Process of coating neurons with a fatty substance (myelin) that enables faster communication between cells

Much of the credit for improvement in efficiency of communication goes to the glial cells, which coat the neural pathways with a fatty substance called *myelin*. This process of **myelination** enables signals to travel faster and more smoothly, permitting the achievement of mature functioning. Myelination begins about halfway through gestation in some parts of the brain and continues into adulthood in others. The pathways related to the sense of touch—the first sense to develop—are myelinated by birth. Myelination of visual pathways, which are slower to mature, begins at birth and continues during the first 5 months

(continued)

in perceiving details, suggesting that they focused more on the meanings of individual words than on the sentence as a whole (Just, Cherkassky, Keller, & Minshew, 2004). Postmortem studies have found fewer neurons in the amygdala, a part of the brain involved in emotion and memory, in the brains of people who had autism (Schumann & Amaral, 2006). People with autism also show deficits in executive function and theory of mind (Zelazo & Müller, 2002).

Autistic disorders run in families and have a strong genetic basis (Constantino, 2003; Ramoz et al., 2004; Rodier, 2000). Monozygotic twins are more concordant for autism than dizygotic twins. Several genes may be involved in cases of varying symptoms and severity (Bespalova & Buxbaum, 2003; Ingram et al., 2000; Ramoz et al., 2004; Rodier, 2000). A variant of a gene located on chromosome 7 has been linked to autism in families that have more than one child with the disorder (Campbell et al., 2006). A large, multi-country study looking for genes involved in autism has implicated a site on chromosome 11 as well as components of the brain's glutamate neurotransmitter system, which plays an important part in wiring the brain during early development (Devlin & Scherer, and the Autism Genome Project Consortium, 2007).

Environmental factors, such as exposure to certain viruses or chemicals, may trigger an inherited tendency toward autism (Rodier, 2000). Certain complications of pregnancy, such as uterine bleeding and vaginal infection seem to be associated with a higher incidence of the condition (Juul-Dam, Townsend, & Courchesne, 2001). So are advanced parental age, first births, threatened fetal loss, epidural anesthesia, induced labour, and Caesarean delivery (Glasson et al., 2004; Reichenberg et al., 2006). Major stress during the 24th to 28th weeks of pregnancy may deform the developing brain (Beversdorf et al., 2001).

Why are autistic children overwhelmingly male? According to one theory, the female brain is predominantly hard-wired for empathy, and the male brain for understanding and building systems. Newborn girls look longer at a face; newborn boys look longer at a mechanical mobile. According to this theory, autism may be an extreme version of the normal male brain. Autistic persons are impaired in emphathizing but very good at systematizing (Baron-Cohen, 2005). In a study of 58 children whose mothers had undergone amniocentesis during pregnancy, high levels of fetal testosterone in amniotic fluid were associated with poorer quality social relationships and more restricted interests at age 4. This finding suggests that high levels of fetal testosterone may be involved in the male vulnerability to autism (Knickmeyer, Baron-Cohen, Raggatt, & Taylor, 2005).

Autism has no known cure, but improvement—sometimes substantial—can occur, especially with early intervention. Some autistic children can be taught to speak, read, and write. Behaviour therapy can help them learn such basic social skills as paying attention, sustaining eye contact, and feeding and dressing themselves (AAP Committee on Children with Disabilities, 2001). However, only about 2 percent of autistic children grow up to live independently; most need some degree of care throughout life. Children with Asperger's syndrome generally fare better (Autism—Part II, 2001).

What's your view?

Have you ever known anyone with autism? If so, in what ways did that person's behaviour seem unusual?

Check it out!

For more information on this topic, go to **www.mcgrawhill.ca/olc/papalia**. For an "inside look at autism," go to **www.autism.org/temple/inside.html**. Temple Grandin, as assistant professor of animal science at Colorado State University, describes her own experiences as an autistic child and the methods that enabled her to direct her energies into constructive activities and a successful career.

---

of life. Pathways related to hearing may begin to be myelinated as early as the fifth month of gestation, but the process is not complete until about age 4. The parts of the cortex that control attention and memory, which are slower to develop, are not fully myelinated until young adulthood. Myelination in an information relay zone of the *hippocampus,* a structure deep in the temporal lobe that plays a key role in memory, and related formations continues to increase until at least age 70 (Benes, Turtle, Khan, & Farol, 1994).

Myelination of sensory and motor pathways, first in the fetus's spinal cord and later, after birth, in the cerebral cortex, may account for the initially evident, and later not evident early reflexes.

Early Reflexes

When you blink at a bright light, your eyelids are acting involuntarily. Such an automatic, innate response to stimulation is called a **reflex behaviour.** Reflex behaviours are controlled by the lower brain centres that govern other involuntary processes, such as breathing and heart rate. These are the parts of the brain most fully myelinated at birth.

reflex behaviours Automatic, involuntary, innate responses to stimulation

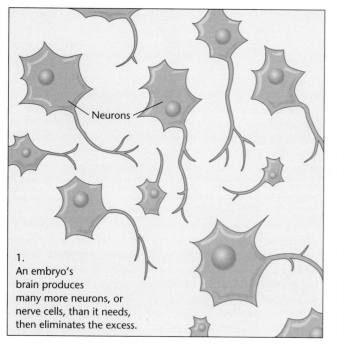

1.
An embryo's brain produces many more neurons, or nerve cells, than it needs, then eliminates the excess.

Neurons

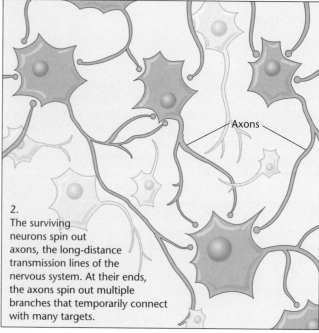

Axons

2.
The surviving neurons spin out axons, the long-distance transmission lines of the nervous system. At their ends, the axons spin out multiple branches that temporarily connect with many targets.

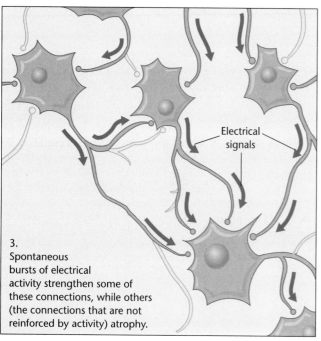

Electrical signals

3.
Spontaneous bursts of electrical activity strengthen some of these connections, while others (the connections that are not reinforced by activity) atrophy.

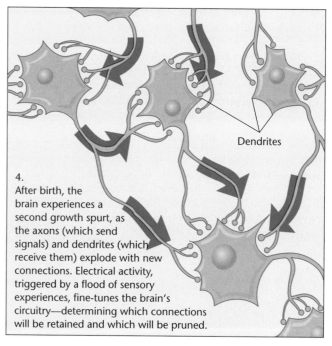

Dendrites

4.
After birth, the brain experiences a second growth spurt, as the axons (which send signals) and dendrites (which receive them) explode with new connections. Electrical activity, triggered by a flood of sensory experiences, fine-tunes the brain's circuitry—determining which connections will be retained and which will be pruned.

Figure 6-6

Wiring the brain: Development of neural connections before and after birth.

Source: Nash, 1997, p. 51.

Reflex behaviours play an important part in stimulating the early development of the central nervous system and muscles.

Human infants have an estimated 27 major reflexes, many of which are present at birth or soon after (Gabbard, 1996; see Table 6-2 for examples). Primitive reflexes, such as sucking, rooting for the nipple, and the Moro reflex (a response to being startled or beginning to fall), are related to instinctive needs for survival and protection. Some primitive reflexes may be part of humanity's evolutionary legacy. One example is the grasping reflex, by which infant monkeys hold on to the hair of their mothers' bodies. As the higher brain centres become active, during the first 2 to 4 months, infants begin to show postural reflexes: reactions to changes in position or balance. For example, infants who

Table 6-2   Early Human Reflexes

Reflex	Stimulation	Baby's Behaviour	Typical Age of Appearance	Typical Age of Disappearance
Moro	Baby is dropped or hears loud noise.	Extends legs, arms, and fingers, arches back, draws back head.	7th month of gestation	3 months
Darwinian (grasping)	Palm of baby's hand is stroked.	Makes strong fist; can be raised to standing position if both fists are closed around a stick.	7th month of gestation	4 months
Tonic neck	Baby is laid down on back.	Turns head to one side, assumes "fencer" position, extends arms and legs on preferred side, flexes opposite limbs.	7th month of gestation	5 months
Babkin	Both of baby's palms are stroked at once.	Mouth opens, eyes close, neck flexes, head tilts forward.	Birth	3 months
Babinski	Sole of baby's foot is stroked.	Toes fan out; foot twists in.	Birth	4 months
Rooting	Baby's cheek or lower lip is stroked with finger or nipple.	Head turns; mouth opens; sucking movements begin.	Birth	9 months
Walking	Baby is held under arms, with bare feet touching flat surface.	Makes steplike motions that look like well-coordinated walking.	1 month	4 months
Swimming	Baby is put into water face down.	Makes well-coordinated swimming movements.	1 month	4 months

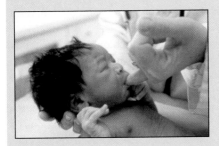

Rooting reflex

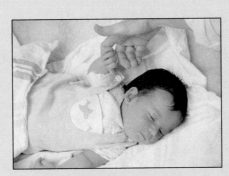

Darwinian reflex

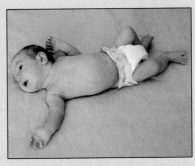

Tonic neck reflex

Moro reflex

Babinski reflex

Walking reflex

Source: Adapted in part from Gabbard, 1996.

are tilted downward extend their arms in the parachute reflex, an instinctive attempt to break a fall.

Locomotor reflexes, such as the walking and swimming reflexes, resemble voluntary movements that do not appear until months after the reflexes have disappeared. As we'll see, there is debate about whether or not locomotor reflexes prepare the way for their later, voluntary counterparts.

Most of the early reflexes become less evident during the first 6 to 12 months. Reflexes that continue to serve protective functions—such as blinking, yawning, coughing, gagging, sneezing, shivering, and the pupillary reflex (dilation of the pupils in the dark)—remain. Disappearance of unneeded reflexes on schedule is a sign that motor pathways in the cortex have been partially myelinated, enabling a shift to voluntary behaviour. Thus we can evaluate a baby's neurological development by seeing whether certain reflexes are present or absent.

Moulding the Brain: The Role of Experience

Although the brain's early development is genetically directed, it can be modified both positively and negatively by environmental experience (Toga et al., 2006). Early experience can have lasting effects on the capacity of the central nervous system to learn and store information (Society for Neuroscience, 2005). Individual differences in intelligence may reflect differences in the brain's ability to develop neural connections in response to experience (Garlick, 2003). The technical term for this malleability, or modifiability, of the brain is **plasticity.** Early synaptic connections, some of which depend on sensory stimulation, refine and stabilize the brain's genetically designed "wiring."

plasticity Modifiability, or "moulding," of the brain through experience

During this formative period, the brain is especially vulnerable. Exposure to hazardous drugs, environmental toxins, or maternal stress before or after birth can threaten the developing brain, and malnutrition can interfere with normal cognitive growth (Rose, 1994; Thompson, 2001). So, too, early abuse or sensory impoverishment may leave an imprint on the brain (J. E. Black, 1998). In one study, a monkey raised until 6 months old with one eyelid closed became permanently blind in that eye, apparently through loss of working connections between that eye and the visual cortex (Society for Neuroscience, 2005). Thus, if certain cortical connections are not made early in life, these circuits may "shut down" forever.

By the same token, enriched experience can spur brain development (Society for Neuroscience, 2005) and even make up for past deprivation (J. E. Black, 1998). Animals raised in toy-filled cages sprout more axons, dendrites, and synapses than animals raised in bare cages (Society for Neuroscience, 2005). Plasticity continues throughout life as neurons change in size and shape in response to environmental experience (Rutter, 2002). Such findings have sparked successful efforts to stimulate the brain development of premature infants (Als et al., 2004) and children with Down syndrome and to help victims of brain damage recover function. And these findings explain why the sensory and cognitive stimulation Anne Sullivan provided was so important in Helen Keller's development.

Early emotional development, too, may depend on experience. Infants whose mothers are severely depressed show less activity in the left frontal lobe, the part of the brain that is involved in positive emotions such as happiness and joy, and more activity in the right frontal lobe, which is associated with negative emotions (Dawson, Frey, Panagiotides, Osterling, & Hessl, 1997; Dawson, Klinger, Panagiotides, Hill, & Spieker, 1992).

Sometimes corrective experience can make up for past deprivation (J. E. Black, 1998). Plasticity continues throughout life as neurons change in size and shape in response to environmental experience (M. C. Diamond, 1988; Pally, 1997). Brain-damaged rats, when raised in an enriched setting, grow more dendritic connections (M. C. Diamond, 1988). Such findings have sparked successful efforts to stimulate the physical and mental development of children with Down syndrome and to help infants and children who have experienced brain damage recover function.

Ethical constraints prevent controlled experiments on the effects of environmental deprivation on human infants. However, the discovery of thousands of infants and young children who had spent virtually their entire lives in overcrowded Romanian orphanages offered an opportunity for a natural experiment (Ames, 1997). Discovered after the fall of the dictator

Nicolae Ceausescu in December 1989, these abandoned children appeared to be starving, passive, and emotionless. They had spent much of their time lying quietly in their cribs or beds, with nothing to look at. They had had little contact with one another or with their caregivers and had heard little conversation or even noise. Most of the 2- and 3-year-olds did not walk or talk, and the older children played aimlessly. PET scans of their brains showed extreme inactivity in the temporal lobes, which regulate emotion and receive sensory input.

Many of these children were adopted by Canadian families. At the time of adoption, all the children showed delayed motor, language, or psychosocial development, and nearly 8 out of 10 were behind in all these areas. Three years later, when compared with children left behind in the Romanian institutions, they showed remarkable progress. Even when compared with Canadian children reared in their own homes from birth, about one-third had no serious problems and were doing well—in a few cases, better than the average home-raised child. Another third—generally those who had been in institutions the longest—still had serious developmental problems. The rest were moving toward average performance and behaviour (Ames, 1997; Morison, Ames, & Chisholm, 1995).

However, another study suggests that age of adoption makes a difference. Among 111 Romanian children adopted in England before age 2, those adopted before age 6 months had largely caught up physically and had made a complete cognitive recovery by age 4, as compared with a control group of English adopted children. However, 85 percent of the English adoptees were more cognitively advanced than the average Romanian child adopted after 6 months of age (Rutter & the English and Romanian Adoptees [ERA] Study Team, 1998). A further study of Romanian children adopted by Canadians showed that those who spent 8 months or more in Romanian orphanages scored lower than non-adopted Canadian-born children in cognitive development, and lower than Romanian children who spent less than 4 months in orphanages before being adopted by Canadians. However, the early adoptees scored lower than Canadian-born children, indicating that prenatal and perinatal environments, genetic factors, and the experience of adoption can influence cognitive development. Better quality adoptive home environments and less time spent in the orphanages were associated with better development (Morison & Ellwood, 2000). Apparently, then, it may take very early environmental stimulation to overcome the effects of extreme deprivation.

Another study looked at social and emotional development in Romanian infants adopted into Wisconsin families. Three and a half years after adoption, these children produced low levels of two hormones, oxytocin and vasopressin, which are critical to the development of social bonds, such as the bond between mother and child (Fries, Ziegler, Kurian, Jacoris, & Pollak, 2005). It may be that there is a critical or sensitive period early in life for this biological mechanism to be established.

What's your view ?

• In view of what is known about the plasticity of the infant brain, should every baby have access to an appropriately stimulating environment? If so, how can this goal be accomplished?

Checkpoint ✔

Can you . . .

✔ Describe important features of early brain development?

✔ Explain the functions of reflex behaviours and why some drop out during the early months?

✔ Discuss how early experience affects brain development?

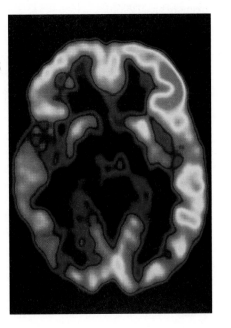

Extreme environmental deprivation in infancy can affect the structure of the brain, resulting in cognitive and emotional problems. A PET scan of a normal child's brain *(left)* shows regions of high *(red)* and low *(blue and black)* activity. A PET scan of the brain of a Romanian orphan institutionalized after birth *(right)* shows little activity.

Early Sensory Capacities

"The baby, assailed by eyes, ears, nose, skin, and entrails at once, feels that all is one great blooming, buzzing confusion," wrote the psychologist William James in 1890. We now know that this is far from true. The developing brain enables newborn infants to make fairly good sense of what they touch, see, smell, taste, and hear; and their senses develop rapidly in the early months of life.

Touch and Pain

Touch seems to be the first sense to develop, and for the first several months it is the most mature sensory system. When a newborn's cheek is stroked near the mouth, the baby responds by trying to find a nipple, probably an evolved survival mechanism (Rakison, 2005). Early signs of this rooting reflex (refer back to Table 6-2) show up in the womb, 2 months after conception. By 32 weeks of gestation, all body parts are sensitive to touch, and this sensitivity increases during the first 5 days of life (Haith, 1986).

Often physicians performing surgery on newborn babies have used no anaesthesia because of a mistaken belief that neonates cannot feel pain, or feel it only briefly. Actually, as we reported in Chapter 4, there is evidence that the capacity for pain perception may emerge by the third trimester of pregnancy (Lee et al., 2005). Furthermore, pain experienced during the neonatal period may sensitize an infant to later pain, perhaps by affecting the neural pathways that process painful stimuli. Circumcised 4- and 6-month-olds have stronger reactions to the pain of vaccination than uncircumcised infants; the reaction is muted among infants who are treated with a painkilling cream before being circumcised (Taddio, Katz, Ilersich, & Koren, 1997). The Canadian Paediatric Society (American Academy of Pediatrics, Committee on Fetus and Newborn and Section on Surgery, Canadian Paediatric Society and Fetus and Newborn Committee, 2006) now maintains that prolonged or severe pain can do long-term harm to newborns, and that pain relief is essential. Although hospitals in Canada routinely use anaesthetic during major surgery for infants, they have used anaesthetic less frequently in minor surgery and in easing post-operative and disease-related pain (Fernandez & Rees, 1994).

Smell and Taste

The senses of smell and taste also begin to develop in the womb. The flavours and odours of foods an expectant mother consumes may be transmitted to the fetus through the amniotic fluid. After birth, a similar transmission occurs through breast milk (Mennella & Beauchamp, 1996b).

A preference for pleasant odours seems to be learned in utero and during the first few days after birth, and the odours transmitted through the mother's breast milk may further contribute to this learning (Bartoshuk & Beauchamp, 1994). This attraction to the fragrance of the mother's milk may be another evolutionary survival mechanism (Rakison, 2005). In a study of French 3- and 4-day-olds, both those who were being breastfed and those who were being formula-fed showed a preference for the odour of human milk (Marlier & Schaal, 2005).

Certain taste preferences seem to be largely innate (Bartoshuk & Beauchamp, 1994). Newborns prefer sweet tastes to sour or bitter ones. The sweeter the fluid, the harder they suck and the more they drink (Haith, 1986). Sweetened water calms crying newborns, whether full-term or 2 to 3 weeks premature—evidence that not only the taste buds themselves (which seem to be fairly well developed by 20 weeks of gestation), but the mechanisms that produce this calming effect are functional before normal term (B. A. Smith & Blass, 1996). An inborn "sweet tooth" may help a baby adapt to life outside the womb, since breast milk is quite sweet. Newborns' rejection of bitter tastes is probably another survival mechanism, since many bitter substances are toxic (Bartoshuk & Beauchamp, 1994).

Taste preferences developed in infancy may last into early childhood. In one study, 4- and 5-year-olds who, as infants, had been fed different types of formula had differing

Most infants begin to eat solid foods after 6 months of age. Even at this age, infants show definite taste preferences. An infant exposed to the flavours of healthy foods through breastfeeding is more likely to accept healthy foods, such as cereal and vegetables.

food preferences (Mennella & Beauchamp, 2002). Exposure to the flavours of healthy foods through breastfeeding may improve acceptance of healthy foods after weaning and later in life (American Heart Association et al., 2006).

Hearing

Hearing, too, is functional before birth; fetuses respond to sounds and seem to learn to recognize them. From an evolutionary perspective, early recognition of voices and language heard in the womb may lay the foundation for the relationship with the mother, which is critical to early survival (Rakison, 2005). As we reported in Chapter 4, three-day-old infants respond to a story heard while in the womb differently from the way they respond to other stories; can distinguish their mother's voice from a stranger's; and prefer their native language to a foreign tongue (DeCasper & Fifer, 1980; DeCasper & Spence, 1986; C. Moon, Cooper, & Fifer, 1993).

Auditory discrimination develops rapidly after birth. Three-day-old infants can distinguish new speech sounds from those they have heard before (L. R. Brody, Zelazo, & Chaika, 1984). At 1 month, babies can distinguish sounds as close as "ba" and "pa" (Eimas, Siqueland, Jusczyk, & Vigorito, 1971).

Because hearing is a key to language development, hearing impairments should be identified as early as possible. Hearing loss occurs in 1 to 3 of 1,000 live births and, if left undetected, can lead to developmental delays (Gaffney et al., 2003). Although there is support for universally testing hearing in newborns (Hyde & Riko, 2000), only 10 percent of Canadian hospitals report having programs for screening newborn hearing (Canadian Working Group on Childhood Hearing, 2001) and the majority screen only high risk infants (Alberta Universal Newborn Hearing Screening Project, 2001–2004).

Sight

Vision is the least developed sense at birth. Some visual capabilities are present at birth and others require time and experience to mature. A great deal of visual development takes place during the first year, but different visual functions mature at different rates (Gwiazda & Birch, 2001). Newborns are capable of attending to objects in the environment, looking at edges, contours, and curves, and showing preference for the human face. Visual perception and the ability to use visual information—identifying caregivers, finding food, and avoiding dangers—become more important as infants become more alert and active (Rakison, 2005).

The eyes of newborns are smaller than those of adults, the retinal structures are incomplete, and the optic nerve is underdeveloped. A neonate's eyes focus best from about 1 foot (or 30 centimetres) away—just about the typical distance from the face of a person holding a newborn. This focusing distance may have evolved to promote mother–infant bonding. There is some evidence that the ability to recognize faces—specifically, a caregiver's face—may be an innate survival mechanism (Rakison, 2005).

Newborns blink at bright lights. Their peripheral vision is very narrow; it more than doubles between 2 and 10 weeks of age (E. Tronick, 1972). The ability to follow a moving target also develops rapidly in the first months, as does colour perception (Haith, 1986). Four-month-old babies can discriminate among red, green, blue, and yellow (M. Bornstein, Kessen, & Weiskopf, 1976; Teller & Bornstein, 1987).

Vision becomes more acute during the first year, reaching the 20/20 level by about the sixth month (Aslin, 1987). (This measure of vision means that a person can read letters on a specified line on a standard eye chart from 20 feet (or 6 metres) away.) Binocular vision—the use of both eyes to focus, allowing perception of depth and distance—does not usually develop until 4 or 5 months (Bushnell & Boudreau, 1993). Another feature of visual development involves the coordination of visual skills and motor movement. Evidence of the beginnings of eye–hand coordination has been found in neonates as young as 3 to 5 days after birth, whose hand movements towards a ball were influenced by visual contact with the ball (Ennouri & Bloch, 1996). Likewise, the direction of movement of eyes and head begins to become coordinated as early as 2 weeks (Bloch & Carchon, 1992).

Checkpoint

Can you . . .

✔ Give evidence for the early development of the senses?

✔ Tell how breastfeeding plays a part in the development of smell, touch, and taste?

✔ Tell how auditory discrimination in newborns is related to fetal hearing?

✔ List at least three ways in which newborns' vision is underdeveloped?

Guidepost 4

What are some early milestones in motor development, and what are some influences on it?

Motor Development

Babies do not have to be taught such basic motor skills as grasping, crawling, and walking. They just need room to move and freedom to see what they can do. When the central nervous system, muscles, and bones are ready and the environment offers the right opportunities for exploration and practice, babies keep surprising the adults around them with their new abilities.

Milestones of Motor Development

Motor development is marked by a series of "milestones": achievements a child masters before going on to more difficult ones. These milestones are not isolated achievements; they develop systematically, each newly mastered ability preparing a baby to tackle the next. Babies first learn simple skills and then combine them into increasingly complex **systems of action,** which permit a wider or more precise range of movement and more effective control of the environment. In developing the precision grip, for example, an infant first tries to pick things up with the whole hand, fingers closing against the palm. Later the baby masters the pincer grasp, in which thumb and index finger meet at the tips to form a circle, making it possible to pick up tiny objects. In learning to walk, an infant first gains control of separate movements of the arms, legs, and feet before putting these movements together to take that momentous first step.

A number of clinical screening tests, like the Gesell Developmental Schedules (Knobloch, Stevens, & Malone, 1980), have been developed to chart the progress of motor development in children from birth to 3 years. This test, used in Canada, determines whether children are developing normally, and it is sensitive to individual differences, giving information on adaptive, gross motor, fine motor, language, and personal/social areas of development. The **Denver Developmental Screening Test** (Frankenburg, Dodds, Fandal, Kazuk, & Cohrs, 1975), is another test that measures **gross motor skills** (those using large muscles), such as rolling over and catching a ball, and **fine motor skills** (using small muscles), such as grasping a rattle and copying a circle. The Denver test has been criticized largely because of its weaknesses in standardization and norms (Lee & Harris, 2005), which do not reflect the cultural diversity of Canada's population.

As we trace typical progress in head control, hand control, and locomotion, notice how these developments follow the cephalocaudal (head to tail) and proximodistal (inner to outer) principles outlined earlier.

Head Control

At birth, most infants can turn their heads from side to side while lying on their backs. While lying chest down, many can lift their heads enough to turn them. Within the first 2 to 3 months, they lift their heads higher and higher—sometimes to the point where they lose their balance and roll over on their backs. By 4 months of age, almost all infants can keep their heads erect while being held or supported in a sitting position.

Hand Control

Babies are born with a grasping reflex. If the palm of an infant's hand is stroked, the hand closes tightly. At about 3½ months, most infants can grasp an object of moderate size, such as a rattle, but have trouble holding a small object. Next they begin to grasp objects with one hand and transfer them to the other, and then to hold (but not pick up) small objects. Some time between 7 and 11 months, their hands become coordinated enough to pick up a tiny object, such as a pea, using the pincer grasp. After that, hand control becomes increasingly precise. By 15 months, the average baby can build a tower of two cubes. A few months after the third birthday, the average toddler can copy a circle fairly well.

Locomotion

By about 3 months, the average infant is experiencing accidental rolling as a result of reflex behaviour. Over the next 2 months deliberate rolling, first from front to back and

systems of action Increasingly complex combinations of skills, which permit a wider or more precise range of movement and more control of the environment

Denver Developmental Screening Test Screening test given to children 1 month to 6 years old to determine whether they are developing normally

gross motor skills Physical skills that involve the large muscles

fine motor skills Physical skills that involve the small muscles and eye–hand coordination

then from back to front, becomes more under the control of the infant's intentions. The average baby can sit without support by 6 months and can assume a sitting position without help about 2½ months later.

Between 6 and 10 months, most babies begin to get around under their own power by means of various forms of creeping or crawling. This new achievement of self-locomotion has striking cognitive and psychosocial ramifications. Crawling infants become more sensitive to where objects are, how big they are, whether they can be moved, and how they look. Crawling helps babies learn to better judge distances and perceive depth. They learn to look to caregivers for clues as to whether a situation is secure or frightening—a skill known as *social referencing* (Hertenstein & Campos, 2004; see Chapter 8).

By holding onto a helping hand or a piece of furniture, the average baby can stand at a little past 7 months of age. A little more than 4 months later, most babies let go and stand alone. The average baby can stand well about 2 weeks or so before the first birthday.

All these developments are milestones along the way to the major motor achievement of infancy: walking. Humans begin to walk later than other species, possibly because babies' heavy heads and short legs make balance difficult. Again, practice is the most important factor in overcoming these difficulties (Adolph, Vereijken, & Shrout, 2003). For some months before they can stand without support, babies practise "cruising" while holding onto furniture. Soon after they can stand alone well. At about 11½ months, most infants take their first unaided steps. Within a few weeks, soon after the first birthday, the child is walking well and thus achieves the status of toddler.

During the second year, children begin to climb stairs one at a time, putting one foot after another on each step; later they will alternate feet. Walking down stairs comes later. In their second year, toddlers run and jump. By age 3½, most children can balance briefly on one foot and begin to hop.

In the past, many Canadian parents put their babies in mobile walkers in the belief that the babies will learn to walk earlier. Actually, by restricting babies' motor exploration, and sometimes their view of their own movements, walkers may *delay* motor skill development (Siegel & Burton, 1999). Furthermore, walkers can be dangerous. An estimated 197,200 walker-related injuries to children younger than 15 months were treated in U.S. hospital emergency departments between 1990 and 2001, but the number of such injuries decreased markedly after 1994, when stationary activity centres for babies came on the market (Shields & Smith, 2006, p. 19).

In 2004, Canada became the first country to ban the sale, advertising, and importation of infant walkers (Reuters, 2004a). Despite this ban, there are persistent walker-related injuries, with parents continuing to use second-hand walkers (Tan, Lim & Ken, 2003).

Motor Development and Perception

Sensory perception enables infants to learn about themselves and their environment so they can make better judgments about how to navigate in it. Motor experience, together with awareness of their changing bodies, sharpens and modifies their perceptual understanding of what is likely to happen if they move in a certain way. This bidirectional connection between perception and action, mediated by the developing brain, gives infants much useful information about themselves and their world (Adolph & Eppler, 2002).

Sensory and motor activity seem to be fairly well coordinated from birth (Bertenthal & Clifton, 1998). Infants as young as 2 months realize that an object's size and shape are constant, even though it looks smaller if it is farther away (Bower, 1966).

Infants begin reaching for objects at about 4 to 5 months; by 5½ months, they can adapt their reach to moving or spinning objects (Wentworth, Benson, & Haith, 2000). Piaget and other researchers long believed that reaching depended on **visual guidance:** the use of the eyes to guide the movement of the hands (or other parts of the body). Now, research has found that infants in that age group can use other sensory cues to reach for an object. They can locate an unseen rattle by its sound, and they can reach for a glowing object in the dark, even though they cannot see their hands (Clifton, Muir, Ashmead, & Clarkson, 1993). They even can reach for an object based only on their memory of its location (McCarty, Clifton, Ashmead, Lee, & Goubet, 2001). Slightly older infants, 5 to 7½ months old, can grasp a

visual guidance Use of the eyes to guide movements of the hands or other parts of the body

moving, fluorescent object in the dark—a feat that requires awareness, not only of how their own hands move, but also of the object's path and speed, so as to anticipate the likely point of contact (Robin, Berthier, & Clifton, 1996).

Depth perception, the ability to perceive objects and surfaces in three dimensions, depends on several kinds of cues that affect the image of an object on the retina of the eye. These cues involve not only binocular coordination, but also motor control (Bushnell & Boudreau, 1993). *Kinetic cues* are produced by movement of the object or the observer, or both. To find out whether an object is moving, a baby might hold his or her head still for a moment, an ability that is well established by about 3 months.

Sometime between 5 and 7 months, babies respond to such cues as relative size and differences in texture and shading. These cues depend on **haptic perception,** the ability to acquire information by handling objects rather than just looking at them. Haptic perception comes only after babies develop enough eye–hand coordination to reach for objects and grasp them (Bushnell & Boudreau, 1993).

Eleanor and James Gibson's Ecological Theory of Perception

In a classic experiment by Richard Walk and Eleanor Gibson (1961), 6-month-old babies were placed on a plexiglass tabletop laid over a checkerboard pattern that created the illusion of a vertical drop in the centre of the table—a **visual cliff.** Would the infants perceive this illusion of depth? The babies did see a difference between the "ledge" and the "drop." They crawled freely on the "ledge" but avoided the "drop," even when they saw their mothers beckoning from the far side of the table.

How do babies decide whether to move across a "ledge" or down a hill? According to Eleanor Gibson's and James J. Gibson's **ecological theory of perception** (E. J. Gibson, 1969; J. J. Gibson, 1979; Gibson & Pick, 2000), infants size up the "fit," or **affordance,** between their own changing physical attributes (such as arm and leg length, endurance, balance, and strength) and the changing characteristics of their environment. Knowledge of affordances enables babies to make decisions about what they can do in a given situation (Adolph, 2000; Adolph & Eppler, 2002). (Is the ground too rough to walk on? Can I keep my balance if I try?) According to the Gibsons, perceptual learning occurs through a growing ability to differentiate the many features of a rich sensory environment. It is this ability, which may be inborn (Gibson & Walk, 1960), that permits infants and toddlers to recognize affordances and thus to successfully negotiate a terrain.

Locomotor development depends on increasing sensitivity to affordances and is an outcome of both perception and action (Adolph & Eppler, 2002). With experience, babies become better able to gauge the environment in which they move and to act accordingly (Adolph, 2000; Adolph et al., 2003; Adolph & Eppler, 2002). In visual cliff experiments, infants who have been crawling for some time are more likely than novices to avoid the "cliff." Similarly, when faced with actual downward slopes of increasing steepness, infants' judgments become more accurate and their explorations more efficient as they gain practice in crawling. They apparently learn from experience how far they can push their limits without losing their balance (Adolph & Eppler, 2002).

This learning is flexible but posture-specific. Babies who learn how far they can reach for a toy across a gap while in a sitting position must acquire this knowledge anew when they begin to crawl (Adolph, 2000; Adolph & Eppler, 2002). Likewise, when crawling babies who have mastered slopes begin to walk, they have to learn to cope with slopes all over again (Adolph, 1997; Adolph & Eppler, 2002).

How Motor Development Occurs: Thelen's Dynamic Systems Theory

The typical sequence of motor development was traditionally thought to be genetically programmed—a largely automatic, preordained series of steps directed by the maturing brain. Today, many developmental scientists consider this view too simplistic. Instead, according to Esther Thelen (1995; Smith & Thelen, 2003), motor development is a continuous process of interaction between baby and environment.

depth perception Ability to perceive objects and surfaces three-dimensionally

haptic perception Ability to acquire information about properties of objects, such as size, weight, and texture, by handling them

visual cliff Apparatus designed to give an illusion of depth and used to assess depth perception in infants

ecological theory of perception Theory developed by Eleanor and James Gibson, which describes developing motor and perceptual abilities as interdependent parts of a functional system that guides behaviour in varying contexts

affordance In the Gibsons' ecological theory of perception, the fit between a person's physical attributes and capabilities and characteristics of the environment

Thelen pointed to the *walking reflex:* stepping movements a neonate makes when held upright with the feet touching a surface. This behaviour usually disappears by the fourth month. Not until the latter part of the first year, when a baby is getting ready to walk, do such movements appear again. The usual explanation is a shift to cortical control: thus, an older baby's deliberate walking is a new skill masterminded by the developing brain. But, Thelen observed, a newborn's stepping involves the same kinds of movements the neonate makes while lying down and kicking. Why would stepping stop, only to reappear months later, whereas kicking continues? The answer, she suggested, might be that babies' legs become thicker and heavier during the early months but not yet strong enough to carry the increased weight (Thelen & Fisher, 1982, 1983). In fact, when infants who had stopped stepping were held in warm water, which helps support their legs, stepping reappeared. Their ability to produce the movement had not changed—only the physical and environmental conditions that inhibited or promoted it.

No matter how enticing a mother's arms are, this baby is staying away from them. As young as she is, she can perceive depth and wants to avoid falling off what looks like a cliff.

Maturation alone cannot explain such an observation, said Thelen. Development does not have a single, simple cause. Infant and environment form an interconnected, dynamic system, which includes the infant's motivation as well as his muscular strength and position in the environment at a particular moment in time (for example, lying in a crib or being held in a pool). Similarly, when an infant tries to reach for a rattle or mobile, opportunities and constraints presented by the infant's physical characteristics, the intensity of her desire, her energy level, the speed and direction of her arm, and the changing positions of her arm and hand at each point in the process affect whether and how she can achieve the goal. Ultimately, a solution emerges as the baby explores various combinations of movements and selects and assembles those that most efficiently contribute to that end. Furthermore, the solution must be flexible, subject to modification in changing circumstances. Rather than being solely in charge of this process, the maturing brain is only one part of it.

These initial insights grew into Thelen's **dynamic systems theory (DST).** According to dynamic systems theory, *"behaviour emerges in the moment from the self-organization of multiple components"* (Spencer et al., 2006, p. 1523). DST emphasizes four principles: (1) the element of time—not only in the moment a behaviour occurs, but in the effects of behavioural decisions that accumulate over time; (2) the interaction of multiple causes or subsystems; (3) the integration of perception and cognition with action; and (4) the differing developmental pathways of individual children (Smith & Thelen, 2003; Spencer et al., 2006). According to Thelen, normal babies develop the same skills in the same order because they are built approximately the same way and have similar physical challenges and needs. Thus, they eventually discover that walking is more efficient than crawling in most situations. However, this discovery arises from each particular baby's physical characteristics and experience in a particular context. That this is so may explain why some babies learn to walk earlier and differently than others.

Thelen believed that the principles of DST apply in all realms of development. Like a jazz musician, infants improvise their own personal solutions to problems by selecting and integrating multiple patterns or strands of behaviour (Spencer et al., 2006).

dynamic systems theory (DST)
Thelen's theory, which holds that motor development is a dynamic process of active coordination of multiple systems within the infant in relation to the environment

Cultural Influences on Motor Development

Dynamic systems theory includes an emphasis on the context in which development occurs. Thus, although motor development follows a virtually universal sequence, its pace does respond to certain cultural factors. When children are well fed and well cared for and have physical freedom and the chance to explore their surroundings, their motor development is likely to be normal. However, what is normal in one culture may not be in another.

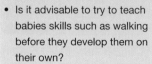

Checkpoint

Can you . . .

✔ Trace a typical infant's progress in head control, hand control, and locomotion, according to the Denver norms?

✔ Discuss how maturation, perception, environmental influence, cultural influences and training relate to early motor development?

What's your view

• Is it advisable to try to teach babies skills such as walking before they develop them on their own?

African babies tend to be more advanced than U.S. and European infants in sitting, walking, and running. In Uganda, for example, babies typically walk at 10 months, as compared with 15 months in Canada and 12 months in the United States (Canadian Paediatric Society, 1999; Gardiner et al., 1998; Gardiner & Kosmitzki, 2005). Asian babies tend to develop these skills more slowly. Such differences may in part be related to ethnic differences in temperament (H. Kaplan & Dove, 1987; see Chapter 8) or may reflect a culture's child-rearing practices (Gardiner et al., 1998).

Some cultures actively encourage early development of motor skills. In many African and West Indian cultures with advanced infant motor development, adults use special "handling routines," such as bouncing and stepping exercises, to strengthen babies' muscles (Hopkins & Westra, 1988). In one study, Jamaican infants, whose mothers used such handling routines daily, sat, crawled, and walked earlier than English infants, whose mothers gave them no such special handling (Hopkins & Westra, 1990).

On the other hand, some cultures discourage early motor development. Children of the Ache in eastern Paraguay do not begin to walk until 18 to 20 months of age—about 5 months later than Canadian babies (H. Kaplan & Dove, 1987). Ache mothers pull their babies back to their laps when the infants begin to crawl away. The Ache mothers closely supervise their babies to protect them from the hazards of nomadic life, and also because the women's primary responsibility is child-raising rather than subsistence labour. Yet, as 8- to 10-year-olds, Ache children climb tall trees, chop branches, and play in ways that enhance their motor skills (H. Kaplan & Dove, 1987). Normal development, then, need not follow the same timetable to reach the same destination.

Guidepost 5

How can we enhance babies' chances of survival and health?

Health

Infancy and toddlerhood are risky times of life, though far less so than they used to be. How many babies die during the first year, and why? What can be done to prevent dangerous or debilitating childhood diseases? How can we ensure that infants and toddlers will live, grow, and develop as they should?

Reducing Infant Mortality

Great strides have been made in protecting the lives of new babies, but these advances are not evenly distributed throughout the population.

Trends in Infant Mortality

In recent decades, prospects for surviving the early years of life have improved in all regions of the world. Worldwide, in 2000 about 8 million infants—more than 1 in 20 born alive—died before their first birthday (Population Reference Bureau, 2005; UNICEF, 2002). Of these deaths, nearly half—about 4 million—occurred during the neonatal period, 3 out of 4 of them in the first week of life, and 2 out of 3 in Africa and Southeast Asia (Lawn, Cousens, & Zupon for the Lancet Neonatal Survival Steering Team, 2005). The primary causes of neonatal death worldwide are preterm delivery (28 percent), sepsis or pneumonia (26 percent), and asphyxiation at birth (23 percent) (Bryce, Boschi-Pinto, Shibuya, and the WHO Child Health Epidemiology Reference Group, 2005). Many of these deaths are preventable, resulting from a combination of poverty, poor maternal health and nutrition, infection, and poor medical care (Lawn et al., 2005; UNICEF, 2003).

infant mortality rate Proportion of babies born alive who die within the first year after birth

In Canada, the **infant mortality rate**—the proportion of babies who die within the first year—is the lowest ever. In 1995 there were 7 deaths in the first year for every 1,000 live male births and 6 for every 1,000 live female births, compared with 15 per 1,000 for males and 12 per 1,000 for females in 1975 (Canadian Institute of Child Health [CICH], 2000). By 2004, the infant mortality rate dropped to 5.3 deaths every 1,000 live births (Statistics Canada, 2007). The overall infant mortality rate in Aboriginal communities has been higher than the Canadian average. In 1995, the rate was 15 deaths for every 1,000 live births (CICH, 2000). However, just as with other groups, infant mortality for Aboriginal

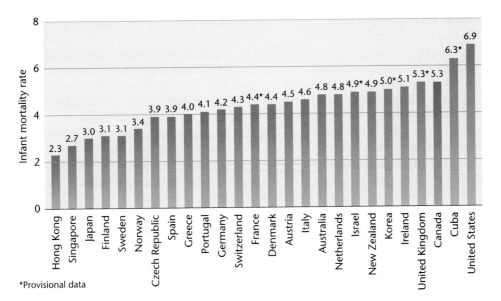

Figure 6-7

Infant mortality rates in industrialized countries, 2003. In recent years most nations, including Canada, have shown dramatic improvement.

Source: Hamilton et al. (2007); Statistics Canada (2007d); United Nations Demographic Yearbook (2003).

*Provisional data

communities is on the decline, with 6.4 infant deaths per 1,000 in the year 2000 (Treasury Board of Canada Secretariat, 2005). Two-thirds of infant deaths take place during the neonatal period (Hoyert, Heron, Murphy, & Kung, 2006; Kochanek & Smith, 2004; Kochanek, Murphy, Anderson, & Scott, 2004). Most likely to die in infancy are babies whose mothers were teenagers, did not finish high school, were unmarried, smoked during pregnancy, had no prenatal care, or had multiple births; and those who were born preterm or of low birth weight (Mathews et al., 2000).

The continuing improvement in infant mortality rates during the 1990s, even at a time when more babies are born perilously small, has been due in part to effective treatment for respiratory distress and to prevention of sudden infant death syndrome (SIDS) (discussed in the next section), as well as to medical advances in keeping very small babies alive and treating sick newborns. Still, in 1997, 1,927 infants died during their first year. Canadian babies, not including Aboriginal infants, have a better chance of reaching their first birthday than babies in many other industrialized countries (see Figure 6-7 above). This comparison, particularly in comparison with the United States, provides an interesting illustration of sociocultural influences on child health. Despite maintaining one of the most technologically advanced medical systems in the world, the United States ranks quite poorly in the world on infant mortality. The higher survival rates of infants in Canada and other industrialized countries compared to the United States may be attributable to free and accessible pre- and postnatal health care (Gardiner et al., 1998).

Perinatal conditions (including low birth weight) were the leading cause of infant deaths in Canada in 1997. Second was birth defects (congenital abnormalities), and third was SIDS; these causes together accounted for 80 percent of all infant deaths. Other significant causes were injury (poisonings and self-inflicted injuries), and nervous system and circulatory problems. SIDS is the greatest cause of death in Aboriginal infants, accounting for 27 percent of total deaths, followed by perinatal conditions (24 percent) and congenital anomalies (19 percent) (CICH, 2000).

For example, there is an increasing prevalence of diabetes in Aboriginal communities in Canada, but the standards of care for this condition among Aboriginal groups do not meet recommended guidelines (Indian and Inuit Health Committee, Canadian Paediatric Society [CPS], 1994). The higher prevalence of high-birth weight babies in Aboriginal communities, compared to non-Aboriginal babies in Canada, might be related to this difficulty (CICH, 2000; CPS, 1994; see Figure 6-8). However, mortality rates in the neonatal period are becoming comparable between

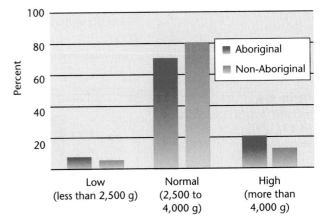

Figure 6-8

Birth weight distribution by ethnic group in Canada (2000–2002). Low–birth weight proportions for Aboriginal refer to off-reserve groups. On-reserve low–birth weight rate is the same as the Canadian Non-Aboriginal average.

Source: Government of Canada (2006).

Aboriginal and non-Aboriginal populations in Canada (CICH, 2000; see Figure 6-9; Treasury Board of Canada Secretariat, 2005).

Although infant mortality has declined for all ethnic groups since 1980, largely as a result of improvements in treatment and care of low–birth weight newborns, disparities have increased—perhaps because such measures have disproportionately benefited infants of European descent (Alexander, Tompkins, Allen, & Hulsey, 2000; CICH, 2000).

Racial or ethnic disparities in access to and quality of health care for minority children (Flores, Olson, & Tomany-Korman, 2005) may help account for differences in mortality, but behavioural factors also may play a part. Obesity, smoking, and alcohol consumption are factors in poor outcomes of pregnancy. Because causes and risk factors for infant mortality vary among ethnic groups, efforts to further reduce infant deaths need to focus on factors specific to each ethnic group (Hesso & Fuentes, 2005).

Sudden Infant Death Syndrome (SIDS)

sudden infant death syndrome
Sudden and unexplained death of an apparently healthy infant

Sudden infant death syndrome (SIDS), sometimes called "crib death," is the sudden death of an infant under 1 year of age in which the cause of death remains unexplained after a thorough investigation that includes an autopsy. In 1998, 154 Canadian babies died as a result of SIDS (CICH, 2000; Public Health Agency of Canada, 2005), making SIDS one of the top three causes of infant death in Canada (Public Health Agency of Canada, 2005).

Although there has been no change in the number of SIDS deaths in Aboriginal populations, there has been a drop in SIDS deaths in the non-Aboriginal population (CICH, 2000).

A number of risk factors, such as being male, and premature or of low birth weight, are associated with SIDS. Often SIDS mothers are young, have received late or no prenatal care, and smoked during pregnancy (Canadian Foundation for the Study of Infant Deaths, the Canadian Institute of Child Health, the Canadian Paediatric Society and Health Canada, 1999, reaffirmed 2000; CICH 2000; USDHHS, 1990). The risk of SIDS may be worsened by poor socio-economic circumstances, but SIDS also strikes infants in advantaged families.

About 20 percent of SIDS deaths occur while the infant is in the care of someone other than the parents (AAP Task Force on Sudden Infant Death Syndrome, 2005), 16.5 percent among infants in child care (Moon, Sprague, & Patel, 2005). Because families who experience one SIDS death often experience another after a later pregnancy, foul play is sometimes suspected. However, the vast majority of these deaths have natural causes (AAP Task Force on Sudden Infant Death Syndrome, 2005). One likely explanation is that women who have experienced a SIDS death tend to have low–birth weight babies, who are especially susceptible to SIDS (Smith, Wood, Pell, & Dobbie, 2005).

It seems likely that SIDS most often results from a combination of factors. An underlying biological defect may make some infants vulnerable during a critical period to certain contributing or triggering experiences, such as prenatal exposure to smoke—an identified risk factor (AAP Task Force on Sudden Infant Death Syndrome, 2005; Canadian Foundation for the Study of Infant Deaths, the Canadian Institute of Child Health, the

Figure 6-9

Neonatal Mortality Rates in Canada, 1979 to 1993

Source: Adapted from CICH, 2000, p. 173.

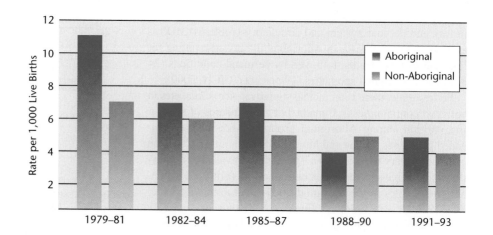

Canadian Paediatric Society and Health Canada, 1999, reaffirmed 2000; Cutz, Perrin, Hackman, & Czegledy-Nagy, 1996; R. P. Ford et al., 1998). The underlying defect may be a delay in maturation of the neural network that is responsible for arousal from sleep in the presence of life-threatening conditions (AAP Task Force on Sudden Infant Death Syndrome, 2005), a disturbance in the brain mechanism that regulates breathing (Tryba, Peña, & Ramirez, 2006), or a genetic factor (Opdal & Rognum, 2004).

At least six gene mutations affecting the heart have been linked to SIDS cases (Ackerman et al., 2001; Cronk et al., 2006; Tester et al., 2006). Nearly 10 percent of victims have mutations or variations in genes associated with irregular heart rhythms (arrhythmias), according to survey of 201 SIDS deaths in a single cohort in Norway (Arnestad et al., 2007; Wang et al., 2007). A gene variant that appears in 1 out of 9 African Americans may help explain the greater incidence of SIDS among babies of African descent (Plant et al., 2006; Weese-Mayer et al., 2004). An elevated level of alpha-fetoprotein in the mother's blood during the second trimester of pregnancy is a predictor of both unexplained stillbirth and SIDS (Smith et al., 2004).

An important clue to what often happens in SIDS has emerged from the discovery of defects in chemical receptors, or nerve endings, in the brain stem, which receive and send messages that regulate breathing, heart beat, body temperature, and arousal. Autopsies of 31 SIDS babies and 10 babies who had died of other causes found that all 31 SIDS babies (but not the other babies) had defects in the brain's ability to use serotonin (Paterson et al., 2006). These defects, which may originate early in fetal life, may prevent SIDS babies from awakening when they are breathing too much stale air containing carbon dioxide trapped under their blankets (Kinney et al., 1995; Panigrahy et al., 2000). This may be especially likely to happen when the baby is sleeping face down. Many SIDS babies may be deficient in a protective mechanism that allows an infant to become aroused enough to turn the head when breathing is restricted (Canadian Foundation for the Study of Infant Deaths, the Canadian Institute of Child Health, the Canadian Paediatric Society and Health Canada, 1999, reaffirmed 2000; Waters, Gonzalez, Jean, Morielli, & Brouillette, 1996). Even in normal, healthy infants, "tummy" sleeping inhibits the swallowing reflex, which protects the airways from choking on an infusion of nasal and digestive fluids (Jeffery, Megevand, & Page, 1999).

Research strongly supports a relationship between SIDS and sleeping on the stomach. Side-sleeping is not safe either, because infants put to bed on their sides often turn onto their stomachs (Canadian Foundation for the Study of Infant Deaths, the Canadian Institute of Child Health, the Canadian Paediatric Society and Health Canada, 1999, reaffirmed 2000; Skadberg, Morild, & Markestad, 1998; J. A. Taylor et al., 1996). SIDS rates fell by as much as 70 percent in some countries following recommendations that healthy babies be put to sleep on their backs.

Sleeping on the back does tend to result in a slight temporary delay in the development of motor skills requiring upper-body strength, such as rolling over, sitting, crawling, and standing. However, these milestones are still attained within the normal age range (Davis, Moon, Sachs, & Ottolini, 1998), and no difference is detectable by 18 months. It is important for infants to have plenty of "tummy time" while awake and supervised, for development of shoulder strength.

Sharing a bed with the mother is a common practice in some cultures; its possible role in preventing or promoting SIDS has been controversial (see Box 6-2).

Doctors recommend that infants *not* sleep on soft surfaces, such as pillows, quilts, or sheepskin, or under loose covers, which, especially when the infant is face down, may increase the risk of overheating or rebreathing (breathing the infant's own exhaled waste products) (AAP Task Force on Sudden Infant Death Syndrome, 2005; see Table 6-3 for a list of the Task Force's recommendations). The risk of SIDS is increased twentyfold when infants sleep in adult beds, sofas, or chairs, or on other surfaces not designed for infants (Scheers, Rutherford, & Kemp, 2003). Studies associate use of pacifiers with lower risk of SIDS (AAP Task Force on Sudden Infant Death Syndrome, 2005; Hauck et al., 2003, 2005; Mitchell, Blair, & L'Hoir, 2006). Contrary to popular reports, studies show no connection between immunizations and SIDS (AAP Task Force on Sudden Infant Death Syndrome, 2005).

Box 6-2 *Sleep Customs*

There is considerable cultural variation in newborns' sleeping arrangements. In many cultures, including many Canadian Aboriginal and immigrant groups, infants sleep in the same room as their mothers for the first few years of life, and frequently in the same bed, making it easier to nurse at night (Broude, 1995). In Canada, many households have a separate bed and a separate room for the infant, reflecting the recommendations of some child-care experts.

Some experts find benefits in the shared sleeping pattern. One research team that has been monitoring sleep patterns of mothers and their 3-month-old infants found that those who sleep together tend to wake each other up during the night and suggested that this may prevent the baby from sleeping too long and too deeply and having long breathing pauses that might be fatal (AAP Task Force on Sudden Infant Death Syndrome, 2005; Baddock, Gallan, Bolton, Williams, & Taylor, 2006; McKenna & Mosko, 1993). However, the American Academy of Pediatrics Task Force on Infant Positioning and SIDS (1997) did not find this evidence persuasive; instead, the Task Force found that, under some conditions, such as the use of soft bedding, or maternal smoking or drug use, bed-sharing can increase the risk of SIDS. Indeed, in a review of medical examiners' investigations of deaths in the St. Louis area between 1994 and 1997, a shared sleep surface was the site of death in nearly half (47.1 percent) of the cases investigated (Kemp et al., 2000). The risk seems to be particularly high when the infant is under 8 to 11 weeks, when more than one person co-sleeps with the baby, or when a bed-sharer has been smoking or drinking alcohol or is overtired (AAP Task Force on Sudden Infant Death Syndrome, 2005). Both the United Kingdom Department of Health and the American Academy of Pediatrics advise that the safest place for an infant to sleep is in a crib in the parents' room for the first 6 months of life (AAP Task Force on Sudden Infant Death Syndrome, 2005).

This is far from a new concern: Medieval church authorities forbade parents to sleep next to their newborns for fear of suffocation (Nakajima & Mayor, 1996). Adult beds are not designed to meet safety standards for infants, as cribs are (Health Canada, 2000). Yet modern-day Japan, where mothers and infants commonly sleep in the same bed, has one of the lowest SIDS rates in the world (Hoffman & Hillman, 1992).

One thing is clear: Bed-sharing promotes breastfeeding. Infants who sleep with their mothers breastfeed about three times longer during the night than infants who sleep in separate beds (McKenna, Mosko, & Richard, 1997). By snuggling up together, mother and baby stay oriented toward each other's subtle bodily signals. Mothers can respond more quickly and easily to an infant's first whimpers of hunger, rather than having to wait until the baby's cries are loud enough to be heard from the next room.

Societal values influence parents' attitudes and behaviours. Throughout this book we will see many ways in which such culturally determined attitudes and behaviours affect children.

What's your view?

In view of preliminary medical evidence that bed-sharing between mother and infant may contribute to SIDS, should mothers from cultures in which sharing a bed is customary be discouraged from doing so?

Check it out!

For more information on this topic, go to **www.mcgrawhill.ca/olc/papalia.**

Death from Injuries

Unintentional injuries are the fourth leading cause of death in infancy in Canada, and the third leading cause of death after the first 4 weeks of life, following SIDS and birth defects (Anderson & Smith, 2005). In 1997, 3 percent of infant deaths in the general Canadian

Table 6-3	Physicians' Recommendations to Prevent SIDS

1. Place infants to sleep on their back (not tummy or side).
2. Use a firm sleep surface.
3. Keep soft objects and loose bedding out of the crib.
4. Do not smoke during pregnancy, and avoid exposing infant to second-hand smoke.
5. Let the infant sleep in his or her own bed, near the mother.
6. Consider offering a pacifier at nap time and bedtime during the first year of life. For breastfed infants, delay introducing the pacifier until 1 month, so that breastfeeding is firmly established.
7. Avoid overheating and overboundling. Infant should be clothed lightly, and room temperature should be comfortable for an adult.
8. Avoid commercial devices that claim to reduce the risk of SIDS. These have not been tested for efficacy or safety.
9. Do not use home monitors to reduce the risk of SIDS; there is no evidence for their effectiveness.
10. Encourage tummy time when the infant is awake and someone is watching.

Source: AAP Task Force on Sudden Infant Death Syndrome (2005).

Box 6-3 *Shaken Baby Syndrome*

The scenario is all too common. A baby, usually 6 weeks to 4 months old, is brought to the emergency room by a parent or caregiver. The infant may show symptoms ranging from lethargy, irritability, breathing problems, tremors, or vomiting and pale or bluish skin to seizures, convulsions, stupor, or coma and may be unable to suck or swallow, make sounds, or follow an object with his or her eyes. However, there is no visible sign of injury, and the parent or caregiver denies knowledge of what caused the condition or claims that the child fell. Closer examination may or may not reveal bruises indicative of abuse, but radiological studies (a CT scan, possibly followed by an MRI) find hemorrhaging of the brain or retina—a result of the infant's having been violently shaken, dropped, or thrown (AAP Committee on Child Abuse and Neglect, 2001; Dowshen, Crowley, & Palusci, 2004; National Center on Shaken Baby Syndrome, 2000; National Institute of Neurological Disorders and Stroke [NINDS], 2006).

Shaken baby syndrome (SBS) is a form of maltreatment, found mainly in children under 2 years and especially in infants. Because a baby has weak neck muscles and a large, heavy head, shaking makes the fragile brain bounce back and forth inside the skull. This causes bruising, bleeding, and swelling and can lead to permanent, severe brain damage, paralysis, or death (AAP, 2001; NINDS, 2006). The damage is even worse when the baby is thrown against a wall or into bed. Head trauma is the leading cause of death in child abuse cases in the United States (Dowshen et al., 2004). The vast majority of these deaths are of babies cared for at home (Wrigley & Dreby, 2005). About 60 percent of the victims are boys, and an estimated 65 to 90 percent of the perpetrators are males—usually either the father or the mother's boyfriend (Dowshen et al., 2004).

Because the milder symptoms of SBS may be mistaken for those of infant colic, feeding problems, or fussiness, the condition is frequently misdiagnosed and underreported (AAP Committee on Child Abuse and Neglect, 2001; King, MacKay, Sirnick, & The Canadian Shaken Baby Study Group, 2003). Incidence estimates range from 600 to 1,400 cases each year in the United States alone. Often these children have suffered previous abuse. About 20 percent die within a few days of being shaken. Survivors may be left with a range of disabilities, from learning and behavioural disorders to neurological injuries, retardation, paralysis, or blindness, or in a permanent vegetative state (King et al., 2003; National Center on Shaken Baby Syndrome, 2000; NINDS, 2006).

Often, victims are difficult to identify, or not provided with medical care (Ward & Bennett, 2003). A 10-year review of 364 cases of shaken baby syndrome in 11 Canadian centres found that 40 percent of victims had no sign of external injury, and 19 percent of the children in the study died. Of the surviving children, 78 percent had continuing health or developmental impairment at the time of their discharge from hospital (King, MacKay, Sirnick, with the Canadian Shaken Baby Study Group, 2003). In another study only 45 percent of cases investigated for shaken baby syndrome were thought to require medical attention (Trocmé, MacMillan, Fallon, & De Marco, 2003).

Why would an adult bring such harm upon a helpless baby? A caregiver who is frustrated or angered by an infant's crying, and who is unable to handle stress or has unrealistic expectations for infant behaviour, may lose control and shake a crying baby in a desperate attempt to quiet the child. If the injured infant becomes drowsy or loses consciousness, the caregiver may think the shaking "worked" and may do it again when the crying resumes. Or the caregiver may put an unconscious baby to bed, hoping the infant will recover, thus missing the opportunity for immediate treatment (AAP Committee on Child Abuse and Neglect, 2001; National Center on Shaken Baby Syndrome, 2000), which could save the child's life (AAP, 2000).

Adults need to know that a baby's crying is normal and is not a reflection on their caregiving skills, that shaking is *never* "okay," and that help is available. (One resource is the National Center on Shaken Baby Syndrome, 888-273-0071.) Parents also need to know that age-appropriate physical play with a baby is *not* injurious (Dowshen et al., 2004; National Center on Shaken Baby Syndrome, 2000).

What's your view?

Have you ever cared for a baby that seemingly would not stop crying? If so, what did you do?

Check it out!

For more information on Shaken Baby Syndrome, go to **http://kidshealth.org/PageManager.jsp?dn=KidsHealth& lic=1&article_set=2178&cat_id=135.** This is the Web site of KidsHealth, an educational site sponsored by the Nemours Foundation. Here you will find a detailed, physician-reviewed article on causes, effects, symptoms, diagnosis, and prognosis of Shaken Baby Syndrome. See also **www.mcgrawhill.ca/olc/papalia.**

population were caused by injury (CICH, 2000), most commonly transport injuries (Public Health Agency of Canada, 2005).

In a 3-year study of injury deaths of infants, based on Canadian national data collected between 1994 and 1997, the greatest cause of injury death was surgery, accounting for 11 deaths per 100,000, followed by falls, at 9 per 100,000 deaths (CICH, 2000). Among the rest, the leading causes of death were from intentional injuries (we discuss child abuse and related fatalities in Chapter 9; see Box 6-3) medical misadventure, being struck, and drug side effects. In Aboriginal communities, 7 percent of infant deaths between 1989 and 1993 resulted from injury (CICH, 2000). Many accidental injuries occur at home. In a study of 990 infants brought to emergency rooms in Kingston, Ontario, by far the most injuries were caused by falls (61.1 percent), followed by ingesting harmful substances (6.6 percent), and then by burns (5.7 percent) (Pickett, Streight, Simpson, & Brison, 2003).

Immunization for Better Health

Such once-familiar and sometimes fatal childhood illnesses as measles, pertussis (whooping cough), and infantile paralysis (polio) are now largely preventable, thanks to the development of vaccines that mobilize the body's natural defences. Unfortunately, many children still are inadequately protected.

Worldwide, an estimated 2 million child deaths were prevented by vaccinations in 2003. During 2002, nearly 2 million (76 percent) of the 2.5 million vaccine-preventable deaths among children less than 5 years old were in Africa and southeast Asia. An estimated 70 to 78 percent of children ages 12 to 23 months worldwide had full routine vaccination coverage between 1990 and 2004. At least 90 percent of European, Western Pacific, and North American children were fully covered, as compared with only 69 percent of southeast Asian children and 66 percent of African children. A Global Immunization Vision Strategy for 2006–2015 seeks to extend routine vaccinations to every eligible person (Department of Immunization, Vaccines, and Biologicals, WHO; United Nations Children's Fund; Global Immunization Division, National Center for Immunization and Respiratory Diseases; & McMorrow, 2006).

Since the development of the Canadian Immunization Guide (Health Canada, 1998), vaccination rates have jumped and the prevalence of vaccine-preventable illnesses has dropped sharply. By 1997, immunization rates for 19- to 35-month-olds had reached 87 percent. Still, many children lack one or more of the recommended shots, and there is substantial variation in coverage (National Advisory Committee on Immunization, 2006; Paterson, Neimanis, Goebel, & Kraftcheck, 2004).

One reason some parents hesitate to immunize their children because of speculation that certain vaccines—particularly the diphtheria-pertussis-tetanus (DPT) and measles-mumps-rubella (MMR) vaccines—may cause autism or other neurodevelopmental disorders, but the preponderance of evidence suggests no reason for this concern (see Box 6-1). Some parents worry that infants receive too many vaccines for their immune system to handle safely. (Today's children routinely receive 11 vaccines and as many as 20 shots by age 2.) Actually, the opposite is true. Multiple vaccines fortify the immune system against a variety of bacteria and viruses and reduce related infections (Offit et al., 2002).

<aside>

What's your view ?

- Who should be primarily responsible for ensuring that children are immunized: parents, community agencies, or government?

Checkpoint

Can you . . .

✔ Summarize trends in infant mortality?

✔ Discuss risk factors, causes, and prevention of sudden infant death syndrome and shaken baby syndrome?

✔ Explain why full immunization of all infants and preschoolers is important?

</aside>

Summary and Key Terms

Growth and Nutrition

Guidepost 1 How do babies grow, and how and what should babies be fed?

- Normal physical growth and sensory and motor development proceed according to the cephalocaudal and proximodistal principles.

- A child's body grows most dramatically during the first year of life; growth proceeds at a rapid but diminishing rate throughout the first 3 years.

- Historic shifts in feeding practices reflected efforts to improve infant survival and health.

- Breastfeeding offers many health advantages and sensory and cognitive benefits. However, the quality of the relationship between parents and infant may be more important than the feeding method.

- Babies should not start solid foods and fruit juices until 6 months of age and should not get cow's milk until 1 year.

- Obese babies are *not* at special risk of becoming obese adults, unless they have obese parents.

The Brain and Reflex Behaviour

Guidepost 2 How does the brain develop, and how do environmental factors affect its early growth?

- The central nervous system controls sensorimotor functioning. Brain growth spurts coincide with changes in cognitive behaviour. Lateralization enables each hemisphere of the brain to specialize in different functions.

- The brain grows most rapidly during the months before and immediately after birth as neurons migrate to their assigned locations, form synaptic connections, and undergo integration and differentiation. Cell death and myelination improve the efficiency of the nervous system.

- Reflex behaviours—primitive, locomotor, and postural—are indications of neurological status. Most early reflexes drop out during the first year as voluntary, cortical control develops.

- Especially during the early period of rapid growth, environmental experience can influence brain development positively or negatively.

  central nervous system (136)   brain growth spurts (136) lateralization (137)   neurons (138)   integration (139) differentiation (139)   cell death (139)   autism (140) myelination (140)   reflex behaviours (141)   plasticity (144)

Early Sensory Capacities

Guidepost 3 How do the senses develop during infancy?

- Sensory capacities, present from birth and even in the womb, develop rapidly in the first months of life. Very young infants can discriminate between stimuli.

- Touch seems to be the first sense to develop and mature. Newborns are sensitive to pain. Smell, taste, and hearing also begin to develop in the uterus.

- Vision is the least developed sense at birth but sharpens within the first 6 months.

Motor Development

Guidepost 4 What are some early milestones in motor development, and what are some influences on it?

- Motor skills develop in a certain sequence, which may depend largely on maturation but also on context, experience, and motivation. Simple skills combine into increasingly complex systems. The Denver Developmental Screening Test assesses gross and fine motor skills as well as linguistic, personality, and social development.

- Depth perception is present at a very early age and is related to motor development.

- Environmental factors, including cultural practices, may affect the pace of early motor development.

- According to Gibson's ecological theory, sensory perception and motor activity are coordinated from birth, helping infants figure out how to navigate in their environment.

- Thelen's dynamic systems theory holds that infants develop motor skills, not by maturation alone, but by active coordination of multiple systems of action within a changing environment.

- Environmental factors, including cultural practices, may affect the pace of early motor development.

  systems of action (148)   Denver Developmental Screening Test (148)   gross motor skills (148)   fine motor skills (148) visual guidance (149)   depth perception (150) haptic perception (150)   visual cliff (150) ecological theory of perception (150)   affordance (150) dynamic systems theory (DST) (151)

Health

Guidepost 5 How can we enhance babies' chances of survival and health?

- Although infant mortality has diminished, it is still disturbingly high for Aboriginal babies. Perinatal conditions and birth defects are the leading causes of death in the first year; for Aboriginal infants, SIDS is the leading cause.

- Sudden infant death syndrome (SIDS) is the third leading cause of death in infants in Canada. Major risk factors are exposure to smoke and sleeping in the prone position.

- Injuries are the fourth leading cause of death.

- Vaccine-preventable diseases have declined as rates of immunization have improved, but many preschoolers are not fully protected.

  infant mortality rate (152)   sudden infant death syndrome (SIDS) (154)

CHAPTER SEVEN

Cognitive Development During the First Three Years

So runs my dream: but what am I?
An infant crying in the night:
An infant crying for the light,
And with no language but a cry.

—Alfred, Lord Tennyson, *In Memoriam,* Canto 54, 1850

Focus *William Erasmus Darwin, Naturalist's Son*

Charles and
"Doddy" Darwin

On December 27, 1839, when the naturalist Charles Darwin was 30 years old, his first baby, William Erasmus Darwin, affectionately known as Doddy, was born. That day— 20 years before the publication of Charles Darwin's *Origin of Species*, which outlined his theory of evolution based on natural selection—the proud father began keeping a diary of observations of his newborn son. It was these notes, published in 1877,* that first called scientific attention to the developmental nature of infant behaviour.

What abilities are babies born with? How do they learn about their world? How do they communicate, first non-verbally and then through language? These were among the questions Darwin set out to answer—questions still central to the study of cognitive development.

Darwin's keen observation illuminates how coordination of physical and mental activity helps an infant adapt to the world— as in this entry written when Doddy was 4 months old:

> Took my finger to his mouth & as usual could not get it in, on account of his own hand being in the way; then he slipped his own back & so got my finger in.—This was not chance & therefore a kind of reasoning. (Diary, p. 12; quoted in Keegan & Gruber, 1985, p. 135)

In Darwin's notes, we can see Doddy developing new cognitive skills through interaction not only with his father's finger, but with other objects as well. The diary depicts a series of encounters with reflected images. In these episodes Doddy gains knowledge, not in sudden bursts or jumps, but through gradual integration of new experience with existing patterns of behaviour. In Darwin's view—as, later, in Piaget's—this was not merely a matter of piling new knowledge upon old; it involved an actual transformation of the way the mind is organized.

When Doddy, at 4½ months, saw his likeness and his father's in a mirror, Darwin noted that the baby "seemed surprised at my voice coming from behind him, my image being in front" (Diary, p. 18; quoted in Keegan & Gruber, 1985, p. 135). Two months later, Doddy apparently had solved the mystery: Now, when his father, standing behind him, made a funny face in the mirror, the infant "was aware that the image . . . was not real & therefore . . . turned round to look" (Diary, pp. 21–22; quoted in Keegan & Gruber, 1985, pp. 135–136).

At first, this newfound understanding did not generalize to other reflective materials. Two weeks later, Doddy seemed puzzled to see his father's reflection in a window. By 9 months, however, the boy realized that "the shadow of a hand, made by a candle, was to be looked for behind, in [the] same manner as in [a] looking glass" (Diary, p. 23; quoted in Keegan & Gruber, 1985, p. 136). His recognition that reflections could emanate from objects behind him now extended to shadows, another kind of two-dimensional image.

Darwin was particularly interested in documenting his son's progress in communication. He believed that language acquisition is a natural process, akin to earlier physical expressions of feelings. Through smiling, crying, laughing, facial expressions, and sounds of pleasure or pain, Doddy managed to communicate quite well with his parents even before uttering his first word. One of his first meaningful verbal expressions was "Ah!"— uttered when he recognized an image in a glass.

● ● ●

Darwin made these observations more than 160 years ago, at a time when infants' cognitive abilities were widely underestimated. We now know—as Darwin inferred from his observations of Doddy—that normal, healthy infants are born with the ability to learn and remember and with a capacity for acquiring and using speech. They use their growing sensory and cognitive capacities to exert control over their behaviour and their world.

In this chapter we look at infants' and toddlers' cognitive abilities from three classic perspectives—behaviourist, psychometric, and Piagetian—and then from three newer perspectives: information processing, cognitive neuroscientific, and social-contextual. We trace the early development of language and discuss how it comes about. Finally, we see how adults help infants and toddlers become more competent with language.

After you have read and studied this chapter, you should be able to answer each of the Guidepost questions that appear at the top of the next page. Look for them again in the margins, where they point to important concepts throughout the chapter. To check your understanding of these Guideposts, review the end-of-chapter summary. Checkpoints located throughout the chapter will help you verify your understanding of what you have read.

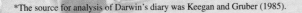

*The source for analysis of Darwin's diary was Keegan and Gruber (1985).

Guideposts for Study

1. What are six approaches to the study of cognitive development?

2. How do infants learn, and how long can they remember?

3. Can infants' and toddlers' intelligence be measured, and how can it be improved?

4. How did Piaget describe early cognitive development, and how have his claims stood up?

5. How can we measure infants' ability to process information, and when do babies begin to think about characteristics of the physical world?

6. What can brain research reveal about the development of cognitive skills?

7. How does social interaction with adults advance cognitive competence?

8. How do babies develop language, and what influences linguistic progress?

Guidepost 1

What are six approaches to the study of cognitive development?

behaviourist approach
Approach to the study of cognitive development that is concerned with basic mechanics of learning

psychometric approach
Approach to the study of cognitive development that seeks to measure the quantity of intelligence a person possesses

Piagetian approach Approach to the study of cognitive development that describes qualitative stages in cognitive functioning

Checkpoint

Can you . . .

✔ Compare six important approaches to the study of cognitive development and identify their goals?

Studying Cognitive Development: Six Approaches

How and when do babies learn to solve problems? How and when does memory develop? What accounts for individual differences in cognitive abilities? Can we measure a baby's intelligence? Can we predict how smart that baby will be in the future? Many investigators have taken one of three classic approaches to the study of such questions:

- The **behaviourist approach** studies the basic *mechanics* of learning. It is concerned with how behaviour changes in response to experience.
- The **psychometric approach** seeks to measure individual differences in *quantity* of intelligence by using intelligence tests. The higher a child scores, the more intelligent she or he is presumed to be.
- The **Piagetian approach** looks at changes, or stages, in the *quality* of cognitive functioning. It is concerned with how the mind structures its activities and adapts to the environment.

During the past few decades, researchers have turned to three newer approaches to add to our knowledge about cognitive development:

- The **information-processing approach** focuses on the processes involved in perception, learning, memory, and problem solving. It seeks to discover what children do with information from the time they encounter it until they use it.
- The **cognitive neuroscience approach** examines the "hardware" of the central nervous system. It seeks to identify what brain structures are involved in specific aspects of cognition.
- The **social-contextual approach** examines the impact of environmental aspects of the learning process, particularly the role of parents and other caregivers.

All six of these approaches help us understand how cognition develops.

Behaviourist Approach: Basic Mechanics of Learning

Babies are born with the ability to learn from what they see, hear, smell, taste, and touch, and they have at least some ability to remember what they learn. Of course, maturation is essential to this process. But while learning theorists recognize maturation as a limiting factor, their main interest is in mechanisms of learning. Because behaviourists do not focus on developmental change, we will discuss this theory here but not in subsequent chapters.

Let's look first at two simple learning processes (introduced in Chapter 2) that behaviourists study: *classical conditioning* and *operant conditioning*. Later we will consider *habituation*, another simple form of learning, which information-processing researchers study.

Classical and Operant Conditioning

Eager to capture Anna's memorable moments on film, her father took pictures of the infant smiling, crawling, and showing off her other achievements. Whenever the flash went off, Anna blinked. One evening when Anna was 11 months old, she saw her father hold the camera up to his eye—and she blinked *before* the flash. She had learned to associate the camera with the bright light, so that the sight of the camera alone activated her blinking reflex.

Anna's blinking (see Figure 7-1) is an example of **classical conditioning,** in which a person learns to make a reflex or involuntary response (in this case, blinking) to a stimulus (the camera) that originally did not provoke the response. Classical conditioning enables infants to anticipate an event before it happens by forming associations between stimuli (such as the camera and the flash) that regularly occur together. Classically conditioned learning will fade, or become *extinct,* if it is not reinforced. Thus, if Anna frequently saw the camera without the flash, she eventually would stop blinking.

In classical conditioning, the learner is passive, absorbing and automatically reacting to stimuli. By contrast, in **operant conditioning**—as when a baby learns that smiling brings loving attention—the learner acts, or operates, on the environment. The infant learns to make a certain response to an environmental stimulus (smiling at sight of the parents) in order to produce a particular effect (parental attention). Researchers often use operant conditioning to study other phenomena, such as memory.

Infant Memory

Can you remember anything that happened to you before you were 2 years old? The chances are you can't. This inability to remember early events is called *infantile amnesia.* One explanation, supported by Piaget (1969) and others, is that early events are not stored in memory because

information-processing approach Approach to the study of cognitive development by observing and analyzing the mental processes involved in perceiving and handling information

cognitive neuroscience approach Approach to the study of cognitive development that links brain processes with cognitive ones

social-contextual approach Approach to the study of cognitive development focusing on environmental influences, particularly of parents and other caregivers

classical conditioning Learning based on associating a stimulus that does not ordinarily elicit a particular response with another stimulus that ordinarily does elicit the response

operant conditioning Learning based on reinforcement or punishment

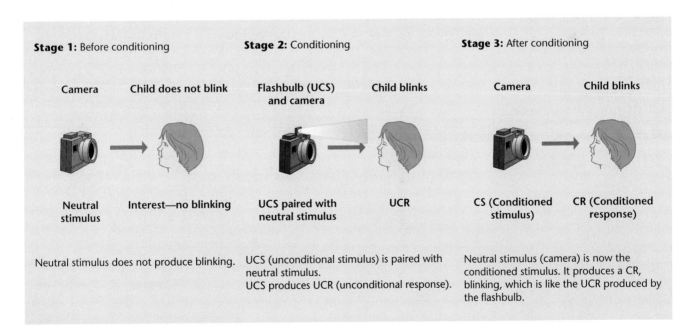

Stage 1: Before conditioning

Camera   Child does not blink

Neutral stimulus   Interest—no blinking

Neutral stimulus does not produce blinking.

Stage 2: Conditioning

Flashbulb (UCS) and camera   Child blinks

UCS paired with neutral stimulus   UCR

UCS (unconditional stimulus) is paired with neutral stimulus.
UCS produces UCR (unconditional response).

Stage 3: After conditioning

Camera   Child blinks

CS (Conditioned stimulus)   CR (Conditioned response)

Neutral stimulus (camera) is now the conditioned stimulus. It produces a CR, blinking, which is like the UCR produced by the flashbulb.

Figure 7-1

Three steps in classical conditioning.

Babies 2 to 6 months old can remember, after a hiatus of 2 days to 2 weeks, that they were able to activate a mobile by kicking; they show this by kicking as soon as they see the mobile.

the brain is not yet developed enough. Freud, by contrast, believed that early memories are stored but are repressed because they are emotionally troubling. Other researchers suggest that children cannot store events in memory until they can talk about them (Nelson, 1992).

Now, research using operant conditioning with non-verbal, age-appropriate tasks suggests that infants' memory processes may not be fundamentally different from those of older children and adults except that infants' retention time is shorter. These studies have found that babies will repeat an action days or weeks later—if they are periodically reminded of the situation in which they learned it (Rovee-Collier, 1999).

In a series of experiments by Carolyn Rovee-Collier and her associates, infants have been operantly conditioned to kick to activate a mobile attached to one ankle by a ribbon. Babies 2 to 6 months old, when again shown the mobiles days or weeks later, repeat the kicking, even though their legs are no longer attached to the mobiles. When the infants see the mobiles, they kick more than before the conditioning, showing that recognition of the mobiles triggers a memory of their initial experience with them (Rovee-Collier, 1996, 1999). In a similar task designed for older infants and toddlers, the child is conditioned to press a lever to make a miniature train go around a track. The length of time a conditioned response can be retained increases with age, from 2 days for 2-month-olds to 13 weeks for 18-month-olds (Hartshorn et al., 1998; Rovee-Collier, 1996, 1999; see Figure 7-2).

Young infants' memory of a behaviour seems to be specifically linked to the original cue. Two- to 6-month-olds will repeat a learned behaviour only when they see the original mobile or train. However, older infants, between 9 and 12 months, will "try out" the behaviour on a different train, if no more than 2 weeks have gone by since the training (Rovee-Collier, 1999).

Context can affect recollection when a memory has weakened. Three-, 9-, and 12-month-olds can initially recognize the mobile or train in a setting different from the one in which they were trained, but not after long delays. Periodic non-verbal reminders through brief exposure to the original stimulus can sustain a memory from early infancy through 1½ to 2 years of age (Rovee-Collier, 1999).

At least one prominent memory researcher disputes the claim that such conditioned memories are qualitatively the same as the memories of older children and adults. From an evolutionary developmental perspective, abilities develop as they can fulfill useful functions in adapting to the environment. The early procedural and perceptual knowledge demonstrated by infants kicking a mobile is not the same as an older child's or adult's explicit memory of specific events. Infancy is a time of great change, and retention of specific experiences is unlikely to be useful for long. This may be one reason that adults do not remember events that occurred when they were infants (Nelson, 2005). Later in this chapter we will discuss brain research that sheds more light on the development of memory in infancy.

Checkpoint ✔

Can you . . .

✔ Give examples of classical and operant conditioning in infants?

✔ Summarize what studies of operant conditioning have shown about infant memory?

Figure 7-2

Maximum number of weeks that infants of varying ages show retention of how to operate either a mobile or a miniature train. Regardless of the task, retention improves with age.

Source: Rovee-Collier, 1999, Fig. 4, p. 83.

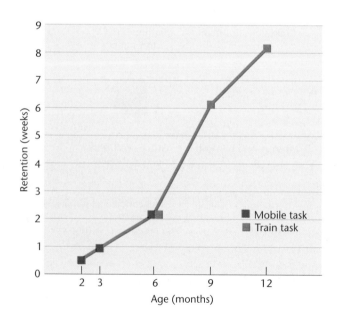

Psychometric Approach: Developmental and Intelligence Testing

When Doddy Darwin, at 4 months, figured out how to get his father's finger into his mouth by moving his own hand out of the way, he showed **intelligent behaviour.** Although there is no scientific consensus on how to define intelligence (Sternberg et al., 2005), most professionals agree that intelligent behaviour is *goal-oriented* and *adaptive:* directed at adjusting to the circumstances and conditions of life. Intelligence enables people to acquire, remember, and use knowledge; to understand concepts and relationships; and to solve problems.

The precise nature of intelligence has been debated for many years, and so has the best way to measure it. The modern intelligence testing movement began in the early twentieth century, when school administrators in Paris asked the psychologist Alfred Binet to devise a way to identify children who could not handle academic work and needed special instruction. The test that Binet and his colleague Theodore Simon developed was the forerunner of psychometric tests that score intelligence by numbers.

Although American tests, like the Stanford-Binet and the WPPSI–III, are used in Canada, their use for Canadian children may not be appropriate. The test norms used to compare individual children's performance do not reflect the make-up of the Canadian population (French, French, & Rutherford, 1999), and the tests could be biased against some ethnic groups in Canada. This bias, which results in systematic differences in scores in groups for which the tests were not originally developed can occur when test items are not well translated (for children with different first languages), when items can mean different things to children from different cultural goups, when the content of questions are not familiar to or are inappropriate for cultural minority children, and when cultural minorities are not included in the standardization groups for the tests (Van de Vijver & Tanzer, 2004).

New Canadians and Aboriginal children could obtain lower scores than they would have achieved if the tests were appropriate to their language backgrounds, cultural experiences, and upbringing (Dolan, 1999; Saklofske & Schwean, 1995; Riddell, 2007). Newer editions, like the Weschler Intelligence Scale for Children–IV, are distributed in Canada with Canadian-based norms (Wechsler, 1996).

The goals of psychometric testing are to quantitatively measure the factors that are thought to make up intelligence (such as comprehension and reasoning), and, from the results of that measurement, to predict future performance (such as school achievement). **IQ (intelligence quotient) tests** consist of questions or tasks that are supposed to show how much of the measured abilities a person has, by comparing that person's performance with that of other test-takers.

For school-age children, as we discuss in Chapter 13, intelligence test scores can predict school performance fairly accurately and reliably. Testing infants and toddlers is another matter.

Testing Infants and Toddlers

Measuring infants' intelligence is virtually impossible, but it is possible to test their cognitive development. Since babies cannot tell us what they know and how they think, the most obvious way to gauge their intelligence is by assessing what they can do. But if they do not grasp a rattle, it is hard to tell whether they do not know how, do not feel like doing it, do not realize what is expected of them, or have simply lost interest.

The **Bayley Scales of Infant Development** (Bayley, 2005) are designed to assess the developmental status of children from 1 month to 3½ years. The Bayley-III (2005) can indicate a child's strengths and weaknesses in each of five developmental domains— *cognitive, language, motor, social-emotional,* and *adaptive behaviour.* An optional *behaviour rating scale* can be completed by the examiner, in part on the basis of information from the child's caregiver. Separate scores, called *developmental quotients* (DQs), are calculated for each scale. DQs are most useful for early detection of emotional disturbances, learning problems, and sensory, neurological, and environmental deficits and in helping parents and professionals plan for a child's needs.

intelligent behaviour Behaviour that is goal-oriented and adaptive to circumstances and conditions of life

Guidepost 3

Can infants' and toddlers' intelligence be measured, and how can it be improved?

IQ (intelligence quotient) tests Psychometric tests that seek to measure intelligence by comparing a test-taker's performance with standardized norms

Bayley Scales of Infant Development Standardized test of infants' mental and motor development

Assessing the Impact of the Home Environment

Home Observation for Measurement of the Environment (HOME) Instrument to measure the influence of the home environment on children's cognitive growth

Intelligence was once thought to be fixed at birth, but we now know that it is influenced by both inheritance and experience. As discussed in Chapter 6, early brain stimulation is a key to future cognitive development. What characteristics of the early home environment may influence measured intelligence and other measures of cognitive development?

Using the **Home Observation for Measurement of the Environment (HOME)** (R. H. Bradley, 1989; Caldwell & Bradley, 1984), trained observers rate the primary caregiver and rate on a yes-or-no checklist the intellectual stimulation and support observed in a child's home. The version for infants and toddlers (see Table 7-1) lasts about one hour. HOME scores after age 2 are significantly correlated with measures of cognitive development (Totsika & Sylva, 2004).

One important factor in HOME is parental responsiveness. HOME gives credit to the parent of an infant or toddler for caressing or kissing the child during an examiner's visit, to the parent of a preschooler for spontaneously praising the child, and to the parent of an older child for answering the child's questions. A longitudinal study found positive correlations between parents' responsiveness to their 6-month-olds and the children's IQs, achievement test scores, and teacher-rated classroom behaviour through age 13 (Bradley, Corwyn, Burchinal, McAdoo, & Coll, 2001).

HOME also assesses the number of books in the home, the presence of playthings that encourage the development of concepts, and parents' involvement in children's play. High scores on all these factors are fairly reliable in predicting children's IQ. In one study, the single most important factor in predicting high intelligence was the mother's ability to create and structure an environment that fostered learning (Stevens & Bakeman, 1985).

Of course, some HOME items may be less culturally relevant in nonwestern than in western families (Bradley, Corwyn, McAdoo, & Coll, 2001). Also we cannot be sure on the basis of HOME and correlational findings that parental responsiveness or an enriched home environment actually increases a child's intelligence. All we can say is that these factors are associated with high intelligence. Intelligent, well-educated parents may be more likely to

Table 7-1	The Infant-Toddler HOME Inventory (ages 0 to 3)	
Name of Subscale	**Description**	**Example Item**
Emotional and verbal responsivity of the primary caregiver (*items* 1–11)	The communicative and affective interactions between the caregiver and the child	Mother spontaneously vocalizes to the child at least twice during visit
		Mother caresses or kisses child at least once during visit
Avoidance of restriction and punishment (*items* 12–19)	How the adult disciplines the child	Primary caregiver (PC) does not shout at child during visit
		PC does not express overt annoyance with or hostility about the child
Organisation of the physical and temporal environment (*items* 20–25)	How the child's time is organized outside the family house. What the child's personal space looks like	When PC is away, care is provided by one of three regular substitutes
		The child's play environment appears safe and free of hazards
Provision of appropriate play materials (*items* 26–34)	Presence of several types of toys available to the child and appropriate for his/her age	Child has one or more large muscle activity toys or pieces of equipment
		Provides equipment appropriate to age, e.g., infant seat, infant rocker, playpen
Parental involvement with the child (*items* 35–40)	How the adult interacts physically with the child	PC tends to keep child within visual range and look at him/her often
		PC talks to child while doing her work
Opportunities for variety in daily stimulation (*items* 40–45)	The way the child's daily routine is designed to incorporate social meetings with people other than the mother	Father provides some care giving everyday. Family visits or receives visits from relatives approximately once a month

Source: Totsika & Sylva (2004).

provide a positive, stimulating home environment; and since they also pass their genes on to their children, there may be a genetic influence as well. (This is an example of a *passive genotype–environment correlation*, described in Chapter 3.) Adoption studies support a genetic influence (Braungart, Fulker, & Plomin, 1992; Coon, Fulker, DeFries, & Plomin, 1990). However, studies of Romanian orphans adopted by Canadian families indicated that orphans' developmental status, including IQ, improved when placed with Canadian adoptive families, particularly in environments rated high on the HOME scale (Morison & Ellwood, 2000).

Other research has identified seven aspects of the early home environment that enable cognitive and psychosocial development and help prepare children for school. These seven conditions are (1) encouraging exploration of the environment; (2) mentoring in basic cognitive and social skills; (3) celebrating developmental advances; (4) guidance in practising and extending skills; (5) protection from inappropriate disapproval, teasing, and punishment; (6) communicating richly and responsively; and (7) guiding and limiting behaviour. The consistent presence of all seven conditions early in life "are causally linked to many areas of brain functioning and cognitive development" (C. T. Ramey & S. L. Ramey, 2003, p. 4). (Table 7-2 lists specific suggestions for helping babies develop cognitive competence.)

Early Intervention

Children who have had limited learning opportunities and low parental expectations are likely to start kindergarten at least two years behind their peers and are unlikely to catch up without special help. **Early intervention** is an effort to prevent or reduce that gap (C. T. Ramey & S. L. Ramey, 2003).

One of the first home-based intervention programs in Canada was started in B.C. in the 1970s, and subsequently spread throughout Canada (Mitchell, Brynelsen, & Holm, 1988).

In Ontario the *Early Years* report, which makes public policy recommendations about early years support for children, demonstrates how intervention in the first 3 years can influence developmental gains more than at any other time in the lifespan (McCain & Mustard, 1999).

Checkpoint ✔

Can you . . .

✔ Tell why developmental tests are sometimes given to infants and toddlers and describe one such widely used test?

✔ Identify aspects of the home environment that may influence intelligence, and explain why such influence is hard to show?

early intervention Systematic process of providing services to help families meet young children's developmental needs

---

Table 7-2	Fostering Competence

Findings from the Harvard Preschool Project, from studies using the HOME scales, and from neurological studies and other research suggest the following guidelines for fostering infants' and toddlers' cognitive development:

1. In the early months, *provide sensory stimulation,* but avoid overstimulation and distracting noises.

2. As babies grow older, *create an environment that fosters learning*—one that includes books, interesting objects (which do not have to be expensive toys), and a place to play.

3. *Respond to babies' signals*. This establishes a sense of trust that the world is a friendly place and gives babies a sense of control over their lives.

4. *Give babies the power to make changes*, through toys that can be shaken, moulded, or moved. Help a baby discover that turning a doorknob opens a door, flicking a light switch turns on a light, and opening a faucet produces running water for a bath.

5. *Give babies freedom to explore*. Do not confine them regularly during the day in a crib, jump seat, or small room, and keep them only for short periods in a playpen. Baby-proof the environment and let them go!

6. *Talk to babies*. They will not pick up language from listening to the radio or television; they need interaction with adults.

7. In talking to or playing with babies, *enter into whatever they are interested in* at the moment instead of trying to redirect their attention to something else.

8. *Arrange opportunities to learn basic skills*, such as labelling, comparing, and sorting objects (say, by size or colour), putting items in sequence, and observing the consequences of actions.

9. *Applaud new skills, and help babies practise and expand them*. Stay nearby but do not hover.

10. *Read to babies in a warm, caring atmosphere from an early age*. Reading aloud and talking about the stories develop preliteracy skills.

11. *Use punishment sparingly*. Do not punish or ridicule results of normal trial-and-error exploration.

Sources: R. R. Bradley & Caldwell, 1982; R. R. Bradley, Caldwell, & Rock, 1988; R. H. Bradley et al., 1989; C. T. Ramey & Ramey, 1998a, 1998b; S. L. Ramey & Ramey, 1992; Staso, quoted in Blakeslee, 1997; J. H. Stevens & Bakeman, 1985; B. L. White, 1971; B. L. White, Kaban, & Attanucci, 1979.

The Mismatch between Opportunity and Investment

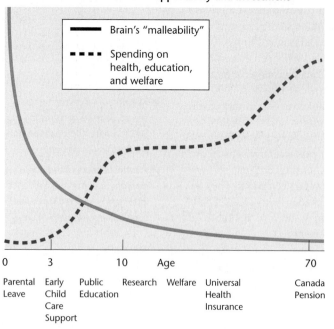

Figure 7-3

The relationship between public expenditures on programs fostering healthy development throughout the life cycle and public expenditures aimed at the critical years of rapid brain development.

Source: Adapted from B. Perry, 2002.

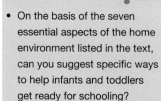

What's your view

• On the basis of the seven essential aspects of the home environment listed in the text, can you suggest specific ways to help infants and toddlers get ready for schooling?

Checkpoint

Can you . . .

✔ Summarize findings about the value of early intervention?

Guidepost 4

How did Piaget describe early cognitive development, and how have his claims stood up?

sensorimotor stage In Piaget's theory, the first stage in cognitive development, during which infants learn through senses and motor activity

In 2001, over half of Canadian children were experiencing some form of child care; about a quarter of whom were in child care centres. This kind of care outside of the home can have beneficial effects in promoting the kinds of skills, like vocabulary, that children need to succeed in school (Dahinten & Willms, 2002). By the time they arrive in Grade 1, they are more ready to learn, and more likely to complete high school than was the case in the past (Ministry of Children and Youth Services, 2005). Nevertheless, as illustrated in Figure 7-3, more public support is needed for programs devoted to learning, behaviour problems, and health for children in the early years to ensure healthy development when brain growth is most rapid.

The program group experienced more growth than the control group in developmental test scores in the first 18 months. By age 3, program children's average IQ was 101, consistent with the general population, but the control children's average IQ was only 84 (C. T. Ramey & S. L. Ramey, 1998).

However, these early gains were not fully maintained. Between the ages of 3 and 8, IQs dropped. Still, scores were higher and more stable among program children than control children, indicating that early intervention can moderate the negative effects of low socio-economic status (Burchinal, Campbell, Bryant, Wasik, & Ramey, 1997). At age 15, the program children continued to outdo the control children on IQ, on reading and math achievement, and were less likely to repeat a school grade (C. T. Ramey et al., 2000).

These findings suggest that early educational intervention can boost cognitive development. The most effective early interventions are those that (1) start early and continue throughout the preschool years; (2) are highly time-intensive (i.e., occupy more hours in a day, or more days in a week, month, or year); (3) provide direct educational experiences, not just parental training; (4) take a comprehensive approach, including health, family counselling, and social services; and (5) are tailored to individual differences and needs (McCain & Mustard, 1999). Studies using IQ are limited because they assume that intelligence involves abilities that are useful in school. Other perspectives on intelligence, such as Howard Gardner's theory of multiple intelligences, propose that there are other important aspects of intelligent behaviour, such as social skills, creativity, and self-knowledge (Chapter 13). Another perspective, that of Jean Piaget, introduced in Chapter 2, examines universal principles underlying the development of intelligence.

Piagetian Approach: The Sensorimotor Stage

Substages of the Sensorimotor Stage

The first of Piaget's four stages of cognitive development (refer back to Table 2-2 in Chapter 2) is the **sensorimotor stage.** During this stage (birth to approximately age 2), infants learn about themselves and their world—as Doddy Darwin seemed to do—through their developing sensory and motor activity. Babies change from creatures who respond primarily through reflexes and random behaviour into goal-oriented toddlers.

The sensorimotor stage consists of six substages (see Table 7-3), which flow from one to another as a baby's **schemes,** organized patterns of behaviour, become more elaborate. During the first five substages, babies learn to coordinate input from their senses and organize their activities in relation to their environment. During the sixth and last substage, they progress from trial-and-error learning to the use of symbols and concepts to solve simple problems.

Substage	Ages	Description	Behaviour
Use of reflexes	birth to 1 month	Infants exercise their inborn reflexes and gain some control over them. They do not coordinate information from their senses. They do not grasp an object they are looking at.	Dorri begins sucking when her mother's breast is in her mouth.
Primary circular reactions	1 to 4 months	Infants repeat pleasurable behaviours that first occur by chance (such as thumb-sucking). Activities focus on infant's body rather than the effects of the behaviour on the environment. Infants make first acquired adaptations; that is, they suck different objects differently. They begin to coordinate sensory information and grasp objects.	When given a bottle, Jesse, who is usually breastfed, is able to adjust his sucking to the rubber nipple.
Secondary circular reactions	4 to 8 months	Infants become more interested in the environment; they repeat actions that bring interesting results (such as shaking a rattle) and prolong interesting experiences. Actions are intentional but not initially goal-directed.	Benjamin pushes pieces of dry cereal over the edge of his high chair tray one at a time and watches each piece as it falls to the floor.
Coordination of secondary schemes	8 to 12 months	Behaviour is more deliberate and purposeful (intentional) as infants coordinate previously learned schemes (such as looking at and grasping a rattle) and use previously learned behaviours to attain their goals (such as crawling across the room to get a desired toy). They can anticipate events.	Nancy pushes the button on her musical nursery rhyme book and "Twinkle, Twinkle, Little Star" plays. She pushes this button over and over again, choosing it instead of the buttons for the other songs.
Tertiary circular reactions	12 to 18 months	Toddlers show curiosity and experimentation; they purposefully vary their actions to see results (for example, by shaking different rattles to hear their sounds). They actively explore their world to determine what is novel about an object, event, or situation. They try out new activities and use trial and error in solving problems.	When Tony's big sister holds his favourite board book up to his crib bars, he reaches for it. His first efforts to bring the book into his crib fail because the book is too wide. Soon, Tony turns the book sideways and hugs it, delighted with his success.
Mental combinations	18 to 24 months	Since toddlers can mentally represent events, they are no longer confined to trial and error to solve problems. Symbolic thought allows toddlers to begin to think about events and anticipate their consequences without always resorting to action. Toddlers begin to demonstrate insight. They can use symbols, such as gestures and words, and can pretend.	Jenny plays with her shape box, searching carefully for the right hole for each shape before trying—and succeeding.

Note: Infants show enormous cognitive growth during Piaget's sensorimotor stage, as they learn about the world through their senses and their motor activities. Note their progress in problem solving and the coordination of sensory information. All ages are approximate

Much of this early cognitive growth comes about through **circular reactions,** in which an infant learns to reproduce pleasurable or interesting events originally discovered by chance. Initially, an activity produces a sensation so enjoyable that the baby wants to repeat it. The repetition then feeds on itself in a continuous cycle in which cause and effect keep reversing (see Figure 7-4). The originally chance behaviour has been consolidated into a new scheme.

In the *first substage* (birth to about 1 month), as neonates exercise their inborn reflexes, they gain some control over them. They begin to engage in a behaviour even when the stimulus that normally elicits it is not present. For example, newborns suck reflexively when their lips are touched. They soon learn to find the nipple even when they are not touched, and they suck at times when they are not hungry. Thus infants modify and extend the scheme for sucking as they begin to initiate activity.

In the *second substage* (about 1 to 4 months), babies learn to repeat a pleasant bodily sensation first achieved by chance (say, sucking their thumbs, as in the first part of Figure 7-4). Piaget called this a *primary circular reaction.* They begin to turn toward sounds, showing the ability to coordinate different kinds of sensory information (vision and hearing).

The *third substage* (about 4 to 8 months) coincides with a new interest in manipulating objects and learning about their properties. Babies engage in *secondary circular*

schemes Piaget's term for organized patterns of behaviour used in particular situations

circular reactions Piaget's term for processes by which an infant learns to reproduce desired occurrences originally discovered by chance

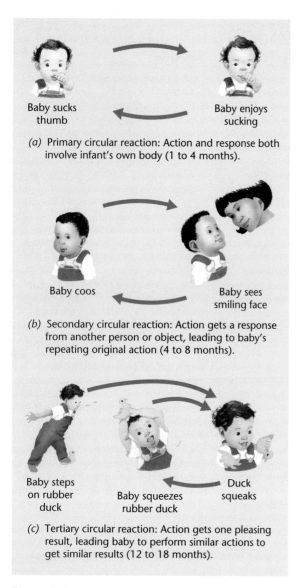

(a) Primary circular reaction: Action and response both involve infant's own body (1 to 4 months).

(b) Secondary circular reaction: Action gets a response from another person or object, leading to baby's repeating original action (4 to 8 months).

(c) Tertiary circular reaction: Action gets one pleasing result, leading baby to perform similar actions to get similar results (12 to 18 months).

Figure 7-4

Primary, secondary, and tertiary circular reactions.

representational ability Piaget's term for capacity to mentally represent objects and experiences, largely through the use of symbols

invisible imitation Imitation with parts of one's body that one cannot see

visible imitation Imitation with parts of one's body that one can see

reactions: intentional actions repeated not merely for their own sake, as in the second substage, but to get results *beyond the infant's own body.* For example, a baby this age will repeatedly shake a rattle to hear its noise, or (as in the second part of Figure 7-4) coo when a friendly face appears, to make the face stay longer.

By the time infants reach the *fourth substage, coordination of secondary schemes* (about 8 to 12 months), they have built on the few schemes they were born with. They have learned to generalize from past experience to solve new problems and to distinguish means from ends. They will crawl to get something they want, grab it, or push away a barrier to it (such as someone else's hand). They try out, modify, and coordinate previous schemes, to find one that works. Thus this substage marks the beginning of complex, goal-directed behaviour.

In the *fifth substage* (about 12 to 18 months), babies begin to experiment with new behaviour to see what will happen. Once they begin to walk, they can more easily explore their environment. They now engage in *tertiary circular reactions, varying* an action to get a similar result, rather than merely *repeating* pleasing behaviour they have accidentally discovered. For example, a toddler may squeeze a rubber duck that squeaked when stepped on, to see whether it will squeak again (as in the third part of Figure 7-4). For the first time, children show originality in problem solving. By trial and error, they try out behaviours until they find the best way to attain a goal.

The *sixth substage, mental combinations* (about 18 months to 2 years) is a transition into the preoperational stage of early childhood. **Representational ability**—the ability to mentally represent objects and actions in memory, largely through symbols such as words, numbers, and mental pictures—blossoms. The ability to manipulate symbols frees children from immediate experience. They can pretend. They can *think* about actions before taking them. They no longer have to go through laborious trial and error to solve problems. Piaget's daughter Lucienne seemed to show representational ability when, in figuring out how to pry open a partially closed matchbox to remove a watch chain, she opened her mouth wider to represent her idea of widening the slit in the box (Piaget, 1936/1952).

During the sensorimotor stage, infants develop certain specific abilities, such as imitation, and knowledge about certain aspects of the physical world; notably, about objects and spatial relationships. Researchers following in Piaget's footsteps have found that some of these developments conform fairly closely to his observations, but others, including representational ability, may occur earlier than Piaget believed possible. (Table 7-4 compares Piaget's views on these and other topics with more recent findings; refer back to this table as you read on.)

Do Imitative Abilities Develop Earlier than Piaget Thought?

Imitation is an important way of learning; it becomes especially valuable toward the end of the first year, as babies try out new skills (Nelson, 2005). Piaget maintained that **invisible imitation**—imitation using parts of the body that a baby cannot see, such as the mouth—develops at about 9 months, after **visible imitation,** the use of hands or feet, for example, which babies can see. Yet in a series of studies by Andrew Meltzoff and M. Keith Moore (1983, 1989), babies less than 72 hours old appeared to imitate adults by opening their mouths and sticking out their tongues—a response that other research has found to disappear by about 2 months of age (Bjorklund & Pellegrini, 2000). According to Meltzoff and Gopnik (1993), this early imitative behaviour reflects an evolved "like me" mechanism; the infant seeks to imitate faces that have the same properties (tongues that can stick out) as his or her own. Meltzoff and Moore (1994) further suggest that infants have an inborn predisposition to

Concept or Skill	Piaget's View	More Recent Findings
Object permanence	Develops gradually between third and sixth substage. Infants in fourth substage (8–12 months) make A, not-B error.	Infants as young as 3½ months (second substage) seem to show object knowledge, though interpretation of findings is in dispute. A, not-B error may persist into second year or longer.
Spatial knowledge	Development of object concept and spatial knowledge is linked to self-locomotion and coordination of visual and motor information.	Research supports Piaget's timetable and relationship of spatial judgments to decline of egocentrism. Link to motor development is less clear.
Causality	Develops slowly between 4 and 12 months, based on infant's discovery, first of effects of own actions and then of effects of outside forces.	Some evidence suggests early awareness of specific causal events in the physical world, but general understanding of causality may be slower to develop.
Number	Depends on use of symbols, which begins in sixth substage (18–24 months).	Infants as young as 5 months may recognize and mentally manipulate small numbers, but interpretation of findings is in dispute.
Categorization	Depends on representational thinking, which develops during sixth substage (18–24 months).	Infants as young as 3 months seem to recognize perceptual categories.
Imitation	Invisible imitation develops around 9 months, deferred imitation after development of mental representations in sixth substage (18–24 months).	Controversial studies have found invisible imitation of facial expressions in newborns and deferred imitation as early as 6 weeks. Deferred imitation of complex activities seems to exist as early as 6 months.

deferred imitation Piaget's term for reproduction of an observed behaviour after the passage of time by calling up a stored symbol of it

elicited imitation Research method in which infants or toddlers are induced to imitate a specific series of actions they have seen but not necessarily done before

> *Checkpoint* ✓
>
> *Can you . . .*
>
> ✔ Summarize major developments during Piaget's sensorimotor stage?
>
> ✔ Explain how primary, secondary, and tertiary circular reactions work?
>
> ✔ Tell why representational ability is important?

imitate human faces—a tendency that may serve the evolutionary purpose of communication with a caregiver (Rakison, 2005). Other researchers have suggested that the tongue thrust may be an early attempt to interact with the mother or simply exploratory behaviour aroused by the sight of an adult tongue (Bjorklund, 1997; S. S. Jones, 1996). In any event, as with some other early capacities, imitation appears to serve a different adaptive purpose for the young infant than for an older infant (Bjorklund & Pellegrini, 2000).

Piaget also held that children under 18 months cannot engage in **deferred imitation** of an act they saw some time before because they have not yet developed the ability to retain mental representations. However, Piaget may have underestimated infants' and toddlers' representational ability because of their limited ability to talk about what they remember. Babies as young as 6 *weeks* have imitated an adult's facial movements after a 24-hour delay, in the presence of the same adult, who this time was expressionless. This suggests that very young babies can retain a mental representation of an event (Meltzoff & Moore, 1994, 1998). Deferred imitation of novel or complex events seems to begin by 6 to 9 months (Meltzoff & Moore, 1998; Bauer, 2002). Thus, the findings on deferred imitation agree with those on operant conditioning (Rovee-Collier, 1999); infants do seem capable of remembering after a delay.

In **elicited imitation,** researchers induce infants and toddlers to imitate a specific series of actions they have seen but not necessarily done before. The initial demonstration may be accompanied by a simple verbal explanation (Bauer, 1996, 2002; Bauer, Wenner, Dropik, & Wewerka, 2000; Bauer, Wiebe, Carver, Waters, & Nelson, 2003). After a one-month delay, with no further demonstration or explanation, more than

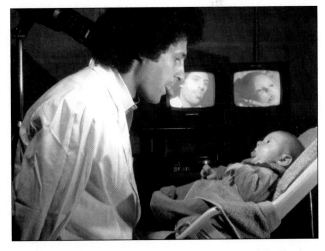

Is this infant imitating the researcher's stuck-out tongue? Studies by Andrew N. Meltzoff suggest that infants as young as 2 weeks are capable of invisible imitation. But other researchers found that only the youngest babies make this response, suggesting that the tongue movement may merely be exploratory behaviour.

40 percent of 9-month-olds can reproduce a simple two-step procedure, such as dropping a toy car down a vertical chute and then pushing the car with a rod to make it roll to the end of a track and turn on a light (Bauer, 2002; Bauer et al., 2003). One study reliably predicted individual differences in performance of this task from scans of the infants' brains as they looked at photos of the same procedure a week after first seeing it. The memory traces of infants who could not repeat the procedure in the right order were less robust, indicating that they had failed to consolidate the memory for long-term storage (Bauer et al., 2003).

Elicited imitation is much more reliable during the second year of life; nearly 8 out of 10 toddlers 13 to 20 months old can repeat an unfamiliar, multistep sequence (such as putting together a metal gong and causing it to ring) as much as a year later (Bauer, 1996; Bauer et al., 2000). Prior practice helps to reactivate children's memories, especially if some new items have been substituted for the original ones (Hayne, Barr, & Herbert, 2003). Four factors seem to determine young children's long-term recall: (1) the number of times a sequence of events has been experienced, (2) whether the child actively participates or merely observes, (3) whether the child is given verbal reminders of the experience, and (4) whether the sequence of events occurs in a logical, causal order (Bauer et al., 2000).

Development of Knowledge about Objects and Space

The ability to perceive the size and shape of objects and to discern their movements may be an early evolved mechanism for avoidance of predators (Rakison, 2005). The *object concept*—the idea that objects have their own independent existence, characteristics, and location in space—is fundamental to an orderly view of physical reality. The object concept is the basis for children's awareness that they themselves exist apart from objects and other people. It is essential to understanding a world full of objects and events. Doddy Darwin's struggle to understand the existence and location of reflective images was part of his development of an object concept.

When Does Object Permanence Develop?

object permanence Piaget's term for the understanding that a person or object still exists when out of sight

One aspect of the object concept is **object permanence,** the realization that an object or person continues to exist when out of sight. This realization allows a child whose parent has left the room to feel secure in the knowledge that the parent still exists and will return. The development of this concept in many cultures can be seen in the game of peekaboo (see Box 7-1).

According to Piaget, object permanence develops gradually during the sensorimotor stage. At first, infants have no such concept. By the third substage, from about 4 to 8 months, they will look for something they have dropped, but if they cannot see it, they act as if it no longer exists. In the fourth substage, about 8 to 12 months, they will look for an object in a place where they first found it after seeing it hidden, even if they later saw it being moved to another place. (Piaget called this the **A, not-B error.**) In the fifth substage, 12 to 18 months, they no longer make this error; they will search for an object in the *last* place they saw it hidden. However, they will *not* search for it in a place where they did not see it hidden. By the sixth substage, 18 to 24 months, object permanence is fully achieved; toddlers will look for an object even if they did not see it hidden.

A, not-B error Tendency, noted by Piaget, for 8- to 12-month-old infants to search for a hidden object in a place where they previously found it, rather than in the place where they most recently saw it being hidden

A study of 48 fourteen-month-olds seems to support the existence of Piaget's fifth substage in the development of object permanence. Even after a 24-hour delay, the babies successfully searched for and found a silver bell in the same place they had seen it hidden. However, when brought to a different or rearranged room, their search was unsuccessful, even if the container in which they had seen the object hidden was still there, and even if the bell itself had been placed on the floor in full view (Moore & Meltzoff, 2004).

A different interpretation of the A, not-B error comes from Esther Thelen's dynamic systems theory (introduced in Chapter 6). The decision where to search for a hidden object, Thelen and her colleagues observed, is not about what babies *know,* but about what they *do,* and why. Infants' reaching behaviour is influenced by multiple processes, including vision, perception, attention, movement, and memory. One factor is how much time has elapsed between the infant's seeing the object hidden in a new place (B) and the infant's reaching for it. If the elapsed time is brief, the infant is more likely to reach for the object

Box 7-1 *Playing Peekaboo*

In rural South Africa, a Bantu mother smiles at her 9-month-old son, covers her eyes with her hands, and asks, *"Uphi?"* (Where?) After 3 seconds, the mother says, "Here!" and uncovers her eyes to the baby's delight. In Tokyo, a Japanese mother plays the same game with her 12-month-old daughter, who shows the same joyous response. In suburban Connecticut, a 15-month-old boy who sees his grandfather for the first time in two months raises his shirt to cover his eyes—as Grandpa did on his previous visit.

Peekaboo is played across diverse cultures, using similar routines (Fernald & O'Neill, 1993). In all cultures in which the game is played,* the moment when the mother or other caregiver reappears is exhilarating. It is marked by exaggerated gestures and voice tones. Infants' pleasure from the immediate sensory stimulation of the game is heightened by their fascination with faces and voices, especially the high-pitched tones the adult usually uses.

The game serves several important purposes. Psychoanalysts say that it helps babies master anxiety when their mother disappears. Cognitive psychologists see it as a way babies play with developing ideas about object permanence. It may also be a social routine that helps babies learn rules that govern conversation, such as taking turns. It may provide practice in paying attention, a prerequisite for learning.

As babies develop the cognitive competency to predict future events, the game takes on new dimensions. Between 3 and 5 months, the baby's smiles and laughter as the adult's face moves in and out of view signal the infant's developing expectation of what will happen next. At 5 to 8 months, the baby shows anticipation by looking and smiling as the adult's voice alerts the infant to the adult's imminent reappearance. By 1 year, babies are no longer merely observers but usually initiate the game, actively engaging adults in play. Now it is the adult who generally responds to the baby's physical or vocal cues, which can become quite insistent if the adult doesn't feel like playing.

To help infants who are learning peekaboo or other games, parents often use *scaffolding* (see Chapter 2). In an 18-month longitudinal study at the University of Montreal, 25 mothers were videotaped playing peekaboo with their babies, using a doll as a prop (Rome-Flanders, Cronk, & Gourde, 1995). The amount and type of scaffolding varied with the infant's age and skill. Mothers frequently tried to attract a 6-month-old's attention to begin the game; this became less and less necessary as time went on. Modelling (performing the peekaboo sequence to encourage a baby to imitate it) also was most frequent at 6 months and decreased significantly by 12 months, when there was an increase in direct verbal instruction ("Cover the doll") as babies became more able to understand spoken language. Indirect verbal instruction ("Where is the doll?"), used to focus attention on the next step in the game, remained constant throughout the entire age range. Reinforcement (showing satisfaction with the infant's performance, for example, by saying "Peekaboo!" when the infant uncovered the doll) was fairly constant from 9 months on. The overall amount of scaffolding dropped substantially at 24 months, by which time most babies have fully mastered the game.

What's your view?

Have you ever played peekaboo periodically with the same infant? If so, did you notice changes with age in the child's participation, as described in this box?

Check it out!

For more information on this topic, go to **www.mcgrawhill.ca/olc/papalia.**

*The cultures included in this report are found in Malaysia, Greece, India, Iran, Russia, Brazil, Indonesia, Korea, and South Africa.

in the new location. When the time interval is longer, however, the perceptual and motor memory of having previously found the object in the old place (A) inclines the infant to search there again, and that inclination grows stronger the more times the object has been found in the same place (Smith & Thelen, 2003; Spencer, Smith, & Thelen, 2001; Spencer et al., 2006).

Other research suggests that Piaget may have underestimated younger infants' grasp of object permanence because of his testing methods. Babies may fail to search for hidden objects because they cannot yet carry out a two-step or two-handed sequence of actions, such as moving a cushion or lifting the cover of a box before grasping the object. When given repeated opportunities, over a period of one to three months, to explore, manipulate, and learn about such a task, infants in the last half of their first year can succeed (Bojczyk & Corbetta, 2004).

When object permanence is tested with a more age-appropriate procedure, in which the object is hidden only by darkness and thus can be retrieved in one motion, infants in the third substage (4 to 8 months) perform surprisingly well. In one study, 6½-month-olds saw a ball drop down a chute and land in one of two spots, each identifiable by a distinctive sound. When the light was turned off and the procedure was repeated, the babies reached for the ball in the appropriate location, guided only by the sound (Goubet & Clifton, 1998). This showed that they knew the ball continued to exist and could tell where it had gone.

Methods based only on infants' looking behaviour eliminate the need for *any* motor activity and thus can be used at very early ages. As we will discuss in the next major section of this chapter, recent, controversial research using information-processing methodology suggests that infants as young as 3 or 4 months old seem not only to have a sense of object permanence but also to understand causality and categorization, to have a rudimentary concept of number, and to know other principles governing the physical world.

What's your view ?

- What comments might Piaget have made about Darwin's diary entries on his son's early cognitive development?

- On the basis of observations by Piaget and the research they inspired, what factors would you consider in designing or purchasing a toy or book for an infant or toddler?

Symbolic Development, Pictorial Competence, and Understanding of Scale

Much of the knowledge people acquire about their world is gained, not through direct observation or experience, but through *symbols,* intentional representations of reality. Learning to interpret symbols is, then, an essential task of childhood. First, however, children must become *symbol-minded:* attentive to symbols and their relationships to the things they represent (DeLoache, 2004). One aspect of symbolic development, studied by Judy DeLoache and her colleagues, is the growth of *pictorial competence,* the ability to understand the nature of pictures (De Loache, Pierroutsakos, & Uttal, 2003).

In studies carried out in both the United States and Africa's Ivory Coast, infants were observed using their hands to explore pictures as if they were objects—feeling, rubbing, patting, or grasping them or attempting to lift a depicted object off the page. This manual exploration of pictures diminishes by 15 months, but not until about 19 months—according to Piaget, the dawn of representational thought—do children show, by pointing at a picture of a bear or telephone while saying its name ("beh" or "teltone"), an understanding that a picture is meant to be a representation, or symbol, of something else (DeLoache et al., 2003; DeLoache, Pierroutsakos, Uttal, Rosengren, & Gottlieb, 1998; Pierroutsakos & DeLoache, 2003).

Although toddlers may spend a good deal of time watching television, they at first seem unaware that what they are seeing is a representation of reality (Troseth, Saylor, & Archer, 2006). In one series of experiments, 2- and 2½-year-olds watched on a video monitor as an adult hid an object in an adjoining room. When taken to the room, the 2½-year-olds found the hidden object easily, but 2-year-olds could not. Yet the younger children did find the object if they had watched through a window as it was being hidden (Troseth & DeLoache, 1998). Apparently, what the 2-year-olds lacked was representational understanding of screen images. In a follow-up experiment, 2-year-olds who were told face to face where to find a hidden toy were able to do so, whereas age-mates who received the same information from a person on video did not (Troseth, Saylor, & Archer, 2006).

Toddlers often make *scale errors*—momentary misperceptions of the relative sizes of symbolic and real objects. In one study, 18- to 36-month-olds were videotaped trying to slide down tiny slides, sit in dollhouse chairs, and squeeze into miniature cars after similar, child-sized objects were removed from their playroom. Such scale errors are clearly distinguishable from pretend play (DeLoache, Uttal, & Rosengren, 2004) and may in part result from lack of impulse control. In addition, the researchers suggested that two different brain systems normally work together during interactions with familiar objects. One system enables the child to recognize and categorize an object ("That's a buggy") and plan what to do with it ("I'm going to lie in it"). A separate system may be involved in perceiving the size of the object and using this information to control actions pertaining to it. Faulty "teamwork" between these immature brain systems is a possible reason for young children's frequent scale errors (DeLoache, 2006).

In one experiment (DeLoache, Uttal, & Rosengren, 2004), toddlers were observed trying to fit into toy cars or slide down miniature slides. Such scale errors may result from lack of impulse control and from lack of coordination between brain systems. One system lets the child recognize an object ("That's a car") and plan what to do with it ("I'm going to sit in it"). A separate system may enable the child to perceive the size of the object and control actions related to it.

According to the **dual representation hypothesis,** it is difficult for toddlers to mentally represent both a symbol (the toy crib or car) and the object it represents at the same time, and so they may confuse the two (DeLoache, 2006; DeLoache et al., 2003). This may be why 2-year-olds tend to have problems interpreting scale models. They can use representational thinking to guide them to the actual location of something shown in a photograph (Suddendorf, 2003), but apparently they think of the model as an object in itself, rather than a representation of something else (DeLoache, 2000).

In one experiment, 2½-year-olds who were told that a "shrinking machine" had shrunk a room to the size of a miniature model were more successful in finding a toy hidden in the room on the basis of its position in the model than were children the same age who were told that the "little room" was just like the "big room." What seems to make the second task harder is that it requires a child to mentally represent both the symbol (the "little room") and its relationship to the thing it stands for (the "big room") at the same time. With the "shrinking machine," children do not have to perform this dual operation, because they are told that the room and the model are one and the same. Three-year-olds do not seem to have this problem with models (DeLoache, Miller, & Rosengren, 1997).

dual representation hypothesis Proposal that children under the age of 3 have difficulty grasping spatial relationships because of the need to keep more than one mental representation in mind at the same time

Evaluating Piaget's Sensorimotor Stage

According to Piaget, the journey from reflex behaviour to the beginnings of thought is a long, slow one. For a year and a half or so, babies learn only from their senses and movements; not until the last half of the second year do they make the breakthrough to conceptual thought. Now, as we have seen, research using simplified tasks and moder tools suggests that certain limitations Piaget saw in infants' early cognitive capabilities, such as object permanence, may instead have reflected immature linguistic and motor skills.

In some ways, then, infants and toddlers seem to be more cognitively competent than Piaget imagined. This does not mean that infants come into the world with minds fully formed. As Piaget observed, immature forms of cognition precede more mature forms. We can see this, for example, in the errors young infants make in searching for hidden objects. However, Piaget may have been mistaken in his emphasis on motor experience as the primary "engine" of cognitive growth. Infants' perceptions are far ahead of their motor abilities, and today's methods enable researchers to make observations and inferences about those perceptions. The relationship between perception and cognition is a major area of investigation, as we will discuss in the next section.

Checkpoint ✔

Can you . . .

✔ Summarize Piaget's views on imitation, object permanence, pictorial competence, and understanding of scale?

✔ Explain why Piaget may have underestimated some of infants' cognitive abilities, and discuss the implications of more recent research?

Information-Processing Approach: Perceptions and Representations

Information-processing research uses new methods to test ideas about cognitive development that sprang from the psychometric and Piagetian approaches. For example, information-processing researchers analyze the separate parts of a complex task, such as Piaget's object search tasks, to figure out what abilities are necessary for each part of the task and at what age these abilities develop. Information-processing researchers also measure, and draw inferences from, what infants pay attention to, and for how long.

Guidepost 5

How can we measure infants' ability to process information, and when do babies begin to think about characteristics of the physical world?

Habituation

At about 6 weeks, Stefan lies peacefully in his crib near a window, sucking a pacifier. It is a cloudy day, but suddenly the sun breaks through, and a shaft of light appears on the end of the crib. Stefan stops sucking for a few moments, staring at the pattern of light and shade. Then he looks away and starts sucking again.

We don't know what was going on in Stefan's mind when he saw the shaft of light, but we can tell by his sucking and looking behaviour at what point he began paying attention and when he stopped. These simple behaviours can be indicators of sensory perception and discrimination and even of future intelligence.

Much information-processing research with infants is based on **habituation,** a type of learning in which repeated or continuous exposure to a stimulus (such as the shaft of light) reduces attention to that stimulus. In other words, familiarity breeds loss of interest.

Researchers study habituation in newborns by repeatedly presenting a stimulus (usually a sound or visual pattern) and then monitoring such responses as heart rate, sucking, eye movements, and brain activity. A baby who has been sucking typically stops when the stimulus is first presented and does not start again until after it has ended. After the same sound or sight has been presented again and again, it loses its novelty and no longer causes the baby to stop sucking. Resumption of uninterrupted sucking shows that the infant has habituated to the stimulus. A new sight or sound, however, will capture the baby's attention and the baby will again stop sucking. This increased response to a new stimulus is called **dishabituation.**

Researchers gauge the efficiency of infants' information processing by measuring how quickly babies habituate to familiar stimuli, how fast their attention recovers when they are exposed to new stimuli, and how much time they spend looking at the new and the old. Efficiency of habituation correlates with later signs of cognitive development, such as a preference for complexity, rapid exploration of the environment, sophisticated play, quick problem solving, and the ability to match pictures. In fact, as we will see, speed of habituation and other information-processing abilities show promise as predictors of intelligence (Bornstein & Sigman, 1986; Colombo, 1993; McCall & Carriger, 1993).

Visual and Auditory Processing Abilities

The amount of time a baby spends looking at different kinds of sights is a measure of **visual preference,** which is based on the ability to make visual distinctions. Babies less than 2 days old prefer curved lines to straight lines, complex patterns to simple patterns, three-dimensional objects to two-dimensional objects, and moving objects to stationary ones—again, possibly an evolved mechanism to enable awareness of predators. Newborns also prefer pictures of faces or facelike configurations to pictures of other things and new sights to familiar ones (Fantz, 1963, 1964, 1965; Fantz, Fagen, & Miranda, 1975; Fantz & Nevis, 1967; Rakison, 2005; Turati, Simion, Milani, & Umilta, 2002). The latter tendency is called *novelty preference.*

Visual recognition memory can be measured by showing an infant two stimuli side by side, one familiar and one novel. A longer gaze at the novel stimulus indicates that the infant recognizes the other stimulus as familiar, as something the infant has seen before. Visual recognition memory depends on comparing incoming information with information the infant already has—in other words, on the ability to form and refer to mental representations (P. R. Zelazo, Kearsley, & Stack, 1995).

Contrary to Piaget's view, habituation and novelty preference studies suggest that at least a rudimentary representational ability exists at birth or very soon after and quickly becomes more efficient. Individual differences in efficiency of information processing reflect the speed with which infants form and refer to such mental images. When shown two sights at the same time, infants who quickly shift attention from one to another tend to have better recognition memory and stronger novelty preference than infants who take longer looks at a single sight (Jankowski, Rose, & Feldman, 2001; Rose, Feldman, & Jankowski, 2001; Stoecker, Colombo, Frick, & Allen, 1998).

Can this baby tell the difference between Raggedy Ann and Raggedy Andy? This researcher may find out by seeing whether the baby has habituated—become used to—one face and then stops sucking on the nipple when a new face appears, showing recognition of the difference.

Auditory discrimination studies also are based on attentional preference. Such studies have found that newborns can tell sounds they have already heard from those they have not. In one study, infants who heard a certain speech sound one day after birth appeared to remember that sound 24 hours later, as shown by a reduced tendency to turn their heads toward the familiar sound and even a tendency to turn away (Swain, Zelazo, & Clifton, 1993). Piaget believed that the senses are unconnected at birth and are only gradually integrated through experience. If so, this integration begins very early. The fact that newborns will look at a source of sound shows that they associate hearing and sight. A more sophisticated ability is **cross-modal transfer,** the ability to use information gained from one sense to guide another—as when a person negotiates a dark room by feeling for the location of familiar objects, or identifies objects by sight after feeling them with eyes closed. In one study, 1-month-old infants showed that they could transfer information gained from sucking (touch) to vision. When the infants saw a rigid object (a hard plastic cylinder) and a flexible one (a wet sponge) being manipulated by a pair of hands, the infants looked longer at the object they had just sucked (Gibson & Walker, 1984).

cross-modal transfer Ability to use information gained by one sense to guide another

Researchers also study how attention itself develops (Colombo, 2001). From about 2 months, the amount of time infants typically gaze at a new sight increases. Between about 2 and 9 months, looking time shortens as infants learn to scan objects more efficiently and shift attention. Later in the first year and into the second, when sustaining attention becomes more voluntary and task oriented, looking time plateaus or increases (Colombo, 2002; Colombo et al., 2004).

The capacity for *joint attention*—which may contribute to social interaction, language acquisition, and the understanding of others' mental states—develops between 10 and 12 months, when babies follow an adults' gaze by looking or pointing in the same direction (Brooks & Meltzoff, 2002, 2005). Joint attention develops slowly during the months of dependence on adult caregivers (Nelson, 2005). In one study, 10- and 11-month-olds' ability to follow an adult's gaze predicted higher language scores eight months later. (Brooks & Meltzoff, 2005). Gaze-following also may be an important step toward understanding the intentions of others (Brooks & Meltzoff, 2005).

Watching television (see Box 7-2) may impede attentional development. In a nationally representative longitudinal study conducted in the United States, the more hours children spent viewing television at ages 1 and 3, the more likely they were to have attentional problems by age 7 (Christakis, Zimmerman, DiGiuseppe, & McCarty, 2004). Children who watched at least 3 hours a day scored lower on cognitive measures at age 6 (Zimmerman & Christakis, 2005).

Information Processing as a Predictor of Intelligence

Because of a weak correlation between infants' scores on developmental tests (such as the Bayley Scales) and their later IQ, many psychologists believed that the cognitive functioning of infants had little in common with that of older children and adults—in other words, that there was a discontinuity in cognitive development. Piaget believed this too. However, when researchers assess how infants and toddlers process information, some aspects of mental development seem to be fairly continuous from birth (McCall & Carriger, 1993). Children who, from the start, are efficient at taking in and interpreting sensory information later score well on intelligence tests. In many longitudinal studies, habituation and attention-recovery abilities during the first 6 months to 1 year of life were moderately useful in predicting childhood IQ. So was visual recognition memory—the ability to distinguish familiar sights from unfamiliar ones when shown both at the same time, as measured by the tendency to look longer at the new (Bornstein & Sigman, 1986; Colombo, 1993; McCall & Carriger, 1993). In one study, a combination of visual recognition memory at 7 months and cross-modal transfer at 1 year predicted IQ at age 11 and also showed a modest (but nonetheless remarkable after 10 years!) relationship to processing speed and memory at that age (Rose & Feldman, 1995, 1997).

Visual reaction time and visual anticipation can be measured by the *visual expectation paradigm.* A series of computer-generated pictures briefly appears, some on the right and some on the left sides of an infant's peripheral visual field. The same sequence of pictures is repeated several times. The infant's eye movements are measured to see how quickly his or her gaze shifts to a picture that has just appeared (reaction time) or to the place where the

Box 7-2 *Do Infants and Toddlers Watch Too Much Television?*

Six-month-old Jenny reclines in her bouncy seat, watching a Baby Einstein DVD. She bounces up and down, claps, and laughs out loud as bright images flash across the screen. Jenny has been watching Baby Einstein videos since she was 5 weeks old.

Jenny is neither precocious nor unusual, according to a nationally representative random-dialed survey of 1,000 parents of preschoolers, sponsored by the Henry J. Kaiser Family Foundation. On a typical day, 59 percent of children under 2 watch television, 42 percent watch a video or DVD, 5 percent use a computer, and 3 percent play video games. These children spend an average of about 2 hours a day in front of a screen, more than twice as much time as they spend being read to (see figure).

An avalanche of media geared to infants and toddlers has occurred since the late 1990s: the first television show targeting children as young as 12 months, computer games with special keyboard toppers for infants as young as 9 months, and educational videotapes and DVDs (with accompanying books, flashcards, and puppets) aimed at infants from 1 to 18 months old. In 2006, creators of the widely respected TV program *Sesame Street* released a series of DVDs for babies as young as 6 months to watch with their parents, and HBO featured a series called "Classical Baby," featuring works of music, art, and dance. The Treehouse channel now offers round-the-clock programming for infants and toddlers.

According to the Kaiser survey, 74 percent of children under 2 watch television, and 26 percent have TV sets in their bedrooms. Two-thirds (66 percent) of children 3 and younger turn on the TV by themselves, 52 percent change channels with a remote device, and 30 percent put in a video or DVD by themselves.

Babies in whose households television is frequently on are more likely to start watching before their first birthday than babies not exposed to such heavy doses of TV. The "heavy watchers" are more likely to watch every day, watch for a longer time, and spend less time being read to. They also are less likely to learn to read by age 6.

All of this flies in the face of recommendations by the American Academy of Pediatrics Committee on Public Education (2001) that children under 2 be discouraged from watching television and instead be engaged in interactive activities that promote brain development, such as talking, playing, singing, and reading with parents. Most parents in the Kaiser survey expressed faith in the educational value of the media and said their children were more likely to imitate positive behaviours, such as sharing and helping, than aggressive behaviours. Parents who value and exhibit positive behaviour tend to steer children toward stories, films, and television programs that depict such behaviour (Singer & Singer, 1998).

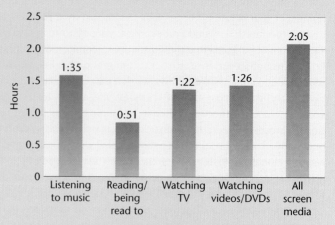

Average amount of time children under 2 spend on media and other activities in a typical day, according to mothers' reports.

Note: These data include only children who participate in these activities.

Source: Rideout et al., 2003.

Further study is needed to find out how heavy exposure to television affects infants and toddlers. Researchers need to investigate such questions as whether the constant presence of background media interferes with the development of physical coordination and language; whether time spent with media takes away time from playing outdoors, reading, or interacting with parents; whether it contributes to a sedentary lifestyle; whether video and computer games help visual and spatial skills or risk eyestrain and ergonomic problems; how various types of media impact cognitive development and attention span; and what is the extent and effect of young children's exposure to noneducational content.

What's your view?

At what age would you let a baby watch television or a videotape or play a computer game, and what restrictions, if any, would you place on such activities?

Check it out!

For more information on this topic, go to **www.kff.org/entmedia 102803nr.cfm** [the Kaiser Foundation report discussed in this box] and **www.mcgrawhill.ca/olc/papalia.**

Source: Unless otherwise referenced, this box is based on Rideout, Vandewater, & Wartella (2003).

infant expects the next picture to appear (anticipation). These measurements are thought to indicate attentiveness and processing speed, as well as the tendency to form expectations on the basis of experience. In a longitudinal study, visual reaction time and visual anticipation at 3½ months correlated with IQ at age 4 (Dougherty & Haith, 1997).

All in all, there is much evidence that the abilities infants use to process sensory information are related to the cognitive abilities intelligence tests measure. Still, we need to be cautious in interpreting these findings. Most of the studies used small samples. Also, the predictability of childhood IQ from measures of habituation and recognition memory is only modest. It is no higher than the predictability from parental education and socio-economic status, and not as high as the predictability from some other infant behaviours, such as early vocalization. Predictions based on information-processing measures alone do not take into account the influence of environmental factors (Colombo & Janowsky, 1998; Laucht, Esser, & Schmidt, 1994; McCall & Carriger, 1993). For example, maternal responsiveness in early infancy seems to play a part in the link between early attentional abilities and cognitive abilities later in childhood (Bornstein & Tamis-LeMonda, 1994) and even at age 18 (Sigman, Cohen, & Beckwith, 1997).

Information Processing and the Development of Piagetian Abilities

As we mentioned in a previous section, new evidence suggests that several of the cognitive abilities Piaget identified as developing toward the end of the sensorimotor stage actually seem to arise much earlier. Research based on infants' visual processing—independent of motor abilities—has given developmental scientists a new window into the timing of such cognitive developments as categorization, causality, object permanence, and number, all of which depend on formation of mental representations (refer back to Table 7-4).

Categorization

Dividing the world into meaningful categories is vital to thinking about objects or concepts and their relationships. It is the foundation of language, reasoning, problem solving, and memory; without it, the world would seem chaotic and meaningless (Rakison, 2005).

According to Piaget, the ability to classify, or group things into categories, does not appear until the sixth sensorimotor substage, around 18 months. Yet, by looking longer at items in a new category, even 3-month-olds seem to know, for example, that a dog is not a cat (Quinn, Eimas, & Rosenkrantz, 1993). Indeed, brain imaging has found that basic components of the neural structures needed to support categorization are functional within the first six months of life (Quinn, Westerlund, & Nelson, 2006). From an evolutionary perspective, infants may be born with a rudimentary ability to discern certain limited categories (such as snakes and spiders) that are dangerous to humans (Rakison, 2005).

For the most part, infants at first seem to categorize on the basis of *perceptual* features, such as shape, colour, and pattern. Toward the end of the first year their categories become *conceptual*, based on real-world knowledge (Oakes, Coppage, & Dingel, 1997), particularly of function (Mandler, 1998a; Mandler & McDonough, 1993, 1996, 1998). In one series of experiments, 10- and 11-month-olds recognized that chairs with zebra-striped upholstery belong in the category of furniture, not animals (Pauen, 2002). In the second year, language becomes a factor in learning to categorize. Hearing an experimenter name an object and/or point out its function can help 14- to 18-month-olds with category formation (Booth & Waxman, 2002).

Causality

An understanding of *causality,* the principle that one event causes another, is important because it "allows people to predict and control their world" (L. B. Cohen, Rundell, Spellman, & Cashon, 1999). Piaget believed that this understanding develops slowly during the first year of life. At about 4 to 6 months, as infants become able to grasp objects, they begin to recognize that they can act on their environment. Thus, said Piaget, the concept of causality is rooted in a dawning awareness of the power of one's own intentions. However, according to Piaget, infants do not yet know that causes must come before effects; and not until close to 1 year do they realize that forces outside of themselves can make things happen.

Some information-processing research suggests that a mechanism for recognizing causality may exist much earlier (Mandler, 1998a), possibly even at birth. Infants 6½ months old have shown by habituation and dishabituation that they seem to see a difference between events that are the immediate cause of other events (such as a brick striking a second brick, which is then pushed out of position) and events that occur with no apparent cause (such as a brick moving away from another brick without having been struck by it) (Leslie, 1982, 1984).

Other researchers have replicated these findings with 6½-month-olds but not with younger infants (L. B. Cohen & Amsel, 1998). These investigators attribute the growth of causal understanding to a gradual improvement in information-processing skills. As infants accumulate more information about how objects behave, they are better able to see causality as a general principle operating in a variety of situations (L. B. Cohen & Amsel, 1998; L. B. Cohen & Oakes, 1993; L. B. Cohen et al., 1999; Oakes, 1994).

Research also has explored infants' expectations about hidden causes. In one experiment, 10- to 12-month-olds looked longer when a human hand emerged from the opposite side of a lighted stage onto which a beanbag had been thrown than when the hand emerged from the same side as the beanbag, suggesting that the infants understood that the hand probably had thrown the beanbag. The infants did *not* have the same reaction when a toy train rather than a hand appeared or when the thrown object was a self-propelled puppet. Thus, infants that age apparently can figure out that (1) an object incapable of self-motion must have a causal agent to set it in motion, and (2) a hand is a more likely causal agent than a toy train (Saxe, Tenenbaum, & Carey, 2005).

Object Permanence

Violation-of-expectations research begins with a familiarization phase, in which infants see an event or series of events happen normally. After the infant is habituated to this procedure, the event is changed in a way that conflicts with (violates) normal expectations. An infant's tendency to look longer at the changed event is interpreted as evidence that the infant recognizes it as surprising.

Using the violation-of-expectations method, Renée Baillargeon and her colleagues claim to have found evidence of object permanence in infants as young as 3½ months. The babies appeared surprised by the failure of a tall carrot that slid behind a screen of the same height to show up in a large notch in the upper part of the screen before appearing again on the other side (Baillargeon & DeVos, 1991; see Figure 7-5).

In other research, the ability to visually follow the path of a ball that briefly passed behind a box was present at 4 months and more firmly established at 6 months (Johnson et al., 2003). Of course, the perception that an object that disappears on one side of a visual barrier looks the same as the object that reappears on the other side does not necessarily imply cognitive knowledge that the object continues to exist behind the barrier (Meltzoff & Moore, 1998).

Number

Some violation-of-expectations research suggests that an understanding of number may begin long before Piaget's sixth substage, when he claimed children first begin to use symbols. In a series of experiments, Karen Wynn (1992) tested whether 5-month-old babies

Figure 7-5

How early do infants show object permanence? In this violation-of-expectations experiment, 3½-month-olds watched a short carrot and then a tall carrot slide along a track, disappear behind a screen, and then reappear. After they became accustomed to seeing these events, the opaque screen was replaced by a screen with a large notch at the top. The short carrot did not appear in the notch when passing behind the screen; the tall carrot, which should have appeared in the notch, also did not. The babies looked longer at the tall than at the short carrot event, suggesting that they were surprised that the tall carrot did not reappear in the notch.

Source: Baillargeon & DeVos, 1991.

Habituation Events

Short carrot event

Tall carrot event

Test Events

Possible event

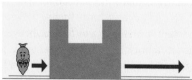

Impossible event

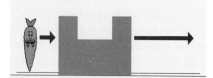

can add and subtract small numbers of objects. The infants watched as Mickey Mouse dolls were placed behind a screen, and a doll was either added or taken away. The screen then was lifted to reveal either the expected number or a different number of dolls. The babies looked longer at surprising "wrong" answers than at expected "right" ones, suggesting (according to Wynn) that they had mentally "computed" the right answers.

According to Wynn, this research suggests that numerical concepts are inborn—that when parents teach their babies numbers, they may merely be teaching them the names ("one, two, three") for *concepts* the babies already know. However, skeptics point out that the idea that these concepts is inborn is mere speculation, since the infants in these studies were already 5 and 6 months old. Furthermore, the infants might simply have been responding *perceptually* to the puzzling presence of a doll they saw removed from behind the screen or the absence of a doll they saw placed there (Haith, 1998; Haith & Benson, 1998). Other researchers suggest that, although infants do seem to discriminate visually between sets of, say, two and three objects, they may merely notice differences in the overall contours, area, or collective mass of sets of objects rather than compare the *number* of objects in the sets (Clearfield & Mix, 1999; Mix, Huttenlocher, & Levine, 2002).

In response to that criticism, McCrink and Wynn (2004) designed an experiment to show that 9-month-olds can add and subtract numbers too large for mere perceptual discrimination. The infants saw five abstract objects go behind an opaque square. Five more objects then appeared and went behind the square. The infants looked longer when the screen dropped to reveal five objects than when it revealed 10. Similarly, when 10 objects went behind the square and five emerged and went away, the infants looked longer when the screen dropped to reveal 10 objects than when it revealed five. The authors concluded that "humans possess an early system that supports numerical combination and manipulation" (p. 780). This experiment does not, however, shed light on whether that system is inborn.

Evaluating Violation-of-Expectations Research

Violation-of-expectations studies and other recent information processing research with infants raises the possibility that at least rudimentary forms of categorization, causal reasoning, object permanence, and numerical understanding may be present in the early months of life.

One proposal is that infants are born with reasoning abilities—*innate learning mechanisms* that help them make sense of the information they encounter—or that they acquire these abilities very early (Baillargeon, 1994a). Some investigators go further, suggesting that infants at birth may already have intuitive *core knowledge* of basic physical principles in the form of specialized brain modules that help infants organize their perceptions and experience (Spelke, 1994, 1998).

However, these interpretations are controversial. In violation-of-expectations studies, does an infant's visual interest in an "impossible" condition reveal a *conceptual* understanding of the way things work or merely a *perceptual* awareness that something unusual has happened? The fact that an infant looks longer at one scene than at another may show only that the infant can see a difference between the two. It does not show what the infant knows about the difference or that the infant is actually surprised. The "mental representation" the infant refers to may be no more than a brief sensory memory of something just seen. It's also possible that an infant, in becoming accustomed to the habituation event, develops the expectations that are then violated by the "surprising" event and did not have such knowledge or expectations before (Goubet & Clifton, 1998; Haith, 1998; Haith & Benson, 1998; Mandler, 1998a; Munakata, 2001; Munakata, McClelland, Johnson, & Siegler, 1997).

Defenders of this research insist that a conceptual interpretation best accounts for the findings (Baillargeon, 1999; Spelke, 1998), but a recent variation on one of Baillargeon's experiments suggests otherwise. In her original research, Baillargeon (1994a) showed infants of various ages a "drawbridge" rotating 180 degrees. When the infants became habituated to the rotation, a barrier was introduced in the form of a box. At 4½ months, infants seemed to show (by longer looking) that they understood that the drawbridge could not move through the entire box (see Figure 7-6). Later investigators replicated the experiment

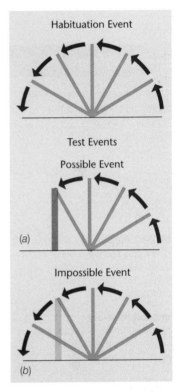

Figure 7-6

Test for infants' understanding of how a barrier works. Infants first become accustomed to seeing a "drawbridge" rotate 180 degrees on one edge. Then a box is placed beside the drawbridge. In the possible event, the drawbridge stops when it reaches the edge of the box. In the impossible events, the drawbridge rotates through part or all of the space occupied by the box. On the basis of how long they stare at each event, 4½-month-old infants seem to know that the drawbridge cannot pass through the entire box (b); but not until 6½ months do infants recognize that the drawbridge cannot pass through 80 percent of the box (a).

Source: Adapted from Baillargeon, 1994.

Checkpoint ✔

Can you . . .

✔ Describe the violation-of-expectations method, tell how and why it is used, and list some criticisms of it?

✔ Discuss four areas in which violation-of-expectations research seems to contradict Piaget's account of development?

Guidepost 6

What can brain research reveal about the development of cognitive skills?

explicit memory Intentional and conscious memory, generally of facts, names, and events; sometimes called *declarative memory*

implicit memory Unconscious recall, generally of habits and skills; sometimes called *procedural memory*

working memory Short-term storage of information being actively processed

Checkpoint ✔

Can you . . .

✔ Identify the brain structures apparently involved in implicit, explicit, and working memory and mention a task made possible by each?

✔ Tell how brain research helps explain Piagetian developments and memory operations?

but eliminated the box. Five-month-olds still looked longer at the 180-degree rotation than at a lesser degree of rotation, even though no barrier was present—suggesting that they simply were demonstrating a preference for greater movement (Rivera, Wakeley, & Langer, 1999). Thus, until further research clarifies these issues, we must be cautious about inferring the existence of adultlike cognitive abilities from data that may have simpler explanations or may represent only partial achievement of mature abilities (Haith, 1998).

Is it plausible that mechanisms to acquire knowledge of physical principles would become functional long before babies can put that knowledge to practical use? According to some evolutionary theorists (Nelson, 2005; Rakison, 2005), the answer is no. Evolutionary principles suggest that people develop various capacities at times of life when they are adaptive, or useful. Thus, infants are endowed at birth with basic attentional, perceptive, and learning abilities that adequately meet their needs for that period of life. It is likely, then, that the ability to find meaning in what they perceive develops later, as do specialized learning abilities for specific domains such as language (Rakison, 2005).

Cognitive Neuroscience Approach: The Brain's Cognitive Structures

Piaget's belief that neurological maturation is a major factor in cognitive development was merely a supposition. Brain growth spurts (periods of rapid growth and development) coincide with changes in cognitive behaviour similar to those Piaget described (Fischer & Rose, 1994, 1995).

Some researchers have used brain scans to determine which brain structures affect which cognitive functions and to chart developmental changes. Brain scans provide physical evidence of the location of two separate long-term memory systems—*explicit* and *implicit*—which acquire and store different kinds of information (Squire, 1992; Vargha-Khadem et al., 1997). **Explicit memory** also called *declarative memory* is conscious or intentional recollection, usually of facts, names, events, or other things that people can state or declare. Delayed imitation of complex behaviours is evidence that declarative memory is developing in late infancy and toddlerhood **Implicit memory,** which develops early in infancy, refers to remembering that occurs without effort or even conscious awareness; it generally pertains to habits and skills, such as knowing how to throw a ball or an infant's kicking upon seeing a familiar mobile (Nelson, 2005).

In early infancy, when the structures responsible for memory storage are not fully formed, memories are relatively fleeting (Serres, 2001). The maturing of the hippocampus, a structure deep in the temporal lobes, along with the development of cortical structures coordinated by the hippocampal formation make longer-lasting memories possible (Bauer, 2002; Bauer et al., 2000, 2003). The hippocampal system continues to develop at least through the fifth year (Serres, 2001).

The *prefrontal cortex* (the large portion of the frontal lobe directly behind the forehead) is believed to control many aspects of cognition. This part of the brain develops more slowly than any other (M. H. Johnson, 1998). During the second half of the first year, the prefrontal cortex and associated circuitry develop the capacity for **working memory**—short-term storage of information the brain is actively processing, or working on. It is in working memory that mental representations are prepared for, or recalled from, storage.

The relatively late appearance of working memory may be largely responsible for the slow development of object permanence, which seems to be seated in a rearward area of the prefrontal cortex (Nelson, 1995). By 12 months, this region may be developed enough to permit an infant to avoid the A, not-B, error by controlling the impulse to search in a place where the object was previously found (Diamond, 1991).

Although memory systems continue to develop beyond infancy, the early emergence of the brain's memory structures underlines the importance of environmental stimulation during the first months of life. Social-contextual theorists and researchers pay particular attention to the impact of environmental influences.

Social-Contextual Approach: Learning from Interactions with Caregivers

Guidepost 7

How does social interaction with adults advance cognitive competence?

Researchers influenced by Vygotsky's socio-cultural theory study how the cultural context affects early social interactions that may promote cognitive competence.

The concept of **guided participation** (Rogoff, 1990, 1998; Rogoff, Mistry, Göncü, & Mosier, 1993) was inspired by Vygotsky's zone of proximal development (refer back to Chapter 2) and his view of learning as a collaborative process. Guided participation refers to interactions with adults that help structure children's activities and bridge the gap between the child's understanding and the adult's. Guided participation often occurs in shared play and in ordinary, everyday activities in which children informally learn the skills, knowledge, and values important in their culture.

In one cross-cultural study (Rogoff et al., 1993), researchers visited the homes of fourteen 1- to 2-year-olds in each of four places: a Mayan town in Guatemala, a tribal village in India, and middle-class urban neighbourhoods in the United States and Turkey. The investigators interviewed caregivers about their child-rearing practices and watched them help the toddlers learn to dress themselves and to play with unfamiliar toys.

Cultural differences affected the types of guided participation the researchers observed. In the Guatemalan town, where toddlers normally saw their mothers sewing and weaving at home to help support the family, and in the Indian village, where they accompanied their mothers at work in the fields, the children customarily played alone or with older siblings while the mother worked nearby. After initial demonstration and instruction, mostly nonverbal, the children took the lead in their own learning, while a parent or other caregiver remained available to help.

The U.S. toddlers, who had full-time homemaker mothers or were in daycare, interacted with their parents in the context of child's play rather than in the parents' work or social worlds. Caregivers spoke with the children as peers and managed and motivated their learning with praise and mock excitement. Turkish families, who were in transition from a rural to an urban way of life, showed a pattern somewhere between the other two.

The cultural context, then, influences the way caregivers contribute to cognitive development. Direct adult involvement in children's play and learning may be better adapted to a middle-class urban community, in which parents or caregivers have more time, greater verbal skills, and possibly more interest in children's play and learning, than in a rural community in a developing country, in which children frequently observe and participate in adults' work activities (Rogoff et al., 1993).

guided participation
Participation of an adult in a child's activity in a manner that helps to structure the activity and to bring the child's understanding of it closer to that of the adult

Checkpoint ✔

Can you . . .

✔ Compare how cultural patterns affect guided participation in toddlers' learning?

Language Development

Guidepost 8

How do babies develop language, and what influences linguistic progress?

Doddy Darwin's use of the word "Ah!" to express his first recognition of his image in a glass is a striking example of the connection between **language,** a communication system based on words and grammar, and cognitive development. Once children know words, they can use them to represent objects and actions. They can reflect on people, places, and things; and they can communicate their needs, feelings, and ideas in order to exert control over their lives. How did language evolve, and how do infants "crack the code" of language?

language Communication system based on words and grammar

The Evolution of Language*

The evolution of language in the human species and its development in each individual illustrate the interaction of all domains of development.

The emergence of human language was made possible by several important physiological adaptations. First, between 10 million and 7 million years ago, the shift from four legs to two was accompanied by an expansion of social groupings. As the brain brought the vocal system under cortical control, it became possible for these groups to adopt distinguishing patterns of utterance and gesture. Imitation of vocalizations and gestures facilitated group cohesion and the linguistic initiation of the young.

*This section is indebted to MacWhinney (2005).

The next step was the development of enough brain storage to commit visual and auditory images and their significance to memory. Beginning about 2 million years ago, the size of the brain gradually tripled. Finally, between 300,000 and 50,000 years ago, with the emergence of *homo sapiens,* or human beings, the brain underwent changes that enabled the systematization of language. People were able to learn, store, and retrieve almost limitless names for things, to combine them into sentences, and to develop principles for grammatical constructions. Four other physiological adaptations—loss of canine teeth, changes in the muscles of the larynx, bending of the vocal tract, and shaping of the tongue muscles—played an important part in the production of speech.

Similarly, each infant acquires language through a combination of physical, cognitive, and social developments. As the physical structures needed to produce sounds mature and the neuronal connections necessary to associate sound and meaning become activated, social interaction motivates and facilitates the communicative nature of speech. Let's look at the typical milestones of language development (see Table 7-5).

Sequence of Early Language Development

prelinguistic speech Forerunner of linguistic speech; utterance of sounds that are not words; includes crying, cooing, babbling, and accidental and deliberate imitation of sounds without understanding their meaning

Before babies can use words, they make their needs and feelings known—as Doddy Darwin did—through sounds that progress from crying to cooing and babbling, then to accidental imitation, and then deliberate imitation. These sounds are known as **prelinguistic speech.** Infants also grow in the ability to recognize and understand speech sounds and to use meaningful gestures. Babies typically say their first word around the end of the first year, and toddlers begin speaking in sentences about 8 months to a year later.

Early Vocalization

Crying is a newborn's only means of communication. Different pitches, patterns, and intensities signal hunger, sleepiness, or anger (Lester & Boukydis, 1985).

Table 7-5	Language Milestones from Birth to 3 Years
Age in Months	**Development**
Birth	Can perceive speech, cry, make some response to sound
1½–3	Coos and laughs
3	Plays with speech sounds
5–6	Recognizes frequently heard sound patterns
6 to 7	Recognizes all phonemes of native language
6–10	Babbles in strings of consonants and vowels
9	Uses gestures to communicate and plays gesture games
9–10	Intentionally imitates sounds
9 to 12	Uses a few social gestures
10–12	No longer discriminates sounds not in own language
9–12	Uses a few social gestures
10–14	Says first word (usually a label for something)
10–18	Says single words
12 to 13	Understands symbolic function of naming; passive vocabulary grows
13	Uses more elaborate gestures
14	Uses symbolic gesturing
16–24	Learns many new words, expanding expressive vocabulary rapidly, going from about 50 words to as many as 400; uses verbs and adjectives
18–24	Says first sentence (two words)
20	Uses fewer gestures; names more things
20–22	Has comprehension spurt
24	Uses many two-word phrases; no longer babbles; wants to talk
30	Learns new words almost every day; speaks in combinations of three or more words; understands very well; makes grammatical mistakes
36	Says up to 1,000 words, 80 percent intelligible; makes some mistakes in syntax

Source: Bates, O'Connell, & Shore, 1987; Capute, Shapiro, & Palmer, 1987; Lalonde & Werker, 1995; Lenneberg, 1969.

Between 6 weeks and 3 months, babies start *cooing* when they are happy—squealing, gurgling, and making vowel sounds like "ahhh." At about 3 to 6 months, babies begin to play with speech sounds, matching the sounds they hear from people around them.

Babbling—repeating consonant-vowel strings, such as "ma-ma-ma-ma"—occurs between 6 and 10 months of age and is often mistaken for a baby's first word. Babbling is not real language, since it does not hold meaning for the baby, but it becomes more word-like. This form of language begins as a result of biological maturation and does not require exposure to language sounds to emerge. It is present in deaf infants, and, although it becomes more complex when reinforced in hearing children during the first year, it drops away in deaf children only to be replaced by manual babbling as they acquire sign language (Meier & Willerman, 1995; Petitto & Marentette, 1991).

Language development continues with accidental *imitation of language sounds* that babies hear and then imitation of themselves making these sounds. At about 9 to 10 months, infants deliberately imitate sounds without understanding them. Once they have a repertoire of sounds, they string them together in patterns that sound like language but seem to have no meaning. Finally, once infants become familiar with the sounds of words and phrases, they begin to attach meanings to them (Fernald, Perfors, & Marchman, 2006; Jusczyk & Hohne, 1997).

Perceiving Language Sounds and Structure

The ability to perceive differences between sounds is essential to language development. As we have seen, this ability is present from or even before birth, and it becomes more refined during the first year of life. In getting ready to understand and use speech, infants first become familiar with the sounds of words and phrases and later attach meanings to them (Jusczyk & Hohne, 1997). Their brains seem to be "preset" to discriminate basic linguistic units, perceive linguistic patterns, and categorize them as similar or different. This complex set of abilities seems to be unique to human infants (Kuhl, 2004).

At first, infants can discriminate the sounds of any language. In time, however, the ongoing process of pattern perception and categorization seems to commit the brain's neural networks to further learning of similar patterns—typically, the patterns of the infant's native language. This *neural commitment* also seems to constrain future learning of non-native language patterns. Babies who lack early exposure to this patterning feature of language—whether spoken or signed—during a critical or sensitive period are unlikely to acquire language normally (Kuhl, 2004; Kuhl, Conboy, Padden, Nelson, & Pruitt, 2005; refer back to Box 1-2 in Chapter 1).

The process apparently begins in the womb. In one experiment, two groups of Parisian women in their 35th week of pregnancy each recited a different nursery rhyme, saying it three times a day for 4 weeks. At the end of that time, researchers played recordings of both rhymes close to the women's abdomens. The fetuses' heart rates slowed when the rhyme the mother had spoken was played, but not for the other rhyme. Since the voice on the tape was not that of the mother, the fetuses apparently were responding to the linguistic sounds they had heard the mother use. This suggests that hearing the "mother tongue" before birth may "pretune" an infant's ears to pick up its sounds (DeCasper, Lecanuet, Busnel, Granier-Deferre, & Maugeais, 1994). In a classic study of basic language sound perception, infants as young as 1 month were able to discriminate between the basic sounds, or phonemes, used in their parents' languages, despite minimal prior exposure to language sounds (Eimas, Siqueland, Jusczyk, & Vigorito, 1971).

By 6 to 7 months of age, hearing babies have learned to recognize the approximately 40 basic sounds, or *phonemes,* of their native language and to adjust to slight differences in the way different speakers form those sounds (Kuhl, Williams, Lacerda, Stevens, & Lindblom, 1992). The ability to discriminate native-language sounds at this age predicts individual differences in language abilities during the second year (Tsao, Liu, & Kuhl, 2004), whereas nonnative sound discrimination does not (Kuhl et al., 2005).

By 10 to 12 months, babies lose their sensitivity to sounds that are not part of the language or languages they usually hear spoken. For example, Japanese infants no longer make a distinction between "ra" and "la," a distinction that does not exist in the Japanese language. Although the ability to perceive nonnative sounds is not entirely lost, the brain no longer routinely discriminates them (Bates, O'Connell, & Shore, 1987; Lalonde & Werker, 1995; Werker, 1989). How does this change occur? One hypothesis, for which there is evidence from behavioural studies and brain imaging, is that infants mentally "compute" the relative frequency of particular phonetic sequences in their language and learn to ignore sequences they infrequently hear (Kuhl, 2004).

During the second half of the first year, babies begin to become aware of the phonological rules of their language—how sounds are arranged in speech. In one series of experiments, 7-month-olds listened longer to "sentences" containing a different order of nonsense sounds (such as "wo fe wo," or ABA) from the order to which the infants had been habituated (such as "ga ti ti," or ABB). The sounds used in the test were different from those used in the habituation phase, so the infants' discrimination must have been based on the patterns of repetition alone. This finding suggests that infants may have a mechanism for discerning abstract rules of sentence structure (Marcus, Vijayan, Rao, & Vishton, 1999). In another series of experiments based on listening time, 9-month-olds appeared to discern patterns of syllabification and pronunciation of initial and final consonants and to apply those patterns to new words that fit or violated them (Saffran & Thiessen, 2003).

Gestures

At 9 months Maika *pointed* to an object, sometimes making a noise to show that she wanted it. Between 9 and 12 months, she learned some *conventional social gestures:* waving bye-bye, nodding her head to mean "yes," and shaking her head to signify "no." By about 13 months, she used more elaborate *representational gestures;* for example, she would hold an empty cup to her mouth to show that she wanted a drink or hold up her arms to show that she wanted to be picked up.

Symbolic gestures, such as blowing to mean "hot," or sniffing to mean "flower," often emerge around the same time as babies say their first words, and they function much like words. By using them, children show an understanding that symbols can refer to specific objects, events, desires, and conditions. Gestures usually appear before children have a vocabulary of 25 words and drop out when children learn the word for the idea they were gesturing and can say it instead (Lock, Young, Service, & Chandler, 1990).

Learning gestures seems to help babies learn to talk. Early gestures often correspond with the words and word combinations children later say (Iverson & Goldin-Meadow, 2005). In one experiment (Goodwyn & Acredolo, 1998), 11-month-olds learned gestures by watching their parents perform them and say the corresponding words. Between 15 and 36 months, when tested on vocal language development, these children outperformed two other groups—one whose parents had only said words and another who had received neither vocal nor gestural training. Gestures, then, can be a valuable alternative or supplement to words, especially during the period of early vocabulary formation.

linguistic speech Verbal expression designed to convey meaning

holophrase Single word that conveys a complete thought

First Words

Doddy Darwin, at 11 months, said his first word—"ouchy"—which he attached to a number of objects. Doddy's development was typical in this respect. The average baby says a first word sometime between 10 and 14 months, initiating **linguistic speech**—verbal expression that conveys meaning. Before long, the baby will use many words and will show some understanding of grammar, pronunciation, intonation, and rhythm. For now, an infant's total verbal repertoire is likely to be "mama" or "dada." Or it may be a simple syllable that has more than one meaning depending on the context in which the child utters it. "Da" may mean "I want that," "I want to go out," or "Where's Daddy?" A word like this, which expresses a complete thought, is called a **holophrase.**

Babies understand many words before they can use them. The first words most babies understand are the ones they are likely to hear most often: their own names and the word *no,* as well as words with special meaning for them. Five-month-olds listen longer to their own

This toddler is communicating with his father by pointing at something that catches his eye. Gesturing seems to come naturally to young children and may be an important part of language learning.

names than to other names (Newman, 2005). Six-month-olds look longer at a video of their mothers when they hear the word *mommy* and of their fathers when they hear *daddy,* suggesting that they are beginning to associate sound with meaning—at least with regard to special people (Tincoff & Jusczyk, 1999). Ten-month-olds attach labels to objects they find interesting, whether those labels are correct or not; 12-month-olds pay attention to cues from adults in learning what an object is called (Pruden, Hirsh-Pasek, Golinkoff, & Hennon, 2006).

By 13 months, most children understand that a word stands for a specific thing or event, and they can quickly learn the meaning of a new word (Woodward, Markman, & Fitzsimmons, 1994). *Passive* (receptive, or understood) vocabulary continues to grow as verbal comprehension gradually becomes faster and more accurate and efficient (Fernald, Perfors, & Marchman, 2006). By 18 months. about 3 out of 4 children can understand 150 words and can say 50 of them (Kuhl, 2004). Children with larger vocabularies and quicker reaction times can recognize spoken words from just the first part of the word. For example, upon hearing "daw" or "ki," they will point to a picture of a dog or kitten (Fernald, Swingley, & Pinto, 2001).

By 14 months, infants can learn to associate words with objects with minimal exposure and no social or contextual support (Werker, Cohen, Lloyd, Casasola, & Stager, 1998). As infants get better at perceiving phonemes in their native languages, and later at learning to associate words and objects, they seem to experience a "functional reorganization" of their language abilities. This reorganization involves dropping their knowledge of details as they move on to increasingly complex language tasks (Werker & Tees, 1999). Examples of this are the loss of phonemes by the end of the first year, and the remarkable abilities of 14-month-olds to associate words and objects. Although 14-month-olds are able to make associations between pairs of words and objects when the words sound distinctly different, they have difficulty making associations when the words sounded similar (Werker et al., 1998). This inattention to phonetic detail, which made it difficult for the infants to carry out the association task, represents a dropping off of detailed language knowledge as a new kind of ability emerges. As children move on to learning more words, the access to phonetic details seems to return to help in distinguishing between words that sound similar (Werker et al., 1999). The same kind of functional reorganization seems to occur when infants learn to produce words, when they fail to pronounce words correctly or consistently, at one point pronouncing "dog" as "gog," and later using the initial "d" sound to mispronounce "truck" as "duck." It is as though infants temporarily lose their capacity to use their established language knowledge when a new language ability begins to emerge. Addition of new words to their expressive (spoken) vocabulary is slower at first. As children come to rely more on words than on gestures to express themselves, the sounds and rhythms of speech grow more elaborate.

Addition of new words to the *expressive* (spoken) vocabulary is slower at first. Then, sometime between 16 and 24 months, a "naming explosion" may occur, though this phenomenon does not appear to be universal (Ganger & Brent, 2004). Within a few weeks, a toddler may go from saying about 50 words to saying about 400 (Bates, Bretherton, & Snyder, 1988). These rapid gains in spoken vocabulary reflect a steady increase in the speed and accuracy of word recognition during the second year of life (Fernald, Pinto, Swingley, Weinberg, & McRoberts, 1998; Fernald et al., 2006).

Nouns seem to be the easiest type of word to learn. In a cross-cultural study, it did not matter whether a family's native language was Spanish, Dutch, French, Hebrew, Italian, Korean, or English; in all these languages, parents reported that their 20-month-old children knew more nouns than any other class of words (Bornstein, Cote et al., 2004). At 24 months, children quickly recognize names of familiar objects in the absence of visual cues (Swingley & Fernald, 2002). At 24 to 36 months, children can figure out the meaning of unfamiliar adjectives from context or from the nouns they modify (Mintz, 2005).

First Sentences

The next important linguistic breakthrough comes when a toddler puts two words together to express one idea ("Dolly fall"). Generally, children do this between 18 and 24 months, about 8 to 12 months after they say their first word. However, this age range varies greatly. Although prelinguistic speech is fairly closely tied to chronological age, linguistic speech is not. Most children who begin talking fairly late catch up eventually—and many make up for lost time by talking nonstop to anyone who will listen! (True delayed language development is further discussed in Chapter 10.)

A child's first sentences typically deal with everyday events, things, people, or activities (Braine, 1976; Rice, 1989; Slobin, 1973). Darwin noted instances in which Doddy expressed his developing moral sense in words. At 27 months the boy gave his sister the last bit of his gingerbread, exclaiming, "Oh, kind Doddy, kind Doddy!"

At first children typically use **telegraphic speech,** consisting of only a few essential words. When Rita says, "Damma deep," she seems to mean "Grandma is sweeping the floor." Children's use of telegraphic speech, and the form it takes, varies, depending on the language being learned (Braine, 1976; Slobin, 1983). Word order generally conforms to what a child hears; Rita does not say "Deep Damma" when she sees her grandmother pushing a broom.

Does the omission of functional words such as *is* and *the* mean that a child does not know these words? Not necessarily; the child may merely find them hard to reproduce. Even during the first year, infants are sensitive to the presence of functional words; at 10½ months, they can tell a normal passage from one in which the functional words have been replaced by similar-sounding nonsense words (Jusczyk, in press).

Sometime between 20 and 30 months, children show increasing competence in **syntax,** the rules for putting sentences together in their language. They become somewhat more comfortable with articles *(a, the)*, prepositions *(in, on)*, conjunctions *(and, but)*, plurals, verb endings, past tense, and forms of the verb to be *(am, are, is)*. They also become increasingly aware of the communicative purpose of speech and of whether their words are being understood (Shwe & Markman, 1997)—a sign of growing sensitivity to the mental lives of others. By age 3, speech is fluent, longer, and more complex; although children often omit parts of speech, they usually get their meaning across well.

Characteristics of Early Speech

Early speech has a character all its own—no matter what language a child is speaking (Slobin, 1971). As we have seen, children *simplify*. They use telegraphic speech to say just enough to get their meaning across ("No drink milk!").

Children *understand grammatical relationships they cannot yet express*. At first, Nina may understand that a dog is chasing a cat, but she cannot string together enough words to express the complete action. Her sentence comes out as "Puppy chase" rather than "Puppy chase kitty."

Children *underextend word meanings*. Lisa's uncle gave her a toy car, which the 13-month-old called her "koo-ka." Then her father came home with a gift, saying, "Look, Lisa, here's a little car for you." Lisa shook her head. "Koo-ka," she said and ran and got the one from her uncle. To her, *that* car—and *only* that car—was a little car, and it took some time before she called any other toy cars by the same name. Lisa was underextending the word car by restricting it to a single object.

Children also *overextend word meanings*. At 14 months, Eddie jumped in excitement at the sight of a grey-haired man on the television screen and shouted, "Gampa!" Eddie was overgeneralizing, or *overextending,* a word; he thought that because his grandfather had grey hair, all grey-haired men could be called "Grandpa." As children develop a larger vocabulary and get feedback from adults on the appropriateness of what they say, they overextend less. ("No, Honey, that man looks a little like Grandpa, but he's somebody else's grandpa, not yours.")

Children *overregularize rules:* They apply them rigidly, not knowing that some rules have exceptions. When John says "mouses" instead of "mice" or Megan says "I thinked" rather than "I thought," this represents progress. Both children initially used the correct forms of these irregular words, but merely in imitation of what they heard. Once children learn the rules for plurals and past tense (a crucial step in learning language), they apply them universally. The next step is to learn the exceptions to the rules, which they generally do by early school age.

Classic Theories of Language Acquisition: The Nature–Nurture Debate

How do children gain access to the secrets of verbal communication? Is linguistic ability learned or inborn? In the 1950s, a debate raged between two schools of thought: one led by B. F. Skinner, the foremost proponent of learning theory, the other by the linguist Noam Chomsky.

telegraphic speech Early form of sentence consisting of only a few essential words

syntax Rules for forming sentences in a particular language

Checkpoint ✔

Can you . . .

✔ Trace the typical sequence of milestones in early language development, pointing out the influence of the language babies hear around them?

✔ Describe five ways in which early speech differs from adult speech?

Skinner (1957) maintained that language learning, like other learning, is based on experience. According to classic learning theory, children learn language through operant conditioning. At first, babies utter sounds at random. Caregivers reinforce the sounds that happen to resemble adult speech with smiles, attention, and praise. Infants then repeat these reinforced sounds. Sounds that are not part of the native language are not reinforced, and the child gradually stops making them. According to social learning theory, babies imitate the sounds they hear adults make and, again, are reinforced for doing so. Word learning depends on selective reinforcement; the word *kitty* is reinforced only when the family cat appears. As this process continues, children are reinforced for speech that is more and more adult-like. Sentence formation is a more complex process: The child learns a basic word order (subject-verb-object—"I want ice cream") and then learns that other words can be substituted in each category ("Daddy eats meat").

Observation, imitation, and reinforcement probably do contribute to language development, but, as Chomsky (1957, 1972) persuasively argued, they cannot fully explain it (Owens, 1996). For one thing, word combinations and nuances are so many and so complex that they cannot all be acquired by specific imitation and reinforcement. Then, caregivers often reinforce utterances that are not strictly grammatical, as long as they make sense. ("Gampa go bye-bye.") Adult speech itself is an unreliable model to imitate, as it is often ungrammatical, containing false starts, unfinished sentences, and slips of the tongue. Also, learning theory does not account for children's imaginative ways of saying things they have never heard—as when 2-year-old Anna described a sprained ankle as a "sprangle" and said she didn't want to go to sleep yet because she wasn't "yawny."

Chomsky's view is called **nativism.** Unlike Skinner's learning theory, nativism emphasizes the active role of the learner. Since language is universal among human beings, Chomsky (1957, 1972) proposed that the human brain has an innate capacity for acquiring language; babies learn to talk as naturally as they learn to walk. He suggested that an inborn **language acquisition device (LAD)** programs children's brains to analyze the language they hear and to figure out its rules. More recently, Chomsky (1995) has sought to identify a simple set of universal principles that underlie all languages, and a single multipurpose mechanism for connecting sound to meaning.

Support for the nativist position comes from newborns' ability to differentiate similar sounds, suggesting that they are "born with perceptual mechanisms that are tuned to the properties of speech" (Eimas, 1985, p. 49). Nativists point out that almost all children master their native language in the same age-related sequence without formal teaching. Furthermore, the brains of human beings, the only animals with fully developed language, contain a structure that is larger on one side than on the other, suggesting that an inborn mechanism for language may be localized in the larger hemisphere—the left for most people. A similar imbalance in the size of this brain structure, the *planum temporale,* has been discovered in chimpanzees, which also show some ability to learn language (Gannon, Holloway, Broadfield, & Braun, 1998). Language lateralization of the brain increases with age, enabling growth in language skills (Szaflarski, Holland, Schmithorst, & Weber-Byars, 2004).

Still, the nativist approach does not explain precisely how such a mechanism operates. It does not tell us why some children acquire language more rapidly and efficiently than others, why children differ in linguistic skill and fluency, or why (as we'll see) speech development appears to depend on having someone to talk with, not merely on hearing spoken language.

Aspects of both learning theory and nativism have been used to explain how deaf babies learn sign language, which is structured much like spoken language and is acquired in the same sequence. Deaf babies of deaf parents seem to copy the sign language they see their parents using, just as hearing babies copy vocal utterances. Using hand motions more systematic and deliberate than those of hearing babies, deaf babies first string together meaningless motions and repeat them over and over in what has been called hand-babbling (Petitto & Marentette, 1991; see Figure 7-7). As parents reinforce these gestures, the babies attach meaning to them (Petitto, Holowka, Sergio, & Ostry, 2001).

However, some deaf children make up their own sign language when they do not have models to follow—evidence that environmental influences alone cannot explain the emergence of linguistic expression (Goldin-Meadow & Mylander, 1998). Since the 1970s,

nativism Theory that human beings have an inborn capacity for language acquisition

language acquisition device (LAD) In Chomsky's terminology, an inborn mechanism that enables children to infer linguistic rules from the language they hear

Figure 7-7

Example of hand-babbling by a non-hearing baby who had been exposed to sign language. The baby repeated this series of hand movements over and over again in sequence. Each motion is comparable to a syllable in a sequence of vocal babbling.

Source: Petitto & Marentette, 1991.

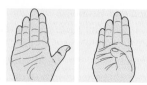

successive waves of Nicaraguan deaf schoolchildren who were being taught only lip-reading in Spanish have developed a true sign language, which has gradually evolved from simple gestures into words and sentences that follow linguistic rules (Senghas & Coppola, 2001; Senghas, Kita, & Ozyürek, 2004). Likewise, Al-Sayyid Bedouin Sign Language, which evolved spontaneously in an isolated village in Israel's Negev desert, has a distinct, systematic grammatical structure unlike that of Israeli Sign Language or of the Arabic dialect spoken by hearing members of the community (Sandler, Meir, Padden, & Aronoff, 2005).

Furthermore, learning theory does not explain the correspondence between the ages at which linguistic advances in both hearing and nonhearing babies typically occur (Padden, 1996; Petitto, Katerelos, et al., 2001; Petitto & Kovelman, 2003). Deaf babies begin hand-babbling between 7 and 10 months of age, about the age when hearing infants begin voice-babbling (Petitto, Holowka, et al., 2001; Petitto & Marentette, 1991). Deaf babies also begin to use sentences in sign language at about the same time that hearing babies begin to speak in sentences (Meier, 1991; Newport & Meier, 1985). This suggests that an inborn language capacity may underlie the acquisition of both spoken and signed language and that advances in both kinds of language are tied to brain maturation.

Most developmentalists today believe that language acquisition, like most other aspects of development, depends on an intertwining of nature and nurture. Children, whether hearing or deaf, probably have an inborn capacity to acquire language, which may be activated or constrained by experience.

Influences on Language Development

What determines how quickly and how well children learn to understand and use language? Research has focused on influences both within and outside the child.

Brain Development

The tremendous brain growth during the early months and years is closely linked with language development. A newborn's cries are controlled by the *brain stem* and *pons,* the most primitive parts of the brain and the earliest to develop (refer back to Figure 6-4 in Chapter 6). Repetitive babbling may emerge with the maturation of parts of the *motor cortex,* which control movements of the face and larynx. Not until early in the second year, when most children begin to talk, do the pathways that link auditory and motor activity mature (Owens, 1996). As we have discussed there is evidence that the development of language actively affects brain networks, committing them to the recognition of native language sounds only (Kuhl, 2004; Kuhl et al., 2005). Cortical regions associated with language continue to develop until at least the late preschool years or beyond—some, not even until adulthood.

In about 98 percent of people, the left hemisphere is dominant for language, though the right hemisphere participates as well (Nobre & Plunkett, 1997; Owens, 1996). Videotapes of babbling babies show that, as in adult speech, the mouth opens more on the right side than on the left. Since the left hemisphere of the brain controls activity on the right side of the body, lateralization of linguistic functions apparently takes place very early in life (Holowka & Petitto, 2002; refer back to Chapter 6). Language lateralization increases into young adulthood, enabling continued growth in language skills (Szaflarski, Holland, Schmithorst, & Weber-Byars, 2004).

Social Interaction: The Role of Parents and Caregivers

As the story of Victor (refer back to Chapter 1 Focus) shows, language is a social act. Parents or other caregivers play an important role at each stage of language development.

Prelinguistic Period At the babbling stage, adults help an infant advance toward true speech by repeating the sounds the baby makes; the baby soon joins in the game and

Checkpoint

Can you . . .

✔ Summarize how learning theory and nativism seek to explain language acquisition, and point out strengths and weaknesses of each theory?

Checkpoint

Can you . . .

✔ Name areas of the brain involved in early language development, and tell the function of each?

✔ Give evidence for plasticity in the brain's linguistic areas?

repeats the sounds back. Parents' imitation of babies' sounds affects the amount of infant vocalization (Goldstein, King, & West, 2003) and the pace of language learning (Hardy-Brown & Plomin, 1985; Hardy-Brown, Plomin, & DeFries, 1981). It also helps babies experience the social aspect of speech, the sense that a conversation consists of taking turns (Kuhl, 2004), an idea most babies seem to grasp at about 7½ to 8 months of age. Even as young as 4 months, babies in a game of peekaboo show sensitivity to the structure of social exchange with an adult (Rochat, Querido, & Striano, 1999; refer back to Box 7-1).

Caregivers may help babies understand spoken words by, for example, pointing to a doll and saying, "Please give me Kermit." If the baby doesn't respond, the adult may pick up the doll and say, "Kermit" encouraging the infant to follow the caregiver's gaze (Kuhl, 2004). In one naturalistic observational study, researchers videotaped 40 mothers playing with their 9-month-old infants at home and rated the mothers' verbal sensitivity. The mother's verbal sensitivity, for example, naming a toy in response to a baby's interest, turned out to be an important predictor of the baby's language comprehension (as reported by the mother) 4 months later (Baumwell, Tamis-LeMonda, & Bornstein, 1997). In one longitudinal study, mothers' responsiveness to 9-month-olds' and, even more so, to 13-month-olds' vocalization and play predicted the timing of language milestones, such as first spoken words and sentences (Tamis-LeMonda, Bornstein, & Baumwell, 2001).

Vocabulary Development When babies begin to talk, parents or caregivers often help them by repeating their first words and pronouncing them correctly. Vocabulary gets a boost when an adult seizes an appropriate opportunity to teach a child a new word. If Jordan's mother says, "This is a ball," when Jordan is looking at the ball, he is more likely to remember the word than if he were playing with something else and she tried to divert his attention to the ball (Dunham, Dunham & Curwin, 1993). Adults help a toddler who has begun to put words together by expanding on what the child says. If Christina says, "Mommy sock," her mother may reply, "Yes, that is Mommy's sock."

Babies learn by listening to what adults say. A strong relationship has appeared between the frequency of various words in mothers' speech and the order in which children learn these words (Huttenlocher, Haight, Bryk, Seltzer, & Lyons, 1991), as well as between mothers' talkativeness and the size of toddlers' vocabularies (Huttenlocher, 1998). Mothers with higher socio-economic status tend to use richer vocabularies and longer utterances, and their 2-year-olds have larger spoken vocabularies (Hoff, 2003)—as much as eight times as large (C. T. Ramey & Ramey, 2003). By age 3, vocabularies of low-income children vary greatly, depending in large part on the diversity of word types they have heard their mothers use, especially around the child's second birthday (Pan, Rowe, Singer, & Snow, 2005).

However, sensitivity and responsiveness to a child's level of development count more than the number of words a mother uses. In a year-long study of 290 low-income families of 2-year-olds, both parents' sensitivity, positive regard for the child, and the cognitive stimulation they provided during play predicted the child's receptive vocabulary and cognitive development at ages 2 and 3 (Tamis-LeMonda et al., 2004).

In households where two languages are spoken, babies achieve similar milestones in each language on the same schedule as children who hear only one language (Petitto, Katerelos, et al., 2001; Petitto & Kovelman, 2003). Bilingual children often use elements of both languages at first, sometimes in the same utterance—a phenomenon called **code mixing.** However, code mixing does not cause them to confuse the two languages (Petitto, Katerelos, et al., 2001; Petitto & Kovelman, 2003). A naturalistic observation in Montreal (Genesee, Nicoladis, & Paradis, 1995) suggests that children as young as 2 in dual-language households differentiate between the two languages, using French, for example, with a predominantly French-speaking father and English with a predominantly English-speaking mother. This ability to shift from one language to another is called **code switching.** (Chapter 13 discusses second-language learning.)

code mixing Use of elements of two languages, sometimes in the same utterance, by young children in households where both languages are spoken

code switching Process of changing one's speech to match the situation, as in people who are bilingual

Child-Directed Speech

You do not have to be a parent to speak "parentese." If, when you talk to an infant or toddler, you speak slowly in a high-pitched voice with exaggerated ups and downs, simplify your speech, exaggerate vowel sounds, and use short words and sentences and much repetition,

child-directed speech (CDS)
Form of speech often used in talking to babies or toddlers; includes slow, simplified speech, a high-pitched tone, exaggerated vowel sounds, short words and sentences, and much repetition; also called *parentese*

you are using **child-directed speech (CDS).** Most adults, and even children, do it naturally. Such "baby talk" may well be universal; it has been documented in many languages and cultures (Kuhl et al., 1997). Apparently this kind of linguistic input helps infants hear the distinguishing features of speech sounds.

Many researchers believe that CDS helps infants learn their native language or at least pick it up faster by exaggerating and directing attention to the distinguishing features of speech sounds (Kuhl et al., 2005). In one cross-cultural observational study, mothers in the United States, Russia, and Sweden were audiotaped speaking to their 2- to 5-month-old infants. Whether the mothers were speaking English, Russian, or Swedish, they produced more exaggerated vowel sounds when talking to the infants than when talking to other adults. At 20 weeks, the babies' babbling contained distinct vowels that reflected the phonetic differences to which their mothers' speech had alerted them (Kuhl et al., 1997).

Other investigators challenge the value of CDS. They contend that babies speak sooner and better if they hear and can respond to more complex adult speech. In fact, some researchers say, children discover the rules of language faster when they hear complex sentences that use these rules more often and in more ways (Gleitman, Newport, & Gleitman, 1984; Oshima-Takane, Goodz, & Derevensky, 1996). Nonetheless, infants themselves prefer to hear simplified speech. This preference is clear before 1 month of age, and it does not seem to depend on any specific experience (Cooper & Aslin, 1990; Kuhl et al., 1997; Werker, Pegg, & McLeod, 1994). Two-day-old infants of both English-speaking and Japanese-speaking parents prefer infant-directed to adult-directed singing (Masataka, 1999). In fact, a McMaster University team found that by 6 months of age infants were able to distinguish between and alter their behaviour in response to lullabies and songs intended for play. This shows that parents may use singing to communicate with and regulate their children's internal states between sleep-oriented and play-oriented emotions (Rock, Trainor, & Addison, 1999).

Social interaction in reading aloud, play, and other daily activities is a key to much of childhood development. Children elicit responses from the people around them and, in turn, react to those responses. In Chapter 8, we look more closely at these bi-directional influences as we explore early psychosocial development.

Checkpoint ✔

Can you . . .

✔ Explain the importance of social interaction and give at least three examples of how parents or caregivers help babies learn to talk?

✔ Assess the arguments for and against the value of child-directed speech (CDS)?

Summary and Key Terms

Studying Cognitive Development: Six Approaches

Guidepost 1 What are six approaches to the study of cognitive development?

- Three classic approaches to the study of cognitive development are the behaviourist, psychometric, and Piagetian approaches.

- Three newer approaches are information processing, cognitive neuroscience, and social-contextual.

- All of these approaches can shed light on how early cognition develops.

    behaviourist approach (162)   psychometric approach (162)
    Piagetian approach (162)   information-processing approach (163)
    cognitive neuroscience approach (163)
    social-contextual approach (163)

Behaviourist Approach: Basic Mechanics of Learning

Guidepost 2 How do infants learn, and how long can they remember?

- Two simple types of learning that behaviourists study are classical conditioning and operant conditioning.

- Rovee-Collier's research suggests that infants' memory processes are much like those of adults, but their memories fade quickly without periodic reminders.

    classical conditioning (163)   operant conditioning (163)

Psychometric Approach: Developmental and Intelligence Testing

Guidepost 3 Can infants' and toddlers' intelligence be measured, and how can it be improved?

- Psychometric tests measure factors presumed to make up intelligence.

- Developmental tests, such as the Bayley Scales of Infant Development, can indicate current functioning but are generally poor predictors of later intelligence.

- Socio-economic status, parenting practices, and the home environment may affect measured intelligence.

- If the home environment does not provide the necessary conditions that pave the way for cognitive competence, early intervention may be needed.

    intelligent behaviour (165)   IQ (intelligence quotient) tests (165)
    Bayley Scales of Infant Development (165)
    Home Observation for Measurement of the Environment
    (HOME) (166)   early intervention (167)

Piagetian Approach:
The Sensorimotor Stage

Guidepost 4 How did Piaget describe early cognitive development, and how have his claims stood up?

- During Piaget's sensorimotor stage, infants' schemes become more elaborate. They progress from primary to secondary to tertiary circular reactions and finally to the development of representational ability, which makes possible deferred imitation, pretending, and problem solving.

- Object permanence develops gradually throughout the sensorimotor stage. Piaget saw the A, not-B, error as a sign of incomplete object knowledge and the persistence of egocentric thought.

- Research suggests that a number of abilities develop earlier than Piaget described. For example, he may have underestimated young infants' grasp of object permanence and their imitative abilities.

**sensorimotor stage (168)   schemes (169)   circular reactions (169)
representational ability (170)   invisible imitation (170)
visible imitation (170)   deferred imitation (171)
elicited imitation (171)   object permanence (172)
A, not-B error (172)   dual representation hypothesis (175)**

Information Processing Approach:
Perceptions and Representations

Guidepost 5 How can we measure infants' ability to process information, and when do babies begin to think about characteristics of the physical world?

- Information-processing researchers measure mental processes through habituation and other signs of visual and perceptual abilities. Contrary to Piaget, such research suggests that representational ability is present virtually from birth.

- Indicators of the efficiency of infants' information processing, such as speed of habituation, tend to predict later intelligence.

- Such information-processing research techniques as habituation, novelty preference, and the violation-of-expectations method have yielded evidence that infants as young as 3½ to 5 months may have a rudimentary grasp of such Piagetian abilities as categorization, causality, object permanence, a sense of number, and an ability to reason about characteristics of the physical world. Some researchers suggest that infants may have innate learning mechanisms for acquiring such knowledge. However, the meaning of these findings is in dispute.

**habituation (176)   dishabituation (176)
visual preference (176)   visual recognition memory (176)
cross-modal transfer (177)   violation-of-expectations (180)**

Cognitive Neuroscience Approach:
The Brain's Cognitive Structures

Guidepost 6 What can brain research reveal about the development of cognitive skills?

- Explicit memory and implicit memory are located in different brain structures.

- Working memory emerges between 6 and 12 months.

- Neurological developments help explain the emergence of Piagetian skills and memory abilities.

**explicit memory (182)   implicit memory (182)
working memory (182)**

Social-Contextual Approach: Learning from Interactions with Caregivers

Guidepost 7 How does social interaction with adults advance cognitive competence?

- Social interactions with adults contribute to cognitive competence through shared activities that help children learn skills, knowledge, and values important in their culture.

guided participation (183)

Language Development

Guidepost 8 How do babies develop language, and what influences linguistic progress?

- The acquisition of language is an important aspect of cognitive development.

- Prelinguistic speech includes crying, cooing, babbling, and imitating language sounds. By 6 months, babies have learned the basic sounds of their language and have begun to link sound with meaning. Perception of categories of sounds in the native language may commit the neural circuitry to further learning in that language only.

- Before they say their first word, babies use gestures.

- The first word typically comes sometime between 10 and 14 months, initiating linguistic speech. A "naming explosion" typically occurs sometime between 16 and 24 months of age.

- The first brief sentences generally come between 18 and 24 months. By age 3, syntax and communicative abilities are fairly well developed.

- Early speech is characterized by simplification, underextending and overextending word meanings, and overregularizing rules.

- Two classic theoretical views about how children acquire language are learning theory and nativism. Today, most developmentalists hold that an inborn capacity to learn language may be activated or constrained by experience.

- Influences on language development include brain maturation and social interaction.

- Family characteristics, such as socio-economic status, adult language use, and maternal responsiveness, affect a childs vocabulary development.

- Children who hear two languages at home generally learn both at the same rate as children who hear only one language, and they can use each language in appropriate circumstances.

- Child-directed speech (CDS) seems to have cognitive, emotional, and social benefits, and infants show a preference for it. However, some researchers dispute its value.

**language (183)   prelinguistic speech (184)   linguistic speech (186)
holophrase (186)   telegraphic speech (188)   syntax (188)
nativism (189)   language acquisition device (LAD) (189)
code mixing (191)   code switching (191)
child-directed speech (CDS) (192)**

CHAPTER EIGHT

Psychosocial Development During the First Three Years

*I'm like a child
trying to do everything
say everything
and be everything
all at once*

—John Hartford, *Life Prayer,* 1971

Focus *Mary Catherine Bateson, Anthropologist**

Mary Catherine
Bateson

Mary Catherine Bateson (b. 1939) is an anthropologist, the daughter of two famous anthropologists: Margaret Mead (refer back to Chapter 2, Focus) and Gregory Bateson, Mead's third husband and research partner. Hers was probably one of the most documented infancies on record—her mother taking notes, her father behind the camera. Margaret Mead's memoir, *Blackberry Winter* (1972), and Mary Catherine Bateson's *With a Daughter's Eye* (1984) together provide a rare and fascinating dual perspective on a child's first 3 years of life.

Cathy—Mead's only child—was born when her mother was 38 years old. Her parents divorced when she was 11. Their work during World War II often necessitated long absences and separations. But during her infancy and toddlerhood, when they were still together, Cathy was the focus of their love and wholehearted attention. Her early recollections include sitting with her parents on a blanket outdoors, being read to on her mother's lap; and watching the two of them hold up their breakfast spoons to reflect the morning light, making a pair of "birds" flash across the walls for her amusement.

To avoid subjecting her to frustration, her parents tried to respond quickly to her needs. Mead arranged her professional commitments around breastfeeding and nursed "on demand," like the mothers in the island cultures she had studied.

Like their friend Erik Erikson, Mead and Bateson placed great importance on the development of trust. They never left Cathy in a strange place with a strange person; she always met a new caregiver in a familiar place. "Her warm responsiveness, her trustingness, and her outgoing interest in people and things . . . set the stage for her expectation that the world was a friendly place" (Mead, 1972, p. 266). As an adult, Catherine observed that, during difficult periods in her life, she often found "resources of faith and strength, a foundation that must have been built in those [first] two years" (Bateson, 1984, p. 35). Yet, as Mead wrote, "How much was temperament? How much was felicitous accident? How much could be attributed to upbringing? We may never know" (1972, p. 268).

Mead tried to avoid overprotectiveness and to let Cathy be herself. Catherine remembers her father pushing her swing so high that he could run under it. Later he taught her to climb tall pine trees, testing every branch for firmness and making sure that she could find her way back down, while her mother, watching,

tried not to show her fear. When Cathy was 2 and her parents' wartime travel increased, they merged their household with that of a friend and colleague, Lawrence Frank. The decision fit in with Mead's belief, gleaned from her studies, that children benefit from having multiple caregivers and learning to adapt to different situations.

The ménage in Frank's brownstone in Greenwich Village included his infant son, Colin, and five older children. "Thus," Catherine writes, "I did not grow up in a nuclear family or as an only child, but as a member of a flexible and welcoming extended family . . . , in which five or six pairs of hands could be mobilized to shell peas or dry dishes." Her summertime memories are of a lakeside retreat in New Hampshire, where "each child was cared for by enough adults so that there need be no jealousy, where the garden bloomed and the evenings ended in song. . . . I was rich beyond other children . . . and yet there were all those partings. There were all those beloved people, yet often the people I wanted most were absent" (Bateson, 1984, pp. 38–39).

● ● ●

In Margaret Mead's and Mary Catherine Bateson's complementary memoirs, we can see how Mead put into practice the beliefs she had developed about child rearing, in part from memories of her own childhood and in part from observations of distant cultures. We see her seeking solutions to a problem that has become increasingly common: child care for children of working parents. And we see a bi-directional influence: how early experiences with parents help shape a child's development, and how a child's needs can shape parents' lives.

This chapter is about the shift from the dependence of infancy to the independence of childhood. We first examine foundations of psychosocial development: emotions, temperament, and early experiences with parents. We consider Erikson's views about the development of trust and autonomy. We look at relationships with caregivers, at the emerging sense of self, and at the foundations of conscience. We explore relationships with siblings and other children and with grandparents. Finally, we consider the increasingly widespread impact of early day care.

After you have read and studied this chapter, you should be able to answer each of the Guidepost questions that appear at the top of the next page. Look for them again in the margins, where they point to important concepts throughout the chapter. To check your understanding of these Guideposts, review the end-of-chapter summary. Checkpoints located throughout the chapter will help you verify your understanding of what you have read.

*Sources of biographical information about Mary Catherine Bateson are Bateson (1984) and Mead (1972).

Guideposts
for Study

1. When and how do emotions develop, and how do babies show them?

2. How do infants show temperamental differences, and how enduring are those differences?

3. How do infants gain trust in their world and form attachments, and how do infants and caregivers "read" each other's non-verbal signals?

4. When and how does the sense of self arise, and how do toddlers exercise autonomy and develop standards for socially acceptable behaviour?

5. When and how do gender differences appear?

6. How do infants and toddlers interact with siblings and other children?

7. How do parental employment and early child care affect infants' and toddlers' development?

Guidepost 1

When and how do emotions develop, and how do babies show them?

emotions Subjective reactions to experience that are associated with physiological and behavioural changes

Foundations of Psychosocial Development

While babies share common patterns of development, they also—from the start—show distinct personalities, which reflect both inborn and environmental influences. From infancy on, personality development is intertwined with social relationships (see Table 8-1).

Emotions

Emotions, such as sadness, joy, and fear, are subjective reactions to experience that are associated with physiological and behavioural changes (Sroufe, 1997). Fear, for example, is accompanied by a faster heartbeat and, often, by self-protective action. A person's

Table 8-1	Highlights of Infants' and Toddlers' Psychosocial Development, Birth to 36 Months
Approximate Age, Months	**Characteristics**
0–3	Infants are open to stimulation. They begin to show interest and curiosity, and they smile readily at people.
3–6	Infants can anticipate what is about to happen and experience disappointment when it does not. They show this by becoming angry or acting warily. They smile, coo, and laugh often. This is a time of social awakening and early reciprocal exchanges between the baby and the caregiver.
6–9	Infants play "social games" and try to get responses from people. They "talk" to, touch, and cajole other babies to get them to respond. They express more differentiated emotions, showing joy, fear, anger, and surprise.
9–12	Infants are intensely preoccupied with their principal caregiver, may become afraid of strangers, and act subdued in new situations. By 1 year, they communicate emotions more clearly, showing moods, ambivalence, and gradations of feeling.
12–18	Toddlers explore their environment, using the people they are most attached to as a secure base. As they master the environment, they become more confident and more eager to assert themselves.
18–36	Toddlers sometimes become anxious because they now realize how much they are separating from their caregiver. They work out their awareness of their limitations in fantasy and in play and by identifying with adults.

Source: Adapted from Sroufe, 1979.

characteristic pattern of emotional reactions begins to develop during infancy and is a basic element of personality. People differ in how often they feel a particular emotion, in the kinds of events that may produce it, in the physical manifestations they show, and in how they act as a result.

Culture influences the way people feel about a situation and the way they show their emotions. For example, some Asian cultures, which stress social harmony, discourage expression of anger but place much importance on shame. The opposite is often true in North American culture, which stresses self-expression, self-assertion, and self-esteem (Cole, Bruschi, & Tamang, 2002).

First Signs of Emotion

Newborns plainly show when they are unhappy. They let out piercing cries, flail their arms and legs, and stiffen their bodies. It is harder to tell when they are happy. During the first month, they become quiet at the sound of a human voice or when they are picked up, and they may smile when their hands are moved together to play pat-a-cake. As time goes by, infants respond more to people—smiling, cooing, reaching out, and eventually going to them.

These early signals or clues to babies' feelings are important steps in development. When babies want or need something, they cry; when they feel sociable, they smile or laugh. When their messages bring a response, their sense of connection with other people grows. Their sense of control over their world grows, too, as they see that their cries bring help and comfort and that their smiles and laughter elicit smiles and laughter in return. They become more able to actively participate in regulating their states of arousal and their emotional life.

Crying Crying is the most powerful way—and sometimes the only way—infants can communicate their needs. Almost all adults around the world respond quickly to a crying infant (Broude, 1995).

Some research has distinguished four patterns of crying (Wolff, 1969): the basic *hunger cry* (a rhythmic cry, which is not always associated with hunger); the *angry cry* (a variation of the rhythmic cry, in which excess air is forced through the vocal cords); the *pain cry* (a sudden onset of loud crying without preliminary moaning, sometimes followed by holding the breath); and the *frustration cry* (two or three drawn-out cries, with no prolonged breath-holding). Current perspectives, particularly among Canadian researchers, on the nature of infant crying, focus on the role of crying as a *sign,* an objective indicator of the child's physical state, such as hunger, fatigue, or pain, or as a *symptom,* or evidence of a medical condition, such as too much or too little crying in potential disabilities. From a developmental perspective, crying can play a third role as a *signal* of the child's developmental status. As a signal, crying functions as a response to—or a form of—communication with a caregiver in a particular context, such as indicating pain (Barr, Hopkins, & Green, 2000). As a way of communicating pain, crying is very adaptive and indicates to caregivers the severity of pain and the effectiveness of pain relief. For example, Taddio, Nulman, Goldbach, Ipp, & Koren (1994) found that an infant's first cry in response to pain typically occurs immediately, whereas after a topical anaesthetic is applied there is a delay between the stimulus and the first cry. Other indicators of pain intensity include the duration of the cry and the pitch of the cry, with more intense pain associated with cries of longer duration and higher pitch (Craig, Gilbert-MacLeod, & Lilley, 2000). A parent's success in interpreting and responding to the infant's cries is important to gaining confidence in parenting and to the infant's development (Leavitt, 1998).

Some parents worry that they will spoil a child by picking up a crying baby. Delays in responding to fussing may help babies learn to deal with minor irritations on their own (Hubbard & van IJzendoorn, 1991). But if parents wait until cries of distress escalate to shrieks of rage, it may become more difficult to soothe the baby; and such a pattern, if experienced repeatedly, may interfere with infants' developing the ability to regulate, or manage, their own emotional state (R. A. Thompson, 1991).

Smiling and Laughing The earliest faint smiles occur spontaneously soon after birth, apparently as a result of subcortical nervous system activity. These involuntary smiles frequently appear during periods of REM sleep (refer back to Chapter 5). They become less frequent during the first 3 months as the cortex matures (Sroufe, 1997).

The earliest *waking* smiles may be elicited by mild sensations, such as gentle jiggling or blowing on the infant's skin. In the second week, a baby may smile drowsily after a feeding. By the third week, most infants begin to smile when they are alert and paying attention to a caregiver's nodding head and voice. At about 1 month, smiles generally become more frequent and more social. During the second month, as visual recognition develops, babies smile more at visual stimuli, such as faces they know (Sroufe, 1997; Wolff, 1963). By 4 months, a spontaneous smile can be elicited by the infant at the sight of a parent, an early indication of cognitive development in the child.

At about the fourth month, infants start to laugh out loud when kissed on the stomach or tickled. As babies grow older, they become more actively engaged in mirthful exchanges. A 6-month-old may giggle in response to the mother making unusual sounds or appearing with a towel over her face; a 10-month-old may laughingly try to put the towel back on her face. This change reflects cognitive development: By laughing at the unexpected, babies show that they know what to expect. By turning the tables, they show a dawning awareness that they can cause things to happen, engage the world around them, and play an active role in beginning interactions with others. Laughter also helps babies discharge tension, such as fear of a threatening object (Sroufe, 1997).

When Do Emotions Appear?

Identifying infants' emotions is a challenge because babies cannot tell us what they feel. Researchers disagree about how many emotions there are, when they arise, and how they should be defined and measured.

Carroll Izard and his colleagues have videotaped infants' facial expressions and have interpreted them as showing joy, sadness, interest, and fear, and to a lesser degree anger, surprise, and disgust (Izard, Huebner, Resser, McGinness, & Dougherty, 1980). Of course, we do not know that these babies actually had the feelings they were credited with, but their facial expressions were remarkably similar to adults' expressions when experiencing these emotions.

Facial expressions are not the only, or necessarily the best, index of infants' emotions; motor activity, body language, and physiological changes are also important indicators. An infant can be fearful without showing a "fear face"; the baby may show fear by turning away or averting the gaze, or by a faster heartbeat, and these signs do not necessarily accompany each other. Different indicators may point to different conclusions about the timing of emergence of specific emotions. In addition, this timetable shows a good deal of individual variation (Sroufe, 1997).

Basic Emotions Emotional development is an orderly process; complex emotions build on earlier, simpler ones. According to one model (Lewis, 1997; see Figure 8-1), soon after birth babies show signs of contentment, interest, and distress. These are diffuse, reflexive, mostly physiological responses to sensory stimulation or internal processes. During the next 6 months or so, these early emotional states differentiate into true emotions: joy, surprise, sadness, disgust, and last, anger and fear—reactions to events that have meaning for the infant. As we'll discuss in the next section, the emergence of these basic, or primary, emotions is related to the biological "clock" of neurological maturation.

Emotions Involving the Self Two types of emotions involving the self are self-conscious emotions and self-evaluating emotions.

Self-conscious emotions, such as embarrassment, empathy, and envy, arise only after children have developed **self-awareness:** the cognitive understanding that they have a recognizable identity, separate and different from the rest of their world. This consciousness of self seems to emerge between 15 and 24 months. Self-awareness is necessary before children can be aware of being the focus of attention, identify with what other "selves" are feeling, or wish they had what someone else has.

self-conscious emotions
Emotions, such as embarrassment, empathy, and envy, that depend on self-awareness

self-awareness Realization that one's existence and functioning are separate from those of other people and things

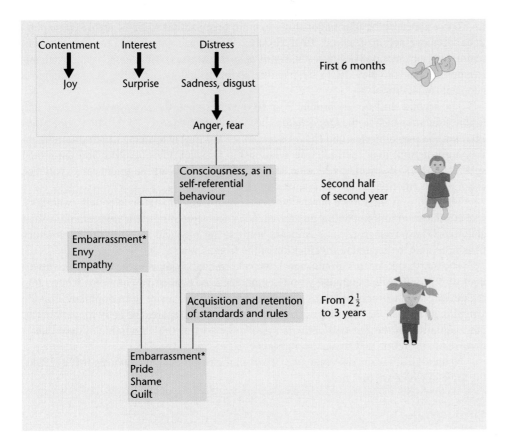

Figure 8-1

Differentiation of emotions during the first 3 years. The primary, or basic, emotions emerge during the first 6 months or so; the self-conscious emotions develop beginning in the second half of the second year, as a result of the emergence of self-awareness (consciousness of self) together with accumulation of knowledge about societal standards and rules.

Note: There are two kinds of embarrassment. The earlier form does not involve evaluation of behaviour and may simply be a response to being singled out as the object of attention. The second kind, evaluative embarrassment, which emerges during the third year, is a mild form of shame.

Source: Adapted from Lewis, 1997, Figure 1, p. 120.

By about age 3, having acquired self-awareness plus a good deal of knowledge about their society's accepted standards, rules, and goals, children become better able to evaluate their own thoughts, plans, desires, and behaviour against what is considered socially appropriate. Only then can they demonstrate the **self-evaluative emotions** of pride, guilt, and shame (Lewis, 1995, 1997, 1998).

Guilt and shame are distinct emotions, even though both may be responses to wrongdoing. Children who fail to live up to behavioural standards may feel guilty (that is, regret their behaviour), but they do not necessarily feel a lack of self-worth, as when they feel ashamed. Their focus is on a bad *act,* not a bad *self* (Eisenberg, 2000).

Empathy: Feeling What Others Feel Empathy—the ability to "put oneself in another person's place" and feel what that person feels, or would be expected to feel, in a particular situation—is thought to arise during the second year. Like guilt, empathy increases with age (Eisenberg, 2000; Eisenberg & Fabes, 1998).

Empathy depends on **social cognition,** the cognitive ability to understand that others have mental states and to gauge their feelings and intentions. Piaget believed that **egocentrism** (inability to see another person's point of view) delays the development of this ability until the concrete operational stage of middle childhood. Other research suggests that social cognition begins much earlier. In one study, 9-month-olds (but not 6-month-olds) reacted differently to a person who was unwilling to give them a toy than to a person who tried to give them a toy but accidentally droppped it. This finding suggests that the older infants had gained some understanding of another person's intentions (Behne, Carpenter, Call, & Tomasello, 2005).

Brain Growth and Emotional Development

The development of the brain after birth is closely connected with changes in emotional life. This is a bi-directional process: Social and emotional experience are not only affected by brain development but can have long-lasting effects on the structure of the brain (Mlot, 1998; Sroufe, 1997).

self-evaluative emotions
Emotions, such as pride, shame, and guilt, that depend on both self-awareness and knowledge of socially accepted standards of behaviour

empathy Ability to put oneself in another person's place and feel what the other person feels

social cognition Ability to understand that other people have mental states and to gauge their feelings and intentions

egocentrism Piaget's term for inability to consider another person's point of view; a characteristic of young children's thought

Checkpoint ✔

Can you . . .

✔ Explain why infants' emotions are difficult to study?

✔ Explain the significance of patterns of crying, smiling, and laughing?

✔ Trace a proposed sequence of emergence of the basic, self-conscious, and evaluative emotions, and explain its connection with cognitive and neurological development?

There appear to be four major shifts in brain organization, which roughly correspond to changes in emotions (Schore, 1994; Sroufe, 1997). During the first 3 months, differentiation of basic emotions begins as the *cerebral cortex* becomes functional, bringing cognitive perceptions into play. REM sleep and reflexive behaviour, including the spontaneous neonatal smile, diminish.

The second shift occurs around 9 or 10 months, when the *frontal lobes* mature and limbic structures such as the *hippocampus* become larger and more adult-like. Connections between the frontal cortex and the *hypothalamus* and limbic system, which process sensory information, may facilitate the relationship between the cognitive and emotional spheres. As these connections become denser and more elaborate, an infant can experience and interpret emotions at the same time.

The third shift takes place during the second year, when infants develop self-awareness, self-conscious emotions, and a greater capacity for regulating their own emotions and activities. These changes, which coincide with greater physical mobility and exploratory behaviour, may be related to myelination of the frontal lobes.

The fourth shift occurs around age 3, when hormonal changes in the autonomic (involuntary) nervous system coincide with the emergence of evaluative emotions. Underlying the development of such emotions as shame may be a shift away from dominance by the *sympathetic system,* the part of the autonomic system that prepares the body for action, and the maturation of the *parasympathetic system,* the part of the autonomic system that is involved in excretion and sexual excitation.

Neurological factors also may play a part in temperamental differences (Mlot, 1998), the topic to which we turn next.

Temperament

Guidepost 2

How do infants show temperamental differences, and how enduring are those differences?

temperament Characteristic disposition, or style of approaching and reacting to situations

"easy" children Children with a generally happy temperament, regular biological rhythms, and a readiness to accept new experiences

Temperament—sometimes defined as a person's characteristic, biologically based way of approaching and reacting to people and situations—has been described as the *how* of behaviour: not *what* people do, but how they go about doing it (Thomas & Chess, 1977). Two toddlers, for example, may be equally able to dress themselves and may be equally motivated, but one may do it more quickly than the other, be more willing to put on a new outfit, and be less distracted if the cat jumps on the bed.

Some researchers look at temperament more broadly. A child may not act the same way in all situations. And temperament may affect not only the way children approach and react to the outside world, but the way they regulate their own mental, emotional, and behavioural functioning (Rothbart et al., 2000).

Temperament has an emotional basis; but while emotions such as fear, excitement, and boredom come and go, temperament is relatively consistent and enduring. Individual differences in temperament, which are thought to derive from a person's basic biological makeup, form the core of a developing personality (Eisenberg, Fabes, Guthrie, & Reiser, 2000).

Studying Temperamental Patterns: The New York Longitudinal Study

In the New York Longitudinal Study (NYLS), a pioneering study on temperament, researchers followed 133 infants into adulthood. The researchers looked at how active the children were; how regular they were in hunger, sleep, and bowel habits; how readily they accepted new people and situations; how they adapted to changes in routine; how sensitive they were to noise, bright lights, and other sensory stimuli; how intensely they responded; whether their mood tended to be pleasant, joyful, and friendly or unpleasant, unhappy, and unfriendly; and whether they persisted at tasks or were easily distracted (A. Thomas, Chess, & Birch, 1968).

Almost two-thirds of the children in the NYLS fell into one of three categories (see Table 8-2). Forty percent were **"easy" children:** generally happy, rhythmic in biological functioning, and accepting of new experiences. This is how Margaret Mead described the infant Cathy. Ten percent were what the researchers called

Seven-month-old Daniel's ready smile and willingness to try a new food are signs of an easy temperament.

Table 8-2	Three Temperamental Patterns (according to the New York Longitudinal Study)	
"Easy" Child	**"Difficult" Child**	**"Slow-to-Warm-Up" Child**
Has moods of mild to moderate intensity, usually positive	Displays intense and frequently negative moods; cries often and loudly; also laughs loudly	Has mildly intense reactions, both positive and negative
Responds well to novelty and change	Responds poorly to novelty and change	Responds slowly to novelty and change
Quickly develops regular sleep and feeding schedules	Sleeps and eats irregularly	Sleeps and eats more regularly than difficult child, less regularly than easy child
Takes to new foods easily	Accepts new foods slowly	Shows mildly negative initial response to new stimuli (a first encounter with a new person, place, or situation)
Smiles at strangers	Is suspicious of strangers	
Adapts easily to new situations	Adapts slowly to new situations	
Accepts most frustrations with little fuss	Reacts to frustration with tantrums	
Adapts quickly to new routines and rules of new games	Adjusts slowly to new routines	Gradually develops liking for new stimuli after repeated, unpressured exposures

Source: Adapted from A. Thomas & Chess, 1984.

"difficult" children: more irritable and harder to please, irregular in biological rhythms, and more intense in expressing emotion. Fifteen percent were **"slow-to-warm-up" children:** mild but slow to adapt to new people and situations (A. Thomas & Chess, 1977, 1984).

Many children (including 35 percent of the NYLS sample) do not fit neatly into any of these three groups. A baby may eat and sleep regularly but be afraid of strangers. A child may be easy most of the time, but not always. Another child may warm up slowly to new foods but adapt quickly to new babysitters (A. Thomas & Chess, 1984). A child may laugh intensely but not show intense frustration, and a child with rhythmic toilet habits may show irregular sleeping patterns (Rothbart et al., 2000). All these variations are normal.

How is Temperament Measured?

Because the complex interviewing and scoring procedures used in the NYLS are cumbersome, many researchers use short-form questionnaires. A parental self-report instrument, the Rothbart Infant Behavior Questionnaire (IBQ) (Gartstein & Rothbart, 2003; Rothbart et al., 2000) focuses on several dimensions of infant temperament similar to those in the NYLS: activity level, positive emotion (smiling and laughing), fear, frustration, soothability, and duration of orienting (a combination of distractibility and attention span) as well as such additional factors as intensity of pleasure, perceptual sensitivity, and attentional shifting. Parents rate their infants with regard to recent concrete events and behaviours ("How often during the past week did the baby smile or laugh when given a toy?" rather than "Does the baby respond positively to new events?").

Although parental ratings are the most commonly used measures of children's temperament, their validity is in question. Studies of twins have found that parents tend to rate a child's temperament by comparison with other children in the family—for example, labelling one child inactive in contrast to a more active sibling (Saudino, 2003a). Still, observations by researchers may reflect biases as well (Seifer, 2003). Parents see their children in a variety of day-to-day situations, whereas a laboratory observer sees only how the child reacts to particular standardized situations. Thus, a combination of methods may provide a more accurate picture of how temperament affects child development (Rothbart & Hwang, 2002; Saudino, 2003a, 2003b).

How Stable is Temperament?

Temperament appears to be largely inborn, probably hereditary (Braungart, Plomin, DeFries, & Fulker, 1992; Emde et al., 1992; Schmitz et al., 1996; A. Thomas & Chess, 1977, 1984), and fairly stable. Newborn babies show different patterns of sleeping, fussing, and activity, and these differences tend to persist (Korner, 1996; Korner et al., 1985).

"difficult" children Children with irritable temperament, irregular biological rhythms, and intense emotional responses

"slow-to-warm-up" children Children whose temperament is generally mild but who are hesitant about accepting new experiences

Studies using the IBQ have found strong links between infant temperament and childhood personality at age 7 (Rothbart et al., 2000, 2001). Other researchers using temperamental types similar to those of the NYLS have studied the extent to which temperament at age 3 predicts personality at ages 18 and 21 (Caspi, 2000; Caspi & Silva, 1995; Newman, Caspi, Moffitt, & Silva, 1997).

That does not mean temperament is fully formed at birth. Temperament develops as various emotions and self-regulatory capacities appear (Rothbart et al., 2000), and can change during the early months in response to parental treatment and other life experiences (Belsky, Fish, & Isabella, 1991; Kagan & Snidman, 2004; Lerner & Galambos, 1985). As Margaret Mead observed, temperament may be affected by culturally influenced child-raising practices. Infants in Malaysia, an island group in Southeast Asia, tend to be less adaptable, more wary of new experiences, and more readily responsive to stimuli than U.S. babies. This may be because Malay parents do not often expose young children to situations that require adaptability, and they encourage infants to be acutely aware of sensations, such as the need for a diaper change (Banks, 1989).

Temperament and Adjustment: "Goodness of Fit"

goodness of fit Appropriateness of environmental demands and constraints to a child's temperament

According to the NYLS, the key to healthy adjustment is **goodness of fit**—the match between a child's temperament and the environmental demands and constraints the child must deal with. If a very active child is expected to sit still for long periods, if a slow-to-warm-up child is constantly pushed into new situations, or if a persistent child is constantly taken away from absorbing projects, tensions may occur.

Caregivers' responses to their children may reflect the amount of control the caregivers think they have over a child's behaviour. In a home observation, parents who saw themselves as having little control over their 12-month-olds were more likely than other parents to play directively with their babies—urging, reminding, restraining, questioning, and correcting them; and mothers who felt and acted this way were more likely to consider their infants "difficult" (Guzell & Vernon-Feagans, 2004).

When caregivers recognize that a child acts in a certain way, not out of willfulness, laziness, stupidity or spite, but largely because of inborn temperament, they may be less likely to feel guilty, anxious, or hostile, to feel a loss of control, or to be rigid or impatient. They can anticipate the child's reactions and help the child adapt—for example, by giving early warnings of the need to stop an activity or, as Mead and Bateson did, by gradually introducing a child to new situations.

Shyness and Boldness: Influences of Biology and Culture

As we have mentioned, temperament seems to have a biological basis. In longitudinal research with about 500 children starting in infancy, Jerome Kagan and his colleagues have studied an aspect of temperament called *inhibition to the unfamiliar,* or shyness, which has to do with how boldly or cautiously the child approaches unfamiliar objects and situations and is associated with certain biological characteristics.

When presented at 4 months with a series of new stimuli, about 20 percent of the infants cried, pumped their arms and legs, and sometimes arched their backs; this group were called "high-reactive." Forty percent (called "low-reactive") showed little distress or motor activity and were more likely to smile spontaneously. The rest either showed little motor activity but became very irritable or showed vigorous motor activity but rarely cried. The researchers hypothesized that these differences might be related to the amygdala, a brain organ that detects and reacts to unfamiliar events and is involved in emotional reactions. High-reactive children may be born with an usually excitable amygdala (Kagan & Snidman, 2004).

At 4½ years, in a play session with two unfamiliar children of the same age and sex, children who had been identified as high-reactive in infancy were more likely to be shy, quiet, and timid, whereas low-reactive children were more likely to be sociable and talkative (Kagan & Snidman, 2004). In addition, the shyer children showed higher and less variable heart rates than bolder children, and the pupils of their eyes dilated more. The boldest children (about 10 to 15 percent) tended to be energetic and spontaneous and to have very low heart rates (Arcus & Kagan, 1995).

Children who had been identified as inhibited or uninhibited seemed to maintain these patterns to some degree during childhood (Kagan, 1997; Kagan & Snidman, 1991a, 1991b), along with specific differences in physiological characteristics. High-reactive (inhibited) children were more likely to have a thin body build, narrow face, and blue eyes, whereas low-reactive (uninhibited) children were taller, heavier, and more often brown-eyed. It may be that the genes that contribute to reactivity and timid or bold behaviour also influence body size and eye colour (Kagan & Snidman, 2004).

Behavioural differences between these two types of children tended to "smooth out" by early adolescence, even though the physiological distinctions remained (Woodward et al., 2001). At their last assessment, at about age 11, about 33 percent of both high- and low-reactives behaved consistent with their infant temperament, but 16 percent of each group did not. However, less than 5 percent of each group developed the behavioural features of the other type. For example, some high-reactive children no longer seemed extremely shy, but they still did not show the relaxed spontaneity characteristic of low-reactives (Kagan & Snidman, 2004).

In a cross-cultural study of Chinese and Canadian 2-year-olds, Canadian mothers of inhibited children tended to be punitive or overprotective, whereas Chinese mothers of such children were warm and accepting and encouraged them to achieve. The Chinese toddlers were significantly more inhibited than the Canadian ones; but because this was a correlational study, we don't know whether the children's temperament was a consequence or a cause of their mothers' treatment, or perhaps a bi-directional effect (Chen et al., 1998). In China, unlike Canada, shyness and inhibition are socially approved; a naturally inhibited Chinese child may be less motivated to come out of his or her shell than a Canadian one, or less subject to parental prodding to do so (Nelson, Hart, Wu, Yang, Roper, & Jin, 2006).

These findings suggest, again, that experience can moderate or accentuate early tendencies. Male toddlers who were inclined to be fearful and shy were more likely to remain so at age 3 if their parents were highly accepting of the child's reactions. If parents encouraged their sons to venture into new situations, the boys tended to become less inhibited (Park, Belsky, Putnam, & Crnic, 1997). Other environmental influences, such as birth order, race/ethnicity, culture, relationships with teachers and peers, and unpredictable events also can reinforce or soften a child's original temperamental bias (Kagan & Snidman, 2004).

Developmental Issues in Infancy

How does a dependent newborn, with a limited emotional repertoire and pressing physical needs, become a 3-year-old with complex feelings, a strong will, and the beginnings of a conscience? Much of this development revolves around issues regarding the self in relation to others.

Developing Trust

For a far longer period than the young of other mammals, human babies are dependent on other people for food, for protection, and for their very lives. How do they come to trust that their needs will be met? According to Erikson (1950), early experiences are the key.

The first of the eight crises, or critical developmental stages, Erikson identified (refer back to Table 2-2 in Chapter 2) is **basic trust versus basic mistrust.** This stage begins in infancy and continues until about 18 months. In these early months, babies develop a sense of the reliability of the people and objects in their world. They need to develop a balance between trust (which lets them form intimate relationships) and mistrust (which enables them to protect themselves). If trust predominates, as it should, children develop the "virtue" of *hope:* the belief that they can fulfill their needs and obtain their desires (Erikson, 1982). If mistrust predominates, children will view the world as unfriendly and unpredictable and will have trouble forming relationships.

The critical element in developing trust is sensitive, responsive, consistent caregiving. Erikson saw feeding time as the setting for establishing the right mix of trust and mistrust.

What's your view

• In Canada, many people consider shyness undesirable. How should a parent handle a shy child? Do you think it is best to accept the child's temperament or try to change it?

Checkpoint

Can you . . .

✔ List and describe nine aspects and three patterns of temperament identified by the New York Longitudinal Study?

✔ Assess evidence for the stability of temperament?

✔ Discuss how temperament can affect social adjustment, and explain the importance of "goodness of fit"?

✔ Give evidence of biological influences on temperament, of the role of parental handling, and of cultural differences?

Guidepost 3

How do infants gain trust in their world and form attachments, and how do infants and caregivers "read" each other's non-verbal signals?

basic trust versus basic mistrust Erikson's first crisis in psychosocial development, in which infants develop a sense of the reliability of people and objects in their world

Diane's sensitivity to Anna's needs contributes to the development of Anna's sense of basic trust—her ability to rely on the people and things in her world. Trust is necessary, according to Erikson, for children to form intimate relationships.

Checkpoint ✔

Can you . . .

✔ Explain the importance of basic trust, and identify the critical element in its development?

attachment Reciprocal, enduring tie between two people—especially between infant and caregiver—each of whom contributes to the quality of the relationship

Strange Situation Laboratory technique used to study attachment

Can the baby count on being fed when hungry, and can the baby therefore trust the mother as a representative of the world? Trust enables an infant to let the mother out of sight "because she has become an inner certainty as well as an outer predictability" (Erikson, 1950, p. 247). This inner trust, in Cathy Bateson, may have formed a solid foundation for more difficult periods ahead.

Developing Attachments

Attachment is a reciprocal, enduring emotional tie between an infant and a caregiver, each of whom contributes to the quality of the relationship. Attachments have adaptive value for babies, ensuring that their psychosocial as well as physical needs will be met (MacDonald, 1998). According to ethological theory (see Chapter 2), infants and parents are biologically predisposed to become attached to each other, and attachment promotes a baby's survival.

Studying Patterns of Attachment

Mary Ainsworth first studied attachment in the early 1950s with John Bowlby after completing her graduate studies at the University of Toronto. Bowlby (1951), on the basis of ethological studies of bonding in animals and observation of disturbed children in a London psychoanalytic clinic, was convinced of the importance of the mother–baby bond; he warned against separating mother and baby without providing good substitute caregiving. Ainsworth, after studying attachment in African babies in Uganda through naturalistic observation in their homes (Ainsworth, 1967), devised the **Strange Situation,** a now-classic laboratory-based technique designed to assess attachment patterns between an infant and an adult. Typically, the adult is the mother (though other adults have taken part as well), and the infant is 10 to 24 months old.

The Strange Situation consists of a sequence of eight episodes, which takes less than half an hour. During that time, the mother twice leaves the baby in an unfamiliar room, the first time with a stranger. The second time she leaves the baby alone, and the stranger comes back before the mother does. The mother then encourages the baby to explore and play again and gives comfort if the baby seems to need it (Ainsworth, Blehar, Waters, & Wall, 1978). Of particular concern is the baby's response each time the mother returns.

When Ainsworth and her colleagues observed 1-year-olds in the Strange Situation and at home, they found three main patterns of attachment: *secure* (the most common category, into which about 60–75 percent of babies fell) and two forms of anxious, or insecure, attachment: *avoidant* (15–25 percent of babies) and *ambivalent, or resistant* (10–15 percent) (Vondra & Barnett, 1999).

Babies with **secure attachment** cry or protest when the mother leaves and greet her happily when she returns. They use her as a secure base, leaving her to go off and explore but returning occasionally for reassurance. They are usually cooperative and relatively free of anger. Babies with **avoidant attachment** rarely cry when the mother leaves, and they avoid her on her return. They tend to be angry and do not reach out in time of need. They dislike being held but dislike being put down even more. Babies with **ambivalent (resistant) attachment** become anxious even before the mother leaves and are very upset when she goes out. When she returns, they show their ambivalence by seeking contact with her while at the same time resisting it by kicking or squirming. Resistant babies do little exploration and are hard to comfort. These three attachment patterns are universal in all cultures in which they have been studied—cultures as different as those in Africa, China, and Israel—though the percentage of infants in each category varies (van IJzendoorn & Kroonenberg, 1988; van IJzendoorn & Sagi, 1999).

Other research (Main & Solomon, 1986) has identified a fourth pattern, **disorganized-disoriented attachment.** Babies with the disorganized pattern often show inconsistent, contradictory behaviours. They greet the mother brightly when she returns but then turn away or approach without looking at her. They seem confused and afraid. This may be the least secure pattern. It is most likely to occur in babies whose mothers are insensitive, intrusive, or abusive (Carlson, 1998). (Table 8-3 describes how babies with each of the four patterns of attachment react to the Strange Situation.)

How Attachment is Established

On the basis of a baby's interactions with the mother, said Bowlby, the baby builds a "working model" of what can be expected from her (Bretherton, 1997). The various patterns of emotional attachment represent different cognitive representations that result in different expectations. As long as the mother continues to act the same way, the model holds up. If her behaviour changes—not just once or twice but consistently—the baby may revise the model, and security of attachment may change.

A baby's working model of attachment is related to Erikson's concept of basic trust. Secure attachment evolves from trust; insecure attachment reflects mistrust. Securely attached babies have learned to trust not only their caregivers but their own ability to get what they need. Thus babies who cry a lot and whose mothers respond by soothing them tend to be securely attached (Del Carmen, Pedersen, Huffman, & Bryan, 1993).

Mothers of securely attached infants and toddlers tend to be sensitive and responsive (Ainsworth et al., 1978; Braungart-Rieker et al., 2001; De Wolff & van IJzendoorn, 1997; Isabella, 1993; NICHD Early Child Care Research Network, 1997a). Equally important

This baby, like most infants, is developing a strong attachment to his mother. Both mother and baby contribute to the security of attachment by their personalities and behaviour and their responsiveness to each other.

secure attachment Pattern in which an infant cries or protests when the primary caregiver leaves and actively seeks out the caregiver upon his or her return

avoidant attachment Pattern in which an infant rarely cries when separated from the primary caregiver and avoids contact upon his or her return

ambivalent (resistant) attachment Pattern in which an infant becomes anxious before the primary caregiver leaves, is extremely upset during his or her absence, and both seeks and resists contact on his or her return

disorganized-disoriented attachment Pattern in which an infant, after being separated from the primary caregiver, shows contradictory behaviours upon his or her return

Table 8-3	Attachment Behaviours in Strange Situation
Attachment Classification	**Behaviour**
Secure	Gloria plays and explores freely when her mother is nearby. She responds enthusiastically when her mother returns.
Insecure-Avoidant	When Sam's mother returns, Sam does not make eye contact or greet her. It is almost as if he has not noticed her return.
Insecure-Resistant	James hovers close to his mother during much of the Strange Situation, but he does not greet her positively or enthusiastically during the reunion episode. Instead, he is angry and upset.
Disorganized/ Disoriented	Erica responds to the Strange Situation with inconsistent, contradictory behaviour. She seems to fall apart, overwhelmed by the stress.

Based on Thompson, 1998, pp. 37–39.

are mutual interaction, stimulation, a positive attitude, warmth and acceptance, and emotional support (De Wolff & van IJzendoorn, 1997; Lundy, 2003).

In a prospective longitudinal study of South African infants at 2 and 18 months, both early and later aspects of the mother–infant relationship influenced security of attachment. Mothers whose infants were insecurely attached at 18 months tended to have been remote (detached) and intrusive or coercive when the infants were 2 months old and to be insensitive and intrusive or coercive when the infants were 18 months. Despite the extreme poverty in which these families lived and the legacy of the apartheid system, an official policy of racial segregation that lasted until the early 1990s, nearly 62 percent of the infants were judged secure, while almost 26 percent were rated as disorganized (Tomlinson, Cooper, & Murray, 2005). By contrast, among institutionalized infants and toddlers in Bucharest, Romania, more than 65 percent were classified as disorganized and only about 19 percent as secure (Zeanah, Smyke, Koga, & Carlson, 2005).

Alternative Methods to Study Attachment

Although much research on attachment has been based on the Strange Situation, some investigators have questioned its validity. The Strange Situation *is* strange; it is also artificial. It asks mothers not to initiate interaction, exposes babies to repeated comings and goings of adults, and expects the infants to pay attention to them. Also, the Strange Situation may be less valid in some nonwestern cultures. Research on Japanese infants, who are less commonly separated from their mothers than Canadian babies, showed high rates of resistant attachment, which may reflect the extreme stressfulness of the Strange Situation for these babies (Miyake, Chen, & Campos, 1985).

Because attachment influences a wider range of behaviours than are seen in the Strange Situation, some researchers have begun to supplement it with methods that enable them to study children in natural settings. The Waters and Deane (1985) Attachment Q-set (AQS) has mothers or other home observers sort a set of descriptive words or phrases ("cries a lot"; "tends to cling") into categories ranging from most to least characteristic of the child and then compare these descriptions with expert descriptions of the prototypical secure child. An analysis of 139 studies found the observer version (but not the maternal report version) a valid measure of attachment security, correlating well with results from the Strange Situation and with measures of maternal sensitivity. The AQS also seems to have cross-cultural validity (van IJzendoorn, Vereijken, Bakermans-Kranenburg, & Riksen-Walraven, 2004). In a study using the AQS, mothers in China, Colombia, Germany, Israel, Japan, Norway, and the United States decribed their children as behaving more like than unlike the "most secure child." Furthermore, the mothers' descriptions of "secure-base" behaviour were about as similar across cultures as within a culture. These findings suggest that the tendency to use the mother as a secure base is universal, though it may take somewhat varied forms (Posada et al., 1995).

The Role of Temperament

How much influence does temperament exert on attachment, and in what ways? Findings vary (Susman-Stillman, Kalkoske, Egeland, & Waldman, 1996; Vaughn et al., 1992). In a study of 6- to 12-month-olds and their families (which used frequent home observations, maternal reports, and Q-sorts in addition to the Strange Situation), both a mother's sensitivity and her baby's temperament influenced attachment patterns (Seifer, Schiller, Sameroff, Resnick, & Riordan, 1996). Some studies have identified frustration levels, amounts of crying, and irritability as predictors of attachment (Calkins & Fox, 1992; Izard, Porges, Simons, Haynes, & Cohen, 1991). Neurological or physiological conditions may underlie temperamental differences in attachment. For example, variability in heart rate is associated with irritability, and heart rate seems to vary more in insecurely attached infants (Izard, Porges, et al., 1991).

A baby's temperament may have not only a direct impact on attachment but also an indirect impact through its effect on the parents. In a series of studies in the Netherlands (van den Boom, 1989, 1994), 15-day-old infants classified as irritable were much more likely than non-irritable infants to be insecurely (usually avoidantly) attached at 1 year.

However, irritable infants whose mostly low-SES mothers received home visits, with instruction on how to soothe their babies, were as likely to be rated as securely attached as the non-irritable infants. Thus infant irritability may prevent the development of secure attachment unless the mother has the skills to cope with the baby's temperament (Rothbart et al., 2000). "Goodness of fit" between parent and child may well be a key to understanding security of attachment.

Intergenerational Transmission of Attachment Patterns

The *Adult Attachment Interview (AAI)* (George, Kaplan, & Main, 1985; Main, 1995; Main, Kaplan, & Cassidy, 1985) is a semi-structured interview that asks adults to recall and interpret feelings and experiences related to their childhood attachments. An analysis of 18 studies using the AAI found that the clarity, coherence, and consistency of responses reliably predicts the security with which the respondent's own child will be attached to him or her (van IJzendoorn, 1995).

The way adults recall early experiences with parents or caregivers affects the way they respond to their own children (Adam, Gunnar, & Tanaka, 2004; Dozier, Stovall, Albus, & Bates, 2001; Pesonen, Raïkkönen, Keltikangas-Järvinen, Strandberg, & Järvenpää, 2003; Slade, Belsky, Aber, & Phelps, 1999). A mother who was securely attached to *her* mother, or who understands why she was insecurely attached, can accurately recognize the baby's attachment behaviours, respond encouragingly, and help the baby form a secure attachment to her (Bretherton, 1990). Mothers who are preoccupied with their past attachment relationships tend to show anger and intrusiveness in interactions with their children. Depressed mothers who dismiss memories of their past attachments tend to be cold and unresponsive to their children (Adam et al., 2004). Parents' attachment history also influences their perceptions of their baby's temperament, and those perceptions may affect the parent-child relationship (Pesonen et al., 2003).

Stranger Anxiety and Separation Anxiety

Sophie used to be a friendly baby, smiling at strangers and going to them, continuing to coo happily as long as someone—anyone—was around. Now, at 8 months, she turns away when a new person approaches and howls when her parents try to leave her with a babysitter. Sophie is experiencing both **stranger anxiety,** wariness of a person she does not know, and **separation anxiety,** distress when a familiar caregiver leaves her.

Separation anxiety and stranger anxiety used to be considered emotional and cognitive milestones of the second half of infancy, reflecting attachment to the mother. However, newer research suggests that although stranger anxiety and separation anxiety are fairly typical, they are not universal. Whether a baby cries when a parent leaves or when someone new approaches may say more about the baby's temperament or life circumstances than about security of attachment (R. J. Davidson & Fox, 1989).

Babies rarely react negatively to strangers before 6 months of age, commonly do so by 8 or 9 months, and do so more and more throughout the rest of the first year (Sroufe, 1997). Even then, however, a baby may react positively to a new person, especially if the mother speaks positively about the stranger (Feinman & Lewis, 1983) or if the person waits a little while and then approaches the baby gradually, gently, and playfully (Sroufe, 1997).

Separation anxiety may be due, not so much to the separation itself, as to the quality of substitute care. When substitute caregivers are warm and responsive and play with 9-month-olds *before* they cry, the babies cry less than when they are with less responsive caregivers (Gunnar, Larson, Hertsgaard, Harris, & Brodersen, 1992). Babies as young as 4 months are capable of distinguishing between adults who have been responsive to them in the past and those who have not been responsive, even if the amount of prior contact has been brief (Bigelow & Birch, 2000).

Stability of care is important. Pioneering work by René Spitz (1945, 1946) on institutionalized children emphasizes the need for substitute care to be as close as possible to good mothering. Research has underlined the value of continuity and consistency in caregiving, so children can form early emotional bonds with their caregivers.

stranger anxiety Wariness of strange people and places, shown by some infants during the second half of the first year

separation anxiety Distress shown by someone, typically an infant, when a familiar caregiver leaves

Today, neither intense fear of strangers nor intense protest when the mother leaves is considered to be a sign of secure attachment. Researchers measure attachment more by what happens when the mother returns than by how many tears the baby sheds at her departure.

Long-term Effects of Attachment

As attachment theory proposes, security of attachment seems to affect emotional, social, and cognitive competence (van IJzendoorn & Sagi, 1997). The more secure a child's attachment to a nurturing adult, the easier it is for the child to eventually become independent of that adult and to develop good relationships with others.

If children, as infants, had a secure base and could count on parents' or caregivers' responsiveness, they are likely to feel confident enough to be actively engaged in their world (Jacobsen & Hofmann, 1997). In a study of 70 fifteen-month-olds, those who were securely attached to their mothers, as measured by the Strange Situation, showed less stress in adapting to child care than did insecurely attached toddlers (Ahnert, Gunnar, Lamb, & Barthel, 2004).

Securely attached toddlers have larger, more varied vocabularies than those who are insecurely attached (Meins, 1998). They also are more sociable (Elicker, Englund, & Sroufe, 1992; Main, 1983). They have more positive interactions with peers, and their friendly overtures are more likely to be accepted (Fagot, 1997). Insecurely attached toddlers tend to show more fear, distress, and anger, whereas securely attached children are more joyful (Kochanska, 2001).

Between ages 3 and 5, securely attached children are likely to be more curious, competent, empathic, resilient, and self-confident, to get along better with other children, and to form close friendships (Arend, Gove, & Sroufe, 1979; Elicker et al., 1992; J. L. Jacobson & Wille, 1986; Waters, Wippman, & Sroufe, 1979; Youngblade & Belsky, 1992). They interact more positively with parents, preschool teachers, and peers and are better able to resolve conflicts (Elicker et al., 1992). They tend to have a more positive self-image (Elicker et al., 1992; Verschueren, Marcoen, & Schoefs, 1996). Their advantages continue. In a French-Canadian laboratory observation, attachment patterns and the emotional quality of 6-year-olds' interactions with their mothers predicted the strength of the children's communicative skills, cognitive engagement, and mastery motivation at age 8 (Moss & St-Laurent, 2001).

Secure attachment seems to prepare children for the intimacy of friendship (Carlson, Sroufe, & Egeland, 2004). In middle childhood and adolescence, securely attached children (at least in western cultures, where most studies have been done) tend to have the closest, most stable friendships (Schneider, Atkinson, & Tardif, 2001; Sroufe, Carlson, & Shulman, 1993).

Insecurely attached infants, by contrast, often have later problems: inhibitions at age 2, hostility toward other children at age 5, and dependency during the school years (Calkins & Fox, 1992; Lyons-Ruth, Alpern, & Repacholi, 1993; Sroufe et al., 1993). Those with disorganized attachment tend to have behaviour problems at all levels of schooling and psychiatric disorders at age 17 (Carlson, 1998). However, it may be that the correlations between attachment in infancy and later development stem, not from attachment itself, but from personality characteristics that affect both attachment and parent–child interactions *after* infancy (Lamb, 1987).

In a longitudinal study of 1,364 families with 1-month-old infants, children who were avoidantly attached at 15 months tended to be rated by their mothers as less socially competent than secure children and by their teachers as more aggressive or anxious during the preschool and school-age years. However, effects of parenting on the children's behaviour during these years was more important than early attachment. Insecure or disorganized children whose parenting had improved were less aggressive in school than those whose parenting did not improve or got worse. Secure children, on the other hand, were relatively immune to parenting that became less sensitive, perhaps because their early working models buoyed them up even under changed conditions. This study suggests that the continuity generally found between attachment and later behaviour can be explained by continuity in the home environment (NICHD Early Child Care Research Network, 2006b).

Checkpoint

Can you . . .

✔ Describe four patterns of attachment?

✔ Discuss how attachment is established, including the roles of mothers and fathers and of the baby's temperament?

✔ Discuss factors affecting stranger anxiety and separation anxiety?

✔ Describe long-term behavioural differences influenced by attachment patterns?

Emotional Communication with Caregivers: Mutual Regulation

Infants are communicating beings; they have a strong drive to interact with others (Striano, 2004). A 1-month-old gazes attentively at the mother's face. At 2 months, in response to the mother's emotional feedback, the infant engages more actively in a mutual exchange of positive emotion. By the third month, the infant becomes more approaching and more playful (Lavelli & Fogel, 2005).

The synchrony of interactions with a caregiver—the ability of both infant and caregiver to respond appropriately and sensitively to each other's mental and emotional states—is known as **mutual regulation.** Infants take an active part in mutual regulation by sending behavioural signals that influence the way caregivers behave toward them (Lundy, 2003). Healthy interaction occurs when a caregiver "reads" a baby's signals accurately and responds appropriately. When a baby's goals are met, the baby is joyful, or at least interested (E. Z. Tronick, 1989). If a caregiver ignores an invitation to play or insists on playing when the baby has signalled "I don't feel like it," the baby may feel frustrated or sad. When babies do not achieve desired results, they keep on sending signals to repair the interaction. Normally, interaction moves back and forth between well-regulated and poorly regulated states, and babies learn from these shifts how to send signals and what to do when their initial signals do not result in a comfortable emotional balance. Mutual regulation helps babies learn to "read" others' behaviour and to develop expectations about it. Even very young infants can perceive emotions expressed by others and can adjust their own behaviour accordingly (Legerstee & Varghese, 2001; Montague & Walker-Andrews, 2001; Termine & Izard, 1988), but they are disturbed when someone—whether the mother or a stranger, and regardless of the reason—breaks off interpersonal contact (Striano, 2004). See Box 8-1.

mutual regulation Process by which infant and caregiver communicate emotional states to each other and respond appropriately

Measuring Mutual Regulation: The "Still-Face" Paradigm

The **"still-face" paradigm** is a research method used to measure mutual regulation in infants from 2 to 9 months old, though infants as young as 1½ months have been found to respond to it (Bertin & Striano, 2006). In the *still-face* episode, which follows a normal face-to-face interaction, the mother suddenly becomes stony-faced, silent, and unresponsive. Then, a few minutes later, she resumes normal interaction (the *reunion* episode). During the still-face episode, infants tend to stop smiling and looking at the mother. They may make faces, sounds, or gestures or may touch themselves, their clothing, or a chair, apparently to comfort themselves or to relieve the emotional stress created by the mother's unexpected behaviour (Cohn & Tronick, 1983; E. Z. Tronick, 1980; 1989; Weinberg & Tronick, 1996).

"still-face" paradigm Research method used to measure mutual regulation in infants 2 to 9 months old

How do infants react during the reunion episode? One study combined a microanalysis of 6-month-olds' facial expressions during this episode with measures of heart rate and nervous system reactivity. The infants' reactions were mixed. On the one hand, they showed even more positive behaviour—joyous expressions and utterances, and gazes and gestures directed toward the mother—than before the still-face episode. On the other hand, the persistence of sad or angry facial expressions, "pick-me-up" gestures, distancing, and indications of stress, as well as an increased tendency to fuss and cry, suggested that while infants welcome the resumption of interaction with the mother, the negative feelings stirred by a breakdown in mutual regulation are not readily eased (Weinberg & Tronick, 1996).

The still-face reaction seems to be similar in eastern and western cultures and in interactions with both fathers and mothers (Braungart-Rieker, Garwood, Powers, & Notaro, 1998; Kisilevsky et al., 1998). Infants whose parents are normally sensitive and responsive to their emotional needs seem better able to comfort themselves and show less negative emotion during the still-face episode and recover more readily during the reunion episode (Braungart-Rieker et al., 2001; Tarabulsy et al., 2003). In cross-cultural experiments, both Chinese and Canadian infants responded similarly to mothers and fathers—and also to strangers—in comparison with control groups that did not experience the still-face episode (Kisilevsky et al., 1998).

What's your view

- Do you see any ethical problems with the still-face paradigm or the Strange Situation? If so, do you think the benefits of these kinds of research are worth the risks?

Box 8-1 *How Postpartum Depression Affects Early Development*

Reading emotional signals lets mothers assess and meet babies' needs; and it lets babies influence or respond to the mother's behaviour toward them. What happens, then, if that communication system seriously breaks down, and what can be done about it?

Postpartum depression—major or minor depression occurring within 4 weeks of giving birth—affects about 14.5 percent of new mothers (Wisner, Chambers, & Sit, 2006), including the actress Brooke Shields, who has written a book about it. First-time mothers are especially at risk, according to a Danish population-based study (Munk-Olsen, Laursen, Pedersen, Mors, & Mortensen, 2006).

Unless treated promptly, postpartum depression may have a negative impact on the way a mother interacts with her baby and on the child's future cognitive and emotional development (Gjerdingen, 2003). Depressed mothers are less sensitive to their infants than nondepressed mothers, and their interactions with their babies are generally less positive (NICHD Early Child Care Research Network, 1999b). Depressed mothers are less likely to interpret and respond to an infant's cries (Donovan, Leavitt, & Walsh, 1998).

Babies of depressed mothers may give up on sending emotional signals and try to comfort themselves by sucking or rocking. If this reaction becomes habitual, babies learn that they have no power to draw responses from other people, that their mothers are unreliable, and that the world is untrustworthy. They also may become depressed themselves (Ashman & Dawson, 2002; Gelfand & Teti, 1995; Teti et al., 1995). We cannot be sure, however, that such infants become depressed through a failure of mutual regulation. They may inherit a predisposition to depression or acquire it prenatally through exposure to hormonal or other biochemical influences.

Infants of depressed mothers tend to show unusual patterns of brain activity, similar to the mothers' own patterns. Within 24 hours of birth, they show relatively less activity in the left frontal region of the brain, which seems to be specialized for "approach" emotions such as joy and anger, and more activity in the right frontal region, which controls "withdrawal" emotions, such as distress and disgust (G. Dawson et al., 1992, 1999; T. Field, 1998a, 1998c; T. Field, Fox, Pickens, Nawrocki, & Soutollo, 1995; N. A. Jones, Field, Fox, Lundy, & Davalos, 1997). Newborns of depressed mothers also tend to have higher levels of stress hormones (Lundy et al., 1999), lower scores on the Brazelton Neonatal Behaviour Assessment Scale, and lower vagal tone, which is associated with attention and learning (T. Field, 1998a, 1998c; N. A. Jones et al., 1998). These findings suggest that a woman's depression during pregnancy may contribute to her newborn's neurological and behavioural functioning.

It may be that a combination of genetic, prenatal, and environmental factors puts infants of depressed mothers at risk. A bidirectional influence may be at work; an infant who does not respond normally may further depress the mother, and her unresponsiveness may in turn increase the infant's depression (T. Field, 1995, 1998a, 1998c; Lundy et al., 1999). Some depressed mothers do maintain good interactions with their infants, and these infants tend to have better emotional regulation than other infants of depressed mothers (Field, Diego, Hernandez-Reif, Schanberg, & Kuhn, 2003). Interactions with a nondepressed adult can help infants compensate for the effects of depressed mothering (T. Field, 1995, 1998a, 1998c).

Children with depressed mothers tend to be insecurely attached (Gelfand & Teti, 1995; Teti et al., 1995). They are likely to grow poorly, to perform poorly on cognitive and linguistic measures, and to have behaviour problems (T. Field, 1998a, 1998c; T. M. Field et al., 1985; Gelfand & Teti, 1995; NICHD Early Child Care Research Network, 1999b; B. S. Zuckerman & Beardslee, 1987). As toddlers these children tend to have trouble suppressing frustration and tension (Cole, Barrett, & Zahn-Waxler, 1992; Seiner & Gelfand, 1995), and in early adolescence they are at risk for violent behaviour (Hay, 2003). The National Longitudinal Study of Children and Youth (NLSCY), showed an increased likelihood of an emotional disorder in Canadian children aged 2 to 3 years whose primary caregiver was depressed. Parental depression was associated with a higher likelihood of emotional disorder, conduct disorder, hyperactivity, and cognitive and relationship problems in children between 4 and 11 years of age (Somers & Willms, 2002; Landy & Tam, 1998).

Antidepressant drugs such as Zoloft (a selective serotonin reuptake inhibitor) and nortriptyline (a tricyclic) appear to be safe and effective for treating postpartum depression (Wisner et al., 2006). Other techniques that may help improve a depressed mother's mood include listening to music, visual imagery, aerobics, yoga, relaxation, and massage therapy (T. Field, 1995, 1998a, 1998c). Massage also can help depressed babies (T. Field, 1998a, 1998b; T. Field et al., 1996), possibly through effects on neurological activity (N. A. Jones et al., 1997). In one study, such mood-brightening measures—plus social, educational, and vocational rehabilitation for the mother and day care for the infant—improved their interaction behaviour. The infants showed faster growth and had fewer pediatric problems, more normal biochemical values, and better developmental test scores than a control group (T. Field, 1998a, 1998b).

What's your view ?

Can you suggest ways to help depressed mothers and babies, other than those mentioned here?

Check it out !

For further information on this topic, go to **www.mcgrawhill. ca/olc/papalia**, or **www.nimh.nih.gov/publicat/depwomenknows. cfm**, a National Institute of Mental Health Web resource called "Depression: What Every Woman Should Know," or **www.nimh. nih.gov/publicat/depresfact.cfm**, a general fact sheet about depression, located on the Web site of the National Institute of Mental Health, which covers women's depression.

Social Referencing

Toward the end of the first year, as infants begin to get around on their own and initiate complex behaviours, they experience an important developmental shift: the ability to participate in person-to-person communication about an external event. They can now engage in *affective sharing,* letting a caregiver know how they feel about a situation or object and reacting to the emotions they discern in the caregiver. These developments are the necessary underpinnings of **social referencing,** the ability to seek out emotional information to guide behaviour (Hertenstein & Campos, 2004). In social referencing, one person forms an understanding of how to act in an ambiguous, confusing, or unfamiliar situation by seeking out and interpreting another person's perception of it. Babies seem to use social referencing when they look at their caregivers upon encountering a new person or toy.

social referencing Understanding an ambiguous situation by seeking out another person's perception of it

Research provides experimental evidence of social referencing at 1 year (Moses, Baldwin, Rosicky, & Tidball, 2001). When exposed to jiggling or vibrating toys fastened to the floor or ceiling, both 12- and 18-month-olds moved closer to or farther from the toys depending on the experimenters' expressed emotional reactions ("Yecch!" or "Nice!"). In a pair of studies, 12-month-olds (but not 10-month-olds) adjusted their behaviour toward certain unfamiliar objects according to nonvocal emotional signals given by an actress on a television screen (Mumme & Fernald, 2003). In another pair of experiments (Hertenstein & Campos, 2004), whether 14-month-olds touched plastic creatures that dropped within their reach was related to the positive or negative emotions they had seen an adult express about the same objects an hour before. Eleven-month-olds responded to such emotional cues if the delay was very brief (3 minutes).

Another advance is in understanding the difference between intentional and unintentional actions. Nine-month-olds (but not 6-month-olds) react differently to a person who is unwilling to give them a toy than to a person who tries to give them a toy but accidentally drops it. This finding suggests that the older infants have gained some understanding of another person's mental state—what Piaget called *theory of mind* (Behne, Carpenter, Call, & Tomasello, 2005; see Chapter 10).

A longitudinal study of 25 infants from age 6 to 12 months in Montreal showed that the use of social referencing as a way of understanding the causes of unfamiliar events grows. Children as young as 6 months used social referencing with their mothers when an object was placed in an unusual place. Social referencing, as a way of getting information about an ambiguous situation, occurred if the infant looked to the mother and back to the object with a puzzled or surprised expression; by the end of the study most of the infants were regularly engaging in this behaviour (Desrochers, Ricard, Decarie, & Allard, 1994).

Social referencing—and the ability to retain information gained from it—may play a role in such key developments of toddlerhood as the rise of self-conscious emotions (embarrassment and pride), the development of a sense of self, and the processes of *socialization* and *internalization,* to which we turn in the remainder of this chapter.

Checkpoint ✔

Can you . . .

✔ Describe how mutual regulation works and explain its importance?

✔ Give examples of how infants seem to use social referencing?

Developmental Issues in Toddlerhood

 Guidepost 4

When and how does the sense of self arise, and how do toddlers exercise autonomy and develop standards for socially acceptable behaviour?

About halfway between their first and second birthdays, babies become toddlers. This transformation can be seen not only in such physical and cognitive skills as walking and talking, but in the ways children express their personalities and interact with others. A toddler becomes a more active, intentional partner in interactions and sometimes initiates them. Caregivers can now more clearly "read" the child's signals. Such "in sync" interactions help toddlers gain communicative skills and social competence and motivate compliance with a parent's wishes (Harrist & Waugh, 2002).

Let's look at three psychological issues that toddlers—and their caregivers—have to deal with: the emerging *sense of self;* the growth of *autonomy,* or self-determination; and the *internalization of behavioural standards.*

The Emerging Sense of Self

The **self-concept** is our image of ourselves—our total picture of our abilities and traits. It describes what we know and feel about ourselves and guides our actions (Harter, 1996, 1998). Children incorporate into their self-image the picture that others reflect back to them.

When and how does the self-concept develop? From a jumble of seemingly isolated experiences (say, from one breastfeeding session to another), infants begin to extract consistent patterns that form rudimentary concepts of self and other. Depending on what kind of care the infant receives and how she or he responds, pleasant or unpleasant emotions become connected with experiences such as sucking that play an important part in the growing concept of the self (Harter, 1998).

Between 4 and 10 months, when infants learn to reach, grasp, and make things happen, they experience a sense of personal *agency,* the realization that they can control external events. At about this time infants develop *self-coherence,* the sense of being a physical whole with boundaries separate from the rest of their world (Harter, 1998). These developments occur in interaction with caregivers in games such as peekaboo (refer back to Box 7-1 in Chapter 7), in which the infant becomes increasingly aware of the difference between self and other ("I see you!").

The emergence of *self-awareness*—conscious knowledge of the self as a distinct, identifiable being—builds on this dawning of perceptual discrimination between self and others (Harter, 1998). In an experiment with 96 four- and nine-month-olds, the infants showed more interest in images of others than of themselves (Rochat & Striano, 2002). This early *perceptual* discrimination may be the foundation of the *conceptual* self-awareness that develops between 15 and 18 months.

Self-awareness can be tested by studying whether an infant recognizes himself or herself in a mirror. In a classic line of research, investigators dabbed rouge on the noses of 6- to 24-month-olds and sat them in front of a mirror. Three-fourths of 18-month-olds and all 24-month-olds touched their red noses more often than before, whereas babies younger than 15 months never did. This behaviour suggests that these toddlers knew they did not normally have red noses and recognized the image in the mirror as their own (Lewis, 1997; Lewis & Brooks, 1974). In a later study, 18- and 24-month-olds were about as likely to touch a sticker on their legs, which was visible only in a mirror, as on their faces (Nielsen, Suddendorf, & Slaughter, 2006). Once children can recognize themselves, they show a preference for looking at their own video image over an image of another child the same age (Nielsen, Dissanayake, & Kashima, 2003).

By 20 to 24 months, toddlers begin to use first-person pronouns, another sign of self-awareness (Lewis, 1997). Between 19 and 30 months, they begin to apply descriptive terms ("big" or "little"; "straight hair" or "curly hair") and evaluative ones ("good," "pretty," or "strong") to themselves. The rapid development of language enables children to think and talk about the self and to incorporate parents' verbal descriptions ("You're so smart!" "What a big boy!") into their own emerging self-image (Stipek, Gralinski, & Kopp, 1990).

Developing Autonomy

As children mature—physically, cognitively, and emotionally—they are driven to seek independence from the very adults to whom they are attached. Erikson (1950) identified the period from about 18 months to 3 years as the second "crisis" in personality development, **autonomy versus shame and doubt,** which is marked by a shift from external control to self-control. Having come through infancy with a sense of basic trust in the world and an awakening self-awareness, toddlers begin to substitute their own judgment for their caregivers'. The "virtue" that emerges during this stage is *will.* Toilet training, which in most children is

This toddler is showing autonomy—the drive to exert her own power over her environment.

completed most rapidly if begun after 27 months (Blum, Taubman, & Nemeth, 2003), is an important step toward autonomy and self-control. So is language; as children are better able to make their wishes understood, they become more powerful and independent.

Since unlimited freedom is neither safe nor healthy, said Erikson, shame and doubt have a necessary place. Toddlers need adults to set appropriate limits, and shame and doubt help them recognize the need for those limits.

The "terrible twos" are a normal manifestation of the drive for autonomy. Toddlers have to test the new notion that they are individuals, that they have some control over their world, and that they have new, exciting powers. They are driven to try out their own ideas, exercise their own preferences, and make their own decisions. This drive typically shows itself in the form of *negativism,* the tendency to shout "No!" just for the sake of resisting authority. Almost all children show negativism to some degree; it usually begins before 2 years of age, tends to peak at about 3½ to 4, and declines by age 6. Parents and other caregivers who view children's expressions of self-will as a normal, healthy striving for independence, not as stubbornness, can help them learn self-control, contribute to their sense of competence, and avoid excessive conflict. (Table 8-4 gives specific, research-based suggestions for dealing with the "terrible twos.")

Many Canadian parents might be surprised to hear that the "terrible twos" are not universal. In some developing countries, the transition from infancy to early childhood is relatively smooth and harmonious (Mosier & Rogoff, 2003; see Box 8-2).

Checkpoint

Can you . . .

✔ Trace the early development of the sense of self?

✔ Describe the conflict of autonomy versus shame and doubt?

✔ Explain why the "terrible twos" are a normal phenomenon, and suggest reasons this transition may not exist in some cultures?

Table 8-4	Dealing with the "Terrible Twos"

The following research-based guidelines can help parents of toddlers discourage negativism and encourage socially acceptable behaviour:

- *Be flexible*. Learn the child's natural rhythms and special likes and dislikes.
- *Think of yourself as a safe harbour,* with safe limits, from which a child can set out and discover the world—and keep coming back for support.
- *Make your home "child-friendly."* Fill it with unbreakable objects that are safe to explore.
- *Avoid physical punishment.* It is often ineffective and may even lead a toddler to do more damage.
- *Offer a choice*—even a limited one—to give the child some control. ("Would you like to have your bath now, or after we read a book?")
- *Be consistent* in enforcing necessary requests.
- *Don't interrupt an activity unless absolutely necessary.* Try to wait until the child's attention has shifted.
- *If you must interrupt, give warning.* ("We have to leave the playground soon.")
- *Suggest alternative activities* when behaviour becomes objectionable. (When Ashley is throwing sand in Keiko's face, say, "Oh, look! Nobody's on the swings now. Let's go over and I'll give you a good push!")
- *Suggest; don't command.* Accompany requests with smiles or hugs, not criticism, threats, or physical restraint.
- *Link requests with pleasurable activities.* ("It's time to stop playing, so that you can go to the store with me.")
- *Remind the child of what you expect:* ("When we go to this playground, we *never* go outside the gate.")
- *Wait a few moments before repeating a request* when a child doesn't immediately comply.
- *Use "time out"* to end conflicts. In a non-punitive way, remove either yourself or the child from a situation.
- *Expect less self-control during times of stress* (illness, divorce, the birth of a sibling, or a move to a new home).
- *Expect it to be harder for toddlers to comply with "do's" than with "don'ts."* "Clean up your room" takes more effort than "Don't write on the furniture."
- *Keep the atmosphere as positive as possible.* Make your child *want* to cooperate.

Source: Haswell, Hock, & Wenar, 1981; Kochanska & Aksan, 1995; Kopp, 1982; Kuczynski & Kochanska, 1995; Power & Chapieski, 1986.

Box 8-2 *Are Struggles with Toddlers Necessary?*

Are the "terrible twos" a normal phase in child development? Many western parents and psychologists think so. Actually, though, this transition does not appear to be universal.

In Zinacantan, Mexico, toddlers do not typically become demanding and resistant to parental control. Instead of asserting independence from their mothers, toddlerhood in Zinacantan is a time when children move from mama's babies toward the new status of "mother's helpers," responsible children who tend a new baby and help with household tasks (Edwards, 1994). A similar developmental pattern seems to occur in Mazahua families in Mexico and among Mayan families in San Pedro, Guatemala. San Pedro parents "do not report a particular age when they expect children to become especially contrary or negative" (Mosier & Rogoff, 2003, p. 1058).

One arena in which issues of autonomy and control appear in western cultures is in sibling conflicts over toys and the way children respond to parental handling of these conflicts. To explore these issues, a cross-cultural study compared 16 San Pedro families with 16 middle-class European-American families in Salt Lake City in the United States. All of the families had toddlers 14 to 20 months old and older siblings 3 to 5 years old. The researchers interviewed each mother about her child-raising practices. They then handed the mother a series of attractive objects (such as nesting dolls and a jumping-jack puppet) and, in the presence of the older sibling, asked the mother to help the toddler operate them, with no instructions about the older child. Researchers who observed the ensuing interactions found striking differences in the way siblings interacted in the two cultures and in the way the mothers viewed and handled sibling conflict.

The older siblings in Salt Lake City often tried to take and play with the objects, but this did not generally happen in San Pedro. Instead, the older San Pedro children would offer to help their younger siblings work the objects, or the two children would play with them together. When there was a conflict over possession of the objects, mothers in both communities were more likely to endorse the toddler's right to have it first, but this tendency was far more characteristic of San Pedro mothers than of Salt Lake City mothers. San Pedro mothers favoured the toddlers 94 percent of the time, even taking an object away from the older child if the younger child wanted it; and the older siblings tended to go along, willingly handing the objects to the toddlers or letting them have the objects from the start. By contrast, in more than one-third of the interactions in Salt Lake City, the mothers tried to treat both children equally, negotiating with them or suggesting that they take turns or share. These observations were consistent

with reports of mothers in both cultures of how they handled such issues at home. San Pedro children are given a privileged position until age 3; then they are expected to willingly cooperate with social expectations.

What explains these cultural contrasts? A possible clue emerged when the mothers were asked at what age children can be held responsible for their actions. Most of the Salt Lake mothers maintained that their toddlers already understood the consequences of touching prohibited objects; several said this understanding arises as early as 7 months. Yet all but one of the San Pedro mothers placed the age of understanding social consequences of actions much later—between 2 and 3 years. Whereas the Salt Lake mothers regarded their toddlers as capable of intentionally misbehaving, most San Pedro mothers did not. More than half of the Salt Lake mothers reporting punishing toddlers for such infractions; none of the San Pedro mothers did. All of the Salt Lake preschoolers were under direct caregiver supervision, much like their toddler siblings, while 11 of the 16 San Pedro preschoolers were already on their own much of the time. The San Pedro preschoolers also had greater household responsibilities.

The researchers suggest that the "terrible twos" may be a phase specific to societies that place individual freedom before the needs of the group. Ethnographic research suggests that, in societies that place higher value on group needs, freedom of choice does exist, but it goes hand in hand with interdependence, responsibility, and expectations of cooperation. Salt Lake parents seem to believe that responsible behaviour develops gradually from engaging in fair competition and negotiations. San Pedro parents seem to believe that responsible behaviour develops rapidly when children are old enough to understand the need to respect others' desires as well as their own.

What's your view ?

From your experience or observation of toddlers, which of the two ways of handling sibling conflict would you expect to be more effective?

Check it out

For more information on this topic, go to **www.mcgrawhill.ca/olc/papalia** or **www.zerotothree.org/.** Here you will find links to a survey of 3,000 parents and other adults about commonly asked questions regarding the handling of young children and a downloadable article on "Cultural Models for Early Caregiving."

Moral Development: Socialization and Internalization

socialization Development of habits, skills, values, and motives shared by responsible, productive members of a society

internalization During socialization, process by which children accept societal standards of conduct as their own

Socialization is the process by which children develop habits, skills, values, and motives that make them responsible, productive members of society. Compliance with parental expectations can be seen as a first step toward compliance with societal standards. Socialization rests on **internalization** of these standards. Children who are successfully socialized no longer merely obey rules or commands to get rewards or avoid punishment; they have made society's standards their own (Grusec & Goodnow, 1994; Kochanska & Aksan, 1995; Kochanska, Tjebkes, & Forman, 1998).

Developing Self-Regulation

Katy, age 2, is about to poke her finger into an electric outlet. In her "child-proofed" apartment, the sockets are covered, but not here in her grandmother's home. When Katy hears her father shout "No!" the toddler pulls her arm back. The next time she goes near an outlet, she starts to point her finger, hesitates, and then says "No." She has stopped herself from doing something she remembers she is not supposed to do. She is beginning to show **self-regulation:** control of her own behaviour to conform to a caregiver's demands or expectations, even when the caregiver is not present.

Self-regulation is the foundation of socialization, and it links all domains of development—physical, cognitive, social, and emotional. Until Katy was physically able to get around on her own, electric outlets posed no hazard. To stop herself from poking her finger into an outlet requires that she consciously understand and remember what her father told her. Cognitive awareness, however, is not enough; restraining herself also requires emotional control. Differences in self-regulation in infants are related to both cognitive performance and emotional responses (Lewis, Koroshegyi, Douglas, & Kampe, 1997).

By "reading" their parents' emotional responses to their behaviour, children continually absorb information about what conduct their parents approve of. As children process, store, and act upon this information, their strong desire to please their parents leads them to do as they know their parents want them to, whether or not the parents are there to see.

Before they can control their own behaviour, children may need to be able to regulate, or control, their *attentional processes* and to modulate negative emotions (Eisenberg, 2000). Attentional regulation enables children to develop willpower and cope with frustration (Sethi, Mischel, Aber, Shoda, & Rodriguez, 2000).

The growth of self-regulation parallels the development of the self-conscious and evaluative emotions, such as empathy, shame, and guilt (Lewis, 1995, 1997, 1998). It requires flexibility and the ability to wait for gratification. When young children want very badly to do something, however, they easily forget the rules; they may run into the street after a ball or take a forbidden cookie. In most children, the full development of self-regulation takes at least 3 years (Kopp, 1982).

Origins of Conscience: Committed Compliance

Before children can develop **conscience,** which includes both emotional discomfort about doing something wrong and the ability to refrain from doing it, they need to have internalized standards. Conscience depends on willingness to do the right thing because a child believes it is right, not (as in self-regulation) just because someone else said so. *Inhibitory control*—conscious, or effortful, control of behaviour, a mechanism of self-regulation that emerges during toddlerhood—may contribute to the underpinnings of conscience by first enabling the child to comply with parental do's and don'ts (Kochanska, Murray, & Coy, 1997).

Grazyna Kochanska (1993, 1995, 1997a, 1997b) and her colleagues have sought the origins of conscience in a longitudinal study of a group of toddlers and mothers in Iowa. Researchers videotaped 103 children ages 26 to 41 months and their mothers playing together with toys for 2 to 3 hours, both at home and in a homelike laboratory setting (Kochanska & Aksan, 1995). After a free-play period, the mother gave the child 15 minutes to put the toys away. The laboratory had a special shelf with other, unusually attractive toys, such as a bubble gum machine, a walkie-talkie, and a music box. The child had been told not to touch anything on the shelf. After about an hour, the experimenter asked the mother to go into an adjoining room, leaving the child alone with the toys. A few minutes later, a woman entered, played with several of the forbidden toys, and then left the child alone again for 8 minutes.

Children were judged to show **committed compliance** if they willingly followed the orders to clean up and not to touch the toys, without reminders or lapses. Committed compliance is related to internalization of parental values and rules (Kochanska, Coy, & Murray, 2001). Children showed **situational compliance** if they needed prompting to obey; their compliance depended on ongoing parental control.

Committed compliance, which seems to be an early form of conscience, is strongly related to internalization of parental values and rules. Children whose mothers rated them

self-regulation A person's independent control of behaviour to conform to understood social expectations

conscience Internal standards of behaviour, which usually control one's conduct and produce emotional discomfort when violated

committed compliance Kochanska's term for wholehearted obedience to a parent's orders without reminders or lapses

situational compliance Kochanska's term for obedience to parent's orders only in the presence of prompting or other signs of ongoing parental control

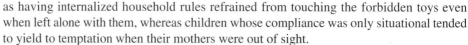

as having internalized household rules refrained from touching the forbidden toys even when left alone with them, whereas children whose compliance was only situational tended to yield to temptation when their mothers were out of sight.

Committed compliance and situational compliance seem to be distinct patterns of behaviour. The two kinds of compliance can be distinguished in children as young as 13 months, but their roots go back to infancy. Committed compliers, who are more likely to be girls than boys, tend to be those who, at 8 to 10 months, could refrain from touching when told "No!" Committed compliance increases with age, while situational compliance decreases (Kochanska et al., 1998).

Factors in the Success of Socialization

The way parents go about their job, together with a child's temperament and the quality of the parent–child relationship, may help predict how hard or easy it will be to socialize a particular child (Kochanska, 1993, 1995, 1997a, 1997b, 2002). Factors in the success of socialization may include security of attachment, observational learning of parents' behaviour, and the mutual responsiveness of parent and child (Kochanska, Aksan, Knaack, & Rhines, 2004; Maccoby, 1992). All these, as well as socio-economic and cultural factors (Harwood, Schoelmerich, Ventura-Cook, Schulze, & Wilson, 1996), may play a part in motivation to comply. However, not all children respond to socialization in the same way. For example, a temperamentally fearful toddler may respond better to gentle reminders than to strong admonitions (Kochanska, Aksan, & Joy, 2007).

Secure attachment and a warm, mutually responsive parent–child relationship seems to foster committed compliance and conscience development. Starting in the child's second year and extending until early school age, researchers observed more than 200 mothers and children in lengthy, naturalistic interactions: caregiving routines, preparing and eating meals, playing, relaxing, and doing household chores. Children who, based on these interactions, were judged to have mutually responsive relationships with their mothers tended to show *moral emotions* such as guilt and empathy; *moral conduct* in the face of strong temptation to break rules or violate standards of behaviour; and *moral cognition*, as judged by their response to hypothetical, age-appropriate moral dilemmas (Kochanska, 2002).

Constructive conflict over a child's misbehaviour—conflict that involves negotiation, reasoning, and resolution—can help children develop moral understanding by enabling them to see another point of view. In one observational study, 2½-year-olds whose mothers gave clear explanations for their requests, compromised, or bargained with the child were better able to resist temptation at age 3 than children whose mothers had threatened, teased, insisted, or given in. Discussion of emotions in conflict situations ("How would you feel if . . .") also led to conscience development, probably by fostering the development of moral emotions (Laible & Thompson, 2002).

Receptive cooperation goes beyond committed compliance. It is a child's eager willingness to cooperate harmoniously with a parent, not only in disciplinary situations, but in a variety of daily interactions, including routines, chores, hygiene, and play. Receptive cooperation enables a child to be an active partner in socialization. In a longitudinal study of 101 seven-month-olds, those who were prone to anger, who received unresponsive parenting, or who were insecurely attached at 15 months tended to be low in receptive cooperation at that age. Children who were securely attached and whose mothers had been responsive to the child during infancy tended to be high in receptive cooperation (Kochanska, Aksan, & Carlson, 2005).

How Different are Baby Boys and Girls?

Being male or female affects how people look, how they move their bodies, and how they work, play, and dress. It influences what they think about themselves and what others think of them. All these characteristics—and more—are included in the word **gender**: what it means to be male or female.

What's your view ?

- In view of Kochanska's research on the roots of conscience, what questions would you ask about the early socialization of anti-social adolescents and adults?

receptive cooperation Kochanska's term for eager willingness to cooperate harmoniously with a parent in daily interactions, including routines, chores, hygiene, and play

gender Significance of being male or female

Checkpoint ✓

Can you . . .

✔ Tell when and how self-regulation develops and how it contributes to socialization?

✔ Distinguish between committed and situational compliance?

✔ Discuss how temperament and parenting practices affect socialization?

Guidepost 5

When and how do gender differences appear?

Gender Differences in Infants and Toddlers

Measurable differences between baby boys and girls are few. Boys are a bit longer and heavier and may be slightly stronger, but, as we mentioned in Chapter 4, they are physically more vulnerable from conception on. Girls are less reactive to stress and more likely to survive infancy (Davis & Emory, 1995; Keenan & Shaw, 1997). Boys' brains at birth are about 10 percent larger than girls' brains, a difference that continues into adulthood (Gilmore et al., 2007). An analysis of a large number of studies found baby boys more active than baby girls, though this difference is not consistently documented (Eaton & Enns, 1986). On the other hand, the two sexes are equally sensitive to touch and tend to teethe, sit up, and walk at about the same ages (Maccoby, 1980). They also achieve the other motor milestones of infancy at about the same times.

One of the earliest *behavioural* differences between boys and girls, appearing between 1 and 2 years of age, is in preferences for toys and play activities and for playmates of the same sex (Campbell, Shirley, Heywood, & Crook, 2000; Serbin et al., 2001; Turner & Gervai, 1995). Boys as young as 17 months tend to play more aggressively than girls (Baillargeon et al., 2007). Between ages 2 and 3, boys and girls tend to say more words pertaining to their own sex (such as "necklace" versus "tractor") than to the other sex (Stennes, Burch, Sen, & Bauer, 2005).

Recently, by using age-appropriate tasks, cognitive psychologists have found evidence that infants begin to perceive differences between males and females long before their behaviour is gender-differentiated and even before they can talk. Habituation studies have found that 6-month-olds respond differently to male and female voices. By 9 to 12 months, infants can tell the difference between male and female faces, apparently on the basis of hair and clothing. During the second year infants begin to associate gender-typical toys, such as dolls, with a face of the correct gender. Boys are slower to develop this knowledge than girls (Martin, Ruble, & Szkrybalo, 2002). In elicited imitation studies (refer back to Chapter 7), 25-month-old boys spend more time imitating "boy" tasks, such as shaving a teddy bear, whereas girls spend about the same amount of time imitating activities associated with each sex (Bauer, 1993).

How Parents Shape Gender Differences

North American parents tend to *think* baby boys and girls are more different than they actually are. In a study of 11-month-old infants who had recently begun crawling, mothers consistently had higher expectations for their sons' success in crawling down steep and narrow slopes than for their daughters. Yet, when tested on the slopes, the baby girls and boys showed identical levels of performance (Mondschein, Adolph, & Tamis-LeMonda, 2000).

Parents also begin to influence boys' and girls' personalities very early. Fathers, especially, promote **gender-typing,** the process by which children learn behaviour that their culture considers appropriate for each sex (Bronstein, 1988). Fathers treat boys and girls more differently than mothers do, even during the first year (M. E. Snow, Jacklin, & Maccoby, 1983). During the second year, fathers talk more and spend more time with sons than with daughters (Lamb, 1981). Mothers talk more, and more supportively, to daughters than to sons (Leaper, Anderson, & Sanders, 1998), and girls at this age tend to be more talkative than boys (Leaper & Smith, 2004). Fathers of toddlers play more roughly with sons and show more sensitivity to daughters (Kelley et al., 1998).

However, a highly physical style of play, characteristic of many fathers in Canada, is not typical of fathers in all cultures. Swedish and German fathers usually do not play with their babies this way (Lamb, Frodi, Frodi, & Hwang, 1982; Parke, Grossman, & Tinsley, 1981). African Aka fathers (Hewlett, 1987) and those in New Delhi, India, also tend to play gently with small children (Roopnarine, Hooper, Ahmeduzzaman, & Pollack, 1993; Roopnarine, Talokder, Jain, Josh, & Srivastav, 1992). Such cross-cultural variations suggest that rough play is *not* a function of male biology, but instead is culturally influenced.

We will discuss gender-typing and gender differences in more depth in Chapter 11.

gender-typing Socialization process by which children learn appropriate gender roles

What's your view

- Should parents try to treat male and female infants and toddlers alike?

Checkpoint

Can you . . .

✔ Compare the roles of fathers and mothers and their influences on gender-typing?

Guidepost 6

How do infants and toddlers interact with siblings and other children?

Contact with Other Children

Although parents exert a major influence on children's lives, relationships with other children—both in the home and out of it—are important, too, from infancy on.

Siblings

If you have brothers or sisters, your relationships with them are likely to be the longest-lasting you'll ever have. They share your roots; they "knew you when," they accepted or rejected the same parental values, and they probably deal with you more candidly than almost anyone else you know. Sibling relationships begin with the birth of a new baby in a household and continue to develop, both positively and negatively, throughout childhood.

The Arrival of a New Baby

Children react in various ways to the arrival of a sibling. To bid for the mother's attention, some suck their thumbs, wet their pants, or use baby talk. Others withdraw. Some suggest taking the baby back to the hospital or flushing it down the toilet. Some take pride in being the "big ones," who can dress themselves, use the potty, and help care for the baby.

Much of the variation in children's adjustment to a new baby may have to do with such factors as the older child's age, the quality of his or her relationship with the mother, and the family atmosphere. A Montreal study of effects on a first-born child of a sibling's birth indicated that younger children show more distress after the birth than older ones. The level of support provided by the mother before and after the birth of a sibling, and degree of support by the father after birth are related to the child's level of distress after the birth (Gottlieb & Mendelson, 1990). Not surprisingly, attachment to the mother often becomes temporarily less secure (Teti, Sakin, Kucera, Corns, & Eiden, 1996).

The birth of a younger sibling may change the way a mother acts toward an older child, at least until the newcomer "settles in." The mother is likely to play less with the older child, to be less sensitive to her or his interests, to give more orders, to have more confrontations, to use physical punishment, and to initiate fewer conversations and games that help develop skills. An older boy, especially, may show temporary behaviour problems (Baydar, Greek, & Brooks-Gunn, 1997; Baydar, Hyle, & Brooks-Gunn, 1997; Dunn, 1985; Dunn & Kendrick, 1982).

On the positive side, the arrival of a baby tends to enhance the older child's language development, perhaps because the child talks more than before with the father and other family members (Baydar, Greek, & Brooks-Gunn, 1997; Baydar, Hyle, & Brooks-Gunn, 1997).

How Siblings Interact

Sibling relationships play a distinct role in socialization, different from the role of relationships with parents or peers (Vandell, 2000). Sibling conflicts can become a vehicle for understanding social relationships (Dunn & Munn, 1985; Ram & Ross, 2001). Lessons and skills learned from interactions with siblings carry over to relationships outside the home (Brody, 1998).

Young children usually become attached to their older brothers and sisters. Although rivalry may be present, so is affection. The more securely attached siblings are to their parents, the better they get along with each other (Teti & Ablard, 1989).

Nevertheless, as babies begin to move around and become more assertive, they can come into conflict with siblings (refer back to Box 8-2).

Babies and toddlers become closely attached to their older brothers and sisters, especially when the older siblings assume a large measure of care for the younger ones.

Sibling conflict increases dramatically after the younger child reaches 18 months of age (Vandell & Bailey, 1992). During the next few months, younger siblings begin to participate more fully in family interactions and become more involved in family disputes. As they do, they become more aware of others' intentions and feelings. They begin to recognize what kind of behaviour will upset or annoy an older brother or sister and what behaviour is considered "naughty" or "good" (Dunn & Munn, 1985).

As this cognitive and social understanding grows, sibling conflict tends to become more constructive, and the younger sibling participates in attempts to reconcile. Constructive conflict helps children recognize each other's needs, wishes, and point of view, and it helps them learn how to fight, disagree, and compromise within the context of a safe, stable relationship (Vandell & Bailey, 1992).

Sociability with Nonsiblings

Although the family is the centre of a baby's social world, infants and—even more so—toddlers show interest in people outside the home, particularly people their own size. During the first few months, they show interest in other babies by looking, smiling, and cooing (T. M. Field, 1978). During the last half of the first year, they increasingly smile at, touch, and babble to another baby, especially when they are not distracted by the presence of adults or toys (Hay, Pedersen, & Nash, 1982).

At about 1 year, when the biggest items on their agenda are learning to walk and to manipulate objects, babies pay more attention to toys and less to other people (T. M. Field & Roopnarine, 1982). This stage does not last long, though; from about 1½ years of age to almost 3, they show more interest in what other children do and increasing understanding of how to deal with them. This insight seems to accompany awareness of themselves as separate individuals. A 10-month-old who holds out a toy to another baby pays no attention to whether the other's back is turned, but an 18-month-old knows when the offer has the best chance of being accepted and how to respond to another child's overtures (Eckerman, Davis, & Didow, 1989; Eckerman & Stein, 1982).

Toddlers learn by imitating one another. Games such as follow-the-leader help toddlers connect with other children and pave the way for more complex games during the preschool years (Eckerman et al., 1989). Imitation of each other's actions leads to more frequent verbal communication (such as "You go in playhouse," "Don't do it!" or "Look at me") which helps peers coordinate joint activity (Eckerman & Didow, 1996). Cooperative activity develops during the second and third years as social understanding grows (Brownell, Ramani, & Zerwas, 2006). As with siblings, conflict, too, can have a purpose: helping children learn how to negotiate and resolve disputes (Caplan, Vespo, Pedersen, & Hay, 1991).

Some children, of course, are more sociable than others, reflecting such temperamental traits as their usual mood, readiness to accept new people, and ability to adapt to change. Sociability is also influenced by experience; babies who spend time with other babies, as in child care, become sociable earlier than those who spend all their time at home alone. They also engage in increasingly complex play with peers. However, this depends on the quality of caregiving and the security of the child's attachment (Howes, 1997).

Children of Working Parents

Parents' work determines more than the family's financial resources. Much of adults' time, effort, and emotional involvement go into their occupations. How do their working and their child care arrangements affect young children? Most research on this subject pertains to mothers' work. (We'll discuss the impact of parents' work on older children in later chapters.)

In 1999, almost 80 percent of mothers with school-aged children, 72 percent of mothers with children aged 3 to 5 years, and 65 percent of women with children younger than 3 years of age were employed (Canadian Council on Social Development, 2001), an increase of over 40 percent over the previous two decades. This change, coupled with an increase in the percentage of Canadian children living with lone parents has increased the demand for child

Checkpoint ✓

Can you . . .

✔ Discuss factors affecting a child's adjustment to a new baby sister or brother?

✔ Describe changes in sibling interaction and sibling conflict during toddlerhood?

✔ Trace changes in sociability during the first 3 years, and state two influences on it?

Guidepost 7

How do parental employment and early child care affect infants' and toddlers' development?

care (Connor & Brink, 1999). Early non-parental child care is now a way of life for most Canadian families, and its impact is the subject of much debate, particularly for government policy-making. In Canada, there is significant government support offered to families for maternal and parental leave, as well as licensing of and financial support for non-parental care (Symons & Carr, 1995). In response to concerns about the importance of parental involvement in child care in the first year, the Canadian government instituted an Employment Insurance policy, which began in January 2001, to provide up to 1 year of financial support to new parents who to stay at home, to be shared between the mother and the father. In addition, Quebec offers substantially improved income for parental leave, which is an important incentive for fathers to stay at home (Tremblay, 2007), as well as support to offset the cost of licensed daycare for children (Canadian Council on Social Development, 2001).

Effects of Parental Employment

What are the short-term and long-term consequences of a mother's going to work during the first 3 years of her child's life? The answer varies.

The National Longitudinal Survey of Children and Youth (NLSCY) showed no relationship between non-parental care and likelihood of learning difficulties in Canadian children. A weak positive relationship was found between number of weeks in the labour force and children's vocabulary: Mothers who were more committed to their careers tended to spend as much time reading to their children, and the combination of the educational benefits of being read to by the parent and being in a higher-income family was related to improved vocabulary in children (Lefebvre & Merigan, 1998). In fact, a Nova Scotia study found that children whose mothers returned to work 6 months after birth were more securely attached than children whose mothers did not work in the first 2 years after birth (Symons, 1998). In addition, the Canadian Transition to Child Care Study found that children of employed mothers who preferred to work and who showed higher levels of sensitivity tended to be more securely attached than children whose mothers preferred to stay at home and who were less sensitive. However, the provision of high quality out-of-home child care tended to reduce the negative outcomes of reduced maternal sensitivity (McKim, Cramer, Stuart, & O'Connor, 1999).

However, a mother's *feelings* about her work situation may make a difference. In a study of 55 white, educated, married mothers of 4- to 6-month-olds, feelings of conflict about going to work (or staying home) reduced mothers' ability to discriminate among different types of cries—an indication of lessened sensitivity and responsiveness to a baby's signals (Donovan et al., 1998).

How does a mother's employment affect the father's relationship with the baby? In an 8-month study of 63 predominantly white, middle-class, employed fathers, the child's tendency to distress and the father's marital satisfaction and involvement in caregiving were more important predictors of men's responsiveness to their infants than whether or not the mother worked outside the home (Grych & Clark, 1999).

In a longitudinal study of 17 infants raised primarily by fathers, the men developed growing confidence in their caregiving skills and responsiveness to the babies' needs. Standardized tests showed the children's emotional, social, and cognitive development to be strong in infancy and beyond. As infants, their social skills were relatively advanced, and they seemed unusually curious and open to stimulation from adults other than their parents (Pruett, 1998).

Longitudinal data on 900 European American children from the National Institute of Child Health and Human Development (NICHD) Study of Early Child Care showed negative effects on cognitive development at 15 months to 3 years when mothers worked 30 or more hours a week by a child's ninth month. Maternal sensitivity, a high-quality home environment, and high-quality child care lessened but did not eliminate these negative effects (Brooks-Gunn, Han, & Waldfogel, 2002).

On the other hand, boys and girls in low-income families tend to benefit academically from the more favourable environment a working mother's

These children in a high-quality group daycare program are likely to do at least as well cognitively and socially as children cared for full time at home. The most important element of infant daycare is the caregiver or teacher, who exerts a strong influence on the children in her care.

income can provide (Chase-Lansdale et al., 2003; Goldberg, Greenberger, & Nagel, 1996; Vandell & Ramanan, 1992). A longitudinal study of an ethnically, socio-economically, and geographically diverse sample of 1,364 children during their first 3 years suggests that the economic and social benefits of maternal employment may outweigh any disadvantages resulting from reduced time with a child. Mothers who worked outside the home compensated for some of their work time by reducing time spent on non-child care activities. Differences in time spent with infants were modestly related to maternal sensitivity but did not seem to affect social or cognitive outcomes. Infants whose mothers spent more time with them did have more stimulating home environments, but so did infants whose mothers spent more time at work. It seems, then, that mothers who are temperamentally prone to be sensitive and to provide stimulating, warm home environments may find ways to do so whether or not they are employed (Huston & Aronson, 2005).

Early Child Care

One factor in the impact of parents working outside the home is the type of substitute care a child receives. About 40 percent of Canadian children between four and five years experience some type of substitute care for part of their week, while their parents study or work outside the home. Unregulated care outside the home is the most common type of substitue care, and only about 12 percent of preschoolers in Canada attend a licensed daycare. Almost 15 percent attend unregulated care outside the home, while 6 percent are cared for at home by a non-relative. Seven percent are cared for by a relative (Kohen, Hertzman & Willms, 2002). Several factors account for the preference by Canadians for unregulated child care, including cost, availability, size, and flexibility. Licensing is an advantage, though, as it ensures that facilities meet criteria for safety, child-to-adult ratios, training of staff, and available resources (Kohen et al., 2002).

With costs of nonrelative care constantly increasing (Iruka & Carver, 2006), affordability and quality of care are pressing issues, especially for low-income families (Marshall, 2004) and parents of children with disabilities (Shonkoff & Phillips, 2000). Unfortunately, most unregulated child care facilities do not meet all recommended guidelines for quality care (Bergen, Reid, & Torelli, 2000; NICHD Early Child Care Research Network, 1998c, 1999a; see Table 8-5). In home settings, where most Canadian babies

Table 8-5	Checklist for Choosing a Good Child-Care Facility

- Is the facility licensed? Does it meet minimum provincial standards for health, fire, and safety? (Many centres and home-care facilities are not licensed or regulated.)
- Is the facility clean and safe? Does it have adequate indoor and outdoor space? Does the facility have small groups, a high adult-to-child ratio, and a stable, competent, highly involved staff?
- Are caregivers trained in child development?
- Are caregivers warm, affectionate, accepting, responsive, and sensitive? Are they authoritative but not too restrictive, and neither too controlling nor merely custodial?
- Does the program promote good health habits?
- Does it provide a balance between structured activities and free play? Are activities age-appropriate?
- Do the children have access to educational toys and materials, which stimulate mastery of cognitive and communicative skills at a child's own pace?
- Does the program nurture self-confidence, curiosity, creativity, and self-discipline?
- Does it encourage children to ask questions, solve problems, express feelings and opinions, and make decisions?
- Does it foster self-esteem, respect for others, and social skills?
- Does it help parents improve their child-rearing skills?
- Does it promote cooperation with public and private schools and the community?

Sources: American Academy of Pediatrics [AAP], 1986; Belsky, 1984; K. A. Clarke-Stewart, 1987; NICHD Early Child Care Research Network, 1996; Norris, Brink, and Mosher, 1999; S. W. Olds, 1989; Scarr, 1998.

stay during the first year of life, quality of care is related to family income; the higher the income, the better the care.

Despite the high demand for quality child care in Canada, child-care arrangements do not always meet the needs of Canadian families (Health Canada, 1999). About 42 percent of regulated daycare spaces were subsidized for low-income families in 1994 (Health Canada, 1999). These subsidies have been reduced in many provinces, with some provincial governments lowering standards for child-care centres, and cutting back on monitoring and enforcement of regulations (Health Canada, 1999; Kohen et al., 2002). These trends indicate that parents need to be particularly careful in choosing daycare facilities for their children. Table 8-5 lists guidelines for judging quality of care.

The most important element in the quality of care is the caregiver; stimulating interactions with responsive adults are crucial to early cognitive, linguistic, and psychosocial development (Burchinal, Roberts, Nabors, & Bryant, 1996; Shonkoff & Phillips, 2000). Low staff turnover is critical; infants need consistent caregiving in order to develop trust and secure attachments. In one longitudinal study, 4-year-olds who had formed secure attachments to child-care providers tended to be more sociable, sensitive, empathic, and better liked than those who were insecurely attached (Howes, Matheson, & Hamilton, 1994).

Isolating Child-Care Effects

Bronfenbrenner's bioecological theory (refer back to Chapter 2) affords a broad perspective on how early child care can affect children's development. Both the family and the child-care setting are microsystems directly affecting the child, but their influences are not fully independent; they are linked through the mesosystem. Parents affect children's child care experience through their selection of particular child care arrangements, which is largely dependent on their means. Child care also may affect family life, for example, when a child learns a new song or game in child care and wants to sing or play it at home. The family–child care mesosystem operates within the exosystem of government policies, subsidies, and regulations that affect the quality and affordability of child care. Above and beyond those specific influences are "the macrosystem of societal beliefs about the desirability of maternal employment and the desired outcomes for children" (Marshall, 2004, p. 167).

Because child care is an integral part of a child's bioecological system, it is difficult to measure its influence alone. It should not be surprising that what look like effects of child care often may be related to family characteristics. After all, stable families with favourable home environments are more able and therefore more likely to place their children in high-quality care. Indeed, parental characteristics are the single best predictor of child-care quality (NICHD Early Child Care Research Network, 2006a). The child's temperament also can affect the impact of child care. Shy children experience greater stress in child care than sociable children (Watamura, Donzella, Alwin, & Gunnar, 2003), and insecurely attached children undergo greater stress than securely attached children when placed in full-time care (Ahnert et al., 2004). Boys are more vulnerable to stress, in child care and elsewhere, than are girls (Crockenberg, 2003).

Data from the NLSCY show that stability of child-care arrangements seems to have an impact on healthy development. Infants and toddlers who experience changes in child-care arrangements (representing about 23 percent of children in the survey who were in non-parental child care) were more likely to be described by their mothers as having poorer mental health and more difficult temperaments than those who did not experience change. As children enter preschool age, those who experience change in child-care arrangements are more likely to have lower vocabulary scores than those who did not experience change. By school age, children who experience child-care change were more likely to have behavioural problems than those who did not experience change (Kohen, Hertzman, & Wiens, 1998). In addition, children from low-income families who experience non-parental daycare outside of the home are more likely to score higher on measures of vocabulary than children from low-income families who are cared for at home (Connor & Brink, 1999; Kohen et al., 2002).

A study of the impact of quality of daycare carried out in Montreal showed that any potential negative effects related to early age of entry into daycare can be offset by the beneficial effects of quality daycare conditions. Long stays at low-quality daycare centres increased the likelihood that children showed anger and defiance in group situations, whereas attendance at high-quality daycare facilities was associated with high levels of interest and positive interactions in groups (Hausfather, Toharia, LaRoche, & Engelsmann, 1997).

A U.S. study conducted by the National Institute of Child Health and Human Development (NICHD) also showed that the quantity and quality of care children receive, as well as the type and stability of care, influence specific aspects of development (Peth-Pierce, 1998; see Table 8-6).

Sometimes family and child-care characteristics work together. For example, the U.S. study found that child care itself has no direct effect on attachment (as measured at 15 months by the Strange Situation), no matter how early infants enter care or how many hours they spend in it. Nor do the stability or quality of care matter, in themselves. However, when unstable, poor quality, or more-than-minimal amounts of child care (10 or more hours a week) are added to the impact of insensitive, unresponsive parenting, insecure attachment is more likely. On the other hand, high-quality care may help to offset insensitive parenting (NICHD Early Child Care Research Network, 1997a).

Quality of care contributes to cognitive and psychosocial development. Children in child-care centres with low child–staff ratios, small group sizes, and trained, sensitive, responsive caregivers who provide positive interactions and language stimulation score higher on tests of language comprehension, cognition, and readiness for school; and their mothers report fewer behaviour problems (NICHD Early Child Care Research Network, 1997c, 1999a, 2000; Kohen et al., 2002). In Canada family income, the home environment, and the amount of mental stimulation the parent provides are even more influential (Lefebvre & Merrigan, 1998; Ryan & Adams, 1998).

It should not be surprising that what on the surface appear to be effects of child care often may be effects of family characteristics. After all, stable families with high incomes and educational backgrounds and favourable home environments are more likely to place their children in high-quality care. It will be illuminating to follow the long-term progress of the NLSCY sample; in some earlier longitudinal studies, apparent early effects of child care faded out during the school years, while family characteristics continued to be important (Lefebvre & Merrigan, 1998; Ryan & Adams, 1998; Scarr, 1997b).

Even if child care may have little long-term effect on most children, those from low-income families or stressful homes do seem to benefit from care that supplies emotional support and cognitive stimulation, which may otherwise be lacking in their lives (Scarr, 1997b). Disadvantaged children in good child-care programs tend not to show the declines in IQ often seen when such children reach school age, they may be more motivated to learn, and experience improved vocabulary skills (AAP, 1986; Belsky, 1984; Bronfenbrenner, Belsky, & Steinberg, 1977; Kohen, Hertzman & Willms, 2002; McCain & Mustard, 1999).

Checkpoint ✔

Can you . . .

✔ Evaluate the impact of parental employment on a baby's well-being?

✔ List at least five criteria for good child care?

✔ Discuss the impact of child care and of family characteristics on emotional, social, and cognitive development?

✔ Point out special considerations regarding child care for low-income and minority children?

Table 8-6	Aspects of Development Affected by Characteristics of Early Child Care*

	Attachment	Parent–Child Relationships	Cooperation	Problem Behaviours	Cognitive Development and School Readiness	Language Development
Quality	•	•		+	+	+
Amount	•	•		•		
Type			•	•	+	+
Stability	•		•			

*Results after taking into account all family and child variables.

+ Consistent effects

• Effects under some conditions

What's your view ?

- In the light of findings about effects of early child care, what advice would you give a new mother about the timing of her return to work and the selection of child care?

To sum up, the findings of studies like the NLSCY and NICHD (NICHD Early Child Care Research Network, 2001a) so far give high-quality child care good marks overall, especially for its impact on cognitive development and interaction with peers. Some observers say that the areas of concern the studies pinpoint—stress levels in infants and toddlers and possible behaviour problems related to amounts of care—might be counteracted by activities that enhance children's attachment to caregivers and peers, emphasize child-initiated learning and internalized motivation, and focus on group social development (Maccoby & Lewis, 2003). The findings support policies that would improve quality of care while enabling parents to reduce the amount of time their children spend in outside care—through flexible workplace hours, and paid parental leave that could be used anytime within the child's first five years (NICHD Child Care Research Network, 2006a).

Impact on Disadvantaged Children and Minorities

Children from low-income families or stressful homes especially benefit from high quality care that supplies cognitive stimulation and emotional support (Scarr, 1997b; Spieker, Nelson, Petras, Jolley, & Barnard, 2003). In a five-year longitudinal study of 451 poor single mothers who were moving from welfare to work, children demonstrated stronger cognitive growth in centre care than in home-based care (Loeb, Fuller, Kagan, & Carrol, 2004). In another study, among more than 14,000 kindergartners, children from poor families gained twice as much from centre-based care in language and mathematics learning as did middle-class children (Loeb, Bridges, Bassock, Fuller, & Rumberger, 2007).

The NICHD study found that the more time a young child spends in nonmaternal care, the greater the risk of problem behaviour (NICHD Early Childhood Research Network, 2003). However, data from a U.S. study of 2,400 randomly selected low-income children in Boston, Chicago, and San Antonio suggest that extensive child care does *not* harm *poor* children's development unless it is of low quality (Votruba-Drzal, Coley, & Chase-Lansdale, 2004). Unfortunately, children from low-income famlies tend to be placed in lower-cost and lower-quality care than children from more affluent families (Marshall, 2004).

However infants and toddlers are cared for, the experiences of the first 3 years lay the foundation for future development. In Part 4, we'll see how young children build on that foundation.

Summary and Key Terms

Foundations of Psychosocial Development

Guidepost 1 When and how do emotions develop, and how do babies show them?

- Emotions serve protective functions.
- Crying, smiling, and laughing are early signs of emotion. Other indices include facial expressions, motor activity, body language, and physiological changes.
- The repertoire of basic emotions seems to be universal, but there are cultural variations in their expression.
- Complex emotions seem to develop from earlier, simpler ones. Self-conscious and evaluative emotions arise after the development of self-awareness.
- Separate but interacting regions of the brain may be responsible for various emotional states.

emotions (196)   self-conscious emotions (198)
self-awareness (198)   self-evaluative emotions (199)

empathy (199)   social cognition (199)
egocentrism (199)

Guidepost 2 How do infants show temperamental differences, and how enduring are those differences?

- Many children seem to fall into three categories of temperament: "easy," "difficult," and "slow-to-warm-up." Temperamental patterns appear to be largely inborn and to have a biological basis. They are generally stable but can be modified by experience.
- Goodness of fit between a child's temperament and environmental demands aids adjustment.
- Cross-cultural differences in temperament may reflect child-raising practices.

temperament (200)   "easy" children (200)
"difficult" children (201)   "slow-to-warm-up" children (201)
goodness of fit (202)

Developmental Issues in Infancy

Guidepost 3 How do infants gain trust in their world and form attachments, and how do infants and caregivers "read" each other's non-verbal signals?

- According to Erikson, infants in the first 18 months experience the first crisis in personality development, basic trust versus basic mistrust. Sensitive, responsive, consistent caregiving is the key to successful resolution of this crisis.

- Research based on the Strange Situation has found four patterns of attachment: secure, avoidant, ambivalent (resistant), and disorganized-disoriented.

- Newer instruments measure attachment in natural settings and in cross-cultural research.

- Attachment patterns may depend on a baby's temperament, as well as on the quality of parenting, and may have long-term implications for development. A parent's memories of childhood attachment can influence his or her own child's attachment.

- Separation anxiety and stranger anxiety may arise during the second half of the first year and appear to be related to temperament and circumstances.

- Mutual regulation enables babies to play an active part in regulating their emotional states.

- A mother's depression, especially if severe or chronic, may have serious consequences for her infant's development.

- Social referencing has been observed by 12 months.

basic trust versus basic mistrust (203) attachment (204) Strange Situation (204) secure attachment (205) avoidant attachment (205) ambivalent (resistant) attachment (205) disorganized-disoriented attachment (205) stranger anxiety (207) separation anxiety (207) mutual regulation (209) "still-face" paradigm (209) social referencing (211)

Developmental Issues in Toddlerhood

Guidepost 4 When and how does the sense of self arise, and how do toddlers exercise autonomy and develop standards for socially acceptable behaviour?

- The self-concept develops between 15 and 18 months and depends on self-awareness.

- Erikson's second stage concerns autonomy versus shame and doubt. Negativism is a normal manifestation of the shift from external control to self-control.

- Socialization, which rests on internalization of societally approved standards, begins with the development of self-regulation.

- A precursor of conscience is committed compliance to a caregiver's demands; toddlers who show committed

compliance tend to internalize adult rules more readily than those who show situational compliance.

- Parenting practices, a child's temperament, the quality of the parent-child relationship, and cultural and socio-economic factors may affect the ease and success of socialization.

self-concept (212) autonomy versus shame and doubt (212) socialization (214) internalization (214) self-regulation (215) conscience (215) committed compliance (215) situational compliance (215) receptive cooperation (216)

How Different are Baby Boys and Girls?

Guidepost 5 When and how do gender differences appear?

- Although significant gender differences typically do not appear until after infancy, parents begin gender-typing boys and girls almost from birth.

gender (216) gender-typing (217)

Contact with Other Children

Guidepost 6 How do infants and toddlers interact with siblings and other children?

- A child's adjustment to a new baby may depend on the child's age, the quality of her or his relationship with the mother, and the family atmosphere.

- Sibling relationships play a distinct role in socialization; what children learn from relations with siblings carries over to relationships outside the home.

- Between 1½ and 3 years of age, children tend to show more interest in other children and increasing understanding of how to deal with them.

Children of Working Parents

Guidepost 7 How do parental employment and early child care affect infants' and toddlers' development?

- In general, parents' workforce participation during a child's first 3 years seems to have little impact on development, but cognitive development may suffer when a mother works 30 or more hours a week by her child's ninth month.

- Substitute child care varies widely in type and quality. The most important element in quality of care is the caregiver.

- Although quality, quantity, stability, and type of care have some influence on psychosocial and cognitive development, the influence of family characteristics seems greater overall.

- Low-income children, especially, benefit from good child care. Minority children may need child care that meets their special needs and is consistent with their family upbringing.

CHAPTER NINE

9

Physical Development and Health in Early Childhood

*Children's playings are not sports and should be deemed as their
most serious actions.*

—Michel de Montaigne, *Essays,* 1575

Focus *Wang Yani, Self-taught Artist**

Wang Yani

Wang Yani (b. 1975) is a gifted young Chinese artist. Now in her 20s, she had her first exhibit in Shanghai at the age of 4 and produced four thousand paintings by the time she turned 6. Since she was 10 her work has been shown throughout Asia and in Europe and the United States.

Yani (her given name)** began painting at 2½. Her father, Wang Shiqiang, was a professional artist and educator. Her father gave her big brushes and large sheets of paper to permit bold strokes. Rather than teach her, he let her learn by doing, in her own way, and always praised her work. In contrast with traditional Chinese art education, which emphasizes conformity and imitation, he allowed his daughter's imagination free rein.

Yani went through the usual stages in preschoolers' drawing, but far more quickly than usual. Her early paintings after the scribble stage were made up of dots, circles, and apparently meaningless lines, which stood for people, birds, or fruit. By the age of 3, she painted recognizable but highly original forms.

Yani's father encouraged her to paint what she saw outdoors near their home in the scenic riverside town of Gongcheng. Like traditional Chinese artists, she did not paint from life but constructed her brightly coloured compositions from mental images of what she had seen. Her visual memory has been called astounding. When she was only 4, her father taught her Chinese characters (letters) of as many as 25 strokes by "writing" them in the air with his finger. Yani immediately put them down on paper.

Her father helped develop her powers of observation and imagery by carrying her on his shoulders as he hiked in the fields and mountains or lying with her in the grass and telling stories about the passing clouds. The pebbles along the riverbank reminded her of the monkeys at the zoo, which she painted over and over between the ages of 3 and 6. Yani made up stories about the monkeys she portrayed. They often represented Yani herself—eating a snack, refereeing an argument among friends, or trying to conquer her fear of her first shot at the doctor's office. Painting, to Yani, was not an objective representation of reality; it was a mirror of her mind, a way to transform her sensory impressions into simple but powerful semi-abstract images onto which she projected her thoughts, feelings, and dreams.

Because of her short arms, Yani's brush strokes at first were short. Her father trained her to hold her brush tightly, by trying to grab it from behind when she was not looking. She learned to paint with her whole arm, twisting her wrist to produce the effect she wanted. As her physical dexterity and experience grew, her strokes became more forceful, varied, and precise: broad, wet strokes to define an animal's shape; fuzzy, nearly dry ones to suggest feathers, fur, or tree bark. The materials she used—bamboo brushes, ink sticks, and rice paper—were traditional, but her style—popularly called *xieyi,* "idea writing"—was not. It was, and remains, playful, free, and spontaneous.

With quick reflexes, a fertile imagination, remarkable visual abilities, strong motivation, and her father's sensitive guidance, Yani's artistic progress has been swift. As a young adult, she is considered an artist of great promise. Yet she herself finds painting very simple: "You just paint what you think about. You don't have to follow any instruction. Everybody can paint" (Zhensun & Low, 1991, p. 9).

● ● ●

Although Wang Yani's artistic growth has been unusual, it rested on typical developments of early childhood: rapid improvement in muscular control and eye–hand coordination. Youngsters in this age group grow more slowly than before, but still at a fast pace; and they make so much progress in muscle development and coordination that they can do much more. Like other children, Yani's gain in fine motor skills was accompanied by a growing cognitive understanding of the world around her—an understanding guided by her powers of observation and memory and her interactions with her father. Together these physical, cognitive, and social influences helped her express her thoughts and emotions through art.

In this chapter, as we look at physical development during the years from 3 to 6, we will see other examples of its interconnection with cognitive and psychosocial development. Nutrition and handedness are influenced by cultural attitudes, and sleep patterns by emotional experiences. Environmental influences, including the parents' life circumstances, affect health and safety. The link between developmental realms is especially evident in the tragic results of child abuse and neglect, poverty, and homelessness; although the most obvious effects may be physical, these conditions affect other aspects of a child's development as well.

After you have read and studied this chapter, you should be able to answer each of the Guidepost questions that appear at the top of the next page. Look for them again in the margins, where they point to important concepts throughout the chapter. To check your understanding of these Guideposts, review the end-of-chapter summary. Checkpoints located throughout the chapter will help you verify your understanding of what you have read.

*Sources of biographical information about Wang Yani were Bond (1989), Costello (1990), Ho (1989), Stuart (1991), and Zhensun & Low (1991).

**In Chinese custom, the given name follows the family name.

1. How do children's bodies change between ages 3 and 6, and what are their nutritional and dental needs?

2. What sleep patterns and problems tend to develop during early childhood?

3. What are the main motor achievements of early childhood, and how does children's artwork show their physical and cognitive maturation?

4. What are the major health and safety risks for children?

5. What are the causes and consequences of child abuse and neglect, and what can be done about it?

Guideposts for Study

Guidepost 1

How do children's bodies change between ages 3 and 6, and what are their nutritional and dental needs?

At age 4½, this boy's 95 cm height is over 3 cm above average but within the normal range.

Aspects of Physiological Development

In early childhood, children slim down and shoot up. They need less sleep than before and are more likely to develop sleep problems. They improve in running, hopping, skipping, jumping, and throwing balls. They also become better at tying shoelaces (in bows instead of knots), drawing with crayons (on paper rather than on walls), and pouring cereal (into the bowl, not onto the floor); and they begin to show a preference for either the right or left hand.

Bodily Growth and Change

At about age 3, children begin to take on the slender, athletic appearance of childhood. As abdominal muscles develop, the toddler potbelly tightens. The trunk, arms, and legs grow longer. The head is still relatively large, but the other parts of the body continue to catch up as body proportions steadily become more adult-like.

The pencil mark on the wall that shows Eve's height at 3 years is 95 cm from the floor, and she now weighs about 13 kg. Her twin brother Isaac, like most boys this age, is a little taller and heavier and has more muscle per kilogram of body weight, whereas Eve, like most girls, has more fatty tissue. Both boys and girls typically grow 5 to 8 cm a year during early childhood and gain 2 to 3 kg annually (see Table 9-1). Boys' slight edge in height and weight continues until the growth spurt of puberty.

These changes in appearance reflect developments inside the body. Muscular and skeletal growth progresses, making children stronger. Cartilage turns to bone at a faster rate than before, and bones become harder, giving the child a firmer shape and protecting

Table 9-1	Physical Growth, Ages 3 to 6 (50th percentile)*			
	Height, Centimetres		**Weight, Kilograms**	
Age	**Boys**	**Girls**	**Boys**	**Girls**
3	93.5	93.0	14	13
3½	99.0	96.0	15	14
4	101.0	99.5	16	15
4½	104.0	103.5	17	16
5	109.0	108.0	18	18
5½	111.5	111.0	20	19
6	114.0	114.0	21	20

*Fifty percent of children in each category are above this height or weight level, and 50 percent are below it.

Source: Kuczmarsld et al., 2000.

the internal organs. These changes, coordinated by the maturing brain and nervous system, promote the development of a wide range of motor skills. The increased capacities of the respiratory and circulatory systems build physical stamina and, along with the developing immune system, keep children healthier.

Nutrition: Preventing Overweight

As in infancy and toddlerhood, proper growth and health depend on good nutrition and adequate sleep (see Box 9-1). However, preschoolers' dietary and sleep needs are quite different from those of infants or toddlers. They are more likely to become overweight, especially if they are not very active, and many develop sleep-related problems. Beginning at age 2, a healthy diet is the same as for adults: primarily fruits and vegetables, whole grains, low-fat and nonfat dairy products, beans, fish, and lean meats (American Heart Association et al., 2006).

Preschoolers eat less in proportion to their size than infants do; as growth slows, they need fewer calories per kilogram of body weight. Preschoolers who are allowed to eat when they are hungry and are not pressured to eat everything given to them are more likely to regulate their own caloric intake than are children fed on schedule (S. L. Johnson & Birch, 1994). In one study of self-regulated feeding, 15 children ages 2 to 5 took in roughly the same number of calories

An obese child is likely to find it hard to keep up with slimmer peers, both physically and socially. Obesity among preschool and school-age children is more common than in the past.

every day for 6 days, even though they often ate very little at one meal and a great deal at another (Birch, Johnson, Andersen, Peters, & Schulte, 1991).

What children eat is a different matter. According to the Canadian Paediatric Society, a quarter of Canadian children are obese, and the major contributing factors are poor diet and lack of exercise (Healthy Active Living Committee, Canadian Paediatric Society, 2002). Young people of all ages eat too much fat and sugar and too few servings of fruits, vegetables, grains, and dairy products. Diets of poor and minority children are especially deficient (Muñoz, Krebs-Smith, Ballard-Barbash, & Cleveland, 1997). Another potential consequence of a poor diet is iron deficiency and iron-deficiency anemia, which affects over 10 percent of children 18 months of age (Nutrition Committee, Canadian Paediatric Society, 1991). To prevent iron deficiency in infants and young children, the Canadian Paediatric Society recommends iron-fortified cereals, formula, and other iron-rich foods for infants after 6 months of age.

Obesity and overweight today is more common among Canadian preschoolers than 20 years ago. According to the NLSCY about one in four children between 2 and 5 years of age are obese (Tucker, Irwin, Bouck & Pollet, 2006), with higher rates in Atlantic Canada than in other regions (Willows et al., 2007, p. 311). Between 1981 and 1996, the prevalence of childhood obesity in Canada tripled (Tremblay & Willms, 2000). In addition, community-based surveys show that obesity and overweight is a significant issue among Aboriginal children, with about 21 percent being overweight and 20 percent obese (Willows et al., 2007). However, across all ethnic groups, the greatest increase in prevalence of overweight is among chldren in low-income families (AAP Committee on Nutrition, 2003; Center for Weight and Health, 2001; Ritchie et al., 2001). Even at age 5, overweight is associated with behavioural problems (Datar & Sturm, 2004a) and low reading and math scores (Datar, Sturm, & Magnabosco, 2004).

Worldwide, an estimated 22 million children under age 5 are obese (Belizzi, 2002). As "junk food" spreads through the developing world, as many as 20 to 25 percent of 4-year-olds in some countries, such as Egypt, Morocco, and Zambia, are overweight or obese—a larger proportion than are malnourished.

A tendency toward obesity can be hereditary, but the main factors driving the obesity epidemic are environmental (AAP, 2004). Excessive weight gain hinges on caloric intake and lack of exercise (AAP Committee on Nutrition, 2003). As growth slows, preschoolers need fewer calories in proportion to their weight than they did before. According to a

Box 9-1 *Helping Children Eat and Sleep Well*

One child refuses to eat anything but peanut butter and jelly sandwiches. Another seems to live on bananas. Mealtimes seem more like art class, as preschoolers make snowmen out of mashed potatoes or lakes out of applesauce, and food remains uneaten on the plate.

Although a diminished appetite in early childhood is normal, many parents make the mistake of insisting that children eat more than they want, setting in motion a contest of wills. Bedtime, too, often becomes an issue ("Daddy, leave the light on! . . . I want a drink of water . . . What's that noise by the window? . . . I'm cold"). When a child delays or has trouble going to sleep or wakes often during the night, parents tend to become irritated, and the entire family feels the strain.

The following research-based suggestions can help make mealtimes and bedtimes pleasanter and children healthier (American Academy of Child and Adolescent Psychiatry [AACAP], 1997; American Academy of Pediatrics [AAP], 1992b; Adams & Rickert, 1989; American Heart Association et al., 2006; Canadian Paediatric Society [CPS], 1999; Graziano & Mooney, 1982; Rolls, Engell, & Birch, 2000; Williams & Caliendo, 1984):

Encouraging Healthy Eating Habits

- Keep a record of what a child eats. The child may in fact be eating enough.
- Serve simple, easily identifiable foods. Preschoolers often balk at mixed dishes like casseroles.
- Serve finger foods as often as possible.
- Introduce only one new food at a time, along with a familiar one the child likes.
- Offer small servings, especially of new or disliked foods; give second helpings if wanted.
- Don't pressure the child to clean the plate.
- After a reasonable time, remove the food and do not serve more until the next meal. A healthy child will not suffer from missing a meal, and children need to learn that certain times are appropriate for eating.
- Give the child a choice of foods containing similar nutrients: rye or whole wheat bread, a peach or an apple, yogourt or milk.
- Encourage a child to help prepare food by making sandwiches or mixing and spooning out cookie dough.
- Have nutritious snacks handy and allow the child to select favourites.
- Turn childish delights to advantage. Serve food in appealing dishes; dress it up with garnishes or little toys; make a "party" out of a meal.
- Don't fight "rituals," in which a child eats foods one at a time, in a certain order.
- Make mealtimes pleasant with conversation on interesting topics, keeping talk about eating itself to a minimum.
- Serve healthy, well-balanced meals offering a wide variety of tastes and textures that children find enjoyable. Prepare foods in a variety of ways.
- Use nutritional information and Canada's Food Guide to Healthy Eating (see www.mcgrawhill.ca/olc/papalia) to help in introducing new foods and working out average amounts.

- Encourage an interest in food by having older children help with shopping.
- Never use food as a reward or punishment.

Helping Children Go to Sleep

- Establish a regular, unrushed bedtime routine—about 20 minutes of quiet activities, such as reading a story, singing lullabies, or having quiet conversation.
- Allow no scary or loud television shows.
- Avoid highly stimulating, active play before bedtime.
- Keep a small night light on if it makes the child feel more comfortable.
- Don't feed or rock a child at bedtime.
- Stay calm but don't yield to requests for "just one more" story, one more drink of water, or one more bathroom trip.
- If you're trying to break a child's habit, offer rewards for good bedtime behaviour, such as stickers on a chart, or simple praise.
- Try putting your child to sleep a little later. Sending a child to bed too early is a common reason for sleep problems.
- If a child's fears about the dark or going to sleep have persisted for a long time, look for a program to help the child learn how to relax, how to substitute pleasant thoughts for frightening ones, and how to cope with stressful situations.

Helping Children Go Back to Sleep

- If a child gets up during the night, take him or her back to bed. Speak calmly, pat the child gently on the back, but be pleasantly firm and consistent.
- After a nightmare, reassure a frightened child and occasionally check in on the child. If frightening dreams persist for more than 6 weeks, consult your doctor.
- After night terrors, do not wake the child. If the child wakes, don't ask any questions. Just let the child go back to sleep.
- Help your child get enough sleep on a regular schedule; over-tired or stressed children are more prone to night terrors.
- Walk or carry a sleepwalking child back to bed. Child-proof your home with gates at the top of stairs and at windows and with bells on the child's bedroom door, so you'll know when she or he is out of bed.

What's your view ?

Have you ever tried to get a young child to eat properly or go to sleep at bedtime? If so, did you find any of the tactics suggested in this box helpful?

Check it out !

For more information on this topic, go to **www.mcgrawhill.ca/olc/papalia** for a link to a parent resource with many useful articles by experts in pediatric sleep disorders and nutrition. Select a topic from the list, search for articles using keywords, or choose one of the experts listed at the Web site.

representative sampling in Glasgow, Scotland, many 3- to 5-year-olds have mostly sedentary lifestyles (Reilly et al., 2004).

As children move through the preschool period, their eating patterns become more environmentally influenced. Whereas 3-year-olds will eat only until they are full, 5-year-olds tend to eat more when a larger portion is put in front of them. Thus, a key to preventing obesity may be to make sure older preschoolers are served appropriate portions—and not to admonish them to clean their plates (Rolls et al., 2000). Preschoolers who are allowed to eat when they are hungry and are not pressured to eat everything given to them are more likely to regulate their own caloric intake than are children fed on a schedule (S. L. Johnson & Birch, 1994). However, children vary in their ability to recognize their internal cues of hunger and fullness and may be influenced by what their parents eat. In a study of 40 families in two child-care facilities, a six-week program designed to teach children to recognize their own cues improved their ability to self-regulate, independent of what they saw their mothers do (Johnson, 2000).

Prevention of overweight in the early years, when excessive weight gain usually begins, is critical; the long-term success of treatment, especially when it is delayed, is limited (AAP Committee on Nutrition, 2003; Quattrin, Liu, Shaw, Shine, & Chiang, 2005). Overweight children, especially those who have overweight parents, tend to become obese adults (AAP Committee on Nutrition, 2003; CPS, 2002; Whitaker et al., 1997), and excess body mass is a threat to health. Early childhood is a good time to treat overweight, when a child's diet is still subject to parental influence or control (Quattrin et al., 2005; Whitaker et al., 1997).

Too little exercise and too much sedentary activity are important factors in overweight. Studies have found that each hour of television preschool children watch increases the risk of overweight, and having a TV set in a child's bedroom further increases the risk (Dennison, Erb, & Jenkins, 2002). Given that the average Canadian child watches about 14 hours of television per week (Canadian Peadiatric Society, 2003), the risk of increased prevalence of overweight and obesity is very real; each additional hour of TV watching above two hours a day increases the likelihood of obesity at age 30 by 7 percent (Viner & Cole, 2005).

To avoid excessive weight and prevent cardiac problems, young children should get no more than 30 percent of their total calories from fat, and less than 10 percent of the total from saturated fat, and as they grow children should be encouraged to eat a variety of kinds of foods with complex carbohydrates and lower-fat foods introduced, and to engage in physical activity (Canadian Paediatic Society, undated). Canadian children's diets include about 35 percent intake from fat, and 13 percent saturated fat (Gibson, MacDonald, & Smit Vanderkooy, 1993). However, current trends in children's dietary habits indicate that their fat consumption is decreasing to the recommended levels (CPS, 2001). Lean meat and dairy foods should remain in the diet to provide protein, iron, and calcium. Milk and other dairy products can now be skim or low-fat (AAP Committee on Nutrition, 1992a). Studies have found no negative effects on height, weight, body mass, or neurological development from a moderately low-fat diet (Rask-Nissilä et al., 2000; Shea et al., 1993).

Over 75 percent of Canadian children in Grade 6 report eating fruits and vegetables daily, although this falls to 70 percent by the time they reach Grade 10 (King, Boyce, & King, 1999). When it comes to less nutritious and fatty foods like french fries, hamburgers, and potato chips, which can be harmful to physical development and contribute to becoming overweight, more Grade 6 boys than girls report eating such food daily (ranging from 10 percent eating hamburgers daily, to 22 percent eating french fries daily). Just over half the number of girls as boys report eating less nutritious foods. People in remote northern communities, particularly Aboriginal people, who are serviced by food mail, are at risk of health problems related to inadequate nutrition, including obesity, respiratory illness, and non–insulin dependent diabetes. The diet in remote communities often consists of convenience foods that are less nutritious than fresh fruits and vegetables that are readily available in less remote centres (CICH, 2000). Obesity is discussed further in Chapters 12 and 15.

Malnutrition

At the other extreme, food-bank use in Canada is on the increase. Forty percent of food-bank users in Canada are children under 18 years of age, yet they make up only a quarter of the population (Wilson & Steinman, 2000; Wilson & Tsoa, 2001). In 2004, about 317,000 foodbank users were children, up from 166,000 Canadian children in 1989 (Canadian Press, 2004).

Nearly half (46 percent) of young children in south Asia, 30 percent in sub-Saharan Africa, 8 percent in Latin America and the Caribbean, and 27 percent worldwide are moderately or severely underweight (UNICEF, 2002). Undernutrition is an underlying cause in more than half of all deaths before age 5 (Bryce, Boschi-Pinto, Shibuya, Black, and the WHO Child Health Epidemiology Reference Group, 2005). Even in Canada, many children live in food-insecure households (Canadian Council on Social Development, 2002).

Because undernourished children usually live in extremely deprived circumstances, the specific effects of malnutrition may be hard to isolate. However, taken together, these deprivations may negatively affect not only growth and physical well-being but cognitive and psychosocial development as well. In an analysis of data on a nationally representative sample of 3,286 six- to 11-year-olds, those whose families had insufficient food were more likely to do poorly on arithmetic tests, to have repeated a grade, to have seen a psychologist, and to have had difficulty getting along with other children (Alaimo, Olson, & Frongillo, 2001). Moreover, cognitive effects of malnutrition may be long lasting. Among 1,559 children born on the island of Mauritius in a single year, those who were undernourished at age 3 had poorer verbal and spatial abilities, reading skills, scholastic ability, and neuropsychological performance than their peers at age 11 (Liu, Raine, Venables, Dalais, & Mednick, 2003).

Effects of malnutrition on growth can be largely reversed with improved diet (Lewit & Kerrebrock, 1997), but the most effective treatments go beyond physical care. A longitudinal study (Grantham-McGregor, Powell, Walker, Chang, & Fletcher, 1994) followed two groups of Jamaican children with low developmental levels who had been hospitalized for severe undernourishment in infancy or toddlerhood and who came from extremely poor, often unstable homes. Health care paraprofessionals played with an experimental group in the hospital and, after discharge, visited them at home every week for three years, showing the mothers how to make toys and encouraging them to interact with their children. Three years after the program stopped, the experimental group's IQs were well above those of a control group who had received only standard medical care (though not as high as those of a third, well-nourished group). Furthermore, the IQs of the experimental group remained higher than those of the control group as much as 14 years after leaving the hospital.

Early education may help counter the effects of undernourishment. In the Jamaican study, the mothers in the experimental group enrolled their children in preschools at earlier ages than did the mothers in the control group. In another Mauritian study, 100 three- to 5-year-olds received nutritional supplements and medical examinations and were placed in special preschools with small classes. At age 17, these children had lower rates of antisocial behaviour and mental health problems than a control group. The effects were greatest among those who had been undernourished to begin with (Raine et al., 2003).

Oral Health

By age 3, all the primary, or deciduous, teeth are in place. The permanent teeth, which will begin to appear at about age 6, are developing.

Use of fluoride and improved dental care have dramatically reduced the incidence of tooth decay since the 1970s (Brown, Wall, & Lazar, 2000), but disadvantaged children still have more untreated cavities than other children (Bloom, Cohen, Vickerie, & Wondimu, 2003; Brown, Wall, & Lazar, 2000). The Canadian Paediatric Society recommends parents use fluoride supplements for children 6 months of age and older in areas that do not fluoridate the water supply, but also to limit the amount of toothpaste used in order to avoid fluorosis. Fluorosis results in pitting and brown staining of the teeth, particularly in the first 6 months (American Academy of Pediatric Dentistry, 2002–2007; Nutrition Committee, Canadian Paediatric Society, 1996). Tooth decay in

Checkpoint ✔

Can you . . .

✔ Describe typical physiological changes between ages 3 and 6?

✔ Summarize preschoolers' dietary needs and explain why overweight, obesity, and tooth decay can become concerns at this age?

✔ Identify effects of malnutrition and factors that may influence its long-term outcome?

early childhood often stems from over-consumption of sweetened milk and juices in infancy, together with lack of regular dental care. A common source of early childhood tooth decay is going to bed with a bottle of milk, juice, or formula—a practice that the Canadian Dental Association recommends that parents avoid (Canadian Dental Association, 2002).

Sleep Patterns and Problems

Guidepost 2

What sleep patterns and problems tend to develop during early childhood?

Sleep patterns change throughout the growing-up years (Iglowstein, Jenni, Molinari, & Largo, 2003; see Figure 9-1), and early childhood has its own distinct rhythms. Young children usually sleep more deeply at night than they will later in life, but most Canadian children still need a daytime nap or quiet rest until about age 5.

Children in different cultures may get the same amount of sleep each day, but its timing may vary. In many traditional cultures, such as the Gusii of Kenya, the Javanese in Indonesia, and the Zuni in New Mexico, young children have no regular bedtime and are allowed to stay up watching adult activities until they are sleepy. Among the Canadian Hare-Chipewyan, 3-year-olds do not take naps but are put to sleep right after dinner and are allowed to sleep as long as they wish in the morning (Broude, 1995).

Young children may develop elaborate routines to put off retiring, and it may take them longer than before to fall asleep. About one-third of preschoolers actively resist going to bed, and more than one-third awake at least once each night (National Sleep Foundation, 2004). Regular, consistent sleep routines can help minimize these problems. Young children who have become accustomed to being put to sleep by feeding or rocking

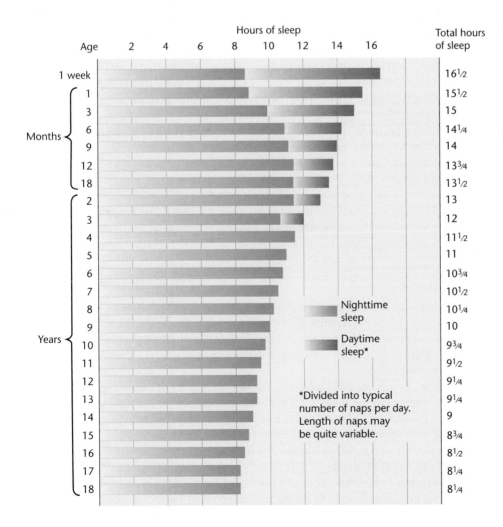

Figure 9-1

Typical sleep requirements in childhood. Unlike infants, who sleep about as long day and night, preschoolers get all or almost all their sleep in one long nighttime period. The number of hours of sleep steadily decreases throughout childhood, but individual children may need more or fewer hours than shown here.

Source: Ferber, 1985.

may find it hard to fall asleep on their own (Hoban, 2004). Bedtime may bring on a form of separation anxiety, and the child may do all she or he can to avoid it. Regular, consistent sleep routines can help minimize this common problem. It is recommended that children past infancy not be put to sleep by feeding or rocking, as this may make it hard for them to fall asleep on their own (American Academy of Child and Adolescent Psychiatry (AACAP), 1997).

Children are likely to want a light left on and to sleep with a favourite toy or blanket (Beltramini & Hertzig, 1983). Such *transitional objects,* used repeatedly as bedtime companions, help a child shift from the dependence of infancy to the independence of later childhood.

Sleep Disturbances and Disorders

About one in 10 parents or caregivers of preschoolers say their child has a sleep problem (National Sleep Foundation, 2004). Sleep disturbances may be caused by accidental activation of the brain's motor control system (Hobson & Silvestri, 1999) or by incomplete arousal from a deep sleep (Hoban, 2004) or may be triggered by disordered breathing or restless leg movements (Guilleminault, Palombini, Pelayo, & Chervin, 2003). These disturbances tend to run in families (AACAP, 1997; Hobson & Silvestri, 1999; Hoban, 2004). In most cases they are only occasional and usually are outgrown. Persistent sleep problems may indicate an emotional, physiological, or neurological condition that needs to be examined.

A child who experiences a *sleep* (or *night*) *terror* appears to awaken abruptly early in the night from a deep sleep in a state of agitation. The child may scream and sit up in bed, breathing rapidly and staring or thrashing about. Yet he is not really awake, quiets down quickly, and the next morning remembers nothing about the episode. Night terrors occur mostly between ages 3 and 13 (Laberge, Tremblay, Vitaro, & Montplaisir, 2000) and affect boys more often than girls (AACAP, 1997; Hobson & Silvestri, 1999).

Walking and talking during sleep are fairly common in early and middle childhood. Although sleepwalking itself is harmless, sleepwalkers may be in danger of hurting themselves (AACAP, 1997; Hoban, 2004; Vgontzas & Kales, 1999). However, it is best not to interrupt sleepwalking or night terrors, as interruptions may confuse and further frighten the child (Hoban, 2004; Vgontzas & Kales, 1999).

Nightmares are quite common, affecting nearly 58 percent of Swedish 5- to 7-year-olds, according to parental reports (Smedje, Broman, & Hetta, 1999). They usually occur toward morning and are often brought on by staying up too late, eating a heavy meal close to bedtime, or overexcitement—for example, from watching an overstimulating television program, seeing a terrifying movie, or hearing a frightening bedtime story (Vgontzas & Kales, 1999). An occasional bad dream is no cause for alarm, but frequent or persistent nightmares, especially those that make a child fearful or anxious during waking hours, may signal excessive stress (Hoban, 2004).

Bedwetting

enuresis Repeated urination in clothing or in bed

Most children stay dry, day and night, by 3 to 5 years of age; but **enuresis,** repeated urination in clothing or in bed, is common, especially at night. About 10 to 15 percent of 5-year-olds, more commonly boys, wet the bed regularly, perhaps while sleeping deeply. More than half outgrow the condition by age 8 without special help (Community Paediatrics Committee, 2005).

Children this age normally recognize the sensation of a full bladder while asleep and awaken to empty it in the toilet. Children who wet the bed do not have this awareness. Fewer than 1 percent of bedwetters have a physical disorder, though they may have a small bladder capacity. Nor is persistent enuresis primarily an emotional, mental, or behavioural problem—though such problems can develop because of the way bedwetters are treated by playmates and family (National [U.S.] Enuresis Society, 1995; Schmitt, 1997).

Enuresis runs in families. About 75 percent of bedwetters have a close relative who also wets the bed, and identical twins are more concordant for the condition than fraternal twins (APA, 1994; Fergusson, Horwood, & Shannon, 1986). The discovery of the approximate site of a gene linked to enuresis (Eiberg, 1995; Eiberg, Berendt, & Mohr, 1995) points to heredity as a major factor, possibly in combination with such other factors as slow motor maturation, allergies, and poor behavioural control (Goleman, 1995b). The gene does not appear to account for occasional bedwetting. Many children who wet the bed are lacking in an anti-diuretic hormone, which concentrates urine during sleep. As a result, they produce more urine than their bladders can hold (National [U.S.] Enuresis Society, 1995).

Children and their parents need to be reassured that enuresis is common and not serious. The child is not to blame and should not be punished. Generally parents need not do anything unless children themselves see bedwetting as a problem. Enuresis that persists beyond 8 to 10 years of age may be a sign of poor self-concept or other psychological problems (Community Paediatrics Committee, 2005).

The most effective treatment is a device to wake the child when he or she begins to urinate by setting off a bell or buzzer. However, the success rate is less than 50 percent, and the devices are most effective with children older than 7 or 8 who are highly motivated to overcome the problem. Drug therapy with desmopressin acetate can be used in special situations, such as camping and sleepovers. Impramine hydrochloride may be used as short-term treatment in distressed older children, if other treatments have been unsuccessful or are contraindicated, but care must be taken to avoid overdose. There is insufficient evidence for routine use of behavioural therapy (Community Paediatrics Committee, 2005).

Motor Development

Children ages 3 to 6 make great advances in motor skills—both **gross motor skills,** which involve the large muscles, such as running and jumping (see Table 9-2), and **fine motor skills,** manipulative skills involving eye–hand and small-muscle coordination, such as buttoning and drawing. They also begin to show a preference for either the right or left hand.

Gross and Fine Motor Skills

At 3, David could walk a straight line and jump a short distance. At 4, he could hop a few steps on one foot. On his fifth birthday, he could jump nearly a metre and hop for 5 metres and was learning to roller skate.

Motor skills such as these do not develop in isolation. The skills that emerge in early childhood build on the achievements of infancy and toddlerhood. As children's bodies change, permitting them to do more, they integrate their new and previously acquired skills into **systems of action,** producing ever more complex capabilities.

In early childhood, development of the sensory and motor areas of the cortex permits better coordination between what children want to do and what they can do. Their bones and muscles are stronger, and their lung capacity is greater, making it possible to run, jump, and climb farther, faster, and better.

Checkpoint ✔

Can you . . .

✔ Discuss age differences and cultural variations in sleep patterns?

✔ Identify four common sleep problems and give recommendations for handling them?

Guidepost 3

What are the main motor achievements of early childhood, and how does children's artwork show their physical and cognitive maturation?

gross motor skills Physical skills that involve the large muscles

fine motor skills Physical skills that involve the small muscles and eye–hand coordination

systems of action Increasingly complex combinations of skills that permit a wider or more precise range of movement and more control of the environment

Table 9-2	Gross Motor Skills in Early Childhood	
3-Year-Olds	**4-Year-Olds**	**5-Year-Olds**
Cannot turn or stop suddenly or quickly	Have more effective control of stopping, starting, and turning	Can start, turn, and stop effectively in games
Can jump a distance of 40 to 60 cm	Can jump a distance of 60 to 80 cm	Can make a running jump of 70 to 90 cm
Can ascend a stairway unaided, alternating feet	Can descend a long stairway alternating feet, if supported	Can descend a long stairway unaided, alternating feet
Can hop, using largely an irregular series of jumps with some variations added	Can hop four to six steps on one foot	Can easily hop a distance of 5 m

Source: Corbin, 1973.

The ability to tie her own shoelaces enables this 5-year-old girl to be more self-reliant.

What's your view ?

- In view of preschool boys' and girls' differing physical and motor development, should parents encourage different kinds of physical activity for boys and girls in that age group?

What's your view ?

- Drawings from children's early pictorial stage show energy and freedom; those from the later pictorial stage show care and accuracy. Why do you think these changes occur? How would you evaluate them?

handedness Preference for using a particular hand

At about 2½, children begin to jump with both feet, a skill they have not been able to master before this time, probably because their leg muscles were not yet strong enough to propel their body weight upward. Hopping is hard to master until about 4 years of age.

Going upstairs is easier than going down; by 3½, most children comfortably alternate feet going up, but not until about 5 do they easily descend that way. Children begin to gallop at about 4, do fairly well by 5, and are quite skilful by 6½. Skipping is harder; although some 4-year-olds can skip, most children cannot do it until age 6 (Corbin, 1973). Of course, children vary in aptitude, depending on their genetic endowment and their opportunities to learn and practise motor skills.

The gross motor skills developed during early childhood are the basis for sports, dancing, and other activities that begin during middle childhood and may continue for a lifetime. There seems to be virtually no limit to the number and kind of motor acts children can learn, at least to some degree, by the age of 6. However, those under 6 are rarely ready to take part in any organized sport. Only 20 percent of 4-year-olds can throw a ball well, and only 30 percent can catch well (AAP Committee on Sports Medicine and Fitness, 1992).

Young children develop best physically when they can be active at an appropriate maturational level in unstructured free play. Parents and teachers can help by offering young children the opportunity to climb and jump on safe, properly sized equipment, by providing balls and other toys small enough to be easily grasped and soft enough not to be harmful, and by offering gentle coaching when a child seems to need help.

Gains in *fine motor skills,* such as tying shoelaces and cutting with scissors, allow young children to take more responsibility for their personal care. At 3, Winnie can pour milk into her cereal bowl, eat with silverware, and use the toilet alone. She can also draw a circle and a rudimentary person—without arms. At 4, Nelson can dress himself with help. He can cut along a line, draw a fairly complete person, make designs and crude letters, and fold paper into a double triangle. At 5, Jean can dress himself without much help, copy a square or triangle, and draw a more elaborate person than before.

Artistic Development

Most 3- to 5-year-olds may not be as accomplished artists as Wang Yani, but with progress in fine motor coordination, they too can use their growing cognitive powers and express themselves emotionally through art. In pioneering research, Rhoda Kellogg (1970) examined more than 1 million drawings by children, half of them under age 6. Since she found drawings by young children similar in different cultures, she concluded that stages in early drawing (see Figure 9-2) reflect maturation of the brain as well as of the muscles.

Two-year-olds *scribble,* and their scribbles are not random. Kellogg identified 20 basic scribbles, such as vertical and zigzag lines, and 17 patterns of placement of scribbles on paper, which appear by age 2.

By age 3, the *shape* stage appears. Now a child draws diagrams in six basic shapes: circles, squares or rectangles, triangles, crosses, Xs, and odd forms. Next, children quickly move on to the *design* stage, in which they combine two basic shapes into a more complex abstract pattern.

Most children enter the *pictorial* stage between ages 4 and 5, though Wang Yani reached it at 3. Early drawings at this stage suggest real-life objects or people; later drawings are better defined. Although most adults see the later drawings as a sign of progress, Kellogg views the switch from abstraction to representation as a fundamental change in the purpose of children's drawing—a move away from a concern with form and design, the primary elements of art—often under the "guidance" of adults who encourage children to portray reality (Kellogg, 1970).

Kellogg quotes artist Pablo Picasso: "Adults should not teach children to draw but should learn from them" (1970, p. 36). Like Wang Yani's father, adults can sustain children's early creativity by letting them draw what they like without imposing suggestions or standards.

Handedness

Handedness, the preference for using one hand over the other, is usually evident by 3 years of age. Since the left hemisphere of the brain, which controls the right side of the body, is

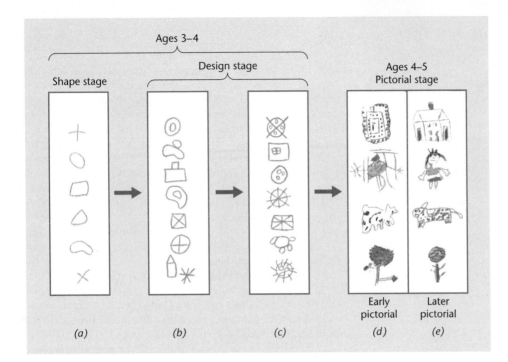

Figure 9-2

Artistic development in early childhood. There is a great difference between the very simple shapes shown in (a) and the detailed pictorial drawings in (e). The challenge for adults is to encourage children's creativity while acknowledging their growing facility in drawing.

Source: Kellogg, 1970.

Ages 3–4

Design stage

Shape stage

Ages 4–5
Pictorial stage

Early pictorial

Later pictorial

(a)   (b)   (c)   (d)   (e)

usually dominant, most people favour their right side. In people whose brains are more symmetrical, the right hemisphere tends to dominate, making them left-handed. Handedness is not always clear-cut; not everybody prefers one hand for every task. Boys are more likely to be left-handed than girls.

Is handedness genetic or learned? That question has been controversial. A new theory proposes the existence of a single gene for right-handedness. According to this theory, people who inherit this gene from either or both parents—about 82 percent of the population—are right-handed. Those who do not inherit the gene still have a 50:50 chance of being right-handed; otherwise they will be left-handed or ambidextrous. Random determination of handedness among those who do not receive the gene could explain why some monozygotic twins have differing hand preferences, as well as why 8 percent of the offspring of two right-handed parents are left-handed. The theory closely predicted the proportion of left-handed offspring in a three-generational sample of families recruited through advertisements (Klar, 1996).

Health and Safety

What used to be a very vulnerable time of life is much safer now. Because of widespread immunization, many of the major diseases of childhood are now fairly rare in industrialized countries. Measles, once a major scourge of childhood, now causes only 4 percent of deaths in children younger than 5 worldwide (Bryce et al., 2005, see Box 9-2). In the non-industrialized world, however, such vaccine-preventable diseases as measles, pertussis (whooping cough), and tuberculosis still take a large toll. Diarrheal infections account for nearly one-fifth of the 11.2 million deaths of children under age 5 in these regions each year (Wegman, 1999).

In Canada, children's death rates from all causes have come down in recent years. Deaths in childhood are relatively few compared with deaths in adulthood, and most are caused by injury rather than illness, particularly during adolescence (see Figure 9-5). Still, environmental influences make this a less healthy time for some children than for others.

Accidental Injuries and Deaths

Because young children are naturally venturesome and often unaware of danger, it is hard for caregivers to protect them from harm without *over*protecting them. By far the

---

Checkpoint ✔

Can you . . .

✔ List at least three gross motor skills and three fine motor skills, and tell when they typically develop?

✔ Identify four stages in young children's drawing?

✔ Tell how brain functioning is related to physical skills and handedness?

 *Guidepost 4*

What are the major health and safety risks for children?

Box 9-2 *Surviving the First Five Years of Life*

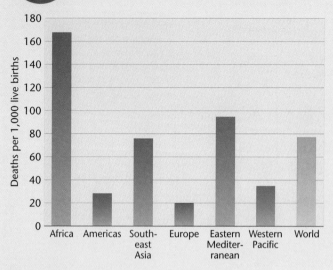

Figure 9-3

Comparative child mortality in six regions of the world, 2002.

Source: WHO, 2003, Figure 1.4.

The chances of a child's living to his or her fifth birthday are substantially better than 38 years ago, but the prospects for survival depend to a great extent on where the child lives. Worldwide, more than 17 million children under 5 died in 1970. Today the number of deaths in this age group has dropped to 10.6 million each year—still far too many (Bryce et al., 2005; WHO, 2003). And, although child mortality has lessened in most parts of the world, these gains have not benefited all children equally.

International efforts to improve child health focus on the first five years because nearly 9 out of 10 deaths of children under age 15 occur during those years. Fully 98 percent of child deaths occur in poor, rural regions of developing countries, where nutrition is inadequate, water is unsafe, and sanitary facilities are lacking; 42 percent of these deaths occur in sub-Saharan Africa and 29 percent in southeast Asia (Bryce et al., 2005; WHO, 2003; see Figure 9-3). A baby born in Sierra Leone is three and a half times more likely to die before age 5 than a child born in India and more than 100 times more likely to die than a child born in Iceland, which has the world's lowest child mortality rate (WHO, 2003).

Worldwide, four major causes of death, accounting for 54 percent of deaths in children younger than 5, are communicable diseases: pneumonia, diarrhea, malaria, and neonatal sepsis or pneumonia (see Figure 9-4). In more than half of these deaths, undernutrition is an underlying cause. Ninety-four percent of deaths from malaria occur in Africa (Bryce et al., 2005).

More advanced developing countries of the Eastern Mediterrean region, Latin America, and Asia are experiencing a shift toward the pattern in more developed countries, where child deaths are most likely to be caused by complications of birth (refer back to Chapter 6). At least 169 countries have shown declines in child mortality in the past three decades. The most striking reduction was in Oman, on the southern end of the Arabian peninsula, from 242 child deaths per 1,000 live births in 1970 to

only 15 per 1,000 in 2002. India and China also have achieved impressive declines. In general, however, the strongest improvement has occurred in rich industrialized nations and in those developing countries where child mortality was already relatively low. Thus, although the mortality gap between the developed and developing world has narrowed, disparities among developing regions have widened (WHO, 2003).

In some African countries, HIV/AIDS is responsible for as many as 6 out of 10 child deaths, often in children who lose their mothers to the disease. Fourteen African countries, after achieving significant reductions in child mortality during the 1970s and 1980s, saw *more* young children die in 2002 than in 1990. On the other hand, eight countries in the region, among them Gabon, Gambia, and Ghana, have reduced child mortality by more than 50 percent since 1970 (WHO, 2003).

In Latin America, the most dramatic reductions in child mortality have taken place in Chile, Costa Rica, and Cuba, where child deaths have dropped more than 80 percent since 1970. In contrast, Haitian children still die at a rate of 133 per 1,000, almost double the rate in Bolivia, which has the next worst mortality record in the Americas (WHO, 2003).

In most countries, with the exception of China, India, Pakistan, and Nepal, boys are more likely to die than girls. In China, where families traditionally prefer boys, young girls have a 33 percent greater risk of dying—often, it has been reported, through abandonment or infanticide (Carmichael, 2004; Hudson & den Boer, 2004; Lee, 2004; Rosenthal, 2003; see Box 11-2 in Chapter 11). Children in poor countries and children of the poor in rich countries are most likely to die young. Survival gains have been slower in rural than in urban areas and, in some countries, such as the United States, have disproportionately benefited those with higher incomes. But even poor U.S. children are less likely to die young than better-off children in Africa (WHO, 2003).

What's your view

What might be done to produce more rapid and more evenly distributed improvements in child mortality throughout the world?

Check it out

For more information on this topic, go to **www.mcgrawhill.ca/olc/papalia.**

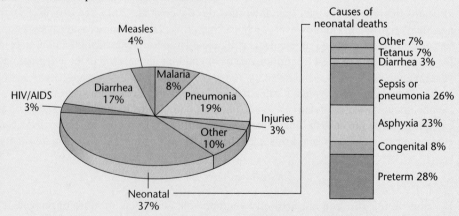

Figure 9-4

Major causes of death in children younger than 5 and in neonates (yearly average, 2000–2003).

Source: Bryce et al., 2005.

most common cause of injury in early childhood is falls, accounting for over 60 percent of all injuries in this age group, based on NLSCY data, and injuries outside the home are becoming more common (Kohen, Soubhi, & Raina, 1999). Although most cuts, bumps, and scrapes are "kissed away" and quickly forgotten, some accidental injuries result in lasting damage or death. Indeed, accidents, drownings and poisonings are the leading causes of death throughout childhood and adolescence in Canada (Canadian Health Network, 2007; Canadian Paediatric Society, 2005–2006; CICH, 2000). Most of these deaths are from motor vehicle injuries, particularly during adolescence (Health Canada, 1998; Rivara, 1999), and fatality rates from these injuries are higher in rural than in urban areas (Kmet & Macarthur, 2006). Deaths from pedestrian injuries have fallen by 65 percent since the late 1970s, but the risk of serious brain damage and lifelong disability from head injuries remains high (Rivara, 1999). Post-traumatic stress disorder is a common, but frequently overlooked, consequence of pedestrian accidents (de Vries et al., 1999).

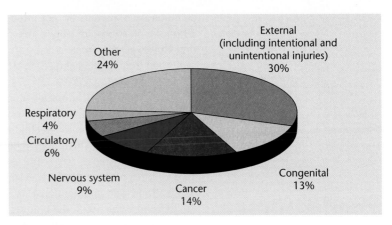

Figure 9-5

Leading causes of death for children aged 1–4 years in Canada, 2004. Total deaths: 286.

Source: Statistics Canada, 2007.

Many kindergartners and first graders walk alone to school, often crossing busy streets without traffic lights, although they do not know how to do this safely (Zeedyk, Wallace, & Spry, 2002). Some children are risk-prone. In one study, 5- and 6-year-olds who tended to take risks in a gambling game were more likely than their peers to say it was safe to cross a busy street between cars without a traffic light or crosswalk (Hoffrage, Weber, Hertwig, & Chase, 2003).

Hospitalization for injury from motor vehicle traffic accidents and other road injuries become more common in childhood. In 1996–1997, 42 out of every 100,000 children aged 5 to 9 years were hospitalized as a result of a traffic accident, and 38 out of every 100,000 children of the same age range were hospitalized after other road injuries (CICH, 2000).

All 10 provinces and three territories require young children in cars to be in specially designed seats or to wear standard seat belts. Four-year-olds who "graduate" from car seats to lap and shoulder belts may need booster seats until they grow bigger. Airbags designed to inflate rapidly so as to protect adults riding in the front seat of a car in high-impact collisions *increase* the risk of fatal injury to children under age 13 by as much as 34 percent (Rivara, 1999). It is safer, therefore, for young children always to ride in the back seat. The number of child deaths in motor vehicle crashes fell each year between 1996 and 2003 as a result of a campaign to keep children out of the front seats of cars (Glassbrenner, Carra, & Nichols, 2005).

The cost to the health-care system of unintentional injury can be staggering ($8.7 billion annually, according to the Canadian Health Network, 2007). Injuries due to falls account for over half of the costs of caring for accidents, according to the British Columbia Injury Research and Prevention Unit (Cloutier & Albert, 2001). The cost of caring for children needing hospitalization due to falls in B.C. is estimated at $108 million per year (Cloutier et al., 2001). Faced with such a situation, health authorities throughout the country are stressing prevention as a way of reducing the monetary and personal costs associated with injuries, including use of bicycle helmets, child safety seats, road safety improvements, smoke alarms, and poison control services (Cloutier et al., 2001).

The ingestion of toxic substances by children under 6 accounts for up to one-half of hospital cases of poisonings (Daws & Kent, 2006). Most poisonings occur in the home. The most common substances reported to Canadian Poison Control centres to have been ingested by children under 5 are acetaminophen, cold medication, multivitamins without iron, rubbing alcohol, nail polish remover, iron, multivitamins with iron, acetylsalicylic acid, camphor, and essential oils (Health Canada, 1998). Because these substances are so commonplace, parents do not often perceive them as highly dangerous (Health Canada, 1998). Medications are responsible for more than half (52 percent) of deaths from poisoning. However, the greatest risks are from swallowing anticonvulsant and antidepressant drugs and iron supplements. Safe storage could prevent many of these deaths (Litovitz et al., 1999; Shannon, 2000).

Laws requiring "childproof" caps on medicine bottles and other dangerous household products, regulation of product safety, mandatory helmets for bicycle riders, and safe storage of firearms have improved child safety. About 23 percent of Canadian households owns a gun. Canada ranks fifth among industrialized countries in firearms deaths among children under 14 years (Cukier, 2000). In 1992, 153 children under 19 years died of firearm injuries. Twenty-three of these deaths were in the 1–14 year age group. The majority of the injuries in this group were unintentional, or were homicides. Since federal gun-control legislation was introduced in 1978, the number of gun-related injuries, particularly suicide, declined (Canadian Paediatric Society, 1996). Recommended changes to gun-control legislation would increase standards for storage of firearms, given that the most common reason given by children for using guns was their accessibility. Making playgrounds safer would be another valuable child-safety measure. An estimated 3 percent of children in daycare are hurt badly enough each year to need medical attention, and about half of accidents at child-care centres occur on playgrounds. Nearly 1 in 5 are from falls, often resulting in skull injury and brain damage (Briss, Sacks, Addiss, Kresnow, & O'Neil, 1994).

Children are less likely to be injured in daycare, however, than in and around the home (Thacker, Addiss, Goodman, Holloway, & Spencer, 1992), where most fatal nonvehicular accidents occur. Children drown in bathtubs, pools, and buckets containing liquids (as well as in lakes, rivers, and oceans); are burned by scalding or in fires or explosions; fall from heights; drink or eat poisonous substances; get caught in mechanical contrivances; and suffocate in traps, such as abandoned refrigerators. Another dangerous place is the supermarket shopping cart (U.S. Consumer Product Safety Commission, 1991). Almost 250 hospitalizations of children under the age of 5 occurring annually in Canada are the result of the child falling off the cart (Canadian Hospitals Injury Reporting and Prevention Program [CHIRPP], 1999). (Table 9-3 summarizes suggestions for reducing accident risks in various settings.)

Health in Context: Environmental Influences

Why do some children have more illnesses or injuries than others? The genetic heritage contributes: Some children seem predisposed toward some medical conditions. But the environment children live in—indeed, the air they breathe—makes a tremendous difference.

Socio-economic Status and Race/Ethnicity

The lower a family's SES, the greater a child's risks of illness, injury, and death (Chen, Matthews, & Boyce, 2002). Poor children are disproportionately minority children (NCHS, 2005), are more likely than other children to have chronic conditions and activity limitations, and to have unmet medical and dental needs. However, the general health of poor children has been improving; between 1984 and 2003, the percentage of poor children in very good or excellent health rose from 62 percent to 71 percent, as compared with 86 to 89 percent for nonpoor children ([U.S.] Federal Interagency Forum on Child and Family Statistics, 2005).

Low income can introduce risks to healthy child development, either directly in limiting the kinds of resources a parent can provide to create an enriched environment for the child, or indirectly through increased stresses that parents experience, which can have detrimental effects on children by reducing the capacity of parents to provide supportive and consistent parenting, and by increasing the likelihood of hostile parenting and parental depression (Lipman, Boyle, Dooley, & Offord, 1998; Ryan & Adams, 1998). Social and governmental initiatives, like the National Child Tax Benefit, which are aimed at reducing the negative effects of low-income, often have limited effectiveness, due to clawbacks of benefits offered to low-income families by provincial governments (Lipman et al., 1998).

Checkpoint ✓

Can you . . .

✔ Tell where and how young children are most likely to be injured, and list ways in which injuries can be avoided?

✔ Compare the health status of young children in developed and developing countries?

Table 9-3	Reducing Accident Risks for Children
Activity	**Precautions**
Bicycling	Helmets reduce risk of head injury by 85 percent and brain injury by 88 percent.
Skateboarding and rollerblading	Children should wear helmets and protective padding on knees, elbows, and wrists.
Using fireworks	Families should not purchase fireworks for home use.
Lawn mowing	Children under 12 should not operate walk-behind mowers; those under 14 should not operate ride-on mowers; small children should not be close to a moving mower.
Swimming	Swimming pools should not be installed in backyards of homes with children under 5; pools already in place need a high fence around all four sides, with gates having high, out-of-reach, self-closing latches. Adults need to watch children very closely near pools, lakes, and other bodies of water.
Playing on a playground	A safe surface under swings, slides, and other equipment can be 25-cm-deep sand, 30-cm-deep wood chips, or rubber outdoor mats; separate areas should be maintained for active play and quiet play, for older and younger children.
Using firearms	Guns should be kept unloaded and locked up, with bullets locked in separate place; children should not have access to keys; adults should talk with children about the risks of gun injury.
Eating	To prevent choking, young children should not eat hard candies, nuts, grapes, and hot dogs (unless sliced lengthwise, then across); food should be cut into small pieces; children should not eat while talking, running, jumping, or lying down.
Ingesting toxic substances	Only drugs and toxic household products with safety caps should be used; toxic products should be stored out of children's reach. Suspected poisoning should be reported immediately to the nearest poison control centre.
Motor vehicles	Young children should sit in approved car seats, in the back seat. Adults should observe traffic laws and avoid aggressive drivers.

Source: Adapted in part from American Academy of Pediatrics (AAP) Committee on Injury and Poison Prevention, 1995a; AAP and Center to Prevent Handgun Violence, 1994; Rivara, 1999; Shannon, 2000.

One reflection of the growing problem of childhood poverty in Canada is the increase in use of food banks across the country. About 41 percent of food bank recipients are children, representing 2 percent of the population, or 57,000 families (Canadian Press, 2004; McIntyre, Connor, & Warren, 2000; Wilson & Tsoa, 2001). This is an indication that food insecurity—inconsistent access to adequate, safe, and nutritionally sound food—is becoming a fact of life for many Canadian children who live in families of limited income facing rising housing costs. As family income deteriorates, food insecurity increases dramatically; increases in number of siblings, parental job loss, and health problems contribute to the likelihood of childhood hunger, and influence the financial circumstances of the family (Tarasuk, 2005). Children who experience the physical and psychological stresses of food insecurity often do poorly in school, experience attention problems, and are at risk of developing psychosocial functioning problems (Doherty, 1997), even after controlling for other factors like age, sex, and education level (Tarasuk, 2005).

Typically, parents go hungry to prevent their children from missing meals, but often are forced to divert funds from food budgets to meet the costs of maintaining adequate housing (Wilson et al., 2001). The income difference between Canadian families who experience frequent hunger and those who experience occasional hunger is $5,000 (McIntyre, Connor, & Warren, 1998). The majority of families using food banks spend more than 30 percent of their incomes on housing, representing those in "core housing need," who are at risk of becoming homeless. The number of homeless families with children is growing across Canada (CICH, 2000). In Toronto alone, it is estimated that

19 percent of homeless people, or 5,300, are children (CICH, 2000; Golden, Currie, Greaves, & Latimer, 1999).

The prevalence of low-income families in urban neighbourhoods has been linked to poor developmental outcomes in children. In a Vancouver study, entire sections of the city have been shown to include higher proportions of children experiencing higher risks of developing multiple problems in physical health, social competence, emotional maturity, and communication skills (Hertzman, 2002). Children in Aboriginal families, in particular, face higher rates of respiratory problems and other infectious diseases, as a function of inadequate housing and crowded living conditions (Public Health Agency of Canada, 2002). Typically, less affluent neighbourhoods that have declining median incomes, and increases in low-income families, single-parent families, and proportion of income spent on rent were associated with higher numbers of developmental risks. Part of the problem has to do with the lower availability of social supports, like child-care facilities and neighbourhood recreation centres in less affluent neighbourhoods.

To combat homelessness, a number of communities and community development groups, like Habitat for Humanity, are building low-income housing units and reclaiming neighbourhoods with the help of federal, provincial, local, foundation, and private financing (Children's Defense Fund, 1998). In addition, the Government of Canada's National Homelessness Initiative was designed to help eradicate homelessness in Canada (Human Resources Development Canada, 2003).

Exposure to Illness

Preschoolers in daycare centres are 2 to 4 times more likely to pick up mild infectious diseases (such as colds, flu, and diarrhea) than are children raised at home. They also have a higher risk of contracting otitis media (middle ear infection), gastrointestinal diseases, and hepatitis A (Nafstad, Hagen, Oie, Magnus, & Jaakkola, 1999; Thacker et al., 1992). However, early mild infections may protect against more serious respiratory illness. In an American longitudinal study of 1,035 Tucson, Arizona, children followed from birth, those who were exposed to older siblings at home or who were in daycare during the first 6 months of life were less likely to develop asthma or frequent wheezing later in childhood (Ball et al., 2000).

Exposure to Smoking

Parental smoking is an important preventable cause of childhood illness and death. The potential damage caused by exposure to tobacco is greatest during the early years of life (DiFranza, Aligne, & Weitzman, 2004), when bodies are still developing. About 2.8 million Canadian children under the age of 15 live with smokers and are exposed to secondhand smoke in the home (Government of Saskatchewan, 2000). Amost a quarter of Canadian mothers report having smoked during pregnancy (Connor & McIntyre, 2002). This could have detrimental long-term effects after birth, with higher likelihood of behavioural and cognitive problems in children of mothers who smoked during pregnancy (Connor & McIntyre, 2002). Secondhand smoke is responsible for 400,000 illnesses in Canadian children every year (Canadian Health Network, 2001). Secondhand smoke contains hundreds of carcinogens, or cancer-causing chemicals and can lead to premature death (Office on Smoking and Health, 2006). Passive exposure increases the risk of contracting a number of medical problems, including bronchitis, serious infectious illnesses, otitis media, burns, and asthma (Allergy Section, Canadian Paediatric Society [CPS], 1986). It also may lead to cancer in adulthood (Aligne & Stoddard, 1997; AAP Committee on Environmental Health, 1997; U.S. Environmental Protection Agency, 1994). The Canadian Paediatric Society recommends that children be raised in a smoke-free environment (CPS Psychosocial Paediatrics Committee, 2001).

Poverty

Poverty is stressful, unhealthy, and dangerous. Low income is the *chief* factor associated with poor health of children and adolescents, over and above race and family structure

(Montgomery, Kiely, & Pappas, 1996; refer back to Table 1-2 in Chapter 1). A commonly used "poverty line" measure is Statistics Canada's low-income cut-off (LICO), which is an income level required for basic needs, adjusted for family size and size of the community in which a family resides. A higher income is typically needed to meet the needs of larger families living in larger urban centres, compared with rural communities. Although social assistance is provided to families in need across Canada, it does not provide families with adequate means to meet their needs. For example, the level of assistance available to a lone-parent family with one child ranges from a low of 50 percent of the LICO in Alberta to a high of 69 percent of the LICO in Newfoundland and Labrador (CICH, 2000).

A growing proportion of children in Canada are poor: In 2003 about 1,250,000 Canadian children under the age of 18 years lived in poverty, almost double the 1981 number of 763,000 children (CICH, 2000; National Anti-Poverty Organization, 2003). This increase occurred despite a 1989 House of Commons resolution to eradicate child poverty in Canada by the year 2000. Although poverty strikes all parts of the population, it besets young families—including working families—and minorities disproportionately.

In all regions of Canada, about 22 percent of children 14 years or younger live in poverty. About half of all immigrant children live in poverty at some time during their early years in Canada, although these children experience fewer emotional and behavioural problems than non-immigrant Canadian children who live in poverty (Beiser, Hou, Hyman, & Tousignant, 2002; National Anti-Poverty Organization, 2003). This likely reflects the readjustment of the family to a new country, which often involves a temporary period of low poverty followed by improved family income (Beiser, Hou, Hyman, & Tousignant, 1998; Smith & Jackson, 2002). About half of Aboriginal children live in poverty, as do 43 percent of visible minorities (CICH, 2000; National Anti-Poverty Organization, 2003). Children with lone parents are also more likely to be in low-income families, particularly when headed by women; 45.4% are poor, compared to 24% of male lone-parent households (National Anti-Poverty Organization, 2003). Despite the challenges of being a lone parent, the developmental outcomes for these children are typically no different from those of other children in low-income families (Chao & Willms, 2002; Lipman, Boyle, Dooley, & Offord, 1998; Willms, 2002).

The health problems of poor children often begin before birth. Many poor mothers do not eat well and do not receive adequate prenatal care; their babies are more likely than babies of more affluent mothers to be of low birth weight or to die in infancy. Poor children who do not eat properly do not grow properly, and thus are weak and susceptible to disease. Many poor families live in crowded, unsanitary housing, and the children may lack adequate supervision, especially when the parents are at work. They are more likely than other children to suffer lead poisoning, hearing and vision loss, and iron-deficiency anemia, as well as such stress-related conditions as asthma, headaches, insomnia, and irritable bowel. They also tend to have more behaviour problems, psychological disturbances, and learning disabilities (J. L. Brown, 1987; Egbuono & Starfield, 1982; Santer & Stocking, 1991; Starfield, 1991).

The Canada Health Act is designed to ensure universal access to medically necessary health services for all Canadians. However, despite the principles of the act, there is evidence that accessibility to health services is not necessarily consistent in all regions. Canadians in remote and northern areas are concerned about limited health services in their communities (Health Canada, 2000). In response, the federal government has started a number of health programs for people living in remote areas. These include the Innovations in Rural and Community Health Initiative, which is designed to improve access to health care and prescription drugs in rural and remote areas, telehealth to improve the delivery of health care, and incentives to attract physicians and other health-care workers to rural communities (Health Canada, 2000).

In addition to the concerns of people living in remote and northern communities, there is evidence that equality of access is not always guaranteed in urban communities. For example, although residents of Winnipeg's poorest neighbourhoods were more likely to see family doctors than were residents of middle- and upper-income neighbourhoods, people in the poor neighbourhoods were less likely to be referred to specialists. In Ontario, people living in lower- and middle-income neighbourhoods were less likely to receive cardiac surgery and more likely to die after being hospitalized with a heart attack, in comparison to residents of wealthier areas (Canadian Institute for Health Information and Statistics Canada, 2000).

Exposure to Pollution

Air pollution, particularly from chemical particles and ozone, is associated with increased risks of death and of chronic respiratory disease. Environmental contaminants may play a role in certain childhood cancers, neurological disorders, attention-deficit hyperactivity disorder, and mental retardation (Goldman et al., 2004; Woodruff et al., 2004). In 2003, 62 percent of children up to age 17 lived in counties that failed to meet one or more national air quality standards, the worst offender being ozone levels (Federal Interagency Forum for Child and Family Statistics, 2005). Poverty and minority status are associated with higher exposure to polluted air (Dilworth-Bart & Moore, 2006). Children tend to spend more time outdoors than adults do and so may have high levels of exposure to airborne traffic and factory exhausts (Schwartz, 2004). Children also appear to be more sensitive than adults to some environmental toxins (Brent & Weitzman, 2004).

More than half of all reported pesticide poisonings occur in children younger than 6 (Weiss, Amler, & Amler, 2004). Children are more vulnerable than adults to chronic pesticide damage (Goldman et al., 2004). In a national survey of human exposure to environmental chemicals, urine levels of dimethylthiophosphate, a chemical produced by metabolism of many organic pesticides, were twice as high in 6- through 11-year-olds as in adults (Centers for Disease Control and Prevention, 2003). There is some, though not definitive, evidence that low-dose pesticide exposure may affect the developing brain (Weiss et al., 2004). Pesticide exposure is greater in children in agricultural and inner-city families (Dilworth-Bart & Moore, 2006). In a study of preschool children in two agricultural communities in Mexico, children in the community that used traditional agricultural methods performed better in several measures of neuropsychological development (such as co-ordination and the ability to draw a person) than children in the other community, which had adopted use of pesticides (Guillette, Meza, Aquilar, Soto, & Garcia, 1998).

Parents can take precautions against pesticide damage by applying pesticides prudently, storing them in their original containers where children cannot reach them, and washing fresh produce before it is eaten. Insect repellants should be applied only to exposed skin and washed off with soap and water when a child comes indoors (Weiss et al., 2004).

Exposure to Lead

Lead poisoning has been called the greatest hazard to the health of children under age 6 (Tesman & Hills, 1994). However, very few cases of lead poisoning occur in Canada in any year. Although the actual number of Canadian children who are suffering from exposure to lead is unknown, about 24 percent of children under 5 years live in houses built before 1960, where hazards from lead in paint and plumbing are more likely than in newer houses (Boyd, 2007).

Children can get lead in the bloodstream from lead-contaminated food or water, from putting contaminated fingers in their mouths, or from inhaling dust in homes or schools where there is lead-based paint. Lead poisoning can seriously interfere with cognitive development and can bring on a variety of neurological and behavioural problems (AAP Committee on Environmental Health, 1998; AAP Committee on Environmental Health, 2005; Federal Interagency Forum for Child and Family Statistics, 2005; Needleman, Riess, Tobin, Biesecker, & Greenhouse, 1996; Tesman & Hills, 1994). Yet it can be completely prevented by removing sources of lead from children's environment (Tesman & Hills, 1994).

The effects on developing brains may be irreversible (Bellinger, 2004). In one study, 42 young adults who had suffered significant lead exposure during infancy and childhood were asked to think of as many verbs as possible to go with a noun, such as "ball." During the task, brain imaging showed that their brains were using an area of the right brain to do this task instead of the regions of the left brain that normally handle language (Yuan et al., 2006). Very high levels of blood lead concentration may cause headaches, abdominal pain, loss of appetite, agitation, or lethargy and eventually vomiting, stupour, and convulsions (AAP Committee on Environmental Health, 2005).

Young children who live in old, dilapidated buildings with peeling lead paint are at risk for lead poisoning, which can adversely affect the developing brain.

Lead exposure and high blood lead-levels have been associated with sensorimotor deficits, lower IQ, and poorer academic achievement. (Which specific areas of cognition are affected is still unclear and may depend on the age of exposure and on socio-economic status.) Lead is strongly linked to such behavioural problems as hyperactivity (see Chapter 13), impulsiveness, irritability, distractibility, and a short attention span (Tesman & Hills, 1994). It is associated with antisocial and delinquent behaviour (Needleman et al., 1996) and can lead to seizures, mental retardation, or death (AAP Committee on Environmental Health, 1993).

There is no safe level of exposure to lead (AAP Committee on Environmental Health, 2005). However, the degree of toxicity depends on the dose, how long a child is exposed, and the child's developmental and nutritional vulnerability (AAP Committee on Environmental Health, 1998). Even low levels of exposure may have detrimental behavioural effects in very young preschoolers, particularly those who have other risk factors, such as poverty and maternal depression (Canfield et al., 2003; Mendelsohn et al., 1998). Moderate lead poisoning can be treated (Ruff, Bijur, Markowitz, Ma, & Rosen, 1993), but reduced exposure may only partially reverse the cognitive effects (Tong, Baghurst, Sawyer, Burns, & McMichael, 1998).

In a five-year longitudinal study, treatment of lead-exposed children decreased blood lead concentrations but proved ineffective in improving psychological, behavioural, and cognitive functioning. Thus, prevention is critical (Rogan et al., 2001). Paint removal can raise lead dust, but professional cleaning and paint stabilization can stop unhealthy exposure. Soil around houses with exterior lead paint and near smokestacks or heavy traffic can be tested, following EPA guidelines (AAP Committee on Environmental Health, 2005).

Maltreatment: Abuse and Neglect

Guidepost 5

What are the causes and consequences of child abuse and neglect, and what can be done about it?

Although most parents are loving and nurturing, some cannot or will not take proper care of their children, and some deliberately hurt or kill them. *Maltreatment,* whether perpetrated by parents or others, is deliberate or avoidable endangerment of a child. Maltreatment takes several forms (U.S. Department of Health and Human Services [USDHHS], 1999a; Trocmé & Wolfe, 2001); any one form is likely to be accompanied by one or more of the others (Belsky, 1993).

In general, *abuse* refers to action that inflicts harm; *neglect* refers to inaction that leads to harm. **Physical abuse** involves injury to the body through punching, beating, kicking, or burning. **Neglect** is failure to meet a child's basic needs, such as food, clothing, medical care, protection, and supervision. **Sexual abuse** is sexual activity involving a child and another person. **Emotional maltreatment** includes acts of abuse or neglect that may cause behavioural, cognitive, emotional, or mental disorders. It may include rejection, terrorization, isolation, exploitation, degradation, ridicule, or failure to provide emotional support, love, and affection. Emotional maltreatment is hard to identify; its effects may not surface immediately and may be difficult to distinguish from signs of emotional disturbance and other developmental problems (USDHHS, 1999a; Trocmé et al., 2001).

physical abuse Action taken to endanger a child involving potential bodily injury

neglect Failure to meet a child's basic needs

sexual abuse Sexual activity involving a child and an older person

emotional maltreatment Action or inaction that may cause behavioural, cognitive, emotional, or mental disorders

Maltreatment: Facts and Figures

The incidence of maltreatment is uncertain. Although Canada has not kept national statistics on child maltreatment, the Canadian Incidence Study of Reported Child Abuse and Neglect (CIS) (Trocmé & Wolfe, 2001) is the first examination of the incidence of child maltreatment in Canada. In the United States, statistics on child maltreatment gathered show a drop in reported cases of child abuse and neglect; the rate per 1,000 children in the U.S. population has dropped from 13.4 chldren in 1990 to 11.9 in 2004 (USDHHS, Administration on Children, Youth, & Families, 2006), but the actual number may be considerably higher (Theodore et al., 2005).

In 2003, 49 percent of investigations of maltreatment in Canada were subtantiated by child-care workers, involving. Over a third (34 percent) involved neglect, particularly failure to supervise leading to physical harm, and almost a quarter (23 percent) involved physical

Checkpoint ✔

Can you . . .

✔ Discuss several environmental influences that endanger children's health and development?

abuse, with inappropriate punishment being most common. Three percent of victims were sexually abused, the most common form being inappropriate touching and fondling, 14 percent of investigations were of cases of emotional harm, and exposure to family violence accounted for 26 percent of substantiated cases of maltreatment (Trocmé, 2005; Trocmé & Wolfe, 2001; Health Canada, 2005).

Child maltreatment is prevalent in Canada with 19 confirmed cases for every 1,000 children. Although boys and girls are equally likely to be victims of maltreatment (Trainor & Mihorean, 2001), an Ontario survey indicates that physical abuse is more prevalent in males (31 percent) than in females (21 percent). However, females are over three times more likely to have been the victims of sexual abuse (13 percent compared to 4 percent for males) (Department of Justice Canada, 2003; Health Canada, 2005; MacMillan, Fleming, Trocmé et al., 1997; Trocmé, 2005).

About 80 percent of adult offenders are the child's parents. However, almost half of sexually abused children were abused by someone other than the child's parent. Other types of abuse are most commonly perpetrated by a parent: 90 percent of cases of neglect are committed by the mother or mother-figure; 90 percent of sexual abuse cases are committed by a male—half of these cases involving the child's father (Health Canada, 2001).

Rates of child homicide and spousal violence in Canada have been dropping over the last decade. However, the rate of spousal abuse is higher in Aboriginal families than in non-Aboriginal families (Trainor & Mihorean, 2001). Although the number of children admitted to shelters has been declining in Canada, the proportion of children who have been abused has grown from 86 percent in 1998 to 91 percent in 2000. Most of these children were under 5 years of age (Trainor & Mihorean, 2001).

Maltreatment has become a major cause of death among young children, and, again, the full incidence of such deaths is unknown. Estimates based on a review of all deaths of children under 11 years old in North Carolina between 1985 and 1994 are that more than 3 times as many child deaths nationally are due to abuse than are officially reported (9,467 as opposed to 2,973). In 63 percent of the North Carolina cases, biological parents were responsible (Herman-Giddens et al., 1999).

Contributing Factors: An Ecological View

As in Bronfenbrenner's bioecological theory, abuse and neglect reflect the interplay of multiple layers of contributing factors involving the family, the community, and the larger society (Health Canada, 2001; USDHHS, 1999a).

Maltreatment by parents is a symptom of extreme disturbance in child rearing, usually aggravated by other family problems, such as poverty, alcoholism, or antisocial behaviour. A disproportionate number of abused and neglected children are in large, poor, or single-parent families, which tend to be under stress and to have trouble meeting children's needs (Sedlak & Broadhurst, 1996). Yet, what pushes one parent over the edge, another may take in stride. Although most neglect occurs in very poor families, most low-income parents do not neglect their children.

Characteristics of Abusive Parents

Many abusers are lonely, unhappy, anxious, depressed, angry, or aggressive. They tend to have low self-esteem and poor impulse control and coping skills. About one-third of abusing parents were abused themselves as children (National Research Council [NRC], 1993b; Schmitt & Kempe, 1983; USDHHS, 1999a; Wolfe, 1985). Substance abuse is a factor in at least one-third of substantiated cases of abuse and neglect (USDHHS, 1999a).

Unlike neglectful parents, who tend to be apathetic, incompetent, irresponsible, or emotionally withdrawn (Wolfe, 1985), abusive parents are overly involved with the child. Often deprived of good parenting themselves, they are greatly upset by behaviour that most parents accept as normal (Reid, Patterson, & Loeber, 1982; Wolfe, 1985). Abuse may begin when a parent who is already anxious, depressed, or hostile tries to control a child physically but loses self-control and ends up shaking or beating the child (USDHHS, 1999a). When parents who had troubled childhoods think poorly of themselves and find negative emotions hard to handle have children who are particularly needy or demanding, who cry a lot, or who are unresponsive, the likelihood of maltreatment increases. These children's greater needs may stem from poor health, "difficult" personalities, or physical disabilities. They are more likely than non-abused children to have been preterm or low–birth weight babies; to be hyperactive, mentally challenged, or physically challenged; or to show behavioural abnormalities (NRC, 1993b; Reid et al., 1982; USDHHS, 1999a).

Abusive parents tend to have marital problems and to fight physically. Their households tend to be disorganized, and they experience more stressful events than other families (Reid et al., 1982; Sedlak & Broadhurst, 1996). Many abusive parents cut themselves off from others, leaving them with no one to turn to in times of stress and no one to see what is happening.

Neighbourhood and Social Support

The outside world can create a climate for family violence. Poverty, unemployment, job dissatisfaction, social isolation, and lack of assistance for the primary caregiver are closely correlated with child and spouse abuse. None of these, however, are determining factors.

What makes one low-income neighbourhood a place where children are highly likely to be maltreated, while another, matched for ethnic population and income levels, is safer? According to NLSCY data, neighbourhood cohesion is an important protective factor in reducing the risk of childhood injury in Canada, while neighbourhood problems like low neighbourhood income, education, and occupation tended to put children at risk of injury. These risk factors interact with child behaviour to increase the likelihood of aggression and oppositional behaviour in children (Soubhi, Raina, & Kohen, 2001). This result is echoed by the outcome of the Vancouver neighbourhood study mentioned above, describing the risks to development in less affluent neighbourhoods (Hertzman, 2002). In one inner-city Chicago neighbourhood, the proportion of children who died from maltreatment (1 death for every 2,541 children) was about twice the proportion in another inner-city neighbourhood. Researchers who interviewed community leaders found a depressed atmosphere in the high-abuse community. Criminal activity was rampant, and facilities for community programs were dark and dreary. This was an environment with "an ecological conspiracy against children" (Garbarino & Kostelny, 1993, p. 213). In the low-abuse neighbourhood, people described their community as a poor but decent place to live. They painted a picture of a neighbourhood with robust social support networks, well-known community services, and strong political leadership. In a community like this, maltreatment is less likely to occur.

Cultural Values and Patterns

Two cultural factors associated with child abuse are societal violence and physical punishment of children. In countries where violent crime is infrequent and children are rarely spanked, such as Japan, China, and Tahiti, child abuse is rare (Celis, 1990).

Section 43 of the Canadian Criminal Code states that "every schoolteacher, parent or person standing in the place of a parent is justified in using force by way of correction toward a pupil or child, as the case may be, who is under his care, if the force does not exceed what is reasonable under the circumstances." Although there have been efforts to change this law, Canadian culture is more accepting of physical punishment than other cultures. Canadian mothers report being more likely to use physical punishment in disciplining their children than Swedish mothers, who live in a culture that does not condone physical punishment (Durrant, Broberg, & Rose-Krasnor, 1999).

Long-term Effects of Maltreatment

Maltreatment can produce grave consequences—not only physical, but emotional, cognitive, and social. The emotional harm that is related to maltreatment includes changes in behaviour (regression and withdrawal from social interactions), sleep and hygiene patterns, and emotions (clinging, crying, and anxiety). In 34 percent of cases of maltreatment in Canada, according to CIS data, evidence of emotional harm was identified, and 21 percent were considered severe enough to warrant treatment (Trocmé et al., 2001). Emotional harm occurs most often in cases of sexual abuse and is also present in many cases of physical abuse, neglect, and emotional maltreatment.

Maltreated children often start speaking late (Coster, Gersten, Beeghly, & Cicchetti, 1989). They are more likely to repeat a grade, to do poorly on cognitive tests, and to have behaviour problems in school (Eckenrode, Laird, & Doris, 1993). They often have disorganized-disoriented attachments to their parents (refer back to Chapter 8) and negative, distorted self-concepts. Deprived of early positive social interactions, they do not develop social skills and have difficulty making friends (Price, 1996). Chronic neglect during early childhood has especially negative effects on later school performance, social relationships, adaptability, and problem solving (NRC, 1993b).

Almost a third of special-needs children in an Alberta study were found to have confirmed histories of maltreatment. Whether the maltreatment is part of the cause of special needs, or a correlate with special needs, it is clear that maltreatment contributes to poor school achievement and is related to behaviour problems in children (Sobsey, 2002).

Maltreated children may become either overly aggressive or withdrawn (USDHHS, 1999a). Physically abused youngsters tend to be fearful, uncooperative, less able to respond appropriately to friendly overtures, and, consequently, less well liked than other children (Coie & Dodge, 1998; Haskett & Kistner, 1991; Salzinger, Feldman, Hammer, & Rosario, 1993).

Although few abused children become delinquent, criminal, or mentally ill, abuse makes it likelier that they will (Dodge, Bates, & Pettit, 1990; NRC, 1993b; Widom, 1989). Teenagers who were abused when they were younger may react by running away, which may be self-protective, or may abuse drugs, which is not (NRC, 1993b).

Consequences of sexual abuse vary with age (see Table 9-4). In a study that followed 68 sexually abused children for 5 years, the abused children showed more disturbed behaviour, had lower self-esteem, and were more depressed, anxious, or unhappy than a control group matched for age and sex. The abused children were also more likely to injure themselves or commit suicide (Swanston, Tebbutt, O'Toole, & Oates, 1997). Sexually abused children may become sexually active at an early age. Among 1,026 African-American first-time mothers, sexual abuse during childhood (but not physical or emotional abuse) was predictive of younger ages of first intercourse and first pregnancy (Fiscella, Kitzman, Cole, Sidora, & Olds, 1998).

Fearfulness and low self-esteem often continue into adulthood. Adults who were sexually abused as children tend to be anxious, depressed, angry, or hostile; to mistrust people;

Table 9-4	Developmentally Related Reactions to Sexual Abuse
Age	**Most Common Symptoms**
Preschoolers	Anxiety
	Nightmares
	Inappropriate sexual behaviour
School-age children	Fear
	Mental illness
	Aggression
	Nightmares
	School problems
	Hyperactivity
	Regressive behaviour
Adolescents	Depression
	Withdrawn, suicidal, or self-injurious behaviours
	Physical complaints
	Illegal acts
	Running away
	Substance abuse

Source: Adapted from Kendall-Tackett, Williams, & Finkelhor, 1993.

to feel isolated and stigmatized; to be sexually maladjusted (Browne & Finkelhor, 1986); and to abuse alcohol or drugs (NRC, 1993b; USDHHS, 1999a).

Emotional maltreatment is more subtle than physical maltreatment, and its effects may be harder to pin down. It has been linked to lying, stealing, low self-esteem, emotional maladjustment, dependency, underachievement, depression, aggression, learning disorders, homicide, and suicide, as well as to psychological distress later in life (S. N. Hart & Brassard, 1987).

Why do some abused children grow up to become antisocial or abusive, while others do not? One possible difference is genetic; some genotypes may be more resistant to trauma than others (Caspi et al., 2002; Jaffee et al., 2005). Research with rhesus monkeys suggests another answer. When baby monkeys who endured high rates of maternal rejection and abuse in the first month of life, their brains produced less serotonin, a brain chemical. Low levels of serotonin are associated with anxiety, depression, and impulsive aggression in humans as well as in monkeys. Abused female monkeys who became abusive mothers had less serotonin in their brains than abused females who did not become abusive mothers. This finding suggests that treatment with drugs that increase serotonin levels early in life may prevent an abused child from growing up to abuse her own children (Maestripieri et al., 2006).

Still, many maltreated children show remarkable resilience, especially if they have been able to form an attachment to a supportive person (Egeland & Sroufe, 1981; Jenkins & Keating, 1998). Above-average intelligence, advanced cognitive abilities, and high self-esteem seem to help. Also important is the child's interpretation of the abuse or neglect. Children who see it as coming from a parent's weaknesses or frustrations seem to cope better than those who take it as parental rejection (Garmezy, Masten, & Tellegen, 1984; Zimrin, 1986).

Few abused children grow up to abuse their own children (Kaufman & Zigler, 1987; USDHHS, 1999a). Abused children who grow up to be *non*abusing parents are likely to have had someone to whom they could turn for help, to have received therapy, and to have good marital or love relationships. They are likely to have been abused by only one parent and to have had a loving, supportive relationship with the other (Egeland, Jacobvitz, & Sroufe, 1988; Kaufman & Zigler, 1987; NRC, 1993b).

Helping Families in Trouble

Since maltreatment is a multifactorial problem, it needs many-pronged solutions. Effective community prevention and intervention should be comprehensive, neighbourhood-based, centred on protecting children, and aimed at strengthening families if possible and removing children if necessary (USDHHS, 1999a).

Some abuse-prevention programs teach basic parenting skills (USDHHS, 1999a; Wolfe, Edwards, Manion, & Koverola, 1988). Other programs offer subsidized daycare, volunteer homemakers, home visitors, and temporary "respite homes" or "relief parents" to take over occasionally. In one program in a semi-rural New York community, first-time unmarried expectant teenage mothers were visited by nurses once a month during pregnancy and then during the child's first 2 years. At the end of that period, there were 80 percent fewer verified cases of abuse and neglect among the nurse-visited children than in a control group; and 15 years later, their mothers were only about half as likely to have been reported as abusers or neglecters (D. L. Olds, Eckenrode, et al., 1997; D. L. Olds, Henderson, et al., 1999).

Provincial and local child protective services agencies investigate reports of child maltreatment; determine what steps, if any, need to be taken; and marshal community resources to help. This may involve helping the family resolve their problems or arranging for alternative care for children who cannot safely remain at home (Larner, Stevenson, & Behrman, 1998; Minister of Public Works and Government Services Canada, 2001; Trocmé, MacLaurin, et al., 2001).

Physicians often identify cases of physical abuse, but even for physicians the signs of abuse can often be difficult to recognize. A retrospective study of children 3 years of age and younger, who experienced abusive head injury showed that the signs of abuse were missed by physicians on initial examination in almost one-third of cases (Jenny, Hymel, Ritzen, Rienert, & Hey, 1999).

Checkpoint ✔

Can you . . .

✔ Define four types of child abuse and neglect?

✔ Discuss the incidence of maltreatment and explain why it is hard to measure?

✔ Identify contributing factors having to do with the child, the family, the neighbourhood, and the wider society?

✔ Give examples of effects of child abuse and neglect?

✔ Describe ways to prevent or stop maltreatment and help its victims?

One way to stop maltreatment is to treat abusers as criminal offenders; people arrested for family violence are less likely to repeat the offence (Bouza, 1990; Sherman & Berk, 1984). Services for abused children and adults include shelters, education in parenting skills, and therapy. Parents Anonymous and other organizations offer free, confidential support groups. Abused children may receive play or art therapy and daycare in a therapeutic environment. In communities where abuse or neglect is widespread, school-based programs can be effective (Trocmé, MacLaurin, et al., 2001).

When authorities remove children from their homes, the usual alternative is foster care, which has increased markedly since the 1980s. Foster care removes a child from immediate danger, but it is often unstable, may also turn out to be an abusive situation, and further alienates the child from the family. It is intended as a temporary emergency measure; but in some cities the average stay is 5 years, often with a series of placements in different homes (NRC, 1993b). However, the growing number of children placed in kinship foster care (31 percent), due in part to a scarcity of traditional foster care homes and an increasing caseload (Berrick, 1998), may make a difference.

The plight of abused and neglected children is one for which society needs to find more effective remedies. Without help, maltreated children often grow up with serious problems, at great cost to themselves and to society, and may continue the cycle of maltreatment when they have children of their own.

Fortunately, few children are maltreated. Preschool children who are in good health and whose basic physical needs are met are able to make major advances in cognitive development, as we'll see in Chapter 10.

Summary and Key Terms

Aspects of Physiological Development

Guidepost 1 How do children's bodies change between ages 3 and 6, and what are their nutritional and dental needs?

- Physical growth increases during the years from 3 to 6, but more slowly than during infancy and toddlerhood. Boys are on average slightly taller, heavier, and more muscular than girls. Internal body systems are maturing, and all primary teeth are present.

- Preschool children generally eat less for their weight than before—and need less—but the prevalence of obesity has increased.

- Tooth decay has decreased since the 1970s but remains a problem among disadvantaged children.

- Thumb-sucking can safely be ignored unless it continues beyond age 4, when permanent teeth begin to develop.

Sleep Patterns and Problems

Guidepost 2 What sleep patterns and problems tend to develop during early childhood?

- Sleep patterns change during early childhood, as throughout life, and are affected by cultural expectations.

- It is normal for preschool children to develop bedtime rituals that delay going to sleep. Prolonged bedtime struggles or persistent sleep terrors or nightmares may indicate emotional disturbances that need attention.

- Bed-wetting is common and is usually outgrown without special help.

enuresis (234)

Motor Development

Guidepost 3 What are the main motor achievements of early childhood, and how does children's artwork show their physical and cognitive maturation?

- Children progress rapidly in gross and fine motor skills and eye–hand coordination, developing more complex systems of action.

- Stages of art production, which appear to reflect brain development and fine motor coordination, are the scribbling stage, shape stage, design stage, and pictorial stage.

- Handedness is usually evident by age 3, reflecting dominance by one hemisphere of the brain.

gross motor skills (235)   fine motor skills (235)   systems of action (235)   handedness (236)

Health and Safety

Guidepost 4 What are the major health and safety risks for children?

- Although major contagious illnesses are rare today in industrialized countries as a result of widespread immunization, preventable disease continues to be a major problem in the non-industrialized world.

- Minor illnesses, such as colds and other respiratory illnesses, are common during early childhood and help build immunity to disease.

- Accidents, most commonly motor vehicle injuries, are the leading cause of death in childhood in Canada. Most fatal non-vehicular accidents occur at home.

- Environmental factors such as exposure to illness, smoking, poverty, and homelessness increase the risks of illness or injury. Lead poisoning can have serious physical, cognitive, and behavioural effects.

Maltreatment: Abuse and Neglect

Guidepost 5   What are the causes and consequences of child abuse and neglect, and what can be done about it?

- The incidence of reported maltreatment of children has dropped in the U.S., but the rate in Canada is higher.

- Forms of maltreatment are physical abuse, neglect, sexual abuse, and emotional maltreatment.

- Characteristics of the abuser or neglecter, the victim, the family, the community, and the larger culture all contribute to child abuse and neglect.

- Maltreatment can interfere with physical, cognitive, emotional, and social development, and its effects can continue into adulthood. Still, many maltreated children show remarkable resilience.

- Preventing or stopping maltreatment may require multi-faceted, coordinated community efforts.

**physical abuse (245)   neglect (245)   sexual abuse (245)
emotional maltreatment (245)**

CHAPTER TEN

Cognitive Development in Early Childhood

Focus *Albert Einstein, Nuclear Physicist**

Albert Einstein

In the public mind, the name Albert Einstein (1879–1955) is synonymous with "genius." His general theory of relativity ("the greatest revolution in thought since Newton"), his discovery of the fundamental principle of quantum physics, and his other contributions to the reshaping of our knowledge of the universe cause him to be considered "one of the greatest physicists of all time" (Whitrow, 1967, p. 1).

Yet the young Einstein hardly seemed destined for intellectual stardom. Born in the German town of Ulm, he was slow in learning to walk and did not begin talking until at least his third year. His parents feared he might be mentally retarded. Einstein himself always insisted that he did not *try* to speak until after the age of 3, skipping babbling and going directly into sentences. Actually, his sentences may have come a bit earlier. When his sister, Maja, was born 4 months before Albert's third birthday, Albert (who had been promised a new baby to play with and apparently thought it would be a toy) reportedly asked in disappointment, "Where are the wheels?"

Regardless of the exact timing, "Albert was certainly a late and reluctant talker" (Brian, 1996, p. 1). The reasons may have had more to do with personality than with cognitive development; he was a shy, taciturn child, whom adults thought backward and other children considered dull. He would not play marbles or soldiers or other games with his peers, but he would crouch for hours, observing an ant colony.

When he started school, he did poorly in most subjects; the headmaster predicted he would never amount to anything. Albert hated the regimentation and rote learning stressed in German schools; he did not have a retentive memory and could not give clear answers to his teachers' questions. He was a daydreamer, his questioning mind occupied with its own speculations. He would not even try to learn anything unless he was interested in it—and then his concentration was intense.

His wonder about the workings of the universe was awakened at the age of 4 or 5, when he was sick in bed and his father gave him a magnetic pocket compass to keep him amused. The boy was astonished: No matter which way he turned the compass, the needle pointed to *N* (for "north"). What controlled its motion? He pestered his Uncle Jacob, who had studied engineering, with questions. His uncle told him about the earth's north and south poles and about magnetic fields, but Albert still was not satisfied. He believed there must be some mysterious force in what appeared to be the empty space around the needle. He carried the

compass around for weeks, trying to figure out its secret. Years later, at the age of 67, he wrote, ". . . this experience made a deep and lasting impression upon me. Something deeply hidden had to be behind things" (Schilpp, 1970, p. 9).

That sense of wonder was reawakened several years later, when Uncle Jacob, noticing that Albert showed an interest in arithmetic, introduced him to algebra and geometry. Albert solved every problem in the books his uncle brought him and then went searching for more. It was that same insatiable curiosity and persistence—what Einstein himself called "a furious impulse to understand" (Michelmore, 1962, p. 24)—that underlay his lifetime quest for scientific knowledge.

● ● ●

Albert Einstein's story touches on several themes of cognitive development in early childhood. One is the variation in normal language development. Second, Einstein's reaction to the compass may have been unusually intense, but it was characteristic of young children's understanding of the physical world—their growing recognition that natural phenomena have causes, but also their tendency to confuse appearance and reality. Einstein's lifelong memory of that incident may shed light on why some kinds of early memories last while others do not. Finally, the underestimation of Einstein's cognitive abilities by his parents and teachers raises issues about how intelligence can best be assessed.

In this chapter, we examine all these aspects of cognitive development in early childhood, as revealed by recent research as well as by such earlier theorists as Piaget and Vygotsky. We see how preschool children's thinking has advanced since toddlerhood and in what ways it is still immature—particularly in understanding of their own mental processes. We look at children's increasing fluency with language and what impact this has on other aspects of cognition, as well as on psychosocial development. We examine memory, drawing on the information processing and social-contextual approaches; and we compare psychometric intelligence tests with assessments based on Vygotsky's theories. Finally, we look at the widening world of preschool and kindergarten.

After you have read and studied this chapter, you should be able to answer each of the Guidepost questions that appear at the top of the next page. Look for them again in the margins, where they point to important concepts throughout the chapter. To check your understanding of these Guideposts, review the end-of-chapter summary. Checkpoints located throughout the chapter will help you verify your understanding of what you have read.

---

*Sources of biographical information about Albert Einstein are Bernstein (1973); Brian (1996); French (1979); Goldsmith, Mackay, & Woudhuysen (1980); Michelmore (1962); Quasha (1980); Schilpp (1970); and Whitrow (1967).

Guideposts for Study

1. What are typical cognitive advances and immature aspects of preschool children's thinking?

2. How does language improve, and what happens when its development is delayed?

3. What memory abilities expand in early childhood?

4. How is preschoolers' intelligence measured, and what factors influence it?

5. What purposes does early childhood education serve, and how do children make the transition to kindergarten?

Guidepost 1

What are typical cognitive advances and immature aspects of preschool children's thinking?

pre-operational stage In Piaget's theory, the second major stage of cognitive development, in which children become more sophisticated in their use of symbolic thought but are not yet able to use logic

Piagetian Approach: The Pre-operational Child

Jean Piaget named early childhood the **pre-operational stage.** The characteristic development in this second major stage of cognitive development, which lasts from approximately ages 2 to 7, is a great expansion in the use of symbolic thought, or representational ability, which first emerges at the end of the sensorimotor stage (refer back to Chapter 7). However, according to Piaget, children cannot think logically until the stage of concrete operations in middle childhood (discussed in Chapter 13).

Let's look at some advances and immature aspects of pre-operational thought (see Tables 10-1 and 10-2), and at recent research findings, some of which challenge Piaget's conclusions.

Advances of Pre-operational Thought

Advances in symbolic thought are accompanied by a growing understanding of space, causality, identities, categorization, and number. Some of these understandings have roots in infancy

Table 10-1	Cognitive Advances During Early Childhood	
Advance	**Significance**	**Example**
Use of symbols	Children do not need to be in sensorimotor contact with an object, person, or event in order to think about it.	Simon asks his mother about the elephants they saw on their trip to the circus several months earlier.
	Children can imagine that objects or people have properties other than those they actually have.	Aidan pretends that a slice of apple is a vacuum cleaner "vrooming" across the kitchen table.
Understanding of identities	Children are aware that superficial alterations do not change the nature of things.	Antonio knows that his teacher is dressed up as a pirate but is still his teacher underneath the costume.
Understanding of cause and effect	Children realize that events have causes.	Seeing a ball roll from behind a wall, Aneko looks behind the wall for the person who kicked the ball.
Ability to classify	Children organize objects, people, and events into meaningful categories.	Emily sorts the pine cones she collected on a nature walk into two piles according to their size: "big" and "little."
Understanding of number	Children can count and deal with quantities.	Lindsay shares some candy with her friends, counting to make sure that each girl gets the same amount.
Empathy	Children become more able to imagine how others might feel.	James tries to comfort his friend when he sees that his friend is upset.
Theory of mind	Children become more aware of mental activity and the functioning of the mind.	Jennifer wants to save some cookies for herself, so she hides them from her brother in a pasta box. She knows her cookies will be safe there because her brother will not look in a place where he doesn't expect to find cookies.

Table 10-2	Limitations of Pre-operational Thought (According to Piaget)	
Limitation	**Description**	**Example**
Centration: inability to decentre	Children focus on one aspect of a situation and neglect others.	Justin teases his younger sister that he has more juice than she does because his juice box has been poured into a tall, skinny glass, but hers has been poured into a short, wide glass.
Irreversibility	Children fail to understand that some operations or actions can be reversed, restoring the original situation.	Justin does not realize that the juice in each glass can be poured back into the juice box from which it came, contradicting his claim that he has more than his sister.
Focus on states rather than transformations	Children fail to understand the significance of the transformation between states.	In the conservation task, Justin does not understand that transforming the shape of a liquid (pouring it from one container into another) does not change the amount.
Transductive reasoning	Children do not use deductive or inductive reasoning; instead they jump from one particular to another and see cause where none exists.	Sarah was mean to her brother. Then her brother got sick. Sarah concludes that she made her brother sick.
Egocentrism	Children assume everyone else thinks, perceives, and feels as they do.	Kara doesn't realize that she needs to turn a book around so that her father can see the picture she is asking him to explain to her. Instead, she holds the book directly in front of her, where only she can see it.
Animism	Children attribute life to objects not alive.	Amanda says that spring is trying to come but winter is saying, "I won't go! I won't go!"
Inability to distinguish appearance from reality	Children confuse what is real with outward appearance.	Courtney is confused by a sponge made to look like a rock. She states that it looks like a rock and it really is a rock.

and toddlerhood; others begin to develop in early childhood but are not fully achieved until middle childhood.

The Symbolic Function

"I want ice cream!" announces Kerstin, age 4, trudging indoors from the hot, dusty backyard. She has not seen anything that triggered this desire—no open freezer door, no television commercial. She no longer needs this kind of sensory cue to think about something. She remembers ice cream, its coldness and taste, and she purposefully seeks it out. This absence of sensory or motor cues characterizes the **symbolic function:** the ability to use symbols, or mental representations—words, numbers, or images to which a person has attached meaning. Having symbols for things helps children to remember and think about them without having them physically present.

Preschool children show the symbolic function through deferred imitation, **pretend play,** and language. *Deferred imitation* (refer back to Chapter 7), which becomes more robust after 18 months, is based on having kept a mental representation of an observed action—as when 3-year-old Bart scolds his little sister, using the same words he heard his father say to the delivery boy who was late in bringing the pizza. In *pretend play* (also called *symbolic play, fantasy play, dramatic play,* or *imaginative play*), which we discuss in Chapter 11, children make an object stand for (symbolize) something else; for example, a doll may represent a child. *Language,* discussed later in this chapter, involves the use of a common system of symbols (words) to communicate.

symbolic function Piaget's term for ability to use mental representations (words, numbers, or images) to which a child has attached meaning

pretend play Play involving imaginary people or situations; also called *fantasy play, dramatic play, or imaginative play*

Understanding of Objects in Space

As reported in Chapter 7, until at least age 3, most children do not reliably grasp the relationships between pictures, maps, or scale models and the objects or spaces they represent. Older preschoolers can use simple maps, and they can transfer the spatial understanding gained from working with models to maps and vice versa (DeLoache, Miller, & Pierrout-sakos, 1998). In a series of experiments, preschoolers were asked to use a simple map to find or place an object at the corresponding location in a similarly shaped but much larger space, such as a rug. Ninety percent of 5-year-olds but only 60 percent of 4-year-olds could do this (Vasilyeva & Huttenlocher, 2004).

Understanding of Causality

transduction Piaget's term for a pre-operational child's tendency to mentally link particular experiences, whether or not there is logically a causal relationship

Although Piaget recognized that toddlers have some understanding of a connection between actions and reactions, he believed that pre-operational children cannot yet reason logically about cause and effect. Instead, he said, they reason by **transduction.** They view one situation as the basis for another situation, often one occurring at about the same time, whether or not there is logically a causal relationship. For example, they may think that their "bad" thoughts or behaviour caused their own or another child's illness or their parents' divorce.

Yet, when tested on situations they can understand, young children do grasp cause and effect. One research team set up a series of experiments using a device called a "blicket detector," rigged to light up and play music only when certain objects (called "blickets") were placed on it. Even 2-year-olds were able to decide, by observing the device in operation, which objects were blickets (because they activated the blicket detector) and which were not (Gopnik, Sobel, Schulz, & Glymour, 2001).

In naturalistic observations of 2½- to 5-year-olds' everyday conversations with their parents, children showed flexible causal reasoning, appropriate to the subject. Types of explanations ranged from physical ("The scissors have to be clean so I can cut better") to social-conventional ("I have to stop now because you said to"). Causal statements were more frequent among older children (Hickling & Wellman, 2001). Preschoolers' unrealistic views about causes of illness may reflect a belief that all causal relationships are equally and absolutely predictable. In one series of experiments, 3- to 5-year-olds, unlike adults, were just as sure that a person who does not wash hands before eating will get sick as they were that a person who jumps up will come down (Kalish, 1998).

Understanding of Identities and Categorization

The world becomes more orderly and predictable as preschool children develop a better understanding of *identities:* the concept that people and many things are basically the same even if they change in form, size, or appearance. This understanding underlies the emerging self-concept.

Categorization, or classification, requires a child to identify similarities and differences. By age 4, many children can classify by two criteria, such as colour and shape. Children use this ability to order many aspects of their lives, categorizing people as "good," "bad," "friend," "non-friend," and so forth. Thus categorization is a cognitive ability that has emotional and social implications.

animism Tendency to attribute life to objects that are not alive

What characteristics distinguish living from non-living things? When Piaget asked young children whether the wind and the clouds were alive, their answers led him to think they were confused about what is alive and what is not. (The tendency to attribute life to objects that are not alive is called **animism.**) But when later researchers questioned 3- and 4-year-olds about something more familiar to them—differences between a rock, a person, and a doll—the children showed they understood that people are alive and rocks and dolls are not (Gelman, Spelke, & Meck, 1983). They did not attribute thoughts or emotions to rocks, and they cited the fact that dolls cannot move on their own as evidence that dolls are not alive.

Of course, plants do not move on their own either, nor do they utter sounds, as most animals do. Yet preschoolers know that both plants and animals can grow and decay and, when injured, can heal themselves (Rosengren, Gelman, Kalish, & McCormick, 1991; Wellman & Gelman, 1998).

Culture can affect such beliefs. In a cross-cultural study, 5- to 9-year-old Israeli children, whose tradition views plants primarily in terms of their usefulness as food, were less likely than U.S. and Japanese children to attribute to plants the qualities of living things, such as respiration, growth, and death. On the other hand, Japanese children were more likely to attribute such qualities to inanimate objects, such as a stone and a chair, which, in their culture, are sometimes viewed as if they were alive and had feelings (Hatano et al., 1993).

Number

As we discussed in Chapter 7, research by Karen Wynn suggests that infants as young as 4½ months have a rudimentary concept of number. They seem to know that if one doll is added to another doll, there should be two dolls, not just one. Other research has found that *ordinality*—the concept of comparing quantities (*more* or *less, bigger* or *smaller*)—seems to begin at around 12 to 18 months and at first is limited to comparisons of very few objects (Siegler, 1998). By age 4, most children have words for comparing quantities. They can say one tree is *bigger* than another, or one cup holds *more* juice than another. They know that if they have one cookie and then get another cookie, they have more cookies than they had before, and that if they give one cookie to another child, they have fewer cookies. Such quantitative knowledge appears to be universal, though it develops at different rates, depending on how important counting is in a particular family or culture (Resnick, 1989; Saxe, Guberman, & Gearhart, 1987). They also can solve numerical ordinality problems ("Megan picked six apples, and Joshua picked four apples; which child picked more?") with up to nine objects (Byrnes & Fox, 1998).

Not until age 3½ or older do most children consistently apply the *cardinality* principle in counting (Wynn, 1990). That is, when asked to count six items, children younger than 3½ tend to recite the number-names (one through six) but not to say how many items there are altogether (six). By age 5, most children can count to 20 or more and know the relative sizes of the numbers 1 through 10. Some can do simple, single-digit addition and subtraction (Siegler, 1998). Children intuitively devise strategies for adding, by counting on their fingers or by using other objects (Naito & Miura, 2001).

By the time they enter school, most children have developed basic "number sense" (Jordan, Kaplan, Oláh, & Locuniak, 2006). This basic level of number skills (see Table 10-3) includes *counting, number knowledge* (ordinality), *number transformations* (simple addition and subtraction), *estimation* ("Is this group of dots more or less than 5?"), and recognition of *number patterns* (2 plus 2 equals 4, and so does 3 plus 1).

SES and preschool experience affect how rapidly children advance in math. By age 4, children from middle-income families have markedly better number skills than low-SES children, and their initial advantage tends to continue. Children whose preschool teachers do a lot of "math talk" (such as asking children to help count days on a calendar) tend to make greater gains (Klibanoff, Levine, Huttenlocher, Vasilyeva, & Hedges, 2006).

Immature Aspects of Pre-operational Thought

According to Piaget, one of the main characteristics of pre-operational thought is **centration:** the tendency to focus on one aspect of a situation and neglect others. He said preschoolers come to illogical conclusions because they cannot **decentre**—think about several aspects of a situation at one time. Centration can limit young children's thinking about both physical and social relationships.

centration In Piaget's theory, tendency of pre-operational children to focus on one aspect of a situation and neglect others

decentre In Piaget's terminology, to think simultaneously about several aspects of a situation

Table 10-3	Key Elements of Number Sense in Children
Area	**Components**
Counting	Grasping one to one correspondence
	Knowing stable order and cardinality principles
	Knowing the count sequence
Number knowledge	Discriminating and coordinating quantities
	Making numerical magnitude comparisons
Number transformation	Simple addition and subtraction
	Calculating in story problems and nonverbal contexts
	Calculating "in the head"
Estimation	Approximating or estimating set sizes
	Using reference points
Number patterns	Copying number patterns
	Extending number patterns
	Discerning numerical relationships

Source: Adapted from Jordan et al., 2006.

Conservation

conservation Piaget's term for awareness that two objects that are equal according to a certain measure remain equal in the face of perceptual alteration so long as nothing has been added to or taken away from either object

A classic example is the failure to understand **conservation,** the fact that two things that are equal remain so if their appearance is altered, so long as nothing is added or taken away. Piaget found that children do not fully grasp this principle until the stage of concrete operations and that they develop different kinds of conservation at different ages. Table 10-4 shows how various dimensions of conservation have been tested.

In one type of conservation task, conservation of liquid, 5-year-old Jeffrey is shown two identical clear glasses, each one short and wide and each holding the same amount of water. Jeffrey is asked, "Is the amount of water in the two glasses equal?" When he agrees, the researcher pours the water in one glass into a third glass, a tall, thin one. Jeffrey is now asked, "Do both glasses contain the same amount of water? Or does one contain more? Why?" In early childhood—even after watching the water being poured out of one of the short, fat glasses into a tall, thin glass or even after pouring it himself—Jeffrey will say that either the taller glass or the wider one contains more water. When asked why, he says, "This one is bigger this way," stretching his arms to show the height or width. Pre-operational children cannot consider height *and* width at the same time. Since they centre on one aspect, they cannot think logically, said Piaget.

irreversibility Piaget's term for a pre-operational child's failure to understand that an operation can go in two or more directions

The ability to conserve is also limited by **irreversibility:** failure to understand that an operation or action can go two or more ways. Once Jeffrey can imagine restoring the original state of the water by pouring it back into the other glass, he will realize that the amount of water in both glasses is the same.

Pre-operational children commonly think as if they were watching a slide show with a series of static frames: They *focus on successive states,* said Piaget, and do not recognize the transformation from one state to another. In the conservation experiment, they focus on the water as it stands in each glass rather than on the water being poured from one glass to another, and so they fail to realize that the amount of water is the same.

Table 10-4	Tests of Various Kinds of Conservation			
Conservation Task	Show Child (and Have Child Acknowledge) that Both Items Are Equal	Perform Transformation	Ask Child	Pre-operational Child Usually Answers
Number	Two equal, parallel rows of candies	Space the candies in one row farther apart.	"Are there the same number of candies in each row or does one row have more?"	"The longer one has more."
Length	Two parallel sticks of the same length	Move one stick to the right.	"Are both sticks the same size or is one longer?"	"The one on the right (or left) is longer."
Liquid	Two identical glasses holding equal amounts of liquid	Pour liquid from one glass into a taller, narrower glass.	"Do both glasses have the same amount of liquid or does one have more?"	"The taller one has more."
Matter (mass)	Two balls of clay of the same size	Roll one ball into a sausage shape.	"Do both pieces have the same amount of clay or does one have more?"	"The sausage has more."
Weight	Two balls of clay of the same weight	Roll one ball into a sausage shape.	"Do both weigh the same or does one weigh more?"	"The sausage weighs more."
Area	Two toy rabbits, two pieces of cardboard (representing grassy fields), with blocks or toys (representing barns on the fields); same number of "barns" on each board	Rearrange the blocks on one piece of board.	"Does each rabbit have the same amount of grass to eat or does one have more?"	"The one with the blocks close together has more to eat."
Volume	Two glasses of water with two equal-sized balls of clay in them	Roll one ball into a sausage shape.	"If we put the sausage back in the glass, will the water be the same height in each glass, or will one be higher?"	"The water in the glass with the sausage will be higher."

Egocentrism

Egocentrism is a form of centration. According to Piaget, young children centre so much on their own point of view that they cannot take in another's. Three-year-olds are not as egocentric as newborn babies; but, said Piaget, they still think the universe centres on them. Egocentrism may help explain why young children (as we will see) sometimes have trouble separating reality from what goes on inside their own heads and why they may show confusion about what causes what. When Jeffrey believes that his "bad thoughts" have made his sister sick, or that he caused his parents' marital troubles, he is thinking egocentrically.

To study egocentrism, Piaget designed the *three-mountain task* (see Figure 10-1). A child sits facing a table that holds three large mounds. A doll is placed on a chair at the opposite side of the table. The investigator asks the child how the "mountains" would look to the doll. Piaget found that young children usually could not answer the question correctly; instead, they described the "mountains" from their own perspective. Piaget saw this as evidence that pre-operational children cannot imagine a different point of view (Piaget & Inhelder, 1967).

However, another experimenter who posed a similar problem in a different way got different results (Hughes, 1975). A child sat in front of a square board divided by "walls" into four sections. A toy police officer stood at the edge of the board; a doll was moved from one section to another. After each move the child was asked, "Can the police officer see the doll?" Then another toy police officer was brought into the action, and the child was told to hide the doll from both officers. Thirty children between ages 3½ and 5 were correct 9 out of 10 times.

Why were these children able to take another person's point of view (the police officer's) when those doing the mountain task were not? It may be because the "police officer" task calls for thinking in more familiar, less abstract ways. Most children do not look at mountains and do not think about what other people might see when looking at one, but most 3-year-olds know about dolls and police officers and hiding. Thus young children may show egocentrism primarily in situations beyond their immediate experience.

Do Young Children Have Theories of Mind?

Piaget (1929) was the first scholar to investigate children's **theory of mind,** their emerging awareness of their own mental processes and those of other people. He asked children such questions as "Where do dreams come from?" and "What do you think with?" On the basis of the answers, he concluded that children younger than 6 cannot distinguish between thoughts or dreams and real physical entities and have no theory of mind. However, more recent research indicates that between ages 2 and 5, children's knowledge about mental processes—their own and others'—grows dramatically (Astington, 1993; Bower, 1993; Flavell, et al., 1995).

Again, methodology seems to have made the difference. Piaget's questions were abstract, and he expected children to be able to put their understanding into words. Contemporary researchers use vocabulary and objects children are familiar with. Instead of talking in generalities, they observe children in everyday activities or give them concrete examples. In this way, we have learned, for example, that 3-year-olds can tell the difference

egocentrism Piaget's term for inability to consider another person's point of view

Checkpoint

Can you . . .

✔ Tell how centration limits preoperational thought?

✔ Give several reasons why preoperational children have difficulty with conservation?

✔ Discuss research that challenges Piaget's views on egocentrism in early childhood?

theory of mind Awareness and understanding of mental processes

Figure 10-1

Piaget's three-mountain task. A pre-operational child is unable to describe the "mountains" from the doll's point of view—an indication of egocentrism, according to Piaget.

between a boy who has a cookie and a boy who is thinking about a cookie; they know which boy can touch, share, and eat it (Astington, 1993).

Let's look at several aspects of theory of mind.

Knowledge about Thinking and Mental States

Between ages 3 and 5, children come to understand that thinking goes on inside the mind; that it can deal with either real or imaginary things; that someone can be thinking of one thing while doing or looking at something else; that a person whose eyes and ears are covered can think about objects; that someone who looks pensive is probably thinking; and that thinking is different from seeing, talking, touching, and knowing (Flavell et al., 1995).

However, preschoolers generally believe that mental activity starts and stops. Not until middle childhood do children know that the mind is continuously active (Flavell, 1993; Flavell et al., 1995). Preschoolers also have little or no awareness that they or other people think in words, or "talk to themselves in their heads," or that they think while they are looking, listening, reading, or talking (Flavell, Green, Flavell, & Grossman, 1997). At the same time, not until age 7 or 8 do most children realize that people who are asleep do *not* engage in conscious mental activity, such as thinking, deciding, and even knowing they are asleep (Flavell, Green, Flavell, & Lin, 1999).

Preschoolers tend to believe they can dream about anything they wish. Five-year-olds show a more adultlike understanding, recognizing that physical experiences, emotions, knowledge, and thoughts can affect the content of dreams. Not until age 11, however, do children fully realize that they cannot control their dreams (Woolley & Boerger, 2002).

Social cognition, the recognition that others have mental states (refer back to Chapter 8), is a distinctly human capacity (Povinelli & Giambrone, 2001) that accompanies the decline of egocentrism and the development of **empathy.** By age 3, children realize that if someone gets what he wants he will be happy, and if not, he will be sad (Wellman & Woolley, 1990). Four-year-olds begin to understand that people have differing beliefs about the world—true or mistaken—and that these beliefs affect their actions.

False Beliefs and Deception

A researcher shows 5-year-old Mariella a candy box and asks what is in it. "Candy," she says. But when Mariella opens the box, she finds crayons, not candy. "What will a child who hasn't opened the box think is in it?" the researcher asks. "Candy!" shouts Mariella, grinning at the joke. When the researcher repeats the same procedure with 3-year-old Bobby, he too answers the first question with "Candy." But after seeing the crayons in the box, when asked what another child would think was in the box, he says, "Crayons." And then he says that he himself originally thought crayons would be in the box (Flavell, 1993; Flavell et al., 1995).

The understanding that people can hold false beliefs flows from the realization that people hold mental representations of reality, which can sometimes be wrong. Three-year-olds, at least in some studies, appear to lack such an understanding (Flavell et al., 1995). An analysis of 178 studies in various countries, using a number of variations on false belief tasks, found this consistent developmental pattern (Wellman & Cross, 2001; Wellman, Cross, & Watson, 2001).

However, other researchers claim that 3-year-olds have at least a rudimentary understanding of false beliefs but may not show it when presented with complicated situations (Hala & Chandler, 1996). When preschoolers were taught to respond to a false-belief task with gestures rather than with words, children near their fourth birthday—but not younger children—did better than on the traditional verbal-response tasks. Thus, gestures may help children on the verge of grasping the idea of false beliefs to make that conceptual leap (Carlson, Wong, Lemke, & Cosser, 2005).

Three-year-olds' failure to recognize false beliefs may stem from egocentric thinking. At that age, children tend to believe that everyone else knows what they know and believes what they do. A child who falls down in the playground at preschool may think his mother knows all about the incident, because he himself does. Three-year-olds also have trouble understanding that their own beliefs can be false (Lillard & Curenton, 1999). In fact, when

The young girl on the right is old enough to know that her cousin needs consoling. Empathy, the ability to understand another person's feelings, begins at an early age.

actually presented with video evidence of their false beliefs, it is interesting that 3-year-old children fail to report what they had once claimed. For example, they continue to hold on to the belief that they had previously thought a candy box contained crayons, despite seeing a video of themselves claiming that the box contained candy (Zelazo & Boseovski, 2001).

Older preschoolers' more advanced understanding of mental representations seems to be related to a decline in egocentrism. Four-year-olds understand that people who see or hear different versions of the same event may come away with different beliefs. Not until about age 6, however, do children realize that two people who see or hear the *same* thing may interpret it differently (Pillow & Henrichon, 1996).

Deception is an effort to plant a false belief in someone else's mind, and it requires a child to suppress the impulse to be truthful. In other words, lying represents cognitive development! Some studies have found that children become capable of deception as early as age 2 or 3, others, at 4 or 5. Children as young as 3 are capable of telling "white lies" to be polite (Talwar & Lee, 2002). The difference may have to do with the means of deception children are expected to use. In a series of experiments, 3-year-olds were asked whether they would like to play a trick on an experimenter by giving a false clue about which of two boxes a ball was hidden in. The children were better able to carry out the deception when asked to put a picture of the ball on the wrong box, or to point to that box with an arrow, than when they pointed with their fingers, which children this age are accustomed to doing truthfully (Carlson, Moses, & Hix, 1998).

Piaget maintained that young children regard all falsehoods—intentional or not— as lies. However, when 3- to 6-year-olds were told a story about a subject close to their experience—the danger of eating contaminated food—and were given a choice between interpreting a character's action as a lie or a mistake, about three-fourths of the children in all age groups characterized it accurately (Siegal & Peterson, 1998). Apparently, then, even 3-year-olds have some understanding of the role of intent in deception. However, understanding that other people can intentionally ignore facts in order to deceive themselves doesn't emerge until 9 years (Johnson, 1997).

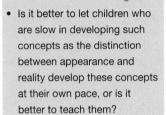

What's your view

- Is it better to let children who are slow in developing such concepts as the distinction between appearance and reality develop these concepts at their own pace, or is it better to teach them?

Distinguishing between Appearance and Reality

According to Piaget, not until about age 5 or 6 do children understand the distinction between what *seems* to be and what *is*. Much research bears him out, though some studies have found this ability beginning to emerge before age 4 (Friend & Davis, 1993; C. Rice, Koinis, Sullivan, Tager-Flusberg, & Winner, 1997).

In one classic series of experiments (Flavell, Green, & Flavell, 1986), 3-year-olds apparently confused appearance and reality in a variety of tests. For example, the experimenters showed preschoolers a red car and then covered it with a filter that made it look black. When the children were asked what colour the car really was, they said, "Black." When the children put on special sunglasses that made milk look green, they said the milk *was* green, even though they had just seen white milk. When an experimenter put on a Halloween mask in front of the children, they thought the experimenter was someone else.

However, when 3-year-olds were shown a sponge that looked like a rock and were asked to help trick someone else into thinking it was a rock, the children were able to make the distinction between the way the sponge looked (like a rock) and what it actually was (a sponge). Apparently, putting the task in the context of a deception helped the children realize that an object can be perceived as other than what it actually is (Rice et al., 1997).

Three-year-olds' difficulty distinguishing appearance from reality may itself be more apparent than real. When children were asked questions about the uses of such objects as a candle wrapped like a crayon, only 3 out of 10 answered correctly. But when asked to respond with actions rather than words ("I want a candle to put on a birthday cake"), 9 out of 10 handed the experimenter the crayon-like candle (Sapp, Lee, & Muir, 2000).

Distinguishing between Fantasy and Reality

Sometime between 18 months and 3 years, children learn to distinguish between real and imagined events. Three-year-olds know the difference between a real dog and a dog in a dream, and between something invisible (such as air) and something imaginary. They can

Box 10-1 *Imaginary Companions*

At 3½, Anna had 23 "sisters" with such names as Och, Elmo, Zeni, Aggie, and Ankie. She often talked to them on the telephone, since they lived about 100 miles away, in the town where her family used to live. During the next year, most of the sisters disappeared, but Och continued to visit, especially for birthday parties. Och had a cat and a dog (which Anna had begged for in vain), and whenever Anna was denied something she saw advertised on television, she announced that she already had one at her sister's house. But when a live friend came over and Anna's mother happened to mention one of her imaginary companions, Anna quickly changed the subject.

All 23 sisters—and some "boys" and "girls" who had followed them—lived only in Anna's imagination, as she well knew. Like an estimated 25 to 65 percent of children between ages 3 and 10 (Woolley, 1997), she created imaginary companions, with whom she talked and played. This normal phenomenon of childhood is seen most often in first-born and only children, who lack the close company of siblings. Like Anna, most children who create imaginary companions have many of them (Gleason, Sebanc, & Hartup, 2000). Girls are more likely than boys to have imaginary "friends," or at least to acknowledge them (Carlson & Taylor, 2005). Girls' imaginary playmates are usually other children, whereas boys' are more often animals (D. G. Singer & Singer, 1990).

Children who have imaginary companions can distinguish fantasy from reality, but in free-play sessions they are more likely to engage in pretend play than are children without imaginary companions (M. Taylor, Cartwright, & Carlson, 1993). They play more happily and more imaginatively than other children and are more cooperative with other children and adults (D. G. Singer & Singer, 1990; J. L. Singer & Singer, 1981); and they do not lack for friends at preschool (Gleason et al., 2000). They are more fluent with language, watch less television, and show more curiosity, excitement, and persistence during play. In one

study, 4-year-olds—regardless of verbal intelligence—who reported having imaginary companions did better on theory-of-mind tasks (such as differentiating between appearance and reality and recognizing false beliefs) than children who did not create such companions (M. Taylor & Carlson, 1997), and these children showed greater emotional understanding three years later. Having imaginary companions remains common in the early school years; almost one-third of the children who reported having had imaginary companions (65 percent of the sample in all) were still playing with them at age 7 (Taylor, Carlson, Maring, Gerow, & Charley, 2004).

Children's relationships with imaginary companions are like peer relationships; they are usually sociable and friendly, in contrast with the nurturing way in which children treat personified objects, such as stuffed animals and dolls (Gleason et al., 2000). Imaginary playmates are good company for an only child like Anna. They provide wish-fulfillment mechanisms ("There was a monster in my room, but Elmo scared it off with magic dust"), scapegoats ("I didn't eat those cookies—Och must have done it!"), displacement agents for the child's own fears ("Aggie is afraid she's going to be washed down the drain"), and support in difficult situations. (One 6-year-old "took" her imaginary companion with her to see a scary movie.)

What's your view?

How should parents respond to children's talk about imaginary companions?

Check it out!

For more information on this topic, go to the Online Learning Centre at **www.mcgrawhill.ca/olc/papalia,** which provides a link to a Web page about children's imaginary companions.

pretend and can tell when someone else is pretending (Flavell et al., 1995). By 3, and, in some cases, by 2 years of age, they know that pretense is intentional; they can tell the difference between trying to do something and pretending to do the same thing (Rakoczy, Tomasello, & Striano, 2004).

Still, the line between fantasy and reality may seem to blur at times. In one study (Harris, Brown, Marriott, Whittall, & Harmer, 1991), 4- to 6-year-olds, left alone in a room, preferred to touch a box holding an imaginary bunny rather than a box holding an imaginary monster, even though most of the children claimed they were just pretending. However, in a partial replication of the study, in which the experimenter stayed in the room and clearly ended the pretense, only about 10 percent of the children touched or looked in either of the boxes, and almost all showed a clear understanding that the creatures were imaginary (Golomb & Galasso, 1995). Thus it is difficult to know, when questioning children about "pretend" objects, whether children are giving serious answers or are keeping up the pretense (M. Taylor, 1997).

Magical thinking in children age 3 and older does *not* seem to stem from confusion between fantasy and reality. Often magical thinking is a way to explain events that do not seem to have obvious realistic explanations (usually because children lack knowledge about them), or simply to indulge in the pleasures of pretending—as with the belief in imaginary companions (see Box 10-1). Children, like adults, generally are aware of the magical nature of such fantasy figures but are more willing to entertain the possibility that they may be real (Woolley, 1997). Magical thinking tends to decline near the end of the preschool period (Woolley, Phelps, Davis, & Mandell, 1999).

All in all, then, the research on various theory-of-mind topics suggests that young children may have a clearer picture of reality than Piaget believed.

Influences on Individual Differences in Theory-of-Mind Development

Some children develop theory-of-mind abilities earlier than others. In part this development reflects brain maturation and general improvements in cognition. What other influences explain these individual differences?

Social competence and language development contribute to an understanding of thoughts and emotions (Cassidy, Werner, Rourke, Zubernis, & Balaraman, 2003). Children whose teachers rate them high on social skills are better able to recognize false beliefs (Watson, Nixon, Wilson, & Capage, 1999). The *kind* of talk a young child hears at home may affect the child's understanding of mental states. Three-year-olds whose mothers talk with them about others' mental states tend to show better theory-of-mind skills (Ruffman, Slade, & Crowe, 2002).

Families that encourage pretend play stimulate the development of theory-of-mind skills. As children play roles, they try to assume others' perspectives. Talking with children about how the characters in a story feel helps them develop social understanding (Lillard & Curenton, 1999). Empathy usually arises earlier in children whose families talk a lot about feelings and causality (Dunn, Brown, Slomkowski, Tesla, & Youngblade, 1991; Dunn, 1991).

Bilingual children, who speak and hear more than one language at home, do somewhat better than children with only one language on certain theory-of-mind tasks (Bialystok & Senman, 2004; Goetz, 2003). Bilingual children know that an object or idea can be represented linguistically in more than one way, and this knowledge may help them see that different people may have different perspectives. Bilingual children also recognize the need to match their language to that of their partner, and this may make them more aware of others' mental states. Finally, bilingual children tend to have better attentional control, and this may enable them to focus on what is true or real rather than on what only seems to be so (Bialystok & Senman, 2004; Goetz, 2003).

Checkpoint ✔

Can you . . .

✔ Give examples of research that challenges Piaget's views on young children's cognitive limitations?

✔ Describe changes between the ages of 3 and 6 in children's knowledge about the way their minds work?

Language Development

Guidepost 2

How does language improve, and what happens when its development is delayed?

Preschoolers are full of questions: "How many sleeps until tomorrow?" "Who filled the river with water?" "Do babies have muscles?" "Do smells come from inside my nose?" Young children's growing facility with language helps them express their own unique view of the world. The child who, at 3, describes how Daddy "hatches" wood (chops with a hatchet), or asks Mommy to "piece" her food (cut it into little pieces) may, by the age of 5, tell her mother, "Don't be ridiculous!" or proudly point to her toys and say, "See how I organized everything?"

Vocabulary

At 3 the average child can use 900 to 1,000 different words and uses about 12,000 each day. By the age of 6, a child typically has a spoken vocabulary of 2,600 words and understands more than 20,000 (Owens, 1996), having learned an average of 9 new words a day since about 1½ years of age (M. L. Rice, 1982). With the help of formal schooling, a youngster's passive, or receptive, vocabulary (words she can understand) will grow four times as large—to 80,000 words—by the time of entry into high school (Owens, 1996).

How do children expand their vocabularies so quickly? Apparently they do it by **fast mapping,** which allows them to absorb the meaning of a new word after hearing it only once or twice in conversation. From the context, children seem to form a quick hypothesis about the meaning of the word and store it in memory. Linguists are not sure how fast mapping works, but it seems likely that children draw on what they know about the rules

fast mapping Process by which a child absorbs the meaning of a new word after hearing it once or twice in conversation

for forming words, about similar words, about the immediate context, and about the subject under discussion.

Names of objects (nouns) seem to be easier to fast map than names of actions (verbs), which are less concrete. Yet one experiment showed that children just under 3 years old can fast map a new verb and apply it to another situation in which the same action is being performed (Golinkoff, Jacquet, Hirsh-Pasek, & Nandakumar, 1996).

Many 3- and 4-year-olds seem able to tell when two words refer to the same object or action (Savage & Au, 1996). They know that a single object cannot have two proper names (a dog cannot be both Spot and Fido). They also know that more than one adjective can apply to the same noun ("Fido is spotted and furry") and that an adjective can be combined with a proper name ("smart Fido!") (Hall & Graham, 1999).

Grammar and Syntax

The ways in which children combine syllables into words and words into sentences grow increasingly sophisticated during early childhood (Owens, 1996). At 3, children typically begin to use plurals, possessives, and past tense and know the difference between *I, you,* and *we*. However, they still make errors of over-regularization because they have not yet learned exceptions to rules (refer back to Chapter 7). Their sentences are generally short and simple, often leaving out small words such as *a* and *the,* but including some pronouns, adjectives, and prepositions. Most of their sentences are declarative ("Kitty wants milk"), but they can ask—and answer—*what* and *where* questions. (*Why* and *how* are harder to grasp.)

Between ages 4 and 5, sentences average 4 to 5 words and may be declarative, negative ("I'm not hungry"), interrogative ("Why can't I go outside?"), or imperative ("Catch the ball!"). Four-year-olds use complex, multi-clause sentences ("I'm eating because I'm hungry") more frequently if their parents often use such sentences (Huttenlocher, Vasilyeva, Cymerman, & Levine, 2000). Children this age tend to string sentences together in long run-on stories (". . . And then . . . And then . . ."). In some respects, comprehension may be immature. For example, 4-year-old Noah can carry out a command that includes more than one step ("Pick up your toys and put them in the cupboard"). However, if his mother tells him "You may watch TV after you pick up your toys," he may process the words in the order in which he hears them and think he can first watch television and then pick up his toys.

By ages 5 to 7, children's speech has become quite adult-like. They speak in longer and more complicated sentences. They use more conjunctions, prepositions, and articles. They use compound and complex sentences and can handle all parts of speech.

Still, while children this age speak fluently, comprehensibly, and fairly grammatically, they have yet to master many fine points of language. They rarely use the passive voice ("I was dressed by Grandpa"), conditional sentences ("If I were big, I could drive the bus"), or the auxiliary verb *have* ("I have seen that lady before") (C. S. Chomsky, 1969). They often make errors because they have not yet learned exceptions to rules. Saying "holded" instead of "held" or "eated" instead of "ate" is a normal sign of linguistic progress. When young children discover a rule, such as adding *-ed* to a verb for past tense, they tend to over generalize—to use it even with words that do not conform to the rule. Eventually, they notice that *-ed* is not always used to form the past tense of a verb. Children are more likely to overgeneralize the use of transitive or intransitive verbs in constructions that call for the other type of verb ("He disappeared it" or "He's hitting") if the verb they are using is not very familiar to them (Brooks, Tomasello, Dodson, & Lewis, 1999).

Training can help children master such syntactical forms. Every school day for two weeks, 72 preschoolers were told narrative stories containing either predominantly active or predominantly passive constructions. When tested the following week, the children who had heard the passive voice stories correctly comprehended and accurately produced more passive sentences (Vasilyeva, Huttenlocher, & Waterfall, 2006).

Pragmatics and Social Speech

As children learn vocabulary, grammar, and syntax, they become more competent in **pragmatics**—the practical knowledge of how to use language to communicate. This

pragmatics The practical knowledge needed to use language for communication

This preschool boy can use his growing vocabulary and knowledge of grammar and syntax to communicate more effectively. He has learned how to ask his father for things, to carry on a conversation, and to tell a story, perhaps about what happened at preschool.

Box 10-2 *Private Speech: Piaget versus Vygotsky*

Anna, age 4, was alone in her room painting. When she finished, she was overheard saying aloud, "Now I have to put the pictures somewhere to dry. I'll put them by the window. They need to get dry now. I'll paint some more dinosaurs."

Private speech—speaking to oneself—is normal and common in childhood, accounting for 20 to 50 percent of what 4- to 10-year-old children say (Berk, 1986a). Two- to 3-year-olds engage in "crib talk," playing with sounds and words. Four- and 5-year-olds use private speech as a way to express fantasies and emotions (Berk, 1992; Small, 1990). Older children "think out loud" or mutter in barely audible tones (see Table 10-5).

Piaget (1962/1923) saw private speech as a sign of cognitive immaturity. Because young children are egocentric, he suggested, they are unable to recognize others' viewpoints and therefore are unable to communicate meaningfully. Instead, they simply vocalize whatever is on their own minds. Another reason young children talk while they do things, said Piaget, is that they do not yet distinguish between words and the actions the words stand for, or symbolize. By the end of the pre-operational stage, with cognitive maturation and social experience, children become less egocentric and more capable of symbolic thought and so discard private speech.

Like Piaget, Vygotsky (1962/1934) believed that private speech helps young children integrate language with thought. However, Vygotsky did not look upon private speech as egocentric. He saw it as a special form of communication: conversation with the self. As such, he said, it serves a very important function in the transition between early social speech (often experienced in the form of adult commands) and inner speech (thinking in words)—a transition toward the internalization of socially derived control of behaviour ("Now I have to put the pictures somewhere to dry").

Research generally supports Vygotsky as to the functions of private speech. In an observational study of 3- to 5-year-olds, 86 percent of the children's remarks were *not* egocentric (Berk, 1986a). The most sociable children and those who engage in the most social speech tend to use the most private speech as well, apparently supporting Vygotsky's view that private speech is stimulated by social experience (Berk, 1986a, 1986b, 1992; Berk & Garvin, 1984; Kohlberg, Yaeger, & Hjertholm, 1968). There also is evidence for the role of private speech in self-regulation, as Anna was doing (Berk & Garvin, 1984; Furrow, 1984). Private speech tends to increase when children are trying to perform difficult tasks, especially without adult supervision (Berk, 1992; Berk & Garvin, 1984).

Vygotsky proposed that private speech increases during the preschool years and then fades away during the early part of middle childhood as children become more able to guide and master their actions. However, the pattern now appears to be more complex than Vygotsky suggested. Some studies have reported no age changes in overall use of private speech; others have found variations in the timing of its decline. The brightest children tend to use it earliest. Whereas Vygotsky considered the need for private speech a universal stage of cognitive development, studies have found a wide range of individual differences, with some children using it very little or not at all (Berk, 1992).

Understanding the significance of private speech has practical implications, especially in school (Berk, 1986a). Talking to oneself or muttering should not be considered misbehaviour; a child may be struggling with a problem, and thinking out loud may help in solving it.

What's your view?

Have you ever seen a child talking to himself or herself? What purpose did the speech seem to serve?

Check it out!

For more information on this topic, go to the Online Learning Centre at **www.mcgrawhill.ca/olc/papalia,** which provides a link to a Web page about private speech, and to **www.iuj.ac.jp/faculty/ mkahmed/privatespeech.html.** This article by Mohammed K. Ahmed of the English Language Program at the International University of Japan applies the concept of private speech to the way adults learn a second language.

---

includes knowing how to ask for things, how to tell a story or joke, how to begin and continue a conversation, and how to adjust comments to the listener's perspective (M. L. Rice, 1982). These are all aspects of **social speech:** speech intended to be understood by a listener. (Box 10-2 discusses **private speech,** talking aloud to oneself with no intent to communicate with others.)

With improved pronunciation and grammar, it becomes easier for others to understand what children say. Most 3-year-olds are quite talkative, and they pay attention to the effect of their speech on others. If people cannot understand them, they try to explain themselves more clearly. Four-year-olds, especially girls, use "parentese" when speaking to 2-year-olds (Owens, 1996; Shatz & Gelman, 1973; refer back to Chapter 7).

Most 5-year-olds can adapt what they say to what the listener knows. They can now use words to resolve disputes, and they use more polite language and fewer direct commands in talking to adults than to other children. Almost half of all 5-year-olds can stick to a conversational topic for about a dozen turns—if they are comfortable with their partner and if the topic is one they know and care about (Owens, 1996).

social speech Speech intended to be understood by a listener

private speech Talking aloud to oneself with no intent to communicate

Checkpoint

Can you . . .

✔ Trace normal progress in 3-
to 6-year-olds' vocabulary,
grammar, syntax, and
conversational abilities?

✔ Give reasons why children of
various ages use private
speech?

Delayed Language Development

The fact that Albert Einstein did not start to speak until he was close to 3 years old may encourage parents of other children whose speech develops later than usual. About 5 to 8 percent of preschool children show speech and language delays (U.S. Preventive Services Task Force, 2006). Boys are more likely than girls to be late talkers (Plomin et al., 1998; U.S. Preventive Services Task Force, 2006).

It is unclear why some children speak late. They do not necessarily lack linguistic input at home. Hearing problems and head and facial abnormalities may be associated with speech and language delays, as are premature birth, family history, socio-economic factors, and other developmental delays (Dale et al., 1998; U.S. Preventive Services Task Force, 2006). Heredity seems to play a major role (Lyytinen, Poikkeus, Laakso, Eklund, & Lyytinen, 2001; Spinath, Price, Dale, & Plomin, 2004). Boys are more likely than girls to be late talkers (Dale et al., 1998; U.S. Preventive Services Task Force, 2006). Children with language delays may have problems in fast mapping; they may need to hear a new word more often than other children do before they can incorporate it into their vocabularies (M. Rice, Oetting, Marquis, Bode, & Pae, 1994).

Like Albert Einstein, many children who speak late—especially those whose comprehension is normal—eventually catch up (Dale, Price, Bishop, & Plomin, 2003; Thal, Tobias, & Morrison, 1991). However, some 40 to 60 percent of children with early language delays, if left untreated, may experience far-reaching cognitive, social, and emotional consequences (U.S. Preventive Services Task Force, 2006).

It is not always easy to predict whether a late talker will need help. In longitudinal, community-based studies of 8,386 two-year-old twins born in England and Wales in 1994 and 1995, only about 40 percent of those reported to have early language delays continued to show language problems at ages 3 and 4 (Dale et al., 2003). Speech and language therapy sometimes can be effective, but samples are generally small and findings vary (U.S. Preventive Services Task Force, 2006).

Table 10-5 | Types of Private Speech

Type	Child's Activity	Examples
Wordplay, repetition	Repeating words and sounds, often in playful, rhythmic recitation	Jean wanders around the room, repeating in a singsong, "Put the mushroom on your head, put the mushroom in your pocket, put the mushroom on your nose."
Solitary fantasy play and speech addressed to non-human objects	Talking to objects, playing roles, producing sound effects for objects	Darryl says, "Ka-powee ka-powee," aiming his finger like a gun. Ashley says in a high-pitched voice while playing in the doll corner, "I'll be better after the doctor gives me a shot. Ow!" she remarks as she pokes herself with her finger (an imaginary needle).
Emotional release and expression	Expressing emotions or feelings directed inward rather than to a listener	Keiko is given a new box of crayons and says to no one in particular, "Wow! Neat!" Rachel is sitting at her desk with an anxious expression on her face, repeating to herself, "My mom's sick, my mom's sick."
Egocentric communication	Communicating with another person, but expressing the information so incompletely or peculiarly that it can't be understood	David and Mark are seated next to one another on the rug. David says to Mark, "It broke," without explaining what or when. Susan says to Ann at the art table, "Where are the paste-ons?" Ann says, "What paste-ons?" Susan shrugs and walks off.
Describing or guiding one's own activity	Narrating one's actions, thinking out loud	Omar sits down at the art table and says to himself, "I want to draw something. Let's see, I need a big piece of paper. I want to draw my cat." Working in her arithmetic workbook, Cathy says to no one in particular, "Six." Then, counting on her fingers, she continues, "Seven, eight, nine, ten. It's ten, it's ten. The answer's ten."
Reading aloud, sounding out words	Reading aloud or sounding out words while reading	While reading a book, Tom begins to sound out a difficult word. "Sherlock Holm-lock," he says slowly and quietly. Then he tries again, "Sher-lock-Holm-lock, Sherlock Holme," he says, leaving off the final s in his most successful attempt.
Inaudible muttering	Speaking so quietly that the words cannot be heard by the observers	Tony's lips move as he works a math problem.

Source: Adapted from Berk & Garvin, 1984.

Preparation for Literacy

To understand what is on the printed page, children first need to master certain prereading skills (Lonigan, Burgess, & Anthony, 2000; Muter, Hulme, Snowling, & Stevenson, 2004). **Emergent literacy** is the development of skills, knowledge, and attitudes that underlie reading and writing. These include such specific skills as the realization that words are composed of distinct sounds, or *phonemes,* and the ability to link phonemes with the corresponding alphabetic letters or combinations of letters (Whitehurst & Lonigan, 1998).

As children learn the skills they will need to translate the written word into speech, they also learn that writing can express ideas, thoughts, and feelings. Preschool children pretend to write by scribbling, lining up their marks from left to right (Brenneman, Massey, Machado, & Gelman, 1996). Later they begin using letters, numbers, and letter-like shapes to represent words, syllables, or phonemes. Often their spelling is so inventive that they may not be able to read it themselves (Whitehurst & Lonigan, 1998)!

Prereading skills can be divided into two types: (1) oral language skills, such as vocabulary, syntax, narrative structure, and the understanding that language is used to communicate; and (2) specific skills that help in decoding the printed word. Among this latter group are the phonological skills of *phonemic awareness,* the realization that words are composed of distinct sounds or *phonemes,* and *phoneme-grapheme correspondence,* the ability to link sounds with the corresponding letters or combinations of letters. Each of these factors seems to have its own independent effect (NICHD Early Child Care Research Network, 2005; Lonigan et al., 2000; Whitehurst & Lonigan, 1998). In a two-year longitudinal study of 90 British school children, the development of word recognition appeared critically dependent on phonological skills, whereas oral language skills such as vocabulary and grammatical skills were more important predictors of reading comprehension (Muter et al., 2004).

Does heredity influence literacy development? Apparently so. In a longitudinal study of 3,052 same-sex twin pairs—about half of them monozygotic and the other half dizygotic—both (1) early preliteracy experience with books or recordings of nursery rhymes or stories and (2) preliteracy knowledge at age 4 (saying the alphabet, knowing letter sounds, sounding out words, knowing word meanings, and recognizing rhymes) showed separate genetic influences that played a role in the children's ability to read and write at age 7 (Oliver, Dale, & Plomin, 2005).

Social interaction can promote emergent literacy. Children are more likely to become good readers and writers if, during the preschool years, parents provide conversational challenges the children are ready for—if they use a rich vocabulary and centre dinner-table talk on the day's activities or on questions about why people do things and how things work (Snow, 1990, 1993).

In a longitudinal study of 24 white, middle-class two-parent families (Reese, 1995), the quality of mother–child conversation at ages 3 and 4—particularly about past events—was a strong predictor of literacy skills prior to entering Grade 1. Most influential was mothers' use of questions and comments that helped children elaborate on events or link them with other incidents.

Reading to children is one of the most effective paths to literacy. According to a U.S. government report, 86 percent of girls and 82 percent of boys are read to at home at least three times a week (Freeman, 2004). Children who are read to from an early age learn that reading and writing move from left to right and from top to bottom and that words are separated by spaces (Siegler, 1998; Whitehurst & Lonigan, 1998). They also are motivated to learn to read. A study of Canadian parents' contributions to literacy skills of children in kindergarten through Grade 2 showed a relationship between reading support and children's scores on reading-related tasks. Children whose parents provided coaching in sounding out words, frequent trips to the local library, and explicit instruction about letters tended to perform better on early reading achievement, letter naming and sounding, and phonological awareness than did children without higher levels of reading support (Evans, 1998). Explicitly emphasizing the connections between phonemes and the spelling patterns that represent language sounds is effective in ensuring children learn basic reading and spelling skills well (Blahman, Fletcher, Clonan, Schatschneider, Francis, Shaywitz, & Shaywitz, 2004).

emergent literacy Preschoolers' development of skills, knowledge, and attitudes that underlie reading and writing

What's your view

- Suppose you wanted to set up a program to encourage preliteracy development in high-risk children. What elements would you include in your program, and how would you judge its success?

Checkpoint

Can you . . .

✔ Discuss possible causes, consequences, and treatment of delayed language development?

✔ Identify two types of prereading skills and explain how social interaction can promote preparation for literacy?

Moderate exposure to educational television can help prepare children for literacy, especially if parents talk with children about what they see. In one study, the more time 3- to 5-year-olds spent watching *Sesame Street,* the more their vocabulary improved (M. L. Rice, Huston, Truglio, & Wright, 1990). In a longitudinal study, the content of television programs viewed at ages 2 and 4 predicted academic skills three years later (Wright et al., 2001).

Information-Processing Approach: Memory Development

Guidepost 3

What memory abilities expand in early childhood?

During early childhood, children show significant improvement in attention and in the speed and efficiency with which they process information; and they begin to form long-lasting memories. Still, young children do not remember as well as older ones. For one thing, young children tend to focus on exact details of an event, which are easily forgotten, whereas older children and adults generally concentrate on the gist of what happened. Also, young children, because of their lesser knowledge of the world, may fail to notice important aspects of a situation, such as when and where it occurred, which could help jog their memory.

Basic Processes and Capacities

encoding Process by which information is prepared for long-term storage and later retrieval

storage Retention of information in memory for future use

retrieval Process by which information is accessed or recalled from memory storage

Information-processing theorists think of memory as a filing system that has three steps, or processes: *encoding, storage,* and *retrieval.* **Encoding** is like putting information in a folder to be filed in memory; it attaches a "code" or "label" to the information so that it will be easier to find when needed. Events are encoded along with information about the context in which they are encountered. **Storage** is putting the folder away in the filing cabinet. **Retrieval** occurs when the information is needed; the child then searches for the file and takes it out. Difficulties in any of these processes can interfere with efficiency.

The way the brain stores information is believed to be universal, though the efficiency of the system varies from one person to another (Siegler, 1998). Information-processing models depict the brain as containing three "storehouses": *sensory memory, working memory,* and *long-term memory.*

sensory memory Initial, brief, temporary storage of sensory information

Sensory memory is a temporary "holding tank" for incoming sensory information. Sensory memory shows little change from infancy on (Siegler, 1998). However, without processing (encoding), sensory memories fade quickly.

working memory Short-term storage of information being actively processed

Information being encoded or retrieved is kept in **working memory,** a short-term "storehouse" for information a person is actively working on: trying to understand, remember, or think about. Brain imaging studies have found that working memory is located partly in the *prefrontal cortex,* the large portion of the frontal lobe directly behind the forehead (Nelson et al., 2000).

The efficiency of working memory is limited by its capacity. Researchers may assess the capacity of working memory by asking children to recall a series of scrambled digits (for example, 2-8-3-7-5-1 if they heard 1-5-7-3-8-2). The capacity of working memory—the number of digits a child can recall—increases rapidly (Cowan, Nugent, Elliott, Ponomarev, & Saults, 1999). At age 4, children usually remember only two digits; at 12 they typically remember six (Zelazo, Müller, Frye, & Marcovitch, 2003).

executive function Conscious control of thoughts, emotions, and actions to accomplish goals or solve problems

The growth of working memory may permit the development of **executive function,** the conscious control of thoughts, emotions, and actions to accomplish goals or solve problems. Executive function enables children to plan and carry out goal-directed mental activity. It probably emerges around the end of an infant's first year and develops in spurts with age. Changes in executive function between ages 2 and 5 enable children to make up and use complex rules for solving problems (Zelazo et al., 2003; Zelazo & Müller, 2002).

central executive In Baddeley's model, element of working memory that controls the processing of information

long-term memory Storage of virtually unlimited capacity that holds information for very long periods

According to a widely used model, a **central executive** controls processing operations in working memory (Baddeley, 1981, 1986, 1992, 1996, 1998). The central executive orders information encoded for transfer to **long-term memory,** a "storehouse" of virtually unlimited capacity that holds information for long periods of time. The central executive also retrieves information from long-term memory for further processing. The central executive can temporarily expand the capacity of working memory by moving information into two separate subsidiary systems while the central executive is occupied with other tasks. One of these subsidiary systems holds verbal information (as in the digit task) and the other, visual/spatial images.

Recognition and Recall

Recognition and *recall* are types of retrieval. **Recognition** is the ability to identify something encountered before (for example, to pick out a missing mitten from a lost-and-found box). **Recall** is the ability to reproduce knowledge from memory (for example, to describe the mitten to someone). Preschool children, like all age groups, do better on recognition than on recall, but both abilities improve with age. The more familiar children are with an item, the better they can recall it. Recall also depends on motivation and on the strategies a child uses to enhance it (Lange, MacKinnon, & Nida, 1989).

Young children often fail to use strategies for remembering—even strategies they already know—unless reminded (Flavell, 1970). This tendency not to generate efficient strategies may reflect lack of awareness of how a strategy would be useful (Sophian, Wood, & Vong, 1995). Older children tend to become more efficient in the spontaneous use of memory strategies, as we discuss in Chapter 13.

recognition Ability to identify a previously encountered stimulus

recall Ability to reproduce material from memory

> *Checkpoint* ✔
>
> *Can you . . .*
>
> ✔ Identify three basic processes and three storehouses of memory and discuss their development?
>
> ✔ Compare preschoolers' recognition and recall ability?

Forming and Retaining Childhood Memories

Memory of experiences in early childhood is rarely deliberate: young children simply remember events that made a strong impression, and most of these early conscious memories seem to be short-lived.

Early Memories: Three Types

One investigator has distinguished three types of childhood memory: *generic, episodic,* and *autobiographical* (Nelson, 1993b). **Generic memory,** which begins at about age 2, produces a **script,** or general outline of a familiar, repeated event without details of time or place. The script contains routines for situations that come up again and again; it helps a child know what to expect and how to act. For example, a child may have scripts for riding the bus to preschool or having lunch at Grandma's house.

Episodic memory is the awareness of having experienced a particular incident that occurred at a specific time and place. Early episodic memories enable young children to build a mental picture of their world by organizing their experience around events (Nelson, 2005). Young children more clearly remember events that are unique or new, like Anna's apple-picking excursion. Three-year-olds may recall details about a trip to the circus for a year or longer (Fivush, Hudson, & Nelson, 1983), whereas generic memories of frequent events (such as going to the park) tend to blur together.

Given a young child's limited memory capacity, episodic memories are temporary. Unless they recur several times (in which case they are transferred to generic memory), they last for a few weeks or months and then fade. As children grow, older memories become obsolete and are replaced by newer, more up-to-date accounts of the child's changing world (Nelson, 2005).

Autobiographical memory refers to memories that form a person's life history. These memories are specific and long-lasting. Not everything in episodic memory becomes part of autobiographical memory—only those memories that have a special, personal meaning to the child (Fivush & Nelson, 2004).

Autobiographical memory generally emerges between ages 3 and 4 and becomes continuous around age 4½, though some people can recall isolated events, such as the birth of a sibling, from age 2 (Howe, 2003; Fivush & Nelson, 2004; Nelson, 2005). One suggested explanation for the relatively late arrival of autobiographical memory (Howe, 2003; Howe & Courage, 1993, 1997) is that children cannot store in memory events about their own lives until they develop a concept of self around which to organize those memories. In a longitudinal study of 58 nineteen-month-olds in Dunedin, New Zealand, those who already

generic memory Memory that produces scripts of familiar routines to guide behaviour

script General remembered outline of a familiar, repeated event, used to guide behaviour

episodic memory Long-term memory of specific experiences or events, linked to time and place

autobiographical memory Memory of specific events in one's own life; a type of episodic memory

recognized themselves in a mirror proved at age 2½ to have better independent memory of earlier events than those whose self-recognition had come later (Harley & Reese, 1999).

Influences on Memory Retention

Why do some early memories, like Einstein's memory of the compass, last longer than others? One factor is the uniqueness of the event. A second factor is children's active participation, either in the event itself or in its retelling or re-enactment.

A third factor is parents' way of talking with children about past events. The emergence of autobiographical memory seems to be linked with the development of language (Fivush & Nelson, 2004; Nelson, 2005). The ability to talk about an event, as Albert Einstein and his uncle Jacob did about the workings of the compass, may affect whether and how the memory is carried into later life (Fivush & Schwarzmueller, 1998). In one study, 2½- to 3-year-olds engaged in pretend play with their mothers about a camping trip, a bird-watching adventure, and the opening of an ice cream shop. Children who jointly handled *and* jointly discussed with their mothers various items connected with these events recalled them better one to three days later than children who had only handled or only discussed the items (Haden, Ornstein, Eckerman, & Didow, 2001).

The way adults talk with a child about a shared experience can influence how well the child will remember it (Cleveland & Reese, 2005; Haden & Fivush, 1996; McGuigan & Salmon, 2004; Reese & Fivush, 1993). When a child becomed stuck, adults with a *repetitive* conversational style tend to repeat their own previous statements or questions. Adults with an *elaborative* style are more likely to move on to a new aspect of the event or add more information. A repetitive-style parent might ask, "Do you remember how we travelled to P.E.I.?" and then, receiving no answer, ask, "How did we get there? We went in the." An elaborative-style parent might instead follow up the first question by saying, "Did we go by car or by plane?" Elaborative parents seem more focused on having a mutually rewarding conversation and affirming the child's responses, whereas repetitive parents are more focused on checking the child's memory performance. Three-year-olds of elaborative-style parents take part in longer conversations about events and remember more details, and they tend to remember the events better at ages 5 and 6 (Reese, Haden, & Fivush, 1993). Even as early as 19 to 32 months, a mother's elaborative reminiscing predicts children's ability to repeat and elaborate on shared memories (Harley & Reese, 1999).

In a study of 3- and 5-year-olds who participated in a staged event (a visit to a "zoo"), elaborative talk a few days *after* the event had greater influence on correct recall two weeks later than did such talk before or during the event. In fact, for 3-year-olds, elaborative talk before or during an event had no more effect on later recall than "empty" talk—talk that conveyed no specific information (McGuigan & Salmon, 2004).

How does elaborative talk enhance recall? Such talk may help a child encode recently experienced information by providing verbal labels for aspects of the event and by giving it an orderly, comprehensible structure. Elaborative talk also may create "boundaries" around children's mental representations of the event, preventing intrusion by irrelevant or distorted information (McGuigan & Salmon, 2004). In one study, at ages 2½ and 3½ children whose mothers had been trained in elaborative techniques recalled richer memories than children of untrained mothers. In addition, at 3½, children who had begun the experiment with higher levels of self-awareness retold their memories more accurately (Reese & Newcombe, in press).

Children also remember better when a parent supports their autonomy and is not controlling. Autonomy-supportive parents follow the child's lead, encouraging the child to continue or expand on what he or she is trying to say. Controlling parents may push the child to talk when she or he doesn't want to, contradict the child, or comment negatively on the child's statements or behavior. In a longitudinal study of 50 New Zealand mothers and children, the children at age 3 were able to give more information about shared memories when their mothers were both elaborative and autonomy-supporting, not controlling. By age 5, the mothers' elaborative questions remained important in eliciting a child's memories, but autonomy support no longer made a difference—perhaps because children that age are more sure of what they remember (Cleveland & Reese, 2005).

Constructing Shared Memories: The Role of Culture

Conversation not only helps children remember; it may be crucial to memory formation. Some investigators influenced by Vygotsky's socio-cultural theory support a **social interaction model,** which holds that children collaboratively construct autobiographical memories with parents or other adults as they talk about shared events (Nelson, 1993a). In reminiscing together, the adult provides a linguistic "scaffold" to help the child focus and organize a memory and compare that memory with what the adult remembers (Fivush & Nelson, 2004). As adults initiate and guide these conversations, children learn how memories are organized in narrative form in their culture (Welch-Ross, 1997). When parents prompt 2- and 3-year-olds with frequent questions about context ("When did you find the pine cone?" "Where did you find it?" "Who was with you?"), children soon learn to include this information (Peterson & McCabe, 1994). When parents of 3-year-olds comment on subjective reactions ("You *wanted* to go on the slide," "It was a *huge* bowl," "Mommy was *wrong*"), the children at 5½ are more likely to weave such comments into their reminiscences (Haden, Haine, & Fivush, 1997).

Culture affects what children remember about an experience and the way parents talk with them about it. In one study (Wang, 2004), 180 European-American and Chinese preschoolers, kindergartners, and second graders were asked such questions as "How did you spend your last birthday?" and "Tell me about a time when your mom or dad scolded you about something." The U.S. children told about particular events; their narratives were longer and more detailed and contained more opinion and emotion than those of the Chinese children. The Chinese children's accounts were shorter and more succinct and centred more on daily routines, group activities, and social interactions and roles. The U.S. children were the chief characters of their stories, whereas the Chinese children shared the "stage" with others. In discussions of shared memories with 3-year-olds, U.S. mothers used elaboration to encourage the child's active participation ("Do you remember when you went swimming at Nana's? What did you do that was really neat?"). Chinese mothers asked leading questions containing most of the content of the memory, and the child added little ("What did you play at the place of skiing? Sat on the ice ship, right?").

Intelligence: Psychometric and Vygotskyan Approaches

One factor that may affect how early children develop both language and memory is intelligence. Let's look at two ways intelligence is measured—through traditional psychometric tests and through newer tests of cognitive potential—and at influences on children's performance.

Traditional Psychometric Measures

Because 3-, 4-, and 5-year-olds are more proficient with language than younger children, intelligence tests can now include more verbal items; and these tests produce more reliable results than the largely non-verbal tests used in infancy. As children approach age 5, there is a higher correlation between their scores on intelligence tests and the scores they will achieve later (Bornstein & Sigman, 1986). IQ tests given near the end of kindergarten are among the best predictors of future school success (Tramontana, et al., 1988).

Although preschool children are easier to test than infants and toddlers, they still need to be tested individually. The two most commonly used individual tests for preschoolers are the Stanford-Binet Intelligence Scale and the Wechsler Preschool and Primary Scale of Intelligence.

The **Stanford-Binet Intelligence Scales,** used for ages 2 and up, takes 45 to 60 minutes to administer. The child is asked to define words, string beads, build with blocks, identify the missing parts of a picture, trace mazes, and show an understanding of numbers. The child's score is supposed to measure fluid reasoning (the ability to solve abstract or novel problems), knowledge, quantitative reasoning, visual-spatial processing, and working memory. The fifth edition, revised in 2003, includes nonverbal methods of testing

social interaction model Model, based on Vygotsky's socio-cultural theory, which proposes that children construct autobiographical memories through conversation with adults about shared events

Checkpoint ✔

Can you . . .

✔ Identify three types of memories in early childhood?

✔ Identify three factors that affect how well a preschool child will remember an event?

✔ Explain how language development may contribute to the onset of autobiographical memory?

✔ Discuss how conversations with adults influence memory construction and retention?

✔ Give an example of how culture influences memories?

Guidepost 4

How is preschoolers' intelligence measured, and what factors influence it?

Stanford-Binet Intelligence Scales Individual intelligence test for ages 2 and up, used to measure knowledge, quantitative reasoning, and working memory

all five of these dimensions of cognition and permits comparisons of verbal and nonverbal performance. In addition to providing a full-scale IQ, the Stanford-Binet yields separate measures of verbal and nonverbal IQ plus composite scores spanning the five cognitive dimensions.

The **Wechsler Preschool and Primary Scale of Intelligence, Revised (WPPSI-III)**, an individual test taking 30 to 60 minutes, has separate levels for ages 2½ to 4 and 4 to 7. It yields separate verbal and performance scores as well as a combined score. The 2002 revision includes new subtests designed to measure both verbal and nonverbal fluid reasoning, receptive versus expressive vocabulary, and processing speed. The WPPSI-III have been restandardized on samples of children representing the population of preschool-age children in the Canada. The WPPSI-III also has been validated for special populations, such as children with intellectual disabilities, developmental delays, language disorders, and autistic disorders.

Intelligence tests, beginning at age 5, tend to be fairly reliable in predicting measured intelligence and school success later in childhood (Bornstein & Sigman, 1986; Neisser et al., 1996). However, despite the widespread use of these tests, fierce controversies remain over what intelligence is and how it can be measured—or whether it can be fairly measured at all (see Chapter 13).

Influences on Measured Intelligence

Many people believe that IQ scores represent a fixed quantity of intelligence a person is born with. That is not so: The score is simply a measure of how well a child can do certain tasks in comparison with others of the same age. Test scores of children in industrialized countries have risen steadily since testing began, forcing test developers to raise standardized norms. This is called the *Flynn effect* (Flynn, 1984, 1987). The reasons for this upward trend are in dispute; it may in part reflect exposure to educational television, preschools, better-educated parents, and a wider variety of experiences, as well as changes in the tests themselves.

How well a particular child does on intelligence tests may be influenced by many factors. These include temperament, the match between cognitive style and the tasks posed, social and emotional maturity, ease in the testing situation, preliteracy or literacy skills, socio-economic status, and ethnic background. (We will examine several of these factors in Chapter 13.)

The degree to which family environment influences a child's intelligence is in question. We do not know how much of parents' influence on intelligence comes from their genetic contribution and how much from the fact that they provide a child's earliest environment for learning. Twin and adoption studies suggest that family life has its strongest influence in early childhood, and this influence diminishes greatly by adolescence (McGue, 1997; Neisser et al., 1996). However, these studies have been done largely with white, middle-class samples; their results may not apply to low-income and nonwhite families (Neisser et al., 1996). In a longitudinal study of low-income African-American children, the influence of the home environment remained substantial—at least as strong as the influence of the mother's IQ (Burchinal et al., 1997).

The correlation between socio-economic status and IQ is well documented (Neisser et al., 1996). Family income is associated with cognitive development and achievement in the preschool years and beyond. Family economic circumstances can exert a powerful influence, not so much in themselves as in the way they affect other factors such as health, stress, parenting practices and the atmosphere in the home (Brooks-Gunn, 2003; Evans, 2004; McLoyd, 1990, 1998; NICHD Early Child Care Research Network, 2005; Rouse, Brooks-Gunn, & McLanahan, 2005; see Chapter 10).

Results from the NLSCY show that among Canadian families, SES has a substantial influence on school achievement in children. Low SES has been shown to be related to lower levels of social support in children, and increased parental depression, higher levels of parental hostility, family dysfunction, and fewer academic skills in children, all of which have significant impacts on children's achievement in school (Ryan & Adams, 1998; Willms, 2002). But socio-economic status is only one of several social and family risk

Giving suggestions and strategies for solving a puzzle or problem—without showing strong approval or disapproval—can foster cognitive growth.

factors. Assessments of 152 children at ages 4 and 13 revealed no single pattern of risk. Instead, a child's IQ was related to *the total number* of such risk factors as the mother's behaviour, mental health, anxiety level, education, and beliefs about children's development; family size and social support; stressful life events; parental occupations; and disadvantaged status. The more risk factors there were, the lower the child's IQ score (Sameroff, Seifer, Baldwin, & Baldwin, 1993).

Why do some economically deprived children do better on IQ tests than others? Both genetic and environmental factors are involved. In a study of 1,116 twin pairs born in England and Wales in 1994 and 1995 and assessed at age 5 (Kim-Cohen, Moffitt, Caspi, & Taylor, 2004), children in deprived families tended, as in other studies, to have lower IQs. However, children with outgoing temperament, warm mothering, and stimulating activities in the home (which, again, may be influenced by parental IQ) tended to do better than other economically deprived children.

Testing and Teaching Based on Vygotsky's Theory

According to Vygotsky, children learn by internalizing the results of their interactions with adults. Adults direct children's learning most effectively in the *zone of proximal development (ZPD),* that is, in tasks children are almost ready to accomplish on their own. The ZPD can be assessed by *dynamic tests* (see Chapter 13), which, according to Vygotskyan theory, provide a better measure of children's intellectual potential than do traditional psychometric tests that measure what children have already mastered.

The ZPD, in combination with the related concept of *scaffolding* (refer back to Chapter 2), can help parents and teachers efficiently guide children's cognitive progress. The less able a child is to do a task, the more direction an adult must give. As the child can do more and more, the adult helps less and less. When the child can do the job alone, the adult takes away the "scaffold" that is no longer needed.

By enabling children to become aware of and monitor their own cognitive processes and to recognize when they need help, parents can help children take responsibility for learning. Prekindergarten children who receive this kind of scaffolding are better able to regulate their own learning when they get to kindergarten (Neitzel & Stright, 2003). In a longitudinal study of 289 families with infants, the skills children developed during interactions with their mothers at 2 and 3½ enabled them, at 4½, to regulate their own goal-directed problem solving and to initiate social interactions. Two-year-olds whose mothers helped maintain the child's interest in an activity—for example, by asking questions, making suggestions or comments, or offering choices—tended, at 3½ and 4½, to show independence in cognitive and social skills, such as solving a problem and initating social interaction (Landry, Smith, Swank, & Miller-Loncar, 2000).

Early Childhood Education

Going to preschool is an important step, widening a child's physical, cognitive, and social environment. Today more 4-year-olds than ever, and even many 3-year-olds, are enrolled in early childhood education. The transition to kindergarten, the beginning of "real school," is another momentous step.

Goals and Types of Preschools

In some countries, such as China, preschools are expected to provide academic preparation for schooling. In contrast, most preschools in Canada and many other western countries traditionally have followed a "child-centred" philosophy stressing social and emotional growth in line with young children's developmental needs—though some, such as those based on the theories of Piaget or the Italian educator Maria Montessori, have a stronger cognitive emphasis.

Montessori preschools are part of a worldwide movement founded by Maria Montessori, the first woman to receive a medical degree in Italy (refer back to Figure 1-1 in Chapter 1).

What's your view

- If you were a preschool or kindergarten teacher, how helpful do you think it would be to know a child's IQ? the child's ZPD?

Checkpoint

Can you . . .

✔ Describe two commonly used individual intelligence tests for preschoolers?

✔ Discuss several influences on measured intelligence?

✔ Explain why an intelligence test score using the ZPD might be significantly different from a traditional psychometric test score?

Guidepost 5

What purposes does early childhood education serve, and how do children make the transition to kindergarten?

The Montessori method enables children to learn independently and undisturbed, at their own pace, as they work with developmentally appropriate materials and self-chosen tasks. Teachers serve merely as "guides," and older children help younger ones. An evaluation of Montessori education in Milwaukee, where urban minority children who apply are randomly selected for enrolment, found that 5-year-old Montessori students were better prepared for elementary school in reading and math than children who attended other schools (Lillard & Else-Quest, 2006).

As part of a debate over how to improve education, pressures have built to offer instruction in basic academic skills in Canadian preschools. Defenders of the traditional developmental approach maintain that academically oriented programs neglect young children's need for exploration and free play and that, although children in such programs may learn more at first, too much teacher-centred instruction may stifle their interest and interfere with self-initiated learning (Elkind, 1986; Zigler, 1987).

Interviews with parents from three First Nations communities in Ontario showed that parents valued play as an appropriate way of learning in early childhood, and had positive attitudes towards play-oriented daycare centres, which they saw as consistent with their cultural values. The parents also stressed the importance of teaching First Nations culture and language in early child education, respect for elders, enhanced parental communication, the need for qualified daycare providers, and the continuation of teaching of culture and language in elementary and secondary schools (Gillis, 1992).

What type of preschool is best for children? Studies in Canada and the United States support a child-centred, developmental approach. One field study (Marcon, 1999) compared 721 randomly selected, predominantly low-income and African-American 4- and 5-year-olds from three types of preschool classrooms in Washington, D.C.: *child-initiated, academically directed,* and *middle-of-the-road* (a blend of the other two approaches). Children from child-initiated programs, in which they actively directed their own learning experiences, excelled in basic academic skills in all subject areas. They also had more advanced motor skills than the other two groups and scored higher than the middle-of-the-road group in behavioural and communicative skills. These findings suggest that a single, coherent philosophy of education may work better than an attempt to blend diverse approaches and that a child-centred approach seems more effective than an academically oriented one.

Compensatory Preschool Programs

The higher the family's socio-economic status, the more likely a child is to be ready for school (Rouse et al., 2005). Children from deprived socio-economic backgrounds often enter school at a considerable disadvantage. They may make as much progress as more advantaged classmates, but because they start out behind, they remain behind (Stipek & Ryan, 1997). It has been estimated that more than two-thirds of children in poor urban areas enter school poorly prepared to learn (Zigler, 1998). Since the 1960s, large-scale programs have been developed to help such children compensate for what they have missed and to prepare them for school.

The best-known compensatory preschool program for 3- and 4-year-old children of low-income families in the United States is Project Head Start, a federally funded program launched in 1965. The goals were to improve physical health, enhance cognitive skills, and foster self-confidence, relationships with others, social responsibility, and a sense of dignity and self-worth for the child and the family.

Head Start is effective in improving school readiness (Ripple et al., 1999), and the most successful Head Start programs have been those with the most parental participation, the best-trained teachers, the lowest staff-to-child ratios, the longest school days and weeks, and the most extensive services. Outcomes are best when the programs last at least 2 years (S. Ramey, 1999).

Has Head Start lived up to its name? Data support its effectiveness in improving school readiness (USDHHS, 2003b). Similarly, children who attend newer state-sponsored programs tend to show better cognitive and

Compensatory preschool education, such as the Aboriginal Head Start program these children are enrolled in, often yields long-lasting gains. Some positive effects of Head Start have held up through high school.

language skills and do better in school than children who do not attend (USDHHS, 2003a). Yet, even though Head Start children make gains in vocabulary, letter recognition, early writing, and early mathematics, their readiness skills remain far below average (USDHHS, 2003b). However, it is not clear that benefits last (Ripple et al., 1999). Although Head Start children do better on intelligence tests than other children from comparable backgrounds, this advantage disappears after the children start school. Nor have Head Start children equalled the average middle-class child in school achievement or on standardized tests (Collins & Deloria, 1983; Zigler & Styfco, 1993, 1994). Still, children from Head Start and other such programs are less likely to be placed in special education or to repeat a grade and are more likely to finish high school than low-income children who did not attend compensatory preschool programs (Neisser et al., 1996).

The Aboriginal Head Start Program (AHS) is an intervention started in 1995 to meet the social and cultural needs of First Nations, Metis, and Inuit children in urban and northern communities across Canada. Funded by Health Canada under the Aboriginal Head Start Initiative, about 100 programs in eight provinces and three northern territories involve 3,000 to 4,000 children from 2½ to 5 years, with the aim of preparing children for elementary school and building understanding and pride in their native culture (Dunning, 2000). The programs are operated as high-quality child-care centres, emphasizing social and cognitive skill development, and include cultural elements with formal involvement of the family and Aboriginal community to promote the retention and growth of Aboriginal cultures and languages. The family and community are integral parts of the AHS; parents work as aids in the classroom, as curriculum planners, kitchen helpers, and custodians, among other roles. All aspects of the children's experiences, including curriculum activities and materials, daily snacks, parent education, and resources, are designed to reflect their traditional culture whenever possible. The key is to develop a connection between Aboriginal language and culture and the educational experiences of the children. Community elders, who are active daily in the AHS centres, maintain a special role in promoting language and culture. Programs like the Waabinong Head Start Family Resource Centre in Sault Ste. Marie (Dunning, 2000), and the Tungasuvvingat Inuit Head Start in Ottawa (Reynolds, 1998), are examples of positive school environments that give parents opportunities to be involved in the decision making of their children's education, and become exposed to their own cultural heritage. For many of the parents, this experience is the first contact with their own language and culture, given their past in the traditional school system. Often parents are beginning to learn their language alongside their children. The AHS programs offer a unique opportunity for Aboriginal youth to develop self-awareness and pride in their own culture and language.

Advocates of compensatory programs say the results point to a need for earlier and longer-lasting intervention (Brooks-Gunn, 2003; Reynolds & Temple, 1998; Zigler & Styfco, 1993, 1994). They say that many economically disadvantaged children need more time and a continuous, predictable learning environment to fully absorb the benefits; and that the transition to formal schooling is a sensitive or critical period, when children need extra support and stability (McCain & Mustard, 1999; Reynolds & Temple, 1998). The Early Years Study showed that more government support was needed to promote development in the first 6 years (McCain & Mustard, 1999). In response to the report's recommendations, the Ontario government has funded community-based Ontario Early Years Centres to provide parents with support and resources to ensure that all children in Ontario have access to enriched environments that support healthy growth (Ministry of Community, Family and Children's Services, 2002).

In 1995, an Early Head Start program began offering child and family development services to low-income families with infants and toddlers in the United States. By 2004, the program was operating in more than 700 communities and serving about 62,000 families (Love et al., 2005). At ages 2 and 3, according to randomized studies, participants scored higher on standardized developmental and vocabulary tests and were at less risk of slow development than children not in the program. At age 3, they were less aggressive, more attentive to playthings, and more positively engaged with their parents. Early Head Start parents were more emotionally supportive, provided more learning and language stimulation, read to their children more, and spanked less. Programs that offered a mix of

Checkpoint ✔

Can you . . .

✔ Assess the benefits of
   compensatory preschool
   education?

✔ Discuss the factors that affect
   adjustment to kindergarten?

centre-based services and home visits showed better results than those that concentrated on one setting or the other (Commissioner's Office of Research and Evaluation and Head Start Bureau, 2001; Love et al., 2002, 2005).

A growing consensus among early childhood educators is that the most effective way to ensure that gains achieved in early intervention and compensatory education programs are maintained is through a *PK-3* approach—a systematic program extending from prekindergarten through third grade. Such a program would (1) offer prekindergarten to all 3- and 4-year olds; (2) require full-day kindergarten; and (3) coordinate and align educational experiences and expectations from prekindergarten through Grade 3 through a sequenced curriculum based on children's developmental needs and abilities and taught by skilled professionals (Bogard & Takanishi, 2005).

The Transition to Kindergarten

Originally a year of transition between the relative freedom of home or preschool and the structure of "real school," kindergarten in Canada has become more like first grade. Children spend less time on self-chosen activities and more time on worksheets and preparing to read. A successful transition to kindergarten lays the foundation for future academic achievement (Schultin, Malone, & Dodge, 2005).

Although some provinces do not require kindergarten, most 5-year-olds attend either a public or private kindergarten; and an increasing number spend a full day in school instead of the traditional half day (National Center for Education Statistics, 2004a). Do children learn more in full-day kindergarten? Initially, they do. According to ongoing longitudinal research on a U.S. nationally representative sample of children who started kindergarten in the fall of 1998, children in full-day public kindergarten are more likely than children in half-day kindergarten to receive daily instruction in prereading skills, math skills, social studies, and science (Walston & West, 2004) and tend to do better through the primary grades (Vecchiotti, 2003; Walston & West, 2004). However, by the end of third grade, amount of time spent in kindergarten makes no substantial difference in reading, math, and science achievement (Rathbun, West, & Germino-Hausken, 2004).

Findings highlight the importance of the preparation a child receives *before* kindergarten. The resources with which children come to kindergarten—preliteracy skills and the richness of the home literacy environment—predict reading achievement in first grade, and these individual differences tend to persist or increase throughout the first four years of school (Denton, West, & Walston, 2003; Rathbun et al., 2004). Children with extensive preschool experience tend to adjust more easily than those who spent little or no time in preschool. Children who start kindergarten with peers they know and like, or who have a "secure base" of ongoing neighbourhood friendships, generally do better (Ladd, 1996).

A study of 200 children in Alberta examined the effects of age of kindergarten entry on academic performance in Grades 1, 3, 6, and 9. Children who were younger when they started kindergarten tended to have higher IQs than the older group, but the children in the younger group were more likely to repeat a school year or need remedial education at some point in their academic careers (Wilgosh, Meyer, & Mueller, 1996).

Some researchers have explored a link between the home environment and a child's adaptation to kindergarten. In a 6-year longitudinal study of 72 couples, beginning in late pregnancy, those who had had happy childhoods, were happily married in the child's early years, and had an authoritative parenting style (see Chapter 11) had children who did better in kindergarten, both socially and academically (P. A. Cowan, Cowan, Schulz, & Heming, 1994).

Emotional and social adjustment affect readiness for kindergarten and strongly predict school success. More important than knowing the alphabet or being able to count to 20, kindergarten teachers say, are the abilities to sit still, follow directions, wait one's turn, and regulate one's own learning (Blair, 2002; Brooks-Gunn, 2003; Raver, 2002). Adjustment to kindergarten can be eased by enabling preschoolers and parents to visit before the start of kindergarten, shortening school days early in the school year, having teachers make home visits, holding parent orientation sessions, and keeping parents informed about what is going on in school (Schultin, Malone, & Dodge, 2005).

About 5 percent of children repeat kindergarten, according to a national longitudinal study of children who first entered kindergarten in 1998-99. Low-SES children, those who did not attend preschool, and those with developmental delays were most likely to repeat kindergarten—typically, in the belief that a second year of kindergarten will help them gain the skills they need to keep up. However, these children still tended to have lower reading and mathematics skills at the end of first grade than those who had spent only one year in kindergarten (Malone, West, Flanagan, & Park, 2006).

Because cutoff birth dates for kindergarten entrance vary among the provinces, children enter kindergarten at ages ranging from 4 to 6. As academic and emotional pressures mount, some parents hold their child back for a year in the belief that the child will then be more ready for kindergarten. Children whose kindergarten entry is delayed do show a modest initial academic advantage, but, by third grade, that advantage typically disappears (Stipek, 2002; Stipek & Byler, 2001).

Proposals have been made to lengthen the school year. When an elementary school in a midsized southeastern city added 30 days to its school year, children who completed kindergarten outperformed their counterparts in a traditional 180-day program on tests of math, reading, general knowledge, and cognitive competence (Frazier & Morrison, 1998).

The burgeoning physical and cognitive skills of early childhood have psychosocial implications, as we'll see in Chapter 11.

Summary and Key Terms

Piagetian Approach: The Pre-operational Child

Guidepost 1   What are typical cognitive advances and immature aspects of preschool children's thinking?

- Children in the pre-operational stage show several important advances, as well as some immature aspects of thought.

- The symbolic function enables children to reflect upon people, objects, and events that are not physically present. It is shown in deferred imitation, pretend play, and language.

- Early symbolic development helps pre-operational children make more accurate judgments of spatial relationships. They can understand the concept of identity, link cause and effect, categorize living and non-living things, and understand principles of counting.

- Centration keeps pre-operational children from understanding principles of conservation. Their logic also is limited by irreversibility and a focus on states rather than transformations.

- Pre-operational children appear to be less egocentric than Piaget thought; they (and even younger children) are capable of empathy.

- The theory of mind, which develops markedly between the ages of 3 and 5, includes awareness of a child's own thought processes, social cognition, understanding that people can hold false beliefs, ability to deceive, ability to distinguish appearance from reality, and ability to distinguish fantasy from reality. Hereditary and environmental influences affect individual differences in theory-of-mind development.

  **pre-operational stage (254)   symbolic function (255)
  pretend play (255)   transduction (256)   animism (256)
  centration (257)   decentre (257)   conservation (258)
  irreversibility (258)   egocentrism (259)   theory of mind (259)
  social cognition (260)   empathy (260)**

Language Development

Guidepost 2   How does language improve, and what happens when its development is delayed?

- During early childhood, vocabulary increases greatly, and grammar and syntax become fairly sophisticated. Children become more competent in pragmatics.

- Private speech is normal and common; it may aid in the shift to self-regulation and usually disappears by age 10.

- Causes of delayed language development are unclear. If untreated, it may have serious cognitive, social, and emotional consequences.

- Interaction with adults can promote emergent literacy.

  **fast mapping (263)   pragmatics (264)   social speech (265)
  private speech (265)   emergent literacy (267)**

Information-Processing Approach: Memory Development

Guidepost 3   What memory abilities expand in early childhood?

- Information-processing models describe three steps in memory: encoding, storage, and retrieval.

- Although sensory memory shows little change with age, the capacity of working memory increases greatly. The central executive controls the flow of information to and from long-term memory.

- At all ages, recognition is better than recall, but both increase during early childhood.

- Early episodic memory is only temporary; it fades or is transferred to generic memory. Autobiographical memory begins at about age 3 or 4 and may be related to early self-recognition ability and language development. According to the social interaction model, children and adults co-construct autobiographical memories by talking about shared experiences.

- Children are more likely to remember unusual activities that they actively participate in. The way adults talk with children about events influences memory formation.

  **encoding (268)   storage (268)   retrieval (268)
  sensory memory (268)   working memory (268)
  executive function (268)   central executive (268)
  long-term memory (268)   recognition (269)
  recall (269)   generic memory (269)   script (269)
  episodic memory (269)   autobiographical memory (269)
  social interaction model (271)**

Intelligence: Psychometric and Vygotskyan Approaches

Guidepost 4   How is preschoolers' intelligence measured, and what factors influence it?

- The two most commonly used psychometric intelligence tests for young children are the Stanford-Binet Intelligence Scales and the Wechsler Preschool and Primary Scale of Intelligence (WPPSI–III).

- Intelligence test scores may be influenced by social and emotional functioning, as well as by parent–child interaction and socio-economic factors.

- Newer tests based on Vygotsky's concept of the zone of proximal development (ZPD) indicate immediate potential for achievement. Such tests, when combined with scaffolding, can help parents and teachers guide children's progress.

  **Stanford-Binet Intelligence Scales (271)
  Wechsler Preschool and Primary Scale of Intelligence
  (WPPSI–III) (272)**

Early Childhood Education

Guidepost 5 What purposes does early childhood education serve, and how do children make the transition to kindergarten?

- Goals of preschool education vary in different cultures. Since the 1970s the academic content of early childhood education programs in Canada has increased.

- Compensatory preschool programs have had positive outcomes, but participants generally have not equalled the performance of middle-class children. Compensatory programs that extend into the primary grades have better long-term results.

- Adjustment to kindergarten may depend on interaction among the child's characteristics and those of the home, school, and neighbourhood environments.

- Many children today attend full-day kindergarten. Success in kindergarten depends in part on emotional and social adjustment and prekindergarten preparation.

CHAPTER ELEVEN

11

Psychosocial Development in Early Childhood

"I love you,"
said a great mother.
"I love you for what you are
knowing so well what you are.
And I love you more yet, child,
deeper yet than ever, child,
for what you are going to be,
knowing so well you are going far,
knowing your great works are ahead,
ahead and beyond,
yonder and far over yet."

—Carl Sandburg, *The People, Yes,* 1936

Focus *Buffy Sainte-Marie, Artist and Educator**

Buffy Sainte-Marie

Buffy Sainte-Marie has made a major impact on Canadian culture and on the lives of countless Aboriginal children throughout North America. Born at the Piapot (Cree) reserve in the Qu'Appelle Valley in Saskatchewan, and raised by adoptive parents (who were themselves part Mi'kmaq) in Maine and Massachusetts, she distinguished herself throughout her life, earning a Ph.D. in fine art, and degrees in oriental philosophy and education.

As a student in the 1960s, she became a highly popular singer and songwriter of folk and protest songs, many of which reflected her experiences as an Aboriginal woman growing up in a mainstream culture that had very inaccurate and misguided understandings of Aboriginal culture, the contributions of Aboriginal peoples to North American society, and the dire need for support for Aboriginal children and youth.

Her hit songs, like "Until It's Time for You to Go," and "Universal Soldier," were focal songs of the 1960s, bringing her great fame and fortune, and were recorded by over 200 artists in 16 languages. In the 1960s, she sought to combine her very successful singing career with contact with Aboriginal communities, striving to find a way to bridge the gap between mainstream and Aboriginal cultures. Thanks to her concerts throughout the world, she had the opportunity to meet with indigenous people in many countries, recognizing many common difficulties that Aboriginal people everywhere face when marginalized by a majority culture. She used her wealth to make a difference in the lives of Aboriginal children in Canada and the United States. She established the Nihewan (a Cree word meaning "talk Cree," or "be your culture") Foundation in 1969, an educational organization dedicated to Aboriginal youth, to prepare children for success in school, and to promote a more accurate understanding of Aboriginal peoples internationally and in their own communities.

In 1976, with the birth of her son, she stopped recording, but later began appearing in television episodes of *Sesame Street,* in which she presented material on Aboriginal culture in North America, reaching young people in Canada, the United States, and around the world with the message that Aboriginal people are an important part of Canadian and American society.

The Nihewan Foundation has expanded to focus on Aboriginal curriculum for elementary school children, with the Cradleboard Teaching Project, which is dedicated to developing teaching

materials on North American Aboriginal cultures. The purpose of the project is to encourage the development of a healthy sense of self-esteem, identity, and pride in Aboriginal children, and to improve relations between indigenous and colonial populations. The project combines traditional Aboriginal culture with high-tech innovations, connecting classrooms of children from Aboriginal and non-Aboriginal communities. In 1993 she helped establish a Juno award category for Aboriginal Canadian music. In recognition of her impact on North American culture she has won many awards and distinctions, including the Order of Canada, and a Lifetime Achievement Award by the American Indian College Fund. She has continued with her love of teaching, teaching digital art as an adjunct professor of fine arts, and combines her concert career with her work with the Cradleboard Teaching Project.

● ● ●

Buffy Sainte-Marie's life as an Aboriginal Canadian growing up in mainstream American society made her recognize the innaccurate perceptions non-Aboriginal people had of the cultures and traditions of Aboriginal peoples throughout North America. She became determined to change those perceptions and is working to ensure that young children in Aboriginal communities have positive educational experiences at a critical point in their development.

The years from ages 3 to 6 are pivotal ones in children's psychosocial development. As children's self-concept grows stronger, they learn what sex they are and begin to act accordingly. Their behaviour also becomes more socially directed.

In this chapter we discuss preschool children's understanding of themselves and their feelings. We see how their identification of themselves as male or female arises and how it affects their behaviour. We describe the activity on which children typically spend most of their time: play. We consider the influence, for good or ill, of what parents do. Finally, we discuss relationships with siblings and other children.

After you have read and studied this chapter, you should be able to answer each of the Guidepost questions that appear at the top of the next page. Look for them again in the margins, where they point to important concepts throughout the chapter. To check your understanding of these Guideposts, review the end-of-chapter summary. Checkpoints throughout the chapter will help you verify your understanding of what you have read.

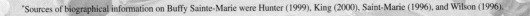

*Sources of biographical information on Buffy Sainte-Marie were Hunter (1999), King (2000), Saint-Marie (1996), and Wilson (1996).

1. How does the self-concept develop during early childhood, and how do children show self-esteem, emotional growth, and initiative?

2. How do boys and girls become aware of the meaning of gender, and what explains differences in behaviour between the sexes?

3. How do preschoolers play, and how does play contribute to and reflect development?

4. How do parenting practices influence development?

5. Why do young children help or hurt others, and why do they develop fears?

6. How do young children get along with—or without—siblings, playmates, and friends?

Guideposts for Study

Guidepost 1

How does the self-concept develop during early childhood, and how do children show self-esteem, emotional growth, and initiative?

self-concept Sense of self; descriptive and evaluative mental picture of one's abilities and traits

The Developing Self

"Who in the world am I? Ah, *that's* the great puzzle," said Alice in Wonderland, after her size had abruptly changed—again. Solving Alice's "puzzle" is a lifelong process of getting to know one's self.

The Self-concept and Cognitive Development

The **self-concept** is our image of ourselves. It is what we believe about who we are—our total picture of our abilities and traits. It is "a *cognitive construction,* . . . a system of descriptive and evaluative representations about the self," which determines how we feel about ourselves and guides our actions (Harter, 1996, p. 207). The sense of self also has a social aspect: Like Buffy Sainte-Marie, who had to deal with the misperceptions about Aboriginal cultures throughout her life, children incorporate into their self-image their growing understanding of how others see them.

The picture of the self comes into focus in toddlerhood, as children develop self-awareness (refer back to Chapter 8). The self-concept becomes clearer and more compelling as a person gains in cognitive abilities and deals with the developmental tasks of childhood, of adolescence, and then of adulthood.

Changes in Self-definition: The 5 to 7 Shift

self-definition Cluster of characteristics used to describe oneself

Changes in *self-definition,* or self-description, reflect self-concept development. Between about ages 5 and 7, as evidenced by changes in **self-definition:** the way children describe themselves typically changes. At age 4, Jason says:

> My name is Jason and I live in a big house with my mother and father and sister, Lisa. I have a kitty that's orange and a television set in my own room. . . . I like pizza and I have a nice teacher. I can count up to 100, want to hear me? I love my dog, Skipper. I can climb to the top of the jungle gym, I'm not scared! Just happy. You can't be happy *and* scared, no way! I have brown hair, and I go to preschool. I'm really strong. I can lift this chair, watch me! (Harter, 1996, p. 208)

The way Jason describes himself is typical of children his age. He talks mostly about concrete, observable behaviours; external characteristics, such as physical features; preferences; possessions; and members of his household. He mentions particular skills (running and climbing) rather than general abilities (being athletic). His self-descriptions are unrealistically positive, and they frequently spill over into demonstrations; what he *thinks* about himself is almost inseparable from what he *does.* Not until age 7 will he describe himself in terms of generalized traits, such as *popular, smart,* or *dumb;* recognize that he can have conflicting emotions; and be self-critical while holding a positive overall self-concept.

What specific changes make up this "age 5 to 7 shift"? A neo-Piagetian analysis (Case, 1985, 1992; Fischer, 1980) describes the 5 to 7 shift as occurring in three steps, which actually form a continuous progression. At 4, Jason is at the first step: His statements about himself are **single representations**—isolated, one-dimensional items. His thinking jumps from particular to particular, without logical connections. At this stage he cannot imagine having two emotions at once ("You can't be happy *and* scared"). He cannot decentre, in part because of his limited working memory capacity, and so he cannot consider different aspects of himself at the same time. His thinking is all-or-nothing. He cannot acknowledge that his **real self,** the person he actually is, is not the same as his **ideal self,** the person he would like to be. So he describes himself as a paragon of virtue and ability.

At about age 5 or 6, Jason moves up to the second step, as he begins to link one aspect of himself to another: "I can run fast, and I can climb high. I'm also strong. I can throw a ball real far, I'm going to be on a team some day!" (Harter, 1996, p. 215) However, these **representational mappings**—logical connections between parts of his image of himself—are still expressed in completely positive, all-or-nothing terms. Since good and bad are opposites, he cannot see how he might be good at some things and not at others.

The third step, *representational systems,* takes place in middle childhood (see Chapter 14), when children begin to integrate specific features of the self into a general, multi-dimensional concept. As all-or-nothing thinking declines, Jason's self-descriptions will become more balanced ("I'm good at hockey but bad at arithmetic").

Cultural Differences in Self-definition

Parents transmit, often through everyday conversations, cultural ideas and beliefs about how to define the self. For example, Chinese parents tend to encourage *interdependent* aspects of the self: compliance with authority, appropriate conduct, humility, and a sense of belonging to the community. European-American parents encourage *independent* aspects of the self: individuality, self-expression, and self-esteem.

A comparative study of 180 European American and Chinese preschoolers, kindergartners, and second graders (Wang, 2004) found that children absorb differing cultural styles of self-definition as early as age 3 or 4, and these differences increase with age. European American children tend to describe themselves in terms of personal attributes and beliefs ("I am big"), whereas Chinese children talk more about social categories and relationships ("I have a sister"). European American children more often describe themselves in terms of personality traits and tendencies ("I'm good at sports"), whereas Chinese children describe specific, overt behaviours ("I play Snowmoon with my neighbour"). European American children tend to put themselves in an unqualifiedly positive light ("I am smart"), whereas Chinese children and adults describe themselves more neutrally ("I sometimes forget my manners"). Thus, differing cultural values influence the way children in each culture perceive and define themselves.

Self-esteem

Self-esteem is the evaluative part of the self-concept, the judgment children make about their overall self-worth. Self-esteem is based on children's growing cognitive ability to describe and define themselves.

Developmental Changes in Self-esteem

Children do not generally articulate a concept of self-worth until about age 8, but younger children often show by their behaviour that they have one. In a study in Belgium (Verschueren, Buyck, & Marcoen, 2001), researchers measured various aspects of 5-year-olds' self-perceptions, such as physical appearance, scholastic and athletic competence, social acceptance, and behavioural conduct. The researchers also used puppets to reveal children's

single representations In neo-Piagetian terminology, first stage in development of self-definition, in which children describe themselves in terms of individual, unconnected characteristics and in all-or-nothing terms

real self The self one actually is

ideal self The self one would like to be

representational mappings In neo-Piagetian terminology, the second stage in development of self-definition, in which a child makes logical connections between aspects of the self but still sees these characteristics in all-or-nothing terms

self-esteem The judgment a person makes about his or her self-worth

---

*This discussion of children's developing understanding of themselves from age 4 on, including their understanding of their emotions, is indebted to Susan Harter (1990, 1993, 1996, 1998).

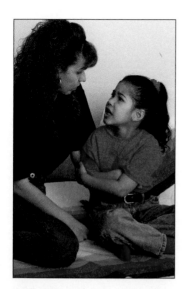

What's your view ?

• Can you think of ways in which your parents or other adults helped you develop self-esteem?

perceptions of what other people think of them. Children's positive or negative self-perceptions at age 5 tended to predict their self-perceptions and socio-emotional functioning at age 8.

Still, before the 5 to 7 shift, young children's self-esteem is not necessarily based on reality. They tend to accept the judgments of adults, who often give positive, uncritical feedback, and thus may overrate their abilities (Harter, 1990, 1993, 1996, 1998). Like the overall self-concept, self-esteem in early childhood tends to be all-or-none: "I am good" or "I am bad" (Harter, 1996, 1998). Not until middle childhood does it become more realistic, as personal evaluations of competence based on internalization of parental and societal standards begin to shape and maintain self-worth (Harter, 1990, 1996, 1998).

Contingent Self-esteem: The "Helpless" Pattern

When self-esteem is high, a child is motivated to achieve. However, if self-esteem is *contingent* on success, children may view failure or criticism as an indictment of their worth and may feel helpless to do better. About one-third to one-half of preschoolers, kindergartners, and first-graders show elements of this "helpless" pattern (Burhans & Dweck, 1995; Ruble & Dweck, 1995). Instead of trying a different way to complete a puzzle, as a child with unconditional self-esteem might do, "helpless" children feel ashamed and give up. They do not expect to succeed, and so they do not try. Whereas older children who fail may conclude that they are "dumb," preschoolers interpret poor performance as a sign of being "bad." Furthermore, this sense of being a bad person may persist into adulthood.

Children whose self-esteem is contingent on success tend to become demoralized when they fail. Often these children attribute poor performance or social rejection to their own personality deficiencies, which they believe they are helpless to change. Rather than trying new strategies, they repeat unsuccessful ones or just give up. Children with noncontingent self-esteem, by contrast, tend to attribute failure or disappointment to factors outside themselves or to the need to try harder. If initially unsuccessful or rejected they persevere, trying new strategies until they find one that works (Erdley, Cain, Loomis, Dumas-Hines, & Dweck, 1997; Harter, 1998; Pomerantz & Saxon, 2001). Children with high self-esteem tend to have parents and teachers who give specific, focused feedback rather than criticize the child as a person ("Look, the tag on your shirt is showing in front," not, "Can't you see your shirt is on backwards?" or "When are you going to learn to dress yourself?").

Understanding and Regulating Emotions

"I hate you!" Maya, age 5, shouts to her mother. "You're a mean mommy!" Angry because her mother sent her to her room for pinching her baby brother, Maya cannot imagine ever loving her mother again. "Aren't you ashamed of yourself for making the baby cry?" her father asks Maya a little later. Maya nods, but only because she knows what response he wants. In truth, she feels a jumble of emotions—not the least of which is feeling sorry for herself.

The ability to understand and regulate, or control, one's feelings is one of the key advances of early childhood (Dennis, 2006). Children who can understand their own emotions are better able to control the way they show them and to be sensitive to how others feel (Garner & Power, 1996). Emotional self-regulation helps children guide their behaviour (Laible & Thompson, 1998) and contributes to their ability to get along with others (Denham et al., 2003). Much of this development occurs during the preschool years.

Preschoolers can talk about their feelings and often can discern the feelings of others, and they understand that emotions are connected with experiences and desires (Saarni, Mumme, & Campos, 1998). They understand that someone who gets what he wants will be happy, and someone who does not get what she wants will be sad (Lagattuta, 2005).

Emotional understanding becomes more complex with age. In one study, 32 largely middle-class 4- through 8-year-olds and 32 adults were asked to tell, for example, how a young boy would feel if his ball rolled into the street and he either retrieved or refrained from retrieving it. The results revealed a "5 to 7 shift" in emotional understanding much like that found for self-concept development. Four- and 5-year-olds tended to believe that the boy would be happy if he got the ball—even though he would be breaking a rule—and unhappy if he didn't. The older children, like the adults, were more inclined to believe that

Being able to control and talk about their emotions is an important step in young children's psychosocial development.

obedience to a rule would make the boy feel good and disobedience would make him feel bad (Lagattuta, 2005).

Understanding Conflicting Emotions

One reason for younger children's confusion about their feelings is that they do not understand that they can experience contrary emotional reactions at the same time, as Maya did toward her mother. Individual differences in understanding conflicting emotions are evident by age 3. In one study, 3-year-olds who could identify whether a face looked happy or sad and who could tell how a puppet felt when enacting a situation involving happiness, sadness, anger, or fear were better able at the end of kindergarten to explain a story character's conflicting emotions. These children tended to come from families that often discussed why people behave as they do (J. R. Brown & Dunn, 1996). Most children acquire a more sophisticated understanding of conflicting emotions during middle childhood (Harter, 1996; see Chapter 14).

Understanding Emotions Directed Toward the Self

Emotions directed toward the self, such as shame and pride, develop during the third year, after children gain self-awareness. These emotions depend on internalization of parental standards of behaviour. But even children a few years older often lack the cognitive sophistication to recognize such emotions and what brings them on.

In one study (Harter, 1993), 4- to 8-year-olds were told two stories. In the first story, a child takes a few coins from a jar after being told not to do so; in the second story, a child performs a difficult gymnastic feat—a flip on the bars. Each story was presented in two versions: one in which a parent sees the child doing the act, and another in which no one sees the child. The children were asked how they and the parent would feel in each circumstance.

The answers revealed a gradual progression in understanding of feelings about the self (Harter, 1996). At ages 4 to 5, children did not say that either they or their parents would feel pride or shame. Instead they used such terms as "worried" or "scared" (for the money jar incident) and "excited" or "happy" (about the gymnastic accomplishment). At 5 to 6, children said their parents would be ashamed or proud of them but did not acknowledge feeling these emotions themselves. At 6 to 7, children said they would feel proud or ashamed, but only if they were observed. At 7 to 8, children acknowledged that even if no one saw them, they would feel ashamed or proud of themselves. By this age, the standards that produce pride and shame appear to be fully internalized. Until that happens, children need the prod of parental observation—a sort of emotional "scaffolding."

Cultural Influences on Emotional Regulation

Culture influences the socialization of emotional expression through interaction with caregivers. In four rural villages in Nepal—two of them populated almost entirely by Brahmans, high-caste Hindus, and the other two by Tamang, a Buddhist minority—researchers compared the way caregivers respond to 3- to 5-year-olds who express shame or anger. In both cultures, social harmony is an important value, but it is achieved in different ways. Brahman caregivers ignore a child's expression of shame, which is considered inappropriate among this high-status group, but deal openly and sympathetically with anger, coaxing the child to control it. The Tamang, on the other hand, rebuke displays of anger but use nurturance and reason to deal with shame (Cole, Tamang, & Shrestha, 2006). Thus, when presented with the same hypothetical upsetting situation (such as someone spilling a drink on their homework), Brahman schoolchildren say they would feel—but control—anger, whereas Tamang children say they would be ashamed of having left their homework near the drink (Cole et al., 2002).

Erikson: Initiative versus Guilt

The need to deal with conflicting feelings about the self is at the heart of the third crisis of personality development identified by Erik Erikson (1950): **initiative versus guilt.** The conflict arises from the growing sense of purpose, which lets a child plan and carry out activities, and the growing pangs of conscience the child may have about such plans.

initiative versus guilt Erikson's third crisis in psychosocial development, in which children balance the urge to pursue goals with moral reservations that may prevent carrying them out

Checkpoint ✔

Can you . . .

✔ Trace self-concept development between ages 3 and 6 and discuss cultural influences on self-definition?

✔ Tell how young children's self-esteem differs from that of school-age children?

✔ Describe how the "helpless pattern" arises and how it can affect children's reactions to failure?

✔ Describe the typical progression in understanding of conflicting emotions and emotions directed toward the self?

✔ Discuss the conflict involved in Erikson's third stage of psychosocial development?

gender identity Awareness, developed in early childhood, that one is male or female

Guidepost 2

How do boys and girls become aware of the meaning of gender, and what explains differences in behaviour between the sexes?

Checkpoint ✔

Can you . . .

✔ Summarize the main behavioural and cognitive differences between boys and girls?

Preschool children can do—and want to do—more and more. At the same time, they are learning that some of the things they want to do meet social approval, while others do not. How do they reconcile their desire to *do* with their desire for approval?

This conflict marks a split between two parts of the personality: the part that remains a child, full of exuberance and a desire to try new things and test new powers, and the part that is becoming an adult, constantly examining the propriety of motives and actions. Children who learn how to regulate these opposing drives develop the "virtue" of *purpose,* the courage to envision and pursue goals without being unduly inhibited by guilt or fear of punishment (Erikson, 1982).

If this crisis is not resolved adequately, said Erikson, a child may turn into an adult who is constantly striving for success or showing off, or who is inhibited and unspontaneous or self-righteous and intolerant, or who suffers from impotence or psychosomatic illness. With ample opportunities to do things on their own—but under guidance and consistent limits—children can attain a healthy balance between the tendency to overdo competition and achievement and the tendency to be repressed and guilt-ridden.

Gender

Gender identity, awareness of one's femaleness or maleness and all it implies in a particular society, is an important aspect of the developing self-concept. How different are young boys and girls? What causes those differences? How do children develop gender identity, and how does it affect their attitudes and behaviour?

Gender Differences

Gender differences are psychological or behavioural differences between males and females. As we discussed in Chapter 8, measurable differences between baby boys and girls are few. Although some gender differences become more pronounced after age 3, boys and girls on average remain more alike than different. Extensive evidence from many studies supports this *gender similarities hypothesis.* Fully 78 percent of gender differences are small to negligible, and some differences, such as in self-esteem, change with age.

Among the larger differences are boys' superior motor performance, especially after puberty, and their moderately greater propensity for physical aggression (Hyde, 2005) beginning at age 2 (Archer, 2004). (Aggression is discussed later in this chapter.) Temperamentally, from infancy on girls are better able to pay attention and to inhibit inappropriate behaviour. Boys are more active and take more intense pleasure in physical activity (Else-Quest, Hyde, Goldsmith, & Van Hulle, 2006).

Cognitive gender differences are few and small (Spelke, 2005). Overall, intelligence test scores show no gender differences (Keenan & Shaw, 1997). This is not surprising, since the most widely used tests are designed to eliminate gender bias (Neisser et al., 1996). Females tend to do better at verbal tasks (but not analogies), at mathematical computation, and at tasks requiring fine motor and perceptual skills, while males excel in most spatial abilities and in abstract mathematical and scientific reasoning (Halpern, 1997). In most studies, these differences do not emerge until elementary school or later (Spelke, 2005). In early childhood and again during pre-adolescence and adolescence, girls tend to use more responsive language, such as praise, agreement, acknowledgment, and elaborating on what someone else has said (Leaper & Smith, 2004).

We need to remember, of course, that gender differences are valid for large groups of boys and girls but not necessarily for individuals. By knowing a child's sex, we cannot predict whether that *particular* boy or girl will be faster, stronger, smarter, more compliant, or more assertive than another child.

Perspectives on Gender Development

What accounts for gender differences, and why do some of them emerge with age? The most influential explanations, until recently, centred on the differing experiences and social expectations that boys and girls meet almost from birth (Halpern, 1997; Neisser et al., 1996).

These experiences and expectations concern three related aspects of gender identity: *gender roles, gender-typing,* and *gender stereotypes.*

Gender roles are the behaviours, interests, attitudes, skills, and personality traits that a culture considers appropriate for males or females. All societies have gender roles. Historically, in most cultures, women have been expected to devote most of their time to caring for the household and children, while men were providers and protectors. Women were expected to be compliant and nurturant; men, to be active, aggressive, and competitive. Today, gender roles in North American and European cultures have become more diverse and more flexible. **Gender-typing** (refer back to Chapter 8), the acquisition of a gender role, takes place early in childhood; but children vary in the degree to which they take on gender roles (Iervolino, Hines, Golombok, Rust, & Plomin, 2005).

Gender stereotypes are preconceived generalizations about male or female behaviour ("All females are passive and dependent; all males are aggressive and independent"). Gender stereotypes pervade many cultures. They are seen to some degree in children as young as 2½ or 3, increase during the preschool years, and reach a peak at age 5 (Campbell, Shirley, & Candy, 2004; Haugh, Hoffman, & Cowan, 1980; Ruble & Martin, 1998; J. E. Williams & Best, 1982). As we might expect from our discussion of self-concept, younger preschoolers often attribute positive qualities to their own sex and negative qualities to the other sex. Still, at this early age *both* boys and girls call boys strong, fast, and cruel, and girls fearful and helpless (Ruble & Martin, 1998).

How do young children acquire gender roles, and why do they adopt gender stereotypes? Are these purely social constructs, or do they reflect underlying biological differences between males and females? Do social and cultural influences create gender differences, or merely accentuate them?

Let's look, then, at five perspectives on gender development (summarized in Table 11-1): *biological, evolutionary developmental, psychoanalytic, social learning,* and *cognitive* approaches. Each of these perspectives can contribute to our understanding; none fully explains why boys and girls turn out differently in some respects and not in others.

gender roles Behaviours, interests, attitudes, skills, and traits that a culture considers appropriate for males and females

gender-typing Socialization process by which children, at an early age, learn appropriate gender roles

gender stereotypes Preconceived generalizations about male or female role behaviour

Biological Approach

The existence of similar gender roles in many cultures suggests that some gender differences, at least, may be biologically based. Indeed, there is some evidence of biological differences that may affect behaviour.

Table 11-1	Five Perspectives on Gender Development		
Theories	**Major Theorists**	**Key Processes**	**Basic Beliefs**
Biological Approach		Genetic, neurological, and hormonal activity	Many or most behavioural differences between the sexes can be traced to biological differences.
Evolutionary Developmental Approach	Charles Darwin	Natural sexual selection	Children develop gender roles in preparation for adult mating and reproductive behaviour.
Psychoanalytic Approach			
Psychosexual theory	Sigmund Freud	Resolution of unconscious emotional conflict	Gender identity occurs when child identifies with same-sex parent.
Social Learning Approach			
Social cognitive theory	Albert Bandura	Observation of models, reinforcement	Child mentally combines observations of multiple models and creates own behavioural variations.
Cognitive Approach			
Cognitive-developmental theory	Lawrence Kohlberg	Self-categorization	Once a child learns she is a girl or he is a boy, child sorts information about behaviour by gender and acts accordingly.
Gender-schema theory	Sandra Bern, Carol Lynn Martin, & Charles F. Halverson	Self-categorization based on processing of cultural information	Child organizes information about what is considered appropriate for a boy or a girl on the basis of what a particular culture dictates, and behaves accordingly. Child sorts by gender because the culture dictates that gender is an important schema.

Scientists have identified more than 50 genes that may explain differences in anatomy and function between the brains of male and female mice. If similar genetic differences exist in humans, then sexual identity may be hardwired into the brain even before sexual organs form and hormonal activity begins (Dewing, Shi, Horvath, & Vilain, 2003).

By age 5, when the brain reaches approximate adult size, boys' brains are about 10 percent larger than girls' brains, mostly because boys have more grey matter in the cerebral cortex, whereas girls have greater neuronal density. What these findings may tell us about brain organization and functioning is unknown (Reiss, Abrams, Singer, Ross, & Denckla, 1996).

We do have evidence that size differences in the *corpus callosum,* the band of tissue joining the right and left hemispheres, are correlated with verbal fluency (Hines, Chiu, McAdams, Bentler, & Lipcamon, 1992). Since girls have a larger corpus callosum, better coordination between the two hemispheres may help explain girls' superior verbal abilities (Halpern, 1997).

Hormones in the bloodstream before or about the time of birth may affect the developing brain. The male hormone testosterone is related to aggressiveness in adult animals, but the relationship in humans is less clear (Simpson, 2001). For one thing, hormonal influences are hard to disentangle from genetic or later environmental ones (Iervolino et al., 2005). In any event, testosterone levels do not appear to be related to aggressiveness in children (Constantino et al., 1993).

Some research focuses on children with unusual hormonal histories. Girls with a disorder called *congenital adrenal hyperplasia (CAH)* have high prenatal levels of *androgens* (male sex hormones). Although raised as girls, they tend to develop into "tomboys," showing preferences for "boys' toys," rough play, and male playmates, as well as strong spatial skills (Berenbaum & Snyder, 1995). *Estrogens* (female sex hormones), on the other hand, seem to have less influence on boys' gender-typed behaviour. Since these studies are natural experiments, they cannot establish cause and effect; other factors besides hormonal differences, such as early interactions with parents, may play a role. Also, hormonal differences may themselves be affected by environmental or other factors. In any case, such atypical patterns of behaviour have not been found in children with normal hormonal variations (Ruble & Martin, 1998).

Perhaps the most dramatic examples of biologically based research have to do with infants born with ambiguous sexual structures that appear to be part male and part female. John Money and his colleagues (Money, Hampson, & Hampson, 1955) developed guidelines for infants born with such disorders. He recommended that the child be assigned as early as possible to the gender that holds the potential for the most nearly normal functioning and for stable gender identity.

In the case of a 7-month-old boy whose penis was accidentally cut off during circumcision, the decision was not made until 17 months to rear the child as a girl, and four months later doctors performed surgical reconstruction (Money & Ehrhardt, 1972). Although initially described as developing into a normal female, the child later rejected female identity and, at puberty, switched to living as a male. After a second surgical reconstruction, he married a woman and adopted her children. This case seems to suggest that gender identity may be rooted in chromosomal structure or prenatal development and cannot easily be changed (Diamond & Sigmundson, 1997)—at least not by waiting until the child is 17 months old.

The only other documented case of this kind had a different outcome. This time, the accident occurred at 2 months, and penile removal and sexual reassignment took place by 7 months. When interviewed at ages 16 and 26, the patient identified as a female, was living as a woman, and had had sexual relationships with both men and women (Bradley, Oliver, Chernick, & Zucker, 1998). Thus assignment of gender—at least during early infancy—may have some flexibility after all.

According to the report of an international conference on intersex disorders, psychosexual development is influenced by a number of factors, including sex-chromosome genes, brain structure, family dynamics, social circumstances, and prenatal androgen exposure. The conferees recommended that decisions about gender assignment of babies with disordered sex development be made carefully but as quickly as thorough diagnostic evaluation and sensitive consultation with parents permits (Houk, Hughes, Ahmed, Lee, and Writing Committee for the International Intersex Consensus Conference Participants, 2006).

Checkpoint ✔

Can you . . .

✔ Assess evidence for biological explanations of gender differences?

Evolutionary Developmental Approach

The evolutionary developmental approach sees gendered behaviour as biologically-based—with a purpose. From this controversial perspective, children's gender roles underlie the evolved mating and childrearing strategies of adult males and females.

According to Darwin's (1871) **theory of sexual selection,** the selection of sexual partners is a response to the differing reproductive pressures that early men and women confronted in the struggle for survival of the species (Wood & Eagly, 2002). The more widely a man can "spread his seed," the greater his chances to pass on his genetic inheritance. Thus, men tend to seek as many partners as possible. They value physical prowess because it enables them to compete for mates and for control of resources and social status, which women value. Because a woman invests more time and energy in pregnancy and can bear only a limited number of children, each child's survival is of utmost importance to her. Thus, she looks for a mate who will remain with her and support their offspring. The need to raise each child to reproductive maturity also explains why women tend to be more caring and nurturant than men (Bjorklund & Pellegrini, 2000; Wood & Eagly, 2002).

According to evolutionary theory, male competitiveness and aggressiveness and female nurturance develop during childhood as preparation for these adult roles. Boys play at fighting; girls play at parenting. In caring for children, women often must put a child's needs and feelings ahead of their own. Thus young girls tend to be better able than young boys to control and inhibit their emotions and to refrain from impulsive behaviour (Bjorklund & Pellegrini, 2000).

If this theory is correct, gender roles should be universal and resistant to change. Evidence in support of the theory is that in all cultures, women tend to be children's primary caregivers, though in some societies this responsibility is shared with the father or others (Wood & Eagly, 2002). Evidence against the theory is men's greater involvement in childraising today than in the past in Canada and other western societies.

Critics of evolutionary theory suggest that society and culture are as important as biology in determining gender roles. Evolutionary theory claims that men's primary role is to provide for subsistence while women's primary role is child care, but in some nonindustrial societies women are the main or equal providers. In an analysis of mating preferences in 37 cultures, women in traditional societies did tend to prefer older men with financial resources, and men to prefer younger women with homemaking skills; but these preferences were less pronounced in more egalitarian societies where women had reproductive freedom and educational opportunities (Wood & Eagly, 2002).

Some evolutionary theorists, therefore, see the evolution of gender roles as a dynamic process. They acknowledge that gender roles (such as men's involvement in child rearing) may change in an environment different from that in which these roles initially evolved (Crawford, 1998).

theory of sexual selection Darwinian theory, which holds that selection of sexual partners is influenced by the differing reproductive pressures that early men and women confronted in the struggle for survival of the species

Psychoanalytic Approach

"Dad, where will you live when I grow up and marry Mommy?" asks Timmy, age 4. From the psychoanalytic perspective, Timmy's question is part of his acquisition of gender identity. That process, according to Freud, is one of **identification,** the adoption of characteristics, beliefs, attitudes, values, and behaviours of the parent of the same sex. Freud and other classical psychoanalytic theorists considered identification an important personality development of early childhood; some social learning theorists also have used the term.

According to Freud, identification will occur for Timmy when he represses or gives up the wish to possess the parent of the other sex (his mother) and identifies with the parent of the same sex (his father). Although this explanation for gender development has been influential, it has been difficult to test. Despite some evidence that preschoolers tend to act more affectionately toward the opposite-sex parent and more aggressively toward the same-sex parent (Westen, 1998), the theory has little research support (Maccoby, 1992). Most developmental psychologists today favour other explanations.

identification In Freudian theory, the process by which a young child adopts characteristics, beliefs, attitudes, values, and behaviours of the parent of the same sex

Social Learning Approach

According to Walter Mischel (1966), a traditional social-learning theorist, children acquire gender roles by imitating models and being rewarded for gender-appropriate behaviour—in other words, by responding to environmental stimuli. Children generally choose models they see as powerful or nurturing. Typically, one model is a parent, often of the same sex, but children also pattern their behaviour after other adults or after peers. Behavioural feedback, together with direct teaching by parents and other adults, reinforces gender-typing. A boy who models his behaviour after his father is commended for acting "like a boy." A girl gets compliments on a pretty dress or hairstyle. In this model, gendered *behaviour precedes gender-knowledge* ("I am rewarded for doing boy things, so I must be a boy").

Since the 1970s, however, studies have cast doubt on the power of same-sex modelling alone to account for gender differences. As cognitive explanations (discussed in the next section) have come to the fore, traditional social learning theory has lost favour (Martin, Ruble, & Szkrybalo, 2002). Albert Bandura's (1986; Bussey & Bandura, 1999) newer **social cognitive theory,** an expansion of social learning theory, incorporates some cognitive elements.

According to social cognitive theory, observation enables children to learn much about gender-typed behaviours before performing them. They can mentally combine observations of multiple models and generate their own behavioural variations. Instead of viewing the environment as a "given," social cognitive theory recognizes that children select or even create their own environments through their choice of playmates and activities. However, critics say that social cognitive theory does not explain how children differentiate between boys and girls before they have a concept of gender, or what initially motivates children to acquire gender knowledge, or how gender norms become internalized—questions that earlier cognitive theories attempt to answer (Martin et al., 2002).

Cognitive Approach

Sarah figures out she is a girl because people call her a girl. She discovers that she will always be a girl. She comes to understand gender the same way she comes to understand everything else: by actively thinking about and constructing her own gender-typing. This is the heart of Lawrence Kohlberg's (1966) cognitive-developmental theory.

Kohlberg's Cognitive-Developmental Theory In Kohlberg's theory, gender knowledge precedes gendered behaviour ("I am a boy, so I like to do boy things"). Children actively search for cues about gender in their social world. As children come to realize which gender they belong to, they adopt behaviours they perceive as consistent with being male or female. Thus, 3-year-old Sarah prefers dolls to trucks because she sees girls playing with dolls and therefore views playing with dolls as consistent with her being a girl. And she plays mostly with other girls, whom she assumes will share her interests (Ruble & Martin, 1998; Martin & Ruble, 2004).

The acquisition of gender roles, said Kohlberg, hinges on **gender constancy,** more recently called *sex-category constancy*—a child's realization that his or her sex will always be the same. Once children achieve this realization, they are motivated to adopt behaviours appropriate to their sex. Gender constancy seems to develop in three stages: *gender identity, gender stability,* and *gender consistency* (Martin et al., 2002; Ruble & Martin, 1998; Szkrybalo & Ruble, 1999). *Gender identity* (awareness of one's own gender and that of others) typically occurs between ages 2 and 3. *Gender stability* comes when a girl realizes that she will grow up to be a woman, and a boy that he will grow up to be a man—in other words, that gender does not change. However, children at this stage may base judgments about gender on superficial appearances (clothing or hairstyle) and stereotyped behaviours. Finally—sometime between ages 3 and 7, or even later—comes *gender consistency:* the realization that a girl remains a girl even if she has a short haircut and wears pants, and a boy remains a boy even if he has long hair and earrings. Once children realize that their behaviour or dress will not affect their sex, they may become less rigid in their adherence to gender norms (Martin et al., 2002).

Much research challenges Kohlberg's view that gender-typing depends on gender constancy. Long before children attain the final stage of gender constancy, they show gender-typed

Anna's enjoyment of her truck shows that she is not restricted in her play by gender stereotypes. According to Bem's gender-schema theory, parents can help their children avoid such sterotypes by encouraging them to pursue their own interests, even when these interests are unconventional for their sex.

preferences (Bussey & Bandura, 1992; Martin & Ruble, 2004; Ruble & Martin, 1998). For example, gender preferences in toys and playmates appear as early as 12 to 24 months. However, these findings do not challenge Kohlberg's basic insight: that gender concepts influence behaviour (Martin et al., 2002).

Today, cognitive-developmental theorists no longer claim that gender constancy must precede gender-typing (Martin et al., 2002). Instead, they suggest, gender-typing may be heightened by the more sophisticated understanding that gender constancy brings (Martin & Ruble, 2004). Each stage of gender constancy increases children's receptivity to gender-relevant information. The achievement of gender identity may motivate children to learn more about gender; gender stability and gender consistency may motivate them to be sure they are acting "like a boy" or "like a girl." Studies have found significant linkage between levels of gender constancy and various aspects of gender development (Martin et al., 2002).

Gender-Schema Theory A second cognitive approach is **gender-schema theory.** Like cognitive-developmental theory, it views children as actively extracting knowledge about gender from their environment *before* engaging in gender-typed behaviour. However, gender-schema theory places more emphasis on the influence of culture. Once children know what sex they are, they develop a concept of what it means to be male or female *in their culture.* Children then match their own behaviour to their culture's view of what boys and girls are "supposed" to be and do. Among the theory's leading proponents are Sandra Bem (1983, 1985, 1993), Carol Lynn Martin, and Charles F. Halverson (Martin & Halverson, 1981; Martin et al., 2002).

One of the key contributions of gender-schema theory is the concept of the gender schema. A *gender schema* (much like Piaget's *schemes*) is a mentally organized network of information about gender that influences behaviour. Gender schemas develop with age in response to experience. Even before they can talk, children organize their observations around the schema of gender because they see that their society classifies people that way: males and females wear different clothes, play with different toys, and use separate bathrooms. Children then generalize this information to other members of the same category. As children's knowledge about gender increases, it influences not only what they do, but also what they pay attention to and remember (Martin et al., 2002).

It has been suggested that gender schemas promote gender stereotypes by leading children to overgeneralize. When a new boy his age moves in next door, 4-year-old Brandon knocks on his door, carrying a toy truck—apparently assuming that the new boy will like the same toys he likes. However, there is little evidence that gender schemas are at the root of stereotyped behaviour (Yunger, Carver, & Perry, 2004). Furthermore, gender-sterotyping does not always become stronger with increased gender knowledge; in fact, the opposite is often true (Bussey & Bandura, 1999).

A current view, which has research support, is that gender-stereotyping rises and then falls in a developmental pattern (Ruble & Martin, 1998; Welch-Ross & Schmidt, 1996). Around ages 4 to 6, when children are constructing and then consolidating their gender schemas, they notice and remember information consistent with these schemas and even exaggerate it. In fact, they tend to *mis*remember information that challenges gender stereotypes, such as photos of a girl sawing wood or a boy cooking, and to insist that the genders in the photos were the other way around (C. L. Martin, Eisenbud, & Rose, 1995; Martin & Ruble, 2004; Ruble & Martin, 1998).

Between ages 5 and 7, children have developed a repertoire of rigid stereotypes about gender that they apply to themselves and others. A boy will pay more attention to what he considers "boys' toys" and a girl to "girls' toys." A boy will expect to do better at "boy things" and a girl, at "girl things." Then, around age 7 or 8, schemas become more complex as children begin to take in and integrate contradictory information, such as the fact that some girls like to play football. As children develop more complex beliefs about gender, they become more flexible in their views about gender roles (Martin & Ruble, 2004; Martin et al., 2002; Ruble & Martin, 1998; M. G. Taylor, 1996; Trautner et al., 2005).

Cognitive approaches to gender development (including social cognitive theory) have made an important contribution by exploring how children think about gender and what they know about it at various ages. However, the various theories differ as to what prompts

gender-schema theory Theory, proposed by Bem, that children socialize themselves in their gender roles by developing a mentally organized network of information about what it means to be male or female in a particular culture

children to enact gender roles and why some children become more strongly gender-typed than others (Bussey & Bandura, 1992, 1999; Martin et al., 2002; Martin & Ruble, 2004; Ruble & Martin, 1998). One important factor, according to both cognitive and social cognitive theorists, may be socialization.

The Role of Socialization

Socialization begins in infancy, long before a conscious understanding of gender begins to form. Gradually, as children begin to regulate their own activities, standards of behaviour become internalized. Children feel good about themselves when they live up to their internal standards and feel bad if they do not. A substantial part of this shift from socially guided control to self-regulation of gender-related behaviour may take place between ages 3 and 4 (Bussey & Bandura, 1992). How do parents, peers, and the media influence this development?

Family Influences When Louisiana Governor Kathleen Blanco's 4-year-old grandson David was asked what he wanted to be when he grew up, he wasn't sure. He shrugged off all his mother's suggestions—firefighter, soldier, policeman, airplane pilot. Finally, she asked whether he'd like to be governor. "Mom," he replied, "I'm a boy!" (Associated Press, 2004a).

David's response illustrates how strong family influences may be, even fostering counterstereotypical preferences. Usually, though, experience in the family seems to reinforce gender-typical preferences and attitudes. We say "seems" because it is difficult to separate parents' genetic influence from the influence of the environment they create. Also, parents may be responding to rather than encouraging children's gender-typed behaviour (Iervolino et al., 2005).

Boys tend to be more strongly gender-socialized concerning play preferences than girls. Parents, especially fathers, generally show more discomfort if a boy plays with a doll than if a girl plays with a truck (Lytton & Romney, 1991; Ruble & Martin, 1998; Sandnabba & Ahlberg, 1999). Girls have more freedom than boys in their clothes, games, and choice of playmates (Miedzian, 1991).

In egalitarian households, the father's role in gender socialization seems especially important (Fagot & Leinbach, 1995). In an observational study of 4-year-olds in British and Hungarian cities, boys and girls whose fathers did more housework and child care were less aware of gender stereotypes and engaged in less gender-typed play (Turner & Gervai, 1995).

Siblings also influence gender development, according to a three-year longitudinal study of 198 first- and secondborn siblings (median ages 10 and 8) and their parents. Secondborns tend to become more like their older siblings in attitudes, personality, and leisure activities, whereas firstborns are more influenced by their parents and less by their younger siblings (McHale, Updegraff, Helms-Erikson, & Crouter, 2001). Young children with an older sibling of the same sex tend to be more gender-typed than those whose older sibling is of the other sex (Iervolino et al., 2005).

Peer Influences Anna, at age 5, insisted on dressing in a new way. She wanted to wear leggings with a skirt over them, and boots—indoors and out. When her mother asked her why, Anna replied, "Because Katie dresses like this—and Katie's the king of the girls!"

Even in early childhood, the peer group is a major influence on gender-typing (Turner & Gervai, 1995). Peers begin to reinforce gender-typed behaviour by age 3, and their influence increases with age. Children show more disapproval of boys who act "like girls" than of girls who are tomboys (Ruble & Martin, 1998). Children who play in same-sex groups tend to be more gender-typed than children who do not (Maccoby, 2002; Martin & Fabes, 2001). Although both 3- and 4-year-olds know what behaviours peers consider gender-appropriate, 4-year-olds more consistently apply these judgments to themselves (Bussey & Bandura, 1992). In a Toronto study of stated preferences for descriptions of fictitious boys and girls, children as young as 5 years preferred fictitious boys or girls whose behaviour was more in keeping with the stereotyped behaviour of the children's own sex. Boys preferred masculine boys and girls, while girls preferred feminine boys and girls (Zucker, Wilson-Smith, Kurita, & Stern, 1995). Generally, however, peer and parental attitudes reinforce each other.

Cultural Influences   A major conduit for the transmission of cultural attitudes toward gender is television. Although women in television programs and commercials are now more likely to be working outside the home and men are sometimes shown caring for children or doing the marketing, for the most part life as portrayed on television continues to be more stereotyped than life in the real world (Coltrane & Adams, 1997; Ruble & Martin, 1998).

Social cognitive theory predicts that children who watch a lot of television will become more gender-typed by imitating the models they see on the screen. Dramatic supporting evidence emerged from a natural experiment in several western Canadian towns, one of which, dubbed "Notel" to protect the anonymity of the participants, obtained access to television transmission for the first time in 1973. Children who had had relatively unstereotyped attitudes in Notel showed marked increases in traditional views 2 years later (Kimball, 1986). In another study, children who watched a series of non-traditional episodes, such as a father and son cooking together, had less stereotyped views than children who had not seen the series (J. Johnston & Ettema, 1982).

Children's books have long been a source of gender stereotypes. Today, the proportion of women as main characters has greatly increased, and children are more frequently shown in nontraditional activities (girls dressing up as pilots or boys helping with laundry). However, women are still shown mostly in domestic roles, whereas men are seldom seen doing housework or caring for children (Gooden, 2001). Fathers, in fact, are largely absent and, when they do appear, are often shown as withdrawn and ineffectual (Anderson & Hamilton, 2005).

Major strengths of the socialization approach include the breadth and multiplicity of processes it examines and the scope for individual differences it reveals. But this very complexity makes it difficult to establish clear causal connections between the way children are raised and the way they think and act. Just what aspects of the home environment and the peer culture promote gender-typing? Underlying this question is a chicken-and-egg problem: Do parents and peers treat boys and girls differently because they *are* different, or because the culture says they *should be* different? Does differential treatment *produce* or *reflect* gender differences? Perhaps, as social cognitive theory suggests, there is a bidirectional relationship. Further research may help to show how socializing agents mesh with children's own tendencies in gender-related attitudes and behaviour.

It seems likely that none of the theories we have discussed has the full answer to how gender identity and gender-typing develop. Today "it is widely acknowledged that . . . cognitive, environmental, and biological factors are all important" (Martin et al., 2002, p. 904). A recent *biosocial theory,* for example, holds that psychological aspects of gender arise from interaction between the physical characteristics of the sexes (such as men's greater physical strength and women's reproductive capacity), their developmental experiences, and the character of the societies in which they live (Wood & Eagly, 2002).

Play: The Business of Early Childhood

Carmen, age 3, pretends that the pieces of cereal floating in her bowl are "fishies" swimming in the milk, and she "fishes," spoonful by spoonful. After breakfast, she puts on her mother's hat, picks up a briefcase, and is a "mommy" going to work. She rides her tricycle through the puddles, comes in for an imaginary telephone conversation, turns a wooden block into a truck and says, "Vroom, vroom!" Carmen's day is one round of play after another.

It would be a mistake to dismiss Carmen's activities as no more than "having fun." Although play may not seem to serve any obvious purpose, it has important current and long-term evolutionary functions (Bjorklund & Pellegrini, 2002; Smith, 2005b; see Box 11-1). Play is the work of the young, and it contributes to all domains of development. Through play, children stimulate the senses, learn how to use their muscles, coordinate sight with movement, gain mastery over their bodies, and acquire new skills. As they sort blocks of

What's your view ?

- Where would you place your own views on the continuum between the following extremes? Explain.

  1. Family A thinks girls should wear only ruffly dresses and boys should never wash dishes or cry.

  2. Family Z treats sons and daughters exactly alike, without making any references to the children's sex.

Checkpoint ✔

Can you . . .

✔ Distinguish among five basic approaches to the study of gender development?

✔ Compare how various theories explain the acquisition of gender roles, and assess the support for each theory?

✔ Assess evidence for biological explanations of gender differences?

✔ Discuss the role of socialization in gender acquisition?

Guidepost 3

How do preschoolers play, and how does play contribute to and reflect development?

Box 11-1 *Does Play Have an Evolutionary Basis?*

Children appear to engage in play for the pure pleasure it brings. Yet, from an evolutionary standpoint, an activity that (1) takes up considerable time and energy, (2) shows a characteristic age progression, peaking in childhood and declining with sexual maturity, (3) is encouraged by parents, and (4) occurs in all cultures would seem to have been naturally selected as having significant benefits for children (Bjorklund & Pellegrini, 2000; Smith, 2005b).

Investigators differ on the value and function of play. One early psychologist, Herbert Spencer (1878/1898), dismissed play as a "useless exercise" of excess energy. The German philosopher Karl Groos (1898, 1901), whose view more closely foreshadows current thinking, argued that play has the essential function of skill practice—indeed, that the main purpose of childhood is for play to occur. G. Stanley Hall (1904/1916) claimed that play serves a cathartic function, allowing children to "play out" primitive human instincts that characterized our evolutionary past.

Today, many psychologists and educators see play as an adaptive activity characteristic of the long period of immaturity and dependence, during which children gain the physical attributes and cognitive and social learning necessary for adult life. Play aids bone and muscle development and gives children a chance to try out and master activities and develop a sense of their own capabilities (Bjorklund & Pellegrini, 2000). Through play, children practice, in a risk-free environment, behaviours and skills they will need in adult life (Hawes, 1996). Animal studies suggest that the evolution of play may be linked to the evolution of intelligence. The most intelligent animals—birds and mammals—play, whereas less intelligent species—fish, reptiles, and amphibians—do not, as far as we can tell (Hawes, 1996).

Parents, according to evolutionary theory, encourage play because the future benefits of children's skill acquisition outweigh any benefits of current productive activity in which children, at their relatively low skill levels, might engage (Smith, 2005b). Gender differences in children's play enable boys and girls to practice adult behaviours important for reproduction and survival (Bjorklund & Pellegrini, 2002; Geary, 1999).

Different types of play serve different adaptive functions. Early locomotor play is common among all mammals and may support brain development. Later, exercise play may help develop muscle strength, endurance, physical skills, and efficiency of movement (Smith, 2005b). Play with objects is found mainly among primates: humans, monkeys, and apes. Object play may have served an evolutionary purpose in the development of tools,

by enabling people to learn the properties of objects and what can be done with them (Bjorklund & Pellegrini, 2002). In premodern societies, the objects used in play can be any materials picked up from the surrounding environment. Object play in such societies tends to focus on developing useful skills, such as making baskets and pounding grain (Smith, 2005b). Young mammals, like human children, engage in social play, such as wrestling and chasing each other. Social play may strengthen social bonds, facilitate cooperation, and lessen aggression (Hawes, 1996).

Unlike other types of play, dramatic play seems to be an almost exclusively human activity. Apes, gorillas, and chimpanzees in captivity have been observed to engage only in simple make-believe play with objects, such as "sipping" from an empty cup. This rudimentary ability may have been the basis for the evolution of true symbolic play in humans, independent of the presence of physical objects (Bjorklund & Pellegrini, 2002; Smith, 2005b).

Dramatic play seems to be universal in humans but is less frequent in societies in which children are expected to participate in adult work (Smith, 2005a). In traditional hunter-gatherer societies, children's pretense focuses on imitating adult subsistence activities such as hunting, fishing, and preparing food. These highly repetitive routines seem to serve primarily as practice for adult activities (Smith, 2005b). As humans began to settle in permanent communities, dramatic play may have evolved so as to practice the changing skills needed for new ways of life. In modern urban industrial societies, themes of dramatic play are highly influenced by the mass media. At least in higher-SES families, dramatic play is encouraged by an abundance of toys, the absence of demands on children to help in subsistence activities, heavy parental involvement in play, and play-based preschool curricula (Smith, 2005a).

Investigators still have much to learn about the functions and benefits of play, but one thing seems clear: the time children spend playing is time well spent.

What's your view

From your observations of children's play, what immediate and long-range purposes does it appear to serve?

Check it out

For more information on this topic, go to **www.mcgrawhill.ca/olc/papalia.**

different shapes, count how many they can pile on each other, or announce that "my tower is bigger than yours," they lay the foundation for mathematical concepts. As they cooperate to build sandcastles or tunnels on the beach, they learn skills of negotiation and conflict resolution (Ginsburg and the Committee on Communications and the Committee on Psychosocial Aspects of Child and Family Health, 2007). Through pretending, they try out roles, cope with uncomfortable emotions, gain understanding of other people's viewpoints, and construct an image of the social world. They develop problem-solving skills, experience the joy of creativity, and become more proficient with language (Bodrova & Leong, 1998; J. I. F. Davidson, 1998; Furth & Kane, 1992; J. E. Johnson, 1998; Nourot, 1998; Singer & Singer, 1990).

Children need plenty of time for free exploratory play. Today, many parents expose young children to enrichment videos and academically oriented playthings. These activities may be valuable in themselves, but not if they interfere with child-directed play. The trend to full-day kindergarten also has markedly reduced time for free play (Ginsburg et al., 2007).

Children of differing ages have differing styles of play, play at different things, and spend different amounts of time in various types of play (Bjorklund & Pellegrini, 2002). Physical play, for example, begins in infancy with apparently aimless rhythmic movements. As gross motor skills improve, preschoolers exercise their muscles by running, jumping, skipping, hopping, and throwing. Toward the end of this period and into middle childhood, *rough-and-tumble play* involving wrestling, kicking, and chasing becomes more common, especially among boys (see Chapter 12).

Particular children have different styles of play, and they play at different things. Researchers categorize children's play by its *cognitive complexity* (what children do when they play) and its *social dimension* (whether they play alone or with others). What can we learn about children by seeing how they play?

Cognitive Levels of Play

Carol, at 3, "talked for" a doll, using a deeper voice than her own. Michael, at 4, wore a kitchen towel as a cape and "flew" around as Batman. These children were engaged in pretend play involving make-believe people or situations.

Pretend play is one of four categories of play identified by Piaget and others as showing increasing levels of cognitive complexity (Piaget, 1951; Smilansky, 1968). The simplest form, which begins during infancy, is active **functional play** involving repetitive muscular movements (such as rolling or bouncing a ball). As gross motor skills improve, preschoolers run, jump, skip, hop, throw, and aim. It consists of repeated practice in large muscular movements, such as rolling a ball (Bjorklund & Pellegrini, 2002).

The second level of cognitive complexity is seen in toddlers' and preschoolers' **constructive play** (using objects or materials to make something, such as a house of blocks or a crayon drawing). Four-year-olds in preschools or daycare centres may spend more than half their time in this kind of play, which becomes more elaborate by ages 5 and 6 (J. E. Johnson, 1998). Children spend an estimated 10 to 15 percent of their time playing with objects, such as blocks (Bjorklund & Pellegrini, 2002).

The third level, which Smilansky called **dramatic play,** also called *fantasy play, pretend play,* or *imaginative play,* rests on the symbolic function, which emerges near the end of the sensorimotor stage (Piaget, 1962). Pretend play typically begins during the last part of the second year, increases during the preschool years, and then declines as school-age children become more involved in the fourth cognitive level of play, *formal games with rules,* such as hopscotch and marbles. Although functional play and constructive play precede dramatic play in Smilanksy's hierarchy, these three types of play often occur at the same ages (Bjorklund & Pellegrini, 2002; Smith, 2005a).

Dramatic play peaks during the preschool years, increasing in frequency and complexity (Bjorklund & Pellegrini, 2002; Smith, 2005a), and then declines as school-age children become more involved in **formal games with rules**—organized games with known procedures and penalties, such as hopscotch and marbles. An estimated 12 to 15 percent of preschoolers' play and 33 percent of kindergartners' is pretend play (Bjorklund & Pellegrini, 2002), but the trend toward academically oriented kindergarten programs may limit the amount of time children can spend in such play (Bergen, 2002; Ginsburg et al., 2007).

Dramatic play at age 2 is largely imitative, often initiated by an adult caregiver and following familiar "scripts" such as feeding a baby (doll) or taking a stuffed animal's temperature. By age 3 or 4, pretense becomes more imaginative and self-initiated. Children may use a block to represent a cup or just imagine the cup (Smith, 2005a).

Children who often play imaginatively tend to cooperate more with other children and to be more popular and more joyful than those who don't (Singer & Singer, 1990). Children who watch a great deal of television tend to play less imaginatively, perhaps because they are accustomed to passively absorbing images rather than generating their own (Howes & Matheson, 1992). Studies have found the quality of dramatic play to be associated

functional play In Piaget's and Smilansky's terminology, the lowest cognitive level of play, involving repetitive muscular movements; also called *locomotor play*

constructive play In Piaget's and Smilansky's terminology, the second cognitive level of play, involving use of objects or materials to make something

dramatic play Play involving imaginary people or situations; also called *fantasy play, pretend play,* or *imaginative play*

formal games with rules Organized games with known procedures, and penalties

with social and linguistic competence (Bergen, 2002). Television also seems to have influenced the kinds of roles preschoolers choose to play. Instead of modelling their dramatic play after real people, they more often pretend to be television adventure heroes (French & Pena, 1991). Pretend play also may further the development of theory-of-mind skills (refer back to Chapter 10). The peak period for pretend play, early childhood, is also the peak period for acquisition of such skills as recognizing false beliefs (Smith, 2005b).

The Social Dimension of Play

In the 1920s, Mildred B. Parten (1932) identified six types of early play, ranging from the least to the most social (see Table 11-2). She found that as children get older, their play tends to become more interactive and more cooperative. At first they play alone, then alongside other children, and finally, together.

Today, however, most researchers now view Parten's characterization of children's play development as too simplistic. Non-social play does not necessarily diminish through the years, to be replaced by social play; instead, children of all ages engage in all of Parten's categories of play. Although solitary active play becomes less common between ages 3 and 6, solitary constructive play does not. Furthermore, playing near other children and watching what they do is often a prelude to joining in their play (K. H. Rubin, Bukowski, & Parker, 1998).

Much non-social play consists of activities that foster cognitive, physical, and social development. In one study of 4-year-olds, some kinds of non-social play, such as *parallel constructive play* (for example, working on puzzles near another child) were most common among children who were good problem solvers, were popular with other children, and were seen by teachers as socially skilled (K. Rubin, 1982). Such play may reflect independence and maturity, not poor social adjustment. Children need some time alone to concentrate on tasks and problems, and some simply enjoy individual activities more than group activities. We need to look, then, at what children *do* when they play, not just at whether they play alone or with someone else (K. H. Rubin et al., 1998). Some investigators have modified Parten's system to more realistically gauge developmental and individual differences in play by assessing both its cognitive and social dimensions (Cheah, Nelson, & Rubin, 2001; Coplan & Rubin, 1998).

What's your view ?

- How do you think use of computers might affect preschool children's cognitive and social development?

Table 11-2	Parten's Categories of Social and Non-social Play
Category	**Description**
Unoccupied behaviour	The child does not seem to be playing, but watches anything of momentary interest.
Onlooker behaviour	The child spends most of the time watching other children play. She talks to them, asking questions or making suggestions, but does not enter into the play. She is definitely observing particular groups of children rather than anything that happens to be exciting.
Solitary independent play	The child plays alone with toys that are different from those used by nearby children and makes no effort to get close to them.
Parallel play	The child plays independently, but among the other children, playing with toys like those used by the other children, but not necessarily playing with them in the same way. Playing *beside* rather than *with* the others, the parallel player does not try to influence the other children's play.
Associative play	The child plays with other children. They talk about their play, borrow and lend toys, follow one another, and try to control who may play in the group. All the children play similarly if not identically; there is no division of labour and no organization around any goal. Each child acts as she or he wishes and is interested more in being with the other children than in the activity itself.
Cooperative or organized supplementary play	The child plays in a group organized for some goal—to make something, play a formal game, or dramatize a situation. One or two children control who belongs to the group and direct activities. By a division of labour, children take on different roles and supplement each other's efforts.

Source: Adapted from Parten, 1932, pp. 249–251.

On the other hand, solitary play can be a sign of shyness, anxiety, fearfulness, or social rejection (Coplan et al., 2004; Henderson, Marshall, Fox, & Rubin, 2004; Spinrad et al., 2004). In two Canadian studies of preschoolers and kindergartners, boys who engaged in solitary *passive* play, drawing pictures or building with blocks while peers played nearby, tended to be shy or maladjusted (Coplan, Gavinski-Molina, Lagacé-Séguin, & Wichman, 2001; Coplan, Prakash, O'Neil, & Armer, 2004).

Reticent play, a combination of Parten's onlooker and unoccupied categories, is often a manifestation of shyness (Coplan et al., 2004). However, such reticent behaviours as playing near other children, watching what they do, or wandering aimlessly may sometimes be a prelude to joining in others' play (K. H. Rubin, Bukowski, & Parker, 1998; Spinrad et al., 2004). In a short-term longitudinal study, preschool children were observed in daily free play. Reticent children, though hesitant to join in other children's play, were well-liked and showed few problem behaviours (Spinrad et al., 2004). Nonsocial play, then, seems to be far more complex than Parten imagined.

One kind of play that does become more social during the preschool years is imaginative play, which shifts from solitary pretending to dramatic play involving other children (K. H. Rubin et al., 1998; Singer & Singer, 1990). Children typically engage in more dramatic play when playing with someone else than when playing alone (Bjorklund & Pellegrini, 2002). Young children follow unspoken rules in organizing dramatic play, staking out territory ("I'm the daddy; you're the mommy"), negotiating ("Okay, I'll be the daddy tomorrow"), or setting the scene ("Watch out—there's a train coming!"). As imaginative play becomes increasingly collaborative, storylines become more complex and more innovative. Dramatic play offers rich opportunities to practise interpersonal and language skills and to explore social roles and conventions (Bergen, 2002; Bodrova & Leong, 1998; Bjorklund & Pellegrini, 2002; Christie, 1991; J. E. Johnson, 1998; Nourot, 1998; Smith, 2005a).

How Gender Influences Play

Boys of all ages engage in more physical play than girls (Bjorklund & Pellegrini, 2002; Smith, 2005b). Boys and girls are equally likely to play with objects, but boys do so more vigorously (Smith, 2005b). Girls tend to use objects for making things, such as puzzles and art projects, whereas boys are more likely to use objects as weapons (Pellegrini & Gustafson, 2005).

A tendency toward sex segregation in play seems to be universal across cultures (Smith, 2005a). It is common among preschoolers as young as 3 and becomes even more common in middle childhood (Maccoby, 1988, 1990, 1994; Ramsey & Lasquade, 1996; Snyder, West, Stockemer, Gibbons, & Almquist-Parks, 1996). Although biology (sex hormones), gender identification, and adult reinforcement all seem to influence gender differences in play, the influence of the peer group may be more powerful (Smith, 2005a). Boys tend to like active, outdoor physical play in large mixed-age groups; girls prefer quiet,

Checkpoint ✔

Can you . . .

✔ Describe four cognitive levels of play, according to Piaget and others, and six categories of social and non-social play, according to Parten?

✔ Explain the connection between the cognitive and social dimensions of play?

Preschool boys and girls prefer different types of play. Boys engage in rough-and-tumble play; girls play more quietly and cooperatively.

harmonious play with one playmate. Boys play spontaneously on sidewalks, streets, or empty lots; girls tend to choose more structured, adult-supervised activities (Benenson, 1993; Bjorklund & Pellegrini, 2002; Fabes, Martin, & Hanish, 2003; Serbin, Moller, Gulko, Powlishta, & Colburne, 1994; Smith, 2005a).

Girls engage in more dramatic play than boys. Boys' pretend play often involves danger or discord and competitive, dominant roles, as in mock battles. Girls' pretend stories generally focus on social relationships and nurturing, domestic roles, as in playing house (Bjorklund & Pellegrini, 2002; Pellegrini & Archer, 2005; Smith, 2005a). However, boys' play is more strongly gender-stereotyped than girls' (Bjorklund & Pellegrini, 2002). Thus, in mixed-sex groups, play tends to revolve around traditionally masculine activities (Fabes et al., 2003).

How Culture Influences Play

The frequency of specific forms of play differs across cultures and is influenced by the play environments adults set up for children, which in turn reflect cultural values (Bodrova & Leong, 1998).

One observational study compared 48 middle-class Korean-American and 48 middle-class Anglo-American children in separate preschools (Farver, Kim, & Lee, 1995). The Anglo-American preschools, in keeping with typical American values, encouraged independent thinking, problem solving, and active involvement in learning by letting children select from a wide range of activities. The Korean-American preschool, in keeping with traditional Korean values, emphasized developing academic skills and completing tasks. The Anglo-American preschools encouraged social interchange among children and collaborative activities with teachers. In the Korean-American preschool, children were allowed to talk and play only during outdoor recess.

Not surprisingly, the Anglo-American children engaged in more social play, whereas the Korean-Americans engaged in more unoccupied or parallel play. Korean-American children played more cooperatively, often offering toys to other children—very likely a reflection of their culture's emphasis on group harmony. Anglo-American children were more aggressive and often responded negatively to other children's suggestions, reflecting the competitiveness of American culture.

Checkpoint ✔

Can you . . .

✔ Tell how gender and culture influence the way children play, and give examples?

Guidepost 4

How do parenting practices influence development?

Parenting

As children gradually become their own persons, their upbringing can be a complex challenge. Parents must deal with small people who have minds and wills of their own, but who still have a lot to learn about what kinds of behaviour work well in a civilized society. How do parents discipline children and teach them self-discipline? Are some ways of parenting more effective than others?

Forms of Discipline

The word *discipline* means "instruction or "training." In the field of child development, **discipline** refers to methods of moulding character and of teaching self-control and acceptable behaviour. It can be a powerful tool for socialization. What forms of discipline work best? Researchers have looked at a wide range of techniques. Although discipline involves imparting knowledge and skill, it is often confused with punishment and control (Psychosocial Paediatrics Committee, Canadian Paediatric Society [CPS], 1997). There are other ways of disciplining children that are more effective than using punishment.

Reinforcement and Punishment

"What are we going to do with that child?" Noel's mother says. "The more we punish him, the more he misbehaves!"

discipline Methods of moulding children's character and of teaching them to exercise self-control and engage in acceptable behaviour

Parents sometimes punish children to stop undesirable behaviour, but children usually learn more from being reinforced for good behaviour. *External* reinforcements may be tangible (candy, money, toys, or gold stars) or intangible (a smile, a word of praise, a hug, extra attention, or a special privilege). Whatever the reinforcement, the child must see it as rewarding and must receive it fairly consistently after showing the desired behaviour. Eventually, the behaviour should provide its own *internal* reward: a sense of pleasure or accomplishment. In Noel's case, his parents often ignore him when he behaves well but scold or spank him when he acts up. In other words, they unwittingly reinforce his *mis*behaviour by giving him attention when he does what they do *not* want him to do.

Still, at times punishment is commonly used. Children may have to be prevented from running out into traffic or hitting another child. Sometimes a child is wilfully defiant. In such situations, punishment, if consistent, immediate, and clearly tied to the offence, may be effective. It should be administered calmly, in private, and aimed at eliciting compliance, not guilt. It is most effective when accompanied by a short, simple explanation (Baumrind, 1996a, 1996b; CPS, 1997). However, the Canadian Paediatric Society recommends against corporal punishment, like disciplinary spanking, and recommends alternatives like time-out and away-from-the-moment reasoning (CPS, 1997).

Imprudent punishment can be counterproductive. Children who are punished harshly and frequently may have trouble interpreting other people's actions and words; they may attribute hostile intentions where none exist (B. Weiss, Dodge, Bates, & Pettit, 1992). Young children who have been punished harshly may later act aggressively, even though the punishment is intended to stop what a parent sees as purposely aggressive behaviour (Nix et al., 1999). Or such children may become passive because they feel helpless. Children may become frightened if parents lose control and may eventually try to avoid a punitive parent, undermining the parent's ability to influence behaviour (Grusec & Goodnow, 1994).

Corporal punishment has been defined as "the use of physical force with the intention of causing a child to experience pain, but not injury, to correct or control the child's behaviour" (Straus, 1994a, p. 4). It can include spanking, hitting, slapping, pinching, shaking (which can be fatal to infants), and other physical acts. Its use is extremely common in Canada and the United States—so much so that it is as a pervasive part of the socialization of many children. Corporal punishment is popularly believed to be more effective than other remedies and to be harmless if done in moderation by loving parents. Corporal punishment is popularly believed to be more effective than other remedies and to be harmless if done in moderation by loving parents (McLoyd & Smith, 2002); but a growing body of evidence suggests that these beliefs are untrue, that corporal punishment can have serious negative consequences, and that it should not be used (MacMillan et al., 1999; Straus, 1999; Straus & Stewart, 1999; see Box 11-2). Outside of the family and despite section 43 of the Canadian Criminal Code, provincial laws like Ontario's Day Nurseries Act prohibit the use of corporal punishment, harsh or degrading measures, or the deprivation of basic needs in disciplining children by daycare workers (Revised Regulations of Ontario, 1990).

corporal punishment Use of physical force with the intention of causing pain, but not injury, to correct or control behaviour

Unlike child abuse, which bears little or no relationship to the child's personality or behaviour, corporal punishment is more frequently used with children who are aggressive and hard to manage, characteristics that may be genetically based (Jaffee et al., 2004). The line between some forms of punishment and physical or emotional abuse is not always easy to draw, but "discipline" clearly becomes abusive when it results in injury to a child. Long-term effects of corporal punishment include lifetime prevalence of anxiety, alcohol abuse, and externalizing behaviour problems (Gray, 2002).

Psychological aggression refers to verbal attacks that may result in psychological harm, such as (1) yelling or screaming, (2) threatening to spank or hit the child, (3) swearing or cursing at the child, (4) threatening to send the child away or kick the child out of the house, and (5) calling the child dumb or lazy. Some psychologists equate the last three categories with emotional abuse. Psychological aggression, like physical aggression (spanking), is almost universal among North American parents. In a nationally representative sampling of 991 parents, 98 percent reported using some form of psychological aggression by the time a child was 5, and about 90 percent thereafter (Straus & Field, 2003).

psychological aggression Verbal attack by a parent that may result in psychological harm to a child

Box 11-2 *The Case Against Corporal Punishment*

"Spare the rod and spoil the child" may sound old-fashioned, but corporal punishment has become a hot issue. Many people still believe that spanking instills respect for authority, motivates good behaviour, and is a necessary part of responsible parenting (Kazdin & Benjet, 2003). Recent court challenges of section 43 of the Canadian Criminal Code, which was ultimately upheld, have made corporal punishment a live issue today. While some professionals view corporal punishment as verging on child abuse (Straus, 1994b); they consider it wrong to inflict pain on children and warn that "violence begets violence" (Kazdin & Benjet, 2003), others defend it as necessary or desirable in moderation, when prudently administered by loving parents (Baumrind, 1996a, 1996b; Baumrind et al., 2002).

At this writing, corporal punishment is banned in Austria, Bulgaria, Croatia, Cyprus, Denmark, Finland, Germany, Hungary, Iceland, Israel, Latvia, Norway, Romania, Sweden, and Ukraine. In the United States, corporal punishment in schools has been outlawed in at least 28 states (Randall, 2005). All states except Minnesota allow parents to administer it, though some insist that it be reasonable, appropriate, moderate, or necessary, and some recognize that excessive corporal punishment can be abusive (Gershoff, 2002). The Supreme Court of Canada in January 2004 ruled out corporal punishment in schools and also forbade it for infants or teenagers in any setting (Center for Effective Discipline, 2005). The United Nations Convention on the Rights of Children opposes all forms of physical violence against children.

Yet in Canada, considered to be a society that is intolerant of physical punishment (Durrant, 1995), an estimated 70 to 90 percent of parents spank their children, and one-third of those report doing so at least once a week (Durrant, Broberg, & Rose-Krasnor, 1999). While over half of Canadians report being spanked, almost three-quarters believe that spanking should be a legal option for parents (Today's Family News, undated; Douglas, 2006). Canadian mothers are more likely than Swedish mothers to spank their children, and the likelihood of spanking is higher if mothers have a positive attitude towards spanking and believe that their children's behaviours are changeable (Durrant et al., 1999). In fact, 80 percent of respondents in a retrospective study of non-abused adults in Ontario reported having experienced some form of corporal punishment as children (MacMillan et al., 1999).

Attitudes of approval of corporal punishment is related to values and common practices in different parts of the world (Douglas, 2006). These attitudes also seem to be related to the degree to which violence in general is tolerated in the family (Douglas, 2006).

Some form of corporal, or bodily, punishment is widely used on infants, and it is virtually universal among parents of toddlers. In interviews with a nationally representative sample of 991 parents in 1995, 35 percent reported using corporal punishment—usually hand slapping—on infants during the previous year, and fully 94 percent on 3- and 4-year-olds. About half of the parents were still hitting children by age 12, one-third at age 14, and 13 percent at age 17 (Straus & Stewart, 1999).*

Why do parents hit children? No doubt, because hitting gets children to comply (Gershoff, 2002). Opponents of corporal punishment are not against disciplining children, but they maintain there are more effective, less risky or harmful ways to do it. A large body of research has consistently found negative outcomes from its use. Apart from the risk of injury to the child, these outcomes include increased physical aggression in childhood and anxiety disorders, depression, alcohol problems, antisocial behaviour, or partner abuse later in life (Gershoff, 2002; MacMillan et al., 1999; Strassberg, Dodge, Pettit, & Bates, 1994).

A child who is spanked is likely to imitate that behaviour. Studies show that children who are spanked tend to become aggressive.

Power Assertion, Induction, and Withdrawal of Love

power assertion Disciplinary strategy to discourage undesirable behaviour through physical or verbal enforcement of parental control

inductive techniques Disciplinary techniques designed to induce desirable behaviour by appealing to a child's sense of reason and fairness

withdrawal of love Disciplinary strategy that may involve ignoring, isolating, or showing dislike for a child

Reinforcement and punishment are not the only ways to influence behaviour. Contemporary research has focused on three broader categories of discipline: *power assertion, induction,* and *temporary withdrawal of love.*

Power assertion is intended to stop or discourage undesirable behaviour through physical or verbal enforcement of parental control; it includes demands, threats, withdrawal of privileges, and spanking. **Inductive techniques** are designed to induce desirable behaviour (or discourage undesirable behaviour) by reasoning with a child; they include setting limits, demonstrating logical consequences of an action, explaining, discussing, and getting ideas from the child about what is fair. **Withdrawal of love** may take the form of ignoring, isolating, or showing dislike for a child. The choice and effectiveness of a disciplinary strategy may depend on the personality of the parent, the personality and age of the child, and the quality of their relationship, as well as on culturally based customs and expectations (Grusec & Goodnow, 1994).

(continued)

Most of this research was cross-sectional or retrospective, and the few longitudinal studies did not consider that the spanked children may have been aggressive in the first place, and that their aggressive behaviour might have led their parents to spank them (Gershoff, 2002). Since 1997 several large, American, nationally representative landmark studies (Brezina, 1999; Gunnoe & Mariner, 1997; Simons, Lin, & Gordon, 1998; Straus, Sugarman, & Giles-Sims, 1997; and Straus & Paschall, 1999) have overcome this defect by taking account of the child's own behaviour at the time of first measurement.

These studies, which included youngsters ranging from age 3 through adolescence, found that corporal punishment is counterproductive: the more a child receives, the more aggressive or antisocial the child's behaviour becomes, and the more likely that child is to show antisocial or other maladaptive behaviour as a child and as an adult (Straus & Stewart, 1999).

Why is this so? One answer is that physical punishment stimulates aggressive behaviour by leading children to imitate the punisher and to consider infliction of pain an acceptable response to problems. Furthermore, as with any punishment, the effectiveness of spanking diminishes with repeated use; children may feel free to misbehave if they are willing to take the consequences. Reliance on physical punishment may weaken parents' authority when children become teenagers and most parents recognize that spanking becomes inappropriate—if not impractical (AAP Committee on Psychosocial Aspects of Child and Family Health, 1998; Gershoff, 2002; McCord, 1996; Psychosocial Paediatrics Committee of the Canadian Paediatric Society, 1997).

Spanking may even inhibit cognitive development, according to data on 2- to 4-year-olds and 5- to 9-year-olds from the U.S. National Longitudinal Study of Youth. Children whose mothers used little or no corporal punishment (such as spanking or hand-slapping) during a 2-week period showed greater cognitive gains than children who received corporal punishment (Straus & Paschall, 1999).

Critics of this research point out that corporal punishment does not occur in isolation; we cannot be sure that the observed outcomes were attributable to it and not to other parental behaviours or family circumstances, such as stressful events, marital discord, lack of parental warmth, or substance abuse (Kazdin & Benjet, 2003). A 6-year study of 1,990 European American, African American, and Hispanic children found that spanking does *not* predict an increase in problem behaviour *if* it is done in the context of a mother's strong emotional support (McLoyd & Smith, 2002). Also, physical discipline is less likely to cause aggression or anxiety in cultures where it is seen as normal, such as in Kenya (Lansford et al., 2005).

Still, the research strongly suggests that frequent or severe corporal punishment is potentially harmful to children. Furthermore, there is no clear line between mild and harsh spanking, and one often leads to the other (Kazdin & Benjet, 2003). Thus, even though no harm from very mild spanking has been established (Larzalere, 2000), it seems prudent to choose other, less risky means of discipline that have *no* potentially adverse effects (Kazdin & Benjet, 2003).

The CPS Psychosocial Paediatrics Committee urges parents to avoid spanking. Instead, the committee suggests such inductive methods as helping children learn to use words to express feelings, giving children choices and helping them evaluate the consequences, and modelling orderly behaviour and collaborative conflict resolution. The committee recommends positive reinforcement to encourage desired behaviours, and verbal reprimands, "time-outs," or removal of privileges to discourage undesired behaviours—all within a positive, supportive, loving parent–child relationship.

What's your view ❓

Did your parents ever spank you? If so, how often and in what kinds of situations? Would you spank, or have you ever spanked, your own child? Why or why not?

Check it out ❗

For more information and relevant links on this topic, go to the Online Learning Centre at **www.mcgrawhill.ca/olc/papalia.**

*Unless otherwise referenced, the material and viewpoint in this box are based on Straus (1999) and Straus & Stewart (1999).

Most parents call upon more than one strategy, depending on the situation. Parents tend to use reasoning to get a child to show concern for others. They use power assertion to stop play that becomes too rough, and they use both power assertion and reasoning to deal with lying and stealing (Grusec & Goodnow, 1994).

The strategy parents choose may depend not only on their belief in its effectiveness but on their confidence that they can carry it out. In one observational study of parental handling of sibling conflicts, mothers were more likely to use inductive techniques, while fathers were more likely to use power-assertive strategies. Still, what both mothers and fathers did most often was not to intervene at all (Perozynski & Kramer, 1999).

An important goal of socialization is to help a child internalize parental teachings in the form of self-discipline. Induction is usually the most effective method, and power assertion the least effective, of getting children to accept parental standards (M. L. Hoffman, 1970a, 1970b). Kindergartners whose mothers reported using reasoning were more likely to see the moral wrongness of behaviour that hurts other people (as opposed to merely breaking rules) than children whose mothers took away privileges (Jagers, Bingham, & Hans, 1996). This may be because removal of privileges encourages children to focus on themselves and their own feelings rather than on the way their behaviour affects others (McCord, 1996).

The effectiveness of parental discipline may hinge on how well the child understands and accepts the parent's message, both cognitively and emotionally (Grusec & Goodnow, 1994). For the child to accept the message, the child has to recognize it as appropriate; so parents need to be fair and accurate, and clear and consistent about their expectations. They need to fit their actions to the misdeed and to the child's temperament and cognitive and emotional level. A child may be more motivated to accept the message if the parents are normally warm and responsive, if they arouse the child's empathy for someone harmed by the misdeed, and if they make the child feel less secure in their affections as a result of the misbehaviour (Grusec & Goodnow, 1994). How well children accept a disciplinary method also may depend on whether the type of discipline used is normative, that is, accepted in the family's culture (Lansford et al., 2005).

One point on which experts agree is that a child interprets and responds to discipline in the context of an ongoing relationship with a parent. Some researchers therefore have looked beyond specific parental practices to overall styles, or patterns, of parenting.

Parenting Styles

Why does Stacy hit and bite the nearest person when she cannot finish a jigsaw puzzle? What makes David sit and sulk when he cannot finish the puzzle, even though his teacher offers to help him? Why does François work on the puzzle for 20 minutes and then shrug and try another? Why are children so different in their responses to the same situation? Temperament is a major factor, of course; but some research suggests that styles of parenting may affect children's competence in dealing with their world.

Diana Baumrind and the Effectiveness of Authoritative Parenting

In her pioneering research, Diana Baumrind (1971, 1996b; Baumrind & Black, 1967) studied 103 preschool children from 95 families. Through interviews, testing, and home studies, she measured how children were functioning, identified three parenting styles, and described typical behaviour patterns of children raised according to each.

Authoritarian parents, according to Baumrind, value control and unquestioning obedience. They try to make children conform to a set standard of conduct and punish them arbitrarily and forcefully for violating it. They are more detached and less warm than other parents. Their children tend to be more discontented, withdrawn, and distrustful.

Permissive parents value self-expression and self-regulation. They make few demands and allow children to monitor their own activities as much as possible. When they do have to make rules, they explain the reasons for them. They consult with children about policy decisions and rarely punish. They are warm, non-controlling, and undemanding. Their preschool children tend to be immature—the least self-controlled and the least exploratory.

Authoritative parents value a child's individuality but also stress social constraints. They have confidence in their ability to guide children, but they also respect children's independent decisions, interests, opinions, and personalities. They are loving and accepting, but also demand good behaviour, are firm in maintaining standards, and are willing to impose limited, judicious punishment when necessary, within the context of a warm, supportive relationship. They explain the reasoning behind their stands and encourage verbal give-and-take. Their children apparently feel secure in knowing both that they are loved and what is expected of them. These preschoolers tend to be the most self-reliant, self-controlled, self-assertive, exploratory, and content.

Eleanor Maccoby and John Martin (1983) added a fourth parenting style—**neglectful, or uninvolved**—to describe parents who, sometimes because of stress or depression, focus on their own needs rather than on those of the child. Neglectful parenting, discussed in Chapter 9, has been linked with a variety of behavioural disorders in childhood and adolescence (Baumrind, 1991; Parke & Buriel, 1998; R. A. Thompson, 1998).

Why does authoritative parenting seem to enhance children's competence? It may be because authoritative parents set sensible expectations and realistic standards. By making

Checkpoint ✔

Can you . . .

✔ Compare various forms of discipline and identify factors that influence their effectiveness?

What's your view ❓

• As a parent, what form of discipline would you favour if your 3-year-old "stole" a cookie from the cookie jar? Refused to take a nap? Hit his little sister? Tell why.

authoritarian Baumrind's term for parenting style emphasizing control and obedience

permissive Baumrind's term for parenting style emphasizing self-expression and self-regulation

authoritative Baumrind's term for parenting style blending respect for a child's individuality with an effort to instill social values

neglectful/uninvolved Maccoby and Martin's term for parents who focus on their own needs rather than on those of the child

clear, consistent rules, they let children know what is expected of them. In authoritarian homes, children are so strictly controlled that often they cannot make independent choices about their own behaviour. In permissive homes, children receive so little guidance that they may become uncertain and anxious about whether they are doing the right thing. In authoritative homes, children know when they are meeting expectations and can decide whether it is worth risking parental displeasure to pursue a goal. These children are expected to perform well, fulfill commitments, and participate actively in family duties as well as family fun. They know the satisfaction of meeting responsibilities and achieving success. Parents who make reasonable demands show that they believe their children can meet them—and that the parents care enough to insist that they do.

The question of how much freedom children should be allowed is a major source of conflict between parents and children in mainstream Canadian culture. Most Canadian parents believe that even preschoolers are entitled to their own opinions and should have control over some aspects of their lives so as to promote competence and self-esteem. However, the precise boundaries where a child's area of autonomy ends and the area of parental control begins are matters of negotiation and may vary among ethnic and socioeconomic groups (Nucci & Smetana, 1996). When conflict arises, an authoritative parent can teach the child positive ways to communicate his or her own point of view and negotiate acceptable alternatives. ("If you don't want to throw away those smelly clam shells you found, where do you think we should keep them?") Internalization of this broader set of skills, not just of specific behavioural demands, may well be a key to the success of authoritative parenting (Grusec & Goodnow, 1994).

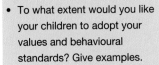

What's your view

- To what extent would you like your children to adopt your values and behavioural standards? Give examples.

Support and Criticisms of Baumrind's Model

Baumrind's work has inspired much research, and the superiority of authoritative parenting (or similar conceptions of parenting style) has repeatedly been supported (Baumrind, 1989; Darling & Steinberg, 1993). For example, a longitudinal study of 585 ethnically and socio-economically diverse families in Tennessee and Indiana from pre-kindergarten through Grade 6 found that four aspects of early supportive parenting—warmth, use of inductive discipline, interest and involvement in children's contacts with peers, and proactive teaching of social skills—predicted children's later behavioural, social, and academic outcomes (Pettit, Bates, & Dodge, 1997). Likewise, the NLSCY found that positive parenting practices were associated with the development of pro-social behaviour in children, and that the effects of responsive parenting on child outcomes become stronger as children get older (Chao & Willms, 2002).

Similar principles apply to teachers and other caregivers. In a low-income daycare centre for 3- to 6-year-olds at risk for developing disruptive behaviour, teachers' laxity (similar to permissive parenting) tended to elicit misbehaviour; and children's misbehaviour, in turn, elicited either laxity or overreactivity (similar in some ways to authoritarian parenting) from the teachers. The results suggest that teachers, like parents, need to learn how to set and enforce firm, consistent, and appropriate rules (Arnold, McWilliams, & Arnold, 1998).

Still, because Baumrind's model seems to suggest that there is one "right" way to raise children well, it has provoked some controversy. Since Baumrind's findings were correlational, they merely establish associations between each parenting style and a particular set of child behaviours. They do not show that different styles of child rearing *cause* children to be more or less competent. Sandra Scarr (1992, 1993), for example, argues that heredity normally exerts a much greater influence than parenting practices.

It is also impossible to know whether the children Baumrind studied were, in fact, raised in a particular style. It may be that some of the better-adjusted children were raised inconsistently, but by the time of the study their parents had adopted the authoritative pattern. Furthermore, parents often behave differently in different situations (Holden & Miller, 1999).

In addition, Baumrind did not consider innate factors, such as temperament, that might have affected children's competence and exerted an influence on the parents. Parents of "easy" children may be more likely to respond to the child in a permissive or authoritative manner, while parents of "difficult" children may become more authoritarian.

Cultural Differences in Parenting Styles

Baumrind's categories reflect the dominant North American view of child development and may be misleading when applied to some cultures or socio-economic groups. Among Chinese parents, for example, obedience and strictness—rather than being associated with harshness and domination—have more to do with caring, concern, and involvement and with maintaining family harmony. Traditional Chinese culture, with its emphasis on respect for elders, stresses adults' responsibility to maintain the social order by teaching children socially proper behaviour. This obligation is carried out through firm and just control and governance of the child and even by physical punishment if necessary (Zhao, 2002). Although Asian immigrant parenting in North America is frequently described as authoritarian, the warmth and supportiveness that characterize Chinese-immigrant family relationships more closely resemble Baumrind's authoritative parenting.

Still, a dichotomy between the individualistic values of western parenting and the collectivist values of Asian parenting may be overly simplistic. In interviews with 64 Japanese mothers of 3- to 6-year-olds (Yamada, 2004), the mothers' descriptions of their parenting practices reflected the search for a balance between granting appropriate autonomy and exercising disciplinary control. The mothers let children make their own decisions within what they saw as the child's personal domain, such as play activities, playmates, and clothing, and this domain enlarged with the child's age. When health, safety, moral issues, or conventional social rules were involved, the mothers set limits or exercised control. When conflicts arose, the mothers used reason rather than power-assertive methods or sometimes gave in to the child, apparently on the theory that the issue wasn't worth struggling over—or that the child might be right after all.

In general, Canadian parents adopt a positive parenting style, characterized by offering support and encouragement to children (Landy & Tam, 1996). Positive parenting approaches are associated with good developmental outcomes in social development and helping behaviour. However, children are particularly vulnerable to poor developmental outcomes if their family situations contain more than several risk factors including family dysfunction, low social support, being in a single-parent family, having a teenage parent, and living in poverty (Willms, 2002). The impact of these factors on child development is typically diminished by positive parenting practices (Landy & Tam, 1996).

The traditional Aboriginal parenting style in Canada is much like Baumrind's permissive style (Neckoway, Brownlee & Castellan, 2007). However, as is the case with the preferred parenting style in families of Asian background, there is no detrimental influence on Aboriginal children's development (Johnson & Cremo, 1995). Among Canadian immigrant groups, there are differences in parenting style, which may reflect differences in social values in the countries of origin. Egyptian Canadians, for example, were found to score higher on measures of authoritarianism and collectivism than were Anglo-Canadians (Rudy & Grusec, 2001). The best predictor of authoritarian parenting style in Egyptian Canadian parents was high levels of collectivism, in comparison to individualism, whereas in Anglo-Canadians the best predictor of authoritarian parenting was a combination of collectivism and lack of warmth (Rudy et al., 2001). It may be misleading, then, to consider parenting styles without looking at the goals parents are trying to achieve and the constraints their life circumstances present.

Special Behavioural Concerns

Three specific issues of especial concern to parents, caregivers, and teachers of preschool children are how to promote altruism, curb aggression, and deal with fears that often arise at this age.

Pro-social Behaviour

Alex, at 3½, responded to two fellow preschoolers' complaints that they did not have enough modelling clay, his favourite plaything, by giving them half of his. Alex was showing **altruism**—acting out of concern for another person with no expectation of reward.

Checkpoint ✔

Can you . . .

✔ Describe and evaluate Baumrind's model of parenting styles?

✔ Discuss how parents' way of resolving conflicts with young children can contribute to the success of authoritative child rearing?

✔ Discuss criticisms of Baumrind's model and cultural variations in parenting styles?

Guidepost 5

Why do young children help or hurt others, and why do they develop fears?

altruism Behaviour intended to help others out of inner concern and without expectation of external reward

Altruistic acts like Alex's often entail cost, self-sacrifice, or risk. Altruism is the heart of **pro-social behaviour,** voluntary activity intended to benefit another.

pro-social behaviour Any voluntary behaviour intended to help others

Even before the second birthday, children often help others, share belongings and food, and offer comfort. Such behaviours may reflect a growing ability to imagine how another person might feel (Zahn-Waxler, Radke-Yarrow, Wagner, & Chapman, 1992). An analysis of 179 studies found increasing evidence of concern for others from infancy throughout childhood and adolescence (Fabes & Eisenberg, 1996). Although girls tend to be more pro-social than boys, the differences are small (Eisenberg & Fabes, 1998).

Is there a pro-social personality or disposition? A longitudinal study that followed 32 four- and 5-year-olds into early adulthood suggests that there is and that it emerges early and remains somewhat consistent throughout life. Preschoolers who were sympathetic and spontaneously shared with classmates tended to show pro-social understanding and empathic behaviour as much as 17 years later. Preschoolers who are shy or withdrawn tend to be less prosocial, perhaps because they hesitate to reach out to others (Coplan et al., 2004).

In a study of pro-social behaviour in children, a team of researchers in Nova Scotia gave children opportunities to share stickers with others, either at no cost to themselves (choosing stickers for themselves and for another person), or at a cost (choosing between taking two stickers or taking one for themselves and giving one to another person). In both cases, 3- and 4-year old children shared, but much more sharing took place in the no-cost condition. When given the choice between immediately receiving a sticker, or waiting awhile to be given a sticker for themselves as well as for another person, older children tended to delay their gratification in order to share, while 3-year-olds tended to choose being given a sticker immediately (Moore, Barresi, & Thompson, 1998).

The family is important as a model and as a source of explicit standards of behaviour (Eisenberg & Fabes, 1998). Genes and environment each contribute to individual differences in pro-social behaviour, an example of gene–environment correlation. This finding comes from a study of 9,319 twin pairs whose pro-social behaviour was rated by parents and teachers at ages 3, 4, and 7. Parents who showed affection and followed positive (inductive) disciplinary strategies tended to encourage their children's natural tendency to pro-social behaviour (Knafo & Plomin, 2006). Parents of pro-social children are typically pro-social themselves. They point out models of pro-social behaviour and steer children toward stories, films, and television programs that depict cooperation, sharing, and empathy and encourage sympathy, generosity, and helpfulness (Singer & Singer, 1998). Relationships with siblings (discussed later in this chapter) provide an important "laboratory" for trying out caring behaviour and learning to see another person's point of view. Peers and teachers also can model and reinforce pro-social behaviour (Eisenberg, 1992; Eisenberg & Fabes, 1998).

Parents encourage pro-social behaviour when they use inductive disciplinary methods instead of power-assertive techniques (Eisenberg & Fabes, 1998). When Sara took candy from a store, her father did not lecture her on honesty, spank her, or tell her what a bad girl she had been. Instead, he explained how the owner of the store would be harmed by her failure to pay for the candy, and he took her back to the store to return it. When such incidents occur, Sara's parents ask, "How do you think Mr. Jones feels?" or, "How would you feel if you were Mr. Jones?"

Motives for pro-social behaviour may change as children grow older and develop more mature moral reasoning (see Chapters 13 and 16). Preschoolers tend to show egocentric motives; they want to earn praise and avoid disapproval. They weigh costs and benefits and consider how they would like others to act toward them. As children grow older, their motives become less self-centred. They adopt societal standards of "being good," which eventually become internalized as principles and values (Eisenberg & Fabes, 1998).

Cultures vary in the degree to which they foster pro-social behaviour. Traditional cultures in which people live in extended family groups and share work seem to foster pro-social values more than cultures that stress individual achievement (Eisenberg & Fabes, 1998).

What's your view ?

• In a society in which "good Samaritans" are sometimes blamed for "butting into other people's business" and sometimes attacked by the very persons they try to help, is it wise to encourage children to offer help to strangers?

Aggression

instrumental aggression
Aggressive behaviour used as a means of achieving a goal

When Peter roughly snatches a ball away from Tommy, he is interested only in getting the ball, not in hurting or dominating Tommy. This is **instrumental aggression,** or aggression used as an instrument to reach a goal—the most common type of aggression in early childhood. Between ages 2½ and 5, children commonly struggle over toys and control of space. Aggression surfaces mostly during social play; children who fight the most also tend to be the most sociable and competent. In fact, the ability to show some instrumental aggression may be a necessary step in social development.

Between ages 2 and 4, as children develop more self-control and become better able to express themselves verbally and to wait for what they want, they typically shift from showing aggression with blows to doing it with words (Coie & Dodge, 1998). However, individual differences remain; children who more frequently hit or grab toys from other children at age 2 are likely to be more physically aggressive at age 5 (Cummings, Iannotti, & Zahn-Waxler, 1989), and children who, as preschoolers, often engaged in violent fantasy play may, at age 6, be prone to violent displays of anger (Dunn & Hughes, 2001).

hostile aggression Aggressive behaviour intended to hurt another person

As aggression declines overall, **hostile aggression**—action intended to hurt another person—proportionately increases (see Chapter 14). Some children do not learn to control aggression; they continue to be destructive and anti-social throughout life (Coie & Dodge, 1998).

Gender Differences in Aggression

Aggression is an exception to the generalization that boys and girls are more similar than different (Hyde, 2005). In all cultures studied, as among most mammals, boys are more physically and verbally aggressive than girls. This gender difference is apparent before age 2 (Archer, 2004; Baillargeon et al., 2007; Pellegrini & Archer, 2005). Research with genetically engineered mice suggests that the SRY gene on the Y chromosome may play a role (Gatewood et al., 2006).

overt, or direct, aggression
Aggression openly directed at its target

relational, or social, aggression Aggression aimed at damaging or interfering with another person's relationships, reputation, or psychological well-being; also called *covert, indirect, or psychological aggression*

However, girls may be more aggressive than they seem; they just show aggressiveness differently (McNeilly-Choque, Hart, Robinson, Nelson, & Olsen, 1996; Putallaz & Bierman, 2004). Boys engage in more **overt aggression,** either instrumental or hostile. Overt aggression, either physical or verbal, is openly directed against its target. Girls tend to practise **relational aggression** (also called *covert, indirect,* or *psychological aggression*). This more subtle kind of aggression consists of damaging or interfering with relationships, reputation, or psychological well-being. It may involve spreading rumours, name-calling, withholding friendship, or excluding someone from a group. It can be either overt or covert (indirect)—for example, making mean faces or ignoring someone. Among preschoolers, it tends to be direct and face-to-face ("You can't come to my party if you don't give me that toy") (Archer, 2004; Brendgen et al., 2005; Crick, Casas, & Nelson, 2002). However, recent trends are showing that gender differences between boys and girls on measures of relational aggression are diminishing (Canadian Council on Learning, 2007) and this trend is reflected in inconsistent findings on gender differences (Merrell, Buchanan, & Tran, 2006).

From an evolutionary perspective, boys' greater overt aggressiveness, like their greater size and strength, may prepare them to compete for a mate (Archer, 2004). Males produce many sperm; females generally produce only one ovum at a time. Males seek to mate as frequently and widely as possible, and they have less investment in each individual offspring; thus they can afford to take the risks of physical aggression. Females are strongly motivated to protect and nurture the few offspring they have; thus they shy away from direct confrontations that could put them at physical risk (Pellegrini & Archer, 2005).

NLSCY data indicate that aggressive girls in Canada experience more difficulty than non-aggressive girls in their family and peer relations, and come from homes with higher levels of ineffective parenting, family violence, and difficulties in relations with parents and with siblings. The types of problems they experience, including emotional, self-concept, and behavioural difficulties, are similar to those of aggressive boys (Pepler & Sedighdeilami, 1998).

Influences on Aggression

Why are some children more aggressive than others?

Biology may play a part. So may temperament: Children who are intensely emotional and low in self-control tend to express anger aggressively (Eisenberg, Fabes, Nyman, Bernzweig, & Pinuelas, 1994). Family relations are also important, particularly for children from lower socio-economic levels: Children from the same family show more similarity in aggression levels than do children from different families (Tremblay et al., 1996; Baillargeon, Tremblay, & Willms, 2002).

Both physical and social aggression have genetic and environmental sources, but their relative influence differs. Among 234 six-year-old twins, physical aggression was 50 to 60 percent heritable; the remainder of the variance was attributable to non-shared environmental influences (unique experiences). Social aggression was much more environmentally influenced; the variance was only 20 percent genetic, 20 percent explained by shared environmental influences, and 60 percent by unshared experiences (Brendgen et al., 2005).

In a classic experiment by Albert Bandura, children who had seen a film of an adult hitting and kicking an inflated clown were more likely to imitate the aggressive behaviour if they had seen the adult being rewarded or experiencing no consequences than if they had seen the adult punished.

A negative early relationship with the mother is an important factor, which may interact with other risk factors, such as low socio-economic status and single parenthood. In longitudinal studies, insecure attachment and lack of maternal warmth and affection in infancy have predicted aggressiveness in early childhood (Coie & Dodge, 1998). Manipulative behaviours such as withdrawal of love and making a child feel guilty or ashamed may foster social aggression (Brendgen et al., 2005). Furthermore, negative parent–child relationships may set the stage for prolonged, destructive sibling conflicts, in which children imitate their parents' hostile behaviour. These coercive family processes (Patterson, 1984) may foster aggressive tendencies. Among 180 low-income 5-year-olds with close-in-age siblings, a combination of rejecting parents (by age 2) and high levels of destructive sibling conflict predicted aggressive or anti-social conduct at home and at school at age 6 (Garcia, Shaw, Winslow, & Yaggi, 2000).

Parents of children who become anti-social often fail to reinforce good behaviour and are harsh or inconsistent, or both, in stopping or punishing misbehaviour (Coie & Dodge, 1998). Parents who back down when confronted with a preschooler's coercive demands (such as whining or shouting when scolded for not going to bed) may reinforce repetition of the undesirable behaviour (G. R. Patterson, 1995). On the other hand, harsh punishment, especially spanking, can backfire; children who are spanked not only suffer frustration, pain, and humiliation (which can be spurs to aggression) but also see aggressive behaviour in an adult model. Manipulative behaviours such as withdrawal of love and making a child feel guilty or ashamed may foster social aggression (Brendgen et al., 2005).

Exposure to real or televised violence can trigger aggression (see Chapter 14). In a study of 431 Head Start participants in an inner-city neighbourhood, parents reported that more than half had witnessed gang activity, drug trafficking, police pursuits and arrests, or people carrying weapons, and some of the children and families had been victimized themselves. These children showed symptoms of distress at home and aggression at school (Farver, Xu, Eppe, Fernandez, & Schwartz, 2005).

Why does witnessing violence lead to aggression? In a classic social learning experiment (Bandura, Ross, & Ross, 1961), 3- to 6-year-olds individually watched adult models play with toys. Children in one experimental group saw the adult play quietly. The model for a second experimental group began to assemble Tinkertoys, but then spent the rest of the 10-minute session punching, throwing, and kicking a life-size inflated doll. A control group did not see any model. After the sessions, the children, who were mildly frustrated by seeing toys they were not allowed to play with, went into another playroom. The children who had seen the aggressive model acted much more aggressively than those in the other groups, imitating many of the same things they had seen the model say and do. The children who had been with the quiet model were less aggressive than the control group. This finding suggests that parents may be able to moderate the effects of frustration by showing non-aggressive behaviour to their children.

Culture and Aggression

How much influence does culture have on aggressive behaviour? One research team asked closely matched samples of 30 Japanese and 30 U.S. middle- to upper-middle-class preschoolers to choose pictured solutions to hypothetical conflicts or stressful situations (such as having one's block tower knocked down, having to stop playing and go to bed, being hit, hearing parents argue, or fighting on a jungle gym). The children also were asked to act out and complete such situations using dolls and props. The U.S. children showed more anger, more aggressive behaviour and language, and less control of emotions than the Japanese children (Zahn-Waxler, Friedman, Cole, Mizuta, & Hiruma, 1996).

These results are consistent with child-rearing values in the two cultures. In Japan, anger and aggression are seen as clashing with the emphasis on harmonious relationships. Japanese mothers are more likely than U.S. mothers to use reasoning and induce guilt, pointing out how aggressive behaviour hurts others. Japanese mothers also show strong disappointment when children fail to meet their behavioural standards. However, the cross-cultural difference in children's anger and aggressiveness was significant even apart from mothers' behaviour, suggesting that temperamental differences also may be at work (Zahn-Waxler et al., 1996).

Fearfulness

Passing fears are common in early childhood. Many 2- to 4-year-olds are afraid of animals, especially dogs. By 6 years, children are more likely to be afraid of the dark. Other common fears are of thunderstorms, doctors, and imaginary creatures (DuPont, 1983; Stevenson-Hinde & Shouldice, 1996). Most of these disappear as children grow older and lose their sense of powerlessness.

Young children's fears stem largely from their intense fantasy life and their tendency to confuse appearance with reality. Sometimes their imaginations become carried away, making them worry about being attacked by a lion or being abandoned. Young children are more likely to be frightened by something that looks scary, such as a cartoon monster, than by something capable of doing great harm, such as a nuclear explosion (Cantor, 1994). For the most part, older children's fears are more realistic and self-evaluative (for example, fear of failing a test), since they know they are being evaluated by others (Stevenson-Hinde & Shouldice, 1996; see Table 11-3).

Fears may come from personal experience or from hearing about other people's experiences (Muris, Merckelbach, & Collaris, 1997). A preschooler whose mother is sick in bed may become upset by a story about a mother's death, even if it is an animal mother. Often fears come from appraisals of danger, such as the likelihood of being bitten by a dog, or are triggered by events, as when a child who was hit by a car becomes afraid to cross the

What's your view ?

• Are there situations in which a child should be encouraged to be aggressive?

Table 11-3	Childhood Fears
Age	**Fears**
0–6 months	Loss of support, loud noises
7–12 months	Strangers; heights; sudden, unexpected, and looming objects
1 year	Separation from parent, toilet, injury, strangers
2 years	Many stimuli, including loud noises (vacuum cleaners, sirens and alarms, trucks, and thunder), animals, dark rooms, separation from parent, large objects or machines, changes in personal environment, unfamiliar peers
3 years	Masks, dark, animals, separation from parent
4 years	Separation from parent, animals, dark, noises (including noises at night)
5 years	Animals, "bad" people, dark, separation from parent, bodily harm
6 years	Supernatural beings (e.g., ghost, witches), bodily injury, thunder and lightning, dark, sleeping or staying alone, separation from parent
7–8 years	Supernatural beings, dark, media events (e.g., news reports on the threat of nuclear war or child kidnapping), staying alone, bodily injury
9–12 years	Tests and examinations in school, school performances, bodily injury, physical appearance, thunder and lightning, death, dark

Source: Adapted from Morris & Kratochwill, 1983; Stevenson-Hinde & Shouldice, 1996.

street. Children who have lived through an earthquake, a kidnapping, or some other frightening event may fear that it will happen again (Kolbert, 1994).

Parents can help prevent children's fears by instilling a sense of trust and normal caution without being too protective, and also by overcoming their own unrealistic fears. They can help a fearful child by reassurance and by encouraging open expression of feelings. Ridicule ("Don't be such a baby!"), coercion ("Pat the nice doggie—it won't hurt you"), and logical persuasion ("The closest bear is 30 kilometres away, locked in a zoo!") are not helpful. Not until elementary school can children tell themselves that what they fear is not real (Cantor, 1994).

Children can also be helped to overcome fears by *systematic desensitization,* a therapeutic technique involving gradual exposure to a feared object or situation. This technique has been used successfully to help children overcome fears ranging from those of snakes to elevators (Murphy & Bootzin, 1973; Sturges & Sturges, 1998).

Relationships with Other Children

Although the most important people in young children's world are the adults who take care of them, relationships with siblings and playmates become more important in early childhood. Virtually every characteristic activity and personality issue of this age, from gender development to pro-social or aggressive behaviour, involves other children. Sibling and peer relationships provide a measuring stick for **self-efficacy,** children's growing sense of capability to master challenges and achieve their goals. By competing with and comparing themselves with other children, they can gauge their physical, social, cognitive, and linguistic competencies and gain a more realistic sense of self (Bandura, 1994).

Siblings—or Their Absence

Ties between brothers and sisters often set the stage for later relationships. Let's look at sibling relationships, and then at children who grow up with no siblings.

Brothers and Sisters

"It's mine!"

"No, it's mine!"

"Well, I was playing with it first!"

The earliest, most frequent, and most intense disputes among siblings are over property rights—who owns a toy or who is entitled to play with it. Although exasperated adults may not always see it that way, sibling disputes and their settlement can be viewed as socialization opportunities, in which children learn to stand up for moral principles. Studies of sibling interactions in Canada have shown that conflict and aggression is common, with conflict around property and possession of objects being the most typical (Perlman & Ross, 1997). Another arena for socialization is joint dramatic play. Siblings who frequently play "let's pretend" develop a history of shared understandings that allow them to more easily resolve issues and build on each other's ideas (Howe et al., 2005).

Despite the frequency of conflict, sibling rivalry is *not* the main pattern between brothers and sisters early in life. While some rivalry exists, so do affection, interest, companionship, and influence. Observations spanning 3½ years, which began when younger siblings were about 1½ years old and the older ones ranged from 3 to 4½, found pro-social and play-oriented behaviours to be more common than rivalry, hostility, and competition (Abramovitch, Corter, & Lando, 1979; Abramovitch, Corter, Pepler, & Stanhope, 1986; Abramovitch, Pepler, & Corter, 1982). Older siblings initiated more behaviour, both friendly and unfriendly; younger siblings tended to imitate the older ones. Siblings got along better when their mother was not with them. (Squabbling can be a bid for parental attention.) As the younger children reached their fifth birthday, the siblings became less physical and more verbal, both in showing aggression (through commands, insults, threats, tattling, put-downs, bribes, and teasing) and in showing care and affection (by compliments and comforting rather than hugs and kisses).

Checkpoint ✔

Can you . . .

✔ Discuss influences that contribute to altruism, aggression, and fearfulness?

Guidepost 6

How do young children get along with—or without—siblings, playmates, and friends?

self-efficacy Sense of one own's capability to master challenges and achieve goals

At least one finding of this research has been replicated in many studies: same-sex siblings, particularly girls, are closer and play together more peaceably than boy-girl pairs (Kier & Lewis, 1998). Because older siblings tend to dominate younger ones, the quality of the relationship is more affected by the emotional and social adjustment of the older child than of the younger (Pike et al., 2005). The quality of relationships with brothers and sisters often carries over to relationships with other children; a child who is aggressive with siblings is likely to be aggressive with friends as well. However, a child who is dominated by an older sibling may be able to take a dominant role with a playmate (Abramovitch et al., 1986), whereas siblings who frequently play amicably together tend to develop pro-social behaviours (Pike, Coldwell, & Dunn, 2005). Children with siblings get along better with kindergarten classmates than do only children (Downey & Condron, 2004).

By the same token, friendships can influence sibling relationships. Older siblings who have experienced a good relationship with a friend before the birth of a new baby are likely to treat their younger siblings better and are less likely to develop anti-social behaviour in adolescence (Kramer & Kowal, 2005). For a young child at risk for behavioural problems, a positive relationship with *either* a sibling or a friend can buffer the effect of a negative relationship with the other (McElwain & Volling, 2005).

The Only Child

Are only children spoiled, selfish, lonely, or maladjusted? That stereotype goes back to some of the early pioneers in psychology. Sigmund Freud claimed that only children were at risk for problems of sexual identity, and G. Stanley Hall maintained that being an only child is damaging (Falbo, 2006). Yet, such apparently well-adjusted public figures as the musician Van Cliburn, and the movie actress Natalie Portman all were only children.

An analysis of 115 studies, "onlies" do comparatively well (Falbo & Polit, 1986; Polit & Falbo, 1987). In occupational and educational achievement and intelligence, they surpass children with siblings. Only children also tend to be more mature and motivated to achieve and to have higher self-esteem. They do not differ, however, in overall adjustment or sociability. Perhaps these children do better because their parents spend more time with them and focus more attention on them, talk to them more, do more with them, and expect more of them than in families with more than one child (Falbo, 2006; Falbo & Polit, 1986; Polit & Falbo, 1987). And, because most children today spend considerable time in play groups, child care, and preschool, only children do not lack opportunities for social interaction with peers. Such factors as genetic predispositions and parents' educational level, SES, emotional health, values, and parenting styles play a much bigger part in a child's development than family size (Falbo, 2006).

Research in China also has produced largely encouraging findings about only children. In 1979, to control an exploding population, the People's Republic of China established an official policy of limiting families to one child each, enforced by a system of rewards and punishments. Although the policy has since been relaxed somewhat, most urban families now have only one child, and most rural families no more than two (Hesketh, Lu, & Xing, 2005). Thus, in many Chinese cities, schoolrooms are almost completely filled with children who have no brothers or sisters. This situation offered researchers a natural experiment: an opportunity to study the adjustment of large numbers of only children.

A review of the literature found no significant differences in behavioural problems (Tao, 1998). Indeed, only children seemed to be at a distinct psychological advantage in a society that favours and rewards such a child. Among 731 urban children and adolescents, those with siblings reported higher levels of fear, anxiety, and depression than only children, regardless of sex or age (Yang et al., 1995).

Among 4,000 third and sixth graders, personality differences between only children and those with siblings—as rated by parents, teachers, peers, and the children themselves—were few. Only children's academic achievement and physical growth were about the same as, or better than, those with siblings (Falbo & Poston, 1993). In a randomized study in Beijing first-grade classrooms (Jiao, Ji, & Jing, 1996), only children outperformed classmates with siblings in memory, language, and mathematics skills. This finding may reflect

Checkpoint ✔

Can you . . .

✔ Explain how the resolution of sibling disputes contributes to socialization?

✔ Tell how birth order and gender affect typical patterns of sibling interaction?

Checkpoint ✔

Can you . . .

✔ Compare development of only children with that of children with siblings?

the greater attention, stimulation, hopes, and expectations that parents shower on a baby they know will be their first and last.

Most of the studies used urban samples. Further research may reveal whether the findings hold up in rural areas and small towns, where children with siblings are more numerous, and whether only children maintain their cognitive superiority as they move through school.

Playmates and Friends

Friendships develop as people develop. Toddlers play alongside or near each other, but not until about age 3 do children begin to have friends. Through friendships and interactions with casual playmates, young children learn how to get along with others. They learn that being a friend is the way to have a friend. They learn how to solve problems in relationships, they learn how to put themselves in another person's place, and they see models of various kinds of behaviour. They learn moral values and gender-role norms, and they practise adult roles.

Choosing Playmates and Friends

Preschoolers usually like to play with children of their own age and sex. In preschool, they tend to spend most of their time with a few other children with whom they have had positive experiences and whose behaviour is like their own. Children who have frequent positive experiences with each other are most likely to become friends (Rubin et al., 1998; Snyder et al., 1996). About 3 out of 4 preschoolers have such mutual friendships (Hartup & Stevens, 1999).

The traits that young children look for in a playmate are similar to the traits they look for in a friend (C. H. Hart, DeWolf, Wozniak, & Burts, 1992). In one study, 4- to 7-year-olds rated the most important features of friendships as doing things together, liking and caring for each other, sharing and helping one another, and to a lesser degree, living nearby or going to the same school. Younger children rated physical traits, such as appearance and size, higher than did older ones and rated affection and support lower (Furman & Bierman, 1983). Preschool children prefer pro-social playmates (C. H. Hart et al., 1992). They reject disruptive, demanding, intrusive, or aggressive children and ignore those who are shy, withdrawn, or tentative (Coplan, et al., 2004; Ramsey & Lasquade, 1996; Roopnarine & Honig, 1985).

Well-liked preschoolers and kindergartners, and those who are rated by parents and teachers as socially competent, generally cope well with anger. They respond directly, in ways that minimize further conflict and keep relationships going. They avoid insults and threats. Unpopular children tend to hit back or tattle (Fabes & Eisenberg, 1992).

Characteristics and Effects of Friendships

Preschoolers act differently with their friends and with other children. They have more positive, pro-social interactions, but also more quarrels and fights (Rubin et al., 1998). Children may become just as angry with a friend as with someone they dislike, but they are more likely to control their anger and express it constructively (Fabes, Eisenberg, Smith, & Murphy, 1996).

Friendships are more satisfying—and more likely to last—when children see them as relatively harmonious and as validating their self-worth. Being able to confide in friends and get help from them is less important at this age than when children are older (Ladd, Kochenderfer, & Coleman, 1996).

Children with friends enjoy school more (Ladd & Hart, 1992). Among 125 kindergartners, those who had friends in their class when they entered in August liked school better 2 months later, and those who kept up these friendships continued to like school better the following May. Children whose friendships are a source of help and self-validation are happier, have more positive attitudes toward school, and feel they can look to classmates for support (Ladd et al., 1996).

Parenting and Popularity

Parenting styles and practices can influence peer relationships. Popular children generally have warm, positive relationships with both mother and father. The parents are likely to be authoritative, and the children to be both assertive and cooperative (Coplan et al., 2004; Isley, O'Neil, & Parke, 1996; Kochanska, 1992; Roopnarine & Honig, 1985). Children whose parents are authoritarian may become shy or withdrawn (Coplan et al., 2004). Children who are insecurely attached or whose parents are harsh, neglectful, or depressed or have troubled marriages are at risk of developing unattractive social and emotional patterns and of being rejected by peers (Rubin et al., 1998).

Children whose parents rely on power-assertive discipline tend to use coercive tactics in peer relations; children whose parents engage in give-and-take reasoning are more likely to resolve conflicts with peers that way (Crockenberg & Lourie, 1996). Children whose parents clearly communicate disapproval rather than anger, as well as strong positive feelings, are more pro-social, less aggressive, and better liked (Boyum & Parke, 1995).

Checkpoint ✔

Can you . . .

✔ Explain how preschoolers choose playmates and friends, how they behave with friends, and how they benefit from friendships?

✔ Discuss how relationships at home can influence relationships with peers?

Summary and Key Terms

The Developing Self

Guidepost 1 How does the self-concept develop during early childhood, and how do children show self-esteem, emotional growth, and initiative?

- The self-concept undergoes major change in early childhood. According to neo-Piagetians, self-definition shifts from single representations to representational mappings. Young children do not see the difference between the real self and the ideal self.

- Culture affects self-definition.

- Self-esteem in early childhood tends to be global and unrealistic, reflecting adult approval

- Understanding of emotions directed toward the self and of simultaneous emotions develops gradually.

- According to Erikson, the developmental conflict of early childhood is initiative versus guilt. Successful resolution of this conflict results in the "virtue" of *purpose*.

  self-concept (282) self-definition (282)
  single representations (283) real self (283)
  ideal self (283) representational mappings (283)
  self-esteem (283) initiative versus guilt (285)

Gender

Guidepost 2 How do boys and girls become aware of the meaning of gender, and what explains differences in behaviour between the sexes?

- Gender identity is an important aspect of the developing self-concept.

- The main gender difference in early childhood is boys' greater aggressiveness. Girls tend to be more empathic and pro-social and less prone to problem behaviour. Some cognitive differences appear early, others not until pre-adolescence or later.

- Children learn gender roles at an early age through gender-typing. Gender stereotypes peak during the preschool years.

- Five major perspectives on gender development are the biological, psychoanalytic, evolutionary, social-learning, and cognitive approaches.

- Evidence suggests that some gender differences may be biologically based.

- In Freudian theory, a child identifies with the same-sex parent after giving up the wish to possess the other parent.

- Evolutionary theory sees children's gender roles as preparation for adult mating behaviour.

- Traditional social-learning theory attributed the learning of gender roles to imitation of models and reinforcement. The expanded social cognitive theory credits cognitive elements as well.

- Cognitive-developmental theory maintains that gender identity develops from thinking about one's gender. Gender constancy enhances the acquisition of gender roles. Gender-schema theory holds that children categorize gender-related information by observing what males and females do in their culture.

- Children also learn gender roles through socialization. Parents, peers, the media, and culture influence gender-typing.

  gender identity (286) gender roles (287)
  gender-typing (287) gender stereotypes (287)
  theory of sexual selection (289) identification (289)
  social cognitive theory (290) gender constancy (290)
  gender-schema theory (291)

Play: The Business of Early Childhood

Guidepost 3 How do preschoolers play, and how does play contribute to and reflect development?

- Play has physical, cognitive, and psychosocial benefits, and may have had evolutionary functions.

- Changes in the types of play children engage in reflect cognitive and social development.

- According to Smilansky, children progress cognitively from functional play to constructive play, dramatic play, and then formal games with rules. Dramatic play becomes increasingly common during early childhood and helps children develop social and cognitive skills. Rough-and-tumble play also begins during early childhood.
- According to Parten, play becomes more social during early childhood. However, later research has found that non-social play is not necessarily immature.
- Children prefer to play with (and play more socially with) others of their sex.
- Cognitive and social aspects of play are influenced by the culturally approved environments adults create for children.

functional play (295)   **constructive play (295)**
dramatic play (295)   **formal games with rules (295)**

Parenting

Guidepost 4   How do parenting practices influence development?

- Discipline can be a powerful tool for socialization.
- Both positive reinforcement and prudently administered punishment can be appropriate tools of discipline within the context of a positive parent–child relationship.
- Power assertion, inductive techniques, and withdrawal of love can each be effective in certain situations. Reasoning is generally the most effective and power assertion the least effective in promoting internalization of parental standards. Spanking and other forms of corporal punishment can have negative consequences.
- Baumrind identified three child-rearing styles: authoritarian, permissive, and authoritative. A fourth style, neglectful or uninvolved, was identified later. Authoritative parents tend to raise more competent children. However, Baumrind's findings may not apply to some cultures or socio-economic groups.

discipline (298)   **corporal punishment (299)**
psychological aggression (299)   **power assertion (300)**
inductive techniques (300)   **withdrawal of love (300)**
authoritarian (302)   **permissive (302)**   **authoritative (302)**
neglectful/uninvolved (302)

Special Behavioural Concerns

Guidepost 5   Why do young children help or hurt others, and why do they develop fears?

- The roots of altruism and pro-social behaviour appear early. This may be an inborn disposition, which can be cultivated by parental modelling and encouragement.
- Instrumental aggression—first physical, then verbal—is most common in early childhood.
- Most children become less aggressive after age 6 or 7, but the proportion of hostile aggression increases. Boys tend to practise overt aggression, whereas girls engage in relational or social aggression.
- Preschool children show temporary fears of real and imaginary objects and events; older children's fears tend to be more realistic.

altruism (304)   **pro-social behaviour (305)**
instrumental aggression (306)   **hostile aggression (306)**
overt, or direct, aggression (306)
relational, or social, aggression (306)

Relationships with Other Children

Guidepost 6   How do young children get along with—or without—siblings, playmates, and friends?

- Sibling and peer relationships contribute to self-efficacy.
- Siblings learn to resolve disputes and negotiate differences.
- Most sibling interactions are positive. Older siblings tend to initiate activities, and younger ones to imitate. Same-sex siblings, especially girls, get along best.
- The kind of relationship children have with siblings often carries over into other peer relationships.
- Only children seem to develop at least as well as children with siblings.
- Preschoolers choose playmates and friends who are like them, and with whom they have positive experiences. Aggressive children are less popular than pro-social children.
- Friends have more positive and negative interactions than other playmates.
- Parenting can affect children's social competence with peers.

self-efficacy (309)

CHAPTER TWELVE

12

Physical Development and Health in Middle Childhood

The healthy human child will keep
Away from home. except to sleep.
Were it not for the common cold.
Our young we never would behold.

—Ogden Nash, *You Can't Get There from Here,* 1957

Focus *Terry Fox, Canadian Hero**

Terry Fox

Terry Fox (1958–1981) was a true Canadian success. Born in Winnipeg and raised in Port Coquitlam, B.C., Terry remembered his childhood as filled with the warmth and closeness of a loving family. His father was a switchman for the Canadian National Railway, and his mother managed a card shop. He had two brothers and a sister.

Terry's intense determination that brought him success in the Marathon of Hope was evident in his childhood. Full of resolution and tenaciousness as a toddler, he would work ceaselessly at projects like stacking blocks until they stayed in place. His patience, evident in his love of long-lasting games and sports in childhood, was an essential quality that he used as a young adult in his struggle to run across Canada to raise funds for cancer research.

Although he was not considered an outstanding student, he ended high school with an A average, having made the school basketball team. In 1977, in his first year at Simon Fraser University, he was diagnosed with a rare form of bone cancer that resulted in the amputation of a leg.

Describing himself as ordinary, he embarked on an extraordinary mission: to run across Canada in an effort to raise money for cancer research. Sponsored by the Canadian Cancer Society, he embarked on his Marathon of Hope in April 1980, dipping his artificial leg in the Atlantic Ocean in St. John's. His prosthesis was rudimentary, causing him discomfort as he ran. He persevered nevertheless. Along the way, his marathon gained momentum in attracting attention across Canada and around the world. Tragically, his cancer reappeared in Thunder Bay, where his run came to an abrupt end in September 1980. His cause was taken up by celebrities who organized a telethon that raised many millions of dollars; he lived long enough to see his dream of a dollar raised for every Canadian for cancer research. His remarkable accomplishment, not only in his run but also in his spirit of determination in raising awareness of the need to support cancer research

was recognized by the many awards he was given: He was made a Companion of the Order of Canada and was awarded the highest honour of the American Cancer Society, the Sword of Hope. He was inducted posthumously into the Sports Hall of Fame and was named Athlete of the Decade by The Sports Network.

He has become a symbol of hope to people around the world, who commemorate his efforts through annual Terry Fox runs for cancer research.

● ● ●

Terry Fox was able to overcome his physical disability and accomplish a remarkable physical feat. His exceptional determination and selflessness, evident from early childhood, allowed him to respond to his physical disability by helping others. In his childhood, his physical competence had cognitive and psychosocial ramifications as well.

Although motor abilities improve less dramatically in middle childhood than before, these years are an important time for the development of the strength, stamina, endurance, and motor proficiency needed for active sports. Despite frequent colds and sore throats, this is a healthy time for most children. Some, however, are not as healthy or fit as they should be, and some have eating problems that can lead to malnutrition or obesity.

In this chapter we will look at normal growth, which depends on proper nutrition and good health. As we explore health concerns, we examine children's understanding of health and illness, which links physical, cognitive, and emotional issues. As children do more, their risk of accidents increases; we examine some ways to lower the risks.

After you have read and studied this chapter, you should be able to answer each of the Guidepost questions that appear at the top of the next page. Look for them again in the margins, where they point to important concepts throughout the chapter. To check your understanding of these Guideposts, review the end-of-chapter summary. Checkpoints located throughout the chapter will help you verify your understanding of what you have read.

*Sources of biographical information about Terry Fox were Brown & Harvey, 1980; Zola, 1984; and Scrivener, 2000.

1. How do school-age children's bodies and brains grow and develop?

2. What are the nutritional and sleep needs of middle childhood?

3. What gains in motor skills typically occur at this age, and what kinds of physical play do boys and girls engage in?

4. What are the principal health, fitness, and safety concerns in middle childhood?

Guideposts for Study

Guidepost 1

How do school-age children's bodies and brains grow and develop?

Aspects of Physical Development

If we were to walk by a typical elementary school just after the 3 o'clock bell, we would see a virtual explosion of children of all shapes and sizes. Tall ones, short ones, husky ones, and skinny ones would be bursting out of the school doors into the open air. We would see that school-age children look very different from children a few years younger.

Height and Weight

Growth during middle childhood slows considerably. Still, although day-by-day changes may not be obvious, they add up to a startling difference between 6-year-olds, who are still small children, and 11-year-olds, many of whom are now beginning to resemble adults.

School-age children grow about 2 to 7 cm each year and gain about 2 to 4 kg or more, doubling their average body weight (Ogden, Fryar, Carroll, & Flegal, 2004). Girls retain somewhat more fatty tissue than boys, a characteristic that will persist through adulthood. The average 10-year-old weighs about 5 kg more than 40 years ago—nearly 39 kg for a boy and 40 kg for a girl (Ogden et al., 2004). Of course, these figures are just averages. Individual children vary widely—so widely that a child of average height at age 7 who did not grow at all for 2 years would still be within the normal limits of height at age 9.

Aboriginal children tend to be heavier at birth and grow heavier at a faster rate than non-Aboriginal children, with about 40 percent of children between 2 and 17 years of age being either overweight or obese (Willows, Johnson & Geoff, 2007). However, heights of Aboriginal children change at about the same rate as in non-Aboriginal children (Indian and Inuit Health Committee, CPS, 1987). Because of the great diversity in growth patterns in Aboriginal communities, doctors are recommended to use standard growth charts to track growth in Aboriginal children (Indian and Inuit Health Committee, CPS, 1987; Willows et al., 2007).

Although most children grow normally, some do not. One type of growth disorder arises from the body's failure to produce enough growth hormone—or sometimes any growth hormone at all. Administration of synthetic growth hormone in such cases can result in rapid growth in height, especially during the first 2 years (Albanese & Stanhope, 1993; Vance & Mauras, 1999).

However, synthetic growth hormone is also being used for children who are much shorter than other children their age, but whose bodies *are* producing normal quantities of the hormone. Although its use is highly controversial (Vance & Mauras, 1999), it was approved by the [U.S.] Food and Drug Administration in 2003 for healthy children whose projected growth rate is too slow to reach a normal adult height (158 cm for men and 148 cm for women). Hormone therapy typically increases adult height only 2.5 to 5.0 cm, and the therapy must be continued daily for 4 to 7 years. However, some children show no response at all. Because the treatment is fairly new, long-term effects are unknown. If unsuccessful, the therapy may do psychological harm by creating unfulfilled expectations or by giving short children the feeling that something is wrong with them (Lee, 2006).

These girls proudly show off a childhood milestone—the normal loss of baby teeth, which will be replaced by permanent ones. Canadian children today have fewer dental cavities than those in the early 1970s, probably owing to better nutrition, widespread use of fluoride, and better dental care.

Tooth Development and Dental Care

Most of the adult teeth arrive early in middle childhood. The primary teeth begin to fall out at about age 6 and are replaced by permanent teeth at a rate of about 4 teeth per year for the next 5 years.

Between 1971–74 and 1988–94, the number of children aged 6 to 18 with untreated cavities dropped nearly 80 percent. Improvements cut across ethnic and socio-economic lines (Brown, Wall, & Lazar, 1999). Much of the improvement in children's dental health is attributed to use of adhesive sealants on the rough, chewing surfaces (L. J. Brown, Kaste, Selwitz, & Furman, 1996).

Brain Development

Brain development during childhood is less dramatic than during infancy, but important changes occur. Brain scans of children studied longitudinally are enabling neuroscientists to map these developmental changes (Blakemore & Choudhury, 2006; Kuhn, 2006).

One such change is a *loss in the density of grey matter* (closely packed neuronal bodies) in certain regions of the cerebral cortex (see Figure 12-1). This process, which reflects pruning of unused dendrites, is balanced by a steady *increase in white matter,* axons or nerve fibres that transmit information between neurons to distant regions of the brain. These connections thicken and myelinate (become insulated), beginning with the frontal lobes and moving toward the rear of the brain. Between ages 6 and 13, striking growth takes place in connections between the temporal and parietal lobes, which deal with sensory functions, language, and spatial understanding. White matter growth in these regions then drops off around the end of the critical period for language learning (Giedd et al., 1999; Kuhn, 2006; National Institute of Mental Health [NIMH], 2001b; Paus et al., 1999). Together these changes increase the speed and efficiency of brain processes.

Whereas the myelination of white matter proceeds from front to back, the loss of grey matter seems to move roughly in the opposite direction. In a longitudinal study of 13 children from ages 4 to 21, the decline in grey matter began between ages 4 and 8 in the regions that support basic sensory and motor activity; then, around ages 11 to 13, moved in a back-to-front direction to the areas of the parietal lobes involved in attention, language, and spatial orientation; and finally, in late adolescence, to the areas of the prefrontal cortex that control reasoning and other higher-order functions. This sequence corresponds roughly to the order in which these parts of the brain developed in human evolution (Gogtay et al., 2004).

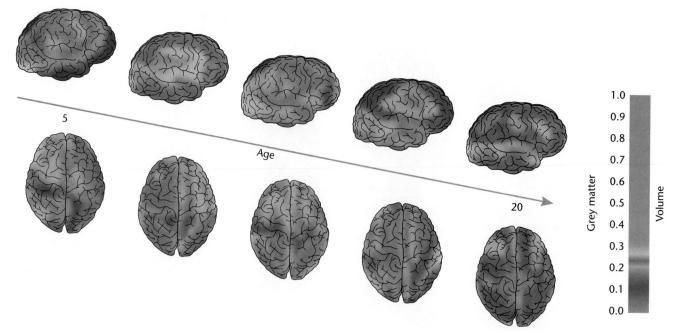

Figure 12-1

Reductions in grey matter density in the cerebral cortex, right side and top views, ages 5 to 20. Losses in grey matter density reflect maturation of various regions of the cortex, permitting more efficient functioning.

Source: Gogtay et al., 2004.

Checkpoint ✔

Can you . . .

✔ Summarize typical growth patterns of boys and girls in middle childhood and give reasons for variations?

✔ Discuss the advisability of administering synthetic growth hormone to short children?

✔ Explain why health of permanent teeth has improved?

✔ Summarize changes in the brain during childhood and discuss their possible effects?

Guidepost 2

What are the nutritional and sleep needs of middle childhood?

Another way neuroscientists measure brain development is by changes in the *thickness* of the cortex. Researchers have observed cortical thickening between 5 and 11 years of age in the regions of the temporal and frontal lobes that handle language. At the same time, thinning occurs in the rear portion of the frontal and parietal cortex in the brain's left hemisphere. This change correlates with improved performance on the vocabulary portion of an intelligence test (Toga et al., 2006).

Developmental changes also have been mapped in the corpus callosum, which links the left and right hemispheres. Progressive myelination of fibres in the corpus callosum leads to more rapid transmission of information between the two hemispheres (Toga et al., 2006). Longitudinal mapping of the corpus callosum from ages 3 to 15 revealed a front-to-back growth pattern (Thompson et al., 2000). Between ages 3 and 6, the most rapid growth occurred in the frontal areas that regulate the planning and organizing of actions. From ages 6 to 11, the most rapid growth was in an area that primarily supports associative thinking, language, and spatial relations; this growth slowed between ages 11 and 15, which may coincide with the end of the critical period that has been proposed for learning a new language.

Sex differences have been found in these patterns of brain development. In a cross-sectional study of 61 boys and 57 girls ages 6 to 17, boys showed markedly greater loss in grey matter and growth in white matter and corpus callosum fibres. Girls showed these changes as well, but at a slower rate (De Bellis et al., 2001).

Nutrition and Sleep

To support their steady growth and constant exertion, school-age children need to eat properly and get enough sleep. Unforturnately, too many children do neither.

Nutritional Needs

Schoolchildren need, on average, 2,400 calories every day—more for older children and less for younger ones (Canada's Food Guide to Healthy Eating, 2007). Breakfast should supply about one-fourth of total calories. Nutritionists recommend a varied diet including plenty of grains, fruits, and vegetables, which are high in natural nutrients, with no more than 30 percent as fat, and 10 percent as saturated fat (CPS and Health Canada, 1994/2001). Canadian children of all ages eat too much fat and sugar and artificially fortified or low-nutrient food (Muñoz et al., 1997; Subar, Krebs-Smith, Cook, & Kahle, 1998).

To avoid overweight and prevent cardiac problems, children (like adults) should get only about 30 percent of their total calories from fat and less than 10 percent of the total from saturated fat (AAP Committee on Nutrition, 1992a; Health Canada, 2007; U.S. Department of Agriculture & USDHHS, 2000). Studies have found no negative effects on height, weight, body mass, or neurological development from a moderately low-fat diet at this age (Rask-Nissilä et al., 2000; Shea et al., 1993). Fruit juice and sweetened beverages should be limited to 227 to 340 ml a day.

As children grow older, pressures and opportunities for unhealthy eating increase. Many children do not eat breakfast, or eat it hurriedly, and get at least one-third of their calories from snacks, including sweetened beverages (American Heart Association et al., 2006). School cafeterias and vending machines often offer unhealthy foods (National [U.S] Center for Education Statistics, 2006). Children frequently eat out, often at fast food restaurants. Many children prepare their own meals and snacks. The media strongly influence children's food choices, and not for the better. Nutrition education in schools can be helpful when combined with parental education and changes in school lunch menus. Changes in food labelling, taxes on unhealthy foods, restrictions on foods provided by government-supported school lunch programs, regulation of food advertising directed toward children, and requiring restaurants to list nutrition information on their menus are among recommendations to encourage healthy nutrition (American Heart Association et al., 2006).

Sleep Patterns and Problems

Sleep needs decline from about 11 hours a day at age 5 to a little more than 10 hours at age 9 and about 9 hours at age 13. Even so, many Canadian children get less sleep than they need. First through fifth graders average 9½ hours a day, short of the recommended 10 to 11 hours. And, as children get older, about 1 in 4 get less sleep on weekends (National Sleep Foundation, 2004). Sleep problems, such as resistance to going to bed, insomnia, and daytime sleepiness are common during these years, in part because many children, as they grow older, are allowed to set their own bedtimes (Hoban, 2004).

More than 40 percent of school-age children have a television set in their bedrooms, and these children get less sleep than other children (National Sleep Foundation, 2004). The more time children spent watching TV, especially at bedtime, the more likely they are to resist going to bed, to be slow in falling asleep, to be anxious around bedtime, and to wake up early (Owens et al., 1999).

A study of sleep patterns of 140 seven- to 12-year-olds in Israel found significant age and gender differences. The older children went to sleep later and slept less (an hour less for 12-year-olds than for 7-year-olds). Older children also reported more morning drowsiness and were more likely to fall asleep during the day. At all ages, children woke up an average of almost twice each night. Girls slept longer and more soundly than boys. Family stress was associated with lower sleep quality (Sadeh, Raviv, & Gruber, 2000).

Although 1 in 5 children in this study experienced significant sleep difficulties, most of them—and their parents—were unaware of them (Sadeh et al., 2000). Similarly, according to a [U.S.] National Sleep Foundation (2004) poll, only 11 percent of parents or caregivers of school-age children think their child has a sleep problem. Yet much higher proportions report that children regularly stall about going to bed (42 percent), have difficulty getting up in the morning (29 percent), snore (18 percent), or awaken at night in need of help or attention (14 percent). In one study, teachers noted that at least 10 percent of kindergarten through fourth-grade students struggled to stay awake in class (Owens, Spirito, McGuinn, & Nobile, 2000).

The prevalence of sleep problems declines between preschool and school age, but earlier sleep problems tend to predict later ones. Children with sleep problems often have allergies, ear infections, or hearing problems. Sleep problems also are highly correlated with psychological and behavioural problems (Stein et al., 2001).

Checkpoint

Can you . . .

✔ Identify nutritional and sleep needs of school-age children and tell why it is important to meet them?

✔ Give reasons why many children do not eat or sleep properly?

Guidepost 3

What gains in motor skills typically occur at this age, and what kinds of physical play do boys and girls engage in?

Motor Development and Physical Play

During the middle years, children's motor abilities continue to improve (see Table 12-1). Children keep getting stronger, faster, and better coordinated—and they derive great pleasure from testing their bodies and learning new skills.

By middle childhood, children in most non-literate and transitional societies go to work, and this along with increased household responsibilities, especially for girls, leaves them little time and freedom to play (Larson & Verma, 1999). In North America, children's lives today are more tightly organized than they were a generation ago. A U.S. nationally representative survey based on time-use diaries found that school-age children spend less time each week on sports and other outdoor activities than in the early 1980s and more hours on schooling and homework, in addition to time spent on television—an average of 12 to 14 hours a week—and on computer activities, which barely existed 20 years ago (Juster, Ono, & Stafford, 2004).

Recess-time Play

Should you come across a couple of schoolboys tumbling over each other, you may hardly be able to tell whether they are fighting or playing except by the expressions on their faces. Such recess-time activities promote growth in agility and social competence and foster adjustment to school (Pellegrini, Kato, Blatchford, & Baines, 2002). About 10 percent of schoolchildren's free play at recess in the early grades consists of **rough-and-tumble play,** vigorous play that involves wrestling, kicking, tumbling, grappling, and sometimes chasing, often accompanied by laughing and screaming (Bjorklund & Pellegrini, 2002).

This kind of play peaks in middle childhood; the proportion typically drops to about 5 percent at age 11, about the same as in early childhood (Bjorklund & Pellegrini, 2002). This kind of play reminds us of our evolutionary heritage; unlike symbolic play, which is distinctly human, rough-and-tumble play was first described in monkeys. Seemingly universal, rough-and-tumble play has been reported in such diverse places as India, Mexico, Okinawa, the Kalahari in Africa, the Philippines, Great Britain, the United States and Canada as well as among most mammals (Bjorklund & Pellegrini, 2002; Humphreys & Smith, 1984). Boys around the world participate in rough-and-tumble play more than girls do, perhaps because of hormonal differences and socialization, and this may be one reason for sex segregation during play (Bjorklund & Pellegrini, 2002; Pellegrini, Kato et al., 2002; Smith, 2005a). From an evolutionary standpoint, rough-and-tumble play has important adaptive benefits: it hones skeletal and muscle development, offers safe practice for hunting and fighting skills, and channels aggression and competition. By age 11,

rough-and-tumble play
Vigorous play involving wrestling, hitting, and chasing, often accompanied by laughing and screaming

Table 12-1	Motor Development in Middle Childhood
Age	**Selected Behaviours**
6	Girls are superior in movement accuracy; boys are superior in forceful, less complex acts. Skipping is possible. Can throw with proper weight shift and step.
7	One-footed balancing without looking becomes possible. Can walk 5 cm-wide balance beams. Can hop and jump accurately into small squares. Can execute accurate jumping-jack exercise
8	Have 5.4-kg pressure on grip strength. Number of games participated in by both sexes is greatest at this age. Can engage in alternate rhythmic hopping in a 2-2, 2-3, or 3-3 pattern. Girls can throw a small ball 12 m.
9	Boys can run 5 m per second. Boys can throw a small ball 21 m.
10	Can judge and intercept pathways of small balls thrown from a distance. Girls can run 5 m per second.
11	Standing broad jump of 1.5 m is possible for boys; 15 cm less for girls.

Source: Adapted from Cratty, 1986.

it often becomes a way to establish dominance within the peer group (Bjorklund & Pellegrini, 2000, 2002; Smith, 2005b).

Organized Sports

When children outgrow rough-and-tumble play and begin playing games with rules, many concentrate on organized, adult-led sports. In Canada, about 60 percent of families participate in common physical activities at least once a week, (Eggertson, 2007). About 53 percent of 6- to 8-year-olds report participating in supervised sports at least once a month, and this number increases to almost 57 percent for children between 9 and 11 years of age. Activity in unsupervised sports is much higher, with 83 percent of the younger group and 85 percent of the older group taking part at least once a month (Offord, Lipman, & Duku, 1998). Too often, parents and coaches pressure children to practise long hours, focus on winning rather than playing the game, criticize children's skills, or offer bribes to make them do well (Wolff, 1993). All these tactics discourage rather than encourage participation. To help children improve their motor skills, organized athletic programs should offer the chance to try a variety of sports, should gear coaching to building skills rather than winning games, and should include as many children as possible rather than concentrating on a few star athletes (American Academy of Pediatrics Committee on Sports Medicine and Committee on School Health, 1989).

Over 50 percent of 6- to 11-year-olds participate in organized afterschool sports, such as soccer. To help children improve motor skills, such programs should emphasize skill-building rather than competition, and should include as many children as possible regardless of ability.

Although it is well established that exercise promotes health and fitness, less than half of Canadian children are active enough to ensure healthy growth (Craig, Cameron, Russell, & Beaulieu, 2001), and the number drops to less than 20 percent for 9- to 12-year-olds (Ahamed, MacDonald, Reed, Naylor, Liu-Ambrose & Mckay, 2007). On average, Canadian children spend 16.5 hours a week in physical activity, with bicycling, swimming, and using playground swings as the top three physical activities (Craig et al., 2001), but girls tend to be less physically active than boys of comparable ages (Ahamed, et al., 2007).

A sound physical education program for *all* children should emphasize skill mastery based on realistic goals, rather than winning or losing. It should include a variety of competitive and recreational sports that can be part of a lifetime fitness regimen, such as tennis, bowling, running, swimming, golf, and skating—but not boxing, which involves direct blows to the head (American Academy of Pediatrics [AAP] Committee on Sports Medicine and Committee on School Health, 1989; AAP Committee on Sports Medicine and Fitness, 1997). Unfortunately, over half of Canadian parents report that their children spend less than the minimum recommended time in physical education classes (Craig et al., 2001), and only 37 percent of Canadian schools offer daily physical education classes, often devoting less than the recommended 10 percent of school time to physical education (Ahamed et al., 2007, Sullivan, 1994).

Besides improving motor skills, regular physical activity has immediate and long-term health benefits: weight control, lower blood pressure, improved cardiorespiratory functioning, and enhanced self-esteem and well-being. Active children tend to become active adults. Thus, organized athletic programs should include as many children as possible rather than concentrating on a few natural athletes and should focus on building skills rather than winning games. Programs should include a variety of sports that can be part of a lifetime fitness regimen, such as tennis, bowling, running, swimming, golf, and skating (AAP Committee on Sports Medicine & Fitness, 1997; Council on Sports Medicine and Fitness and Council on School Health, 2006). Six- to 9-year-olds need more flexible rules, shorter instruction time, and more free time for practice than older children. At this age girls and boys are about equal in weight, height, endurance and motor skill development. Older children are better able to process instruction and learn team strategies, so they are better equipped to engage in team sports (Council on Sports Medicine and Fitness and Council on School Health, 2006).

Checkpoint ✔

Can you . . .

✔ Explain the evolutionary significance of rough-and-tumble play?

✔ Tell how boys' and girls' recess-time activities differ?

✔ Tell what proportion of children remain physically active as they get older and what types of physical play they engage in?

✔ Explain the importance of adequate exercise and give some recommendations for parents?

Guidepost 4

What are the principal health, fitness, and safety concerns in middle childhood?

Health and Safety

The development of vaccines for major childhood illnesses has made middle childhood a relatively safe time of life. Since immunizations are required for school admission, children this age are likely to be protected. The death rate in these years is the lowest in the lifespan. Still, many children get too little exercise to maintain physical fitness; some suffer from acute or chronic medical conditions; and some are injured in accidents.

Overweight and Body Image

Overweight in children has become a major health issue in Canada. The proportion of children ages 7 to 13 who are obese more than tripled between 1981 and 1996—from 5 percent to nearly 17 percent for boys and 15 percent for girls (Tremblay & Willms, 2000). By 2010, if current trends continue, nearly half the children in North and South America, 39 percent in Europe, and 20 percent in China will be overweight (Wang & Lobstein, 2006). A child whose *body mass index,* or *BMI* (weight in comparison with height) was in the 95th percentile (that is, higher than that of 95 percent of children of the same age and sex in a standardized sample) was considered obese. Furthermore, standards have become more lenient, obscuring the full extent of the problem.

Boys are more likely to be overweight than girls (Ogden et al., 2006). Although overweight has increased in all ethnic groups (Center for Weight and Health, 2001), it is most prevalent among Aboriginal children in Canada (over 40 percent) (Willows et al., 2007).

body image Descriptive and evaluative beliefs about one's appearance

Unfortunately, children who try to lose weight are not always the ones who need to do so. Concern with **body image**—how one believes one looks—begins to be important early in middle childhood, especially for girls, and may develop into eating disorders that become more common in adolescence (see Chapter 15). Playing with Barbie dolls may be an influence in that direction (see Box 12-1).

Causes of Overweight

As we reported in Chapters 3 and 9, overweight (or obesity) often results from an *inherited tendency,* aggravated by too little exercise and too much, or the wrong kinds of, food (American Academy of Pediatrics [AAP] Committee on Nutrition, 2003; Chen et al., 2004). Researchers have identified several genes that seem to be involved in obesity (Clément et al., 1998; Jackson et al., 1997; Montague et al., 1997; Ristow, Muller-Wieland, Pfeiffer, Krone, & Kahn, 1998). One of these genes governs production of a brain protein called *leptin,* which seems to help regulate body fat. A defect in this gene, originally found in mice, can disrupt appetite control (Campfield, Smith, Guisez, Devos, & Burn, 1995; Friedman & Halaas, 1998; Halaas et al., 1995; Kristensen et al., 1998; Pelleymounter et al., 1995; Zhang et al., 1994). A mutation in the human gene for leptin has been found in two young cousins who had been extremely obese from an early age and whose leptin level was very low (Montague et al., 1997). Other researchers have found a natural hormone that stimulates the production of fat cells (Forman et al., 1995; Kliewer et al., 1995). Such research may lead to identification and treatment of children predisposed to obesity.

Children who spend many hours watching television tend to be overweight. They are likely to get too little exercise and eat too many fattening snacks.

Environment is also influential, since children tend to eat the same kinds of foods and develop the same kinds of habits as the people around them. Although children of all ages eat too much fat and sugar and too few healthful foods, diets of poor and minority children are especially unbalanced (Muñoz et al., 1997). Aboriginal people living in remote northern communities are at risk of obesity and related health problems, particularly diabetes, because of lack of access to nutritious food. The food needs of these communities are supplemented by a food mail service, but the typical diet tends to be high in fat, sugar, and salt, which contributes to the prevalence of obesity (CIHC, 2000). Children living in families of low socio-economic status are also at higher risk for childhood obesity (Canadian Task Force on the Periodic Health Examination, 1994). Children are more likely to be overweight if they have overweight parents or other relatives. As we mentioned earlier in this chapter, poor nutrition, encouraged by media advertising and wide availability of snack foods and beverages, also contributes (Council on Sports Medicine and Fitness and Council on School

Box 12-1 *Do Barbie Dolls Affect Girls' Body Image?*

"I looked at a Barbie doll when I was 6 and said, 'This is what I want to look like,'" the model Cindy Jackson said on CBS News (2004). "I think a lot of little 6-year-old girls or younger even now are looking at that doll and thinking, 'I want to be her.'"

Barbie is the bestselling fashion doll around the world and the favourite toy of many young girls. Yet Barbie's body proportions are "unrealistic, unattainable, and unhealthy" (Dittmar, Halliwell, & Ive, 2006, p. 284). Fewer than 1 in 100,000 women actually have Barbie's body proportions; her waist, as compared to her bust size, is 39 percent smaller than that of a woman with the eating disorder anorexia (see Chapter 15).

By age 6, studies show, many girls wish to be thinner than they are. According to Bandura's social-cognitive theory, Barbie dolls are role models for young girls, transmitting a cultural ideal of beauty. The media reinforce this ideal. Girls who do not measure up may experience *body dissatisfaction*—negative thoughts about their bodies, leading to low self-esteem.

To test Barbie's effect on young girls' body image, researchers read aloud picture books to 162 English girls, ages 5½ to 8½. One group saw picture stories about Barbie; control groups saw stories about a full-figured fashion doll called Emme or about no doll (Dittmar et al., 2006). Afterward, the girls completed questionnaires in which they were asked to agree or disagree with such statements as "I'm pretty happy about the way I look" and "I really like what I weigh." The girls also were given line drawings of an assortment of female figures. Each girl was asked to colour in the figure whose body looked most like her own, as well as the figures that showed the way she wanted to look, now and when she grew up.

The findings were striking. Among the youngest girls (ages 5½ to 6½), a single exposure to the Barbie picture book significantly lowered body esteem and increased the discrepancy between actual and ideal body size. This did not happen with the girls who saw the Emme book or no doll. The effect of Barbie on body image was even stronger on 6½- to 7½-year-olds. However, the findings for the oldest group, ages 7½ to 8½, were completely different: pictures of Barbie had no direct effect on body image at this age. What accounts for this difference? Girls up to age 7 may be in a sensitive period in which they acquire idealized images of beauty. As girls grow older, they may internalize the ideal of thinness as part of their emerging identity. Once the ideal is internalized, its power no longer depends on direct exposure to the original role model (Dittmar et al., 2006).

On the other hand, it may be that girls simply outgrow Barbie. In another study (Kuther & McDonald, 2004), sixth- through eighth-grade girls were asked about their childhood experiences with Barbie. All the girls had owned at least two Barbie dolls but said they no longer played with them. Looking back, some of the girls saw Barbie as a positive influence: "She is like the perfect person . . . that everyone wants to be like." But most of the young people, girls and boys alike, saw Barbie as an unrealistic role model for girls:

- "Barbie dolls provide a false stereotype . . . as it is physically impossible to attain the same body size. . . . There wouldn't be enough room for organs and other necessary things."
- "Barbie has this perfect body and now every girl is trying to have her body because they are so unhappy with themselves."

Barbie now has a major competitor: Bratz, an ultra-thin doll with a large round face, sassy mouth, and heavy makeup. Longitudinal research will help determine whether fashion dolls such as Barbie and Bratz have a lasting impact on body image.

What's your view

If you had (or have) a young daughter, would you allow her to play with Barbie dolls? Why or why not?

Check it out

For more information on this topic, go to **www.mcgrawhill.ca/olc/papalia**.

Health, 2006). On a typical day, more than 30 percent of a nationally representative sample of 6,212 children and adolescents reported eating fast foods high in fat, carbohydrates, and sugar additives (Bowman, Gortmaker, Ebbeling, Pereira, & Ludwig, 2004). Eating out is one culprit; children who eat outside the home consume an estimated 200 more calories a day than when the same foods are eaten at home (French, Story, & Jeffery, 2001).

Inactivity may be a major factor in the sharp rise in obesity (Freedman et al., 1997; Harrell, Gansky, Bradley, & McMurray, 1997). As we have mentioned, school-age children today spend less time than the children of 20 years ago in outdoor play and sports (Juster et al., 2004). There is a negative correlation between *activity level* and weight. Although the [U.S.] National Association of State Boards of Education recommends 150 minutes of physical education each week for elementary students, the average school offers it only two to three times a week for a total of 85 to 98 minutes (National Center for Education Statistics, 2006). Yet, one additional hour of physical education per week in kindergarten and first grade could reduce by half the number of overweight girls that age (Datar & Sturm, 2004b).

Outside of school, many children are not as active as they should be. According to one U.S. survey, 22.6 percent of 9- to 13-year-olds engage in *no* free-time physical activity (Duke et al., 2003). Pre-adolescent girls in ethnic minorities, children with disabilities, children who live in public housing, and children in unsafe neighbourhoods where facilities for outdoor exercise are lacking are most likely to be sedentary (Council on Sports Medicine and Fitness and Council on School Health, 2006).

Excessive television viewing contributes to overweight. Children who watch TV 5 hours a day are 4.6 times as likely to be overweight as those who watch no more than 2 hours daily (Institute of Medicine, 2005).

Why is Childhood Overweight a Serious Concern?

Being overweight is a decided disadvantage for school-age children. In a longitudinal study of 1,456 primary students in Victoria, Australia, children classified as overweight or obese fell behind their classmates in physical and social functioning by age 10 (Williams, Wake, Hesketh, Maher, & Waters, 2005). When 106 severely obese children and adolescents were asked to rate their health-related quality of life (for example, their ability to walk more than one block, to sleep well, to get along with others, and to keep up in school), they reported significant impairment as compared with healthy peers (Schwimmer, Burwinkle, & Varni, 2003).

Overweight children often suffer emotionally and may compensate by indulging themselves with treats, making their physical and social problems even worse. These children are at risk for behaviour problems, depression, and low self-esteem (AAP Committee on Nutrition, 2003; Datar & Sturm, 2004a; Mustillo et al., 2003). They commonly have medical problems, including high blood pressure (discussed in the next section), high cholesterol, and high insulin levels (AAP Committee on Nutrition, 2003; National Center for Health Statistics [NCHS], 2004).

Overweight children tend to become obese adults, at risk for high blood pressure, heart disease, orthopedic problems, and diabetes. Indeed, childhood overweight may be a stronger predictor of some diseases than adult overweight (AAP Committee on Nutrition, 2003; AAP, 2004; Li et al., 2004; Center for Weight and Health, 2001; Must, Jacques, Dallal, Bajema, & Dietz, 1992). Even children in the upper half of the *normal* weight range are more likely than their peers to become overweight or obese in adulthood (Field, Cook, & Gillman, 2005). In one longitudinal study, girls who were overweight before puberty were 7.7 times as likely as their peers to be overweight as adults (Must et al., 2005).

Prevention and Treatment of Overweight

Prevention of weight gain is easier, less costly, and more effective than treating overweight (Center for Weight and Health, 2001; Council on Sports Medicine and Fitness and Council on School Health, 2006). Effective weight-management programs should include efforts of parents, schools, physicians, communities, and the larger culture (Krishnamoorthy, Hart, & Jelalian, 2006; see Table 12-2). Less time in front of television and computers, changes in food labelling and advertising, healthier school meals, education to help children make better food choices, and more time spent in physical education would help (AAP, 2004). Parents can make exercise a family activity by hiking or playing ball together, building strength on playground equipment, walking whenever possible, using stairs instead of elevators, and limiting television. Parents should watch children's eating and activity patterns and address excessive weight gain *before* a child becomes severely overweight (AAP Committee on Nutrition, 2003). A 2004 U.S. federal law (Public Law 108-265) requires that every school receiving federal funding for school lunches or breakfasts must set goals for healthy nutrition, physical activity, and wellness promotion with emphasis on prevention of childhood obesity.

Treatment of overweight should begin early, involve the family, and promote permanent changes in lifestyle, not weight loss alone (Barlow & Dietz, 1998; Canadian Task Force on the Periodic Health Examination, 1994; Miller-Kovach, 2003). During a 12-week experiment with 10 obese 8- to 12-year-olds, those whose television viewing was limited to the amount of time they spent pedalling an exercise bicycle watched much less television and showed significantly greater reductions in body fat than a control group (Faith et al., 2001).

Table 12-2	A Coordinated Strategy to Stop the "Overweight Epidemic"

What federal, provincial, or local governments can do:

- Give ministries of education and school boards authority over all foods available in schools—in vending machines and after-school programs as well as in the cafeteria.
- Publish nutritional guidelines for all foods and beverages sold in schools.
- Give Health Canada authority to establish guidelines for advertising of "junk foods" aimed at children.
- Sponsor media campaigns to promote healthy nutrition and physical activity.
- Support community programs that foster an active environment, for example, road projects that accommodate bicycles and pedestrians.
- Tax soft drinks and snack foods and partially subsidize the cost of fresh fruits and vegetables.

What communities can do:

- Offer after-school recreational programs emphasizing physical activity and classes in cooking, nutrition, health, and fitness.
- Develop pedestrian-friendly neighbourhoods with shops and grocery stores within walking distance.

What health care professionals can do:

- Identify and track children and adolescents at risk for obesity due to genetic and environmental factors.
- Calculate body mass index annually for children and adolescents and refer to a weight control specialist those who are overweight or at risk of overweight.
- Encourage parents and caregivers to promote healthy eating by offering nutritious snacks, letting children eat what they want within appropriate limits, and modelling healthy food choices.
- Promote physical activity, including unstructured play time.
- Recommend limiting screen time to a maximum of 2 hours a day.
- Give parents information on appropriate nutrition and advise families on adopting healthier lifestyles.

What private industry can do:

- Offer employee medical benefits that include preventive coverage.
- Develop healthy products that are attractive to children.
- Offer incentives for healthy eating.
- Use television advertising aimed at children to promote healthy products.

What schools can do:

- Develop school wellness policies in partnership with the local school board, parents, students, physical education teachers, and health care professionals.
- Provide healthier foods in the cafeteria, vending machines, and school stores.
- Make sure that all children spend at least 30 minutes a day in moderate to vigorous physical activity.
- Eliminate advertising of low-nutrient foods on scoreboards and at school functions.

What parents can do:

- Make sure children are offered healthy foods and get plenty of outdoor play time.
- Limit food choices.
- Limit television time and video games to 2 hours a day, and monitor what children watch.
- Provide healthy role models.

Source: Adapted from Krishnamoorthy, Hart, & Jelalian, 2006.

Overweight and Childhood Hypertension

Hypertension (high blood pressure) once was relatively rare in childhood, but it has been termed an "evolving epidemic" of cardiovascular risk, especially among ethnic minorities (Sorof, Lai, Turner, Poffenbarger, & Portman, 2004, p. 481). In nationally representative samples of U.S. children and adolescents ages 8 to 17, average blood pressure rose between 1988 and 2000, in part due to increases in overweight (Muntner, He, Cutler, Wildman, & Whelton, 2004). A series of screenings of 5,102 children ages 10 to 19 in eight Houston public schools found an estimated 4.5 percent prevalence of hypertension, with overweight the major contributing factor (Sorof et al., 2004). A study of 3,293 Canadian adolescents showed similar results, especially among those with lower fitness levels (Flouris, Canham, Faught & Klentrou, 2007).

Weight reduction through dietary modification and regular physical activity is the primary treatment for overweight-related hypertension. If blood pressure does not come

hypertension High blood pressure

Checkpoint ✓

Can you . . .

✔ Discuss why childhood obesity has increased, how it can affect adult health, and how it can be treated?

acute medical conditions
Occasional illnesses that last a short time

activity limitations Chronic conditions that continually restrict everyday behaviours

chronic medical conditions
Physical, behavioural, and/or emotional conditions that require special health services

down, drug treatment can be considered. However, care must be taken in prescribing such drugs, as their long-term effects on children are unknown—as are the long-term consequences of untreated hypertension in children (National High Blood Pressure Education Program Working Group on High Blood Pressure in Children and Adolescents, 2004).

Medical Conditions

Illness in middle childhood tends to be brief. **Acute medical conditions**—occasional, short-term conditions, such as infections, allergies, and warts—are common. Six or seven bouts a year with colds, flu, or viruses are typical at this age, as germs pass among children at school or at play (Behrman, 1992).

As children's experience with illness increases, so does their understanding of the causes of health and illness and of how people can promote their own health (Crisp, Ungerer, & Goodnow 1996). From a Piagetian perspective, children's understanding of health and illness is tied to cognitive development. As they mature, their explanations for disease change. Before middle childhood, children are egocentric; they believe that illness is magically produced by human actions, often their own ("I was a bad boy, so now I feel bad"). Later they explain all diseases—only a little less magically—as the doing of all-powerful germs. As children approach adolescence, they see that there can be multiple causes of disease, that contact with germs does not automatically lead to illness, and that people can do much to keep healthy.

According to the National Population Health Survey (CIHC, 2000), 7.7 percent of Canadians between birth and age 19 years have **activity limitations** and **chronic medical conditions:** physical, developmental, behavioural, and/or emotional conditions requiring special health services. Children with special health needs spend three times as many days sick in bed and miss school three times as often as other children (Newacheck et al., 1998).

Socio-economic status plays an important part in children's health. Poor children (living in families below the low-income cut-off (Statistics Canada, 1994)) and those living with a single parent are more likely than other children to have chronic conditions (Newacheck et al., 1998). These disadvantaged children tend to be in fair or poor health, to have been hospitalized, and to have health-related limitations on activities. Why is this so? Parents with higher socio-economic status tend to know more about good health habits and have better access to preventive health care, and two-parent families tend to have higher incomes and more wholesome diets than single-parent families (Collins & LeClere, 1997). Also, parents of children with special needs experience difficulty finding adequate care for them, which would permit the parents to find full- or part-time work (CIHC, 2000; Irwin & Lero, 1997). Another factor in variations in health care is differing beliefs and attitudes about health and healing among cultural and ethnic groups (Yu, Huang, & Singh, 2004; see Box 12-2).

Children with chronic conditions tend to be remarkably resilient. Few show problems in mental health, behaviour, or schooling (AAP Committee on Children with Disabilities and Committee on Psychosocial Aspects of Child and Family Health, 1993). However, by adolescence, some mental-health indicators like history of abuse, emotional distress, and low self-esteem are more likely to be found in children with chronic illness than in children without health problems (CIHC, 2000). Still, certain conditions—such as vision and hearing problems, stuttering, asthma, and AIDS—can greatly affect everyday living.

In Canada, 15 percent of children and 20 percent of adolescents live with a chronic medical condition (Miller, Recsky, & Armstrong, 2004). Let's look at some chronic conditions that affect everyday living.

Vision and Hearing Problems

Most children in middle childhood have keener vision than when they were younger. Children under 6 years old tend to be far-sighted. By age 6, vision is typically more acute; and because the two eyes are better coordinated, they can focus better.

About 10 to 15 percent of Canadian preschool children experience some visual problem, with up to 5 percent experiencing amblyopia, and 5 percent experiencing strebismus. About 15 percent of Canadian preschoolers experience short-term hearing problems, and 3 percent experience persistent hearing difficulties (Feightner, 1994). Current screening guidelines may miss many children with very high frequency impairments. This is of concern,

Box 12-2 *How Cultural Attitudes Affect Health Care*

One morning Buddi Kumar Rai, a university-educated resident of Badel, a remote hill village in Nepal, carried his 2½-year-old daughter, Kusum, to the shaman, the local "medicine man." Kusum's little face was sobre, her usually golden complexion pale, and her almond-shaped eyes droopy from the upper-respiratory infection she had been suffering the past week, complete with fever and a hacking cough.

Two days before, Kusum had been in her father's arms when he had slipped and fallen backwards off a veranda to the ground about a metre below, still tightly holding his little daughter. Neither was hurt, but little Kusum had screamed in fright.

Now the shaman told Buddi that Kusum's illness was due to that fright. He prescribed incantations and put a mark, a charcoal smudge the size of a loonie, on the child's forehead to drive away the evil spirit that had entered her body when she had her scare.

Adherence to ancient beliefs about illness is common in many parts of the industrialized world, where many people cling to beliefs that are at odds with mainstream scientific and medical thinking. To provide better medical care to members of various ethnic minorities, policy-makers need to understand the cultural beliefs and attitudes that influence what people do, what decisions they make, and how they interact with the broader society.

Many cultures see illness and disability as a form of punishment inflicted upon someone who has transgressed (as did Buddi in failing to pray to the river god), has done something wrong in a previous life, or is paying for an ancestor's sin. Another belief, common in Latin America and Southeast Asia, is that an imbalance of elements in the body causes illness and the patient has to re-establish his or her own equilibrium. Other groups tend to attribute disease to such causes as the evil eye, grief and loss, exposure to drafts, and eating the wrong combination of foods.

In many societies people believe that a severely disabled child will not survive. Since there is no hope, they do not expend time, effort, or money on the child—which often creates a self-fulfilling prophecy. Such a belief makes it nearly impossible for parents to plan realistically for the child's future. In some religious households, parents hold out hope for a miracle and refuse surgery or other treatment.

Of course, standard medical practice in Canada is also governed by a cultural belief system. Here, parents are asked to make decisions about their child without consulting members of the extended family, as would be done in many other cultures. To foster independence and self-sufficiency, parents are discouraged from "babying" a disabled child. People from other cultures may not respond well to mainstream Canadian values: Parents may feel a need to consult their own parents about medical decisions and may not consider it important, for example, for a disabled daughter to become self-supporting.

Professionals need to explain clearly, whenever possible in the family's language, what course of treatment they recommend, why they favour it, and what they expect to happen. Such concern can help prevent incidents like one that occurred when an Asian mother became hysterical as an American nurse took her baby to get a urine sample. The mother had had three children taken from her in Cambodia. None had returned.

This Peruvian healer treats a child by traditional methods, such as herbs and incantations. In many Latin American cultures, such practices are believed to cure illness by restoring the natural balance of elements in the body.

Sources: S. W. Olds, 2002; Groce & Zola, 1993.

What's your view

How would Piaget interpret the belief in some cultures that illness and disabilities are punishments for human actions? Does such a belief suggest that Piaget's theory is limited in its applicability to non-industrialized cultures?

Check it out

For more information on this topic, go to **www.mcgrawhill.ca/olc/papalia.**

Sources: S. W. Olds (2002); Groce & Zola (1993).

since even slight hearing loss can affect communication, behaviour, and social relationships (Niskar et al., 1998).

Stuttering

Stuttering—involuntary, frequent repetition or prolongation of sounds or syllables—interferes with social functioning. As stutterers become frustrated and anxious about ordinary conversation, their self-esteem plummets. It usually begins between ages 2 and 5

stuttering Involuntary, frequent repetition or prolongation of sounds or syllables

(Büchel & Sommer, 2004). By fifth grade, it is four times more common in boys than in girls. Five percent of children stutter for a period of 6 months or more, but three-quarters of these recover by late childhood, leaving about 1 percent with a long-term problem (Stuttering Foundation, 2006).

Stuttering is now widely regarded as a neurological condition. It sometimes results from brain damage (for example, head trauma or a stroke). The more common type, *persistent developmental stuttering (PDS)*, is especially noticeable at the beginning of a word or phrase or in long, complex sentences. The concordance rate is about 70 percent for monozygotic twins, 30 percent for dizygotic twins, and 18 percent for same-sex siblings, suggesting a genetic component. It seems likely that two factors are at work in PDS. The basic cause may be a structural or functional disorder of the central nervous system. This may then be reinforced by parental reactions to the stuttering, which may make the child nervous or anxious about speaking (Büchel & Sommer, 2004).

There is no known cure for stuttering, but speech therapy can help a child talk more easily and fluently (Stuttering Foundation, 2006). If stutterers become frustrated or anxious about their speech, they may learn to avoid speaking as much as possible. On the other hand, the actor Bruce Willis treated himself by joining a drama club, which forced him to speak before an audience (Büchel & Sommer, 2004). Many other famous people, including the actress Julia Roberts and the actor James Earl Jones, have succeeded despite this disability.

Asthma

asthma A chronic respiratory disease characterized by sudden attacks of coughing, wheezing, and difficulty in breathing

Asthma, a chronic respiratory disease, is the primary cause of childhood disability, affecting an estimated 845,000 Canadian children. Its prevalence has increased from 2 percent of individuals younger than 19 years in 1978 to 12 percent in 1996 (CICH, 2000), and by 1999 the prevalence among children less than 10 years of age was 20 percent (Argles & Greer, 2004). Asthma is increasing worldwide (Asher et al., 2006) but may have plateaued in parts of the western world, including Canada (Eder, Ege, & von Mutius, 2006; Hertzen & Haahtela, 2005). Apparently allergy-based, it is characterized by sudden attacks of coughing, wheezing, and difficulty in breathing; and it can be fatal. These symptoms reflect an extreme narrowing of the airways when a sufferer inhales certain substances, such as smoke (Eder et al., 2006). Although about 20 Canadian children die from asthma per year (Department of Environmental Health, 2003), this rate is unacceptable given that asthma is a fully treatable disease; however, the asthma mortality rate has been decreasing since 1987 (Health Canada, 2001).

The cause of the asthma explosion is unknown, but a genetic predisposition is likely to be involved (Eder et al., 2006). Some experts point to environmental factors: tightly insulated houses that intensify exposure to environmental toxins and allergens (Habbick, Pizzichini, Taylor, Rennie, Senthilselvan, & Sears, 1999; Health Canada, 2001; Nugent, 1999; Sly, 2000; Stapleton, 1998), such as tobacco smoke, moulds, and insect droppings. Allergies to household pets also have been suggested as risk factors (Bollinger, 2003; Etzel, 2003; Lanphear, Aligne, Auinger, Weitzman, & Byrd, 2001). Findings regarding these proposed causes, except for smoke exposure, are inconclusive. However, indoor exposure to allergens may contribute to the *persistence* of symptoms in children who already have asthma (Eder et al., 2006). In one study of 174 asthmatic schoolchildren, exposure to higher levels of dust mites and nitrogen dioxide, a product of unflued gas appliances, was linked to worsened asthma symptoms (Nitschke et al., 2006). A one-year program to reduce indoor allergens and tobacco smoke in the homes of children with asthma significantly reduced asthma symptoms and asthma-related illnesses (Morgan et al., 2004). Increasing evidence points to an association between obesity and asthma, perhaps because of an underlying lifestyle factor related to both conditions. Asthma also has been linked to the use of antibiotics (Eder et al., 2006).

Poor, minority children, especially boys, are most likely to be affected, as are children in single-parent families (Newacheck & Halfon, 2000; Stapleton, 1998). Twenty-two percent of children with asthma report limited activity for 1 to 5 days per year, and 13 percent report 6 or more days of restricted activity (Health Canada, 2001). A 1999 survey found asthma accounting for 20 percent absenteeism from school (Glaxo Wellcome, 2000)—almost twice as often as children with other chronic ailments (Newacheck & Halfon, 2000).

Some of this sickness may be avoidable; most children with moderate to severe asthma—especially young children from poor families—do not get adequate treatment (Glaxo Wellcome, 2000; Halterman, Aligne, Auinger, McBride, & Szilagyi, 2000).

Attacks tend to follow severely stressful events, such as illness, parental separation or divorce, the death of a grandparent, a close friend moving away, or becoming a victim of bullying (Sandberg, Järvenpää, Penttinen, Paton, & McCann, 2004). Children with asthma may be at risk for social and psychological problems (Berz, Murdock, & Mitchell, 2005).

Many children get inadequate treatment (Halterman, Aligne, Auinger, McBride, & Szilagyi, 2000; Shields, Comstock, & Weiss, 2004). In a randomized, controlled study of 134 asthmatic inner-city children ages 8 to 16, use of the Internet to educate patients and their families in symptom monitoring and medication led to improved compliance and reduced symptoms (Dorsey & Schneider, 2003).

HIV and AIDS

Worldwide, an estimated 2.2 million children under age 15 are living with the human immunodeficiency virus (HIV) (UNAIDS/WHO, 2004). These children are at high risk of developing AIDS (acquired immune deficiency syndrome), if they have not done so already. In 2004, 510,000 children under 15 died of AIDS (UNAIDS/WHO, 2004).

Seventy-eight percent of these children acquired the AIDS virus from their mothers, almost all of them in the uterus, during delivery, or through breast milk (Bureau of HIV/AIDS, STD and TB, Centre for Infectious Disease Prevention and Control [CIDPC], 2001; refer back to Chapter 4). However, treatment has greatly reduced the likelihood of mother–child transmission, so that even though the number of children born to HIV-positive mothers has increased since 1989, the number of newborns infected with HIV has remained constant (CIDPC, 2001). About 3 to 4 pregnant women in 10,000 are found to be HIV-positive each year in Canada. Since December 1998, as reported by the CPS in 2000, 924 Canadian babies were born to HIV-infected women, 325 were HIV positive, and 107 have died of AIDS (Infectious Diseases and Immunization Committee, Canadian Paediatric Society, 2000). Between 1984 and 2002, of the 1,584 infants who were exposed to HIV from their mothers 420 have been confirmed as being infected (Public Health Agency of Canada, 2004).

Prospects for survival and health of children born with HIV infection have improved greatly due to antiretroviral therapy (AAP Committee on Pediatric AIDS, 2000; Gortmaker et al., 2001; Lee et al., 2006). Although some of these children develop full-blown AIDS by their first or second birthday, others live for years without apparent effects (European Collaborative Study, 1994; Grubman et al., 1995; Nielsen et al., 1997; Nozyce et al., 1994). Genetic factors may affect the immune system's response to the virus, causing symptoms to develop more slowly in some children than in others (Singh et al., 2003).

Most children infected with HIV who reach school age function normally, though their quality of life may be affected, especially if they are not getting antiretroviral treatment (Lee et al., 2006). Because there is virtually no risk of infecting classmates, children who carry the AIDS virus do not need to be isolated. They should be encouraged to participate in all school activities, including athletics, to the extent they are able (AAP Committee on Sports Medicine and Fitness, 1999; AAP Committee on Pediatric AIDS, 2000).

Because symptoms may not appear until a disease has progressed to the point of causing serious long-term complications, early detection is important. Regular, school-based screening and treatment, together with programs that promote abstention from or postponement of sexual activity, responsible decision making, and ready availability of condoms for those who are sexually active may have some effect in controlling the spread of sexually transmitted diseases (AAP Committee on Adolescence, 1994; Alan Guttmacher Institute (AGI), 1994; Cohen, Nsuami, Martin, & Farley, 1999; Rotheram-Borus & Futterman, 2000).

Diabetes

About 6 percent of Canadians are affected by diabetes (Montour, MacAulay, & Adelson, 1989). However, there has been a dramatic increase in non-insulin-dependent diabetes among Aboriginal children in some communities, which concerns pediatricians and Aboriginal groups (Evers, 1987; Montour et al., 1989; Zinman, 2006). Until 1940, diabetes

What's your view ?

- Medical evidence shows virtually no evidence that children with HIV infection who are symptom-free can transmit the virus to others except through bodily fluids. Yet many parents are afraid to have their children go to school with a child who is HIV-positive. Can you suggest ways to deal with this problem?

Many accidental injuries occur on school playgrounds. By wearing protective helmets when bicycling or roller skating, these children are dramatically reducing their risk of head injury.

was a rare condition among Aboriginal children, but its prevalence has grown since that time (Dean, Mundy, & Moffatt, 1992; Indian and Inuit Health Committee, CPS, 1994). An important factor involved in the outset of the disease is obesity, and programs are under way to increase public awareness to promote physical fitness in Aboriginal children in communities across Canada. Unfortunately, the needed medical care is often not provided because of the lack of trained health-care educators and practitioners who are members of Aboriginal communities (Indian and Inuit Health Committee, CPS, 1994).

Accidental Injuries

As in early childhood, accidental injuries are the leading cause of death among school-age Canadian children (Anderson & Smith, 2003; Kochanek et al., 2004). In a 9-year study of 96,359 children born in Alberta, 21 percent suffered at least one injury each year, and 73 percent had repeat injuries during the study period. Boys were more likely to be injured than girls and to have repeat injuries (Spady, Saunders, Schopflocher, & Svenson, 2004).

The hospitalization rate due to injury is about 700 per 100,000 children under 5 years of age. This rate drops to about 560 for children 5 to 9 years of age, and 660 for children aged 10 to 14 years. Injury is the leading cause of death for all children (CIHC, 2000). Most hospital visits by children are due to accidents resulting from playground injuries (Canadian Institute for Health Information [CIHI], 2007). Over 50 percent of playground injuries involve bone fractures, and 22 percent are head injuries (CIHI, 2007).

Injury-related deaths in Aboriginal children are three times the national average. Accounting for 25 percent of fatalities in Aboriginal populations (Health Canada, 1999; Canadian Institute of Health Research, 2002). The most common type of injury requiring hospitalization involves falls (CIHC, 2000). An important aspect of determining severity of accidental injury is measuring the pain associated with the injury. Great strides in this area have been made by Canadian researchers, who have identified effective ways of uncovering fine-grained measures, but are hampered by habituation to chronic pain over time (McGrath, 1996).

Bicycle injuries also account for a substantial proportion of hospitalizations among Canadian children. About a third of all cases of bicycle-related injuries in hospitals are children and youth between 5 and 14 years of age (CIHI, undated). Almost 60 percent of these injuries were bone-related, while 27 percent involved head injuries. Although the proportion of head injuries from bicycle accidents is declining (CIHI, undated).

The dangers of riding a bicycle can be reduced dramatically by using helmets (D. C. Thompson, Rivara, & Thompson, 1996). Slightly more than half of all children aged 12 and younger regularly wear bicycle helmets while riding bicycles or tricycles, though the rate varies across Canada due to variations in provincial regulations on helmet use (Canadian Institute of Child Health (CICH), 2000). Protective headgear is also vital for football, roller skating, roller blading, skateboarding, scooter riding, horseback riding, hockey, speed sledding, and tobogganing. For soccer, protective goggles and mouth guards may help reduce head and facial injuries. "Heading" the ball should be minimized because of the danger of brain injury, and aggressive or violent infractions of rules should be dealt with strongly (AAP Committee on Sports Medicine and Fitness, 2000).

There is a relationship between income and injury for boys. Male children in low-income families tend to be more susceptible to injury than males in high-income families (CIHC, 2000). This may be due to unsafe housing conditions and neighbourhoods that lack the facilities to provide safe playgrounds and recreational activities (CIHC, 2000).

Most injuries experienced by children younger than 5 years took place in the home, while playing. The same is true of children 5 to 9 years of age, but now a substantial

Checkpoint

Can you . . .

✔ Distinguish between acute and chronic medical conditions, and discuss how chronic conditions can affect everyday life?

✔ Identify factors that increase the risks of accidental injury?

✔ Explain why socially disadvantaged children tend to have more health problems than their peers?

proportion of injuries occur in the school. By the time children reach 10 to 14 years of age, most injuries take place in school, followed by the home, and sports and recreational environments. Although most injuries continue to occur while children are playing, a large percentage now occur while they are engaged in organized sports activities. This indicates that children, parents, and coaches need to be better informed about safety equipment, safe play, and sporting behaviours (CIHC, 2000).

One reason for some accidents is children's immaturity, both cognitive (preventing them from being aware of some dangers) and emotional (leading them to take dangerous risks). We discuss cognitive development in middle childhood in Chapter 13 and emotional and social development in Chapter 14.

Summary and Key Terms

Aspects of Physical Development

Guidepost 1 How do school-age children's bodies annd brains grow and develop?

- Physical development is less rapid in middle childhood than in earlier years. Wide differences in height and weight exist.

- Children with retarded growth due to growth-hormone deficiency may be given synthetic growth hormone. Although the hormone is sometimes prescribed for short children who do *not* have hormone deficiency, extreme caution is advised in such cases.

- The permanent teeth arrive in middle childhood. Dental health has improved, in part because of the use of sealants on chewing surfaces.

- Brain growth continues during childhood with a gradual increase in white matter and decrease in grey matter. The corpus callosum connecting the two hemispheres becomes progressively myelinated.

Nutrition and Sleep

Guidepost 2 What are the nutritional and sleep needs of middle childhood?

- Proper nutrition is essential for normal growth and health.

- Malnutrition can affect all aspects of development.

- Most children do not get enough sleep, and may have sleep problems.

Motor Development and Physical Play

Guidepost 3 What gains in motor skills typically occur at this age, and what kinds of physical play do boys and girls engage in?

- Because of improved motor development, boys and girls in middle childhood can engage in a wide range of motor activities.

- About 10 percent of schoolchildren's play, especially among boys, is rough-and-tumble play.

- Informal, spontaneous play helps develop physical and social skills.

- Many children engage in organized, competitive sports.

- A sound physical education program should aim at skill development for all children and should emphasize enjoyment and lifelong fitness rather than competition.

rough-and-tumble play (320)

Health and Safety

Guidepost 4 What are the principal health, fitness, and safety concerns in middle childhood?

- Middle childhood is a relatively healthy period; most children are immunized against major illnesses, and the death rate is the lowest in the lifespan. However, many children, especially girls, do not meet fitness standards.

- Concern with body image, especially among girls, may lead to eating disorders.

- Overweight, which is increasingly common among Canadian children, is influenced by genetic and environmental factors and can be prevented more easily than it can be treated.

- Respiratory infections and other acute medical conditions are common. Chronic conditions such as asthma are most prevalent among poor children.

- Children's understanding of health and illness is related to their cognitive level. Cultural beliefs affect expectations of health care.

- Vision becomes keener during middle childhood, but a minority of children have defective vision or hearing.

- Stuttering is fairly common but usually not permanent.

- Most children who are HIV-positive function normally in school and should not be excluded from any activities of which they are physically capable.

- Accidents are the leading cause of death in middle childhood. Use of helmets and other protective devices and educating children, parents, and coaches about safe equipment and practices during play and sports can greatly reduce injuries.

body image (322) hypertension (325) acute medical conditions (326) activity limitations (326) chronic medical conditions (326) stuttering (327) asthma (328)

CHAPTER THIRTEEN

Cognitive Development in Middle Childhood

Focus *Akira Kurosawa, Master Filmmaker**

Akira Kurosawa

The Japanese filmmaker Akira Kurosawa (1910–1998), who wrote and directed such classics as the Academy Award–winning *Rashomon* (1951) and *Seven Samurai* (1954), has been called a cinematographic genius. Kurosawa uses the screen as if it were a canvas. Artistic intelligence—an unerring sense of composition, form, colour, and texture—pervades his scenes.

In his mid-20s, as an apprentice to the great film director Kajiro Yamamoto, he was a quick study. Assigned to write scenarios, the talented novice came up with idea after idea. "He is completely creative," Yamamoto said of him (Richie, 1984, p. 12).

Yet, as a child, during his first 2 years at a Westernized school in Tokyo, Kurosawa remembers being a slow learner. Because he had trouble following the lessons, he just sat quietly, trying to amuse himself. Finally his teacher moved Akira's desk and chair away from the other students and frequently aroused snickers with such comments as "Akira probably won't understand this, but . . ." (Kurosawa, 1983, p. 8).

That initial school experience left an indelible mark on Kirosawa. He felt isolated and miserable. Then, toward the end of his second year of school, his family moved to another part of the city, and he was transferred to a traditional Japanese school. His new classmates, with their close-shaved heads, duck-cloth trousers, and wooden clogs, made fun of Akira's long hair and European-style clothing. The youngest of seven children, Akira had been a crybaby; now he became a laughingstock.

It was in Grade 3 that he came out of his intellectual and emotional fog. The strongest catalyst for this change was his teacher, a man named Tachikawa. In art class, instead of having all the students copy a picture and giving the top grade to the closest imitation, as was the custom, he let the children draw whatever they liked. Akira became so carried away that he pressed on his coloured pencils until they broke, and then he licked his fingertips and smeared the colours all over the paper. When Mr. Tachikawa held up Akira's drawing, the class laughed boisterously. But the teacher lavished it with praise and gave it the highest grade.

"From that time on," Kurosawa later wrote, ". . . I somehow found myself hurrying to school in anticipation on the days when we had art classes. . . . I became really good at drawing. At the same time my marks in other subjects suddenly began to improve. By the time Mr. Tachikawa left . . . , I was the president of my class, wearing a little gold badge with a purple ribbon on my chest" (1983, p. 13).

Academically, his performance was uneven: the best in his class in the subjects he liked, he did barely passable work in science and math. Still, he graduated as valedictorian. According to former classmate Uekusa Keinosuke, who became a scriptwriting colleague, "He certainly was not the little-genius type who merely gets good grades" but a "commanding" figure who became popular seemingly without effort (Richie, 1984, p. 10).

It was Mr. Tachikawa who introduced Akira to the fine arts and to film. Akira's father and his older brother Heigo discussed great literature with him and took him to Japanese vaudeville and Western movies.

Even after Mr. Tachikawa left the school, Akira and his friend Uekusa would go to the teacher's home and sit around talking for hours. So strong was Akira's spirit by this time that when Mr. Tachikawa's conservative successor lambasted one of his paintings, the boy simply made up his mind to "work so hard that this teacher would never be able to criticize me again" (Kurosawa, 1983, p. 25).

• • •

We can learn several lessons from Akira Kurosawa's school experience. First, children—even highly gifted ones—develop at different rates. A late bloomer should not be expected to progress as fast as a more precocious child. Second, Kurosawa's story illustrates the strong impact a teacher can have and how the influences of home and school interact. Finally, we see once again the tie-in between cognitive and psychosocial development. The flowering of Kurosawa's cognitive and social competence followed closely upon Mr. Tachikawa's move to boost his self-esteem. As Kurosawa later wrote, "When someone is told over and over again that he's no good at something, he loses more and more confidence and eventually does become poor at it. Conversely, if he's told he's good at something, his confidence builds and he actually becomes better at it" (1983, p. 40).

School is a major formative experience in middle childhood, impinging on every aspect of development. Even today, when many children go to preschool and most go to kindergarten, the start of Grade 1 is a milestone—a sign that a child has entered a new stage of development. During the next few years, children typically gain in self-confidence as they read, think, talk, play, and imagine in ways that were well beyond them only a few years before.

In this chapter we examine cognitive advances during the first 5 or 6 years of formal schooling, from about ages 6 to 11. Entry into Piaget's stage of concrete operations enables children to think logically and to make more mature moral judgments. As children improve in memory and problem solving, intelligence tests become more accurate in predicting school performance. The abilities to read and write open the door to a wider world. We describe all these changes, and we examine the controversies over IQ testing, homework, mathematics instruction, and bilingual education. Finally, we examine influences on school achievement and how schools try to meet special educational needs.

After you have read and studied this chapter, you should be able to answer each of the Guidepost questions that appear at the top of the next page. Look for them again in the margins, where they point to important concepts throughout the chapter. To check your understanding of these Guideposts, review the end-of-chapter summary. Checkpoints located throughout the chapter will help you verify your understanding of what you have read.

*Sources of biographical information about Akira Kurosawa are Goodwin (1994), Kurosawa (1983), and Richie (1984).

Guideposts for Study

1. How do school-age children's thinking and moral reasoning differ from those of younger children?

2. What advances in information-processing skills occur during middle childhood?

3. How accurately can schoolchildren's intelligence be measured?

4. How do communicative abilities expand during middle childhood?

5. What factors influence school achievement?

6. How do schools meet special needs?

Guidepost 1

How do school-age children's thinking and moral reasoning differ from those of younger children?

concrete operations Third stage of Piagetian cognitive development (approximately from ages 7 to 12), during which children develop logical but not abstract thinking

Piagetian Approach: The Concrete Operational Child

At about age 7, according to Piaget, children enter the stage of **concrete operations,** when they can use mental operations to solve concrete (actual) problems. Children now can think logically because they can take multiple aspects of a situation into account. However, children are still limited to thinking about real situations in the here and now.

Cognitive Advances

Children in the stage of concrete operations can perform many tasks at a much higher level than they could in the pre-operational stage (see Table 13-1). They have a better understanding

Table 13-1	Advances in Selected Cognitive Abilities During Middle Childhood
Ability	**Example**
Spatial thinking	Danielle can use a map or model to help her search for a hidden object and can give someone else directions for finding the object. She can find her way to and from school, can estimate distances, and can judge how long it will take her to go from one place to another.
Cause and effect	Douglas knows which physical attributes of objects on each side of a balance scale will affect the result (i.e., number of objects matters but colour does not). He does not yet know which spatial factors, such as position and placement of the objects, make a difference.
Categorization	Elena can sort objects into categories, such as shape, colour, or both. She knows that a subclass (roses) has fewer members than the class of which it is a part (flowers).
Seriation and transitive inference	Catherine can arrange a group of sticks in order, from the shortest to the longest, and can insert an intermediate-size stick into the proper place. She knows that if one stick is longer than a second stick, and the second stick is longer than a third, then the first stick is longer than the third.
Inductive and deductive reasoning	Dara can solve both inductive and deductive problems and knows that inductive conclusions (based on particular premises) are less certain than deductive ones (based on general premises).
Conservation	Stacy, at age 7, knows that if a clay ball is rolled into a sausage, it still contains the same amount of clay (conservation of substance). At age 9, she knows that the ball and the sausage weigh the same. Not until early adolescence will she understand that they displace the same amount of liquid if dropped in a glass of water.
Number and mathematics	Kevin can count in his head, can add by counting up from the smaller number, and can do simple story problems.

of spatial concepts, of causality, of categorization, of inductive and deductive reasoning, of conservation, and of number.

Space and Causality

Why can many 6- or 7-year-olds find their way to and from school, whereas most younger children cannot? One reason is that children in the stage of concrete operations can better understand spatial relationships. They have a clearer idea of how far it is from one place to another and how long it will take to get there, and they can more easily remember the route and the landmarks along the way. Experience plays a role in this development: A child who walks to school becomes more familiar with the neighbourhood outside the home.

Both the ability to use maps and models and the ability to communicate spatial information improve with age (Gauvain, 1993). So do judgments about cause and effect. When 5-to 12-year-olds were asked to predict how levers and balance scales would perform under varying conditions, the older children gave more correct answers than the younger children. Children understood the influence of physical attributes (the number of objects on each side of a scale) earlier than they recognized the influence of spatial factors (the distance of objects from the centre of the scale) (Amsel, Goodman, Savoie, & Clark, 1996).

Categorization

Categorization now includes such sophisticated abilities as *seriation, transitive inference,* and *class inclusion*. Children show that they understand **seriation** when they can arrange objects in a series according to one or more dimensions, such as weight (lightest to heaviest) or colour (lightest to darkest). By 7 or 8, children can grasp the relationships among a group of sticks on sight and arrange them in order of size (Piaget, 1952).

seriation Ability to order items along a dimension

Transitive inference is the ability to recognize a relationship between two objects by knowing the relationship between each of them and a third object. Catherine is shown three sticks: a yellow one, a green one, and a blue one. She is shown that the yellow stick is longer than the green one, and the green one is longer than the blue. Without physically comparing the yellow and blue sticks, she knows that the yellow one is longer than the blue one (Chapman & Lindenberger, 1988; Piaget & Inhelder, 1967).

transitive inference Understanding of the relationship between two objects by knowing the relationship of each to a third object

Class inclusion is the ability to see the relationship between a whole and its parts. If pre-operational children are shown a bunch of 10 flowers—seven roses and three carnations—and are asked whether there are more roses or more flowers, they are likely to say there are more roses, because they are comparing the roses with the carnations rather than with the whole bunch. Not until the stage of concrete operations do children come to realize that roses are a subclass of flowers and that, therefore, there cannot be more roses than flowers (Flavell, 1963; Flavell et al., 2002). However, even 3-year-olds show a rudimentary awareness of class inclusion, depending on the type of task, the practical cues they receive, and their familiarity with the categories of objects they are tested on (Johnson, Scott, & Mervis, 1997).

class inclusion Understanding of the relationship between a whole and its parts

Inductive and Deductive Reasoning

According to Piaget, children in the stage of concrete operations use only **inductive reasoning.** Starting with observations about particular members of a class of people, animals, objects, or events, they then draw general conclusions about the class as a whole. ("My dog barks. So does Terry's dog and Melissa's dog. So it looks as if all dogs bark.") Inductive conclusions must be tentative because it is always possible to come across new information (a dog that does not bark) that does not support the conclusion.

inductive reasoning Type of logical reasoning that moves from particular observations about members of a class to a general conclusion about that class

Deductive reasoning, which Piaget believed does not develop until adolescence, starts with a general statement (premise) about a class and applies it to particular members of the class. If the premise is true of the whole class, and the reasoning is sound, then the conclusion must be true: "All dogs bark. Spot is a dog. Spot barks."

deductive reasoning Type of logical reasoning that moves from a general premise about a class to a conclusion about a particular member or members of the class

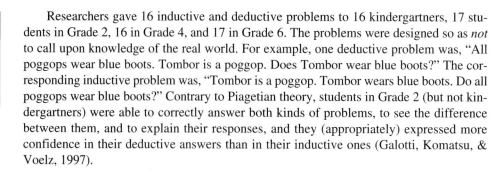

What's your view ?

- How can parents and teachers help children improve their reasoning ability?

horizontal décalage Piaget's term for inability to transfer learning about one type of conservation to other types, which causes a child to master different types of conservation tasks at different ages

Checkpoint ✔

Can you . . .

✔ Identify six kinds of cognitive abilities that emerge or strengthen during middle childhood, and explain how?

✔ Name three principles that help school-aged children understand conservation, and explain why children master different kinds of conservation at different ages?

✔ Give examples of how neurological development and schooling can affect ability to perform on Piagetian tasks?

Researchers gave 16 inductive and deductive problems to 16 kindergartners, 17 students in Grade 2, 16 in Grade 4, and 17 in Grade 6. The problems were designed so as *not* to call upon knowledge of the real world. For example, one deductive problem was, "All poggops wear blue boots. Tombor is a poggop. Does Tombor wear blue boots?" The corresponding inductive problem was, "Tombor is a poggop. Tombor wears blue boots. Do all poggops wear blue boots?" Contrary to Piagetian theory, students in Grade 2 (but not kindergartners) were able to correctly answer both kinds of problems, to see the difference between them, and to explain their responses, and they (appropriately) expressed more confidence in their deductive answers than in their inductive ones (Galotti, Komatsu, & Voelz, 1997).

Conservation

In solving various types of conservation problems, children in the stage of concrete operations can work out the answers in their heads; they do not have to measure or weigh the objects.

If one of two identical clay balls is rolled or kneaded into a different shape—say, a long, thin "sausage,"—Felipe, who is in the stage of concrete operations, will say that the ball and the "sausage" still contain the same amount of clay. Stacy, who is in the preoperational stage, is deceived by appearances. She says the long, thin roll contains more clay because it looks longer.

Felipe, unlike Stacy, understands the principle of *identity:* he knows the clay is still the same clay, even though it has a different shape. He also understands the principle of *reversibility:* he knows he can change the sausage back into a ball. And he can *decentre:* he can focus on both length and width. He recognizes that although the ball is shorter than the "sausage," it is also thicker. Stacy centres on one dimension (length) while excluding the other (thickness).

Typically, children can solve problems involving conservation of substance, like this one, by about age 7 or 8. However, in tasks involving conservation of weight—in which they are asked, for example, whether the ball and the "sausage" weigh the same—children typically do not give correct answers until about age 9 or 10. In tasks involving conservation of volume—in which children must judge whether the "sausage" and the ball displace an equal amount of liquid when placed in a glass of water—correct answers are rare before age 12.

Piaget's term for this inconsistency in the development of different types of conservation is **horizontal décalage.** Children's thinking at this stage is so concrete, so closely tied to a particular situation, that they cannot readily transfer what they have learned about one type of conservation to another type, even though the underlying principles are the same.

Number and Mathematics

By age 6 or 7, many children can count in their heads. They also learn to *count on:* to add 5 and 3, they start counting at 5 and then go on to 6, 7, and 8 to add the 3. It may take 2 or 3 more years for them to perform a comparable operation for subtraction, but by age 9 most children can either count up from the smaller number or down from the larger number to get the answer (Resnick, 1989).

Children also become more adept at solving simple story problems, such as: "Peter went to the store with $5 and spent $2 on candy. How much did he have left?" When the original amount is unknown ("Peter went to the store, spent $2 and had $3 left. How much did he start out with?"), the problem is harder because the operation needed to solve it (addition) is not as clearly indicated. Few children can solve this kind of problem before age 8 or 9 (Resnick, 1989).

Research with minimally schooled people in non-industrialized countries suggests that the ability to add develops nearly universally and often intuitively, through concrete experience in a cultural context (Guberman, 1996; Resnick, 1989). These intuitive procedures are different from those

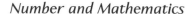

Are there more red checkers or black checkers? This girl counting the checkers is solving a Piagetian conservation task. Because the red checkers are more spread out, a pre-operational child would say there are more of them. A child in the stage of concrete operations will count, as this girl is doing, and say there are equal numbers of each colour.

taught in school. In a study of Brazilian street vendors ages 9 to 15, a researcher acting as a customer says, "I'll take two coconuts." Each one costs 40 cruzeiros; she pays with a 500-cruzeiros bill and asks, "What do I get back?" The child counts up from 80: "Eighty, 90, 100 . . . " and gives the customer 420 cruzeiros. However, when this same child is given a similar problem in the classroom ("What is 500 minus 80?"), he arrives at the wrong answer by incorrectly using a series of steps learned in school (Carraher, Schliemann, & Carraher, 1988). This suggests that teaching math through concrete applications, not only through abstract rules, may be more effective.

Some intuitive understanding of fractions seems to exist by age 4 (Mix, Levine, & Huttenlocher, 1999), as children show when they deal a deck of cards or distribute portions of pizza (Frydman & Bryant, 1988; Sophian, Garyantes, & Chang, 1997). However, children tend not to think about the quantity a fraction represents; instead, they focus on the numerals that make it up. Thus they may say that ½ plus ⅓ equals ⅖. Also difficult for many children to grasp at first is the fact that ½ is bigger than ¼—that the smaller fraction (¼) has the larger denominator (Siegler, 1998; Sophian & Wood, 1997).

The ability to estimate progresses with age. When asked to place 24 numbers along a line from 0 to 100, almost all kindergartners exaggerate the differences between low numbers and minimize the distances between high numbers. Most second graders produce number lines that are more evenly spaced (Siegler & Booth, 2004). Second, fourth, and sixth graders show a similar progression in producing number lines from 0 to 1,000 (Siegler & Opfer, 2003), most likely reflecting the experience older children gain in dealing with larger numbers. Besides improving in *number line estimation,* school-age children also improve in three other types of estimation: *computational estimation,* such as estimating the sum in an addition problem; *numerosity estimation,* estimating the number of candies in a jar; and *measurement estimation,* estimating the length of a line (Booth & Siegler, 2006).

Influences of Neurological Development and Schooling

Piaget maintained that the shift from the rigid, illogical thinking of younger children to the flexible, logical thinking of older ones depends on both neurological maturation and experience in adapting to the environment. Support for a neurological basis of conservation of volume comes from scalp measurements of brain activity during a conservation task. Children who had achieved conservation of volume showed brainwave patterns different from those of children who had not yet achieved it, suggesting that they may have been using different brain regions for the task (Stauder, Molenaar, & Van der Molen, 1993).

Today's schoolchildren may not be advancing through Piaget's stages as rapidly as their parents did. When 10,000 British 11- and 12-year-olds were tested on conservation of volume and weight, their performance was two to three years behind that of their counterparts 30 years earlier (Shayer, Ginsburg, & Coe, 2007). These results suggest that today's schoolchildren may be getting too much drilling on the three Rs and not enough hands-on experience with the way materials behave.

Moral Reasoning

To draw out children's moral thinking, Piaget (1932) would tell them a story about two little boys: "One day Augustus noticed that his father's inkpot was empty and decided to help his father by filling it. While he was opening the bottle, he spilled a lot of ink on the table cloth. The other boy, Julian, played with his father's inkpot and spilled a little ink on the cloth." Then Piaget would ask, "Which boy was naughtier, and why?"

Children younger than 7 usually considered Augustus naughtier, since he made the bigger stain. Older children recognized that Augustus meant well and made the large stain by accident, whereas Julian made a small stain while doing something he should not have been doing. Immature moral judgments, Piaget concluded, centre only on the degree of offence; more mature judgments consider intent.

Piaget (1932; Piaget & Inhelder, 1969) proposed that moral reasoning develops in three stages. Children move gradually from one stage to another, at varying ages.

The first stage (approximately ages 2 to 7, corresponding with the preoperational stage) is based on *rigid obedience to authority.* Because young children are egocentric,

What's your view

- Do you agree that intent is an important factor in morality?
- How does the criminal justice system reflect this view?

they cannot imagine more than one way of looking at a moral issue. They believe that rules cannot be bent or changed, that behaviour is either right or wrong, and that any offence (like Augustus') deserves punishment, regardless of intent.

The second stage (ages 7 or 8 to 10 or 11, corresponding with the stage of concrete operations) is characterized by *increasing flexibility*. As children interact with more people and come into contact with a wider range of viewpoints, they begin to discard the idea that there is a single, absolute standard of right and wrong and to develop their own sense of justice based on fairness or equal treatment for all. Because they can consider more than one aspect of a situation, they can make more subtle moral judgments, such as taking into consideration the intent behind Augustus' and Julian's behaviour.

Around age 11 or 12, when children may become capable of formal reasoning, the third stage of moral development arrives. The belief that everyone should be treated alike gives way to the ideal of *equity*, of taking specific circumstances into account. Thus, a child of this age might say that a 2-year-old who spilled ink on the tablecloth should be held to a less demanding moral standard than a 10-year-old who did the same thing.

Current perspectives are beginning to challenge the traditional view that children pass through universal stages of moral development. Instead, children as young as 6 years of age have been shown to be sensitive to the context and domain of moral issues. In a study of 72 Canadian children, Helwig and Jasiobedzka (2001) found that using simple tasks that did not require responses to open-ended questions, 6-year-old children were as capable as 8- and 10-year-old children in evaluating fairness of just and unjust laws, and reasoning about the consequences of violating socially unjust laws. In fact children as young as 3 years are capable of understanding the nature of psychological harm in making moral judgments, though they tend to focus on the outcome of the act rather than the intention of the act, which older children tend to do (Helwig, Zelazo, & Wilson, 2001). Earlier research on moral reasoning might reflect children's developing abilities to articulate abstract moral principles, rather than their basic moral reasoning abilities (Helwig et al., 2001).

We discuss Lawrence Kohlberg's theory of moral reasoning, which builds on Piaget's, in Chapter 16.

Checkpoint ✔

Can you . . .

✔ Describe Piaget's three stages of moral development and explain their link to cognitive maturation?

Information-Processing Approach: Attention, Memory, and Planning

Guidepost 2

What advances in information-processing skills occur during middle childhood?

executive function Conscious control of thoughts, emotions, and actions to accomplish goals or solve problems

As children move through the school years, they make steady progress in their abilities to process and retain information. They understand more about how memory works, and this knowledge enables them to use strategies, or deliberate plans, to help them remember. All of these interrelated developments are central to **executive function,** the conscious control of thoughts, emotions, and actions to accomplish goals or solve problems (Luna et al., 2004; NICHD Early Child Care Research Network, 2005d; Zelazo & Müller, 2002). In addition, as their knowledge expands, they become more aware of what kinds of information are important to pay attention to and remember. School-age children also understand more about how memory works, and this knowledge enables them to plan and use strategies, or deliberate techniques, to help them remember.

How Do Executive Skills Develop?

The gradual development of executive function from infancy through adolescence accompanies the development of the brain, in particular, the *prefrontal cortex,* the region that enables planning, judgment, and decision making (Lamm, Zelazo, & Lewis, 2006). As unneeded synapses are pruned away and pathways become myelinated, *processing speed*—usually measured by reaction time—improves dramatically, especially in girls (Camarata & Woodcock, 2006; Luna, Garver, Urban, Lazar, & Sweeney, 2004). Faster, more efficient processing increases the amount of information children can keep in working memory, enabling complex thinking and goal-directed planning (Flavell et al., 2002; Luna et al., 2004).

The home environment, too, contributes to the development of executive skills. In a longitudinal study of 700 children from infancy on, the quality of the family environment, especially between ages 4½ and 6—including such factors as available resources, cognitive stimulation, and maternal sensitivity—predicted attentional and memory performance in first grade (NICHD Early Child Care Research Network, 2005d).

School-age children develop planning skills by making decisions about their own everyday activities. Parenting practices and culture affect the pace at which children are allowed to do this. In a three-year longitudinal study of 79 European American and 61 Latino children in a southwestern U.S. city, the responsibility for planning children's informal activities gradually shifted between second and fourth grades from parent to child, and this change was reflected in improved ability to plan classroom work. This shift occurred at an earlier age for European American children than for Latino children. More acculturated Latino parents let boys (but not girls) plan their own activities earlier than did nonacculturated Latino parents (Gauvain & Perez, 2005).

Completing a science fair project and displaying the results, as this student is doing, promotes the use of higher-level thinking.

Working Memory Span

The efficiency of working memory increases greatly in middle childhood, laying the foundation for a wide range of cognitive skills. What changes produce that vast improvement? In one study, 120 British 6- to 10-year-olds were asked to perform complex memory span tasks involving computerized visual and verbal images. Improvements both in processing speed and in storage capacity were found to underlie the development of working memory in this age group (Bayliss, Jarrold, Baddeley, Gunn, & Leigh, 2005).

Metamemory: Understanding Memory

Between ages 5 and 7, the brain's frontal lobes may undergo significant development and reorganization, making improved recall and **metamemory,** knowledge about the processes of memory, possible (Janowsky & Carper, 1996).

metamemory Understanding of processes of memory

From kindergarten through Grade 5, children advance steadily in understanding of memory (Flavell et al., 1993; Kreutzer, Leonard, & Flavell, 1975). Kindergartners and first-graders know that people remember better if they study longer, that people forget things with time, and that relearning something is easier than learning it for the first time. By Grade 3, children know that some people remember better than others and that some things are easier to remember than others.

Mnemonics: Strategies for Remembering

Devices to aid memory are called **mnemonic strategies.** The most common mnemonic strategy among both children and adults is use of *external memory aids.* Other common mnemonic strategies include *rehearsal, organization,* and *elaboration* (see Table 13-2).

mnemonic strategies Techniques to aid memory

Writing down a telephone number, making a list, setting a timer, and putting a library book by the front door are examples of **external memory aids:** prompting by something outside the person. Saying a telephone number over and over after looking it up, so as not to forget it before dialing, is a form of **rehearsal,** or conscious repetition. **Organization** is mentally placing information into categories (such as animals, furniture, vehicles, and clothing) to make it easier to recall. In **elaboration,** children associate items with something else, such as an imagined scene or story. To remember to buy lemons, ketchup, and napkins, for example, a child might imagine a ketchup bottle balanced on a lemon, with a pile of napkins handy to wipe up spilled ketchup.

external memory aids Mnemonic strategies using something outside the person

rehearsal Mnemonic strategy to keep an item in working memory through conscious repetition

organization Mnemonic strategy of categorizing material to be remembered

elaboration Mnemonic strategy of making mental associations involving items to be remembered

As children get older, they develop better strategies, use them more effectively, and tailor them to meet specific needs (Bjorklund, 1997; see Table 13-2). When taught to use a strategy, older children are more likely to apply it spontaneously to other situations (Flavell et al., 2002). Children often use more than one strategy for a task and choose different kinds of strategies for different problems (Coyle & Bjorklund, 1997).

Table 13-2	Four Common Memory Strategies		
Strategy	**Definition**	**Development in Middle Childhood**	**Example**
External memory aids	Prompting by something outside the person	5- and 6-year-olds can do this, but 8-year-olds are more likely to think of it.	Dana makes a list of the things she has to do today.
Rehearsal	Conscious repetition	6-year-olds can be taught to do this; 7-year-olds do it spontaneously.	Ian says the letters in his spelling words over and over until he knows them.
Organization	Grouping by categories	Most children do not do this until at least age 10, but younger children can be taught to do it.	Luis recalls the animals he saw in the zoo by thinking first of the mammals, then the reptiles, then the amphibians, then the fish, and then the birds.
Elaboration	Associating items to be remembered with something else, such as a phrase, scene, or story	Older children are more likely to do this spontaneously and remember better if they make up their own elaboration; younger children remember better if someone else makes it up.	Yolanda remembers the lines of the musical staff (E, G, B, D, F) by associating them with the phrase "Every good boy does fine."

Selective Attention

School-age children can concentrate longer than younger children and can focus on the information they need and want while screening out irrelevant information. For example, they can summon up the appropriate meaning of a word they read and suppress other meanings that do not fit the context (Simpson & Foster, 1986; Simpson & Lorsbach, 1983). Students in Grade 5 are better able than those in Grade 1 to keep discarded information from re-entering working memory and vying with other material for attention (Harnishfeger & Pope, 1996). This growth in *selective attention*—the ability to deliberately direct one's attention and shut out distractions—may hinge on the executive skill of *inhibitory control,* the voluntary suppression of unwanted responses (Luna et al., 2004).

The increasing capacity for selective attention is believed to be due to neurological maturation and is one of the reasons memory improves during middle childhood (Bjorklund & Harnishfeger, 1990; Harnishfeger & Bjorklund, 1993). Older children may make fewer mistakes in recall than younger ones because they are better able to select what they want to remember and what they can forget (Lorsbach & Reimer, 1997).

Information Processing and Piagetian Tasks

Improvements in information processing may help explain the advances Piaget described. For example, 9-year-olds may be better able than 5-year-olds to find their way to and from school because they can scan a scene, take in its important features, and remember objects in context, in the order in which the children encountered them (Allen & Ondracek, 1995).

Improvements in memory may contribute to the mastery of conservation tasks. Young children's working memory is so limited that, even if they are able to master the concept of conservation, they may not be able to remember all the relevant information (Siegler & Richards, 1982). They may forget that two differently shaped pieces of clay were originally identical. Gains in short-term memory may contribute to the ability to solve problems like this in middle childhood.

Robbie Case (1985, 1992), a neo-Piagetian theorist (refer back to Chapter 2), suggests that as a child's application of a concept or scheme becomes more automatic, it frees space in working memory to deal with new information. This may help explain horizontal

Checkpoint

Can you . . .

✔ Explain the importance of executive function and how it develops?

✔ Identify at least three specific ways in which information processing improves during middle childhood?

✔ Explain the value of selective attention and metamemory?

✔ Name four common mnemonic aids and discuss developmental differences in their use?

✔ Give examples of how improved information processing may help explain cognitive advances Piaget described?

décalage: Children may need to become comfortable enough with one kind of conservation to use it without conscious thought before they can extend and adapt that scheme to other kinds of conservation.

Psychometric Approach: Assessment of Intelligence

Guidepost 3

How accurately can schoolchildren's intelligence be measured?

Intelligence tests (or IQ tests) are called **aptitude tests:** they claim to measure the capacity to learn, as contrasted with **achievement tests,** which assess how much children have already learned in various subject areas.

Traditional Group and Individual Tests

The original IQ tests, such as those of Alfred Binet and Theodore Simon (see Chapter 7), were designed to be given to individuals, and their modern versions still are used that way. The first group tests, developed during World War I to screen army recruits for appropriate assignments, became models for the group tests now given in schools. As both individual and group tests have been refined, their developers have turned from the original emphasis on general intelligence to more sophisticated distinctions among various kinds of abilities and have sought to adapt the tests to special needs (Anastasi & Urbina, 1997; Daniel, 1997).

One popular group test, the **Otis-Lennon School Ability Test (OLSAT8)** has levels for kindergarten through Grade 12. Children are asked to classify items, to show an understanding of verbal and numerical concepts, to display general information, and to follow directions. Separate scores for verbal comprehension, verbal reasoning, pictorial reasoning, figural reasoning, and quantitative reasoning can identify strengths and weaknesses.

The most widely used individual test is the **Wechsler Intelligence Scale for Children (WISC–IV).** This test for ages 6 through 16 measures verbal and performance abilities, yielding separate scores for each, as well as a total score. With separate subtest scores, it is easier to pinpoint a child's strengths and to diagnose specific problems. For example, if a child does well on verbal tests (such as general information and basic arithmetic operations) but poorly on performance tests (such as doing a puzzle or drawing the missing part of a picture), the child may be slow in perceptual or motor development. A child who does well on performance tests but poorly on verbal tests may have a language problem. Another commonly used individual test is the Stanford-Binet Intelligence Scales, Fifth Edition (see Chapter 10).

The most commonly used intelligence tests in Canada are produced in the United States. This can be a problem because many items may not be appropriate measures of intelligence of Canadian children (for example, using imperial measures instead of metric for arithmetic problems, or items requiring knowledge of U.S. culture and history, rather than Canadian). In addition, developers of American tests use American representative samples of children as the basis for developing norms against which individual children's scores are compared. The characteristics of the U.S. samples are different enough from the Canadian population to raise concerns about the appropriateness of using American norms for Canadian children. Canadian children score differently from American children (Weiss, Saklofske, Prifitera, Chen, & Hildebrand, 1999); for example, Aboriginal children might be at a disadvantage on tests that rely heavily on verbal abilities (Scaldwell, Frame, & Cookson, 1985). Canadian norms have been developed for the WISC (Wechsler, 1996; 2003), as have ways of using the test, appropriate for Canadian children, to look at different aspects of intelligence (Saklofske, Caravan, & Schwartz, 2000; Weiss et al., 1999).

The IQ Controversy

The use of psychometric intelligence tests is controversial. On the positive side, because IQ tests have been standardized and widely used, there is extensive information about

aptitude tests Tests that measure children's general intelligence, or capacity to learn

achievement tests Tests that assess how much children know in various subject areas

Otis-Lennon School Ability Test (OLSAT8) Group intelligence test for kindergarten through Grade 12

Wechsler Intelligence Scale for Children (WISC–IV) Individual intelligence test for schoolchildren, which yields verbal and performance scores as well as a combined score

their norms, validity, and reliability (see Chapters 2 and 7). IQ scores during middle childhood are fairly good predictors of school achievement, especially for highly verbal children, and scores are more reliable than during the preschool years. In fact, IQ at age 11 has been found to predict length of life, functional independence late in life, and the presence or absence of dementia (Starr, Deary, Lemmon, & Whalley, 2000; Whalley & Deary, 2001; Whalley et al., 2000).

But are IQ tests fair? Critics claim that the tests underestimate the intelligence of children who are in ill health or, for one reason or another, do not do well on tests (Anastasi, 1988; Ceci, 1991; Sternberg, 2004). Because the tests are timed, they equate intelligence with speed and penalize a child who works slowly and deliberately. Their appropriateness for diagnosing learning disabilities has been questioned (Benson, 2003).

A more fundamental criticism is that IQ tests infer intelligence from what children already know; and much of this knowledge is derived from schooling or culture, and thus the tests cannot measure native ability. As we'll see, it is virtually impossible to design a test that requires no prior knowledge. Further, the tests are validated against measures of achievement, such as school performance, which are affected by such factors as schooling and culture (Sternberg, 2004, 2005). As we will discuss in a subsequent section, there is also controversy over whether intelligence is a single, general ability or whether there are types of intelligence not captured by IQ tests. For these and other reasons, there is strong disagreement over how accurately these tests assess children's intelligence.

Influences on Intelligence

As we discussed in Chapter 3, both heredity and environment influence intelligence. Keeping in mind the controversy over whether IQ tests actually measure intelligence, let's look more closely at these influences.

Genes and Brain Development

Brain imaging research shows a moderate correlation between brain size or amount of grey matter and general intelligence, especially reasoning and problem solving abilities (Gray & Thompson, 2004). One study found that the amount of grey matter in the frontal cortex is largely inherited, varies widely among individuals, and is linked with differences in IQ (Thompson, Cannon, et al., 2001). A later study suggests that the key is not the *amount* of grey matter a child has at a certain age, but rather the *pattern of development* of the prefrontal cortex, the seat of executive function and higher-level thinking. In children of average IQ, the prefrontal cortex is relatively thick at age 7, peaks in thickness by age 8, and then gradually thins as unneeded connections are pruned. In the most intelligent 7-year-olds, by contrast, the cortex does not peak in thickness until age 11 or 12. The prolonged thickening of the prefrontal cortex may represent an extended critical period for developing high-level thinking circuits (Shaw et al., 2006).

Although reasoning, problem solving, and executive function are linked to the prefrontal cortex, other brain regions under strong genetic influence contribute to intelligent behaviour. So does the speed and reliabiity of transmission of "messages" in the brain. Environmental factors, such as the family, schooling, and culture, also play a part; but heritability of intelligence (the degree to which individual differences in intelligence are genetically caused) increases with age as children select or create environments that fit their genetic tendencies (Gray & Thompson, 2004).

Influence of Schooling on IQ

Schooling does seem to increase tested intelligence (Ceci & Williams, 1997; Neisser et al., 1996). In one study, differences in IQ between identical twins raised in different homes were directly related to the amount of education each twin had had (Bronfenbrenner, 1979). Children whose school entrance was significantly delayed (as happened, for example, in South Africa due to a teacher shortage and in the Netherlands during the Nazi occupation) lost as many as 5 IQ points per year, and some of these losses were never recovered (Ceci & Williams, 1997).

IQ scores also drop during summer vacation (Ceci & Williams, 1997). Among a national sample of 1,500 children, language, spatial, and conceptual scores improved much more between October and April, the bulk of the school year, than between April and October, which includes summer vacation and the beginning and end of the school year (Huttenlocher, Levine, & Vevea, 1998).

Influence of Race/Ethnicity on IQ

Ethnicity also affects test scores, inspiring claims that the tests are unfair to minorities. Although there is a great deal of individual diversity, Aboriginal children tend to score lower than non-Aboriginal children on standardized measures of IQ, particularly on tests involving verbal intelligence (Beiser & Gotowiec, 2000). On the other hand, Inuit children in Arctic Quebec have been found to score higher than U.S. norms on a non-verbal intelligence test (the Raven's Coloured Progressive Matrices, measuring analytic intelligence), and similar to their non-Inuit counterparts in southern Quebec (Wright, Taylor, & Ruggiero, 1996). In the United States, African-Americans on average score about 15 points lower than white children and show a comparable lag on school achievement tests. However, Asian-Americans, who typically do better than other groups on academic achievement, do not seem to have a significant edge in IQ—a reminder of the limited predictive power of intelligence testing (Neisser et al., 1996).

What accounts for ethnic differences in IQ? Some writers have argued that part of the cause is genetic (Herrnstein & Murray, 1994; Jensen, 1969; Rushton & Jensen, 2005). However, while there is strong evidence of a genetic influence on *individual* differences in intelligence, there is *no* direct evidence that differences among ethnic, cultural, or racial groups are hereditary (Gray & Thompson, 2004; Neisser et al., 1996; Sternberg et al., 2005). Instead, many studies attribute ethnic differences in IQ largely or entirely to inequalities in environment (Nisbett, 1998, 2005)—in income, nutrition, living conditions, health, parenting practices, early child care, intellectual stimulation, schooling, culture, or other circumstances such as the effects of oppression and discrimination that can affect self-esteem, motivation, and academic performance. Environmental differences also affect readiness for school (Rouse et al., 2005), which, in turn, affects measured intelligence as well as achievement.

The recent narrowing of the gap between white and black children's test scores in the U.S. parallels an improvement in the life circumstances and educational opportunities of many African-American children (Nisbett, 2005). In addition, as we discussed in Chapter 7, some early intervention programs have had significant success in raising disadvantaged children's IQs (Nisbett, 2005). With improvements in educational opportunities in Canada, such as those offered by the Aboriginal Head Start program, it is likely that the gaps reported between Aboriginal and non-Aboriginal children will similarly diminish.

In a study of Aboriginal children, when IQ scores were adjusted for differences between Aboriginal and non-Aboriginal children in prenatal maternal health, English-language skills, socio-economic status, and parental attitudes towards school and cultural separation, the differences were virtually eliminated (Beiser et al., 2000). With better health care, socio-economic status, and educational opportunities for Aboriginal groups, the disparity in IQ scores will probably be reduced or eliminated.

The strength of genetic influence itself appears to vary with socioeconomic status. In a longitudinal study of 319 pairs of twins followed from birth, the genetic influence on IQ scores at age 7 among children from impoverished families was close to zero and the influence of environment was strong, whereas among children in affluent families the opposite was true. In other words, high SES strengthens genetic influence, whereas low SES tends to override it (Turkheimer, Haley, Waldron, D'Onofrio, & Gottesman, 2003). Still, although socio-economic status and IQ are strongly related, SES does not seem to explain the entire intergroup variance in IQ (Neisser et al., 1996; Suzuki & Valencia, 1997).

Influence of Culture on IQ

Some critics attribute ethnic differences in IQ to **cultural bias:** a tendency to include questions that use vocabulary or call for information or skills more familiar or meaningful to

cultural bias Tendency of intelligence tests to include items calling for knowledge or skills more familiar or meaningful to some cultural groups than to others

Can you . . .

✔ Name and describe two traditional intelligence tests for schoolchildren?

✔ Discuss influences on measured intelligence and explanations that have been advanced for differences in the performance of children of various racial/ethnic and cultural groups?

culture-free Describing an intelligence test that, if it were possible to design, would have no culturally linked content

culture-fair Describing an intelligence test that deals with experiences common to various cultures, in an attempt to avoid cultural bias

culture-relevant Describing an intelligence test that takes into account the adaptive tasks children face in their culture

theory of multiple intelligences Gardner's theory that each person has several distinct forms of intelligence

some cultural groups than to others (Sternberg, 1985a, 1987), particularly in established market economies in the industrialized world (Sternberg, Grigorenko, & Bundy, 2001). These critics argue that intelligence tests are built around the dominant thinking style and language of white people of European ancestry, putting minority children at a disadvantage (Heath, 1989; Helms, 1992).

Culture, language, and socio-economic status differences (Beiser et al., 2000) may well explain the lower IQs of Aboriginal children, who tend to do better on performance tasks than on verbal tasks (Neisser et al., 1996). Language may play a part in the black–white differential in the United States as well; some test items may be confusing to children who hear black English rather than standard English at home. Cultural bias also may affect the testing situation. For example, a child from a culture that stresses sociability and cooperation may be handicapped taking a test alone (Kottak, 1994). Still, while cultural bias may play a part in some children's performance, controlled studies have failed to show that it contributes substantially to overall group differences in IQ (Neisser et al., 1996).

Test developers have tried to design **culture-free** tests—tests with no culture-linked content—by posing tasks that do not require language, such as tracing mazes, putting the right shapes in the right holes, and completing pictures; but they have been unable to eliminate all cultural influences. Test designers also have found it virtually impossible to produce **culture-fair** tests consisting only of experiences common to people in various cultures. Robert Sternberg (2004) maintains that intelligence and culture are inextricably linked. Behaviour seen as intelligent in one culture may be viewed as foolish in another. For example, when given a sorting task, North Americans would be likely to place a robin under the category of birds, whereas the Kpelle people in North Africa would consider it more intelligent to place the robin in a functional category (flying things) (Cole, 1998). Thus a test of intelligence developed in one culture may not be equally valid in another. Furthermore, the schooling offered in a culture may prepare a child to do well in certain tasks and not in others, and the competencies taught and tested in school are not necessarily the same as the practical skills needed to succeed in everyday life (Sternberg, 2004, 2005).

Sternberg (2004) defines *successful intelligence* as the skills and knowledge needed for success within a particular social and cultural context. The mental processes that underlie intelligence may be the same across cultures, says Sternberg, but their products may be different—and so should the means of assessing performance. Sternberg proposes **culture-relevant** tests that take into account the adaptive tasks that confront children in particular cultures.

Is There More than One Intelligence?

Another serious criticism of IQ tests is that they focus almost entirely on abilities that are useful in school. They do *not* cover other important aspects of intelligent behaviour, such as common sense, social skills, creative insight, and self-knowledge. Yet these abilities, in which some children with modest academic skills excel, may become equally or more important in later life (Gardner, 1993; Sternberg, 1985a, 1987) and may even be considered separate forms of intelligence. Two of the chief advocates of this position are Howard Gardner and Robert Sternberg.

Gardner's Theory of Multiple Intelligences

In his **theory of multiple intelligences,** Howard Gardner (1993) defines *intelligence* as the ability to solve problems or create culturally valued products. He maintains that people have at least eight separate kinds of intelligence. Conventional intelligence tests tap only three of these "intelligences": *linguistic, logical-mathematical,* and, to some extent, *spatial.* The other four, which are not reflected in IQ scores, are *musical, bodily-kinesthetic, interpersonal,* and *intrapersonal.* Gardner (1998, 1999) recently added an eighth intelligence, *naturalist intelligence,* to his original list. (See Table 13-3 for definitions and examples of fields in which each "intelligence" is useful.)

High intelligence in one area is not necessarily accompanied by high intelligence in any of the others. A person may be extremely gifted in art (a spatial ability), precision of

Table 13-3	Eight Intelligences, According to Gardner	
Intelligence	**Definition**	**Fields or Occupations Where Used**
Linguistic	Ability to use and understand words and nuances of meaning	Writing, editing, translating
Logical-mathematical	Ability to manipulate numbers and solve logical problems	Science, business, medicine
Musical	Ability to perceive and create patterns of pitch and rhythm	Musical composition, conducting
Spatial	Ability to find one's way around in an environment and judge relationships between objects in space	Architecture, carpentry, city planning
Bodily-kinesthetic	Ability to move with precision	Dancing, athletics, surgery
Interpersonal	Ability to understand and communicate with others	Teaching, acting, politics
Intrapersonal	Ability to understand the self	Counselling, psychiatry, spiritual leadership
Naturalist	Ability to distinguish species	Hunting, fishing, farming, gardening, cooking

Source: Based on Gardner, 1993, 1998.

movement (bodily-kinesthetic), social relations (interpersonal), or self-understanding (intrapersonal), but not have a high IQ. The various intelligences also develop at different rates. For example, logical-mathematical ability tends to develop earlier and to decline more quickly in late life than interpersonal ability.

Gardner would assess each intelligence directly by observing its products—how well a child can tell a story, remember a melody, or get around in a strange area. Extended observation could reveal strengths and weaknesses so as to help children realize their potential, rather than to compare individuals (Gardner, 1995; Scherer, 1985). Of course, such assessments would be far more time-consuming and more open to observer bias than paper and pencil tests.

Sternberg's Triarchic Theory of Intelligence

Sternberg's (1985a, 2004) **triarchic theory of intelligence** embraces three elements, or aspects, of intelligence: *componential, experiential,* and *contextual.* A person may be strong in one, two, or all three.

- The **componential element** is the *analytic* aspect of intelligence; it determines how efficiently people process information. It tells people how to solve problems, how to monitor solutions, and how to evaluate the results.
- The **experiential element** is *insightful;* it determines how people approach novel or familiar tasks. It allows people to compare new information with what they already know and to come up with new ways of putting facts together—in other words, to think originally.
- The **contextual element** is *practical;* it determines how people deal with their environment. It is the ability to size up a situation and decide what to do: adapt to it, change it, or get out of it.

According to Sternberg, everyone has these three kinds of abilities to a greater or lesser extent. A person may be strong in one, two, or all three.

Conventional IQ tests measure mainly componential ability; and since this ability is the kind most school tasks require, it's not surprising that the tests are fairly good predictors of school performance. Their failure to measure experiential (insightful) or contextual (practical) intelligence, says Sternberg, may explain why they are less useful in predicting

What's your view

- Which of Gardner's "intelligences" are you strongest in?
- Did your education include a focus on any of these aspects?

triarchic theory of intelligence Sternberg's theory describing three types of intelligence: componential (analytical ability), experiential (insight and originality), and contextual (practical thinking)

componential element Sternberg's term for the analytic aspect of intelligence

experiential element Sternberg's term for the insightful aspect of intelligence

contextual element Sternberg's term for the practical aspect of intelligence

tacit knowledge Sternberg's term for information that is not formally taught or openly expressed, but is necessary to get ahead

Sternberg Triarchic Abilities Test (STAT) Test to measure componential, experiential, and contextual intelligence

success in the outside world. In studies in Usenge, Kenya and among Yup'ik Inuit children in southwestern Alaska, children's **tacit knowledge** of such practical matters as medicinal herbs, hunting, fishing, and preserving plants—information gleaned informally, not explicitly taught—showed no correlation with conventional measures of intelligence (Grigorenko et al., 2004; Sternberg, 2004; Sternberg et al., 2001).

The **Sternberg Triarchic Abilities Test (STAT)** (Sternberg, 1993) seeks to measure each of the three aspects of intelligence—analytic, creative, and practical—through multiple-choice and essay questions in three domains: *verbal, quantitative,* and *figural* (or spatial). For example, a test of practical-quantitative intelligence might be to solve an everyday math problem having to do with buying tickets to a ball game or following a recipe for making cookies. A creative-verbal item might ask children to solve deductive reasoning problems that start with factually false premises (such as, "Money falls off trees"). An analytical-figural item might ask children to identify the missing piece of a figure.

Validation studies have found correlations between the STAT and several other tests of critical thinking, creativity, and practical problem solving. As predicted, the three kinds of abilities are only weakly correlated with each other (Sternberg, 1997; Sternberg & Clinkenbeard, 1995).

New Directions in Intelligence Testing

The STAT is only one of several new directions in intelligence testing. Other new diagnostic and predictive tools are based on neurological research and information processing theory. The second edition of the **Kaufman Assessment Battery for Children (K-ABC-II)** (Kaufman & Kaufman, 1983, 2003), an individual test for ages 3 to 18, is designed to evaluate cognitive abilities in children with diverse needs (such as autism, hearing impairments, and language disorders) and from varying cultural and linguistic backgrounds. It has subtests that minimize verbal instructions and responses. It also has items with limited cultural content.

Kaufman Assessment Battery for Children (K-ABC-II) Nontraditional individual intelligence test designed to provide fair assessments of minority children and children with disabilities

Dynamic tests based on Vygotsky's theories emphasize potential rather than present achievement. These tests, which seek to capture the dynamic nature of intelligence, offer an alternative to traditional "static" tests that measure a child's current abilities. Dynamic tests contain items up to two years above a child's current level of competence. Examiners help the child when necessary by asking leading questions, giving examples or demonstrations, and offering feedback; thus, the test itself is a learning situation. The difference between the items a child can answer alone and the items the child can answer with help is the child's zone of proximal development (ZPD) (refer back to Chapter 2).

By pointing to what a child is ready to learn, dynamic testing may give teachers more useful information than does a psychometric test and can aid in designing interventions to help children progress. It can be particularly effective with disadvantaged children and with children in nonwestern cultures (Grigorenko & Sternberg, 1998; Rutland & Campbell, 1996; Sternberg, 2005). However, the ZPD has had little experimental validation (Grigorenko & Sternberg, 1998) and may be inherently difficult to measure precisely.

Despite such innovations, it seems likely that conventional psychometric intelligence tests will continue to dominate the field for some time to come (Daniel, 1997). They are widely entrenched, heavily researched, and readily available, and their developers continue to respond to criticisms with each new revision, seeking to better reflect the abilities of children from various cultural and linguistic backgrounds. Rather than rely on a single score, competent practitioners assess *patterns* of performance along with clinical observations to provide a better picture of the whole child. The results can guide the development of appropriate teaching strategies for a particular child (Benson, 2003).

Checkpoint ✔

Can you . . .

✔ Compare Gardner's and Sternberg's theories, and name and describe specific abilities each proposed?

✔ Describe several new types of intelligence tests?

Guidepost 4

How do communicative abilities expand during middle childhood?

Language and Literacy

Language abilities continue to grow during middle childhood. Children are now better able to understand and interpret oral and written communication and to make themselves understood.

Vocabulary, Grammar, and Syntax

As vocabulary grows during the school years, children use increasingly precise verbs to describe an action *(hitting, slapping, striking, pounding)*. They learn that a word like *run* can have more than one meaning, and they can tell from the context which meaning is intended. They learn, not only to use many more words, but to select the right word for a particular use. *Simile* and *metaphor,* figures of speech in which a word or phrase that usually designates one thing is compared or applied to another, become increasingly common (Owens, 1996; Vosniadou, 1987). Although grammar is quite complex by age 6, children during the early school years rarely use the passive voice (as in "The sidewalk is being shovelled"), verb tenses that include the auxiliary *have* ("I have already shovelled the sidewalk"), and conditional sentences ("If Barbara were home, she would help shovel the sidewalk") (C. S. Chomsky, 1969).

Children's understanding of rules of *syntax* (how words are organized into phrases and sentences) becomes more sophisticated with age (Chomsky, 1969). For example, most children under 5 or 6 years old think the sentences "John promised Bill to go shopping" and "John told Bill to go shopping" both mean that Bill is the one to go to the store. Many 6-year-olds have not yet learned how to interpret constructions such as the one in the first sentence, even though they know what a promise is and can use and understand the word correctly in other sentences. By age 8, most children can interpret the first sentence correctly, and by age 9 virtually all children can. They now look at the meaning of a sentence as a whole instead of focusing on word order alone.

Sentence structure continues to become more elaborate. Older children use more subordinate clauses ("The boy *who delivers the newspapers* rang the doorbell"), and they now look at the semantic effect of a sentence as a whole, rather than focusing on word order as a signal of meaning. Still, some constructions, such as clauses beginning with *however* and *although,* do not become common until early adolescence (Owens, 1996).

Pragmatics: Knowledge about Communication

Children's major area of linguistic growth during the school years is in **pragmatics:** the practical use of language to communicate.* Pragmatics include both conversational and narrative skills.

Good conversationalists probe by asking questions before introducing a topic with which the other person may not be familiar. They quickly recognize a breakdown in communication and do something to repair it. There are wide individual differences in such conversational skills; some 7-year-olds are better conversationalists than some adults (Anderson, Clark, & Mullin, 1994). There also are gender differences. In one study, 120 middle-class London fourth-graders worked in pairs to solve a mathematical problem. When boys and girls worked together, boys tended to use more controlling statements and to make more negative interruptions, whereas girls phrased their remarks in a more tentative, conciliatory way. Children's communication was more collaborative when working with a partner of their own sex (Leman, Ahmed, & Ozarow, 2005).

When first-graders tell stories, they usually do not make them up; they are more likely to relate a personal experience. Most 6-year-olds can retell the plot of a short book, movie, or television show. They are beginning to describe motives and causal links.

By Grade 2, children's stories become longer and more complex. Fictional tales often have conventional beginnings and endings ("Once upon a time . . ." and "They lived happily ever

pragmatics The practical knowledge needed to use language for communication

School-age children's use of language is more sophisticated than before. They are better able to tell stories and secrets and to make themselves understood.

*This section is largely indebted to Owens (1996).

after," or simply "The end"). Word use is more varied than before, but characters do not show growth or change, and plots are not fully developed.

Older children usually "set the stage" with introductory information about the setting and characters, and they clearly indicate changes of time and place during the story. They construct more complex episodes than younger children do, but with less unnecessary detail. They focus more on the characters' motives and thoughts, and they think through how to resolve problems in the plot.

Literacy

Learning to read and write frees children from the constraints of face-to-face communication. Now they have access to the ideas and imagination of people in faraway lands and long-ago times. Once children can translate the marks on a page into patterns of sound and meaning, they can develop increasingly sophisticated strategies to understand what they read. They also learn that they can use written words to express ideas, thoughts, and feelings.

Reading

decoding Process of phonetic analysis by which a printed word is converted to spoken form before retrieval from long-term memory

visually-based retrieval Process of retrieving the sound of a printed word upon seeing the word as a whole

phonetic, or code-emphasis, approach Approach to teaching reading that emphasizes decoding of unfamiliar words

whole-language approach Approach to teaching reading that emphasizes visual retrieval and use of contextual clues

Children can identify a printed word in two contrasting ways. One is called **decoding:** the child "sounds out" the word, translating it from print to speech before retrieving it from long-term memory. To do this, the child must master the phonetic code that matches the printed alphabet to spoken sounds. The second method is **visually-based retrieval:** the child simply looks at the word and then retrieves it.

Traditionally, most children learned to read by mastering a **phonetic** code that matches the printed alphabet to spoken sounds that can be combined into words. A child who knows this code can "sound out," and thus "decode," unfamiliar words. Teaching methods that stress phonics take a **code emphasis** approach.

The **whole-language approach** (sometimes called *literature-based* or *process-oriented*), is based on very different principles. Whole-language advocates believe that children can learn to read and write naturally, through discovery, much as they learn to understand and use speech. They claim that phonetic instruction hampers this natural process by obscuring the purpose of written language—to communicate meaning—and produces readers who can decode but cannot comprehend.

The whole-language method emphasizes *visually based retrieval:* The child looks at a whole word and then retrieves it from memory, with the help of contextual cues if necessary. Whole-language programs are built around real literature and open-ended, student-initiated activities, in contrast with the more explicit, teacher-directed tasks involved in phonics instruction. Proponents argue that children learn to read better—and enjoy it more—if they see written language as a way to gain information and express ideas and feelings, not as a system of isolated sounds and syllables that must be learned by memorization and drill.

Despite the popularity of the whole-language approach, reviews of the literature have found little support for its claims (Stahl, McKenna, & Pagnucco, 1994; Stahl & Miller, 1989). Critics hold it largely responsible for the failure of many schoolchildren to learn to read well—or even to want to read. A survey of 18,185 students in Grades 1 to 6 found that attitudes toward reading—both recreational and academic—worsen from Grade 1 on, especially among boys, who may prefer sports or other activities (McKenna, Kear, & Ellsworth, 1995).

Critics claim that whole-language teaching encourages children to skim through a text, guessing at words and their meaning, without trying to correct reading or spelling errors as long as the results "make sense." They say that reading, unlike talking, is a skill that must be taught; the brain is not programmed to acquire it. A long line of research supports the importance of phonemic awareness (the ability to analyze and manipulate sounds in words) and early phonics training as keys to reading proficiency (Hatcher, Hulme, & Ellis, 1994; Liberman & Liberman, 1990; National Reading Panel, 2000). In a comparison of whole language and an instructional approach that uses more direct instruction (the

"Bridge" program, which uses icons to facilitate word identification), in inner-city children in Toronto who were at risk of reading failure, the Bridge group showed better reading scores at the end of Grade 1 and Grade 2 (Biemiller & Siegel, 1997).

The most effective way to teach reading—according to a comprehensive research review by the National Reading Panel, a U.S. congressionally mandated independent panel of experts—is by developing strong phonetic skills (phonetic awareness and phonics) along with methods to improve fluency and comprehension. The panel highlighted the value of *systematic* phonics instruction—teaching a planned sequence of phonics elements rather than merely pointing them out as they appear in a text. Children can become fluent by reading aloud frequently with guidance and feedback (Ehri et al., 2001; National Reading Panel, 2000).

How do students gain in comprehension—the goal of reading?

The developmental processes that improve reading comprehension during the school years are similar to those that improve memory. As word recognition becomes faster and more automatic, children can focus on the meaning of what they read and look for inferences and connections. **Metacognition**—awareness of what is going on in their own minds—helps children monitor their understanding of what they read. It also helps them develop strategies to clear up any problems—such strategies as rereading difficult passages, reading more slowly, trying to visualize what is being described, and thinking of examples. Children learn to adjust their reading speed and attention to the importance and difficulty of the material. As their store of knowledge grows, they can more readily check new information against what they already know (Siegler, 1998).

metacognition Awareness of a person's own mental processes

Like the mechanics of reading (decoding), comprehension may best be taught through a variety of approaches. The National Reading Panel suggests that vocabulary be learned both directly and indirectly, as children encounter words in text. Repeated exposure to the same words helps; so may computerized programs that link words with their definitions. Using word processors for writing may improve children's reading: reading instruction is most effective when combined with writing (National Reading Panel, 2000).

Techniques to help students recall, summarize, and ask questions about what they read can enhance comprehension (National Reading Panel, 2000). Some school programs help children develop interpretive strategies through literary discussion. Teachers model effective strategies (such as making associations with prior knowledge, summarizing, visualizing relationships, and making predictions) and coach students on how to select and use them (R. Brown & Pressley, 1994; R. Brown, Pressley, Schuder, & Van Meter, 1994).

A balanced literacy approach used by effective teachers (Pressley, Wharton-McDonald, Mistretta-Hampston, & Echevarria, 1998) combines in about equal measure instruction in word reading and comprehension with literature-rich activities. These include extensive reading, writing about what was read, and the opportunity for students to select their own reading material from a variety of types and difficulty levels that are matched to the students' own ability (Guthrie, Schafer, & Huang, 2001; Pressley, 1998). This approach results in superior outcomes in reading achievement, in both advantaged and disadvantaged groups, and engages children in reading (Guthrie et al., 2001; Pressley, 1998), and it is advocated by the Canadian Psychological Association (Simner, 1993; 1998).

Efforts to improve the teaching of reading seem to be paying off. The 1998 National Assessment of Educational Progress showed significant increases in average reading scores in Grades 4, 8, and 12 since 1994—the first time all three grades' averages have risen since the nationwide testing program began in 1971.

An assessment of reading abilities of 46,000 13- and 16-year-old students in all provinces and territories of Canada was carried out in 1994 and 1998 by the School Achievement Indicators Program (Council of Ministers of Education, Canada [CMEC], 1999). Results showed that 13- and 16-year-olds in 1994 and 1998 maintained expected reading levels between the two testing periods. However, writing scores improved significantly between the two measurement periods for both age groups (CMEC, 1999).

Children who have early reading difficulties are not necessarily condemned to reading failure. One longitudinal study followed the progress of 146 low-income children whose first grade reading scores fell below the 30th percentile. Thirty percent of the children showed steady movement toward average reading skills from second through fourth grade. The children who improved the most were those who, as kindergartners, had shown relatively strong emergent literacy skills (refer back to Chapter 10) and better classroom behaviour, which permitted them to pay attention and benefit from instruction (Spira, Bracken, & Fischel, 2005). Another longitudinal study of low-income 4- to 6-year-olds found consistent associations between social skills and literacy achievement in first, third, and fifth grades (Miles & Stipek, 2006).

Writing

The acquisition of writing skill goes hand in hand with the development of reading. Writing is difficult for young children, and early compositions are usually quite short. Unlike conversation, which offers constant feedback, writing provides no immediate sign of how well the child has met his or her communicative goals (Siegler, 1998).

Young children, whose thinking is still somewhat egocentric, have difficulty separating what they know about a topic from what they can expect their readers to know, and they have trouble finding errors in their own work. As children get older and can take more than one perspective, they spend more time planning their writing so as to present it in a way that their audience will understand (Siegler, 1998).

In the typical classroom, children are discouraged from discussing their work with other children. This practice is based on the belief that children, especially friends, will distract one another. Research based on Vygotsky's social interaction model of language development suggests that this is not so.

In one study, Grade 4 students progressed more when they wrote with other children, especially friends. Children, working in pairs, wrote stories with more solutions to problems, more explanations and goals, and fewer errors in syntax and word use than did children working alone. Friends, working as a team, elaborated on each other's ideas and posed alternative ones (Daiute, Hartup, Sholl, & Zajac, 1993).

What makes collaboration between friends so fruitful? Friends understand each other's needs, abilities, and likely behaviours. They can expect reciprocal commitment, and they are more comfortable and trusting; thus they may be more willing to take intellectual risks (Hartup, 1996a, 1996b).

Efforts to improve the teaching of reading and writing in Canadian schools seem to be paying off. As an indicator, Canadian fourth-graders were found to score higher than their counterparts in any of eight other G-8 industrialized countries except England on an international literacy test (Sen, Partelow, & Miller, 2005).

Checkpoint ✔

Can you . . .

✔ Summarize improvements in language skills during middle childhood?

✔ Compare the phonetic and whole-language methods of teaching reading, and discuss how comprehension improves?

✔ Explain why writing is harder for younger children than for older ones?

✔ Summarize trends in reading and writing achievement?

The Child in School

School is a major formative experience, as it was for Akira Kurosawa, affecting every aspect of development. In school, children gain knowledge, skills, and social competence, stretch their bodies and minds, and prepare for adult life. Worldwide, more children are going to school than ever before. In highly developed countries such as Canada, the United States, France, Germany, Italy, Japan, and the United Kingdom, participation in elementary education is almost universal (Sen, Partelow, & Miller, 2005). Worldwide, however, 103.5 million primary-age children—57 percent of them girls—are *not* in school, and in nearly one-third of 91 countries reporting, less than 75 percent of students reach fifth grade (UNESCO, 2004).

Early school experiences are critical in setting the stage for future success or failure in school and in adult life (Feinstein & Bynner, 2004). Let's look at the first-grade experience and at influences on school achievement. In the next major section we'll consider how schools educate children with special needs.

Entering Grade 1

"What will the teacher be like?" 6-year-old Julia wonders as she walks up the steps to her new school, wearing her new backpack. "Will the work be too hard? Will the kids like me? What games will we play at recess?"

Even today, when many children go to preschool and most go to kindergarten, children often approach the start of Grade 1 with a mixture of eagerness and anxiety. The first day of "regular" school is a milestone—a sign of the developmental advances that make this new status possible.

To make the most academic progress, a child needs to be involved in what is going on in class (Valeski & Stipek, 2001). Interest, attention, and active participation were associated with achievement test scores and, even more so, with teachers' marks from Grade 1 through at least Grade 4 (K. L. Alexander, Entwisle, & Dauber, 1993). Since patterns of classroom behaviour seem to be established in Grade 1, this crucial year offers a "window of opportunity" for parents and teachers to help a child form good learning habits.

In a U.S. national longitudinal study, first graders at risk of school failure—either because of low SES or academic, attentional, or behavioural problems—progressed as much as their low-risk peers when teachers offered strong instructional and emotional support. Such support took the form of frequent literacy instruction, evaluative feedback, engaging students in discussions, responding to their emotional needs, encouraging responsibility, and creating a positive classroom atmosphere (Hamre & Pianta, 2005).

Checkpoint ✔

Can you . . .

✔ Explain the impact of the Grade 1 experience on a child's school career, and identify factors that affect success in Grade 1?

Influences on School Achievement: An Ecological Analysis

As Bronfenbrenner's bioecological theory would predict, in addition to children's own characteristics, each level of the context of their lives influences how well they do in school—from the immediate family to what goes on in the classroom to the messages children receive from peers and from the larger culture (such as "It's not cool to be smart"). Let's look at this web of influences. (We discuss the influence of culture on student motivation in Chapter 16.)

Self-Efficacy Beliefs

Students who are high in *self-efficacy*—who believe that they can master schoolwork and regulate their own learning—are more likely to succeed than students who do not believe in their own abilities (Bandura, Barbaranelli, Caprara, & Pastorelli, 1996; Zimmerman, Bandura, & Martinez-Pons, 1992). Self-regulated learners set challenging goals and use appropriate strategies to achieve them. They try hard, persist despite difficulties, and seek help when necessary. Students who do not believe in their ability to succeed tend to become frustrated and depressed—feelings that make success more elusive. When Akira Kurosawa's self-efficacy increased, he began to shine in school.

Gender

Girls tend to do better in school than boys; they are less likely to repeat grades, have fewer school problems, and outperform boys in national reading and writing assessments (Freeman, 2004). In one study, fifth- and seventh-grade girls got better math grades than boys but did no better on math achievement tests. The explanation for the girls' better grades may lie in the way they approached schoolwork. Girls tended to aim for mastery of the subject matter, whereas boys were more interested in how smart they looked in class. Girls had better classroom behaviour and adopted more effective strategies for learning. However, girls had less confidence in their abilities, an important factor in performance on achievement tests (Kenney-Benson, Pomerantz, Ryan, & Patrick, 2006). On the other hand, in a study of more than 8,000 males and females ranging from 2 to 90 years old, girls and women tended to do better than boys and men on timed tests (Camarata & Woodcock, 2006).

Boys' advantage in spatial skills has been widely noted, but a study of 547 urban second- and third-graders found that socio-economic status makes a difference. Although middle- and high-SES boys did better than their female counterparts on spatial tasks, low-SES boys did not, perhaps because higher-SES boys are more likely to engage in spatially-oriented activities such as building with Legos and playing video games (Levine, Vasilyeva, Lourenco, Newcombe, & Huttenlocher, 2005).

The family is an important influence on school achievement. A child who takes the major responsibility for doing homework can benefit from a parent's active interest—and an occasional helping hand.

Parenting Practices

Parents of achieving children create an environment for learning. They provide a place to study and to keep books and supplies; they set times for meals, sleep, and homework; they monitor how much television their children watch and what their children do after school; and they show interest in their children's lives by talking with them about school and being involved in school activities. Children whose parents are involved in their schools do better in school (Hill & Taylor, 2004).

Parents' perceived self-efficacy—their belief in their ability to promote their children's academic growth—affects their success in doing so. Parents who are economically secure and who have high aspirations for their children and a strong sense of parental efficacy tend to have children with high academic goals and achievement (Bandura et al., 1996).

How do parents motivate children to do well? Some use *extrinsic* (external) means—giving children money or treats for good grades or punishing them for bad ones. Others encourage children to develop *intrinsic* (internal) motivation by praising them for ability and hard work. Intrinsic motivation seems more effective. In fact, some educators claim that even praise should be used sparingly, as it shifts the focus from the child's own motivation to the need to please others (Aldort, 1994). In a study of 77 students in Grades 3 and 4, those who were interested in the work itself did better in school than those who mainly sought grades or parents' approval (Miserandino, 1996).

Parenting styles may affect motivation. In one study, the highest achieving students in Grade 5 had *authoritative* parents. These children were curious and interested in learning; they liked challenging tasks and enjoyed solving problems by themselves. *Authoritarian* parents, who kept after children to do their homework, supervised closely, and relied on extrinsic motivation, tended to have lower-achieving children. So did children of *permissive* parents, who were uninvolved and did not seem to care how the children did in school (G. S. Ginsburg & Bronstein, 1993). Quality of attachment is also related to academic achievement. In a longitudinal study of 108 French-Canadian school-age children, Moss and St-Laurent (2001) found that children who were securely attached their mothers at 6 years of age tended to have higher scores than their insecurely attached peers on measures of school achievement at 8 years of age.

Socio-economic Status

Socio-economic status can be a powerful factor in educational achievement—not in and of itself, but through its influence on such factors as family atmosphere, choice of neighbourhood, and parenting practices (Evans, 2004; National Research Council [NRC], 1993a;

Rouse et al., 2005). Children of poor parents are more likely to experience negative home and school atmospheres, stressful events, and unstable, chaotic households (Evans, 2004; Felner et al., 1995). SES can affect parents' ability to provide an environment that enhances learning (G. H. Brody, Stoneman, & Flor, 1995; G. H. Brody, Flor, & Gibson, 1999; Rouse et al., 2005). In a nationally representative study of children who entered kindergarten in 1998, achievement gaps between advantaged and disadvantaged students widened during the first four years of schooling (Rathbun, West, & Germino-Hausken, 2004); and in a longitudinal study of 11,200 British children born in 1970, low SES increased the likelihood that early progress would not be maintained (Feinstein & Bynner, 2004).

Socio-economic status, then, does not itself determine school achievement. Other factors, like age of entry into kindergarten, and the experience of a highly stimulating home environment are strong influences. Younger children in an Alberta study of kindergarteners were later more likely to be held back a year or need remedial help, but were more likely to have higher IQ scores than older children (Wilgosh et al., 1996; see Chapter 10). The results also showed no relationship between SES and later school achievement (Wilgosh et al., 1996). The difference comes from its effects on family life. In a longitudinal study, 8-year-olds whose home environment was cognitively stimulating had higher intrinsic motivation for academic learning at ages 9, 10, and 13 than children who lived in less stimulating homes. This was true over and above effects of SES (Gottfried, Fleming, & Gottfried, 1998). Similar patterns were found in the NLSCY (Lipman, Offord, Dooley & Boyle, 2002).

How can some young people from disadvantaged homes and neighbourhoods do well in school and improve their condition in life? One factor is **social capital:** the networks of community resources children and families can draw upon (J. S. Coleman, 1988). In a three-year experimental antipoverty intervention in which working poor parents received wage supplements and subsidies for child care and health insurance, their school-age children's academic achievement and behaviour improved in comparison with a control group who did not participate (Huston et al., 2001). Two years after the families had left the program, the impact on school achievement and motivation held steady, especially for older boys, though the effect on social and problem behaviour declined (Huston et al., 2005).

social capital Family and community resources on which a person or family can draw

Peer Acceptance

As we discuss in Chapter 14, children who are liked and accepted by peers tend to do better in school. Among 248 fourth-graders, those whose teachers reported that they were not liked by peers had poorer academic self-concepts and more symptoms of anxiety or depression in fifth grade and lower reading and math grades in sixth grade. Early teacher identification of children who exhibit social problems could lead to interventions that would improve such children's academic as well as emotional and social outcomes (Flook, Repetti, & Ullman, 2005).

The Educational System

How can school best enhance children's development? Throughout the twentieth century, conflicting educational philosophies, along with historical events, brought great swings in educational theory and practice—from the "three R's" (reading, 'riting, and 'rithmetic), to "child-centred" methods that focused on children's interests, and then, when competition from Russia and then from Japan loomed and test scores plummeted, back to the "basics." In the 1980s, a series of governmental and educational commissions in the U.S. proposed plans for improvement, ranging from more homework (see Box 13-1) to a longer school day and school year to a total reorganization of schools and curricula.

Today, many educators recommend teaching children in the primary grades by integrating subject matter fields and building on children's natural interests and talents: teaching reading and writing, for example, in the context of a social studies project or teaching math concepts through the study of music. They favour cooperative projects, hands-on problem solving, and close parent–teacher cooperation (Rescorla, 1991). (Box 13-2 discusses the current controversy over the best way to teach math.)

Many contemporary educators also emphasize a "fourth R": reasoning. Children who are taught thinking skills in the context of academic subject matter perform better on

Checkpoint

Can you . . .

✔ Tell how self-efficacy beliefs and parenting practices can influence school success?

✔ Discuss the impact of socio-economic status and peer acceptance on school achievement?

What's your view

- Which approach to education do you favour for children in the primary grades: instruction in the "basics," a more flexible, child-centred curriculum, or a combination of the two?

Box 13-1 *The Homework Debate*

The homework debate is far from new. Historical swings in homework use have reflected shifts in educational philosophy (Cooper, 1989; Gill & Schlossman, 1996).

During the nineteenth century, the mind was considered a muscle, and homework a means of exercising it. But anti-homework crusaders argued that assignments lasting far into the evening endangered children's physical and emotional health and interfered with family life. By the 1940s, "progressive," child-centred education held sway, and homework had lost favour (Gill & Schlossman, 1996).

In the 1950s, when the Soviet Union's Sputnik launch brought calls for more rigorous science and math education, "More homework!" became a battle cry in campaigns to upgrade educational standards (Cooper, 1989).

By 1997, according to one survey, students in Grades 1 through 3 were spending about 2 hours a week on homework, three times as much as in 1981 (Hofferth & Sandberg, 1998). Child psychologists report an increase in homework-related anxieties (Winerip, 1999). A survey of Canadian adolescents showed that teenagers in homes with Internet access spend 8 hours a week on average on homework (Canadian Council on Social Development [CCSD], 2001). This is an increase by about an hour in comparison with 1998, and represents more time spent using computers. The average time spent researching on the Internet in order to complete school assignments is 2 hours each week. The majority of parents see this as beneficial to their children, with about 90 percent reporting that Internet access has had a positive impact on their children. However, because Internet access at home is more likely for high-SES children, the benefits of Internet access are more likely to be available to children in higher-income families (CCSD, 2001).

Homework advocates claim that it disciplines the mind, develops good work habits, improves retention, and lets students cover more ground than they could in the classroom alone. Homework is a bridge between home and school, increasing parental involvement. Opponents claim that too much homework leads to boredom, anxiety, or frustration, puts unnecessary pressure on children, discourages intrinsic motivation, and usurps time from other worthwhile activities. They say that parental "help" can be counterproductive if parents become overly intrusive or use teaching methods that conflict with those taught at school (Cooper, 1989). Once again, some critics (Kralovec & Buell, 2000) want to ban homework, at least for young children.

Research supports a balanced view, recognizing that homework can improve achievement and long-term success, but also has costs (Larson & Verma, 1999). A comprehensive review of nearly 120 studies found that the value of homework depends on many factors, including the age, ability, and motivation of the child; the amount and purpose of homework; the home situation; and classroom follow-up. The older the child, the more effective homework can be. While it has strong benefits for high school students, it has only moderate benefits for junior high school students (and then only if limited to 2 hours a night), and virtually no benefits for elementary school students

as compared with in-class study. Homework seems to work best when assignments are not overly complicated or completely unfamiliar, when material is spread out over several assignments, and when the need for parental involvement (which varies in effectiveness and can create tension at home) is kept to a minimum (Cooper, 1989).

Junior high and high school students who spend more time on homework tend to get better grades (Cooper et al., 1998; Cooper, Valentine, Nye, & Lindsay, 1999), but this is less true at the elementary level. The more homework younger children get, the more negatively they feel toward it. In a survey of 709 students in Grades 2 to 12, about one-third of lower-grade students said they typically did not finish their homework. Even in the upper grades, students who received lengthy assignments tended not to complete them (Cooper et al., 1998).

Homework, then, has value—but only in moderation and when geared to students' developmental levels. Homework serves different purposes at different ages. For young children, it can develop good study habits and an understanding that learning can take place at home as well as in school. In junior high, a mix of mandatory and voluntary homework can promote academic goals and motivate children to pursue studies that interest them. In high school, homework can provide opportunities for practice, review, and integration of what is being learned at school (Cooper, 1989).

Should parents help with homework? In an 18-month study of 166 fourth- through sixth-graders, mothers tended to give "intrusive support"—helping with or checking homework without being asked—when their children were uncertain about their performance or when the mothers were worried about it. Intrusive support tended to help low achievers improve but sometimes fostered failure, perhaps because the learning was not internalized (Pomerantz & Eaton, 2001). In a study of 109 eight- to 12-year-olds, mothers who helped with homework tended to see their children as helpless and to become irritated and annoyed. However, this did not affect the mothers' positive feelings for their children or to undermine the children's motivation and emotional functioning (Pomerantz, Wang, & Ng, 2005).

Assignments in the elementary grades should be short and easy enough for children to succeed. Research-based recommendations range from one to three 15-minute assignments a week in the primary grades to four or five assignments a week, each lasting 75 to 120 minutes, in Grades 10 to 12. Instead of grading homework, teachers should use it to diagnose learning problems (Cooper, 1989).

What's your view ?

How much homework do you think is appropriate for children of various ages?

Check it out !

For more information on this topic, go to **www.mcgrawhill.ca/olc/papalia**.

Should children learn math by rules and formulas, or by manipulating coloured blocks or pie-shaped segments to illustrate mathematical concepts? By memorizing and drilling in the multiplication tables, or by using computer simulations and relating math problems to real life?

These questions have spurred heated argument between proponents of traditional "skill-and-drill" math teaching and advocates of the newer *constructivist math* (or *whole math*), in which children actively construct their own mathematical concepts. This approach came into nationwide use after 1989, when the National Council of Teachers of Mathematics (NCTM) issued new standards of instruction based on constructivist principles.

The new standards de-emphasized basic skills. Instead, they stressed understanding how mathematics works. Rather than passively absorb rules from a teacher or textbook, children were to discover mathematical concepts for themselves, often on the basis of intuitive learning gleaned from telling time, playing board games, dealing with money, and other everyday experiences. Instead of arriving at precise answers to a problem such as 19 × 6, children were encouraged to make rough estimates from more familiar relationships, such as 20 × 5.

Much like older arguments about reading instruction, the math wars split educators into opposing camps. Many parents called the new curriculum "dumbed down" or "fuzzy math." They complained that their children could not add, subtract, multiply, divide, or do simple algebra. They questioned how well teachers could handle the new materials and methods—indeed, how well the teachers themselves understood the principles their students were groping to discover (Jackson, 1997a, 1997b).

The reforms were widely pronounced a failure. And then, the first scientific studies on their effectiveness proved generally favourable. A study of 2,369 urban algebra students found that following the NCTM standards did not hurt students' performance on traditional tests and improved the performance of middle school students (Mayer, 1998). A study of elementary school students bore out the constructivist belief that children learn best by analyzing problems, figuring out *why* an answer is right or wrong (Siegler, 1995). And while the constructivist approach has been criticized as inappropriate for diverse school populations, a randomized study of 104 low-achieving, mostly poor and minority students in Grades 3 and 4 found otherwise. Students taught by problem-solving and/or peer collaboration outperformed students taught by more traditional methods on computation and word problems (Ginsburg-Block & Fantuzzo, 1998).

In the Third International Mathematics and Science Study (TIMSS) in 1998, Canadian Grade 12 students scored higher than the average of 21 competing nations on math literacy and higher than any of the other G-8 countries (McConaghy, 1998). However, immigrant children tended to score lower than native-born children in Canada. One explanation is that the poorer English language skills of first-generation immigrant children were contributing to difficulties in learning mathematics in English-language classrooms (Huang, 2000). The 2002 report of mathematics achievement by the CMEC showed mathematics scores, particularly in problem solving, improved between 1997 and 2001, and that children were performing at higher than expected levels (CMEC, 2002).

As in the reading wars, both sides of the math wars may have merit, and the best approach may be a combination of old and new approaches. That is what the NCTM (2000) advocates with the issuance of its revised standards. The revision strives for a balance between conceptual understanding and mathematical procedures and re-emphasizes accuracy, efficiency, and fluency in basic computational skills. In 2003, math scores on the U.S. National Assessment of Educational Progress rose sharply to their highest levels since the test began in 1990 (National Center for Education Statistics [NCES], 2004a). In 2005 they inched higher. The percentage of fourth graders scoring at or above the basic level of achievement increased by 30 points since 1990, from 50 to 80 percent; and the percentage of eighth graders at that level increased 17 points, from 52 to 69 percent. However, only 36 percent of fourth graders and 30 percent of eighth graders were judged "proficient" in 2005 (NCES, 2005a).

A further step "back to the basics" is the NCTM's (2006) issuance of "curriculum focal points." To help teachers and students wade through the dozens of topics set forth in curriculum standards, the focal points specify the most important skills students need to learn in each grade.

What's your view?

Based on your own experience, which method of teaching math do you think would be more effective, or would you advocate a combination of both?

Check it out!

For more information on this topic, go to **www.mcgrawhill.ca/olc/papalia.**

---

intelligence tests and in school (R. D. Feldman, 1986; Sternberg, 1984, 1985a, 1985b). Everyday activities can also be routes to enhancing thinking skills (see Table 13-4).

Research on Sternberg's triarchic theory suggests that students learn better when taught in a variety of ways, emphasizing creative and practical skills as well as memorization and critical thinking (Sternberg, Torff, & Grigorenko, 1998).

The School Environment Children learn better and teachers teach better in a comfortable, healthful school environment. Most educators consider small class size a key factor, especially in the early grades, but findings on this point are mixed (Schneider, 2002). A longitudinal

Table 13-4	Everyday Ways to Enhance Children's Thinking Skills

- When reading to children, ask open-ended questions (beginning with what, why, and how).
- Help children find the most important points in what they read, see, or hear.
- Ask children to compare new information with what they already know. Identifying commonalities and differences can help children organize information, which helps them think as well as remember.
- Teach children not to accept a statement that contradicts common knowledge without reliable proof.
- Encourage children to write. Putting thoughts on paper forces them to organize their thoughts. Projects may include keeping a journal, writing a letter to a famous person, and presenting an argument to parents (say, for an increase in allowance or a special purchase or privilege).
- Encourage children to think imaginatively about what they have learned. ("How do you think the soldiers in the First World War felt at the Battle of Vimy Ridge? What do you suppose they wore?")
- When writing a poem or drawing a picture, encourage children to produce a first version and then to polish or revise it.
- Show children how to approach a problem by identifying what they do and don't know about it, by designing a plan to solve it, by carrying out the plan, and then by deciding whether it has worked.
- Ask children to invent a new product, such as a gadget to ease a household chore.
- Teach children such skills as reading a map and using a microscope, and provide opportunities to practise them.

Sources: Marzano & Hutchins, 1987; Maxwell, 1987.

study of 11,600 kindergarten and primary students in Tennessee public elementary schools found lasting academic benefits for students randomly assigned to classes of about 15 students in kindergarten through third grade, and—especially for low-SES students—greater likelihood of finishing high school (Finn, Gerber, & Boyd-Zaharias, 2005; Krueger, 2003; Krueger & Whitmore, 2000).

However, in most places "small" classes are larger than that. In classroom observations of 890 first-graders, classes with 25 students or less tended to be more social and interactive (with a bit more disruptive behaviour) and to enable higher quality instruction and emotional support. Students in these classes tended to score higher on standardized achievements tests and beginning reading skills (NICHD Early Childhood Research Network, 2004b).

social promotion Policy in which children are automatically promoted from one grade to another even if they do not meet academic standards for the grade they are completing

Current Educational Developments When the Chicago public schools in 1996 ended **social promotion,** the practice of promoting children who do not meet academic standards, many observers hailed the change. However, some educators maintain that the alternative— forcing failing students to go to summer school before they can graduate, or to repeat a grade—is shortsighted (Bronner, 1999). Although retention in some cases can be a "wake-up call," more often it is the first step on a remedial track that leads to lowered expectations, poor performance, and ultimately dropping out of school (J. M. Fields & Smith, 1998; Lugaila, 2003; McLeskey, Lancaster, & Grizzle, 1995; Temple, Reynolds, & Miedel, 2000). A number of countries with well-regarded educational systems, such as Denmark, Sweden, Norway, Japan, and South Korea, have automatic promotion policies. Indeed, studies by University of Chicago researchers found that Chicago's retention policy did *not* improve third graders' test scores, hurt sixth graders' scores, and greatly increased eighth grade and high school dropout rates for retained students (Nagaoka & Roderick, 2004; Roderick et al., 2003).

Many educators say the only real solution to a high failure rate is to identify at-risk students early and intervene *before* they fail (Bronner, 1999). In a longitudinal study of students in kindergarten through to Grade 8 in the Chicago schools, retained students did more poorly on math and reading-achievement tests than peers who had been promoted, and also did more poorly in math than their new, younger classmates (McCoy & Reynolds, 1999). In a second study of the same sample, those who had been in a high-quality early childhood education program were less likely to be held back in school or to drop out of high school (Temple, Reynolds, & Miedel, 2000).

Some parents, unhappy with their public schools or seeking a particular style of education, are choosing charter schools (in Alberta; Bezeau, 2006) or homeschooling. Charter schools tend to be smaller than regular public schools and have a unique philosophy, curriculum, structure, or organizational style. Although parents are generally satisfied with their charter schools, studies of their effects on student outcomes have had mixed results (Braun, Jenkins, & Grigg, 2006; Bulkley & Fisler, 2002; Center for Education Reform, 2004; Detrich, Phillips, & Durett, 2002; National Assessment of Educational Progress, 2004; Schemo, 2004). With homeschooling, Alberta provides some funding to parents, while other provinces, like British Columbia require parents to register their children with public schools. The public school then provides children with evaluation and assessment services (Bezeau, 2006). The main reason why parents choose homeschooling, based on a national survey, is concern about poor or unsafe learning environments in the schools, and the choice to provide religious education (Princiotta & Chapman, 2006).

Computer and Internet Use In 2003, about 91 percent of children and adolescents used computers at home or at school, and about 59 percent used the Internet. Girls and boys spend about the same amount of time on computer and Internet use (Day, Janus, & Davis, 2005; DeBell & Chapman, 2006). Figure 13-1 shows the percentages of children of all ages who use computers at home for various purposes.

Computer literacy and the ability to navigate the Internet are opening new possibilities for individualized instruction, global communication, and early training in independent research skills. However, this tool poses dangers. First is the risk of exposure to harmful or inappropriate material. Second, students need to learn to evaluate critically information they find in cyberspace and to separate facts from opinion and advertising. Finally, a focus on "visual literacy" could divert financial resources from other areas of the curriculum.

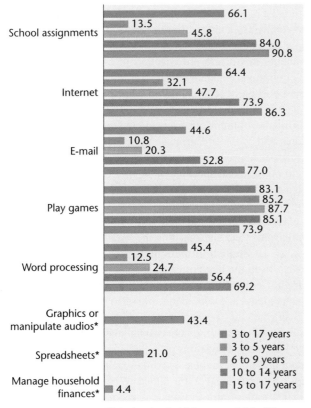

*Asked only of children ages 15 to 17.

Figure 13-1

Percentage of U.S. children ages 3 to 17 who use computers at home for various purposes, 2003.

Source: Day, Janus, & Davis, 2005; Data from U.S. Census Bureau, current Population Survey, October 2003.

Educating Children with Special Needs

Public schools have a tremendous job educating children of varying abilities from all sorts of families and cultural backgrounds. They also must educate children who have special needs: Aborignal and immigrant children for whom the school's language of instruction is a second language, those who have learning problems, and those who are gifted, talented, or creative.

Needs of Aboriginal Children

Although the proportion of Aboriginal students attending band-operated schools has risen dramatically (Frideres, 1998), more has to be done to improve academic achievement and self-image of Aboriginal children. The number of Aboriginal children completing elementary school has risen from 63 to 76 percent between 1981 and 1991. During this same time, the percentage completing high school has risen from 29 to 43 percent (Frideres, 1998). However, in urban areas, less than 20 percent of Aboriginal students complete secondary school, compared to over 80 percent of non-Aboriginal students (Bonneau, Ee & Lauzon, 2006). According to the 2001 Aboriginal Peoples Survey, almost three-quarters of Metis students completed elementary or high school (Metis Health in Canada, 2004). The gaps between Aboriginal and non-Aboriginal completion rates are narrowing. However, self-perceived competence in the classroom is low, and contributes to difficulties that Aboriginal children experience when they attend majority-culture schools (Beiser, Sack, Manson, Redshirt, & Dion, 1998). Efforts to close achievement gaps and to address the unique cultural and spiritual needs of Aboriginal children, programs such as Aboriginal Head Start, the inclusion of Aboriginal cultural knowledge, content, and perspectives, and the use of Aboriginal languages in public schools is also increasing (Burnaby, 1996; Children Resource and Research Unit, 1998 CICH, 2000; Kanu, 2005). Promoting the use of Aboriginal languages may have significant psychosocial benefits (Hallett, Chandler, & Lalonde, 2007).

Second (Additional)-Language Education

Canada is an officially bilingual, French and English, multicultural nation, which celebrates its ethnic diversity as a cultural mosaic. Educating students to ensure proficiency in both official languages is encouraged in schools. Outside of Quebec, over 50 percent of public school students in Canada are enrolled in either French immersion or regular French-language programs (Canadian Council on Social Development, 2001). With rising immigration, the proportion of schoolchildren who speak languages other than English or French at home has risen from 13 percent in 1991 to 16 percent in 1996 (CICH, 2000), with Ontario and British Columbia experiencing the greatest increases. Similar trends exist in the United States and Western European countries, and schools there are also under pressure to meet the special needs of immigrant children. Whereas a main goal of most U.S. programs is to help non-English-speaking students learn English well enough to compete academically with native English speakers (NCES, 1996), the aim of Canadian and European programs is to help preserve students' cultural identity. The federal policy on multiculturalism was designed to ensure that every ethno-cultural group in Canada is able to maintain and enhance its cultural identity and values within the broader Canadian society (Friesen, 1995).

Some schools use an **English-immersion** approach, in which immigrant children are immersed in English from the beginning, in special classes. Other schools have adopted programs of **bilingual education,** in which children are taught in two languages, first learning in their native language with others who also speak it, and then switching to regular classes in English when they become more proficient in it. These programs can encourage children to become **bilingual** (fluent in two languages) and to feel pride in their cultural identity. **Heritage Language Programs** provide language and culture classes as a way for children to maintain and improve their native language abilities, and by doing so demonstrate that children's native languages are valued. When a child's first language is used and valued in schools, learning of an additional, or second, language and academic achievement are enhanced (Swain & Lapkin, 1991; Genesee, 1987; Hakuta, 1986).

Checkpoint ✔

Can you . . .

✔ Identify some ways of addressing cultural differences in the classroom?

Guidepost 6

How do schools meet special needs?

English immersion Approach to teaching English as an additional (second) language in which instruction is presented only in English

bilingual education System of teaching non-English-speaking children in their native language while they learn English, and later switching to all-English instruction

bilingual Fluent in two languages

Heritage Language Program Language classes given in the regular school day for children of immigrant background, designed to promote the home language and culture

Advocates of early English-immersion claim that the sooner children are exposed to English and the more time they spend speaking it, the better they learn it (Rossel & Ross, 1986). Support for this view comes from findings that the effectiveness of additional-language learning declines from early childhood through late adolescence (Newport, 1991). On the other hand, proponents of bilingual programs claim that children progress faster academically in their native language and later make a smoother transition to all-English classrooms (Padilla et al., 1991). Some educators maintain that the English-only approach stunts children's cognitive growth; because foreign-speaking children can understand only simple English at first, the curriculum must be watered down, and children are less prepared to handle complex material later (Collier, 1995).

One of Canada's success stories is **French immersion,** which began in Montreal in the 1960s (Lambert & Tucker, 1972) and has spread across the country since. The program uses French as the language of instruction to English-speaking students living in English communities. Many studies have shown that French immersion is an effective way of teaching second-language skills to children. What is its effect on English-language skills? Research on French immersion has shown no negative effects on native language proficiency and academic achievement (Genesee, 1991), and longitudinal studies have demonstrated that, relative to those of non-immersion children, first-language skills seem to be enhanced by Grade 3 when basic proficiency in French is attained (Swain & Lapkin, 1991). These benefits continue through to at least Grade 6, even when French immersion students are compared with students in enriched English programs (Turnbull, Hart & Lapkin, 2003).

Statistical analyses of multiple studies conclude that children in bilingual programs typically outperform those in all-English programs on tests of English proficiency (Krashen & McField, 2005). Most successful was a third, less common approach: **two-way,** or **dual-language learning,** in which English-speaking and foreign-speaking children learn together in their own and each other's languages. This approach avoids any need to place minority children in separate classes. By valuing both languages equally, it helps build self-esteem and thus improve school performance. An added advantage is that English speakers learn a foreign language at an early age, when they can acquire it most easily (Collier, 1995; W. P. Thomas & Collier, 1997, 1998). These findings echo earlier ones: The more bilingually proficient children are, the higher their cognitive and linguistic achievement—as long as school personnel value bilingualism and the second language is added at no sacrifice to the first (Diaz, 1983; Padilla et al., 1991).

A study of minority-language students in French-immersion programs in Ontario examined how well these children, who were also fluent in English, learned French in comparison with children whose first language was English. On all measures of grammar and oral language performance, minority-language students were superior to students of English background, while English-background students did better on measures of lexical (vocabulary) knowledge (Bild & Swain, 1989). The results indicate that learning a third language might be facilitated by other language learning—in this case, first learning of English by minority-language students. In a later study, students with a minority language and who read and write in their minority language were found to do better than English-background and non-literate minority-language students on most measures of French proficiency (Swain & Lapkin, 1991). Literacy, rather than oral language proficiency, in a minority language seemed to have a positive impact in learning a third language.

When bilingualism rises to the level of *biliteracy* (proficiency in reading and writing two languages), which makes possible full participation in both cultures, we see the most positive effects (Huang, 1995).

Children with Learning Problems

Some children, like Akira Kurosawa, are late bloomers when it comes to schoolwork. An unfortunate minority have serious learning problems.

Intellectual Disability

Intellectual disability (mental retardation) is a clinical term for significantly subnormal cognitive functioning. In some fields like early childhood education and social work, the

French immersion Approach to teaching French as a second language in which English-speaking children are given instruction in French only

two-way (dual-language) learning Approach to second-language education in which English speakers and non-English speakers learn together in their own and each other's languages

Checkpoint ✓

Can you . . .

✔ Describe and evaluate various types of second-language education?

intellectual disability (mental retardation) Significantly subnormal cognitive functioning preferred term is *mentally challenged.* It is indicated by an IQ of about 70 or less, coupled with a deficiency in age-appropriate adaptive behaviour (such as communication, social skills, and self-care), appearing before age 18 (Kanaya, Scullin, & Ceci, 2003). Both IQ and behaviour are considered in making a diagnosis. Fewer than 1 percent of children are mentally retarded (National Center for Health Statistics [NCHS], 2004; Woodruff et al., 2004), about three boys for every two girls (American Psychiatric Association [APA], 1994).

In 30 to 50 percent of cases the cause of mental retardation is unknown. Known causes include genetic disorders, traumatic accidents, prenatal exposure to infection or alcohol, and environmental exposure to lead or high levels of mercury (Woodruff et al., 2004). Many cases of retardation may be preventable through genetic counselling, prenatal care, amniocentesis, routine screening and health care for newborns, and nutritional services for pregnant women and infants.

With a supportive and stimulating early environment and continued help and guidance, many children with intellectual disability can expect a reasonably good outcome. Most can benefit from schooling. Intervention programs have helped many adults with mild or moderate mental retardation and those considered "borderline" (with IQs ranging from 70 up to about 85) to hold jobs, live in the community, and function fairly well in society. Those with profound intellectual disability need constant care and supervision, usually in institutions. For some, daycare centres, hostels for retarded adults, and home-making services for caregivers can be less costly and more humane alternatives.

Learning Disabilities

Nelson Rockefeller, former vice-president of the United States, had so much trouble reading that he ad libbed speeches instead of using a script. Rockefeller is one of many eminent persons, including the World War II hero General George Patton, the inventor Thomas Edison, the actor Whoopi Goldberg, the sculptor Auguste Rodin, and Leonardo da Vinci (Aaron & Guillemard, 1993) who reportedly have suffered from **dyslexia,** a developmental reading disorder in which reading achievement is substantially below the level predicted by IQ or age.

dyslexia Developmental disorder in which reading achievement is substantially lower than predicted by IQ or age

learning disabilities (LDs) Disorders that interfere with specific aspects of learning and school achievement

Dyslexia is the most commonly diagnosed of a large number of **learning disabilities (LDs),** disorders that interfere with specific aspects of school achievement, resulting in performance substantially lower than would be expected given a child's age, intelligence, and amount of schooling (APA, 1994). A growing number of children are classified as learning disabled (LD) (T. D. Snyder, Hoffman, & Geddes, 1997). A growing number of children—5 percent of the school population—are served by programs for students with LDs (National Center for Learning Disabilities, 2004b).

Children with LDs often have near-average to higher-than-average intelligence and normal vision and hearing, but they seem to have trouble processing sensory information. A review of quantitative genetic research concluded that the genes most responsible for the high heritability of the most common LDs—language impairment, reading disability, and mathematical disability—are also responsible for normal variations in learning abilities and that genes that affect one type of disability are also likely to affect other types. However, genes specific to particular learning disabilities also play a role (Plomin & Kovas, 2005). Environmental factors may include complications of pregnancy or birth, injuries after birth, nutritional deprivation, and exposure to lead (National Center for Learning Disabilities, 2004b).

Children with LDs tend to be less task oriented and more easily distracted than other children; they are less well organized as learners and less likely to use memory strategies (Feagans, 1983). Learning disabilities can have devastating effects on self-esteem as well as on the report card.

Four out of five children with LDs have dyslexia. Estimates of its prevalence range from 5 to 17.5 percent of the school population. It is generally considered to be a chronic, persistent medical condition. It is heritable and runs in families (S. E. Shaywitz, 1998; 2003). It hinders the development of oral as well as written language skills and may cause problems with reading, writing, spelling, grammar, and understanding speech (National Center for Learning Disabilities, 2004a). Reading disability is more frequent in boys than in girls (Rutter et al., 2004).

The term *dyslexia* used to mean "mirror-reading" (saying "was" for "saw"), but now refers to any type of reading problem. Most cases are believed to result from a neurological defect in processing speech sounds: an inability to recognize that words consist of smaller units of sound, which are represented by printed letters. This defect in phonological processing makes it hard to decode words. Dyslexic children may also be weak in short-term verbal memory and other linguistic and cognitive skills (Morris et al., 1998; S. E. Shaywitz, 1998; 2003). Brain imaging has revealed differences or underactivity in the regions of the brain activated during the processing of spoken and written language in dyslexic as compared with normal readers (Breier et al., 2003; Casanova et al., 2005; Eden et al., 2004; Shaywitz, 2003) and significantly reduced volumes of grey matter in persons with familial dyslexia (Brambati et al., 2004). Several identified genes contribute to these abnormalities (Meng et al., 2005; Kere et al., 2005).

The biology of dyslexia may vary by culture. In brain imaging studies, Chinese children used different parts of the brain in reading than English speakers do, and different parts were affected by dyslexia. This finding is not surprising, as the Chinese language is not phonological but instead relies on memory of visual symbols. About 2 to 7 percent of Chinese children are dyslexic (Sick, Perfetti, Jin, & Tan, 2004).

Many children—and even adults—with dyslexia can be taught to read through systematic phonological training. However, the process does not become automatic, as it does with most readers (Eden et al., 2004; S. E. Shaywitz, 1998, 2003).

Hyperactivity and Attention Deficits

Attention-deficit/hyperactivity disorder (ADHD) has been called the most common mental disorder in childhood (Wolraich et al., 2005). It affects an estimated 2 to 11 percent or more of school-age children worldwide (Zametkin & Ernst, 1999c) However, its prevalence is in dispute. Some research suggests that it may be underestimated (Rowland et al., 2002). On the other hand, some physicians warn that the disorder may be overdiagnosed, resulting in unnecessary overmedication of children whose parents or teachers do not know how to control them (Elliott, 2000). ADHD diagnosis rates vary greatly by gender, ethnicity, geographic area, and other contextual factors and may in part be related to pressures on children to succeed in school (Schneider & Eisenberg, 2006).

It is marked by persistent inattention, distractibility, impulsivity, low tolerance for frustration, and a great deal of activity at the wrong time and the wrong place, such as the classroom (APA, 1994; Woodruff et al., 2004). Boys are three to four times as likely to be diagnosed as girls (Barkley, 1998b; USDHHS, 1999c; Zametkin & Ernst, 1999). More than 1 in 4 children with learning disabilities has ADHD (Roush, 1995; Zametkin, 1995).

The disorder has two different sets of symptoms. Some children are inattentive but not hyperactive; others show the reverse pattern (USDHHS, 1999c). However, in 85 percent of cases, the two kinds of behaviour go together (Barkley, 1998a). Because these characteristics appear to some degree in most children some practitioners question whether ADHD is actually a distinct neurological or psychological disorder (Bjorklund & Pellegrini, 2002; Furman, 2005). However, most experts agree that there is cause for concern when they are unusually frequent and so severe that they interfere with the child's functioning in school and in daily life (AAP Committee on Children with Disabilities and Committee on Drugs, 1996; Barkley, 1998b; USDHHS, 1999c).

Many studies have linked ADHD to abnormalities in the prefrontal cortex and impairment of executive function (Zelazo & Müller, 2002). Children with ADHD have unusually small brain structures in the cortical regions that regulate attention and impulse control (Sowell et al., 2003). They tend to forget responsibilities, to speak aloud rather than give themselves silent directions, to be frustrated or angered easily, and to give up when they don't see how to solve a problem. Parents and teachers may be able to help these children by breaking down tasks into small "chunks," providing frequent prompts about rules and time, and giving frequent, immediate rewards for small accomplishments (Barkley, 1998b).

ADHD has a substantial genetic basis, with heritability approaching 80 percent (APA, 1994; Barkley, 1998b; Elia, Ambrosini, & Rapoport, 1999; USDHHS, 1999c; Zametkin, 1995; Zametkin & Ernst, 1999). Symptoms of ADHD may be products of gene-environment interaction. In one study, exposure to high levels of lead impaired executive function, but only in children with certain variations of a gene that helps regulate brain levels of

attention-deficit/hyperactivity disorder (ADHD) Syndrome characterized by persistent inattention and distractibility, impulsivity, low tolerance for frustration, and inappropriate overactivity

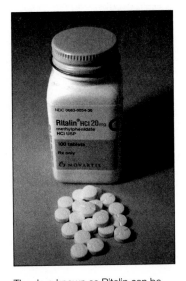

The drug known as Ritalin can be effective in treating attention-deficit/hyperactivity disorder (ADHD), but its long-term effects are unknown. Some physicians warn that Ritalin may be overprescribed, resulting in overmedication of children.

dopamine, a brain chemical essential for attention and cognition (Froehlich, Lamphear, Dietrich, Cory-Slechta, & Kahn, 2006). Birth complications that may play a part in ADHD include prematurity, a prospective mother's alcohol or tobacco use, and oxygen deprivation (Barkley, 1998b; Thapar et al., 2003; USDHHS, 1999c; Woodruff et al., 2004).

Most children diagnosed with ADHD continue to show symptoms as adolescents. Problems with impulse control and hyperactivity often decline, but inattention persists. Academic problems, cumulative family stress, and troubled peer relationships become more apparent (Whalen, Jamner, Henker, Delfino, & Lozano, 2002; Wolraich et al., 2005). Although symptoms tend to decline with age, ADHD often persists into adolescence and adulthood and, if untreated, can lead to excessive injuries, academic problems, anti-social behaviour, risky driving, substance abuse, and anxiety or depression and other personality disorders (Barkley, 1998b; Barkley, Murphy, & Kwasnik, 1996; Elia et al., 1999; McGee, Partridge, Williams, & Silva, 1991; Molina & Pelham, 2003; USDHHS, 1999c; Whalen et al., 2002; Wolraich et al., 2005; Wender, 1995; Zametkin, 1995). ADHD sometimes continues into adulthood; it affects an estimated 4 percent of adults worldwide (Wilens, Faraone, & Biederman, 2004).

ADHD is often managed with drugs, sometimes combined with behavioural therapy, counselling, training in social skills, and special classroom placement. A British Columbia study found that there were significant disparities in the prevalence of Ritalin prescriptions across the regions of the province, and that children from lower-SES families were more likely to be prescribed Ritalin than children from more prosperous families (Miller, 2001).

Contrary to the popular impression that drug treatment is dramatically increasing among children, 2.9 percent of the child population were treated with stimulant drugs such as Ritalin in 2002, as compared with 2.7 percent in 1997 (Zuvekas, Vitello, & Norquist, 2006). The number of Ritalin pills dispensed in Canada has increased dramatically, more than doubling between 1994 and 1998 (CICH, 2000). In a 14-month randomized study of 579 children with ADHD, a carefully monitored program of Ritalin treatment, alone or in combination with behaviour modification, was more effective than the behavioural therapy alone or standard community care (MTA Cooperative Group, 1999). However, the superior benefits of the program diminished during the following 10 months (MTA Cooperative Group, 2004a). A side effect of the combined treatment was slower growth in height and weight (MTA Cooperative Group, 2004b). Furthermore, long-term effects of Ritalin are unknown (Wolraich et al., 2005). Because of known cardiovascular risks of stimulant drugs, In 2006 the Drug Safety and Risk Management Advisory Committee of the Food and Drug Administration recommended that a warning accompany these drugs (Nissen, 2006).

Educating Children with Disabilities

Unlike the United States, which has national legislation ensuring appropriate education for all children with disabilities, Canada has no such national legislation. However, policies for appropriate education for children with disabilities are being enacted by provinces and territories. In general, where there are provisions for providing appropriate services, an individual education plan is designed for each child, with parental involvement. Children are educated in the "least restrictive environment" appropriate to their needs: that means, whenever possible, the regular classroom. Many of these students can be served by "inclusion" programs, in which they are integrated with non-disabled children for all or part of the day. Inclusion can help children with disabilities learn to get along in society and can let non-disabled children know and understand people with disabilities. About 16 percent of all school-age children in Canada have a disability (Winzer, 1996), 25 percent of whom are educated outside of the regular school system (Wizner, 1997). Although most educators favour integrating children with disabilities into regular classrooms, two general approaches have emerged. The first is mainstreaming integration, which involves providing complete services to meet the needs of children with disabilities in the least restrictive environment possible. The second approach is inclusive integration in regular classrooms in children's neighbourhood schools, which would eliminate any segregation of children with disabilities from the regular classroom, and would involve altering the physical structure of schools to accommodate children with disabilites. Most provinces and territories currently favour implementing the mainstreaming integration approach (Doré, Wagner, Brunet, & Bélanger, 1999).

What's your view

• Long-term effects of drug treatment for ADHD are unknown, and leaving the condition untreated also carries risks. If you had a child with ADHD, what would you do?

Checkpoint

Can you . . .

✔ Describe the causes and prognoses for three common types of conditions that interfere with learning?

A potential problem with inclusion is that children with learning disabilities may be evaluated by unrealistic standards, resulting in their being held back and made to repeat grades. This has already happened on a large scale in some schools, despite evidence that retention is ineffective even with children of normal abilities (McLeskey et al., 1995).

Gifted Children

Akira Kurosawa was not the only gifted person who was considered backward as a child. Sir Isaac Newton, who discovered gravity, did poorly in grade school. Thomas Edison, inventor of the light bulb, was told as a boy that he was too stupid to learn. The British prime minister Winston Churchill failed sixth grade. The great operatic tenor Enrico Caruso was told as a child that he could not sing.

Giftedness, like intelligence, is hard to define and measure. Educators disagree on who qualifies as gifted and on what basis, and what kinds of educational programs these children need. Another source of confusion is that creativity and artistic talent are sometimes viewed as aspects or types of giftedness and sometimes as independent of it (Gardner, 2000; Hunsaker & Callahan, 1995).

This deaf girl learns in a class with hearing children through the aid of a special teacher who communicates with her in sign language.

Identifying Gifted Children

The traditional criterion of giftedness is high general intelligence, as shown by an IQ score of 130 or higher. This definition tends to exclude highly creative children (whose unusual answers often lower their test scores), children from minority groups (whose abilities may not be well developed, though the potential is there), and children with specific aptitudes (who may be only average or even show learning problems in other areas). Most provinces and school boards have therefore adopted a broader definition, which includes children who have shown high *potential* or *achievement* in one or more of the following: general intellect, specific aptitude (such as in mathematics or science), creative or productive thinking, leadership, talent in the arts (such as painting, writing, music, or acting), and psychomotor ability (Cassidy & Hossler, 1992). Many school boards now use multiple criteria for admission to programs for the gifted, including achievement test scores, grades, classroom performance, creative production, parent and teacher nominations, and student interviews; but IQ remains an important, and sometimes the determining, factor (Reis, 1989). An estimated 6 percent of the student population are considered gifted (NAGC, undated).

Some children are "globally gifted." Others excel, say, in math but not in reading, or may be talented in art but have a below normal IQ or be uninterested in academics. As Gardner suggested, they may have "intelligences" in some areas but not in others. Thus, programs that rely on IQ to identify gifted children may miss those who are unevenly gifted. Instead, some experts say, it makes more sense to place children in special programs tailored to their particular gifts, including the arts as well as academics (Winner, 2000).

What Causes Giftedness?

Psychologists who study the lives of extraordinary achievers find that high levels of performance require strong intrinsic motivation and years of rigorous training (Bloom, 1985; Czikszentmihalyi, 1996; Gardner, 1993; Gruber, 1981; Keegan, 1996). However, motivation and training will not produce giftedness unless a child is endowed with unusual ability (Winner, 2000). Conversely, children with innate gifts are unlikely to show exceptional achievement without motivation and hard work (Achter & Lubinski, 2003).

Gifted children tend to grow up in enriched family environments with much intellectual or artistic stimulation. Their parents recognize and often devote themselves to nurturing the children's gifts but also give their children an unusual degree of independence. Parents of gifted children typically have high expectations and are hard workers and high achievers

Checkpoint ✔

Can you . . .

✔ Discuss the impact of provincial and territorial requirements for the education of children with disabilities?

Checkpoint ✔

Can you . . .

✔ Tell how gifted children are identified?

Mahito Takahashi of New Jersey made a perfect score in a worldwide mathematics Olympiad and has won close to 200 other awards. A well-rounded youngster, he sings in a chamber choir and acted in a school production of Shakespeare's *Romeo and Juliet*. The key to helping such children achieve lies in recognizing and nurturing their natural gifts.

themselves. But although parenting can enhance the development of gifts, it cannot create them (Winner, 2000).

Brain research suggests that gifted children "are born with unusual brains that enable rapid learning in a particular domain" (Winner, 2000, p. 161). For example, children with mathematical, musical, and artistic gifts tend to have unusual activity in the right hemisphere while doing tasks normally done by the left. They are also more likely to be left-handed (Winner, 2000).

Lewis M. Terman and the Lives of Gifted Children

A classic longitudinal study of gifted children began in 1921, when Lewis M. Terman (who brought the Binet intelligence test to the United States) identified more than 1,500 California children with IQs of 135 or higher. The study demolished the widespread stereotype of the bright child as a puny, pasty-faced bookworm. These children were taller, healthier, better coordinated, better adjusted, and more popular than the average child (Wallach & Kogan, 1965), and their cognitive, scholastic, and vocational superiority has held up for nearly 80 years (Terman & Oden, 1959).

On the other hand, none of Terman's sample grew up to be Einsteins or Kurosawas, and those with the highest IQs became no more illustrious than those who were only moderately gifted. This lack of a close correlation between childhood giftedness and adult eminence has been supported by later research (Winner, 1997).

Terman's findings about the physical and psychological health of gifted children have been confirmed by later, more controlled studies (Achter & Lubinski, 2003). However, *profoundly* gifted children (often defined as having 180 IQ or higher) are more likely to have social and emotional difficulties than the less highly gifted. Feeling "different" and socially isolated, they may try to hide their gifts. This is a strong argument for placing these children in classes or groups with others like themselves (Winner, 2000).

Defining and Measuring Creativity

In Kurosawa's directorial debut in *Sanshiro Saguto* in 1943, he surprised audiences and critics by combining traditional Japanese samurai themes with tension-building techniques from American action movies. Throughout his career, innovation was his hallmark.

One definition of *creativity* is the ability to see things in a new light—to produce something never seen before or to discern problems others fail to recognize and find new and unusual solutions. High creativity and high academic intelligence (or IQ) do not necessarily go hand in hand. Classic research found only modest correlations (Anastasi & Schaefer, 1971; Getzels, 1964, 1984; Getzels & Jackson, 1962, 1963).

convergent thinking Thinking aimed at finding the one "right" answer to a problem

divergent thinking Thinking that produces a variety of fresh, diverse possibilities

J. P. Guilford (1956, 1959, 1960, 1967, 1986) distinguished between two kinds of thinking: *convergent* and *divergent*. **Convergent thinking**—the kind IQ tests measure—seeks a single correct answer; **divergent thinking** comes up with a wide array of fresh possibilities. Tests of creativity call for divergent thinking. The Torrance Tests of Creative Thinking (Torrance, 1966, 1974; Torrance & Ball, 1984), among the most widely known tests of creativity, include such tasks as listing unusual uses for a paper clip, completing a figure, and writing down what a sound brings to mind.

One problem with many of these tests is that the score depends partly on speed, which is not a hallmark of creativity. Moreover, although the tests yield fairly reliable results, there is dispute over whether they are valid—whether they identify children who are creative in everyday life (Anastasi, 1988; Mansfield & Busse, 1981; Simonton, 1990). As Guilford recognized, divergent thinking may not be the only, or even the most important, factor in creative performance.

Educating Gifted Children

Most provinces have special programs for the gifted; about 6 percent of public school children participate (Winzer, 1996). They generally follow one of two approaches: *enrichment* or *acceleration*. **Enrichment** broadens and deepens knowledge and skills through extra classroom activities, research projects, field trips, or coaching by experts. **Acceleration,** often recommended for highly gifted children, speeds up their education by early school entrance, by grade skipping, by placement in fast-paced classes, or by advanced courses in specific subjects.

enrichment Approach to educating the gifted that broadens and deepens knowledge and skills through extra activities, projects, field trips, or mentoring

acceleration Approach to educating the gifted, which moves them through a curriculum at an unusually rapid pace

Moderate acceleration does not seem to harm social adjustment, at least in the long run (Winner, 1997). A 30-year study of 3,937 young people who took advanced placement (AP; accelerated) courses in high school found that they were more satisfied with their school experience and ultimately achieved more than equally gifted young people who did not take AP courses (Bleske-Rechek, Lubinski, & Benbow, 2004).

Julian Stanley: Seeking and Nurturing the Profoundly Gifted In 1971 Julian Stanley founded the Study of Mathematically Gifted Youth (SMPY) at Johns Hopkins University. Highly intelligent and highly motivated 12- and 13-year-olds who qualify can take advanced summer courses at participating universities and can apply for very early college entrance.

Whereas Terman selected children in the top 1 percent of intellectual ability, Stanley looked for profoundly gifted young people in the top 0.001 percent—1 in 10,000. Rather than take IQ as a criterion, Stanley used college entrance examinations, primarily the SAT, to identify children capable of exceptional reasoning in math. Later the program was extended to children profoundly gifted in verbal intelligence (Achter & Lubinski, 2003; Lubinski, Webb, Morelock, & Benbow, 2001).

How did Stanley's "finds" turn out? By early adulthood, among 320 SMPY participants, several already had won significant awards and had noteworthy literary, scientific, or technical accomplishments. The vast majority said that accelerating their education had promoted their academic progress and social-emotional development (Lubinski et al., 2001).

By their mid-thirties, more than half of 380 SMPY participants had earned doctor's degrees, twice the rate found in studies of persons in the top 1 percent of cognitive ability (Lubinski, Benbow, Webb, & Bleske-Rechek, 2006). More SMPY men than women had gone into math and science careers, but the women who did not do so obtained similar proportions of advanced degrees and high level careers in other fields, such as law and medicine, where they could use their advanced reasoning skills (Lubinski & Benbow, 2006). As compared with a control group of graduate students from top universities, the SMPY group achieved exceptional career success, higher incomes, and similar life satisfaction (Lubinski et al., 2006). However, even in this group, not everyone was a top achiever—again underlining the importance of motivation and effort (Achter & Lubinski, 2003).

There is no firm dividing line between being gifted and not being gifted, creative and not creative. All children benefit from being encouraged in their areas of interest and ability. What we learn about fostering intelligence, creativity, and talent in the most able children may help all children make the most of their potential. The degree to which they do this will affect their self-concept and other aspects of personality, as we discuss in Chapter 14.

Checkpoint ✓

Can you . . .

✔ Tell why identification of gifted children is an issue?

✔ Discuss the relationships between giftedness and life achievements, and between IQ and creativity?

✔ Describe two approaches to education of gifted children?

What's your view ❓

• Would you favour strengthening, cutting back, or eliminating special educational programs for gifted students?

Summary and Key Terms

Piagetian Approach: The Concrete Operational Child

Guidepost 1 How do school-age children's thinking and moral reasoning differ from those of younger children?

• A child from about age 7 to age 12 is in the stage of concrete operations. Children are less egocentric than before and are more proficient at tasks requiring logical reasoning, such as spatial thinking, understanding of causality, categorization, inductive and deductive reasoning, conservation, and working with numbers. However, their reasoning is largely limited to the here and now.

• Cultural experience, as well as neurological development, seems to contribute to the rate of development of conservation and other Piagetian skills.

• According to Piaget, moral development is linked with cognitive maturation and occurs in three stages in which children move from strict obedience to authority toward more autonomous judgments based first on fairness and later on equity.

concrete operations (334)   seriation (335)   transitive inference (335)   class inclusion (335)   inductive reasoning (335)   deductive reasoning (335)   horizontal décalage (336)

Information-Processing Approach: Attention, Memory, and Planning

Guidepost 2 What advances in information-processing skills occur during middle childhood?

- Information-processing models describe three steps in memory: encoding, storage, and retrieval.
- Executive function—including attentional, memory, and planning skills—improves during middle childhood as a result of pruning of neurons in the prefrontal cortex.
- Processing speed, inhibitory control, selective attention, working memory capacity, metamemory, metacognition, and use of mnemonic strategies are specific skills that improve during the school years.
- Gains in information processing may help explain the advances Piaget described.

executive function (338) metamemory (339) mnemonic strategies (339) external memory aids (339) rehearsal (339) organization (339) elaboration (339)

Psychometric Approach: Assessment of Intelligence

Guidepost 3 How accurately can schoolchildren's intelligence be measured?

- The intelligence of school-age children is assessed by group or individual tests. Although intended as aptitude tests, they are validated against measures of achievement.
- IQ tests are fairly good predictors of school success but may be unfair to some children.
- Differences in IQ among ethnic groups appear to result to a considerable degree from socio-economic and other environmental differences. Schooling seems to increase measured intelligence.
- Attempts to devise culture-free or culture-fair tests have been unsuccessful.
- IQ tests tap only three of the "intelligences" in Howard Gardner's theory of multiple intelligences. According to Robert Sternberg's triarchic theory, IQ tests mainly measure the componential element of intelligence, not the experiential and contextual elements.
- New directions in intelligence testing include the Sternberg Triarchic Abilities Tests (STAT) and the Kaufman Assessment Battery for Children (K-ABC-II), and dynamic tests based on Vygotskyan theory.

aptitude tests (341) achievement tests (341) Otis-Lennon School Ability Test (OLSAT8) (341) Wechsler Intelligence Scale for Children (WISC–IV) (341) cultural bias (343) culture-free (344) culture-fair (344) culture-relevant (344) theory of multiple intelligences (344) triarchic theory of intelligence (345) componential element (345) experiential element (345) contextual element (345) tacit knowledge (346) Sternberg Triarchic Abilities Test (STAT) (346) Kaufman Assessment Battery for Children (K-ABC-II) (346)

Language and Literacy

Guidepost 4 How do communicative abilities expand during middle childhood?

- Use of vocabulary, grammar, and syntax become increasingly sophisticated, but the major area of linguistic growth is in pragmatics.
- Metacognition contributes to progress in reading.
- Despite the popularity of whole-language programs, early phonics training is a key to reading proficiency.
- Interaction with peers fosters development of writing skills.

pragmatics (347) decoding (348) visually-based retrieval (348) phonetic, or code-emphasis, approach (348) whole-language approach (348) metacognition (349)

The Child in School

Guidepost 5 What factors influence school achievement?

- Because schooling is cumulative, the foundation laid in first grade is very important.
- Children's self-efficacy beliefs affect school achievement.
- Parents influence children's learning by becoming involved in their schooling, motivating them to achieve, and transmitting attitudes about learning.
- Socio-economic status can influence parental beliefs and practices that, in turn, influence achievement. Poor families whose children do well in school tend to have more social capital than poor families whose children do not do well.
- The school environment and class size affect learning.
- Current educational issues and innovations include the amount of homework assigned, methods of teaching math, social promotion, charter schools, homeschooling, and computer literacy.

social capital (353) social promotion (356)

Educating Children with Special Needs

Guidepost 6 How do schools meet special needs?

- Innovative programs for Aboriginal education aim to address disparities in academic achievement.
- Methods of second-language education are controversial. Issues include speed and facility with English, long-term achievement in academic subjects, and pride in cultural identity.
- French immersion, a Canadian innovation, is effective in teaching French in English-language communities, while at the same time not adversely affecting English-language proficiency or academic achievement.
- Three frequent sources of learning problems are intellectual disability (mental retardation), learning disabilities (LDs), and attention-deficit/hyperactivity disorder (ADHD). Dyslexia is the most common learning disability.

- In Canada, all children with disabilities are entitled to a free, appropriate education. However, because there is no national legislation, the specific provisions for educating children with disabilities vary from province to province. In general, children must be educated in the least restrictive environment possible, often in the regular classroom.

- An IQ of 130 or higher is a common standard for identifying gifted children. Broader definitions include creativity, artistic talent, and other attributes and rely on multiple criteria for identification. Minorities are under-represented in programs for the gifted.

- In Terman's classic longitudinal study of gifted children, most turned out to be well adjusted and successful, but not outstandingly so.

- Creativity and IQ are *not* closely linked. Tests of creativity seek to measure divergent thinking, but their validity has been questioned.

- Special educational programs for gifted, creative, and talented children stress enrichment or acceleration.

English-immersion (358)   bilingual education (358) bilingual (358)   Heritage Language Program (358) French immersion (359)   two-way (dual-language) learning (359)   intellectual disability (mental retardation) (359)   dyslexia (360)   learning disabilities (LDs) (360)   attention-deficit/hyperactivity disorder (ADHD) (361)   convergent thinking (364)   divergent thinking (364)   enrichment (365)   acceleration (365)

CHAPTER FOURTEEN

Psychosocial Development in Middle Childhood

Have you ever felt like nobody?
Just a tiny speck of air.
When everyone's around you,
And you are just not there.

—Karen Crawford, age 9

Focus *Marian Anderson, Operatic Trailblazer**

Marian Anderson

The African-American contralto Marian Anderson (1902–1993) had—in the words of the great Italian conductor Arturo Toscanini—a voice heard "once in a hundred years." She was also a pioneer in breaking racial barriers. Turned away by a music school in her hometown of Philadelphia, she studied voice privately and in 1925 won a national competition to sing with the New York Philharmonic. When she was refused the use of a concert hall in Washington, D.C., First Lady Eleanor Roosevelt arranged for her to sing on the steps of the Lincoln Memorial. The unprecedented performance on Easter Sunday, 1939, drew 75,000 people and was broadcast to millions. Several weeks later, Marian Anderson was the first black singer to perform at the White House. But not until 1955 did Anderson, at age 57, become the first person of her race to sing with New York's Metropolitan Opera.

A remarkable story lies behind this woman's "journey from a single rented room in South Philadelphia" (McKay, 1992, p. xxx). It is a story of nurturing family ties—bonds of mutual support, care, and concern that extended from generation to generation.

Marian Anderson was the eldest of three children of John and Annie Anderson. Two years after her birth, the family left their one-room apartment to move in with her father's parents and then into a small rented house nearby.

At the age of 6, Marian joined the junior choir at church. There she made a friend, Viola Johnson, who lived across the street from the Andersons. Within a year or two, they sang a duet together—Marian's first public performance.

When Marian was 10, her beloved father died, and the family again moved in with his parents, his sister, and her two daughters. Marian's grandfather had a steady job. Her grandmother took care of all the children, her aunt ran the house, and her mother contributed by cooking dinners, working as a cleaning woman, and taking in laundry, which Marian and her sister Alyce delivered.

The most important influence in Marian Anderson's life was the counsel, example, and spiritual guidance of her hardworking, unfailingly supportive mother. Annie Anderson placed great importance on her children's schooling and saw to it that they didn't skimp on homework. Even when she was working full time, she cooked their dinner every night, and she taught Marian to sew her own clothes. "Not once can I recall . . . hearing Mother lift her voice to us in anger . . . ," Marian wrote. "She could be firm, and we learned to respect her wishes" (Anderson, 1992, p. 92).

When Marian Anderson became a world-renowned concert artist, she often returned to her old neighbourhood in Philadelphia. Her mother and sister Alyce shared a modest house, and the other sister, Ethel, lived next door with her son.

"It is the pleasantest thing in the world to go into that home and feel its happiness, . . . " the singer wrote. "They are all comfortable, and they cherish and protect one another. . . . I know that it warms [Mother] to have her grandson near her as he grows up, just as I think that when he gets to be a man, making his own life, he will have pleasant memories of his home and family" (1992, p. 93). In 1992, Marian Anderson—widowed, childless, and frail at age 95—went to live with that nephew, James DePriest, then music director of the Oregon Symphony. She died of a stroke at his home the following year.

• • •

Marian Anderson experienced significant cultural changes, but one thing that never changed was the strong, supportive network of relationships that sustained her and her family. The kind of household a child lives in, and the relationships within the household, can have profound effects on psychosocial development in middle childhood, when children are developing a stronger sense of what it means to be responsible, contributing members, first of a family, and then of society. The family is part of a web of contextual influences, including the peer group, the school, and the neighbourhood in which the family lives. Marian Anderson's first friend, her church choir, and the neighbours for whom she did odd jobs to earn the price of a violin all played parts in her development.

In this chapter, we trace the rich and varied emotional and social lives of school-age children. We see how children develop a more realistic concept of themselves and how they become more independent, self-reliant, and in control of their emotions. Through being with peers they make discoveries about their own attitudes, values, and skills. Still, as Anderson's story shows, the family remains a vital influence. Children's lives are affected, not only by the way parents approach the task of child raising, but by whether and how they are employed, by the family's economic circumstances, and by its structure, or composition—whether the child lives with one parent or two; whether or not the child has siblings, and how many; and whether or not the household includes other relatives, such as Anderson's grandparents, aunt, and cousins. Although most children are emotionally healthy, some have mental health problems; we look at several of these. We also describe resilient children, who emerge from the stresses of childhood healthier and stronger.

After you have read and studied this chapter, you should be able to answer each of the Guidepost questions that appear at the top of the next page. Look for them again in the margins, where they point to important concepts throughout the chapter. To check your understanding of these Guideposts, review the end-of-chapter summary. Checkpoints throughout the chapter will help you verify your understanding of what you have read.

---

*The chief source of biographical material about Marian Anderson and her family was Anderson (1992). Some details come from Kernan (1993) and from obituaries published in *Time* (April 19, 1993), *People Weekly, The New Yorker,* and *Jet* (April 26, 1993).

1. How do the self-concept and self-esteem change in middle childhood, and how do school-age children show emotional growth?

2. What are the effects of family atmosphere and family structure, and what part do siblings play in children's development?

3. How do relationships with peers change in middle childhood, and what factors influence popularity and aggressive behaviour?

4. What are some common mental health problems of childhood, and how do children respond to the stresses of modern life?

Guideposts for Study

Guidepost 1

How do the self-concept and self-esteem change in middle childhood, and how do school-age children show emotional growth?

representational systems In neo-Piagetian terminology, the third stage in development of self-definition, characterized by breadth, balance, and the integration and assessment of aspects of the self

industry versus inferiority Erikson's fourth critical alternative of psychosocial development, in which children must learn the productive skills their culture requires or else face feelings of inferiority

Checkpoint

Can you . . .

✔ From a neo-Piagetian perspective, tell how the self-concept develops in middle childhood as compared with early childhood?

✔ Compare Erikson's and Harter's views about sources of self-esteem?

The Developing Self

The cognitive growth that takes place during middle childhood enables children to develop more complex concepts of themselves and to grow in emotional understanding and control.

Self-concept Development

Around age 7 or 8, children reach the third of the neo-Piagetian stages of self-concept development. Judgments about the self become more realistic and balanced as children form **representational systems:** broad, inclusive self-concepts that integrate various aspects of the self (Harter, 1993, 1996, 1998).

"At school I'm feeling pretty smart in certain subjects, Language Arts and Social Studies," says 8-year-old Lisa. "I got A's in these subjects on my last report card and was really proud of myself. But I'm feeling really dumb in Arithmetic and Science, particularly when I see how well the other kids are doing. . . . I still like myself as a person, because Arithmetic and Science just aren't that important to me. How I look and how popular I am are more important" (Harter, 1996, p. 208).

Lisa's self-description shows that she can focus on more than one dimension of herself. She has outgrown an all-or-nothing, black-or-white self-definition; she recognizes that she can be "smart" in certain subjects and "dumb" in others. Her self-descriptions are more balanced; she can verbalize her self-concept better, and she can weigh different aspects of it ("How I look and how popular I am are more important"). She can compare her *real self* with her *ideal self* and can judge how well she measures up to social standards in comparison with others. All of these changes contribute to the development of self-esteem, her assessment of her *global self-worth* ("I like myself as a person").

Self-esteem

A major determinant of self-esteem, according to Erikson (1982), is children's view of their capacity for productive work. The central issue of middle childhood is **industry versus inferiority.** Children need to learn skills valued in their society. Arapesh boys in New Guinea learn to make bows and arrows; Arapesh girls learn to plant, weed, and harvest. Inuit children in Canada learn to hunt and fish. Children in industrialized countries learn to read, write, count, and use computers. Like Marian Anderson, many children learn household skills and help out with odd jobs.

The "virtue" that develops with successful resolution of this stage is *competence,* a view of the self as able to master skills and complete tasks. If children feel inadequate in comparison with their peers, they may retreat to the protective embrace of the family. If, on the other hand, they become too industrious, they may neglect social relationships and turn into "workaholics."

Parents strongly influence beliefs about competence. In a longitudinal study of 514 U.S. middle-class children, parents' beliefs about their children's competence in math and sports were strongly associated with the children's beliefs (Fredricks & Eccles, 2002).

Middle childhood, according to Erikson, is a time for learning the skills one's culture considers important. In driving geese to market, this Vietnamese girl is developing a sense of competence and gaining self-esteem.

Emotional Growth

As children grow older, they are more aware of their own and other people's feelings. They can better regulate their emotional expression in social situations, and they can respond to others' emotional distress (Saarni et al., 1998).

By age 7 or 8, children typically feel shame and pride, and they have a clearer idea of the difference between guilt and shame (Harris, Olthof, Meerum Terwogt, & Hardman, 1987; Olthof, Schouten, Kuiper, Stegge, & Jennekens-Schinkel, 2000). These emotions, which depend on awareness of the implications of their actions and on what kind of socialization children have received, affect their opinion of themselves (Harter, 1993, 1996). Children can also verbalize conflicting emotions. As Lisa says, "Most of the boys at school are pretty yukky. I don't feel that way about my little brother Jason, although he does get on my nerves. I love him but at the same time, he also does things that make me mad. But I control my temper. I'd be ashamed of myself if I didn't" (Harter, 1996, p. 208).

By middle childhood, children are aware of their culture's "rules" for emotional expression (Cole, Bruschi, & Tamang, 2002). Children learn what makes them angry, fearful, or sad and how other people react to a display of these emotions, and they learn to adapt their behaviour accordingly. Kindergartners believe that a parent can make a child less sad by telling the child to stop crying, or can make a child less afraid of a dog by telling the child there is nothing to be afraid of. Sixth graders know that an emotion may be suppressed, but it still exists (Rotenberg & Eisenberg, 1997).

Emotional self-regulation involves effortful (voluntary) control of emotions, attention, and behaviour (Eisenberg et al., 2004). Children low in effortful control tend to become visibly angry or frustrated when interrupted or prevented from doing something they want to do. Children with high effortful control can stifle the impulse to show negative emotion at inappropriate times. Effortful control may be temperamentally based but generally increases with age. Low effortful control may predict later behaviour problems (Eisenberg et al., 2004).

Pro-social Behaviour

School-age children generally become more empathic and more inclined to pro-social behaviour. Pro-social children tend to act appropriately in social situations, to be relatively free from negative emotion, and to cope with problems constructively (Eisenberg, Fabes, & Murphy, 1996). Parents who acknowledge children's feelings of distress and help them deal with the source of their distress foster empathy, pro-social development, and social skills (Bryant, 1987; Eisenberg et al., 1996). When parents respond with disapproval or

Checkpoint ✔

Can you . . .

✔ Identify some aspects of emotional growth in middle childhood and tell how parental treatment may affect children's handling of negative emotions?

✔ Tell ways in which pro-social behaviour increases in middle childhood?

punishment, emotions such as anger and fear may become more intense and may impair social adjustment (Fabes, Leonard, Kupanoff, & Martin, 2001), or the child may become secretive and anxious about these negative feelings. As children approach early adolescence, parental intolerance of negative emotion may heighten parent-child conflict (Eisenberg, Fabes, et al., 1999). As we'll see in the next section, this is one of many ways in which the family environment affects children's development.

Guidepost 2

What are the effects of family atmosphere and family structure, and what part do siblings play in children's development?

The Child in the Family

School-age children spend more time away from home than when they were younger and become less close to their parents (Hofferth, 1998). They also spend more time at school and on studies and less time at family meals than 20 years ago (Juster et al., 2004). In Canada, parents are less likely to be involved in playing with children as children get older; over three-quarters of parents of children between 1 and 4 years reporting playing with their children, while only 20 percent of parents of 13 to 17 year old adolescents report playing actively with their children (Canadian Fitness and Lifestyle Research Institute, 2000).

To understand the child in the family we need to look at the family environment—its atmosphere and structure. These in turn are affected by what goes on beyond the walls of the home. As Bronfenbrenner's theory describes (refer back to Chapter 2), additional layers of influence—including parents' work and socio-economic status and societal trends such as urbanization, changes in family size, divorce, and remarriage—help shape the family environment and, thus, children's development.

Beyond these influences are cultural experiences and values that define rhythms of family life and roles of family members. Children generally are socialized differently in ethnic minority families and in white families. For example, although there are more similarities than differences, Aboriginal parents tend to have a more liberal approach to child rearing than do non-Aboriginal parents (Gfellner, 1990). Children are often involved in decision-making in the family because they are regarded as independent persons who are free to explore their own environment (Neckoway, Brownlee, & Castellan, 2007). In addition, the way in which children are brought up in immigrant families might be reflected in values that children express, in comparison with their non-immigrant peers. In an Ottawa-Hull study of children from different ethnic groups, differences in values were found. Although English, French, and Italian 10- to 12-year-olds demonstrated similar perspectives on self-esteem, children of English background had an individualist orientation, children of French background had a family orientation, and children of Italian background were most peer-oriented (Lortie-Lussier, & Fellers, 1991). The experience that children of Italian background have of assimilating into mainstream culture may be reflected in these outcomes (Lortie-Lussier et al., 1991).

As we look at the child in the family, then, we need to be aware of outside influences that affect the family.

Family Atmosphere

The most important influences of the family environment on children's development come from the atmosphere within the home. Is it supportive and loving or conflict ridden? One contributing factor is how well parents handle school-age children's growing need—and ability—to make their own decisions. Another factor is the family's economic situation. How does parents' work affect children's well-being? Does the family have enough financial resources to provide for basic needs?

Parenting Issues: Co-regulation and Discipline

co-regulation Transitional stage in the control of behaviour in which parents exercise general supervision and children exercise moment-to-moment self-regulation

During the course of childhood, control of behaviour gradually shifts from parents to child. Middle childhood is the transitional stage of **co-regulation,** in which parent and child share power: Parents oversee a child's behaviour, but children exercise moment-to-moment self-regulation (Maccoby, 1984). In problems with peers, for example, parents now rely less on direct management or supervision and more on consultation and discussion with their own child (Parke & Buriel, 1998). Children are more apt to follow their parents' wishes or advice when they recognize that the parents are fair and are concerned about the child's welfare and that they may "know better" because of experience. It also helps if parents try to defer to children's maturing judgment and take strong stands only on important issues (Maccoby, 1984).

The shift to co-regulation affects how parents handle discipline (Maccoby, 1984; Roberts, Block, & Block, 1984). Parents of school-age children are more likely to use inductive techniques that include reasoning. For example, 8-year-old Jared's father points out how his actions affect others: "Hitting Jermaine hurts him and makes him feel bad." In other situations, Jared's parents may appeal to his self-esteem ("What happened to the helpful boy who was here yesterday?"), sense of humour ("If you go one more day without a bath, we'll know when you're coming without looking!"), moral values ("A big, strong boy like you shouldn't sit on the train and let an old person stand"), or appreciation ("Aren't you glad that your father cares enough to remind you to wear boots so that you won't catch a cold?"). Above all, Jared's parents let him know he must bear the consequences of his behaviour ("No wonder you missed the school bus today—you stayed up too late last night! Now you'll have to walk to school").

In one longitudinal study in Finland, 196 kindergartners were followed until second grade. Children whose mothers used guilt-producing disciplinary methods ("I'm so-o-o disappointed in you!") but also were highly affectionate tended to develop behaviour problems—perhaps because the mothers communicated inconsistent messages or kept the children too emotionally dependent on maternal approval (Aunola & Nurmi, 2005).

The way parents and children resolve conflicts may be more important than the specific outcomes. If family conflict is constructive, it can help children see the need for rules and standards. They also learn what kinds of issues are worth arguing about and what strategies can be effective (A. R. Eisenberg, 1996). However, as children become pre-adolescents and their striving for autonomy becomes more insistent, the quality of family problem solving often deteriorates (Vuchinich, Angelelli, & Gatherum, 1996).

Although school-age children spend less time at home than before, parents who enjoy being with their children tend to raise children who feel good about themselves—and about their parents.

Checkpoint

Can you . . .

✔ Describe how co-regulation works and how discipline and the handling of family conflict change during middle childhood?

Effects of Parents' Work

With 66.4 percent of all Canadian women with children under 6 years of age employed (Statistics Canada, Labour Force Survey, 2007), many children are unlikely to have any memory of a time when their mothers were *not* working for pay. For children between the ages of 6 and 15 years, 78.2 percent of Canadian mothers are working outside of the home (Statistics Canada, Labour Force Survey, 2007).

In general, the more satisfied a mother is with her employment status, the more effective she is likely to be as a parent (Parke & Buriel, 1998). However, the impact of a mother's work outside the home depends on many factors, including the child's age, sex, temperament, and personality; whether the mother works full- or part-time; why she is working; whether she has a supportive or unsupportive mate, or none; the family's socio-economic status; and the kind of care the child receives before and/or after school (Parke & Buriel, 1998). Often a single mother like Marian Anderson's must work to stave off economic disaster. How her working affects her children may hinge on how much time and energy she has left over to spend with them and what sort of role model she provides (B. L. Barber & Eccles, 1992)—clearly, a positive one in Annie Anderson's case.

How well parents keep track of their children may be more important than whether the mother is employed (Crouter, MacDermid, McHale, & Perry-Jenkins, 1990). Some children are supervised after school by babysitters or relatives; some go to structured programs, either at school or in child-care settings. Like good child care for preschoolers, good after-school programs have relatively low enrolment, low child–staff ratios, and well-educated staff (Rosenthal & Vandell, 1996). Children, especially boys, in organized after-school programs marked by flexible programming and a positive emotional climate tend to adjust better and do better in school (Pierce, Hamm, & Vandell, 1999).

"Latchkey" children who care for themselves after school while parents work, like this brother and sister, should be mature, responsible, and resourceful and should know how to get help in an emergency.

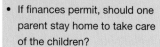

What's your view ?

• If finances permit, should one parent stay home to take care of the children?

About 9 percent of school-aged children and 23 percent of early adolescents are reported to be in *self-care,* regularly caring for themselves at home without adult supervision (Hofferth & Jankuniene, 2000; NICHD Early Childhood Research Network, 2004). This arrangement is advisable only for older children who are mature, responsible, and resourceful and know how to get help in an emergency—and, even then, only if a parent stays in touch by telephone.

Poverty and Parenting

More than 1.2 million, or 1 in 6 of children in Canada lived in poverty (below the Statistics Canada low-income cut-off for their communities) in 2003, about the same as in 1989 (Campaign 2000, 2005; CICH, 2000). However, some groups of children in Canada experience a much higher rate of poverty than the average; the rate is 1 in 3 for children in Aboriginal, immigrant, and visible minority groups (Canadian Nurses Association, 2005) The experience of poverty is more frequent for children younger than 7 years (25 percent) compared to children between 7 and 17 years (19 percent) (CICH, 2000). The rate of poverty is dramatically higher for lone-mother families, consistent at about 60 percent from 1981 to 1997 (CICH, 2000). However, the depth of poverty, how far below the low-income cut-off (LICO), is greater for two-parent families than for lone-mother families.

Poverty can harm children's development through its impact on parents' emotional state and parenting practices and on the home environment they create (Evans, 2004; NICHD Early Child Care Research Network, 2005a).

Vonnie McLoyd's (1990, 1998) ecological analysis of the effects of poverty traces a route that leads to adult psychological distress, to effects on child rearing, and finally to emotional, behavioural, and academic problems in children. Parents who live in poor housing (or have none), who have lost their jobs, who are worried about their next meal, and who feel a lack of control over their lives are likely to become anxious, depressed, or irritable. They may become less affectionate with, and less responsive to, their children. They may discipline inconsistently, harshly, and arbitrarily. They may ignore good behaviour and pay attention only to misbehaviour. The children, in turn, tend to become depressed themselves, to have trouble getting along with peers, to lack self-confidence, and to engage in anti-social acts (Brooks-Gunn, Britto, & Brady, 1999; McLoyd, 1990, 1998; Mistry et al., 2002).

The effects of *persistent* poverty can be complex. In another U.S. longitudinal study of 1,364 families of mixed SES, transitory poverty during the first four years of a child's life was less damaging to long-term cognitive and social development than later or chronic poverty(NICHD Early Child Care Research Network, 2005a). However, what seemed to be most damaging to children were family characteristics that may accompany poverty— an unstimulating home environment, lack of maternal sensitivity, unstable adult relationships, psychiatric problems, and violent or criminal behaviour.

Poverty can sap parents' confidence in their ability to affect their children's development. Lack of financial resources also can make it harder for mothers and fathers to support each other in parenting. Lone-parent families working for minimum wage in 1996 had to work between a low of 61 hours, in British Columbia, and high of 80 hours per week, in Manitoba, to reach the LICO (CICH, 2000). For two-parent families with two children, the number of hours of work per week ranged from 89 to 118 hours, to reach the LICO. Families working under these conditions experience great stress, which can create difficulties for healthy family functioning. A solution to this problem would be to raise the minimum wage in order to allow parents better opportunities to maintain work and family responsibilities (CICH, 2000).

However, this bleak picture is not etched in stone. Parents who can turn to relatives (as Annie Anderson did) or to community representatives for emotional support, help with child care, and child-rearing information often can parent their children more effectively. These positive factors work to counteract the negative effects of poverty in Canada, and add to a child's resiliency in the face of the risks to healthy development, as found in the National Longitudinal Survey of Children and Youth. In fact, multiple risk factors are more likely to have a negative effect on development than a single risk factor like poverty

(Landy & Tam, 1998; Willms, 2002). Also, some children are more adaptable than others; their temperament enables them to cope more successfully with a stressful environment (Ackerman, Kogos, Youngstrom, Schoff, & Izard, 1999).

Family Structure

Family structure in Canada has changed dramatically in recent decades. In earlier generations, the vast majority of children grew up in traditional families, with two biological parents or two parents who had adopted one or more children in infancy. Today, although about 2 out of 3 children under 18 live with two married biological, adoptive, or stepparents, that proportion represents a dramatic decline over the past two decades (Canadian Council on Social Development, 2001; Statistics Canada, 2007; see Figure 14-1). During this period, there has been an increase in common-law families, as well as families headed by lone parents. There are also a growing number of other non-traditional families, including lone-parent families (18.3 percent of all families in Canada in 2006 were lone-parent families, and of these 80 percent were female-headed, and 20 percent were male-headed; Statistics Canada, 2007). Among two-parent families, are new structures, including common-law families, blended families (resulting from divorce and remarriage), gay and lesbian families, and grandparent-headed families (Statistics Canada, 2007). How do these various family structures affect children?

Other things being equal, children tend to do better in families with two continuously married parents than in cohabiting, divorced, lone-parent, or stepfamilies, or when the child is born outside of marriage. The distinction is even stronger for children growing up with two *happily* married parents. These children tend to experience a higher standard of living, more effective parenting, more cooperative co-parenting, closer relationships with both (especially fathers) and fewer stressful events (Amato, 2005).

However, the parents' relationship, the quality of their parenting, and their ability to create a favourable family atmosphere may affect children's adjustment more than their marital status (Amato, 2005; Bray & Hetherington, 1993; Bronstein et al., 1993; D. A. Dawson, 1991). Adoptive children in two-parent families are equally advantaged as biological children in such families (Hamilton, Cheng, & Powell, 2007).

A father's frequent and positive involvement with his child, from infancy on, is directly related to the child's well-being and physical, cognitive, and social development (Cabrera et al., 2000; Kelley, Smith, Green, Berndt, & Rogers, 1998; Shannon, Tamis-LeMonda, London, & Cabrera, 2002).

Adoptive Families

Adoption is found in all cultures throughout history. It is not only for infertile people; single people, older people, gay and lesbian couples, and people who already have biological children have become adoptive parents. Famous adoptees include the singer Buffy Sainte-Marie, and writer Lucy Maud Montgomery, and hockey legend Stan Mikita.

Adoptions usually take place through public or private agencies. Agency adoptions are supposed to be confidential, with no contact between the birth mother and the adoptive parents, and the identity of the birth mother is kept secret. However, in recent years independent adoptions, made by agreement between birth parents and adoptive parents, have become more common than in the past. Often these are *open adoptions*, in which the parties share information or have direct contact. Studies suggest that the presumed risks of open adoption, such as fear that a birth mother who

Checkpoint ✔

Can you . . .

✔ Identify ways in which parents' work can affect children?

✔ Discuss effects of poverty on child raising?

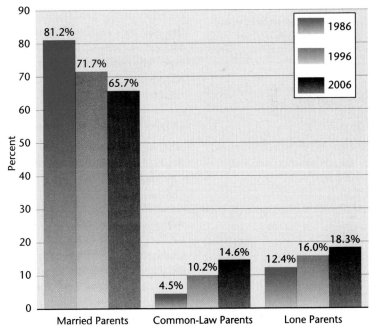

Figure 14-1

The proportion of children aged 14 years and under living with married, common-law, and lone parents. The proportion of married parent families has decreased over the past two decades, while the proportion of common-law and lone parent families has increased in Canada.

Source: Statistics Canada, 2007.

knows her child's whereabouts will try to reclaim the child, are overstated (Grotevant, McRoy, Elde, & Fravel, 1994). In a survey of 1,059 California adoptive families, whether an adoption was open bore no relation to the children's adjustment or to the parents' satisfaction with the adoption, both of which were very high (Berry, Dylla, Barth, & Needell, 1998).

Adopting a child carries special challenges: integrating the adopted child into the family, explaining the adoption to the child, helping the child develop a healthy sense of self, and perhaps eventually helping the child find and contact the biological parents. Data from a national longitudinal study show that adoptive parents invest just as much energy and resources in their children as biological parents do—perhaps to compensate for the special challenges of being adopted (Hamilton, Cheng, & Powell, 2007). A review of the literature found few significant differences in adjustment between adopted and nonadopted children (Haugaard, 1998). Children adopted in infancy are least likely to have adjustment problems (Sharma, McGue, & Benson, 1996b). Any problems that do occur may surface during middle childhood, when children become more aware of differences in the way families are formed, or in adolescence, particularly for boys (Freeark et al., 2005).

Cognitively, adoption is usually beneficial. An analysis of 62 studies of a total of 17,767 adopted children found that they scored higher on IQ tests and performed better in school than siblings or peers who remained in the birth family or in institutional care. Their IQ scores also equaled those of their adoptive siblings and nonadopted peers, but their school performance and language abilities tended to lag, and they were more likely to develop learning problems and to be referred for special education (van IJzendoorn & Juffer, 2005; van IJzendoorn, Juffer, & Poelhuis, 2005).

A growing number of Canadian families are adopting children from other countries. Between 2000 and 2004, about 10,000 children were adopted from abroad (Human Resources and Social Development Canada, 2007). Rules governing intercountry adoption vary among provinces and territories, but they involve the principles of The Hague Convention on Protection of Children and Co-operation in Respect of Intercountry Adoption to ensure that the best interests of adoptive children are protected.

Does foreign adoption entail special problems? Aside from the possibility of malnourishment or other serious medical conditions in children from developing countries (Bosch et al., 2003), a number of studies find no significant problems with children's psychological adjustment, school adjustment and performance, or observed behaviour at home or in the way they cope with being adopted (Levy-Shiff, Zoran, & Shulman, 1997; Sharma, McGue, & Benson, 1996a). However, not all international adoptions proceed so smoothly, especially when the children have experienced substandard care or are older at the time of adoption (refer back to the discussion of children adopted from Romanian orphanages in Chapter 6).

When Parents Divorce

Although the annual number of divorces in Canada has increased fivefold in the past 3 decades, the rate has remained constant in recent years at about 37 percent (Health Canada, 1999; CBC News, 2004; Statistics Canada, 2005b). How do children in these families adjust?

Adjusting to Divorce Divorce is stressful for children. First there is the stress of marital conflict and then of parental separation and the departure of one parent, usually the father. Children may not fully understand what is happening. Divorce is, of course, stressful for the parents as well and may negatively affect their parenting. The family's standard of living is likely to drop; and, if a parent moves away, a child's relationship with the noncustodial parent may suffer (Kelly & Emery, 2003). A divorced parent's remarriage can increase the stress on children, renewing feelings of loss (Ahrons & Tanner, 2003; Amato, 2003).

Children's emotional or behavioural problems may reflect the level of parental conflict *before* the divorce (Amato, 2005). In a longitudinal study of almost 11,000 Canadian children, those whose parents later divorced showed more anxiety, depression, or antisocial behaviour than those whose parents stayed married (Strohschein, 2005). If predivorce parental discord is chronic, overt, or destructive, children may be as well, or better, off after a divorce (Amato, 2003, 2005; Amato & Booth, 1997).

A child's adjustment to divorce may depend in part on the child's age or maturity, gender, temperament, and psychosocial adjustment before the divorce. Younger children tend to be more anxious about divorce, have less realistic perceptions of what caused it, and are more likely to blame themselves. However, they may adapt more quickly than older children, who better understand what is going on. School-age children are sensitive to parental pressures and loyalty conflicts and, like younger children, may fear abandonment and rejection. Boys find it harder to adjust than girls do and are more susceptible to social and conduct problems (Amato, 2005; Hetherington et al., 1998; Hines, 1997; Parke & Buriel, 1998).

Custody, Visitation, and Co-Parenting Children do better after divorce if the custodial parent is warm, supportive, and authoritative, monitors the child's activities, and holds age-appropriate expectations; if parental conflict subsides; and if the nonresident parent maintains close contact and involvement (Ahrons & Tanner, 2003; Kelly & Emery, 2003).

In most divorce cases, the mother gets custody, though paternal custody is a growing trend (Meyer & Garasky, 1993). Children living with divorced mothers adjust better when the father pays child support, which may be a barometer of the tie between

Although paternal custody is still relatively rare, it is a growing trend. Whether or not a father has custody, as this man does, his son is likely to adjust better if his father remains involved in his life.

father and child and also of cooperation between the ex-spouses (Amato & Gilbreth, 1999; Kelly & Emery, 2003). Many children of divorce say that losing contact with a father is one of the most painful results of divorce (Fabricius, 2003). However, frequency of contact with the father is not as important as the quality of the father-child relationship and the level of parental conflict. Children who are close to their nonresident fathers and whose fathers are authoritative parents tend to do better in school and are less likely to have behaviour problems (Amato & Gilbreth, 1999; Kelly & Emery, 2003).

In a U.S. national sample of 354 divorced families, *cooperative co-parenting*—active consultation between a mother and a nonresident father on parenting decisions—led to more frequent contact between father and child, and this, in turn, led to better father-child relationships and more responsive fathering (Sobolewski & King, 2005). Unfortunately, cooperative parenting is not the norm (Amato, 2005). Parent education programs that teach separated or divorced couples how to prevent or deal with conflict, keep lines of communication open, develop an effective co-parenting relationship, and help children adjust to divorce have been introduced in many courts with measurable success (Wolchik et al., 2002).

Joint custody, custody shared by both parents, can be advantageous if the parents can cooperate, as both parents can continue to be closely involved with the child. When parents have joint *legal* custody, they share the right and responsibility to make decisions regarding the child's welfare. When parents have joint *physical* custody (which is less common), the child lives part time with each of them. An analysis of 33 studies found that children in either legal or physical joint custody were better adjusted and had higher self-esteem and better family relationships than children in sole custody. In fact, the joint custody children were as well-adjusted as children in nondivorced families (Bauserman, 2002). It is likely, though, that couples who choose joint custody are those that have less conflict.

Long-term Effects Most children of divorce adjust reasonably well. Still, children with divorced parents tend to have modestly lower levels of cognitive, social, and emotional well-being than children whose parents stay together (Amato, 2005). In adolescence, divorce increases the risk of antisocial behaviour, difficulties with authority figures (Amato, 2003, 2005; Kelly & Emery, 2003), and dropping out of school (McLanahan & Sandefur, 1994). According to some research, 25 percent of children of divorce reach adulthood with serious social, emotional, or psychological problems, as compared with 10 percent of children whose parents stay together (Hetherington & Kelly, 2002). As adults, they tend to have lower SES, lower psychological well-being, and a greater chance of having a birth outside marriage. Their marriages tend to be of poorer quality and are more likely to end in divorce (Amato, 2005).

The anxiety connected with parental divorce may surface as children enter adulthood and try to form intimate relationships of their own (Amato, 2003; Wallerstein, Lewis, & Blakeslee, 2000). Having experienced their parents' divorce, some young adults are afraid of making commitments that might end in disappointment and are intent on protecting their independence (Glenn & Marquardt, 2001; Wallerstein & Corbin, 1999). However, much depends on how young people resolve and interpret the experience of parental divorce. Some, who saw a high degree of conflict between their parents, are able to learn from that negative example and to form highly intimate relationships themselves (Shulman, Scharf, Lumer, & Maurer, 2001).

Divorce may have consequences for later generations. In a 20-year longitudinal study of a random sample of 2,033 married persons in the United States, the children of those who divorced tended to have lower educational levels, more instability in their own marriages, and increased tension with their own children than those whose parents had remained married. The children of these "children of divorce" (the grandchildren of the original respondents) also tended to have lower educational levels and more marital discord as well as weaker bonds with their parents (Amato & Cheadle, 2005).

Living in a One-Parent Family

One-parent families result from divorce or separation, unwed parenthood, or death. The number of lone-parent families in Canada almost doubled between 1961 and 1991, from 11 percent to 20 percent (Health Canada, 1999). In 2004 lone parent families represented about 16 percent of all families in Canada (Statistics Canada, 2005). Today a child has at least a 50-percent chance of living with only one parent at some point (Bianchi, 1995; Hines, 1997; NCES, 1998b), with 3 in 10 children experiencing lone parenthood before the age of 10 (Department of Justice Canada, 2005).

In 1998, about more than 5 out of 6 Canadian children who lived with a single parent lived with their mothers, but about 1 in 6 single-parent families was headed by the father (Lapierre-Adamcyk, 1999), and more recently the ratio has changed to reflect a growing proportion of father-headed lone-parent families (currently about 20 percent; Public Health Agency of Canada, 2003) apparently due largely to an increase in the number of fathers having custody after divorce (Fields, 2004; Garasky & Meyer, 1996; U.S. Bureau of the Census, 1998).

Although children in single-parent families do fairly well overall, they tend to lag socially and educationally behind peers in two-parent families. This is true of both children born out of wedlock and those whose parents are divorced. Studies on children who experience a parent's death have mixed results, but overall, they suggest that these children are at risk for more problems than children who grow up with two married parents but less problems than those who are born to unwed mothers or whose parents divorce (Amato, 2005).

What explains these findings? It is possible that people who become lone parents out of wedlock or through divorce have personality traits or adjustment problems that "select" them into single parenthood and also make them less effective parents. However, the weight of the evidence is otherwise. Children living with a lone parent are exposed to many stressful experiences. For one thing, they tend to be economically disadvantaged; 37 percent of children living with an unmarried mother and 16 percent of children living with an unmarried father live in poverty (Kreider & Fields, 2005). Because their parents are struggling to maintain the household, these children often receive poorer parenting. Losing contact with a parent or observing conflict and hostility between parents can produce emotional insecurity. In many cases, moving to a new neighbourhood and changing schools can be upsetting (Amato, 2005). Children living with married parents tend to have more daily interaction with their parents, are read to more often, progress more steadily in school, and participate more in extracurricular activities than children living with a single parent (Lugaila, 2003).

However, negative outcomes for children in one-parent families are far from inevitable. The child's age and level of development, the family's financial circumstances, whether there are frequent moves, and a nonresident father's involvement make a difference (Amato, 2005; Seltzer, 2000). In a U.S. longitudinal study of 1,500 white, black, and Hispanic families with 6- and 7-year-old children, the mother's educational and ability level and, to a lesser extent, family income and the quality of the home environment accounted for any negative effects of single parenting on academic performance and behaviour (Ricciuti, 1999, 2004).

Because lone parents often lack the resources needed for good parenting, potential risks to children in these families might be reduced or eliminated through increased access to economic, social, educational, and parenting support. Children of lone parents do better on measures of math and science achievment, for example, in countries with supportive family policies such as child and family allowances, tax benefits to single parents, maternity leave, and released time from work (Pong et al., 2003).

Living in a Cohabiting Family

Cohabiting families are similar in many ways to married families, but the parents tend to be more disadvantaged. They have less income and education, report poorer relationships, and have more mental health problems. Thus, it is not surprising that children living with parents who are cohabiting experience higher levels of conduct disorder, and engage in more aggressive behaviour than children in non-cohabiting households. This pattern might be related to less effective socialization processes by cohabiting parents (Wu, Hou & Schimmele, 2006).

Furthermore, cohabiting families are more likely to break up than married families. Although about 40 percent of unwed mothers are living with the child's father at the time of birth, 25 percent of cohabiting parents are no longer together one year later, and 31 percent break up after five years (Amato, 2005).

Living in a Stepfamily

Children in divorced families typically spend 5 years in a single-parent home, usually the mother's, before she remarries. Outside of Quebec, about 70 percent of divorced men, and 58 percent of divorced women remarry. Remarriage is more prevalent among divorced immigrants than among Canadian-born divorced people. In Quebec, remarriage is less common than in other parts of the country because of a higher preferrence for cohabitation (Ambert, 2005). Eighty-two percent of children in remarriages live with their biological mother and a stepfather (CICH, 2000). About half of the 503,000 stepfamilies in Canada involve parents in common-law relationships, (Statistics Canada, 2002b). Many unwed mothers marry men who were not the father of their children (Amato, 2005), thus forming step-, or blended, families.

Adjusting to a new stepparent may be stressful. A child's loyalties to an absent or dead parent may interfere with forming ties to a stepparent (Amato, 2005). Many stepchildren maintain ties with their noncustodial parents. Noncustodial mothers tend to keep in touch more than do noncustodial fathers and offer more social support (Gunnoe & Hetherington, 2004).

Some studies have found that boys—who often have more trouble than girls in adjusting to divorce and living with a single mother—benefit from a stepfather. A girl, on the other hand, may find the stepfather a threat to her independence and to her close relationship with her mother (Bray & Hetherington, 1993; Hetherington, 1987; Hetherington et al., 1989; Hetherington et al., 1998; Hines, 1997). In a longitudinal study of a nationally representative

This girl has two fathers—and both obviously dote on the child. Contrary to popular stereotypes, children living with homosexual parents are no more likely than other children to have social or psychological problems or to turn out to be homosexual themselves.

sample of U.S. adults, mothers who remarried or formed new cohabiting relationships tended to use gentler discipline than mothers who remained single, and their children reported better relationships with them. On the other hand, supervision was greater in stable single-mother families (Thomson, Mosley, Hanson, & McLanahan, 2001).

Among 173 university students of mixed ethnicity in a large midwestern U.S. city, those raised in stepfamilies tended to report lower well-being than those raised in intact families, and they also were less likely to recall having been securely attached. Thus, attachment quality may help explain why people from stepfamilies tend not to fare as well emotionally, socially, and psychologically as those from intact families (Love & Murdock, 2004).

Living with Gay or Lesbian Parents

Although the number of children of gay and lesbian parents in Canada is unknown (Dundas & Kaufman, 2000), about 9 percent of the approximately 45,300 same sex couples in Canada are raising children (Statistics Canada, 2006a). Of those, more are raised by female couples (about 16 percent of couples) than by male couples (about 3 percent) (Statistics Canada, 2006a). Some are raising children born of previous heterosexual relationships. Others conceive by artificial means, become foster parents, or adopt children (C. J. Patterson, 1997).

A considerable body of research has examined the development of children of gays and lesbians, including physical and emotional health, intelligence, adjustment, sense of self, moral judgment, and social and sexual functioning, and has indicated no special concerns (APA, 2004). There is *no* consistent difference between homosexual and heterosexual parents in emotional health or parenting skills and attitudes; and where there are differences, they tend to favour gay and lesbian parents (Brewaeys, Ponjaert, Van Hall, & Golombok, 1997; Meezan & Rauch, 2005; Pawelski et al., 2006; Perrin and AAP Committee on Psychosocial Aspects of Child and Family Health, 2002; Wainright, Russell, & Patterson, 2004).

Openly gay or lesbian parents usually have positive relationships with their children, and the children are no more likely than children raised by heterosexual parents to have emotional, social, academic, or psychological problems (APA, 2004; Chan, Raboy, & Patterson, 1998; Gartrell, Deck, Rodas, Peyser, & Banks, 2005; Meezan & Rauch, 2005; Mooney-Somers & Golombok, 2000; Golombok et al., 2003; Wainright et al., 2004). Furthermore, children of gays and lesbians are no more likely to be homosexual themselves or to be confused about their gender than are children of heterosexuals (Anderssen, Amlie, & Ytteroy, 2002; Golombok et al., 2003; Meezan & Rauch, 2005; Pawelski et al., 2006; Wainright et al., 2004). However, many children of gays and lesbians are teased, and they often seek to hide information about their parents to avoid ridicule (Meezan and Rauch, 2005).

Such findings can have social policy implications for legal decisions on custody and visitation disputes, foster care, and adoptions. In the face of controversy over gay and lesbian marriage or civil unions, with its implications for the security of children, several U.S. states have considered or adopted legislation sanctioning second-parent adoption by same-sex partners. To promote the economic and emotional well-being of children of these partnerships, the American Academy of Pediatrics supports a right to civil marriage for gays and lesbians (Pawelski et al., 2006) as is the case in Canada and legislative and legal efforts to permit a partner in a same-sex couple to adopt the other partner's child (AAP Committee on Psychosocial Aspects of Child and Family Health, 2002).

Living with Grandparents

In many developing societies, such as those in Latin America and Asia, and in some minority communities in Canada extended-family households predominate, and resident grandparents play an integral role in the family. In Thailand and Taiwan, about 40 percent of the population ages 50 and over live in the same household with a minor grandchild, and half of those with grandchildren ages 10 or younger—usually grandmothers—provide care for the child (Kinsella & Velkoff, 2001). Most children in technologically advanced countries like Canadian grow up in *nuclear families* limited to parents and siblings, and many grandparents live far away or are busy with careers or other interests. Over 90 percent of 10-year-old children have at least one living grandparent (Rosenthal & Gladstone, 2000).

Yet, in both types of societies, a growing number of grandparents are their grandchildren's sole or primary caregivers. One reason, in developing countries, is rural parents'

Checkpoint ✔

Can you . . .

✔ Discuss the impact of parental divorce on children and how living in a lone-parent household can affect children's well-being?

✔ Identify some special issues and challenges of a stepfamily?

✔ Summarize findings on outcomes of children raised by gay and lesbian parents?

migration to urban areas to find work. In sub-Saharan Africa, the AIDS epidemic has left many orphans whose grandparents step into the parents' place (Kinsella & Velkoff, 2001). Such "skip-generation" families exist in all regions of the world, including Canada (Fuller-Thomson, 2005).

In Canada, an increasing number of grandparents are serving as "parents by default" for children whose parents are unable to care for them—often as a result of substance abuse, intervention by child-welfare agencies, or maternal incarceration (Fuller-Thomson, 2005). Between 1991 and 2001, the number of grandparent-headed families increased by 20 percent, and most of these grandparents were female. Approximately 16,500 Canadian families are headed by a grandparent (Fuller-Thomson, 2005), caring for about 28,000 or 0.5 percent of all Canadian chidren (Statistics Canada, 2007). About 17 percent of these families are headed by Aboriginal grandparents. Many grandparent-headed families are on fixed incomes (Hudnall, 2001), and about a third are in dire financial straits (Casper & Bryson, 1998; Fuller-Thomson, 2005; Minkler & Fuller-Thomson, 2005), and 57 percent of the grandparents are out of the workforce (Fuller-Thomson, 2005). Many of the grandparent-caregivers (mostly grandmothers) are widowed or divorced (Hudnall, 2001).

Most grandparents who take on the responsibility to raise their grandchildren do it because they love the children and do not want them placed in a stranger's foster home. However, the age difference can become a barrier, and both generations may feel cheated out of their traditional roles (Crowley, 1993; Larsen, 1990-1991). Also, aging grandparents may lack the stamina to keep up with an active child. About a third of the grandparents who head families in Canada have a disability (Fuller-Thomson, 2005).

Grandparents who do not become foster parents or gain custody have no legal status. They may face many practical problems, from enrolling the child in school and gaining access to academic records. Like working parents, working grandparents need good, affordable child care and family-friendly workplace policies, such as time off to care for a sick child.

Checkpoint ✔

Can you . . .

✔ Discuss the challenges involved in grandparents raising grandchildren?

Sibling Relationships

In remote rural villages of Asia, Africa, Oceania, and Central and South America, it is common to see older girls caring for three or four younger siblings. In such a community, older siblings have an important, culturally defined role. Parents train children early to teach younger sisters and brothers how to gather firewood, carry water, tend animals, and grow food. Younger siblings absorb intangible values, such as respecting elders and placing the welfare of the group above that of the individual (Cicirelli, 1994). In industrialized societies such as in Canada, parents generally try not to "burden" older children with the regular care of siblings (Weisner, 1993). When older siblings do teach younger ones, this usually happens informally and not as an established part of the social system (Cicirelli, 1994).

The number of siblings in a family and their spacing, birth order, and gender often determine roles and relationships. The larger number of siblings in non-industrialized societies helps the family carry on its work and provide for aging members. In industrialized societies, siblings tend to be fewer and farther apart in age, making it easier for parents to pursue careers or other interests and to focus more resources and attention on each child (Cicirelli, 1994).

Two longitudinal studies, one in England and one in Pennsylvania, based on naturalistic observation of siblings and mothers and interviews with the mothers, found that changes in sibling relationships were most likely to occur when one sibling was between ages 7 and 9. Both mothers and children often attributed these changes to outside friendships, which led to jealousy and competitiveness or loss of interest in, and intimacy with, the sibling. Sometimes the younger sibling's growing assertiveness played a part (Dunn, 1996). Nevertheless, a study of 40 children in Grades 5 to 6 in Quebec found important links between the quality of relationships with siblings and the children's own social and emotional development. The presence of a warm relationship with a sibling was

These Inuit boys in a northern fishing camp enjoy caring for a baby brother. Children in many societies tend to have regular responsibility for siblings.

associated with high levels of emotional understanding and self-disclosure. On the other hand, children who reported not trusting or not getting emotional support from a sibling were less likely to confide with the sibling (Howe, Aquan-Asee, Bukowski, Lehoux, & Rinaldi, 2001). This may lead to a pattern of interaction that provides few opportunities to build warmth and trust with a sibling (Howe et al., 2001).

Sibling relations are a laboratory for conflict resolution. Siblings are impelled to make up after quarrels, since they know they will see each other every day. They learn that expressing anger does not end a relationship. Children are more apt to squabble with same-sex siblings; two brothers quarrel more than any other combination (Cicirelli, 1976, 1995).

Siblings influence each other, not only *directly,* through their own interactions, but also *indirectly* through their impact on each other's relationship with the parents. Parents' experience with an older sibling influences their expectations and treatment of a younger one (Brody, 2004). Conversely, behaviour patterns a child establishes with parents tend to "spill over" into the child's behaviour with siblings. In a study of 101 English families, when the parent-child relationship was warm and affectionate, siblings tended to have positive relationships as well. When the parent-child relationship was conflictual, sibling conflict was more likely (Pike et al., 2005).

The Child in the Peer Group

In middle childhood the peer group comes into its own. Groups form naturally among children who live near one another or go to school together and often consist of children of the same racial or ethnic origin and similar socio-economic status. Children who play together are usually close in age and of the same sex (Hartup, 1992; Pellegrini et al., 2002).

How does the peer group influence children? What determines their acceptance by peers and their ability to make friends?

Positive and Negative Effects of Peer Relations

Children benefit from doing things with peers. They develop skills needed for sociability and intimacy, they enhance relationships, and they gain a sense of belonging. They are motivated to achieve, and they attain a sense of identity. They learn leadership and communication skills, cooperation, roles, and rules (Zarbatany, Hartmann, & Rankin, 1990).

As children begin to move away from parental influence, the peer group opens new perspectives and frees them to make independent judgments. In comparing themselves with others their age, children can gauge their abilities more realistically and gain a clearer sense of self-efficacy. The peer group helps children learn how to get along in society—how to adjust their needs and desires to those of others, when to yield, and when to stand firm. The peer group also offers emotional security. It is reassuring for children to find out that they are not alone in harbouring thoughts that might offend an adult.

On the negative side, peer group may reinforce **prejudice:** unfavourable attitudes toward "outsiders," especially members of certain racial or ethnic groups. A study done in Montreal found signs of prejudice in a sample of 254 English-speaking boys and girls in kindergarten through Grade 6 (Powlishta, Serbin, Doyle, & White, 1994). The children were given brief descriptions of positive and negative traits (such as *helpful, smart, mean,* and *naughty*) and were asked whether one or both of two cartoon children—one English-speaking and the other French-speaking—would be likely to possess each trait. A similar procedure was followed with male and female figures (using gender stereotypes such as *ambitious* and *gentle*) and figures of overweight and normal-weight children. The researchers also asked the children which of two pictured children they would like to play with.

In general, children showed biases in favour of children like themselves, but these biases (except for a preference for children of the same sex) diminished with age and cognitive development. Girls were more biased with regard to gender, and boys with regard to ethnicity. However, individual differences were significant, and a child who was highly prejudiced in one respect was not necessarily prejudiced in another. Similarly, a study

Checkpoint

Can you . . .

✔ Compare the roles and responsibilities of siblings in industrialized and non-industrialized countries?

✔ Discuss how siblings affect each other's development?

Guidepost 3

How do relationships with peers change in middle childhood, and what factors influence popularity and aggressive behaviour?

prejudice Unfavourable attitude toward members of certain groups outside one's own, especially racial or ethnic groups

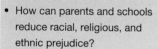
What's your view

• How can parents and schools reduce racial, religious, and ethnic prejudice?

conducted with Aboriginal and non-Aboriginal children in Northern Ontario showed that children tended to maintain same-race trust expectancies. Both Aboriginal and non-Aboriginal children expected children in the other group to be less likely to be trustworthy or to keep secrets and promises. This pattern tended to break down in children who attended schools that were mixed-race (Rotenberg & Cerda, 1995).

Prejudice and discrimination can do real damage. In a U.S. five-year longitudinal study of 714 African American 10- to 12-year-olds, those who saw themselves as targets of discrimination tended to show depressive symptoms or conduct problems during the next five years (Brody et al., 2006).

The peer group also can foster anti-social tendencies. Pre-adolescent children are especially susceptible to pressure to conform. It is usually in the company of peers that some children shoplift and begin to use drugs (Hartup, 1992). Of course, some degree of conformity to group standards is healthy. It is unhealthy when it becomes destructive or prompts young people to act against their own better judgment.

Checkpoint ✔

Can you . . .

✔ Tell what characteristics members of a peer group tend to have in common?

✔ Identify positive and negative effects of the peer group?

✔ Discuss gender differences in peer-group activities and relationships?

Gender Differences in Peer-group Relationships

Boys' and girls' peer groups engage in different types of activities. Groups of boys more consistently pursue gender-typed activities. They play in large groups with well-defined leadership hierarchies and engage in more competitive and rough-and-tumble play. Girls have more intimate conversations characterized by pro-social interactions and shared confidences (Rose & Rudolph, 2006). Also, girls are more likely than boys to engage in "cross-gender" activities, such as team sports (McHale, Kim, Whiteman, & Crouter, 2004).

Boys are apt to receive less emotional support from their friends than girls do. Girls tend to seek social connections and are more sensitive to others' distress. They are more likely than boys to worry about their relationships, to express emotions, and to seek emotional support (Rose & Rudolph, 2006).

Why do children segregate themselves by sex and engage in such different activities? One obvious reason is that males and females differ in body size, strength, and energy. Boys need more space and more physical exercise to build physical fitness. Another explanation is that same-sex peer groups help socialize children for their future roles as competitors or nurturers (Pellegrini & Archer, 2005). Same-sex peer groups help children learn gender-appropriate behaviours and incorporate gender roles into their self-concept. In a two-year study of 106 ethnically diverse third- through seventh-graders, a sense of being typical of one's gender and being content with that gender contributed to self-esteem and well-being, whereas feeling pressure—from parents, peers, or oneself—to conform to gender stereotypes lessened well-being (Yunger, Carver, & Perry, 2004).

Popularity

Popularity becomes more important in middle childhood. Schoolchildren whose peers like them are likely to be well adjusted as adolescents. Those who have trouble getting along with peers are more likely to develop psychological problems, drop out of school, or become delinquent (Hartup, 1992; Kupersmidt & Coie, 1990; Morison & Masten, 1991; Newcomb, Bukowski, & Pattee, 1993).

Popularity can be measured in two ways, and the results may differ. Researchers measure *sociometric popularity* by asking children which peers they like most and least; *perceived popularity* is measured by asking children which children are best liked by their peers.

Sociometric studies have identified five *peer status groups: popular* (youngsters who receive many positive nominations), *rejected* (those who receive many negative nominations), *neglected* (those who receive few nominations of either kind), *controversial* (those who receive many positive and many negative nominations), and *average* (those who do not receive an unusual number of nominations of either kind).

Sociometrically popular children typically have good cognitive abilities, are high achievers, are good at solving social problems, help other children, and are assertive without being disruptive or aggressive. They are kind, trustworthy, cooperative, loyal, and self-disclosing and provide emotional support. Their superior social skills make others enjoy being with them (Cillessen & Mayeux, 2004; LaFontana & Cillessen, 2002; Masten & Coatsworth, 1998). On the other hand, as we will discuss in a subsequent section, some school-aged children with *perceived* popularity, that is, high status, may be dominant, arrogant, and aggressive. Children with perceived popularity tend to be physically attractive and to have athletic and, to a lesser extent, academic ability (Cillessen & Mayeux, 2004; LaFontana & Cillessen, 2002).

Children can be *un*popular (either rejected or neglected) for many reasons. Some unpopular children are aggressive; others are hyperactive, inattentive, or withdrawn (Dodge, Coie, Pettit, & Price, 1990; Masten & Coatsworth, 1998; Newcomb et al., 1993; A. W. Pope, Bierman, & Mumma, 1991). Still others act silly and immature or anxious and uncertain. Unpopular children are often insensitive to other children's feelings and do not adapt well to new situations (Bierman, Smoot, & Aumiller, 1993). Some show undue interest in being with groups of the other sex (Sroufe, Bennett, Englund, Urban, & Shulman, 1993). Some unpopular children *expect* not to be liked, and this becomes a self-fulfilling prophecy (Rabiner & Coie, 1989).

It is often in the family that children acquire behaviours that affect popularity (Masten & Coatsworth, 1998). Authoritative parents tend to have more popular children than authoritarian parents (Dekovic & Janssens, 1992). Children of authoritarian parents who punish and threaten are likely to threaten or act mean with other children. They are less popular than children whose authoritative parents reason with them and try to help them understand how another person might feel (C. H. Hart, Ladd, & Burleson, 1990).

In both western and Chinese cultures, sociability and cooperativeness are associated with social and school adjustment, whereas aggression is generally associated with peer rejection and adjustment problems. In both cultures boys tend to be more aggressive and to have more problems in school than girls (Chen, Cen, Li, & He, 2005). One cultural difference is in the social acceptance of shy, sensitive children (see Box 14-1).

Friendship

Children may spend much of their free time in groups, but only as individuals do they form friendships. Popularity is the peer group's opinion of a child, but friendship is a two-way street.

Children look for friends who are like them in age, sex, ethnicity, and interests. The strongest friendships involve equal commitment and mutual give-and-take. Even unpopular children can make friends; but they have fewer friends than popular children and tend to find friends among younger children, other unpopular children, or children in a different class or a different school (George & Hartmann, 1996; Hartup, 1992, 1996a, 1996b; Newcomb & Bagwell, 1995).

With their friends, children learn to communicate and cooperate. They help each other weather stressful transitions. The inevitable quarrels help children learn to resolve conflicts (Hartup, 1992, 1996a, 1996b; Hartup & Stevens, 1999; Newcomb & Bagwell, 1995). Friendship seems to help children feel good about themselves, though it's also likely that children who feel good about themselves have an easier time making friends. Peer rejection and friendlessness in middle childhood have long-term effects. In one longitudinal study, fifth graders who had no friends were more likely than their classmates to have low self-esteem in young adulthood and to show symptoms of depression (Bagwell, Newcomb, & Bukowski, 1998).

Children's concepts of friendship, and the ways they act with their friends, change with age, reflecting cognitive and emotional growth. Preschool friends play together, but friendship among school-age children is deeper and more stable. Children cannot be or have true friends until they achieve the cognitive maturity to consider other people's views and needs as well as their own (Hartup, 1992; Hartup & Stevens, 1999; Newcomb & Bagwell, 1995).

On the basis of interviews with more than 250 people between ages 3 and 45, Robert Selman (1980; Selman & Selman, 1979) traced changing conceptions of friendship through

Checkpoint

Can you . . .

✔ Compare two measures of popularity and discuss reasons for unpopularity?

✔ Describe characteristics of popular and unpopular children, and tell how they vary?

✔ Identify family and cultural influences on popularity?

Checkpoint

Can you . . .

✔ Distinguish between popularity and friendship?

✔ List characteristics children look for in friends?

✔ Tell how age and gender affect friendship?

Box 14-1 *Popularity: A Cross-cultural View*

How does culture affect popularity? Would a child who is popular in one culture be equally popular in another? Researchers compared 480 students in Grades 2 and 4 in Shanghai, with 296 children the same ages in Ontario (X. Chen, Rubin, & Sun, 1992). Although the two samples were quite different—for example, none of the Canadian children came from peasant families, but many of the Chinese children did—both samples were representative of school-age children in the two countries.

The researchers assessed the children's popularity by two kinds of peer perceptions. The children filled out a sociometric rating telling which three classmates they most and least liked to be with and which three classmates were their best friends. The results showed that certain traits are valued similarly in both cultures. A sociable, cooperative child is likely to be popular in both China and Canada, and an aggressive child is likely to be rejected in both countries. However, one important difference emerged: shy, sensitive children are well liked in China, but not in Canada. This is not surprising. Chinese children are encouraged to be cautious, to restrain themselves, and to inhibit their urges; thus a quiet, shy youngster is considered well behaved. In a North American culture, by contrast, such a child is likely to be seen as socially immature, fearful, and lacking in self-confidence. A related study of Grades 3 and 4 children in Toronto and Taipei, Taiwan, showed that children reported both closeness and conflict in their friendships in both cultures. However, there was less reported conflict among friends in Taiwan than in Canada. This may reflect negative attitudes towards the expression of conflict in Chinese culture (Benjamin, Schneider, Greenman, & Hum, 2001).

A follow-up study to the Shanghai study at ages 8 and 10 (X. Chen, Rubin, & Li, 1995) again found that shy, sensitive Chinese children were popular with peers. They also were rated by teachers as socially competent, as leaders, and as academic achievers. However, by age 12, an interesting twist had occurred: Shy, sensitive Chinese children were no longer popular. They tended to be rejected by their peers, just as in North American cultures.

It may be, then, that shyness and sensitivity take on different social meanings in China as children enter adolescence, when peer relationships become more important and adult approval becomes less so. As in Canada, a shy early adolescent may lack the assertiveness and communication skills needed to establish and maintain strong peer relationships.

This research suggests that the influence of culture may be tempered by developmental processes that are more or less universal. Even in China, with its strong tradition of obedience to authority, the influence of adult social standards may wane as children's urge to make their own independent judgments of their peers asserts itself.

A more recently published study concerning younger children points to effects of social change resulting from the radical restructuring of China's economic system, particularly since the late 1990s. During that time China has shifted from a completely

During middle childhood, shy, sensitive children are better liked in China than in European and North American cultures, because they are considered well behaved. Children this age tend to accept adult standards of behaviour.

collectivist system toward a more competitive, technologically advanced market economy with its associated individualistic values.

In the current study (Chen, Cen, Li, & He, 2005), researchers administered sociometric measures and peer assessments of social functioning to three cohorts of third- and fourth-graders in Shanghai schools in 1990, 1998, and 2002. They examined the children's school records and teacher ratings. As in the earlier studies, pro-social behaviour was associated with social status and school achievement, whereas aggression was generally associated with peer rejection and adjustment problems. However, a striking change emerged with regard to shyness/sensitivity. In the 1990 cohort, shy children were accepted by peers and were high in academic achievement, leadership, and teacher-rated competence. By 2002, the results were just the reverse: shy children tended to be rejected by peers, to be depressed, and to be rated by teachers as low in competence. The results for the 1998 cohort were mixed, likely reflecting the attitudes of a society in transition. These findings suggest that the social acceptability of shy children is closely related to cultural norms. In the quasi-capitalistic society that China has become, social assertiveness and initiative may be more highly appreciated and encouraged than in the past, and shyness and sensitivity may lead to social and psychological difficulties for children

What's your view

How would you advise parents of a shy, sensitive child who complains of being rejected by other children?

Check it out

For more information on this topic, go to **www.mcgrawhill.ca/olc/papalia** which will direct you to relevant links.

five overlapping stages (see Table 14-1). He found that most school-age children are in Stage 2 (reciprocal friendship based on self-interest). Older children, from about age 9 up, may be in Stage 3 (intimate, mutually shared relationships).

School-age children distinguish "best friends," "good friends," and "casual friends" on the basis of how intimate they are and how much time they spend together (Hartup &

Table 14-1   Selman's Stages of Friendship

Stage	Description	Example
Stage 0: Momentary playmateship (ages 3 to 7)	On this *undifferentiated* level of friendship, children are egocentric and have trouble considering another person's point of view; they tend to think only about what they want from a relationship. Most very young children define their friends in terms of physical closeness and value them for material or physical attributes.	"She lives on my street," or "He has the Power Rangers."
Stage 1: One-way assistance (ages 4 to 9)	On this *unilateral* level, a "good friend" does what the child wants the friend to do.	"She's not my friend anymore, because she wouldn't go with me when I wanted her to," or "He's my friend because he always says yes when I want to borrow his eraser."
Stage 2: Two-way fair-weather cooperation (ages 6 to 12)	This *reciprocal* level overlaps Stage 1. It involves give-and-take but still serves many separate self-interests, rather than the common interests of the two friends.	"We are friends; we do things for each other," or "A friend is someone who plays with you when you don't have anybody else to play with."
Stage 3: Intimate, mutually shared relationships (ages 9 to 15)	On this *mutual* level, children view a friendship as having a life of its own. It is an ongoing, systematic, committed relationship that incorporates more than doing things for each other. Friends become possessive and demand exclusivity.	"It takes a long time to make a close friend, so you really feel bad if you find out that your friend is trying to make other friends too."
Stage 4: Autonomous interdependence (beginning at age 12)	In this *interdependent* stage, children respect friends' needs for both dependency and autonomy.	"A good friendship is a real commitment, a risk you have to take; you have to support and trust and give, but you have to be able to let go too."

Source: Selman, 1980; Selman & Selman, 1979.

hostile aggression Aggressive behaviour intended to hurt another person

instrumental aggression Aggressive behaviour used as a means of achieving a goal

Stevens, 1999). Children this age typically have three to five "best" friends with whom they spend most of their free time, but they usually play with only one or two at a time (Hartup, 1992; Hartup & Stevens, 1999).

School-age girls care less about having many friends than about having a few close friends they can rely on; boys have more friendships, but they tend to be less intimate and affectionate (Furman, 1982; Furman & Buhrmester, 1985; Hartup & Stevens, 1999).

School-age friends often share secrets—and laughs—as Anna and her friend Christina are doing.

Aggression and Bullying

During the school years, aggression declines and changes in form (Coie & Dodge, 1998). **Hostile aggression** (aggression aimed at hurting its target) becomes more common than **instrumental aggression** (aggression aimed at achieving an objective), the hallmark of the preschool period (Coie & Dodge, 1998). The National Longitudinal Survey of Children and Youth found that 3.5 percent of Canadian children aged 2 to 4 years are physically aggressive, as indicated in a survey of the person most knowledgeable about the child (PMK). By the time they reach the ages of 5 to 11 years, 3.3 percent of boys and only 0.6 percent of girls are identified as physically aggressive by the PMK (Baillargeon, Tremblay, & Willms, 1999). Especially among girls, *overt* aggression (physical force or verbal threats) largely gives way to *relational*, or social, aggression ("putting down" or spreading rumours about another person, teasing, manipulating, and bidding for control; refer back to Chapter 8). A high level of physical aggression may lead to a high level of social aggression, which is less likely to be punished (Brendgen et al., 2005).

Nine-year-olds and older children recognize such behaviour as aggressive; they realize that it stems from anger and is aimed at hurting others (Crick, Bigbee, & Howes, 1996; Galen & Underwood, 1997).

A small minority of children do not learn to control physical aggression (Coie & Dodge, 1998). These children tend to have social and psychological problems, but it is not clear whether aggression causes these problems or is a response to them, or both (Crick & Grotpeter, 1995). Highly aggressive children often egg each other on to anti-social acts. Thus, school-age boys who are physically aggressive may become juvenile delinquents in adolescence (Broidy et al., 2003).

Gender Differences in Aggressiveness

As we discussed in Chapter 11, from an early age boys are more physically aggressive, whereas relational (or social) aggression seems to be more typical of girls. As children grow older, gender differences in the amount of physical aggression remain. However, gender differences in relational aggression seem to increase from ages 6 to 17, peaking between ages 11 and 17 (Archer, 2004). Some researchers suggest that relational aggression may be no more frequent in girls than in boys, but its consequences may be more serious for girls, who tend to be more preoccupied with relationships than boys are (Cillessen & Mayeux, 2004; Crick et al., 2002).

Sex-segregated peer groups are the context within which these gender differences develop. Boys tend to be especially aggressive when a group is forming, as they compete for dominance. Later, once their status is achieved, they seek to reconcile with their former adversaries. Girls seek status through more manipulative means involving indirect or relational aggression (Pellegrini & Archer, 2005).

As we have already mentioned, aggressors tend to be personally disliked, but physically aggressive boys and some relationally aggressive girls are perceived as among the most popular in the classroom (Cillessen & Mayeux, 2004; Rodkin, Farmer, Pearl, & Van Acker, 2000). In a study of peer-rejected fourth graders, aggressive boys tended to gain in social status by the end of fifth grade, suggesting that behaviour shunned by younger children may be seen as "cool" or glamorous by pre-adolescents (Sandstrom & Coie, 1999). In a longitudinal study of a multi-ethnic group of 905 urban fifth through ninth graders, physical aggression became less disapproved as children moved into adolescence, and relational aggression was increasingly reinforced by high status among peers (Cillessen & Mayeux, 2004).

Types of Aggression and Social Information Processing

What makes children act aggressively? One answer may lie in the way they process social information: what features of the social environment they pay attention to, and how they interpret what they perceive (Crick & Dodge, 1994, 1996).

Instrumental (or *proactive*) aggressors view force and coercion as effective ways to get what they want. They act deliberately, not out of anger. In social learning terms, they are aggressive because they expect to be rewarded; and when they *are* rewarded, their belief in the effectiveness of aggression is reinforced (Crick & Dodge, 1996). By contrast, a child who is accidentally bumped in line may push back angrily, assuming that the other child bumped her on purpose. This is an example of hostile, or *reactive,* aggression. Such children often have a **hostile attribution bias;** they see other children as trying to hurt them, and they strike out in retaliation or self-defence (Crick & Dodge, 1996; de Castro, Veerman, Koops, Bosch, & Monshouwer, 2002; Waldman, 1996).

Children who seek dominance and control may react aggressively to threats to their status, which they may attribute to hostility (de Castro et al., 2002; Erdley et al., 1997). Rejected children and those exposed to harsh parenting also tend to have a hostile attribution bias (Coie & Dodge, 1998; Masten & Coatsworth, 1998; Weiss, Dodge, Bates, & Pettit, 1992). Since people often *do* become hostile toward someone who acts aggressively toward them, a hostile bias may set in motion a cycle of aggression (de Castro et al., 2002). Hostile attribution bias becomes more common between ages 6 and 12 (Aber, Brown, & Jones, 2003).

hostile attribution bias Tendency for someone to perceive others as trying to hurt him or her and to strike out in retaliation or self-defence

Both instrumental and hostile aggressors need help in altering the way they process social information so that they do not interpret aggression as either useful or justified. *Instrumental* aggression tends to stop if it is not rewarded (Crick & Dodge, 1996). Adults can help children curb *hostile* aggression by teaching them how to recognize when they are getting angry and how to control their anger. In a New York City school study, children exposed to a conflict resolution curriculum that involved discussion and group role playing showed less hostile attribution bias, less aggression, fewer behaviour problems, and more effective responses to social situations than children who had not participated in the program (Aber et al., 2003).

Does Media Violence Stimulate Aggression?

Children see an enormous amount of violence on television. Canadian children watch television about 14 hours per week (CPS, 1999; Statistics Canada, 2006b).

About 6 out of 10 U.S. television programs portray violence, usually glamorized, glorified, or trivialized (Yokota & Thompson. 2000), in addition to the constant, repetitive news coverage of natural disasters and violent acts (American Academy of Child & Adolescent Psychiatry, 2002). Among 50 major televised sporting events, such as the Superbowl, 49 percent of commercial breaks contained at least one commercial showing unsafe behaviour or violence (Tamburro, Gordon, D'Apolito, & Howard, 2004). Music videos disproportionately feature violence against women and blacks. The motion picture, music, and video game industries aggressively market violent, adult-rated products to children (AAP Committee on Public Education, 2001b).

Because of the high proportion of their time that children spend with media, the images they see can become primary role models and sources of information about how people behave in the real world. The vast preponderance of experimental, longitudinal, epidemiological, and cross-cultural studies supports a causal relationship between media violence and aggressive behaviour in childhood, adolescence, and adulthood. In fact, the strongest single correlate of violent behaviour is previous exposure to violence (AAP Committee on Public Education, 2001b; Anderson, Berkowitz et al., 2003; Anderson, Huston, Schmitt, Linebarger, & Wright, 2001; Huesmann, Moise-Titus, Podolski, & Eron, 2003).

How does media violence lead to long-term aggressiveness? It provides visceral thrills without showing the human cost and leads children to view aggression as acceptable. Children who see both heroes and villains achieving their aims through violence are likely to conclude that force is an effective way to resolve conflicts. They may learn to take violence for granted and may be less likely to intervene when they see it. The more realistically violence is portrayed, the more likely it is to be accepted (AAP Committee on Public Education, 2001b; Anderson, Berkowitz et al., 2003). Furthermore, each hour that children spend watching violent television reduces time spent with friends. Thus, violent TV fare may set off a cycle in which frequent viewers become more aggressive, and their behaviour leads to social isolation and, in turn, to viewing more violent television (Bickham & Rich, 2006).

Children are more vulnerable than adults to the influence of televised violence (AAP Committee on Public Education, 2001b; Coie & Dodge, 1998). Classic social learning research suggests that children imitate filmed models even more than live ones (Bandura, Ross, & Ross, 1963). The influence is stronger if the child believes the violence on the screen is real, identifies with the violent character, finds that character attractive, and watches without parental supervision or intervention (Anderson, Berkowitz et al., 2003; Coie & Dodge, 1998). Highly aggressive children are more strongly affected by media violence than are less aggressive children (Anderson, Berkowitz et al., 2003).

The long-term influence of televised violence is greater among school-age children than at earlier ages (Eron & Huesmann, 1986). Among 427 children whose viewing habits were studied at age 8, the best predictor of aggressiveness at age 19 was the degree of violence in the shows they had watched as children (Eron, 1980, 1982). In a follow-up study, the amount of television viewed at age 8 and the preference among boys for violent shows predicted the severity of criminal offences at age 30 (Huesmann, 1986; Huesmann & Eron, 1984).

Checkpoint ✔

Can you . . .

✔ Tell how aggression changes in form during middle childhood and how social information processing and televised violence can contribute to it?

Less research has been done on effects of newer, interactive media, such as video games and the Internet, but initial studies suggest that "effects of child-initiated virtual violence may be more profound than those of passive media, such as television." Rather than merely let a child observe rewards for violent behaviour, violent video games "place the child in the role of the aggressor and reward him or her for successful violent behaviour" (AAP Committee on Public Education, 2001b, pp. 1223–1224). In experimental studies, young people, after playing video games, have shown decreases in pro-social behaviour and increases in aggressive thoughts and violent retaliation to provocation (Anderson, 2000).

Media-induced aggressiveness can be minimized by cutting down on television use and by parental monitoring and guidance of the shows children watch (Anderson, Berkowitz et al., 2003). The American Academy of Pediatrics Committee on Public Education (2001b) recommends that parents limit children's media exposure to 1 to 2 hours a day. Third and fourth graders who participated in a six-month curriculum aimed at motivating them to monitor and reduce the time they spent on television, videotapes, and video games showed significant decreases in peer-rated aggression, as compared with a control group (Robinson, Wilde, Navracruz, Haydel, & Varady, 2001).

The Canadian Paediatric Society (1999) and the American Psychological Association (1993) have called for a major effort to reduce violence on television. In 1996, the U.S. Congress enacted a law requiring all new television sets to be equipped with an electronic blocking device, the "V" chip, developed in Canada, that parents can use to screen out objectionable programs. The law also prods the networks to devise a violence rating system (Mifflin, 1996). Canadian television is encoded for the "V" chip. Although electronic blocking devices are useful in filtering out unwanted programming, they can create a false sense of security in parents who might believe that all violent programs are being eliminated. As a result, the Canadian Paediatric Society encourages parents to monitor their children's television viewing (Canadian Paediatric Society, 1999).

What's your view ?

• What can and should be done about children's exposure to violent television programs?

bullying Aggression deliberately and persistently directed against a particular target, or victim, typically one who is weak, vulnerable, and defenceless

Bullies and Victims

Aggression becomes **bullying** when it is deliberately, persistently directed against a particular target: a victim who, typically, is weak, vulnerable, and defenceless. Bullying can be physical (hitting, punching, kicking, or taking of personal belongings), verbal (name calling or threatening), or psychological (isolating and gossiping) (Veenstra et al., 2005). Twenty-four percent of primary schools, 42 percent of middle schools, and 21 percent of high schools report student bullying at school at least once a week (Guerino, Hurwitz, Noonan, & Kaffenberger, 2006). Bullying also is a problem in other industrialized countries, such as England and Japan (Hara, 2002; Kanetsuna & Smith, 2002; Ruiz & Tanaka, 2001). In Japan and Korea, school bullying has been associated with a growing wave of student suicide and suicidal thoughts and behaviour (Kim, Koh, & Leventhal, 2005; Rios-Ellis, Bellamy, & Shoji, 2000).

Most bullies are boys (Veenstra et al., 2005) who tend to victimize other boys; female bullies tend to target other girls (Pellegrini & Long, 2002). Male bullies tend to use physical force (overt aggression) and to select either boys or girls as victims. Female bullies use verbal or psychological means (relational aggression) and are more likely to victimize other girls (Boulton, 1995; CICH, 2000; Nansel et al., 2001). Patterns of bullying and victimization may become established as early as kindergarten; as tentative peer groups form, aggressors soon get to know which children make the easiest "marks." Bullying and aggression peak during the transition to middle school. During this transition, boys use bullying as a way to establish dominance in the peer group. Unlike the pattern for bullying, the likelihood of *being* bullied decreases steadily. As children get older, most of them may learn how to discourage bullying, leaving a smaller "pool" of available victims (Pellegrini & Long, 2002; P. K. Smith & Levan, 1995).

Bullying tends to peak in the middle grades. Boys are more likely to use overt aggression; girls, relational aggression.

A study of Canadian children in Grades 4 to 6 showed boys to be more likely to report using physical aggression than girls to resolve conflicts. Although no gender differences were found in children's reports of using relational aggression, those children who did report using this form of aggression were more likely to indicate that they were concerned about avoiding trouble and maintaining relationships with their peer group than did children who reported using physical aggression in conflict resolution (Delveaux & Daniels, 2000).

Both bullies and victims exhibit psychological problems, and both tend to be disliked. In fact, about half of bullies say they are victims as well, and they function more poorly than either bullies or victims. Bullies are aggressive, impulsive, hostile, domineering, antisocial, and uncooperative, though they describe themselves as making friends easily. In keeping with the theory of hostile attribution bias, they may claim to pick on their victims because they were provoked (Veenstra et al., 2005).

Risk factors for victimization seem to be similar across cultures (Schwartz, Chang, & Farver, 2001). Victims "do not fit in." They tend to be anxious and submissive and to cry easily, or to be argumentative and provocative (Hodges, Boivin, Vitaro, & Bukowski, 1999; Olweus, 1995; Veenstra et al., 2005). Victims are apt to have low self-esteem, though it is not clear whether low self-esteem leads to or follows from victimization. Male victims tend to be physically weak (Boulton & Smith, 1994; Olweus, 1995). Children who are bullied may develop such behaviour problems as hyperactivity and overdependence, and they may become more aggressive themselves (Schwartz, McFadyen-Ketchum, Dodge, Pettit, & Bates, 1998). Having a best friend seems to provide some protection against victimization (Hodges et al., 1999). Among 5,749 Canadian children, those who were overweight were most likely to become either victims or bullies (Janssen, Craig, Boyce, & Pickett, 2004).

Victims of bullying may develop behaviour problems, such as hyperactivity. They may become more aggressive themselves or may become depressed (Schwartz, McFadyen-Ketchum, Dodge, Pettit, & Bates, 1998; Veenstra et al., 2005). Bullies are at increased risk of delinquency, crime, or alcohol abuse. In the wave of school shootings since 1994, the perpetrators often had been victims of bullying (Anderson, Kaufman et al., 2001).

A longitudinal study using naturalistic observation of bullying in Toronto schools showed that although peers were present most of the time, they intervened in only 19 percent of bullying incidents. When they did intervene, the intervention was usually effective in stopping the bullying. The interventions tended to involve aggression when they were directed towards the bully, and non-aggressive when directed to the victim, or the victim–bully pair. Children were more likely to intervene when the victim and bully were the same sex as the child who was intervening (Hawkins, Pepler, & Craig, 2001).

Bullying can be stopped or prevented. Programs like "I am Safe" in Canada and "Steps to Respect" in the U.S. aim to reduce bullying by using a variety of strategies, which include (1) increasing staff awareness and responsiveness to bullying, (2) teaching students social and emotional skills, and (3) fostering socially responsible beliefs. A randomized controlled study of 1,023 third- to sixth-graders found a reduction in playground bullying and argumentative behaviour and an increase in harmonious interactions among children who received the program, as well as less bystander incitement to bullying (Frey et al., 2005).

Mental Health

Although most children have a fairly high level of emotional adjustment, at least 1 in 10 children and adolescents has a diagnosed mental illness severe enough to cause some impairment, according to recent estimates (Leslie, Newman, Chesney, & Perrin, 2005). Among the mental health illnesses identified in children between the ages of 4 and 11 years are hyperactivity, conduct disorder, and emotional disorders, according to parent reports (CICH, 2000). More boys than girls experience such disorders, with about 1 in 4 boys and less than 1 in 5 girls being identified with one or more mental health problems (CICH, 2000). About 3 percent of children in this age group experienced social impairment as a result of their problems (Offord & Lipman, 1996). Diagnosis of mental disorders

Guidepost 4

What are some common mental health problems of childhood, and how do children respond to the stresses of modern life?

in children is important because they can lead to psychiatric disorders in adulthood (Kim-Cohen et al., 2003). In fact, half of all cases of mental disorders begin by age 14 (Kessler et al., 2005).

Common Emotional Disturbances

Children with emotional, behavioural, and developmental problems tend to be an underserved group. Compared with other children who have special health-care needs, they are more likely to have conditions that affect their daily activities and cause them to miss school. They often have chronic physical conditions. Many of them lack adequate health insurance and have unmet health care needs (Bethell et al., 2005).

A reported 55.7 percent of children diagnosed with emotional, behavioural, and developmental problems have *disruptive conduct disorders:* aggression, defiance, or anti-social behaviour. Almost all the rest (43.5 percent) have *anxiety* or *mood disorders:* feeling sad, depressed, unloved, nervous, fearful, or lonely (Bethell et al., 2005).

Disruptive Conduct Disorders

Temper tantrums and defiant, argumentative, hostile, deliberately annoying behaviour—common among 4- and 5-year-olds—typically are outgrown by middle childhood. When such a pattern of behaviour persists until age 8, children (usually boys) may be diagnosed with **oppositional defiant disorder (ODD),** a pattern of defiance, disobedience, and hostility toward adult authority figures. Children with ODD constantly fight, argue, lose their temper, snatch things, blame others, are angry and resentful, have few friends, are in constant trouble in school, and test the limits of adults' patience (APA, 2000; National Library of Medicine, 2004).

Some children with ODD also have **conduct disorder (CD),** a persistent, repetitive pattern, beginning at an early age, of aggressive, anti-social acts, such as truancy, setting fires, habitual lying, fighting, bullying, theft, vandalism, assaults, and drug and alcohol use (APA, 2000; National Library of Medicine, 2003). Up to 10 percent of boys and 9 percent of girls aged 4 to 11 years in Canada demonstrate symptoms of conduct disorder, according to parents' reports (Offord & Lipman, 1996), and the rates vary by age and type of CD identified (Children's Mental Health Ontario, 2001). Some 11- to 13-year-olds progress from conduct disorder to criminal violence—mugging, rape, and break-ins—and by age 17 may be frequent, serious offenders (Coie & Dodge, 1998). Between 25 and 50 percent of these highly anti-social children become anti-social adults (USDHHS, 1999b).

What determines whether a particular child with anti-social tendencies will become severely and chronically anti-social? Neurobiological deficits, such as weak stress-regulating mechanisms, may fail to warn children to restrain themselves from dangerous or risky behaviour. Such deficits may be genetically influenced or may be brought on by adverse environments such as hostile parenting or family conflict, or both (van Goozen, Fairchild, Snoek, & Harold, 2007). (In Chapter 17 we further discuss roots of anti-social behaviour and juvenile delinquency.)

School Phobia and Other Anxiety Disorders

Children with **school phobia** have an unrealistic fear of going to school. Some children have realistic reasons to fear going to school: a sarcastic teacher, overly demanding work, or a bully in the school yard. In such cases, the environment may need changing, not the child (Kochenderfer & Ladd, 1996). True school phobia may be a type of **separation anxiety disorder,** a condition involving excessive anxiety for at least four weeks concerning separation from home or from people to whom the child is attached.

Although separation anxiety is normal in infancy, when it persists in older children it is cause for concern. Separation anxiety disorder affects some 4 percent of children and young adolescents and may persist through the college years. These children often come from close-knit, caring families. They may develop the disorder spontaneously or after a stressful event, such as the death of a pet, an illness, or a move to a new school (APA, 2000;

oppositional defiant disorder (ODD) Pattern of behaviour, persisting into middle childhood, marked by negativity, hostility, and defiance

conduct disorder (CD) Repetitive, persistent pattern of aggressive, anti-social behaviour violating societal norms or the rights of others

school phobia Unrealistic fear of going to school, may be a form of *separation anxiety disorder* or *social phobia*

separation anxiety disorder Condition involving excessive, prolonged anxiety about separation from home or from people to whom a child is attached

Harvard Medical School, 2004a). Many children with separation anxiety also show symptoms of depression (USDHHS, 1999b).

Sometimes school phobia may be a form of **social phobia,** or *social anxiety:* extreme fear and/or avoidance of social situations, such as speaking in class or meeting an acquaintance on the street. Social phobia affects about 5 percent of children. It runs in families, so there is likely a genetic component. Often these phobias are triggered by traumatic experiences, such as a child's mind going blank after being called on in class (Beidel & Turner, 1998). Social anxiety tends to increase with age, whereas separation anxiety decreases (Costello et al., 2003).

Some children have a **generalized anxiety disorder,** not focused on any specific aspect of their lives. These children worry about just about everything: school grades, storms, earthquakes, hurting themselves on the playground, or the amount of gas in the tank. They tend to be self-conscious, self-doubting, and excessively concerned with meeting the expectations of others. They seek approval and need constant reassurance, but their worry seems independent of performance or of how they are regarded by others (APA, 1994; Harvard Medical School, 2004a; USDHHS, 1999b).

Far less common is **obsessive-compulsive disorder (OCD).** Sufferers from this disorder may be obsessed by repetitive, intrusive thoughts, images, or impulses (often involving irrational fears) or may show compulsive behaviours, such as constant hand-washing, or both (APA, 2000; Harvard Medical School, 2004a; USDHHS, 1999b).

Anxiety disorders of these types are among the most prevalent mental health problems in Canada for children and adolescents (Antony & Swinson, 1996; Eggertson, 2005). They tend to run in families (Harvard Medical School, 2004a), and are twice as common among girls as among boys. The heightened female vulnerability to anxiety begins as early as age 6. Females are also more susceptible to depression, which is similar to anxiety in some ways and often goes hand-in-hand with it (Lewinsohn, Gotlib, Lewinsohn, Seeley, & Allen, 1998). Both anxiety and depression may involve a neurologically based *behaviour inhibition system:* apprehensiveness, diminished motor activity, and watchful waiting for anticipated danger. A tendency to anxiety and depression may stem from early experiences that make children feel a lack of control over what happens around them (Chorpita & Barlow, 1998; Harvard Medical School, 2004a).

Childhood Depression

"Nobody likes me" is a common complaint among school-age children, who tend to be popularity-conscious; but a prolonged sense of friendlessness may be one sign of **childhood depression:** a disorder of mood that goes beyond normal, temporary sadness. At any given time, between 14 and 38 percent of 4- to 11-year-old children have symptoms of depression, as reported by parents (CICH, 2000). Depression is estimated to occur in 2 percent of elementary school children (NCHS, 2004). Symptoms include inability to have fun or concentrate, fatigue, extreme activity or apathy, crying, sleep problems, feelings of worthlessness, weight change, physical complaints, or frequent thoughts about death or suicide. Any five of these symptoms, lasting at least 2 weeks, may point to depression (APA, 1994). If symptoms persist, the child should be given psychological help. Depression may lead to an attempted suicide and often signals the beginning of a recurrent problem that, if present during adolescence, is likely to persist into adulthood (Birmaher, 1998; Birmaher et al., 1996; Cicchetti & Toth, 1998; Kye & Ryan, 1995; USDHHS, 1999c; Weissman et al., 1999).

The exact causes of childhood depression are unknown, but depressed children tend to come from families with high levels of parental depression, anxiety, substance abuse, or anti-social behaviour. The atmosphere in such families may increase children's risk of depression (Cicchetti & Toth, 1998; USDHHS, 1999b).

Depression often emerges during the transition to middle school and may be related to academic pressures (Cicchetti & Toth, 1998). The prevalence of depression increases during adolescence. Three percent of 12- to 14-year olds in Canada experience a major depression episode, and this number grows to 6 percent for boys and 12 percent for girls between 15 and 19 years of age (CICH, 2000). Adolescent girls, like adult women, are especially subject to depression (Birmaher et al., 1996; Cicchetti & Toth, 1998).

Researchers have found two specific genes related to depression. The gene 5-HTT helps to control the brain chemical serotonin and affects mood. In a longitudinal study of 847 people born in the same year in Dunedin, New Zealand, those who had two short versions of this gene were more likely to become depressed than those who had two long versions (Caspi et al., 2003). A short form of another gene, SERT-s, which also controls serotonin, is associated with enlargement of the pulvinar, a brain region involved in negative emotions (Young et al., in press).

Children as young as 5 or 6 can accurately report depressed moods and feelings that forecast later trouble, from academic problems to major depression and ideas of suicide (Ialongo, Edelsohn, & Kellam, 2001). Depression often emerges during the transition to middle school and may be related to stiffer academic pressures (Cicchetti & Toth, 1998), weak self-efficacy beliefs, and lack of personal investment in academic success (Rudolph, Lambert, Clark, & Kurlakowsky, 2001). Depression becomes more prevalent during adolescence (Costello et al., 2003; see Chapter 15).

Aboriginal children show a pattern of depression different from that of non-Aboriginal children, as demonstrated in the Flower of Two Soils study (Beiser, Sack, Manson, Redshirt, & Dion, 1998). In Grade 2, non-Aboriginal children report higher levels of depression compared to Aboriginal children, and this difference gradually decreases in magnitude until Grade 4, when the difference disappears. However, there is a high rate of depression among Aboriginal adolescents (Sack, Beiser, Baker-Brown, & Redshirt, 1994).

Any child may be sad or lonely at times, but sadness that lasts two weeks or more and is accompanied by such symptoms as fatigue, apathy, sleep problems, and inability to concentrate may be a sign of depression.

Treatment Techniques

Psychological treatment for emotional disturbances can take several forms. In **individual psychotherapy,** a therapist sees a child one-on-one, to help the child gain insights into his or her personality and relationships and to interpret feelings and behaviour. Such treatment may be helpful at a time of stress, such as the death of a parent or parental divorce, even when a child has not shown signs of disturbance. Child psychotherapy is usually more effective when combined with counselling for the parents.

In **family therapy,** the therapist sees the family together, observes how members interact, and points out both growth-producing and growth-inhibiting or destructive patterns of family functioning. Sometimes the child whose problem brings the family into therapy is, ironically, the healthiest member, responding openly to a troubled family situation. Therapy can help parents confront their own conflicts and begin to resolve them. This is often the first step toward resolving the child's problems as well.

Behaviour therapy, or *behaviour modification* (refer back to Chapter 2), is a form of psychotherapy that uses principles of learning theory to eliminate undesirable behaviours or to develop desirable ones. A statistical analysis of many studies found that psychotherapy is generally effective with children and adolescents, but behaviour therapy is more effective than non-behavioural methods. Results are best when treatment is targeted to specific problems and desired outcomes (Weisz, Weiss, Han, Granger, & Morton, 1995). *Cognitive behavioural therapy,* which seeks to change negative thoughts through gradual exposure, modelling, rewards, or "talking" to oneself has proven the most effective treatment for anxiety disorders in children and adolescents (Harvard Medical School, 2004a).

When children have limited verbal and conceptual skills or have suffered emotional trauma, **art therapy** can help them describe what is troubling them without the need to put their feelings into words. The child may express deep emotions through choice of colours and subjects to depict (Kozlowska & Hanney, 1999). Observing how a family plans, carries out, and discusses an art project can reveal patterns of family interactions (Kozlowska & Hanney, 1999).

In **play therapy,** a child plays freely while a therapist occasionally comments, asks questions, or makes suggestions. Play therapy has proven effective with a variety of emotional, cognitive, and social problems, especially when consultation with parents or other close family members is part of the process (Athansiou, 2001; Bratton & Ray, 2002; Leblanc & Ritchie, 2001; Ryan & Needham, 2001; Wilson & Ryan, 2001).

individual psychotherapy Psychological treatment in which a therapist sees a troubled person one-on-one

family therapy Psychological treatment in which a therapist sees the whole family together to analyze patterns of family functioning

behaviour therapy Therapeutic approach using principles of learning theory to encourage desired behaviours or eliminate undesired ones; also called *behaviour modification*

art therapy Therapeutic approach that allows a child to express troubled feelings without words, using a variety of art materials and media

play therapy Therapeutic approach in which a child plays freely while a therapist observes and occasionally comments, asks questions, or makes suggestions

drug therapy Administration of drugs to treat emotional disorders

Checkpoint

Can you . . .

✔ Identify causes and symptoms of disruptive behaviour disorders, anxiety disorders, and childhood depression?

✔ Describe and evaluate five common types of therapy for emotional disorders?

✔ Tell why drug therapy is controversial?

The use of **drug therapy**—antidepressants, stimulants, tranquilizers, and antipsychotic medications—to treat childhood emotional disorders is controversial. The rate of prescriptions for antipsychotic medications for children and adolescents has increased over the past two decades (Olfson, Blanco, Liu, Moreno, & Laje, 2006). Sufficient research on the effectiveness and safety of many of these drugs, especially for children, is lacking (Murray, de Vries, & Wong, 2004; USDHHS, 1999b; Wong, Murray, Camilleri-Novak, & Stephens, 2004; Zito et al., 2003). An exception is the use of Ritalin to treat attention-deficit hyperactivity disorder (refer back to Chapter 13).

The use of *selective serotonin reuptake inhibitors (SSRIs)* to treat obsessive-compulsive, depressive, and anxiety disorders increased rapidly in the 1990s (Leslie et al., 2005) but has since decreased about 20 percent (Daly, 2005). Some studies show moderate risks of suicidal thought and behaviour for children and adolescents under antidepressant treatment, whereas others show no significant added risk (Hammad, Laughren, & Racoosin, 2006; Simon, Savarino, Operskalski, & Wang, 2006) or lessened risk (Simon, 2006). The U.S. Food and Drug Administration in 2004 concluded that antidepressant use can lead to suicidal behaviour in children and adolescents, especially in the early months of treatment (Leslie, Newman, Chesney, & Perrin, 2005). (Use of antidepressant drugs for adolescent depression is discussed in Chapter 15.)

Stress and Resilience

Stressful events are part of childhood, and most children learn to cope. Stress that becomes overwhelming, however, can lead to psychological problems. Severe stressors, such as kidnapping or child abuse, may have long-term effects on physical and psychological well-being. Yet some children show remarkable resilience in surmounting such ordeals.

Stresses of Modern Life

The child psychologist David Elkind (1981, 1984, 1986, 1997) has called today's child the "hurried child." He warns that the pressures of modern life are forcing children to grow up too soon and are making their childhood too stressful. Today's children are expected to succeed in school, to compete in sports, and to meet parents' emotional needs. Children are exposed to many adult problems on television and in real life before they have mastered the problems of childhood. They know about sex and violence, and they often must shoulder adult responsibilities. Many children move frequently and have to change schools and leave old friends (Fowler, Simpson, & Schoendorf, 1993; G. A. Simpson & Fowler, 1994). The tightly scheduled pace of life also can be stressful (Hofferth & Sandberg, 1998). Yet children are not small adults. They feel and think like children, and they need the years of childhood for healthy development.

Given how much stress children are exposed to, it should not be surprising it has increased greatly (Twenge, 2000). Fears of danger and death are the most consistent fears of children at all ages (Gullone, 2000; Silverman, La Greca, & Wasserstein, 1995). This intense anxiety about safety may reflect the high rates of crime and violence in the larger society—including the presence of street gangs and violence in schools (DeVoe, Peter, Noonan, Snyder, & Baum, 2005). In 2003–2004, 94 percent of middle schools and 74 percent of primary schools in the U.S. reported incidents of violent crime, such as rape, robbery, and physical attacks with or without weapons (Guerino et al., 2006).

Findings about children's fears have been corroborated in a wide range of developed and developing societies, including the United States, Australia, China, the United Kingdom, Israel, Italy, Nigeria, and Northern Ireland, in addition to Canada. Poor children—who may see their environment as threatening—tend to be more fearful than children of higher socio-economic status (Gullone, 2000; Ollendick, Yang, King, Dong, & Akande, 1996). Children who grow up surrounded by violence often have trouble concentrating and sleeping. Some become aggressive, and some come to take brutality for granted. Many do not allow themselves to become attached to other people, for fear of more hurt and loss (Garbarino et al., 1992, 1998).

Children are more susceptible than adults to psychological harm from a traumatic event such as war or terrorism, and their reactions vary with age (Wexler, Branski, & Kerem, 2006; see Table 14-2). Younger children, who do not understand why the event occurred, tend to focus on the consequences. Older children are more aware of, and worried about, the underlying forces that caused the event (Hagan et al., 2005).

The impact of a traumatic event is also influenced by the type of event, how much exposure children have to it, and how much they and their families and friends are personally affected. Human-caused disasters, such as terrorism and war, are much harder on children psychologically than natural disasters, such as earthquakes and floods. Exposure to graphic news coverage can worsen the effects (Wexler et al., 2006; Table 14-2). Most children who watched news coverage of the September 11, 2001, terrorist attacks on New York and Washington, DC, experienced profound stress, even if they were not directly affected (Walma & van der Molen, 2004).

Children's responses to a traumatic event typically occur in two stages: *first,* fright, disbelief, denial, grief, and relief if their loved ones are unharmed; *second,* several days or weeks later, developmental regression and signs of emotional distress—anxiety, fear, withdrawal, sleep disturbances, pessimism about the future, or play related to themes of the event. If symptoms last for more than a month, the child should receive counselling (Hagan et al., 2005).

For some children, the effects of a traumatic event may remain for years. Children who have been exposed to war or terrorism have high rates of depression, disruptive behaviours, and unexplained, recurring physical symptoms. If they and their household have been personally affected, physical pain and loss of home and family may compound the psychological effects (Wexler et al., 2006). Parents' responses to a violent event or disaster and the way they talk with a child about it strongly influence the child's ability to recover (NIMH, 2001a). Box 14-2 gives suggestions for talking with children about terrorism and war.

Table 14-2	Children's Age-Related Reactions to Trauma
Age	**Typical Reactions**
5 years or less	Fear of separation from parent
	Crying, whimpering, screaming, trembling
	Immobility or aimless motion
	Frightened facial expressions
	Excessive clinging
	Regressive behaviours (thumbsucking, bed-wetting, fear of dark)
6 to 11 years	Extreme withdrawal
	Disruptive behaviour
	Inability to pay attention
	Stomachaches or other symptoms with no physical basis
	Declining school performance, refusal to go to school
	Depression, anxiety, guilt, irritability, or emotional numbing
	Regressive behaviour (nightmares, sleep problems, irrational fears, outbursts of anger or fighting)
12 to 17 years	Flashbacks, nightmares
	Emotional numbing, confusion
	Avoidance of reminders of the traumatic event
	Revenge fantasies
	Withdrawal, isolation
	Substance abuse
	Problems with peers, anti-social behaviour
	Physical complaints
	School avoidance, academic decline
	Sleep disturbances
	Depression, suicidal thoughts

Source: NIMH, 2001a.

Box 14-2 *Talking to Children about Terrorism and War*

In today's world, parents are faced with the challenge of explaining violence, terrorism, and war to children. Although difficult, these conversations are extremely important. They give parents an opportunity to help their children feel more secure and understand the world in which they live. The following information can be helpful to parents when discussing these issues.

Listen to Children

1. Create a time and place for children to ask their questions. Don't force children to talk about things until they're ready.
2. Remember that children tend to personalize situations. For example, they may worry about friends or relatives who live in a city or province associated with incidents or events.
3. Help children find ways to express themselves. Some children may not be able to talk about their thoughts, feelings, or fears. They may be more comfortable drawing pictures, playing with toys, or writing stories or poems directly or indirectly related to current events.

Answer Children's Questions

1. Use words and concepts your child can understand. Make your explanation appropriate to your child's age and level of understanding. Don't overload a child with too much information.
2. Give children honest answers and information. Children will usually know if you're not being honest.
3. Be prepared to repeat explanations or have several conversations. Some information may be hard to accept or understand. Asking the same question over and over may be your child's way of asking for reassurance.
4. Acknowledge and support your child's thoughts, feelings, and reactions. Let your child know that you think their questions and concerns are important.
5. Be consistent and reassuring, but don't make unrealistic promises.
6. Avoid stereotyping groups of people by race, nationality, or religion. Use the opportunity to teach tolerance and explain prejudice.
7. Remember that children learn from watching their parents and teachers. They are very interested in how you respond to events. They learn from listening to your conversations with other adults.
8. Let children know how you are feeling. It's OK for them to know if you are anxious or worried about events. However, don't burden them with your concerns.
9. Don't confront your child's way of handling events. If a child feels reassured by saying that things are happening "very far away," it's usually best not to disagree. The child may need to think about events this way to feel safe.

Provide Support

1. Don't let children watch lots of violent or upsetting images on TV. Don't let children watch lots of violent or upsetting images on TV. Repetitive frightening images or scenes can be very disturbing, especially to young children.

2. Help children establish a predictable routine and schedule. Children are reassured by structure and familiarity. School, sports, birthdays, holidays, and group activities take on added importance during stressful times.
3. Coordinate information between home and school. Parents should know about activities and discussions at school. Teachers should know about the child's specific fears or concerns.
4. Children who have experienced trauma or losses may show more intense reactions to tragedies or news of war or terrorist incidents. These children may need extra support and attention.
5. Watch for physical symptoms related to stress. Many children show anxiety and stress through complaints of physical aches and pains.
6. Watch for possible preoccupation with violent movies or war theme video/computer games.
7. Children who seem preoccupied or very stressed about war, fighting, or terrorism should be evaluated by a qualified mental health professional. Other signs that a child may need professional help include ongoing trouble sleeping, persistent upsetting thoughts, fearful images, intense fears about death, and trouble leaving their parents or going to school. The child's physician can assist with appropriate referrals.
8. Help children communicate with others to express themselves at home. Some children may want to write letters to the prime minister, premier, mayor, local newspaper, or grieving families.
9. Let children be children. They may not want to think or talk a lot about these events. It is OK if they'd rather play ball, climb tress, or ride their bike, etc.

War and terrorism are not easy for anyone to comprehend or accept. Understandably, many young children feel confused, upset, and anxious. Parents, teachers, and caring adults can help by listening and responding in an honest, consistent, and supportive manner. Most children, even those exposed to trauma, are quite resilient. Like most adults, they can and do get through difficult times and go on with their lives. By creating an open environment where they feel free to ask questions, parents can help them cope and reduce the likelihood of emotional difficulties.

What's your view?

Which of the suggestions in this box do you think would be most helpful in talking with a child about a war or terrorist attack? Why?

Check it out!

For more information on this topic, go to **www.mcgrawhill.ca/olc/papalia** which provides a link to a Web site that includes information on talking to children about terrorism and war.

Source: American Academy of Child & Adolescent Psychiatry, 2003.

Coping with Stress: The Resilient Child

Resilient children, like Marian Anderson, are those who weather circumstances that would blight most others, who maintain their composure and competence under challenge or threat, or who bounce back from traumatic events. These children do not possess mysterious qualities. They simply have managed, despite adverse circumstances, to hold onto the basic systems and resources that promote positive development in normal children (Masten, 2001; see Table 14-3). The two most important **protective factors,** which seem to help children overcome stress and contribute to resilience, are good *family relationships* and *cognitive functioning* (Masten & Coatsworth, 1998).

Resilient children are likely to have good relationships and strong bonds with at least one supportive parent (Pettit et al., 1997) or caregiver. If not, the child may be close to at least one other caring, competent adult (Masten & Coatsworth, 1998).

Resilient children tend to have high IQs and to be good problem solvers. Their superior information-processing skills may help them cope with adversity, protect themselves, regulate their behaviour, and learn from experience. They may attract the interest of teachers, who can act as guides, confidants, or mentors (Masten & Coatsworth, 1998). They may even have protective genes, which may buffer the effects of an unfavorable environment (Caspi et al., 2003; Kim-Cohen, Moffitt, Caspi, & Taylor, 2004).

Other frequently cited protective factors (Eisenberg et al., 2004; Eisenberg et al., 1997; Masten et al., 1990; Masten & Coatsworth, 1998; E. E. Werner, 1993) include:

- *The child's temperament or personality:* Resilient children are adaptable, friendly, well liked, independent, and sensitive to others. They are competent and have high self-esteem. They are creative, resourceful, independent, and pleasant to be with. When under stress, they can regulate their emotions by shifting attention to something else.
- *Reduced risk:* Children who have been exposed to only one of a number of factors strongly related to psychiatric disorder (such as parental discord, low social status, a disturbed mother, a criminal father, and experience in foster care or an institution) are often better able to overcome stress than children who have been exposed to more than one risk factor.
- *Compensating experiences:* A supportive school environment or successful experiences in studies, in sports, in music, or with other children or adults can help make up for a destructive home life.

All this does not mean that bad things that happen in a child's life do not matter. In general, children with unfavourable backgrounds have more problems in adjustment than

resilient children Children who weather adverse circumstances, function well despite challenges or threats, or bounce back from traumatic events

protective factors Influences that reduce the impact of early stress and tend to predict positive outcomes

What's your view

- How can adults contribute to children's resilience? Give examples.

Table 14-3	Characteristics of Resilient Children and Adolescents
Source	**Characteristic**
Individual	Good intellectual functioning
	Appealing, sociable, easygoing disposition
	Self-efficacy, self-confidence, high self-esteem
	Talents
	Faith
Family	Close relationship to caring parent figure
	Authoritative parenting: warmth, structure, high expectations
	Socio-economic advantages
	Connections to extended supportive family networks
Extra-familial context	Bonds to pro-social adults outside the family
	Connections to pro-social organizations
	Attending effective schools

Source: Masten & Coatsworth, 1998, p. 212.

Figure 14-2

Prevalence of Mental Health Outcomes in New Immigrant and National Populations.

Source: Adapted from Beiser, Hou, et al., 1998.

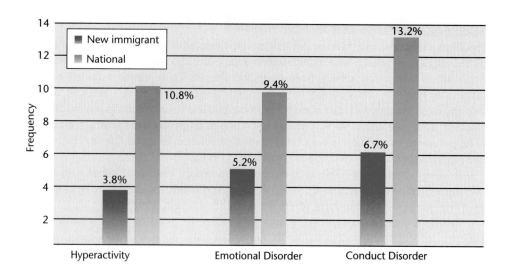

children with more favourable backgrounds. Some outwardly resilient children may suffer internal distress that may have long-term consequences (Masten & Coatsworth, 1998). Still, what is heartening about these findings is that negative childhood experiences do not necessarily determine the outcome of a person's life and that many children have the strength to rise above the most difficult circumstances (Jenkins and Keating, 1998). In an interesting reversal of expected trends, immigrant children to Canada experience better mental health than Canadian children, despite the fact that a larger proportion of immigrant children live in poverty, as shown in Figure 14-2 above. It seems that immigrant families provide adequate emotional support and stability to children, despite low income levels in the first years after immigration to Canada (Beiser, Hou, Hyman, & Tousignant, 1998; Human Resources Development Canada, 2002).

Adolescence, too, is a stressful, risk-filled time—more so than middle childhood. Yet most adolescents develop the skills and competence to deal with the challenges they face, as we'll see in Part 6.

Checkpoint ✔

Can you . . .

✔ Explain Elkind's concept of the "hurried child"?

✔ Name the most common sources of stress, fear, and anxiety in children?

✔ Identify protective factors that contribute to resilience?

Summary and Key Terms

The Developing Self

Guidepost 1 How do the self-concept and self-esteem change in middle childhood, and how do school-age children show emotional growth?

- The self-concept becomes more realistic during middle childhood, when, according to neo-Piagetian theory, children form representational systems.

- According to Erikson, the chief source of self-esteem is children's view of their productive competence. This "virtue" develops through resolution of the crisis of industry versus inferiority. According to Susan Harter's research, however, self-esteem arises primarily from social support and self-evaluation.

- School-age children have internalized shame and pride and can better understand and control negative emotions.

- Empathy and pro-social behaviour increase.

- Emotional growth is affected by parents' reactions to displays of negative emotions.

  representational systems (370)   industry versus inferiority (370)

The Child in the Family

Guidepost 2 What are the effects of family atmosphere and family structure, and what part do siblings play in children's development?

- School-age children spend less time with parents and are less close to them than before; but relationships with parents continue to be important. Culture influences family relationships and roles.

- The family environment has two major components: family structure and family atmosphere. Family atmosphere includes both emotional tone and economic well-being.

- Development of co-regulation may affect the way a family handles conflicts and discipline.

- The impact of mothers' employment depends on many factors concerning the child, the mother's work and her feelings about it; whether she has a supportive partner; the family's socio-economic status; and the kind of care the child receives.

- Parents living in persistent poverty may have trouble providing effective discipline and monitoring and emotional support.

- Many children today grow up in nontraditional family structures. Children tend to do better in traditional two-parent families than in divorced families, single-parent families, and stepfamilies. The structure of the family, however, is less important than its effects on family atmosphere.

- The amount of conflict in a marriage and the likelihood of its continuing after divorce may influence whether children are better off if the parents stay together.

- Children living with only one parent are at heightened risk of behavioural and academic problems, in part related to socio-economic status.

- Remarriages are more likely to fail than first marriages. Boys tend to have more trouble than girls in adjusting to divorce and single-parent living but tend to adjust better to the mother's remarriage.

- Studies have found positive outcomes in children living with gay or lesbian parents.

- Adopted children are generally well adjusted, though they face special challenges.

- The roles and responsibilities of siblings in nonindustrialized societies are more structured than in industrialized societies.

- Siblings learn about conflict resolution from their relationships with each other. Relationships with parents affect sibling relationships.

  co-regulation (372)

The Child in the Peer Group

Guidepost 3 How do relationships with peers change in middle childhood, and what factors influence popularity and aggressive behaviour?

- The peer group becomes more important in middle childhood. Peer groups generally consist of children who are similar in age, sex, ethnicity, and socio-economic status and who live near one another or go to school together.

- The peer group helps children develop social skills, allows them to test and adopt values independent of parents, gives them a sense of belonging, and helps develop the self-concept. It also may encourage conformity and prejudice.

- Popularity influences self-esteem and future adjustment. Popular children tend to have good cognitive abilities and social skills. Behaviours that affect popularity may be derived from family relationships and cultural values.

- Intimacy and stability of friendships increase during middle childhood. Boys tend to have more friends, whereas girls have closer friends.

- During middle childhood, aggression typically declines. Relational aggression becomes more common than overt aggression. Also, instrumental aggression generally gives way to hostile aggression, often with a hostile bias. Highly aggressive children tend to be unpopular, but this may change as children move into adolescence.

- Aggressiveness promoted by exposure to televised violence can extend into adult life.

- Middle childhood is a prime time for bullying; patterns may be established in kindergarten. Victims tend to be weak and submissive or argumentative and provocative and to have low self-esteem.

  prejudice (382)   hostile aggression (386)   instrumental aggression (386)   hostile attribution bias (387)   bullying (389)

Mental Health

Guidepost 4 What are some common mental health problems of childhood, and how do children respond to the stresses of modern life?

- Common emotional and behavioural disorders among school-age children include disruptive behavioural disorders, anxiety disorders, and childhood depression.

- Treatment techniques include individual psychotherapy or family therapy, behaviour therapy, art therapy, play therapy, and drug therapy. Often therapies are used in combination.

- As a result of the pressures of modern life, many children experience stress. Children tend to worry about school, health, and personal safety.

- Resilient children are better able than others to withstand stress. Protective factors involve cognitive ability, family relationships, personality, degree of risk, and compensating experiences.

  oppositional defiant disorder (ODD) (391)
  conduct disorder (CD) (391)   school phobia (391)
  separation anxiety disorder (391)   social phobia (392)
  generalized anxiety disorder (392)
  obsessive-compulsive disorder (392)
  childhood depression (392)   individual psychotherapy (393)
  family therapy (393)   behaviour therapy (393)
  art therapy (393)   play therapy (393)   drug therapy (394)
  resilient children (397)   protective factors (397)

CHAPTER FIFTEEN

Physical Development and Health in Adolescence

What I like in my adolescents is that they have not yet hardened. We all confuse hardening and strength. Strength we must achieve, but not callousness.

—Anaïs Nin, *The Diaries of Anaïs Nin*, Vol. IV, 1971

Focus *Anne Frank, Diarist of the Holocaust**

Anne Frank

For her 13th birthday on June 12, 1942, Anne Frank's parents gave her a diary. This small, cloth-covered volume was the first of several notebooks in which Anne recorded her experiences and reflections during the next 2 years. Little did she dream that her jottings would become one of the most famous published accounts by victims of the Holocaust during World War II.

Anne Frank (1929–1945), her parents, Otto and Edith Frank, and her older sister, Margot, were German Jews who fled to Amsterdam after Hitler came to power in 1933, only to see the Netherlands fall to Nazi conquest 7 years later. In the summer of 1942, when the Nazis began rounding up Dutch Jews for deportation to concentration camps, the family went into hiding on the upper floors of the building occupied by Otto Frank's pharmaceutical firm. Behind a door concealed by a movable cupboard, a steep stairway led to the four rooms Anne called the "Secret Annexe." For 2 years, they stayed in those confined quarters with a couple named "Van Daan," their 15-year-old son, "Peter," and a middle-aged dentist, "Albert Dussel,"** who shared Anne's room. Then, on August 4, 1944, German and Dutch security police raided the "Secret Annexe" and sent its occupants to concentration camps, where all but Anne's father died.

Anne's writings, published by Otto Frank after the war, describe the life the fugitives led. During the day they had to be completely quiet so as not to alert people in the offices below. They saw no one except a few trusted Christian helpers who risked their lives to bring food, books, newspapers, and essential supplies. To venture outside—which would have been necessary to replace Anne's quickly outgrown clothes or to correct her worsening nearsightedness—was unthinkable.

The diary reveals the thoughts, feelings, daydreams, and mood swings of a high-spirited, introspective adolescent coming to maturity under traumatic conditions. Anne wrote of her concern about her "ugly" appearance, of her wish for "a real mother who understands me," and of her adoration for her father (Frank, 1958, pp. 36, 110). She expressed despair at the adults' constant criticism of her failings and at her parents' apparent favouritism toward her sister. She wrote about her fears, her urge for independence, her hopes for a return to her old life, and her aspirations for a writing career.

As tensions rose in the "Secret Annexe," Anne lost her appetite and began taking antidepressant medication. But as time went on, she became less self-pitying and more serious-minded. When she thought back to her previous carefree existence, she felt like a different person from the Anne who had "grown wise within these walls" (p. 149).

She was deeply conscious of her sexual awakening: "I think what is happening to me is so wonderful, and not only what can be seen on my body, but all that is taking place inside. . . . Each time I have a period . . . I have the feeling that . . . I have a sweet secret, and . . . I always long for the time that I shall feel that secret within me again" (pp. 115–116).

Anne originally had regarded Peter as shy and gawky—a not-very-promising companion; but eventually she began visiting his attic room for long, intimate talks and finally, her first kiss. Her diary records the conflict between her stirring sexual passion and her strict moral upbringing.

One of the last diary entries is dated July 15, 1944, less than 3 weeks before the raid and 8 months before Anne's death in the concentration camp at Bergen-Belsen: ". . . in spite of everything, I still believe that people are really good at heart. . . . I hear the ever approaching thunder, which will destroy us too, I can feel the suffering of millions and yet, if I look up into the heavens, I think that it will all come right, that this cruelty too will end, and that peace and tranquillity will return again" (p. 233).

● ● ●

The moving story of Anne Frank's tragically abbreviated adolescence points up the insistent role of biology and its interrelationships with inner and outer experience. Anne's "coming of age" occurred under highly unusual conditions. Yet her normal physical maturation went on, along with a host of cognitive and psychosocial changes heightened by her stressful circumstances.

In this chapter, we describe the physical transformations of adolescence and how they affect young people's feelings. We consider the impact of early and late maturation. We discuss health issues associated with this time of life, and we examine two serious problems: maltreatment and teenage suicide.

After you have read and studied this chapter, you should be able to answer each of the Guidepost questions that appear at the top of the next page. Look for them again in the margins, where they point to important concepts throughout the chapter. To check your understanding of these Guideposts, review the end-of-chapter summary. Checkpoints located throughout the chapter will help you verify your understanding of what you have read.

*Sources of biographical information about Anne Frank were Bloom (1999); Frank (1958, 1995), Lindwer (1991), Müller (1998), and Netherlands State Institute for War Documentation (1989). Page references are to the 1958 paperback version of the diary.
**Fictional names Anne invented for use in her diary.

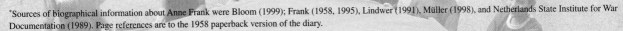

1. What is adolescence, and what opportunities and risks does it entail?

2. What physical changes do adolescents experience, and how do these changes affect them psychologically?

3. What brain developments occur during adolescence, and how do they affect adolescent behaviour?

4. What are some common health problems and health risks of adolescence, and how can they be prevented?

Guideposts for Study

Guidepost 1

What is adolescence, and what opportunities and risks does it entail?

adolescence Developmental transition between childhood and adulthood entailing major physical, cognitive, and psychosocial changes

puberty Process by which a person attains sexual maturity and the ability to reproduce

Adolescence: A Developmental Transition

Rituals to mark a child's "coming of age" are common in many societies. For example, Apache tribes celebrate a girl's first menstruation with a 4-day ritual of sunrise-to-sunset chanting. In most modern societies, the passage from childhood to adulthood is marked, not by a single event, but by a long period known as **adolescence**—a developmental transition that involves physical, cognitive, emotional, and social changes and takes varying forms in different social, cultural, and economic settings (Larson & Wilson, 2004).

An important physical change is the onset of **puberty,** the process that leads to sexual maturity, or fertility—the ability to reproduce.* Traditionally, adolescence and puberty were thought to begin at the same time, around age 13, but, as we will discuss, physicians in some western societies now see pubertal changes before age 10. In this book, we define adolescence as encompassing the years between 11 and 19 or 20.

Adolescence as a Social Construction

Adolescence is a social construction. In pre-industrial societies, children entered the adult world when they matured physically or when they began a vocational apprenticeship. Not until the twentieth century was adolescence defined as a separate stage of life in the western world. Today, adolescence is global (see Box 15-1). In most parts of the world, entry into adulthood takes longer and is less clear-cut than in the past. Puberty begins earlier than it used to; and entrance into a vocation occurs later, often requiring longer periods of education or vocational training to prepare for adult responsibilities. Marriage with its attendant responsibilities typically comes later as well. Adolescents spend much of their time in their own world, largely separate from that of adults (Larson & Wilson, 2004).

Adolescence: A Time of Risks and Opportunities

Early adolescence (approximately ages 11 or 12 to 14), the transition out of childhood, offers opportunities for growth—not only in physical dimensions, but also in cognitive and social competence, autonomy, self-esteem, and intimacy. This period also carries great risks. Some young people have trouble handling so many changes at once and may need help in overcoming dangers along the way. Adolescence is a time of increasing divergence between the majority of young people, who are headed for a fulfilling and productive adulthood, and a sizable minority (about 1 out of 5) who will be dealing with major problems (Offer, Kaiz, Ostrov, & Albert, 2002; Offer, Offer, & Ostrov, 2004; Offer & Schonert-Reichl, 1992).

*Some people use the term *puberty* to mean the end of sexual maturation and refer to the process as *pubescence,* but our usage conforms to that of most psychologists today.

Box 15-1 *The Globalization of Adolescence*

Young people today live in a global neighbourhood, a web of interconnections and interdependencies. Goods, capital, information, electronic images, songs, entertainment, and fads sweep almost instantaneously around the planet. The historical and cultural forces that influence adolescents' lives often arise from events oceans away. Western youth dance to Latin music and watch Japanese films, western movies undermine the system of arranged marriage in Africa, and Arabic girls draw their images of romance from Indian cinema. Maori youth in New Zealand listen to African American rap music to symbolize their separation from adult society.

Adolescence is no longer solely a western phenomenon. Globalization and modernization have set in motion societal changes the world over. Among these changes are urbanization, longer and healthier lives, reduced birth rates, and smaller families. Earlier puberty and later marriage are increasingly common. More women and fewer children work outside the home. The rapid spread of advanced technologies has made knowledge a prized resource. Young people need more schooling and skills to enter the labour force. Together these changes result in an extended transitional phase between childhood and adulthood.

Puberty in less developed countries traditionally was marked by initiation rites such as circumcision. Today adolescents in these countries are increasingly identified by their status as students removed from the working world of adults. In this changing world, new pathways are opening up for them. They are less apt to follow in their parents' footsteps and to be guided by their advice. If they work, they are more likely to work in factories than on the family farm.

This does *not* mean that adolescence is the same the world over. The strong hand of culture shapes its meaning differently in different societies. Adolescents' choices are influenced by parents, teachers, friends, and broader societal institutions, conditions, and values. In Canada, adolescents tend to spend less time with their parents than before and confide in them less, despite the growing trend for young people to prolong living in the parental home (Statistics Canada, 2007). In India, adolescents may wear western clothing and use computers, but they maintain strong family ties, and their life decisions often are influenced by traditional Hindu values. In western countries, teenage girls strive to be as thin as possible. In Niger and other African countries, obesity is considered beautiful, and girls try to fatten themselves with steroids and growth hormones. Furthermore, the progress of modernization and globalization is uneven. For adolescents in poor, developing countries—and for the rural and urban poor everywhere—opportunities and choices are more limited than in advanced technological societies.

In many nonwestern countries, adolescent boys and girls seem to live in two separate worlds. In parts of the Middle East, Latin America, Africa, and Asia, puberty brings more restrictions on girls, whose virginity must be protected to uphold family status and ensure their marriageability. They are closely watched and are not allowed to go out in public alone. Girls who

In many cultures, special celebrations herald entrance to puberty. These 9-year-old schoolgirls in Tehran celebrate the ceremony of Taqlif, which marks their readiness to begin the religious duties of Islam.

are suspected of sexual activity or even of flirting with boys—may be ostracized, whipped, or killed by their fathers and brothers. Boys, on the other hand, gain more freedom and mobility, and their sexual exploits are tolerated by parents and admired by peers.

Puberty also heightens preparation for gender roles, which, for girls in most parts of the world, means preparation for domestic roles. In Laos, a girl may spend two and a half hours a day husking, washing, and steaming rice. In Istanbul, a girl must learn the proper way to serve tea when a suitor comes to call. Whereas boys are expected to prepare for adult work and to maintain family honour, adolescent girls in many less developed countries, such as rural regions of China, do not even go to school because the skills they would learn would be of no use after they married. Instead they are expected to spend most of their time helping at home. As a result, they have less opportunity to develop independent thinking and decision-making. Boys, on the other hand, face greater risks of harm or death due to violence, accidents, and suicide.

This traditional pattern is changing in some parts of the developing world, as women's employment and self-reliance become financial necessities. During the past quarter-century, the advent of public education has enabled more girls to go to school. In East and Southwest Asia, as many girls as boys now enroll in high school (but not in university). Being able to go to school has broken down some of the taboos and restrictions on girls' activities, has given them wider exposure to contexts and role models outside the family, and has increased their options for the future. Better educated girls tend to marry later and have

(continued)

Box 15-1 *The Globalization of Adolescence* (continued)

fewer children, which enables them to seek skilled employment in the new technological society.

In many other developing countries, however, girls' education still lags or differs from that of boys. In Saudi Arabia, girls go to separate schools, where they spend less time on academic studies and more on cooking, sewing, and child care. In many places schoolgirls still carry a heavy burden of domestic work at home. Even after completing their schooling, girls' employment opportunities are more limited than boys'.

Cultural change is complex; it can be both liberating and challenging. Today's adolescents are charting a new course, not always certain where it will lead. We will further discuss how globalization affects adolescents in Chapters 16 and 17.

What's your view ?

Can you think of examples from your own experience of how globalization affects adolescents?

Check it out !

For more information on the globalization of adolescence, go to **www.mcgrawhill.ca/olc/papalia,** and **http://www.unfpa.org/adolescents/about.htm.** This Web page, part of the Web site of the United Nations Population Fund, contains an article on "Adolescent Realities in a Changing World."

Source: Larson & Wilson, 2004.

Checkpoint ✔

Can you . . .

✔ Explain why adolescence is a social construction?

✔ Point out similarities and differences among adolescence in various parts of the world?

✔ Identify risky behaviour patterns common during adolescence?

Canadian adolescents today face greater hazards to their physical and mental well-being than did their counterparts in earlier years (Petersen, 1993; Takanishi, 1993). Among these hazards are early pregnancy and child-bearing (see Chapter 17) and high death rates from accidents, homicide, and suicide (CICH, 2000; National Center for Health Statistics [NCHS], 1998a). Behaviour patterns that contribute to these risks, such as heavy drinking, drug abuse, sexual and gang activity, motorcycling without helmets, and use of firearms, are established early in adolescence (Petersen, 1993; Rivara & Grossman, 1996). As we will see, such risky behaviours may reflect immaturity of the adolescent brain. However, young people who have supportive connections with parents, school, and community tend to develop in a positive, healthful way (Youngblade et al., 2007).

Large national surveys of youth reveal encouraging trends. Since the 1990s, adolescents have high levels of life satisfaction (Statistics Canada, 1999); have become less likely to use alcohol, tobacco, or marijuana; to ride in a car without wearing a seatbelt or to ride with a driver who has been drinking; to carry weapons; to have sexual intercourse or to have it without condoms; or to attempt suicide (CDC, 2006). Avoidance of such risky behaviours increases the chances that young people will come through the adolescent years in good physical and mental health.

Guidepost 2

What physical changes do adolescents experience, and how do these changes affect them psychologically?

adrenarche Maturation of adrenal glands

gonadarche Maturation of testes or ovaries

Puberty: The End of Childhood

Puberty involves dramatic biological changes. These changes are part of a long, complex process of maturation that begins even before birth, and their psychological ramifications may continue into adulthood.

How Puberty Begins: Hormonal Changes

Puberty results from heightened production of sex-related hormones, which occurs in two stages: **adrenarche,** the maturing of the adrenal glands, followed a few years later by **gonadarche.**

First, beginning around age 7 or 8, the adrenal glands located above the kidneys secrete gradually increasing levels of androgens, principally *dehydroepiandrosterone* (DHEA) (Susman & Rogol, 2004). DHEA plays a part in the growth of pubic, axillary (armpit), and facial hair, as well as in faster body growth, oilier skin, and the development of body odour. By age 10, levels of DHEA are 10 times what they were between ages 1 and

4. In several studies, adolescent boys and girls—whether homosexual or heterosexual—recalled their earliest sexual attraction as having taken place at age 9 or 10 (McClintock & Herdt, 1996).

The maturing of the sex organs triggers a second burst of DHEA production, which then rises to adult levels (McClintock & Herdt, 1996). In this second stage, gonadarche, a girl's ovaries step up their output of estrogen, which stimulates growth of female genitals and development of breasts and pubic and underarm hair. In boys, the testes increase the manufacture of androgens, particularly testosterone, which stimulate growth of male genitals, muscle mass, and body hair. Boys and girls have both types of hormones, but girls have higher levels of estrogen, and boys have higher levels of androgens. In girls, testosterone influences growth of the clitoris as well as of the bones and of pubic and axillary hair.

The precise time when this rush of hormonal activity begins seems to depend on reaching a critical amount of body fat necessary for successful reproduction. Thus, girls with a higher percentage of body fat in early childhood and those who experience unusual weight gain between ages 5 and 9 tend to show earlier pubertal development (Davison, Susman, & Birch, 2003). Studies suggest that leptin, a hormone identified as having a role in overweight, may trigger the onset of puberty by signalling the brain that sufficient fat has accumulated. An accumulation of leptin in the bloodstream may stimulate the hypothalamus to signal the pituitary gland, which in turn, may signal the sex glands to increase their secretion of hormones (Chehab, Mounzih, Lu, & Lim, 1997; Clément et al., 1998; O'Rahilly, 1998; Strobel, Camoin, Ozata, & Strosberg, 1998; Susman & Rogol, 2004). Scientists have identified a gene, *GPR54*, on chromosome 19 that is essential for this development to occur (Seminara et al., 2003).

Some research attributes the heightened emotionality and moodiness of early adolescence, so apparent in Anne Frank's diary, to these hormonal developments. Indeed, negative emotions such as distress and hostility as well as symptoms of depression in girls, do tend to rise as puberty progresses (Susman & Rogol, 2004). However, other influences, such as sex, age, temperament, and the timing of puberty, may moderate or even override hormonal ones (Buchanan, Eccles, & Becker, 1992).

The Apache Indians of the southwestern United States celebrate a girl's entrance into puberty with a 4-day ritual that includes special clothing, a symbolic blanket, and singing from sunrise to sunset.

Table 15-1	Usual Sequence of Physiological Changes in Adolescence
Female Characteristics	**Age of First Appearance**
Growth of breasts	7–13
Growth of pubic hair	7–14
Body growth	9.5–14.5
Menarche	10–16.5
Underarm hair	About 2 years after appearance of pubic hair
Increased output of oil- and sweat-producing glands (which may lead to acne)	About the same time as appearance of underarm hair
Male Characteristics	**Age of First Appearance**
Growth of testes, scrotal sac	10–13.5
Growth of pubic hair	12–16
Body growth	10.5–16
Growth of penis, prostate gland, seminal vesicles	11–14.5
Change in voice	About the same time as growth of penis
First ejaculation of semen	About 1 year after beginning of growth of penis
Facial and underarm hair	About 2 years after appearance of pubic hair
Increased output of oil- and sweat-producing glands (which may lead to acne)	About the same time as appearance of underarm hair

Timing, Signs, and Sequence of Puberty and Sexual Maturation

Changes that herald puberty now typically begin at age 8 in girls and age 9 in boys (Susman & Rogol, 2004), but a wide range of ages exists for various changes (see Table 15-1 above). Recently, pediatricians have seen a significant number of girls with breast budding before their eighth birthday (Slyper, 2006). The pubertal process typically takes about 3 to 4 years for both sexes.

Primary and Secondary Sex Characteristics

primary sex characteristics
Organs directly related to reproduction, which enlarge and mature during adolescence

secondary sex characteristics
Physiological signs of sexual maturation (such as breast development and growth of body hair) that do not involve the sex organs

The **primary sex characteristics** are the organs necessary for reproduction. In the female, the sex organs include the ovaries, fallopian tubes, uterus, clitoris, and vagina. In the male, they include the testes, penis, scrotum, seminal vesicles, and prostate gland. During puberty, these organs enlarge and mature.

The **secondary sex characteristics** (see Table 15-2) are physiological signs of sexual maturation that do not directly involve the sex organs, for example, the breasts of females and the broad shoulders of males. Other secondary sex characteristics are changes in the voice and skin texture, muscular development, and the growth of pubic, facial, axillary, and body hair.

Table 15-2	Secondary Sex Characteristics
Girls	**Boys**
Breasts	Pubic hair
Pubic hair	Axillary (underarm) hair
Axillary (underarm) hair	Muscular development
Changes in voice	Facial hair
Changes in skin	Changes in voice
Increased width and depth of pelvis	Changes in skin
Muscular development	Broadening of shoulders

These changes unfold in a sequence that is much more consistent than their timing, though it does vary somewhat. One girl may develop breasts and body hair at about the same rate; in another girl, body hair may reach adultlike growth a year or so before breasts develop. Similar variations in pubertal status (degree of pubertal development) and timing occur among boys. Let's look more closely at these changes.

Signs of Puberty

The first external signs of puberty typically are breast tissue and pubic hair in girls and enlargement of the testes in boys (Susman & Rogol, 2004). A girl's nipples enlarge and protrude, the *areolae* (the pigmented areas surrounding the nipples) enlarge, and the breasts assume first a conical and then a rounded shape. Some adolescent boys experience temporary breast enlargement, much to their distress; however, this is normal and may last up to 18 months.

Pubic hair, at first straight and silky, eventually becomes coarse, dark, and curly. It appears in different patterns in males and females. Adolescent boys are usually happy to see hair on the face and chest; but girls are usually dismayed at the appearance of even a slight amount of hair on the face or around the nipples, though this is normal.

The voice deepens, especially in boys, partly in response to the growth of the larynx and partly in response to the production of male hormones. The skin becomes coarser and oilier. Increased activity of the sebaceous glands may give rise to pimples and blackheads. Acne is more common in boys and seems related to increased amounts of testosterone.

The Adolescent Growth Spurt

In Anne Frank's diary, she made rueful references to her physical growth—to shoes she could no longer get into and vests "so small that they don't even reach my tummy" (p. 71). Anne clearly was in the **adolescent growth spurt**—a rapid increase in height, weight, muscle and bone growth that occurs during puberty.

The adolescent growth spurt generally begins in girls between ages 9½ and 14½ (usually at about 10) and in boys, between 10½ and 16 (usually at 12 or 13). It typically lasts about 2 years; soon after it ends, the young person reaches sexual maturity. Both growth hormone and the sex hormones (androgens and estrogen) contribute to this normal pubertal growth (Susman & Rogol, 2004).

Because girls' growth spurt usually occurs 2 years earlier than that of boys, girls between ages 11 and 13 tend to be taller, heavier, and stronger than boys the same age. After their growth spurt, boys are again larger, as before. Girls usually reach full height at age 15 and boys by age 17. The rate of muscular growth peaks at age 12½ for girls and 14½ for boys (Gans, 1990).

Boys and girls grow differently, not only in rate of growth, but also in form and shape. A boy becomes larger overall: his shoulders wider, his legs longer relative to his trunk, and his forearms longer relative to his upper arms and his height. A girl's pelvis widens to make child-bearing easier, and layers of fat are deposited under the skin, giving her a more rounded appearance. Fat accumulates twice as rapidly in girls as in boys (Susman & Rogol, 2004).

Because each of these changes follows its own time-table, parts of the body may be out of proportion for a while. The result is the familiar teenage gawkiness Anne noticed in Peter Van Daan, which accompanies unbalanced, accelerated growth.

These striking physical changes have psychological ramifications. Most young teenagers are more concerned about their appearance than about any other aspect of themselves, and some do not like what they see in the mirror. As we will discuss in a subsequent section, these attitudes can lead to eating problems.

adolescent growth spurt Sharp increase in height and weight that precedes sexual maturity

From ages 11 to 13, girls are, on the average, taller, heavier, and stronger than boys, who reach their adolescent growth spurt later than girls do.

Signs of Sexual Maturity: Sperm Production and Menstruation

The maturation of the reproductive organs brings the beginning of menstruation in girls and the production of sperm in boys. The principal sign of sexual maturity in boys is the production of sperm. The first ejaculation, or **spermarche,** occurs at an average age of 13. A boy may wake up to find a wet spot or a hardened, dried spot on the sheets—the result of a *nocturnal emission,* an involuntary ejaculation of semen (commonly referred to as a *wet dream*). Most adolescent boys have these emissions, sometimes in connection with an erotic dream.

The principal sign of sexual maturity in girls is *menstruation,* a monthly shedding of tissue from the lining of the womb—what Anne Frank called her "sweet secret." The first menstruation, called **menarche,** occurs fairly late in the sequence of female development (refer back to Table 15-1). On average, girls in Canada first menstruate shortly before their 13th birthday. However, the normal timing of menarche can vary from ages 10 to 16½.

Influences on Timing of Puberty

Puberty is an evolved mechanism to maximize the chances of successful reproduction, and it is still evolving in response to environmental circumstances and demands (Susman & Rogol, 2004). On the basis of historical sources, developmental scientists have found a **secular trend**—a trend that spans several generations—in the onset of puberty: a drop in the ages when puberty begins and when young people reach adult height and sexual maturity. The trend, which also involves increases in adult height and weight, began about 100 years ago. It has occurred in Canada, the United States, western Europe, and Japan (Anderson, Dallal, & Must, 2003).

One proposed explanation for the secular trend is a higher standard of living. Children who are healthier, better nourished, and better cared for might be expected to mature earlier and grow bigger. Thus, the average age of sexual maturity is earlier in developed countries than in developing ones. A contributing factor in North America during the last part of the twentieth century may be the increase in overweight among young girls (S. E. Anderson et al., 2003), but the evidence for this hypothesis is inconclusive. Another proposed factor is changes in lifestyle and nutrition that produce insulin resistance, increasing the risk of diabetes and heart disease (Slyper, 2006).

A combination of genetic, physical, emotional, and contextual influences may affect the timing of menarche (Graber, Brooks-Gunn, & Warren, 1995). Twin studies have documented the heritability of age of menarche (Mendle et al., 2006). Other research has found that the age of a girl's first menstruation tends to be similar to that of her mother *if* nutrition and standard of living remain stable from one generation to the next (Susman & Rogol, 2004). Bigger girls and those whose breasts are more developed tend to menstruate earlier (Moffitt, Caspi, Belsky, & Silva, 1992). So do girls who have low SES or have psychological problems (Mendle et al., 2006). In several studies, family conflict was associated with early menarche, whereas parental warmth, harmonious family relationships, and paternal involvement in child rearing were related to later menarche (Mendle et al., 2006).

The relationship with the father seems particularly important. In one longitudinal study, girls who, as preschoolers, had had close, supportive relationships with their parents—especially with an affectionate, involved father—entered puberty later than girls whose parental relationships had been cold or distant or those who were raised by single mothers (Ellis, McFadyen-Ketchum, Dodge, Pettit, & Bates, 1999). In another study, the presence of a stepfather was more closely associated with early menarche than the absence of a father (Ellis & Garber, 2000).

How might family relationships affect pubertal development? One suggestion is that human males, like some animals, may give off *pheromones,* odourous chemicals that attract mates. As a natural incest-prevention mechanism, sexual development may be inhibited in girls who are heavily exposed to their fathers' pheromones, as would happen in a close father-daughter relationship. On the other hand, frequent exposure to the pheromones of unrelated adult males, such as a stepfather or a single mother's boyfriend, may speed up pubertal development (Ellis & Garber, 2000). Because both a father's absence and early pubertal timing have been identified as risk factors for sexual promiscuity and teenage pregnancy, the father's early presence and active involvement may be important to girls' healthy sexual development (Ellis et al., 1999).

Another explanation is that both a father's tendency toward family abandonment and his daughter's tendency toward early puberty and precocious sexual activity may stem from a shared gene: a sex-linked variant of the androgen receptor (AR) gene, which is carried on the X chromosome of affected fathers and can be transmitted to daughters but not to sons. Among 121 men and 164 unrelated women, men with this allele tended to be aggressive, impulsive, and sexually promiscuous. Women with the same allele tended to have had early menarche and to have experienced parental divorce and father absence before age 7 (Comings, Muhleman, Johnson, & MacMurray, 2002). This hypothesis needs to be tested more directly by genetic analysis of absent fathers and their biological daughters.

Psychological Effects of Early and Late Maturation

The effects of early and late maturation vary in boys and girls, and the timing of maturation tends to predict adolescent mental health and health-related behaviours in adulthood (Susman & Rogol, 2004). Research on early maturing boys has had mixed results. Some studies found that most boys like to mature early, and those who do so seem to gain in self-esteem (Alsaker, 1992). They tend to be more poised, relaxed, good-natured, and popular and less impulsive than late maturers, and also more cognitively advanced. In contrast, other studies have found early maturing boys to be more anxious or aggressive, more worried about being liked, more cautious, more reliant on others, and more bound by rules and routines (Ge, Conger, & Elder, 2001b; Graber, Lewinsohn, Seeley, & Brooks-Gunn, 1997; R. T. Gross & Duke, 1980). Some early maturers may have trouble living up to expectations that they will act as mature as they look. Late maturing boys, on the other hand, have been found to feel more inadequate, self-conscious, rejected, and dominated; to be more dependent, aggressive, insecure, or depressed; to have more conflict with parents and more trouble in school; and to have poorer social and coping skills (Graber et al., 1997; Mussen & Jones, 1957).

Girls are generally happier if their timing is about the same as that of their peers. Early maturing girls tend to be less sociable, less expressive, and less poised; more introverted and shy; and more negative about menarche than later maturing girls (Livson & Peskin, 1980; Ruble & Brooks-Gunn, 1982; Stubbs, Rierdan, & Koff, 1989). Perhaps because they feel rushed into confronting the pressures of adolescence before they are ready (Susman & Rogol, 2004), they are more vulnerable to psychological distress. They are more likely to associate with anti-social peers (Ge, Conger, & Elder, 1996). They may have a poor body image and lower self-esteem than later maturing girls (Alsaker, 1992; Graber et al., 1997; Simmons, Blyth, Van Cleave, & Bush, 1979). Early maturing girls are at increased risk of anxiety and depression, disruptive behaviour, eating disorders, early smoking, drinking, and substance abuse, precocious sexual activity, early pregnancy, and attempted suicide (Deardorff, Gonzalez, Christopher, Roosa, & Millsap, 2005; Dick, Rose, Viken, & Kaprio, 2000; Graber et al., 1997; Japel, Tremblay, Mcduff & Willms, 2002; Susman & Rogol, 2004). However, this is less true of girls with no history of behaviour problems (Susman & Rogol, 2004). Among both boys and girls, early maturers tend to be vulnerable to risky behaviour and the influence of deviant peers (D. P. Orr & Ingersoll, 1995; Susman & Rogol, 2004).

It is hard to generalize about the psychological effects of pubertal timing because they depend on how the adolescent and other people in his or her world interpret the accompanying changes. Effects of early or late maturation are most likely to be negative when adolescents are much more or less developed than their peers; when they do not see the changes as advantageous; and when several stressful events, such as the advent of puberty and the transition to junior high school, occur at about the same time (Petersen, 1993; Simmons, Blyth, & McKinney, 1983).

Contextual factors such as ethnicity, school, and neighbourhood can make a diffrence. Early maturing girls are more likely to show problem behaviour in mixed-gender schools than in all-girl schools and in disadvantaged urban communities as compared with rural or middle-class urban communities (Caspi et al., 1993; Dick et al., 2000; Ge et al., 2002).

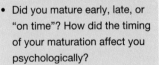

What's your view

- Did you mature early, late, or "on time"? How did the timing of your maturation affect you psychologically?

Checkpoint

Can you . . .

✔ Tell how puberty begins and how its timing and length vary?

✔ Identify typical pubertal changes in boys and girls, and factors that affect psychological reactions to these changes?

Guidepost 3

What brain developments occur during adolescence, and how do they affect adolescent behaviour?

The Adolescent Brain

Not long ago, most scientists believed that the brain is fully mature by puberty. Now brain imaging studies reveal that the adolescent brain is still a work in progress. Dramatic changes in brain structures involved in emotions, judgment, organization of behaviour, and self-control take place between puberty and young adulthood. These findings may help explain teenagers' tendency toward emotional outbursts and risky behaviour (ACT for Youth, 2002) and raise questions about the extent to which adolescents should be held legally responsible for their actions.

Adolescents process information about emotions differently than adults do. In one line of research, researchers scanned adolescents' brain activity while they identified emotions on pictures of faces on a computer screen. Early adolescents (ages 11 to 13) tended to use the amygdala, a small, almond-shaped structure deep in the temporal lobe that is heavily involved in emotional and instinctual reactions (refer back to Figure 6-4 in Chapter 6). Older adolescents, like adults, were more likely to use the frontal lobes, which handle planning, reasoning, judgment, emotional regulation, and impulse control and thus permit more accurate, reasoned judgments. This suggests a possible reason for some early adolescents' unwise choices, such as substance abuse and sexual risk taking: immature brain development may permit feelings to override reason and may keep some adolescents from heeding warnings that seem logical and persuasive to adults (Baird et al., 1999; Yurgelon-Todd, 2002). Underdevelopment of frontal cortical systems associated with motivation, impulsivity, and addiction may help explain adolescents' thrill and novelty seeking and also may explain why many adolescents find it hard to focus on long-term goals (Bjork et al., 2004; Chambers, Taylor, & Potenza, 2003).

To understand the immaturity of the adolescent brain, we need to look at changes in the structure and composition of the frontal cortex. In Chapter 12, we summarized two important childhood brain developments. First, a steady increase in white matter (nerve fibres that connect distant portions of the brain) permits faster transmission of information. In adolescence, this process continues in the frontal lobes (ACT for Youth, 2002; Blakemore & Choudhury, 2006; Kuhn, 2006; NIMH, 2001b). Second, the pruning of unused dendritic connections during childhood results in a reduction in density of grey matter (nerve cells), increasing the brain's efficiency. This process begins in the rear portions of the brain and moves forward. For the most part, however, it has not yet reached the frontal lobes.

A major spurt in production of grey matter in the frontal lobes begins around puberty. After the growth spurt, the density of grey matter declines greatly, particularly in the prefrontal cortex, as unused synapses (connections between neurons) are pruned and those that remain are strengthened (ACT for Youth, 2002; Blakemore & Choudhury, 2006; Kuhn, 2006; NIMH, 2001b). Thus, by mid- to late adolescence young people have fewer but stronger, smoother, and more effective neuronal connections, making cognitive processing more efficient (Kuhn, 2006).

Even more than in childhood, cognitive stimulation in adolescence makes a critical difference in the brain's development. The process is bidirectional: A young person's activities and experiences determine which neuronal connections will be retained and strengthened, and this in turn supports further cognitive growth in those areas (Kuhn, 2006).

Because the adolescent brain is still developing, teenagers can exert some control over that development. Adolescents who "'exercise' their brains by learning to order their thoughts, understand abstract concepts, and control their impulses are laying the neural foundations that will serve them for the rest of their lives" (ACT for Youth, 2002, p. 1).

Checkpoint

Can you . . .

✔ Describe two major changes in the adolescent brain?

✔ Identify immature features of the adolescent brain, and explain how this immaturity can affect behaviour?

Physical and Mental Health

Guidepost 4

What are some common health problems and health risks of adolescence, and how can they be prevented?

Nine out of 10 of early and mid-adolescents consider themselves healthy, according to an international school-based survey of more than 120,000 adolescents 11, 13, and 15 years old in Canada and 27 other industrialized countries under auspices of the World Health Organization (WHO) (Scheidt, Overpeck, Wyatt, & Aszmann, 2000).*

---

*The other countries were Belgium, Czech Republic, Denmark, England, Estonia, Finland, France, Germany, Greece, Greenland, Hungary, Republic of Ireland, Israel, Latvia, Lithuania, Northern Ireland, Norway, Poland, Portugal, Russian Federation, Scotland, Slovak Republic, Spain, Sweden, Switzerland, the United States, and Wales.

Despite their general good health, many younger adolescents—especially girls—report frequent health problems and symptoms, such as headache, stomach ache, backache, nervousness, and feeling tired, lonely, or "low." Such reports are most common in Canada and the United States, perhaps because life in those cultures tends to be fast-paced and stressful (King, Boyce, & King, 1999; Scheidt et al., 2000). About 7 percent of males and 8 percent of females between the ages of 10 and 19 in Canada experience disabilities that result in a limitation in their daily activities (CICH, 2000).

Health Problems and Health-related Behaviours

Many health problems are preventable, stemming from lifestyle or poverty. In industrialized countries, according to the WHO survey, adolescents from less affluent families tend to report poorer health and more frequent symptoms. More affluent adolescents tend to have healthier diets and to be more physically active (Mullan & Currie, 2000).

In Canada and the United States, across ethnic and social-class lines, many early adolescents use drugs, drive while intoxicated, and become sexually active, and these types of risky behaviours increase throughout the teenage years (see Figure 15-1) (CICH, 2000; Health Canada, 1999a; King et al., 1999; Adlaf, Begin, & Sawka, 2005; Statistics Canada, 2005). Adolescents whose families have been disrupted by parental separation or death are more likely to start these activities early and to engage in them more frequently during the next few years (Millstein et al., 1992). Boys and girls who enter puberty early or whose cognitive maturation comes late are especially prone to risky behaviour (Orr & Ingersoll, 1995).

Adolescents are less likely than younger children to see a physician regularly; they more frequently go to school-based health centres (CICH, 2000; Health Canada, 1999a; King et al., 1999). Young people who do not receive needed care are at increased risk of physical and mental health problems, including frequent smoking and drinking (Ford, Bearman, & Moody, 1999). Although all Canadian youth have health services universally available to them, accessibility may vary, depending on level of awareness of health services, or on ability to reach those services, which is especially serious to those living in remote locations (Health Canada, 1999a). Adolescents with mental health problems are more likely to turn to family or friends (if anyone) than to professionals (Offer & Schonert-Reichl, 1992).

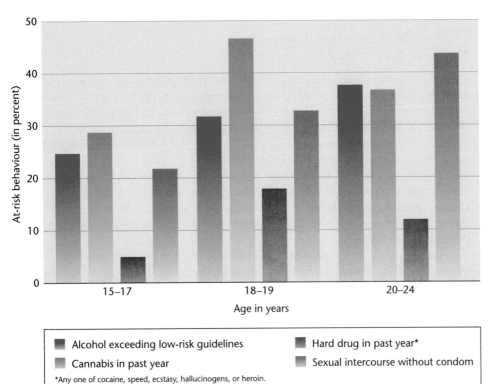

Figure 15-1

Age-specific rates for prevalence of some high-risk behaviours.

Source: Adapted from Adlaf, Begin, & Sawka (2005); Statistics Canada (2005).

Alcohol exceeding low-risk guidelines   Hard drug in past year*

Cannabis in past year   Sexual intercourse without condom

*Any one of cocaine, speed, ecstasy, hallucinogens, or heroin.

Let's look at several specific health concerns: physical fitness, sleep needs, eating disorders, drug abuse, and causes of death in adolescence.

Physical Activity

Exercise—or lack of it—affects both physical and mental health. It improves strength and endurance, helps build healthy bones and muscles, helps control weight, reduces anxiety and stress, and increases self-confidence. Even moderate physical activity has health benefits if done regularly for at least 30 minutes on most, and preferably all, days of the week. A sedentary lifestyle that carries over into adulthood may result in increased risk of obesity, diabetes, heart disease, and cancer (Canadian Paediatric Society [CPS] Advisory Committee on Healthy Active Living for Children and Youth, 2002; Carnethon, Gulati, & Greenland, 2005; Centers for Disease Control and Prevention [CDC], 2000a; National [U.S.] Institutes of Health [NIH] Consensus Development Panel on Physical Activity and Cardiovascular Health, 1996; NCHS, 2004; Nelson & Gordon-Larsen, 2006; Troiano, 2002).

Many boys and, especially, girls become less active during adolescence. Adolescents in Canada rank in the mid-range, compared to other industrialized countries, on exercise duration, but Canada ranks highest, next to Denmark, in proportion of males who play computer games for 4 or more hours a week—an indicator that although many Canadian adolescents are spending a great deal of time in physical activity, the frequency is dropping and the proportion of adolescents engaged in sedentary activities is rising (King et al., 1999). The proportion of Canadian Grade 10 students who report exercising two or more times a week outside of school hours dropped from 83 to 75 percent for males and from 59 to 54 percent for females between 1990 and 1998 (King et al., 1999). Participation in physical education classes, as measured in a 2004 survey, in Grades 10, 11, and 12 is 50, 43 and 36 percent respectively; an overall drop of about 13 percent in comparison to participation rates 6 years before. In addition, only 25 percent of high school students participated in inter-school sports (Canadian Association for Health, Physical Education Recreation and Dance, 2006; Kleiner, Nolin, & Chapman, 2004; Snyder & Hoffman, 2002). Currently, primary school children get as little as 30 minutes of physical education weekly, and physical-education is not a required course after Grade 10 in most provinces. Although Canada's physical activity guidelines recommend 90 minutes of daily vigourous activity for healthy growth and development, many children are not meeting this requirement (Canadian Association for Health, Physical Education Recreation and Dance, 2006). Only about a third of Canadian youth are active enough for optimal health (Health Canada, 1999a).

Sleep Needs

Sleep deprivation among adolescents has been called an epidemic (Hansen et al., 2005). In the WHO study, an average of 40 percent of adolescents (mostly boys) in 28 industrialized countries reported morning sleepiness at least once a week, and 22 percent said they are sleepy most days (Scheidt et al., 2000). About 25 percent of Canadian adolescents report having trouble getting to sleep more than once a week, and girls tend to have more difficulties in falling asleep than boys (King et al., 1999).

Children generally go to sleep later and sleep less on school days the older they get. The average adolescent who slept more than 10 hours at night at age 9 gets less than 8 hours' sleep at age 16 (Hoban, 2004). Students who work 20 or more hours a week also tend to "burn the candle at both ends." As a result, many adolescents doze or sleep in class (Millman et al., 2005).

Actually, adolescents need as much or more sleep than when they were younger (Hoban, 2004; Iglowstein, Jenni, Molinari, & Largo, 2003). "Sleeping in" on weekends does not make up for the loss of sleep on school nights (Hoban, 2004; Sadeh, Raviv, & Gruber, 2000). A pattern of late bedtimes and oversleeping in the mornings can contribute to insomnia, a problem that often begins in late childhood or adolescence. Daytime naps worsen the problem (Hoban, 2004).

Sleep deprivation can sap motivation and cause irritability, and concentration and school performance can suffer (Millman et al., 2005). In a longitudinal study of 2,259 middle school students, sixth-graders who slept less than their peers were more likely to show depressive symptoms and to have low self-esteem (Fredriksen, Rhodes, Reddy, & Way, 2004). Sleepiness also can be deadly for adolescent drivers. Studies have found that young people ages 16 to 29 are most likely to be involved in crashes caused by the driver falling asleep (Millman et al., 2005).

Why do adolescents stay up late? They may need to do homework, want to talk on the phone with friends or surf the Web, or wish to act "grown up." However, physiological changes are also important (Sadeh et al., 2000). The timing of secretion of the hormone *melatonin* is a gauge of when the brain is ready for sleep. After puberty, this secretion takes place later at night (Carskadon, Acebo, Richardson, Tate, & Seifer, 1997). Thus, adolescents *need* to go to bed later and get up later than younger children. Yet most secondary schools start earlier than elementary schools. Their schedules are out of sync with students' biological rhythms (Hoban, 2004). Teenagers tend to be least alert and most stressed early in the morning and more alert in the afternoon (Hansen et al., 2005). Starting school later, or at least offering difficult courses later in the day, would help improve students' concentration (Crouter & Larson, 1998).

Checkpoint

Can you . . .

✔ Summarize the status of adolescents' health and list prevalent health problems?

✔ Explain why physical activity is important in adolescence?

✔ Explain why adolescents often get too little sleep and how sleep deprivation can affect them?

Nutrition and Eating Disorders

Canadian adolescents have less healthy diets than those in most other industrialized countries. They eat fewer fruits and vegetables and more sweets, chocolate, soft drinks, and other "junk" foods, which are high in cholesterol, fat, and calories, and low in nutrients (CICH, 2000; King et al., 1999; Vereecken & Maes, 2000) Adolescents who regularly watch television consume the most junk food (Hickman et al., 2000). Deficiencies of calcium, zinc, and iron are common at this age (Bruner, Joffe, Duggan, Casella, & Brandt, 1996; Lloyd et al., 1993).

Although poor nutrition is most common in economically depressed or isolated populations, it also may result from concern with body image and weight control (Vereecken & Maes, 2000). Eating disorders, including obesity or overweight, are most prevalent in industrialized societies, where food is abundant and attractiveness is equated with slimness; but eating disorders appear to be increasing in nonwestern countries as well (Makino, Tsuboi, & Dennerstein, 2004).

Obesity/Overweight

The average teenage girl needs about 2,200 calories per day; the average teenage boy needs about 2,800. Many adolescents eat more calories than they expend and thus accumulate excess body fat.

Obesity and overweigh are the most common outcomes of eating difficulties in Canada. The prevalence of obesity/overweight in Canadians between 7 and 13 years has more than doubled between 1981 and 1996, and 70 percent of obese adolescents become obese adults (CPS, 2002); 13.5 percent of boys and 11.8 percent of girls in this age range are in the 95th percentiles of body mass, based on age- and sex-norm data from 1981 (Tremblay & Willms, 2000). Over the past 25 years, the largest increase in rates of obesity occurred among adolescents between 12 and 17 years of age, tripling from 3 percent to 9 percent, most commonly among males (Statistics Canada, 2005).

Some causes of obesity—too little physical activity and poor eating habits—are within a person's control. Adolescents who eat fruits and vegetables five or more times a day, about 4 in 10, were less likely to be overweight or obese than those who consumed them less frequently. For individuals between 6 and 17 years of age, the chances of being overweight or obese increase as time spent watching television, playing video games, and using the computer increases (Statistics Canada, 2006). Although about 64 percent of Canadian Grade 10 students report eating fruit and vegetables at least once a day, about 10 percent eat french fries or potato chips daily, and 23 percent eat candy or chocolate bars daily (King et al., 1998).

Overweight teenagers tend to be in poorer health than their peers and are more likely to have functional limitations, such as difficulty attending school, performing household chores, or engaging in strenuous activity or personal care (Swallen, Reither, Haas, & Meier, 2005). They are at heightened risk of high cholesterol, hypertension, and diabetes (NCHS, 2005). Obese teenagers tend to become obese adults, subject to physical, social, and psychological risks (Gortmaker, Must, Perrin, Sobol, & Dietz, 1993). Being overweight in adolescence can lead to life-threatening chronic conditions in adulthood, even if the excess weight is lost (Must et al., 1992).

Genetic and other factors having nothing to do with willpower or lifestyle choices seem to put some young people at risk for overweight (refer back to Chapters 3 and 9). Among these factors are faulty regulation of metabolism (Morrison et al., 2005) and, at least in girls, depressive symptoms and having obese parents (Stice, Presnell, Shaw, & Rohde, 2005). Family functioning seems to be related to obesity in Canadian girls: Obese girls tend to rate their families as having lower levels of cohesion, expressiveness, and democratic style than non-obese girls, while obese boys did not differ from normal-weight boys on ratings of family style (Mendelson, White, & Schliecker, 1995). In such cases, targeted, early prevention efforts are advisable (Morrison et al., 2005; Stice et al., 2005).

Weight-loss programs that use behavioural modification techniques to help adolescents make changes in diet and exercise have had some success. For many pre-adolescents and adolescents, however, dieting may be counterproductive. In a prospective three-year study of 8,203 girls and 6,769 boys ages 9 to 14, those who dieted gained more weight than those who did *not* diet (Field et al., 2003). Use of sibutramine, a weight-loss medication usually used with adults, in conjunction with behavioural modification may improve results, but more study is needed on the drug's safety and efficacy with this age group (Berkowitz, Wadden, Tershakovec, & Cronquist, 2003).

Body Image and Eating Disorders

Sometimes a determination *not* to become obese can result in graver problems than obesity itself. Concern with body image may lead to obsessive efforts at weight control (Davison & Birch, 2001; Vereecken & Maes, 2000). This pattern is more common among girls than among boys and is less likely to be related to actual weight problems.

Because of girls' normal increase in body fat during puberty, many girls, especially if they are advanced in pubertal development, become unhappy about their appearance, reflecting the cultural emphasis on women's physical attributes (Susman & Rogol, 2004). Girls' dissatisfaction with their bodies increases over the course of early to mid-adolescence, while boys, who are becoming more muscular, become more satisfied with their bodies (Feingold & Mazella, 1998; Rosenblum & Lewis, 1999; Swarr & Richards, 1996). By age 15, more than half the girls sampled in 16 countries were dieting or thought they should be (Vereecken & Maes, 2000). Surveys of Canadian adolescents show that more females than males express dissatisfaction with their body shape or size, to diet, or felt the need to lose weight (Croll, 2005; King et al., 1999).

According to a large prospective cohort study, parental attitudes and media images play a greater part than peer influences in encouraging weight concerns. Girls who try to look like the unrealistically thin models they see in the media tend to develop excessive concern about weight. In addition, both girls and boys who believe that thinness is important to their parents, especially to their fathers, tend to become constant dieters (Field et al., 2001).

Body image problems are often overlooked by medical practitioners. Among 208 adolescent inpatients at a psychiatric hospital who were not being specifically treated for such problems, one-third were found to have severe weight and body image concerns, and they tended to be more anxious, depressed, and suicidal than the other mentally ill adolescents (Dyl, Kittler, Phillips, & Hunt, 2006).

Excessive concern with weight control and body image may be signs of *anorexia nervosa* or *bulimia nervosa,* which involve abnormal patterns of food intake. Both disorders involve abnormal patterns of food intake (Harvard Medical School, 2002b), such as erratic eating, self-starvation, or binge eating followed by either self-induced vomiting or use of laxatives to "purge" the system. Ironically, such radical weight control efforts can result in weight *gain* rather than loss because such practices alter normal appetite and metabolic patterns (Stice et al., 2005).

As chronic disorders, anorexia affects an estimated 1 to 2 percent of females in Canada, and bulimia affects 3 to 5 percent (CICH, 2000). Although most victims are adolescent girls and young women, about 5 to 15 percent are male (Andersen, 1995). Anorexia and bulimia tend to run in families, suggesting a possible genetic basis. Other apparent causes are neurochemical, developmental, and social-cultural (Becker et al., 1999; "Eating Disorders–Part I, Part II," 1997; Kendler et al., 1991). These disorders are especially common among girls driven to excel in ballet, competitive swimming, long-distance running, figure skating, and gymnastics ("Eating Disorders–Part II," 1997; Martínez-González et al., 2003; Skolnick, 1993). Body-esteem, which reflects self-satisfaction and self-evaluations of body weight, physical appearance, and perceptions of others' evaluations of one's body and appearance (Mendelson, Mendelson, & White, 2001), has been found to be positively related to global self-worth in Canadian children between 8 and 12 years of age (Mendelson, White, & Mendelson, 1996), as well as in adolescents (Mendelson, Mendelson, & Andrews, 2000). Males tend to have higher body-esteem than females (Mendelson et al., 1996; Mendelson et al., 2000).

Anorexia Nervosa

Anorexia nervosa is a disorder typically beginning in adolescence and characterized by an obsessive preoccupation with being thin. There are two types of anorexia. One is characterized by self-starvation, often accompanied by compulsive, excessive exercise. The other type involves binge eating, purging, or both (Yager & Andersen, 2005). Anorexics have a distorted body image; though they are at least 15 percent below natural body weight (McGilley & Pryor, 1998), they think they are too fat. An estimated 0.5 percent of adolescent girls and young women and a smaller but growing percentage of boys and men in western countries have anorexia (AAP Committee on Adolescence, 2003; Martínez-González et al., 2003). In a large study of Swedish twins, for example, the prevalence of the disorder was 1.2 percent in women and 0.29 percent in men in 2002 (Bulik et al., 2006).

anorexia nervosa Eating disorder characterized by self-starvation

Anorexia has the highest death rate and the highest suicide rate of any mental disorder (Bulik et al., 2006; Crow, 2006). Medical complications affect almost every organ in the body (Yager & Andersen, 2005). Among the early warning signs are: determined, secret dieting; dissatisfaction after losing weight; setting new, lower weight goals after reaching an initial desired weight; excessive exercising; interruption of regular menstruation; hair loss; low body temperature; and growth of soft, fuzzy body hair.

The causes of anorexia probably are multifactorial (Yager & Andersen, 2005). It is estimated to be 56 percent heritable (Bulik et al., 2006). A variant of a gene that may lead to decreased feeding signals has been found in anorexic patients (Vink et al., 2001). In addition, certain complications of birth increase the risk of developing anorexia. These include maternal anemia, diabetes, and death of a portion of the placenta. Risk factors during the neonatal period include heart problems, low body temperature, tremors, and low reactivity (Favaro, Tenconi, & Santonastaso, 2006). People with anorexia tend to have reduced blood flow to certain parts of the brain, including an area thought to control visual self-perception and appetite (Gordon, Lask, Bryantwaugh, Christie, & Timini, 1997).

Personality may play a role. Young people with anorexia often are good students, described by their parents as "model" children. They may be withdrawn or depressed and may engage in repetitive, perfectionist behaviour. Other suggested causes are anxiety disorders, a family history of depression and obesity, and familial, peer, and cultural pressures to be slender (Yager & Andersen, 2005).

Because anorexia is potentially life threatening, the immediate goal of treatment is to get patients to eat and gain weight. Therapy should focus on educating the patient and the family about the disorder, its risks, and the benefits of treatment and on reducing unhealthful attitudes (Yager & Andersen, 2005). Patients may be given drugs

Anorexics have an unrealistic body image. Despite the evidence of their mirrors, they think they are too fat.

to inhibit vomiting and to treat associated medical problems. Psychotherapy—either behavioural or cognitive—has had some success in getting patients to put on weight. Outcomes tend to be better when the family is involved (Yager & Andersen, 2005). Lack of access to interdisciplinary health teams, and limits in funding for supports by some provincial health plans can make treatment more difficult (Adolescent Medicine Committee, Canadian Paediatric Society, 1998).

Patients who show signs of severe malnutrition, are resistant to treatment, show medical danger signs or poor motivation, or do not make progress on an outpatient basis may be admitted to a hospital, where they can be given 24-hour nursing. Once their weight is stabilized, patients may enter less intensive daytime care that includes ongoing psychotherapy; but if they fail to sustain their weight, they should be rehospitalized (McCallum & Bruton, 2003; Yager & Andersen, 2005). About 50 to 70 percent of anorexia patients make a full recovery; the process may take 5 to 7 years (Yager & Andersen, 2005).

Bulimia Nervosa

In **bulimia nervosa,** a person regularly goes on huge eating binges within a short time, usually 2 hours or less, and then tries to undo the high caloric intake by self-induced vomiting, strict dieting or fasting, engaging in excessively vigorous exercise, or taking laxatives, enemas, or diuretics to purge the body. These episodes occur at least twice a week for at least 3 months (APA, 1994).

Bulimia differs from the binging-and-purging form of anorexia in that people with bulimia are not abnormally underweight. Some people move back and forth between anorexia and bulimia as their eating and weight patterns change (McGilley & Pryor, 1998). Nevertheless, the two are separate disorders. A related *binge eating disorder* involves frequent binging but without subsequent fasting, exercise, or vomiting; it is the most prevalent eating disorder among Canadian adults and is a factor in the rise in obesity (Hudson, Hiripi, Pope, & Kessler, 2007).

Bulimia and binge eating disorder are much more common than anorexia. About 3 percent of women and 0.3 percent of men have developed bulimia or binge eating disorder at some time in their lives, and much larger numbers have an occasional episode (Harvard Medical School, 2002b; McGilley & Pryor, 1998). Unlike anorexia, there is little evidence of bulimia either historically or in cultures not subject to Western influence. The reasons may be that binge eating, unlike anorexia, requires an abundance of food, and purging would be difficult to hide without modern plumbing (Keel & Klump, 2003).

People with bulimia are obsessed with their weight and shape. They become overwhelmed with shame, self-contempt, and depression over their eating habits. They have low self-esteem (as do people with anorexia), and a history of wide weight fluctuation, dieting, or frequent exercise (Kendler et al., 1991).

Like anorexia, bulimia appears to be multifactorial in origin (McGilley & Pryor, 1998). Bulimia seems to be related to low levels of the brain chemical serotonin ("Eating Disorders—Part I," 1997; K. A. Smith, Fairburn, & Cowen, 1999). It may share genetic roots with major depression or with phobias and panic disorder (Keel et al., 2003). There also may be is a psychoanalytic explanation: people with bulimia are thought to crave food to satisfy their hunger for love and attention ("Eating Disorders—Part I," 1997. As with anorexia, certain complications of birth or the early days of life are associated with bulimia: partial placental death, low birth weight and length, low neonatal reactivity, and early difficulties with eating (Favaro et al., 2006).

Cognitive behavioural therapy is the most effective treatment for bulimia. Patients keep daily diaries of their eating patterns and are taught ways to avoid the temptation to binge. Because these patients are at risk for depression and suicide, antidepressant drugs may be combined with psychotherapy (Harvard Medical School, 2002b; McCallum & Bruton, 2003). Fluoxetine has had well-documented success in treating bulimia (Crow, 2006). Recovery rates from bulimia average 50 percent after 6 months to 5 years (Harvard Medical School, 2002b). However, some 30 percent of patients quickly relapse, and as many as 40 percent have continuing symptoms (McGilley & Pryor, 1998).

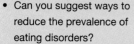

Use and Abuse of Drugs

Although the great majority of adolescents do not abuse drugs, a significant minority do (see Figure 15-2). The longest-running school survey of Canadian adolescents, the 30-year Ontario Student Drug Use and Health Survey carried out by the Centre for Addiction and Mental Health (CAMH), found that in comparison with their peak periods of usage, the use of most illicit drugs, along with cigarettes and alcohol, have dropped in recent years among adolescents (Adlaf & Paglia-Boak, 2007; see Figure 15-2). Only the frequency of use of solvents has shown no change (Adlaf et al., 2007).

Substance abuse is harmful use of alcohol or other drugs. Abuse can lead to **substance dependence** (addiction), which may be physiological or psychological, or both, and is likely to continue into adulthood. Addictive drugs are especially dangerous for adolescents because they stimulate parts of the brain that are changing in adolescence (Chambers et al., 2003). In 2003–2004, about 6 percent of young people ages 12 to 17 were identified as needing treatment for alcohol use and more than 5 percent as needing treatment for illicit drug use (National Survey on Drug Use and Health [NSDUH], 2006c).

Trends in Drug Use

Use of illicit drugs among Canadian adolescents increased during the 1990s, but has shown a gradual decline in recent years (Adlaf & Paglia-Boak, 2007; see Figure 15-2). More males than females are drug users (Tjepkema, 2004). The major increase in the 1990s was in the use of hashish/marijuana, with the use of cocaine, amphetamines, and LSD slowly increasing. This trend has slowly been reversing in recent years (Adlaf et al., 2007). An exception is solvent use, which declined during the 1990s, but has shown a recent increase. The trends in drug use have been accompanied by a decrease in the use of beer, wine, and liquor, as well as a significant decrease in smoking.

Many of these findings come from a series of surveys of over 6,000 students in all regions of Canada, which represents the Canadian component of a World Health Organization cross-national study, called Health Behaviour in School-Aged Children. Ten other countries—Denmark, England, France, Germany, Greece, Norway, Poland, Sweden, Switzerland, and the United States—participated in the study (King et al., 1999). These surveys probably underestimate adolescent drug use since they do not reach high school dropouts, who are likely to have higher rates. Continued progress in eliminating drug abuse

substance abuse Repeated, harmful use of a substance, usually alcohol or other drugs

substance dependence Addiction (physical, psychological, or both) to a harmful substance

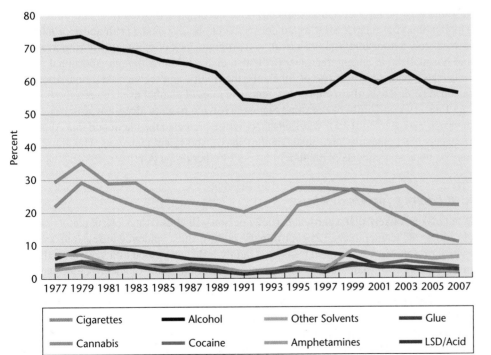

Figure 15-2

Percentage of adolescents from Grades 7, 9, and 11 in Ontario reporting using drugs at least once during the past year. In general, the current rates of drug use are lower than earlier peak periods.

Source: Adlaf and Paglia-Boak, 2007.

is slow because new drugs are continually introduced or rediscovered by a new generation, and young people do not necessarily generalize the adverse consequences of one drug to another (Johnston et al., 2006).

As indicated in a 1998 survey, about 4 percent of Canadian adolescents have used MDMA ("ecstasy") (King et al., 1999). Ecstasy is a hallucinatory, amphetamine-like drug, one of several relatively low-cost "club drugs" popular at nightclubs, bars, and night-long "raves" or "trances." In a Canadian Rave Population study MDMA was the most prevalent drug used by the 10.2 percent of adolescents trying drugs other than alcohol or cannabis (Gross, Barrett, Shestowsky & Pihl, 2002). It can cause long-term brain damage and other physical and psychological problems. Short-term problems—rapid heart rate, sweating, muscle spasms, and high fever—are complicated by the factors associated with raves, including high temperatures, vigorous activity, and dehydration; the use of ecstasy has resulted in deaths in Canada (Rieder, 2002).

Although illicit drug use has declined, nonmedical use of prescription drugs, such as sedatives, stimulants, tranquilizers, and narcotic pain relievers, particularly OxyContin, remains at high levels (Adlaf et al., 2007). In 2007, 2 percent of adolescents reported using OxyContin, 1 percent reported using stimulants prescribed for ADHD, and 21 percent reported using prescription narcotic pain relievers at least once in the past 12 months (Adlaf et al., 2007). A new trend is the abuse of nonprescription cough and cold medications, with between 4 and 6 percent of U.S. high-school students reporting taking medicines containing dextromethorphan (DXM), a cough suppressant, to get high within the past year (Johnston et al., 2007).

Inhalants are chemical vapours that adolescents sniff to get high, often from common household products such as glues, solvents, gasoline, butane, and aerosols. Because they are inexpensive and easy to obtain, they are most often used by younger students. Sniffing can damage hearing, brain, bone marrow, liver, and kidneys and also can cause oxygen depletion, heart failure, and death. Inhalant use has been on the decline, along with growing peer disapproval of its use (L. D. Johnston et al., 2000). However, for some Canadian populations, including Aboriginal youth, inhalant use is a serious problem (Coleman, Charles, & Collins, 2001), with up to 60 percent of youth in some communities reporting their use (Dell, Dell & Hopkins, 2005). A retrospective study of 78 Aboriginal youth, who had received treatment for inhalant abuse in the National Breakthrough Inhalant Abuse Program, tailored for Aboriginal youth, at a treatment centre in western Canada, showed that many came from isolated and low-income families that experienced violence and histories of substance abuse. The average age of solvent use was 9.7 years, and typically gasoline was the most common inhalant, often accompanied by alcohol and other drugs. The likelihood of relapse after treatment seemed to be associated with abuse of inhalants immediately before admission to a treatment program, lack of motivation during treatment, and hospitalization during treatment (Coleman et al., 2001). Although Aboriginal adolescents show higher rates of use of inhalants, marijuana, and tobacco than non-Aboriginal matched adolescents, there are no differences in rates of alcohol use between these groups (Gfellner, 1994). Family background factors involving parents' drug-use attitudes and behaviours, and peer attitudes toward substance abuse predicted the likelihood that Aboriginal teenagers used inhalants, marijuana, and tobacco. Aboriginal teenagers who abuse drugs may be bypassing the use of alcohol in favour of other drugs (Gfellner, 1994).

Risk Factors for Drug Abuse

What makes it likely that a particular young person will abuse drugs? Risk factors include: (1) "difficult" temperament, (2) poor impulse control and a tendency to seek out sensation (which may have a biochemical basis), (3) family influences (such as a genetic predisposition to alcoholism, parental use or acceptance of drugs, poor or inconsistent parenting practices, family conflict, and troubled or distant family relationships), (4) early and persistent behaviour problems, particularly aggression, (5) academic failure and lack of commitment to education, (6) peer rejection, (7) association with drug users, (8) alienation and rebelliousness, (9) favourable attitudes toward drug use, and (10) early initiation into drug use (Hawkins, Catalano, & Miller, 1992; Johnson, Hoffmann, & Gerstein, 1996; Masse &

Tremblay, 1997; USDHHS, 1996b). The more risk factors that are present, the greater the chance that an adolescent or young adult will abuse drugs.

Let's look more closely at alcohol, marijuana, and tobacco, the three drugs most popular with adolescents, and at influences on their use.

Alcohol, Marijuana, and Tobacco

Alcohol, marijuana, and tobacco use among teenagers has followed a trend roughly parallel to that of harder drug use, with a dramatic rise during most of the 1990s followed by a smaller, gradual decline (Johnston et al., 2006; see Figure 15-2).

Alcohol is a potent, mind-altering drug with major effects on physical, emotional, and social well-being. Its use is a very serious problem in many countries (Gabhainn & François, 2000). According to a recent survey of Canadian youth, 62 percent of 15- to 17-year-olds, 91 percent of 18- and 19-year-olds, and 90 percent of 20- to 24-year-olds said they had consumed alcohol at least once during the past year (Adlaf, Begin, & Sawka, 2005).

Adolescents are more vulnerable than adults to both immediate and long-term negative effects of alcohol on learning and memory (White, 2001). In one study, 15- and 16-year-old alcohol abusers who stopped drinking showed cognitive impairments weeks later in comparison with nonabusing peers (Brown, Tapert, Granholm, & Delis, 2000).

Despite the decline in *marijuana* use, it is still by far the most widely used illicit drug in Canada (Adlaf et al., 2007; see Figure 15-2). Marijuana smoke typically contains more than 400 carcinogens. Heavy use can damage the brain, heart, lungs, and immune system and cause nutritional deficiencies, respiratory infections, and other physical problems. It may lessen motivation, interfere with daily activities, and cause family problems. Marijuana use also can impede memory, thinking speed, and learning. It can cut down perception, alertness, attention span, judgment, and the motor skills needed to drive a vehicle and thus can contribute to traffic accidents (Macdonald, Mann, Chipman, & Anglin-Bodrug, 2004; Messinis, Krypianidou, Maletaki, & Papathanasopoulos, 2006; National Institute on Drug Abuse [NIDA], 1996; Solowij et al., 2002). Both alcohol and marijuana use can harm academic performance (NSDUH, 2006a).

Contrary to common belief, marijuana use may be addictive (Tanda, Pontieri, & DiChiara, 1997) and tends to lead to hard drug use (Lynskey et al., 2003). Addictive drugs are especially dangerous for adolescents because they stimulate parts of the brain that are still changing (Chambers et al., 2003).

Adolescent *tobacco* use is a less widespread problem in Canada than in most other industrialized countries (Gabhainn & François, 2000), with more girls than boys admitting to smoking daily (King et al., 1999). Smoking rates have declined by one-third to more than one-half among Canadian eighth- to- twelfth-graders since the mid-1990s (King et al., 1999; Patton et al., 2005; Adlaf et al., 2007).

A randomized, controlled trial found nicotine replacement therapy plus behavioural skills training effective in helping adolescents stop smoking. After 10 weeks of treatment, 28 percent of teens who got a nicotine patch had quit completely. After six months, only 7 percent were completely smoke-free, but most cut down to a few cigarettes a day or less (Killen et al., 2004).

It is hoped that, as a result of government initiatives to educate young smokers about the health hazards of smoking—including legislated changes to health warnings on cigarette packages, restrictions on where smoking is permitted in public places, and an increase in government taxes on cigarette purchases—the decline in smoking among youth will continue.

Dangers of Early Initiation

Drug use often begins when children enter middle school, where they become more vulnerable to peer pressure. Fourth to sixth graders may start using cigarettes, beer, and inhalants and, as they get older, move on to marijuana or harder drugs (National Parents' Resource Institute for Drug Education, 1999). The earlier young people start using a drug, the more frequently they are likely to use it and the greater their tendency to abuse it.

Checkpoint ✔

Can you . . .

✔ Summarize recent trends in drug use among adolescents?

✔ Discuss risk factors and influences connected with use of drugs, specifically alcohol, marijuana, and tobacco?

✔ Tell why early initiation into substance use is dangerous?

The average age for starting to drink is 13 to 14, and some children start earlier. In 2003, nearly 28 percent of underage drinkers had a drink before age 13 (Faden, 2006). Young people who begin drinking early tend to have behaviour problems or to have siblings who are alcohol-dependent (Kuperman et al., 2005). Those who start drinking before age 15 are more than five times more likely to become alcohol dependent or alcohol abusers than those who do not start drinking until age 21 or later (Substance Abuse and Mental Health Services Administration (SAMHSA), 2004).

Adolescents who begin smoking by age 11 are twice as likely as other young people to engage in risky behaviours, such as riding in a car with a drinking driver; carrying knives or guns to school; using inhalants, marijuana, or cocaine; and planning suicide. Early use of alcohol and marijuana also are associated with multiple risk behaviours (DuRant, Smith, Kreiter, & Krowchuk, 1999).

Influences on Smoking and Drinking

Peer influence on both smoking and drinking has been documented extensively (Center on Addiction and Substance Abuse at Columbia University [CASA], 1996; Cleveland & Wiebe, 2003). As with hard drugs, the influence of older siblings and their friends increases the likelihood of tobacco and alcohol use (Rende, Slomkowski, Richardson, & Niaura, 2005). Adolescents who believe that their parents disapprove of smoking are less likely to smoke (Sargent & Dalton, 2001). Rational discussions with parents can counteract harmful influences and discourage or limit drinking (Austin, Pinkleton, & Fujioka, 2000; Turrisi et al., 2000).

The omnipresence of substance use in the media is an important influence. Movies that depict smoking increase early initiation of smoking (Charlesworth & Glantz, 2005). In a U.S. national longitudinal survey, 10- to 15-year-olds who watched at least 4 or 5 hours of television each day were 5 to 6 times more likely to start smoking within the next 2 years than those who watched less than 2 hours a day (Gidwani, Sobol, DeJong, Perrin, & Gortmaker, 2002). A random sample of major motion pictures found a decline in depiction of smoking from 10.7 incidents per hour in 1950 to 4.9 in 1980–1982, but by 2002 portrayals of smoking had reverted to 1950 levels (Glantz, Kacirk, & McCulloch, 2004).

Depression

In view of the desperate situation in which Anne Frank found herself, it is not surprising that she needed to take an antidepressant. Even in normal surroundings, the prevalence of depression increases during adolescence. In 2004, 9 percent of young people ages 12 to 17 had experienced at least one episode of major depression, and only about 40 percent of them had been treated (NSDUH, 2005). Depression in young people does not necessarily appear as sadness but as irritability, boredom, or inability to experience pleasure. One reason it needs to be taken seriously is the danger of suicide (Brent & Birmaher, 2002).

Adolescent girls, especially early maturing girls, are more subject to depression than adolescent boys (Brent & Birmaher, 2002; Ge, Conger, & Elder, 2001; NSDUH, 2005; Stice et al., 2001). This gender difference may be related to biological changes connected with puberty; studies show a correlation between advancing puberty status and depressive symptoms (Susman & Rogol, 2004). Other possible factors are the way girls are socialized (Birmaher et al., 1996) and their greater vulnerability to stress in social relationships (Ge et al., 2001; USDHHS, 1999c).

In addition to female gender, risk factors for depression include anxiety, fear of social contact, stressful life events, chronic illnesses such as diabetes or epilepsy, parent-child conflict, abuse or neglect, alcohol and drug use, sexual activity, and having a parent with a history of depression. Alcohol and drug use and sexual activity are more likely to lead to depression in girls than in boys (Brent & Birmaher, 2002; Hallfors, Waller, Bauer, Ford, & Halpern, 2005; NSDUH, 2005; Waller et al., 2006). Body-image problems and eating disturbances can aggravate depressive symptoms (Stice & Bearman, 2001).

Depressed adolescents who do not respond to outpatient treatment or who have substance dependence or psychosis or seem suicidal may need to be hospitalized. At least 1 in

Marijuana is the most widely used illicit drug in Canada; almost half of Grade 10 students say they have tried it.

5 persons who experience bouts of depression in childhood or adolescence are at risk for bipolar disorder, in which depressive episodes ("low" periods) alternate with "high" periods characterized by increased energy, euphoria, grandiosity, and risk taking (Brent & Birmaher, 2002). Even adolescents with depressive symptoms not severe enough for a diagnosis of depression are at elevated risk of depression and suicidal behaviour by age 25, according to a 25-year longitudinal study of 1,265 New Zealand children (Fergusson, Horwood, Ridder, & Beautrais, 2005).

SSRIs are the only type of antidepressant medication currently approved for children and adolescents (refer back to Chapter 14). However, as with the use of SSRIs for children, there is concern about the safety of these medications for adolescents. As we mentioned in Chapter 14, the U.S. Food and Drug Administration requires a warning to accompany their distribution and sale (Leslie, Newman, Chesney, & Perrin, 2005).

The only other treatment option is psychotherapy. An analysis of all available studies found modest short-term effectiveness of psychotherapy, cognitive or noncognitive, with effects lasting no more than a year (Weisz, McCarty, & Valeri, 2006). In view of the greater effectiveness of antidepressant medicine, especially fluoxetine, the Society for Adolescent Medicine supports its use for adolescents when clinically warranted and closely monitored, despite the risk (Lock, Walker, Rickert, & Katzman, 2005).

Abuse and Neglect

Maltreatment of adolescents is much less widely discussed than maltreatment of younger children, but it does exist. Of the almost 136,000 children found by agencies to be victims of substantiated or indicated abuse or neglect in 1998, 18.5 children per 1,000 were boys between the ages of 12 and 15 years, and 25.1 per 1,000 were girls in the same age range, according to the Canadian Incidence Study of Reported Child Abuse and Neglect (Trocmé et al., 2001). Most cases involve neglect, exposure to domestic violence, and physical abuse. Emotional maltreatment, and sexual abuse are less common (Public Health Agency of Canada, 2003).

A longitudinal study in Calgary tracked 290 females on a variety of psychological and social factors from age 3 to age 13, and measured the incidence of maltreatment up to the age of 16. Results showed that early neurological problems, difficult temperament, mothers' stress, low income, poor attachment, and disrupted family were associated with higher likelihood of maltreatment (Bagley & Mallick, 2000).

Unlike younger children who are abused, teenagers are more likely to fight back or run away (Sedlak & Broadhurst, 1996). Physically abused teenagers are often perceived as bearing at least part of the blame for provoking parents; they are more likely than other adolescents to use violence against parents and siblings.

Although abuse of teenagers is less likely to result in death or severe injury than abuse of younger children, it can have serious long-term results. Sexually abused teenagers are more likely than their peers to engage in early or heavy sexual activity; to become pregnant or delinquent; to abuse alcohol or other drugs; to be confused about their sexual identity; to be depressed or anxious; and to attempt suicide. Physically abused teenagers also tend to be anxious and depressed. They may show severe behavioural, academic, and sleeping problems; self-destructive or reckless actions; involvement in prostitution or heavy drug use; or suicidal tendencies (Council on Scientific Affairs of the American Medical Association, 1993; Schissel & Fedec, 1999).

Death in Adolescence

Not every death in adolescence is as poignant as Anne Frank's. Still, death this early in life is always tragic, and (unlike Anne's) usually accidental (CICH, 2000; Hoyert, Heron, Murphy, & Kung, 2006; USDHHS, 1999b)—but not entirely so. The frequency of car crashes, handgun deaths, and suicide in this age group reflects a violent culture, as well as adolescents' inexperience and immaturity, which often lead to risk taking and carelessness.

Deaths from Vehicle Accidents and Firearms

Motor vehicle collisions are the leading cause of death among Canadian teenagers; they account for more than half of all deaths of 10- to 14-year-olds (Canadian Council on Social Development, 2001). The risk of collision is greater among 16- to 19-year-olds than for any other age group and especially so among 16- and 17-year olds who have recently started to drive (McCartt, 2001; Miniño, Anderson, Fingerhut, Boudreault, & Warner, 2006; National Center for Injury Prevention and Control [NCIPC], 2004). Collisions are more likely to be fatal when teenage passengers are in the vehicle, probably because adolescents tend to drive more recklessly in the presence of peers (Chen, Baker, Braver, & Li, 2000). In 2002, 29 percent of drivers ages 15 to 20 who died in motor crashes had been drinking alcohol, and 77 percent of those were not wearing seat belts (National Highway Traffic Safety Administration, 2003).

Death rates for this age group have dropped 52 percent between 1975 and 1995, despite the high percentage of youth in Canada (12 percent) who report drinking and driving at least once in the previous year. This percentage is higher than any other age group, excepting the 20- to 24-year-old group (CICH, 2000). Although the death rate for males is higher than for females, the gap is narrowing (CICH, 2000). Some provinces have adopted graduated licensing systems, which allow beginning drivers to drive only with supervision at first, and lift the restrictions gradually.

Firearm-related deaths of 15- to 19-year-olds (including homicide, suicide, and accidental deaths) are far more common in the United States than in Canada and other industrialized countries. Nevertheless, in Canada gun-related injury is the third leading cause of death for Canadian youth between 15 and 24 years, after vehicle accidents and suicide brought on by other means (Wilkins, 2005).

Suicide

Although the frequency of suicide is low for Canadian youth, the rate has increased dramatically for males over several decades (CICH, 2000; Task Force on Suicide in Canada, 1994), and the rate is higher in Canada than in the United States (Leenaars & Lester, 1990; 1995). Currently, the rate of completed suicides for youth between 15 and 19 years is 19 per 100,000 males and 4 per 100,000 females (CICH, 2000), accounting for 24 percent of all deaths among 15- to 24-year-olds (Canadian Mental Health Association, 2006). However, women tended to attempt suicide more frequently than males, with 265 women and 98 men per 100,000 being hospitalized for suicide attempts in 1996 to 1997, and street youth are more likely to attempt suicide than youth in school (Canadian Mental Health Association, 2006; CICH, 2000).

Although suicide affects all ethnic groups, the suicide death rate for Aboriginal males between 15 and 24 years of age is about five times higher, at 126 per 100,000, than it is for non-Aboriginal males of the same age range, and the rate is 35 per 100,000 Aboriginal females (CICH, 2000). The suicide rate among Inuit youth is among the highest in the world, over 10 times the national average in Canada (Health Canada, 2006). One possible explanation for the higher prevalence may be related to the link between cultural continuity and Aboriginal suicide rates; with added numbers of protective cultural factors in a community—like self-governance, land claims negotiations, and local control over educational and health services—rates of youth suicide decrease (CICH, 2000). Other factors that have been associated with suicide attempts among Inuit youth in particular are substance abuse, recent alcohol abuse, life event stressors, and the presence of a psychiatric problem (Kirmayer, Boothroyd, & Hodgins, 1998). The increased likelihood of suicide for individuals whose identity has been undermined by radical cultural change is particularly relevant for Aboriginal youth in Canada (Chandler & Lalonde, 1998; 1995). Given the wide variations of experience among Aboriginal communities, some bands show higher suicide rates than others, with some communities showing rates that are 800 times the national average, while other bands have virtually no suicide (Chandler et al., 1998). One possible explanation for these differences is cultural rehabilitation and preservation: Aboriginal communities that have taken steps to preserve and rehabilitate their own cultures have dramatically lower suicide rates (Chandler et al., 1998).

Young people who consider or attempt suicide tend to have histories of emotional illness. They are likely to be either perpetrators or victims of violence and to have school

Checkpoint ✔

Can you . . .

✔ Discuss factors affecting gender differences in adolescent depression?

✔ Tell how maltreatment of adolescents differs from maltreatment of younger children?

✔ Name the leading causes of death among adolescents, and discuss the dangers of firearm injury?

✔ Assess risk factors and prevention programs for teenage suicide?

Box 15-2 *Preventing Teenage Suicide*

What can be done to stem the alarming rise in suicide among young people? Many people intent on killing themselves keep their plans secret, but others send out signals well in advance. An attempt at suicide is sometimes a call for help, and some people die because they are more successful than they intended to be.

Warning signs include withdrawal from relationships; talking about death, the hereafter, or suicide; giving away prized possessions; drug or alcohol abuse; personality changes, such as a rise in anger, boredom, or apathy; unusual neglect of appearance; difficulty concentrating at work or in school; staying away from work, school, or other usual activities; complaints of physical problems when nothing is organically wrong; and eating or sleeping much more or much less than usual. Friends or family may be able to help by talking to a young person about his or her suicidal thoughts to bring them out in the open; telling others who are in a position to do something—the person's parents or spouse, other family members, a close friend, a therapist, or a counsellor; and showing the person that she or he has other options besides death, even though none of them may be ideal.

Telephone hotlines are the most common type of suicide intervention for adolescents, but their effectiveness appears to be minimal (Borowsky et al., 2001; Garland & Zigler, 1993). School-based screening programs have proliferated in recent years and have their advocates (Friedman, 2006). Although some observers worry that such programs may "put ideas in young people's heads," a randomized controlled trial of 2,342 high school students in New York state found *no* basis for that concern (Gould et al., 2005). However, there is little evidence that such programs reduce the risk of suicide or motivate adolescents who are contemplating suicide to seek help (Harvard Medical School, 2003c) Equally important is to attack the risk factors through programs to reduce substance abuse, violence, and access to guns and to strengthen families and improve parenting skills (Borowsky et al., 2001; Garland & Zigler, 1993).

Suicide intentions are sometimes accompanied by warning signs, such as withdrawal, as ways of calling out for help.

What's your view

Have you ever experienced any of the warning signs described in this box? What would you do if a close friend or family member showed one or more of these signs?

Check it out

For more information on this topic, go to **www.mcgrawhill.ca/olc/papalia,** which will direct you to links to statistics about suicide and to prevention materials.

---

problems, academic or behavioural. Many have suffered from maltreatment in childhood and have severe problems with relationships. They tend to think poorly of themselves, to feel hopeless, and to have poor impulse control and low tolerance for frustration and stress. These young people are often alienated from their parents and have no one outside the family to turn to. They also tend to have attempted suicide before or to have friends or family members who did so (Borowsky et al., 2001; Brent & Mann, 2006; Garland & Zigler, 1993; Johnson et al., 2002; NIMH, 1999a; "Suicide—Part I," 1996; Swedo et al., 1991). Alcohol plays a part in half of all teenage suicides (AAP Committee on Adolescence, 2000). Perhaps the key factor is a tendency toward impulsive aggression. Postmortem and imaging studies of the brains of persons who have attempted or completed suicide have identified neurocognitive deficits in executive function, risk assessment, and problem solving (Brent & Mann, 2006). Protective factors that reduce the risk of suicide include a sense of connectedness to family and school, emotional well-being, and academic achievement (Borowsky et al., 2001).

Box 15-2 discusses ways of preventing suicide.

Protective Factors: Health in Context

Checkpoint

Can you . . .

✔ Identify factors that tend to protect adolescents from health risks?

Adolescents' physical development, like that of younger children, does not occur in a vacuum. Young people live and grow in a social world. As we have pointed out throughout this book, the influences of the family and school environments, particularly, play an important part in physical and mental health.

A study of 12,118 students in Grades 7 through 12 in a random sample of 134 schools across the United States (Resnick et al., 1997) took a broad overview of risk factors and protective factors affecting four major aspects of adolescent health and well-being: emotional distress and suicidal behaviour; involvement in violence (fighting or threats or use of weapons); use of cigarettes, alcohol, and marijuana; and sexuality (including age of sexual initiation and any history of pregnancy). The students completed questionnaires and had 90-minute home interviews; during the sensitive portions of the interview, the young people listened to the questions through earphones and entered their answers on laptop computers. The adolescents' school administrators also filled out questionnaires.

The findings emphasize the interconnectedness of physical, cognitive, emotional, and social development. Perceptions of connectedness to others, both at home and at school, consistently affect young people's health and well-being in all domains. The findings underline the importance of parents' spending time with, and being available to, their children. Even more important, however, is an adolescent's sense that parents and teachers are warm and caring and that they have high expectations for the adolescent's achievement. These findings are clear and consistent with other research: Adolescents who are getting emotional support at home and are doing well in school have the best chance of avoiding the health hazards of adolescence.

Despite the perils of adolescence, most young people emerge from these years with a mature, healthy body and a zest for life. While their bodies have been developing, their minds have continued to develop too, as we will see in Chapter 16.

Summary and Key Terms

Adolescence: A Developmental Transition

Guidepost 1 What is adolescence, and what opportunities and risks does it entail?

- Adolescence is the transition from childhood to adulthood. Neither its beginning nor its end is clearly marked in industrialized societies; it lasts about a decade, between ages 11 or 12 and the late teens or early twenties.
- In some nonwestern cultures, "coming of age" is signified by special rites.
- Adolescence is full of opportunities for physical, cognitive, and psychosocial growth, but also of risks to healthy development. Risky behaviour patterns, such as drinking alcohol, drug abuse, sexual and gang activity, and use of firearms tend to be established early in adolescence. About 4 out of 5 young people experience no major problems.

  adolescence (402) puberty (402)

Puberty: The End of Childhood

Guidepost 2 What physical changes do adolescents experience, and how do these changes affect them psychologically?

- Puberty is triggered by hormonal changes, which may affect moods and behaviour. Puberty takes about 4 years, typically begins earlier in girls than in boys, and ends when a person can reproduce.
- Primary sex characteristics (the reproductive organs) enlarge and mature during puberty. Secondary sex characteristics also appear.
- During puberty, both boys and girls undergo an adolescent growth spurt. A secular trend toward earlier attainment of adult height and sexual maturity began about 100 years ago, probably because of improvements in living standards.
- The principal signs of sexual maturity are production of sperm (for males) and menstruation (for females). Spermarche typically occurs at age 13. Menarche occurs, on average, between the ages of 12 and 13 in Canada.
- Sexual attraction seems to begin at about age 10, when the adrenal glands increase their hormonal output.
- Teenagers, especially girls, tend to be sensitive about their physical appearance. Girls who mature early tend to adjust less easily than early maturing boys.

  adrenarche (404) gonadarche (404) primary sex characteristics (406) secondary sex characteristics (406) adolescent growth spurt (407) spermarche (408) menarche (408) secular trend (408)

The Adolescent Brain

Guidepost 3 What brain developments occur during adolescence, and how do they affect adolescent behaviour?

- The adolescent brain is not yet fully mature. Adolescents process information about emotions with the amygdala, whereas adults use the frontal lobe. Thus, adolescents tend to make less accurate, less reasoned judgments.
- A wave of overproduction of grey matter, especially in the frontal lobes, is followed by pruning of excess dendrites. Continuing myelination of the frontal lobes facilitates maturation of cognitive processing.
- Underdevelopment of frontal cortical systems connected with motivation, impulsivity, and addiction may help explain adolescents' tendency toward risk taking.
- Because of their developing brains, adolescents are particularly vulnerable to effects of alcohol and addictive drugs.

Physical and Mental Health

Guidepost 4 What are some common health problems and health risks of adolescence, and how can they be prevented?

- For the most part, the adolescent years are relatively healthy. Health problems are often are associated with poverty or a risk-taking lifestyle. Adolescents are less likely than younger children to get regular medical care.
- Many adolescents, especially girls, do not engage in regular vigorous physical activity.
- Many adolescents do not get enough sleep because the high school schedule is out of sync with their natural body rhythms.
- Three common eating disorders in adolescence are obesity, anorexia nervosa, and bulimia nervosa. All can have serious long-term effects. Anorexia and bulimia affect mostly girls. Outcomes for bulimia tend to be better than for anorexia.
- Adolescent substance abuse and dependence have lessened in recent years; still, drug use often begins as children move into middle school.
- Marijuana, alcohol, and tobacco are the most popular drugs with adolescents. All involve serious risks.
- Maltreatment of adolescents can lead to serious behaviour problems.
- Leading causes of death among adolescents include motor vehicle accidents, gun-related injury, and suicide.

  anorexia nervosa (415) bulimia nervosa (416) substance abuse (417) substance dependence (417)

CHAPTER SIXTEEN

Cognitive Development in Adolescence

I should place [the prime of a life] at between fifteen and sixteen. It is then, it always seems to me, that his vitality is at its highest: he has greatest sense of the ludicrous and least sense of dignity. After that time, decay begins to set in.

—Evelyn Waugh, *age 16, in a school debate,* 1920

Focus *Nelson Mandela, Freedom Fighter**

Nelson Mandela

Rolihlahla, the name Nelson Mandela's father gave him at his birth in 1918, means "stirring up trouble." And that is exactly what Mandela did throughout his long and finally successful struggle to topple apartheid, South Africa's rigid system of racial separation and subjugation.

Mandela's election as his country's first black president in April 1994—only 4 years after his emergence from 28 years behind bars for conspiring to overthrow the white-dominated government—was the realization of a dream formed in his youth. It was a dream kindled as Mandela sat quietly listening to his tribal elders reminisce about a bygone era of self-government more than a century earlier, before the coming of white people—an era of peace, freedom, and equality.

"The land . . . belonged to the whole tribe and there was no individual ownership whatsoever," Mandela told the court that sentenced him to prison in 1962. "There were no classes, no rich or poor and no exploitation of man by man. . . . The council was so completely democratic that all members of the tribe could participate in its deliberations. Chief and subject, warrior and medicine man, all took part" (Meer, 1988, p. 12). Mandela recognized that his forebears' way of life would not be viable in the modern world. But the vision of a society "in which none will be held in slavery or servitude, and in which poverty, want and insecurity shall be no more" served as a lifelong inspiration.

Mandela has royal blood: One of his ancestors ruled his Thembu tribe, and his father was chief of Mvezo, a small, isolated village in Transkei where Mandela was born. Mandela seems to have inherited his "proud rebelliousness" and "stubborn sense of fairness" (Mandela, 1994, p. 6): Not long after his birth, his father, a counsellor to tribal kings, was deposed for refusing to honour a summons to appear before the local British magistrate. For standing on his traditional prerogatives and defying the magistrate's authority, Mandela's father paid with his lands and fortune.

Mandela's mother, his father's third of four wives, moved with her baby and his three sisters to the nearby village of Qunu, where they grew up in a compound of mud huts. The family raised all their own food—cows and goats for milk, and mealies (a form of corn), which his mother ground between two stones to make bread or boiled over an open fire. At 5, Mandela became a herd boy, driving sheep and cattle through the fertile grasslands. His was a simple life, governed for the most part by the time-honoured rules of his tribe. But his mother, who had become a Christian, had him baptized in the Methodist church; and at 7, he became the first member of his family to go to school. It was his first teacher who gave him his English name, Nelson.

When Mandela was 9, his father died, and his life changed completely. His mother sent him to live at the tribal headquarters at Mqhekezweni. The acting regent, who owed his position to Mandela's father, had offered to become his guardian and raise him as his own son.

As Mandela grew into adolescence, he observed tribal meetings, where any member could speak and the regent listened quietly before summing up the consensus. This style of leadership deeply impressed Mandela and influenced his own demeanour as a leader in later years. He also watched his guardian preside over council meetings to which minor chiefs brought disputes to be tried. His fascination with the presentation of cases and the cross-examination of witnesses planted the seeds of an ambition to be a lawyer—an ambition he eventually fulfilled. From the visiting chiefs and headmen, he heard tales about early African warriors who had fought against European domination. These stories stirred his interest in his people's history and laid the groundwork for his political activism.

At the age of 16, Mandela underwent circumcision, the traditional ritual by which a boy becomes recognized as a man and a participant in tribal councils. At the concluding ceremony, the main speaker, Chief Meligqili, struck a discordant note. The promise of manhood, he said, was an empty one in a land where Africans were a conquered people. "Among these young men," he said, "are chiefs who will never rule because we have no power to govern ourselves; soldiers who will never fight for we have no weapons to fight with; scholars who will never teach because we have no place for them to study. The abilities, the intelligence, the promise of these young men will be squandered in their attempt to eke out a living doing the simplest, most mindless chores for the white man. These gifts [we give them] today are naught, for we cannot give them the greatest gift of all, which is freedom and independence." Although Mandela did not appreciate it at the time, that speech sparked his political awakening.

● ● ●

The formative influences of Mandela's adolescent years helped shape his moral and political thinking and his life's work. The lessons he had learned about leadership and about his people's past glory stood him in good stead as he directed the resistance to an increasingly repressive regime, first in the streets and then from his island prison. Those lessons remained with him as he eventually managed to negotiate a new nonracial constitution and free elections—accomplishments for which he received a Nobel Peace Prize in 1993.

In this chapter, we first examine the Piagetian stage of formal operations, which makes it possible for a young person like Nelson Mandela to visualize an ideal world. We also look at what David Elkind has identified as some immature aspects of adolescents' thought and at their moral development. Finally, we explore practical aspects of cognitive growth—issues of school and vocational choice.

After you have read and studied this chapter, you should be able to answer each of the Guidepost questions that appear at the top of the next page. Look for them again in the margins, where they point to important concepts throughout the chapter. To check your understanding of these Guideposts, review the end-of-chapter summary. Checkpoints located throughout the chapter will help you verify your understanding of what you have read.

*The main sources of biographical information about Nelson Mandela's youth are Benson (1986), Hargrove (1989), Harwood (1987), Mandela (1994), and Meer (1988).

Guideposts for Study

Guidepost 1

How do adolescents' thinking and use of language differ from younger children's?

formal operations In Piaget's theory, the final stage of cognitive development, characterized by the ability to think abstractly

Aspects of Cognitive Maturation

Adolescents not only look different from younger children; they also think differently. Their speed of information processing continues to increase, though not as dramatically as in middle childhood. Although their thinking may remain immature in some ways, they are capable of abstract reasoning and sophisticated moral judgments, and they can plan more realistically for the future.

Piaget's Stage of Formal Operations

Adolescents enter what Piaget called the highest level of cognitive development—**formal operations**—when they develop the capacity for abstract thought. This development, usually around age 11, gives them a new, more flexible way to manipulate information. No longer limited to the here and now, they can understand historical time and extraterrestrial space. They can use symbols for symbols (for example, letting the letter X stand for an unknown numeral) and thus can learn algebra and calculus. They can better appreciate metaphor and allegory and thus can find richer meanings in literature. They can think in terms of what *might* be, not just what *is*. They can imagine possibilities and can form and test hypotheses.

As Nelson Mandela did during his adolescence, people in the stage of formal operations can integrate what they have learned in the past with the challenges of the present and make plans for the future. Thought at this stage has a flexibility not possible in the stage of concrete operations. The ability to think abstractly has emotional implications, too. Earlier, a child could love a parent or hate a classmate. Now "the adolescent can love freedom or hate exploitation. . . . The possible and the ideal captivate both mind and feeling" (H. Ginsburg & Opper, 1979, p. 201).

Hypothetical-Deductive Reasoning

To appreciate the difference formal reasoning makes, let's follow the progress of a typical child in dealing with a classic Piagetian problem, the pendulum problem.* The child, Adam, is shown the pendulum—an object hanging from a string. He is then shown how he can change any of four factors: the length of the string, the weight of the object, the height from which the object is released, and the amount of force he may use to push the object. He is asked to figure out which factor or combination of factors determines how fast the pendulum swings. (This and other Piagetian tasks for assessing the achievement of formal operations are pictured in Figure 16-1.)

When Adam first sees the pendulum, he is not yet 7 years old and is in the preoperational stage. Unable to formulate a plan for attacking the problem, he tries one thing after another in a hit-or-miss manner. First he puts a light weight on a long string and

---

*This description of age-related differences in the approach to the pendulum problem is adapted from H. Ginsburg and Opper (1979).

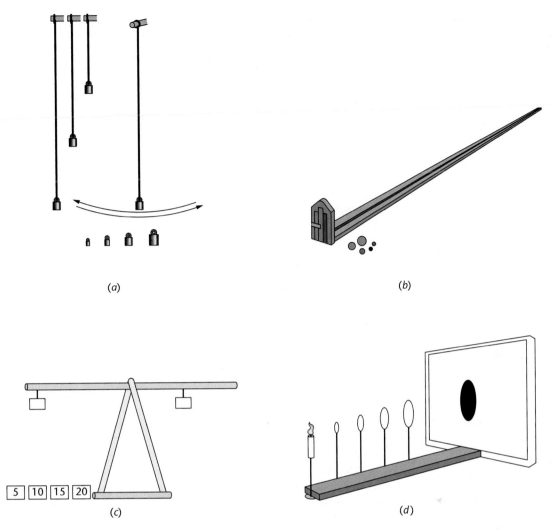

Figure 16-1

Piagetian tasks for measuring attainment of formal operations. (a) Pendulum. The pendulum's string can be shortened or lengthened, and weights of varying sizes can be attached to it. The student must determine what variables affect the speed of the pendulum's swing. (b) Motion in a horizontal plane. A spring device launches balls of varying sizes, which roll in a horizontal plane. The student must predict their stopping points. (c) Balance beam. A balance scale comes with weights of varying sizes, which can be hung at different points along the crossbar. The student must determine what factors affect whether or not the scale will balance. (d) Shadows. A board containing a row of peg holes is attached perpendicularly to the base of a screen. A light source and rings of varying diameters can be placed in the holes, at varying distances from the screen. The student must produce two shadows of the same size, using different-sized rings.

Source: Adapted from Small, 1990, Fig. 8-12.

pushes it; then he tries swinging a heavy weight on a short string; then he removes the weight entirely. Not only is his method random; he also cannot understand or report what has happened.

Adam next encounters the pendulum at age 10, when he is in the stage of concrete operations. This time, he discovers that varying the length of the string and the weight of the object affects the speed of the swing. However, because he varies both factors at the same time, he cannot tell which is critical or whether both are.

Adam is confronted with the pendulum for a third time at age 15, and this time he goes at the problem systematically. He designs an experiment to test all the possible hypotheses, varying one factor at a time—first, the length of the string; next, the weight of the object; then the height from which it is released; and finally, the amount of force used—each time holding the other three factors constant. In this way, he is able to determine that only one factor—the length of the string—determines how fast the pendulum swings.

Adam's solution of the pendulum problem shows that he has arrived at the stage of formal operations. He is now capable of **hypothetical-deductive reasoning.** He can develop

hypothetical-deductive reasoning Ability, believed by Piaget to accompany the state of formal operations, to develop, consider, and test hypotheses

a hypothesis and can design an experiment to test it. He considers all the relationships he can imagine and goes through them systematically, one by one, to eliminate the false and arrive at the true. Hypothetical-deductive reasoning gives him a tool to solve problems, from fixing the family car to constructing a political theory as Nelson Mandela did as a leader of the anti-apartheid movement.

What brings about the shift to formal reasoning? Piaget attributed it to a combination of brain maturation and expanding environmental opportunities. Both are essential: Even if young people's neurological development has advanced enough to permit formal reasoning, they can attain it only with appropriate environmental stimulation.

As with the development of concrete operations, schooling and culture seem to play a role in addition to bio-neurological maturation—as Piaget (1972) ultimately recognized. When adolescents in New Guinea and Rwanda were tested on the pendulum problem, none were able to solve it. On the other hand, Chinese children in Hong Kong, who had been to British schools, did at least as well as North American or European children. Schoolchildren in Central Java and New South Wales also showed some formal operational abilities (Gardiner & Kosmitzki, 2005). Apparently, this kind of thinking is a learned ability that is not equally necessary or equally valued in all cultures.

Knowing what questions to ask and what strategies work are keys to hypothetical-deductive reasoning. When 30 low-performing urban sixth-graders were asked to investigate factors in earthquake risk, those who received a suggestion to focus on one variable at a time made more valid inferences than those who were not given the suggestion (Kuhn & Dean, 2005). This result demonstrates that hypothetical-deductive reasoning can be taught and learned.

Evaluating Piaget's Theory

Although adolescents *do* tend to think more abstractly than younger children, there is debate about the precise age at which this advance occurs (Eccles, Wigfield, & Byrnes, 2003). Piaget's own writings provide many examples of children displaying aspects of scientific thinking well before adolescence. At the same time, Piaget seems to have *over*-estimated some older children's abilities. Many late adolescents and adults—perhaps one-third to one-half—seem incapable of abstract thought as Piaget defined it (Gardiner & Kosmitzki, 2005; Kohlberg & Gilligan, 1971; Papalia, 1972), and even those who are capable of abstract thinking do not always use it.

Piaget, in most of his early writings, paid little attention to individual differences, to variations in a child's performance of different kinds of tasks, or to social and cultural influences (Flavell et al., 1993). In his later years, Piaget himself "came to view his earlier model of the development of children's thinking, particularly formal operations, as flawed because it failed to capture the essential *role of the situation* in influencing and constraining . . . children's thinking" (Brown, Metz, & Campione, 1996, pp. 152–153).

Piaget's concept of formal operations as the apex of mature thought may be too narrow. Neo-Piagetian research suggests that adolescent thought processes are more flexible and varied. The type of thinking young people use is closely tied to what they are thinking *about,* as well as to the context of a problem and the kinds of information and thought a culture considers important (Case & Okamoto, 1996; Kuhn, 2006).

Furthermore, Piaget's theory does not adequately consider such cognitive advances as gains in information-processing capacity, accumulation of knowledge and expertise in specific fields, and the role of *metacognition,* the awareness and monitoring of one's own mental processes and strategies (Flavell et al., 2002). This ability to "think about what one is thinking about" and, thus, to manage one's own mental processes—in other words, enhanced executive function—may be the chief advance of adolescent thought, the result of changes occurring in the adolescent brain (Kuhn, 2006).

Elkind: Immature Characteristics of Adolescent Thought

We have seen how children develop from egocentric beings whose interest extends not much farther than the nipple to persons capable of solving abstract problems and imagining ideal societies. Yet in some ways adolescents' thinking seems strangely immature.

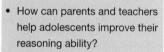

What's your view

- How can parents and teachers help adolescents improve their reasoning ability?

Checkpoint

Can you . . .

✔ Explain the difference between formal operational and concrete operational thinking, as exemplified by the pendulum problem?

✔ Cite factors influencing adolescents' development of formal reasoning?

✔ Evaluate Piaget's theory of formal operations?

They may be rude to adults, they have trouble making up their minds what to wear each day, and they often act as if the whole world revolved around them.

According to the psychologist David Elkind (1984, 1998), such behaviour stems from adolescents' inexperienced ventures into formal operational thought. This new way of thinking, which fundamentally transforms the way they look at themselves and their world, is as unfamiliar to them as their reshaped bodies, and they sometimes feel just as awkward in its use. As they try out their new powers, they may sometimes stumble, like an infant learning to walk.

This immaturity of thinking manifests itself in at least six characteristic ways, according to Elkind:

Argumentativeness—usually with parents—is a typical characteristic of adolescent thought, according to David Elkind.

1. *Idealism and criticalness:* As adolescents envision an ideal world, they realize how far the real world, for which they hold adults responsible, falls short. They become super-conscious of hypocrisy in public life; with their sharpened verbal reasoning, they relish magazines and entertainers that attack public figures with satire and parody. Convinced that they know better than adults how to run the world, they frequently find fault with their parents and other authority figures.

2. *Argumentativeness:* Adolescents are constantly looking for opportunities to try out their newfound formal reasoning abilities. They often become argumentative as they marshal facts and logic to build a case for, say, staying out later than their parents think they should.

3. *Indecisiveness:* Adolescents can keep many alternatives in mind at the same time, yet may lack effective strategies for choosing among them. They may have trouble making up their minds even about such simple things as what to wear and whether to go to the mall with a friend or to the computer to work on a school assignment.

4. *Apparent hypocrisy:* Young adolescents often do not recognize the difference between expressing an ideal, such as conserving energy, and making the sacrifices necessary to live up to it, such as driving less often.

5. *Self-consciousness:* Once they are in the stage of formal operations, adolescents can think about thinking—their own and other people's. However, in their preoccupation with their own mental state, adolescents often assume that everyone else is thinking about the same thing they are thinking about: themselves. A teenage girl may be mortified if she wears "the wrong thing" to a party, thinking that everyone else must be looking askance at her. Elkind refers to this self-consciousness as the **imaginary audience,** a conceptualized "observer" who is as concerned with a young person's thoughts and behaviour as he or she is. The imaginary audience fantasy is especially strong in the early teens but persists to a lesser degree into adult life.

6. *Specialness and invulnerability:* Elkind uses the term **personal fable** to denote a belief by adolescents that they are special, that their experience is unique, and that they are not subject to the rules that govern the rest of the world ("Other people get hooked from taking drugs, not me," or, "No one has ever been as deeply in love as I am"). According to Elkind, this special form of egocentrism underlies much risky, self-destructive behaviour. Like the imaginary audience, the personal fable continues in adulthood. It is the personal fable, says Elkind, that persuades people to take such everyday risks as driving a car despite statistics on highway deaths. Perhaps Elkind would say that it was in part the personal fable that led Nelson Mandela to engage in dangerous insurrectionary activities against a brutal dictatorship.

imaginary audience Elkind's term for an observer who exists only in an adolescent's mind and is as concerned with the adolescent's thoughts and actions as the adolescent is

personal fable Elkind's term for conviction that one is special, unique, and not subject to the rules that govern the rest of the world

The concepts of the imaginary audience and the personal fable have been widely accepted, but their validity as distinct earmarks of adolescence has little independent research support. In some studies of the personal fable, adolescents were *more* likely than university students or adults to see themselves as vulnerable to certain risks, such as alcohol and other drug problems, rather than *less* likely, as the personal fable would predict (Quadrel, Fischoff, & Davis, 1993).

It has been suggested that the imaginary audience and personal fable, rather than constituting universal features of adolescents' cognitive development, may be related to specific social experiences. For example, contrary to the personal fable, in a study of 2,694 urban black adolescents treated at an outpatient clinic in Washington, D.C., about 7 percent of the boys and more than 5 percent of the girls said they believed they would die within the next 2 years. Those who reported taking health risks or being exposed to risky behaviour such as weapon carrying were as much as 5.6 times more likely to hold such beliefs than those who had not seen or engaged in such behaviour. It is not clear whether these adolescents take risks because, living in dangerous neighbourhoods, they expect their lives to be short or whether they expect to die early because of the chances they take (Valadez-Meltzer, Silber, Meltzer, & D'Angelo, 2005).

Language Development

Children's use of language reflects their level of cognitive development. School-age children are quite proficient in use of language, but adolescence brings further refinements. Vocabulary continues to grow as reading matter becomes more adult. By ages 16 to 18 the average young person knows approximately 80,000 words (Owens, 1996).

With the advent of formal thought, adolescents can define and discuss such abstractions as *love, justice,* and *freedom.* They more frequently use such terms as *however, otherwise, anyway, therefore, really,* and *probably* to express logical relations between clauses or sentences. They become more conscious of words as symbols that can have multiple meanings; they take pleasure in using irony, puns, and metaphors (Owens, 1996).

Adolescents also become more skilled in *social perspective-taking,* the ability to understand another person's point of view and level of knowledge and to tailor their own speech accordingly. This ability is essential in order to persuade or just to engage in polite conversation. It undoubtedly helped Nelson Mandela in his eventually successful negotiations with his country's repressive rulers.

Conscious of their audience, adolescents speak a different language with peers and with adults (Owens, 1996; see Box 16-1). Teenage slang is part of the process of developing an independent identity separate from parents and the adult world (see Chapter 17). In creating such expressions as "That's sweet!" and "dabomb," young people use their new-found ability to play with words "to define their generation's unique take on values, tastes, and preferences" (Elkind, 1998, p. 29).

Changes in Information Processing in Adolescence

Changes in the way adolescents process information reflect the maturation of the brain's frontal lobes and may help explain the cognitive advances Piaget described. Which neural connections wither and which become strengthened is highly responsive to experience. Thus, progress in cognitive processing varies greatly among individual adolescents (Kuhn, 2006).

Researchers have identified two broad categories of measurable change in information processing: *structural change* and *functional change* (Eccles et al., 2003).*

Structural Change

Structural changes in adolescence may include (1) growth of information-processing capacity and (2) an increase in the amount of knowledge stored in long-term memory.

The capacity of working memory, which enlarges rapidly in middle childhood, may continue to increase during adolescence. The expansion of working memory enables older adolescents to deal with complex problems or decisions involving multiple pieces of information.

Information stored in long-term memory can be declarative, procedural, or conceptual. **Declarative knowledge** ("knowing that . . .") consists of all the factual knowledge a person has acquired (for example, knowing that $2 + 2 = 4$ and that John A. MacDonald was

Checkpoint ✔

Can you . . .

✔ Describe Elkind's six proposed aspects of immature adolescent thought, and explain how they may grow out of the transition to formal operational thought?

declarative knowledge Acquired factual knowledge stored in long-term memory

---

*Unless otherwise referenced, the discussion in these sections is indebted to Eccles et al., 2003.

Box 16-1 *"Pubilect": The Dialect of Adolescence*

"We're tight!"

"It's all good!"

"Chill!"

"Let's bounce!"

Adolescents' conversation is mainly about the people and events in their everyday world (Labov, 1992). They use slang (non-standard speech) to label people ("player" or "hottie"), to pronounce judgments ("That's cool!"), and to describe alcohol or drug-related activity ("She's twisted" or "He's blazed").

The Canadian linguist Marcel Danesi (1994),* argues that adolescent speech is more than just slang (which, of course, adults can use, too). Instead, it constitutes a dialect of its own: pubilect, "the social dialect of puberty" (p. 97). Pubilect is more than an occasional colourful expression. It is the primary mode of verbal communication among teenagers, by which they differentiate themselves from adults. As they approach puberty, youngsters absorb this dialect from slightly older peers. Like any other linguistic code, pubilect serves to strengthen group identity and to shut outsiders (adults) out. Teenage vocabulary is characterized by rapid change. Although some of its terms have entered common discourse, adolescents keep inventing new ones all the time.

Analyses of recorded samples of adolescent conversation reveal several key features of pubilect. First, it is an *emotive* code. Through exaggerated tone, slow and deliberate delivery, prolonged stress, accompanying gestures, and vulgar interjections, it draws attention to feelings and attitudes ("Yeah, riiight!" "Well, duuuh!"). The use of fillers, such as the word *like,* as well as the typical pattern of narrative intonation, in which each phrase or sentence seems to end with a question mark, reflects unconscious uncertainty and serves to draw the listener into the speaker's state of mind.

A second feature of pubilect is its *connotative* function. Teenagers coin descriptive words (or extend the meaning of existing words) to convey their view of their world and the people in it—often, in highly metaphorical ways. A person does not need a dictionary to figure out the meanings of such expressions as "space cadet" and "ditz." Such terms provide a ready lexicon for quick, automatic value judgments about others.

In Canada, there is not just a single youth culture, but many subcultures. Vocabulary may differ by gender, ethnicity, age, geographical region, neighbourhood (city, suburban, or rural) and type of school (public or private) (Labov, 1992). Also, pubilect is *clique-coded:* It varies from one clique to another. "Druggies" and "jocks" engage in different kinds of activities, which form the main subjects of their conversation. This talk, in turn, cements bonds within the clique. Males use verbal duelling to assert power. Contenders for leadership trade insults and clever retorts in an effort to symbolically gain the upper hand in front of the group.

A study of teenage speech patterns in Naples, Italy, suggests that similar features may emerge "in any culture where teenagerhood constitutes a distinct social category" (Danesi, 1994, p. 123). Neapolitan teenagers use "mmmm" much as U.S. teenagers use "like": "Devo, mmmm, dire che, mmmm, non capisco, mmmm, . . ." ("I have, mmmm, to say that, mmmm, I don't understand, mmmm, . . ."). Exaggerated tone and rising intonation at the ends of phrases are also common. The Italian young people have terms roughly equivalent to the English "cool" (*togo*), "loser" (*grasta*), and "dork" or "nerd" (*secchione*). Other investigators report that adolescents in Milan, Bologna, and other northern Italian cities speak "the language of rock and roll." This cultural borrowing—the result of wide dissemination of English-language television channels, such as MTV—may well be creating a "symbolic universe" for teenagers around the world (Danesi, 1994, p. 123).

What's your view?

- Can you remember "pubilect" expressions from your own adolescence?
- When and why did you use such expressions?
- What was their effect on others your age? On adults?

Check it out

For more information on this topic, go to **www.mcgrawhill.ca/olc/papalia.**

*Unless otherwise referenced, the source of this discussion is Danesi, 1994.

Canada's first prime minister). **Procedural knowledge** (knowing how to . . .") consists of all the skills a person has acquired, such as being able to multiply and divide and drive a car. **Conceptual knowledge** ("knowing why") is an understanding of, for example, why an algebraic equation remains true if the same amount is added or subtracted from both sides.

procedural knowledge Acquired skills stored in long-term memory

conceptual knowledge Acquired interpretive understandings stored in long-term memory

Functional Change

Processes for obtaining, handling, and retaining information are *functional* aspects of cognition. Among these are learning, remembering, and reasoning, all of which improve during adolescence.

Among the most important functional changes are: (1) a continued increase in processing speed (Kuhn, 2006), and (2) further development of *executive function* (refer back to Chapter 13), which includes such skills as selective attention, decision making, inhibitory control of impulsive responses, and management of working memory. These skills seem to develop at varying rates (Blakemore & Choudbury, 2006; Kuhn, 2006). In one study, researchers tested processing speed, inhibitory control, and working memory in 245 eight- to 30-year-olds by measuring their eye movements in response to cognitive tasks. For example, participants were told to remember the location of a light that appeared in their peripheral field of vision while keeping their eyes focused on the centre and then, after the light went out, to look at the spot where it had been seen. Adolescents reached adult-level performance in response inhibition at age 14, processing speed at 15, and working memory at 19. Although each process appears to mature independently, each seems to aid in the development of the others (Luna et al., 2004).

However, improvements observed in laboratory situations do not necessarily carry over to real life, where behaviour depends in part on motivation and emotion regulation. Many older adolescents make poorer real-world decisions than younger adolescents do. In the game Twenty Questions, the object is to ask as few yes or no questions as necessary to discover the identity of a person, place, or thing by systematically narrowing down the categories within which the answer might fall. In one study (Drumm & Jackson, 1996), high school students, especially boys, showed a greater tendency than either early adolescents or college students to jump to guessing the answer. This pattern of guesswork may reflect a penchant for impulsive, risky behaviour. As we discussed in Chapter 15, adolescents' rash judgments may be related to immature brain development, which may permit feelings to override reason.

Checkpoint ✔

Can you . . .

✔ Identify several characteristics of adolescents' language development that reflect cognitive advances?

✔ Name two major kinds of changes in adolescents' cognitive processing, and give examples of each?

Guidepost 2

On what basis do adolescents make moral judgments, and how does pro-social behaviour vary?

Moral Development

As children grow older and attain higher cognitive levels, they become capable of more complex reasoning about moral issues. Their tendencies toward altruism and empathy increase as well. Adolescents are better able than younger children to take another person's perspective, to solve social problems, to deal with interpersonal relationships, and to see themselves as social beings. All of these tendencies foster moral development.

Let's look at Lawrence Kohlberg's groundbreaking theory of moral reasoning, at Carol Gilligan's influential work on moral development in women and girls, and at research on pro-social behaviour in adolescence.

Kohlberg's Theory of Moral Reasoning

A woman is near death from cancer. A druggist has discovered a drug that doctors believe might save her. The druggist is charging $2,000 for a small dose—10 times what the drug costs him to make. The sick woman's husband, Heinz, borrows from everyone he knows but can scrape together only $1,000. He begs the druggist to sell him the drug for $1,000 or let him pay the rest later. The druggist refuses, saying, "I discovered the drug and I'm going to make money from it." Heinz, desperate, breaks into the man's store and steals the drug. Should Heinz have done that? Why or why not? (Kohlberg, 1969).

Heinz's problem is the most famous example of Lawrence Kohlberg's approach to studying moral development. Starting in the 1950s, Kohlberg and his colleagues posed hypothetical dilemmas like this one to 75 boys ages 10, 13, and 16, and continued to question them periodically for more than 30 years. At the heart of each dilemma was the concept of justice. By asking respondents how they arrived at their answers, Kohlberg, like Piaget, concluded that the way people look at moral issues reflects cognitive development.

Kohlberg's Levels and Stages

Moral development in Kohlberg's theory bears some resemblance to Piaget's (refer back to Chapter 13), but Kohlberg's model is more complex. On the basis of thought processes shown by responses to his dilemmas, Kohlberg (1969) described three levels of moral reasoning, each divided into two stages (see Table 16-1):

- *Level I:* **Preconventional morality.** People act under external controls. They obey rules to avoid punishment or reap rewards, or act out of self-interest. This level, said Kohlberg, is typical of children ages 4 to 10.

preconventional morality First level of Kohlberg's theory of moral reasoning, in which control is external and rules are obeyed in order to gain rewards or avoid punishment, or out of self-interest

| Table 16-1 | Kohlberg's Six Stages of Moral Reasoning |

Levels	Stages of Reasoning	Typical Answers to Heinz's Dilemma
Level I: Preconventional morality (ages 4 to 10)	*Stage 1: Orientation toward punishment and obedience.* "What will happen to me?" Children obey rules to avoid punishment. They ignore the motives of an act and focus on its physical form (such as the size of a lie) or its consequences (for example, the amount of physical damage).	*Pro:* "He should steal the drug. It isn't really bad to take it. It isn't as if he hadn't asked to pay for it first. The drug he'd take is worth only $200; he's not really taking a $2,000 drug." *Con:* "He shouldn't steal the drug. It's a big crime. He didn't get permission; he used force and broke and entered. He did a lot of damage and stole a very expensive drug."
	Stage 2: Instrumental purpose and exchange. "You scratch my back, I'll scratch yours." Children conform to rules out of self-interest and consideration for what others can do for them. They look at an act in terms of the human needs it meets and differentiate this value from the act's physical form and consequences.	*Pro:* "It's all right to steal the drug, because his wife needs it and he wants her to live. It isn't that he wants to steal, but that's what he has to do to save her." *Con:* "He shouldn't steal it. The druggist isn't wrong or bad; he just wants to make a profit. That's what you're in business for—to make money."
Level II: Conventional morality (ages 10 to 13 or beyond)	*Stage 3: Maintaining mutual relations, approval of others, the golden rule.* "Am I a good boy or girl?" Children want to please and help others, can judge the intentions of others, and develop their own ideas of what a good person is. They evaluate an act according to the motive behind it or the person performing it, and they take circumstances into account.	*Pro:* "He should steal the drug. He is only doing something that is natural for a good husband to do. You can't blame him for doing something out of love for his wife. You'd blame him if he didn't love his wife enough to save her. *Con:* "He shouldn't steal. If his wife dies, he can't be blamed. It isn't because he's heartless or that he doesn't love her enough to do everything that he legally can. The druggist is the selfish or heartless one."
	Stage 4: Social concern and conscience. "What if everybody did it?" People are concerned with doing their duty, showing respect for higher authority, and maintaining the social order. They consider an act always wrong, regardless of motive or circumstances, if it violates a rule and harms others.	*Pro:* "You should steal it. If you did nothing, you'd be letting your wife die. It's your responsibility if she dies. You have to take it with the idea of paying the druggist." *Con:* "It is a natural thing for Heinz to want to save his wife, but it's still always wrong to steal. He knows he's taking a valuable drug from the man who made it."
Level III: Postconventional morality (early adolescence, or not until young adulthood, or never)	*Stage 5: Morality of contract, of individual rights, and of democratically accepted law.* People think in rational terms, valuing the will of the majority and the welfare of society. They generally see these values as best supported by adherence to the law. While they recognize that there are times when human need and the law conflict, they believe it is better for society in the long run if they obey the law.	*Pro:* "The law wasn't set up for these circumstances. Taking the drug in this situation isn't really right, but it's justified." *Con:* "You can't completely blame someone for stealing, but extreme circumstances don't really justify taking the law into your own hands. You can't have people stealing whenever they are desperate. The end may be good, but the ends don't justify the means."
	Stage 6: Morality of universal ethical principles. People do what they as individuals think is right, regardless of legal restrictions or the opinions of others. They act in accordance with internalized standards, knowing that they would condemn themselves if they did not.	*Pro:* "This is a situation that forces him to choose between stealing and letting his wife die. In a situation where the choice must be made, it is morally right to steal. He has to act in terms of the principle of preserving and respecting life." *Con:* "Heinz is faced with the decision of whether to consider the other people who need the drug just as badly as his wife. Heinz ought to act not according to his feelings for his wife, but considering the value of all the lives involved."

Source: Adapted from Kohlberg, 1969; Lickona, 1976.

- *Level II:* **Conventional morality (or morality of conventional role conformity).** People have internalized the standards of authority figures. They are concerned about being "good," pleasing others, and maintaining the social order. This level is typically reached after age 10; many people never move beyond it, even in adulthood.
- *Level III:* **Postconventional morality (or morality of autonomous moral principles).** People recognize conflicts between moral standards and make their own judgments on the basis of principles of right, fairness, and justice, as Nelson Mandela did during adulthood. People generally do not reach this level of moral reasoning until at least early adolescence, or more commonly in young adulthood, if ever.

Kohlberg later added a transitional level between Levels II and III, when people no longer feel bound by society's moral standards but have not yet developed rationally derived principles of justice. Instead, they base their moral decisions on personal feelings.

In Kohlberg's theory, it is the reasoning underlying a person's response to a moral dilemma, not the answer itself, that indicates the stage of moral development. As illustrated in Table 16-1, two people who give opposite answers may be at the same stage if their reasoning is based on similar factors.

Some adolescents, and even some adults, remain at Kohlberg's Level I. Like young children, they seek to avoid punishment or satisfy their own needs. Most adolescents, and most adults, seem to be at Level II, usually in Stage 3. They conform to social conventions, support the status quo, and do the "right" thing to please others or to obey the law. (For Nelson Mandela, the event that triggered his emergence from this stage was his circumcision ceremony at age 16, when he listened to the shocking speech that challenged the morality of the system into which he was being initiated.) Often adolescents show periods of apparent disequilibrium when advancing from one level to another (Eisenberg & Morris, 2004) or fall back on other ethical systems, such as religious prescriptions, rather than Kohlberg's justice-based one (Thoma & Rest, 1999).

Before people can develop a fully principled (Level III) morality, Kohlberg said, they must recognize the relativity of moral standards. Many young people question their earlier moral views when they enter high school or university or college or the world of work and encounter people whose values, culture, and ethnic background are different from their own. Still, very few people reach a level where they can choose among differing moral standards. In fact, at one point Kohlberg questioned the validity of Stage 6, morality based on universal ethical principles, because so few people seem to attain it. Later, he proposed a seventh, "cosmic" stage, in which people consider the effect of their actions not only on other people but on the universe as a whole (Kohlberg, 1981; Kohlberg & Ryncarz, 1990).

Evaluating Kohlberg's Theory

Kohlberg, building on Piaget, inaugurated a profound shift in the way we look at moral development. Instead of viewing morality solely as the attainment of control over self-gratifying impulses, investigators now study how children and adults base moral judgments on their growing understanding of the social world.

Research has supported some aspects of Kohlberg's theory but has left others in question. The American boys whom Kohlberg and his colleagues followed through adulthood progressed through Kohlberg's stages in sequence, and none skipped a stage. Their moral judgments correlated positively with age, education, IQ, and socio-economic status (Colby, Kohlberg, Gibbs, & Lieberman, 1983). More recent research, however, has cast doubt on the delineation of some of Kohlberg's stages (Eisenberg & Morris, 2004). A study of children's judgments about laws and lawbreaking suggests that some children can reason flexibly about such issues as early as age 6 (Helwig & Jasiobedzka, 2001).

One reason the ages attached to Kohlberg's levels are so variable is that people who have achieved a high level of cognitive development do not always reach a comparably high level of moral development. A certain level of cognitive development is *necessary* but not *sufficient* for a comparable level of moral development. Thus, other processes

Early adolescent girls have more intimate social relationships than early adolescent boys and are more concerned about caring for others. This may help explain why girls in this age group tend to score higher than boys on moral judgments.

besides cognition must be at work. Some investigators suggest that moral activity is motivated not only by abstract considerations of justice, but also by such emotions as empathy, guilt, and distress and the internalization of pro-social norms (Eisenberg & Morris, 2004; Gibbs, 1991, 1995; Gibbs & Schnell, 1985). It also has been argued that Kohlberg's Stages 5 and 6 cannot fairly be called the most mature stages of moral development because they restrict "maturity" to a select group of people given to philosophical reflection (J. C. Gibbs, 1995).

Furthermore, there is not always a clear relationship between moral reasoning and moral behaviour. People at postconventional levels of reasoning do not necessarily act more morally than those at lower levels. Other factors, such as specific situations, conceptions of virtue, and concern for others contribute to moral behaviour (Colby & Damon, 1992; Fischer & Pruyne, 2003). Perhaps one problem is the remoteness from young people's experience of such dilemmas as the "Heinz" situation. (Box 16-2 describes adolescents' moral judgments on everyday issues.) Generally speaking, however, adolescents who are more advanced in moral reasoning do tend to be more moral in their behaviour as well as better adjusted and higher in social competence, whereas anti-social adolescents tend to use less mature moral reasoning (Eisenberg & Morris, 2004).

A practical problem in using Kohlberg's system is its time-consuming testing procedures. The standard dilemmas need to be presented to each person individually and then scored by trained judges. One alternative is the Defining Issues Test (DIT), in which students rate and rank a list of statements rather than being asked to articulate the issues and arguments involved (Rest, 1975; Rest, Deemer, Barnett, & Spickelm, 1986). The DIT can be given quickly to a group and scored objectively. However, the DIT may tend to overestimate the degree of moral development (Rest et al., 1999).

Influence of Parents and Peers Neither Piaget nor Kohlberg considered parents important to children's moral development, but more recent research emphasizes parents' contribution in both the cognitive and the emotional realms. Adolescents with supportive, authoritative parents who stimulate them to question and expand on their moral reasoning tend to reason at higher levels (Eisenberg & Morris, 2004).

Peers also affect moral reasoning by talking with each other about moral conflicts. Having more close friends, spending quality time with them, and being perceived as a leader are associated with higher moral reasoning (Eisenberg & Morris, 2004).

What's your view

- Can you think of a time when you, or someone you know, acted contrary to his or her own moral judgment? Why do you think this happened?

Box 16-2 *How Do Psychosocial Issues Affect Adolescents' Moral Judgments?*

How many adolescents face the problem of having to get a rare and expensive medicine for a mortally ill spouse? Not many do. And yet, Kohlberg's theory of moral development is based on responses to dilemmas like this. Today some researchers are instead interviewing adolescents about moral issues they are likely to confront in everyday life, such as whether and how a bystander should respond to aggression, under what circumstances it might be all right to break a school rule, and whether to admit someone from a minority group to an exclusive club. The findings suggest that psychosocial issues, such as the needs for peer acceptance and personal autonomy, may be important factors in adolescents' moral choices.

In one study (Tisak & Tisak, 1996), interviewers asked 111 working-class and middle-class 10-, 12-, and 14-year-olds in rural Ohio what a person their age *would* do and *should* do, and why, when witnessing a good friend or a younger sibling hit or push someone, tear a book, or break a game. The answers fell into five main categories: (1) *looking out for others' welfare* ("He [the victim] will get hurt if she [the bystander] doesn't do something to stop it"), (2) *helping the aggressor avoid punishment* ("She will get in trouble if she continues to hit"), (3) *family responsibility* ("He is supposed to make sure his brother doesn't do that"), (4) *maintaining solidarity with friends* ("She will lose her as a friend [if she intervenes]"), and (5) *importance of the consequences* ("Why should she do anything, it's not important").

Older participants were less concerned about the welfare of the victim than about maintaining solidarity with the aggressor or helping him or her avoid punishment, perhaps reflecting adolescents' growing need for peer acceptance. However, they were less inclined to expect or favour *any* intervention, perhaps because they felt that the aggressor and the victim should be able to resolve the dispute themselves. Respondents of all ages thought a bystander would be more likely to stop a sibling's aggression than a friend's and had a greater obligation to do so. Girls were more apt to expect a bystander to intervene, though boys were just as likely to think it would be wrong not to. This finding may reflect girls' greater confidence in their ability to influence a peer's behaviour.

In another study, 120 students from Grades 5, 7, 9, and 11 were asked about the legitimacy of school rules (Smetana & Bitz, 1996). Both pre-adolescents and adolescents agreed that three kinds of conduct should be regulated: (1) *immoral* behaviour violating the rights and welfare of others, such as stealing, fighting, or failing to return textbooks; (2) *unconventional* behaviour violating customary standards, such as acting up in class, swearing, coming late, or talking back to the teacher; and (3) *imprudent* behaviour, such as smoking, drinking, taking drugs, and eating junk food for lunch. The young people viewed *personal* behaviour, such as whom to sit next to and talk to, choice of clothing or hairstyle, and eating or reading comics in class, as matters to decide for themselves.

The respondents were almost evenly split in their judgments about behaviour that is customarily regulated in school but not in other contexts, such as kissing a boyfriend or girlfriend in the hall, leaving class without permission, keeping forbidden items in a school locker, and passing notes to friends in class. As compared with Grade 5 students, older participants were more likely to view this kind of behaviour as a matter of personal discretion rather than a proper subject for regulation. Adolescents' views about the legitimacy of rules were important predictors of how often they broke the rules, according to their own and teachers' reports.

In a third study (Phinney & Cobb, 1996), 120 European-American and Hispanic-American students in Grades 5, 8, and 11 were asked how they would respond to a Hispanic or European-American student's request to join an exclusive school club in which all the members were of the other ethnic group. In half of the cases, the hypothetical applicant was of the same ethnic group as the respondent; in the other half, of the other ethnic group.

About three-quarters of the students favoured accepting the applicant, mainly out of *fairness* ("Everybody should be treated the same") or *concern with individual welfare* ("So they won't hurt her feelings"). Other reasons were *upholding social principles* ("If they choose their own people, then they're never going to get along with each other") and the benefits of *cultural diversity* ("They can get to meet new people . . . learn about different cultures"). Less than 10 percent favoured excluding the outsider, citing the *right of club members* to select their associates ("They're the ones who started this club and . . . they should have the right . . . to choose who they want") or *cultural barriers* ("If they start speaking Spanish, she's going to feel left out").

In contrast to these two groups, who strongly held to their views when challenged, about 12 percent of the respondents (mostly students in Grades 5 and 8) originally favoured admission but switched when the interviewer suggested that "some people" would consider exclusion appropriate. The original reasons given by those who switched were largely pragmatic rather than principled ("Let him in, otherwise it'll cause a lot of tension").

Ethnicity did not affect the decisions but did seem to influence the reasons. European-American students tended to appeal to rights of free choice and rules ("The school says they could choose their own members") as reasons for exclusion, Hispanics to cultural barriers. Girls also tended to refer to rules. In line with Kohlberg's theory, older adolescents who favoured inclusion were more likely than younger ones to show awareness of the impact on the social order ("If you start getting your own little groups . . . that hurts the country").

What's your view?

What would be your answers to the three issues presented here, and why?

Check it out!

For more information on this topic, go to **www.mcgrawhill.ca/olc/papalia,** which will direct you to a Web site with links to a character education reading list and many projects and reports about character education.

Cross-cultural Validity It is doubtful how accurately Kohlberg's system represents moral reasoning in non-western cultures (Eisenberg & Morris, 2004). Older people in non-western countries do tend to score at higher stages than younger people. However, people in non-western cultures rarely score above Stage 4 (Edwards, 1981; Nisan & Kohlberg, 1982; Snarey, 1985), suggesting that some aspects of Kohlberg's model may not fit the cultural values of these societies. For example, children 7, 9, and 11 years old, in Taiwan, mainland China, and Canada were read stories about child characters telling lies. In Taiwan and mainland China, older children expressed positive opinions about lying to mask good deeds that they had done, whereas children at all ages in Canada had negative attitudes about lying. These results demonstrate an emphasis on modesty and self-effacing behaviour in Chinese traditional values (Lee, Xu, Fu, Cameron, & Chen, 2001).

Gilligan's Theory: An Ethic of Care

On the basis of research on women, Carol Gilligan (1982) asserted that Kohlberg's theory is oriented toward values more important to men than to women. Gilligan claimed that women see morality not so much in terms of justice and fairness as of responsibility to show caring and avoid harm. They focus on not turning away from others rather than on not treating others unfairly (Eisenberg & Morris, 2004).

Research has not found much support for Gilligan's claim of a male bias in Kohlberg's stages (Brabeck & Shore, 2003; Jaffee & Hyde, 2000), and she has since modified her position. However, research *has* found small gender differences in care-related moral reasoning among adolescents in some cultures (Eisenberg & Morris, 2004). For example, early adolescent girls in the United States tend to emphasize care-related concerns more than boys do, especially when tested with open-ended questions ("How important is it to keep promises to a friend?") or self-chosen moral dilemmas related to their own experience (Garmon, Basinger, Gregg, & Gibbs, 1996). This may be because girls generally mature earlier and have more intimate social relationships (Garmon et al., 1996; Skoe & Diessner, 1994). In an analysis of 113 studies, girls and women were more likely to think in terms of care and boys and men in terms of justice, but these differences were small (Jaffee & Hyde, 2000).

Aside from possible gender differences, some researchers have studied prosocial (similar to care-oriented) moral reasoning as an alternative to Kohlberg's justice-based system. Pro-social moral reasoning is reasoning about moral dilemmas in which one person's needs or desires conflict with those of others in situations in which social rules or norms are unclear or nonexistent. In a longitudinal study that followed children into early adulthood, prosocial reasoning based on personal reflection about consequences and on internalized values and norms increased with age, whereas reasoning based on such stereotypes as "it's nice to help" decreased from childhood into the late teens (Eisenberg & Morris, 2004).

Pro-social Behaviour and Volunteer Activity

Just as adolescents' moral reasoning is more sophisticated and shows more concern about others than that of younger children, pro-social behaviour typically increases from childhood through adolescence (Eisenberg & Morris, 2004). Girls tend to show more pro-social behaviour than boys (Eisenberg & Fabes, 1998), and this difference becomes more pronounced in adolescence (Fabes, Carlo, Kupanoff, & Laible, 1999).

Girls tend to see themselves as more empathic and pro-social than boys do, and parents of girls emphasize social responsibility more than parents of sons (Eisenberg & Morris, 2004). In a large-scale study, this was true of 18-year-olds in seven countries—Australia, United States, Sweden, Hungary, Czech Republic, Bulgaria, and Russia (Flannagan, Bowes, Jonsson, Csapo, & Sheblanova, 1998). As with younger children, parents who use inductive discipline are more likely to have prosocial adolescents than parents who use power-assertive techniques.

About half of all adolescents engage in some sort of community service or volunteer activity. These pro-social activities enable adolescents to become involved in adult society, to explore their potential roles as part of the community and to link their developing

Checkpoint ✔

Can you . . .

✔ List Kohlberg's levels and
stages, and discuss factors
that influence how rapidly
children and adolescents
progress through them?

✔ Evaluate Kohlberg's theory
with regard to the role of
emotion and socialization,
parent and peer influences,
and cross-cultural validity?

✔ Explain the difference between
Gilligan's and Kohlberg's
standards of moral reasoning,
and discuss gender effects?

✔ Discuss individual differences
in prosocial behaviour, such
as volunteering?

sense of identity to civic involvement. Adolescent volunteers tend to be outgoing and to have a high degree of self-understanding and commitment to others. Girls tend to volunteer more than boys, and adolescents with high SES volunteer more than those with lower SES (Eisenberg & Morris, 2004). Students who engage in volunteer work outside of school tend, as adults, to be more engaged in their communities than those who do not (Eccles, 2004).

Educational and Vocational Issues

School is a central organizing experience in most adolescents' lives. It offers opportunities to learn information, master new skills, and sharpen old ones; to participate in sports, the arts, and other activities; to explore vocational choices; and to be with friends. It widens intellectual and social horizons. Some adolescents, however, experience school not as an opportunity but as one more hindrance on the road to adulthood. The school experience can have profound effects, not only on cognitive development, but on psychosocial adjustment and even on physical health. In Canada, as in all other industrialized countries and in some developing countries as well, more students finish high school than ever before, and many enroll in higher education (Eccles et al., 2003; OECD, 2004). In 2006, 84 percent of Canadian youth had received a high school diploma or equivalent credential (OECD, 2006). Among the 30 member countries of the Organisation for Economic Cooperation and Development (OECD, 2004), average levels of educational attainment range from only 7.4 years of schooling in Mexico to 13.8 years in Norway.

Canada, with about 45 percent of the adult population having completed either college or university, is on the high end of this international comparison. Canadian adolescents, on average, do better on academic achievement tests, measuring skills such as mathematics, than adolescents in many other OECD countries (Council of Ministers of Education (Canada) & OECD, 2006).

Let's examine influences on school achievement. Then we'll look at why some young people drop out of school, and what penalties they pay. Finally, we'll consider planning for higher education and vocations.

Influences on School Achievement

Guidepost 3

What influences affect
adolescents' school success and
their educational and vocational
planning and preparation?

The proportion of adolescents staying in school is rising: In 1980–81, 68 percent of young people were students, and currently that has risen to 84 percent (CICH, 2000; Canadian Council on Learning, 2005).

Students who like school do well in school and are likely to remain in school (Samdal & Dür, 2000). As in the elementary grades, such factors as socio-economic status, and the nature of the home environment influence school achievement in adolescence. Other factors include gender, ethnicity, parenting practices, peer influence, quality of schooling, and—perhaps first and foremost—students' motivation to learn.

Student Motivation and Self-Efficacy

In western countries, including Canada, educational practices are based on the assumption that students are, or can be, motivated to learn. Educators emphasize the value of intrinsic motivation—the student's desire to learn for the sake of learning (Larson & Wilson, 2004). Unfortunately, many Canadian students are *not* self-motivated, and motivation often declines as they enter high school. Many are bored, some resist learning or give up easily, and some (as we will discuss later) drop out of school (Eccles, 2004; Larson & Wilson, 2004).

According to Albert Bandura (Bandura, Barbaranelli, Caprara, & Pastorelli, 1996; Zimmerman, Bandura, & Martinez-Pons, 1992), whose social-cognitive theory we discussed in Chapters 2 and 11, students who are high in *self-efficacy*—who believe that they can master academic material and regulate their own learning—are more likely to try to achieve and more likely to succeed than students who do not believe in their own abilities. In a study of 116 ninth and tenth graders in two U.S. high schools, students' perceived self-efficacy predicted the social studies grades they expected and achieved. Students' goals were influenced by their parents' goals for them, but students' beliefs about their own abilities were more influential (Zimmerman et al., 1992). In a longitudinal study of 140 eighth graders, students' self-discipline was twice as important as IQ in accounting for their grades and achievement test scores and for selection into a competitive high school program at the end of the year (Duckworth & Seligman, 2005).

In many cultures, education is *not* based on personal motivation but on such factors as duty (India), submission to authority (Islamic countries), and participation in the family and community (sub-Saharan Africa). In the countries of East Asia, students are expected to learn, not for the value of learning, but to meet family and societal expectations of perfection. Learning is expected to require intense effort, and students who fail or fall behind feel obligated to try again. This may help explain why, in international comparisons in science and math, East Asian students substantially surpass most other students. On the other hand, East Asian cultures tend to encourage passive, uncritical conformity and suppress creativity. And, because of the heavy reliance on competitive testing to select students for continued education and careers, students tend to show high levels of anxiety, stress, and depression (Larson & Wilson, 2004). In developing countries, issues of motivation pale in the light of social and economic barriers to education: inadequate or absent schools and educational resources, the need for child labour to support the family, barriers to schooling for girls or cultural subgroups, and early marriage (Larson & Wilson, 2004). Thus, as we discuss factors in educational success, which are drawn largely from studies in Canada, the U.S., and other western countries, we need to remember that they do not apply to all cultures.

Importance of SES and Related Family Characteristics

High socio-economic status is an important predictor of academic success, according to a study of 15-year-olds' mathematical literacy in 20 relatively high-income countries (Hampden-Thompson & Johnston, 2006). In all countries, students with at least one postsecondary-educated parent performed better than students whose parents had lower educational levels. A similar gap occurred between students whose parents had high occupational status and those whose parents were of middle or low occupational status. Having more than 200 books in the home also was associated with higher scores. All of these are indicators of socio-economic status. Living in a two-parent family—another key predictor of math competence in all 20 countries—also was related to SES. In addition to family SES, the neighbourhood SES, as well as the average SES of a classroom can have their own influences on student achievement, according to the NLSCY (Frempong & Willms, 2002; Willms, 1996).

When a school has a predominance of low-income children, negative effects of low socio-economic status tend to spread through the school population, affecting student achievement (Pong, 1997). Still, many young people from disadvantaged neighbourhoods do well in school and improve their condition in life. What may make the difference is **social capital:** the family and community resources children can draw upon. Parents who invest time and effort in their children and who have a strong network of community support build the family's social capital (J. S. Coleman, 1988).

social capital Family and community resources on which a person or family can draw

Gender

Internationally, in 2000, girls were better readers than boys in all of 43 participating countries. Boys were ahead in mathematical literacy in about half of the countries, though these gender differences were smaller (OECD, 2004). Adolescent boys and girls score about the same on standardized tests in most subject-matter areas (Freeman, 2004; Sen et al., 2005). Boys have had a slight edge on standardized tests of math and science, but this gender gap appears to be shrinking as girls take equally challenging math and science courses and do as well or better in them (Spelke, 2005). Girls do better than boys on assessments of reading and writing (Freeman, 2004; Sen et al., 2005).

Regardless of test scores, girls tend to have more confidence in their academic abilities than boys do. They like school a little better, earn better grades, and are more likely to graduate from high school and to plan to attend and finish college and graduate or professional schools. Boys are more likely than girls to be underachievers, to be assigned to special or remedial education, and to be expelled or drop out of school (Eccles et al., 2003; Freeman, 2004). Teachers tend to discipline boys more harshly than girls but give more favourable attention to high-achieving boys than to high-achieving girls. Boys are more likely than girls to be encouraged to take honours courses, to apply to top colleges or universities, and to aim for challenging careers (Eccles et al., 2003).

Parenting Styles and Peer Influence

In western cultures, the benefits of authoritative parenting continue to affect school achievement during adolescence (Baumrind, 1991). A study of 525 adolescents in Quebec found that parenting practices and involvement were more strongly related to school grades than were family characteristics (Deslandes, Potvin, & Leclerc, 1999).

Authoritative parents urge adolescents to look at both sides of issues, welcome their participation in family decisions, and admit that children sometimes know more than parents. These parents strike a balance between making demands and being responsive. Their children receive praise and privileges for good grades; poor grades bring encouragement to try harder and offers of help.

Authoritarian parents, by contrast, tell adolescents not to argue with or question adults and tell them they will "know better when they are grown up." Good grades bring admonitions to do even better; poor grades may be punished by reduced allowances or "grounding." *Permissive parents* seem indifferent to grades, make no rules about watching television, do not attend school functions, and neither help with nor check their children's homework. These parents may not be neglectful or uncaring; they may, in fact, be nurturant. They may simply believe that teenagers should be responsible for their own lives.

What accounts for the academic success of authoritatively raised adolescents? Authoritative parents' greater involvement in schooling may be a factor, as well as their encouragement of positive attitudes toward work. A more subtle mechanism, consistent with findings on self-efficacy, may be parents' influence on how children explain success or failure. In a study of 2,353 high school students in California and Wisconsin, those who saw their parents as non-authoritative were more likely than their peers to attribute poor grades to external causes or to low ability—forces beyond their control—rather than to their own efforts. A year later, such students tended to pay less attention in class and to spend less time on homework (Glasgow et al., 1997). Thus a sense of helplessness associated with non-authoritative parenting may become a self-fulfilling prophecy, discouraging students from trying to succeed.

Peer influence may help explain the downward trend in academic motivation and achievement that begins for many students in early adolescence. In a longitudinal study of students entering an urban middle school, motivation and grades declined, on average, during seventh grade. Students whose peer group were high achievers showed less decline in achievement and enjoyment of school, whereas those who associated with low achievers showed greater declines (Ryan, 2001).

Recent Immigration

A large proportion of the school population in Canada comprises children of immigrants. According to information collected from the National Longitudinal Survey of Children and Youth, these students do as well as their non-immigrant schoolmates on a variety of educational measures including reading, writing, mathematics, and overall academic aptitude, particularly if the parents' first language is either English or French. For those whose parents' first language is not one of Canada's official languages, the children

Even though adolescents are more independent than younger children, the home atmosphere continues to influence school achievement. Parents help not only by monitoring homework but by taking an active interest in other aspects of teenagers' lives. Children of authoritative parents who discuss issues openly and offer praise and encouragement tend to do best in school.

do as well as non-immigrant children on all measures except reading, on which they tend to perform lower. However, on average, these students catch up to their peers on reading by the time they turn 13 (Worswick, 2001). These results indicate that children of recent immigrants are adapting well to the Canadian school system, despite the economic difficulties that immigrant families often face when they arrive in Canada.

The School

The quality of a school strongly influences student achievement (Frempong & Willms, 2002). A good middle school or high school has an orderly, safe environment; an active, energetic principal; a stable teaching staff, and a positive sense of community. It also offers opportunities for extracurricular activities, which keep students engaged and prevent them from getting into trouble after school. Teachers trust, respect, and care about students and have high expectations for them as well as confidence in their own ability to help students succeed (Eccles, 2004).

Adolescents are more satisfied with school if they are allowed to participate in making rules and feel support from teachers and other students (Samdal & Dür, 2000) and if the curriculum and instruction are meaningful and appropriately challenging and fit their interests, skill level, and needs (Eccles, 2004). In a survey of 452 suburban sixth graders, the students' perceptions of their teachers' fairness, expectations, modelling of academic motivation, rule setting, and negative feedback explained significant variances in student motivation, behaviour, and achievement. High expectations were the most consistent positive predictor of students' goals and interests, and negative feedback was the most consistent negative predictor of academic performance and classroom behaviour (Wentzel, 2002). Compared with students in other countries, Canadian students report being relatively satisfied with school, although the number claiming to enjoy school drops as they progress through higher grades. Good relations with parents, and good general health are linked with positive feelings towards school. On the other hand, more students are skipping classes, and bullying by boys and girls is a common occurrence in Canadian schools, making school a place where a small but significant number of students feel unsafe (King, Boyce, & King, 1999).

A decline in academic motivation and achievement often begins with the transition from the intimacy and familiarity of elementary school to the larger, more pressured, and less supportive environment of junior high school (Eccles, 2004).

These high school graduates are taking an important step toward their future careers. Today, more young people in Canada than ever before graduate from high school.

Dropping Out of High School

Although more Canadian youths are completing high school than ever before, in 2004–2005 about 12 percent of young men and 7 percent of young women between the ages of 20 and 24 have not completed high school (Canadian Council on Learning, 2005). The trend, however, over time, has indicated improvements in educational attainment across language groups in Canada. The major language groups in Canada, Anglophone, Francophone, and Allophone (individuals whose first languages are neither English nor French) have all shown dramatic decreases in percentage with less than high-school education, and increases in percentage completing a university degree (Corbeil, 2003; see Figure 16-2). Despite the drop, the proportion is high, considering that high school graduation, for most purposes, is a minimum requirement for labour force entry. Aboriginal youth tend to drop out of high school more than non-Aboriginal youth, but the dropout rate has also declined sharply in recent years (Canadian Council on Learning, 2005). Still, the higher school-leaving rate among Aboriginal students compared to non-Aboriginal students might be a reflection of the failings of the public school system to be sensitive to Aboriginal values and needs (Rabson, 2001). The differences continue through to higher education: 4 percent of the Aboriginal population have university education, compared to 19 percent of non-Aboriginal people (Canadian Education Statistics Council, 2000). In addition, low-income students are 4 times more likely to drop out than high-income students (Laird, DeBell, & Chapman, 2006).

Why are poor and minority adolescents more likely to drop out? One reason may be ineffective schooling: low teacher expectations or differential treatment of these students;

Figure 16-2

(a) Trends in the percentages of individuals aged 15 years and over who have less than Grade 9 education, by language grouping, showing declines in all language groups over the last 30 years;
(b) Percentages of individuals who have completed a university degree, by language grouping, showing increases in all language groups.

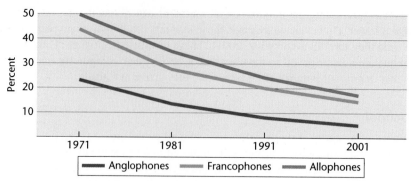

Source: Statistics Canada, Censuses of Population.

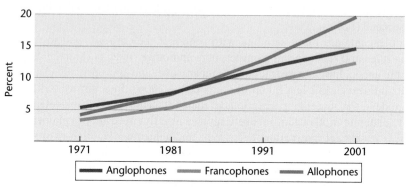

Source: Statistics Canada, Censuses of Population.

Checkpoint

Can you . . .

✔ Explain how self-efficacy beliefs, and how schools in various cultures can contribute to adolescents' motivation to learn?

✔ Assess the influences of personal qualities, SES, gender, ethnicity, parents, and peers on academic achievement?

✔ Give examples of educational practices that can help high school students succeed?

✔ Discuss trends in high school completion and causes and effects of dropping out?

✔ Explain the importance of active engagement in schooling?

less teacher support than at the elementary level; and the perceived irrelevance of the curriculum to culturally underrepresented groups. In schools that use ability tracking, students in low-ability or non-universitiy/college tracks often have inferior educational experiences. Placed with peers who are equally alienated, they tend to have feelings of incompetence and negative attitudes toward school and to engage in problem behaviours, both within and outside of school (Eccles, 2004).

Society suffers when young people do not finish school. Dropouts are more likely to be unemployed or to have low incomes (Statistics Canada, 2002), to end up on welfare, and to become involved with drugs, crime, and delinquency. They also tend to be in poorer health (Laird et al., 2006; NCES, 2001, 2003, 2004).

Having low grades does not seem to be the only reason for students to drop out of high school: 47 percent of all school leavers had an average of B or more as reported in the 1999 Youth in Transition Survey of Canadian Adolescents (Bowlby et al., 2002). Although the majority of Canadian dropouts lived in two-parent families during high school, students in single-parent and remarried households—even relatively affluent ones—are more likely to drop out than students living with both parents (Bowlby et al., 2002; Finn & Rock, 1997; Zimiles & Lee, 1991). Frequent moves may contribute to the effects of family instability, and changing schools may reduce a family's social capital. Families that move a lot generally have weaker social connections, know less about the children's school, and are less able to make wise decisions about schooling (Teachman, Paasch, & Carver, 1996). According to the Youth in Transition Survey, Canadian high school leavers were less likely to have friends who went on to post-secondary education, and were more likely to skip classes, drink alcohol regularly, and abuse drugs (Bowlby et al., 2002).

A longitudinal study that followed 3,502 disadvantaged eighth graders into early adulthood points up the difference success in high school can make (Finn, 2006). Of this group, 21 percent ("successful completers") successfully completed high school, and 52 percent ("marginal completers") did but received below average grades or test scores. The remaining 27 percent ("noncompleters") dropped out. As young adults, successful completers were most likely and noncompleters least likely to obtain post-secondary education, to have jobs, and to be consistently employed.

An important factor distinguishing the successful completers in this study was *active engagement:* the "attention, interest, investment, and effort students expend in the work of school" (Marks, 2000, p. 155). On the most basic level, active engagement means coming to class on time, being prepared, listening and responding to the teacher, and obeying school rules. A second level of engagement consists of getting involved with the coursework—asking questions, taking the initiative to seek help when needed, or doing extra projects. Both levels of active engagement tend to pay off in positive school performance (Finn & Rock, 1997). Family encouragement, small class size, and a warm, supportive school environment promote active engagement.

What's your view ?

• How can parents, educators, and societal institutions encourage young people to finish high school successfully?

Preparing for Higher Education or Vocations

Coming from an initially humble background and with a racist system stacked against him, Nelson Mandela made up his mind early to be a lawyer so he could help his people. He followed through on that ambition and the education it took to achieve it.

How do young people develop career goals? How do they decide whether or not to go to college or university and, if not, how to enter the world of work? Many factors enter in, including individual ability and personality, education, socio-economic and ethnic background, the advice of school counsellors, life experiences, and societal values. Let's look at some influences on educational and vocational aspirations. Then we'll look at what provisions exist for young people who do not plan to go to college or university. And we'll discuss the pros and cons of outside work for high school students.

Influences on Students' Aspirations

Students' self-efficacy beliefs—their confidence in their educational and vocational prospects—shape the occupational options they consider and the way they prepare for careers (Bandura, Barbaranelli, Caprara, & Pastorelli, 2001; Bandura et al., 1996). The adjustment from school to work can be particularly stressful for some young people. Among Canadian adolescents, the difficulties that are often experienced in making the transition from school to work may be rooted in negative attitudes about themselves, the work they do, and poor social and decision-making skills (Sankey, 1995).

Parents' values with regard to academic achievement influence adolescents' values and occupational goals (Jodl, Michael, Malanchuk, Eccles, & Sameroff, 2001). This influence is especially apparent among children of East Asian immigrant families, who strongly value education. Although high school graduates from immigrant families in general are as likely to go on to college or university as peers from Canadian-born families, the proportion of children of East Asian families who do so (96 percent) is much higher than among some other immigrant groups (Fuligni & Witkow, 2004).

Despite the greater flexibility in career goals today, gender—and gender-stereotyping—may influence vocational choice (Eccles et al., 2003). Girls and boys in Canada are now equally likely to plan careers in math and science (Andres, 2002); but boys are much more likely to earn post-secondary degrees in engineering, physics, and computer science (Andres, 2002; OECD, 2004), whereas girls are still more likely to go into nursing, social welfare professions, and teaching (Eccles et al., 2003). Much the same is true in other industrialized countries (OECD, 2004).

The educational system itself may act as a brake on vocational aspirations. Students who can memorize and analyze tend to do well on intelligence tests and in classrooms where teaching is geared to those abilities. Thus, as predicted by the tests, these students are achievers in a system that stresses the abilities in which they happen to excel. Students whose strength is in creative or practical thinking—areas critical to success in certain fields—never get a chance to show what they can do (Sternberg, 1997). Recognition of a broader range of "intelligences" (refer back to Chapter 13), combined with more flexible teaching and career counselling, could allow more students to meet their education goals and enter the occupations they desire so as to make the contributions of which they are capable.

Conventional approaches to career counselling are sometimes inappropriate, particularly for Aboriginal youth for whom goals and values may be incompatible with those of

Is this career counsellor influenced by the student's gender in advising him about possible career choices? Even though there is little or no overall difference between boys and girls in mathematical or verbal ability, many school counsellors still steer young people into gender-typed careers.

mainstream counselling techniques (Neumann, McCormick, Amundson, & McLean, 2000). One attempt at a solution to the need for a culturally sensitive career-counselling approach is the First Nations Career-Life Planning Model, which is designed to integrate traditional values of connection with family, community, and culture within the process of guiding an individual's career decision-making. By involving family and community members in career counselling, and offering the option of including traditional practices of prayer, smudge ceremony, use of talking stick or eagle feather, the process has been found to be effective and meaningful to the young people involved (Neumann et al., 2000).

Guiding Students Not Bound for College or University

Most industrialized countries offer some kind of structured guidance to non-college-or-university-bound students. Germany, for example, has an apprenticeship system, in which high school students go to school part time and spend the rest of the week in paid on-the-job training supervised by an employer-mentor (Hopfensperger, 1996).

Whatever vocational training programs do exist for the approximately 38 percent of high school graduates who do *not* immediately go on to college or university (NCES, 2003) tend to be less comprehensive than the German model and less closely tied to the needs of businesses and industries. Most young people get necessary training on the job or in community college courses. Many, ignorant about the job market, do not obtain the skills they need. Others take jobs beneath their abilities. Some do not find work at all (NRC, 1993a).

In some communities, demonstration programs help in the school-to-work transition. The most successful ones offer instruction in basic skills, counselling, peer support, mentoring, apprenticeship, and job placement (NRC, 1993a). In 1996, the federal government established the department of Human Resources and Social Development, with the aim of improving the employment prospects of Canadians by developing initiatives like vocational training programs, in co-operation with provincial authorities.

Adolescents in the Workplace

Youth employment is not a simple issue. In much of the developing world, such as in India, youth employment is an entrenched system vital to family subsistence. Working with the family in the fields or at home is part of a child's normal socialization. However, the conditions of employment for young adolescents are changing with globalization and urbanization. Young people may work as apprentices to a craftsman, as factory labourers, as live-in domestic servants, or as street vendors. Others assist parents at their jobs (Larson & Wilson,

2004). In many cases, they are bound by informal employment agreements. The ILO (2002) estimates that 5.7 million children and young adolescents are in bonded or forced labour.

About 46 percent of Canadian youth work part time while going to school (Statistics Canada, 2006), and most of these have low-level, repetitive jobs in which they do not learn skills useful later in life (Health Canada 1999). According to some research, teenagers who work are no more independent in making financial decisions and are unlikely to earn any more money as adults than those who do not hold jobs during high school. By assuming adult burdens they are not yet ready to deal with, young people may miss out on the opportunity to explore their interests and to develop close relationships. Outside work may require a stressful juggling of other commitments and cut down on active involvement in school (Greenberger & Steinberg, 1986). Long hours of work may undermine

This young man—one of approximately 38 percent of Canadian high school graduates who do not immediately go on to university or college—is learning electronics servicing and repair. Vocational training, to be effective, must be tied to the current needs of the job market.

school performance and increase the likelihood of dropping out (Larson & Verma, 1999; NCES, 1987). Most high school students who choose not to work prefer to focus on school work or other activities (Statistics Canada, 2006). Among Canadian youth, dropout rates are lowest (7 percent) for those who work a moderate number of hours per week (10 to 19), while the highest dropout rate (21 percent) is found among those who work the equivalent of a full-time job (30 hours or more). A surprising finding is that there is a substantial dropout rate (14 percent) for those who do not work at all (Bowlby et al., 2002; Statistics Canada, 2006).

Researchers disagree over whether part-time work is beneficial to high school students (by helping them develop real-world skills and a work ethic) or detrimental (by distracting them from long-term educational and occupational goals).

Some of the alleged harmful effects of work for students may be overstated (Mortimer, 2003). In a four-year longitudinal study of how ninth graders use their time, most of the students who worked also were heavily engaged in school and other activities (Shanahan & Flaherty, 2001). The number of hours a student worked did not seem to reduce self-esteem, mental health, or mastery motivation. Working had no effect on homework time or grades until senior year, when students who worked more than 20 hours a week tended to do less homework than other students. Even so, their grades and achievement motivation did not suffer. And students who worked fewer than 20 hours had *higher* grades than those who did not work at all.

Other research suggests that working students fall into two groups: those who are on an accelerated path to adulthood, and those who make a more leisurely transition, balancing schoolwork, paid jobs, and extracurricular activities. The "accelerators" work more than 20 hours a week during high school and spend little time on school-related leisure activities. Precocious exposure to an adult world may lead them into early alcohol and drug use, sexual activity, and delinquent behaviour. Many of these adolescents have relatively low SES; they tend to look for full-time work right after high school and not to obtain college degrees. Intensive work experience in high school improves their prospects for work and income after high school, but not for long-term occupational attainment. The "balancers," by contrast, often come from more privileged backgrounds. For them, the effects of part-time work seem entirely benign. Work helps them to gain a sense of responsibility, independence, and self-confidence and to appreciate the value of work but does not deter them from their educational paths. These young people are more likely to earn a four-year university degree, which opens the door to better long-term occupational prospects. If they engage in risky behaviours, they do not do so until after high school, and these activities are less likely to interfere with future attainments (Staff et al., 2004).

Checkpoint ✓

Can you . . .

✔ Discuss influences on educational and vocational aspirations and planning?

✔ Weigh factors in the value of part-time work for high school students?

For high school students who must or choose to work outside of school, then, the effects are more likely to be positive if they try to limit working hours and remain engaged in school activities. Cooperative educational programs that enable students to work part time as part of their school program may be especially protective (Staff et al., 2004).

Vocational planning is one aspect of an adolescent's search for identity. The question "What shall I do?" is very close to "Who shall I be?" People who feel they are doing something worthwhile, and doing it well, feel good about themselves. Those who feel that their work does not matter—or that they are not good at it—may wonder about the meaning of their lives. A prime personality issue in adolescence, which we discuss in Chapter 17, is the effort to define the self.

Summary and Key Terms

Aspects of Cognitive Maturation

Guidepost 1 How do adolescents' thinking and use of language differ from younger children's?

- People in Piaget's stage of formal operations can engage in hypothetical-deductive reasoning. They can think in terms of possibilities, deal flexibly with problems, and test hypotheses.

- Since environmental stimulation plays an important part in attaining this stage, not all people become capable of formal operations; and those who are capable do not always use it.

- Piaget's proposed stage of formal operations does not take into account such developments as accumulation of knowledge and expertise, gains in information-processing capacity, and the growth of metacognition. Piaget also paid little attention to individual differences, between-task variations, and the role of the situation.

- According to Elkind, immature thought patterns can result from adolescents' inexperience with formal thinking. These thought patterns include idealism and criticalness, argumentativeness, indecisiveness, apparent hypocrisy, self-consciousness, and an assumption of specialness and invulnerability. Research has cast doubt on the special prevalence of the latter two patterns during adolescence.

- Research has found both structural and functional changes in adolescent cognition, which reflect developments in the adolescent brain. Structural changes include increases in information processing capacity, in the amount of knowledge in long-term memory, and in the capacity of working memory. Functional changes include progress in learning, remembering, and reasoning.

- Vocabulary and other aspects of language development, especially those related to abstract thought, such as social perspective-taking, improve in adolescence. Adolescents enjoy wordplay and create their own "dialect."

formal operations (428)   hypothetical-deductive reasoning (429) imaginary audience (431)   personal fable (431)   declarative knowledge (432)   procedural knowledge (433)   conceptual knowledge (433)

Moral Development

Guidepost 2 On what basis do adolescents make moral judgments, and how does pro-social behaviour vary?

- According to Kohlberg, moral reasoning is based on a developing sense of justice and growing cognitive abilities. Kohlberg proposed that moral development progresses from external control to internalized societal standards to personal, principled moral codes.

- Kohlberg's theory has been criticized on several grounds, including failure to credit the roles of emotion, socialization, and parental guidance. The applicability of Kohlberg's system to women and girls and to people in non-industrialized cultures has been questioned. Research has found no significant gender differences in moral reasoning as measured by Kohlbergian methods.

- Gilligan proposed an alternative theory of moral development based on an ethic of caring, rather than justice.

- Pro-social behaviour continues to increase during adolescence, especially among girls. Many adolescents engage in volunteer community service.

   preconventional morality (434)   conventional morality (or morality of conventional role conformity) (436) postconventional morality (or morality of autonomous moral principles) (436)

Educational and Vocational Issues

Guidepost 3 What influences affect adolescents' school success and their educational and vocational planning and preparation?

- Academic motivation, socio-economic status, parental involvement, parenting styles, cultural and peer influences, and quality of schooling affect educational achievement. Self-efficacy beliefs and parental and peer attitudes can influence motivation to achieve. Poor families whose children do well in school tend to have more social capital than poor families whose children do not do well.

- Although most Canadians graduate from high school, the dropout rate is higher among poor and Aboriginal students and among those not living with both parents. Active engagement in studies is an important factor in keeping adolescents in school.

- Educational and vocational aspirations are influenced by several factors, including self-efficacy beliefs, parental values, and gender.

- High school graduates who do not immediately go on to college or university can benefit from vocational training.

- Part-time work seems to have both positive and negative effects on educational, social, and occupational development. The long-term effects tend to be best when working hours are limited.

   social capital (441)

CHAPTER SEVENTEEN

Psychosocial Development in Adolescence

This face in the mirror
stares at me
demanding Who are you? What will you become?
And taunting. You don't even know.
Chastened. I cringe and agree
and then
because I'm still young.
I stick out my tongue.

—Eve Merriam, "Conversation with Myself," 1964

Focus *David Suzuki, Naturalist**

David Suzuki

David Suzuki is one of Canada's best-known scientists. A spokesperson for ecology, he speaks out about the impact of science and industry on the environment. He and his twin sister were born in Vancouver just before the Second World War. His first memory is of his father planning a camping trip with him and taking him out to buy a pup tent; his father setting up the tent on the floor of the store to make sure it was just right for the two of them. The trip was the start of Suzuki's life-long love of nature, and what helped commit him to become a naturalist.

His ethnic background combined with the political events of his childhood later led to early experience with family displacement and injustice. His carefree childhood in B.C. came to a sudden halt when he and his family were forced to stay in an internment camp during the Second World War, a product of mass hysteria following the bombing of Pearl Harbor and the invoking of the War Measures Act in 1941. During that time in Canada, all people of Japanese descent were considered enemies of Canada, and all their property was confiscated. The years he spent with his family in a camp in the interior of B.C. helped to foster his love of and fascination with nature.

After the war, Suzuki's family moved to Ontario, where his parents worked as farm labourers. He excelled in high school, but felt like an outsider. His competitiveness in trying to be better than his classmates, a result of wishing to free his family from poverty, contributed to his feeling like an outsider: He was non-white in a white-dominated school environment, non-athletic, and intelligent. However, in his family he was lavished a great deal of attention, being the only male in a traditional Japanese family. His father urged him to excel, and to develop public speaking skills. He won a speaking contest in Grade 9, and competed in high school debating. He would fill his room with insect and fish specimens in his growing interest in biology. His success in high school led to a scholarship at Amherst College in Massachusetts, where he rose to the challenges of high expectations not only in educational but also in cultural and athletic pursuits. There a mentor who supervised his initial work introduced him to genetics.

He went on to earn a Ph.D. in biology at the University of Chicago, and returned to Canada to work as a geneticist at U.B.C. This work became a passion to him, which resulted in significant contributions to science, substantial research support, and the leadership of a 20-person research team. He received many awards for his outstanding work as a scientist and came to the attention of the national media. Bringing science to Canadians in television programs such as *The Nature of Things,* he has become a spokesperson for and interpreter of science, speaking out against the misuses of science and urging the nation to focus on the responsibilities and ethics of genetic research. He promotes the importance and relevance of the balanced perspectives of Aboriginal values, manifested in the relationships that Aboriginal communities across Canada maintain with the natural world, seeing the earth not as a resource to be exploited but rather as an integral part of their identities. Suzuki urges all Canadians to adopt these values, as the only way to survive in a healthy and sustainable world.

David Suzuki remains committed to hard work and the power of human reason to change our culture and behaviour. His commitment to social justice and ecology was spurred on by his father's conviction to be a good Canadian citizen despite poor treatment by the Canadian government during the Second World War. This conveyed to David the same strong conviction to stand up for what he believes in.

• • •

Adolescence is a time of both opportunities and risks. Teenagers are on the threshold of love, of life's work, and of participation in adult society. Yet adolescence is also a time when some young people engage in behaviour that closes off their options and limits their possibilities. Today, research is increasingly focusing on how to help young people avoid hazards that can keep them from fulfilling their potential. What helped David Suzuki—in addition to the influence of his hardworking father's love of nature, his mother, sisters, and adult mentors—were his talent and his passion for preserving nature, which ultimately enabled him to channel his drive, energy, audacity, and intelligence in a positive direction.

In Chapter 16 we looked at some physical and cognitive factors that contribute to an adolescent's sense of self, such as appearance and school achievement. In this chapter, we turn to psychosocial aspects of the quest for identity. We discuss how adolescents come to terms with their sexuality. We consider how teenagers' burgeoning individuality expresses itself in relationships with parents, siblings, and peers. We examine sources of anti-social behaviour and ways of reducing the risks of adolescence to make it a time of positive growth and expanding possibilities. Finally, we compare adolescents' views of themselves and their lives around the world.

After you have read and studied this chapter, you should be able to answer each of the Guidepost questions that appear at the top of the next page. Look for them again in the margins, where they point to important concepts throughout the chapter. To check your understanding of these Guideposts, review the end-of-chapter summary. Checkpoints located throughout the chapter will help you verify your understanding of what you have read.

*Sources of biographical information about David Suzuki were Knowles, 1995; Suzuki, 2000, Webb, 1991, and Wideman, 1990.

1. How do adolescents form an identity, and what roles do gender and ethnicity play?

2. What determines sexual orientation, what sexual practices are common among adolescents, and what leads some to engage in risky sexual behaviour?

3. How do adolescents relate to parents, siblings, and peers?

4. What causes anti-social behaviour, and what can be done to reduce the risk of juvenile delinquency?

5. How do various cultures define what it means to become an adult, and what markers confer that status?

Guidepost 1

How do adolescents form an identity, and what roles do gender and ethnicity play?

identity In Erikson's terminology, a coherent conception of the self made up of goals, values, and beliefs to which a person is solidly committed

identity versus identity confusion Erikson's fifth crisis of psychosocial development, in which an adolescent seeks to develop a coherent sense of self, including the role she or he is to play in society; also called *identity versus role confusion*

The Search for Identity

The search for **identity,** which Erikson defined as confidence in one's inner continuity amid change, comes into focus during the teenage years. Adolescents' cognitive development now enables them to construct a "theory of the self" (Elkind, 1998). As Erikson (1950) emphasized, a teenager's effort to make sense of the self is not "a kind of maturational malaise." It is part of a healthy, vital process that builds on the achievements of earlier stages—on trust, autonomy, initiative, and industry—and lays the groundwork for coping with the crises of adult life.

Erikson: Identity versus Identity Confusion

The chief task of adolescence, said Erikson (1968), is to confront the crisis of **identity versus identity confusion** (or *identity versus role confusion*), to become a unique adult with a coherent sense of self and a valued role in society. The identity crisis is seldom fully resolved in adolescence; issues concerning identity crop up again and again throughout adult life.

Erikson's concept of the identity crisis was based on his own life and his research on adolescents in various societies. Growing up in Germany as the son of a Danish mother and a Jewish adoptive father, Erikson had felt confusion about his identity. He never knew his biological father; he floundered before settling on a vocation; and when he came to the United States, he needed to redefine his identity as an immigrant. All these issues found echoes in the identity crises he observed among disturbed adolescents, soldiers in combat, and members of minority groups (Erikson, 1968, 1973; L. J. Friedman, 1999).

Identity, according to Erikson, forms as young people resolve three major issues: the choice of an *occupation,* the adoption of *values* to believe in and live by, and the development of a satisfying *sexual identity.* During middle childhood, children acquire skills needed for success in their culture. As adolescents, they need to find constructive ways to use these skills. When young people have trouble settling on an occupational identity—or when their opportunities are artificially limited—they are at risk of behaviour with serious negative consequences, such as criminal activity or early pregnancy.

According to Erikson, the *psychosocial moratorium*—the "time out" period that adolescence provides—allows young people search for commitments to which they can be faithful. These youthful commitments may shape a person's life for years to come. David Suzuki's commitments were to develop his abilities as a scientist and to help improve the natural world by promoting values that would ensure the survival of the earth. The extent to which young people remain faithful to commitments, as Suzuki did, influences their ability to resolve the identity crisis.

Adolescents who satisfactorily resolve that crisis develop the "virtue" of *fidelity:* sustained loyalty, faith, or a sense of belonging to a loved one or to friends and companions.

Fidelity also can mean identification with a set of values, an ideology, a religion, a political movement, a creative pursuit, or an ethnic group (Erikson, 1982).

Fidelity is an extension of trust. In infancy, it is important for trust of parents to outweigh mistrust; in adolescence, it becomes important to be trustworthy oneself. In addition, adolescents now extend their trust to mentors or loved ones. In sharing thoughts and feelings, an adolescent clarifies a tentative identity by seeing it reflected in the eyes of the beloved. However, these adolescent "intimacies" differ from mature intimacy, which involves greater commitment, sacrifice, and compromise.

Erikson saw the prime danger of this stage as identity or role confusion, which can greatly delay reaching psychological adulthood. (He himself did not resolve his own identity crisis until his mid-20s.) Some degree of identity confusion is normal, however. According to Erikson, it accounts for the seemingly chaotic nature of much adolescent behaviour and for teenagers' painful self-consciousness. Cliquishness and intolerance of differences, both hallmarks of adolescence, are defences against identity confusion.

Erikson's theory describes male identity development as the norm. According to Erikson, a man is not capable of real intimacy until after he has achieved a stable identity, whereas women define themselves through marriage and motherhood (something that may have been truer when Erikson developed his theory than it is today). Thus, said Erikson, women (unlike men) develop identity *through* intimacy, not before it. As we'll see, this male orientation of Erikson's theory has prompted criticism. Still, Erikson's concept of the identity crisis has inspired much valuable research.

Mastering the challenge of rappelling may help this adolescent girl assess her abilities, interests, and desires. According to Erikson, this process of self-assessment helps adolescents resolve the crisis of identity versus identity confusion.

Marcia: Identity Status—Crisis and Commitment

Kate, Andrea, Nick, and Mark are all about to graduate from high school. Kate has considered her interests and her talents and plans to become an engineer. She has narrowed her choices to three universities that offer good programs in this field.

Andrea knows exactly what she is going to do with her life. Her mother, a union leader at a plastics factory, has arranged for Andrea to enter an apprenticeship program there. Andrea has never considered doing anything else.

Nick, on the other hand, is agonizing over his future. Should he attend a community college or join the armed forces? He cannot decide what to do now or what he wants to do eventually.

Mark still has no idea of what he wants to do, but he is not worried. He figures he can get some sort of a job and make up his mind about the future when he is ready.

These four young people are involved in identity formation. What accounts for the differences in the way they go about it, and how will these differences affect the outcome? According to research by the psychologist James E. Marcia (1966, 1980), these students are in four different states of ego (self) development, or **identity statuses,** which seem to be related to certain aspects of personality.

Through 30-minute, semi-structured *identity-status interviews* (Kroger, 2003; see Table 17-1), Marcia found four types of identity status: *identity achievement, foreclosure, moratorium,* and *identity diffusion.* The four categories differ according to the presence or absence of **crisis** and **commitment,** the two elements Erikson saw as crucial to forming identity.

Marcia defines *crisis* as a period of conscious decision making, and *commitment* as a personal investment in an occupation or system of beliefs (ideology). He found relationships between identity status and such characteristics as anxiety, self-esteem, moral reasoning, and patterns of behaviour. Building on Marcia's theory, other researchers have

identity statuses Marcia's term for states of ego development that depend on the presence or absence of crisis and commitment

crisis Marcia's term for period of conscious decision making related to identity formation

commitment Marcia's term for personal investment in an occupation or system of beliefs

Table 17-1   Identity-Status Interview

Sample Questions	Typical Answers for the Four Statuses
About occupational commitment: "How willing do you think you'd be to give up going into _____ if something better came along?"	*Identity achievement.* "Well, I might, but I doubt it. I can't see what 'something better' would be for me."
	Foreclosure. "Not very willing. It's what I've always wanted to do. The folks are happy with it and so am I."
	Moratorium. "I guess if I knew for sure, I could answer that better. It would have to be something in the general area— something related . . ."
	Identity diffusion. "Oh, sure. If something better came along, I'd change just like that."
About ideological commitment: "Have you ever had any doubts about your religious beliefs?"	*Identity achievement.* "Yes, I started wondering whether there is a God. I've pretty much resolved that now. The way it seems to me is . . ."
	Foreclosure. "No, not really; our family is pretty much in agreement on these things."
	Moratorium. "Yes, I guess I'm going through that now. I just don't see how there can be a God and still so much evil in the world . . ."
	Identity diffusion. "Oh, I don't know. I guess so. Everyone goes through some sort of stage like that. But it really doesn't bother me much. I figure that one religion is about as good as another!"

Source: Adapted from Marcia, 1966.

identified other personality and family variables related to identity status (see Table 17-2). Here is a thumbnail sketch of people in each identity status:

identity achievement Identity status, described by Marcia, which is characterized by commitment to choices made following a crisis, a period spent in exploring alternatives

foreclosure Identity status, described by Marcia, in which a person who has not spent time considering alternatives (that is, has not been in crisis) is committed to other people's plans for his or her life

1. **Identity achievement** *(crisis leading to commitment).* Kate has resolved her identity crisis. During the crisis period, she devoted much thought and some emotional struggle to major issues in her life. She has made choices and expresses strong commitment to them. Her parents have encouraged her to make her own decisions; they have listened to her ideas and given their opinions without pressuring her to adopt them. Kate is thoughtful but not so introspective as to be unable to act. She has a sense of humour, functions well under stress, is capable of intimate relationships, and holds to her standards while being open to new ideas. Research in a number of cultures has found people in this category to be more mature and more competent in relationships than people in the other three (Marcia, 1993).

2. **Foreclosure** *(commitment without crisis).* Andrea has made commitments, not as a result of a crisis, which would involve questioning and exploring possible choices,

Table 17-2   Family and Personality Factors Associated with Adolescents in Four Identity Statuses*

Factor	Identity Achievement	Foreclosure	Moratorium	Identity Diffusion
Family	Parents encourage autonomy and connection with teachers; differences are explored within a context of mutuality.	Parents are overly involved with their children; families avoid expressing differences.	Adolescents are often involved in an ambivalent struggle with parental authority.	Parents are laissez-faire in child-rearing attitudes; are rejecting or not available to children.
Personality	High levels of ego development, moral reasoning, self-certainty, self-esteem, performance under stress, and intimacy.	Highest levels of authoritarianism and stereotypical thinking, obedience to authority, dependent relationships, low level of anxiety.	Most anxious and fearful of success; high levels of ego development, moral reasoning, and self-esteem.	Mixed results, with low levels of ego development, moral reasoning, cognitive complexity, and self-certainty; poor cooperative abilities.

*These associations have emerged from a number of separate studies. Since the studies have all been correlational, rather than longitudinal, it is impossible to say that any factor caused placement in any identity status.

Source: Kroger, 1993.

but by accepting someone else's plans for her life. She is happy and self-assured, perhaps even smug and self-satisfied, and she becomes dogmatic when her opinions are questioned. She has close family ties, is obedient, and tends to follow a powerful leader (like her mother), who accepts no disagreement

3. **Moratorium** *(crisis with no commitment yet).* Nick is in crisis, struggling with decisions. He is lively, talkative, self-confident, and scrupulous, but also anxious and fearful. He is close to his mother but also resists her authority. He wants to have a girlfriend but has not yet developed a close relationship. He will probably come out of his crisis eventually with the ability to make commitments and achieve identity.

4. **Identity diffusion** *(no commitment, no crisis).* Mark has not seriously considered options and has avoided commitments. He is unsure of himself and tends to be uncooperative. His parents do not discuss his future with him; they say it's up to him. People in this category tend to be unhappy. They are often lonely because they have only superficial relationships.

These categories are not stages; they represent the status of identity development at a particular time, and they are likely to change in any direction as young people continue to develop (Marcia, 1979). When middle-aged people look back on their lives, they most commonly trace a path from foreclosure to moratorium to identity achievement (Kroger & Haslett, 1991). From late adolescence on, as Marcia proposed, more and more people are in moratorium or achievement: seeking or finding their own identity. About half of late adolescents remain in foreclosure or diffusion, but when development does occur, it is typically in the direction Marcia described (Kroger, 2003). Furthermore, although people in foreclosure seem to have made final decisions, that is often not so.

Gender Differences in Identity Formation

Much research supports Erikson's view that, for women, identity and intimacy develop together. Rather than view this pattern as a departure from a male norm, however, some researchers see it as pointing to a weakness in Erikson's theory, which, they claim, is based on male-centred Western concepts of individuality, autonomy, and competitiveness. According to Carol Gilligan (1982, 1987a, 1987b; L. M. Brown & Gilligan, 1990), the female sense of self develops not so much through achieving a separate identity as through establishing relationships. Girls and women, says Gilligan, judge themselves on their handling of their responsibilities and on their ability to care for others as well as for themselves.

Some developmental scientists question how different the male and female paths to identity really are—especially today—and suggest that individual differences may be more important than gender differences (Archer, 1993; Marcia, 1993). Indeed, Marcia (1993) argues that an ongoing tension between independence and connectedness is at the heart of all of Erikson's psychosocial stages for *both* men and women. In research on Marcia's identity statuses, few gender differences have appeared (Kroger, 2003).

However, the development of self-esteem during adolescence seems to support Gilligan's view. Male self-esteem tends to be linked with striving for individual achievement, whereas female self-esteem depends more on connections with others (Thorne & Michaelieu, 1996).

The preponderance of evidence suggests that adolescent girls have lower self-esteem, on average, than adolescent boys, though this finding has been controversial. Several large, recent studies find that self-esteem drops during adolescence, more rapidly for girls than for boys, and then rises gradually into adulthood. These changes may be due in part to body image and other anxieties associated with puberty and with the transitions to junior high or middle school and high school (Robins & Trzesniewski, 2005). As we will see, the pattern seems to be different among minorities.

Ethnic Factors in Identity Formation

In 1971, the federal government announced a policy of multiculturalism, which was designed to safeguard the right of every ethnic group in Canada to maintain and develop its own values and culture (Freisen, 1993, 1995). Despite official policy supporting the growth of cultural diversity in Canada, the process of forming an identity for adolescent

moratorium Identity status, described by Marcia, in which a person is currently considering alternatives (in crisis) and seems headed for commitment

identity diffusion Identity status, described by Marcia, which is characterized by absence of commitment and lack of serious consideration of alternatives

What's your view

- Which of Marcia's identity statuses do you think you fit into as an adolescent?
- Has your identity status changed since then? If so, how?

immigrants and members of some ethnic minorities can be difficult. This is particularly relevant when the values of the ethnic group, such as the case of a culture that emphasizes the community, are different from those of mainstream Canadian society, which emphasizes the individual.

What happens to young people's identity when the values of their ethnic community conflict with those of the larger society—for example, when Aboriginal adolescents are expected to participate in a ceremony on a day when they are also supposed to be in school? Or when young people face and perhaps internalize (take into their own value system) prejudice against their own ethnic group? Or when discrimination limits their occupational choices, as it did for David Suzuki's father during the Second World War? All these situations can lead to identity confusion.

Identity formation is especially complicated for young people in minority groups. In fact, for some adolescents ethnicity may be central to identity formation. As Erikson (1968) pointed out, an "oppressed and exploited minority" may come to see themselves in the negative way the majority see them (p. 303). This is called *self-hatred.* Even in a more tolerant society in which ethnic minorities have become more assertive, skin colour and other physical features, language differences, and stereotyped social standing can be extremely influential in moulding minority adolescents' self-concept. At a time when adolescents want to fit in—when they are painfully self-conscious about physical differences—minority adolescents cannot help but stand out (Spencer & Dornbusch, 1998).

With nearly double the number of immigrant young people between the ages of 6 and 15 arriving in Canada in 1997, compared to 1987 (Canadian Council on Social Development, 2001), the process of forming an identity can be difficult for many Canadian youth. Almost two-thirds do not speak either official language on arrival, and more than half of recent immigrant children are members of visible minorities (Canadian Council on Social Development, 2002). However, children who have arrived in Canada since 1986 have reported more close friends than children who immigrated in earlier years (Canadian Council on Social Development, 2002).

Teenagers have wider social networks and more mobility than younger children, and greater cognitive awareness of cultural attitudes and distinctions. Caught between two cultures, many minority youth are keenly conscious of conflicts between the values stressed at home and those dominant in the wider society. Despite positive appraisals by parents, teachers, community, and peers, minority adolescents' self-perceptions may, as Erikson noted, reflect negative views of their group by the majority culture. With the scale of diversity among Aboriginal cultures in Canada (see Chapter 1), it is difficult to draw general conclusions about identity formation among young Aboriginal people in Canada. However, the shared history of these groups may be related to some of the difficulties many young Aboriginal people face in identity formation. Disruption of traditional ways of life through a history of colonization, relocation to reserves, separation from families and abuse in residential schools, and efforts at assimilation have dealt a severe blow to the maintenance of strong cultural identities in many communities. More recent introduction of mass media and other economic and political changes has introduced additional challenges to the development of an Aboriginal identity for young people, who are exposed to a large variety of influences and rapid cultural changes (Kirmayer et al., 2000).

A study of Chinese immigrant youth in Toronto showed that higher levels of social support and the presence of both parents in the life of the adolescent predicted more successful adaptation to Canadian culture, as indicated by good academic achievement, and low levels of conflict with parents (Leung, 2001).

For many young people in minority groups, race or ethnicity is central to identity formation. Following Marcia's model, some research has identified four ethnic identity statuses (Phinney, 1998):

1. *Diffuse:* Anastasia has done little or no exploration of her ethnicity and does not clearly understand the issues involved.
2. *Foreclosed:* Kwame had done little or no exploration of his identity but has clear feelings about it. These feelings may be positive or negative, depending on the attitudes he absorbed at home.

Identity development can be especially complicated for young people from minority groups. Ethnicity—and the conflicts with the dominant culture it entails—may play a central part in their self-concept.

3. *Moratorium:* Cho-san has begun to explore her ethnicity but is confused about what it means to her.
4. *Achieved:* Mario has explored his identity and understands and accepts his ethnicity.

A study of 940 African American adolescents, college students, and adults found evidence of all four identity statuses in each age group. Only 27 percent of the adolescents were in the "achieved" group, as compared with 47 percent of the college students and 56 percent of the adults. Instead, adolescents were more likely to be in moratorium (42 percent), still exploring what it means to be African American. Twenty-five percent of the adolescents were in foreclosure, with feelings about African American identity based on their family upbringing. All three of these groups (achieved, in moratorium, and foreclosed) reported more positive regard for being African American than the 6 percent of adolescents who were "diffused" (neither committed nor exploring). Those of any age who were in the "achieved" status were most likely to view race as central to their identity (Yip, Seaton, & Sellers, 2006).

Another model focuses on three aspects of racial/ethnic identity: *connectedness* to one's own racial/ethnic group, *awareness of racism,* and *embedded achievement,* the belief that academic achievement is a part of group identity. A longitudinal study of low-income minority youth found that all three aspects of identity appear to stabilize and even to increase slightly by midadolescence. Thus racial/ethnic identity may buffer tendencies toward a drop in grades and connection to school during the transition from middle school to high school (Altschul, Oyserman, & Bybee, 2006). On the other hand, perceived discrimination during the transition to adolescence can interfere with positive identity formation and lead to conduct problems or depression. Protective factors are nurturant, involved parenting, pro-social friends, and strong academic performance (Brody et al., 2006).

A 3-year longitudinal study of 420 African American, Latino American, and European American adolescents looked at two dimensions of ethnic identity: *group esteem* (feeling good about one's ethnicity) and *exploration of the meaning of ethnicity* in one's life. Group esteem rose during both early and middle adolescence, especially for African Americans and Latinos, whose group esteem was lower to begin with. Exploration of the meaning of ethnicity increased only in middle adolescence, perhaps reflecting the transition from relatively homogeneous neighbourhood elementary or junior high schools into more ethnically diverse high schools. Interactions with members of other ethnic groups may stimulate young people to curiosity about their own ethnic identity (French, Seidman, Allen, & Aber, 2006).

The term **cultural socialization** refers to parental practices that teach children about their racial or ethnic heritage, promote cultural customs and traditions, and promote racial/ethnic and cultural pride. Adolescents who have experienced cultural socialization tend to have stronger and more positive ethnic identity than those who have not (Hughes et al., 2006).

Place of birth of adolescent members of minority groups can have an influence on identity and self-esteem, likely based on differences in life experience (Lay & Verkuyten, 1999). A study of 31 Chinese adolescents who were Canadian-born, and 31 Chinese adolescents who immigrated to Canada, all living in Toronto, found that the foreign-born adolescents tended to identify themselves as Chinese, rather than Chinese-Canadian. The foreign-born adolescents tended to perceive themselves as being separate from the larger Canadian culture, regarded their ethnicity as more important, and were more likely to relate the collectivist values of their ethnic identities to their own self-identities than did the Canadian-born adolescents (Lay et al., 1999).

Particularly vulnerable to difficulties in forming healthy identity are child refugees, many of whom have settled in Canada. Particular problems they face, in addition to adapting to life in a new and often unfamiliar culture, include dealing with the trauma of war, persecution, dangerous escapes, and prolonged periods of settlement in refugee camps, many having witnessed killings, torture, and other atrocities (Fantino & Colak, 2001).

Sexuality

Seeing oneself as a sexual being, recognizing one's sexual orientation, coming to terms with sexual stirrings, and forming romantic or sexual attachments are all parts of achieving

cultural socialization Parental practices that teach children about their racial/ethnic heritage and promote cultural practices and cultural pride

Checkpoint ✓

Can you . . .

✔ List the three major issues involved in identity formation, according to Erikson?

✔ Describe four types of identity status found by Marcia?

✔ Discuss how gender and ethnicity can affect identity formation

 Guidepost 2

What determines sexual orientation, what sexual practices are common among adolescents, and what leads some to engage in risky sexual behaviour?

sexual identity. This urgent awareness of sexuality is an important aspect of identity formation, profoundly affecting self-image and relationships. Although this process is biologically driven, its expression is in part culturally defined.

During the twentieth century a major change in sexual attitudes and behaviour in Canada and other industrialized countries brought more widespread acceptance of premarital sex, homosexuality, and other previously disapproved forms of sexual activity. With widespread access to the Internet, casual sex with fleeting cyber-acquaintances who "hook up" through online chat rooms or singles' meeting sites has become common. Cell phones, e-mail, and instant messaging make it easy for adolescents to arrange these hook-ups with disembodied strangers, insulated from adult scrutiny. All of these changes have brought increased concerns about sexual risk taking. On the other hand, the AIDS epidemic has led many young people to abstain from sexual activity outside of committed relationships or to engage in "safer" sexual practices.

Sexual Orientation and Identity

sexual orientation Gender focus of consistent sexual, romantic, and affectionate interest, either heterosexual, homosexual, or bisexual

Although present in younger children, it is in adolescence that a person's **sexual orientation** generally becomes a pressing issue: whether that person will consistently be sexually, romantically, and affectionately attracted to persons of the other sex *(heterosexual)* or of the same sex *(homosexual)* or of both sexes *(bisexual)*. Heterosexuality predominates in nearly every known culture throughout the world. The prevalence of homosexual orientation varies widely, depending upon how it is defined and measured. Depending on whether it is measured by sexual or romantic *attraction or arousal* (as in the definition we just gave) or by sexual *behaviour* or by sexual *identity,* the rate of homosexuality in the North American population ranges from 1 to 21 percent (Savin-Williams, 2006; Statistics Canada, 2004).

Many young people have one or more homosexual experiences as they are growing up, but isolated experiences or even occasional homosexual attractions or fantasies do not determine sexual orientation. Social stigma may bias such self-reports, underestimating the prevalence of homosexuality and bisexuality.

Origins of Sexual Orientation

Much research on sexual orientation has focused on efforts to explain homosexuality. Although homosexuality was once considered a mental illness, several decades of research have found no association between sexual orientation and emotional or social problems (American Psychological Association, undated; C. J. Patterson, 1992, 1995a, 1995b). These findings eventually led the psychiatric profession to stop classifying homosexuality as a mental disorder.

Sexual orientation seems to be partly genetic (Diamond & Savin-Williams, 2003). The first full genome-wide scan for male sexual orientation has identified three stretches of DNA on chromosomes 7, 8, and 10 that appear to be involved (Mustanski et al., 2005). However, because identical twins are not perfectly concordant for sexual orientation, nongenetic factors also must play a part. Different combinations of causes may operate in different individuals, and this may account for individual differences in the age at which same-sex attraction first appears (Diamond & Savin-Williams, 2003).

The more older brothers a man has, the more likely he is to be gay—but only if they are biological brothers. In an analysis of 905 men and their biological, adoptive, half-, or stepsiblings, the only significant factor in whether a man was heterosexual or homosexual was the number of times his mother had previously given birth to boys. Each older biological brother increased the chances of homosexuality in a younger brother by 33 percent. This phenomenon may

Although sexual orientation may well be shaped before birth or very early in life, it is in adolescence that it becomes a pressing issue. In 2002, Marc Hall, an Ontario high school student, challenged his school's decision to prevent him from attending his end-of-year formal with his boyfriend.

be a cumulative immune-like response to the presence of successive "foreign" male fetuses in the womb (Bogaert, 2006).

One researcher has reported a difference in the size of the hypothalamus, a brain structure that governs sexual activity, in heterosexual and gay men. However, it is not known whether this difference arises before birth or later (LeVay, 1991). In brain-imaging studies on the effects of pheromones, odours that attract mates, the odour of male sweat activated the hypothalamus in gay men much as it did in heterosexual women. Similarly, lesbian women, like straight men, reacted more positively to female pheromones than to male ones, though the effect was smaller (Savic, Berglund, & Lindström, 2005; Savic, Berglund, & Lindström, 2006). However, we do not know whether these differences are a cause of homosexuality or an effect of it.

Homosexual and Bisexual Identity Development

Despite the increased acceptance of homosexuality in Canada, many adolescents who openly identify as gay, lesbian, or bisexual feel isolated in a hostile environment. They may be subject to discrimination and even violence (CICH, 2000; C. J. Patterson, 1995b). Others may be reluctant to disclose their sexual orientation, even to their parents, for fear of strong disapproval or a rupture in the family (Hillier, 2002; C. J. Patterson, 1995b). They may find it difficult to meet and identify potential same-sex partners. Thus, homosexuals' recognition and expression of their sexual identity is more complex and follows a less defined timetable than for heterosexuals (Diamond & Savin-Williams, 2003).

There is no single route to the development of gay, lesbian, or bisexual identity and behaviour. Because of the lack of socially sanctioned ways to explore their sexuality, many gay and lesbian adolescents experience identity confusion (Sieving, Oliphant, & Blum, 2002). Gay, lesbian, and bisexual youth who are unable to establish peer groups that share their sexual orientation may struggle with the recognition of same-sex attractions (Bouchey & Furman, 2003; Furman & Wehner, 1997).

One model for the development of gay or lesbian sexual identity proposes the following sequence: (1) awareness of same-sex attraction (beginning at ages 8 to 11); (2) same-sex sexual behaviours (ages 12 to 15); (3) identification as gay or lesbian (ages 15 to 18); (4) disclosure to others (ages 17 to 19); and (5) development of same-sex romantic relationships (ages 18 to 20). However, this model may not accurately reflect the experience of younger gay men, many of whom feel freer than in the past to openly declare their sexual orientation; of lesbian and bisexual women, whose sexual identity development may be slower, more flexible, and more tied to emotional and situational factors than that of homosexual men; and of ethnic minorities, whose traditional communities and cultures may espouse strong religious beliefs or sterotypical gender roles, leading to internal and family conflict (Diamond, 1998, 2000; Diamond & Savin-Williams, 2003; Dubé & Savin-Williams, 1999).

Checkpoint ✔

Can you . . .

✔ Discuss theories and research regarding origins of sexual orientation?

✔ Discuss homosexual identity and relationship formation?

Sexual Behaviour

Internationally, there are wide variations in timing of sexual initiation, according to a survey sponsored by the World Health Organization (WHO), and another by the Canadian National Population Health Survey (Statistics Canada, 1998; Maticka-Tyndale, 2001; Maticka-Tyndale et al., 2001; Ross & Wyatt, 2000). The percentage of 15-year-old women who report having first intercourse is greater in Canada (about 25 percent) than in France (20 percent), Israel (11 percent), and Poland (14 percent), but it is less than the rate in the United States (38 percent). On the other hand, fewer 15-year-old Canadian men (about 20 percent) report having had sexual intercourse than 15-year-old men in the nine countries studied by the WHO (Finland, France, Hungary, Israel, Latvia, Northern Ireland, Poland, Scotland, and the United States). Although earlier male initiation is the norm in most cultures, in Canada more women than men report having had sexual intercourse by age 15 (Maticka-Tyndale et al., 2001). In Canada, the average age that teenagers, both male and female, report having sex for the first time is 16.5 years. Whereas about 28 percent of teens aged 15 to 17 report having sexual intercourse at least once, this number rises to 80 percent by age 20 to 24 years. In a 2005 survey, about 40 percent of male youth and 30 percent of female youth reported having more than one sexual partner in the past year (The Society of Obstetricians and Gynaecologists of Canada, 2006). Still, about one young person in four does not have intercourse during the teens (Maticka-Tyndale, McKay, & Barrett, 2001).

In Canada, after a steady rise since the 1970s, the median age of first intercourse has been constant at age 16.5 for men and women (Maticka-Tyndale et al., 2001). More Canadian boys postponed their first experience of sexual intercourse in 2002, compared with 1989, and the proportion of youth reporting having multiple partners has also dropped (Dorrance & Peterson, 2003).

Sexual Risk Taking

Two major concerns about adolescent sexual activity are the risks of contracting sexually transmitted diseases and, for heterosexual activity, of pregnancy. Most at risk are young people who start sexual activity early, have multiple partners, do not use contraceptives, and have inadequate information—or misinformation—about sex (Abma et al., 1997). Other risk factors are living in a socio-economically disadvantaged community, substance use, anti-social behaviour, and association with deviant peers. Parental monitoring can help reduce these risks (Baumer & South, 2001; Capaldi, Stoolmiller, Clark, & Owen, 2002).

Why do some adolescents become sexually active at an early age? Various factors—including early entrance into puberty, poverty, poor school performance, lack of academic and career goals, a history of sexual abuse or parental neglect, and cultural or family patterns of early sexual experience—may play a part (CICH, 2000; Garriguet, 2005; Klein & Committee on Adolescence, 2005; see Table 17-3). For example, a survey of British Columbia girls in Grades 7 to 12 showed that those who thought they looked older than their peers were more likely to report having sexual intercourse then those who thought they looked the same age as their peers (CICH, 2000). The absence of a father, especially early in life, is a strong factor (Ellis et al., 2003). Teenagers who have close, warm relationships with their mothers are more likely to delay sexual activity. So are those who perceive that their mothers disapprove of such activity (Jaccard & Dittus, 2000; Sieving, McNeely, & Blum, 2000). Other reasons teenagers give for *not* yet having had sex are that it is against their religion or morals and that they do not want to get (or get a girl) pregnant (Abma, Martinez, Mosher, & Dawson, 2004).

One of the most powerful influences is perception of peer group norms. Young people often feel under pressure to engage in activities they do not feel ready for. In a nationally representative survey of youth in the U.S., nearly one-third of 15- to 17-year-olds, especially boys, said they had experienced pressure to have sex (Kaiser Family Foundation et al., 2003).

According to the Canadian Youth Sexual Health and HIV/AIDS Study, a survey of over 10,000 Canadian youth in Grades 7, 9, and 11, (Boyce et al., 2003; 2006) more girls than boys reported being coerced into having sex. Twelve percent of Grade 9 girls and

Table 17-3	Some Factors Associated with Timing of First Intercourse	
	Factors Associated with Early Age	**Factors Associated with Later Age**
Timing of puberty	Early	Late
Personality style and behaviour	Risk taking, impulsive	Traditional values, religious orientation
	Depressive symptoms Anti-social or delinquent	Pro-social or conventional behaviour
Substance use	Use of drugs, alcohol, tobacco	Non-use
Education	Fewer years of schooling	More years of schooling; valuing academic achievement
Family structure	Single-parent family	Two-parent family
Socio-economic status	Disadvantaged	Advantaged

Source: Dubé & Savin-Williams, 1999; B. C. Miller & Moore, 1990; Sonenstein, Pleck, & Ku, 1991.

17 percent of Grade 11 girls reported being pressured to have sex when they did not want it, compared to only 5 percent of boys in each grade. In another study, 10 percent of girls reported having sex because they "didn't know how to say no" or "I did not give consent" (Canadian Women's Foundation, 2005). Seven out of 10 women whose first intercourse took place before age 13 report that it was unwanted or not voluntary (AGI, 1999a).

As adolescents have become more aware of the risks of sexual activity, the percentage who have ever had intercourse has declined, especially among boys (Abma et al., 2004). However, noncoital forms of genital sexual activity, such as oral and anal sex and mutual masturbation, are common. Many heterosexual teens do not regard these activities as "sex" but as substitutes for, or precursors of, sex, or even as abstinence (Remez, 2000). In one U.S. national survey, just over half of teenage boys and girls reported having given or received oral sex, more than had had vaginal intercourse (Mosher et al., 2005).

Use of Contraceptives

The use of contraceptives among teenagers has increased since 1990 (Abma et al., 2004). About 83 percent of girls and 91 percent of boys in one survey said they had used contraception the most recent time they had sex (Abma et al., 2004). Teens who, in their first relationship, delay intercourse, discuss contraception before having sex, or use more than one method of contraception are more likely to use contraceptives consistently throughout that relationship (Manlove, Ryan, & Franzetta, 2003).

The best safeguard for sexually active teens is the regular use of condoms, which give some protection against STDs as well as against pregnancy. Condom use has increased in recent years, as has use of the pill and new hormonal and injectable methods of contraception or combinations of methods (Abma et al., 2004). Still, in 2003, only 63 percent of sexually active U.S. high school students reported having used condoms the last time they had intercourse (Klein & Committee on Adolescence, 2005). In Canada the likelihood that adolescents use condoms declines as they get older; also, for females, those who start having intercourse in early adolescence are less likely to use condoms than those who begin intercourse later (Rotermann, 2005; see Figure 17-1). Adolescents who start using prescription contraceptives often stop using condoms, not realizing that they leave themselves unprotected against STDs (Klein & Committee on Adolescence, 2005).

Almost one-quarter of Canadian sexually active high school women and about one-third of sexually active high school men report two or more sex partners in a year (Maticka-Tyndale, 2001; Rotermann, 2005). About 13 percent of female 15- to 19-year-olds and 19 percent of males in the same age range who had two or more sex partners did not use condoms—an activity that places them at risk of developing sexually transmitted diseases (CICH, 2000). Studies of Canadian adolescent compliance in contraceptive use show that of those women who begin using oral contraceptives, only 49 percent continue to use them after 12 months. The factors that predicted compliance were being in a higher grade at school, being a non-smoker, and having the father's support for using birth control (Kalagian, Delmore, Loewen, & Busca, 1998). In a study of Canadian adolescent use of condoms, although 75 percent indicated at the outset that they would always use condoms,

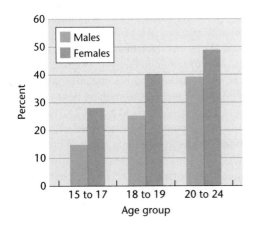

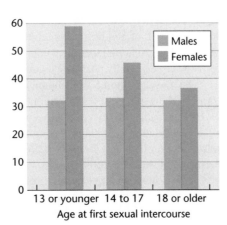

Figure 17-1

Percentage of sexually active young people in 2003 reporting that they did not use a condom the last time they had sexual intercourse a) by age; b) by age of first intercourse. With age, the likelihood that adolescents use condoms drops. Also, females who started having intercourse at the beginning of their teens are less likely to use condoms than males or females who started having intercourse at later ages.

Source: Rotermann, 2005.

only 42 percent reported using condoms in their last three experiences of intercourse. The factors that predicted having sex without a condom included having a negative attitude towards condoms, and having a weaker intention to use condoms (Richardson, Beazley, Delaney, & Langille, 1997). The proportion of youth having sex without adequate protection drops between Grade 9, with 51 percent of boys using condoms, and Grade 11, with 42 percent of boys using condoms (Boyce et al., 2003).

Where Do Teenagers Get Information about Sex?

Adolescents get their information about sex primarily from friends, parents, sex education in school, and the media (Kaiser Family Foundation et al., 2003). Adolescents who can talk about sex with older siblings as well as with parents are more likely to have positive attitudes toward safe sexual practices (Kowal & Pike, 2004). Today's teenagers tend to know more about sex than their predecessors did. In 1995, about 96 percent of 18- to 19-year-olds (as compared with only 80 percent of 25- to 29-year-olds and 65 percent of 35- to 39-year-olds) reported having had formal sex instruction. This instruction typically covered birth control methods, sexually transmitted diseases, safe sex to prevent HIV infection, and how to say no to sex (Abma et al., 1997).

This is important because teenagers who are knowledgeable about sex are more likely to use contraceptives and to use them consistently (Ku, Sonenstein, & Pleck, 1992; Louis Harris & Associates, 1986; Luster & Small, 1994). They are also more likely to postpone sexual intimacy—the most effective means of birth control (Conger, 1988; Jaslow, 1982). Teenagers who can go to their parents or other adults with questions about sex and those who get sex education from school or community programs have a better chance of avoiding pregnancy and other risks connected with sexual activity (see Box 17-1).

Unfortunately, many teenagers get much of their "sex education" from the media, which present a distorted view of sexual activity, associating it with fun, excitement, competition, danger, or violence and rarely showing the risks of unprotected sex. In a 2-year longitudinal survey of 12 to 14-year-olds, exposure to a heavy diet of sexual content in the media accelerated students' sexual activity and their likelihood of engaging in early intercourse (Brown et al., 2006).

Sexually Transmitted Diseases (STDs)

Sexually transmitted diseases (STDs) are diseases spread by sexual contact. Table 17-4 summarizes some common STDs: their causes, most frequent symptoms, treatment, and consequences.

Rates in Canada are typical of those in most Western countries, with the exception of the United States, which has among the highest rates of STDs in the industrialized world (Maticka-Tyndale, 2001). The chief reasons for the prevalence of STDs among teenagers are early sexual activity, which increases the likelihood of having multiple high-risk partners, failure to use condoms or to use them regularly and correctly, and, for women, the tendency to have sex with older partners (CDC, 2000c).

STDs are most likely to develop undetected in adolescent girls. In a *single* unprotected sexual encounter with an infected partner, a girl runs a 1-percent risk of acquiring HIV, a 30-percent risk of acquiring genital herpes, and a 50-percent risk of acquiring gonorrhea (AGI, 1999a). Although teenagers tend to view oral sex as less risky than intercourse, a number of STDs, especially pharyngeal gonorrhea, can be transmitted in that way (Remez, 2000).

The most common STD is human papilloma virus (HPV), which sometimes produces warts on the genitals. It is the leading cause of cervical cancer in women. A new vaccine for HPV is highly effective when given routinely to 11- and 12-year-old girls (CDC Davison of Media Relations, 2006). Also common among young people is trichomoniasis, a parasitic infection that may be passed along by moist towels and bathing suits (Weinstock, Berman, & Cates, Jr., 2004).

Genital herpes simplex is a chronic, recurring, often painful, and highly contagious disease caused by a virus. This condition can be fatal to a person with a deficiency of the immune system or to the newborn infant of a mother who has an outbreak at the time of

What's your view ?

- How can adolescents be helped to avoid or change risky sexual behaviour?

Checkpoint

Can you . . .

✔ Cite trends in sexual activity among adolescents?

✔ Identify factors that increase or decrease the risks of sexual activity?

sexually transmitted diseases (STDs) Diseases spread by sexual contact

Box 17-1 *Preventing Teenage Pregnancy*

Teenage pregnancy rates in Canada dropped during the 1990s and into the 2000s, currently at about 20 pregnancies per 1,000 adolescent women between 15 and 17 years, and they are lower than in many other industrialized countries, where adolescents begin sexual activity just as early or earlier—half as high as in the United States, and equal to England (Canadian Women's Foundation, 2005; Maticka-Tyndale, 2001) (Figure 17-2).

Experts disagree about the causes of teenage pregnancy. Some observers point to such factors as the reduced stigma on unwed motherhood, media glorification of sex, the lack of a clear message that sex and parenthood are for adults, the influence of childhood sexual abuse, and failure of parents to communicate with children. The European experience suggests the importance of two other factors: sex education and access to birth control (AAP Committee on Adolescence, 1999).

Europe's industrialized countries have long provided universal, comprehensive sex education—as has Canada. Canadian programs, following the Canadian Guidelines for Sexual Health Education (Health Canada, 1994), encourage young teenagers to delay intercourse but also aim to improve contraceptive use among adolescents who are sexually active. Such programs include education about sexuality and acquisition of skills for making responsible sexual decisions and communicating with partners. They provide information about risks and consequences of teenage pregnancy, about birth control methods, and about where to get medical and contraceptive help (Health Canada, 1994; McKay & Barrett, 1999; Sieccan [Sex Information and Education Council of Canada], 2000). Programs aimed at adolescent boys emphasize the wisdom of delaying fatherhood and the need to take responsibility when it occurs (Children's Defense Fund, 1998).

Of course, parents are young people's first and often best teachers. Teenagers whose parents have talked with them about sex from an early age, have communicated healthy attitudes, and have been available to answer questions tend to wait longer for sexual activity (J. J. Conger, 1988; Jaslow, 1982). However, many adolescents are uncomfortable talking about sex with parents. Peer counselling can be effective; teenagers often heed peers when they might not pay attention to the same advice from an older person (Jay, DuRant, Shoffitt, Linder, & Litt, 1984).

An important component of pregnancy prevention in European countries is access to reproductive services. Contraceptives are provided free to adolescents in Britain, France, Sweden, and, in many cases, the Netherlands. Sweden showed a fivefold reduction in the teenage birth rate following introduction of birth control education, free access to contraceptives, and free abortion on demand (Bracher & Santow, 1999).

In Canada, although sex education is widely available in public schools, students have complained that not enough information is provided on sexual feelings, alternatives and choices in sexuality, and ways to obtain confidential information and contraception (Maticka-Tyndale, 2001). In addition, some measures, like knowledge about the fatality of AIDs, knowledge about sexual health has declined since 1989 (Dorrance & Peterson, 2003).

The problem of teenage pregnancy requires a multi-faceted solution. It must include programs and policies to encourage postponing or refraining from sexual activity. But it must also recognize that many young people do become sexually active

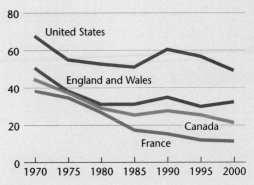

Figure 17-2

Trends in teenage birth rates per 1,000 girls ages 15 to 19 in selected western countries. The Canadian teenage birth rate has fallen since 1990, and it remains lower than in England and Wales, and the United States.

Source: Bernstein, 2004. Based on data from Centers for Disease Control and Prevention, Alan Guttmacher Institute, and Child Trends Databank.

and need education and information to prevent pregnancy and infection (AGI, 1999b). Ultimately, it requires attention to underlying factors that put teenagers and families at risk: reducing poverty, school failure, behavioural and family problems, and expanding employment, skills training, and family life education (AGI, 1994; Children's Defense Fund, 1998; Health Canada, 1994; Kirby, 1997). Programs for preschoolers and elementary school students have shown that comprehensive early intervention can reduce teenage pregnancy (Hawkins, Catalano, Kosterman, Abbott, & Hill, 1999; Schweinhart et al., 1993).

Because adolescents with high aspirations are less likely to become pregnant, programs that motivate young people to achieve and raise their self-esteem have had some success. Teen Outreach Program (TOP), which began in 1978, helps teenagers make decisions, handle emotions, and deal with peers and adults. The program also includes community service. By encouraging students to select a volunteer activity, the program helps them see themselves as autonomous and competent. Among 1,600 students in TOP and 1,600 in a control group, TOP participants had about half the risk of pregnancy or school suspension and 60 percent of the risk of failure of nonparticipants (Allen & Philliber, 2001). This is evidence that teenage pregnancy and school failure are not isolated problems but are part of a larger developmental picture.

What's your view ?

If you were designing a school-based or community-based sexuality education program, what would you include? Do you favour programs that provide contraceptives to teenagers?

Check it out !

For more information on this topic, go to **www.mcgrawhill.ca/ olc/papalia,** which provides links to relevant Web sites concerning teen pregnancy.

Table 17-4　Common Sexually Transmitted Diseases

Disease	Cause	Symptoms: Male	Symptoms: Female	Treatment	Consequences if Untreated
Chlamydia	Bacterial infection	Pain during urination, discharge from penis	Vaginal discharge, abdominal discomfort[†]	Tetracycline or erythromycin	Can cause pelvic inflammatory disease or eventual sterility
Trichomoniasis	Parasitic infection, sometimes passed on in moist objects such as towels and bathing suits	Often absent	May be absent, or may include vaginal discharge, discomfort during intercourse, odour, painful urination	Oral antibiotic	May lead to abnormal growth of cervical cells
Gonorrhea	Bacterial infection	Discharge from penis, pain during urination[*]	Discomfort when urinating, vaginal discharge, abnormal menses[†]	Penicillin or other antibiotics	Can cause pelvic inflammatory disease or eventual sterility; can also cause arthritis, dermatitis, and meningitis
HPV (genital warts)	Human papiloma virus	Painless growths that usually appear on penis, but may also appear on urethra or in rectal area[*]	Small, painless growths on genitals and anus; may also occur inside the vagina without external symptoms[*]	Removal of warts; but infection often reappears	May be associated with cervical cancer. In pregnancy, warts enlarge and may obstruct birth canal.
Herpes	Herpes simplex virus	Painful blisters anywhere on the genitalia, usually on the penis[*]	Painful blisters on the genitalia, sometimes with fever and aching muscles; women with sores on cervix may be unaware of outbreaks[*]	No known cure, but controlled with antiviral drug acyclovir	Possible increased risk of cervical cancer
Hepatitis B	Hepatitis B virus	Skin and eyes become yellow	Same as in men	No specific treatment; no alcohol	Can cause liver damage, chronic hepatitis
Syphilis	Bacterial infection	In first stage, reddish-brown sores on the mouth or genitalia, or both, which may disappear, though the bacteria remain; in the second, more infectious stage, a widespread skin rash[*]	Same as in men	Penicillin or other antibiotics	Paralysis, convulsions, brain damage, and sometimes death
AIDS (acquired immune deficiency syndrome)	Human immunodeficiency virus (HIV)	Extreme fatigue, fever, swollen lymph nodes, weight loss, diarrhea, night sweats, susceptibility to other diseases[*]	Same as in men	No known cure; protease inhibitors and other drugs appear to extend life	Death, usually due to other diseases, such as cancer

[*]May be asymptomatic

[†]Often asymptomatic

delivery. There is no cure, but the antiviral drug acyclovir can prevent active outbreaks. The incidence of genital herpes has increased dramatically during the past three decades. Hepatitis B remains a prominent STD despite the availability of a preventive vaccine for more than 20 years (Weinstock et al., 2004).

The most common *curable* STDs are chlamydia and gonorrhea (Maticka-Tyndale, 2001; Wong, Singh, Hansen, & McMahon, 2004). These diseases, if undetected and untreated, can lead to severe health problems, including, in women, to pelvic inflammatory disease (PID), a serious abdominal infection.

The human immunodeficiency virus (HIV), which causes AIDS, is transmitted through bodily fluids (mainly blood and semen), usually by sharing of intravenous drug needles or by sexual contact with an infected partner. The virus attacks the body's immune system, leaving a person vulnerable to a variety of fatal diseases. Symptoms of AIDS, which include extreme fatigue, fever, swollen lymph nodes, weight loss, diarrhea, and night sweats, may not appear until 6 months to 10 or more years after initial infection.

Worldwide, of the 4.1 million new HIV infections each year, about half are in young people ages 15 to 24 (UNAIDS, 2006). Although the prevalence of AIDS among Canadian youth is small compared to adults (approximately 3.4 percent of all cases), it is a cause for concern as many young people with undetected HIV go unreported (CICH, 2000). In addition, there is a growing proportion of Aboriginal youth with AIDS, compared to non-Aboriginal youth; 26 percent of Aboriginal people who were HIV-positive were under 30 years of age, compared to 17.6 percent of non-Aboriginal HIV-positive counterparts (Public Health Agency of Canada, 2004b, 2006). As of now, AIDS is incurable, but increasingly the related infections that kill people are being stopped with antiviral therapy, including protease inhibitors (Palella et al., 1998; Weinstock et al., 2004). A Danish study found the young patients diagnosed with HIV have an estimated median survival of more than 35 years (Lohse et al., 2007).

Because symptoms may not appear until a disease has progressed to the point of causing serious long-term complications, early detection is important. Regular, school-based screening and treatment, together with programs that promote abstention from or postponement of sexual activity, responsible decision making, and ready availability of condoms for those who are sexually active may have some effect in controlling the spread of STDs (AAP Committee on Adolescence, 1994; AGI, 1994; Cohen, Nsuami, Martin, & Farley, 1999; Rotheram-Borus & Futterman, 2000). There is *no* evidence that education about condom use and availability contributes to increased sexual activity (Klein & Committee on Adolescence, 2005).

Checkpoint ✔

Can you . . .

✔ Identify and describe the most common sexually transmitted diseases?

✔ List risk factors for developing an STD during adolescence, and describe effective prevention methods?

Teenage Pregnancy and Childbearing

In Canada in 1997, the pregnancy rate for teenagers was 42.7 pregnancies for every 1,000 women between the ages of 15 and 19 (Statistics Canada, 2000), which had declined over the previous 3 years. By 2003, the rate was 35.7 per 1,000 (CTV, 2007). The U.S. rate, although also declining, is about double the Canadian rate (CTV, 2007). The Canadian pregnancy rate is higher for older adolescents (about 69 per 1,000 women between ages 18 and 19), reflecting their higher likelihood of being sexually active than younger women.

Many pregnant girls are inexperienced: 50 percent had their first intercourse within the past 6 months (AGI, 1994; Children's Defense Fund, 1998; Ventura, Mathews, & Curtin, 1999). Some were coerced or sexually abused: About 1 in 5 infants born to unmarried minors are fathered by men at least 5 years older than the mother (AGI, 1999a).

The proportion of adolescents giving birth has fallen although the number of abortions has been constant over the past several years prior to 1997. In that year, the percentage of teenage pregnancies that were aborted (50.3 percent) surpassed the number of live births (46.8 percent). The remaining pregnancies ended in miscarriage (Statistics Canada, 2000). Of the 33,000 teens who become pregnant each year, 18,000 choose to end their pregnancies (CTV, 2007). More than 40 percent of Canadian women report having been pregnant at least once before the age of 20 (Klein & Committee on Adolescence, 2005).

During the 1990s, teenage pregnancy and birthrates fell to below 1970s levels, reflecting the trends toward decreased sexual activity and, more so, toward increased use of contraceptives (CTV, 2007). The regions of Canada that had the highest teenage pregnancy rates were the northern regions and prairie provinces. In the Northwest Territories (including Nunavut) the rate was 123 pregnancies per 1,000 teenage women, and over 60 per 1,000 in the Yukon and in Manitoba. The highest rates of abortion were in the northern regions and in Ontario, while

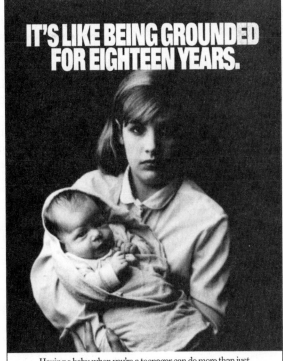

IT'S LIKE BEING GROUNDED FOR EIGHTEEN YEARS.

Having a baby when you're a teenager can do more than just take away your freedom, it can take away your dreams.

THE CHILDREN'S DEFENSE FUND

To teenagers, one of the most persuasive arguments against sexual risk-taking is the danger that pregnancy will ruin their lives. Teenage girls respond better when the advice comes from other girls close to their own age.

the lowest rates were in Prince Edward Island and New Brunswick (CTV, 2007; Statistics Canada, 2000). About 84 percent of births to adolescent mothers in Canada were to unwed teens, a rate that has increased over the last four decades (Dahinten & Willms, 2002). While past teenage pregnancies typically resulted in marriage or putting the child up for adoption, today most pregnant teenagers choose abortion or single parenthood (Daly & Sobol, 1993).

Teenage pregnancies often have poor outcomes. Many of the mothers are impoverished and poorly educated, and risk poor health. Many do not eat properly or do not gain enough weight. Their babies are likely to be premature or dangerously small and are at heightened risk of neonatal death, disability, or health problems (AAP Committee on Adolescence, 1999; Adoption, and Dependent Care, 2001; AGI, 1999a; Children's Defense Fund, 1998, 2004; Dahinten & Willms, 2002; Klein & Committee on Adolescence, 2005; Maticka-Tyndale, 2001; Menacker et al., 2004).

Babies of more affluent teenage mothers are also at risk. Among more than 134,000 U.S. white, largely middle-class girls and women, 13- to 19-year-olds were more likely than 20- to 24-year-olds to have low–birth weight babies, even when the mothers were married and well educated and had adequate prenatal care. Good prenatal care apparently cannot always overcome the biological disadvantage inherent in being born to a still-growing girl whose own body may be competing with the developing fetus for vital nutrients (Fraser et al., 1995).

Teenage unwed mothers and their families are likely to suffer financial hardship. Child support laws are spottily enforced, court-ordered payments are often inadequate, and many young fathers cannot afford them. Adolescent fathers often have poor school records, high dropout rates, and limited financial resources and income potential. Even if they want to be involved in their children's lives, they may not know how (AAP Committee on Adolescence, 1999).

Teenage mothers are likely to drop out of school and to have repeated pregnancies. They and their partners may lack the maturity, skills, and social support to be good parents. Their children, in turn, are likely to have developmental and academic problems, to be depressed, to engage in substance abuse and early sexual activity, and to become adolescent parents themselves (Dahinten & Willms, 2002; Klein & Committee on Adolescence, 2005). However, these outcomes are far from inevitable. Several long-term studies find that, two decades after giving birth, most former adolescent mothers are not on welfare; many have finished high school and secured steady jobs, and do not have large families. Comprehensive adolescent pregnancy and home visitation programs seem to contribute to good outcomes (Klein & Committee on Adolescence, 2005).

In Canada, although many children from single-parent families have difficulties as infants, by the time they begin school any differences that might have existed in social, emotional, or cognitive development between children of teenage mothers and those of older mothers disappear (Maticka-Tyndale, 2001).

Guidepost 3

How do adolescents relate to parents, siblings, and peers?

Relationships with Family and Peers

Age becomes a powerful bonding agent in adolescence. Adolescents spend more time with peers and less with family. However, most teenagers' fundamental values (like David Suzuki's) remain closer to their parents' than is generally realized (Offer & Church, 1991). Even as adolescents turn to peers for companionship and intimacy, they look to parents for a "secure base" from which they can try their wings (Laursen, 1996). The most secure adolescents have strong, supportive relationships with parents who are attuned to the way the young people see themselves, who permit and encourage their strivings for independence, and who provide a safe haven in times of emotional stress (Allen et al., 2003; Laursen, 1996).

Is Adolescent Rebellion a Myth?

The teenage years have been called a time of **adolescent rebellion,** involving emotional turmoil, conflict within the family, alienation from adult society, reckless behaviour, and rejection of adults' values. Yet school-based research on adolescents the world over suggests that only about 1 in 5 teenagers fits this pattern (Offer & Schonert-Reichl, 1992).

adolescent rebellion Pattern of emotional turmoil, characteristic of a minority of adolescents, which may involve conflict with family, alienation from adult society, reckless behaviour, and rejection of adult values

The idea of adolescent rebellion may have been born in the first formal theory of adolescence, that of the psychologist G. Stanley Hall. Hall (1904/1916) believed that young people's efforts to adjust to their changing bodies and to the imminent demands of adulthood usher in a period of "storm and stress," which produces conflict between the generations. Sigmund Freud (1935/1953) and his daughter, Anna Freud (1946), described "storm and stress" as universal and inevitable, growing out of a resurgence of early sexual drives toward the parents.

However, the anthropologist Margaret Mead (1928, 1935; see Chapter 2: Focus), who studied adolescence in Samoa and other South Pacific islands, concluded that when a culture provides a gradual, serene transition from childhood to adulthood, "storm and stress" is not typical. Although her research in Samoa was later challenged (Freeman, 1983), her observation was eventually supported by research in 186 pre-industrial societies (Schlegel & Barry, 1991).

Full-fledged rebellion now appears to be uncommon even in industrialized countries, at least among middle-class youngsters who are in school. Most young people feel close to and positive about their parents, share similar opinions on major issues, and value their parents' approval (J. P. Hill, 1987; King et al., 1999; Offer et al., 1989; Offer, Ostrov, Howard, & Atkinson, 1988). Furthermore, contrary to a popular belief, apparently well-adjusted adolescents are not "ticking time bombs" set to "explode" later in life. In a 34-year longitudinal study of 67 fourteen-year-old suburban boys, the vast majority adapted well to their life experiences (Offer, Offer, & Ostrov, 2004). The relatively few deeply troubled adolescents tended to come from disrupted families and, as adults, continued to have unstable family lives and to reject cultural norms. Those raised in intact two-parent homes with positive family atmosphere tended to sail through adolescence with no serious problems and, as adults, to have solid marriages and lead well-adjusted lives (Offer, Kaiz, Ostrov, & Albert, 2002).

Still, adolescence can be a tough time for young people and their parents. Family conflict, depression, and risky behaviour are more common than during other parts of the life span (Arnett, 1999; Petersen et al., 1993). Negative emotionality and mood swings are most intense during early adolescence, perhaps due to the stress connected with puberty. By late adolescence, emotionality tends to become more stable (Larson, Moneta, Richards, & Wilson, 2002).

As Canadian youth get older, their relationships with parents, particularly in trust and expectations, worsens. About half of Grade 10 girls and one-third of Grade 10 boys agree that there are times when they would like to leave home. Most value their parents' opinions of them, but parents' expectations of school performance were felt to be too high by about a third of adolescents in Grade 10. Young people tend to find it easier to communicate with their mothers rather than their fathers. Canadian parents are slightly more distanced from their children than parents in many European countries (King et al., 1999). These results reflect similar ones from a study of "connectedness" between adolescents and their families in British Columbia (CICH, 2000). Feeling that the relationship is close, is caring, and fosters a sense of belonging indicates a high level of connectedness. The highest level of connectedness in young people is reported by 12-year-olds. Connectedness drops off steeply as young people progress through adolescence, until 17 years of age, when only 9 percent of young people report high levels of connectedness (CICH, 2000; Public Health Agency of Canada, 2004). This can have serious consequences, because high levels of connectedness are correlated with low levels of risk behaviours such as early sexual activity, and alcohol and drug abuse.

Recognizing that adolescence may be a difficult time can help parents and teachers put troubling behaviour in perspective. But adults who assume that adolescent turmoil is normal and necessary may fail to heed the signals of the occasional young person who needs special help.

Changing Time Use and Changing Relationships

One way to assess changes in adolescents' relationships with the important people in their lives is to see how they spend their discretionary time. The amount of time adolescents spend with families declines dramatically between ages 10 and 18, from 35 percent to 14 percent of waking hours (Larson, Richards, Moneta, Holmbeck, & Duckett, 1996).

What's your view

- Can you think of values you hold that are different from those of your parents? How did you come to develop these values?

Disengagement is not a rejection of the family but a response to developmental needs. Early adolescents often retreat to their rooms; they seem to need time alone to step back from the demands of social relationships, regain emotional stability, and reflect on identity issues (Larson, 1997).

Cultural variations in time use reflect varying cultural needs, values, and practices (Verma & Larson, 2003). Young people in tribal or peasant societies spend most of their time producing bare necessities of life and have much less time for socializing than adolescents in technologically advanced societies (Larson & Verma, 1999). In some postindustrial societies such as Korea and Japan, where the pressures of schoolwork and family obligations are strong, adolescents have relatively little free time. To relieve stress, they spend their time in passive pursuits, such as watching television and "doing nothing" (Verma & Larson, 2003). In India's family-centred culture, on the other hand, middle-class urban eighth-graders spend 39 percent of their waking hours with family and report being happier when with their families than eighth-graders in North America do. For these young people, the task of adolescence is not to separate from the family but to become more integrated with it. Similar findings have been reported in Indonesia, Bangladesh, Morocco, and Argentina (Larson & Wilson, 2004). By comparison, North American adolescents have a good deal of discretionary time, most of which they spend with peers, increasingly of the other sex (Juster et al., 2004; Larson & Seepersad, 2003; Verma & Larson, 2003).

As adolescents get older, they often find it progressively difficult to talk to their parents, with more difficulty communicating with fathers than with mothers. About two-thirds of Grade 10 students find it easy or very easy to talk with their mothers, while 55 percent of boys, and only 33 percent of girls, find it easy or very easy to talk with their fathers. Mothers appear to be more approachable than fathers for Canadian adolescents (King et al., 1999; Public Health Agency of Canada, 2002). In addition, about half of Grade 10 students feel that their parents understand them, with more boys than girls feeling this way (King et al., 1999).

Interviews with 377 adolescents in Canada, Belgium, and Italy showed that Italian teenagers tended to maintain closer ties with their families, whereas friends occupied a more central position for Canadian adolescents. Belgian teenagers tended to maintain close ties with both family members and friends (Claes, 1998). It is likely that differences in cultural contexts and practices account for these differences: Parents seem to play a larger role in organizing daily life and behaving in ways that foster closeness in Italy, compared to Canada and Belgium. Despite these differences, there were similarities in relations. Friends emerged as important aspects of the social life of teens in all cultures, and the participants tended to have closer relations with their mothers than with their fathers (Claes, 1998).

With such variations in mind, let's look more closely at relationships with parents, and then with siblings and peers.

Adolescents and Parents

Just as adolescents feel tension between dependency on their parents and the need to break away, parents often have mixed feelings, too. They want their children to be independent, yet they find it hard to let go. Parents have to walk a fine line between giving adolescents enough independence and protecting them from immature lapses in judgment. These tensions often lead to family conflict, and parenting styles can influence its shape and outcome. Effective parental monitoring depends on how much adolescents let parents know about their daily lives, and this may depend on the atmosphere parents have established. Also, as with younger children, teenagers' relationships with parents are affected by the parents' life situation—their work and marital and socio-economic status.

Family Conflict and Individuation

Most arguments between adolescents and parents concern mundane personal matters—chores, schoolwork, dress, money, curfews, dating, and friends—rather than issues of health and safety or right and wrong (Adams & Laursen, 2001; Steinberg, 2005). The emotional intensity of these conflicts—out of all proportion with the subject matter—may reflect the underlying process of **individuation,** the adolescent's struggle for autonomy and

individuation Adolescent's struggle for autonomy and differentiation, or personal identity

differentiation, or personal identity. An important aspect of individuation is carving out boundaries of control between the self and others (Nucci, Hasebe, & Lins-Dyer, 2005).

Family conflict is most frequent during early adolescence but most intense in mid-adolescence (Laursen, Coy, & Collins, 1998). By Grade 10, 29 percent of males and 36 percent of females in Canada feel that they have a lot of arguments with their parents (King et al., 1999). The frequency of strife in early adolescence may be related to the strains of puberty and the need to assert autonomy. The more highly charged arguments in mid-adolescence and, to a lesser extent, in late adolescence may reflect the emotional strains that occur as adolescents try their wings. The reduced frequency of conflict in late adolescence may signify adjustment to the momentous changes of the teenage years and a renegotiation of the balance of power between parent and child (Fuligni & Eccles, 1993; Laursen et al., 1998; Molina & Chassin, 1996; Steinberg, 1988), enlarging the boundaries of what is considered the adolescent's own business (Steinberg, 2005). A study of Canadian adolescents showed that the nature of the conflict changes as teenagers develop. Arguments about chores, appearance, and politeness typically decrease between Grades 6 and 8, while conflict over finances increase (Galambos & Almeida, 1992).

The level of family discord may depend largely on family atmosphere. Among 335 two-parent rural midwestern U.S. families with teenagers, conflict declined during early to middle adolescence in warm, supportive families but worsened in hostile, coercive, or critical families (Rueter & Conger, 1995).

What's your view ?

• What kinds of issues caused the most conflict in your family when you were a teenager, and how were they resolved?

• If you lived with both parents, were your conflicts more with one parent than with the other? Did your mother and father handle such issues similarly or differently?

Parenting Styles and Parental Authority

As we mentioned in Chapter 16, authoritative parenting continues to foster healthy development (Baumrind, 1991, 2005). Most adolescents (like David Suzuki) "excel in most areas of their lives when they simply feel that they come from a loving home with responsive parents" (Gray & Steinberg, 1999, p. 584). Parents who show disappointment in teenagers' misbehaviour are more effective in motivating responsible behaviour than parents who punish harshly (Krevans & Gibbs, 1996). Overly strict, authoritarian parenting may be especially counterproductive as children enter adolescence and want to be treated more as adults. When parents do not adjust, an adolescent may reject parental influence and seek peer support and approval at all costs (Fuligni & Eccles, 1993).

Authoritative parents insist on important rules, norms, and values but are willing to listen, explain, and negotiate (Lamborn, Mounts, Steinberg, & Dornbusch, 1991). They exercise appropriate control over a child's conduct (*behavioural control*) but not over the child's feelings, beliefs, and sense of self (*psychological control*) (Steinberg & Darling, 1994). Psychological control, exerted through such emotionally manipulative techniques as withdrawal of love, can harm adolescents' psychosocial development and mental health (Steinberg, 2005). (Table 17-5 is a checklist used for adolescents' self-reports on parents' use of psychological control.) Parents who are psychologically controlling tend to be unresponsive to their children's growing need for *psychological autonomy*, the right to their own thoughts and feelings (Steinberg, 2005).

Authoritative parenting seems to bolster an adolescent's self-image. A survey of 8,700 U.S. students in Grades 9 to 12 concluded that "the more involvement, autonomy granting, and structure that adolescents perceive from their parents, the more positively teens evaluate their own general conduct, psychosocial development, and mental health" (Gray & Steinberg, 1999, p. 584). When adolescents thought their parents were trying to dominate their psychological experience, their emotional health suffered more than when parents tried to control their behaviour. Teens whose parents were firm in enforcing behavioural rules had more self-discipline and fewer behaviour problems than those with more permissive parents. Those whose parents granted them psychological autonomy tended to become self-confident and competent in both the academic and social realms.

Problems arise when parents overstep what adolescents perceive as appropriate bounds of legitimate parental authority. The existence of a mutually agreed personal domain in which authority belongs to the adolescent has been

The warmth and acceptance this mother shows to her son are characteristic of an authoritative parenting style. Authoritative parents set reasonable rules about, for example, what time a child must come home, but are willing to listen to and respect the child's point of view. Authoritative parenting may be especially effective as children enter adolescence and want to be treated more like adults.

Table 17-5	Psychological Control Scale—Youth Self-Report

Ratings:

1 = Not like her (him); 2 = Somewhat like her (him); 3 = A lot like her (him)

My Mother (Father) is a person who . . .

changes the subject, whenever I have something to say.

finishes my sentences whenever I talk.

often interrupts me.

acts like she (he) knows what I'm thinking or feeling.

would like to be able to tell me how to feel or think about things all the time.

is always trying to change how I feel or think about things.

blames me for other family members' problems.

brings up my past mistakes when she (he) criticizes me.

tells me that I am not a loyal or good member of the family.

tells me of all the things she (he) had done for me.

says, if I really cared for her (him), I would not do things that cause her (him) to worry.

is less friendly with me, if I do not see things her (his) way.

will avoid looking at me whn I have disappointed her (him).

if I have hurt her (his) feelings, stops talking to me until I please her (him) again.

often changes his (her) moods when with me.

goes back and forth between being warm and critical toward me.

Source: Adapted from Barber, 1996.

found in various cultures and social classes from Japan to Brazil. This domain expands as parents and adolescents continually renegotiate its boundaries (Nucci et al., 2005).

Parental Monitoring and Adolescents' Self-disclosure

Young people's growing autonomy and the shrinking areas of perceived parental authority redefine the types of behaviour adolescents are expected to disclose to parents (Smetana, Crean, & Campione-Barr, 2005; see Table 17-6). In a study of 276 ethnically diverse suburban ninth and twelfth graders, both adolescents and parents saw *prudential* behaviour related to health and safety (such as smoking, drinking, and drug use) as most subject to disclosure, followed by *moral* issues (such as lying), *conventional* issues (such as bad manners or swearing), and *multifaceted* or "borderline" issues (such as seeing an R-rated movie), which lie at the boundary between *personal* matters and one of the other categories. Both adolescents and parents saw *personal* matters (such as how teens spend their time and

Table 17-6	Items Used to Assess Perceived Areas of Parental vs. Adolescent Authority				
Moral Items	**Conventional Items**	**Prudential Items**	**Multifaceted Items**	**Multifaceted Friendship**	**Personal Items**
Stealing money from parents	Not doing assigned chores	Smoking cigarettes	Not cleaning bedroom	When to start dating	Sleeping late on weekends
Hitting siblings	Talking back to parents	Drinking beer or wine	Getting ears peirced with multiple holes	Staying over at a friend's house	Choosing how to spend allowance money
Lying to parents	Using bad manners	Doing drugs	Staying out late	Seeing friends whom parents don't like	Choosing own clothes or hairstyles
Breaking a promise to parents	Cursing	Having sex	Watching cable TV	Seeing friends rather than going out with family	Choice of music

Source: Adapted from Smetana, Crean, & Campione-Barr, 2005.

money) as least subject to disclosure. However, for each type of behaviour parents were more inclined to expect disclosure than adolescents were to do it. This discrepancy diminished between ninth and twelfth grades as parents modified their expectations to fit adolescents' growing maturity (Smetana, Metzger, Gettman, & Campione-Barr, 2006).

In a study of 690 Belgian adolescents, young people were more willing to disclose information about themselves when parents maintained a warm, responsive family climate in which adolescents were encouraged to speak openly and when parents provided clear expectations without being overly controlling (Soenens, Vansteenkiste, Luyckx, & Goossens, 2006)—in other words, when parenting was authoritative. Adolescents, especially girls, tend to have closer, more supportive relationships with their mothers than with their fathers, and girls confide more in their mothers (Smetana et al., 2006).

Family Structure and Family Atmosphere

Many adolescents today live in families that are very different from families of a few decades ago. Many parents are single; some are remarried. Most work outside the home. How do these family situations affect adolescents?

Adolescents, like younger children, are sensitive to the atmosphere in the family home. In a longitudinal study of 451 adolescents and their parents, changes in marital distress or marital conflict—either for better or worse—predicted corresponding changes in adolescents' adjustment (Cui, Conger, & Lorenz, 2005). In other studies, adolescent boys and girls whose parents later divorced showed more academic, psychological, and behavioural problems *before* the breakup than peers whose parents did not later divorce (Sun, 2001).

Adolescents living with their continuously married parents tend to have significantly less behavioural problems than those in any other family structure (single-parent, cohabiting, or stepfamilies), according to data from a major U.S. national longitudinal study. An important factor is father involvement. High-quality involvement by a nonresident father helps a great deal, but not as much as the involvement of a father living in the home (Carlson, 2006).

Adolescents in cohabiting families, like younger children, tend to have greater behavioural and emotional problems than adolescents in married families; and, when one of the cohabiting parents is not the biological parent, school engagement suffers as well. For adolescents, unlike younger children, these effects are independent of economic resources, parental well-being, or effectiveness of parenting, suggesting that parental cohabitation itself may be more troublesome for adolescents than for younger children (Brown, 2004).

On the other hand, a multiethnic study of 12- and 13-year-old children of single mothers—first assessed when the children were 6 and 7 years old—found no negative effects of single parenting on school performance and no greater risk of problem behaviour. What mattered most were the mother's educational level and ability, family income, and the quality of the home environment (Ricciuti, 2004). This finding suggests that negative effects of living in a single-parent home can be offset by positive factors, like engagement with the parent (Lipman et al., 2002).

Mothers' Employment and Economic Stress

The impact of a mother's work outside the home may depend on whether there are two parents or only one in the household. Often a single mother must work to stave off economic disaster; how her working affects her teenage children may hinge on how much time and energy she has left over to spend with them, how well she keeps track of their whereabouts, and what kind of role model she provides. A longitudinal study of 819 ten- to 14-year-olds from low-income urban families points up the importance of the type of care and supervisions adolescents receive after school. Those who are on their own, away from home, tend to become involved in alcohol and drug use and in misconduct in school, especially if they have an early history of problem behaviour. However, this is less likely to happen when parents monitor their children's activities and neighbours are actively involved (Coley, Morris, & Hernandez, 2004).

Studies of Canadian families show that when parents feel overworked, parent–child conflict tends to rise. Mothers who feel overloaded tend to become less caring and accepting, and their children often show behaviour problems (Galambos, Sears, Almeida, &

Kolaric, 1995). When mothers are stressed, tensions between adolescents and fathers increase as well (Almeida & McDonald, 1998).

A mother's work status helps shape adolescents' attitudes toward women's roles (Galambos, Petersen, & Lenerz, 1988). In a study of adolescents' attitudes towards work, 14-year-olds in dual-earner families tended to have higher levels of respect towards their mothers' and fathers' work, when the work was seen as resulting in less strain and depersonalization along with more satisfaction for the parents (Galambos & Sears, 1998). Teenage sons of working mothers tend to have more flexible attitudes toward gender roles when they have warm relationships with their mothers, and teenage daughters show non-stereotypical attitudes when their mothers are happy with their dual roles (Galambos et al., 1988). Surprisingly, some of the strongest gender-typing occurs in families with full-time employed mothers. Gender divisions may be more egalitarian during the week, when everyone is occupied with work or school. On weekends, however, girls—like their mothers—do a larger share of the housework and of care of younger siblings (Crouter & Maguire, 1998).

As we have discussed earlier, a major problem in many single-parent families is lack of money. In a U.S. national longitudinal study, adolescent children of low-income single mothers were negatively affected by their mother's unstable employment or being out of work for 2 years. The adolescents were more likely to drop out of school and to experience declines in self-esteem and mastery (Kalil & Ziol-Guest, 2005). Furthermore, family economic hardship during adolescence can affect adult well-being. The degree of risk depends on whether parents see their situation as stressful; whether that stress interferes with family relationships; and how much it affects children's educational and occupational attainments (Sobolewski & Amato, 2005).

On the other hand, many adolescents in economically distressed families may benefit from accumulated social capital—the support of kin and community. In 51 poor, urban African-American families in which teenagers were living with their mothers, grandmothers, or aunts, women who had strong kinship networks exercised firmer control and closer monitoring while granting appropriate autonomy, and their teenage charges were more self-reliant and had fewer behaviour problems (R. D. Taylor & Roberts, 1995).

Adolescents and Siblings

As adolescents begin to separate from their families and spend more time with peers, they have less time and less need for the emotional gratification they used to get from the sibling bond. Adolescents are less close to siblings than to either parents or friends, are less influenced by them, and become even more distant as they move through adolescence (Laursen, 1996).

Changes in sibling relationships may well precede similar changes in the relationship between adolescents and parents: more independence on the part of the younger person and less authority exerted by the older person. As children approach high school, their relationships with their siblings become progressively more equal. Older siblings exercise less power over younger ones, and younger siblings no longer need as much supervision. As relative age differences shrink, so do differences in competence and independence (Buhrmester & Furman, 1990).

Older and younger siblings tend to have different feelings about their changing relationship. As the younger sibling grows up, the older one may look on a newly assertive younger brother or sister as a pesky annoyance. Younger siblings still tend to look up to older ones—as Jackie Robinson did to his brother Mack—and try to feel more "grown up" by identifying with and emulating them (Buhrmester & Furman, 1990). In a 5-year longitudinal study of 227 Latino and African American families, sibling relationships under certain circumstances had important effects on the younger sibling. In single-mother homes, a warm and nurturing relationship with an older sister tended to prevent a younger sister from engaging in substance use and risky sexual behaviour. On the other hand, having a domineering older sister tended to increase a younger sibling's high-risk sexual behaviour (East & Khoo, 2005). As we mentioned in Chapter 15, older siblings may influence a younger one to smoke, drink, or use drugs (Pomery et al., 2005; Rende et al., 2005). In a longitudinal study of 206 boys and

Checkpoint ✔

Can you . . .

✔ Identify factors that affect conflict with parents and adolescents' self-disclosure?

✔ Discuss the impact on adolescents of parenting styles and of marital status, mothers' employment, and economic status?

What's your view ❓

• If you have one or more brothers or sisters, did your relationships with them change during adolescence?

Sibling relationships become more equal as the younger sibling approaches or reaches adolescence and the relative difference in age diminishes. Even so, this younger sister still looks up to her "big sister" and may try to emulate her.

their younger siblings, younger siblings "hanging out" with an anti-social older brother were at serious risk for adolescent anti-social behaviour, drug use, sexual behaviour, and violence, regardless of parental discipline (Snyder, Bank, & Burraston, 2005).

Peers and Friends

Checkpoint ✔

Can you . . .

✔ Describe typical changes in sibling relationships during adolescence?

An important source of emotional support during the complex transition of adolescence, as well as a source of pressure for behaviour that parents may deplore, is a young person's growing involvement with peers. The peer group is a source of affection, sympathy, understanding, and moral guidance; a place for experimentation; and a setting for achieving autonomy and independence from parents. It is a place to form intimate relationships that serve as "rehearsals" for adult intimacy.

The influence of peers normally peaks at ages 12 to 13 and declines during middle and late adolescence. At age 13 or 14, popular adolescents may engage in mildly anti-social behaviours, such as trying drugs or sneaking into a movie without paying, so as to demonstrate to their peers their independence from parental rules (Allen, Porter, McFarland, Marsh, & McElhaney, 2005). However, attachment to peers in early adolescence is not likely to forecast real trouble unless the attachment is so strong that the young person is willing to give up obeying household rules, doing schoolwork, and developing his or her own talents in order to win peer approval and popularity (Fuligni et al., 2001).

In one study that demonstrated the influence of peers on risk-taking, 306 adolescents, college-age youth, and young adults played a video game called "Chicken." The younger participants were more likely to take risks and make risky decisions than the older ones. For all ages groups, risk-taking was higher in the company of peers than alone, but this was more true of younger participants than of adults (Gardner & Steinberg, 2005).

In childhood, most peer interactions are *dyadic,* or one-to-one, though somewhat larger groupings begin to form in middle childhood. As children move into adolescence, *cliques*—structured groups of friends who do things together—become more important. A third, and larger, type of grouping, *crowds,* which does not normally exist before adolescence, is based not on personal interactions but on reputation, image, or identity. Crowd membership is a social construction, a set of labels by which young people divide the social map based on neighbourhood, ethnicity, socio-economic status, or other factors. All three of these levels of peer groupings may exist simultaneously, and some may overlap in membership, which may change over time (Brown & Klute, 2003).

Friendships

The intensity and importance of friendships and the amount of time spent with friends are probably greater in adolescence than at any other time in the life span. Friendships tend to become more reciprocal, more equal, and more stable; those that are not may lose importance or be abandoned.

Adolescents, like younger children, tend to choose friends who are like them, and friends influence each other to become even more alike (Berndt, 1982; Berndt & Perry, 1990). Friends tend to have similar academic attitudes and performance and similar levels of drug use (Hamm, 2000), and they may influence each other either toward pro-social activity (Barry & Wentzel, 2005) or toward risky or problem behaviour. Alternatively, the qualities that lead friends to choose each other may lead them to develop in similar directions. By controlling for these selection effects, a one-year longitudinal study of 1,700 adolescent friendship pairs found that friends' influence on binge drinking and sexual activity was fairly weak (Jaccard, Blanton, & Dodge, 2005).

Friends are not necessarily of the same race: A study of inter-ethnic friendships of young adolescents in Toronto showed that most friends of students belong to other ethnic groups (Smith & Schneider, 2000). Although East-Asian students rated their same-ethnicity friendships as being of higher quality than their friendships with members of other ethnic groups, students of European, West-Indian, and East-Indian backgrounds indicated no differences in ratings of quality of friendships with members of different ethnic backgrounds. Friends do tend to have similar academic attitudes and performance and, especially, similar levels of drug use (Hamm, 2000) and to have similar status within the peer group (Berndt & Perry, 1990).

A stress on intimacy, loyalty, and sharing marks a transition toward adultlike friendships. Adolescents begin to rely more on friends than on parents for intimacy and support, and they share confidences more than younger friends do (Berndt & Perry, 1990; Buhrmester, 1990, 1996; Hartup & Stevens, 1999; Laursen, 1996). Girls' friendships tend to be more intimate than boys', with frequent sharing of confidences (Brown & Klute, 2003). Intimacy with same-sex friends increases during early to mid-adolescence, after which it typically declines as intimacy with the other sex grows (Laursen, 1996).

The increased intimacy of adolescent friendship reflects cognitive, as well as emotional, development. Adolescents are now better able to express their private thoughts and feelings. They can also more readily consider another person's point of view, and so it is easier for them to understand a friend's thoughts and feelings. Increased intimacy also reflects early adolescents' concern with getting to know themselves. Confiding in a friend helps young people explore their own feelings, define their identity, and validate their self-worth. Friendship provides a safe place to venture opinions, admit weaknesses, and get help with problems (Buhrmester, 1996).

The capacity for intimacy is related to psychological adjustment and social competence. Adolescents who have close, stable, supportive friendships generally have a high opinion of themselves, do well in school, are sociable, and are unlikely to be hostile, anxious, or d pressed (Berndt & Perry, 1990; Buhrmester, 1990; Hartup & Stevens, 1999). They also tend to have established strong bonds with parents (Brown & Klute, 2003). A bi-directional process seems to be at work: Good friendships foster adjustment, which in turn fosters good friendships.

Loneliness is a common experience in adolescence, particularly in the absence of intimate friendships. There seem to be cultural differences in how loneliness is experienced by adolescents. In a survey of how adolescents experience loneliness, differences were found in comparisons between 100 Canadian and 206 Portuguese teenagers. In response to questions on experiences of loneliness, Canadian youth report more extreme feelings of emotional distress, social inadequacy and alienation, and interpersonal isolation than Portuguese youth (Rokach & Neto, 2001). These differences may reflect differences in how the individual and community interact in the two cultures. In Portuguese society the community provides support and a sense of belonging for the individual, whereas Canadian society emphasizes individual resources in finding support and a sense of belonging, with loneliness perceived as an example of individual failure (Rokach et al., 2001).

Cliques

Cliques may exist among pre-adolescent children but are a more prominent feature of early adolescence. As expanded circles of friends, they usually consist of young people of the same age, gender, and ethnicity. However, membership in cliques tends to be based not only on personal affinity but on popularity, or social status. A person may belong to more than one clique or to no clique, and the membership of a clique may be stable or shifting (Brown & Klute, 2003).

The dynamics of clique membership in pre-adolescence are highly status-based, especially among girls. The members with highest status are acknowledged leaders with the ultimate say over who is in and who is out. Cliques themselves form a hierarchy; higher-status cliques are most desirable to outsiders but maintain the tightest control over membership (Adler & Adler, 1995). In early adolescence this social control may become somewhat less rigid (Brown & Klute, 2003).

The clique structure can seem harsh to outsiders, but it effectively serves the purpose of "redirecting young people's priorities from childhood to adolescent social norms. It sends a blunt message as to who is in charge of the peer social system (peers, rather than adults) and provides unequivocal information about how to proceed within that system" (Brown & Klute, 2003, p. 341). It also can create emotional distress among those who are less than successful in negotiating the system (Brown & Klute, 2003).

Crowds

Leonard Bernstein's musical *West Side Story* vividly illustrates the power of adolescent crowds. Crowd labels are cognitive designations for a feature that members of the crowd have in common, such as neighbourhood (west siders or south siders), ethnic background (Puerto Ricans or Italians), peer status (snobs or nobodies), or abilities, interests, or life-style (brains, jocks, druggies). The specific categories by which adolescents describe their social landscape may vary from one community to another.

Crowds serve several purposes. They help adolescents establish their identity and re-inforce allegiance to the behavioural norms of ethnic or socioeconomic groups. As *West Side Story* dramatizes, being part of a crowd makes it easier to establish relationships with peers in the same crowd and harder to do so with outsiders. As with cliques, crowd affilia-tion tends to become looser as adolescence progresses (Brown & Klute, 2003).

Romantic Relationships

Romantic relationships are a central part of most adolescents' social worlds. They contrib-ute to the development of both intimacy and identity. Because they tend to involve sexual contact, they also entail risks of pregnancy, STDs, and sometimes of sexual victimization, where 1 out of 11 Canadian high school students report being a victim of dating violence (Health Canada, 2007). Breakups with romantic partners are among the strongest predic-tors of depression and suicide (Bouchey & Furman, 2003).

With the onset of puberty, most heterosexual boys and girls begin to think about and interact more with members of the other sex. Typically they move from mixed groups or group dates to one-on-one romantic relationships that involve passion and a sense of com-mitment (Bouchey & Furman, 2003; Furman & Wehner, 1997).

Romantic relationships tend to become more intense and more intimate across adoles-cence (Bouchey & Furman, 2003). Early adolescents think primarily about how a romantic relationship may affect their status in the peer group (Bouchey & Furman, 2003). They pay little or no attention to attachment or support needs, such as help, caring, and nurturance, and their attention to sexual needs is limited to how to engage in sexual activity and which activities to engage in (Bouchey & Furman, 2003; Furman & Wehner, 1997).

In mid-adolescence, most young people have at least one exclusive partner lasting for several months to about a year, and the effect of the choice of partner on peer status tends to become less important (Furman & Wehner, 1997). In interviews with 1,316 junior high and high school students, boys revealed less confidence than girls about these early roman-tic relationships. Girls' greater ease in romantic relationships may be an extension of their greater intimacy in same-sex friendships (Giordano, Longmore, & Manning, 2006).

By age 16, adolescents interact with and think about romantic partners more than about parents, friends, or siblings (Bouchey & Furman, 2003). Not until late adolescence or early adulthood, though, do romantic relationships begin to meet the full gamut of emo-tional needs that such relationships can serve and then only in relatively long-term rela-tionships (Furman & Wehner, 1997).

Relationships with parents and peers may affect the quality of romantic relationships. The parents' marriage or romantic relationship may serve as a model for their adolescent child. The peer group forms the context for most romantic relationships and may affect an adolescent's choice of a partner and the way the relationship develops (Bouchey & Furman, 2003).

Anti-social Behaviour and Juvenile Delinquency

What influences young people to engage in—or refrain from—violence (see Box 17-2) or other anti-social acts? What determines whether or not a juvenile delinquent will grow up to be a hardened criminal? By what processes do anti-social tendencies develop? How do "problem behaviours" escalate into chronic delinquency? What determines whether a juve-nile delinquent will grow up to be a hardened criminal? As we mentioned in Chapter 14, an interaction between environmental and genetic or biological risk factors may underlie much anti-social behaviour (van Goozen, Fairchild, Snoek, & Harold, 2007).

Checkpoint ✔

Can you . . .

✔ List several functions of the peer group in adolescence?

✔ Discuss important features of adolescent friendships, cliques, and crowds?

✔ Describe developmental changes in romantic relationships?

Guidepost 4

What causes anti-social behaviour, and what can be done to reduce the risk of juvenile delinquency?

Box 17-2 *An Epidemic of Youth Violence*

On April 20, 1999, 18-year-old Eric Harris and 17-year-old Dylan Klebold entered Columbine High School in Littleton, Colorado, wearing black trench coats and carrying a rifle, a semi-automatic pistol, two sawed-off shotguns, and more than 30 homemade bombs. Laughing and taunting, they began spraying bullets at fellow students, killing 12 classmates and one teacher before fatally shooting themselves.

The massacre in Littleton was not an isolated event. In 2004–2005, 21 young people ages 5 to 18 were victims of school killings in the U.S. But while the occasional youth killing may make the headlines, such crimes as forcible rape, robbery, and assault are much more prevalent. In 2004 students ages 12 to 18 in the U.S. were victims of about 1.4 million nonfatal crimes at school, 107,000 of them serious. In 2005, 10 percent of male high school students and 6 percent of female students reported being threatened or injured by a weapon on school property. Six percent of the students, including 10 percent of boys, admitted to carrying weapons on school property (Dinkes, Forrest Cataldi, Kena, & Baum, 2006). A high proportion of delinquent youth, who are disproportionately ethnic/racial minorities, die violent deaths (Teplin, McClelland, Abram, & Mileusnic, 2005).

School violence is not a peculiarly American phenomenon. In Canada similar incidents in Taber, Alberta and Dawson College in Montreal have occurred. In a Japanese elementary school in June 2004, an 11-year-old girl stabbed her 12-year-old classmate to death after an argument over messages sent each other over the Internet—one of several such incidents in recent years ("Japan in shock at school murder," 2004). In a survey of 161,082 students in 35 western countries, 37 to 69 percent of the boys and 13 to 32 percent of the girls reported fighting, usually with friends or relatives. The lowest prevalence of fighting for both boys and girls was in Finland; the highest prevalence was in Eastern or Central European countries. In all countries, fighting and weapon carrying were associated with risks of serious injury (Pickett et al., 2005).

The massacre in Littleton was one of a string of incidents that add up to what has been called an epidemic of youth violence. Eight days after the Columbine massacre, a 14-year-old former student at W. R. Myers High School in Taber, Alberta, entered the school with a sawed-off rifle hidden under a parka, killing one student and seriously wounding another. The former student was a victim of bullying and was unpopular with his schoolmates. Victims of bullying in Canada have taken their own lives, as was the case of Hamed Sastoh, in Surrey, B.C., in March 2000, and Dawn-Marie Wesley, in Mission, B.C., in November 2000. Both were 14 years old, and both left suicide notes referring to their despair at being victims of bullying.

Why do some young people engage in such destructive behaviour? One answer lies in the immaturity of the adolescent brain, particularly the prefrontal cortex, which is critical to judgment and impulse suppression (refer back to Chapter 15). Another answer is availability of guns in a culture that "romanticizes gunplay" (Weinberger, 2001, p. 2).

Youth violence is strongly related to the presence of gangs at school (NCES, 2003; "Youth Violence," 2001). The brutal murder of Reena Virk, in Victoria, B.C., on November 14, 1997, is a horrific example of the brutality of gang violence, in which six teenage girls and a teenage boy beat their victim unconscious and left her to drown. For many adolescents, gangs satisfy unfulfilled needs for identity, connection, and a sense of power and control. For young people who lack positive family relationships, a gang can become a substitute family. Gangs promote a sense of "us-versus-them." Violence against outsiders strengthens bonds of loyalty and support within the gang (Staub, 1996).

Teenage violence and anti-social behaviour have roots in childhood. Children, especially boys, who are aggressive in elementary school tend to be violently anti-social in adolescence (Broidy et al., 2003). However, teenage violence is not limited to boys. Kindergarten girls in Montreal who showed patterns of highly disruptive behaviours during childhood were more likely to be diagnosed with conduct disorder as adolescents than those who showed little evidence of disruptive behaviours in childhood (Coté, Zoccolillo, Tremblay, Nagin, & Vitaro, 2001). Although fewer girls than boys report engaging in violent acts, as found in a survey of 962 Calgary high school students (Paetsch & Bertrand, 1999), the characteristics of female perpetrators of violence may be different from those of males. Case studies of six female offenders showed that they had negative opinions of themselves, had life experiences in which women were devalued, and in which violence was considered justified because victims provoke the assailants, particularly in cases of victims perceived to be threatening assailants' relationships with males (Artz, 1998). Children raised in a rejecting or coercive atmosphere or in an overly permissive or chaotic one tend to behave aggressively, and the hostility they evoke in others increases their own aggression. Their negative self-image prevents them from succeeding at school or developing other constructive interests, and they generally associate with peers who reinforce their anti-social attitudes and behaviour (Staub, 1996). Boys in poor, unstable inner-city neighbourhoods with high crime rates and low community involvement and neighbourhood support are most likely to become involved in violence (Tolan et al., 2003), but the shootings at Columbine show that even middle-class students in a suburban school are not immune.

Adolescents are more likely to commit violence if they have witnessed or have been victims of neighbourhood violence or have been exposed to media violence (Brookmeyer, Henrich, &

Becoming a Delinquent: Genetic and Neurological Factors

Anti-social behaviour tends to run in families. Analyses of many studies have concluded that genes influence 40 to 50 percent of the variation in anti-social behaviour within a population, and 60 to 65 percent of the variation in aggressive anti-sociality (Rhee & Waldman, 2002; Tackett, Krueger, Iacono, & McGue, 2005).

(continued)

Stone, 2005; Pearce, Jones, Schwab-Stone, & Ruchkin, 2003). As we discussed in Chapter 14, a steady diet of media violence can breed aggression, and adolescents are no exception (Johnson, Cohen, Smailes, Kasen, & Brook, 2002). Parental support tends to buffer the negative effects of exposure to violence, especially for boys; girls' own pro-social tendencies have a buffering effect (Brookmeyer et al., 2005; Pearce et al., 2003).

Psychologists point to potential warning signs that might avert future tragedies. Adolescents who are likely to commit violence often refuse to listen to authority figures, such as parents and teachers; ignore the feelings and rights of others; mistreat people; rely on violence or threatened violence to solve problems; and believe that life has treated them unfairly. They often look older than their peers. They tend to do poorly in school; cut classes or play truant; be held back or suspended or drop out; use alcohol, inhalants, and/or drugs; join gangs; and fight, steal, or destroy property (Resnick et al., 1997; Smith-Khuri et al., 2004; "Youth Violence," 2001). Harris and Klebold showed several of these characteristics.

Of course, not all youngsters who grow up in difficult circumstances become violent. Factors that contribute to resilience (refer back to Chapter 14) include positive role models; a close, trusting bond with a parent or other adult; supportive relationships with teachers and peers; development of self-esteem and self-efficacy; strong social skills; ability to take refuge in hobbies, work, or creative pursuits; and a sense of control over one's life (American Psychological Association, undated; Jenkins & Keating, 1998).

Fortunately, despite occasional widely publicized tragedies such as the ones in Littleton and Taber, there are signs that the epidemic of youth violence is abating. Incidents of self-reported physical fighting and injury are dropping (Brener, Simon, Krug, & Lowry, 1999). Recent statistics show that youth crime in general, and youth violence in particular, is decreasing in Canada (The John Howard Society of Newfoundland, 1998).

Successful preventive programs have given parents help in reducing the stress of child raising (American Psychological Association, undated) and training in socialization skills. Cooperative learning practices in schools and multicultural education can create a sense of community and reduce the us-versus-them mentality. Giving young people substantial responsibilities and the opportunity to participate in making rules can help them understand how the individual's behaviour affects the group (Staub, 1996). There is evidence that social-skills training for young offenders in Canada may reduce the likelihood of repeated violent behaviour (Cunliffe, 1992).

Suggestions for parents include: limiting and monitoring television viewing; encouraging participation in sports and other supervised after-school activities; using non-physical methods of discipline, such as grounding; and teaching young people to stand up against violence when they see it (American Psychological Association and AAP, 1996).

What's your view

What methods for controlling youth violence seem to you most likely to work?

Check it out

For more information and links to relevant Web sites on this topic, go to **www.mcgrawhill.ca/olc/papalia.**

Neurobiological deficits, particularly in the portions of the brain that regulate reactions to stress, may help explain why some children become anti-social children and adolescents. As a result of these neurological deficits, which may result from the interaction of genetic factors or difficult temperament with adverse early environments, children may not receive or heed normal warning signals to restrain impulsive or reckless behaviour (van Goozen et al., 2007).

Becoming a Delinquent: How Family, Peer, and Community Influences Interact

Young people with anti-social tendencies tend to gravitate to others like themselves and reinforce each other's anti-social behaviour.

As Bronfenbrenner's theory would suggest, anti-social behaviour is influenced by multileveled, interacting factors ranging from micro-system influences, such as parent-child hostility, poor parenting practices, and peer deviance, to macrosystem influences, such as community structure and neighbourhood social support (Buehler, 2006; Tolan, Gorman-Smith, & Henry, 2003). This network of interacting influences begins to be woven early in childhood.

Parents shape pro-social or anti-social behaviour through their responses to children's basic emotional needs (Krevans & Gibbs, 1996; Staub, 1996). Parents of children who become anti-social may have failed to reinforce good behaviour in early childhood and been harsh or inconsistent—or both—in punishing misbehaviour (Coie & Dodge, 1998; Snyder, Cramer, Afrank, & Patterson, 2005). Through the years these parents may not have been closely and positively involved in their children's lives (G. R. Patterson, DeBaryshe, & Ramsey, 1989). The children may get payoffs for anti-social behaviour: when they act up, they may gain attention or get their own way. These early negative patterns pave the way for negative peer influences that promote and reinforce anti-social behaviour (Collins et al., 2000; B. B. Brown, Mounts, Lamborn, & Steinberg, 1993).

By early adolescence, open hostility may exist between parent and child. When constant criticism, angry coercion, or rude, uncooperative behaviour characterizes parent-child interactions, the child tends to show aggressive behaviour problems, which worsen the parent-child relationship (Buehler, 2006). Ineffective parenting can leave younger siblings to the powerful influence of a deviant older brother, especially if the siblings are close in age (Snyder, Bank, & Burraston, 2005).

The choice of anti-social peers is affected mainly by environmental factors (Iervolino et al., 2002). Young people gravitate to others brought up like themselves who are similar in school achievement, adjustment, and pro-social or anti-social tendencies (Collins et al., 2000; B. B. Brown, Mounts, Lamborn, & Steinberg, 1993). As in childhood, anti-social adolescents tend to have anti-social friends, and their anti-social behaviour increases when they associate with each other (Dishion, McCord, & Poulin, 1999; Hartup & Stevens, 1999; Vitaro, Tremblay, Kerr, Pagani, & Bukowski, 1997). The way anti-social teenagers talk, laugh, or smirk about rule breaking and nod knowingly among themselves seems to constitute a sort of "deviancy training" (Dishion et al., 1999). These "problem children" continue to elicit ineffective parenting, which predicts delinquent behaviour and association with deviant peer groups or gangs (Simons, Chao, Conger, & Elder, 2001; Tolan et al., 2003).

Authoritative parenting can help young people internalize standards that may insulate them against negative peer influences and open them to positive ones (Collins et al., 2000). Improved parenting during adolescence can reduce delinquency by discouraging association with deviant peers (Simons et al., 2001). Adolescents whose parents know where they are and what they are doing are less likely to engage in delinquent acts (Laird, Pettit, Bates, & Dodge, 2003) or to associate with deviant peers (Lloyd & Anthony, 2003).

Family economic circumstances may influence the development of anti-social behaviour. Persistent economic deprivation can undermine sound parenting by depriving the family of social capital. Poor children are more likely than other children to commit anti-social acts, and those whose families are continuously poor tend to become more anti-social with time. Conversely, when families rise from poverty while a child is still young, the child is no more likely to develop behaviour problems than a child whose family was never poor (Macmillan, McMorris, & Kruttschnitt, 2004).

Weak neighbourhood social organization in a disadvantaged community can influence delinquency through its effects on parenting behaviour and peer deviance (Chung & Steinberg, 2006). *Collective efficacy* the strength of social connections within a neighbourhood and the extent to which residents monitor or supervise each other's children—can influence outcomes in a positive direction (Sampson, 1997). A combination of nurturant, involved parenting and collective efficacy can discourage adolescents from association with deviant peers (Brody et al., 2001).

Long-term Prospects

The vast majority of young people who engage in anti-social behaviours or even in violence do not become adult criminals (Kosterman, Graham, Hawkins, Catalano, & Herrenkohl, 2001; Moffitt, 1993). Delinquency peaks at about age 15 and then declines, as most adolescents and their families come to terms with young people's need to assert independence.

Teenagers who do not see positive alternatives are more likely to adopt a permanently anti-social lifestyle (Elliott, 1993). Those most likely to persist in violence are boys who had early anti-social influences. Least likely to persist are boys and girls who were early school achievers and girls who showed early pro-social development (Kosterman et al., 2001). Because adolescents' character is still in flux, many developmental psychologists deplore trends toward transferring juvenile offenders from the juvenile court system, which is aimed at rehabilitation, to criminal courts where they are tried and sentenced as adults (Steinberg, 2000; Steinberg & Scott, 2003).

Preventing and Treating Delinquency

Because juvenile delinquency has roots early in childhood, so should preventive efforts. To be most successful, interventions should attack the multiple factors that can lead to delinquency.

Adolescents who have taken part in certain early childhood intervention programs are less likely to get in trouble than their equally underprivileged peers who did not have these early experiences (Yoshikawa, 1994; Zigler, Taussig, & Black, 1992). Effective programs are those that target high-risk urban children and last at least two years during the child's first five years of life. They influence children directly, through high-quality day care or education, and at the same time indirectly, by offering families assistance and support geared to their needs (Berrueta-Clement et al., 1985; Berrueta-Clement, Schweinhart, Barnett, & Weikart, 1987; Schweinhart et al., 1993; Seitz, 1990; Yoshikawa, 1994; Zigler et al., 1992).

These programs operate on Bronfenbrenner's mesosystem by affecting interactions between the home and the school or child-care centre. The programs also go one step further to the exosystem, by creating supportive parent networks and linking parents with such community services as prenatal and postnatal health care and educational and vocational counselling (Yoshikawa, 1994; Zigler et al., 1992). Through their multi-pronged approach, these interventions have an impact on several early risk factors for delinquency.

Once children reach adolescence, especially in poor, crime-ridden neighbourhoods, interventions need to focus on spotting troubled adolescents and preventing gang recruitment (Tolan et al., 2003). Successful programs boost parenting skills through better monitoring, behavioural management, and neighbourhood social support.

Programs such as teen hangouts and summer camps for behaviourally disturbed youth can be counterproductive because they bring together groups of deviant youth who tend to reinforce each other's deviancy. More effective programs—Scouts, sports, and church activities—integrate deviant youth into the nondeviant mainstream. Structured, adult-monitored or school-based activities after school, on weekend evenings, and in summer, when adolescents are most likely to be idle and to get in trouble, can reduce their exposure to settings that encourage anti-social behaviour (Dodge, Dishion, & Lansford, 2006).

As David Suzuki's experience shows, getting teenagers involved in constructive activities like camping during their free time can pay long-range dividends (Larson, 1998). Participation in extracurricular school activities tends to cut down on dropout and criminal arrest rates among high-risk boys and girls (Mahoney, 2000). Table 17-7 lists examples of effective programs to discourage deviancy.

What's your view ?

• How should society deal with youthful offenders?

Table 17-7 Effective Measures to Discourage Deviant Behaviour

Mental Health

1. Individually administered treatment
2. Family-based interventions
3. Mentoring programs such as Big Brothers/Big Sisters

Education

1. Universal, environment-centred programs that focus on school-wide reform, including:
   a. Clearly explicated expectations for student and staff behaviour;
   b. Consistent utilization of proactive school discipline strategies;
   c. Active monitoring of "hot spots" for behaviour problems; and
   d. Improved systems to monitor student achievement and behaviour.
2. Universal classroom programs to build social competence
3. School-wide positive behaviour support
4. Individual behaviour support plan for each student
5. Improved training in behaviour management practices for classroom teachers
6. Consultation and support for classroom teachers
7. Matching deviant youth with well-adjusted peers (e.g., coaching)
8. Proactive prevention programs that shape student "morals" and encourage responsible decision-making

Juvenile Justice and Child Welfare

1. Multidimentional Treatment Foster Care
2. Intensive Protective Supervision
3. Sending delinquent youth to programs that serve the general population of youth in their neighbourhoods (e.g., Boys and Girls Clubs)
4. Community rather than custodial settings
5. Interpersonal skills training
6. Individual counselling
7. Treatment administered by mental health professionals
8. Early diversion programs
9. Victim-Offender Mediation
10. Teen court programs

Community Programming

1. Public or private organizations, open to all youth, that provide structure and adult involvement (e.g., religious groups, service clubs, Scouts, Boys and Girls Clubs)
2. School-based extracurricular activities
3. Encouragement of commitments outside of gangs (e.g., to jobs, family roles, military service, mentors)
4. Early childhood interventions such as the Perry Preschool program
5. Job Corps (e.g., "Katimavik")
6. Policing programs that target high-crime neighbourhoods where high-risk youth congregate
7. Community efforts to reduce marginalization of specific groups of youth

One multi-faceted intervention, called Equipping Youth to Help One Another (EQUIP), uses daily, adult-guided mutual peer support groups to teach each other how to manage anger, make moral decisions, and learn social skills (Gibbs, Potter, Barriga, & Liau, 1996; Gibbs, Potter, Goldstein, & Brendtro, 1998). Among 57 male juvenile offenders in a medium-security correctional facility, EQUIP participants improved significantly in conduct within the institution and had lower repeat offence rates during the first year after release than control groups that did not have the training (Leeman, Gibbs, & Fuller, 1993).

Another program, developed in Edmonton, called the High Risk Recognition Program, aims to reduce the likelihood of repetition of delinquent behaviours by adolescents (Howell & Enns, 1995). The program is based on the notion that risk factors, like social pressure, feelings of retaliation or revenge, self-gratification or pleasure seeking, lead to reoffending. Teaching young offenders about those risk factors, showing them how to monitor their daily activities for the presence of the risk factors, and helping them to develop coping strategies for those factors, equips young offenders to avoid repeating delinquent behaviours.

Fortunately, the great majority of adolescents do not get into serious trouble. Those who do show disturbed behaviour can—and should—be helped. With love, guidance, and support, adolescents can avoid risks, build on their strengths, and explore their possibilities as they approach adult life.

Emerging Adulthood

In modern western societies, entrance into adulthood takes longer and follows more varied routes than in the past. Before the mid-twentieth century, a young man just out of high school could, in short order, obtain a stable job, marry, and start a family. For a young woman, the chief route to adulthood was marriage, which occurred as soon as she could find a suitable mate. Now, the technological revolution has made higher education or specialized training increasingly essential. The gender revolution has brought more women into the workforce and broadened female roles (Furstenberg, Rumbaut, & Settersten, Jr., 2005; Fussell & Furstenberg, 2005). Today the road to adulthood may be marked by multiple milestones—entering college or university (full or part time), working (full or part time), moving away from home, getting married, and having children—and the order and timing of these transitions varies (Schulenberg, O'Malley, Bachman, & Johnston, 2005). Thus, some developmental scientists suggest that the period from the late teens through the mid- to late twenties has become a distinct period of the life course, **emerging adulthood**—a time when young people are no longer adolescents but have not yet become fully adult (Arnett, 2000, 2004; Furstenberg et al., 2005).

In the minds of many people today, the onset of adulthood is marked, not so much by external criteria such as driving, voting, and work, as by such internal indicators as a sense of autonomy, self-control, and personal responsibility. It is more a state of mind than a discrete event (Shanahan, Porfeli, & Mortimer, 2005).

Since the 1990s, surveys of emerging adults (mostly white, urban, and middle class) have repeatedly come up with three top criteria for adulthood: "accepting responsibility for oneself, making independent decisions, and becoming financially independent"—criteria that reflect North American society's values of individualism and self-sufficiency (Arnett & Galambos, 2003, p. 92). A study of 97 Canadian first-year university students indicated that the majority of emerging adults experience personal growth during this period, particularly in three areas: relating to others, optimism in new opportunities and possibilities, and personal strength in overcoming adversity (Gottlieb, Sill, & Newby-Clark, 2007). In studies of Israelis, Argentinians, U.S. minority groups, and Mormons, those same criteria for adulthood were most widely expressed. However, emerging adults in those cultures also mentioned criteria reflecting collectivistic values. In Israel, universal military service is an important marker of adulthood (Mayseless & Scharf, 2003). Young Argentines, who have experienced severe economic crises and high unemployment in recent years, emphasize family responsibilities more than work (Facio & Micocci, 2003). Mormons cite religious rites of passage, such as being admitted to men's or women's organizations of their church (Nelson, 2003).

African Americans, Latinos, and Asian Americans are more likely than European Americans to mention criteria involving obligations to others (such as supporting one's family), recognized role transitions (such as marriage), and complying with social norms (such as avoiding illegal drug use). African Americans and Latinos who come from lower-SES families tend to believe they have reached adulthood at an earlier age than do European and Asian Americans, probably because of greater and earlier family responsibilities (Arnett, 2003).

As research on this topic continues, it will be interesting to see what adulthood means in rural, nonwesternized cultures, which tend to hold more strongly collectivist values.

Checkpoint

Can you . . .

✔ Explain how family, peer, and community influences may interact to promote anti-social behaviour and delinquency?

✔ Give examples of types of programs that have been successful in preventing or stopping delinquency and other anti-social behaviour?

Guidepost 5

How do various cultures define what it means to become an adult, and what markers confer that status?

emerging adulthood Proposed transitional period between adolescence and adulthood, usually extending from the late teens through the mid-twenties

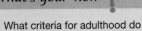

What's your view

• What criteria for adulthood do you consider most relevant?

• Do you think those criteria are influenced by the culture in which you live or grew up?

Checkpoint ✔

Can you . . .

✔ Explain the concept of emerging adulthood, and tell why it applies to modern westernized societies?

✔ Discuss cultural conceptions of what it means to be an adult?

The normal developmental changes in the early years of life are obvious and dramatic signs of growth. The infant lying in the crib becomes an active, exploring toddler. The young child enters and embraces the worlds of school and society. The adolescent, with a new body and new awareness, prepares to step into adulthood.

Growth and development do not screech to a stop after adolescence. People change in many ways throughout adulthood. Human beings continue to shape their own development, as they have been doing since birth. What occurs in a child's world is significant, but it is not the whole story. We each continue to write our own story of human development for as long as we live.

Summary and Key Terms

The Search for Identity

Guidepost 1 How do adolescents form an identity, and what roles do gender and ethnicity play?

- A central concern during adolescence is the search for identity, which has occupational, sexual, and values components. Erik Erikson described the psychosocial crisis of adolescence as the conflict of identity versus identity confusion. The "virtue" that should arise from this crisis is *fidelity*.

- James Marcia, in research based on Erikson's theory, described four identity statuses with differing combinations of crisis and commitment: identity achievement, foreclosure, moratorium, and identity diffusion.

- Self-esteem tends to fall during adolescence, especially for girls, but not for minority youth.

- Ethnicity is an important part of identity. Minority adolescents seem to go through stages of ethnic identity development much like Marcia's identity statuses.

   **identity (452)   identity versus identity confusion (452)
   identity statuses (453)   crisis (453)   commitment (453)
   identity achievement (454)   foreclosure (454)
   moratorium (455)   identity diffusion (455)
   cultural socialization (457)**

Sexuality

Guidepost 2 What determines sexual orientation, what sexual practices are common among adolescents, and what leads some to engage in risky sexual behaviour?

- Sexual orientation appears to be influenced by an interaction of biological and environmental factors and may be at least partly genetic.

- Teenage sexual activity is more prevalent and more accepted than in the past, but it involves risks of pregnancy and sexually transmitted diseases (STDs). Adolescents at greatest risk are those who begin sexual activity early, have multiple partners, do not use contraceptives, and are ill-informed about sex.

- The course of homosexual identity and relationship development may vary with cohort, gender, and ethnicity.

- Rates of STDs in Canada are increasing, and are especially high among adolescents. STDs are more likely to develop undetected in girls than in boys.

- Teenage pregnancy and birthrates in Canada have declined. Most of these births are to unmarried mothers.

- Teenage pregnancy and childbearing often have negative outcomes. Teenage mothers and their families tend to suffer ill health and financial hardship, and the children often suffer from ineffective parenting.

   **sexual orientation (458)   sexually transmitted diseases
   (STDs) (462)**

Relationships with Family and Peers

Guidepost 3 How do adolescents relate to parents, siblings, and peers?

- Although relationships between adolescents and their parents are not always smooth, full-scale adolescent rebellion is unusual. For the majority of teens, adolescence is a fairly smooth transition. For the minority who seem more deeply troubled, it can predict a troubled adulthood.

- Adolescents spend an increasing amount of time with peers, but relationships with parents continue to be close and influential.

- Conflict with parents tends to be most frequent during early adolescence and most intense during middle adolescence. The intensity of minor conflicts may reflect the process of individuation.

- Authoritative parenting is associated with the most positive outcomes. Behavioural control normally diminishes across adolescence; psychological control, which suppresses a young person's emotional autonomy, does not.

- Effective parental monitoring depends on adolescents' self-disclosure, which is influenced by the quality of the parent-child relationship.

- Effects of divorce, single parenting, and maternal employment on adolescents' development depend on such factors as how closely parents monitor adolescents' activity and the quality of the home environment.

- Economic stress affects relationships in both lone-parent and two-parent families.

- Relationships with siblings tend to become more distant during adolescence, and the balance of power between older and younger siblings becomes more equal.
- The influence of the peer group is strongest in early adolescence. Adolescents who are rejected by peers tend to have the greatest adjustment problems. Peer relationships fall into three categories: friendships, cliques, and crowds.
- Friendships, especially among girls, become more intimate and supportive in adolescence. Cliques are highly status-based; crowds are based on common features, such as ethnicity or SES.
- Romantic relationships involve several roles and develop with age and experience.

adolescent rebellion (466)   individuation (468)

Anti-social Behaviour and Juvenile Delinquency

Guidepost 4 What causes anti-social behaviour, and what can be done to reduce the risk of juvenile delinquency?

- Anti-social behaviour is associated with multiple interacting risk factors, including genes, neurological deficits, ineffective parenting, school failure, peer influence, and low socio-economic status.
- Programs that attack environmental risk factors from an early age have had success in preventing juvenile delinquency.

Emerging Adulthood

Guidepost 5 How do various cultures define what it means to become an adult, and what markers confer that status?

- A new transitional period called emerging adulthood has developed in westernized cultures in recent years.
- Emerging adults in various westernized cultures hold similar views of what defines entrance into adulthood. The most widely accepted criteria are individualistic ones having to do with self-sufficiency and independence. However, some cultures also embrace collectivistic criteria, such as family responsibilities and conformity with social norms.

emerging adulthood (481)

Glossary

A

A, not-B error Tendency, noted by Piaget, for 8- to 12-month-old infants to search for a hidden object in a place where they previously found it, rather than in the place they most recently saw it being hidden

acceleration Approach to educating the gifted, which moves them through a curriculum at an unusually rapid pace

accommodation Piaget's term for changes in a cognitive structure to include new information

achievement tests Tests that assess how much children know in various subject areas

acquired immune deficiency syndrome (AIDS) Viral disease that undermines effective functioning of the immune system

activity limitations Chronic conditions that continually restrict everyday behaviours

acute medical conditions Occasional illnesses that last a short time

adaptation Piaget's term for adjustment to new information about the environment

adolescence Developmental transition between childhood and adulthood entailing major physical, cognitive, and psychosocial changes

adolescent growth spurt Sharp increase in height and weight that precedes sexual maturity

adolescent rebellion Pattern of emotional turmoil, characteristic of a minority of adolescents, which may involve conflict with family, alienation from adult society, reckless behaviour, and rejection of adult values

adrenarche Maturation of adrenal glands

affordance In the Gibsons' ecological theory of perception, the fit between a person's physical attributes and capabilities and characteristics of the environment

alleles Two or more alternative forms of a gene that can occupy the same position on paired chromosomes and affect the same trait

altruism Behaviour intended to help others out of inner concern and without expectation of external reward

ambivalent (resistant) attachment Pattern in which an infant becomes anxious before the primary caregiver leaves, is extremely upset during his or her absence, and both seeks and resists contact on his or her return

[...]fe to objects that are not alive

anorexia nervosa Eating disorder characterized by self-starvation

anoxia Lack of oxygen, which may cause brain damage

Apgar scale Standard measurement of a newborn's condition; it assesses *a*ppearance, *p*ulse, *g*rimace, *a*ctivity, and *r*espiration

aptitude tests Tests that measure children's general intelligence, or capacity to learn

art therapy Therapeutic approach that allows a child to express troubled feelings without words, using a variety of art materials and media

assimilation Piaget's term for incorporation of new information into an existing cognitive structure

asthma A chronic respiratory disease characterized by sudden attacks of coughing, wheezing, and difficulty in breathing

attachment Reciprocal, enduring tie between two people—especially between infant and caregiver—each of whom contributes to the quality of the relationship

attention-deficit/hyperactivity disorder (ADHD) Syndrome characterized by persistent inattention and distractibility, impulsivity, low tolerance for frustration, and inappropriate overactivity

authoritarian Baumrind's term for parenting style emphasizing control and obedience

authoritative Baumrind's term for parenting style blending respect for a child's individuality with an effort to instill social values

autism Pervasive developmental disorder of the brain, characterized by lack of normal social interaction, impaired communication and imagination, and repetitive, obsessive behaviours

autobiographical memory Memory of specific events in one's own life; a type of episodic memory

autonomy versus shame and doubt Erikson's second crisis in psychosocial development, in which children achieve a balance between self-determination and control by others

autosomes The 22 pairs of chromosomes not related to sexual expression

avoidant attachment Pattern in which an infant rarely cries when separated from the primary caregiver and avoids contact upon his or her return

B

basic trust versus basic mistrust Erikson's first crisis in psychosocial development, in which infants develop a sense of the reliability of people and objects in their world

Bayley Scales of Infant Development Standardized test of infants' mental and motor development

behaviour therapy Therapeutic approach using principles of learning theory to encourage desired behaviours or eliminate undesired ones; also called *behaviour modification*

behavioural genetics Quantitative study of relative hereditary and environmental influences

behaviourism Learning theory that emphasizes the predictable role of environment in causing observable behaviour

behaviourist approach Approach to the study of cognitive development that is concerned with basic mechanics of learning

bilingual Fluent in two languages

bilingual education System of teaching non-English-speaking children in their native language while they learn English, and later switching to all-English instruction

bioecological theory Bronfenbrenner's approach to understanding processes and contexts of development

birth trauma Injury sustained at the time of birth

body image Descriptive and evaluative beliefs about one's appearance

brain growth spurts Periods of rapid brain growth and development

Brazelton Neonatal Behavioural Assessment Scale (NBAS) Neurological and behavioural test to measure neonate's responses to the environment

bulimia nervosa Eating disorder in which a person regularly eats huge quantities of food and then purges the body by laxatives, induced vomiting, fasting, or excessive exercise

bullying Aggression deliberately and persistently directed against a particular target, or victim, typically one who is weak, vulnerable, and defenceless

C

Caesarean delivery Delivery of a baby by surgical removal from the uterus

canalization Limitation on variance of expression of certain inherited characteristics

caregiver–infant bond The feeling of close, caring connection between the caregiver and his or her newborn

case study Study covering a single case or life

cell death Elimination of excess brain cells to achieve more efficient functioning

central executive In Baddeley's model, element of working memory that controls the processing of information

central nervous system Brain and spinal cord

centration In Piaget's theory, tendency of pre-operational children to focus on one aspect of a situation and neglect others

cephalocaudal principle Principle that development proceeds in a head-to-tail direction; that is, upper parts of the body develop before lower parts

child development Scientific study of processes of change and stability from conception through adolescence

child-directed speech (CDS) Form of speech often used in talking to babies or toddlers; includes slow, simplified speech, a high-pitched tone, exaggerated vowel sounds, short words and sentences, and much repetition; also called *parentese*

childhood depression Mood disorder characterized by such symptoms as a prolonged sense of friendlessness, inability to have fun or concentrate, fatigue, extreme activity or apathy, feelings of worthlessness, weight change, physical complaints, and thoughts of death or suicide

chromosomes Coils of DNA that carry the genes

chronic medical conditions Physical, behavioural, and/or emotional conditions that require special health services

chronosystem Bronfenbrenner's term for effects of time on other developmental systems

circular reactions Piaget's term for processes by which an infant learns to reproduce desired occurrences originally discovered by chance

class inclusion Understanding of the relationship between a whole and its parts

classical conditioning Learning based on associating a stimulus that does not ordinarily elicit a particular response with another stimulus that ordinarily does elicit the response

clone *(verb)* To make a genetic copy of an individual; *(noun)* a genetic copy of an individual

code mixing Use of elements of two languages, sometimes in the same utterance, by young children in households where both languages are spoken

code switching Process of changing one's speech to match the situation, as in people who are bilingual

cognitive development Patterns of change in mental abilities, such as learning, attention, memory, language, thinking, reasoning, and creativity

cognitive neuroscience Study of links between neural processes and cognitive abilities

cognitive neuroscience approach Approach to the study of cognitive development that links brain processes with cognitive ones

cognitive perspective View that thought processes are central to development

cognitive-stage theory Piaget's theory that children's cognitive development advances in a series of four stages involving qualitatively distinct types of mental operations

cohort Group of people who share a similar experience, such as growing up at the same time and in the same place

commitment Marcia's term for personal investment in an occupation or system of beliefs

committed compliance Kochanska's term for wolehearted obedience to a parent's orders without reminders or lapses

componential element Sternberg's term for the analytic aspect of intelligence

conceptual knowledge Acquired interpretive understandings stored in long-term memory

concordant Term describing twins who share the same trait or disorder

concrete operations Third stage of Piagetian cognitive development (approximately from ages 7 to 12), during which children develop logical but not abstract thinking

conduct disorder (CD) Repetitive, persistent pattern of aggressive, anti-social behaviour violating societal norms or the rights of others

conscience Internal standards of behaviour, which usually control one's conduct and produce emotional discomfort when violated

conservation Piaget's term for awareness that two objects that are equal according to a certain measure remain equal in the face of perceptual alteration so long as nothing has been added to or taken away from either object

constructive play In Piaget's and Smilansky's terminology, the second cognitive level of play, involving use of objects or materials to make something

contextual element Sternberg's term for the practical aspect of intelligence

contextual perspective View of development that sees the individual as inseparable from the social context

control group In an experiment, a group of people similar to the people in the experimental group who do not receive the treatment whose effects are to be measured

conventional morality (*or morality of conventional role conformity*) Second level in Kohlberg's theory of moral reasoning, in which the standards of authority figures are internalized

convergent thinking Thinking aimed at finding the one "right" answer to a problem

co-regulation Transitional stage in the control of behaviour in which parents exercise general supervision and children exercise moment-to-moment self-regulation

corporal punishment Use of physical force with the intention of causing pain, but not injury, to correct or control behaviour

correlational study Research design intended to discover whether a statistical relationship between variables exists

crisis Marcia's term for period of conscious decision making related to identity formation

critical period Specific time when a given event, or its absence, has the greatest impact on development

cross-modal transfer Ability to use information gained by one sense to guide another

cross-sectional study Study design in which people of different ages are assessed on one occasion

cultural bias Tendency of intelligence tests to include items calling for knowledge or skills more familiar or meaningful to some cultural groups than to others

cultural socialization Parental practices that teach children about their racial/ethnic heritage and promote cultural practices and cultural pride

culture A society's or group's total way of life, including customs, traditions, beliefs, values, language, and physical products—all learned behaviour passed on from parents to children

culture-fair Describing an intelligence test that deals with experiences common to various cultures, in an attempt to avoid cultural bias

culture-free Describing an intelligence test that, if it were possible to design, would have no culturally linked content

culture-relevant Describing an intelligence test that takes into account the adaptive tasks children face in their culture.

D

decentre In Piaget's terminology, to think simultaneously about several aspects of a situation declarative knowledge Acquired factual knowledge stored in long-term memory

decoding Process of phonetic analysis by which a printed word is converted to spoken form before retrieval from long-term memory

deductive reasoning Type of logical reasoning that moves from a general premise about a class to a conclusion about a particular member or members of the class

deferred imitation Piaget's term for reproduction of an observed behaviour after the passage of time by calling up a stored symbol of it

Denver Developmental Screening Test Screening test given to children 1 month to 6 years old to determine whether they are developing normally

deoxyribonucleic acid (DNA) Chemical that carries inherited instructions for the formation and function of body cells

dependent variable In an experiment, the condition that may or may not change as a result of changes in the independent variable

depth perception Ability to perceive objects and surfaces three-dimensionally

developmental priming mechanisms Aspects of the home environment that seem necessary for normal cognitive and psychosocial development

differentiation Process by which neurons acquire specialized structure and function

"difficult" children Children with irritable temperament, irregular biological rhythms, and intense emotional responses

discipline Methods of moulding children's character and of teaching them to exercise self-control and engage in acceptable behaviour

dishabituation Increase in responsiveness after presentation of a new stimulus; compare *habituation*

disorganized-disoriented attachment Pattern in which an infant, after being separated from the primary caregiver, shows contradictory behaviours upon his or her return

divergent thinking Thinking that produces a variety of fresh, diverse possibilities

dizygotic (two-egg) twins Twins conceived by the union of two different ova (or a single ovum that has split) with two different sperm cells; also called *fraternal twins*

dominant inheritance Pattern of inheritance in which, when a child receives contradictory alleles, only the dominant one is expressed

Down syndrome Chromosomal disorder characterized by moderate-to-severe mental retardation

dramatic play Play involving imaginary people or situations; also called *fantasy play*, *pretend play*, or *imaginative play*

drug therapy Administration of drugs to treat emotional disorders

dual representation hypothesis Proposal that children under the age of 3 have difficulty grasping spatial relationships because of the need to keep more than one mental representation in mind at the same time

dynamic systems theory (DST) Thelen's theory, which holds that motor development is a dynamic process of active coordination of multiple systems within the infant in relation to the environment

dyslexia Developmental disorder in which reading achievement is substantially lower than predicted by IQ or age

E

early intervention Systematic provision of therapeutic and educational services to families to help meet young children's developmental needs

"easy" children Children with a generally happy temperament, regular biological rhythms, and a readiness to accept new experiences

ecological theory of perception Theory developed by Eleanor and James Gibson, which describes developing motor and perceptual abilities as interdependent parts of a functional system that guides behaviour in varying contexts

egocentrism Piaget's term for inability to consider another person's point of view; a characteristic of young people's thought

elaboration Mnemonic strategy of making mental associations involving items to be remembered

electronic fetal monitoring Mechanical monitoring of fetal heartbeat during labour and delivery

elicited imitation Research method in which infants or toddlers are induced to imitate a specific series of actions they have seen but not necessarily done before

embryonic stage Second stage of gestation (2 to 8 weeks), characterized by rapid growth and development of major body systems and organs

emergent literacy Preschoolers' development of skills, knowledge, and attitudes that underlie reading and writing

emerging adulthood Proposed transitional period between adolescence and adulthood, usually extending from the late teens through the mid-twenties

emotional maltreatment Action or inaction that may cause behavioural, cognitive, emotional, or mental disorders

emotions Subjective reactions to experience that are associated with physiological and behavioural changes

empathy Ability to put oneself in another person's place and feel what that person feels

encoding Process by which information is prepared for long-term storage and later retrieval

English immersion Approach to teaching English as an additional (second) language in which instruction is presented only in English

enrichment Approach to educating the gifted that broadens and deepens knowledge and skills through extra activities, projects, field trips, or mentoring

enuresis Repeated urination in clothing or in bed

environment Totality of nonhereditary, or experiential, influences on development

epigenesis Mechanism that turns genes on or off and determines functions of body cells

episodic memory Long-term memory of specific experiences or events, linked to time and place

equilibration Piaget's term for the tendency to seek a stable balance among cognitive elements

ethnic gloss Overgeneralization about an ethnic or cultural group that blurs or obscures variations within the group or overlaps with other such groups

ethnic group Group united by ancestry, race, religion, language, and/or national origins, which contribute to a sense of shared identity

ethnographic study In-depth study of a culture, which uses a combination of methods including participant observation

ethological perspective View of development that focuses on biological and evolutionary bases of behaviour

ethology Study of distinctive adaptive behaviours of species of animals that have evolved to increase survival of the species

evolutionary psychology Application of Darwinian principles of natural selection and survival of the fittest to individual behaviour

evolutionary/sociobiological perspective View of human development that focuses on evolutionary and biological bases of social behaviour

executive function Conscious control of thoughts, emotions, and actions to accomplish goals or solve problems

exosystem Bronfenbrenner's term for linkages between two or more settings, one of which does not contain the child

experiential element Sternberg's term for the insightful aspect of intelligence

experiment Rigorously controlled, replicable procedure in which the researcher manipulates variables to assess the effect of one on the other

experimental group In an experiment, the group receiving the treatment under study

explicit memory Intentional and conscious memory, generally of facts, names, and events; sometimes called *declarative memory*

extended family Kinship network of parents, children, and other relatives, sometimes living together in an *extended-family household*

external memory aids Mnemonic strategies using something outside the person

F

family therapy Psychological treatment in which a therapist sees the whole family together to analyze patterns of family functioning

fast mapping Process by which a child absorbs the meaning of a new word after hearing it once or twice in conversation

fertilization Union of sperm and ovum fuse to produce a zygote; also called *conception*

fetal alcohol syndrome (FAS) Combination of mental, motor, and developmental abnormalities affecting the offspring of some women who drink heavily during pregnancy

fetal stage Final stage of gestation (from 8 weeks to birth), characterized by increased detail of body parts and greatly enlarged body size

fine motor skills Physical skills that involve the small muscles and eye–hand coordination

fontanels Soft spots on head of young infant

foreclosure Identity status, described by Marcia, in which a person who has not spent time considering alternatives (that is, has not been in crisis) is committed to other people's plans for his or her life

formal games with rules Organized games with known procedures, and penalties

formal operations In Piaget's theory, the final stage of cognitive development, characterized by the ability to think abstractly

French immersion Approach to teaching French as a second language in which English-speaking children are given instruction in French only

functional play In Piaget's and Smilansky's terminology, the lowest cognitive level of play, involving repetitive muscular movements; also called *locomotor play*

G

gateway drugs Drugs such as alcohol, tobacco, and marijuana, the use of which tends to lead to use of more addictive drugs

gender Significance of being male or female

gender constancy Awareness that one will always be male or female; also called *sex-category constancy*

gender identity Awareness, developed in early childhood, that one is male or female

gender roles Behaviours, interests, attitudes, skills, and traits that a culture considers appropriate for males and females

gender-schema theory Theory, proposed by Bem, that children socialize themselves in their gender roles by developing a mentally organized network of information about what it means to be male or female in a particular culture

gender stereotypes Preconceived generalizations about male or female role behaviour

gender-typing Socialization process by which children, at an early age, learn appropriate gender roles

generalized anxiety disorder Anxiety not focused on any single target

generic memory Memory that produces scripts of familiar routines to guide behaviour

genes Small segments of DNA located in specific positions on particular chromosomes

genetic code Sequence of base pairs within DNA, which determine inherited characteristics

genetic counselling Clinical service that advises couples of their probable risk of having children with hereditary defects

genetic testing Procedure for ascertaining genetic makeup to identify predispositions to hereditary diseases or disorders

genotype Genetic makeup of a person, containing both expressed and unexpressed characteristics

genotype–environment correlation Tendency of certain genetic and environmental influences to reinforce each other; may be passive, reactive (evocative), or active; also called *genotype–environment covariance*

genotype–environment interaction The portion of phenotypic variation that results from the reactions of genetically different individuals to similar environmental conditions

germinal stage First 2 weeks of prenatal development, characterized by rapid cell division, increasing complexity and differentiation, and implantation in the wall of the uterus

gonadarche Maturation of testes or ovaries

goodness of fit Appropriateness of environmental demands and constraints to a child's temperament

gross motor skills Physical skills that involve the large muscles

guided participation Participation of an adult in a child's activity in a manner that helps to structure the activity and to bring the child's understanding of it closer to that of the adult

H

habituation Type of learning in which familiarity with a stimulus reduces, slows, or stops a response; Compare *dishabituation*

handedness Preference for using a particular hand

haptic perception Ability to acquire information about properties of objects, such as size, weight, and texture, by handling them

heredity Inborn influences or traits inherited from biological parents

heritability Statistical estimate of contribution of heredity to individual differences in a specific trait within a given population

Heritage Language Program Language classes given in the regular school day for children of immigrant background, designed to promote the home language and culture

heterozygous Possessing differing alleles for a trait

historical generation A group of people strongly influenced by a major historical event during their formative period

holophrase Single word that conveys a complete thought

Home Observation for Measurement of the Environment (HOME) Instrument to measure the influence of the home environment on children's cognitive growth

homozygous Possessing two identical alleles for a trait

horizontal décalage Piaget's term for inability to transfer learning about one type of conservation to other types, which causes a child to master different types of conservation tasks at different ages

hostile aggression Aggressive behaviour intended to hurt another person

hostile attribution bias Tendency for someone to perceive others as trying to hurt him or her and to strike out in retaliation or self-defence

human genome Complete sequence or mapping of genes in the human body and their locations

hypertension High blood pressure

hypotheses Possible explanations for phenomena, used to predict the outcome of research

hypothetical-deductive reasoning Ability, believed by Piaget to accompany the state of formal operations, to develop, consider, and test hypotheses

I

ideal self The self one would like to be

identification In Freudian theory, the process by which a young child adopts characteristics, beliefs, attitudes, values, and behaviours of the parent of the same sex

identity In Erikson's terminology, a coherent conception of the self made up of goals, values, and beliefs to which a person is solidly committed

identity achievement Identity status, described by Marcia, which is characterized by commitment to choices made following a crisis, a period spent in exploring alternatives

identity diffusion Identity status, described by Marcia, which is characterized by absence of commitment and lack of serious consideration of alternatives

identity statuses Marcia's term for states of ego development that depend on the presence or absence of crisis and commitment

identity versus identity confusion Erikson's fifth crisis of psychosocial development, in which an adolescent seeks to develop a coherent sense of self, including the role she or he is to play in society; also called *identity versus role confusion*

imaginary audience Elkind's term for an observer who exists only in an adolescent's mind and is as concerned with the adolescent's thoughts and actions as the adolescent is

implicit memory Unconscious recall, generally of habits and skills; sometimes called *procedural memory*

imprinting Instinctive form of learning in which, during a critical period in early development, a young animal forms an attachment to the first moving object it sees, usually the mother

incomplete dominance Pattern of inheritance in which a child receives two different alleles, resulting in partial expression of a trait

independent variable In an experiment, the condition over which the experimenter has direct control

individual differences Differences among children in characteristics, influences, or developmental outcomes

individual psychotherapy Psychological treatment in which a therapist sees a troubled person one-on-one

individuation Adolescent's struggle for autonomy and differentiation, or personal identity

inductive reasoning Type of logical reasoning that moves from particular observations about members of a class to a general conclusion about that class

inductive techniques Disciplinary techniques designed to induce desirable behaviour by appealing to a child's sense of reason and fairness

industry versus inferiority Erikson's fourth critical alternative of psychosocial development, in which children must learn the productive skills their culture requires or else face feelings of inferiority

infant mortality rate Proportion of babies born alive who die within the first year after birth

infertility Inability to conceive after 12 months of trying

information-processing approach Approach to the study of cognitive development by observing and analyzing the mental processes involved in perceiving and handling information

initiative versus guilt Erikson's third crisis in psychosocial development, in which children balance the urge to pursue goals with moral reservations that may prevent carrying them out

instrumental aggression Aggressive behaviour used as a means of achieving a goal

integration Process by which neurons coordinate the activities of muscle groups

intellectual disability (mental retardation) Significantly subnormal cognitive functioning

intelligent behaviour Behaviour that is goal-oriented and adaptive to circumstances and conditions of life

internalization During socialization, process by which children accept societal standards of conduct as their own

invisible imitation Imitation with parts of one's body that one cannot see

IQ (intelligence quotient) tests Psychometric tests that seek to measure intelligence by comparing a test-taker's performance with standardized norms

irreversibility Piaget's term for a pre-operational child's failure to understand that an operation can go in two or more directions

K

Kaufman Assessment Battery for Children (K-ABC-II) Non-traditional individual intelligence test designed to provide fair assessments of minority children and children with disabilities

L

laboratory observation Research method in which all participants are observed in the same situation, under controlled conditions

language Communication system based on words and grammar

language acquisition device (LAD) In Chomsky's terminology, an inborn mechanism that enables children to infer linguistic rules from the language they hear

lanugo Fuzzy prenatal body hair, which drops off within a few days after birth

lateralization Tendency of each of the brain's hemispheres to have specialized functions

learning disabilities (LDs) Disorders that interfere with specific aspects of learning and school achievement

learning perspective View of development that holds that changes in behaviour result from experience, or adaptation to the environment

linguistic speech Verbal expression designed to convey meaning

literacy Ability to read and write

longitudinal study Study design to assess changes in a sample over time

long-term memory Storage of virtually unlimited capacity that holds information for very long periods

low birth weight Weight of less than 2,500 g at birth because of prematurity or being small for date

M

macrosystem Bronfenbrenner's term for overall cultural patterns

maturation Unfolding of a natural sequence of physical and behavioural changes, including readiness to master new abilities

mechanistic model Model that views development as a passive, predictable response to stimuli

meconium Fetal waste matter, excreted during the first few days after birth

menarche Girl's first menstruation

mental retardation Significantly subnormal cognitive functioning

mesosystem Bronfenbrenner's term for linkages of two or more microsystems

metacognition Awareness of a person's own mental processes

metamemory Understanding of processes of memory

microgenetic study Study design that allows researchers to directly observe change by repeated testing over a short time

microsystem Bronfenbrenner's term for a setting in which a child interacts with others every day, face to face

mnemonic strategies Techniques to aid memory

monozygotic (one-egg) twins Twins resulting from the division of a single zygote after fertilization; also called *identical twins*

morality of constraint First of Piaget's two stages of moral development, characterized by rigid, egocentric judgments

morality of cooperation Second of Piaget's two stages of moral development, characterized by flexible judgments and formation of one's own moral code

moratorium Identity status, described by Marcia, in which a person is currently considering alternatives (in crisis) and seems headed for commitment

multifactorial transmission Combination of genetic and environmental factors to produce certain complex traits

mutations Permanent alterations in genes or chromosomes that may produce harmful characteristics

mutual regulation Process by which infant and caregiver communicate emotional states to each other and respond appropriately

myelination Process of coating neurons with a fatty substance (myelin) that enables faster communication between cells

N

nativism Theory that human beings have an inborn capacity for language acquisition

natural, or prepared, childbirth Methods of childbirth that use instruction, breathing exercises, and social support to induce controlled physical responses to uterine contractions and reduce fear and pain

natural selection According to Darwin's theory of evolution, process by which characteristics that promote survival of a species are reproduced in successive generations, and characteristics that do not promote survival die out

naturalistic observation Research method in which behaviour is studied in natural settings without intervention or manipulation

neglect Failure to meet a child's basic needs

neglectful/uninvolved Maccoby and Martin's term for parents who focus on their own needs rather than on those of the child

neonatal jaundice Condition, in many newborn babies, caused by immaturity of liver and evidenced by yellowish appearance; can cause brain damage if not treated promptly

neonatal period First 4 weeks of life, a time of transition from intrauterine dependency to independent existence

neonate Newborn baby, up to 4 weeks old

neurons Nerve cells

niche-picking Tendency of a person, especially after early childhood, to seek out environments compatible with his or her genotype

non-normative Characteristic of an unusual event that happens to a particular person, or a typical event that happens at an unusual time of life

non-shared environmental effects The unique environment in which each child grows up, consisting of distinctive influences or influences that affect one child differently from another

normative Characteristic of an event that occurs in a similar way for most people in a group

nuclear family Kinship and household unit made up of parents and their natural or adopted children

O

obesity Extreme overweight in relation to age, sex, height, and body type; sometimes defined as having a body mass index (weight-for-height) at or above the 85th or 95th percentile of growth curves for children of the same age and sex

object permanence Piaget's term for the understanding that a person or object still exists when out of sight

observational learning Learning through watching the behaviour of others

obsessive-compulsive disorder Anxiety aroused by repetitive, intrusive thoughts, images, or impulses, often leading to compulsive ritual behaviours

operant conditioning Learning based on reinforcement or punishment

operational definitions Definitions stated in terms of operations or procedures used to produce or measure a phenomenon

oppositional defiant disorder (ODD) Pattern of behaviour, persisting into middle childhood, marked by negativity, hostility, and defiance

organismic model Model that views development as internally initiated by an active organism and as occurring in a sequence of qualitatively different stages

organization Mnemonic strategy of categorizing material to be remembered

organization Piaget's term for integration of knowledge into systems

Otis-Lennon School Ability Test (OLSAT8) Group intelligence test for kindergarten through Grade 12

overt, or direct, aggression Aggression openly directed at its target

P

participant observation Research method in which the observer lives with the people or participates in the activity being observed

parturition Process of uterine, cervical, and other changes, usually lasting about 2 weeks, preceding childbirth

patchwork self Elkind's term for a sense of identity constructed by substituting other people's attitudes, beliefs, and commitments for one's own

perinatal Period from 28 weeks' gestation to 7 days after birth

permissive Baumrind's term for parenting style emphasizing self-expression and self-regulation

personal fable Elkind's term for conviction that one is special, unique, and not subject to the rules that govern the rest of the world

phenotype Observable characteristics of a person

phonetic, or code-emphasis, approach Approach to teaching reading that emphasizes decoding of unfamiliar words.

physical abuse Action taken to endanger a child involving potential bodily injury

physical development Growth of body and brain, including patterns of change in sensory capacities, motor skills, and health

Piagetian approach Approach to the study of cognitive development that describes qualitative stages in cognitive functioning

plasticity Modifiability, or "moulding," of the brain through experience

play therapy Therapeutic approach in which a child plays freely while a therapist observes and occasionally comments, asks questions, or makes suggestions

polygenic inheritance Pattern of inheritance in which multiple genes at different sites on chromosomes affect a complex trait

postconventional morality (or morality of autonomous moral principles) Third level in Kohlberg's theory of moral reasoning, in which people follow internally held moral principles and can decide among conflicting moral standards

postmature Referring to a fetus not yet born as of 2 weeks after the due date or 42 weeks after the mother's last menstrual period

power assertion Disciplinary strategy to discourage undesirable behaviour through physical or verbal enforcement of parental control

pragmatics The practical knowledge needed to use language for communication

preconventional morality First level of Kohlberg's theory of moral reasoning, in which control is external and rules are obeyed in order to gain rewards or avoid punishment, or out of self-interest

prejudice Unfavourable attitude toward members of certain groups outside one's own, especially racial or ethnic groups

prelinguistic speech Forerunner of linguistic speech; utterance of sounds that are not words; includes crying, cooing, babbling, and accidental and deliberate imitation of sounds without understanding their meaning

pre-operational stage In Piaget's theory, the second major stage of cognitive development, in which children become more sophisticated in their use of symbolic thought but are not yet able to use logic

pretend play Play involving imaginary people or situations; also called *fantasy play, dramatic play,* or *imaginative play*

preterm (premature) infants Infants born before completing the 37th week of gestation

primary sex characteristics Organs directly related to reproduction, which enlarge and mature during adolescence

private speech Talking aloud to oneself with no intent to communicate

procedural knowledge Acquired skills stored in long-term memory

pro-social behaviour Any voluntary behaviour intended to help others

protective factors Influences that reduce the impact of early stress and tend to predict positive outcomes

proximodistal principle Principle that development proceeds from within to without; that is, parts of the body near the centre develop before the extremities

psychoanalytic perspective View of development as shaped by unconscious forces

psychological aggression Verbal attack by a parent that may result in psychological harm to a child

psychometric approach Approach to the study of cognitive development that seeks to measure the quantity of intelligence a person possesses

psychosexual development In Freudian theory, an unvarying sequence of stages of personality development during infancy, childhood, and adolescence, in which gratification shifts from the mouth to the anus and then to the genitals

psychosocial development (1) Pattern of change in emotions, personality, and social relationships; (2) In Erikson's eight-stage theory, the socially and culturally influenced process of development of the ego, or self

puberty Process by which a person attains sexual maturity and the ability to reproduce

punishment In operant conditioning, a stimulus that discourages repetition of a behaviour

Q

qualitative change Change in kind, structure, or organization, such as the change from nonverbal to verbal communication

qualitative research Research that involves the interpretation of nonnumerical data, such as subjective experiences, feelings, or beliefs

quantitative change Change in number or amount, such as in height, weight, or size of vocabulary

quantitative research Research that deals with objectively measurable data

quantitative trait loci (QTL) Interaction of multiple genes, each with effects of varying size, to produce a complex trait

R

random assignment Assignment of participants in an experiment to groups in such a way that each person has an equal chance of being placed in any group

random selection Achieving representativeness by allowing each person in a population an equal and independent chance of being chosen

reaction range Potential variability, depending on environmental conditions, in the expression of a hereditary trait

real self The self one actually is

recall Ability to reproduce material from memory

receptive cooperation Kochanska's term for eager willingness to cooperate harmoniously with a parent in daily interactions, including routines, chores, hygiene, and play

recessive inheritance Pattern of inheritance in which a child receives identical recessive alleles, resulting in expression of a nondominant trait

reciprocal determinism Bandura's concept that behaviour is determined bidirectionally, by the child and the environment acting on each other

reciprocity System of mutually binding, mutually responsive relationships into which a child is socialized

recognition Ability to identify a previously encountered stimulus

reflex behaviours Automatic, involuntary, innate responses to stimulation

rehearsal Mnemonic strategy to keep an item in working memory through conscious repetition

reinforcement In operant conditioning, a stimulus that encourages repetition of a desired behaviour

relational, or social, aggression Aggression aimed at damaging or interfering with another person's relationships, reputation, or psychological well-being; also called *covert, indirect,* or *psychological aggression*

representational ability Piaget's term for capacity to mentally represent objects and experiences, largely through the use of symbols

representational mappings In neo-Piagetian terminology, the second stage in development of self-definition, in which a child makes logical connections between aspects of the self

but still sees these characteristics in all-or-nothing terms

representational systems In neo-Piagetian terminology, the third stage in development of self-definition, characterized by breadth, balance, and the integration and assessment of aspects of the self

resilient children Children who weather adverse circumstances, function well despite challenges or threats, or bounce back from traumatic events

retrieval Process by which information is accessed or recalled from memory storage

risk factors Conditions that increase the likelihood of a negative developmental outcome

rough-and-tumble play Vigorous play involving wrestling, hitting, and chasing, often accompanied by laughing and screaming

S

sample Group of participants chosen to represent the entire population under study

scaffolding Temporary support to help a child master a task

schemes Piaget's term for organized patterns of behaviour used in particular situations

schizophrenia Mental disorder marked by loss of contact with reality; symptoms include hallucinations and delusions

school phobia Unrealistic fear of going to school, may be a form of *separation anxiety disorder* or *social phobia*

scientific method System of established principles and processes of scientific inquiry

script General remembered outline of a familiar, repeated event, used to guide behaviour

secondary sex characteristics Physiological signs of sexual maturation (such as breast development and growth of body hair) that do not involve the sex organs

secular trend Trend that can be seen only by observing several generations, such as the trend toward earlier attainment of adult height and sexual maturity, which began a century ago

secure attachment Pattern in which an infant cries or protests when the primary caregiver leaves and actively seeks out the caregiver upon his or her return

self-awareness Realization that one's existence and functioning are separate from those of other people and things

self-concept Sense of self; descriptive and evaluative mental picture of one's abilities and traits

self-conscious emotions Emotions, such as embarrassment, empathy, and envy, that depend on self-awareness

self-definition Cluster of characteristics used to describe oneself

self-efficacy Sense of one's own capability to master challenges and achieve goals

self-esteem The judgment a person makes about his or her self-worth

self-evaluative emotions Emotions, such as pride, shame, and guilt, that depend on both self-awareness and knowledge of socially accepted standards of behaviour

self-fulfilling prophecy False expectation or prediction of behaviour that tends to come true because it leads people to act as if it already were true

self-regulation A person's independent control of behaviour to conform to understood social expectations

sensitive periods Times in development when a person is particularly open to certain kinds of experiences

sensorimotor stage In Piaget's theory, the first stage in cognitive development, during which infants learn through sensory and motor activity

sensory memory Initial, brief, temporary storage of sensory information

separation anxiety Distress shown by someone, typically an infant, when a familiar caregiver leaves

separation anxiety disorder Condition involving excessive, prolonged anxiety about separation from home or from people to whom a child is attached

sequential study Study design that combines cross-sectional and longitudinal techniques

seriation Ability to order items along a dimension

sex chromosomes Pair of chromosomes that determines sex: XX in the normal female, XY in the normal male

sex-linked inheritance Pattern of inheritance in which certain characteristics carried on the X chromosome inherited from the mother are transmitted differently to her male and female offspring

sexual abuse Sexual activity involving a child and an older person

sexual orientation Gender focus of consistent sexual, romantic, and affectionate interest, either heterosexual, homosexual, or bisexual

sexually transmitted diseases (STDs) Diseases spread by sexual contact

single representations In neo-Piagetian terminology, first stage in development of self-definition, in which children describe themselves in terms of individual, unconnected characteristics and in all-or-nothing terms

situational compliance Kochanska's term for obedience to parent's orders only in the presence of prompting or other signs of ongoing parental control

"slow-to-warm-up" children Children whose temperament is generally mild but who are hesitant about accepting new experiences

small-for-gestational age infants Infants whose birth weight is less than that of 90 percent of babies of the same gestational age, as a result of slow fetal growth

social capital Family and community resources on which a person or family can draw

social cognition Ability to understand that others have mental states and to judge their feelings and intentions

social cognitive theory Albert Bandura's expansion of social learning theory; holds that children learn gender roles through socialization

social construction Concept about the nature of reality, based on societally shared perceptions or assumptions

social-contextual approach Approach to the study of cognitive development focusing on environmental influences, particularly of parents and other caregivers

social interaction model Model, based on Vygotsky's socio-cultural theory, which proposes that children construct autobiographical memories through conversation with adults about shared events

social learning theory Theory that behaviours are learned by observing and imitating models; also called *social cognitive theory*

social phobia Extreme fear and/or avoidance of social situations

social promotion Policy in which children are automatically promoted from one grade to another even if they do not meet academic standards for the grade they are completing

social referencing Understanding an ambiguous situation by seeking out another person's perception of it

social speech Speech intended to be understood by a listener

socialization Development of habits, skills, values, and motives shared by responsible, productive members of a society

socio-cultural theory Vygotsky's theory of how contextual factors affect children's development

socio-economic status (SES) Combination of economic and social factors describing an individual or family, including income, education, and occupation

spermarche Boy's first ejaculation

spontaneous abortion Natural expulsion from the uterus of an embryo or fetus that cannot survive outside the womb; also called *miscarriage*

Stanford-Binet Intelligence Scale Individual intelligence test for ages 2 and up, used to measure knowledge, quantitative, reasoning, and working memory

state of arousal An infant's physiological and behavioural status at a given moment in the periodic daily cycle of wakefulness, sleep, and activity

Sternberg Triarchic Abilities Test (STAT) Test to measure componential, experiential, and contextual intelligence

stillbirth The death of a fetus at or after the 20th week of gestation

"still-face" paradigm Research method used to measure mutual regulation in infants 2 to 9 months old

storage Retention of information in memory for future use

Strange Situation Laboratory technique used to study attachment

stranger anxiety Wariness of strange people and places, shown by some infants during the second half of the first year

stuttering Involuntary, frequent repetition or prolongation of sounds or syllables

substance abuse Repeated, harmful use of a substance, usually alcohol or other drugs

substance dependence Addiction (physical, psychological, or both) to a harmful substance

sudden infant death syndrome Sudden and unexplained death of an apparently healthy infant

symbolic function Piaget's term for ability to use mental representations (words, numbers, or images) to which a child has attached meaning

syntax Rules for forming sentences in a particular language

systems of action Increasingly complex combinations of skills, which permit a wider or more precise range of movement and more control of the environment

T

tacit knowledge Sternberg's term for information that is not formally taught or openly expressed, but is necessary to get ahead

telegraphic speech Early form of sentence consisting of only a few essential words

temperament Characteristic disposition, or style of approaching and reacting to situations

teratogenic Capable of causing birth defects

theory Coherent set of logically related concepts that seeks to organize, explain, and predict data

theory of mind Awareness and understanding of mental processes

theory of multiple intelligences Gardner's theory that each person has several distinct forms of intelligence

theory of sexual selection Darwinian theory, which holds that selection of sexual partners is influenced by the differing reproductive pressures that early men and women confronted in the struggle for survival of the species

transduction Piaget's term for a preoperational child's tendency to mentally link particular experiences, whether or not there is logically a causal relationship

transitive inference Understanding of the relationship between two objects by knowing the relationship of each to a third object

triarchic theory of intelligence Sternberg's theory describing three types of intelligence: componential (analytical ability), experiential (insight and originality), and contextual (practical thinking)

two-way (dual-language) learning Approach to second-language education in which English speakers and non-English speakers learn together in their own and each other's languages

U

ultrasound Prenatal medical procedure using high-frequency sound waves to detect the outline of a fetus and its movements, in order to determine whether a pregnancy is progressing normally

V

vernix caseosa Oily substance on a neonate's skin that protects against infection

violation-of-expectations Research method in which dishabituation to a stimulus that conflicts with previous experience is taken as evidence that an infant recognizes the new stimulus as surprising

visible imitation Imitation with parts of one's body that one can see

visual cliff Apparatus designed to give an illusion of depth and used to assess depth perception in infants

visual guidance Use of the eyes to guide movements of the hands or other parts of the body

visually-based retrieval Process of retrieving the sound of a printed word upon seeing the word as a whole.

visual preference Tendency of infants to spend more time looking at one sight than another

visual recognition memory Ability to distinguish a familiar visual stimulus from an unfamiliar one when shown both at the same time

W

Wechsler Intelligence Scale for Children (WISC–III) Individual intelligence test for schoolchildren, which yields verbal and performance scores as well as a combined score

Wechsler Preschool and Primary Scale of Intelligence (WPPSI–III) Individual intelligence test for children ages 2½ to 7, which yields verbal and performance scores as well as a combined score

whole-language approach Approach to teaching reading that emphasizes visual retrieval and use of contextual clues

withdrawal of love Disciplinary strategy that may involve ignoring, isolating, or showing dislike for a child

working memory Short-term storage of information being actively processed

Z

zone of proximal development (ZPD) Vygotsky's term for the difference between what a child can do alone and with help

zygote One-celled organism resulting from fertilization

Bibliography

Aaron, P. G., & Guillemard, J.-C. (1993). Artists as dyslexics. In D. M. Willows, R. S. Kruk, & E. Corcos (Eds.), *Visual processes in reading and reading disabilities* (pp. 393–415). Hillsdale, NJ: Lawrence Erlbaum Associates.

Abbey, A., Andrews, F. M., & Halman, J. (1992). Infertility and subjective well-being: The mediating roles of self-esteem, internal control, and interpersonal conflict. *Journal of Marriage and the Family, 54*, 408–417.

Aber, J. L., Brown, J. L., & Jones, S. M. (2003). Developmental trajectories toward violence in middle childhood: Course, demographic differences, and response to school-based intervention. *Developmental Psychology, 39*, 324–348.

Abma, J. C., Chandra, A., Mosher, W. D., Peterson, L., & Piccinino, L. (1997). Fertility, family planning, and women's health: New data from the 1995 National Survey of Family Growth. *Vital Health Statistics, 23*(19). Washington, DC: National Center for Health Statistics.

Abma, J. C., Martinez, G. M., Mosher, W. D., & Dawson, B. S. (2004). Teenagers in the United States: Sexual activity, contraceptive use, and childbearing, 2002. *Vital Health Statistics, 23*(24). Washington, DC: National Center for Health Statistics.

Abramovitch, R., Corter, C., & Lando, B. (1979). Sibling interaction in the home. *Child Development, 50*, 997–1003.

Abramovitch, R., Corter, C., Pepler, D., & Stanhope, L. (1986). Sibling and peer interactions: A final follow-up and comparison. *Child Development, 57*, 217–229.

Abramovitch, R., Pepler, D., & Corter, C. (1982). Patterns of sibling interaction among preschool-age children. In M. E. Lamb (Ed.), *Sibling relationships: Their nature and significance across the lifespan.* Hillsdale, NJ: Erlbaum.

Abrams, B., & Parker, J. D. (1990). Maternal weight gain in women with good pregnancy outcome. *Obstetrics and Gynecology, 76*(1), 1–7.

Achter, J. A., & Lubinski, D. (2003). Fostering exceptional development in intellectually talented populations. In W. B. Walsh (Ed.), *Counseling psychology and optimal human functioning* (pp. 279–296). Mahwah, NJ: Erlbaum.

Ackerman, B. P., Kogos, J., Youngstrom, E., Schoff, K., & Izard, C. (1999). Family instability and the problem behaviors of children from economically disadvantaged families. *Developmental Psychology, 35*(1), 258–268.

Ackerman, M. J., Siu, B. L., Sturner, W. Q., Tester D. J., Valdivia, C. R., Makielski, J. C., & Towbin, J. A. (2001). Postmortem molecular analysis of SCN5A defects in sudden infant death syndrome. *Journal of the American Medical Association, 286*, 2264–2269.

Acs, G., Shulman, R., Ng, M. W., & Chussid, S. (1999). Tooth decay may slow child's growth. *Pediatric Dentistry, 21*, 109–113.

ACT for Youth Upstate Center of Excellence. (2002). *Adolescent brain development. Research facts and findings.* [A collaboration of Cornell University, University of Rochester, and the NYS Center for School Safety.] Retrieved March 23, 2004, from http://www.human.cornell.edu/actforyouth.

Adair, J. (2001). Ethics of psychological research: New policies; continuing issues; new concerns. *Canadian Psychology, 42*, 25–37.

Adam, E. K., Gunnar, M. R., & Tanaka, A. (2004). Adult attachment, parent emotion, and observed parenting behavior: Mediator and moderator models. *Child Development, 75*, 110–122.

Adams, G. R., & Berzonsky, M. D. (eds.). (2003). *Blackwell handbook of adolescence* (pp. 313–329). Oxford, UK: Blackwell Publishers.

Adams, L. A., & Rickert, V. I. (1989). Reducing bedtime tantrums: Comparison between positive routines and graduated extinction. *Pediatrics, 84*, 756–761.

Adams, R., & Laursen, B. (2001). The organization and dynamics of adolescent conflict with parents and friends. *Journal of Marriage and the Family, 63*, 97–110.

Adlaf, E. M., & Paglia-Boak, A. (2007). *Drug Use Among Ontario Students 1977-2007: Detailed OSDUHS Findings.* CAMH Research Document Series No. 20. Toronto, ON: CAMH. Retrieved November 27, 2007 from http://www.camh.net/Research/Areas_of_research/Population_Life_Course_Studies/OSDUS/OSDUHS2007_DrugDetailed_final.pdf.

Adlaf, E. M., Begin, P., & Sawka, E. (Eds.). (2005). *Canadian Addiction Survey (CAS): A national survey of Canadians' use of alcohol and other drugs: Prevalence of use and related harms: Detailed report.* Ottawa: Canadian Centre of Substance Abuse.

Adler, P. A., & Adler, P. (1995). Dynamics of inclusion and exclusion in preadolescent cliques. Social Psychology Quarterly, 58, 145–162.

Adolescent Medicine Committee, Canadian Paediatric Society. (1998). Eating disorders in adolescents: Principles of diagnosis and treatment. *Paediatrics and Child Health, 3*, 189–192.

Adolph, K. E. (2000). Specificity of learning: Why infants fall over a veritable cliff. *Psychological Science, 11*, 290–295.

Adolph, K. E., & Eppler, M. A. (2002). Flexibility and specificity in infant motor skill acquisition. In J. Fagen & H. Hayne (Eds.), *Progress in infancy research* (vol. 2, pp. 121–167). Mahwah, NJ: Lawrence Erlbaum Associates.

Adolph, K. E., Vereijken, B., & Shrout, P. E. (2003). What changes in infant walking and why. *Child Development, 74*, 475–497.

Ahamed, Y., MacDonald, H., Reed, K., Naylor, P., Liu-Ambrose, T. & McKay, H. (2007). School-based physical activity does not compromise children's academic performance. *Medicine & Science in Sports & Exercise, 39*, 371–376.

Ahnert, L., Gunnar, M. R., Lamb, M. E., & Barthel, M. (2004). Transition to child care: Associations with infant-mother attachment, infant negative emotion and corticol elevation. *Child Development, 75*, 639–650.

Ahnert, L., Pinquart, M., & Lamb, M. E. (2006). Security of children's relationships with nonparental care providers: A meta-analysis. *Child Development, 74*, 664–679.

Ahrons, C. R., & Tanner, J. L. (2003). Adult children and their fathers: Relationship changes 20 years after parental divorce. *Family Relations, 52*, 340–351.

Ainsworth, M. D. S. (1967). *Infancy in Uganda: Infant care and the growth of love.* Baltimore: Johns Hopkins University Press.

Ainsworth, M. D. S., Blehar, M. C., Waters, E., & Wall, S. (1978). *Patterns of attachment: A psychological study of the strange situation.* Hillsdale, NJ: Erlbaum.

Alaimo, K., Olson, C. M., & Frongillo, E. A. (2001). Food insufficiency and American school-aged children's cognitive, academic, and psychosocial development. *Pediatrics, 108*, 44–53.

Alan Guttmacher Institute (AGI). (1994). *Sex & America's teenagers.* New York: Author.

Alan Guttmacher Institute (AGI). (1999a). *Facts in brief: Teen sex and pregnancy.* Retrieved January 31, 2000, from http://www.agi_usa.org/pubs/fb_teen_sex.html#sfd.

Alan Guttmacher Institute (AGI). (1999b). *Occasional report: Why is teenage pregnancy declining? The roles of abstinence, sexual activity and contraceptive use.* Retrieved January 31, 2000, from http://www.agi-usa.org/pubs/or_teen_preg_decline.html.

Alati, R., Al Mamun, A., Williams, G. M., O'Callaghan, M., Najman, J. M., & Bor, W. (2006). In utero alcohol exposure and prediction of alcohol disorders in early adulthood: A birth cohort study. *Archives of General Psychiatry, 63*(9), 1009–1016.

Albanese, A., & Stanhope, R. (1993). Growth and metabolic data following growth hormone treatment of children with intrauterine growth retardation. *Hormone Research, 39*, 8–12.

Alberta Universal Newborn Hearing Screening Project, 2001–2004. Retrieved from www.babynear.ucalgary.ca on July 15, 2007.

Aldort, N. (1994, summer). Getting out of the way. *Mothering,* 38–43.

Alexander, G. R., Tompkins, M. E., Allen, M. C., & Hulsey, T. C. (2000). Trends and racial differences in birth weight and related survival. *Maternal and Child Health Journal, 3*, 71–79.

Alexander, K. L., Entwisle, D. R., & Dauber, S. L. (1993). First-grade classroom behavior: Its short- and long-term consequences for school performance. *Child Development, 64*, 801–814.

Aligne, C. A., & Stoddard, J. J. (1997). Tobacco and children: An economic evaluation of the medical effects of parental smoking. *Archives of Pediatric and Adolescent Medicine, 151*, 648–653.

Allen, G. L., & Ondracek, P. J. (1995). Age-sensitive cognitive abilities related to children's acquisition of spatial knowledge. *Developmental Psychology, 31*, 934–945.

Allen, J. P., & Philliber, S. (2001). Who benefits most from a broadly targeted prevention program? Differential efficacy across populations in the Teen Outreach Program. *Journal of Community Psychology, 29*, 637–655.

Allen, J. P., McElhaney, K. B., Land, D. J., Kuperminc, G. P., Moore, C. W., O'Beirner-Kelly, H., et al. (2003). A secure base in adolescence: Markers of attachment security in the mother-adolescent relationship. *Child Development, 74*, 292–307.

Allen, J. P., Porter, M. R., McFarland, F. C., Marsh, P., & McElhaney, K. B. (2005). The two faces of adolescents' success with peers: Adolescent popularity, social adaptation, and deviant behavior. *Child Development, 76,* 747–760.

Allergy Section, Canadian Paediatric Society [CPS]. (1986). Secondhand cigarette smoke worsens symptoms in children with asthma. *Canadian Medical Association Journal, 135,* 321–323.

Almeida, D. M., & McDonald, D. (1998). Weekly rhythms of parents' work stress, home stress, and parent–adolescent tension. In A. Crouter & R. Larson (Eds.), *Temporal rhythms in adolescence: Clocks, calendars, and the coordination of daily life* (pp. 69–82). *[New Directions in Child and Adolescent Development, 82.]* San Francisco: Jossey-Bass.

Als, H., Duffy, F. H., McAnulty, G. B., Rivkin, M. J., Vajapeyam, S., Mulkern, R. V., Warfield, S. K., Huppi, P. S., Butler, S. C., Conneman, N., Fischer, C., and Eichenwald, E. C. (2004). Early experience alters brain function and structure. *Pediatrics, 113,* 846–857.

Alsaker, F. D. (1992). Pubertal timing, overweight, and psychological adjustment. *Journal of Early Adolescence, 12*(4)*,* 396–419.

Altschul, I., Oyserman, D., & Bybee, D. (2006). Racial-ethnic identity in mid-adolescence: Content and change as predictors of academic achievement. *Child Development, 77,* 1155–1169.

Amato, P. R. (2003). Reconciling divergent perspectives: Judith Wallerstein, quantitative family research, and children of divorce. *Family Relations, 52,* 332–339.

Amato, P. R. (2005). The impact of family formation change on the cognitive, social, and emotional well-being of the next generation. *Future of Children, 15,* 75–96.

Amato, P. R., & Booth, A. (1997). *A generation at risk: Growing up in an era of family upheaval.* Cambridge, MA: Harvard University Press.

Amato, P. R., & Cheadle, J. (2005). The long reach of divorce: Divorce and child well-being across three generations. *Journal of Marriage and Family, 67,* 191–206.

Amato, P. R., & Gilbreth, J. G. (1999). Nonresident fathers and children's well-being: A meta-analysis. *Journal of Marriage and the Family, 61,* 557–573.

Ambert, A. (2005). Divorce: Facts, causes and consequences. Retrieved August 17, 2007 from http://www.vifamily.ca/library/cft/divorce_05.html#Children.

American Academy of Child and Adolescent Psychiatry (AACAP). (1997). Children's sleep problems. [Fact sheet] No. 34. (Available from the AACAP, 3615 Wisconsin Ave., N. W., Washington, DC, 20016–3007.)

American Academy of Child and Adolescent Psychiatry (AACAP). (2002). Children and the news. *Facts for Families* #67. Retrieved April 24, 2005, from http://www.aacap.org/publications/ factsfam/67.htm.

American Academy of Pediatric Dentistry. (2002–2007). Enamel Fluorosis. Retrieved July 25, 2007 from http://www.aapd.org/publications/brochures/fluorosis.asp.

American Academy of Pediatrics (AAP). (1986). *Positive approaches to day care dilemmas: How to make it work.* Elk Grove Village, IL: Author.

American Academy of Pediatrics (AAP). (1989a, November). The facts on breast feeding [Fact sheet]. (Available from AAP, 141 Northwest Point Blvd., Elk Grove Village, IL, 60007–1098.)

American Academy of Pediatrics (AAP). (1989b). Follow-up on weaning formulas. *Pediatrics, 83,* 1067.

American Academy of Pediatrics (AAP). (1992a, January 15). AAP proposes handgun ban, other measures to curb firearm deaths, injuries [News release]. Elk Grove Village, IL: Author.

American Academy of Pediatrics (AAP). (1992b, spring). Bedtime doesn't have to be a struggle. Healthy Kids, pp. 4–10.

American Academy of Pediatrics (AAP). (1998). Policy statement on female genital mutilation. *Pediatrics, 102,* 153–156.

American Academy of Pediatrics (AAP). (2004, September 30). American Academy of Pediatrics (AAP) supports Institute of Medicine's (IOM) childhood obesity recommendations. Press release.

American Academy of Pediatrics (AAP) and Center to Prevent Handgun Violence. (1994). *Keep your family safe from firearm injury.* Washington, DC: Center to Prevent Handgun Violence.

American Academy of Pediatrics (AAP) Committee on Adolescence & Committee on Early Childhood, Adoption, and Dependent Care. (2001). Care of adolescent parents and their children. *Pediatrics, 107,* 429–434.

American Academy of Pediatrics (AAP) Committee on Adolescence. (1994). Sexually transmitted diseases. *Pediatrics, 94,* 568–572.

American Academy of Pediatrics (AAP) Committee on Adolescence. (1999). Adolescent pregnancy—Current trends and issues: 1998. *Pediatrics, 103,* 516–520.

American Academy of Pediatrics (AAP) Committee on Adolescence. (2000). Suicide and suicide attempts in adolescents. *Pediatrics, 105*(4)*,* 871–874.

American Academy of Pediatrics (AAP) Committee on Adolescence. (2003). Policy statement: Identifying and treating eating disorders. *Pediatrics, 111,* 204–211.

American Academy of Pediatrics (AAP) Committee on Bioethics. (2001). Ethical issues with genetic testing in pediatrics. *Pediatrics, 107*(6)*,* 1451–1455.

American Academy of Pediatrics (AAP) Committee on Child Abuse and Neglect. (2001). Shaken baby syndrome: Rotational cranial injuries—Technical report. *Pediatrics, 108,* 206–210.

American Academy of Pediatrics (AAP) Committee on Children with Disabilities. (2001). The pediatrician's role in the diagnosis and management of autistic spectrum disorder in children. *Pediatrics, 107*(5)*,* 1221–1226.

American Academy of Pediatrics (AAP) Committee on Children with Disabilities and Committee on Drugs. (1996). Medication for children with attentional disorders. *Pediatrics, 98,* 301–304.

American Academy of Pediatrics (AAP) Committee on Children with Disabilities and Committee on Psychosocial Aspects of Child and Family Health. (1993). Psychosocial risks of chronic health conditions in childhood and adolescence. *Pediatrics, 92,* 876–877.

American Academy of Pediatrics (AAP) Committee on Environmental Health. (1997). Environmental tobacco smoke: A hazard to children. *Pediatrics, 99,* 639–642.

American Academy of Pediatrics (AAP) Committee on Environmental Health. (1998). Screening for elevated blood lead levels. *Pediatrics, 101,* 1072–1078.

American Academy of Pediatrics (AAP) Committee on Environmental Health. (2005). Lead exposure in children: Prevention, detection, and management. *Pediatrics, 116,* 1036–1046.

American Academy of Pediatrics (AAP) Committee on Fetus and Newborn and American College of Obstetricians and Gynecologists (ACOG) Committee on Obstetric Practice. (1996). Use and abuse of the Apgar score. *Pediatrics, 98,* 141–142.

American Academy of Pediatrics (AAP) Committee on Fetus and Newborn & American College of Obstetricians and Gynecologists (ACOG) Committee on Obstetric Practice. (2006). The Apgar score. *Pediatrics, 117,* 1444–1447.

American Academy of Pediatrics (AAP) Committee on Genetics. (1999). Folic acid for the prevention of neural tube defects. *Pediatrics, 104,* 325–327.

American Academy of Pediatrics (AAP) Committee on Injury and Poison Prevention. (2001a). Bicycle helmets. *Pediatrics, 108*(4)*,* 1030–1032.

American Academy of Pediatrics (AAP) Committee on Injury and Poison Prevention and Committee on Sports Medicine and Fitness. (1999). Policy statement: Trampolines at home, school, and recreational centers. *Pediatrics, 103,* 1053–1056.

American Academy of Pediatrics (AAP) Committee on Injury and Poison Prevention. (1995a). Bicycle helmets. *Pediatrics, 95,* 609–610.

American Academy of Pediatrics (AAP) Committee on Nutrition. (1992a). Statement on cholesterol. *Pediatrics, 90,* 469–473.

American Academy of Pediatrics (AAP) Committee on Nutrition. (1992b). The use of whole cow's milk in infancy. *Pediatrics, 89,* 1105–1109.

American Academy of Pediatrics (AAP) Committee on Nutrition. (2003). Prevention of pediatric overweight and obesity. *Pediatrics, 112,* 424–430.

American Academy of Pediatrics (AAP) Committee on Pediatric Research. (2000). Race/ethnicity, gender, socioeconomic status—Research exploring their effects on child health: A subject review. *Pediatrics, 105,* 1349–1351.

American Academy of Pediatrics (AAP) Committee on Psychosocial Aspects of Child and Family Health. (1998). Guidance for effective discipline. *Pediatrics, 101,* 723–728.

American Academy of Pediatrics (AAP) Committee on Psychosocial Aspects of Child and Family Health & Committee on Adolescence. (2001). Sexuality education for children and adolescence. Pediatrics, 108(2), 498–502.

American Academy of Pediatrics (AAP) Committee on Public Education. (2001). Policy statement: Children, adolescents, and television. *Pediatrics, 107,* 423–426.

American Academy of Pediatrics (AAP) Committee on Public Education (2001b). Policy statement: Children, adolescents, and television. *Pediatrics, 107,* 423–426.

American Academy of Pediatrics (AAP) Committee on Quality Improvement. (2002). Making Advances Against Jaundice in Infant Care (MAJIC). Retrieved October 25, 2002, from http://www/ aap.org/visit/majic.htm.

American Academy of Pediatrics (AAP) Committee on Sports Medicine and Fitness. (1992). Fitness, activity, and sports participation in the preschool child. *Pediatrics, 90,* 1002–1004.

American Academy of Pediatrics (AAP) Committee on Sports Medicine and Fitness. (1997). Participation in boxing by children, adolescents, and young adults. *Pediatrics, 99,* 134–135.

American Academy of Pediatrics (AAP) Committee on Sports Medicine and Fitness. (2001). Risk of injury from baseball and softball in children. *Pediatrics, 107*(4)*,* 782–784.

American Academy of Pediatrics (AAP) Committee on Sports Medicine and Committee on School Health. (1989). Organized athletics for preadolescent children. *Pediatrics, 84,* 583–584.

American Academy of Pediatrics (AAP) Committee on Substance Abuse. (2001). Tobacco's toll: Implications for the pediatrician. *Pediatrics, 107,* 794–798.

American Academy of Pediatrics (AAP) Section on Breastfeeding. (2005). Breastfeeding and the use of human milk. *Pediatrics, 115,* 496–506.

American Academy of Pediatrics (AAP) Task Force on Infant Positioning and SIDS. (1997). Does bed sharing affect the risk of SIDS? *Pediatrics, 100,* 272.

American Academy of Pediatrics Task Force on Sudden Infant Death Syndrome. (2005). The changing concept of sudden infant death syndrome: Diagnostic coding shifts, controversies regarding sleeping environment, and new variables to consider in reducing risk. *Pediatrics, 116,* 1245–1255.

American Heart Association, Gidding, S. S., Dennison, B. A., Birch, L. L., Daniels, S. R., Gilman, M. W., Lichtenstein, A. H., Rattay, K. T., Steinberger, J., Stettler, N., & Van Horn, L. (2006). Dietary recommendations for children and adolescents: A guide for practitioners. *Pediatrics, 117,* 544–559.

American Psychiatric Association (APA). (1994). *Diagnostic and statistical manual of mental disorders* (4th ed.). Washington, DC: Author.

American Psychiatric Association (APA). (2000). *Diagnostic and statistical manual of mental disorders* (4th ed., Text Revision). Washington, DC: Author.

American Psychological Association. (1993). *Violence and youth: Psychology's response* (Vol. 1). Summary report of the American Psychological Association Commission on Violence and Youth. Washington, DC: Author.

American Psychological Association. (n.d.). *Answers to your questions about sexual orientation and homosexuality* [Brochure]. Washington, DC: Author.

American Psychological Association (APA). (2004, July). *Resolution on sexual orientation, parents, and children.* Retrieved January 23, 2007, from http://www.apa.org/pi/lgbc/policy/parents.html.

American Psychological Association and American Academy of Pediatrics (AAP). (1996). Raising children to resist violence: What you can do? Retrieved September 23, 2002, from www.apa.org/pi/pii/raisingchildren.html.

American Psychological Association Commission on Violence and Youth. (1994). *Reason to hope.* Washington, DC: Author.

Ames, E. W. (1997). *The development of Romanian orphanage children adopted to Canada: Final report* (National Welfare Grants Program, Human Resources Development, Canada). Burnaby, BC: Simon Fraser University, Psychology Department.

Ammenheuser, M. M., Berenson, A. B., Babiak, A. E., Singleton, C. R., & Whorton, E. B. (1998). Frequencies of hprt mutant lymphocytes in marijuana-smoking. *Mutation Research, 403,* 55–64.

Amsel, E., Goodman, G., Savoie, D., & Clark, M. (1996). The development of reasoning about causal and noncausal influences on levers. *Child Development, 67,* 1624–1646.

Ananth, C. V., Liu, S., Kinzler, W. L., & Kramer, M. S. (2005). Stillbirths in the United States, 1981–2000: An age, period, and cohort analysis. *American Journal of Public Health, 95,* 2213–2217.

Anastasi, A. (1988). *Psychological testing* (6th ed.). New York: Macmillan.

Anastasi, A., & Schaefer, C. E. (1971). Note on concepts of creativity and intelligence. *Journal of Creative Behavior, 3,* 113–116.

Anastasi, A., & Urbina, S. (1997). *Psychological testing* (7th ed.). Upper Saddle River, NJ: Prentice-Hall.

Andersen, A. E. (1995). Eating disorders in males. In K. D. Brownell & C. G. Fairburn (Eds.), *Eating disorders and obesity: A comprehensive handbook* (pp. 177–187). New York: Guilford.

Anderson, A. H., Clark, A., & Mullin, J. (1994). Interactive communication between children: Learning how to make language work in dialog. *Journal of Child Language, 21,* 439–463.

Anderson, A. M., Wohlfahrt, J., Christens, P., Olsen, J., & Melbye, M. (2000). Maternal age and fetal loss: Population based register linkage study. *British Medical Journal, 320,* 1708–1712.

Anderson, C. (2000). *The impact of interactive violence on children.* Statement before the Senate Committee on Commerce, Science, and Transportation, 106th Congress, 1st session.

Anderson, C. A., Berkowitz, L., Donnerstein, E., Huesmann, L. R., Johnson, J. D., Linz, D., Malamuth, N. M., & Wartella, E. (2003). The influence of media violence on youth. *Psychological Science in the Public Interest, 4,* 81–110.

Anderson, D. A., & Hamilton, M. (2005). Gender role stereotyping of parents in children's picture books: The invisible father. *Sex Roles, 52,* 145–151.

Anderson, D. R., Huston, A. C., Schmitt, K. L., Linebarger, D. L., & Wright, J. C. (2001). Early childhood television viewing and adolescent behavior. *Monographs of the Society for Research in Child Development,* Serial No. 264, *66*(1).

Anderson, M. (1992). *My Lord, what a morning.* Madison: University of Wisconsin Press.

Anderson, M., Kaufman, J., Simon, T. R., Barrios, L., Paulozzi, L., Ryan, G., Hammond, R., Modzeleski, W., Feucht, T., Potter, L., & the School-Associated Violent Deaths Study Group. (2001). School-associated violent deaths in the United States, 1994–1999. *Journal of the American Medical Association, 286*(21), 2695–2702.

Anderson, P., Doyle, L. W., & the Victorian Infant Collaborative Study Group (2003). *Journal of the American Medical Association, 289,* 3264–3272.

Anderson, R. N., & Smith, B. L. (2003). Deaths: Leading causes for 2001. *National Vital Statistics Reports, 52*(9). Hyattsville, MD: National Center for Health Statistics.

Anderson, R. N., & Smith, B. L. (2005). Deaths: Leading causes for 2002. *National Vital Statistics Reports, 53*(17). Hyattsville, MD: National Center for Health Statistics.

Anderson, S. E., Dallal, G. E., & Must, A. (2003). Relative weight and race influence average age at menarche: Results from two nationally representative surveys of U.S. girls studied 25 years apart. *Pediatrics 2003, 111,* 844–850.

Anderson, W. F. (1998). Human gene therapy. *Nature, 392*(Suppl.), 25–30.

Andersson, N., Amlie, C., & Ytteroy, E. A. (2002). Outcomes for children with lesbian or gay parents: A review of studies from 1978 to 2000. *Scandinavian Journal of Psychology, 43*(4), 335–351.

Andres, L. (2002). Policy research issues for Canadian youth: Transition experiences of young women. Applied Research Branch: Strategic Policy: Human Resources Development Canada. Retrieved August 27, 2007 from http://www.hrsdc.gc.ca/en/cs/sp/hrsd/prc/publications/research/2002–000143/SP-555-11-02E.pdf.

Antonarakis, S. E., & Down Syndrome Collaborative Group. (1991). Parental origin of the extra chromosome in trisomy 21 as indicated by analysis of DNA polymorphisms. *New England Journal of Medicine, 324,* 872–876.

Antony, M. M., & Swinson, R. P. (1996). *Anxiety disorders and their treatment: A critical review of the evidence-based literature.* Ottawa: Health Canada.

AOM (Association of Ontario Midwives). (n.d.). What is a midwife? Retrieved October 22, 2007 from www.aom.on.ca/About/What_is_a_Midwife.aspx.

Apgar, V. (1953). A proposal for a new method of evaluation of the newborn infant. *Current Research in Anesthesia and Analgesia, 32,* 260–267.

Arbuckle, T. E., Savitz, D. A., Mery, L. S., & Curtis, K. M. (1999). Exposure to phenoxy herbicides and the risk of spontaneous abortion. *Epidemiology, 10,* 752–760.

Arbuckle, T. E., Schrader, S. M., Cole, D., Hall, J. C., Bancej, C. M., Turner L. A., & Claman P. (1999). 2,4-Doichlorophenoxyacetic acid residues in semen of Ontario farmers. *Reproductive Toxicology, 13,* 421–429.

Archer, J. (2006). Sex differences in aggression in real-world settings: A meta-analytic review. *Review of General Psychology, 8,* 291–322.

Archer, S. L. (1993). Identity in relational contexts: A methodological proposal. In J. Kroger (Ed.), *Discussions on ego identity* (pp. 75–99). Hillsdale, NJ: Erlbaum.

Arcus, D., & Kagan, J. (1995). Temperament and craniofacial variation in the first two years. *Child Development, 66,* 1529–1540.

Arend, R., Gove, F., & Sroufe, L. A. (1979). Continuity of individual adaptation from infancy to kindergarten: A predictive study of ego-resiliency and curiosity in preschoolers. *Child Development, 50,* 950–959.

Argles, J. & Greer, L. (2004). Ontario study first population-wide look at childhood asthma in Canada 35% increase in the number of children with asthma. Sick Kids, Retrieved on August 7, 2007 from http://www.sickkids.ca/mediaroom/custom/asthma04.asp.

Arias, E., MacDorman, M. F., Strobino, D. M., & Guyer, B. (2003). Annual summary of vital statistics—2002. *Pediatrics, 112,* 1215–1230.

Ariès, P. (1962). *Centuries of childhood.* New York: Random House.

Armson, B. A. (2007). Is planned cesarean childbirth a safe alternative? *Canadian Medical Association Journal, 176,* 475–476.

Arnestad, M., Crotti, L., Rognum, T. O., Insolia, R., Pedrazzini, M., Ferrandi, C., Vege, A., Wang, D. W., Rhodes, T. E., George, A. L., Schwartz, P. J. (2007). Prevalence of long-qt syndrome gene variants in sudden infant death syndrome. *Circulation, 115,* 361–367.

Arnett, J. J. (1999). Adolescent storm and stress, reconsidered. *American Psychologist, 54,* 317–326.

Arnett, J. J. (2000). Emerging adulthood: A theory of development from the late teens through the twenties. *American Psychologist, 55,* 469–480.

Arnett, J. J. (2003). Conceptions of the transition to adulthood among emerging adults in American ethnic groups. In J. J. Arnett & N. L. Galambos (Eds.), *Exploring cultural conceptions of the transition to adulthood. New Directions for Child and Adolescent Development, 100,* 63–75.

Arnett, J. J., & Galambos, N. L. (2003). Culture and conceptions of adulthood. In J. J. Arnett

& N. L. Galambos (eds.). Exploring cultural conceptions of the transition to adulthood. *New Directions for Child and Adolescent Development, 100,* 91–98.

Arnold, D. H., McWilliams, L., & Arnold, A. H. (1998). Teacher discipline and child misbehavior in day care: Untangling causality with correlational data. *Developmental Psychology, 34*(2), 276–287.

Arslanoglu, S. Moro, G. E. & Ziegler, E. E. (2006). Adjustable fortification of human milk fed to preterm infants: Does it make a difference? *Journal of Perinatology, 26,* 614–621.

Artz, S. (1998). Where have all the school girls gone? Violent girls in the school yard. *Child and Youth Care Forum, 27,* 77–109.

Asher, M. I., Montefort, S., Björkstén, B., Lai, C. K., Strachan, D. P., Weiland, S. K., Williams, H., & the ISAAC Phase Three Study Group. (2006). Worldwide time trends in the prevalence of symptoms of asthma, allergic rhinoconjunctivitis, and eczema in childhood: ISAAC phases one and three repeat multicountry cross-sectional surveys. *Lancet, 368,* 733–743.

Ashman, S. B., & Dawson, G. (2002). Maternal depression, infant psychobiological development, and risk for depression. In S. H. Goodman, & I. H. Gotlib (Eds.), *Children of depressed parents: Mechanisms of risk and implications for treatment* (pp. 37–58). Washington, DC, American Psychological Association.

Associated Press. (2004a, November 22). *Boys have no place in politics: 4-year-old.* AP Newswire.

Associated Press. (2007, January 15). *Louise Brown, world's first "test-tube" baby, gives birth.*

Astington, J. W. (1993). *The child's discovery of the mind.* Cambridge, MA: Harvard University Press.

Astington, J. W., & Jenkins, J. M. (1999). A longitudinal study of the relation between language and theory-of-mind development. *Developmental Psychology, 35,* 1311–1320.

Athansiou, M. S. (2001). Using consultation with a grandmother as an adjunct to play therapy. *Family Journal—Consulting and Therapy for Couples and Families, 9,* 445–449.

Aunola, K., & Nurmi, J.-E. (2005). The role of parenting styles in children's problem behavior. Child Development, 76, 1144–1159.

Austin, E. W., Pinkleton, B. E., & Fujioka, Y. (2000). The role of interpretation processes and parental discussion in the media's effects on adolescents' use of alcohol. *Pediatrics, 105*(2), 343–349.

Autism and Developmental Disabilities Monitoring Network Surveillance Year 2002 Principal Investigators. (2007, February 9). Prevalence of autism spectrum disorders—Autism and Developmental Disabilities Monitoring Network, 14 sites, United States, 2002. Morbidity and Mortality Weekly Report, Surveillance Summaries, 56(*SS01*), 12–28.

Autism—Part II. (1997, April). *The Harvard Mental Health Letter,* 1–4.

Autism—Part II. (2001, July). *The Harvard Mental Health Letter, 18*(1), 1–4.

Aylward, G. P., Pfeiffer, S. I., Wright, A., & Verhulst, S. J. (1989). Outcome studies of low birth weight infants published in the last decade: A meta-analysis. *Journal of Pediatrics, 115,* 515–520.

Azar, B. (2002a, January). At the frontier of science. *Monitor on Psychology,* 40–41.

Babu, A., & Hirschhorn, K. (1992). *A guide to human chromosome defects (Birth Defects:*

Original Article Series, 28[2]). White Plains, NY: March of Dimes Birth Defects Foundation.

Baddeley, A. (1996). Exploring the central executive. *Quarterly Journal of Experimental Psychology: Human Experimental Psychology* (Special Issue: Working Memory), *49A,* 5–28.

Baddeley, A. (1998). Recent developments in working memory. *Current Opinion in Neurobiology, 8,* 234–238.

Baddeley, A. D. (1981). The concept of working memory: A view of its current state and probable future development. *Cognition, 10,* 17–23.

Baddeley, A. D. (1986). *Working memory.* London: Oxford University Press.

Baddeley, A. D. (1992). Working memory. *Science, 255,* 556–559.

Baddock, S. A., Galland, B. C., Bolton, D. P. G., Williams, S. M., & Taylor, B. J. (2006). Differences in infant and parent behaviors during routine bed sharing compared with cot sleeping in the home setting. *Pediatrics, 117,* 1599–1607.

Baer, J. S., Sampson, P. D., Barr, H. M., Connor, P. D., & Streissguth, A. P. (2003). A 21-year longitudinal analysis of the effects of prenatal alcohol exposure on young adult drinking. *Archives of General Psychiatry, 60,* 377–385.

Bagley, C., & Mallick, K. (2000). Prediction of sexual, emotional, and physical maltreatment and mental health outcomes in a longitudinal cohort of 290 adolescent women. *Child Maltreatment, 5,* 218–227.

Bagwell, C. L., Newcomb, A. F., & Bukowski, W. M. (1998). Preadolescent friendship and peer rejection as predictors of adult adjustment. *Child Development, 69,* 140–153.

Baillargeon, R. (1994). How do infants learn about the physical world? *Current Directions in Psychological Science, 3,* 133–140.

Baillargeon, R. (1999). Young infants' expectations about hidden objects. *Developmental Science, 2,* 115–132.

Baillargeon, R. H., Zoccolillo, M., Keenan, K., Côté, S., Pérusse, D., Wu, H.-X., Boivin, M., & Tremblay, R. E. (2007). Gender differences in physical aggression: A prospective population-based survey of children before and after 2 years of age. *Developmental Psychology, 43,* 13–26.

Baillargeon, R., & DeVos, J. (1991). Object permanence in young infants: Further evidence. *Child Development, 62,* 1227–1246.

Baillargeon, R., Tremblay, R. E., & Willms, J. D. (1999). *The prevalence of physical aggression in Canadian children: A multi-group latent class analysis of data from the first collection cycle (1994–1995) of the NLSCY.* Catalogue No. MP32-30/00-2E. Ottawa: Applied Research Branch, Strategic Policy, Human Resources Development Canada.

Baillargeon, R., Tremblay, R. & Willms, J. D. (2002). Physical aggression among toddlers does it run in families? In Willms, J. D. *Vulnerable Children.* (Pg. 121–130). University of Alberta Press.

Baird, A. A., Gruber, S. A., Fein, D. A., Maas, L. C., Steingard, R. J., Renshaw, P. F., Cohen, B. M., & Yurgelon-Todd, D. A. (1999). Functional magnetic resonance imaging of facial affect recognition in children and adolescents. *Journal of the American Academy of Child and Adolescent Psychiatry, 38,* 195–199.

Baker, M. (2001). *Families: Changing trends in Canada.* Toronto: McGraw-Hill Ryerson.

Balercia, G., Mosca, F., Mantero, F., Boscaro, M., Mancini, A., Ricciardo-Lamonica, G., & Littarru, G. (2004). Coenzyme

q(10) supplementation in infertile men with idiopathic asthenozoospermia: An open, uncontrolled pilot study. *Fertility and Sterility, 81,* 93–98.

Ball, T. M., Castro-Rodriguez, J. A., Griffith, K. A., Holberg, C. J., Martinez, F. D., & Wright, A. L. (2000). Siblings, day-care attendance, and the risk of asthma and wheezing during childhood. *New England Journal of Medicine, 343,* 538–543.

Bandura, A. (1977). *Social learning theory.* Englewood Cliffs, NJ: Prentice-Hall.

Bandura, A. (1986). *Social foundations of thought and action: A social cognitive theory.* Englewood Cliffs, NJ: Prentice-Hall.

Bandura, A. (1989). Social cognitive theory. In R. Vasta (Ed.), *Annals of child development.* Greenwich, CT: JAI.

Bandura, A. (1994). Self-efficacy. In V. S. Ramachaudran (Ed.), *Encyclopedia of Human Behavior* (Vol. 4, pp. 71–81). New York: Academic Press.

Bandura, A., & Walters, R. H. (1963). *Social learning and personality development.* New York: Holt, Rinehart, & Winston.

Bandura, A., Barbaranelli, C., Caprara, G. V., & Pastorelli, C. (1996). Multifaceted impact of self-efficacy beliefs on academic functioning. *Child Development, 67,* 1206–1222.

Bandura, A., Barbaranelli, C., Caprara, G. V., & Pastorelli, C. (2001). Self efficacy beliefs as shapers of children's aspirations and career trajectories. *Child Development 72*(1), 187–206.

Bandura, A., Ross, D., & Ross, S. A. (1961). Transmission of aggression through imitation of aggressive models. *Journal of Abnormal and Social Psychology, 63,* 575–582.

Bandura, A., Ross, D., & Ross, S. A. (1963). Imitation of film-mediated aggressive models. *Journal of Abnormal and Social Psychology, 66,* 3–11.

Banks, E. (1989). Temperament and individuality: A study of Malay children. *American Journal of Orthopsychiatry, 59,* 390–397.

Barber, B. K. 1996. Parental psychological control: Revisiting a neglected construct. *Child Development, 67,* 3296–3319.

Barber, B. L., & Eccles, J. S. (1992). Long-term influence of divorce and single parenting on adolescent family- and work-related values, behaviors, and aspirations. *Psychological Bulletin, 111*(1), 108–126.

Barker, D. J., & Lackland, D. T. (2003). Prenatal influences on stroke mortality in England and Wales. *Stroke: A Journal of Cerebral Circulation, 34,* 1598–1602.

Barkley, R. A. (1998a, February). How should attention deficit disorder be described? *Harvard Mental Health Letter,* 8.

Barkley, R. A. (1998b, September). Attention-deficit hyperactivity disorder. *Scientific American,* 66–71.

Barkley, R. A., Murphy, K. R., & Kwasnik, D. (1996). Motor vehicle competencies and risks in teens and young adults with attention deficit hyperactivity disorder. *Pediatrics, 98,* 1089–1095.

Barlow, S. E., & Dietz, W. H. (1998). Obesity evaluation and treatment: Expert committee recommendations. *Pediatrics, 102*(3), e29. Retrieved from http://www.pediatrics.org/cgi/content/full/102/3/e29.

Barnes, J., Sutcliffe, A., Ponjaert, I., Loft, A., Wennerholm, U., Tarlatzis, V., & Bonduelle, M. (2003, July). The European study of 1,523 ICSI/IVF versus naturally conceived 5-year-old children and their families: Family functioning and socioemotional development. Paper presented at conference of European

Society of Human Reproduction and Embryology, Madrid.

Baron-Cohen, S. (2005). The essential difference: The male and female brain. *Phi Kappa Phi Forum, 85*(1), 23–26.

Barr, R. G., Hopkins, B., & Green, J. A. (2000). Crying as a sign, a symptom and a signal: Evolving concepts of crying behavior. In R. G. Barr, B. Hopkins, & J. A. Green (Eds.), *Crying as a sign, a symptom, and a signal: Clinical, emotional and developmental aspects of infant and toddler crying* (pp. 1–7). London: MacKeith Press.

Barry, C. M., & Wentzel, K. R. (2006). Friend influence on prosocial behavior: The role of motivational factors and friendship characteristics. *Developmental Psychology, 42,* 153–163.

Barthel, J. (1982, May). Just a normal, naughty three-year-old. *McCall's,* pp. 78, 136–144.

Bartoshuk, L. M., & Beauchamp, G. K. (1994). Chemical senses. *Annual Review of Psychology, 45,* 419–449.

Basso, O., & Baird, D. D. (2003). Infertility and preterm delivery, birth weight, and Caesarean section: A study within the Danish National Birth Cohort. *Human Reproduction, 18,* 2478–2484.

Bates, E., Bretherton, I., & Snyder, L. (1988). *From first words to grammar: Individual differences and dissociable mechanisms.* New York: Cambridge University Press.

Bates, E., O'Connell, B., & Shore, C. (1987). Language and communication in infancy. In J. D. Osofsky (Ed.), *Handbook of infant development* (2nd ed.). New York: Wiley.

Bateson, M. C. (1984). *With a daughter's eye: A memoir of Margaret Mead and Gregory Bateson.* New York: William Morrow & Co.

Bauer, P. J. (1993). Memory for gender-consistent and gender-inconsistent event sequences by twenty-five-month-old children. *Child Development, 64,* 285–297.

Bauer, P. J. (1996). What do infants recall of their lives? Memory for specific events by one- to two-year-olds. *American Psychologist, 51,* 29–41.

Bauer, P. J. (2002). Long-term recall memory: Behavioral and neurodevelopmental changes in the first 2 years of life. *Current Directions in Psychological Science, 11,* 137–141.

Bauer, P. J., Wenner, J. A., Dropik, P. L., & Wewerka, S. S. (2000). Parameters of remembering and forgetting in the transition from infancy to early childhood. *Monographs of the Society for Research in Child Development,* Serial No. 263, *65*(4). Malden, MA: Blackwell Publishers.

Bauer, P. J., Wiebe, S. A., Carver, L. J., Waters, J. M., & Nelson, C. A. (2003). Developments in long-term explicit memory late in the first year of life: Behavioral and electrophysiological indices. *Psychological Science, 14,* 629–635.

Bauman, L. J., Silver, E. J., & Stein, R. E. K. (2006). Cumulative social disadvantage and child health. *Pediatrics, 117,* 1321–1328.

Baumer, E. P., & South, S. J. (2001). Community effects on youth sexual activity. *Journal of Marriage and the Family, 63,* 540–554.

Baumrind, D. (1971). Harmonious parents and their preschool children. *Developmental Psychology, 41,* 92–102.

Baumrind, D. (1989). Rearing competent children. In W. Damon (Ed.), *Child development today and tomorrow* (pp. 349–378). San Francisco: Jossey-Bass.

Baumrind, D. (1991). Parenting styles and adolescent development. In J. Brooks-Gunn, R. Lerner, & A. C. Peterson (Eds.), *The*

encyclopedia of adolescence (pp. 746–758). New York: Garland.

Baumrind, D. (1996a). A blanket injunction against disciplinary use of spanking is not warranted by the data. *Pediatrics, 88,* 828–831.

Baumrind, D. (1996b). The discipline controversy revisited. *Family Relations, 45,* 405–414.

Baumrind, D. (2005). Patterns of parental authority and adolescent autonomy. In J. Smetana (Ed.), *Changing boundaries of parental authority during adolescence: New directions for child and adolescent development, 108* (pp. 61–70). San Francisco: Jossey-Bass.

Baumrind, D., & Black, A. E. (1967). Socialization practices associated with dimensions of competence in preschool boys and girls. *Child Development, 38,* 291–327.

Baumrind, D., Larzelere, R. E., & Cowan, P. A. (2002). Ordinary physical punishment: Is it harmful? Comment on Gershoff (2002). *Psychological Bulletin, 128,* 580–589.

Baumwell, L., Tamis-LeMonda, C. S., & Bornstein, M. H. (1997). Maternal verbal sensitivity and child language comprehension. *Infant Behavior and Development, 20,* 247–258.

Bauserman, R. (2002). Child adjustment in joint-custody versus sole-custody arrangements: A meta-analytic review. *Journal of Family Psychology, 16,* 91–102.

Baydar, N., Greek, A., & Brooks-Gunn, J. (1997). A longitudinal study of the effects of the birth of a sibling during the first 6 years of life. *Journal of Marriage and the Family, 59,* 939–956.

Baydar, N., Hyle, P., & Brooks-Gunn, J. (1997). A longitudinal study of the effects of the birth of a sibling during preschool and early grade school years. *Journal of Marriage and the Family, 59,* 957–965.

Bayley, N. (2005). *Bayley Scales of Infant Development, Third Ed.* (Bayley-III). New York: Harcourt Brace.

Bayliss, D. M., Jarrold, C., Baddeley, A. D., Gunn, D. M., & Leigh, E. (2005). Mapping the developmental constraints on working memory span performance. *Developmental Psychology, 41*(4), 579–597.

BC Centre for Disease Control. Poisoning in British Columbia. *BC Medical Journal, 48,* 35 Retrieved July 25, 2007 from http://www.bcma. org/public/bc_medical_journal/BCMJ/2006/ jan_feb_2006/cdc.asp.

Bearman, P. S., & Bruckner, H. (2001). Promising the future: Virginity pledges and first intercourse. *American Journal of Sociology, 106,* 859–913.

Bech, B. H., Nohr, E. A., Vaeth, M., Henriksen, T. B., & Olsen, J. (2005). Coffee and fetal death: A cohort study with prospective data. *American Journal of Epidemiology, 162*(10), 983–990.

Becker, A. E., Grinspoon, S. K., Klibanski, A., & Herzog, D. B. (1999). Eating disorders. *New England Journal of Medicine, 340,* 1092–1098.

Behne, R., Carpenter, M., Call, J., & Tomasello, M. (2005). Unwilling versus unable: Infants' understanding of intentional action. *Developmental Psychology, 41,* 328–337.

Behrman, R. E. (1992). *Nelson textbook of pediatrics* (13th ed.). Philadelphia: Saunders.

Beidel, D. C., & Turner, S. M. (1998). *Shy children, phobic adults: Nature and treatment of social phobia.* Washington, DC: American Psychological Association.

Beiser, M., & Gotowiec, A. (2000). Accounting for native/non-native differences in IQ scores. *Psychology in the Schools, 37,* 237–252.

Beiser, M., Hou, F., Hyman, I., & Tousignant, M. (1998). *Growing up Canadian: A study of new immigrant children.* Report No. W-98-24E. Ottawa: Applied Research Branch, Strategic Policy, Human Resources Development Canada.

Beiser, M., Hou, F., Hyman, I., & Tousignant, M. (2002). Poverty, family process, and the mental health of immigrant children in Canada. *American Journal of Public Health, 92,* 220–227.

Beiser, M., Sack, W., Manson, S. M., Redshirt, R., & Dion, R. (1998). Mental health and the academic performance of First Nations and majority-culture children. *American Journal of Orthopsychiatry, 68,* 455–467.

Bekedam, D. J., Engelsbe1, S., Mol, B. W., Buitendijk, S. E., & van der Pal-de Bruin, K. M. (2002). Male predominance in fetal distress during labor. *American Journal of Obstetrics and Gynecology, 187,* 1605–1607.

Belizzi, M. (2002, May). *Obesity in children— What kind of future are we creating?* Presentation at the Fifty-Fifth World Health Assembly Technical Briefing, Geneva.

Bellamy, L. (2004). More children live a divided life. Retrieved on August 17 2007 from http://www.theage.com.au/ articles/2004/05/22/1085176040565.html

Bellinger, D. (2004). Lead. *Pediatrics, 113,* 1016–1022.

Belsky, J. (1984). Two waves of day care research: Developmental effects and conditions of quality. In R. Ainslie (Ed.), *The child and the day care setting.* New York: Praeger.

Belsky, J. (1993). Etiology of child maltreatment: A developmental-ecological analysis. *Psychological Bulletin, 114,* 413–434.

Belsky, J., Fish, M., & Isabella, R. (1991). Continuity and discontinuity in infant negative and positive emotionality: Family antecedents and attachment consequences. *Developmental Psychology, 27,* 421–431.

Belsky, J., Vandell, D. L., Burchinal, M., Clarke-Stewart, K. A., McCartney, K., Owen, M. T., and the NICHD Early Child Care Research Network. (in press). Are there long-term effects of early child care? *Child Development, 78,* 681–701.

Beltramini, A. U., & Hertzig, M. E. (1983). Sleep and bedtime behavior in preschool-aged children. *Pediatrics, 71,* 153–158.

Bem, S. L. (1983). Gender schema theory and its implications for child development: Raising gender-aschematic children in a gender-schematic society. *Signs, 8,* 598–616.

Bem, S. L. (1993). *The lenses of gender: Transforming the debate on sexual inequality.* New Haven, CT: Yale University Press.

Bendersky, M., & Lewis, M. (1998). Arousal modulation in cocaine-exposed infants. *Developmental Psychology, 34,* 555–564.

Benenson, J. F. (1993). Greater preference among females than males for dyadic interaction in early childhood. *Child Development, 64,* 544–555.

Benes, F. M., Turtle, M., Khan, Y., & Farol, P. (1994). Myelination of a key relay zone in the hippocampal formation occurs in the human brain during childhood, adolescence, and adulthood. *Archives of General Psychiatry, 51,* 447–484.

Benjamin, W. J., Schneider, B. H., Greenman, P. S., & Hum, M. (2001). Conflict and childhood friendship in Taiwan and Canada. *Canadian Journal of Behavioural Science, 33,* 203–211.

Benoit, C. & Carroll, D. (2005). Midwifery in Canada. Museum of Civilization: 2005 Nursing Exhibit Update. Retrieved July 10, 2007 from http://web.uvic.ca/~cbenoit/ MidwiferyFlyer0903.pdf.

Benson, E. (2003). Intelligent intelligence testing. *Monitor on Psychology, 43*(2), 48–51.

Benson, M. (1986). *Nelson Mandela: The man and the movement.* New York: Norton.

Berenbaum, S. A., & Snyder, E. (1995). Early hormonal influences on childhood sex-typed activity and playmate preferences: Implications for the development of sexual orientation. *Developmental Psychology, 31,* 31–42.

Bergeman, C. S., & Plomin, R. (1989). Genotype-environment interaction. In M. Bornstein & J. Bruner (Eds.), *Interaction in human development* (pp. 157–171). Hillsdale, NJ: Erlbaum.

Bergen, D. (2002). The role of pretend play in children's cognitive development. *Early Childhood Research & Practice, 4*(1). Retrieved from http://ecrp.uiuc.edu/v4n1/bergen.html

Bergen, D., Reid, R., & Torelli, L. (2000). *Educating and caring for very young children: The infant-toddler curriculum.* Washington, DC: National Association for the Education of Young Children.

Berk, L. E. (1986a). Development of private speech among preschool children. *Early Child Development and Care, 24,* 113–136.

Berk, L. E. (1986b). Private speech: Learning out loud. *Psychology Today, 20*(5), 34–42.

Berk, L. E. (1992). Children's private speech: An overview of theory and the status of research. In R. M. Diaz & L. E. Berk (Eds.), *Private speech: From social interaction to self-regulation* (pp. 17–53). Hillsdale, NJ: Erlbaum.

Berk, L. E., & Garvin, R. A. (1984). Development of private speech among low-income Appalachian children. *Developmental Psychology, 20,* 271–286.

Berkowitz, G. S., Skovron, M. L., Lapinski, R. H., & Berkowitz, R. L. (1990). Delayed childbearing and the outcome of pregnancy. *New England Journal of Medicine, 322,* 659–664.

Berkowitz, R. I., Stallings, V. A., Maislin, G., & Stunkard, A. J. (2005). Growth of children at high risk of obesity during the first 6 years of life: Implications for prevention. *American Journal of Clinical Nutrition, 81,* 140–146.

Berkowitz, R. I., Wadden, T. A., Tershakovec, A. M., & Cronquist, J. L. (2003). Behavior therapy and sibutramine for the treatment of adolescent obesity: A randomized controlled trial. *Journal of the American Medical Association, 289,* 1805–1812.

Berndt, T. J. (1982). The features and effects of friendship in early adolescence. *Child Development, 53,* 1447–1460.

Berndt, T. J., & Perry, T. B. (1990). Distinctive features and effects of early adolescent friendships. In R. Montemayor, G. R. Adams, & T. P. Gullotta (Eds.), *From childhood to adolescence: A transitional period?* (Vol. 2, pp. 269–287). Newbury Park, CA: Sage.

Bernier, L. & Gregoire, D. (2004). Reproductive and therapeutic cloning, germline therapy, and purchase of gametes and embryos: comments on Canadian legislation governing reproductive technologies. *Journal Medical Ethics, 30,* 527–532.

Bernstein, J. (1973). *Einstein.* New York: Viking.

Bernstein, N. (2004, March 7). Behind fall in pregnancy, a new teenage culture of restraint. *New York Times,* pp. 1, 36–37.

Bernstein, P. S. (2003). Achieving equity in women's and perinatal health. *Medscape Ob/Gyn & Women's Health, 8.* Posted 12/12/03.

Berrick, J. D. (1998). When children cannot remain home: Foster family care and kinship care. *The Future of Children, 8,* 72–87.

Berrueta-Clement, J. R., Schweinhart, L. J., Barnett, W. S., & Weikart, D. P. (1987). The effects of early educational intervention on crime and delinquency in adolescence and early adulthood. In J. D. Burchard & S. N. Burchard (Eds.), *Primary prevention of psychopathology: Vol. 10. Prevention of delinquent behavior* (pp. 220–240). Newbury Park, CA: Sage.

Berrueta-Clement, J. R., Schweinhart, L. J., Barnett, W. S., Epstein, A. S., & Weikart, D. P. (1985). *Changed lives: The effects of the Perry Preschool Program on youths through age 19.* Ypsilanti, MI: High/Scope.

Berry, M., Dylla, D. J., Barth, R. P., & Needell, B. (1998). The role of open adoption in the adjustment of adopted children and their families. *Children and Youth Services Review, 20,* 151–171.

Berry, N., Jobanputra, V., & Pal, H. (2003). Molecular genetics of schizophrenia: A critical review. *Journal of Psychiatry and Neuroscience, 28,* 415–429.

Berry, R. J., Li, Z., Erickson, J. D., Li, S., Moore, C. A., Wang, H., Mulinare, J., Zhao, P., Wong, L.-Y. C., Gindler, J., Hong, S.-X., & Correa, A. for the China–U.S. Collaborative Project for Neural Tube Defect Prevention. (1999). Prevention of neural-tube defects with folic acid in China. *New England Journal of Medicine, 341,* 1485–1490.

Bertenthal, B. I., & Clifton, R. K. (1998). Perception and action. In W. Damon (Ed.-in-Chief), D. Kuhn & R. S. Siegler (Vol. Eds.), *Handbook of child psychology, Vol. 2: Cognition perception, and language* (pp. 51–102). New York: Wiley.

Bertin, E., & Striano, T. (2006). The still face response in newborn, 1.5-, and 3-month-old infants. *Infant Behavior and Development, 29,* 294–297.

Berz, J. B., Murdock, K. K., & Mitchell, D. K. (2005). Children's asthma, internalizing problems, and social functioning: An urban perspective. *Journal of Child and Adolescent Psychiatric Nursing, 18*(4), 181–197.

Bespalova, I. N., & Buxbaum, J. D. (2003). Disease susceptibility genes for autism. *Annals of Medicine, 35,* 274–281.

Bethell, T. N. (2005, April). What's the big idea? There's more than one solution for Social Security. Here are nine ways to keep the system solvent. *AARP Bulletin,* pp. 22–26.

Betran, A. P., Merialdi, M., Lauer, J. A., Bing-Shaun, W., Thomas, J., Van Look, P. & Wagner, M. (2007). Rates of caesarean section: Analysis of global, regional and national estimates. *Paediatric and Perinatal Epidemiology, 21,* 98–113.

Beversdorf, D. Q., Manning, S. E., Anderson, S. L., Nordgren, R. E., Walters, S. E., Cooley, W. C., et al. (2001, November 10–15). Timing of prenatal stressors and autism. Presentation at the 31st Annual Meeting of the Society for Neuroscience, San Diego.

Bezeau, L. M. (2006). Home schooling, private schools, and charter schools. In Educational Administration for Canadian Teachers. Retrieved August 10, 2007 from http://www.unb.ca/education/bezeau/eact/eact.html

Bialystok, E., & Senman, L. (2004). Executive processes in appearance-reality tasks: The role of inhibition of attention and symbolic representation. *Child Development, 75,* 562–579.

Bianchi, S. M. (1995). The changing demographic and socioeconomic characteristics of single parent families. *Marriage and Family Review, 20*(1–2), 71–97.

Biason-Lauber, A., Konrad, D., Navratil, F., & Schoenle, E. J. (2004). A WNT4 mutation associated with Mullerian-duct regression and virilization in a 46, XX woman. *New England Journal of Medicine, 351,* 792–798.

Bickham, D., & Rich, M. (2006). Is television viewing associated with social isolation?: Roles of exposure time, viewing context, and violent content. *Archives of Pediatrics and Adolescent Medicine, 160,* 387–392.

Biemiller, A., & Siegel, L. S. (1997). A longitudinal study of the effects of the Bridge reading program for children at risk for reading failure. *Learning Disability Quarterly, 20,* 83–92.

Bierman, K. L., Smoot, D. L., & Aumiller, K. (1993). Characteristics of aggressive-rejected, aggressive (non-rejected), and rejected (non-aggressive) boys. *Child Development, 64,* 139–151.

Bigelow, A. E., & Birch, S. A. J. (2000). The effects of contingency in previous interactions on infants' preference for social partners. *Infant Behavior & Development, 22,* 367–382.

Bild, E.-R., & Swain, M. (1989). Minority language students in a French immersion programme: Their French proficiency. *Journal of Multilingual and Multicultural Development, 10,* 255–274.

Birch, L. L., Johnson, S. L., Andersen, G., Peters, J. C., & Schulte, M. C. (1991). The variability of young children's energy intake. *New England Journal of Medicine, 324,* 232–235.

Birmaher, B. (1998). Should we use antidepressant medications for children and adolescents with depressive disorders? *Psychopharmacology Bulletin, 34,* 35–39.

Birmaher, B., Ryan, N. D., Williamson, D. E., Brent, D. A., Kaufman, J., Dahl, R. E., Perel, J., & Nelson, B. (1996). Childhood and adolescent depression: A review of the past 10 years. *Journal of the American Academy of Child, 35,* 1427–1440.

Bjork, J. M., Knutson, B., Fong, G. W., Caggiano, D. M., Bennett, S. M., & Hommer, D. W. (2004). Incentive-elicited brain activities in adolescents: Similarities and differences from young adults. *The Journal of Neuroscience, 24,* 1793–1802.

Bjorklund, D. F. (1997). The role of immaturity in human development. *Psychological Bulletin, 122,* 153–169.

Bjorklund, D. F., & Pellegrini, A. D. (2000). Child development and evolutionary psychology. *Child Development, 71,* 1687–1708.

Bjorklund, D. F., & Harnishfeger, K. K. (1990). The resources construct in cognitive development: Diverse sources of evidence and a theory of inefficient inhibition. *Developmental Review, 10,* 48–71.

Bjorklund, D. F., & Pellegrini, A. D. (2002). *The origins of human nature: Evolutionary developmental psychology.* Washington, DC: American Psychological Association.

Blachman, B., Schatschneider, C., Fletcher, J. M., Francis, D. J., Clonan, S. M., Shaywitz, B., & Shaywitz, S. (2004). Effects of intensive reading remediation for the second and third graders and a 1-year follow-up. *Journal of Educational Psychology, 96,* 444–461.

Black, J. E. (1998). How a child builds its brain: Some lessons from animal studies of neural plasticity. *Preventive Medicine, 27,* 168–171.

Black, M. M., & Krishnakumar, A. (1998). Children in low-income, urban settings: Interventions to promote mental health and well-being. *American Psychologist, 53,* 636–646.

Black, R. E., Morris, S. S., & Bryce, J. (2003). Where and why are 10 million children dying each year? *The Lancet, 361,* 2226–2234.

Blair, C. (2002). School readiness: Integrating cognition and emotion in a neurobiological conceptualization of children's functioning at school entry. *American Psychologist, 57,* 111–127.

Blakemore, S., & Choudhury, S. (2006). Development of the adolescent brain: Implications for executive function and social cognition. Journal of Child Psychology and Psychiatry, 47(3), 296–312.

Blakeslee, S. (1997, April 17). Studies show talking with infants shapes basis of ability to think. New York Times, p. D21.

Bleske-Rechek, A, Lubinski, D., & Benbow, C. P. (2004). Meeting the educational needs of special populations. Advanced placement's role in developing exceptional human capital. Psychological Sciences, 15, 217–224.

Bloch, H., & Carchon, I. (1992). On the onset of eye–head coordination in infants. Behavioural Brain Research, 49, 85–90.

Bloom, B. (1985). Developing talent in young people. New York: Ballantine.

Bloom, B., Cohen, R. A., Vickerie, J. L., & Wondimu, E. A. (2003). Summary health statistics for U.S. children: National Health Interview Survey, 2001. Vital and Health Statistics, 10(216). Hyattsville, MD: National Center for Health Statistics.

Bloom, H. (Ed.). (1999). A scholarly look at The Diary of Anne Frank. Philadelphia: Chelsea.

Blum, N. J., Taubman, B., & Nemeth, N. (2003). Relationship between age at initiation of toilet training and duration of training: A prospective study. Pediatrics, 111, 810–814.

Bocskay, K. A., Tang, D., Orjuela, M. A., Liu, X., Warburton, D. P., & Perera, F. P. (2005). Chromosomal aberrations in cord blood are associated with prenatal exposure to carcinogenic polycyclic aromatic hydrocarbons. Cancer Epidemiology Biomarkers and Prevention, 14, 506–511.

Bodrova, E., & Leong, D. J. (1998). Adult influences on play: The Vygotskian approach. In D. P. Fromberg & D. Bergen (Eds.), Play from birth to twelve and beyond: Contexts, perspectives, and meanings (pp. 277–282). New York: Garland.

Bogaert, A. F. (2006). Biological versus nonbiological older brothers and men's sexual orientation. Proceedings of the National Academy of Sciences, 103, 10771–10774.

Bogard, K., & Takaneshi, R. (2005). PK-3: An aligned and coordinated approach to education for children 3 to 8 years old. Social Policy Report, 19, 3–23.

Bojczyk, K. E., & Corbetta, D. (2004). Object retrieval in the 1st year of life: Learning effects of task exposure and box transparency. Developmental Psychology, 40, 54–66.

Bollinger, M. B. (2003). Involuntary smoking and asthma severity in children: Data from the Third National Health and Nutrition Examination Survey (NHANES III). Pediatrics, 112, 471.

Bond, C. A. (1989, September). A child prodigy from China wields a magical brush. Smithsonian, 20, pp. 70–79.

Bonham, V. L., Warshauer-Baker, E., & Collins, F. S. (2005). Race and ethnicity in the genome era. American Psychologist, 60, 9–15.

Bonneau, C., Ee, B. & Lauzon, J. (2006). First nations learners and extracurricular activities: Barriers and bridges to participation. Educational Insights, (10). Retrieved August 13 2006 from http://www.ccfi.educ.ubc.ca/publication/insights/v10n01/articles/bonneau.html

Booth, A. E., & Waxman, S. (2002). Object names and object functions serve as cues to categories for infants. Developmental Psychology, 38, 948–957.

Booth, J. L., & Siegler, R. S. (2006). Developmental and individual differences in pure numerical estimation. Developmental Psychology, 41, 189–201.

Bornstein, M. H. & Cote, L. R. with Maital, S., Painter, K., Park, S. Y., Pascual, L., Pecheux, M. G., Ruel, J., Venuti, P., and Vyt, A. (2004). Cross-linguistic analysis of vocabulary in young children: Spanish, Dutch, French, Hebrew, Italian, Korean, and American English. Child Development, 75, 1115–1139.

Bornstein, M. H., & Sigman, M. D. (1986). Continuity in mental development from infancy. Child Development, 57, 251–274.

Bornstein, M. H., & Tamis-LeMonda, C. S. (1994). Antecedents of information processing skills in infants: Habituation, novelty responsiveness, and cross-modal transfer. Infant Behavior and Development, 17, 371–380.

Bornstein, M., Kessen, W., & Weiskopf, S. (1976). The categories of hue in infancy. Science, 191, 201–202.

Borowsky, I. A., Ireland, M., & Resnick, M. D. (2001). Adolescent suicide attempts: Risks and protectors. Pediatrics, 107(3), 485–493.

Bosch, J., Sullivan, S.,Van Dyke, D. C., Su, H., Klockau, L., Nissen, K., Blewer, K., Weber, E., & Eberly, S. S. (2003). Promoting a healthy tomorrow here for children adopted from abroad. Contemporary Pediatrics, 20(2), 69–86.

Botkin, J. R., Clayton, E. W., Fost, N. C., Burke, W., Murray, T. H., Baily, M. A., Wilfond, B., Berg, A., & Ross, L. F. (2006). Newborn screening technology: Proceed with caution. Pediatrics, 117, 1793–1799.

Botto, L. D., Moore, C. A., Khoury, M. J., & Erickson, J. D. (1999). Neural-tube defects. New England Journal of Medicine, 341, 1509–1519.

Bouchard, T. J. (1994). Genes, environment, and personality. Science, 264, 1700–1701.

Bouchard, T. J. (2004). Genetic in?uence on human psychological traits: A survey. Current Directions in Psychological Science, 13, 148–154.

Bouchey, H. A. & Furman, W. (2003). Dating and romantic experiences in adolescence. In

Boulton, M. J., & Smith, P. K. (1994). Bully/victim problems in middle-school children: Stability, self-perceived competence, peer perception, and peer acceptance. British Journal of Developmental Psychology, 12, 315–329.

Boutin, P., Dina, C., Vasseur, F., Dubois, S. S., Corset, L., Seron, K., et al. (2003). GAD2 on chromosome 10 is a candidate gene for human obesity. Public Library of Science Biology, 1(3), E68.

Bouza, A. V. (1990). The police mystique: An insider's look at cops, crime, and the criminal justice system. New York: Plenum.

Bower, B. (1993). A child's theory of mind. Science News, 144, 40–42.

Bower, T. G. R. (1966). The visual world of infants. Scientific American, 215, 80–92.

Bowlby, J. (1951). Maternal care and mental health. Bulletin of the World Health Organization, 3, 355–534.

Bowlby, J. (1969). Attachment and loss: Vol. I. Attachment. London: Hogarth Press & the Institute of Psychoanalysis.

Bowlby, J. W., & McMullen, K. (2002). At a crossroads: First results for the 18- to 20-year-old cohort of the Youth in Transition Survey. Catalogue No. 81-591-XIE. Ottawa: Human Resources Development Canada and Statistics Canada.

Bowman, S. A., Gortmaker, S. L., Ebbeling, C. B., Pereira, M. A., Ludwig, D. S. (2004). Effects of fast food consumption on energy intake and diet quality among children in a national household survey. Pediatrics, 113, 112–118.

Boyce, W., Doherty, M., Fortin, C, & Mackinnon, D. (2003). Canadian Youth, Sexual Health and HIV/ AIDS Study: Factors influencing knowledge, attitudes and behaviours. Toronto, ON: Council of Ministers of Education.

Boyce, W., Doherty-Poirier, M., MacKinnon, D., Fortin, C., Saab, H., King, M., & Gallupe, O. (2006). Sexual health of Canadian youth: Findings from the Canadian Youth, Sexual Health and HIV/AIDS Study. Canadian Journal of Human Sexuality, 15, 59–68.

Boyd, D. R. (2007). U.S. far ahead of Canada on lead contaminants. The Hamilton Spectator. Retrieved July 26, 2007 from http://www.hamiltonspectator.com/NASApp/cs/ContentServer?pagename=hamilton/Layout/Article_Type1&c=Article&cid=1173674131247&call_pageid=1020420665036&col=1112188062581

Boyd, S. (1994). Women and illicit drug use. Retrieved July 22, 2007 from www.drugtext.org/library/articles/94539.htm

Boyle, M. H., & Lipman, E. L. (1998). Do places matter? A multilevel analysis of geographic variations in child behaviour in Canada. Catalogue No. W-98-16E. Ottawa: Applied Research Branch, Strategic Policy, Human Resources Development Canada.

Boyle, M. H., Georgiades, K., Racine, Y., & Mustard, C. (2007). Neighborhood and family influences on educational attainment: Results from the Ontario Child Health Study follow-up 2001. Child Development, 78, 168–189.

Boyles, S. (2002, January 27). Toxic landfills may boost birth defects. WebMD Medical News. Retrieved February 5, 2007, from http://www.webmd.com/content/article/25/3606_1181.htm

Boyum, L. A., & Parke, R. D. (1995). The role of family emotional expressiveness in the development of children's social competence. Journal of Marriage and the Family, 57, 593–608.

Brabeck, M. M., & Shore, E. L. (2003). Gender differences in intellectual and moral development? The evidence refutes the claims. In J. Demick and C. Andreoletti (Eds.), Handbook of adult development (pp. 351–368). NY: Plenum Press.

Bracher, G., & Santow, M. (1999). Explaining trends in teenage childbearing in Sweden. Studies in Family Planning, 30, 169–182.

Bradley, R. H. (1989). Home measurement of maternal responsiveness. In M. H. Bornstein (Ed.), Maternal responsiveness: Characteristics and consequences (New Directions for Child Development 43). San Francisco: Jossey-Bass.

Bradley, R. H., Caldwell, B. M., Rock, S. L., Ramey, C. T., Barnard, K. E., Gray, C., Hammond, M. A., Mitchell, S., Gottfried, A. W., Siegel, L., & Johnson, D. L. (1989). Home environment and cognitive development in the first 3 years of life: A collaborative study involving six sites and three ethnic groups in North America. Developmental Psychology, 25, 217–235.

Bradley, R. H., Corwyn, R. F., Burchinal, M., McAdoo, H. P., & Coll, C. G. (2001). The home environment of children in the United States: Part II: Relations with behavioral development through age thirteen. Child Development, 72(6), 1868–1886.

Bradley, R. H., Corwyn, R. F., McAdoo, H. P., & Coll, C. G. (2001). The home environment of children in the United States: Part I: Variation by age, ethnicity, and poverty status. Child Development, 72(6), 1844–1867.

Bradley, R., & Caldwell, B. (1982). The consistency of the home environment and its relation to child development. International Journal of Behavioral Development, 5, 445–465.

Bradley, R., Caldwell, B., & Rock, S. (1988). Home environment and school performance: A ten-year follow-up and examination of three models of environmental action. *Child Development, 59,* 852–867.

Bradley, S., J., Oliver, G. D., Chernick, A. B., & Zuker, K. J. (1998). Experiment of nurture: Ablatio penis at 2 months, sex reassignment at 7 months, and a psychosexual follow-up in young adulthood. *Pediatrics, 102*(1), e9.

Braine, M. (1976). Children's first word combinations. *Monographs of the Society for Research in Child Development, 41*(1, Serial No. 164).

Brambati, S. M., Termine, C., Ruffino, M., Stella, G., Fazio, F., Cappa, S. F., & Perani, D. (2004). Regional reductions of gray matter volume in familial dyslexia. *Neurology, 63,* 742–745.

Brass, L. M., Isaacsohn, J. L., Merikangas, K. R., & Robinette, C. D. (1992). A study of twins and stroke. *Stroke, 23*(2), 221–223.

Bratton, S. C., & Ray, D. (2002). Humanistic play therapy. In D. J. Cain (Ed.), *Humanistic psychotherapies: Handbook of research and practice* (pp. 369–402). Washington, DC: American Psychological Association.

Braun, H., Jenkins, F., & Grigg, W. (2006). *A closer look at charter schools using hierarchical linear modeling* (NCES 2006-460). Washington, DC: U.S. Government Printing Office.

Braungart, J. M., Fulker, D. W., & Plomin, R. (1992). Genetic mediation of the home environment during infancy: A sibling adoption study of the HOME. *Developmental Psychology, 28,* 1048–1055.

Braungart, J. M., Plomin, R., DeFries, J. C., & Fulker, D. W. (1992). Genetic influence on tester-rated infant temperament as assessed by Bayley's Infant Behavior Record: Nonadoptive and adoptive siblings and twins. *Developmental Psychology, 28,* 40–47.

Braungart-Rieker, J. M., Garwood, M. M., Powers, B. P., & Wang, X. (2001). Parental sensitivity, infant affect, and affect regulation: Predictors of later attachment. *Child Development, 72,* 252–270.

Braungart-Rieker, J., Garwood, M. M., Powers, B. P., & Notaro, P. C. (1998). Infant affect and affect regulation during the still-face paradigm with mothers and fathers: The role of infant characteristics and parental sensitivity. *Developmental Psychology, 34*(6), 1428–1437.

Bray, J. H., & Hetherington, E. M. (1993). Families in transition: Introduction and overview. *Journal of Family Psychology, 7,* 3–8.

Brazelton, T. B. (1973). *Neonatal Behavioral Assessment scale.* Philadelphia: Lippincott.

Brazelton, T. B. (1984). *Neonatal Behavioral Assessment Scale.* Philadelphia: Lippincott.

Brazelton, T. B., & Nugent, J. K. (1995). *Neonatal Behavioral Assessment Scale* (3rd ed.). Cambridge, England: Cambridge University Press.

Breier, J. I., Simos, P. G., Fletcher, J. M., Castillo, E. M., Zhang, W., & Papanicolaou, A. C. (2003). Abnormal activation of temporoparietal language areas during phonetic analysis in children with dyslexia. *Neuropsychology, 17,* 610–621.

Brendgen, M., Dionne, G., Girard, A., Boivin, M., Vitaro, F., & Perusse, D. (2005). Examining genetic and environmental effects on social aggression: A study of 6-year-old twins. *Child Development, 76,* 930–946.

Brendgen, M., Little, T. D., & Krappmann, L. (2000). Rejected children and their friends: A shared evaluation of friendship quality? *Merrill-Palmer Quarterly, 46,* 45–70.

Brener, N. D., Simon, T. R., Krug, E. G., & Lowry, R. (1999). Recent trends in violence-related behaviors among high school students in the United States. *Journal of the American Medical Association, 282,* 440–446.

Brenneman, K., Massey, C., Machado, S. F., & Gelman, R. (1996). Young children's plans differ for writing and drawing. *Cognitive Development, 11,* 397–419.

Brent, D. A., & Birmaher, B. (2002). Adolescent depression. *New England Journal of Medicine, 347,* 667–671.

Brent, D. A., & Mann, J. J. (2006). Familial pathways to suicidal behavior—Understanding and preventing suicide among adolescents. *New England Journal of Medicine, 355,* 2719–2721.

Brent, R. L. & Weitzman, M. (2004). The current state of knowledge about the effects, risks, and science of children's environmental exposures. *Pediatrics, 113,* 1158–1166.

Bretherton, I. (1990). Communication patterns, internal working models, and the intergenerational transmission of attachment relationships. *Infant Mental Health Journal, 11*(3), 237–252.

Bretherton, I. (1997). Bowlby's legacy to developmental psychology. *Child Psychiatry and Human Development, 28,* 33–43.

Brewaeys, A., Ponjaert, I., Van Hall, V. E., & Golombok, S. (1997). Donor insemination: Child development and family functioning in lesbian mother families. *Human Reproduction, 12,* 1349–1359.

Brezina, T. (1999). Teenage violence toward parents as an adaptation to family strain: Evidence from a national survey of male adolescents. *Youth & Society, 30,* 416–444.

Brian, D. (1996). *Einstein: A life.* New York: Wiley.

Brin, D. J. (2004). The use of rituals in grieving for a miscarriage or stillbirth. *Women & Therapy, 27,* 123–132.

Briss, P. A., Sacks, J. J., Addiss, D. G., Kresnow, M., & O'Neil, J. (1994). A nationwide study of the risk of injury associated with day care center attendance. *Pediatrics, 93,* 364–368.

Brody, G. H. (1998). Sibling relationship quality: Its causes and consequences. *Annual Review of Psychology, 49,* 1–24.

Brody, G. H. (2004). Siblings' direct and indirect contributions to child development. *Current Directions in Psychological Science, 13,* 124–126.

Brody, G. H., Chen, Y.-F., Murry, V. M., Ge, X., Simons, R. L., Gibbons, F. X., Gerrard, M., & Cutrona, C. E. (2006). Perceived discrimination and the adjustment of African American youths: A five-year longitudinal analysis with contextual moderation effects. *Child Development, 77* (5), 1170–1189.

Brody, G. H., Flor, D. L., & Gibson, N. M. (1999). Linking maternal efficacy beliefs, developmental goals, parenting practices, and child competence in rural single-parent African American families. *Child Development, 70*(5), 1197–1208.

Brody, G. H., Ge, X., Conger, R., Gibbons, F. X., Murry, V. M., Gerrard, M., et al. (2001). The influence of neighborhood disadvantage, collective socialization, and parenting on African American children's affiliation with deviant peers. *Child Development, 72*(4), 1231–1246.

Brody, G. H., Kim, S., Murry, V. M., & Brown, A. C. (2004). Protective longitudinal paths linking child competence to behavioral problems among African American siblings. *Child Development, 75,* 455–467.

Brody, G. H., Stoneman, Z., & Flor, D. (1995). Linking family processes and academic competence among rural African American

youths. *Journal of Marriage and the Family, 57,* 567–579.

Brody, J. E. (1995, June 28). Preventing birth defects even before pregnancy. *New York Times,* p. C10.

Brody, L. R., Zelazo, P. R., & Chaika, H. (1984). Habituation-dishabituation to speech in the neonate. *Developmental Psychology, 20,* 114–119.

Broidy, L. M., Tremblay, R. E., Brame, B., Fergusson, D., Horwood, J. L., Laird, R., Moffitt, T. E., Nagin, D. S., Bates, J. E., Dodge, K. A., Loeber, R., Lyam, D. R., Pettit, G. S., & Vitaro, F. (2003). Developmental trajectories of childhood disruptive behaviors and adolescent delinquency: A six-site cross-national study. *Developmental Psychology, 39,* 222–245.

Bronfenbrenner, U. (1979). *The ecology of human development.* Cambridge, MA: Harvard University Press.

Bronfenbrenner, U. (1986). Ecology of the family as a context for human development: Research perspectives. *Developmental Psychology, 22,* 723–742.

Bronfenbrenner, U. (1994). Ecological models of human development. In T. Husen & T. N. Postlethwaite (Eds.), *International encyclopedia of education* (2nd ed., Vol. 3, pp. 1643–1647). Oxford: Pergamon Press/Elsevier Science.

Bronfenbrenner, U., Belsky, J., & Steinberg, L. (1977). *Daycare in context: An ecological perspective on research and public policy.* Review prepared for Office of the Assistant Secretary for Planning and Evaluation, U.S. Department of Health, Education, and Welfare.

Bronfenbrenner, U., & Morris, P. A. (1998). The ecology of developmental processes. In W. Damon (Series Ed.) & R. Lerner (Vol. Ed.), *Handbook of child psychology: Vol. 1. Theoretical models of human development* (5th ed., pp. 993–1028). New York: Wiley.

Bronner, E. (1999, January 22). Plans to ask schools to deny promotion rekindles debate. New York Times. Retrieved September 24, 2002, from http://query.nytimes.com/search/abstract?res=F00D17F935540C718EDDA80894D1494D81

Bronstein, P. (1988). Father–child interaction: Implications for gender role socialization. In P. Bronstein & C. P. Cowan (Eds.), *Fatherhood today: Men's changing role in the family.* New York: Wiley.

Bronstein, P., Clauson, J., Stoll, M. F., & Abrams, C. L. (1993). Parenting behavior and children's social, psychological, and academic adjustment in diverse family structures. *Family Relations, 42,* 268–276.

Brookmeyer, K. A., Henrich, C. C., & Schwab-Stone, M. (2005). Adolescents who witness community violence: Can parent support and prosocial cognitions protect them from committing violence? *Child Development, 76,* 917–929.

Brooks, P. J., Tomasello, M., Dodson, K., and Lewis, L. B. (1999). Young children's overgeneralizations with fixed transitivity verbs. *Child Development, 70,* 1325–1337.

Brooks, R., & Meltzoff, A. N. (2002). The importance of eyes: How infants interpret adult looking behavior. *Developmental Psychology, 38,* 958–966.

Brooks, R., & Meltzoff, A. N. (2005). The development of gaze following and its relation to language. *Developmental Science, 8,* 535–543.

Brooks-Gunn, J. (2003). Do you believe in magic? What can we expect from early childhood intervention programs? *SRCD Social Policy Report, 17*(1).

Brooks-Gunn, J., & Duncan, G. J. (1997). The effects of poverty on children. *The Future of Children, 7,* 55–71.

Brooks-Gunn, J. & Duncan-Johnson, A. (2006). G. Stanley Hall's contribution to science, practice and policy: The child study, parent education, and child welfare movements. *History of Psychology, 9,* 247–258.

Brooks-Gunn, J., Britto, P. R., & Brady, C. (1999). Struggling to make ends meet: Poverty and child development. In M. E. Lamb (Ed.), *Parenting and child development in "nontraditional" families* (pp. 279–304). Mahwah, NJ: Erlbaum.

Brooks-Gunn, J., Duncan, G. J., Leventhal, T., & Aber, J. L. (1997). Lessons learned and future directions for research on the neighborhoods in which children live. In J. Brooks-Gunn, G. J. Duncan, & J. L. Aber (Eds.), *Neighborhood poverty: Context and consequences for children* (Vol. 1, pp. 279–297). New York: Russell Sage Foundation.

Brooks-Gunn, J., Han, W.-J., & Waldfogel, J. (2002). Maternal employment and child cognitive outcomes in the first three years of life: The NICHD study of early child care. *Child Development, 73,* 1052–1072.

Brooks-Gunn, J., Klebanov, P. K., Liaw, F., & Spiker, D. (1993). Enhancing the development of low-birthweight, premature infants: Changes in cognition and behavior over the first three years. *Child Development, 64,* 736–753.

Brooks-Gunn, J., McCarton, C. M., Casey, P. H., et al. (1994). Early intervention in low-birthweight premature infants: Results through age 5 years from the Infant Health Development Program. *Journal of the American Medical Association, 272,* 1257–1262.

Broude, G. J. (1995). *Growing up: A cross-cultural encyclopedia.* Santa Barbara, CA: ABC-CLIO.

Brown, A. L., Metz, K. E., & Campione, J. C. (1996). Social interaction and individual understanding in a community of learners: The influence of Piaget and Vygotsky. In A. Tryphon & J. Voneche (Eds), *Piaget-Vygotsky: The social genesis of thought* (pp. 145–170). Hove, England: Psychology/Erlbaum (UK) Taylor & Francis.

Brown, A. S., Begg, M. D., Gravenstein, S., Schaefer, C. A., Wyatt, R. J., Bresnahan, M., Babulas, V. P., & Susser, E. S. (2004). Serologic evidence of prenatal influence in the etiology of schizophrenia. *Archives of General Psychiatry, 61,* 774–780.

Brown, A. S., Tapert, S. F., Granholm, E., & Delis, D. C. (2000). Neurocognitive functioning of adolescents: Effects of protracted alcohol use. *Alcoholism: Clinical and Experimental Research, 24,* 164–171.

Brown, B. (1999). Optimizing expression of the common human genome for child development. *Current Directions in Psychological Science, 8*(2), 37–41.

Brown, B. B., Mounts, N., Lamborn, S. D., & Steinberg, L. (1993). Parenting practices and peer group affiliation in adolescence. *Child Development, 64,* 467–482.

Brown, J. D., L'Engle, K. L., Pardun, C. J., Guo, G., Kenneavy, K., & Jackson, C. (2006). Sexy media matter: Exposure to sexual content in music, movies, television, and magazines predicts black and white adolescents' sexual behavior. *Pediatrics, 117,* 1018–1027.

Brown, J. L. (1987). Hunger in the U.S. *Scientific American, 256*(2), 37–41.

Brown, J. R., & Dunn, J. (1996). Continuities in emotion understanding from three to six years. *Child Development, 67,* 789–802.

Brown, J., & Harvey, G. (1980). *Terry Fox: A pictorial tribute to the Marathon of Hope.* Don Mills, ON: General Publishing Co. Limited.

Brown, L. J., Kaste, L. M., Selwitz, R. H., & Furman, L. J. (1996). Dental caries and sealant usage in U.S. children, 1988–1991. *Journal of the American Dental Association, 127,* 335–343.

Brown, L. J., Wall, T. P., & Lazar, V. (1999). Trends in untreated cavities in permanent teeth of children 6 to 18 years old. *Journal of the American Dental Association, 130,* 1637–1644.

Brown, L. M., & Gilligan, C. (1990, April). *The psychology of women and the development of girls.* Paper presented at the Laurel-Harvard Conference on the Psychology of Women and the Education of Girls, Cleveland, OH.

Brown, N. M. (1990). Age and children in the Kalahari. *Health and Human Development Research, 1,* 26–30.

Brown, P. (1993, April 17). Motherhood past midnight. *New Scientist,* pp. 4–8.

Brown, R., & Pressley, M. (1994). Self-regulated reading and getting meaning from text: The transactional strategies instruction model and its ongoing validation. In D. Schunk & B. Zimmerman (Eds.), *Self-regulation of learning and performance: Issues and educational applications* (pp. 155–179). Hillsdale, NJ: Erlbaum.

Brown, R., Pressley, M., Schuder, T., & Van Meter, P. (1994). *A quasi-experimental validation of transactional strategies instruction with previously low-achieving grade-2 readers.* Buffalo and Albany: State University of New York.

Brown, S. L. (2004). Family structure and child well-being: The significance of parental cohabitation. *Journal of Marriage and Family, 66,* 351–367.

Brown, S. S. (1985). Can low birth weight be prevented? *Family Planning Perspectives, 17*(3), 112–118.

Browne, A., & Finkelhor, D. (1986). Impact of child sexual abuse: A review of research. *Psychological Bulletin, 99*(1), 66–77.

Brownell, C. A., Ramani, G. B., & Zerwas, S. (2006). Becoming a social partner with peers: Cooperation and social understanding in one- and two-year-olds. Child Development, 77, 803–821.

Bruner, A. B., Joffe, A., Duggan, A. K., Casella, J. F., & Brandt, J. (1996). Randomised study of cognitive effects of iron supplementation in non-anaemic iron-deficient adolescent girls. *Lancet, 348,* 992–996.

Brunson, K. L., Kramar, E., Lin, B., Chen, Y., Colgin, L. L., Yanagihara, T. K., Lynch, G., & Baram, T. Z. (2005). Mechanisms of late-onset cognitive decline after early-life stress. *Journal of Neuroscience, 25*(41), 9328–9338.

Bryant, B. K. (1987). Mental health, temperament, family, and friends: Perspectives on children's empathy and social perspective taking. In N. Eisenberg & J. Strayer (Eds.), *Empathy and its development* (pp. 245–270). Cambridge, UK: Cambridge University Press.

Bryce, J., Boschi-Pinto, C., Shibuya, K., & the WHO Child Health Epidemiology Reference Group. (2005). WHO estimates of the causes of death in children. *Lancet, 365,* 1147–1152.

Buchanan, C. M., Eccles, J. S., & Becker, J. B. (1992). Are adolescents the victims of raging hormones: Evidence for activational effects of hormones on moods and behavior at adolescence. *Psychological Bulletin, 111,* 62–107.

Büchel, C., & Sommer, M. (2004). Unsolved mystery: What causes stuttering? *PLoS Biology, 2,* 0159–0163.

Buckner, J. C., Bassuk, E. L., Weinreb, L. F., & Brooks, M. G. (1999). Homelessness and its relation to the mental health and behavior of low-income school-age children. *Developmental Psychology, 35*(1), 246–257.

Buehler, C. (2006). Parents and peers in relation to early adolescent problem behavior. *Journal of Marriage and Family, 68,* 109–124.

Buhrmester, D. (1990). Intimacy of friendship, interpersonal competence, and adjustment during preadolescence and adolescence. *Child Development, 61,* 1101–1111.

Buhrmester, D. (1996). Need fulfillment, interpersonal competence, and the developmental contexts of early adolescent friendship. In W. M. Bukowski, A. F. Newcomb, & W. W. Hartup (Eds.), *The company they keep: Friendship in childhood and adolescence* (pp. 158–185). New York: Cambridge University Press.

Buhrmester, D., & Furman, W. (1990). Perceptions of sibling relationships during middle childhood and adolescence. *Child Development, 61,* 138–139.

Bulik, C. M., Sullivan, P. F., Tozzi, F., Furberg, H., Lichenstein, P., & Petersen, N. L. (2006). Prevalence, heritability, and prospective risk factors for anorexia nervosa. *Archives of General Psychiatry, 63,* 305–312.

Bulkley, K., & Fisler, J. (2002). A decade of charter schools: From theory to practice. Philadelphia: Consortium for Policy Research in Education, Graduate School of Education. University of Pennsylvania.

Bullock, M., Gelman, R., & Baillargeon, R. (1982). The development of causal reasoning. In W. J. Friedman (Ed.), *The developmental psychology of time* (pp. 209–254). New York: Academic.

Bunikowski, R., Grimmer, I., Heiser, A., Metze, B., Schafer, A., & Obladen, M. (1998). Neurodevelopmental outcome after prenatal exposure to opiates. *European Journal of Pediatrics, 157,* 724–730.

Burchinal, M. R., Campbell, F. A., Bryant, D. M., Wasik, B. H., & Ramey, C. T. (1997). Early intervention and mediating processes in cognitive performance of children of low-income African American families. *Child Development, 68,* 935–954.

Burchinal, M. R., Roberts, J. E., Nabors, L. A., & Bryant, D. M. (1996). Quality of center child care and infant cognitive and language development. *Child Development, 67,* 606–620.

Burhans, K. K., & Dweck, C. S. (1995). Helplessness in early childhood: The role of contingent worth. *Child Development, 66,* 1719–1738.

Burnaby, B. (1996). Aboriginal language maintenance, development, and enhancement: A review of the literature. In G. Cantoni (Editor) *Stabilizing Indigenous Languages.* Tucson, AZ: Center for Excellence in Education. Retrieved November 20, 2007 from http://www.ncela.gwu.edu/pubs/stabilize/i-needs/aboriginal.htm#N_4_.

Burns, B. J., Phillips, S. D., Wagner, H. R., Barth, R. P., Kolko, D. J., Campbell, Y., & Landsverk, J. (2004). Mental health need and access to mental health services by youths involved with child welfare: A national survey. *Journal of the American Academy of Child & Adolescent Psychiatry, 43,* 960–970.

Burt, A., Annest, J. L., Ballesteros, M. F., & Budnitz, D. S. (2006). Nonfatal, unintentional medication exposures among young children—United States, 2001–2003. *Morbidity and Mortality Weekly Report, 55,* 1–5.

Burt, R. D., Vaughan, T. L., & Daling, J. R. (1988). Evaluating the risks of cesarean section: Low Apgar score in repeat C-section and vaginal deliveries. *American Journal of Public Health, 78,* 1312–1314.

Bushnell, E. W., & Boudreau, J. P. (1993). Motor development and the mind: The potential role of motor abilities as a determinant of aspects of perceptual development. *Child Development, 64,* 1005–1021.

Bussey, K., & Bandura, A. (1992). Self-regulatory mechanisms governing gender development. *Child Development, 63,* 1236–1250.

Bussey, K., & Bandura, A. (1999). Social cognitive theory of gender development and differentiation. *Psychological Review, 106,* 676–713.

Byrne, M., Agerbo, E., Ewald, H., Eaton, W. W., & Mortensen, P. B. (2003). Parental age and risk of schizophrenia. *Archives of General Psychiatry, 60,* 673–678.

Byrnes, J. P., & Fox, N. A. (1998). The educational relevance of research in cognitive neuroscience. *Educational Psychology Review, 10,* 297–342.

Bystron, I., Rakic, P., Molnar, Z., & Blakemore, C. (2006). The first neurons of the human cerebral cortex. *Nature Neuroscience, 9*(7), 880–886.

Cabrera, N. J., Tamis-LeMonda, C. S., Bradley, R. H., Hofferth, S., & Lamb, M. E. (2000). Fatherhood in the twenty-first century. *Child Development, 71,* 127–136.

Caelli, K., Downie, J., & Letendre, A. (2002). Parents' experiences of midwife-managed care following the loss of a baby in a previous pregnancy. *Journal of Advanced Nursing, 39,* 127–136.

Caldji, C., Diorio, J., & Meaney, M. J. (2003). Variations in maternal care alter GABA(A) receptor subunit expression in brain regions associated with fear. *Neuropsychopharmacology, 28,* 1950–1959.

Caldwell, B. M., & Bradley, R. H. (1984). *Home observation for measurement of the environment.* Unpublished manuscript, University of Arkansas at Little Rock.

Calkins, S. D., & Fox, N. A. (1992). The relations among infant temperament, security of attachment, and behavioral inhibition at twenty-four months. *Child Development, 63,* 1456–1472.

CAM (Canadian Association of Midwives). (2006). Across Canada. Retrieved October 22, 2007 from www.canadianmidwives.org/across_canada.htm.

Camarata, S., & Woodcock, R. (2006). Sex differences in processing speed: Developmental effects in males and females. *Intelligence, 34*(3), 231–252.

Campaign 2000. (2005). Decision Time for Canada: Let's Make Poverty History: 2005 Report Card on Child Poverty in Canada. Toronto: Author. Retrieved January 14, 2008 from www.campaign2000.ca/rc/rc05/05NationalReportCard.pdf.

Campbell, A., Shirley, L., & Candy, J. (2004). A longitudinal study of gender-related cognition and behaviour. *Developmental Science, 7,* 1–9.

Campbell, A., Shirley, L., Heywood, C., & Crook, C. (2000). Infants' visual preference for sex-congruent babies, children, toys, and activities: A longitudinal study. *British Journal of Developmental Psychology, 18,* 479–498.

Campbell, D. B., Sutcliffe, J. S., Ebert, P. J., Militerni, R., Bravaccio, C., Trillo, S., et al. (2006). A genetic variant that disrupts MET transcription is associated with autism. *Proceedings of the National Academy of Sciences of the United States of America, 103*(45), 16834–16839.

Campfield, L. A., Smith, F. J., Guisez, Y., Devos, R., & Burn, P. (1995). Recombinant mouse OB protein: Evidence for a peripheral signal linking adiposity and central neural networks. *Science, 269,* 546–549.

Campos, J., Bertenthal, B., & Benson, N. (1980, April). *Self-produced locomotion and the extraction of form invariance.* Paper presented at the meeting of the International Conference on Infant Studies, New Haven, CT.

Canada Health Network. National drowning prevention week. Retrieved July 25, 2007 from http://www.canadian-health-network.ca/servlet/ContentServer?cid=1042668267588&pagename=CHN-RCS/Page/HEHPageTemplate&c=Page&lang=En.

Canada's Food Guide to Healthy Eating. (2007). Calorie countdown fun. Retrieved on August 7, 2007 from http://www.nms.on.ca/Elementary/calorie_countdown_fun.htm.

Canadian Association for Health, Physical Education Recreation and Dance. (2006). Phys-ed enrolment wanes after grade 9, study says. Retrieved August 21, 2007 from http://www.cahperd.ca/eng/story_detail.cfm?id=218.

Canadian Association of Food Banks. (2006). Hunger count 2006. Retrieved on August 7, 2007 from http://www.cafb-acba.ca/documents/2006_HungerCount_EN_designed.pdf.

Canadian Council on Children's Social Development. (2001). The progress of Canada's children. Retrieved on August 7, 2007 from http://www.ccsd.ca/pubs/2001/pcc2001/hl.htm.

Canadian Council on Learning. (2005). Good news: Canada's high school dropout rates are falling. Retrieved August 26, 2007 from http://www.ccl-cca.ca/CCL/Reports/LessonsInLearning/LiL-16Dec2005.htm.

Canadian Council on Learning. (2007). State of learning in Canada: No time for complacency. Report on learning in Canada 2007. Ottawa, ON: Author. Retrieved November 20, 2007 from http://www.ccl-cca.ca/NR/rdonlyres/5ECAA2E9-D5E4-43B9-94E4-84D6D31BC5BC/0/NewSOLR_Report.pdf.

Canadian Council on Social Development (2001). *The progress of Canada's children.* Ottawa: Author.

Canadian Council on Social Development. (2002). Highlights: The progress of Canada children 2002. Retrieved August 29, 2007 from http://www.ccsd.ca/pubs/2002/pcc02/hl.htm.

Canadian Council on Social Development. (2007). *A demographic profile of Canada.* Retrieved June 29, 2007, from http://www.ccsd.ca/factsheets/demographics/.

Canadian Dental Association (2002). *Early childhood tooth decay.* Retrieved July 27, 2002, from www.cda-adc.ca

Canadian Education Statistics Council. (2000). *Education indicators in Canada: Report of the Pan-Canadian education indicators program 1999.* Toronto: Author.

Canadian Fitness and Lifestyle Research. (2000). Results of the 2000 physical activity monitor. Retrieved August 14, 2007 from http://www.cflri.ca/eng/provincial_data/pam2000/canada.php.

Canadian Foundation for the Study of Infant Deaths, the Canadian Institute of Child Health, the Canadian Paediatric Society and Health Canada. (1999, reaffirmed 2000). Reducing the risk of sudden infant death syndrome in Canada. *Paediatrics & Child Health, 4,* 223–224.

Canadian Health Network. (2001). *What can I do to ensure clean smoke-free air for my family and myself?* Retrieved September 20, 2002, from http://canadian-health-network.ca/faq-faq/tobacco-tabagisme/9e.html.

Canadian Hospitals Injury Reporting and Prevention Program. (1999). *Injuries associated with shopping carts.* Retrieved September 20, 2002, from http://www.hc-sc.gc.ca/pphb-dgspsp/injury-bles/chirpp/injrep-rapbles/shpcrt_e.html.

Canadian Institute for Health Information (CICI). (Undated). Hospitalizations due to bicycle-related injuries among children and youth down 15% in five years, reports CIHI. Retrieved on August 7, 2007 from http://secure.cihi.ca/cihiweb/dispPage.jsp?cw_page=media_28apr2004_e.

Canadian Institute for Health Information (CIHI). (2007). 23 children visit an Ontario ER daily due to playground injuries, Canada. Retrieved on August 7, 2007 from http://www.medicalnewstoday.com/articles/77307.php.

Canadian Institute for Health Information and Statistics Canada. (2000). *Health care in Canada 2000: A first annual report.* Catalogue No. 82-222-XIE. Ottawa: Author.

Canadian Institute of Child Health [CICH]. (2000). *The health of Canada's children: A CICH profile* (3rd ed.). Ottawa: Author.

Canadian Institute of Health Research: Institute of Aboriginal Peoples' Health (IAPH). (2002). Five-year strategic plan: 2002 to 2007. Retrieved on August 7, 2007 from http://www.cihr-irsc.gc.ca/e/32823.html.

Canadian Mental Health Association. (2006). Suicide. Retrieved August 23, 2007 from http://www.ontario.cmha.ca/content/about_mental_illness/suicide.asp?cID=3965.

Canadian Nurses Association. (2005). Children's health and nursing: A summary of the issues. Retrieved on August 16, 2007 from http://www.cna-nurses.ca/CNA/documents/pdf/publications/BG2_Childrens_Health_and_Nursing_e.pdf

Canadian Paediatric Society Advisory Committee on Healthy Active Living for Children and Youth. (2002). Healthy active living for children and youth. *Paediatrics and Child Health, 7,* 339–345.

Canadian Paediatric Society and Health Canada (1994/2001). *Nutrition recommendations update: Dietary fat and children.* Ottawa: Canadian Paediatric Society.

Canadian Paediatric Society Psychosocial Paediatrics Committee. (2001, February). Smoking and your child: What parents should know. *Paediatrics & Child Health, 6* (2). Retrieved September 20, 2002, from http://www.pulsus.com/Paeds/06_02/contents.htm.

Canadian Paediatric Society, Dietitians of Canada and Health Canada. (1998). *Nutrition for healthy term infants.* Ottawa: Minister of Public Works and Government Services.

Canadian Paediatric Society. (1996). Prevention of firearm deaths in Canadian children and adolescents. *Paediatrics & Child Health, 1,* 231–233.

Canadian Paediatric Society. (1999). *Well Beings: A guide to promote the physical health, safety and emotional well being of children in child care centres and family day care homes,* 2nd edition. Ottawa: Author.

Canadian Paediatric Society. (1999a). *Being well.* Ottawa: Author.

Canadian Paediatric Society. (1999b). Children and the media. *Paediatrics & Child Health, 4,* 350–354.

Canadian Paediatric Society. (1999c). *Well beings: A guide to promote the physical health, safety and emotional well being of children in*

child care centres and family day care homes (2nd ed.). Ottawa, ON: Author.

Canadian Paediatric Society. (2001). *Nutrition Recommendations Update … Dietary Fat and Children: Report of the Joint Working Group of the Canadian Paediatric Society (CPS) and Health Canada*, Reference No. N94-01. Ottawa: Author.

Canadian Paediatric Society. (2005–2006). Building blocks: Annual report. Retrieved July 25, 2007 from http://www.cps.ca/English/Publications/Reports/AnnualReport.pdf.

Canadian Paediatric Society. (Undated) Nutrition recommendations update: Dietary fat and children. Retrieved July 25, 2007 from http://www.cps.ca/english/statements/N/n94-01.htm.

Canadian Perinatal Surveillance System. (2000). *Canadian perinatal health report, 2000.* Ottawa: Health Canada.

Canadian Press. (2004). Food bank use by B.C. children up 42 percent. Retrieved July 25, 2007 from www.ctv.ca/servlet/ArticleNews/story/CTVNews/1100172223116_98/?hub=Canada

Canadian Sugar Institute. (2005). Healthy eating. Retrieved on August 7, 2007 from http://www.sugar.ca/english/educators/sugarsandhealth.cfm#top

Canadian Task Force on the Periodic Health Examination. (1994). Periodic health examination, 1994 update: 1. Obesity in childhood. *Canadian Medical Association Journal, 150,* 871–879.

Canadian Women's Foundation. (2005). Girls in Canada 2005. Retrieved September 2, 2007 from http://www.canadianwomen.org/newsite/PDFs/EN/CWF-GirlsCanada-Report05.pdf

Canadian Working Group on Childhood Hearing. (2001). *Notice from the Canadian Working Group on Childhood Hearing to interested consumer groups.* Ottawa: Health Canada. Retrieved July 16, 2002, from http://www.hc-sc.gc.ca/pphb-dgspsp/rhs-ssg/index.html.

Canfield, R. L., Henderson, C. R., Cory- Slechta, D. A., Cox, C., Jusko, T. A., & Lanphear, B. P. (April 17, 2003). Intellectual impairment in children with blood lead concentrations below 10 adolescence to young adulthood: Prevalence, prediction, and association with STD contraction. *Developmental Psychology, 38,* 394–406.

Cannon, T. D., Hennah, W., van Erp, T. G. M., Thompson, P. M., Lonnqvistt, J., Huttenen, M., Gasperoni, T., Tuulio-Henriksson, A., Pirkola, T., Toga, A. W., Kaprio, J., Mazziotta, J., & Peltonen, L. (2005). Association of DISC1/TRAX haplotypes with schizophrenia, reduced prefrontal gray matter, and impaired short- and long-term memory. *Archives of General Psychiatry, 62,* 1205–1213.

Cantor, J. (1994). Confronting children's fright responses to mass media. In D. Zillman, J. Bryant, & A. C. Huston (Eds.), *Media, children, and the family: Social scientific, psychoanalytic, and clinical perspectives* (pp. 139–150). Hillsdale, NJ: Erlbaum.

Cao, A., Saba, L., Galanello, R., & Rosatelli, M. C. (1997). Molecular diagnosis and carrier screening for thalassemia. *Journal of the American Medical Association, 278,* 1273–1277.

Cao, X.-Y., Jiang, X.-M., Dou, Z.-H., Rakeman, M. A., Zhang, M.-L., O'Donnell, K., Ma, T., Amette, K., DeLong, N., & DeLong, G. R. (1994). Timing of vulnerability of the brain to iodine deficiency in endemic cretinism. *New England Journal of Medicine, 331,* 1739–1744.

Capaldi, D. M., Stoolmiller, M., Clark, S., & Owen, L. D. (2002). Heterosexual risk behaviors in at-risk young men from early adolescence to young adulthood: Prevalence, prediction, and STD contraction. *Developmental Psychology, 38,* 394–406.

Caplan, M., Vespo, J., Pedersen, J., & Hay, D. F. (1991). Conflict and its resolution in small groups of one- and two-year olds. *Child Development, 62,* 1513–1524.

Capute, A. J., Shapiro, B. K., & Palmer, F. B. (1987). Marking the milestones of language development. *Contemporary Pediatrics, 4*(4), 24.

Carlson, E. A. (1998). A prospective longitudinal study of attachment disorganization/disorientation. *Child Development, 69*(4), 1107–1128.

Carlson, E. A., Sroufe, L. A., & Egeland, B. (2004). The construction of experience: A longitudinal study of representation and behavior. *Child Development, 75,* 66–83.

Carlson, M. J. (2006). Family structure, father involvement, and adolescent behavioral outcomes. *Journal of Marriage and Family, 68,* 137–154.

Carlson, S. M., & Taylor, M. (2005). Imaginary companions and impersonated characters: Sex differences in children's fantasy play. *Merrill-Palmer Quarterly, 51*(1), 93–118.

Carlson, S. M., Moses, L. J., & Hix, H. R. (1998). The role of inhibitory processes in young children's difficulties withdeception and false belief. *Child Development, 69*(3), 672–691.

Carlson, S. M., Wong, A., Lemke, M., & Cosser, C. (2005). Gesture as a window in children's beginning understanding of false belief. *Child Development, 76,* 73–86.

Carmichael, M. (2004, January 26). In parts of Asia, sexism is ingrained and gender selection often means murder. No girls, please. *Newsweek,* p. 50.

Carnethon, M. R., Gulati, M., & Greenland, P. (2005). Prevalence and cardiovascular disease correlates of low cardiorespiratory fitness in adolescents and adults. *Journal of the American Medical Association, 294,* 2981–2988.

Carpenter, M., Akhtar, N., & Tomasello, M. (1998). Fourteen- through 18-month-old infants differentially imitate intentional and accidental actions. *Infant Behavior and Development, 21,* 315–330.

Carraher, T. N., Schliemann, A. D., & Carraher, D. W. (1988). Mathematical concepts in everyday life. In G. B. Saxe & M. Gearhart (Eds.), Children's mathematics. *New Directions in Child Development, 41,* 71–87.

Carrel, L., & Willard, B. F. (2005). X-inactivation profile reveals extensive variability in X-linked gene expression in females. *Nature, 434,* 400–404.

Carroll, D., & Benoit, C. (spring, 2001). Aboriginal midwifery in Canada: Blending traditional and modern forms. *Network Magazine, 4*(3). Retrieved July 14, 2002, from http://www.cwhn.ca/network-reseau/4-3/4-3pg2.html

Carskadon, M. A., Acebo, C., Richardson, G. S., Tate, B. A., & Seifer, R. (1997). Long nights protocol: Access to circadian parameters in adolescents. *Journal of Biological Rhythms, 12,* 278–289.

Carson, J. L., & Parke, R. D. (1996). Reciprocal negative affect in parent–child interactions and children's peer competency. *Child Development, 67,* 2217–2226.

Carter, R. C., Jacobson, S. W., Molteno, C. D., Chiodo, L. M., Viljoen, D., & Jacobson, J. L. (2005). Effects of prenatal alcohol exposure on infant visual acuity. *The Journal of Pediatrics, 147*(4), 473–479.

Casaer, P. (1993). Old and new facts about perinatal brain development. *Journal of Child Psychology and Psychiatry, 34*(1), 101–109.

Casanova, M. F., Christensen, J. D., Giedd, J., Rumsey, J. M., Garver, D. L., & Postel, G. C. (2005). Magnetic response imaging of brain asymmetries in dyslexic patients. *Journal of Child Neurology, 20,* 842–847.

Case, R. (1985). *Intellectual development: Birth to adulthood.* Orlando, FL: Academic Press.

Case, R. (1992). Neo-Piagetian theories of child development. In R. Sternberg & C. Berg (Eds.), *Intellectual development* (pp. 161–196). New York: Cambridge University Press.

Case, R., & Okamoto, Y. (1996). The role of central conceptual structures in the development of children's thought. *Monographs of the Society for Research in Child Development, 61*(1–2, Serial No. 246).

Case, R., Demetriou, A., Platsidou, M. & Kazi, S. (2001). Integrating concepts and tests of intelligence from the differential and developmental traditions. *Intelligence, 29,* 307–336.

Casey, B. M., McIntire, D. D., & Leveno, K. J. (2001). The continuing value of the Apgar score for the assessment of newborn infants. *New England Journal of Medicine, 344,* 467–471.

Casper, L. M. (1997). My daddy takes care of me: Fathers as care providers. *Current Population Report*s (P70-59). Washington, DC: U.S. Bureau of the Census.

Casper, L. M., & Bryson, K. R. (1998). *Co-resident grandparents and their grandchildren: Grandparent maintained families* (Population Division Working Paper No. 26). Washington, DC: U.S. Bureau of the Census.

Caspi, A. M., Lyman, D., Moffitt, T. E., & Silva, P. A. (1993). Unraveling girls' delinquency: Biological, dispositional, and contextual contributions to adolescent misbehavior. *Developmental Psychology, 29,* 19–30.

Caspi, A., McClay, J., Moffitt, T. E., Mill, J., Martin, J., Craig, I. W., et al. (2002). Role of genotype in the cycle of violence in maltreated children. *Science, 297,* 851–854.

Cassidy, J., & Hossler, A. (1992). State and federal definitions of the gifted: An update. *Gifted Child Quarterly, 15,* 46–53.

Cassidy, K. W., Werner, R. S., Rourke, M., Zubernis, L. S., & Balaraman, G. (2003). The relationship between psychological understanding and positive social behaviors. *Social Development, 12,* 198–221.

Cattanach, B. M., & Kirk, M. (1985). Differential activity of maternally and paternally derived chromosome regions in mice. *Nature, 315,* 496–498.

Caughey, A. B., Hopkins, L. M., & Norton, M. E. (2006). Chorionic villus sampling compared with amniocentesis and the difference in the rate of pregnancy loss. *Obstetrics and Gynecology, 108,* 612–616.

Cavazanna-Calvo, M., Hacein-Bey, S., de Saint Basile, G., Gross, F., Yvon, E., Nusbaum, P., Selz, F., Hue, C., Certain, S., Casanova, J. L., Bousso, P., Deist, F. L., & Fischer, A. (2000). Gene therapy of human severe combined immunodeficiency (SCID)-X1 disease. *Science, 288,* 669–672.

CBC News. (2004). Fewer Canadian marriages end in divorce. Retrieved on August 16, 2007 from http://www.cbc.ca/canada/story/2004/05/04/divorce040504.html.

CBS News. (2004). Becoming Barbie: Living dolls. Retrieved September 27, 2007, from http://www.cbsnews.com/stories/2004/07/29/48hours/main632909.shtml.

Ceci, S. J. (1991). How much does schooling influence general intelligence and its cognitive components? A reassessment of the evidence. *Developmental Psychology, 27,* 703–722.

Ceci, S. J., & Williams, W. M. (1997). Schooling, intelligence, and income. *American Psychologist, 52*(10), 1105–1058.

Celis, W. (1990, Aug. 16). More states are laying school paddle to rest. *New York Times,* pp. A1, B12.

CEMAT Group, 1998: The Canadian Early and Mid-Trimester Amniocentesis Trial (CEMAT) Group. (1998). Randomised trial to assess safety and fetal outcome of early and midtrimester amniocentesis. *The Lancet, 351,* 242–247.

Center for Autism Research. (n.d.). MRI research. Retrieved May 10, 2006, from http://www.courchesneautismlab.org/mri.html.

Center for Education Reform. (2004, August 17). *Comprehensive data discounts New York Time account; reveals charter schools performing at or above traditional schools.* (CER Press Release). Retrieved September 17, 2004, from http://www.edreform.com/index.cfm/fuseAction =document&documentId=1806.

Center for Weight and Health (2001). *Pediatric overweight: A review of the literature: Executive summary.* Berkeley, CA: University of California at Berkeley.

Center on Addiction and Substance Abuse at Columbia University (CASA). (1996, June). *Substance abuse and the American woman.* New York: Author.

Centers for Disease Control and Prevention (CDC) Office of Media Relations. (2006, June 29). CDC's advisory committee recommends human papillomavirus virus vaccination. (Press release). Atlanta, GA: Author.

Centers for Disease Control and Prevention (CDC). (2000a). *CDC's guidelines for school and community programs: Promoting lifelong physical activity.* Retrieved May 26, 2000, from http://www.cdc.gov/nccdphp/dash/phactaag.htm

Centers for Disease Control and Prevention (CDC). (2004). National, state, and urban area vaccination coverage among children aged 19–36 months—United States, 2003. Morbidity and Mortality Weekly Report, 53, 658–661.

Centers for Disease Control and Prevention. (2005a). *Assisted reproductive technology: Home.* Retrieved January 25, 2006, from http://www.cdc.gov/ART/

Centers for Disease Control and Prevention (CDC). (2006a). Achievements in public health: Reduction in perinatal transmission of HIV infection—United States, 1985–2005. *Morbidity and Mortality Weekly Report, 55*(21), 592–597.

Centers for Disease Control and Prevention. (2006b). Improved national prevalence estimates for 18 selected major birth defects—United States, 1999–2001. *Morbidity and Mortality Weekly Report, 54*(51 & 52), 1301–1305.

Centers for Disease Control and Prevention (CDC). (2006c). Recommendations to improve preconception health and health care—United States. *Morbidity and Mortality Weekly Report, 55*(RR06), 1–23.

Chambers, C. D., Hernandez-Diaz, S., Van Marter, L. J., Werler, M. M., Louik, C., Jones, K. L., & Mitchell, A. A. (2006). Selective serotonin-reuptake inhibitors and risk of persistent pulmonary hypertension of the newborn. *New England Journal of Medicine, 354,* 579–587.

Chambers, R. A., Taylor, J. R., & Potenza, M. N. (2003). Developmental neurocircuitry of motivation in adolescence: A critical period of addiction vulnerability. *American Journal of Psychiatry, 160,* 1041–1052.

Chan, R. W., Raboy, B., & Patterson, C. J. (1998). Psychosocial adjustment among children conceived via donor insemination by lesbian and heterosexual mothers. *Child Development, 69,* 443–457.

Chandler, M. J., & Lalonde, C. (1995). The problem of self-continuity in the context of rapid personal and cultural change. In A. Oosterwegel & R. A. Wcklund (Eds.), *The self in European and North American culture: Development and processes.* NATO advanced science institutes series (pp. 45–63). Dordrecht, The Netherlands: Kluwer Academic Publishers.

Chandler, M. J., & Lalonde, C. (1998). Cultural continuity as a hedge against suicide in Canada's First Nations. *Transcultural Psychiatry, 35,* 191–219.

Channel 3000 News. (1998). *First test tube baby turns 20: Louise Brown 'no different' from peers.* Retrieved September 23, 2002, from http://www.channel3000.com/news/stories/news-980725-121445.html

Chao, R. K. & Willms, J. D. (2002). The effects of parenting practices on children's outcomes. In Willms, J. D. *Vulnerable Children* (pg. 149–166). University of Alberta Press.

Chapman, M., & Lindenberger, U. (1988). Functions, operations, and décalage in the development of transitivity. *Developmental Psychology, 24,* 542–551.

Charlesworth, A., & Glantz, S. A. (2005). Smoking in the movies increases adolescent smoking: A review. *Pediatrics, 116,* 1516–1528.

Chase-Lansdale, P. L., Moffitt, R. A., Lohman, B. J., Cherlin, A. J., Coley, R. L., Pittman, L. D., Rolf, J., & Votruba-Drzal, E. (2003). Mothers' transitions from welfare to work and the well-being of preschoolers and adolescents. *Science, 299*(5612), 1548–1552.

Cheah, C. S. L., Nelson, L. J., & Rubin, K. H. (2001). Nonsocial play as a risk factor in social and emotional development. In A. Goencue & E. L. Klein (Eds.), *Children in play, story, and school* (pp. 39–71). New York: The Guildford Press.

Chehab, F. F., Mounzih, K., Lu, R., & Lim, M. E. (1997, January 3). Early onset of reproductive function in normal female mice treated with leptin. *Science, 275,* 88–90.

Chen, A., & Rogan, W. J. (2004). Breastfeeding and the risk of postneonatal death in the United States. *Pediatrics, 113,* e435–e439.

Chen, E., Matthews, K. A., & Boyce, W. T. (2002). Socioeconomic differences in children's health: How and why do these relationships change with age? *Psychological Bulletin, 128,* 295–329.

Chen, L., Baker S. P., Braver, E. R., & Li, G. (2000). Carrying passengers as a risk factor for crashes fatal to 16- and 17-year-old drivers. *Journal of the American Medical Association, 283*(12), 1578–1582.

Chen, W., Li, S., Cook, N. R., Rosner, B. A., Srinivasan, S. R., Boerwinkle, E., et al. (2004). An autosomal genome scan for loci influencing longitudinal burden of body mass index from childhood to young adulthood in white sibships: The Bogalusa Heart Study. *International Journal of Obesity, 28,* 462–469.

Chen, X., Cen, G., Li, D., & He, Y. (2005). Social functioning and adjustment in Chinese children: The imprint of historical time. *Child Development, 76,* 182–195.

Chen, X., Hastings, P. D., Rubin, K. H., Chen, H., Cen, G., & Stewart, S. L. (1998). Child-rearing attitudes and behavioral inhibition in Chinese and Canadian toddlers: A cross-cultural study. *Developmental Psychology, 34*(4), 677–686.

Chen, X., He. Y., De Oliveira, A. M., Lo Coco, A., Zappulla, C., Kaspar, V., Schneider, B., Valdivia, I. A., Tse, H. C. & De Souzza, A. (2004). Loneliness and social adaptation in Brazilian, Canadian, Chinese and Italian children: A multi-national comparative study. *Journal of Child Psychology and Psychiatry, 45,* 1373–1384.

Chen, X., Rubin, K. H., & Li, Z. (1995). Social functioning and adjustment in Chinese children: A longitudinal study. *Developmental Psychology, 31,* 531–539.

Chen, X., Rubin, K. H., & Sun, Y. (1992). Social reputation and peer relationships in Chinese and Canadian children: A cross-cultural study. *Child Development, 63,* 1336–1343.

Cheruku, S. R., Montgomery-Downs, H. E., Farkas, S. L., Thoman, E. B., Lammi-Keefe C. J. (2002). Higher maternal plasma docosahexaenoic acid during pregnancy is associated with more mature neonatal sleep-state patterning. *American Journal of Clinical Nutrition, 76,* 608–613.

Chess, S., & Thomas, A. (1982). Infant bonding: Mystique and reality. *American Journal of Orthopsychiatry, 52*(2), 213–222.

Children's Defense Fund. (1998). *The state of America's children yearbook, 1998.* Washington, DC: Author.

Children's Defense Fund. (2000). *The state of America's children yearbook, 2000.* Washington, DC: Author.

Children's Defense Fund. (2004). *The state of America's children 2004.* Washington, DC: Author.

Children's Mental Health Ontario. (2001). Children and adolescents with conduct disorder: Findings from the literature and clinical consultation in Ontario. Retrieved August 17, 2007 from http://www.kidsmentalhealth.ca/documents/EBP_conduct_disorder_findings.pdf

Children's Resource and Research Unit (1998). *Early Childhood Care and Education in Canada: Provinces and Territories.* Toronto, ON: Author. Retrieved October 17, 2007 from http://www.childcarecanada.org/pt98/pdf/Prov&Terr98.pdf.

Chiriboga, C. A., Brust, J. C. M., Bateman, D., & Hauser, W. A. (1999). Dose-response effect of fetal cocaine exposure on newborn neurologic function. *Pediatrics, 103,* 79–85.

Chomitz, V. R., Cheung, L. W. Y., & Lieberman, E. (1995). The role of lifestyle in preventing low birth weight. *The Future of Children, 5*(1), 121–138.

Chomsky, C. S. (1969). *The acquisition of syntax in children from five to ten.* Cambridge, MA: MIT Press.

Chomsky, N. (1957). *Syntactic structures.* The Hague: Mouton.

Chomsky, N. (1972). *Language and mind* (2nd ed.). New York: Harcourt Brace Jovanovich.

Chomsky, N. (1995). *The minimalist program.* Cambridge, MA: MIT Press.

Chorpita, B. P., & Barlow, D. H. (1998). The development of anxiety: The role of control in the early environment. *Psychological Bulletin, 124,* 3–21.

Christakis, D. A., Zimmerman, F. J., DiGiuseppe, D. L., & McCarty, C. A. (2004). Early television exposure and subsequent attentional problems in children. *Pediatrics, 113,* 708–713.

Christian, M. S., & Brent, R. L. (2001). Teratogen update: Evaluation of the reproductive and developmental risks of caffeine. *Teratology, 64*(1), 51–78.

Christie, J. F. (1991). *Psychological research on play: Connections with early literacy development.* Albany: State University of New York Press.

Christie, J. F. (1998). Play as a medium for literacy development. In D. P. Fromberg & D. Bergen (Eds.), *Play from birth to twelve and beyond: Contexts, perspectives, and meanings* (pp. 50–55). New York: Garland.

Chugani, H. T. (1998). A critical period of brain development: Studies of cerebral glucose utilization with PET. *Preventive Medicine, 27,* 184–187.

Chung, I. W. (2006). A cultural perspective on emotions and behavior: An empathetic pathway to examine intergenerational conflicts in Chinese Immigrant Families. *Families in Society, 87,* 366–376.

Chung. H. L., & Steinberg, L. (2006). Relations between neighborhood factors, parenting behaviors, peer deviance, and delinquency among serious juvenile offenders. *Developmental Psychology, 42,* 319–331.

Cicchetti, D., & Toth, S. L. (1998). The development of depression in children and adolescents. *American Psychologist, 53,* 221–241.

Cicirelli, V. G. (1976). Family structure and interaction: Sibling effects on socialization. In M. F. McMillan & S. Henao (Eds.), *Child psychiatry: Treatment and research.* New York: Brunner/Mazel.

Cicirelli, V. G. (1994). Sibling relationships in cross-cultural perspective. *Journal of Marriage and the Family, 56,* 7–20.

Cicirelli, V. G. (1994, November). *Sibling relationships over the life course.* Paper presented at the 49th Annual Scientific Meeting of the Gerontological Society of America, Atlanta, GA.

Cicirelli, V. G. (1995). *Sibling relationships across the life span.* New York: Plenum Press.

CIHI (Canadian Institute for Health Information). (2007). Giving birth in Canada: Regional trends from 2001–2002 to 2005–2006. Ottawa, ON: Author.

Cillessen, A. H. N., & Mayeux, L. (2004). From censure to reinforcement: Developmental changes in the association between aggression and social status. *Child Development, 75,* 147–163.

Claes, M. (1998). Adolescents' closeness with parents, siblings, and friends in three countries: Canada, Belgium, and Italy. *Journal of Youth and Adolescence, 27,* 165–184.

Clark, A. G., Glanowski, S., Nielsen, R., Thomas, P. D., Kejariwal, A., Todd, M. A., Tanenbaum, D. M., Civello, D., Lu, F., Murphy, B., Ferriera, S., Wang, G., Zheng, X., White, T. J., Sninsky, J. J., Adams, M. D., & Cargill, M. (2003). Inferring non-neutral evolution from human-chimp-mouse orthologous gene trios. *Science, 302,* 1960–1963.

Clarke-Stewart, K. A. (1987). Predicting child development from day care forms and features: The Chicago study. In D. A. Phillips (Ed.), *Quality in child care: What does the research tell us?* (Research Monographs of the National Association for the Education of Young Children). Washington, DC: National Association for the Education of Young Children.

Clayton, E. W. (2003). Ethical, legal, and social implications of genomic medicine. *New England Journal of Medicine, 349,* 562–569.

Clayton, R., & Heard, D. (Eds.). (1994). *Elvis up close: In the words of those who knew him best.* Atlanta, GA: Turner.

Clearfield, M. W., & Mix, K. S. (1999). Number versus contour length in infants' discrimination of small visual sets. *Current Directions in Psychological Science, 10,* 408–411.

Clément, K., Vaisse, C., Lahlou, N., Cabrol, S., Pelloux, V., Cassuto, D., Gourmelen, M., Dina, C., Chambaz, J., Lacorte, J.-M., Basdevant, A., Bougnères, P., Lebouc, Y., Froguel, P., & Guy-Grand, B. (1998). A mutation in the human leptin receptor gene causes obesity and pituitary dysfunction. *Nature, 392,* 398–401.

Cleveland, E., & Resse, E. (2005). Maternal structure and autonomy support in conversations about the past: Contributions to children's autobiographical memory. *Development Psychology, 41,* 376–388.

Cleveland, H. H., & Wiebe, R. P. (2003). The moderation of adolescent-to-peer similarity in tobacco and alcohol use by school level of substance use. *Child Development, 74,* 279–291.

Clifton, R. K., Muir, D. W., Ashmead, D. H., & Clarkson, M. G. (1993). Is visually guided reaching in early infancy a myth? *Child Development, 64,* 1099–1110.

Cloutier, E. & Albert, T. (2001). *Economic burden of unintentional injury in British Columbia.* Vancouver: BC Injury Research and Prevention Unit.

Cnattingius, S., Bergstrom, R., Lipworth, L., & Kramer, M. S. (1998). Prepregnancy weight and the risk of adverse pregnancy outcomes. *New England Journal of Medicine, 338,* 147–152.

Cnattingius, S., Signorello, L. B., Anneré, G., Clausson, B., Ekbom, A., Ljunger, E., Blot, W. J., McLaughlin, J. K., Petersson, G., Rane, A., & Granath, F. (2000). Caffeine intake and the risk of first-trimester spontaneous abortion. *New England Journal of Medicine, 343*(25), 1839–1845.

Cohen, D. A., Nsuami, M., Martin, D. H., & Farley, T. A. (1999). Repeated school-based screening for sexually transmitted diseases: A feasible strategy for reaching adolescents. *Pediatrics, 104*(6), 1281–1285.

Cohen, L. B., & Amsel, L. B. (1998). Precursors to infants' perception of the causality of a simple event. *Infant Behavior and Development, 21,* 713–732.

Cohen, L. B., & Oakes, L. M. (1993). How infants perceive a simple causal event. *Developmental Psychology, 29,* 421–433.

Cohen, L. B., Rundell, L. J., Spellman, B. A., & Cashon, C. H. (1999). Infants' perception of causal chains. *Current Directions in Psychological Science, 10,* 412–418.

Cohn, J. F., & Tronick, E. Z. (1983). Three-month-old infants' reaction to simulated maternal depression. *Child Development, 54,* 185–193.

Coie, J. D., & Dodge, K. A. (1998). Aggression and antisocial behavior. In W. Damon (Series Ed.) & N. Eisenberg (Vol. Ed.), *Handbook of child psychology: Vol. 3. Social, emotional, and personality development* (5th ed., pp. 780–862). New York: Wiley.

Colby, A., & Damon, W. (1992). *Some do care: Contemporary lives of moral commitment.* New York: Free Press.

Colby, A., Kohlberg, L., Gibbs, J., & Lieberman, M. (1983). A longitudinal study of moral development. *Monographs of the Society for Research in Child Development, 48*(1–2, Serial No. 200).

Cole, M. (1998). *Cultural psychology: A once and future discipline.* Cambridge, MA: Belknap.

Cole, P. M., Barrett, K. C., & Zahn-Waxler, C. (1992). Emotion displays in two-year-olds during mishaps. *Child Development, 63,* 314–324.

Cole, P. M., Bruschi, C. J., & Tamang, B. L. (2002). Cultural differences in children's emotional reactions to difficult situations. *Child Development, 73*(3), 983–996.

Cole, P. M., Tamang, B. L., & Shrestha, S. (2006). Cultural variations in the socialization of young children's anger and shame. *Child Development, 77*(5), 1237–1251.

Coleman, H., Charles, G., & Collins, J. (2001). Inhalant use by Canadian Aboriginal youth. *Journal of Child & Adolescent Substance Abuse, 10*(3), 1–20.

Coleman, J. S. (1988). Social capital in the creation of human capital. *American Journal of Sociology, 94*(Suppl. 95), S95–S120.

Colen, C. G., Geronimus, A. T., Bound, J., & James, S. A. (2006). Maternal upward socioeconomic mobility and black-white disparities in infant birthweight. *American Journal of Public Health, 96,* 2032–2039.

Coley, R. L., Morris, J. E., & Hernandez, D. (2004). Out-of-school care and problem behavior trajectories among low-income adolescents: Individual, family, and neighborhood characteristics as added risks. *Child Development, 75,* 948–965.

Collier, V. P. (1995). Acquiring a second language for school. *Directions in Language and Education, 1*(4), 1–11.

Collins, J. A. & Van Steirteghem, A. (2004). Overall prognosis with current treatment of infertility. *Human Reproduction, 10,* 309–316.

Collins, J. G., & LeClere, F. B. (1997). *Health and selected socioeconomic characteristics of the family: United States, 1988–90* (DHHS No. PHS 97–1523). Washington, DC: U.S. Government Printing Office.

Collins, R. C., & Deloria, D. (1983). Head Start research: A new chapter. *Children Today, 12*(4), 15–19.

Collins, W. A., Maccoby, E. E., Steinberg, L., Hetherington, E. M., & Bornstein, M. H. (2000). Contemporary research in parenting: The case for nature and nurture. *American Psychologist, 55,* 218–232.

Colliver, J. D., Kroutil, L. A., Dai, L., & Gfroerer, J. C. (2006). Misuse of prescription drugs: Data from the 2002, 2003, and 2004 National Surveys on Drug Use and Health (DHHS Publication No. SMA 06-4192, Analytic Series A-28). Rockville, MD: Substance Abuse and Mental Health Services Administration, Office of Applied Studies.

Colombo, J. (1993). *Infant cognition: Predicting later intellectual functioning.* Thousand Oaks, CA: Sage.

Colombo, J. (2001). The development of visual attention in infancy. *Annual Review of Psychology, 52,* 337–367.

Colombo, J. (2002). Infant attention grows up: The emergence of a developmental cognitive neuroscience perspective. *Current Directions in Psychological Science, 11,* 196–200.

Colombo, J., Kannass, K. N., Shaddy, J., Kundurthi, S., Maikranz, J. M., Anderson, C. J., Bkaga, O. M., & Carlson, S. E. (2004). Maternal DHA and the development of attention in infancy and toddlerhood. *Child Development, 75,* 1254–1267.

Coltrane, S., & Adams, M. (1997). Work-family imagery and gender stereotypes: Television and the reproduction of difference. *Journal of Vocational Behavior, 50,* 323–347.

Comings, D. E., Muhleman, D., Johnson, J. P., & MacMurray, J. P. (2002). Parent-daughter transmission of the androgen receptor gene as an explanation of the effect of father absence on age of menarche. *Child Development, 73*(4), 1046–1051.

Commissioner's Office of Research and Evaluation and Head Start Bureau, Department of Health and Human Services. (2001). Building their futures: How Early Head Start programs are enhancing the lives of infants and toddlers in low-income families. Summary report. Washington, DC: Author.

Committee on Obstetric Practice. (2002). ACOG committee opinion: Exercise during pregnancy and the postpartum period. *International Journal of Gynaecology & Obstetrics, 77*(1), 79–81.

Community Paediatrics Committee, Canadian Paediatrics Society. (2005). Management of primary nocturnal enuresis. *Paediatrics and Child Health, 10,* 611–614.

Conde-Agudelo, A., Rosas-Bermúdez, A., & Kafury-Goeta, A. C. (2006). Birth spacing and risk of adverse perinatal outcomes: A meta-analysis. *Journal of the American Medical Association, 295,* 1809–1823.

Conel, J. L. (1959). *The postnatal development of the human cerebral cortex.* Cambridge, MA: Harvard University Press.

Conger, J. J. (1988). Hostages to fortune: Youth, values, and the public interest. *American Psychologist, 43*(4), 291–300.

Connor, S. K. & Mcintyre, L. (2002). The Effects of Smoking and Drinking During Pregnancy. In Willms, J. D. *Vulnerable Children* (pp. 131–148). Edmonton, AB: The University of Alberta Press.

Connor, S., & Brink, S. (1999). *The impacts of non-parental care on child development.* Ottawa: Applied Research Branch, Strategic Policy, Human Resources Development Canada.

Constantino, J. N. (2003). Autistic traits in the general population: A twin study. *Archives of General Psychiatry, 60,* 524–530.

Constantino, J. N., Grosz, D., Saenger, P., Chandler, D. W., Nandi, R., & Earls, F. J. (1993). Testosterone and aggression in children. *Journal of the Academy of Child and Adolescent Psychiatry, 32,* 1217–1222.

Cook, C. & Willms, J. D. (2002). Balancing work and family life. In Willms, J. D. *Vulnerable Children.* Edmonton, AB: The University of Alberta Press.

Coon, H., Fulker, D. W., DeFries, J. C., & Plomin, R. (1990). Home environment and cognitive ability of 7-year-old children in the Colorado Adoption Project: Genetic and environmental etiologies. *Developmental Psychology, 26,* 459–468.

Cooper, H. (1989, November). Synthesis of research on homework. *Educational Leadership,* 85–91.

Cooper, H., Lindsay, J. J., Nye, B., & Greathouse, S. (1998). Relationships among attitudes about homework, amount of homework assigned and completed, and student achievement. *Journal of Educational Psychology, 90,* 70–83.

Cooper, H., Valentine, J. C., Nye, B., & Lindsay, J. J. (1999). Relationships between five after-school activities and academic achievement. *Journal of Educational Psychology, 91*(2), 369–378.

Cooper, R. P., & Aslin, R. N. (1990). Preference for infant-directed speech in the first month after birth. *Child Development, 61,* 1584–1595.

Cooper, W. O., Hernandez-Diaz, S., Arbogast, P. G., Dudley, J. A., Dyer, S., Gideon, P. S., Hall, K., & Ray, W. A. (2006). Major congenital formations after first-trimester exposure to ACE inhibitors. *New England Journal of Medicine, 354,* 2443–2451.

Coping with Life. (Undated). Retrieved August 21 2007 from http://www.phac-aspc.gc.ca/dca-dea/publications/pdf/hbsc_05ch5_e.pdf

Coplan, R. J., & Rubin, K. H. (1998). Social play. In D. P. Fromberg & D. Bergen (Eds.), *Play from birth to twelve and beyond: Contexts, perspectives, and meanings* (pp. 368–377). New York: Garland.

Coplan, R. J., Gavinski-Molina, M., Lagacè-Sèguin, D. G., & Wichman, C. (2001). When girls versus boys play alone: Nonsocial play and adjustment in kindergarten. *Developmental Psychology, 37*(4), 464–474.

Coplan, R. J., Prakash, K., O'Neil, K., & Armer, M. (2004). Do you "want" to play? Distinguishing between conflicted-shyness and social disinterest in early childhood. *Developmental Psychology, 40,* 244–258.

Corbeil, J.-P. (2003). 30 years of education: Canada's language groups. *Canadian Social Trends.* Statistics Canada Catalogue No. 11-008, p. 8–12.

Corbet, A., Long, W., Schumacher, R., Gerdes, J., Cotton, R., & the American Exosurf Neonatal Study Group 1. (1995). Double-blind developmental evaluation at 1-year corrected age of 597 premature infants with birth weight from 500 to 1,350 grams enrolled in three placebo-controlled trials of prophylactic synthetic surfactant. *Journal of Pediatrics, 126,* S5–S12.

Corbin, C. (1973). *A textbook of motor development.* Dubuque, IA: Wm. C. Brown Publishers.

Cornelius, M. D., & Day, N. L. (2000). The effects of tobacco use during and after pregnancy on exposed children. *Alcohol Research and Health, 24,* 242–249.

Correa, A., Botto, L., Liu, V., Mulinare, J., & Erickson, J. D. (2003). Do multivitamin supplements attenuate the risk for diabetes-associated birth defects? *Pediatrics, 111,* 1146–1151.

Costello, E. J., Compton, S. N., Keeler, G., & Angold, A. (2003). Relationship between poverty and psychopathology: A natural experiment. *Journal of the American Medical Association, 290,* 2023–2029.

Costello, S. (1990, December). Yani's monkeys: Lessons in form and freedom. *School Arts,* pp. 10–11.

Coster, W. J., Gersten, M. S., Beeghly, M., & Cicchetti, D. (1989). Communicative functioning in maltreated toddlers. *Developmental Psychology, 25,* 1020–1029.

Coté, S, Zoccolillo, M., Tremblay, R. E., Nagin, D., & Vitaro, F. (2001). Predicting girls' conduct disorder in adolescence from childhood trajectories of disruptive behaviors. *Journal of the American Academy of Child and Adolescent Psychiatry, 40,* 678–684.

Council of Ministers of Education (Canada) & OECD. (2006). *Country Profile for Canada.* Toronto, ON: Council of Ministers of Education (Canada).

Council of Ministers of Education, Canada. (1999). *School achievement indicators program: 1998 report on reading and writing assessment.* Toronto: Author.

Council of Ministers of Education, Canada. (2002). *School achievement indicators program: Mathematics III.* Toronto: Author.

Council on Scientific Affairs of the American Medical Association. (1993). Adolescents as victims of family violence. *Journal of the American Medical Association, 276,* 1850–1856.

Council on Sports Medicine and Fitness and Council on School Health. (2006). Active healthy living: Prevention of childhood obesity through increased physical activity. *Pediatrics, 117,* 1834–1842.

Cowan, N., Nugent, L. D., Elliott, E. M., Ponomarev, I., & Saults, J. S. (1999). The role of attention in the development of short-term memory: Age differences in the verbal span of apprehension. *Child Development, 70,* 1082–1097.

Cowan, P. A., Cowan, C. P., Schulz, M. S., & Heming, G. (1994). Prebirth to preschool family factors in children's adaptation to kindergarten. In R. D. Parke & S. G. Kellam (Eds.), *Exploring family relationships with other social contexts. Family research consortium: Advances in family research* (pp. 75–114). Hillsdale, NJ: Erlbaum.

Coyle, T. R., & Bjorklund, D. F. (1997). Age differences in, and consequences of, multiple- and variable-strategy use on a multitrial sort-recall task. *Developmental Psychology, 33,* 372–380.

CPS Joint Statement: Canadian Foundation for the Study of Infant Deaths, the Canadian Institute of Child Health, the Canadian Paediatric Society and Health Canada (1999). Reducing the risk of sudden infant death syndrome in Canada. *Paediatrics & Child Health, 4,* 223–224.

Craig, C. L., Cameron, C., Russell, S. J., & Beaulieu, A. (2001). *Increasing physical activity: Supporting children's participation.* Ottawa, ON: Canadian Fitness and Lifestyle Research Institute.

Craig, K. D., Gilbert-MacLeod, C. A., & Lilley, C. M. (2000). Crying as an indicator of pain in infants. In R. G. Barr, B. Hopkins, & J. A. Green (Eds.), *Crying as a sign, a symptom, and a signal: Clinical, emotional and developmental aspects of infant and toddler crying* (pp. 23–40). London: MacKeith Press.

Crain-Thoreson, C., & Dale, P. S. (1992). Do early talkers become early readers? Linguistic precocity, preschool language, and emergent literacy. *Developmental Psychology, 28,* 421–429.

Crary, D. (2007, January 6). After years of growth, foreign adoptions by Americans decline sharply. *Associated Press.*

Crawford, C. (1998). Environments and adaptations: Then and now. In C. Crawford & D. L. Krebs (Eds.), *Handbook of evolutionary psychology: Ideas, issues, and applications* (pp. 275–302). Mahwah, NJ: Erlbaum.

Crawford, J. (2002). Obituary: The Bilingual Ed Act, 1968–2002. *Rethinking Schools Online.* Retrieved August 26, 2006, from http://www.rethinkingschool.org/special reports/bilingual/Bill64.shtml

Crawford, J. (in press). The decline of bilingual education: How to reverse a troubling trend? *International Multilingual Research Journal.*

Crick, N. R., & Dodge, K. A. (1994). A review and reformulation of social information-processing mechanisms in children's social adjustment. *Psychological Bulletin, 115,* 74–101.

Crick, N. R., & Dodge, K. A. (1996). Social information-processing mechanisms in reactive and proactive aggression. *Child Development, 67,* 993–1002.

Crick, N. R., & Grotpeter, J. K. (1995). Relational aggression, gender, and social-psychological adjustment. *Child Development, 66,* 710–722.

Crick, N. R., Bigbee, M. A., & Howes, C. (1996). Gender differences in children's normative beliefs about aggression: How do I hurt thee? Let me count the ways. *Child Development, 67,* 1003–1014.

Crick, N. R., Casas, J. F., & Nelson, D. A. (2002). Toward a more comprehensive understanding of peer maltreatment: Studies of relational victimization. *Current Directions in Psychological Science, 11*(3), 98–101.

Crisp, J., Ungerer, J. A., & Goodnow, J. J. (1996). The impact of experience on children's understanding of illness. *Journal of Pediatric Psychology, 21,* 57–72.

Crockenberg, S. C. (2003). Rescuing the baby from the bathwater: How gender and temperament influence how child care affects child development. *Child Development, 74,* 1034–1038.

Crockenberg, S., & Lourie, A. (1996). Parents' conflict strategies with children and children's conflict strategies with peers. *Merrill-Palmer Quarterly, 42,* 495–518.

Croll, J. (2005). Body image and adolescents. Retrieved on August 21, 2007 from http://www.epi.umn.edu/let/pubs/img/adol_ch13.pdf

Cronk, L. B., Ye, B., Tester, D. J., Vatta, M., Makielski, J. C., & Ackerman, M. J. (2006, May). *Identification of CAV3-encoded caveolin-3 mutations in sudden infant death syndrome.* Presentation at Heart Rhythm 2006, the 27th Annual Scientific Sessions of the Heart Rhythm Society, Boston.

Crouter, A., & Larson, R. (Eds.). (1998). *Temporal rhythms in adolescence: Clocks, calendars, and the coordination of daily life (New Directions in Child and Adolescent Development, 82).* San Francisco: Jossey-Bass.

Crouter, A. C., & Maguire, M. C. (1998). Seasonal and weekly rhythms: Windows into variability in family socialization experiences in early adolescence. In A. C. Crouter & R. Larson (Eds.), *Temporal rhythms in adolescence: Clocks, calendars, and the coordination of daily life (New Directions for Child and Adolescent Development, 82).* San Francisco: Jossey-Bass.

Crouter, A. C., MacDermid, S. M., McHale, S. M., & Perry-Jenkins, M. (1990). Parental monitoring and perception of children's school performance and conduct in dual- and single-earner families. *Developmental Psychology, 26,* 649–657.

Crow, S. J. (2006). Fluoxetine treatment of anorexia nervosa: Important but disappointing results. *Journal of the American Medical Association, 295,* 2659–2660.

Crowley, S. L. (1993, October). Grandparents to the rescue. *AARP Bulletin,* pp. 1, 16–17.

CTV.ca. (2007). Teen pregnancy rate at all-time low, study finds. Retrieved September 3, 2007 from http://www.ctv.ca/servlet/ArticleNews/story/CTVNews/20070518/teen_pregnancy_070518?s_name=&no_ads=

Cui, M., Conger, R. D., & Lorenz, F. O. (2005). Predicting change in adolescent adjustment from change in marital problems. *Developmental Psychology, 41,* 812–823.

Cukier, W. (2000). Firearms regulation: Canada in the international context. *Public Health Agency of Canada: Chronic Diseases in Canada, 19.* Retrieved July 25, 2007 from http://www.phac-aspc.gc.ca/publicat/cdic-mcc/19-1/d_e.html.

Cummings, E. M., Iannotti, R. J., & Zahn-Waxler, C. (1989). Aggression between peers in early childhood: Individual continuity and developmental change. *Child Development, 60,* 887–895.

Cunliffe, T. (1992). Arresting youth crime: A review of social skills training with young offenders. *Adolescence, 27,* 891–900.

Cunningham, F. G., & Leveno, K. J. (1995). Childbearing among older women: The message is cautiously optimistic. *New England Journal of Medicine, 333,* 1002–1004.

Curtin, S. C., & Martin, J. A. (2000). Births: Preliminary data for 1999. *National Vital Statistics Reports, 48*(14). Hyattsville, MD: National Center for Health Statistics.

Curtin, S. C., & Park, M. M. (1999). *Trends in the attendant, place, and timing of births, and in the use of obstetric interventions: United States, 1989–97* (National Vital Statistics

Reports, 47[27]). Hyattsville, MD: National Center for Health Statistics.

Curtiss, S. (1977). *Genie.* New York: Academic Press.

Cutting, A. L., & Dunn, J. (1999). Theory of mind, emotion understanding, language, and family background: Individual differences and interrelations. *Child Development, 70,* 853–865.

Cutz, E., Perrin, D. G., Hackman, R., & Czegledy-Nagy, E. N. (1996). Maternal smoking and pulmonary neuroendocrine cells in sudden infant death syndrome. *Pediatrics, 88,* 668–672.

Czikszentmihalyi, M. (1996). *Creativity: Flow and the psychology of discovery and invention.* New York: HarperCollins.

D'Alton, M. E., & DeCherney, A. H. (1993). Prenatal diagnosis. *New England Journal of Medicine, 32*(2), 114–120.

Dahinten, V. S. & Willms, J. D. (2002). The effects fo adolescent child-bearing on children's outcomes. In Willms, J. D. *Vulnerable Children.* (Pg. 229–258). University of Alberta Press.

Daiute, C., Hartup, W. W., Sholl, W., & Zajac, R. (1993, March). *Peer collaboration and written language development: A study of friends and acquaintances.* Paper presented at the meeting of the Society for Research in Child Development, New Orleans.

Dale, P. S., Price, T. S., Bishop, D. V. M., & Plomin, R. (2003). Outcomes of early language delay: I. Predicting persistent and transient language difficulties at 3 and 4 years. *Journal of Speech, Language, and Hearing Research, 46,* 544–560.

Dale, P. S., Simonoff, E., Bishop, D. V. M., Eley, T. C., Oliver, B., Price, T. S., et al. (1998). Genetic influence on language delay in two-year-old children. Nature Neuroscience, 1, 324–328.

Daley, P. (2003, July 19). "Miracle baby" speaks of life after the test tube. *The Age.* Retrieved July 22, 2007 from http://www.theage.com.au/articles/2003/07/18/1058035200790.html.

Daly, K. J. and Sobol, M. P. (1993). *Adoption in Canada: Final report, National Adoption Study.* Guelph, ON: University of Guelph.

Daly, R., (2005). Drop in youth antidepressant use prompts call for FDA monitoring. *Psychiatric News, 40*(19), 18.

Danesi, M. (1994). *Cool: The signs and meanings of adolescence.* Toronto: University of Toronto Press.

Daniel, M. H. (1997). Intelligence testing: Status and trends. *American Psychologist, 52,* 1038–1045.

Darling, N., & Steinberg, L. (1993). Parenting style as context: An integrative model. *Psychological Bulletin, 113,* 487–496.

Darlington, R. B. (1991). The long-term effects of model preschool programs. In L. Okagaki & R. J. Sternberg (Eds.), *Directors of development: Influences on the development of children's thinking.* Hillsdale, NJ: Erlbaum.

Darwin, C. (1995). *The origin of species.* New York: Gramercy. (Original work published 1859.)

Datar, A., & Sturm, R. (2004a). Childhood overweight and parent- and teacher-reported behavior problems. *Archives of Pediatric and Adolescent Medicine, 158,* 804–810.

Datar, A., & Sturm, R. (2004b). Duke Physical education in elementary school and body mass index: Evidence from the Early Childhood Longitudinal Study. *American Journal of Public Health, 94,* 1501–1507.

Datar, A., Sturm, R., & Magnabosco, J. L. (2004). Childhood overweight and academic performance: National study of kindergartners and first-graders. *Obesity Research, 12,* 58–68.

David and Lucile Packard Foundation. (2004). Children, families, and foster care: Executive summary. *The Future of Children, 14*(1). Available: http://www.futureofchildren.org

Davidson, J. I. F. (1998). Language and play: Natural partners. In D. P. Fromberg & D. Bergen (Eds.), *Play from birth to twelve and beyond: Contexts, perspectives, and meanings* (pp. 175–183). New York: Garland.

Davidson, R. J., & Fox, N. A. (1989). Frontal brain asymmetry predicts infants' response to maternal separation. *Journal of Abnormal Psychology, 948*(2), 58–64.

Davis, B. E., Moon, R. Y., Sachs, H. C., & Ottolini, M. C. (1998). Effects of sleep position on infant motor development. *Pediatrics, 102,* 1135–1140.

Davis, D. L., Gottlieb, M. B., & Stampnitzky, J. R. (1998). Reduced ratio of male to female births in several industrial countries. *Journal of the American Medical Association, 279,* 1018–1023.

Davis, M., & Emory, E. (1995). Sex differences in neonatal stress reactivity. *Child Development, 66,* 14–27.

Davison, K. K., Susman, E. J., & Birch, L. L. (2003). Percent body fat at age 5 predicts earlier pubertal development among girls at age 9. *Pediatrics, 111,* 815–821.

Daws, D., & Kent, D.A. (2006). Poisoning in British Columbia. *BC Medical Journal, 48,* 35. Retrieved November 12, 2007 from www.bcma.org/public/bc_medical_journal/bcmj/2006/jan_feb_2006/cdc.asp.

Dawson, D. A. (1991). Family structure and children's health and well-being: Data from the 1988 National Health Interview Survey on child health. *Journal of Marriage and the Family, 53,* 573–584.

Dawson, G., Frey, K., Panagiotides, H., Osterling, J., & Hessl, D. (1997). Infants of depressed mothers exhibit atypical frontal brain activity: A replication and extension of previous findings. *Journal of Child Psychology & Allied Disciplines, 38,* 179–186.

Dawson, G., Frey, K., Panagiotides, H., Yamada, E., Hessl, D. and Osterling, J. (1999). Infants of depressed mothers exhibit atypical frontal electrical brain activity during interactions with mother and with a familiar nondepressed adult. *Child Development, 70,* 1058–1066.

Dawson, G., Klinger, L. G., Panagiotides, H., Hill, D., & Spieker, S. (1992). Frontal lobe activity and affective behavior of infants of mothers with depressive symptoms. *Child Development, 63,* 725–737.

Day, J. C., Janus, A., & Davis, J. (2005). Computer and Internet use in the United States: 2003. *Current Population Reports* (P23-208). Washington, DC: U.S. Census Bureau.

De Bellis, M. D., Keshavan, M. S., Beers, S. R., Hall, J., Frustaci, K., Masalehdan, A., Noll, J., & Boring, A. M. (2001). Sex differences in brain maturation during childhood and adolescence. *Cerebral Cortex, 11,* 552–557.

de Castro, B. O., Veerman, J. W., Koops, W., Bosch, J. D., & Monshouwer, H. J. (2002). Hostile attribution of intent and aggressive behavior: A meta-analysis. *Child Development, 73,* 916–934.

Dean, H. J., Mundy, R. L., & Moffatt, M. (1992). Non-insulin-dependent diabetes mellitus in Indian children in Manitoba. *Canadian Medical Association Journal, 148,* 147.

Deardorff, J., Gonzales, N. A., Christopher, S., Roosa, M. W., & Millsap, R. E. (2005). Early puberty and adolescent pregnancy: The influence of alcohol use. *Pediatrics, 116,* 1451–1456.

Deaths: Injuries, 2002. *National Vital Statistics Reports, 54*(10). Hyattsville MD: National Center for Health Statistics.

DeBell, M., & Chapman, C. (2006). *Computer and Internet use by students in 2003: Statistical analysis report* (NCES 2006-065). Washington, DC: National Center for Education Statistics.

DeCasper, A. J., & Fifer, W. P. (1980). Of human bonding: Newborns prefer their mothers' voices. *Science, 208,* 1174–1176.

DeCasper, A. J., & Spence, M. J. (1986). Prenatal maternal speech influences newborns' perceptions of speech sounds. *Infant Behavior and Development, 9,* 133–150.

DeCasper, A. J., Lecanuet, J. P., Busnel, M. C., Granier-Deferre, C., & Maugeais, R. (1994). Fetal reactions to recurrent maternal speech. *Infant Behavior and Development, 17,* 159–164.

Dekovic, M., & Janssens, J. M. A. M. (1992). Parents' child-rearing style and child's sociometric status. *Developmental Psychology, 28,* 925–932.

Del Carmen, R. D., Pedersen, F. A., Huffman, L. C., & Bryan, Y. E. (1993). Dyadic distress management predicts subsequent security of attachment. *Infant Behavior and Development, 16,* 131–147.

Dell, C. A., Dell, D. E. & Hopkins, C. (2005). Resiliency and holistic inhalant abuse treatment. *Journal of Aboriginal Health.* Retrieved August 22 2007 from http://www.naho.ca/english/documents/JournalVol2No1ENG3abusetreatment.pdf

DeLoache, J. S. (2000). Dual representation and young children's use of scale models. *Child Development, 71,* 329–338.

DeLoache, J. S. (2004). Becoming symbol-minded. *Trends in Cognitive Science, 8,* 66–70.

DeLoache, J. S. (2006). Mindful of symbols. *Scientific American Mind, 17,* 70–75.

DeLoache, J. S., Miller, K. F., & Pierroutsakos, S. L. (1998). Reasoning and problem solving. In D. Kuhn & R. S. Siegler (Eds.), *Handbook of child psychology: Vol. 2. Cognition, perception, and language* (5th ed., pp. 801–850). New York: Wiley.

DeLoache, J. S., Pierroutsakos, S. L., & Uttal, D. H. (2003). The origins of pictorial competence. *Current Directions in Psychological Science, 12,* 114–118.

DeLoache, J. S., Uttal, D. H., & Rosengren, K. S. (2004). Scale errors offer evidence for a perception-action dissociation early in life. *Science, 304,* 1027–1029.

DeLoache, J., & Gottlieb, A. (2000). If Dr. Spock were born in Bali: Raising a world of babies. In J. DeLoache & A. Gottlieb (Eds.), *A world of babies: Imagined childcare guides for seven societies* (pp. 1–27). New York: Cambridge University Press.

Delveaux, K. D., & Daniels, T. (2000). Children's social cognitions: Physically and relationally aggressive strategies and children's goals in peer conflict situations. *Merrill-Palmer Quarterly, 46,* 672–691.

Denham, S. A., Blair, K. A., DeMulder, E., Levitas, J., Sawyer, K., Auerbach-Major, S., & Queenan, P. (2003). Preschool emotional competence: Pathway to social competence? *Child Development, 74,* 238–256.

Dennis, T. (2006). Emotional self-regulation in preschoolers: The interplay of child approach reactivity, parenting, and control capacities. *Developmental Psychology, 42,* 84–97.

Dennis, W. (1936). A bibliography of baby biographies. *Child Development, 7,* 71–73.

Dennison, B. A., Erb, T. A., & Jenkins, P. L. (2002). Television viewing and television

in bedroom associated with overweight risk among low-income preschool children.

Denton, K., West, J., & Walston, J. (2003). Reading—young children's achievement and classroom experiences: Findings from The Condition of Education 2003. Washington, DC: National Center for Education Statistics.

Department of Environmental Health. (2003). Environmental risk factors for asthma in children. Health Effects Review. Retrieved on August 7, 2007 from http://www.ijc.org/rel/pdf/04_asthma-winter2003.pdf

Department of Immunization, Vaccines, and Biologicals, World Health Organization; United Nations Children's Fund; Global Immunization Division, National Center for Immunization and Respiratory Diseases (proposed); & McMorrow, M. (2006). Vaccine preventable deaths and the global immunization vision and strategy, 2006–2015. *Morbidity and Mortality Weekly Report, 55,* 511–515.

Department of Justice Canada. (1996). Selected statistics on Canadian families and family law: Second Edition. Retrieved from www.justice.gc.ca/en/ps/sup/pub/selstats2000/chap1.html#LPF on July 22, 2007.

Department of Justice Canada. (2003). *Child Abuse: A Fact Sheet* [Online] Ottawa: Author. Retrieved October 12, 2007 from http://www.justice.gc.ca/en/ps/fm/childafs.html

Department of Justice Canada (2004). *Assisted Human Reproduction Act.* Retrieved July 22, 2007 from http://laws.justice.gc.ca/en/ShowFullDoc/cs/A-13.4///en

Department of Justice Canada. (2005). When parents separate: Further findings from the national longitudinal survey of children and youth: 2004-FCY-6E. Retrieved August 17, 2007 from http://justicecanada.ca/en/ps/pad/reports/2004-FCY-6/chap2.html

Deslandes, R., Potvin, P., & Leclerc, D. (1999). Family characteristics as predictors of school achievement: Parental involvement as a mediator. *McGill Journal of Education, 34,* 135–153.

Desrochers, S., Ricard, M., Decarie, T.-G., & Allard, L. (1994). Developmental synchrony between social referencing and Piagetian sensorimotor causality. *Infant Behavior and Development, 17,* 303–309.

Detrich, R., Phillips, R., & Durett, D. (2002). Critical issue: Dynamic debate— determining the evolving impact of charter schools. North Central Regional Educational Laboratory. Retrieved from http://www.ncrel.org/sdrs/areas/issues/ envrnmnt/go/go800.htm

Devaney, B., Johnson, A., Maynard, R., & Trenholm, C. (2002). *The evaluation of abstinence education programs funded under Title V, Section 510: Interim report.* Washington, DC: U.S. Department of Health and Human Services.

Devlin, B., Scherer, S., & the Autism Genome Project Consortium. (2007, February 18). Mapping autism risk loci using genetic linkage and chromosomal rearrangements. Retrieved February 20, 2007, from http://www.nature.com/ng/journal/vaop/ncurrent/abs1985.html.

DeVoe, J. F., Peter, K., Noonan, M., Snyder, T. D., Baum, K. & U. S. Departments of Education and Justice. (2005). *Indicators of school crime and safety: 2005* (NCES 2006-001/NCJ210697). Washington, DC: U.S. Government Printing Office.

deVries, A. P. J., Kassam-Adams, N., Cnaan, A., Sherman-Slate, E., Gallagher, P. R., & Winston, F. K. (1999). Looking beyond the physical injury: Posttraumatic stress disorder

in children and parents after pediatric traffic injury. *Pediatrics, 104,* 1293–1299.

Dewing, P., Shi, T., Horvath, S., & Vilain, E. (2003). Sexually dimorphic gene expression in mouse brain precedes gonadal differentiation. *Molecular Brain Research, 118,* 82–90.

Dexema, D. S. (2006). Conducting ethical research in pediatrics: A brief historical overview and review of pediatric regulations. *The Journal of Pediatrics, 149,* S3–S11.

Dey, A. N., Schiller, J. S., & Tai, D. A. (2004). Summary health statistics for U.S. children: National Health Interview Survey, 2002. *Vital Health Statistics 10* (221). Bethesda, MD: National Center for Health Statistics.

Diamond, A. (1991). Neuropsychological insights into the meaning of object concept development. In S. Carey & R. Gelman (Eds.), *Epigenesis of mind* (pp. 67–110). Hillsdale, NJ: Erlbaum.

Diamond, L. M. (1998). Development of sexual orientation among adolescent and young adult women. *Developmental Psychology, 34*(5), 1085–1095.

Diamond, L. M. (2000). Sexual identity, attractions, and behavior among young sexual-minority women over a 2-year period. *Developmental Psychology, 36,* 241–250.

Diamond, L. M., & Savin-Williams, R. C. (2003). The intimate relationships of sexual-minority youths. In G. R. Adams & M. D. Berzonsky (Eds.), *Blackwell handbook of adolescence* (pp. 393–412). Malden, MA: Blackwell.

Diamond, M. C. (1988). *Enriching heredity.* New York: Free Press.

Diamond, M., & Sigmundson, H. K. (1997). Sex reassignment at birth: Long-term review and clinical implications. *Archives of Pediatric and Adolescent Medicine, 151,* 298–304.

Diaz, R. M. (1983). Thought and two languages: The impact of bilingualism on cognitive development. *Review of Research in Education, 10,* 23–54.

Dick, D. M., Rose, R. J., Viken, R. J., & Kaprio, J. (2000). Pubertal timing and substance use: Association between and within families across late adolescence. *Developmental Psychology, 36*(2), 180–189.

Dietert, R. R. (2005). Developmental immunotoxicology (DIT): Is DIT testing necessary to ensure safety? Proceedings of the 14th Immunotoxicology Summer School, Lyon, France, October 2005, 246–257.

DiFranza, J. R., & Lew, R. A. (1995, April). Effect of maternal cigarette smoking on pregnancy complications and sudden infant death syndrome. *Journal of Family Practice, 40,* 385–394.

DiFranza, J. R., Aligne, C. A., & Weitzman, M. (2004). Prenatal and postnatal environmental tobacco smoke exposure and children's health. *Pediatrics, 113,* 1007–1015.

Dilworth-Bart, J. E., & Moore., C. F. (2006). Mercy mercy me: Social injustice and the prevention of environmental pollutant exposures among ethnic minority and poor children. (2006). *Child Development, 77*(2), 247–265.

DiMarco, M. A., Menke, E. M., & McNamara, T. (2001). Evaluating a support group for perinatal loss. *MCN American Journal of Maternal and Child Nursing, 26,* 135–140.

Dingfelder, S. (2004). Programmed for psychopathology? Stress during pregnancy may increase children's risk for mental illness, researchers say. *Monitor on Psychology, 35*(2), 56–57.

Dinkes, R., Forrest Cataldi, E., Kena, G., & Baum, K. (2006). *Indicators of school crime and safety: 2006* (NCES 2007003). National Center for Education Statistics. Retrieved

January 30, 2007, from http://nces.ed.gov/pubsearch/pubsinfo.asp?pubid=2007003

DiPietro, J. A. (2004). The role of prenatal maternal stress in child development. *Current Directions in Psychological Science, 13*(2), 71–74.

DiPietro, J. A., Caulfield, L. E., Costigan, K. A., Merialdi, M., Nguyen, R. H. N., Zavaleta, N., & Gurewitsch, E. D. (2004). Fetal neurobehavioral development: A tale of two cities. *Developmental Psychology, 40,* 445–456.

DiPietro, J. A., Hodgson, D. M., Costigan, K. A., & Johnson, T. R. B. (1996). Fetal antecedents of infant temperament. *Child Development, 67,* 2568–2583.

DiPietro, J. A., Hodgson, D. M., Costigan, K. A., Hilton, S. C., & Johnson, T. R. B. (1996). Fetal neurobehavioral development. *Child Development, 67,* 2553–2567.

DiPietro, J. A., Novak, M. F. S. X., Costigan, K. A., Atella, L. D., & Reusing, S. P. (in press). Maternal psychological distress during pregnancy in relation to child development at age two. *Child Development, 77,* 573–587.

DiPietro, J., Hilton, S., Hawkins, M., Costigan, K., & Pressman, E. (2002). Maternal stress and affect influences fetal neurobehavioral development. *Developmental Psychology, 38,* 659–668.

Dishion, T. J., McCord, J., & Poulin, F. (1999). When intervention harms. *American Psychologist, 54,* 755–764.

Dittmar, H., Halliwell, E., & Ive, S. (2006). Does Barbie make girls want to be thin? The effect of experimental exposure to images of dolls on the body image of 5- to 8-year-old girls. *Developmental Psychology, 42,* 283–292.

Dlugosz, L., Belanger, K., Helienbrand, K., Holfard, T. R., Leaderer, B., & Bracken, M. B. (1996). Maternal caffeine consumption and spontaneous abortion: A prospective cohort study. *Epidemiology, 7,* 250–255.

Dodge, K. A., Bates, J. E., & Pettit, S. G. (1990). Mechanisms in the cycle of violence. *Science, 250,* 1678–1683.

Dodge, K. A., Coie, J. D., Pettit, G. S., & Price, J. M. (1990). Peer status and aggression in boys' groups: Developmental and contextual analysis. *Child Development, 61,* 1289–1309.

Dodge, K. A., Dishion, T. J., & Lansford, J. E. (2006). Deviant peer influences in intervention and public policy for youth. *Social Policy Report, XX,* 3–19.

Doherty, G. (1997). *Zero to six: The basics for school readiness.* Report No. R-97-8E. Ottawa: Applied Research Branch, Strategic Policy, Human Resources Development Canada.

Dolan, B. (1999). From the field: Cognitive profiles of First Nations and Caucasian children referred for psychoeducational assessment. *Canadian Journal of School Psychology, 15,* 63–71.

Donovan, W. L., Leavitt, L. A., & Walsh, R. O. (1998). Conflict and depression predict maternal sensitivity to infant cries. *Infant Behavior and Development, 21,* 505–517.

Doré, R., Wagner, S., Brunet, J.-P., & Bélanger, N. (1999). *School integration of children with a disability in provinces and territories in Canada.* Commissioned paper submitted for the February 1999 PCERA Symposium. Retrieved September 20, 2002, from http://www.cmec.ca/stats/pcera/compaper/98-52en.pdf

Dorrance, N. & Peterson, L. (2003). National study of adolescent sexual health yields mixed results. Retrieved September 2, 2007 from http://qnc.queensu.ca/story_loader.php?id=3f5dedd7530e6

Dorsey, M. J., and Schneider, L. C. (2003). Improving asthma outcomes and self-management behaviors of inner-city children. *Pediatrics, 112,* 474.

Dougherty, T. M., & Haith, M. M. (1997). Infant expectations and reaction time as predictors of childhood speed of processing and IQ. *Developmental Psychology, 33,* 146–155.

Douglas, E. (2006). Familial violence socialization in childhood and later life approval of corporal punishment: A cross-cultural perspective. *American Journal of Orthopsychiatry, 76,* 23–30.

Downey, D. B., & Condron, D. J. (2004). Playing well with others in kindergarten: The benefit of siblings at home. *Journal of Marriage and Family, 66,* 333–350.

Dowshen, S., Crowley, J., & Palusci, V. J. (2004). Shaken baby/shaken impact syndrome. Retrieved February 17, 2007, from http://www.kidshealth.org/parent/medical/brain/shaken.html

Dozier, M., Stovall, K. C., Albus, K. E., & Bates, B. (2001). Attachment for infants in foster care: The role of caregiver state of mind. *Child Development, 72,* 1467–1477.

Dreher, M. C., Nugent, K., & Hudgins, R. (1994). Prenatal marijuana exposure and neonatal outcomes in Jamaica: An ethnographic study. *Pediatrics, 93,* 254–260.

Driedger, L. (2000). *Mennonites in the global village.* Toronto: University of Toronto Press.

Drug Policy Alliance. (2004, June 23). *South Carolina v. McKnight.* Retrieved April 6, 2005, from http://www.drugpolicy.org/law/womenpregnan/mcknight/

Drumm, P., & Jackson, D. W. (1996). Developmental changes in questioning strategies during adolescence. *Journal of Adolescent Research, 11,* 285–305.

Dubé, E. M., & Savin-Williamn, R. C. (1999). Sexual identity development among ethnic sexual-minority youths. *Developmental Psychology, 35*(6), 1389–1398.

Dube, S. R., Anda, R. F., Felitti, V. J., Chapman, D. P., Williamson, D. F., & Giles, W. H. (2001). Childhood abuse, household dysfunction, and the risk of attempted suicide throughout the life span: Findings from the Adverse Childhood Experiences Study. *Journal of the American Medical Association, 286*(24), 3089–3096.

Dubowitz, H. (1999). The families of neglected children. In M. E. Lamb (Ed.), *Parenting and child development in "nontraditional" families* (pp. 372–345). Mahwah, NJ: Erlbaum.

Duenwald, M. (2003, July 15). After 25 years, new ideas in the prenatal test tube. *New York Times.* Retrieved July 22, 2007, from http://www.nytimes.com

Duke, J., Huhman, M., & Heitzler, C. (2003). Physical activity levels among children aged 9–13 years—United States, 2002. *Morbidity and Mortality Weekly Report, 52,* 785–788.

Duncan, G. J., & Brooks-Gunn, J. (1997). Income effects across the life span: Integration and interpretation. In G. J. Duncan & J. Brooks-Gunn (Eds.), *Consequences of growing up poor* (pp. 596–610). New York: Russell Sage Foundation.

Dundas, S., & Kaufman, M. (2000). The Toronto lesbian family study. *Journal of Homosexuality, 40,* 65–79.

Dundy, E. (1985). *Elvis and Gladys.* New York: Dell.

Dunham, P. J., Dunham, F., & Curwin, A. (1993). Joint-attentional states and lexical acquisition at 18 months. *Developmental Psychology, 29,* 827–831.

Dunn, J. (1985). *Sisters and brothers.* Cambridge, MA: Harvard University Press.

Dunn, J. (1991). Young children's understanding of other people: Evidence from observations within the family. In D. Frye & C. Moore (Eds.), *Children's theories of mind: Mental states and social understanding.* Hillsdale, NJ: Erlbaum.

Dunn, J. (1996). Sibling relationships and perceived self-competence: Patterns of stability between childhood and early adolescence. In A. J. Sameroff & M. M. Haith (Eds.), *The five to seven year shift: The age of reason and responsibility* (pp. 253–269). Chicago: University of Chicago Press.

Dunn, J., & Hughes, C. (2001). "I got some swords and you're dead!": Violent fantasy, antisocial behavior, friendship, and moral sensibility in young children. *Child Development, 72,* 491–505.

Dunn, J., & Kendrick, C. (1982). *Siblings: Love, envy and understanding.* Cambridge, MA: Harvard University Press.

Dunn, J., & Munn, P. (1985). Becoming a family member: Family conflict and the development of social understanding in the second year. *Child Development, 56,* 480–492.

Dunn, J., Brown, J., Slomkowski, C., Tesla, C., & Youngblade, L. (1991). Young children's understanding of other people's feelings and beliefs: Individual differences and antecedents. *Child Development, 62,* 1352–1366.

Dunning, P. (2000). Aboriginal head start. *Education Canada, 39*(4), 38–39.

Dunson, D. (2002). *Late breaking research session. Increasing infertility with increasing age: Good news and bad news for older couples.* Paper presented at 18th Annual Meeting of the European Society of Human Reproduction and Embryology, Vienna.

Dunson, D. B., Colombo, B., & Baird, D. D. (2002). Changes with age in the level and duration of fertility in the menstrual cycle. *Human Reproduction, 17,* 1399–1403.

DuPont, R. L. (1983). Phobias in children. *Journal of Pediatrics, 102,* 999–1002.

DuRant, R. H., Smith, J. A., Kreiter, S. R., & Krowchuk, D. P. (1999). The relationship between early age of onset of initial substance use and engaging in multiple health risk behaviors among young adolescents. *Archives of Pediatrics & Adolescent Medicine, 153,* 286–291.

Durrant, J. E. (1995). Culture, corporal punishment, and child abuse. In K. Covell (Ed.), *Readings in child development: A Canadian perspective.* (pp. 28–48). Toronto: Nelson.

Durrant, J. E., Broberg, A. G., & Rose-Krasnor, L. (1999). Predicting mother's use of physical punishment during mother–child conflicts in Sweden and Canada. In C. C. Piotrowski & P. D. Hastings (eds.), *Conflict as a context for understanding maternal beliefs about child rearing and children's misbehaviour. (New Directions for Child and Adolescent Development, 86).* San Francisco: Jossey-Bass Publishers.

Dwyer, T., Ponsonby, A. L., Blizzard, L., Newman, N. M., & Cochrane, J. A. (1995). The contribution of changes in the prevalence of prone sleeping position to the decline in sudden infant death syndrome in Tasmania. *Journal of the American Medical Association, 273,* 783–789.

Dyl, J., Kittler, J., Phillips, K. A., & Hunt, J. I. (2006). Body dysmorphic disorder and other clinically significant body image concerns in adolescent psychiatric inpatients: Prevalence and clinical characteristics. *Child Psychiatry and Human Development, 36*(4), 369–382.

Dzakpasu, S., Joseph, K. S., Kramer, M. S., & Allen, A. C. (2000). The Matthew Effect: Infant mortality in Canada and internationally. *Pediatrics, 106,* 1–5.

East, P. L., & Khoo, S. T. (2005). Longitudinal pathways linking family factors and sibling relationship qualities to adolescent substance use and sexual risk behaviors. *Journal of Family Psychology, 19,* 571–580.

Eating disorders—Part I. (1997, October). *The Harvard Mental Health Letter,* pp. 1–5.

Eating disorders—Part II. (1997, November). *The Harvard Mental Health Letter,* pp. 1–5.

Eaton, W. O., & Enns, L. R. (1986). Sex differences in human motor activity level. *Psychological Bulletin, 100,* 19–28.

Eccles, A. (1982). *Obstetrics and gynaecology in Tudor and Stuart England.* Kent, OH: Kent State University Press.

Eccles, J. S. (2004). Schools, academic motivation, and stage-environment fit. In R. M. Lerner & L. Steinberg (Eds.), *Handbook of adolescent development* (2nd ed., pp. 125–153). Hoboken, NJ: Wiley.

Eccles, J. S., Wigfield, A., & Byrnes, J. (2003). Cognitive development in adolescence. In Weiner, I. B. (Ed.), R. M. Lerner, M.A. Easterbrooks, and J. Mistry (Vol Eds.), *Handbook of psychology: Vol. 6. Developmental psychology.* New York: John Wiley and Sons.

Echeland, Y., Epstein, D. J., St-Jacques, B., Shen, L., Mohler, J., McMahon, J. A., & McMahon, A. P. (1993). Sonic hedgehog, a member of a family of putative signality molecules, is implicated in the regulation of CNS polarity. *Cell, 75,* 1417–1430.

Eckenrode, J., Laird, M., & Doris, J. (1993). School performance and disciplinary problems among abused and neglected children. *Developmental Psychology, 29,* 53–62.

Eckerman, C. O., & Didow, S. M. (1996). Nonverbal imitation and toddlers' mastery of verbal means of achieving coordinated action. *Developmental Psychology, 32,* 141–152.

Eckerman, C. O., & Stein, M. R. (1982). The toddler's emerging interactive skills. In K. H. Rubin & H. S. Ross (Eds.), *Peer relationships and social skills in childhood.* New York: Springer-Verlag.

Eckerman, C. O., Davis, C. C., & Didow, S. M. (1989). Toddlers' emerging ways of achieving social coordination with a peer. *Child Development, 60,* 440–453.

Eddleman, K. A., Malone, F. D., Sullivan, L., Dukes, K., Berkowitz, R. L., & Kharbutli, Y., (2006). Pregnancy loss rates after midtrimester amniocentesis. *Obstetrics and Gynecology, 108*(5), 1067–1072.

Eden, G. F., Jones, K. M., Cappell, K., Gareau, L., Wood, F. B., Zeffiro, T. A.. et al., (2004). Neural changes following remediation in adult developmental dyslexia. *Neuron, 44,* 411–422.

Eder, W., Ege, M. J., & von Mutius, E. (2006). The asthma epidemic. *New England Journal of Medicine, 355,* 2226–2235.

Edwards, C. P. (1981). The comparative study of the development of moral judgment and reasoning. In R. Monroe, R. Monroe, & B. B. Whiting (Eds.), *Handbook of cross-cultural human development.* New York: Garland.

Edwards, C. P. (1994, April). Cultural relativity meets best practice, or, anthropology and early education, a promising friendship. Paper presented at the meeting of the American Educational Research Association, New Orleans.

Edwards, K. I. (1993). Obesity, anorexia, and bulimia. *Clinical Nutrition, 77,* 899–909.

Egan, M. F., Straub, R. E., Goldberg, T. E. Yakub I., Callicott, J. H., Hariri, A. R., Mattay, V. S., Bertolino, A., Hyde, T. M., Shannon-Weickert, C., Akil, M., Crook, J., Vakkalanka, R. K., Balkissoon, R., Gibbs, R. A., Kleinman, J. E., Weinberger, D. R. (2004). Variation in GRM3 affects cognition, prefrontal glutamate, and risk for schizophrenia. *Proceedings of the National Academy of Sciences (USA), 101*(34), 12604–12609.

Egbuono, L., & Starfield, B. (1982). Child health and social status. *Pediatrics, 69,* 550–557.

Egeland, B., & Sroufe, L. A. (1981). Attachment and early maltreatment. *Child Development, 52,* 44–52.

Egeland, B., Jacobvitz, D., & Sroufe, L. A. (1988). Breaking the cycle of abuse. *Child Development, 59,* 1080–1088.

Eggertson, L. (2005). Children's mental health service neglected: Kirby. *Canadian Medical Association Journal, 173,* 471.

Eggertson, L. (2007). Physicians challenge Canada to make children, youth a priority. *Canadian Medical Association, 176,* 1602–1604.

Ehri, L. C., Nunes, S. R., Willows, D. M., Schuster, B. V., Zoreh, Y. Z., & Shanahan, T. (2001). Phonemic awareness instruction helps children learn to read: Evidence from the National Reading Panel's meta-analysis. *Reading Research Quarterly, 36,* 250–287.

Eiberg, H. (1995). Nocturnal enuresis is linked to a specific gene. *Scandinavian Journal of Urology and Nephrology, 173*(Supplement), 15–17.

Eiberg, H., Berendt, I., & Mohr, J. (1995). Assignment of dominant inherited nocturnal enuresis (ENUR1) to chromosome 13q. *Nature Genetics, 10,* 354–356.

Eiger, M. S., & Olds, S. W. (1999). *The complete book of breastfeeding* (3rd ed.). New York: Workman.

Eimas, P. (1985). The perception of speech in early infancy. *Scientific American, 252*(1), 46–52.

Eimas, P., Siqueland, E., Jusczyk, P., & Vigorito, J. (1971). Speech perception in infants. *Science, 171,* 303–306.

Eisenberg, A. R. (1996). The conflict talk of mothers and children: Patterns related to culture, SES, and gender of child. *Merrill-Palmer Quarterly, 42,* 438–452.

Eisenberg, N. (1992). *The caring child.* Cambridge, MA: Harvard University Press.

Eisenberg, N. (2000). Emotion, regulation, and moral development. *Annual Review of Psychology, 51,* 665–697.

Eisenberg, N., & Fabes, R. A. (1998). Prosocial development. In W. Damon (Series Ed.) & N. Eisenberg (Vol. Ed.), *Handbook of child psychology: Vol. 3. Social, emotional, and personality development* (5th ed., pp. 701–778). New York: Wiley.

Eisenberg, N., & Morris, A. D. (2004). Moral cognitions and prosocial responding in adolescence. In R. M. Lerner & L. Steinberg (Eds.), *Handbook of adolescent psychology* (2nd ed.) (pp. 155–188). Hoboken, NJ: Wiley.

Eisenberg, N., Fabes, R. A., & Murphy, B. C. (1996). Parents' reactions to children's negative emotions: Relations to children's social competence and comforting behavior. *Child Development, 67,* 2227–2247.

Eisenberg, N., Fabes, R. A., Guthrie, I. K., & Reiser, M. (2000). Dispositional emotionality and regulation: Their role in predicting quality of social functioning. *Journal of Personality and Social Psychology, 78,* 136–157.

Eisenberg, N., Fabes, R. A., Nyman, M., Bernzweig, J., & Pinuelas, A. (1994). The relations of emotionality and regulation to children's anger-related reactions. *Child Development, 65,* 109–128.

Eisenberg, N., Fabes, R. A., Shepard, S. A., Guthrie, I. K., Murphy, B. C., & Reiser, M. (1999). Parental reactions to children's negative emotions: Longitudinal relations to quality of children's social functioning. *Child Development, 70*(2), 513–534

Eisenberg, N., Guthrie, I. K., Fabes, R. A., Reiser, M., Murphy, B. C., Holgren, R., Maszk, P., & Losoya, S. (1997). The relations of regulation and emotionality to resiliency and competent social functioning in elementary school children. *Child Development, 68,* 295–311.

Eisenberg, N., Spinrad, T. L., Fabes, R. A., Reiser, M., Cumberland, A., Shepard, S. A., Valiente, C., Losoya, S. H., Guthrie, I. K., & Thompson, M. (2004). The relations of effortful control and impulsivity to children's resiliency and adjustment. *Child Development, 75,* 25–46.

Elia, J., Ambrosini, P. J., & Rapoport, J. L. (1999). Treatment of Attention-Deficit-Hyperactivity Disorder. *New England Journal of Medicine, 340,* 780–788.

Elicker, J., Englund, M., & Sroufe, L. A. (1992). Predicting peer competence and peer relationships in childhood from early parent–child relationships. In R. Parke & G. Ladd (Eds.), *Family–peer relationships: Modes of linkage* (pp. 77–106). Hillsdale, NJ: Erlbaum.

Elkind, D. (1981). *The hurried child.* Reading, MA: Addison-Wesley.

Elkind, D. (1984). *All grown up and no place to go.* Reading, MA: Addison-Wesley.

Elkind, D. (1986). *The miseducation of children: Superkids at risk.* New York: Knopf.

Elkind, D. (1997). *Reinventing childhood: Raising and educating children in a changing world.* Rosemont, NJ: Modern Learning Press.

Elkind, D. (1998). *All grown up and no place to go.*Reading, MA: Addison-Wesley.

Elliott, D. S. (1993). Health enhancing and health compromising lifestyles. In S. G. Millstein, A. C. Petersen, & E. O. Nightingale (Eds.), *Promoting the health of adolescents: New directions for the twenty-first century* (pp. 119–145). New York: Oxford University Press.

Elliott, V. S. (2000, November 20). Doctors caught in middle of ADHD treatment controversy: Critics charge that medications are being both under- and overprescribed. *AMNews.* Retrieved April 21, 2005, from http://www.ama-assn.org/amednews/2000/11/ 20/hlsb1120.htm

Ellis, B. J., & Garber, J. (2000). Psychosocial antecedents of variation in girls' pubertal timing: Maternal depression, stepfather presence, and marital family stress. *Child Development, 71*(2), 485–501.

Ellis, B. J., Bates, J. E., Dodge, K. A., Fergusson, D. M., Horwood, L. J., Pettit, G. S., & Woodward, L. (2003). Does father-absence place daughters at special risk for early sexual activity and teenage pregnancy? *Child Development, 74,* 801–821.

Ellis, B. J., McFadyen-Ketchum, S., Dodge, K. A., Pettit, G. S., & Bates, J. E. (1999). Quality of early family relationships and individual differences in the timing of pubertal maturation in girls: A longitudinal test of an evolutionary model. *Journal of Personality and Social Psychology, 77,* 387–401.

Else-Quest, N. M., Hyde, J. S., Goldsmith, H. H., & Van Hulle, C. A. (2006). Gender differences in temperament: A meta-analysis. *Psychological Bulletin, 132,* 33–72.

Eltzschig, H. K., Lieberman, E. S., & Camann, W. R. (2003). Regional anesthesia and analgesia for labor and delivery. *New England Journal of Medicine, 348,* 319–332.

Emde, R. N., Plomin, R., Robinson, J., Corley, R., DeFries, J., Fulker, D. W., Reznick, J. S., Campos, J., Kagan, J., & Zahn-Waxler, C. (1992). Temperament, emotion, and cognition at 14 months: The MacArthur longitudinal twin study. *Child Development, 63,* 1437–1455.

Engle, P. L., & Breaux, C. (1998). Fathers' involvement with children: Perspectives from developing countries. *Social Policy Report, 12*(1), 1–21.

Enloe, C. F. (1980). How alcohol affects the developing fetus. *Nutrition Today, 15*(5), 12–15.

Ennouri, K., & Bloch, H. (1996). Visual control of hand approach movements in new-borns. *British Journal of Developmental Psychology, 14,* 327–338.

Eogan, M.A., Geary, M. P., O'Connell, M. P., & Keane, D. P. (2003). Effect of fetal sex on labour and delivery: Retrospective review. *British Medical Journal, 326,* 137.

Erdley, C. A., Cain, K. M., Loomis, C. C., Dumas-Hines, F., & Dweck, C. S. (1997). Relations among children's social goals, implicit personality theories, and responses to social failure. *Developmental Psychology, 33,* 263–272.

Erikson, E. H. (1950). *Childhood and society.* New York: Norton.

Erikson, E. H. (1968). *Identity: Youth and crisis.* New York: Norton.

Erikson, E. H. (1973). The wider identity. In K. Erikson (Ed.), *In search of common ground: Conversations with Erik H. Erikson and Huey P. Newton.* New York: Norton.

Erikson, E. H. (1982). *The life cycle completed.* New York: Norton.

Erikson, E. H., Erikson, J. M., & Kivnick, H. Q. (1986). *Vital involvement in old age: The experience of old age in our time.* New York: Norton.

Eriksson, P. S., Perfilieva, E., Björk-Eriksson, T., Alborn, A., Nordborg, C., Peterson, D. A., & Gage, F. H. (1998). Neurogenesis in the adult human hippocampus. *Nature Medicine, 4,* 1313–1317.

Eron, L. D. (1980). Prescription for reduction of aggression. *American Psychologist, 35,* 244–252.

Eron, L. D. (1982). Parent–child interaction, television violence, and aggression in children. *American Psychologist, 37,* 197–211.

Eron, L. D., & Huesmann, L. R. (1986). The role of television in the development of prosocial and antisocial behavior. In D. Olweus, J. Block, & M. Radke-Yarrow (Eds.), *The development of antisocial and prosocial behavior: Research, theories, and issues.* New York: Academic.

Etzel, R. A. (2003). How environmental exposures influence the development and exacerbation of asthma. *Pediatrics, 112*(1): 233–239.

European Collaborative Study. (1994). Natural history of vertically acquired human immunodeficiency virus-1 infection. *Pediatrics, 94,* 815–819.

Evans, G. W. (2004). The environment of childhood poverty. *American Psychologist, 59,* 77–92.

Evans, J. (1998, November). "Princesses are not into war 'n things, they always scream and run off": Exploring gender stereotypes in picture books. *Reading,* pp. 5–11.

Evans, M. A. (1998). Parental involvement in beginning reading: Preliminary report from a three-year longitudinal study. *Canadian Journal of School Psychology, 14,* 11–20.

Evers, S. (1987). The prevalence of diabetes in Indians and Caucasians living in Southwestern

Ontario. *Canadian Journal of Public Health, 78,* 240–243.

Fabes, R. A., & Eisenberg, N. (1992). Young children's coping with interpersonal anger. *Child Development, 63,* 116–128.

Fabes, R. A., & Eisenberg, N. (1996). *An examination of age and sex differences in prosocial behavior and empathy.* Unpublished data, Arizona State University.

Fabes, R. A., Eisenberg, N., Smith, M. C., & Murphy, B. C. (1996). Getting angry at peers: Associations with liking of the provocateur. *Child Development, 67,* 942–956.

Fabes, R. A., Leonard, S. A., Kupanoff, K., & Martin, C. L. (2001). Parental coping with children's negative emotions: Relations with children's emotional and social responding. *Child Development, 72,* 907–920.

Fabes, R. A., Martin, C. L., & Hanish, L. D. (2003, May). Young children's play qualities in same-, other-, and mixed-gender peer groups. *Child Development, 74*(3), 921–932.

Fabricius, W. V. (2003). Listening to children of divorce: New findings that diverge from Wallerstein, Lewis, and Blakeslee. *Family Relations, 52,* 385–394.

Facio, A., & Micocci, F. (2003). Emerging adulthood in Argentina. In J. J. Arnett & N. L. Galambos (Eds.), *Exploring cultural conceptions of the transition to adulthood. New Directions for Child and Adolescent Development, 100,* 21–32.

Faden, V. B. (2006). Trends in initiation of alcohol use in the United States: 1975–2003. *Alcoholism: Clinical and Experimental Research. 30*(6), 1011–1022.

Fagot, B. I., & Leinbach, M. D. (1995). Gender knowledge in egalitarian and traditional families. *Sex Roles, 32,* 513–526.

Faith, M. S., Berman, N., Heo, M., Pietrobelli, A., Gallagher, D., Epstein, L. H., Eiden, M. T., & Allison, D. B. (2001). Effects of contingent television on physical activity and television viewing in obese children. *Pediatrics, 107,* 1043–1048.

Falbo, T. (2006). *Your one and only: Educational psychologist dispels myths surrounding only children.* Retrieved July 20, 2006, from http://www.utexas.edu/features/archive/2004/single.htm

Falbo, T., & Polit, D. F. (1986). Quantitative review of the only child literature: Research evidence and theory development. *Psychological Bulletin, 100*(2), 176–189.

Falbo, T., & Poston, D. L. (1993). The academic, personality, and physical outcomes of only children in China. *Child Development, 64,* 18–35.

Faltermayer, C., Horowitz, J. M., Jackson, D., Lofaro, L., Maroney, T., Morse, J., Ramirez, A., & Rubin, J. C. (1996, August 5). Where are they now? *Time,* p. 18.

Fantino, A. M., & Colak, A. (2001). Refugee children in Canada: Searching for identity. *Child Welfare, 80,* 587–596.

Fantz, R. L. (1963). Pattern vision in newborn infants. *Science, 140,* 296–297.

Fantz, R. L. (1964). Visual experience in infants: Decreased attention to familiar patterns relative to novel ones. *Science, 146,* 668–670.

Fantz, R. L. (1965). Visual perception from birth as shown by pattern selectivity. In H. E. Whipple (Ed.), New issues in infant development. *Annals of the New York Academy of Science, 118,* 793–814.

Fantz, R. L., & Nevis, S. (1967). Pattern preferences and perceptual-cognitive development in early infancy. *Merrill-Palmer Quarterly, 13,* 77–108.

Fantz, R. L., Fagen, J., & Miranda, S. B. (1975). Early visual selectivity. In L. Cohen

& P. Salapatek (Eds.), *Infant perception: From sensation to cognition: Vol. 1. Basic visual processes* (pp. 249–341). New York: Academic Press.

Farver, J. A. M., Kim, Y. K., & Lee, Y. (1995). Cultural differences in Korean-and Anglo-American preschoolers' social interaction and play behavior. *Child Development, 66,* 1088–1099.

Farver, J. A. M., Xu, Y., Eppe, S., Fernandez, A., & Schwartz, D. (2005). Community violence, family conflict, and preschoolers' socioemotional functioning. *Developmental Psychology, 41,* 160–170.

Fauth, R.C., Leventhal, T., & Brooks-Gunn, J. (2005). Early impacts of moving from poor to middle-class neighborhoods on low-income youth. *Applied Developmental Psychology, 26,* 415–439.

Favaro, A., Tenconi, E., & Santonastaso, P. (2006). Perinatal factors and the risk of developing anorexia nervosa and bulimia nervosa. *Archives of General Psychiatry 63*(1), 82–88.

Feagans, L. (1983). A current view of learning disabilities. *Journal of Pediatrics, 102*(4), 487–493.

Fearon, P., O'Connell, P., Frangou, S., Aquino, P., Nosarti, C., Allin, M., Taylor, M., Stewart, A., Rifkin, L., & Murray, R. (2004). Brain volume in adult survivors of very low birth weight: A sibling-controlled study. *Pediatrics, 114,* 367–371.

Federal Bureau of Investigation. (1995, December). *Juveniles and violence* (updated). Washington, DC: Author.

Federal Interagency Forum on Child and Family Statistics. (2006). *America's children in brief: Key national indicators of well-being, 2006.* Washington, DC: U.S. Government Printing Office.

Feightner, J. W. (1994). Routine preschool screening for visual and hearing problems. In Canadian Task Force on the Periodic Health Examination. *Canadian guide to clinical preventative health care* (pp. 298–304). Ottawa: Health Canada.

Feingold, A., & Mazzella, R. (1998). Gender differences in body image are increasing. *Psychological Science, 9*(3), 190–195.

Feinman, S., & Lewis, M. (1983). Social referencing at ten months: A second-order effect on infants' responses. *Child Development, 54,* 878–887.

Feinstein, L., & Bynner, J. (2004). The importance of cognitive development in middle childhood for adult socioeconomic status, mental health, and problem behavior. *Child Development, 75,* 1329–1339.

Feldman, R. & Eidelman, A. I. (2005). Does a triplet birth pose a special risk for infant development? Assessing cognitive development in relation to intrauterine growth and mother-infant interaction across the first 2 years. *Pediatrics, 114,* 443–452.

Feldman, R. D. (1986, April). What are thinking skills? *Instructor,* pp. 62–71.

Felner, R. D., Brand, S., DuBois, D. L., Adan, A. M., Mulhall, P. F., & Evans, E. G. (1995). Socioeconomic disadvantage, proximal environmental experiences, and socioemotional and academic adjustment in early adolescence: Investigation of a mediated effect. *Child Development, 66,* 774–792.

Ferber, R. (1985). *Solve your child's sleep problems.* New York: Simon & Schuster.

Ferber, S. G. & Makhoul, I. R. (2004). The effect of skin-to-skin contact (Kangaroo Care) shortly after birth on the neurobehavioral responses of the term newborn: A randomized, controlled trial. *Pediatrics, 113,* 858–865.

Fergusson, D. M., Horwood, L. J., & Shannon, F. T. (1986). Factors related to the age of attainment of nocturnal bladder control: An 8-year longitudinal study. *Pediatrics, 78,* 884–890.

Fergusson, D. M., Horwood, L. J., Ridder, E. M., Beautrais, A. L. (2005). Sub-threshold depression in adolescence and mental health outcomes in adulthood. *Archives of General Psychiatry, 62*(1), 66–72.

Fernald, A., & O'Neill, D. K. (1993). Peekaboo across cultures: How mothers and infants play with voices, faces, and expectations. In K. MacDonald (Ed.), *Parent–child play* (pp. 259–285). Albany: State University of New York Press.

Fernald, A., Perfors, A., & Marchman, V. A. (2006). Picking up speed in understanding: Speech processing efficiency and vocabulary growth across the second year. *Developmental Psychology, 42,* 98–116.

Fernald, A., Pinto, J. P., Swingley, D., Weinberg, A., & McRoberts, G. W. (1998). Rapid gains in speed of verbal processing by infants in the 2nd year. *Psychological Science, 9*(3), 228–231.

Fernald, A., Swingley, D., & Pinto, J. P. (2001). When half a word is enough: Infants can recognize spoken words using partial phonetic information. *Child Development, 72*(4), 1003–1015.

Fernandez, C. V., & Rees, E. P. (1994). Pain management in Canadian level 3 neonatal intensive care units. *Canadian Medical Association Journal, 150,* 499–504.

Field, A. E., Austin, S. B., Taylor, C. B., Malspeis, S., Rosner, B., Rockett, H. R., Gillman, M. W., & Colditz, G. A. (2003). Relation between dieting and weight change among preadolescents and adolescents. *Pediatrics, 112*(4), 900–906.

Field, A. E., Camargo, C. A., Taylor, B., Berkey, C. S., Roberts, S. B., & Colditz, G. A. (2001). Peer, parent, and media influence on the development of weight concerns and frequent dieting among preadolescent and adolescent girls and boys. *Pediatrics, 107*(1), 54–60.

Field, A. E., Cook, N. R., & Gillman, M. W. (2005). Weight status in childhood as a predictor of becoming overweight or hypertensive in early adulthood. *Obesity Research, 13,* 163–169.

Field, T. (1995). Infants of depressed mothers. *Infant Behavior and Development, 18,* 1–13.

Field, T. (1998a). Emotional care of the at-risk infant: Early interventions for infants of depressed mothers. *Pediatrics, 102,* 1305–1310.

Field, T. (1998b). Massage therapy effects. *American Psychologist, 53,* 1270–1281.

Field, T. (1998c). Maternal depression effects on infants and early intervention. *Preventive Medicine, 27,* 200–203.

Field, T. M. (1978). Interaction behaviors of primary versus secondary caretaker fathers. *Developmental Psychology, 14,* 183–184.

Field, T. M. (1986). Interventions for premature infants. *Journal of Pediatrics, 109*(1), 183–190.

Field, T. M., & Roopnarine, J. L. (1982). Infant–peer interaction. In T. M. Field, A. Huston, H. C. Quay, L. Troll, & G. Finley (Eds.), *Review of human development.* New York: Wiley.

Field, T. M., Sandberg, D., Garcia, R., Vega-Lahr, N., Goldstein, S., & Guy, L. (1985). Pregnancy problems, postpartum depression, and early infant–mother interactions. *Developmental Psychology, 21,* 1152–1156.

Field, T., Diego, M., Hernandez-Reif, M., Schanberg, S., & Kuhn, C (2003). Depressed mothers who are "good interaction" partners versus those who are withdrawn or intrusive. *Infant Behavior & Development, 26,* 238–252.

Field, T., Fox, N. A., Pickens, J., Nawrocki, T., & Soutollo, D. (1995). Right frontal EEG activation in 3- to 6-month-old infants of depressed mothers. *Developmental Psychology, 31,* 358–363.

Field, T., Hernandez-Reif, M., & Freedman, J. (2004). Stimulation programs for preterm infants. *Social Policy Report, 18*(1), 1–19.

Fields, J. (2003). Children's living arrangements and characteristics: March 2002. *Current Population Reports* (p. 20–547). Washington, DC: U.S. Bureau of the Census.

Fields, J. (2004). America's families and living arrangements: 2003. *Current Population Reports* (P20–553). Washington, DC: U.S. Census Bureau.

Fields, J. M., & Smith, K. E. (1998, April). *Poverty, family structure, and child well-being: Indicators from the SIPP* (Population Division Working Paper No. 23, U.S. Bureau of the Census). Paper presented at the Annual Meeting of the Population Association of America, Chicago.

Fifer, W. P., & Moon, C. M. (1995). The effects of fetal experience with sound. In J. P. Lecanuet, W. P. Fifer, N. A. Krasnegor, & W. P. Smotherman (Eds.), *Fetal development: A psychobiological perspective* (pp. 351–366). Hillsdale, NJ: Erlbaum.

Finn, J. D. (2006). *The adult lives of at-risk students: The roles of attainment and engagement in high school* (NCES 2006-328). Washington, DC: U.S. Department of Education, National Center for Education Statistics.

Finn, J. D., & Rock, D. A. (1997). Academic success among students at risk for dropout. *Journal of Applied Psychology, 82,* 221–234.

Finn, J. D., Gerber, S. B., & Boyd-Zaharias, J. (2005). Small classes in the early grades, academic achievement, and graduating from high school. *Journal of Educational Psychology, 97,* 214–223.

Fiore, E. (2003). Multiple births and the rising rate of preterm delivery. *Contemporary Ob/Gyn, 48,* 67–77.

Fiscella, K., Kitzman, H. J., Cole, R. E., Sidora, K. J., & Olds, D. (1998). Does child abuse predict adolescent pregnancy? *Pediatrics, 101,* 620–624.

Fischer, K. W. (1980). A theory of cognitive development: The control and construction of hierarchies of skills. *Psychological Review, 87,* 477–531.

Fischer, K. W., & Pruyne, E. (2003). Reflective thinking in adulthood. In J. Demick & C. Andreoletti (Eds.) *Handbook of adult development.* New York: Plenum Press.

Fischer, K. W., & Rose, S. P. (1994). Dynamic development of coordination of components in brain and behavior: A framework for theory and research. In G. Dawson & K. W. Fischer (Eds.), *Human behavior and the developing brain* (pp. 3–66). New York: Guilford.

Fischer, K. W., & Rose, S. P. (1995, fall). Concurrent cycles in the dynamic development of brain and behavior. *SRCD Newsletter,* pp. 3–4, 15–16.

Fisher, C. B., Hoagwood, K., Boyce, C., Duster, T., Frank, D. A., Grisso, T., Levine, R. J., Macklin, R., Spencer, M. B., Takanishi, R., Trimble, J. E., & Zayas, L. H. (2002). Research ethics for mental health science involving ethnic minority children and youth. *American Psychologist, 57,* 1024–1040.

Fivush, R., & Nelson, K. (2004). Culture and language in the emergence of autobiographical memory. *Psychological Science, 15,* 573–577.

Fivush, R., Hudson, J., & Nelson, K. (1983). Children's long-term memory for a novel event: An exploratory study. *Merrill-Palmer Quarterly, 30,* 303–316.

Flavell, J. (1963). *The developmental psychology of Jean Piaget.* New York: Van Nostrand.

Flavell, J. H. (1970). Developmental studies of mediated memory. In H. W. Reese & L. P. Lipsitt (Eds.), *Advances in child development and behavior* (Vol. 5, pp. 181–211). New York: Academic.

Flavell, J. H., Green, F. L., & Flavell, E. R. (1986). Development of knowledge about the appearance–reality distinction. *Monographs of the Society for Research in Child Development, 51* (1, Serial No. 212).

Flavell, J. H., Green, F. L., & Flavell, E. R. (1995). Young children's knowledge about thinking. *Monographs of the Society for Research in Child Development, 60*(1, Serial No. 243).

Flavell, J. H., Green, F. L., Flavell, E. R., & Grossman, J. B. (1997). The development of children's knowledge about inner speech. *Child Development, 68,* 39–47.

Flavell, J. H., Green, F. L., Flavell, E. R., & Lin, N. T. (1999). Development of children's knowledge about unconsciousness. *Child Development, 70,* 396–412.

Flavell, J. H., Miller, P. H., & Miller, S. A. (1993). *Cognitive development.* Englewood Cliffs, NJ: Prentice-Hall.

Flavell, J. H., Miller, P. H., & Miller, S. A. (2002). *Cognitive development.* Englewood Cliffs, NJ: Prentice-Hall.

Flinn, M. V., & Ward, C. V. (2005). Ontogeny and the evolution of the social child. In B. J. Flook, L., Repetti, R. L., & Ullman, J. B. (2005). Classroom social experiences as predictors of academic performance. *Developmental Psychology, 41,* 319–327.

Flook, L., Repetti, R. L., & Ullman, J. B. (2005). Classroom social experiences as predictors of academic performance. *Developmental Psychology, 41,* 319–327.

Flores, G., Fuentes-Afflick, E., Barbot, O., Carter-Pokras, O., Claudio, L., Lara, M., McLaurin, J. A., Pachter, L., Gomez, F. R., Mendoza, F., Valdez, R. B., Villarruel, A. M., Zambrana, R. E., Greenberg, R., & Weitzman, M. (2002). The health of Latino children: Urgent priorities, unanswered questions, and a research agenda. *Journal of the American Medical Association, 288,* 82–90.

Flores, G., Olson, L, & Tomany-Korman, S. C. (2005). Racial and ethnic disparities in early childhood health and health care. *Pediatrics, 115,* e183–e193.

Flouris, A. D., Canham, C. H., Faught, B. E. & Klentrou, P. (2007). Prevalence of cardiovascular disease risk in Ontario adolescents. *Archives of Disease in Childhood, 92,* 521–523.

Flynn, J. R. (1984). The mean IQ of Americans: Massive gains 1932 to 1978. *Psychological Bulletin, 95,* 29–51.

Flynn, J. R. (1987). Massive IQ gains in 14 nations: What IQ tests really measure. *Psychological Bulletin, 101,* 171–191.

Flynn, M.A.T., McNeil, D.A., Maloff, B., Mutasingwa, D., Wu, M., Ford, C., & Tough, S.C. (2006). Reducing obesity and related chronic disease risk in children and youth: A synthesis of evidence with 'best practice' recommendations. *Obesity Reviews, 7 (s1),* 7–66.

Fontanel, B., & d'Harcourt, C. (1997). *Babies, history, art, and folklore.* New York: Abrams.

Ford, C. A., Bearman, P. S., & Moody, J. (1999). Foregone health care among adolescents.

Journal of the American Medical Association, 282(23), 2227–2234.

Ford, R. P., Schluter, P. J., Mitchell, E. A., Taylor, B. J., Scragg, R., & Stewart, A. W. (1998). Heavy caffeine intake in pregnancy and sudden infant death syndrome (New Zealand Cot Death Study Group). *Archives of Disease in Childhood, 78*(1), 9–13.

Forman, B. M., Thotonoz, P., Chen, J., Brun, R. P., Spiegelman, B. M., & Evans, R. M. (1995). 15-deoxy-delta 12, 14-prostaglandin J2 is a ligand for the adopocyte determination factor PPAR gamma. *Cell, 83*, 803–812.

Fowler, M. G., Simpson, G. A., & Schoendorf, K. C. (1993). Families on the move and children's health care. *Pediatrics, 91*, 934–940.

Fraga, C. G., Motchnik, P. A., Shigenaga, M. K., Helbock, H. J., Jacob, R. A., & Ames, B. N. (1991). Ascorbic acid protects against endogenous oxidative DNA damage in human sperm. *Proceedings of the National Academy of Sciences of the United States, 88*, 11003–11006.

Fraga, M., F., Ballestar, E., Paz, M. F., Ropero, S., Setien, F., Ballestar, M. L., Heine-Suñer, D., Cigudosa, J. C., Urioste, M., Benitez, J., Boix-Chornet, M., Sanchez-Aguilera, Ling, C., Carlsson, E., Poulsen, P., Vaag, A., Zarko, S., Spector, T. D., Yue-Zhong, W., Plass, C. & Esteller, M. (2005). Epigenetic differences arise during the lifetime of monozygotic twins. *Proceedings of the National Academy of Sciences, USA, 102*, 10604–10609.

Frank, A. (1958). *The diary of a young girl* (B. M. Mooyaart-Doubleday, Trans.). New York: Pocket.

Frank, A. (1995). *The diary of a young girl: The definitive edition* (O. H. Frank & M. Pressler, Eds.; S. Massotty, Trans.). New York: Doubleday.

Frank, D. A., Augustyn, M., Knight, W. G., Pell, T., & Zuckerman, B. (2001). Growth, development, and behavior in early childhood following prenatal cocaine exposure. *Journal of the American Medical Association, 285*, 1613–1625.

Frankenburg, W. K., Dodds, J. B., Fandal, A. W., Kazuk, E., & Cohrs, M. (1975). *The Denver Developmental Screening Test: Reference manual.* Denver: University of Colorado Medical Center.

Fraser, A. M., Brockert, J. F., & Ward, R. H. (1995). Association of young maternal age with adverse reproductive outcomes. *New England Journal of Medicine, 332*(17), 1113–1117.

Frazier, J. A., & Morrison, F. J. (1998). The influence of extended-year schooling on growth of achievement and perceived competence in early elementary school. *Child Development, 69*, 495–517.

Fredricks, J. A., & Eccles, J. S. (2002). Children's competence and value beliefs from childhood through adolescence: Growth trajectories in two male-sex-typed domains. *Developmental Psychology, 38*, 519–533.

Fredriksen, K., Rhodes, J., Reddy, R., & Way, N. (2004). Sleepless in Chicago: Tracking the effects of adolescent sleep loss during the middle-school years. *Child Development, 75*, 84–95.

Freeark, K., Rosenberg, E. B., Bornstein, J., Jozefowicz-Simbeni, D., Linkevich, M., & Lohnes, K. (2005). Gender differences and dynamics shaping the adoption life cycle: Review of the literature and recommendations. *American Journal of Orthopsychiatry, 75*, 86–101.

Freedman, D. S., Srinivasan, S. R., Valdez, R. A., Williamson, D. F., & Berenson, G. S. (1997). Secular increases in relative weight and adiposity among children over two decades: The Bogalusa Heart Study. *Pediatrics, 88*, 420–426.

Freeman, C. (2004). *Trends in educational equity of girls & women: 2004* (NCES 2005016). Washington, DC: National Center for Education Statistics.

Freeman, D. (1983). *Margaret Mead and Samoa: The making and unmaking of an anthropological myth.* Cambridge, MA: Harvard University Press.

Frempong, G. & Willms, J. D. (2002). Can school quality compensate for socioeconomic disadvantage? In Willms, J. D. *Vulnerable Children.* (Pg. 277–304). University of Alberta Press.

French, A. P. (Ed.). (1979). *Einstein: A centenary volume.* Cambridge, MA: Harvard University Press.

French, C. D., French, F., & Rutherford, P. J. (1999). Applications of the WPPSI–R with a Canadian sample. *Canadian Journal of School Psychology, 15*, 1–10.

French, J., & Pena, S. (1991). Children's hero play of the 20th century: Changes resulting from television's influence. *Child Study Journal, 21*, 79–94.

French, S. A., Story, M., & Jeffery, R. W. (2001). Environmental influences on eating and physical activity. *Annual Review of Public Health, 22*, 309–335.

French, S. E., Seidman, E., Allen, L., & Aber, J. L. (2006). The development of ethnic identity during adolescence. *Developmental Psychology, 42*, 1–10.

Freud, A. (1946). *The ego and the mechanisms of defense.* New York: International Universities Press.

Freud, S. (1953). *A general introduction to psychoanalysis* (J. Riviere, Trans.). New York: Perma-books. (Original work published 1935)

Freud, S. (1964a). New introductory lectures on psycho-analysis. In J. Strachey (Ed. & Trans.), *The standard edition of the complete psychological works of Sigmund Freud* (Vol. 22). London: Hogarth. (Original work published 1933)

Freud, S. (1964b). An outline of psycho-analysis. In J. Strachey (Ed. & Trans.), *The standard edition of the complete psychological works of Sigmund Freud* (Vol. 23). London: Hogarth. (Original work published 1940)

Frey, K. S., Hirschstein, M. K., Snell, J. L., Edstrom, L. V. S., MacKenzie, E P., and Broderick, C. J. (2005). Reducing playground bullying and supporting beliefs: An experimental trial of the Steps to Respect program. *Developmental Psychology, 41*, 479–491.

Frideres, J. S. (1998). *Aboriginal peoples in Canada: Contemporary conflicts.* Scarborough, ON: Prentice Hall Allyn and Bacon Canada.

Fried, P. A. (2002). Conceptual issues in behavioral teratology and their application in determining long-term consequences of prenatal marihuana exposure. *Journal of Child Psychology and Psychiatry, 43*, 81–102.

Fried, P. A., & Smith, A. M. (2001). A literature review of the consequences of prenatal marijuana exposure: An emerging theme of a deficiency in aspects of executive function. *Neurotoxicology and Teratology, 23*, 1–11.

Fried, P. A., & Watkinson, B. (2001). Differential effects on facets of attention in adolescents prenatally exposed to cigarettes and marihuana. *Neurotoxicology and Teratology, 23*, 421–430.

Fried, P. A., James, D. S., & Watkinson, B. (2001). Growth and pubertal milestones during adolescence in offspring prenatally exposed to cigarettes and marihuana. *Neurotoxicology and Teratology, 23*, 431–436.

Fried, P. A., Watkinson, B., & Willan, A. (1984). Marijuana use during pregnancy and decreased length of gestation. *American Journal of Obstetrics and Gynecology, 150*, 23–27.

Friedman, J. M., & Halaas, J. L. (1998). Leptin and the regulation of body weight in mammals. *Nature, 395*, 763–770.

Friedman, L. J. (1999). *Identity's architect.* New York: Scribner.

Friedman, R. A. (2006). The changing face of teenage drug abuse-The trend toward prescription drugs. *New England Journal of Medicine, 354*, 1448–1450.

Friend, M., & Davis, T. L. (1993). Appearance–reality distinction: Children's understanding of the physical and affective domains. *Developmental Psychology, 29*, 907–914.

Fries, A. B. W., Ziegler, T. E., Kurian, J. R., Jacoris, S., & Pollak, S. D. (2005). Early experiences in humans is associated with changes in neuropeptides critical for regulating social behavior. *Proceedings of the National Academy of Sciences, USA, 102*, 17237–17240.

Friesen, J. W. (1993). *When cultures clash: Case studies in multiculturalism.* Calgary, AB: Detselig Enterprises.

Friesen, J. W. (1995). Multicultural education as a component of formal socialization. In K. Covell (Ed.), *Readings in child development: A Canadian perspective* (pp. 172–184). Toronto: Nelson Canada.

Frith, U. (1989). *Autism: Explaining the enigma.* Oxford: Basil Blackwell.

Froehlich, T. E., Lamphear, B. P., Dietrich, K. N., Cory-Slechta, D. A., & Kahn, R. S. (2006, May). *Effects of DRD4, lead, and sex on ADHD-related executive function.* Paper presented at the annual meeting of the Pediatric Academic Societies, San Francisco.

Fromkin, V., Krashen, S., Curtiss, S., Rigler, D., & Rigler, M. (1974). The development of language in Genie: Acquisition beyond the "critical period." *Brain and Language, 15*(9), 28–34.

Frydman, O., & Bryant, P. (1988). Sharing and the understanding of number equivalence by young children. *Cognitive Development, 3*, 323–339.

Fuligni, A. J., & Eccles, J. S. (1993). Perceived parent–child relationships and early adolescents' orientation toward peers. *Developmental Psychology, 29*, 622–632.

Fuligni, A. J., Eccles, J. S., Barber, B. L., & Clements, P. (2001). Early adolescent peer orientation and adjustment during high school. *Developmental Psychology, 37*(1), 28–36.

Fuligni, A. J., & Witkow, M. (2004). The postsecondary educational progress of youth from immigrant families. *Journal of Research on Adolescence, 14*, 159–183.

Fuller-Thomson, E. (2005). Grandparents raising grandchildren in Canada: A profile of skipped generation families (SEDAP Research Paper No. 132). Hamilton, ON: McMaster University. Retrieved October 1, 2007 from http://socserv. mcmaster.ca/sedap/p/sedap132.pdf

Furman, L. (2005). What is attention-deficit hyperactivity disorder (ADHD)? *Journal of Child Neurology, 20*, 994–1003.

Furman, L., Taylor, G., Minich, N., & Hack, M. (2003). The effect of maternal milk on neonatal morbidity of very low birth-weight infants. *Archives of Pediatrics and Adolescent Medicine, 157*, 66–71.

Furman, W. (1982). Children's friendships. In T. M. Field, A. Huston, H. C. Quay, L. Troll, & G. E. Finley (Eds.), *Review of human development.* New York: Wiley.

Furman, W., & Bierman, K. L. (1983). Developmental changes in young children's conception of friendship. *Child Development, 54,* 549–556.

Furman, W., & Buhrmester, D. (1985). Children's perceptions of the personal relationships in their social networks. *Developmental Psychology, 21,* 1016–1024.

Furman, W., & Wehner, E. A. (1997). Adolescent romantic relationships: A developmental perspective. In S. Shulman & A. Collins (Eds.), Romantic relationships in adolescence: Developmental perspectives. *New Directions for Child and Adolescent Development, 78,* 21–36.

Furstenberg, Jr., F. F., Rumbaut, R. G., & Settersten, Jr., R. A. (2005). On the frontier of adulthood: Emerging themes and new directions. In R. A. Settersten, Jr., F. F. Furstenberg, Jr., & R. G. Rumbaut (Eds.), *On the frontier of adulthood: Theory, research, and public policy* (pp. 3–25). (John D. and Catherine T. MacArthur Foundation Series on Mental Health and Development, Research Network on Transitions to Adulthood and Public Policy.) Chicago: University of Chicago Press.

Furth, H. G., & Kane, S. R. (1992). Children constructing society: A new perspective on children at play. In H. McGurk (Ed.), *Childhood social development: Contemporary perspectives* (pp. 149–173). Hove: Erlbaum.

Fussell, E., & Furstenberg, F. (2005). The transition to adulthood during the twentieth century: Race, nativity, and gender. In R. A. Settersten, Jr., F. F. Furstenberg, Jr., & R. G. Rumbaut (Eds.), *On the frontier of adulthood: Theory, research, and public policy* (pp. 29–75). (John D. and Catherine T. MacArthur Foundation Series on Mental Health and Development, Research Network on Transitions to Adulthood and Public Policy.) Chicago: University of Chicago Press.

Gabbard, C. P. (1996). *Lifelong motor development* (2nd ed.). Madison, WI: Brown and Benchmark.

Gabhainn, S., & François, Y. (2000). Substance use. In C. Currie, K. Hurrelmann, W. Settertobulte, R. Smith, & J. Todd (Eds.), *Health behaviour in school-aged children: A WHO cross-national study (HBSC) international report* (pp. 97–114). WHO Policy Series: Healthy Policy for Children and Adolescents, Series No. 1.

Gaffney, M., Gamble, M., Costa, P., Holstrum, J., & Boyle, C. (2003). Infants tested for hearing loss—United States, 1999–2001. *Morbidity and Mortality Weekly Report, 51,* 981–984.

Galambos, N. L., & Almeida, D. M. (1992). Does parent–adolescent conflict increase in early adolescence? *Journal of Marriage and the Family, 54,* 737–747.

Galambos, N. L., & Sears, H. A. (1998). Adolescents' perceptions of parents' work and adolescents' work values in two-earner families. *Journal of Early Adolescence, 18,* 397–420.

Galambos, N. L., Petersen, A. C., & Lenerz, K. (1988). Maternal employment and sex typing in early adolescence: Contemporaneous and longitudinal relations. In A. D. Gottfried & A. W. Gottfried (Eds.), *Maternal employment and children's development: Longitudinal research.* New York: Plenum.

Galambos, N. L., Sears, H. A., Almeida, D. M., & Kolaric, G. C. (1995). Parents' work overload and problem behavior in young adolescents. *Journal of Research on Adolescence, 5*(2), 201–223.

Galan, J. J., De Felici, M., Buch, B., Rivero, M. C., Segura, A., Royo, J. L., Cruz, N., Real, L. M. & Ruiz, A. (2006). Association of genetic markers within the KIT and KITLG genes with human male infertility. *Human Reproduction, 21,* 3185–3192.

Galen, B. R., & Underwood, M. K. (1997). A developmental investigation of social aggression among children. *Developmental Psychology, 33,* 589–600.

Galotti, K. M., Komatsu, L. K., & Voelz, S. (1997). Children's differential performance on deductive and inductive syllogisms. *Developmental Psychology, 33,* 70–78.

Ganger, J. & Brent, M. R. (2004). Reexamining the vocabulary spurt. *Developmental Psychology, 40,* 621–632.

Gannon, P. J., Holloway, R. L., Broadfield, D. C., & Braun, A. R. (1998). Asymmetry of chimpanzee planum temporale: Humanlike pattern of Wernicke's brain language homolog. *Science, 279,* 22–222.

Gans, J. E. (1990). *America's adolescents: How healthy are they?* Chicago: American Medical Association.

Garasky, S., & Meyer, D. R. (1996). Reconsidering the increase in father-only families. *Demography, 33,* 385–393.

Garbarino, J., & Kostelny, K. (1993). Neighborhood and community influences on parenting. In T. Luster & L. Okagaki (Eds.), *Parenting: An ecological perspective* (pp. 203–226). Hillsdale, NJ: Erlbaum.

Garbarino, J., Dubrow, N., Kostelny, K., & Pardo, C. (1992). *Children in danger: Coping with the consequences of community violence.* San Francisco: Jossey-Bass.

Garbarino, J., Dubrow, N., Kostelny, K., & Pardo, C. (1998). *Children in danger: Coping with the consequences of community violence.* San Francisco: Jossey-Bass.

Garcia, M. M., Shaw, D. S., Winslow, E. B., & Yaggi, K. E. (2000). Destructive sibling conflict and the development of conduct problems in young boys. *Developmental Psychology, 36*(1), 44–53.

Gardiner, H. W. & Kosmitzki, C. (2005). *Lives across cultures: Cross-cultural human development.* Boston: Allyn & Bacon.

Gardiner, H. W., Mutter, J. D., & Kosmitzki, C. (1998). *Lives across cultures: Cross-cultural human development.* Boston: Allyn and Bacon.

Gardner, H. (1993). *Frames of mind: The theory of multiple intelligences.* New York: Basic. (Original work published 1983)

Gardner, H. (1995). Reflections on multiple intelligences: Myths and messages. *Phi Delta Kappan,* pp. 200–209.

Gardner, H. (1998). Are there additional intelligences? In J. Kane (Ed.), *Education, information, and transformation: Essays on learning and thinking.* Englewood Cliffs, NJ: Prentice-Hall.

Gardner, H. (1999). *Intelligence reframed: Multiple intelligences for the 21st century.* New York: Basic Books.

Gardner, H. (2000). The giftedness matrix: A developmental perspective. In R. C. Friedman & B. M. Shore (Eds.), *Talents unfolding: Cognition and development.* Washington, DC: APA.

Gardner, M., & Steinberg, L. (2005). Peer influence on risk taking, risk preference, and risky decision making in adolescence and adulthood: An experimental study. *Developmental Psychology, 41,* 625–635.

Garland, A. F., & Zigler, E. (1993). Adolescent suicide prevention: Current research and social policy implications. *American Psychologist, 48*(2), 169–182.

Garlick, D. (2003). Integrating brain science research with intelligence research. *Current Directions in Psychological Science, 12,* 185–192.

Garmezy, N., Masten, A., & Tellegen, A. (1984). The study of stress and competence in children: A building block for developmental psychopathology. *Child Development, 55,* 97–111.

Garmon, L. C., Basinger, K. S., Gregg, V. R., & Gibbs, J. C. (1996). Gender differences in stage and expression of moral judgment. *Merrill-Palmer Quarterly, 42,* 418–437.

Garner, D. M. (1993). Pathogenesis of anorexia nervosa. *Lancet, 341,* 1631–1635.

Garner, P. W., & Power, T. G. (1996). Preschoolers' emotional control in the disappointment paradigm and its relation to temperament, emotional knowledge, and family expressiveness. *Child Development, 67,* 1406–1419.

Garriguet, D. (2005). Early sexual intercourse. *Health Reports, 16,* 9–18.

Gartrell, N., Deck, A., Rodas, C., Peyser, H., & Banks, A. (2005). The National Lesbian Family Study: Interviews with the 10-year-old children. *American Journal of Orthopsychiatry, 75,* 518–524.

Gartstein, M.A., & Rothbart, M. K. (2003). Studying infant temperament via the Revised Infant Behavior Questionnaire. *Infant Behavior & Development, 26,* 64–86.

Gatewood, J. D., Wills, A., Shetty, S., Xu, J., Arnold, A. P., Burgoyne, P. S., & Rissman, E. F. (2006). Sex chromosome complement and gonadal sex influence aggressive and parental behaviors in mice. *Journal of Neuroscience, 26,* 2335–2342.

Gauvain, M. (1993). The development of spatial thinking in everyday activity. *Developmental Review, 13,* 92–121.

Gauvain, M., & Perez, S. M. (2005). Parent-child participation in planning children's activities outside of school in European American and Latino families. *Child Development, 76,* 371–383.

Gazzaniga, M. S. (Ed.). (2000). *The new cognitive neurosciences* (2nd ed.). Cambridge, MA: The MIT Press.

Ge, X., Conger, R. D., & Elder, G. H. (2001). Pubertal transition, stressful life events, and the emergence of gender differences in adolescent depressive symptoms. *Developmental Psychology, 37*(3), 404–417.

Geary, D. C. (1999). Evolution and developmental sex differences. *Current Directions in Psychological Science, 8*(4), 115–120.

Geen, R. (2004). The evolution of kinship care: Policy and practice. In David and Lucile Packard Foundation, Children, families, and foster care. *The Future of Children, 14*(1). Retrieved from http://www.futureofchildren.org.

Geier, D. A., & Geier, M. R. (2006). Early downward trends in neurodevelopmental disorders following removal of thimerosal-containing vaccines. *Journal of American Physicians and Surgeons, 11*(1), 8–13.

Gelfand, D. M., & Teti, D. M. (1995, November). How does maternal depression affect children? *The Harvard Mental Health Letter,* p. 8.

Gelis, J. (1991). *History of childbirth: Fertility, pregnancy, and birth in early modern Europe.* Boston: Northeastern University Press.

Gelman, R., Spelke, E. S., & Meck, E. (1983). What preschoolers know about animate and inanimate objects. In D. R. Rogers & J. S. Sloboda (Eds.), *The acquisition of symbolic skills* (pp. 297–326). New York: Plenum.

Genbacev, O. D., Prakobphol, A., Foulk, R. A., Krtolica, A. R., Ilic, D., Singer, M. S., Yang, Z.-Q., Kiessling, L. L., Rosen, S. D., & Fisher, S. J. (2003). Trophoblash Lselectin-mediated adhesion at the maternalfetal interface. *Science, 299*, 405–408.

Genesee, F. (1987). *Learning through two languages: Studies of immersion and bilingual education.* Cambridge, MA: Newbury House.

Genesee, F. (1991). Second language learning in school settings: Lessons from immersion. In A. G. Reynolds (Ed.), *Bilingualism, multiculturalism, and second language learning: The McGill conference in honour of Wallace E. Lambert* (pp. 183–201). Hillsdale, NJ: Lawrence Erlbaum Associates.

Genesee, F., Nicoladis, E., & Paradis, J. (1995). Language differentiation in early bilingual development. *Journal of Child Language, 22*, 611–631.

George, C., Kaplan, N., & Main, M. (1985). *The Berkeley Adult Attachment Interview.* Unpublished protocol, Department of Psychology, University of California, Berkeley, CA.

George, T. P., & Hartmann, D. P. (1996). Friendship networks of unpopular, average, and popular children. *Child Development, 67*, 2301–2316.

Gershoff, E. T. (2002). Corporal punishment by parents and associated child behaviors and experiences: A meta-analytic and theoretical review. *Psychological Bulletin, 128*, 539–579.

Getzels, J. W. (1964). Creative thinking, problem-solving, and instruction. In *Yearbook of the National Society for the Study of Education* (Pt. 1, pp. 240–267). Chicago: University of Chicago Press.

Getzels, J. W., & Jackson, P. W. (1962). *Creativity and intelligence: Explorations with gifted students.* New York: Wiley.

Getzels, J. W., & Jackson, P. W. (1963). The highly intelligent and the highly creative adolescent: A summary of some research findings. In C. W. Taylor & F. Baron (Eds.), *Scientific creativity: Its recognition and development* (pp. 161–172). New York: Wiley.

Gfellner, B. M. (1990). Culture and consistency in ideal and actual child-rearing practices: A study of Canadian Indian and white parents. *Journal of Comparative Family Studies, 21*, 413–423.

Gfellner, B.M. (1994). A matched-group comparison of drug use and problem behavior among Canadian Indian and White adolescents. *Journal of Early Adolescence, 14*, 24–48.

Gibbs, J. C. (1991). Toward an integration of Kohlberg's and Hoffman's theories of moral development. In W. M. Kurtines & J. L. Gewirtz (Eds.), *Handbook of moral behavior and development: Advances in theory, research, and application* (Vol. 1). Hillsdale, N.J.: Erlbaum.

Gibbs, J. C. (1995). The cognitive developmental perspective. In W. M. Kurtines & J. L. Gewirtz (Eds.), *Moral development: An introduction.* Boston: Allyn & Bacon.

Gibbs, J. C., & Schnell, S. V. (1985). Moral development "versus" socialization. *American Psychologist, 40*(10), 1071–1080.

Gibbs, J. C., Potter, G. B., Barriga, A. Q., & Liau, A. K. (1996). Developing the helping skills and prosocial motivation of aggressive adolescents in peer group programs. *Aggression and Violent Behavior, 1*(3), 283–305.

Gibbs, J. C., Potter, G. C., Goldstein, A. P., & Brendtro, L. K. (1998). How EQUIP programs help youth change. *Reclaiming Children and Youth, 7*(2), 117–122.

Gibson, E. J. (1969). *Principles of perceptual learning and development.* New York: Appleton-Century-Crofts.

Gibson, E. J., & Pick, A. D. (2000). *An ecological approach to perceptual learning and development.* New York: Oxford University Press.

Gibson, E. J., & Walk, R. D. (1960). The "visual cliff." *Scientific American, 202*, 64–71.

Gibson, E. J., & Walker, A. S. (1984). Development of knowledge of visual–tactual affordances of substance. *Child Development, 55*, 453–460.

Gibson, J. J. (1979). *The ecological approach to visual perception.* Boston: Houghton-Mifflin.

Gibson, R. S., MacDonald, C. A., & Smit Vanderkooy, P. D. (1993). Dietary fat patterns of some Canadian preschool children in relation to indices of growth, iron, zinc and dietary status. *Journal of the Canadian Dietary Association, 54*, 33–37.

Gidwani, P. P., Sobol, A., DeJong, W., Perrin, J. M., & Gortmaker, S. L. (2002). Television viewing and initiation of smoking among youth. *Pediatrics, 110*, 505–508.

Giedd, J. N., Blumenthal, J., Jeffries, N. O., Castellanos, F. X., Zijdenbos, A., Paus, T., Evans, A. C., & Rapoport, J. L. (1999). Brain development during childhood and adolescence: A longitudinal MRI study. *Nature Neuroscience, 2*, 861–863.

Gilbert, S. (1998, May 19). Benefits of assistant for childbirth go far beyond the birthing room. *New York Times*, p. F7.

Gilbert, W. M., Nesbitt, T. S., & Danielsen, B. (1999). Childbearing beyond age 40: Pregnancy outcome in 24,032 cases. *Obstetrics and Gynecology, 93*, 9–14.

Gill, B., & Schlossman, S. (1996). "A sin against childhood": Progressive education and the crusade to abolish homework, 1897–1941. *American Journal of Education, 105*, 27–66.

Gilligan, C. (1982). *In a different voice: Psychological theory and women's development.* Cambridge, MA: Harvard University Press.

Gilligan, C. (1987a). Adolescent development reconsidered. In E. E. Irwin (Ed.), *Adolescent social behavior and health.* San Francisco: Jossey-Bass.

Gilligan, C. (1987b). Moral orientation and moral development. In E. F. Kittay & D. T. Meyers (Eds.), *Women and moral theory* (pp. 19–33). Totowa, NJ: Rowman & Littlefield.

Gillis, J. (1992). Views of Native parents about early childhood education. *Canadian Journal of Native Education, 19*, 73–81.

Gilmore, J., Lin, W., Prastawa, M. W., Looney, C. B., Vetsa, Y. S. K., Knickmeyer, R. C., et al. (2007). Regional gray matter growth, sexual dimorphism, and cerebral asymmetry in the neonatal brain. *Journal of Neuroscience, 27*(6), 1255–1260.

Ginsburg, G. S., & Bronstein, P. (1993). Family factors related to children's intrinsic/extrinsic motivational orientation and academic performance. *Child Development, 64*, 1461–1474.

Ginsburg, H., & Opper, S. (1979). *Piaget's theory of intellectual development* (2nd ed.). Englewood Cliffs, NJ: Prentice-Hall.

Ginsburg, K., & Committee on Communications and the Committee on Psychosocial Aspects of Child and Family Health, American Academy of Pediatrics (AAP). (2007). *Pediatrics, 119*, 182–191.

Ginsburg-Block, M. D., & Fantuzzo, J. W. (1998). An evaluation of the relative effectiveness of NCTM standards-based interventions for low-achieving urban elementary students. *Journal of Educational Psychology, 90*, 560–569.

Giscombé, C. L. & Lobel, M. (2005). Explaining disproportionately high rates of adverse birth outcomes among African Americans: The impact of stress, racism, and related factors in pregnancy. *Psychological Bulletin, 131*, 662–683.

Giusti, R. M., Iwamoto, K., & Hatch, E. E. (1995). Diethylstilbestrol revisited: A review of the long-term health effects. *Annals of Internal Medicine, 122*, 778–788.

Gjerdingen, D. (2003). The effectiveness of various postpartum depression treatments and the impact of antidepressant drugs on nursing infants. *Journal of American Board of Family Practice, 16*, 372–382.

Glantz, S A., Kacirk, K. W., & McCulloch, C. (2004). Back to the future: Smoking in movies in 2002 compared with 1950 levels. *American Journal of Public Health, 94*, 261–263.

Glaser, D. (2000). Child abuse and neglect and the brain: A review. *Journal of Child Psychiatry, 41*, 97–116.

Glasgow, K. L., Dornbusch, S. M., Troyer, L., Steinberg, L., & Ritter, P. L. (1997). Parenting styles, adolescents' attributions, and educational outcomes in nine heterogeneous high schools. *Child Development, 68*, 507–529.

Glassbrenner, D., Carra, J. S., & Nichols, J. (2005). Recent estimates of safety belt use. *Journal of Safety Research, 35*(2), 237–244.

Glasson, E. J., Bower, C., Petterson, B., de Klerk, N., Chaney, G., & Hallmayer, J. F. (2004). Perinatal factors and the development of autism: A population study. *Archives of General Psychiatry, 61*, 618–627.

Glaxo Wellcome Inc. (2000). *Asthma in Canada: A landmark survey.* Mississauga, ON: Author.

Gleason, T. R., Sebanc, A. M., & Hartup, W. W. (2000). Imaginary companions of preschool children. *Developmental Psychology, 36*, 419–428.

Gleitman, L. R., Newport, E. L., & Gleitman, H. (1984). The current status of the motherese hypothesis. *Journal of Child Language, 11*, 43–79.

Glenn, N., & Marquardt, E. (2001). *Hooking up, hanging out, and hoping for Mr. Right: College women on dating and mating today.* New York: Institute for American Values.

Goetz, P. J. (2003). The effects of bilingualism on theory of mind development. *Bilingualism: Language and Cognition, 6*, 1–15.

Gogtay, N., Giedd, J. N., Lusk, L., Hayashi, K. M., Greenstein, D., Vaituzis, A. C., Nugent, T. F., III, Herman, D. H., Clasen, L. S., Toga, A. W., Rapoport, J. L., & Thompson, P. M. (2004). Dynamic mapping of human cortical development during childhood through early adulthood. *Proceedings of the National Academy of Sciences, USA, 101*, 8174–8179.

Golden, A., Currie, W. H., Greaves, E., & Latimer, E. J. (1999). *Taking responsibility for homelessness: An action plan for Toronto—Report of the mayor's homelessness action task force.* Toronto: Access Toronto.

Goldenberg, R. L., & Rouse, D. J. (1998). Prevention of premature labor. *New England Journal of Medicine, 339*, 313–320.

Goldenberg, R. L., & Tamura, T. (1996). Prepregnancy weight and pregnancy outcome. *Journal of the American Medical Association, 275*, 1127–1128.

Goldenberg, R. L., Tamura, T., Neggers, Y., Copper, R. L., Johnston, K. E., DuBard, M. B., & Hauth, J. C. (1995). The effect of zinc supplementation on pregnancy outcome. *Journal of the American Medical Association, 274*, 463–468.

Goldin-Meadow, S., & Mylander, C. (1998). Spontaneous sign systems created by deaf children in two cultures. *Nature, 391,* 279–281.

Goldman, A. (1981). *Elvis.* New York: McGraw-Hill.

Goldsmith, M., Mackay, A., & Woudhuysen, J. S. (Eds.). (1980). *Einstein: The first hundred years.* Oxford: Pergamon.

Goldstein, M., King, A., & West, M. (2003). Social interaction shapes babbling: Testing parallels between birdsong and speech. *Proceedings of the National Academy of Sciences, USA, 100,* 8030–8035.

Goleman, D. (1995). *Emotional intelligence: Why it can matter more than IQ.* New York: Bantam.

Goleman, D. (1995, July 1). A genetic clue to bed-wetting is located: Researchers say discovery shows the problem is not emotions! *New York Times,* p. 8.

Golinkoff, R. M., Jacquet, R. C., Hirsh-Pasek, K., & Nandakumar, R. (1996). Lexical principles may underlie the learning of verbs. *Child Development, 67,* 3101–3119.

Golomb, C., & Galasso, L. (1995). Make believe and reality: Explorations of the imaginary realm. *Developmental Psychology, 31,* 800–810.

Golombok, S., MacCallum, F., & Goodman, E. (2001). The "test-tube" generation: Parent-child relationships and the psychological well-being of in vitro fertilization children at adolescence. *Child Development, 72,* 599–608.

Golombok, S., MacCallum, F., Goodman, E., & Rutter, M. (2002). Families with children conceived by donor insemination: A follow-up at age twelve. *Child Development, 73,* 952–968.

Golombok, S., Murray, C., Jadva, V., MacCallum, F., & Lycett, E. (2004). Families created through surrogacy arrangements: Parent-child relationships in the 1st year of life. *Developmental Psychology, 40,* 400–411.

Golombok, S., Perry B., Burston, A., Murray, C., Mooney-Summers, J., Stevens, M., & Golding, J. (2003). Children with lesbian parents: A community study. *Developmental Psychology, 39,* 20–33.

Gonzales, N. A., Cauce, A. M., & Mason, C. A. (1996). Interobserver agreement in the assessment of parental behavior and parent-adolescent conflict: African American mothers, daughters, and independent observers. *Child Development, 67,* 1483–1498.

Gooden, A. M. (2001). Gender representation in Notable Children's picture books: 1995–1999. *Sex Roles: A Journal of Research.* Retrieved April 20, 2005, from http://www.?ndarticles.com/p/articles/mi m2294/is_2001_July/ai_81478076.

Goodman, G. S., Emery, R. E., & Haugaard, J. J. (1998). Developmental psychology and law: Divorce, child maltreatment, foster care, and adoption. In W. Damon (Series Ed.), I. E. Sigel & K. A. Renninger (Vol. Eds.), *Handbook of child psychology* (Vol. 4, pp. 775–874). New York: Wiley.

Goodwin, J. (1994). *Akira Kurosawa and intertextual cinema.* Baltimore: Johns Hopkins University Press.

Goodwyn, S. W., & Acredolo, L. P. (1998). Encouraging symbolic gestures: A new perspective on the relationship between gesture and speech. In J. M. Iverson & S. Goldin-Meadow (Eds.), *The nature and functions of gesture in children's communication* (pp. 61–73). San Francisco: Jossey-Bass.

Gootman, E. (2007, January 22). Taking middle schoolers out of the middle. *New York Times,* p. A1.

Gootman, E., & Herszenhorn, D. M. (2005, May 3). Getting smaller to improve the big

picture. *New York Times.* Retrieved May 3, 2005, from http://www.nytimes.com/1005/05/03/nyregion/03small.html.

Gopnik, A., Sobel, D. M., Schulz, L. E., & Glymour, C. (2001). Causal learning mechanisms in very young children: Two-, three-, and four-year-olds infer causal relations from patterns of variation and covariation. *Developmental Psychology, 37*(5), 620–629.

Gordon, I., Lask, B., Bryantwaugh, R., Christie, D., & Timini, S. (1997). Childhood onset anorexia nervosa: Towards identifying a biological substrate. *International Journal of Eating Disorders, 22*(2), 159–165.

Gorman, K. S., & Pollitt, E. (1996). Does schooling buffer the effects of early risk? *Child Development, 67,* 314–326.

Gorman, M. (1993). Help and self-help for older adults in developing countries. *Generations, 17*(4), 73–76.

Gortmaker, S. L., Hughes, M., Cervia, J., Brady, M., Johnson, G. M., Seage, G. R., Song, L. Y., Dankner, W. M., & Oleske, J. M. for the Pediatric AIDS Clinical Trial Group Protocol 219 Team. (2001). Effect of combination therapy including protease inhibitors on mortality among children and adolescents infected with HIV-1. *New England Journal of Medicine, 345*(21), 1522–1528.

Gortmaker, S. L., Must, A., Perrin, J. M., Sobol, A. M., & Dietz, W. H. (1993). Social and economic consequences of overweight in adolescence and young adulthood. *New England Journal of Medicine, 329,* 1008–1012.

Gosden, R. G., & Feinberg, A. P. (2007). Genetics and epigenetics—nature's pen-and-pencil set. *New England Journal of Medicine, 356,* 731–733.

Gottfried, A. E., Fleming, J. S., & Gottfried, A. W. (1998). Role of cognitively stimulating home environment in children's academic intrinsic motivation: A longitudinal study. *Child Development, 69,* 1448–1460.

Gottlieb, B. H., Sill, E., & Newby-Clark, I. R. (2007). Types and precipitants of growth and decline in emerging adulthood. *Journal of Adolescent Research, 22,* 132–155.

Gottlieb, G. (1991). Experiential canalization of behavioral development theory. *Developmental Psychology, 27*(1), 4–13.

Gottlieb, G. (2007). Probabilistic epigenesis. *Developmental Science, 10,* 1–11.

Gottlieb, L. N., & Mendelson, M. J. (1990). Parental support and firstborn girls' adaptation to the birth of a sibling. *Journal of Applied Developmental Psychology, 11,* 29–48.

Gottman, J. M., & Notarius, C. I. (2000). Decade review: Observing marital interaction. *Journal of Marriage and the Family, 62,* 927–947.

Goubet, N., & Clifton, R. K. (1998). Object and event representation in 6 1/2-month-old infants. *Developmental Psychology, 34,* 63–76.

Gould, E., Reeves, A. J., Graziano, M. S. A., & Gross, C. G. (1999). Neurogenesis in the neocortex of adult primates. *Science, 286,* 548–552.

Gould, M. S., Marrocco, F. A., Kleinman, M., Thomas, J. G., Mostkoff, K., Cote, J., & Davies, M. (2005). Evaluating iatrogenic risk of youth suicide screening programs: A randomized controlled trial. *Journal of the American Medical Association, 293,* 1635–1643.

Government Canada (n.d.). *Tri-Council Policy Statement: Ethical Conduct for Research Involving Humans: Section 6. Research Involving Aboriginal Peoples.* Retrieved July 20, 2007 from www.pre.ethics.gc.ca/english/policystatement/section6.cfm.

Government of Canada (2006). The well-being of Canada's young children. Retrieved September 17, 2007, www.socialunion.ca/well_being.pdf.

Government of Saskatchewan. (2000). *Secondhand tobacco smoke health risks: Infants and children at home.* Retrieved September 20, 2002, from http://www.health.gov.sk.ca/rr_2ndhandsmoke_ic.html

Graber, J. A., Brooks-Gunn, J., & Warren, M. P. (1995). The antecedents of menarcheal age: Heredity, family environment, and stressful life events. *Child Development, 66,* 346–359.

Graber, J. A., Lewinsohn, P. M., Seeley, J. R., & Brooks-Gunn, J. (1997). Is psychopathology associated with the timing of pubertal development? *Journal of the American Academy of Child and Adolescent Psychiatry, 36,* 1768–1776.

Grady, B. (2002, December). *Miscarriage: The need to grieve.* Retrieved April 9, 2006, from http://www.parenting-plus.com/newsletter_0212.htm.

Grant, A. (1996). *No end of grief: Indian residential schools in Canada.* Winnipeg, MB: Pemmican Publications, Inc.

Grantham-McGregor, S., Powell, C., Walker, S., Chang, S., & Fletcher, P. (1994). The long-term follow-up of severely malnourished children who participated in an intervention program. *Child Development, 65,* 428–439.

Gray, C. (2002). Pediatricians taking new look at corporal-punishment issue. *Canadian Medical Association, 166,* 793.

Gray, J. R., & Thompson, P. M. (2004). Neurobiology of intelligence: Science and ethics. *Neuroscience, 5,* 471–492.

Gray, M. R., & Steinberg, L. (1999). Unpacking authoritative parenting: Reassessing a multidimensional construct. *Journal of Marriage and the Family, 61,* 574–587.

Graziano, A. M., & Mooney, K. C. (1982). Behavioral treatment of "nightfears" in children: Maintenance and improvement at 21/2 to 3-year follow-up. *Journal of Counseling and Clinical Psychology, 50,* 598–599.

Grech, V., Vassallo-Agius, P. & Savona-Ventura, C. (2003). Secular trends in sex ratios at birth in North America and Europe over the second half of the 20th century. *Epidemial Community Health, 57,* 612–615.

Greenberger, E., & Steinberg, L. (1986). *When teenagers work.* New York: Basic Books.

Greene, M. F. (2002). Outcomes of very low birth weight in young adults. *New England Journal of Medicine, 346*(3), 146–148.

Greene, M. L., & Way, N. (2005). Self-esteem trajectories among ethnic minority adolescents: A growth curve analysis of the patterns and predictors of change. *Journal of Research on Adolescence, 15,* 151–178, 161–168.

Greenfield, P. M., & Childs, C. P. (1978). Understanding sibling concepts: A developmental study of kin terms in Zinacanten. In P. R. Dasen, (Ed.), *Piagetian psychology* (pp. 335–358). New York: Gardner.

Greenhouse, L. (2000a, February 29). Program of drug-testing pregnant women draws review by the Supreme Court. *New York Times,* p. A12.

Greenhouse, L. (2000b, September 9). Should a fetus's well-being override a mother's rights? *New York Times,* pp. B9, B11.

Grigorenko, E. L., & Sternberg, R. J. (1998). Dynamic testing. *Psych Bulletin, 124,* 75–111.

Grigorenko, E. L., Meier, E., Lipka, J., Mohatt, G., Yanez, E., & Sternberg, R. J. (2004). Academic and practical intelligence: A case study of the Yup'ik in Alaska. *Learning and Individual Differences, 14*(4), 183–207.

Groos, K. (1898). *The play of animals.* New York: Appleton.

Gross, R. T., & Duke, P. (1980). The effect of early versus late physical maturation on adolescent behavior. [Special issue: I. Litt (Ed.), Symposium on adolescent medicine.] *Pediatric Clinics of North America, 27,* 71–78.

Gross, S. R., Barrett, S. P., Shestowsky, J. S. & Pihl, R. O. (2002). Ecstasy and drug consumption patterns: A Canadian rave population study. Canadian Psychiatric Association. Retrieved on August 22, 2007 from http://ww1.cpa-apc.org:8080/Publications/Archives/CJP/2002/August/originalResearchEcstasy1.asp.

Grotevant, H. D., McRoy, R. G., Elde, C. L., & Fravel, D. L. (1994). Adoptive family system dynamics: Variations by level of openness in the adoption. *Family Process, 33*(2), 125–146.

Gruber, H. (1981). *Darwin on man: A psychological study of scientific creativity* (2nd ed.). Chicago: University of Chicago Press.

Grubman, S., Gross, E., Lerner-Weiss, N., Hernandez, M., McSherry, G. D., Hoyt, L. G., Boland, M., & Oleske, J. M. (1995). Older children and adolescents living with perinatally acquired human immunodeficiency virus. *Pediatrics, 95,* 657–663.

Grunau, R. E., Whitfield, M. F., & Petrie, J. (1994). Pain sensitivity and temperament in extremely low-birth-weight premature toddlers and preterm and full-term controls. *Pain, 58,* 341–346.

Grunau, R. V., Kearney, S. M., & Whitfield, M. F. (1990). Language development at 3 years in pre-term children of birth weight below 1000 g. *British Journal of Disorders of Communication, 25,* 173–182.

Grusec, J. E., & Goodnow, J. J. (1994). Impact of parental discipline methods on the child's internalization of values: A reconceptualization of current points of view. *Developmental Psychology, 30,* 4–19.

Grusec, J. E., Goodnow, J. J., & Kuczynski, L. (2000). New directions in analyses of parenting contributions to children's acquisition of values. *Child Development, 71,* 205–211.

Grych, J. H., & Clark, R. (1999). Maternal employment and development of the father–infant relationship in the first year. *Developmental Psychology, 35,* 893–903.

Guberman, S. R. (1996). The development of everyday mathematics in Brazilian children with limited formal education. *Child Development, 67,* 1609–1623.

Guerino, P., Hurwitz, M. D, Noonan, M. E., & Kaffenberger, S. M. (2006). *Crime, violence, discipline, and safety in U.S. public schools: Findings from the School Survey on Crime and Safety: 2003-2004* (NCES 2007-303). Washington, DC: National Center for Education Statistics.

Guilford, J. P. (1956). Structure of intellect. *Psychological Bulletin, 53,* 267–293.

Guilford, J. P. (1959). Three faces of intellect. *American Psychologist, 14,* 469–479.

Guilford, J. P. (1960). Basic conceptual problems of the psychology of thinking. *Proceedings of the New York Academy of Sciences, 91,* 6–21.

Guilford, J. P. (1967). *The nature of human intelligence.* New York: McGraw-Hill.

Guilford, J. P. (1986). *Creative talents: Their nature, uses and development.* Buffalo, NY: Bearly.

Guilleminault, C., Palombini, L., Pelayo, R., & Chervin, R. D. (2003). Sleeping and sleep terrors in prepubertal children: What triggers them? *Pediatrics, 111,* pp. e17–e25.

Guillermoprieto, A. (1996, December 2). Little Eva. *The New Yorker,* pp. 98–106.

Guillette, E. A., Meza, M. M., Aquilar, M. G., Soto, A. D., & Garcia, I. E. (1998). An anthropological approach to the evaluation of pre-school children exposed to pesticides in Mexico. *Environmental Health Perspectives, 106,* 347–353.

Gullone, E. (2000). The development of normal fear: A century of research. *Clinical Psychology Review, 20,* 429–451.

Gunby, J., Daya, S., & IVF Directors Group of the Canadian Fertility and Andrology Society. (2006). Assisted reproductive technologies (ART) in Canada: 2002 results from the Canadian ART Register, *Fertility and Sterility, 86,* 1356–1364.

Gunnar, M. R., Larson, M. C., Hertsgaard, L., Harris, M. L., & Brodersen, L. (1992). The stressfulness of separation among nine-month-old infants: Effects of social context variables and infant temperament. *Child Development, 63,* 290–303.

Gunnoe, M. L., & Hetherington, E. M. (2004). Stepchildren's perceptions of noncustodial mothers and noncustodial fathers: Differences in socioemotional involvement and associations with adolescent adjustment problems. *Journal of Family Psychology, 18,* 555–563.

Gunnoe, M. L., & Mariner, C. L. (1997). Toward a developmental-contextual model of the effects of parental spanking on children's aggression. *Archives of Pediatric and Adolescent Medicine, 151,* 768–775.

Guralnick, P. (1994). *Last train to Memphis: The rise of Elvis Presley.* Boston: Little, Brown.

Guthrie, J. T., Schafer, W. D., & Huang, C.-W. (2001). Benefits of opportunity to read and balanced instruction on the NAEP. *The Journal of Educational Research, 94,* 145–162.

Guttmann, A., Dick, P., & To, T. (2004). Infant hospitalization and maternal depression, poverty and single parenthood–a population-based study. *Child: Care, Health & Development, 30,* 67–75.

Guyer, B., Hoyert, D. L., Martin, J. A., Ventura, S. J., MacDorman, M. F., & Strobino, D. M. (1999). Annual summary of vital statistics—1998. *Pediatrics, 104,* 1229–1246.

Guzell, J. R., & Vernon-Feagans, L. (2004). Parental perceived control over caregiving and its relationship to parent–infant interaction. *Child Development, 75,* 134–146.

Guzick, D. S., Carson, S. A., Coutifaris, C., Overstreet, J. W., Factor-Litvak, P., Steinkampf, M. P., Hill, J. A., Mastroianni, L., Buster, J. E., Nakajima, S. T., Vogel, D. L., & Canfield, R. E. (1999). Efficacy of superovulation and intrauterine insemination in the treatment of infertility. *New England Journal of Medicine, 340,* 177–183.

Gwiazda, J. & Birch, E. E. (2001). Perceptual development: Vision. In B. E. Goldstein (Ed.), *Blackwell handbook of perception.* (pp. 636–668). Oxford: Blackwell Publishers.

Habbick, B. F., Pizzichini, M. M. M., Taylor, B., Rennie, D., Senthilselvan, A., & Sears, M. R. (1999). Prevalence of asthma, rhinitis and eczema among children in 2 Canadian cities: The international study of asthma and allergies in childhood. *Canadian Medical Association Journal, 160,* 1824–1828.

Hack, M., Flannery, D. J., Schluchter, M., Cartar, L., Borawski, E., & Klein, N. (2002). Outcomes in young adulthood for very low-birth-weight infants. *New England Journal of Medicine, 346*(3), 149–157.

Hack, M., Youngstrom, E. A., Cartar, L., Schluchter, M., Taylor, H. G., Flannery, D., et al. (2004). Behavioral outcomes and

evidence of psychopathology among very low birth weight infants at age 20 years. *Pediatrics, 114,* 932–940.

Haddow, J. E., Palomaki, G. E., Allan, W. C., Williams, J. R., Knight, G. J., Gagnon, J., O'Heir, C. E., Mitchell, M. L., Hermos, R. J., Waisbren, S. E., Faix, J. D., & Klein, R. Z. (1999). Maternal thyroid deficiency during pregnancy and subsequent neuropsychological development of the child. *New England Journal of Medicine, 341,* 549–555.

Haddow, J. E., Palomaki, G. E., Knight, G. J., Williams, J., Polkkiner, A., Canick, J. A., Saller, D. N., & Bowers, G. B. (1992). Prenatal screening for Down's syndrome with use of maternal serum markers. *New England Journal of Medicine, 327,* 588–593.

Haden, C. A., & Fivush, F. (1996). Contextual variation in maternal conversational styles. *Merrill-Palmer Quarterly, 42,* 200–227.

Haden, C. A., Haine, R. A., & Fivush, R. (1997). Developing narrative structure in parent–child reminiscing across the preschool years. *Developmental Psychology, 33,* 295–307.

Haden, C. A., Ornstein, P. A., Eckerman, C. O., & Didow, S. M. (2001). Mother child conversational interactions as events unfold: Linkages to subsequent remembering. *Child Development, 72*(4), 1016–1031.

Hagan, J. F., Committee on Psychosocial Aspects of Child and Family Health, & Task Force on Terrorism. (2005). Psychosocial implications of disaster or terrorism on children: A guide for pediatricians. *Pediatrics, 116,* 787–796.

Haig, D. (1993). Genetic conflicts in human pregnancy. *Quarterly Review of Biology, 68,* 495–532.

Haig, D., & Westoby, M. (1989). Parent-specific gene expression and the triploid endosperm. *American Naturalist, 134,* 147–155.

Haight, W. L., Wang, X., Fung, H. H., Williams, K., & Mintz, J. (1999). Universal, developmental, and variable aspects of young children's play: A cross-cultural comparison of pretending at home. *Child Development, 70*(6), 1477–1488.

Haith, M. M. (1986). Sensory and perceptual processes in early infancy. *Journal of Pediatrics, 109*(1), 158–171.

Haith, M. M. (1998). Who put the cog in infant cognition? Is rich interpretation too costly? *Infant Behavior and Development, 21*(2), 167–179.

Haith, M. M., & Benson, J. B. (1998). Infant cognition. In D. Kuhn & R. S. Siegler (Eds.), *Handbook of Child Psychology: Vol. 2. Cognition, perception, and language* (5th ed., pp. 199–254). New York: Wiley.

Hakuta, K. (1986). *The mirror of language: The debate on bilingualism.* New York: Basic Books.

Hala, S., & Chandler, M. (1996). The role of strategic planning in accessing false-belief understanding. *Child Development, 67,* 2948–2966.

Halaas, J. L., Gajiwala, K. S., Maffei, M., Cohen, S. L., Chait, B. T., Rabinowitz, D., Lallone, R. L., Burley, S. K., & Friedman, J. M. (1995). Weight reducing effects of the plasma protein encoded by the obese gene. *Science, 269,* 543–546.

Hall, D. G., & Graham, S. A. (1999). Lexical form class information guides word-to-object mapping in preschoolers. *Child Development, 70,* 78–91.

Hall, G. S. (1916). *Adolescence.* New York: Appleton. (Original work published 1904.)

Hallett, D., Chandler, M.J., & Lalonde, C.E. (2007). Aboriginal language knowledge and youth suicide. *Cognitive Development, 22,* 392–399.

Hallfors, D. D., Waller, M. W., Bauer, D., Ford, C. A., & Halpern, C. T. (2005). Which comes first in adolescence—sex and drugs or depression? *American Journal of Preventive Medicine, 29,* 163–170.

Halpern, D. F. (1997). Sex differences in intelligence: Implications for education. *American Psychologist, 52*(10), 1091–1102.

Halpern, S. H., Leighton, B. L., Ohlsson, A., Barrett, J. F. R., & Rice, A. (1998). Effect of epidural vs. parenteral opioid analgesia on the progress of labor. *Journal of the American Medical Association, 280,* 2105–2110.

Halterman, J. S., Aligne, A., Auinger, P., McBride, J. T., & Szilagyi, P. G. (2000). Inadequate therapy for asthma among children in the United States. *Pediatrics, 105*(1), 272–276.

Hamilton, L., Cheng, S., & Powell, B. (2007). Adoptive parents, adaptive parents: Evaluating the importance of biological ties for parental investment. *American Sociological Review, 72,* 95–116.

Hammad, T. A., Laughren, T., & Racoosin, J. (2006). Suicidality in pediatric patients treated with antidepressant drugs. *Archives of General Psychiatry, 63,* 332–339.

Hampden-Thompson, G., & Johnston, J. S. (2006). Variation in the relationship between nonschool factors and student achievement on international assessments (NCES 2006-014). Washington, DC: U. S. Department of Education, National Center for Education Statistics.

Hampson, J. G., Money, J., & Hampson, J. L. (1956). Hermaphrodism: Recommendations concerning case management. *Journal of Clinical Endocrinology & Metabolism, 16*(4), 547–556.

Hamre, B. K., & Pianta, R.C. (2005). Can instructional and emotional support in the first-grade classroom make a difference for children at risk of school failure? *Child Development, 76,* 949–967.

Handmaker, N. S., Rayburn, W. F., Meng, C., Bell, J. B., Rayburn, B. B., & Rappaport, V. J. (2006). Impact of alcohol exposure after pregnancy recognition on ultrasonographic fetal growth measures. *Alcoholism: Clinical and Experimental Research, 30,* 892–898.

Hanley, W. B. (2005). Newborn screening in Canada—Are we out of step? *Paediatrics and Child Health, 10,* 203–207.

Hansen, D., Lou, H. C., & Olsen, J. (2000). Serious life events and congenital malformations: A national study with complete follow-up. *Lancet, 356,* 875–880.

Hansen, M., Janssen, I., Schiff, A., Zee, P. C., & Dubocovich, M. L. (2005). The impact of school daily schedule on adolescent sleep. *Pediatrics, 115,* 1555–1561.

Hara, H. (2002). Justifications for bullying among Japanese school children. *Asian Journal of Social Psychology, 5,* 197–204.

Hardy, R., Kuh, D., Langenberg, C., & Wadsworth, M. E. (2003). Birth weight, childhood social class, and change in adult blood pressure in the 1946 British birth cohort. *Lancet, 362,* 1178–1183.

Hardy-Brown, K., & Plomin, R. (1985). Infant communicative development: Evidence from adoptive and biological families for genetic and environmental influences on rate differences. *Developmental Psychology, 21,* 378–385.

Hardy-Brown, K., Plomin, R., & DeFries, J. C. (1981). Genetic and environmental influences on rate of communicative development in the

first year of life. *Developmental Psychology, 17,* 704–717.

Hareven, T. (1986). Historical changes in the family and the life course: Implications for child development. In A. M. Smuts & J. W. Hagen (Eds.), History and research in child development: *Monographs of the Society for Research in Child Development, 50,* (4–5, Serial No. 211), 8–23.

Hargrove, J. (1989). *Nelson Mandela: South Africa's silent voice of protest.* Chicago: Children's Press.

Harley, K. and Reese, E. (1999). Origins of autobiographical memory. *Developmental Psychology, 35,* 1338–1348.

Harlow, H. F., & Harlow, M. K. (1962). The effect of rearing conditions on behavior. *Bulletin of the Menninger Clinic, 26,* 213–224.

Harlow, H. F., & Zimmerman, R. R. (1959). Affectional responses in the infant monkey. *Science, 130,* 421–432.

Harmon, A. (2005, November 20). The problem with an almost-perfect genetic world. *New York Times.* Retrieved November 20, 2005, from http://www.nytimes.com/2005/11/20/weekinreview/20harmon.html?ex=1142053200&en=c6c3a9ec0867ef48&ei=5070Harris, G. (2005, March 3). Gene therapy is facing a crucial hearing. *New York Times.* Retrieved March 3, 2005, from http://www.nytimes.com/2005/03/03/politics/ 03gene.html.

Harnishfeger, K. K., & Bjorklund, D. F. (1993). The ontogeny of inhibition mechanisms: A renewed approach to cognitive development. In M. L. Howe & R. P. Pasnak (Eds.), *Emerging themes in cognitive development* (Vol. 1, pp. 28–49). New York: Springer-Verlag.

Harnishfeger, K. K., & Pope, R. S. (1996). Intending to forget: The development of cognitive inhibition in directed forgetting. *Journal of Experimental Psychology, 62,* 292–315.

Harrell, J. S., Gansky, S. A., Bradley, C. B., & McMurray, R. G. (1997). Leisure time activities of elementary school children. *Nursing Research, 46,* 246–253.

Harris, G. (2005, March 3). Gene therapy is facing a crucial hearing. *New York Times.* Retrieved March 3, 2005, from http://www.nytimes.com/2005/03/03/politics/03gene.html.

Harris, P. L., Brown, E., Marriott, C., Whittall, S., & Harmer, S. (1991). Monsters, ghosts, and witches: Testing the limits of the fantasy–reality distinction in young children. In G. E. Butterworth, P. L. Harris, A. M. Leslie, & H. M. Wellman (Eds.), *Perspective on the child's theory of mind.* Oxford: Oxford University Press.

Harris, P. L., Olthof, T., Meerum Terwogt, M., & Hardman, C. (1987). Children's knowledge of situations that provoke emotion. *International Journal of Behavioral Development, 10,* 319–343.

Harrison, A. O., Wilson, M. N., Pine, C. J., Chan, S. Q., & Buriel, R. (1990). Family ecologies of ethnic minority children. *Child Development, 61,* 347–362.

Harrist, A. W., & Waugh, R. M. (2002). Dyadic synchrony: Its structure and function in children's development. *Developmental Review, 22,* 555–592.

Hart, C. H., DeWolf, M., Wozniak, P., & Burts, D. C. (1992). Maternal and paternal disciplinary styles: Relations with preschoolers' playground behavioral orientation and peer status. *Child Development, 63,* 879–892.

Hart, C. H., Ladd, G. W., & Burleson, B. R. (1990). Children's expectations of the outcome of social strategies: Relations with sociometric

status and maternal disciplinary style. *Child Development, 61,* 127–137.

Hart, C. H., Nelson, D. A., Robinson, C. C., Olsen, S. F., & McNeilly-Choque, M. K. (1998). Overt and relational aggression in Russian nursery-school-age children: Parenting style and marital linkages. *Developmental Psychology, 34,* 687–697.

Hart, S. N., & Brassard, M. R. (1987). A major threat to children's mental health: Psychological maltreatment. *American Psychologist, 42*(2), 160–165.

Harter, S. (1990). Causes, correlates, and the functional role of global self-worth: A life-span perspective. In J. Kolligan & R. Sternberg (Eds.), *Competence considered: Perceptions of competence and incompetence across the life-span* (pp. 67–97). New Haven: Yale University Press.

Harter, S. (1993). Developmental changes in self-understanding across the 5 to 7 shift. In A. Sameroff & M. Haith (Eds.), *Reason and responsibility: The passage through childhood.* Chicago: University of Chicago Press.

Harter, S. (1996). Developmental changes in self-understanding across the 5 to 7 shift. In A. J. Sameroff & M. M. Haith (Eds.), *The five to seven year shift: The age of reason and responsibility* (pp. 207–235). Chicago: University of Chicago Press.

Harter, S. (1998). The development of self-representations. In W. Damon (Series Ed.) & N. Eisenberg (Vol. Ed.), *Handbook of child psychology: Vol. 3. Social, emotional, and personality development* (5th ed., pp. 553–617). New York: Wiley.

Hartshorn, K., Rovee-Collier, C., Gerhardstein, P., Bhatt, R. S., Wondoloski, R. L., Klein, P., Gilch, J., Wurtzel, N., & Campos-de-Carvalho, M. (1998). The ontogeny of long-term memory over the first year-and-a-half of life. *Developmental Psychobiology, 32,* 69–89.

Hartup, W. W. (1992). Peer relations in early and middle childhood. In V. B. Van Hasselt & M. Hersen (Eds.), *Handbook of social development: A lifespan perspective* (pp. 257–281). New York: Plenum.

Hartup, W. W. (1996a). The company they keep: Friendships and their developmental significance. *Child Development, 67,* 1–13.

Hartup, W. W. (1996b). Cooperation, close relationships, and cognitive development. In W. M. Bukowski, A. F. Newcomb, & W. W. Hartup (Eds.), *The company they keep: Friendship in childhood and adolescence* (pp. 213–237). New York: Cambridge University Press.

Hartup, W. W., & Stevens, N. (1999). Friendships and adaptation across the life span. *Current Directions in Psychological Science, 8,* 76–79.

Harvard Medical School. (2002b, July). Treatment of bulimia and binge eating. *Harvard Mental Health Letter, 19*(1), pp. 1–4.

Harvard Medical School. (2003c, June). Confronting suicide, Part II. *Harvard Mental Health Letter, 19*(12), 1–5.

Harvard Medical School. (2004a, December). Children's fears and anxieties. *Harvard Mental Health Letter, 21*(6), 1–3.

Harwood, R. (1987). *Mandela.* New York: New American Library.

Harwood, R. L., Schoelmerich, A., Ventura-Cook, E., Schulze, P. A., & Wilson, S. P. (1996). Culture and class influences on Anglo and Puerto Rican mothers' beliefs regarding long-term socialization goals and child behavior. *Child Development, 67,* 2446–2461.

Haskins, R. (1989). Beyond metaphor: The efficacy of early childhood education. *American Psychologist, 44*(2), 274–282.

Haswell, K., Hock, E., & Wenar, C. (1981). Oppositional behavior of preschool children: Theory and prevention. *Family Relations, 30*, 440–446.

Hatano, G., Siegler, R. S., Richards, D. D., Inagaki, K., Stavy, R., & Wax, N. (1993). The development of biological knowledge: A multi-national study. *Cognitive Development, 8*, 47–62.

Hatcher, P. J., Hulme, C., & Ellis, A. W. (1994). Ameliorating early reading failure by integrating the teaching of reading and phonological skills: The phonological linkage hypothesis. *Child Development, 65*, 41–57.

Hauck, F. R., Herman, S. M., Donovan, M., Iyasu, S., Moore, C. M., Donoghue, E., et al. (2003). Sleep environment and the risk of sudden infant death syndrome in an urban population: The Chicago Infant Mortality Study. *Pediatrics, 111*, 1207–1214.

Hauck, F. R., Omojokun, O. O., & Siadaty, M. S. (2005). Do pacifiers reduce the risk of sudden infant death syndrome? A meta-analysis. *Pediatrics, 116*, e716–e723.

Haugaard, J. J. (1998). Is adoption a risk factor for the development of adjustment problems? *Clinical Psychology Review, 18*, 47–69.

Haugh, S., Hoffman, C., & Cowan, G. (1980). The eye of the very young beholder: Sex typing of infants by young children. *Child Development, 51*, 598–600.

Hausfather, A., Toharia, A., LaRoche, C., & Engelsmann, F. (1997). Effects of age of entry, daycare quality, and family characteristics on preschool behavior. *Journal of Child Psychology and Psychiatry, 38*, 441–448.

Hawes, A. (1996). Jungle gyms: The evolution of animal play. *ZooGoer, 25*(1). Retrieved July 18, 2006, from http://nationalzoo.si.edu/Publications/ZooGoer.1996/1/junglegyms.cfm.

Hawkins, D. L., Pepler, D. J., & Craig, W. M. (2001). Naturalistic observations of peer interventions in bullying. *Social Development, 10*, 512–527.

Hawkins, J. (1999). Trends in anesthesiology during childbirth. *Anesthesiology, 91*, A1060.

Hawkins, J. D., Catalano, R. F., & Miller, J. Y. (1992). Risk and protective factors for alcohol and other drug problems in adolescence and early adulthood: Implications for substance abuse programs. *Psychological Bulletin, 112*(1), 64–105.

Hawkins, J. D., Catalano, R. F., Kosterman, R., Abbott, R., & Hill, K. G. (1999). Preventing adolescent health-risk behaviors by strengthening protection during childhood. *Archives of Pediatrics and Adolescent Medicine, 153*, 226–234.

Hay, D. (2003). Pathways to violence in the children of mothers who were depressed post partum. *Developmental Psychology, 39*, 1083–1094.

Hay, D. F., Pedersen, J., & Nash, A. (1982). Dyadic interaction in the first year of life. In K. H. Rubin & H. S. Ross (Eds.), *Peer relationships and social skills in children.* New York: Springer.

Hayes, A., & Batshaw, M. L. (1993). Down syndrome. *Pediatric Clinics of North America, 40*, 523–535.

Hayne, H., Barr, R., & Herbert, J. (2003). The effect of prior practice on memory reactivation and generalization. *Child Development, 74*, 1615–1627.

Health Canada. (1994). *Canadian guidelines for sexual health education.* Ottawa: Minister of Supply and Services.

Health Canada. (1998a). *Canadian immunization guide* (5th ed.). Ottawa: Author.

Health Canada. (1998b). *For the Safety of Canadian Children and Youth.* Ottawa: Author.

Health Canada. (1999a). *Healthy development of children and youth: The role of the determinants of health.* Catalogue No. H39-501/1999E. Ottawa: Author.

Health Canada. (1999b). *Aboriginal peoples and the AIDS epidemic in Canada.* Ottawa: Health Canada Laboratory Centre for Disease Control. Retrieved August 10, 2002, from http://caan.ca/Epi/Dev/Design/Epi-Update.pdf

Health Canada. (2000a) *Crib safety.* Ottawa: Author.

Health Canada. (2000b). *Family-centred maternity and newborn care: National guidelines* (4th ed.). Ottawa: Minister of Public Works and Government Services.

Health Canada. (2000c). *Perinatal health indicators for Canada: A resource manual.* Ottawa: Minister of Public Works and Government Services Canada.

Health Canada. (2000d). *Rural health.* Retrieved September 20, 2002, from http://www.hc-sc.gc.ca/english/media/releases/2000/2000_61ebk2.htm

Health Canada. (2001a). *A conceptual and epidemiological framework for child maltreatment surveillance.* Ottawa: Minister of Public Works and Government Services Canada.

Health Canada. (2001b). *Respiratory disease in Canada.* Ottawa: Author.

Health Canada. (2002). *Congenital Anomalies in Canada–A Perinatal Health Report.* Ottawa: Minister of Public Works and Government Services Canada.

Health Canada (2004). *Canadian Perinatal Health Report 2003.* Ottawa: Minister of Public Works and Government Services Canada. Available at: www.phac-aspc.gc.ca/publicat/cphr-rspc03/index.html.

Health Canada. (2005). Child maltreatment: A public health issue. Retrieved July 26, 2007 from http://www.hc-sc.gc.ca/sr-sr/pubs/hpr-rpms/bull/2004-9-child-enfant/method_e.html.

Health Canada. (2006). First Nations & Inuit: Suicide prevention. Retrieved on August 23, 2007 from http://www.hc-sc.gc.ca/fnih-spni/promotion/suicide/index_e.html.

Health Canada. (2007). Dating violence. Retrieved September 3, 2007 from www.childtrendsdatabank.org/pdf/66_PDF.pdf.

Health Canada. (2007). *Eating Well with Canada's Food Guide: A Resource for Educators and Communicators.* Ottawa, ON: Ministry of Health.

Heath, S. B. (1989). Oral and literate tradition among black Americans living in poverty. *American Psychologist, 44*, 367–373.

Heffner, L. J. (2004). Advanced maternal age—how old is too old? *New England Journal of Medicine, 351*, 1927–1929.

Helgason, A., & Lund, K. E. (2001). Environmental tobacco smoke exposure of young children: Attitudes and health-risk awareness in the Nordic countries. *Nicotine and Tobacco Research, 3*, 341–345.

Helms, J. E. (1992). Why is there no study of cultural equivalence in standardized cognitive ability testing? *American Psychologist, 47*, 1083–1101.

Helms, J. E., Jernigan, M., & Macher, J. (2005). The meaning of race in psychology and how to change it: A methodological perspective. *American Psychologist, 60*, 27–36.

Helwig, C. C., & Jasiobedzka, U. (2001). The relation between law and morality: Children's reasoning about socially beneficial and unjust laws. *Child Development, 72*, 1382–1393.

Helwig, C. C., Zelazo, P. D., & Wilson, M. (2001). Children's judgments of psychological harm in normal and noncanonical situations. *Child Development, 72*, 66–81.

Henderson, H. A., Marshall, P. J., Fox, N. A., & Rubin, K. H. (2004). Psychophysiological and behavioral evidence for varying forms and functions of nonsocial behavior in preschoolers. *Child Development, 75*, 251–263.

Henrich, C. C., Brown, J. L., & Aber, J. L. (1999). Evaluating the effectiveness of school-based violence prevention: Developmental approaches. *Social Policy Report, SRCD, 13*(3), 1-16.

Herman-Giddens, M. E., Brown, G., Verbiest, S., Carlson, P. J., Hooten, E. G., Howell, E., & Butts, J. D. (1999). Underascertainment of child abuse mortality in the United States. *Journal of the American Medical Association, 282*, 463–467.

Hernandez, D. J. (1997). Child development and the social demography of childhood. *Child Development, 68*, 149–169.

Hernandez, D. J. (2004, Summer). Demographic change and the life circumstances of immigrant families. In R. E. Behrman (Ed.), *Children of immigrant families* (pp. 17–48). *The Future of Children, 14*(2).

Herrmann, H. J., & Roberts, M. W. (1987). Preventive dental care: The role of the pediatrician. *Pediatrics, 80*, 107–110.

Herrnstein, R. J., & Murray, C. (1994). *The bell curve: Intelligence and class structure in American life.* New York: Free Press.

Hertenstein, M. J., & Campos, J. J. (2004). The retention effects of an adult's emotional displays on infant behavior. *Child Development, 75*, 595–613.

Hertzen, V. & Haahtela, T. (2005). Signs of reversing trends in prevalence of asthma. *Allergy, 60*, 283–292.

Hertzman, C. (2002). *Leave no child behind! Social exclusion and child development.* Toronto: The Laidlaw Foundation.

Hesketh, T., Lu, L. & Xing, Z. W. (2005). The effect of China's one-child policy after 25 years. *New England Journal of Medicine, 353*, 1171–1176.

Hesso, N. A., & Fuentes, E. (2005). Ethnic differences in neonatal and postneonatal mortality. *Pediatrics, 115*, e44–e51.

Hetherington, E. M. (1987). Family relations six years after divorce. In K. Pasley & M. Ihinger-Tallman (Eds.), *Remarriage and parenting today: Research and theory.* New York: Guilford.

Hetherington, E. M., & Kelly, J. (2002). *For better or worse: Divorce reconsidered.* New York: Norton.

Hetherington, E. M., Bridges, M., & Insabella, G. M. (1998). What matters? What does not? Five perspectives on the association between marital transitions and children's adjustment. *American Psychologist, 53*, 167–184.

Hetherington, E. M., Stanley-Hagan, M., & Anderson, E. (1989). Marital transitions: A child's perspective. *American Psychologist, 44*, 303–312.

Hetzel, B. S. (1994). Iodine deficiency and fetal brain damage. *New England Journal of Medicine, 331*, 1770–1771.

Hewlett, B. S. (1987). Intimate fathers: Patterns of paternal holding among Aka pygmies. In M. E. Lamb (Ed.), *The father's role: Cross-cultural perspectives* (pp. 295–330). Hillsdale, NJ: Erlbaum.

Hewlett, B. S. (1992). Husband–wife reciprocity and the father–infant relationship among Aka pygmies. In B. S. Hewlett (Ed.), *Father–child relations: Cultural and biosocial contexts* (pp. 153–176). New York: de Gruyter.

Hewlett, B. S., Lamb, M. E., Shannon, D., Leyendecker, B., & Schölmerich, A. (1998). Culture and early infancy among central African foragers and farmers. *Developmental Psychology, 34*(4), 653–661.

Hickling, A. K., & Wellman, H. M. (2001). The emergence of children's causal explanations and theories: Evidence from everyday conversations. *Developmental Psychology, 37*(5), 668–683.

Hickman, M., Roberts, C., & de Matos, M. G. (2000). Exercise and leisure time activities. In C. Currie, K. Hurrelmann, W. Settertobulte, R. Smith, & J. Todd (Eds.), *Health and health behaviour among young people.* WHO Policy Series: Healthy Policy for Children and Adolescents, Series No. 1. (pp. 73–82).

Hill, J. L., Waldfogel, J., Brooks-Gunn, J., & Han, W.-J. (2005). Maternal employment and child development: A fresh look using newer methods. *Developmental Psychology, 41*, 833–850.

Hill, J. P. (1987). Research on adolescents and their families: Past and prospect. In E. E. Irwin (Ed.), *Adolescent social behavior and health.* San Francisco: Jossey-Bass.

Hill, N. E., & Taylor, L. C. (2004). Parental school involvement and children's academic achievement: Pragmatics and issues. *Current Directions in Psychological Science, 13*, 161–168.

Hillier, L. (2002). "It's a catch-22": Same-sex-attracted young people on coming out to parents. In S. S. Feldman & D. A. Rosenthal, (Eds.), Talking sexuality. *New Directions for Child and Adolescent Development, 97*, 75–91.

Hinckley, A. F., Bachard, A. M., & Reif, J. S. (2005). Late pregnancy exposures to disinfection by-products and growth-related birth outcomes. *Environmental Health Perspectives, 113*, 1808–1813.

Hinds, T. S., West, W. L., Knight, E. M., & Harland, B. F. (1996). The effect of caffeine on pregnancy outcome variables. *Nutrition Reviews, 54*, 203–207.

Hines, A. M. (1997). Divorce-related transitions, adolescent development, and the role of the parent–child relationship: A review of the literature. *Journal of Marriage and the Family, 59*, 375–388.

Hines, M., Chiu, L., McAdams, L. A., Bentler, M. P., & Lipcamon, J. (1992). Cognition and the corpus callosum: Verbal fluency, visual spatial ability, language lateralization related to midsagittal surface areas of the corpus callosum. *Behavioral Neuroscience, 106*, 3–14.

Hirsch, H. V., & Spinelli, D. N. (1970). Visual experience modifies distribution of horizontally and vertically oriented receptive fields in cats. *Science, 168*, 869–871.

Hitchins, M. P., & Moore, G. E. (2002, May 9). Genomic imprinting in fetal growth and development. *Expert Reviews in Molecular Medicine.* Retrieved November 21, 2006, from http://www.expertreviews.org/0200457Xh.htm.

Hitlin, S., Brown, J. S., & Elder, G. H. (2006). Racial self-categorization in adolescence: Multiracial development and social pathways. *Child Development, 77*, 1298–1308.

Ho, W. C. (1989). *Yani: The brush of innocence.* New York: Hudson Hills.

Hoban, T. F. (2004). Sleep and its disorders in children. *Seminars in Neurology, 24*, 327–340.

Hobson, J. A., & Silvestri, L. (1999, February). Parasomnias. *Harvard Mental Health Letter*, pp. 3–5.

Hodges, E. V. E., Boivin, M., Vitaro, F., & Bukowski, W. M. (1999). The power of friendship: Protection against an escalating cycle of peer victimization. *Developmental Psychology, 35*, 94–101.

Hoff, E. (2003). The specificity of environmental influence: Socioeconomic status affects early vocabulary development via maternal speech. *Child Development, 74*, 1368–1378.

Hofferth, S. L. (1998). *Healthy environments, healthy children: Children in families* (Report of the 1997 Panel Study of Income Dynamics, Child Development Supplement). Ann Arbor: University of Michigan Institute for Social Research.

Hofferth, S. L., & Sandberg, J. (1998). *Changes in American children's time, 1981–1997* (Report of the 1997 Panel Study of Income Dynamics, Child Development Supplement). Ann Arbor: University of Michigan Institute for Social Research.

Hoffman, H. J., & Hillman, L. S. (1992). Epidemiology of the sudden infant death syndrome: Maternal, neonatal, and postneonatal risk factors. *Clinics in Perinatology, 19*, 717–737.

Hoffman, M. L. (1970a). Conscience, personality, and socialization techniques. *Human Development, 13*, 90–126.

Hoffman, M. L. (1970b). Moral development. In P. H. Mussen (Ed.), *Carmichael's manual of child psychology* (Vol. 2, 3rd ed., pp. 261–360). New York: Wiley.

Hoffman, M. L., & Hoffman, L. W. (Eds.). (1964). *Review of child development research.* New York: Russell Sage Foundation.

Hoffrage, U., Weber, A., Hertwig, R., & Chase, V. M. (2003). How to keep children safe in traffic: Find the daredevils early. *Journal of Experimental Psychology: Applied, 9*, 249–260.

Hofman, P. L., Regan, F., Jackson, W. E., Jefferies, C., Knight, D. B., Robinson, E. M., & Cutfield, W. S. (2004). Premature birth and later insulin resistance. *New England Journal of Medicine, 351*, 2179–2186.

Holden, G. W., & Miller, P. C. (1999). Enduring and different: A meta-analysis of the similarity in parents' child rearing. *Psychological Bulletin, 125*, 223–254.

Holloway, S. D. (1999). Divergent cultural models of child rearing and pedagogy in Japanese preschools. *New Directions for Child and Adolescent Development, 83*, 61–75.

Holowka, S., & Petitto, L. A. (2002). Left hemisphere cerebral specialization for babies while babbling. *Science, 297*, 1515.

Holsti, L., Grunau, R. V. E., & Whitfield, M. F. (2002). Developmental coordination disorder in extremely low birth weight children at nine years. *Journal of Developmental and Behavioral Pediatrics, 23*, 9–15.

Hopfensperger, J. (1996, April 15). Germany's fast track to a career. *Minneapolis Star-Tribune*, pp. A1, A6.

Hopkins, B., & Westra, T. (1988). Maternal handling and motor development: An intracultural study. *Genetic, Social and General Psychology Monographs, 14*, 377–420.

Hopkins, B., & Westra, T. (1990). Motor development, maternal expectations and the role of handling. *Infant Behavior and Development, 13*, 117–122.

Horbar, J. D., Wright, E. C., Onstad, L., & the Members of the National Institute of Child Health and Human Development Neonatal Research Network. (1993). Decreasing mortality associated with the introduction of surfactant therapy: An observational study of neonates weighing 601 to 1300 grams at birth. *Pediatrics, 92*, 191–196.

Horwood, L. J., & Fergusson, D. M. (1998). Breastfeeding and child achievement. [Electronic version]. *Pediatrics, 101*(1). Retrieved January 5, 1998, from http://www.pediatrics.org/cgi/content/full/101/1/e9.

Houk, C. P., Hughes, I. A., Ahmed, S. F., Lee, P. A., & Writing Committee for the International Intersex Consensus Conference Participants. (2006). Summary of Consensus Statement on Intersex Disorders and their Management. *Pediatrics, 118*, 753–757.

Howe, M. L. (2003). Memories from the cradle. *Current Directions in Psychological Science, 12*, 62–65.

Howe, M. L., & Courage, M. L. (1993). On resolving the enigma of infantile amnesia. *Psychological Bulletin, 113*, 305–326.

Howe, M. L., & Courage, M. L. (1997). The emergence and early development of autobiographical memory. *Psychological Review, 104*, 499–523.

Howe, N., Aquan-Assee, J., Bukowski, W. M., Lehoux, P. M., & Rinaldi, C. M. (2001). Siblings as confidants: Emotional understanding, relationship warmth, and sibling self-disclosure. *Social Development, 10*, 439–454.

Howe, N., Petrakos, H., Rinaldi, C. M., & LeFebvre, R. (2005). "This is a bad dog, you know...": Constructing shared meanings during sibling pretend play. *Child Development, 76*, 783–794.

Howe, R. B. (1995). Evolving policy on children's rights in Canada. In K. Covell (Ed.), *Readings in child development* (pp. 3–27). Toronto: Nelson.

Howell, A. J., & Enns, R. A. (1995). A high risk recognition program for adolescents in conflict with the law. *Canadian Psychology, 36*, 149–161.

Howell, R. R. (2006). We need expanded newborn screening. *Pediatrics, 117*, 1800–1805.

Howes, C. (1997). Teacher-sensitivity, children's attachment and play with peers. *Early Education and Development, 8*, 41–49.

Howes, C., & Matheson, C. C. (1992). Sequences in the development of competent play with peers: Social and social pretend play. *Developmental Psychology, 28*, 961–974.

Howes, C., Matheson, C. C., & Hamilton, C. E. (1994). Maternal, teacher, and child care history correlates of children's relationships with peers. *Child Development, 65*, 264–273.

Hoyert, D. L., Heron, M. P., Murphy, S. L., & Kung, H. C. (2006). Deaths: Final data for 2003. *National Vital Statistics Reports, 54*(13). Hyattsville, MD: National Center for Health Statistics.

Hoyert, D. L., Mathews, T. J., Menacker, F., Strobino, D. M., & Guyer, B. (2006). Annual summary of vital statistics: 2004. *Pediatrics, 117*, 168–183.

Huang, G. G. (1995). Self-reported biliteracy and self-esteem: A study of Mexican American 8th graders. *Applied Psycholinguistics, 16*, 271–291.

Huang, G. G. (2000). Mathematics achievement by immigrant children: A comparison of five English-speaking countries. *Education Policy Analysis Archives, 8*(25). Retrieved May 3, 2002, from http://epaa.asu.edu/epaa

Hubbard, F. O. A., & van IJzendoorn, M. H. (1991). Maternal unresponsiveness and infant crying across the first 9 months: A naturalistic longitudinal study. *Infant Behavior and Development, 14*, 299–312.

Hudnall, C. E. (2001, November). "Grand" parents get help: Programs aid aging caregivers and youngsters. *AARP Bulletin, 9,* 12–13.

Hudson, J. I., Hiripi, E., Pope, H. G., Jr., & Kessler, R. C. (2007). The prevalence and correlates of eating disorders in the national comorbidity survey replication. *Biological Psychiatry, 61(3),* 348–358.

Hudson, V. M., & den Boer, A. M. (2004). *Bare branches: Security implications of Asia's surplus male population.* Cambridge, MA: MIT Press.

Huebner, C. E., & Meltzoff, A. N. (2005). Intervention to change parent-child reading style: A comparison of instructional methods. *Applied Developmental Psychology, 26,* 296–313.

Huesmann, L. R. (1986). Psychological processes promoting the relation between exposure to media violence and aggressive behavior by the viewer. *Journal of Social Issues, 42,* 125–139.

Huesmann, L. R., & Eron, L. D. (1984). Cognitive processes and the persistence of aggressive behavior. *Aggressive Behavior, 10,* 243–251.

Huesmann, L. R., Moise-Titus, J., Podolski, C. L., & Eron, L. (2003). Longitudinal relations between children's exposure to TV violence and their aggressive and violent behavior in young adulthood: 1977–1992. *Developmental Psychology, 39,* 201–221.

Hughes, C. and Cutting, A. L. (1999). Nature, nurture, and individual differences in early understanding of mind. *Psychological Science, 10,* 429–432.

Hughes, D., Rodriguez, J., Smith, E. P., Johnson, D. J., Stevenson, H. C., & Spicer, P. (2006). Parents' ethnic-racial socialization practices: A review of research and directions for future study. *Developmental Psychology, 42,* 747–770.

Hughes, I. A. (2004). Female development—all by default? *New England Journal of Medicine, 351,* 748–750

Hughes, M. (1975). *Egocentrism in preschool children.* Unpublished doctoral dissertation, Edinburgh University, Edinburgh.

Huizink, A. C., Mulder, E. J. H., & Buitelaar, J. K. (2004). Prenatal stress and risk for psychopathology: Specific effects or induction of general susceptibility? *Psychological Bulletin 130,* 80–114.

Huizink, A., Robles de Medina, P., Mulder, E., Visser, G., & Buitelaar, J. (2002). Psychological measures of prenatal stress as predictors of infant temperament. *Journal of the American Academy of Child & Adolescent Psychiatry, 41,* 1078–1085.

Hujoel, P. P., Bollen, A.-M., Noonan, C. J., & del Aguila, M.A. (2004). Antepartum dental radiography and infant low birth weight. *Journal of the American Medical Association, 291,* 1987–1993.

Human Resources and Social Development Canada. (2002). Investing in our youth for a skilled workforce. Quarterly Labour Market and Income Review-June 2002. Retrieved August 28 2007 from http://www.hrsdc.gc.ca/en/cs/sp/hrsd/prc/publications/quarterlies/2002-000061/page03.shtml.

Human Resources and Social Development Canada. (2003). Section 3 Children (Aged 0-14). In Disability in Canada: A 2001 Profile. Retrieved August 13, 2007 from http://www.hrsdc.gc.ca/en/hip/odi/documents/PALS/PALS001.shtml.

Human Resources and Social Development Canada. (2007). Intercountry adoption services. Retrieved on August 16, 2007 from http://www.hrsdc.gc.ca/en/hip/sd/ias/intercountry_adoption.shtml.

Human Resources Development Canada. (1996). *Growing up in Canada. National longitudinal survey of children and youth.* Ottawa: HRDC.

Human Resources Development Canada. (2002). More immigrant children enjoy good mental health than Canadian children. Bulletin: Special edition on child development. Retrieved September 20, 2002, from http://www.hrdc-drhc.gc.ca/sp-ps/arb-dgra/publications/bulletin/child_dev/chi_dev13.shtml.

Human Resources Development Canada (2003). National Homelessness Initiative Evaluation.

Humphreys, A. P., & Smith, P. K. (1984). Rough-and-tumble in preschool and playground. In P. K. Smith (Ed.), *Play in animals and humans.* Oxford: Blackwell.

Humphreys, G. W. (2002). Cognitive neuroscience. In H. Pashler, & D. Medin (Eds.), *Steven's handbook of experimental psychology* (3rd ed.), *Vol. 2: Memory and cognitive processes* (pp. 77–112). New York: John Wiley & Sons, Inc.

Hunsaker, S. L., & Callahan, C. M. (1995). Creativity and giftedness: Published instrument uses and abuses. *Gifted Child Quarterly, 39(2),* 110–114.

Hunt, C. E. (1996). Prone sleeping in healthy infants and victims of sudden infant death syndrome. *Journal of Pediatrics, 128,* 594–596.

Hunter, S. (1999). *Visual and performing artists: Women in profile.* New York: Crabtree Publishing Company.

Hurst, L. (2007). Sexually transmitted diseases surging. Retrieved August 22, 2007 from http://www.thestar.com/article/245612.

Huston, A. C. & Aronson, S. R. (2005). Mothers' time with infant and time in employment as predictors of mother-child relationships and children's early development. *Child Development, 76,* 467-482.

Huston, A. C., Duncan, G. J., McLoyd, V. C., Crosby, D. A., Ripke, M. N., Weisner, T. S., & Eldred, C. A. (2005). Impacts on children of a policy to promote employment and reduce poverty for low-income parents: New hope after 5 years. *Developmental Psychology, 41,* 902–918.

Huston, H. C., Duncan, G. J., Granger, R., Bos, J., McLoyd, V., Mistry, R., Crosby, D., Gibson, C., Magnuson, K., Romich, J., and Ventura, A. (2001). Work-based antipoverty programs for parents can enhance the performance and social behavior of children. *Child Development, 72(1),* 318–336.

Huttenlocher, J. (1998). Language input and language growth. *Preventive Medicine, 27,* 195–199.

Huttenlocher, J., Haight, W., Bryk, A., Seltzer, M., & Lyons, T. (1991). Early vocabulary growth: Relation to language input and gender. *Developmental Psychology, 27,* 236–248.

Huttenlocher, J., Levine, S., & Vevea, J. (1998). Environmental input and cognitive growth: A study using time-period comparisons. *Child Development, 69,* 1012–1029.

Huttenlocher, J., Vasilyeva, M., Cymerman, E., & Levine, S. (2000). *Language input and child language.* Unpublished manuscript.

Hwang, S. J., Beaty, T. H., Panny, S. R., Street, N. A., Joseph, J. M., Gordon, S., McIntosh, I., & Francomano, C. A. (1995). Association study of transforming growth factor alpha (TGFa) TaqI polymorphism and oral clefts: Indication of gene-environment interaction in a population-based sample of infants with birth defects. *American Journal of Epidemiology, 141,* 629–636.

Hyde, J. S. (2005). The gender similarity hypothesis. *American Psychologist, 60,* 581–592.

Hyde, M. L., & Riko, K. (2000). Design and evaluation issues in Universal Newborn Hearing Screening Programs. *Journal of Speech Language Pathology and Audiology, 24,* 102–118.

Ialongo, N. S., Edelsohn, G., & Kellam, S. G. (2001). A further look at the prognostic power of young children's reports of depressed mood and feelings. *Child Development, 72,* 736–747.

Iamsafe.ca. (2006). Who we are. Retrieved on August 17, 2007 from http://iamsafe.ca/aboutus_en.php.

Iervolino, A. C., Pike, A., Manke, B., Reiss, D., Hetherington, E. M., & Plomin, R. (2002). Genetic and environmental influences in adolescent peer socialization: Evidence from two genetically sensitive designs. *Child Development, 73(1),* 162–174.

Iervolino, A. C., Hines, M., Golombok, S. E., Rust, J., & Plomin, R. (2005). Genetic and environmental influences on sex-types behavior during the preschool years. *Child Development, 76,* 826–840.

Iglowstein, I., Jenni, O. G., Molinari, L., & Largo, R. H. (2003). Sleep duration from infancy to adolescence: Reference values and generational trends. *Pediatrics, 111,* 302–307.

Ikonomidou, C., Bittigau, P., Ishimaru, M. J., Wozniak, D. F., Koch, C., Genz, K., Price, M. T., Stefovska, V., Horster, F., Tenkova, T., Dikranian, K., & Olney, J. W. (2000). Ethanol-induced apoptotic neurodegeneration and fetal alcohol syndrome. *Science, 287,* 1056–1060.

Impagnatiello, F. Guidotti, A. R., Pesold, C. Dwivedi, Y., Caruncho, H., Pisu, M. G., Uzonov, D. P., Smalheiser, N. R., Davis, J. M., Pandey, G. N., Pappas, G. D., Tueting, P., Sharma, R. P., & Costa, E. (1998). A decrease of reelin expression as a putative vulnerability factor in schizophrenia. *Proceedings of the National Academy of Science, 95,* 15718–15723.

Indian and Inuit Health Committee, Canadian Paediatric Society. (1987). Growth charts for Indian and Inuit children. *Canadian Medical Association Journal, 136,* 118–119.

Indian and Inuit Health Committee, Canadian Paediatric Society. (1994). Diabetes and the First Nations. *The Canadian Journal of Paediatrics, 1,* 222–224.

Infante-Rivard, C., Fernández, A., Gauthier, R., David, M., & Rivard, G. E. (1993). Fetal loss associated with caffeine intake before and during pregnancy. *Journal of the American Medical Association, 270,* 2940–2943.

Infectious Diseases and Immunization Committee, Canadian Paediatric Society. (2001). Measles-mumps-rubella vaccine and autistic spectrum disorder: A hypothesis only. *Paediatrics & Child Health, 6,* 387–389.

Ingels, S. J., Planty, M., & Bozick, R. (2005). *A profile of the American high school senior in 2004: A first look. Initial results from the first follow-up of the Education Longitudinal Study of 2002 (ELS:2002).* (NCES 2006348). Jessup, MD: National Center for Education Statistics.

Ingersoll, E. W., & Thoman, E. B. (1999). Sleep/wake states of preterm infants: Stability, developmental change, diurnal variation, and relation with care giving activity. *Child Development, 70,* 1–10.

Ingoldsby, B.B., & Smith, S.R. (2005). Public school teachers' perspectives on the contemporary Hutterite family. *Journal of Comparative Family Studies, 36,* 249–265.

Ingram, J. L., Stodgell, C. S., Hyman, S. L., Figlewicz, D. A., Weitkamp, L. R., & Rodier, P. M. (2000). Discovery of allelic variants of

HOXA1 and HOXB1: Genetic susceptibility to autism spectrum disorders. *Teratology, 62,* 393–406.

Institute of Medicine (IOM) National Academy of Sciences. (1993, November). *Assessing genetic risks: Implications for health and social policy.* Washington, DC: National Academy of Sciences.

Institute of Medicine of the National Academies. (2005). *Preventing childhood obesity: Health in the balance.* Washington, DC: Author.

International Committee for Monitoring Assisted Reproductive Technologies (ICMART). (2006, June). *2002 World report on ART.* Report released at meeting of the European Society of Human Reproduction and Embryology, Prague.

International Human Genome Sequencing Consortium. (2004). Finishing the euchromatic sequence of the human genome. *Nature, 431,* 931–945.

International Labour Office (ILO). (2002). *Every child counts: New global estimates on child labour.* Geneva, Switzerland: Author.

Iruka, I. U., & Carver, P. R. (2006). Initial results from the 2005 NHDS Early Childhood Program Participation Survey (NCES 2006–075). Washington, DC: National Center for Education Statistics.

Irwin, S. H., & Lero, D. S. (1997). *In our way: Child care barriers to full workforce participation experience by parents of young children with special needs and potential remedies.* Cape Breton: Breton Books.

Isabella, R. A. (1993). Origins of attachment: Maternal interactive behavior across the first year. *Child Development, 64,* 605–621.

Isley, S., O'Neil, R., & Parke, R. (1996). The relation of parental affect and control behaviors to children's classroom acceptance: A concurrent and predictive analysis. *Early Education and Development, 7,* 7–23.

Iverson, G. L., Lange, R. T. & Viljoen, H. (2006). Comparing the Canadian and American WAIS-III Normative Systems in Inpatient neuropsychiatry and forensic psychiatry. *Canadian Journal of Behavioral Science, 38,* 348–353.

Iverson, J. M., & Goldin-Meadow, S. (2005). Gesture paves the way for language development. *Psychological Science, 16,* 367–371.

Izard, C. E., Huebner, R. R., Resser, D., McGinness, G. C., & Dougherty, L. M. (1980). The young infant's ability to produce discrete emotional expressions. *Developmental Psychology, 16,* 132–140.

Izard, C. E., Porges, S. W., Simons, R. F., Haynes, O. M., & Cohen, B. (1991). Infant cardiac activity: Developmental changes and relations with attachment. *Developmental Psychology, 27,* 432–439.

Jaccard, J., & Dittus, P. J. (2000). Adolescent perceptions of maternal approval of birth control and sexual risk behavior. *American Journal of Public Health, 90,* 1426–1430.

Jaccard, J., Blanton, H., & Dodge, T. (2005). Peer influences on risk behavior: An analysis of the effects of a close friend. *Developmental Psychology, 41,* 135–147.

Jackson, A. (1997a). The math wars: California battles it out over mathematics Education Reform (Part I). *Notices of the AMS.* Retrieved January 22, 1999, from http://www.ams.org/notices/199706/comm-calif.html

Jackson, A. (1997b). The math wars: California battles it out over mathematics Education Reform (Part II). *Notices of the AMS.* Retrieved January 22, 1999, from http://www.ams.org/notices/199708/comm-calif2.html

Jackson, R. S., Creemers, J. W. M., Ohagi, S., Raffin-Sanson, M. L., Sanders, L., Montague, C. T., Hutton, J. C., & O'Rahilly, S. (1997). Obesity and impaired prohormone processing associated with mutations in the human prohormone convertase 1 gene. *Nature Genetics, 16,* 303–306.

Jacobsen, T., & Hofmann, V. (1997). Children's attachment representations: Longitudinal relations to school behavior and academic competency in middle childhood and adolescence. *Developmental Psychology, 33,* 703–710.

Jacobson, J. L., & Wille, D. E. (1986). The influence of attachment pattern on developmental changes in peer interaction from the toddler to the preschool period. *Child Development, 57,* 338–347.

Jacobson, S. W., Chiodo, L. M., & Jacobson, J. L. (1999). Breast-feeding effects on intelligence quotient in 4- and 11-year-old children. *Pediatrics 103*(5). Retrieved September 23, 2002, from http://www.pediatrics.org/cgi/content/full/103/5/e71.

Jaffee, S. R., Caspi, A., Moffitt, T. E., Dodge, K. A., Rutter, M., Taylor, A., et al. (2005). Nature X nature: Genetic vulnerabilities interact with physical maltreatment to promote conduct problems. *Developmental Psychopathology, 17,* 67–84.

Jaffee, S. R., Caspi, A., Moffitt, T. E., Polo-Tomas, M., Price, T. S., & Taylor, A. (2004). The limits of child effects: Evidence for genetically mediated child effects on corporal punishment but not on physical maltreatment. *Developmental Psychology, 40,* 1047–1058.

Jaffee, S., & Hyde, J. S. (2000). Gender differences in moral orientation: A meta-analysis. *Psychological Bulletin, 126,* 703–726.

Jagers, R. J., Bingham, K., & Hans, S. L. (1996). Socialization and social judgments among inner-city African-American kindergartners. *Child Development, 67,* 140–150.

Jain, T., Missmer, S. A., & Hornstein, M. D. (2004). Trends in embryo-transfer practice and in outcomes of the use of assisted reproductive technology in the United States. *New England Journal of Medicine, 350,* 1639–1645.

Jamieson, C. E. (2001). *Genetic testing for late onset diseases: Current research practices and analysis of policy development.* Working Paper 01–02. Ottawa: Health Canada Policy Research Communications Unit.

Jamieson, C. E. (2001). *Genetic testing for late onset diseases: In-depth thematic analysis of policy and jurisdictional issues.* Health Policy Working Paper Series, Working Paper 01-03. Ottawa: Minister of Public Works and Government Services Canada. Retrieved November 11, 2007 from www.hc-sc.gc.ca/sr-sr/alt_formats/iacb-dgiac/pdf/pubs/hpr-rps/wp-dt/2001-0103-genet-analys/2001-0103-genet-analys_e.pdf.

Jankowiak, W. (1992). Father–child relations in urban China. *Father–child relations: Cultural and bisocial contexts* (pp. 345–363). New York: de Gruyter.

Jankowski, J. J., Rose, S. A., & Feldman, J. F. (2001). Modifying the distribution of attention in infants. *Child Development, 72,* 339–351.

Janowsky, J. S., & Carper, R. (1996). Is there a neural basis for cognitive transitions in school-age children? In A. J. Sameroff & M. M. Haith (Eds.), *The five to seven year shift: The age of reason and responsibility* (pp. 33–56). Chicago: University of Chicago Press.

Janssen, I., Craig, W. M., Boyce, W. F., & Pickett, W. (2004). Associations between overweight and obesity with bullying behaviors in school-aged children. *Pediatrics, 113,* 1187–1194.

Janssen, P. A., Klein, M. C., Harris, S. J., Soolsma, J. & Seymour, L. C. (2000). Single room maternity care and client satisfaction. *Birth, 27,* 235–243.

Japan in shock at school murder. (2004, June 2). BBC News. Retrieved June 2, 2004, from http://news.bbc.co.uk/go/pr/fr/-/1/hi/world/asia-pacific/3768983.stm.

Japel, C., Tremblay, R., Mcduff, P. & Willms, J. D. (2002). Pre-adolescent girls and the onset of puberty. In Willms, J. D. *Vulnerable Children.* (Pg. 305–316). University of Alberta Press.

Jaslow, C. K. (1982). *Teenage pregnancy* (ERIC/CAPS Fact Sheet). Ann Arbor, MI: Counseling and Personnel Services Clearing House.

Javaid, M. K., Crozier, S. R., Harvey, N. C., Gale, C. R., Dennison, E. M., Boucher, B. J., Arden, N. K., Godfrey, K. M., Cooper, C., & Princess Anne Hospital Study Group. (2006). Maternal vitamin D status during pregnancy and childhood bone mass at age 9 years: A longitudinal study. *Lancet, 367*(9504), 36–43.

Jay, M. S., DuRant, R. H., Shoffitt, T., Linder, C. W., & Litt, I. F. (1984). Effect of peer counselors on adolescent compliance in use of oral contraceptives. *Pediatrics, 73,* 126–131.

Jeffery, H. E., Megevand, M., & Page, M. (1999). Why the prone position is a risk factor for sudden infant death syndrome. *Pediatrics, 104,* 263–269.

Jeffords, J. M., & Daschle, T. (2001). Political issues in the genome era. *Science, 291,* 1249–1251.

Jenkins, J. J. & Astington, J. W. (1996). Cognitive factors and family structure associated with theory of mind development in young children. *Developmental Psychology, 32,* 70–78.

Jenkins, J., & Keating, D. (1998). *Risk and resilience in six- and ten-year-old children.* Catalogue No. W-98-23E. Ottawa: Applied Research Branch, Strategic Policy, Human Resources Development Canada.

Jenkins, J., & Keating, D. (1999). *Risk and resilience in six- and ten-year-old children.* Retrieved September 23, 2002, from http://www.hrdc-drhc.gc.ca/sp-ps/arb-dgra/publications/research/1999docs/w-98-23e.pdf

Jenny, C., Hymel, K.P., Ritzen, A., Reinert, S. E., & Hay, T. C. (1999). Analysis of missed cases of abusive head trauma. *Journal of the American Medical Association, 281,* 621–626.

Jensen, A. R. (1969). How much can we boost IQ and scholastic achievement? *Harvard Educational Review, 39,* 1–123.

Ji, B. T., Shu, X. O., Linet, M. S., Zheng, W., Wacholder, S., Gao, Y. T., Ying, D. M., & Jin, F. (1997). Paternal cigarette smoking and the risk of childhood cancer among offspring of nonsmoking mothers. *Journal of the National Cancer Institute, 89,* 238–244.

Jiao, S., Ji, G., & Jing, Q. (1996). Cognitive development of Chinese urban only children and children with siblings. *Child Development, 67,* 387–395.

Jodl, K. M., Michael, A., Malanchuk, O., Eccles, J. S., & Sameroff, A. (2001). Parents' roles in shaping early adolescents' occupational aspirations. *Child Development 72*(4), 1247–1265.

Johnson, D. J., Jaeger, E., Randolph, S. M., Cauce, A. M., Ward, J., & National Institute of Child Health and Human Development Early Child Care Research Network (2003). Studying the effects of early child care experiences on the development of children of color in the United States: Toward a more inclusive research agenda. *Child Development, 74,* 1227–1244.

Johnson, E. (1997). Children's understanding of epistemic conduct in self-deception and other false belief stories. *Child Development, 68,* 1117–1132.

Johnson, J. E. (1998). Play development from ages four to eight. In D. P. Fromberg & D. Bergen (Eds.), *Play from birth to twelve and beyond: Contexts, perspectives, and meanings* (pp. 145–153). New York: Garland.

Johnson, J. G., Cohen, P., Gould, M. S., Kasen, S., Brown, J., & Brook, J. S. (2002). Childhood adversities, interpersonal difficulties, and risk for suicide attempts during late adolescence and early adulthood. *Archives of General Psychiatry, 59,* 741–749.

Johnson, J. G., Cohen, P., Smailes, E. M., Kasen, S., & Brook, J. S. (2002). Television viewing and aggressive behavior during adolescence and adulthood. *Science, 295,* 2468–2471.

Johnson, J., Canning, J., Kaneko, T., Pru, J. K., & Tilly, J. L. (2004). Germline stem cells and follicular renewal in the postnatal mammalian ovary. *Nature, 428,* 145–150.

Johnson, K. E., Scott, P., & Mervis, C. B. (1997). Development of children's understanding of basic-subordinate inclusion relations. *Developmental Psychology, 33,* 745–763.

Johnson, M. H. (1998). The neural basis of cognitive development. In D. Kuhn & R. S. Siegler (Eds.), *Handbook of Child Psychology: Vol. 2. Cognition, perception, and language* (5th ed., pp. 1–49). New York: Wiley.

Johnson, M. H. (1999). Developmental cognitive neuroscience. In M. Bennett (Ed.), *Developmental psychology: Achievements and prospects* (pp. 147–164). Philadelphia, PA: Psychology Press/Taylor & Francis.

Johnson, M. H. (2001). Functional brain development during infancy. In G. Bremner & A. Fogel (Eds.), *Handbooks of developmental psychology: Blackwell handbook of infant development* (pp. 169–190). Malden, MA: Blackwell Publishers.

Johnson, N., & Cremo, E. (1995). Socialization and the Native family. In K. Covell (Ed.), *Readings in child development: A Canadian perspective* (pp. 159–171). Toronto: Nelson.

Johnson, R. A., Hoffmann, J. P., & Gerstein, D. R. (1996). *The relationship between family structure and adolescent substance use* (DHHS Publication No. SMA 96–3086). Washington, DC: U.S. Department of Health and Human Services.

Johnson, S. L. (2000). Improving preschoolers' self-regulation of energy intake. *Pediatrics, 106,* 1429–1435.

Johnson, S. L., & Birch, L. L. (1994). Parents' and children's adiposity and eating styles. *Pediatrics, 94,* 653–661.

Johnston, J., & Ettema, J. S. (1982). *Positive images: Breaking stereotypes with children's television.* Newbury Park, CA: Sage.

Johnston, L. D., O'Malley, P. M., & Bachman, J. G. (2000). *The Monitoring the Future results on adolescent drug use. Overview of key findings 1999.* USDHSS, PHS, NIDA, NIH Publication number 00-490. Bethesda, MD: National Institute on Drug Abuse.

Johnston, L. D., O'Malley, P. M., Bachman, J. G., & Schulenberg, J. E. (2007). *Monitoring the future national results on adolescent drug use: Overview of key findings, 2006* (NIH Publication No. 07-6202). Bethesda, MD: National Institute on Drug Abuse.

Jones, H. W., & Toner, J. P. (1993). The infertile couple. *New England Journal of Medicine, 329,* 1710–1715.

Jones, N. A., Field, T., Fox, N. A., Davalos, M., Lundy, B., & Hart, S. (1998). Newborns of mothers with depressive symptoms are physiologically less developed. *Infant Behavior & Development, 21*(3), 537–541.

Jones, N. A., Field, T., Fox, N. A., Lundy, B., & Davalos, M. (1997). EEG activation in one-month-old infants of depressed mothers. *Development and Psychopathology, 9,* 491–505..

Jones, S. S. (1996). Imitation or exploration? Young infants' matching of adults' oral gestures. *Child Development, 67,* 1952–1969.

Jordan, N. C., Kaplan, D., Olah, L. N., & Locunia, M. N. (2006). Number sense growth in kindergarten: A longitudinal investigation of children at risk for mathematics difficulties. *Child Development, 77,* 153–175.

Joseph, K. S., Huang, L., Liu, S., Ananth, C. V., Allen, A., Sauve, R., & Kramer, M. S. (2007). Reconciling the high rates of preterm and postterm birth in the United States. *Obstetrics & Gynecology, 109,* 813–822.

Joseph, K. S., Marcoux, S., Ohlsson, A., Liu, S., Allen, A. C., Kramer, M. S., & Wen, S. W. (2001). Changes in stillbirth and infant mortality associated with increases in preterm birth among twins. *Pediatrics, 108,* 1055–1061.

Juszczyk, P. W. (2003). The role of speech perception capacities in early language acquisition. In M. T. Banich & M. Mack (Eds.), *Mind, brain, and language: Multidisciplinary perspectives.* Mahwah, NJ: Erlbaum.

Juszczyk, P. W., & Hohne, E. A. (1997). Infants' memory for spoken words. *Science, 277,* 1984–1986.

Just, M. A., Cherkassky, V. L., Keller, T. A., & Minshew, N. J. (2004). Cortical activation and synchronization during sentence comprehension in high-functioning autism: Evidence of underconnectivity. *Brain, 127,* 1811–1821.

Just, M. A., Cherkassky, V. L., Keller, T. A., Kana, R. K., & Minshew, N. J. (2007). Functional and anatomical cortical underconnectivity in autism: Evidence from an fMRI study of an executive function task and corpus callosum morphometry. *Cerebral Cortex, 17,* 951–961.

Juster, F. T., Ono. H., & Stafford, F. P. (2004). *Changing times of American youth: 1981–2003 (Child Development Supplement).* Ann Arbor, MI: University of Michigan Institute for Social Research.

Juul-Dam, N., Townsend, J., & Courchesne, E. (2001). Prenatal, perinatal, and neonatal factors in autism, pervasive developmental disorder—not otherwise specified, and the general population. *Pediatrics, 107*(4), e63.

Kaback, M., Lim-Steele, J., Dabholkar, D., Brown, D., Levy, N., & Zeiger, K., for the International TSD Data Collection Network. (1993). Tay-Sachs disease: Carrier screening, prenatal diagnosis, and the molecular era. *Journal of the American Medical Association, 270,* 2307–2315.

Kagan, J. (1997). Temperament and the reactions to unfamiliarity. *Child Development, 68,* 139–143.

Kagan, J., & Snidman, N. (1991a). Infant predictors of inhibited and uninhibited behavioral profiles. *Psychological Science, 2,* 40–44.

Kagan, J., & Snidman, N. (1991b). Temperamental factors in human development. *American Psychologist, 46,* 856–862.

Kagan, J., & Snidman, N. (2004). *The long shadow of temperament.* Cambridge, MA: Belknap.

Kail, R. (1991). Processing time declines exponentially during childhood and adolescence. *Developmental Psychology, 27,* 259–266.

Kail, R. (1997). Processing time, imagery, and spatial memory. *Journal of Experimental Child Psychology, 64,* 67–78.

Kaiser Family Foundation, Hoff, T., Greene, L., & Davis, J. (2003). *National survey of adolescents and young adults: Sexual health knowledge, attitudes and experiences.* Menlo Park, CA: Henry J. Kaiser Foundation.

Kalagian, W., Delmore, T., Loewen, I., & Busca, C. (1998). Adolescent oral contraceptive use: Factors predicting compliance at 3 and 12 months. *The Canadian Journal of Human Sexuality, 7,* 1–8.

Kalil, A., & Ziol-Guest, K. M. (2005). Single mothers' employment dynamics and adolescent well-being. *Child Development, 76,* 196–211.

Kalish, C. W. (1998). Young children's predictions of illness: Failure to recognize probabilistic cause. *Developmental Psychology, 34*(5), 1046–1058.

Kanaya, T., Scullin, M. H., & Ceci, S. J. (2003). The Flynn effect and U.S. policies: The impact of rising IQ scores on American society via mental retardation diagnoses. *American Psychologist, 58,* 778–790.

Kanetsuna, T., & Smith, P. K. (2002). Pupil insight into bullying and coping with bullying: A bi-national study in Japan and England. *Journal of School Violence, 1,* 5–29.

Kanu, Y. (2005). Teachers' perceptions of the integration of Aboriginal culture into the high school curriculum. *Alberta Journal of Educational Research, 51,* 50–68.

Kaplan, H., & Dove, H. (1987). Infant development among the Ache of East Paraguay. *Developmental Psychology, 23,* 190–198.

Katzman, R. (1993). Education and prevalence of Alzheimer's disease. *Neurology, 43,* 13–20.

Kaufman, A. S., & Kaufman, N. L. (1983). *Kaufman assessment battery for children: Administration and scoring manual.* Circle Pines, MN: American Guidance Service.

Kaufman, A. S., & Kaufman, N. L. (2003). *Kaufman Assessment Battery for Children* (2nd ed.). Circle Pines, MN: American Guidance Service.

Kaufman, J., & Zigler, E. (1987). Do abused children become abusive parents? *American Journal of Orthopsychiatry, 57*(2), 186–192.

Kazdin, A. E., & Benjet, C. (2003). Spanking children: Evidence and issues. *Current Directions in Psychological Science, 12,* 99–103.

Keegan, R. T. (1996). Creativity from childhood to adulthood: A difference of degree and not of kind. *New Directions for Child Development, 72,* 57–66.

Keegan, R. T., & Gruber, H. E. (1985). Charles Darwin's unpublished "Diary of an Infant": An early phase in his psychological work. In G. Eckardt, W. G. Bringmann, & L. Sprung (Eds.), *Contributions to a history of developmental psychology: International William T. Preyer Symposium* (pp. 127–145). Berlin: Walter de Gruyter.

Keel, P. K., & Klump, K. L. (2003). Are eating disorders culture-bound syndromes? Implications for conceptualizing their etiology. *Psychological Bulletin, 129,* 747–769.

Keenan, K., & Shaw, D. (1997). Developmental and social influences on young girls' early problem behavior. *Psychological Bulletin, 121*(1), 95–113.

Kelleher, K. J., Casey, P. H., Bradley, R. H., Pope, S. K., Whiteside, L., Barrett, K. W., Swanson, M. E., & Kirby, R. S. (1993). Risk factors and outcomes for failure to thrive in low birth weight preterm infants. *Pediatrics, 91,* 941–948.

Keller, B. (1999, February 24). A time and place for teenagers. Education Week on the WEB. Retrieved March 11, 2004, from http://www.edweek.org/ew/vol-18/24studen.h18.

Keller, H. (1905). *The story of my life.* New York: Grosset & Dunlap.

Keller, H. (1920). *The world I live in.* New York: Century. (Original work published 1908)

Keller, H. (1929). *The bereaved.* New York: Leslie Fulenwider, Inc.

Kelley, M. L., Smith, T. S., Green, A. P., Berndt, A. E., & Rogers, M. C. (1998). Importance of fathers' parenting to African-American toddler's social and cognitive development. *Infant Behavior & Development, 21,* 733–744.

Kellogg, N., & the Committee on Child Abuse and Neglect. (2005). The evaluation of sexual abuse in children. *Pediatrics, 116*(2), 506–512.

Kellogg, R. (1970). Understanding children's art. In P. Cramer (Ed.), *Readings in developmental psychology today.* Delmar, CA: CRM.

Kelly, A. M., Wall, M., Eisenberg, M., Story, M., & Neumark-Sztainer, D. (2004). High body satisfaction in adolescent girls: Association with demographic, socio-environmental, personal, and behavioral factors. *Journal of Adolescent Health, 34,* 129.

Kelly, J. B., & Emery, R. E. (2003). Children's adjustment following divorce: Risk and resiliency perspectives. *Family Relations, 52,* 352–362.

Kemp. J. S., Unger, B., Wilkins, D., Psara, R. M., Ledbetter, T. L., Graham, M. A., Case, M., and Thach, B. T. (2000). Unsafe sleep practices and an analysis of bedsharing among infants dying suddenly and unexpectedly: Results of a four-year, population-based, death-scene investigation study of sudden infant death and related syndromes. *Pediatrics, 106*(3), e41.

Kendall-Tackett, K. A., Williams, L. M., & Finkelhor, D. (1993). Impact of sexual abuse on children: A review and synthesis of recent empirical studies. *Psychological Bulletin, 113*(1), 164–180.

Kendler, K. S., MacLean, C., Neale, M., Kessler, R., Heath, A., & Eaves, L. (1991). The genetic epidemiology of bulimia nervosa. *American Journal of Psychiatry, 148,* 1627–1637.

Kenney-Benson, G. A., Pomerantz, E. M., Ryan, A. M., & Patrick, H. (2006). Sex differences in math performance: The role of children's approach to schoolwork. *Developmental Psychology, 42,* 11–26.

Kere, J., Hannula-Jouppi, K., Kaminen-Ahola, N., Taipale, M., Eklund, R., Nopola-Hemmi, J., & Kaariainen, H. (2005, October). *Identification of the dyslexia susceptibility gene for DYX5 on chromosome 3.* Paper presented at the American Society of Human Genetics meeting, Salt Lake City, UT.

Kernan, M. (1993, June). The object at hand. *Smithsonian,* pp. 14–16.

Kerns, K. A., Don, A., Mateer, C. A., & Streissguth, A. P. (1997). Cognitive deficits in nonretarded adults with fetal alcohol syndrome. *Journal of Learning Disabilities, 30,* 685–693.

Kessler, R. C., Berglund, P., Demler, O., Jin, R., Merikangas, K. R., & Walters, E. E. (2005). Lifetime prevalence and age-of-onset distributions of *DSM-IV* disorders in the National Comorbidity Survey Replication. *Archives of General Psychiatry, 62,* 593–602.

Khoury, M. J., McCabe, L. L., & McCabe, E. R. B. (2003). Population screening in the age of genomic medicine. *New England Journal of Medicine, 348,* 50–58.

Kier, C., & Lewis, C. (1998). Preschool sibling interaction in separated and married families: Are same-sex pairs or older sisters more sociable? *Journal of Child Psychology and Psychiatry, 39,* 191–201.

Killen, J. D., Robinson, T. N., Ammerman, S., Hayward, C., Rogers, J., Stone, C., et al. (2004). Randomized clinical trial of the efficacy of bupropion combined with nicotine patch in the treatment of adolescent smokers. *Journal of Consulting and Clinical Psychology, 72,* 729–735.

Kim, J., Peterson, K. E., Scanlon, K. S., Fitzmaurice, G. M., Must, A., Oken, E., Rifas-Shiman, S. L., Rich-Edwards, J. W., & Gillman, M. W. (2006). Trends in overweight from 1980 through 2001 among preschool-aged children enrolled in a health maintenance organization. *Obesity, 14*(7), 1107–1112.

Kim, Y. S., Koh, Y.-J., & Leventhal, B. (2005). School bullying and suicidal risk in Korean middle school students. *Pediatrics, 115,* 357–363.

Kimball, M. M. (1986). Television and sex-role attitudes. In T. M. Williams (Ed.), *The impact of television: A natural experiment in three communities* (pp. 265–301). Orlando, FL: Academic Press.

Kim-Cohen, J., Caspi, A., Moffitt, T. E., Harrington, H., Milne, B. J., & Poulton, R. (2003). Prior juvenile diagnoses in adults with mental disorder: Developmental follow-back of a prospective-longitudinal cohort. *Archives of General Psychiatry, 60,* 709–717.

Kim-Cohen, J., Moffitt, T. E., Caspi, A., & Taylor, A. (2004). Genetic and environmental processes in young children's resilience and vulnerability to socioeconomic deprivation. *Child Development, 75,* 651–668.

King, A. J. C., Boyce, W. F., & King, M. A. (1999). *Trends in the health of Canadian youth.* Ottawa: Health Canada.

King, A., Beazley, R., Warren, W., Hankins, C., Robertson, A., & Radford, J. (1988). *Canada youth and AIDS study.* Kingston, ON: Social Program Evaluation Group, Queen's University.

King, B. M. (1996). *Human sexuality today.* Englewood Cliffs, NJ: Prentice-Hall.

King, C. (2000). From cradleboard to motherboard: Buffy Sainte-Marie's interactive multimedia curriculum transforms Native American studies. *Teaching Tolerance, 17,* 10–13.

King, C., Siegel, M., Celebucki, C., & Connolly, G. N. (1998). Adolescent exposure to cigarette advertising in magazines. *Journal of the American Medical Association, 279,* 1–520.

King, W. J., MacKay, M., Sirnick, A., & the Canadian Shaken Baby Study Group. (2003). Shaken baby syndrome in Canada: Clinical characteristics and outcomes of hospital cases. *Canadian Medical Association Journal, 168,* 155–159.

Kinney, H. C., Filiano, J. J., Sleeper, L. A., Mandell, F., Valdes-Dapena, M., & White, W. F. (1995). Decreased muscarinic receptor binding in the arcuate nucleus in Sudden Infant Death Syndrome. *Science, 269,* 1446–1450.

Kinsbourne, M. (1994). Sugar and the hyperactive child. *New England Journal of Medicine, 330,* 355–356.

Kinsella, K., & Velkoff, V. A. (2001). *An aging world: 2001.* U.S. Census Bureau, Series P95/01–1. Washington, DC: U.S. Government Printing Office.

Kinsman, S., Romer, D., Furstenberg, F. F., & Schwarz, D. F. (1998). Early sexual initiation: The role of peer norms. *Pediatrics, 102,* 1185–1192.

Kirby, D. (1997). *No easy answers: Research findings on programs to reduce teen pregnancy.*

Washington, DC: National Campaign to Prevent Teen Pregnancy.

Kirkham, C., Harris, S. & Grzybowski, S. Evidence-based prenatal care: Part II. Third-trimester care and prevention of infectious diseases. *American Family Physician, 71,* 1555–1560.

Kirmayer, L. J., Boothroyd, L. J., & Hodgins, S. (1998). Attempted suicide among Inuit youth: Psychosocial correlates and implications for prevention. *Canadian Journal of Psychiatry, 43,* 816–822.

Kirmayer, L. J., Brass, G. M., & Tait, C. L. (2000). The mental health of Aboriginal peoples: Transformations of identity and community. *Canadian Journal of Psychiatry, 45,* 607–616.

Kisilevsky, B. S., Hains, S. M. J., Lee, K., Muir, D. W., Xu, F., Fu, G., Zhao, Z. Y., & Yang, R. L. (1998). The still-face effect in Chinese and Canadian 3- to 6-month-old infants. *Developmental Psychology, 34*(4), 629–639.

Kisilevsky, B. S., Hains, S. M J., Lee, K., Xie, X., Huang, H., Ye, H. H., Zhang, K., & Wang, Z. (2003). Effects of experience on fetal voice recognition. *Psychological Science, 14,* 220–224.

Kisilevsky, B. S., Muir, D. W., & Low, J. A. (1992). Maturation of human fetal responses to vibroacoustic stimulation. *Child Development, 63,* 1497–1508.

Klar, A. J. S. (1996). A single locus, RGHT, specifies preference for hand utilization in humans. In *Cold Spring Harbor Symposia on Quantitative Biology* (Vol. 61, pp. 59–65). Cold Spring Harbor, NY: Cold Spring Harbor Laboratory Press.

Klaus, M. H., & Kennell, J. H. (1982). *Parent–infant bonding* (2nd ed.). St. Louis, MO: Mosby.

Klaus, M. H., & Kennell, J. H. (1997). The doula: An essential ingredient of childbirth rediscovered. *Acta Paediatrica, 86,* 1034–1036.

Klebanov, P. K., Brooks-Gunn, J., & McCormick, M. C. (2001). Maternal coping strategies and emotional distress: Results of an early intervention program for low birth weight young children. *Developmental Psychology, 37*(5), 654–667.

Klein, J. D., & the American Academy of Pediatrics Committee on Adolescence. (2005). Adolescent pregnancy: Current trends and issues. *Pediatrics, 116,* 281–286.

Kleiner, B., Nolin, M. J., & Chapman, C. (2004). *Before- and after-school care, programs, and activities of children in kindergarten through eighth grade: 2001. Statistical analysis report* (NCES 2004–008). Washington, DC: National Center for Education Statistics.

Klibanoff, R. S., Levine, S. C., Huttenlocher, J., Vasilyeva, M., & Hedges, L. V. (2006). Preschool children's mathematical knowledge: The effect of teacher "math talk." *Developmental Psychology, 42,* 59–69.

Kliewer, S. A., Lenhard, J. M., Willson, T. M., Patel, I., Morris, D. C., & Lehmann, J. M. (1995). A prostaglandin JZ metabolite binds peroxisome proliferator-activated receptor gamma and promotes adipocyte differentiation. *Cell, 83,* 813–819.

Kmet, L. & Macarthur, C. (2006). Urban-rural differences in motor vehicle crash fatality and hospitolization rates among children and youth. *Accident Analysis and Prevention, 38,* 122–127.

Knafo, A., & Plomin, R. (2006). Parental discipline and affection and children's prosocial behavior: Genetic and environmental links. *Journal of Personality and Social Psychology, 90,* 147–164.

Knoblock, H., Stevens, F., & Malone, A. F. (1980). *Manual of developmental diagnosis: The administration and interpretation of the revised Gesell and Amatruda developmental and neurologic examination.* New York: Harper & Row.

Knowles, D. W. (1995). The development of giftedness. In K. Covell (Ed.), *Readings in child development: A Canadian perspective* (pp. 237–261). Toronto: Nelson Canada.

Knudsen, E. I. (1999). Early experience and critical periods. In M. J. Zigmond (Ed.), *Fundamental neuroscience* (pp. 637–654). San Diego, CA: Academic.

Kochanek, K. D., & Smith, B. L. (2004). Deaths: Preliminary data for 2002. *National Vital Statistics Reports, 52*(13). Hyattsville, MD: National Center for Health Statistics.

Kochanek, K. D., Murphy, S. L., Anderson, R. N., & Scott, C. (2004). Deaths: Final data for 2002. *National Vital Statistics Reports, 53*(5). Hyattsville, MD: National Center for Health Statistics.

Kochanska, G. (1992). Children's interpersonal influence with mothers and peers. *Developmental Psychology, 28*, 491–499.

Kochanska, G. (1993). Toward a synthesis of parental socialization and child temperament in early development of conscience. *Child Development, 64*, 325–437.

Kochanska, G. (1995). Children's temperament, mothers' discipline, and security of attachment: Multiple pathways to emerging internalization. *Child Development, 66*, 597–615.

Kochanska, G. (1997a). Multiple pathways to conscience for children with different temperaments: From toddlerhood to age 5. *Developmental Psychology, 33*, 228–240.

Kochanska, G. (1997b). Mutually responsive orientation between mothers and their young children: Implications for early socialization. *Child Development, 68*, 94–112.

Kochanska, G. (2001). Emotional development in children with different attachment histories: The first three years. *Child Development, 72*, 474–490.

Kochanska, G. (2002). Mutually responsive orientation between mothers and their young children: A context for the early development of conscience. *Current Directions in Psychological Science, 11*, 191–195.

Kochanska, G., & Aksan, N. (1995). Mother–child positive affect, the quality of child compliance to requests and prohibitions, and maternal control as correlates of early internalization. *Child Development, 66*, 236–254.

Kochanska, G., Aksan, N., Knaack, A., & Rhines, H. M. (2004). Maternal parenting and children's conscience: Early security as moderator. *Child Development, 75*, 1229–1242.

Kochanska, G., Aksan, N., & Carlson, J. J. (2005). Temperament, relationships, and young children's receptive cooperation with their parents. *Developmental Psychology, 41*, 648–660.

Kochanska, G., Aksan, N., & Joy, M. E. (2007). Children's fearfulness as a moderator of parenting in early socialization: Two longitudinal studies. *Developmental Psychology, 43*, 222–237.

Kochanska, G., Coy, K. C., & Murray, K. T. (2001). The development of self-regulation in the first four years of life. *Child Development, 72*(4), 1091–1111.

Kochanska, G., Murray, K., & Coy, K. C. (1997). Inhibitory control as a contributor to conscience in childhood: From toddler to early school age. *Child Development, 68*, 263–277.

Kochanska, G., Tjebkes, T. L., & Forman, D. R. (1998). Children's emerging regulation of conduct: Restraint, compliance, and internalization from infancy to the second year. *Child Development, 69*(5), 1378–1389.

Kochenderfer, B. H., & Ladd, G. W. (1996). Peer victimization: Cause or consequence of school maladjustment? *Child Development, 67*, 1305–1317.

Koenig, L. B., McGue, M., Krueger, R. F., & Bouchard, T. J. (2005). Genetic and environmental influences on religiousness: Findings for retrospective and current religiousness ratings. *Journal of Personality, 73*, 471–488.

Kogan, M. D., Martin, J. A., Alexander, G. R., Kotelchuck, M., Ventura, S. J., & Frigoletto, F. D. (1998). The changing pattern of prenatal care utilization in the United States, 1981–1995, using different prenatal care indices. *Journal of the American Medical Association, 279*, 1623–1628.

Kogan, M. D., Newacheck, P. W., Honberg, L., & Strickland, B. (2005). Association between underinsurance and access to care among children with special health care needs in the United States. *Pediatrics, 116*, 1162–1169.

Kohen, D. E., Hertzman, C., & Brooks-Gunn, J. (1998). *Neighbourhood influences on children's school readiness.* Catalogue No. W-98-15E. Ottawa: Applied Research Branch, Strategic Policy, Human Resources Development Canada.

Kohen, D. E., Soubhi, H., & Raina, P. (1999). *A Canadian picture of maternal reports of childhood injuries.* Vancouver: BC Injury Research and Prevention Unit.

Kohen, D., Hertzman, C. & Willms, J. D. (2002). The importance of quality child care. In Willms, J. D. *Vulnerable Children* (pp. 261–276). Edmonton, AB: The University of Alberta Press.

Kohen, D., Hertzman, C., & Wiens, M. (1998). *Environmental changes and children's competencies.* Working Paper W-98-25E. Ottawa: Applied Research Branch, Human Resources Development Canada.

Kohlberg, L. (1966). A cognitive-developmental analysis of children's sex-role concepts and attitudes. In E. E. Maccoby (Ed.), *The development of sex differences.* Stanford, CA: Stanford University Press.

Kohlberg, L. (1969). Stage and sequence: The cognitive-developmental approach to socialization. In D. A. Goslin (Ed.), *Handbook of socialization theory and research.* Chicago: Rand McNally.

Kohlberg, L. (1981). *Essays on moral development.* San Francisco: Harper & Row.

Kohlberg, L., & Gilligan, C. (1971, fall). The adolescent as a philosopher: The discovery of the self in a postconventional world. *Daedalus,* pp. 1051–1086.

Kohlberg, L., & Ryncarz, R. A. (1990). Beyond justice reasoning: Moral development and consideration of a seventh stage. In C. N. Alexander & E. J. Langer (Eds.), *Higher stages of human development* (pp. 191–207). New York: Oxford University Press.

Kohlberg, L., Yaeger, J., & Hjertholm, E. (1968). Private speech: Four studies and a review of theories. *Child Development, 39*, 691–736.

Kolata, G. (1988, March 29). Fetuses treated through umbilical cords. *New York Times,* p. C3.

Kolata, G. (2003). Using genetic tests, Ashkenazi Jews vanquish a disease. *New York Times.* Retrieved July 22, 2007, from http://www.nytimes.com.

Kolbert, E. (1994, January 11). Canadians curbing TV violence. *New York Times,* pp. C15, C19.

Kolder, V. E., Gallagher, J., & Parsons, M. T. (1987). Court-ordered obstetrical interventions. *New England Journal of Medicine, 316*, 1192–1196.

Kopp, C. B. (1982). Antecedents of self-regulation. *Developmental Psychology, 18*, 199–214.

Koren, G., Pastuszak, A., & Ito, S. (1998). Drugs in pregnancy. *New England Journal of Medicine, 338*, 1128–1137.

Korner, A. (1996). Reliable individual differences in preterm infants' excitation management. *Child Development, 67*, 1793–1805.

Korner, A. F., Zeanah, C. H., Linden, J., Berkowitz, R. I., Kraemer, H. C., & Agras, W. S. (1985). The relationship between neonatal and later activity and temperament. *Child Development, 56*, 38–42.

Kosterman, R., Graham, J. W., Hawkins, J. D., Catalano, R. F., & Herrenkohl, T. I. (2001). Childhood risk factors for persistence of violence in the transition to adulthood: A social development perspective. *Violence & Victims. Special Issue: Developmental Perspectives on Violence and Victimization, 16*(4), 355–369.

Kottak, C. P. (1994). *Cultural anthropology.* New York: McGraw-Hill.

Kowal, A. K., & Pike, L. B. (2004). Sibling influences on adolescents' attitudes toward safe sex practices. *Family Relations, 53*, 377–384.

Kozlowska, K., & Hanney, L. (1999). Family assessment and intervention using an interactive art exercise. *Australia and New Zealand Journal of Family Therapy, 20*(2), 61–69.

Kralovec, E., & Buell, J. (2000). *The end of homework.* Boston: Beacon.

Kramer, L., & Kowal, A. K. (2005). Sibling relationship quality from birth to adolescence: The enduring contributions of friends. *Journal of Family Psychology, 19*, 503–511.

Kramer, L., Perozynski, L. A., & Chung, T. (1999). Parental responses to sibling conflict: The effects of development and parent gender. *Child Development, 70*(6), 1401–1414.

Kramer, M. S., Platt, R., Yang, H., Joseph, K. S., Wen, S. W., Morin, L., & Usher, R. H. (1998). Secular trends in preterm birth: A hospital-based cohort study. *Journal of the American Medical Association, 280*, 1849–1854.

Krashen, S., & McField, G. (2005, November/December). What works? Reviewing the latest evidence on bilingual education. *Language Learner, 1*(2), 7–10, 34.

Krauss, S., Concordet, J. P., & Ingham, P. W. (1993). A functionally conserved homolog of the Drosophila segment polarity gene hh is expressed in tissues with polarizing activity in zebrafish embryos. *Cell, 75*, 1431–1444.

Kravetz, J. D., & Federman, D. G. (2002). Cat-associated zoonoses. *Archives of Internal Medicine, 162*, 1945–1952.

Kreider, R. M., & Fields, J. (2005). *Living arrangements of children: 2001.* Current Population Reports, (P70-104). Washington, DC: U. S. Census Bureau.

Kreutzer, M., Leonard, C., & Flavell, J. (1975). An interview study of children's knowledge about memory. *Monographs of the Society for Research in Child Development, 40*(1, Serial No. 159).

Krevans, J., & Gibbs, J. C. (1996). Parents' use of inductive discipline: Relations to children's empathy and prosocial behavior. *Child Development, 67*, 3263–3277.

Krishnamoorthy, J. S., Hart, C., & Jelalian, E. (2006). The epidemic of childhood obesity:

Review of research and implications for public policy. *Society for Research in Child Development (SRCD) Social Policy Report,* 20(2).

Kristensen, P., Judge, M. E., Thim, L., Ribel, U., Christjansen, K. N., Wulff, B. S., Clausen, J. T., Jensen, P. B., Madsen, O. D., Vrang, N., Larsen, P. J., & Hastrup, S. (1998). Hypothalamic CART is a new anorectic peptide regulated by leptin. *Nature, 393,* 72–76.

Kroger, J. (1993). Ego identity: An overview. In J. Kroger (Ed.), *Discussions on ego identity* (pp. 1–20). Hillsdale, NJ: Erlbaum.

Kroger, J. (2003). Identity development during adolescence. In G. R. Adams & M. D. Berzonsky. (Eds.), *Blackwell handbook of adolescence* (pp. 205–226). Malden, MA: Blackwell.

Kroger, J., & Haslett, S. J. (1991). A comparison of ego identity status transition pathways and change rates across five identity domains. *International Journal of Aging and Human Development, 32,* 303–330.

Krueger, A. B. (February 2003). Economic considerations and class size. *The Economic Journal, 113,* F34–F63.

Krueger, A. B., & Whitmore, D. M. (April 2000). The effect of attending a small class in the early grades on college-test taking and middle school test results: Evidence from Project STAR. NBER Working Paper No. W7656.

Ku, L. C., Sonenstein, F. L., & Pleck, J. H. (1992). The association of AIDS education and sex education with sexual behavior and condom use among teenage men. *Family Planning Perspectives, 24,* 100–106.

Kuczmarski, R. J., Ogden, C. L., Grummer-Strawn, L. M., Flegal, K. M., Guo, S. S., Wei, R., Mei, Z., Curtin, L. R., Roche, A. F., & Johnson, C. L. (2000). CDC growth charts: United States. *Advance Data,* No. 314. Centers for Disease Control and Prevention, U.S. Department of Health and Human Services.

Kuczynski, L., & Kochanska, G. (1995). Function and content of maternal demands: Developmental significance of early demands for competent action. *Child Development, 66,* 616–628.

Kuhl, P. K. (2004). Early language acquisition: Cracking the speech code. *Nature Reviews Neuroscience, 5,* 831–843.

Kuhl, P. K., Andruski, J. E., Chistovich, I. A., Chistovich, L. A., Kozhevnikova, E. V., Ryskina, V. L., Stolyarova, E. I., Sundberg, U., & Lacerda, F. (1997). Cross-language analysis of phonetic units in language addressed to infants. *Science, 277,* 684–686.

Kuhl, P. K., Conboy, B. T., Padden, D., Nelson, T., & Pruitt, J. (2005). Early speech perception and later language development: Implications for the "critical period." *Language Learning and Development, 1,* 237–264.

Kuhl, P. K., Williams, K. A., Lacerda, F., Stevens, K. N., & Lindblom, B. (1992). Linguistic experience alters phonetic perception in infants by 6 months of age. *Science, 255,* 606–608.

Kuhn, D. (2006). Do cognitive changes accompany developments in the adolescent brain? *Perspectives on Psychological Science, 1,* 59–67.

Kuhn. D., & Dean, D. (2005). Is developing scientific thinking all about learning to control variables? *Psychological Science, 16,* 866–870.

Kuperman, S., Chan, G., Kramer, J. R., Bierut, L., Buckholz, K. K., Fox, L., et al. (2005). Relationship of age of first drink to child behavioral problems and family psychopathology. *Alcoholism: Clinical and Experimental Research, 29(10),* 1869–1876.

Kupersmidt, J. B., & Coie, J. D. (1990). Preadolescent peer status, aggression, and school adjustment as predictors of externalizing problems in adolescence. *Child Development, 61,* 1350–1362.

Kurjak, A., Kupesic, S., Matijevic, R., Kos, M., & Marton, U. (1999). First trimester malformation screening. *European Journal of Obstetrics, Gynecology, and Reproductive Biology (E4L), 85,* 93–96.

Kurosawa, A. (1983). *Something like an autobiography* (A. E. Bock, Trans.). New York: Vintage.

Kuther, T., & McDonald, E. (2004). Early adolescents' experiences with, and views of, Barbie. *Adolescence, 39,* 39–51.

Kuxhaus, D. (November 1, 1997). Sniffing mother came out of fog, took back her life. *Winnipeg Free Press,* A12.

Kye, C., & Ryan, N. (1995). Pharmacologic treatment of child and adolescent depression. *Child and Adolescent Psychiatric Clinics of North America, 4,* 261–281.

Laberge, L., Tremblay, R. E., Vitaro, F., & Montplaisir, J. (2000). Development of parasomnias from childhood to early adolescence. *Pediatrics, 106,* 67–74.

Labov, T. (1992). Social and language boundaries among adolescents. *American Speech, 67,* 339–366.

Ladd, G. W. (1996). Shifting ecologies during the 5 to 7 year period: Predicting children's adjustment during the transition to grade school. In A. J. Sameroff & M. M. Haith (Eds.), *The five to seven year shift: The age of reason and responsibility* (pp. 363–386). Chicago: University of Chicago Press.

Ladd, G. W., & Colter, B. S. (1988). Parents' management of preschoolers' peer relations: Is it related to children's social competence? *Developmental Psychology, 24,* 109–117.

Ladd, G. W., & Hart, C. H. (1992). Creating informal play opportunities: Are parents' and preschoolers' initiations related to children's competence with peers? *Developmental Psychology, 28,* 1179–1187.

Ladd, G. W., Kochenderfer, B. J., & Coleman, C. C. (1996). Friendship quality as a predictor of young children's early school adjustment. *Child Development, 67,* 1103–1118.

LaFontana, K. M., & Cillessen, A. H. N. (2002). Children's perceptions of popular and unpopular peers: A multi-method assessment. *Developmental Psychology, 38,* 635–647.

Lagattuta, K. H. (2005). When you shouldn't do what you want to do: Young children's understanding of desires, rules, and emotions. *Child Development, 76,* 713–733.

Lagercrantz, H., & Slotkin, T. A. (1986). The "stress" of being born. *Scientific American, 254(4),* 100–107.

Laible, D. J., & Thompson, R. A. (1998). Attachment and emotional understanding in preschool children. *Developmental Psychology, 34(5),* 1038–1045.

Laible, D. J., & Thompson, R. A. (2002). Mother-child conflict in the toddler years: Lessons in emotion, morality, and relationships. *Child Development, 73,* 1187–1203.

Laird, J., Lew, S., DeBell, M., & Chapman, C. (2006). Dropout rates in the United States: 2002 and 2003 (NCES 2006-062). Washington, DC: U. S. Department of Education, National Center for Education Statistics.

Laird, R. D., Pettit, G. S., Bates, J. E., & Dodge, K. A. (2003). Parents' monitoring relevant knowledge and adolescents' delinquent behavior: Evidence of correlated developmental changes and reciprocal influences. *Child Development, 74,* 752–768.

Lalonde, C. E., & Werker, J. F. (1995). Cognitive influences on cross-language speech perception in infancy. *Infant Behavior and Development, 18,* 459–475.

Lamason, R. L.; Mohideen, Manzoor-Ali P. K.; Mest, J. R.; Wong, A, C.; Norton, H. L.; Arcs, M. C., et al. (2005). SLC24A5, a putative cation exchanger, affects pigmentation in zebrafish and humans. *Science, 310,* 1782–1786.

Lamb, M. E. (1981). The development of father–infant relationships. In M. E. Lamb (Ed.), *The role of the father in child development* (2nd ed.). New York: Wiley.

Lamb, M. E. (1983). Early mother–neonate contact and the mother–child relationship. *Journal of Child Psychology & Psychiatry & Allied Disciplines, 24,* 487–494.

Lamb, M. E. (1987). Predictive implications of individual differences in attachment. *Journal of Consulting and Clinical Psychology, 55(6),* 817–824.

Lamb, M. E., Frodi, A. M., Frodi, M., & Hwang, C. P. (1982). Characteristics of maternal and paternal behavior in traditional and non-traditional Swedish families. *International Journal of Behavior Development, 5,* 131–151.

Lambert, W. E., & Tucker, G. R. (1972). *The bilingual education of children: The St. Lambert experiment.* Rowley, MA: Newbury House.

Lamborn, S. D., Mounts, N. S., Steinberg, L., & Dornbusch, S. M. (1991). Patterns of competence and adjustment among adolescents from authoritative, authoritarian, indulgent, and neglectful families. *Child Development, 62,* 1049–1065.

Lamm, C., Zelazo, P. D., & Lewis, M. D. (2006). Neural correlates of cognitive control in childhood and adolescence: Disentangling the contributions of age and executive function. *Neuropsychologia, 44,* 2139–2148.

Landesman-Dwyer, S., & Emanuel, I. (1979). Smoking during pregnancy. *Teratology, 19,* 119–126.

Landon, M. B., Hauth, J. C., Leveno, K. J., Spong, C. Y., Leindecker, S., Varner, M. W., Moawad, A. H., Caritis, S. N., Harper, M., Wapner, R. J., Sorokin, Y., Miodovnik, M., Carpenter, M., Peaceman, A. M., O'Sullivan, M. J., Sibai, B., Langer, O., Thorp, J. M., Ramin, S. M., Mercer, B. M., & Gabbe, S. G., for the National Institute of Child Health and Human Development Maternal-Fetal Medicine Units Network. (2004). Maternal and perinatal outcomes associated with a trial of labor after prior cesarean delivery. *New England Journal of Medicine, 351,* 2581–2589.

Landry, S. H., Smith, K. E., Swank, P. R., & Miller Loncar, C. L. (2000). Early maternal and child influences on children's later independent cognitive and social functioning. *Child Development, 71,* 358–375.

Landy, S., & Tam, K. K. (1996). Yes, parenting does make a difference to the development of children in Canada. In Human Resources Development Canada & Statistics Canada, *Growing up in Canada. National Longitudinal Survey of Children and Youth.* Ottawa: Author.

Landy, S., & Tam, K. K. (1998). *Understanding the contribution of multiple risk factors on child development at various ages.* Catalogue No. W-98-22E. Ottawa: Applied Research Branch, Strategic Policy, Human Resources Development Canada.

Lane, H. (1976). *The wild boy of Aveyron.* Cambridge, MA: Harvard University Press.

Lange, G., MacKinnon, C. E., & Nida, R. E. (1989). Knowledge, strategy, and motivational contributions to preschool children's object recall. *Developmental Psychology, 25,* 772–779.

Lanphear, B. P. Aligne, C. A., Auinger, P., Weitzman, M., & Byrd, R. S. (2001). Residential exposure associated with asthma in U.S. children. *Pediatrics, 107,* 505–511.

Lansford, J. E., Chang, L., Dodge, K. A., Malone, P. S., Oburu, P., Palmérus, K., Bacchini, D., Pastorelli, C., Bombi, A. S., Zelli, A., Tapanya, S., Chaudhary, N., Deater-Deckard, K., Manke, B., & Quinn, N. (2005). Physical discipline and children's adjustment: Cultural normativeness as a moderator. *Child Development, 76,* 1234–1246.

Lansford, J. E., Dodge, K. A., Pettit, G. S., Bates, J. E., Crozier, J., & Kaplow, J. (2002). A 12-year prospective study of the long-term effects of early child physical maltreatment on psychological, behavioral, and academic problems in adolescence. *Archives of Pediatric and Adolescent Medicine, 156*(8), 824–830.

Lapham, E. V., Kozma, C., & Weiss, J. O. (1996). Genetic discrimination: Perspectives of consumers. *Science, 274,* 621–624.

Lapierre-Adamcyk, E. (1999). *Family status from the children's perspective. Canadian families at the approach of the year 2000.* Ottawa: Statistics Canada.

Larivée, S., Normandeau, S., & Parent, S. (2000). The French connection: Some contributions of French-language research in the post-Piagetian era. *Child Development, 71,* 823–839.

Larner, M. B., Stevenson, C. S., & Behrman, R. E. (1998). Protecting children from abuse and neglect: Analysis and recommendations. *The Future of Children, 8,* 4–22.

Larsen, D. (1990, December–1991, January). Unplanned parenthood. *Modern Maturity,* 32–36.

Larson, R. (1998). Implications for policy and practice: Getting adolescents, families, and communities in sync. In A. Crouter & R. Larson (Eds.), *Temporal rhythms in adolescence: Clocks, calendars, and the coordination of daily life* (*New Directions in Child and Adolescent Development, 82,* pp. 83–88). San Francisco: Jossey-Bass.

Larson, R. W. (1997). The emergence of solitude as a constructive domain of experience in early adolescence. *Child Development, 68,* 80–93.

Larson, R. W., & Verma, S. (1999). How children and adolescents spend time across the world: Work, play, and developmental opportunities. *Psychological Bulletin, 125,* 701–736.

Larson, R. W., Moneta, G., Richards, M. H., & Wilson, S. (2002). Continuity, stability, and change in daily emotional experience across adolescence. *Child Development, 73,* 1151–1165.

Larson, R. W., Richards, M. H., Moneta, G., Holmbeck, G., & Duckett, E. (1996). Changes in adolescents' daily interactions with their families from ages 10 to 18: Disengagement and transformation. *Developmental Psychology, 32,* 744–754.

Larson, R., & Seepersad, S. (2003). Adolescents' leisure time in the United States: Partying, sports, and the American experiment. In S. Verma & R. Larson (Eds.), *Examining adolescent leisure time across cultures: Developmental opportunities and risks. New Directions for Child and Adolescent Development, 99,* 53–64.

Larson, R., & Wilson, S. (2004). Adolescents across place and time: Globalization and the changing pathways to adulthood. In R. M. Lerner & L. Steinberg (Eds.), *Handbook of adolescent psychology* (2nd ed.) (pp. 299–331). Hoboken, NJ: Wiley.

Larzalere, R. E. (2000). Child outcomes of nonabusive and customary physical punishment by parents: An updated literature review. *Clinical Child and Family Psychology Review, 3,* 199–221.

Lash, J. P. (1980). *Helen and teacher: The story of Helen Keller and Anne Sullivan Macy.* New York: Delacorte.

Laucht, M., Esser, G., & Schmidt, M. H. (1994). Contrasting infant predictors of later cognitive functioning. *Journal of Child Psychology and Psychiatry, 35,* 649–652.

Laursen, B. (1996). Closeness and conflict in adolescent peer relationships: Interdependence with friends and romantic partners. In W. M. Bukowski, A. F. Newcomb, & W. W. Hartup (Eds.), *The company they keep: Friendship in childhood and adolescence* (pp. 186–210). New York: Cambridge University Press.

Laursen, B., Coy, K. C., & Collins, W. A. (1998). Reconsidering changes in parent–child conflict across adolescence: A meta-analysis. *Child Development, 69,* 817–832.

Lavelli, M. & Fogel, A. (2005). Developmental changes in the relationship between the infant's attention and emotion during early face-to-face communication: The 2-month transition. *Developmental Psychology, 41,* 265–280.

Law, K. L., Stroud, L. R., LaGasse, L. L., Niaura, R., Liu, J., & Lester, B. (2003). Smoking during pregnancy and newborn neurobehavior. *Pediatrics, 111,* 1318–1323.

Lawn, J. E., Cousens, S., & Zupan, J., for the Lancet Neonatal Survival Steering Team. (2005). 4 million neonatal deaths: When? Where? Why? *The Lancet, 365,* 891–900.

Lawson, C. (1993, October 4). Celebrated birth aside, teen-ager is typical now. *New York Times,* p. A18.

Lay, C., & Verkuyten, M. (1999). Ethnic identity and its relation to personal self-esteem: A comparison of Canadian-born and foreign-born Chinese adolescents. *Journal of Social Psychology, 139,* 288–299.

Leacy, F. H. (Ed.) (1983). *Historical statistics of Canada* (2nd ed.). Ottawa: Statistics Canada.

Leaper, C., & Smith, T. E. (2004). A meta-analytic review of gender variations in children's language use: Talkativeness, affiliative speech, and assertive speech. *Developmental Psychology, 40,* 993–1027.

Leaper, C., Anderson, K. J., & Sanders, P. (1998). Moderators of gender effects on parents' talk to their children: A meta-analysis. *Developmental Psychology, 34*(1), 3–27.

Leavitt, L. A. (1998). Research perspectives: Mothers' sensitivity to infant signals. *Pediatrics, 102,* 1247–1249.

Leblanc, M., & Ritchie, M. (2001). A meta-analysis of play therapy outcomes. *Counseling Psychology Quarterly, 14,* 149–163.

Lecanuet, J. P., Granier-Deferre, C., & Busnel, M.-C. (1995). Human fetal auditory perception. In J. P. Lecanuet, W. P. Fifer, N. A. Krasnegor, & W. P. Smotherman (Eds.), *Fetal development: A psychobiological perspective* (pp. 239–262). Hillsdale, NJ: Erlbaum.

LeDoux, J. (1989). Cognitive and emotional interactions in the brain. *Cognition and Emotion, 3,* 265–289.

Lee, F. R. (2004, July 3). Engineering more sons than daughters: Will it tip the scales toward war? *New York Times,* pp. A17, A19.

Lee, G. M., Gortmaker, S. L., McIntosh, K., Hughes, M. D., Oleske, J. M., & Pediatric

AIDS Clinical Trials Group Protocol 219C Team. (2006). Quality of life for children and adolescents: Impact of HIV infection and antiretroviral treatment. *Pediatrics, 117,* 273–283.

Lee, K., Xu, F., Cameron, C. A., & Chen, S. (2001). Taiwan and Mainland Chinese and Canadian children's categorization and evaluation of lie- and truth-telling: A modesty effect. *British Journal of Developmental Psychology, 19,* 525–542.

Lee, L. S. & Harriss, S. R. (2005). Psychometric properties and standardization samples of four screening tests for infants and young children: A review. *Pediatric Physical Therapy, 17,* 140–147.

Lee, M. M. (2006). Idiopathic short stature. *New England Journal of Medicine, 354,* 2576–2582.

Lee, S. J., Ralston, H. J. P., Drey, E. A., Partridge, J. C., & Rosen, M.A. (2005). Fetal pain: A systematic multidisciplinary review of the evidence. *Journal of the American Medical Association, 294,* 947–954.

Leeman, L. W., Gibbs, J. C., & Fuller, D. (1993). Evaluation of a multi-component group treatment program for juvenile delinquents. *Aggressive Behavior, 19,* 281–292.

Leenaars, A. A., & Lester, D. (1990). Suicide in adolescents: A comparison of Canada and the United States. *Psychological Reports, 67,* 867–873.

Leenaars, A. A., & Lester, D. (1995). The changing suicide pattern in Canadian adolescents and youth, compared to their American counterparts. *Adolescence, 30,* 539–548.

Lefebvre, P., & Merrigan, P. (1998). *Family background, family income, maternal work and child development.* Catalogue No. W-98-12E. Ottawa: Applied Research Branch, Strategic Policy, Human Resources Development Canada.

Legerstee, M., & Varghese, J. (2001). The role of maternal affect mirroring on social expectancies in three-month-old infants. *Child Development, 72,* 1301–1313.

Leibel, R. L. (1997). And finally, genes for human obesity. *Nature Genetics, 16,* 218–220.

Leman, P. J., Ahmed, S., & Ozarow, L. (2005). Gender, gender relations, and the social dynamics of children's conversations. *Developmental Psychology, 41,* 64–74.

Lenneberg, E. H. (1967). *Biological functions of language.* New York: Wiley.

Lenneberg, E. H. (1969). On explaining language. *Science, 164*(3880), 635–643.

Lerner, J. V., & Galambos, N. L. (1985). Maternal role satisfaction, mother–child interaction, and child temperament: A process model. *Child Development, 21,* 1157–1164.

Lesch, K. P., Bengel, D., Heils, A., Sabol, S. Z., Greenberg, B. D., Petri, S., Benjamin, J., Müller, C. R., Hamer, D. H., & Murphy, D. L. (1996). Association of anxiety-related traits with a polymorphism in the serotonin transporter gene regulatory region. *Science, 274,* 1527–1531.

Leslie, A. M. (1982). The perception of causality in infants. *Perception, 11,* 173–186.

Leslie, A. M. (1984). Spatiotemporal continuity and the perception of causality in infants. *Perception, 13,* 287–305.

Leslie, L. K., Newman, T. B., Chesney, J., & Perrin, J. M. (2005). The Food and Drug Administration's deliberations on antidepressant use in pediatric patients. *Pediatrics, 116,* 195–204.

Lester, B. M., & Boukydis, C. F. Z. (1985). *Infant crying: Theoretical and research perspectives.* New York: Plenum.

Lester, B. M., & Dreher, M. (1989). Effects of marijuana use during pregnancy on newborn cry. *Child Development, 60,* 765–771.

Leung, C. (2001). The sociocultural and psychological adaptation of Chinese migrant adolescents in Australia and Canada. *International Journal of Psychology, 36,* 8–19.

LeVay, S. (1991). A difference in hypothalamic structure between heterosexual and homosexual men. *Science, 253,* 1034–1037.

Leve, L. D., & Fagot, B. I. (1997). Gender-role socialization and discipline processes in one- and two-parent families. *Sex Roles, 36,* 1–21.

Leventhal, T., & Brooks-Gunn, J. (2000). The neighborhoods they live in: The effects of neighborhood residence on child and adolescent outcomes. *Psychological Bulletin, 126*(2), 309–337.

Leventhal, T., & Brooks-Gunn, J. (2003). Children and youth in neighborhood contexts. *Current Directions in Psychological Science, 12,* 27–31.

LeVine, R. A. (1974). Parental goals: A cross-cultural view. *Teacher College Record, 76,* 226–239.

LeVine, R. A. (1989). Human parental care: Universal goals, cultural strategies, individual behavior. In R. A. LeVine, P. M. Miller, & M. M. West (Eds.), *Parental behavior in diverse societies* (pp. 3–12). San Francisco: Jossey-Bass.

LeVine, R. A. (1994). *Child care and culture: Lessons from Africa.* Cambridge, England: Cambridge University Press.

Levine, S. C., Vasilyeva, M., Lourenco, S. E., Newcombe, N. S., & Huttenlocher, J. (2005). Socioeconimic status modifies the sex differences in spatial skills. *Psychological Science, 16,* 841–845.

Leviton, A., & Cowan, L. (2002). A review of the literature relating caffeine consumption by women to their risk of reproductive hazards. *Food & Chemical Toxicology, 40*(9), 1271–1310.

Levitt, M. J., Guacci-Franco, N., & Levitt, J. L. (1993). Convoys of social support in childhood and early adolescence: Structure and function. *Developmental Psychology, 29,* 811–818.

Levron, J., Aviram, A., Madgar, I., Livshits, A., Raviv, G., Bider, D., Hourwitz, A., Barkai, G., Goldman, B., & Mashiach, S. (1998, October). *High rate of chromosomal aneupoloidies in testicular spermatozoa retrieved from azoospermic patients undergoing testicular sperm extraction for in vitro fertilization.* Paper presented at the 16th World Congress on Fertility and Sterility and the 54th annual meeting of the American Society for Reproductive Medicine, San Francisco, CA.

Levy-Shiff, R., Zoran, N., & Shulman, S. (1997). International and domestic adoption: Child, parents, and family adjustment. *International Journal of Behavioral Development, 20,* 109–129.

Lewinsohn, P. M., Gotlib, I. H., Lewinsohn, M., Seeley, J. R., & Allen, N. B. (1998). Gender differences in anxiety disorders and anxiety symptoms in adolescents. *Journal of Abnormal Psychology, 107,* 109–117.

Lewis, M. (1995). Self-conscious emotions. *American Scientist, 83,* 68–78.

Lewis, M. (1997). The self in self-conscious emotions. In S. G. Snodgrass & R. L. Thompson (Eds.), *The self across psychology: Self-recognition, self-awareness, and the self-concept* (Vol. 818, pp. 118–142). New York: The New York Academy of Sciences, Annals of the New York Academy of Sciences.

Lewis, M. (1998). Emotional competence and development. In D. Pushkar, W. Bukowski, A. E. Schwartzman, D. M. Stack, & D. R. White (Eds.), *Improving competence across the lifespan* (pp. 27–36). New York: Plenum.

Lewis, M. D., Koroshegyi, C., Douglas, L., & Kampe, K. (1997). Age-specific associations between emotional responses to separation and cognitive performance in infancy. *Developmental Psychology, 33,* 32–42.

Lewis, M., & Brooks, J. (1974). Self, other, and fear: Infants' reaction to people. In H. Lewis & L. Rosenblum (Eds.), *The origins of fear: The origins of behavior* (Vol. 2). New York: Wiley.

Lewit, E., & Kerrebrock, N. (1997). Population-based growth stunting. *The Future of Children, 7*(2), 149–156.

Li, H. Z. (2002). Culture, gender and self-close-others connectedness in Canadian and Chinese samples. *European Journal of Social Psychology, 32,* 93–104.

Li, R., Chase, M., Jung, S., Smith, P. J. S., Loeken, M. R. (2005). Hypoxic stress in diabetic pregnancy contributes to impaired embryo gene expression and defective development by inducing oxidative stress. *American Journal of Physiology: Endocrinology and Metabolism, 289,* 591–599.

Li, X., Li, S., Ulusoy, E., Chen, W., Srinivasan, S. R., & Berenson, G. S. (2004). Childhood adiposity as a predictor of cardiac mass in adulthood. *Circulation, 110,* 3488–3492.

Liaw, F., & Brooks-Gunn, J. (1993). Patterns of low-birth-weight children's cognitive development. *Developmental Psychology, 29,* 1024–1035.

Liberman, I. Y., & Liberman, A. M. (1990). Whole language vs. code emphasis: Underlying assumptions and their implications for reading instruction. *Annals of Dyslexia, 40,* 51–76.

Lickliter, R., & Honeycutt, H. (2003). Developmental dynamics: Toward a biologically plausible evolutionary psychology. *Psychological Bulletin, 129,* 819–835.

Lie, E., & Newcombe, N. S. (1999). Elementary school children's explicit and implicit memory for faces of preschool classmates. *Developmental Psychology, 35,* 102–112.

LifeSiteNews.com. (2004). StatsCan Reveals Canada's Birth Rate Continues to Drop: At All-Time Low. Retrieved July 6, 2007 from http://www.lifesite.net/ldn/2004/apr/04041905.html.

Lillard, A., & Curenton, S. (1999). Do young children understand what others feel, want, and know? *Young Children, 54*(5), 52–57.

Lillard, A., & Else-Quest, N. (2006). The early years: Evaluating Montessori education. *Science, 313,* 1893–1894.

Lin, S. S., & Kelsey, J. L. (2000). Use of race and ethnicity in epidemiological research: Concepts, methodological issues, and suggestions for research. *Epidemiologic Reviews, 22*(2), 187–202.

Lindwer, W. (1991). *The last seven months of Anne Frank* (A. Meersschaert, Trans.). New York: Pantheon.

Linnet, K. M., Wisborg, K., Obel, C., Secher, N. J., Thomsen, P. H., Agerbo, E., et al. (2005). Smoking during pregnancy and the risk of hyperkinetic disorder in offspring. *Pediatrics, 116,* 462–467.

Linney, J. A., & Seidman, E. (1989). The future of schooling. *American Psychologist, 44*(2), 336–340.

Lipman, E. L., Boyle, M. H., Dooley, M. D., & Offord, D. R. (1998). *Children and lone-mother families: An investigation of factors influencing child well-being.* Report No. W-98-11E. Ottawa: Applied Research Branch, Strategic Policy, Human Resources Development Canada.

Lipman, E. L., Offord, D. R., Dooley, M. D. & Boyle, M. H. (2002). Children's outcomes in differing types of single-parent families. In Willms, J. D. *Vulnerable Children.* (pg. 229–242). University of Alberta Press.

Litovitz, T. L., Klein-Schwartz, W., Caravati, E. M., Youniss, J., Crouch, B., & Lee, S. (1999). Annual report of the American Association of Poison Control Centers Toxic Exposure Surveillance System. *American Journal of Emergency Medicine, 17,* 435–487.

Littleton, H., Breitkopf, C., & Berenson, A. (2006, August 13). *Correlates of anxiety symptoms during pregnancy and association with perinatal outcomes: A meta-analysis.* Presentation at the 114th annual convention of the American Psychological Association, New Orleans.

Liu, J., Raine, A., Venables, P. H., Dalais, C., and Mednick, S. A. (2003). Malnutrition at age 3 years and lower cognitive ability at age 11 years. *Archives of Pediatric and Adolescent Medicine, 157,* 593–600.

Liu, S., Heaman, Kramer, M. S., Demissie, K., Wen, S. W. & Marcoux, S. (2002). Length of hospital stay, obstetric conditions at childbirth, and maternal readmission: A population-based cohort study. *American Journal of Obstetrics & Gynaecology, 187,* 681–687.

Livson, N., & Peskin, H. (1980). Perspectives on adolescence from longitudinal research. In J. Adelson (Ed.), *Handbook of adolescent psychology.* New York: Wiley.

Lloyd, J. J., & Anthony, J. C. (2003). Hanging out with the wrong crowd: How much difference can parents make in an urban environment? *Journal of Urban Health, 80,* 383–399.

Lloyd, T., Andon, M. B., Rollings, N., Martel, J. K., Landis, J. R., Demers, L. M., Eggli, D. F., Kieselhorst, K., & Kulin, H. E. (1993). Calcium supplementation and bone mineral density in adolescent girls. *Journal of the American Medical Association, 270,* 841–844.

Lock, A., Young, A., Service, V., & Chandler, P. (1990). Some observations on the origin of the pointing gesture. In V. Volterra & C. J. Erting (Eds.), *From gesture to language in hearing and deaf children.* New York: Springer.

Lockwood, C. J. (2002). Predicting premature delivery—no easy task. *New England Journal of Medicine, 346,* 282–284.

Loeb, S., Bridges, M., Bassock, D., Fuller, B., & Rumberger, R.W. (2007). How Much Is too Much? The Influence of Preschool Centers on Children's Social and Cognitive Development. *Economics of Education Review, 26,* 52–66.

Loeb, S., Fuller, B., Kagan, S. L., & Carrol, B. (2004). Child care in poor communities: Early learning effects of type, quality, and stability. *Child Development, 75,* 47–65.

Lohse, N., Hansen, A. E., Pedersen, G., Kronborg, G., Gerstoft, J., Sorensen, H. T., Vaeth, M., & Obel, N. (2007). Survival of persons with and without HIV infection in Denmark, 1995–2005. *Annals of Internal Medicine, 146,* 87–95.

Longnecker, M. P., Klebanoff, M. A., Zhou, H., & Brock, J. W. (2001). Association between maternal serum concentration of the DDT metabolite DDE and preterm and small-for-gestational-age babies at birth. *Lancet, 358,* 110–114.

Lonigan, C. J., Burgess, S. R., & Anthony, J. L. (2000). Development of emergent literacy and early reading skills in preschool children: Evidence from a latent-variable longitudinal study. *Developmental Psychology, 36,* 593–613.

Lorenz, K. (1957). Comparative study of behavior. In C. H. Schiller (Ed.), *Instinctive behavior.* New York: International Universities Press.

Lorsbach, T. C., & Reimer, J. F. (1997). Developmental changes in the inhibition of previously relevant information. *Journal of Experimental Child Psychology, 64,* 317–342.

Lortie-Lussier, M. & Feller, G. L. (1991). Self–ingroup relationships: Their variations among Canadian pre-adolescents of English, French, and Italian origin. *Journal of Cross-Cultural Psychology, 22,* 458–471.

Louis Harris & Associates. (1986). *American teens speak: Sex, myths, TV and birth control: The Planned Parenthood poll.* New York: Planned Parenthood Federation of America.

Louise Brown: From miracle baby to regular teen. (1994, February 7). *People Weekly,* p. 12.

Louise Brown: The world's first "test-tube baby" ushered in a revolution in fertility. (1984, March). *People Weekly,* p. 82.

Love, J. M., Kisker, E. E., Ross, C. M., Schochet, P. Z., Brooks-Gunn, J., Paulsell, D., Boller, K., Constantine, J., Vogel, C., Fuligni, A. S., & Brady-Smith, C. (2002). *Making a difference in the lives of infants and toddlers and their families: The impacts of Early Head Start: Executive Summary.* Washington, DC: U.S. Department of Health and Human Services.

Love, J. M., Kisker, E. E., Ross, C., Raikes, H., Constantine, J., Boller, K., Brooks-Gunn, J., Chazan-Cohen, R., Tarullo, L. B., Brady-Smith, C., Fuligni, A. S., Schochet, P. Z., Paulsell, D., & Vogel, C. (2005). The effectiveness of Early Head Start for 3-year-old children and their parents: Lessons for policy and programs. *Developmental Psychology, 41,* 885–901.

Love, K. M., & Murdock, B. (2004). Attachment to parents and psychological well-being: An examination of young adult college students in intact families and stepfamilies. *Journal of Family Psychology, 18,* 600–608.

Lozoff, B., Klein, N. K., Nelson, E. C., McClish, D. K., Manuel, M., & Chacon, M. E. (1998). Behavior of infants with iron-deficiency anemia. *Child Development, 69*(1), 24–36.

Lubell, K. M., Swahn, M. H., Crosby, A. E., & Kegler, S. R. (2004). Methods of suicide among persons aged 10–19 years—United States, 1992–2001. *Morbidity and Mortality Weekly Report, 53,* 471–474.

Lubinski, D., & Benbow, C. P. (2006). Study of Mathematically Precocious Youth (SMPY) after 35 years: Uncovering antecedents for the development of math-science expertise. *Perspectives on Psychological Science, 1,* 316–343.

Lubinski, D., Benbow, C. P., Webb, R. M., & Bleske-Recek, A. (2006). Tracking exceptional human capital over two decades. *Psychological Sciences, 17,* 104–109.

Lubinski, D., Webb, M. R., Morelock, M. J., & Benbow, C. P. (2001). Top 1 in 10,000: A 10-year follow-up of the profoundly gifted. *Journal of Applied Psychology, 86,* 718–729.

Lugaila, T. A. (2003). A child's day: 2000 (Selected indicators of child well-being). *Current Population Reports* (P70-89). Washington, DC: U.S. Census Bureau.

Luke, B., Mamelle, N., Keith, L., Munoz, F., Minogue, J., Papiernik, E., Johnson, T. R., & Timothy, R. B. (1995). The association between occupational factors and preterm birth: A United States nurses' study. *American Journal of Obstetrics and Gynecology, 173,* 849–862.

Luna, B., Garver, K. E., Urban, T. A., Lazar, N. A., & Sweeney, J. A. (2004). Maturation of cognitive processes from late childhood to adulthood. *Child Development, 75,* 1357–1372.

Lundy, B. L. (2003). Father- and mother-infant face-to-face interactions: Differences in mind-related comments and infant attachment? *Infant Behavior & Development, 26,* 200–212.

Lundy, B. L., Jones, N. A., Field, T., Nearing, G., Davalos, M., Pietro, P. A., Schanberg, S., & Kuhn, C. (1999). Prenatal depression effects on neonates. *Infant Behavior and Development, 22,* 119–129.

Luster, T., & Small, S. A. (1994). Factors associated with sexual risk-taking among adolescents. *Journal of Marriage and the Family, 56,* 622–632.

Luthar, S. S., & Latendresse, S. J. (2005). Children of the affluence: Challenges to well-being. *Current Directions in Psychological Science, 14,* 49–53.

Lutke, J. (2000). Works in progress: The meaning of success for individuals with FAS/E. In J. Kleinfeld, B. Morse, & S. Wescott (Eds.), *Fanastic Antone grows up: Adolescents and adults with fetal alcohol syndrome.* Fairbanks, AK: University of Alaska Press.

Lynskey, M. T., Heath, A. C., Bucholz, K. K., Slutske, W. S., Madden, P. A. F., Nelson, E. C., Statham, D. J., & Martin, N. G. (2003). Escalation of drug use in early-onset cannabis users versus co-twin controls. *Journal of the American Medical Association, 289,* 427–433.

Lyons-Ruth, K., Alpern, L., & Repacholi, B. (1993). Disorganized infant attachment classification and maternal psychosocial problems as predictors of hostile-aggressive behavior in the preschool classroom. *Child Development, 64,* 572–585.

Lytton, H., & Romney, D. M. (1991). Parents' differential socialization of boys and girls: A meta-analysis. *Psychological Bulletin, 109*(2), 267–296.

Lyytinen, P., Poikkeus, A., Laakso, M., Eklund, K., & Lyytinen, H. (2001). Language development and symbolic play in children with and without familial risk for dyslexia. *Journal of Speech, Language, and Hearing Research, 44,* 873–885.

Maccoby, E. (1980). *Social development.* New York: Harcourt Brace Jovanovich.

Maccoby, E. E. (1984). Middle childhood in the context of the family. In W. A. Collins (Ed.), *Development during middle childhood.* Washington, DC: National Academy.

Maccoby, E. E. (1988). Gender as a social category. *Developmental Psychology, 24,* 755–765.

Maccoby, E. E. (1990). Gender and relationships: A developmental account. *American Psychologist, 45*(11), 513–520.

Maccoby, E. E. (1992). The role of parents in the socialization of children: An historical overview. *Developmental Psychology, 28,* 1006–1017.

Maccoby, E. E. (1994). Commentary: Gender segregation in childhood. In C. Leaper (Ed.), *Childhood gender segregation: Causes and consequences* (New Directions for Child Development, 65, pp. 87–97). San Francisco: Jossey-Bass.

Maccoby, E. E. (2002). Gender and group process: A developmental perspective. *Current Directions in Psychological Science, 11,* 54–58.

Maccoby, E. E., & Lewis, C. C. (2003). Less day care or different day care? *Child Development, 74,* 1069–1075.

Maccoby, E. E., & Martin, J. A. (1983). Socialization in the context of the family: Parent–child interaction. In P. H. Mussen (Series Ed.) & E. M. Hetherington (Vol. Ed.), *Handbook of child psychology: Vol. 4. Socialization, personality, and social development* (pp. 1–101). New York: Wiley.

MacDonald, K. (1988). The interfaces between developmental psychology and evolutionary biology. In K. MacDonald (Ed.), *Sociobiological perspectives on human development* (pp. 3–23). New York: Springer-Verlag.

MacDonald, K. (1998). Evolution and development. In A. Campbell & S. Muncer (Eds.), *Social development* (pp. 21–49). London: UCL Press.

Macdonald, S., Mann, R.E., Chipman, M., & Anglin-Bodrug, K. (2004). Collisions and traffic violations of alcohol, cannabis and cocaine abuse clients before and after treatment. *Accident Analysis and Prevention, 36,* 795–800.

Mackey, K., Arnold, M. L., & Pratt, M. W. (2001). Adolescents' stories of decision making in more and less authoritative families: Representing the voices of parents in narrative. *Journal of Adolescent Research, 16,* 243–268.

MacKinnon-Lewis, C., Starnes, R., Volling, B., & Johnson, S. (1997). Perceptions of parenting as predictors of boys' sibling and peer relations. *Developmental Psychology, 33,* 1024–1031.

Macmillan, C., Magder, L. S., Brouwers, P., Chase, C., Hittelman, J., Lasky, T., et al. (2001). Head growth and neurodevelopment of infants born to HIV-1–infected drug-using women. *Neurology, 57,* 1402–1411.

MacMillan, H. L., Fleming, J. E., Trocmé, N., Boyle, M. H., Wong, M., Racine, Y. A., Beardslee, W. R., & Offord, D. R. (1997). Prevalence of child physical and sexual abuse in the community: Results from the Ontario health supplement. *Journal of the American Medical Association, 278*(2), 131–135.

MacMillan, H. L., Jamieson, E., & Walsh, C. (2003). Reported contact with child protection services among those reporting child physical and sexual abuse: Results from a community survey. *Child Abuse & Neglect, 27,* 1397–1408.

MacMillan, H. M., Boyle, M. H., Wong, M. Y.-Y., Duku, E. K., Fleming, J. E., & Walsh, C. A. (1999). Slapping and spanking in childhood and its association with lifetime prevalence of psychiatric disorders in a general population sample. *Canadian Medical Association Journal, 161,* 805–809.

Macmillan, R., McMorris, B. J., & Kruttschnitt, C. (2004). Linked lives: Stability and change in maternal circumstances and trajectories of antisocial behavior in children. *Child Development, 75,* 205–220.

MacWhinney, B. (2005). Language evolution and human development. In B. J. Ellis & D. F. Bjorklund (Eds.), Origins of the social mind: Evolutionary psychology and child development (pp. 383–410). New York: Guilford.

Maestripieri, D., Higley, J. D., Lindell, S. G., Newman, T. K., McCormack, K. M., & Sanchez, M. M. (2006). Early maternal rejection affects the development of monoaminergic systems and adult abusive parenting in rhesus macaques. *Behavioral Neuroscience, 120*(5), 1017–1024.

Mahoney, J. L. (2000). School extracurricular activity participation as a moderator in the development of antisocial patterns. *Child Development, 71*(2), 502–516.

Main, M. (1983). Exploration, play, and cognitive functioning related to infant–mother attachment. *Infant Behavior and Development, 6,* 167–174.

Main, M. (1995). Recent studies in attachment: Overview, with selected implications for clinical work. In S. Goldberg, R. Muir, & J. Kerr (Eds.), *Attachment theory: Social, developmental, and clinical perspectives* (pp. 407–470). Hillsdale, NJ: Analytic Press.

Main, M., & Solomon, J. (1986). Discovery of an insecure, disorganized/disoriented attachment pattern: Procedures, findings, and implications for the classification of behavior. In M. Yogman & T. B. Brazelton (Eds.), *Affective development in infancy.* Norwood, NJ: Ablex.

Main, M., Kaplan, N., & Cassidy, J. (1985). Security in infancy, childhood and adulthood: A move to the level of representation. In I. Bretherton & E. Waters (Eds.), Growing points in attachment. *Monographs of the Society for Research in Child Development, 50*(1–20), 66–104.

Makino, M., Tsuboi, K., and Dennerstein, L. (2004). Prevalence of eating disorders: A comparison of Western and non-Western countries. *Medscape General Medicine, 6*(3). Retrieved September 27, 2004, from http://www.medscape.com/ viewarticle/487413.

Malaspina, D., Harlap, S., Fennig, S., Heiman, D., Nahon, D., Feldman, C., et al. (2001). Advancing paternal age and the risk of schizophrenia. *Archives of General Psychiatry, 58,* 361–371.

Malone, F. D., Canick, J. A., Ball, R. H., Nyberg, D. A., Comstock, C. H., Bukowski, R., Berkowitz, R. L., Gross, S. J., Dugoff, L., Craigo, S. D., Timor-Tritsch, I. E., Carr, S. R., Wolfe, H. M., Dukes, K., Bianchi, D. W., Rudnicka, A. R., Hackshaw, A. K., Lambert-Messerlian, G., Wald, N. J., & D'Alton, M. E. (2005). First-trimester or second-trimester screening, or both, for Down's syndrome. *New England Journal of Medicine, 353,* 2001–2011.

Malone, L. M., West, J., Flanagan, K. D., & Park, J. (2006). *Statistics in brief: The early reading and mathematics achievement of children who repeated kindergarten or who began school a year late* (NCES 2006-064). Washington, DC: National Center for Education Statistics.

Mandela, N. (1994). *Long walk to freedom: The autobiography of Nelson Mandela.* Boston: Little, Brown.

Mandler, J. (1998). The rise and fall of semantic memory. In M. A. Conway, S. E. Gathercole, & C. Cornoldi (Eds.), *Theories of memory* (Vol. 2). East Sussex, England: Psychology Press.

Mandler, J. M. (1998a). Representation. In D. Kuhn & R. S. Siegler (Eds.), *Handbook of child psychology: Vol. 2: Cognition, perception, and language* (5th ed., pp. 255–308). New York: Wiley.

Mandler, J. M., & McDonough, L. (1993). Concept formation in infancy. *Cognitive Development, 8,* 291–318.

Mandler, J. M., & McDonough, L. (1996). Drinking and driving don't mix: Inductive generalization in infancy. *Cognition, 59,* 307–335.

Mandler, J. M., & McDonough, L. (1998). Cognition across the life span: On developing a knowledge base in infancy. *Developmental Psychology, 34,* 1274–1288.

Manlove, J., Ryan, S., & Franzetta, K. (2003). Patterns of contraceptive use within teenagers' first sexual relationships. *Perspectives on Sexual and Reproductive Health, 35,* 246–255.

Mansfield, R. S., & Busse, T. V. (1981). *The psychology of creativity and discovery: Scientists and their work.* Chicago: Nelson-Hall.

March of Dimes Birth Defects Foundation. (1987). *Genetic counseling: A public health information booklet* (Rev. ed.). White Plains, NY: Author.

March of Dimes Birth Defects Foundation. (2004). *Marijuana: What you need to know.* Retrieved October 29, 2004, from http://www.marchofdimes.com/pnhec/159_4427.asp.

March of Dimes Foundation. (2002). *Toxoplasmosis.* (Fact Sheet). Wilkes-Barre, PA: Author.

Marcia, J. E. (1966). Development and validation of ego identity status. *Journal of Personality and Social Psychology, 3*(5), 551–558.

Marcia, J. E. (1979, June). *Identity status in late adolescence: Description and some clinical implications.* Address given at symposium on identity development, Rijksuniversitat Groningen, Netherlands.

Marcia, J. E. (1980). Identity in adolescence. In J. Adelson (Ed.), *Handbook of adolescent psychology.* New York: Wiley.

Marcia, J. E. (1993). The relational roots of identity. In J. Kroger (Ed.), *Discussions on ego identity* (pp. 101–120). Hillsdale, NJ: Erlbaum.

Marcon, R. A. (1999). Differential impact of preschool models on development and early learning of inner-city children: A three-cohort study. *Developmental Psychology, 35*(2), 358–375.

Marcus, G. F., Vijayan, S., Rao, S. B., & Vishton, P. M. (1999). Rule learning by seven-month-old infants. *Science, 283,* 77–80.

Markoff, J. (1992, October 12). Miscarriages tied to chip factories. *New York Times,* pp. A1, D2.

Marks, H. (2000). Student engagement in instructional activity: Patterns in the elementary, middle, and high school years. *American Education Research Journal, 37,* 153–184.

Marlier, L. & Schaal, B. (2005). Human newborns prefer human milk: Conspecific milk odor is attractive without postnatal exposure. *Child Development, 76,* 155–168.

Marling, K. A. (1996). *Graceland: Going home with Elvis.* Cambridge, MA: Harvard University Press.

Marlow, N., Wolke, D., Bracewell, M. A., & Samara, M., for the EPICure Study Group. (2005). Neurologic and developmental disability at six years of age after extremely preterm birth.

Marshall, N. L. (2004). The quality of early child care and children's development. *Current Directions in Psychological Science, 13,* 165–168.

Martens, P. J., Phillips, S. J., Cheang, M. S., Rosolowich, V., & Breastfeeding Promotion Steering Committee of Manitoba. (2000). How baby-friendly are Manitoba hospitals? The provincial infant feeding study. *Canadian Journal of Public Health, 91,* 51–57.

Martin, C. L., Eisenbud, L., & Rose, H. (1995). Children's gender-based reasoning about toys. *Child Development, 66,* 1453–1471.

Martin, C. L., & Fabes, R. A. (2001). The stability and consequences of young children's same-sex peer interactions. *Developmental Psychology, 37,* 431–446.

Martin, C. L., & Halverson, C. F. (1981). A schematic processing model of sex typing and stereotyping in children. *Child Development, 52,* 1119–1134.

Martin, C. L., Ruble, D. N., & Szkrybalo, J. (2002). Cognitive theories of early gender development. *Psychological Bulletin, 128,* 903–933.

Martin, C. L., & Ruble, D. (2004). Children's search for gender cues: Cognitive perspectives on gender development. *Current Directions in Psychological Science, 13,* 67–70.

Martin, J. A., Hamilton, B. E., Sutton, P. D., Ventura, S. J., Menacker, F., & Munson, M. L. (2003). Births: Final data for 2002. *National Vital Statistics Reports, 52*(10). Hyattsville, MD: National Center for Health Statistics.

Martin, J. A., Hamilton, B. E., Sutton, P. D., Ventura, S. J., Menacker, F., & Munson, M. L. (2005). Births: Final data for 2003. *National Vital Statistics Reports, 54*(2). Hyattsville, MD: National Center for Health Statistics.

Martin, J. A., Hamilton, B. E., Sutton, P. D., Ventura, S. J., Menacker, F., & Kirmeyer, S. (2006). Births: Final data for 2004. *National Vital Statistics Reports, 55*(1). Hyattsville, MD: National Center for Health Statistics.

Martin, J. A., Hamilton, B. E., Sutton, P. D., Ventura, S. J., Menacker, F., & Kirmeyer, S. (2006). Births: Final data for 2004. *National Vital Statistics Reports, 55*(1). Hyattsville, MD: National Center for Health Statistics

Martin, N., & Montgomery, G. (2002, March 18). *Is having twins, either identical or fraternal, in someone's genes? Is there a way to increase your chances of twins or is having twins just luck?* Retrieved March 7, 2006, from http://genepi.qimr.edu.au/Scientific American_Twins.html.

Martin, R., Noyes, J., Wisenbaker, J., & Huttunen, M. (2000). Prediction of early childhood negative emotionality and inhibition from maternal distress during pregnancy. *Merrill-Palmer Quarterly, 45,* 370–391.

Martínez-González, M. A., Gual, P., Lahortiga, F., Alonso, Y., de Irala-Estévez, J., & Cervera, S. (2003). Parental factors, mass media influences, and the onset of eating disorders in a prospective population-based cohort. *Pediatrics, 111,* 315–320.

Marwick, C. (1997). Health care leaders from drug policy group. *Journal of the American Medical Association, 278,* 378.

Marwick, C. (1998). Physician leadership on national drug policy finds addiction treatment works. *Journal of the American Medical Association, 279,* 1149–1150.

Marzano, R. J., & Hutchins, C. L. (1987). *Thinking skills: A conceptual framework* (ERIC Document Reproduction Service No. ED 266436).

Masataka, N. (1999). Preference for infant-directed signing in 2-day-old hearing infants of deaf parents. *Developmental Psychology, 35,* 1001–1005.

Masse, L. C., & Tremblay, R. E. (1997). Behavior of boys in kindergarten and the onset of substance use during adolescence. *Archives of General Psychiatry, 54,* 62–68.

Masten, A. S. (2001). Ordinary magic: Resilience processes in development. *American Psychologist, 56,* 227–238.

Masten, A. S., & Coatsworth, J. D. (1998). The development of competence in favorable and unfavorable environments: Lessons from research on successful children. *American Psychologist, 53,* 205–220.

Masten, A., Best, K., & Garmezy, N. (1990). Resilience and development: Contributions from the study of children who overcome adversity. *Development and Psychopathology, 2,* 425–444.

Mathews, T. J., & Ventura, S. J. (1997). *Birth and fertility rates by educational attainment: United States, 1994* (Monthly Vital Statistics Report, 45[10, Suppl.], DHHS Publication No. PHS

97-1120). Hyattsville, MD: National Center for Health Statistics.

Mathews, T. J., Curtin, S. C., & MacDorman, M. F. (2000). Infant mortality statistics from the 1998 period linked birth/infant death data set. *National Vital Statistics Reports, 48*(12). Hyattsville, MD: National Center for Health Statistics.

Mathias, R. (1999). Tracking trends in teen drug abuse over the years. *NIDA Notes (National Institute on Drug Abuse), 14*(1), p. S8.

Maticka-Tyndale, E. (2001). Sexual health and Canadian youth: How do we measure up? *The Canadian Journal of Human Sexuality, 10,* 1–16.

Maticka-Tyndale, E., McKay, A., & Barrett, M. (2001). Teenage sexual and reproductive behavior in developed countries: Country report for Canada. Occasional Report No. 4. New York: The Alan Guttmacher Institute.

Maxwell, L. (1987, January). *Eight pointers on teaching children to think* (Research in Brief No. IS 87-104 RIB). Washington, DC: U.S. Department of Education, Office of Educational Research and Improvement.

May, K. A., & Perrin, S. P. (1985). Prelude: Pregnancy and birth. In S. M. H. Hanson & F. W. Bozett (Eds.), *Dimensions of fatherhood.* Beverly Hills, CA: Sage.

Mayer, D. P. (1998). Do new teaching standards undermine performance on old tests? *Educational Evaluation and Policy Analysis, 20,* 53–73.

Mayo Clinic. (2005, December 7). *Infertility.* Retrieved October 4, 2007, from www. mayoclinic.com/health/infertility/DS00310.

Mayo Clinic. (2007, February 22). Early symptoms of pregnancy: What happens right away. Retrieved July 23, 2007, from http://www.mayoclinic.com/health/symptoms-of-pregnancy/PR00102.

Mayseless, O., & Scharf, M. (2003). What does it mean to be an adult? The Israeli experience. In J. J. Arnett & N. L. Galambos (Eds.), Exploring cultural conceptions of the transition to adulthood. *New Directions for Child and Adolescent Development, 100,* 5–20.

McCain, M., & Mustard, J. F. (1999). *The early years: Reversing the real brain drain.* Toronto: Ontario Children's Secretariat.

McCall, R. B., & Carriger, M. S. (1993). A meta-analysis of infant habituation and recognition memory performance as predictors of later IQ. *Child Development, 64,* 57–79.

McCallum, K. E., & Bruton, J. R. (2003). The continuum of care in the treatment of eating disorders. *Primary Psychiatry, 10*(6), 48–54.

McCarton, C. M., Brooks-Gunn, J., Wallace, I. F., Bauer, C. R., Bennett, F. C., Bernbaum, J. C., Broyles, S., Casey, P. H., McCormick, M. C., Scott, D. T., Tyson, J., Tonascia, J., & Meinert, C. L., for the Infant Health and Development Program Research Group. (1997). Results at age 8 years of early intervention for low-birth-weight premature infants. *Journal of the American Medical Association, 277,* 126–132.

McCartt, A. T. (2001). Graduated driver licensing systems: Reducing crashes among teenage drivers. *Journal of the American Medical Association, 286,* 1631–1632.

McCarty, M. E., Clifton, R. K., Ashmead, D. H., Lee, P., & Goubet, N. (2001). How infants use vision for grasping objects. *Child Development, 72,* 973–987.

McClearn, G. E., Johansson, B., Berg, S., Pedersen, N. L., Ahern, F., Petrill, S. A., & Plomin, R. (1997). Substantial genetic influence on cognitive abilities in twins 80 or more years old. *Science, 276,* 1560–1563.

McClintock, M. K., & Herdt, G. (1996). Rethinking puberty: The development of sexual attraction. *Current Directions in Psychological Science, 5*(6), 178–183.

McConaghy, T. (1998). Canada's participation in TIMSS. *Phi Delta Kappan, 79,* 793–800.

McCord, J. (1996). Unintended consequences of punishment. *Pediatrics, 88,* 832–834.

McCormick, M. C., Brooks-Gunn, J., Buka, S. L., Goldman, J., Yu, J., Salganik, M., Scott, D. T., Bennett, F. C., Kay, L. L., Bernbaum, J. C., Bauer, C. R., Martin, C., Woods, E. R., Martin, A., & Casey, P. H. (2006). Early intervention in low birth weight premature infants: Results at 18 years of age for the Infant Health and Development Program. *Pediatrics, 117,* 771–780.

McCormick, M. C., McCarton, C., Brooks-Gunn, J., Belt, P., & Gross, R. T. (1998). The infant health and development program: Interim summary. *Journal of Developmental and Behavioral Pediatrics, 19,* 359–371.

McCoy, A. R., & Reynolds, A. J. (1999). Grade retention and school performance: An extended investigation. *Journal of School Psychology, 37,* 273–298.

McCrink, K., & Wynn, K. (2004). Large-number addition and subtraction by 9-month-old infants. *Psychological Science, 15,* 776–781.

McDaniel, M., Paxson, C., & Waldfogel, J. (2006). Racial disparities in childhood asthma in the United States: Evidence from the National Health Interview Survey, 1997 to 2003. *Pediatrics, 117,* 868–877.

McElwain, N. L., & Volling, B. L. (2005). Preschool children's interactions with friends and older siblings: Relationship specificity and joint contributions to problem behavior. *Journal of Family Psychology, 19,* 486–496.

McGauhey, P. J., Starfield, B., Alexander, C., & Ensminget, M. E. (1991). Social environment and vulnerability of low birth weight children: A social-epidemiological perspective. *Pediatrics, 88,* 943–953.

McGee, R., Partridge, F., Williams, S., & Silva, P. A. (1991). A twelve-year follow-up of preschool hyperactive children. *Journal of the American Academy of Child and Adolescent Psychiatry, 30,* 224–232.

McGilley, B. M., & Pryor, T. L. (1998). Assessment and treatment of bulimianervosa. *American Family Physician, 57*(11), 2743–2750.

McGrath, P. J. (1996). There is more to pain measurement in children than "ouch." *Canadian Psychology, 37,* 63–75.

McGue, M. (1997). The democracy of the genes. *Nature, 388,* 417–418.

McGuffin, P., Owen, M. J., & Farmer, A. E. (1995). Genetic basis of schizophrenia. *Lancet, 346,* 678–682.

McGuffin, P., Riley, B., & Plomin, R. (2001). Toward behavioral genomics. *Science, 291,* 1232–1249.

McGuigan, F. & Salmon, K. (2004). The time to talk: The in?uence of the timing of adult-child talk on children's event memory. *Child Development, 75,* 669–686.

McHale, S. M., Kim, J., Whiteman, S., & Crouter, A. C. (2004). Links between sex-typed time use in middle childhood and gender development in early adolescence. *Developmental Psychology, 40,* 868–881.

McHale, S. M., Updegraff, K. A., Helms-Erikson, H., & Crouter, A. C. (2001). Sibling influences on gender development in middle childhood and early adolescence: A longitudinal study. *Developmental Psychology, 37,* 115–125.

McIntyre, L., Connor, S., & Warren, J. (1998). *A glimpse of child hunger in Canada.* Report No. W-98-26E. Ottawa: Applied Research Branch, Strategic Policy, Human Resources Development Canada.

McIntyre, L., Connor, S. K., & Warren, J. (2000). Child hunger in Canada: Results of the 1994 National Longitudinal Survey of Children and Youth. *Canadian Medical Association Journal, 163,* 961–965.

McKay, A., & Barrett, M. (1999). Pre-service sexual health education training of elementary, secondary, and physical health education teachers in Canadian faculties of education. *Canadian Journal of Human Sexuality, 8,* 91–101.

McKay, N. Y. (1992). Introduction. In M. Anderson, *My Lord, what a morning* (pp. ix–xxxiii). Madison: University of Wisconsin Press.

McKenna, J. J., & Mosko, S. (1993). Evolution and infant sleep: An experimental study of infant–parent co-sleeping and its implications for SIDS. *Acta Paediatrica, 389*(Suppl.), 31–36.

McKenna, J. J., Mosko, S. S., & Richard, C. A. (1997). Bedsharing promotes breastfeeding. *Pediatrics, 100,* 214–219.

McKenna, M. C., Kear, D. J., & Ellsworth, R. A. (1995). Children's attitudes toward reading: A national survey. *Reading Research Quarterly, 30,* 934–956.

McKim, M. K., Cramer, K. M., Stuart, B., & O'Connor, D. L. (1999). Infant care decisions and attachment security: The Canadian Transition to Child Care Study. *Canadian Journal of Behavioural Science, 31,* 92–106.

McKusick, V. A. (2001). The anatomy of the human genome. *Journal of the American Medical Association, 286*(18), 2289–2295.

McLanahan, S., & Sandefur, G. (1994). *Growing up with a single parent.* Cambridge, MA: Harvard University Press.

McLeod, R., Boyer, K., Karrison, T., Kasza, K., Swisher, C., Roizen, N., Jalbrzikowski, J., Remington, J., Heydemann, P., Noble, A. J., Mets, M., Holfels, E., Withers, S., Latkany, P., Meier, P., & Toxoplasmosis Study Group. (2006). Outcome of treatment for congenital toxoplasmosis, 1981–2004: The national collaborative Chicago-based, congenital toxoplasmosis study. *Clinical Infectious Diseases: An Official Publication of the Infectious Diseases Society of America, 42*(10), 1383–1394.

McLeskey, J., Lancaster, M., & Grizzle, K. L. (1995). Learning disabilities and grade retention: A review of issues with recommendations for practice. *Learning Disabilities Research & Practice, 10,* 120–128.

McLoyd, V. C. (1990). The impact of economic hardship on black families and children: Psychological distress, parenting, and socioemotional development. *Child Development, 61,* 311–346.

McLoyd, V. C. (1998). Socioeconomic disadvantage and child development. *American Psychologist, 53,* 185–204.

McLoyd, V. C., & Smith, J. (2002). Physical discipline and behavior problems in African American, European American, and Hispanic children: Emotional support as a moderator. *Journal of Marriage and Family, 64,* 40–53.

McMahon, M. J., Luther, E. R., Bowes, W. A., & Olshan, A. F. (1996). Comparison of a trial of labor with an elective second cesarean section. *New England Journal of Medicine, 335,* 689–695.

McNeilly-Choque, M. K., Hart, C. H., Robinson, C. C., Nelson, L. J., & Olsen, S. F. (1996). Overt and relational aggression on the playground: Correspondence among different informants. *Journal of Research in Childhood Education, 11,* 47–67.

McQuillan, J., Greil, A. L., White, L., & Jacob, M. C. (2003). Frustrated fertility: Infertility and psychological distress among women. *Journal of Marriage and Family, 65,* 1007–1018.

Mead, M. (1928). *Coming of age in Samoa.* New York: Morrow.

Mead, M. (1930). *Growing up in New Guinea.* New York: Blue Ribbon.

Mead, M. (1935). *Sex and temperament in three primitive societies.* New York: Morrow.

Mead, M. (1972). *Blackberry winter: My earlier years.* New York: Morrow.

Meeks, J. J., Weiss, J., & Jameson, J. L. (2003, May). Dax1 is required for testis formation. *Nature Genetics, 34,* 32–33.

Meezan, W., & Rauch, J. (2005). Gay marriage, same-sex parenting, and America's children. *Future of Children, 15,* 97–115.

Meier, D. (1995). *The power of their ideas.* Boston: Beacon.

Meier, R. (1991, January–February). Language acquisition by deaf children. *American Scientist, 79,* 60–70.

Meier, R.P., & Willerman, R. (1995). Prelinguistic gesture in deaf and hearing infants. In J. S. Reilly & K. Emmory (eds.), *Language, Gesture, and Space.* (391–409). Hillsdale, NJ: Lawrence Erlbaum Associates, Inc.

Meins, E. (1998). The effects of security of attachment and maternal attribution of meaning on children's linguistic acquisitional style. *Infant Behavior and Development, 21,* 237–252.

Meis, P. J., Klebanoff, M., Thom, E., Dombrowski, M. P., Sibai, B., Moawad, A. H., Spong, C. Y., Hauth, J. C., Miodovnik, M., Varner, M. W., Leveno, K. J., Caritis, S. N., Iams, J. D., Wapner, R. J., Conway, D., O'Sullivan, M. J., Carpenter, M., Mercer, B., Ramin, S. M., Thorp, J. M., Peaceman, A. M., Gabbe, S., & National Institute of Child Health and Human Development Maternal-Fetal Medicine Units Network. (2003). Prevention of recurrent preterm delivery by 17 alpha-hydroxyprogesterone caproate. *New England Journal of Medicine, 348,* 2379–2385.

Meltzoff, A., & Gopnik, A. (1994). The role of imitation in understanding persons and developing a theory of mind. In D.J. Cohen, S. Baron-Cohen, & H. Tager-Flusberg (Eds.). *Understanding other minds: Perspectives from autism.* (pp. 335–366). New York: Oxford University Press.

Meltzoff, A. N., & Gopnik, A. (1993). The role of imitation in understanding persons and developing a theory of mind. In S. Baron-Cohen, H. Tager-Flusberg, & D. J. Cohen (Eds.), *Understanding other minds: Perspectives from autism* (pp. 335–366). New York: Oxford University Press.

Meltzoff, A. N., & Moore, M. K. (1983). Newborn infants imitate adult facial gestures. *Child Development, 54,* 702–709.

Meltzoff, A. N., & Moore, M. K. (1989). Imitation in newborn infants: Exploring the range of gestures imitated and the underlying mechanisms. *Developmental Psychology, 25,* 954–962.

Meltzoff, A. N., & Moore, M. K. (1994). Imitation, memory, and the representation of persons. *Infant Behavior and Development, 17,* 83–99.

Meltzoff, A. N., & Moore, M. K. (1998). Object representation, identity, and the paradox of early permanence: Steps toward a new

framework. *Infant Behavior & Development, 21,* 201–235.

Menacker, F., Martin, J. A., MacDorman, M. F., & Ventura, S. J. (2004). Births to 10–14 year-old mothers, 1990–2002: Trends and health outcomes. *National Vital Statistics Reports, 53*(7). Hyattsville, MD: National Center for Health Statistics.

Mendelsohn, A. L., Dreyer, B. P., Fierman, A. H., Rosen, C. M., Legano, L. A., Kruger, H. A., Lim, S. W., & Courtlandt., C. D. (1998). Low-level lead exposure and behavior in early childhood. *Pediatrics, 101*(3), e10. Retrieved September 24, 2002, from http://www.pediatrics.org/cgi/content/full/101/3/e10.

Mendelson, B. K., Mendelson, M. J., & White, D. R. (2001). Body-esteem scale for adolescents and adults. *Journal of Personality Assessment, 76,* 90–106.

Mendelson, B. K., White, D. R., & Mendelson, M. J. (1996). Self-esteem and body esteem: Effects of gender, age, and weight. *Journal of Applied Developmental Psychology, 17,* 321–346.

Mendelson, B. K., White, D. R., & Schliecker, E. (1995). Adolescents' weight, sex, and family functioning. *International Journal of Eating Disorders, 17,* 73–79.

Mendelson, M. J., Mendelson, B. K., & Andrews, J. (2000). Self-esteem, body esteem, and body-mass in late adolescence: Is a competence x importance model needed? *Journal of Applied Developmental Psychology, 21,* 249–266.

Mendle, J., Turkheimer, E., D'Onofrio, B. M., Lynch, S. K., Emery, R. E., Slutske, W. S., & Martin, N. G. (2006). Family structure and age at menarche: A children-of-twins approach. *Developmental Psychology, 42,* 533–542.

Menegaux, F., Baruchel, A., Bertrand, Y., Lescoeur, B., Leverger, G., Nelken, B., Sommelet, D., Hemon, D., & Clavel, J. (2006). Household exposure to pesticides and risk of childhood acute leukaemia. *Occupational and Environmental Medicine, 63*(2), 131–134.

Meng, H., Smith, S. D., Hager, K., Held, M., Liu, J., Olson, R. K., et al. (2005, October). A deletion in DCDC2 on 6p22 is associated with reading disability. Paper presented at the American Society of Human Genetics meeting, Salt Lake City, UT.

Menken, J., Trussell, J., & Larsen, U. (1986). Age and infertility. *Science, 233,* 1389–1394.

Mennella, J. A., & Beauchamp, G. K. (1996a). The early development of human flavor preferences. In E. D. Capaldi (Ed.), *Why we eat what we eat: The psychology of eating* (pp. 83–112). Washington, DC: American Psychological Association.

Mennella, J. A., & Beauchamp, G. K. (1996b). The human infants' response to vanilla flavors in mother's milk and formula. *Infant Behavior and Development, 19,* 13–19.

Mennella, J. A., & Beauchamp, G. K. (2002). Flavor experiences during formula feeding are related to preferences during childhood. *Early Human Development, 68,* 71–82.

Ment, L. R., Vohr, B., Allan, W., Katz, K. H., Schneider, K. C., Westerveld, M., Duncan, C. C., & Makuch, R. W. (2003). Changes in cognitive function over time in very low-birth-weight infants. *Journal of the American Medical Association, 289,* 705–711.

Merrell, K. W., Buchanan, R., & Tran, O. K. (2006). Relational aggression in children and adolescents: A review with implications for school settings. *Psychology in the Schools, 43,* 345–360.

Messinger, D. S., Bauer, C. R., Das, A., Seifer, R., Lester, B. M., Lagasse, L. L., Wright, L. L., Shankaran, S., Bada, H. S., Smeriglio, V. L., Langer, J. C., Beeghly, M., & Poole, W. K. (2004). The maternal lifestyle study: Cognitive, motor, and behavioral outcomes of cocaine-exposed and opiate-exposed infants through three years of age. *Pediatrics, 113,* 1677–1685.

Messinis, L., Krypianidou, A., Maletaki, S., & Papathanasopoulos, P. (2006). Neuropsychological deficits in long-term cannabis users. *Neurology, 66,* 737–739.

Metis Health in Canada. (2004). Aboriginal peoples survey APSI (1991) and APS II (2001). Retrieved August 13, 2007 from http://www.naho.ca/MHC_Site/B/survey.html.

Meyer, D. R., & Garasky, S. (1993). Custodial fathers: Myths, realities, and child support policy. *Journal of Marriage and the Family, 55,* 73–89.

Michelmore, P. (1962). *Einstein: Profile of the man.* London: Frederick Muller, Ltd.

Miedzian, M. (1991). *Boys will be boys: Breaking the link between masculinity and violence.* New York: Doubleday.

Mifflin, L. (1996, February 15). 4 networks plan a ratings system for their shows. *New York Times,* pp. A1, C24.

Migeon, B. R. (2006). The role of X inactivation and cellular mosaicism in women's health and sex-specific disorders. *Journal of the American Medical Association, 295,* 1428–1433.

Mikkola, K., Ritari, N., Tommiska, V., Salokorpi, T., Lehtonen, L., Tammela, O., Paakkonen, L., Olsen, P., Korkman, M., & Fellman, V. for the Finnish ELBW Cohort Study Group. (2005). Neurodevelopmental outcome at 5 years of age of a national cohort of extremely low birth weight infants who were born in 1996–1997. *Pediatrics, 116,* 1391–1400.

Milberger, S., Biederman, J., Faraone, S. V., Chen, L., & Jones, J. (1996). Is maternal smoking during pregnancy a risk factor for attention hyperactivity disorder in children? *American Journal of Psychiatry, 153,* 1138–1142.

Miles, S. B., & Stipek, D. (2006). Contemporaneous and longitudinal associations between social behavior and literacy achievement in a sample of low-income elementary school children. *Child Development, 77,* 103–117.

Millar, W. J., Wadhera S., & Nimrod C. (1992). Multiple births: Trends and patterns in Canada, 1974–1990. *Health Reports, 4,* 223–250.

Miller, A. (2001). Prescription of methylphenidate to children and youth, 1990–1996. *Canadian Medical Association Journal, 165,* 1489–1494.

Miller, A. R., Recsky, M. A. & Armstrong, R. W. (2004). Responding to the needs of children with chronic health conditions in an era of health services reform. *Canadian Medical Association, 171,* 1366–1367.

Miller, B. C., & Moore, K. A. (1990). Adolescent sexual behavior, pregnancy, and parenting: Research through the 1980s. *Journal of Marriage and the Family, 52,* 1025–1044.

Miller, B. C., Fan, X., Christensen, M., Grotevant, H. D., & van Dulmen, M. (2000). Comparisons of adopted and nonadopted adolescents in a large, nationally representative sample. *Child Development, 71,* 1458–1473.

Miller, F., Jenkins, J. & Keating, D. (2002). Parenting and Children's Behavior Problems. In Willms, J. D. *Vulnerable Children* (pp. 167–182). Edmonton, AB: The University of Alberta Press.

Miller, J. R. (1996). *Singwauk's vision: A history of Native residential schools.* Toronto: University of Toronto Press.

Miller, M. W., Astley, S. J., & Clarren, S. K. (1999). Number of axons in the corpus callosum of the mature macaca nemestrina: Increases caused by prenatal exposure to ethanol. *Journal of Comparative Neurology, 412,* 123–131.

Miller-Kovach, K. (2003). Childhood and adolescent obesity: A review of the scientific literature. Weight Watchers International: Unpublished ms.

Millman, R. P., Working Group on Sleepiness in Adolescents/Young Adults, & AAP Committee on Adolescents. (2005). Excessive sleepiness in adolescents and young adults: Causes, consequences, and treatment strategies. *Pediatrics, 115,* 1774–1786.

Mills, J. L., Holmes, L. B., Aarons, J. H., Simpson, J. L., Brown, Z. A., Jovanovic-Peterson, L. G., Conley, M. R., Graubard, B. I., Knopp, R. H., & Metzger, B. E. (1993). Moderate caffeine use and the risk of spontaneous abortion and intrauterine growth retardation. *Journal of the American Medical Association, 269,* 593–597.

Millstein, S. G., Irwin, C. E., Adler, N. E., Cohn, L. D., Kegeles, S. M., & Dolcini, M. M. (1992). Health-risk behaviors and health concerns among young adolescents. *Pediatrics, 89,* 422–428.

Milunsky, A. (1992). *Heredity and your family's health.* Baltimore: Johns Hopkins University Press.

Minister of Public Works and Government Services Canada. (2001). *Federal/provincial/territorial early childhood development agreement: Report on Government of Canada activities and expenditures 2000–2001.* Ottawa: Author.

Ministry of Children and Youth Services. (2005). Best start: Ontario's plan for early learning and child care. Retrieved from www.children.gov. on.ca/NR/CS/BestStart/ActionPlan.pdf on July 17, 2007.

Ministry of Community, Family and Children's Services. (2002). *Early years challenge fund.* Toronto: Queen's Printer for Ontario.

Minkler, M., & Fuller-Thomson, E. (2005). African American grandparents raising grandchildren: A national study using the Census 2000 American Community Survey. *Journal of Gerontology: Social Sciences, 60B,* S82–S92.

Mintz, T. H. (2005). Linguistic and conceptual influences on adjective acquisition in 24- to 36-month-olds. *Developmental Psychology, 41,* 17–29.

Miotti, P. G., Taha, T. E. T., Kumwenda, N. I., Broadhead, R., Mtimavalye, L. A. R., Van der Hoeven, L., Chiphangwi, J. D., Liomba, G., & Biggar, R. J. (1999). HIV transmission through breastfeeding: A study in Malawi. *Journal of the American Medical Association, 282,* 744–749.

Mischel, W. (1966). A social learning view of sex differences in behavior. In E. Maccoby (Ed.), *The development of sex differences* (pp. 57–81). Stanford, CA: Stanford University Press.

Miserandino, M. (1996). Children who do well in school: Individual differences in perceived competence and autonomy in above-average children. *Journal of Educational Psychology, 88*(2), 203–214.

Misra, D. P., & Guyer, B. (1998). Benefits and limitations of prenatal care: From counting visits to measuring content. *Journal of the American Medical Association, 279,* 1661–1662.

Mistry, R. S., Vandewater, E. A., Huston, A. C., & McLoyd, V. (2002). Economic well-being and children's social adjustment: The role of family process in an ethnically diverse low income sample. *Child Development, 73,* 935–951.

Mitchell, D., Brynelsen, D., & Holm, M. (1988). Evaluating the process of early intervention programmes. *Irish Journal of Psychology, 9,* 235–248.

Mitchell, E. A., Blair, P. S., & L'Hoir, M. P. (2006). Should pacifiers be recommended to prevent sudden infant death syndrome? *Pediatrics, 117,* 1755–1758.

Mix, K. S., Huttenlocher, J., & Levine, S. C. (2002). Multiple cues for quantification in infancy: Is number one of them? *Psychological Bulletin, 128,* 278–294.

Mix, K. S., Levine, S. C., & Huttenlocher, J. (1999). Early fraction calculation ability. *Developmental Psychology, 35,* 164–174.

Miyake, K., Chen, S., & Campos, J. (1985). Infants' temperament, mothers' mode of interaction and attachment in Japan: An interim report. In I. Bretherton & E. Waters (Eds.), Growing points of attachment theory and research. *Monographs of the Society for Research in Child Development, 50*(1–2, Serial No. 109), 276–297.

Mlot, C. (1998). Probing the biology of emotion. *Science, 280,* 1005–1007.

Moawad, A. H., Caritis, S. N., Harper, M., Wapner, R. J., Sorokin, Y., Miodovnik, M., Carpenter, M., Peaceman, A. M., O'Sullivan, M. J., Sibai, B., Langer, O., Thorp, J. M., Ramin, S. M., Mercer, B. M., & National Institute of Child Health and Human Development Maternal-Fetal Medicine Units Network. (2006). Maternal morbidity associated with multiple repeat cesarean deliveries. *Obstetrics and Gynecology, 107*(6), 1226–1232.

Modell, J. (1989). *Into one's own: From youth to adulthood in the United States, 1920–1975.* Berkeley: University of California Press.

Moffitt, T. E. (1993). Adolescent-limited and life-course persistent antisocial behavior: A developmental taxonomy. *Psychological Review, 100,* 674–701.

Moffitt, T. E., Caspi, A., Belsky, J., & Silva, P. A. (1992). Childhood experience and the onset of menarche: A test of a sociobiological model. *Child Development, 63,* 47–58.

Molina, B. S. G., & Chassin, L. (1996). The parent–adolescent relationship at puberty: Hispanic ethnicity and parent alcoholism as moderators. *Developmental Psychology, 32,* 675–686.

Molina, B. S. G., & Pelham, W. E., Jr. (2003). Childhood predictors of adolescent substance use in a longitudinal study of children with ADHD. *Journal of Abnormal Psychology, 112,* 497–507.

Mondschein, E. R., Adolph, K. E., & Tamis-Lemonda, C. S. (2000). Gender bias in mothers' expectations about infant crawling. *Journal of Experimental Child Psychology. Special Issue on Gender, 77,* 304–316.

Money, J., & Ehrhardt, A. A. (1972). *Man and woman/Boy and girl.* Baltimore, MD: Johns Hopkins University Press.

Money, J., Hampson, J. G., & Hampson, J. L. (1955). Hermaphroditism recommendations concerning assignment of sex, change of sex, and psychotic management. *Bulletin of Johns Hopkins Hospital, 97,* 284–300.

Montague, C. T., Farooqi, I. S., Whitehead, J. P., Soos, M. A., Rau, H., Wareham, N. J., Sewter, C. P., Digby, J. E., Mohammed, S. N., Hurst, J. A., Cheetham, C. H., Earley, A. R., Barnett, A. H., Prins, J. B., & Orahilly, S. (1997). Congenital leptin deficiency is associated with severe early onset obesity in humans. *Nature, 387,* 903–908.

Montague, D. P. F., & Walker-Andrews, A. S. (2001). Peekaboo: A new look at infants' perception of emotion expressions. *Developmental Psychology, 37,* 826–838.

Montgomery, L. E., Kiely, J. L., & Pappas, G. (1996). The effects of poverty, race, and family structure on U.S. children's health: Data from the NHIS, 1978 through 1980 and 1989 through 1991. *American Journal of Public Health, 86,* 1401–1405.

Moon, C., & Fifer, W. P. (1990, April). *Newborns prefer a prenatal version of mother's voice.* Paper presented at the biannual meeting of the International Society of Infant Studies, Montreal.

Moon, C., Cooper, R. P., & Fifer, W. P. (1993). Two-day-olds prefer their native language. *Infant Behavior and Development, 16,* 495–500.

Moon, R. Y., Sprague, B. M., & Patel, K. M. (2005). Stable prevalence but changing risk factors for sudden infant death syndrome in child care settings in 2001. *Pediatrics, 116,* 972–977.

Mooney-Somers, J., & Golombok, S. (2000). Children of lesbian mothers: From the 1970s to the new millennium. *Sexual and Relationship Therapy 15*(2), 121–126.

Moore, C., Barresi, J., & Thompson, C. (1998). The cognitive basis of future-oriented prosocial behavior. *Social Development, 7,* 198–218.

Moore, M. K., & Meltzoff, A. N. (2004). Object permanence after a 24-hr delay and leaving the locale of disappearance: The role of memory, space, and identity. *Developmental Psychology, 40,* 606–620.

Moore, S. E., Cole, T. J., Poskitt, E. M. E., Sonko, B. J., Whitehead, R. G., McGregor, I. A., & Prentice, A. M. (1997). Season of birth predicts mortality in rural Gambia. *Nature, 388,* 434.

Moretti, M. E., Lee, A., Ito, S. (2000). Which drugs are contraindicated during breastfeeding? Practice guidelines. *Canadian Family Physician, 46,* 1753–1757.

Morgan, B., Maybery, M., & Durkin, K. (2003). Weak central coherence, poor joint attention, and low verbal ability: Independent deficits in early autism. *Developmental Psychology, 39,* 646–656.

Morgan, W. J., Crain, E. F., Gruchalla, R. S., O'Connor, G. T., Kattan, M., Evans, R., Stout, J., Malindzak, G., Smartt, E., Plaut, M., Walter, M., Vaughan, B., & Mitchell, H. for the Inner-City Asthma Study Group. (2004). Results of a home-based environmental intervention among urban children with asthma. *New England Journal of Medicine, 351,* 1068–1080.

Morison, P., & Masten, A. S. (1991). Peer reputation in middle childhood as a predictor of adaptation in adolescence: A seven-year follow-up. *Child Development, 62,* 991–1007.

Morison, S. J., & Ellwood, A.-L. (2000). Resiliency in the aftermath of deprivation: A second look at the development of Romanian orphanage children. *Merrill-Palmer Quarterly, 46,* 717–737.

Morison, S. J., Ames, E. W., & Chisholm, K. (1995). The development of children adopted from Romanian orphanages. *Merrill-Palmer Quarterly Journal of Developmental Psychology, 41,* 411–430.

Morris, R. D., Stuebing, K. K., Fletcher, J. M., Shaywitz, S. E., Lyon, G. R., Shankweiler, D. P., Katz, L., Francis, D. J., & Shaywitz, B. A. (1998). Subtypes of reading disability: Variability around a phonological core. *Journal of Educational Psychology, 90,* 347–373.

Morris, R., & Kratochwill, T. (1983). *Treating children's fears and phobias: A behavioral approach.* Elmsford, NY: Pergamon.

Morrison, J. A., Friedman, L. A., Harlan, W. R., Harlan, L. C., Barton, B. A., Schreiber, G. B., & Klein, D. J. (2005). Development of the metabolic syndrome in black and white adolescent girls. *Pediatrics, 116,* 1178–1182.

Morse, J. M., & Field, P. A. (1995). *Qualitative research methods for health professionals.* Thousand Oaks, CA: Sage.

Mortensen, E. L., Michaelson, K. F., Sanders, S. A., & Reinisch, J. M. (2002). The association between duration of breastfeeding and adult intelligence. *Journal of the American Medical Association, 287,* 2365–2371.

Mortensen, P. B., Pedersen, C. B., Westergaard, T., Wohlfahrt, J., Ewald, H., Mors, O., Andersen, P. K., & Melbye, M. (1999). Effects of family history and place and season of birth on the risk of schizophrenia. *New England Journal of Medicine, 340,* 603–608.

Mortimer, J. (2003). *Working and growing up in America.* Cambridge, MA: Harvard University Press.

Moses, L. J., Baldwin, D. A., Rosicky, J. G., & Tidball, G. (2001). Evidence for referential understanding in the emotions domain at twelve and eighteen months. *Child Development, 72,* 718–735.

Mosier, C. E., & Rogoff, B. (2003). Privileged treatment of toddlers: Cultural aspects of individual choice and responsibility. *Developmental Psychology, 39,* 1047–1060.

Moss, E., & St-Laurent, D. (2001). Attachment at school age and academic performance. *Developmental Psychology, 37,* 863–874.

Msall, M. S. E. (2004). Developmental vulnerability and resilience in extremely preterm infants. *Journal of the American Medical Association, 292,* 2399–2401.

MTA Cooperative Group. (1999). A 14-month randomized clinical trial of treatment strategies for attention-deficit/hyperactivity disorder. *Archives of General Psychiatry, 56,* 1073–1986.

MTA Cooperative Group. (2004a). National Institute of Mental Health multimodal treatment study of ADHD follow-up: Changes in effectiveness and growth after the end of treatment. *Pediatrics, 113,* 762–769.

MTA Cooperative Group. (2004b). National Institute of Mental Health multimodal treatment study of ADHD follow-up: 24-month outcomes of treatment strategies for attention-deficit/hyperactivity disorder. *Pediatrics, 113,* 754–762.

Mullan, D., & Currie, C. (2000). Socioeconomic equalities in adolescent health. In C. Currie, K. Hurrelmann, W. Settertobulte, R. Smith, & J. Todd (Eds.), *Health and health behaviour among young people: A WHO cross-national study (HBSC) international report* (pp. 65–72). WHO Policy Series: Healthy Policy for Children and Adolescents, Series No. 1.

Müller, M. (1998). *Anne Frank: The biography.* New York: Holt.

Mulrine, A. (2004, February 2). Coming of age in ancient times. *U.S. News & World Report.* Retrieved July 17, 2007, from http://www.usnews.com/usnews/culture/ articles/040202/2child.htm.

Multiple Births Canada. (2000). Incidence of multiple births. Retrieved July 6, 2007 from www.multiplebirthscanada.org/english/ documents/factsheets/incidenceofmb.pdf.

Multiple Births Canada. (2005). Low birth weight and preterm multiple births: A Canadian profile. Retrieved from www.multiplebirthscanada.org/english/documents/ low_birth_bro_final2005.pdf on July 10, 2007.

Mumme, D. L., & Fernald, A. (2003). The infant as onlooker: Learning from emotional reactions observed in a television scenario. *Child Development, 74,* 221–237.

Munakata, Y., McClelland, J. L., Johnson, M. J., & Siegler, R. S. (1997). Rethinking infant knowledge: Toward an adaptive process account of successes and failures in object permanence tasks. *Psychological Review, 104,* 686–714.

Munk-Olsen, T., Laursen, T. M., Pedersen, C. B., Mors, O., & Mortensen, P. B. (2006). New parents and mental disorders: A population-based register study. *Journal of the American Medical Association, 296,* 2582–2589.

Muñoz, K. A., Krebs-Smith, S. M., Ballard-Barbash, R., & Cleveland, L. E. (1997). Food intakes of U.S. children and adolescents compared with recommendations. *Pediatrics, 100,* 323–329.

Muntner, P., He, J., Cutler, J. A., Wildman, R. P., & Whelton, P. K. (2004, May 5). Trends in blood pressure among children and adolescents. *Journal of the American Medical Association, 291,* 2107–2113.

Murchison, C., & Langer, S. (1927). Tiedemann's observations on the development of the mental facilities of children. *Journal of Genetic Psychology, 34,* 205–230.

Muris, P., Merckelbach, H., & Collaris, R. (1997). Common childhood fears and their origins. *Behaviour Research and Therapy, 35,* 929–937.

Murphy, C. C., Schei, B., Myhr, T. L., & Du Mont, J. (2001). Abuse: A risk factor for low birth weight? A systematic review and meta-analysis. *Canadian Medical Association Journal, 164,* 1567–72.

Murphy, C. M., & Bootzin, R. R. (1973). Active and passive participation in the contact desensitization of snake fear in children. *Behavior Therapy, 4,* 203–211.

Murray, M. L., deVries, C. S., and Wong, I. C. K. (2004). A drug utilisation study of anti-depressants in children and adolescents using the General Practice Research data base. *Archives of the Diseases of Children, 89,* 1098–1102.

Mussen, P. H., & Jones, M. C. (1957). Self-conceptions, motivations, and interpersonal attitudes of late- and early-maturing boys. *Child Development, 28,* 243–256.

Must, A., Jacques, P. F., Dallal, G. E., Bajema, C. J., & Dietz, W. H. (1992). Long-term morbidity and mortality of overweight adolescents: A follow-up of the Harvard Growth Study of 1922 to 1935. *New England Journal of Medicine, 327*(19), 1350–1355.

Must, A., Naumova, E. N., Phillips, S. M., Blum, M., Dawson-Hughes, B., & Rand, W. M. (2005). Childhood overweight and maturational timing in the development of adult overweight and fatness: The Newton Girls Study and its follow-up. *Pediatrics, 116,* 620-627.

Mustanski, B. S., DuPree, M. G., Nievergelt, C. M., Bocklandt, S., Schork, N. J., & Hamer, D. H. (2005). A genomewide scan of male sexual orientation. *Human Genetics, 116,* 272–278.

Mustillo, S., Worthman, C., Erkanli, A., Keeler, G., Angold, A., & Costello, E. J. (2003). Obesity and psychiatric disorder: Developmental trajectories. *Pediatrics, 111,* 851–859.

Muter, V., Hulme, C., Snowling, M. J., & Stevenson, J. (2004). Phonemes, rimes, vocabulary, and grammatical skill as foundations of early reading development: Evidence from a longitudinal study. *Developmental Psychology, 40,* 665–681.

Naeye, R. L., & Peters, E. C. (1984). Mental development of children whose mothers smoked during pregnancy. *Obstetrics and Gynecology, 64,* 601.

Nafstad, P., Hagen, J. A., Oie, L., Magnus, P., & Jaakkola, J. J. K. (1999). Day care and respiratory health. *Pediatrics, 103,* 753–758.

Nagaoka, J., & Roderick, M. (April 2004). *Ending social promotion: The effects of retention.* Chicago: Consortium on Chicago School Research.

Nagaraja, J., Menkedick, J., Phelan, K. J., Ashley, P., Zhang, X., & Lanphear, B. P. (2005). Deaths from residential injuries in US children and adolescents, 1985-1997. *Pediatrics, 116,* 454–461.

Naito, M., & Miura, H. (2001). Japanese childrens' numerical competencies: Ageand school-related influences on the development of number concepts and addition skills. *Developmental Psychology, 37,* 217–230.

Nakajima, H., & Mayor, F. (1996). Culture and health. *World Health, 49*(2), 13–15.

Nansel, T. R., Overpeck, M., Pilla, R. S., Ruan, W. J., Simons-Morton, B., & Scheidt, P. (2001). Bullying behaviors among U.S. youth: Prevalence and association with psychosocial adjustment. *Journal of the American Medical Association, 285,* 2094–2100.

Nash, J. M. (1997, February 3). Fertile minds. *Time,* pp. 49–56.

Nathanielsz, P. W. (1995). The role of basic science in preventing low birth weight. *The Future of Our Children, 5*(1), 57–70.

National Advisory Committee on Immunization. (2006). *Canadian Immunization Guide,* Seventh Edition. Ottawa: Public Health Agency of Canada, Infectious Disease and Emergency Preparedness Branch, Centre for Infectious Disease Prevention and Control.

National Anti-Poverty Organization. (2003). The face of poverty in canada: An overview. Retrieved July 25, 2007 from http://oafb.ca/ portal/images/pdfs/Poverty_Canada/Face%20of %20Poverty%20in%20Canada%202003.pdf.

National Assessment of Educational Progress: The Nation's Report Card. (2004). *America's charter schools: Results from the NAEP 2003 Pilot Study* (NCES 2005-456). Jessup, MD: U.S. Department of Education.

National Association for Gifted Children (NAGC). (undated). *Frequently asked questions.* Retrieved April 22, 2006, from http://www.nagc.org/index.aspx?id=548.

National Center for Education Statistics (NCES). (1987). *Who drops out of high school? From high school and beyond.* Washington, DC: U.S. Department of Education, Office of Educational Research and Improvement.

National Center for Education Statistics (NCES). (1996). *Education indicators: An international perspective* (NCES 96-003). Washington, DC: U.S. Department of Education.

National Center for Education Statistics (NCES). (1998b, June). *Nonresident fathers can make a difference in children's school performance* (Issue Brief, NCES 98-117). Washington, DC: U.S. Department of Education, Office of Educational Research and Improvement.

National Center for Education Statistics (NCES). (2001). *The condition of education*

2001 (Publication No. 2001–072). Washington, DC: U.S. Government Printing Office.

National Center for Education Statistics (NCES). (2003). *The condition of education, 2003* (Publication No. 2003–067). Washington, DC: Author.

National Center for Education Statistics (NCES). (2004a). *National assessment of educational progress: The nation's report card. Mathematics highlights 2003* (NCES 2004–451). Washington, DC: U.S. Department of Education.

National Center for Education Statistics (NCES). (2004a). *The condition of education 2004* (NCES 2004–077). Washington, DC: U.S. Government Printing Office.

National Center for Education Statistics (NCES). (2004b). *National assessment of educational progress: The nation's report card. Mathematics highlights 2003* (NCES 2004–451). Washington, DC: U.S. Department of Education.

National Center for Education Statistics (NCES). (2004c). *National assessment of educational progress: The nation's report card. Reading highlights 2003* (NCES 2004–452). Washington, DC: U.S. Department of Education.

National Center for Education Statistics. (2005a). Children born in 2001—First results from the base year of Early Childhood Longitudinal Study, Birth Cohort (ECLS-B). Retrieved November 19, 2004, from http://nces. ed.gov/pubs2005/children/index.asp.

National Center for Education Statistics. (2006). *Calories in, calories out: Food and exercise in public elementary schools, 2005* (NCES 2006-057). Washington, DC: Author.

National Center for Health Statistics (NCHS). (1998). *Health, United States, 1998 with socioeconomic status and health chartbook.* Hyattsville, MD: Author.

National Center for Health Statistics (NCHS). (1999). Abstract adapted from *Births: Final data for 1999* by Mid Atlantic Parents of Multiples.

National Center for Health Statistics (NCHS). (1999). *Health, United States, 1999* (DHS Publication No. PHS 99–1232). Hyattsville, MD: Author.

National Center for Health Statistics (NCHS). (2000a). *2 to 20 years: Boys stature-for-age and weight-for-age percentiles.* Retrieved December 4, 2002, from http://www.cdc. gov/growthcharts

National Center for Health Statistics (NCHS). (2000b). *2 to 20 years: Girls stature-for-age and weight-for-age percentiles.* Retrieved December 4, 2002, from http://www.cdc.gov/growthcharts

National Center for Health Statistics (NCHS). (2004). *Health, United States, 2004 with chart-book on trends in the health of Americans* (DHHS Publication No. 2004-1232). Hyattsville, MD: National Center for Health Statistics.

National Center for Health Statistics (NCHS). (2005). *Health, United States, 2005* (DHHS Publication No. 2005-1232). Hyattsville, MD: Author.

National Center for Injury Prevention and Control (NCIPC). (2004). Fact sheet: Teen drivers. Retrieved May 7, 2004, from http://www.cdc.gov/ncip.

National Center for Learning Disabilities (2004a). *Dyslexia: Learning disabilities in reading.* Fact sheet.Retrieved May 30, 2004, from http://www.ld.org/LDInfoZone/InfoZone_ FactSheet_Dyslexia.cfm.

National Center for Learning Disabilities (2004b). *LD at a glance.* Fact sheet. Retrieved May 30, 2004, from http://www.ld.org/LDInfoZone/InfoZone_ FactSheet_LD.cfm.

National Center on Shaken Baby Syndrome. (2000). SBS questions. Retrieved from http://www.dontshake.com/sbsquestions.html.

National Coalition for the Homeless. (2004, May). *Who is homeless?* NCH Fact Sheet 3. Washington, DC: Author.

National Commission for the Protection of Human Subjects of Biomedical and Behavioral Research. (1978). *Report.* Washington, DC: Author.

National Council of Teachers of Mathematics. (2000). *Principles and standards for school mathematics.* Reston, VA: National Council of Teachers of Mathematics.

National Council of Teachers of Mathematics (NCTM). (2006). *Curriculum focal points for prekindergarten through grade 8 mathematics.* Reston, VA: Author.

National Enuresis Society. (1995). *Enuresis.* [Fact sheet].

National High Blood Pressure Education Program Working Group on High Blood Pressure in Children and Adolescents. (2004). The fourth report on the diagnosis, evaluation, and treatment of high blood pressure in children and adolescents. *Pediatrics, 114*(2-Supp.), 555–576.

National Highway Traffic Safety Administration. (2003). *Traffic safety facts 2002: Young drivers.* Washington, DC: Author.

National Institute of Child Health and Development (NICHD). (1997; updated 1/12/00). [Fact sheet] Sudden Infant Death Syndrome. Retrieved January 30, 2001, from http://www.nichd.nih.gov/sids/sids_fact.htm

National Institute of Mental Health (NIMH). (1999a, April). Suicide facts. Washington, DC: Author. Retrieved September 24, 2002, from http://www.nimh.nih.gov/research/suifact.htm

National Institute of Mental Health (NIMH). (2001a). *Helping children and adolescents cope with violence and disasters: Fact sheet* (NIH Publication No., 01-3518). Bethesda, MD: Author.

National Institute of Mental Health (NIMH). (2001b). *Teenage brain: A work in progress.* Retrieved March 11, 2004, from http://www.nimh.gov/publicat/ teenbrain.cfm.

National Institute of Neurological Disorders and Stroke (NINDS). (2007). Asperger syndrome information page. Retrieved May 24, 2007, from http://www.ninds.nih.gov/disorders/asperger/asperger.htm.

National Institute on Drug Abuse (NIDA). (1996). *Monitoring the future.* Washington, DC: National Institutes of Health.

National Institutes of Health (NIH) Consensus Development Panel on Physical Activity and Cardiovascular Health. (1996). Physical activity and cardiovascular health. *Journal of the American Medical Association, 276,* 241–246.

National Institutes of Health Consensus Development Panel. (2001). National Institutes of Health Consensus Development conference statement: Phenylketonuria screening and management. October 16–18, 2000. *Pediatrics, 108*(4), 972–982.

National Library of Medicine. (2003). Medical encyclopedia: Conduct disorder. Retrieved April 23, 2005, from http://www.nlm.nih.gov/medlineplus/ency/article/000919.htm.

National Library of Medicine. (2004). Medical Encyclopedia: Oppositional defiant disorder. Retrieved April 23, 2005, from http://www.nlm.nih.gov/medlineplus/ency/ article/001537.htm.

National Parents' Resource Institute for Drug Education. (1999, September 8). *PRIDE surveys, 1998–99 national summary: Grades 6–12.* Bowling Green, KY: Author.

National Reading Panel. (2000). *Report of the National Reading Panel: Teaching children to read: An evidence-based assessment of the scientific research literature on reading and its implications for reading instruction: Reports of the subgroups.* Washington, DC: National Institute of Child Health and Human Development.

National Research Council (NRC). (1993a). *Losing generations: Adolescents in high-risk settings.* Washington, DC: National Academy Press.

National Research Council (NRC). (1993b). *Understanding child abuse and neglect.* Washington, DC: National Academy Press.

National Sleep Foundation. (2004). *Sleep in America.* Washington, DC: Author.

National Survey on Drug Use and Health (NSDUH). (2006a). Academic performance and substance use among students aged 12 to 17: 2002, 2003, and 2004. *The NSDUH Report* (Issue 18). Rockville, MD: Office of Applied Statistics, Substance Abuse and Mental Health Services, U. S. Department of Health and Human Services.

National Survey on Drug Use and Health (NSDUH). (2006c). Substance use treatment need among adolescents: 2003–2004. *The NSDUH* Report (Issue 24). Rockville, MD: Office of Applied Statistics, Substance Abuse and Mental Health Services, U. S. Department of Health and Human Services.

National Television Violence Study. (1995). *Scientific Papers: 1994–1995.* Studio City, CA: Mediascope.

National Television Violence Study: Key findings and recommendations. (1996, March). *Young Children, 51*(3), 54–55.

Natural Science and Engineering Research Council. (2000). *Tri-Council policy statement: Ethical conduct for research involving humans.* Retrieved September 20, 2002, from http://www.nserc.ca/programs/ethics/english/policy.htm

Nduati, R., John, G., Mbori-Ngacha, D., Richardson, B., Overbaugh, J., Mwatha, A., Ndinya-Achola, J., Bwayo, J., Onyango, F. E., Hughes, J., & Kreiss, J. (2000). Effect of breastfeeding and formula feeding on transmission of HIV-i. A randomized clinical trial. *Journal of the American Medical Association, 283*(9), 1167–1174.

Nebraska Symposium on Motivation. (1984). Psychology and gender. Lincoln: University of Nebraska Press.

Neckoway, R., Brownlee, K. & Castellan, B. (2007). Is attachment theory consistent aboriginal parenting realities? *First Peoples Child & Family Review, 3,* 65–74.

Needleman, H. L., Riess, J., Tobin, M. J., Biesecker, G. E., & Greenhouse, J. B. (1996). Bone lead levels and delinquent behavior. *Journal of the American Medical Association, 275,* 363–369.

Nef, S. Verma-Kurvari, S., Merenmies, J., Vassallt, J.-D., Efstratiadis, A., Accili, D., & Parada, L. F. (2003). Testis determination requires insulin receptor family function in mice. *Nature, 426,* 291–295.

Neisser, U., Boodoo, G., Bouchard, T. J., Jr., Boykin, A. W., Brody, N., Ceci, S. J., Halpern, D. F., Loehlin, J. C., Perloff, R., Sternberg, R. J., & Urbina, S. (1996). Intelligence: Knowns and unknowns. *American Psychologist, 51*(2), 77–101.

Neitzel, C., & Stright, A. D. (2003). Relations between parents' scaffolding and children's academic self-regulation: Establishing a foundation of self-regulatory competence. *Journal of Family Psychology, 17,* 147–159.

Nelson, C. A. (1995). The ontogeny of human memory: A cognitive neuroscience perspective. *Developmental Psychology, 31,* 723–738.

Nelson, C. A., Monk, C. S., Lin, J., Carver, L. J., Thomas, K. M., & Truwit, C. L. (2000). Functional neuroanatomy of spatial working memory in children. *Developmental Psychology, 36,* 109–116.

Nelson, K. (1992). Emergence of autobiographical memory at age 4. *Human Development, 35,* 172–177.

Nelson, K. (1993a). Events, narrative, memory: What develops? In C. Nelson (Ed.), *Memory and affect in development: The Minnesota Symposia on Child Psychology* (Vol. 26, pp. 1–24). Hillsdale, NJ: Erlbaum.

Nelson, K. (1993b). The psychological and social origins of autobiographical memory. *Psychological Science, 47,* 7–14.

Nelson, K. (2005). Evolution and development of human memory systems. In B. J. Ellis & D. F. Bjorklund (Eds.), *Origins of the social mind: Evolutionary psychology and child development* (pp. 319–345). New York: Guilford.

Nelson, K. B., Dambrosia, J. M., Ting, T. Y., & Grether, J. K. (1996). Uncertain value of electronic fetal monitoring in predicting cerebral palsy. *New England Journal of Medicine, 334,* 613–618.

Nelson, L. J. (2003). Rites of passage in emerging adulthood: Perspectives of young Mormons. In J. J. Arnett and N. L. Galambos (Eds.), Exploring cultural conceptions of the transition to adulthood. *New Directions for Child and Adolescent Development, 100,* 33–49.

Nelson, L. J., & Marshall, M. F. (1998). *Ethical and legal analyses of three coercive policies aimed at substance abuse by pregnant women.* Report published by the Robert Wood Johnson Substance Abuse Policy Research Foundation.

Nelson, L. J., Hart, C. H., Wu, B., Yang, C., Jin, S. & Roper, S. O. (2006). Relations between Chineese mothers' parenting practices and social withdrawal in early childhood. *International Journal of Behavioral Development, 30,* 261–271.

Nelson, M. C., & Gordon-Larsen, P. (2006). Physical activity and sedentary behavior patterns are associated with selected adolescent risk behaviors. *Pediatrics, 117,* 1281–1290.

Netherlands State Institute for War Documentation. (1989). *The diary of Anne Frank: The critical edition* (D. Barnouw & G. van der Stroom, Eds.; A. J. Pomerans & B. M. Mooyaart-Doubleday, Trans.). New York: Doubleday.

Neugebauer, R., Hoek, H. W., & Susser, E. (1999). Prenatal exposure to wartime famine and development of antisocial personality disorder in early adulthood. *Journal of the American Medical Association, 282,* 455–462.

Neumann, H., McCormick, R. M., Amundson, N. E., & McLean, H. B. (2000). Career counselling First Nations youth: Applying the First Nations Career-Life Planning Model. *Canadian Journal of Counselling, 34,* 172–185.

Neville, A. (n.d.). The emotional and psychological effects of miscarriage. Retrieved July 23, 2007 from http://www.opendoors.com.au/pregnancyD.htm.

Newacheck, P. W., Strickland, B., Shonkoff, J. P., Perrin, J. M., McPherson, M., McManus, M., Lauver, C., Fox, H., & Arango, P. (1998). An epidemiologic profile of children with special health care needs. *Pediatrics, 102,* 117–123.

Newcomb, A. F., & Bagwell, C. L. (1995). Children's friendship relations: A meta-analytic review. *Psychological Bulletin, 117*(2), 306–347.

Newcomb, A. F., Bukowski, W. M., & Pattee, L. (1993). Children's peer relations: A meta-analytic review of popular, rejected, neglected, controversial, and average sociometric status. *Psychological Bulletin, 113,* 99–128.

Newcombe, N., & Fox, N. A. (1994). Infantile amnesia: Through a glass darkly. *Child Development, 65,* 31–40.

Newman, D. L., Caspi, A., Moffitt, T. E., & Silva, P. A. (1997). Antecedents of adult interpersonal functioning: Effects of individual differences in age 3 temperament. *Developmental Psychology, 33,* 206–217.

Newman, R. S. (2005). The cocktail party effect in infants revisited: Listening to one's name in noise. *Developmental Psychology, 41,* 352–362.

Newport, E. L. (1991). Contrasting conceptions of the critical period for language. In S. Carey & R. Gelman (Eds.), *The epigenesis of mind: Essays on biology and cognition.* Hillsdale, NJ: Erlbaum.

Newport, E. L., Bavelier, D., & Neville, H. J. (2001). Critical thinking about critical periods: Perspectives on a critical period for language acquisition. In Dupoux, E. (Ed.), *Language, brain, and cognitive development: Essays in honor of Jacques Mehler* (pp. 481–502). Cambridge, MA: The MIT Press.

Newport, E., & Meier, R. (1985). The acquisition of American Sign Language. In D. Slobin (Ed.), *The crosslinguistic study of language acquisition* (Vol. 1, pp. 881–938). Hillsdale, NJ: Erlbaum.

Newschaffer, C. J., Falb, M. D., & Gurney, J. G. (2005). National autism prevalence trends from United States special education data. *Pediatrics, 115,* e277–e282.

Newson, J., Newson, E., & Mahalski, P. A. (1982). Persistent infant comfort habits and their sequelae at 11 and 16 years. *Journal of Child Psychology and Psychiatry, 23,* 421–436.

NICHD Early Child Care Research Network & Duncan, G. J. (2003). Modeling the impacts of child care quality on children's preschool cognitive development. *Child Development, 74,* 1454–1475.

NICHD Early Child Care Research Network. (1996). Characteristics of infant child care: Factors contributing to positive caregiving. *Early Childhood Research Quarterly, 11,* 269–306.

NICHD Early Child Care Research Network. (1997a). The effects of infant child care on infant–mother attachment security: Results of the NICHD study of early child care. *Child Development, 68,* 860–879.

NICHD Early Child Care Research Network. (1998c, November). *When child-care classrooms meet recommended guidelines for quality.* Paper presented at the meeting of the National Association for the Education of Young People.

NICHD Early Child Care Research Network. (1999a). Child outcomes when child care center classes meet recommended standards for quality. *American Journal of Public Health, 89,* 1072–1077.

NICHD Early Child Care Research Network. (1999b). Chronicity of maternal depressive symptoms, maternal sensitivity, and child functioning at 36 months. *Developmental Psychology, 35,* 1297–1310.

NICHD Early Child Care Research Network. (2000). The relation of child care to cognitive and language development. *Child Development, 71,* 960–980.

NICHD Early Child Care Research Network. (2003). Does amount of time spent in child care predict socioemotional adjustment during the transition to kindergarten? *Child Development, 74,* 976–1005.

NICHD Early Child Care Research Network (2004). Are child developmental outcomes related to before- and afterschool care arrangement? Results from the NICHD Study of Early Child Care. *Child Development 75,* 280–295.

NICHD Early Child Care Research Network. (2004b). Does class size in first grade relate to children's academic and social performance or observed classroom processes? *Developmental Psychology, 40,* 651–664.

NICHD Early Child Care Research Network. (2005a). Duration and developmental timing of poverty and children's cognitive and social development from birth through third grade. *Child Development, 76,* 795–810.

NICHD Early Child Care Research Network. (2005d). Predicting individual differences in attention, memory, and planning in first graders from experiences at home, child care, and school. *Developmental Psychology, 41,* 99–114.

NICHD Early Child Care Research Network. (2006a). Child-care effect sizes for the NICHD study of early child care and youth development. *American Psychologist, 61,* 99–116.

NICHD Early Child Care Research Network. (2006b). Infant-mother attachment classification: Risk and protection in relation to changing maternal caregiving quality. *Developmental Psychology, 42,* 38–58.

Nielsen, K., McSherry, G., Petru, A., Frederick, T., Wara, D., Bryson, Y., Martin, N., Hutto, C., Ammann, A. J., Grubman, S., Oleske, J., & Scott, G. B. (1997). A descriptive survey of pediatric human immunodeficiency virus-infected long-term survivors. *Pediatrics, 99.* Retrieved September 24, 2002, from http://www.pediatrics.org/cgi/content/full/99/4/e4

Nielsen, M., Dissanayake, C., & Kashima, Y. (2003). A longitudinal investigation of self-other discrimination and the emergence of mirror self-recognition. *Infant Behavior & Development, 26,* 213–226.

Nielsen, M., Suddendorf, T., & Slaughter, V. (2006). Mirror self-recognition beyond the face. *Child Development, 77,* 176–185.

Nisan, M., & Kohlberg, L. (1982). Universality and variation in moral judgment: A longitudinal and cross-sectional study in Turkey. *Child Development, 53,* 865–876.

Nisbett, R. E. (1998). Race, genetics, and IQ. In C. Jencks & M. Phillips (Eds.), *The Black-White test score gap* (pp. 86–102). Washington, DC: Brookings Institution.

Nisbett, R. E. (2005). Heredity, environment, and race differences in IQ: A commentary on Rushton and Jensen (2005). *Psychology, Public Policy, and Law, 11,* 302–310.

Nishimura, H., Hashikawa, K., Doi, K., Iwaki, T., Watanabe, Y., Kusuoka, H., Nishimura, T., & Kubo, T. (1999). Sign language "heard" in the auditory cortex. *Nature, 397,* 116.

Niskar, A. S., Kieszak, S. M., Holmes, A., Esteban, E., Rubin, C., & Brody D. J. (1998). Prevalence of hearing loss among children 6 to 19 years of age: The third National Health and Nutrition Examination Survey. *Journal of the American Medical Association, 279,* 1071–1075.

Nissen, S. E. (2006). ADHD drugs and cardiovascular risk. *New England Journal of Medicine, 354,* 1445–1448.

Nitschke, M., Pilotto, L S., Attewell, R. G., Smith, B. J., Pisaniello, D., Martin, J., Ruffin, R. E., & Hiller, J. E. (2006). Cohort study of indoor nitrogen dioxide and house dust mite exposure in asthmatic children. *Journal of Occupational and Environmental Medicine, 48*(5), 462–469.

Nix, R. L., Pinderhughes, E. E., Dodge, K. A., Bates, J. E., Pettit, G. S., & McFadyen-Ketchum, S. A. (1999). The relation between mothers' hostile attribution tendencies and children's externalizing behavior problems: The mediating role of mothers' harsh discipline practices. *Child Development, 70*(4), 896–909.

Nobre, A. C., & Plunkett, K. (1997). The neural system of language: Structure and development. *Current Opinion in Neurobiology, 7,* 262–268.

Noirot, E., & Algeria, J. (1983). Neonate orientation towards human voice differs with type of feeding. *Behavioral Processes, 8,* 65–71.

Norris, C., Brink, S., & Mosher, P. (1999). *Measuring non-parental care in the NLSCY: Content and process issues.* Technical Paper T-00-1E. Ottawa: Applied Research Branch, Strategic Policy, Human Resources Development Canada.

Norris, S. (2001). *In brief. Reproductive infertility: Prevalence, causes, trends, and treatments.* Report No. PRB 00-32E. Ottawa: Parliamentary Research Branch, Library of Parliament. Retrieved November 11, 2007 from http://dsp-psd.pwgsc.gc.ca/Collection-R/LoPBdP/EB-e/prb0032-e.pdf.

Norwitz, E. R., Schust, D. J., & Fisher, S. J. (2001). Implantation and the survival of early pregnancy. *New England Journal of Medicine, 345*(19), 1400–1408.

Notzon, F. C. (1990). International differences in the use of obstetric interventions. *Journal of the American Medical Association, 263*(24), 3286–3291.

Nourot, P. M. (1998). Sociodramatic play: Pretending together. In D. P. Fromberg & D. Bergen (Eds.), *Play from birth to twelve and beyond: Contexts, perspectives, and meanings* (pp. 378–391). New York: Garland.

Nova Scotia Student Drug Use Survey. (2002). Retrieved August 22 2007 from http://www.gov.ns.ca/health/downloads/2002_NSDrugHighlights.pdf.

Nozyce, M., Hittelman, J., Muenz, L., Durako, S. J., Fischer, M. L., & Willoughby, A. (1994). Effect of perinatally acquired human immunodeficiency virus infection on neurodevelopment in children during the first two years of life. *Pediatrics, 94,* 883–891.

Nucci, L., & Smetana, J. G. (1996). Mothers' concepts of young children's areas of personal freedom. *Child Development, 67,* 1870–1886.

Nucci, L., Hasebe, Y., & Lins-Dyer, M. T. (2005). Adolescent psychological well-being and parental control. In J. Smetana (Ed.), *Changing boundaries of parental authority during adolescence: New directions for child and adolescent development, no. 108.* (pp. 17–30). San Francisco: Jossey-Bass.

Nugent, J. K., Keefer, C., O'Brien, S., Johnson, L., & Blanchard, Y. (2005). *The Newborn Behavioral Observation System.* Brazelton Institute, Children's Hospital, Boston.

Nugent, J. K., Lester, B. M., Greene, S. M., Wieczorek-Deering, D., & O'Mahony, P. (1996). The effects of maternal alcohol consumption and cigarette smoking during pregnancy on acoustic cry analysis. *Child Development, 67,* 1806–1815.

Nugent, T. (1999, September). At risk: 4 million students with asthma: Quick access to rescue inhalers critical for schoolchildren. *AAP News,* pp. 1, 10.

Nutrition Committee, Canadian Paediatric Society. (1991). Meeting the iron needs of infants and young children: An update. *Canadian Medical Association Journal, 144,* 1451–1454.

Nutrition Committee, Canadian Paediatric Society. (1995). Nutrient needs and feeding of premature infants. *Canadian Medical Association Journal, 152,* 1765–1785.

Nutrition Committee, Canadian Paediatric Society. (1996). The use of fluoride in infants and children. *Paediatrics & Child Health, 1,* 131–134.

Nybo Andersen, A. M., Wohlfahrt, J., Christens, P., Olsen, J., & Melbye, M. (2000). Maternal age and fetal loss: population based register linkage study. *British Medical Journal, 320,* 1708–1712.

O'Brien, C. M., & Jeffery, H. E. (2002). Sleep deprivation, disorganization and fragmentation during opiate withdrawal in newborns. *Pediatric Child Health, 38,* 66–71.

O'Connor, T., Heron, J., Golding, J., Beveridge, M., & Glover, V. (2002). Maternal antenatal anxiety and children's behavioural/emotional problems at 4 years. *British Journal of Psychiatry, 180,* 502–508.

O'Rahilly, S. (1998). Life without leptin. *Nature, 392,* 330–331.

Oakes, L. M. (1994). Development of infants' use of continuity cues in their perception of causality. *Developmental Psychology, 30,* 869–879.

Oakes, L. M., Coppage, D. J., & Dingel, A. (1997). By land or by sea: The role of perceptual similarity in infants' categorization of animals. *Developmental Psychology, 33,* 396–407.

Ochieng, B. M. W. (2003). Minority ethnic families and family-centred care. *Journal of Child Health Care, 7,* 123–132.

Ochsner, K. N., & Lieberman, M. D. (2001). The emergence of social cognitive neuroscience. *American Psychologist, 56,* 717–734.

OECD. (2006). *Education at a Glance 2006: Draft OECD Briefing Note for Canada. Paris: OECD Directorate for Education.* Retrieved October 24, 2007 from http://www.oecd.org/dataoecd/52/1/37392733.pdf.

Offer, D., & Church, R. B. (1991). Generation gap. In R. M. Lerner, A. C. Petersen, & J. Brooks-Gunn (Eds.), *Encyclopedia of adolescence* (pp. 397–399). New York: Garland.

Offer, D., & Schonert-Reichl, K. A. (1992). Debunking the myths of adolescence: Findings from recent research. *Journal of the American Academy of Child and Adolescent Psychiatry, 31,* 1003–1014.

Offer, D., Kaiz, M., Ostrov, E., & Albert, D. B. (2002). Continuity in family constellation. *Adolescent and Family Health, 3,* 3–8.

Offer, D., Offer, M. K., & Ostrov, E. (2004). *Regular guys: 34 years beyond adolescence.* Dordrecht, Netherlands: Kluwer Academic.

Offer, D., Ostrov, E., & Howard, K. I. (1989). Adolescence: What is normal? *American Journal of Diseases of Children, 143,* 731–736.

Offer, D., Ostrov, E., Howard, K. I., & Atkinson, R. (1988). *The teenage world: Adolescents' self-image in ten countries.* New York: Plenum.

Office of the Auditor General of Canada. (2003). Report of the Commissioner of the Environment and Sustainable Development: Pesticide Use in Canada. Retrieved July 26, 2007 from http://www.oag-bvg.gc.ca/domino/reports.nsf/html/c20031001xe02.html.

Office on Smoking and Health, Centers for Disease Control and Prevention. (2006). *The health consequences of involuntary exposure to tobacco smoke: A report of the surgeon-general* (No. 017-024-01685-3). Washington, DC: U. S. Department of Health and Human Services.

Offit, P. A., Quarles, J., Gerber, M. A., Hackett, C. J., Marcuse, E. K., Kollman, T. R., Gellin, B. G., & Landry, S. (2002). Addressing parents' concerns: Do multiple vaccines overwhelm or weaken the infant's immune system? *Pediatrics, 109,* 124–129.

Offord, D. R., & Lipman, E. L. (1996). Emotional and behavioural problems. In Human Resources Development Canada and Statistics Canada. *Growing up in Canada: National Longitudinal Survey of Children and Youth.* Ottawa: Author.

Offord, D. R., Lipman, E. L., & Duku, E. K. (1998). *Sports, the arts and community programs: Rates and correlates of participation.* Working Paper W-98-18E. Ottawa: Applied Research Branch, Strategic Policy, Human Resources Development Canada.

Ofori, B., Oraichi, D., Blais, L., Rey, E., & Berard, A. (2006). Risk of congenital anomalies in pregnant users of non-steroidal anti-inflammatory drugs: A nested case-control study. Birth Defects Research: Part B. *Developmental and Reproductive Toxicology, 77*(4), 268–279.

Ogden, C. L., Carroll, M. D., Curtin, L. R., McDowell, M. A., Tabak, C. J., & Flegal, K. M. (2006). Prevalence of overweight and obesity in the United States, 1999-2004. *Journal of the American Medical Association, 295,* 1549–1555.

Ogden, C. L., Fryar, C. D., Carroll, M. D., & Flegal, K. M. (2004). Mean body weight, height, and body mass index, United States 1960–2002. Advance data from *Vital and Health Statistics,* No. 347. Hyattsville, MD: National Center for Health Statistics.

Oken, E., Wright, R. O., Kleinman, K. P., Bellinger, D., Amarasiriwardena, C. J., Hu, H., Rich-Edwards, J. W., & Gillman, M. W. (2005). Maternal fish consumption, hair mercury, and infant cognition in a U.S. cohort. *Environmental Health Perspectives, 113*(10), 1376–1380.

Olds, D. L., Eckenrode, J., Henderson, C. R., Jr, Kitzman, H., Powers, J., Cole, R., Sidora, K., Morris, P., Pettitt, L. M., & Luckey, D. (1997). Long-term effects of home visitation on maternal life course and child abuse and neglect: Fifteen-year follow-up of a randomized trial. *Journal of the American Medical Association, 278,* 637–643.

Olds, D. L., Henderson, C. R., & Tatelbaum, R. (1994a). Intellectual impairment in children of women who smoke cigarettes during pregnancy. *Pediatrics, 93,* 221–227.

Olds, D. L., Henderson, C. R., & Tatelbaum, R. (1994b). Prevention of intellectual impairment in children of women who smoke cigarettes during pregnancy. *Pediatrics, 93,* 228–233.

Olds, D. L., Henderson, C. R., Klitzman, H. J., Eckenrode, J. J., Cole, R. E., & Tatelbaum, R. C. (1999). Prenatal and infancy home visitation by nurses: Recent findings. *The Future of Children, 9,* 44–65.

Olds, S. W. (1989). *The working parents' survival guide.* Rocklin, CA: Prima.

Olds, S. W. (2002). *A balcony in Nepal: Glimpses of a Himalayan village.* Lincoln, NE: ASJA Books, an imprint of iUniverse.

Olfson, M., Blanco, C., Liu, L., Moreno, C., Laje, G. (2006). National trends in the outpatient treatment of children and adolescents with antipsychotic drugs. *Archives of General Psychiatry, 63,* 679–685.

Oliver, B. R., Dale, P. S., & Plomin, R. (2005). Predicting literacy at age 7 from preliteracy at age 4: A longitudinal genetic analysis. *Psychological Science, 16,* 861–865.

Ollendick, T. H., Yang, B., King, N. J., Dong, Q., & Akande, A. (1996). Fears in American, Australian, Chinese, and Nigerian children and adolescents: A crosscultural study. *Journal of Child Psychology and Psychiatry, 37,* 213–220.

Olthof, T., Schouten, A., Kuiper, H., Stegge, H., & Jennekens-Schinkel, A. (2000). Shame and guilt in children: Differential situational antecedents and experiential correlates. *British Journal of Developmental Psychology, 18,* 51–64.

Olweus, D. (1995). Bullying or peer abuse at school: Facts and intervention. *Current Directions in Psychological Science, 4,* 196–200.

Opdal, S. H. & Rognum, T. O. (2004). The sudden infant death syndrome gene: Does it exist? *Pediatrics, 114,* e506–e512.

Orenstein, P. (2002, April 21). Mourning my miscarriage. Retrieved from http://www.NYTimes.com.

Organization for Economic Cooperation and Development (OCED). (2004). Education at a glance: OECD indicators—2004. *Education & Skills, 2004* (14), 1–456.

Orr, D. P., & Ingersoll, G. M. (1995). The contribution of level of cognitive complexity and pubertal timing to behavioral risk in young adolescents. *Pediatrics, 95*(4), 528–533.

Oshima-Takane, Y., Goodz, E., & Derevensky, J. L. (1996). Birth order effects on early language development: Do secondborn children learn from overheard speech? *Child Development, 67,* 621–634.

Ossorio, P., & Duster, T. (2005). Race and genetics: Controversies in biomedical, behavioral, and forensic sciences. *American Psychologist, 60,* 115–128.

Owen, C. G., Martin, R. M., Whincup, P. H., Smith, G. D., & Cook, D. G. (2005). Effects of infant feeding on the risk of obesity across the life course: A quantitative review of published evidence. *Pediatrics, 115,* 1367–1377.

Owen, C. G., Whincup, P. H., Odoki, K., Gilg, J. A., & Cook, D. G. (2002). Infant feeding and blood cholesterol: A study in adolescents and a systematic review. *Pediatrics, 110,* 597–608.

Owens, J., Maxim, R., McGuinn, M., Nobile, C., Msall, M., & Alario, A. (1999). Television-viewing habits and sleep disturbances in school children. *Pediatrics, 104*(3), e27.

Owens, J., Spirito, A., McGuinn, N., & Nobile, C. (2000). Sleep habits and sleep disturbance in elementary school children. *Developmental and Behavioral Pediatrics, 21,* 27–3.

Owens, R. E. (1996). *Language development* (4th ed.). Boston: Allyn and Bacon.

Padilla, A. M., Lindholm, K. J., Chen, A., Durán, R., Hakuta, K., Lambert, W., & Tucker, G. R. (1991). The English-only movement: Myths, reality, and implications for psychology. *American Psychologist, 46*(2), 120–130.

Paetsch, J. J., & Bertrand, L. D. (1999). Victimization and delinquency among Canadian youth. *Adolescence, 34,* 351–367.

Palda, V. A., Guise, J. & Wathen, N. C., with the Canadian Task Force on Preventative Health Care. (2004). Interventions to promote breast-feeding: applying the evidence in clinical practice. *CMAJ Canadian Medical Association Journal, 170,* 976–978.

Palella, F. J., Delaney, K. M., Moorman, A. C., Loveless, M. O., Fuhrer, J., Satten, G. A., Aschman, D. J., Holmberg, S. D., & the HIV Outpatient Study investigators. (1998). Declining morbidity and mortality among patients with advanced human immunodeficiency virus infection. *New England Journal of Medicine, 358,* 853–860.

Palkovitz, R. (1985). Fathers' birth attendance, early contact, and extended contact with their newborns: A critical review. *Child Development, 56,* 392–406.

Pally, R. (1997). How brain development is shaped by genetic and environmental factors. *International Journal of Psycho-Analysis, 78,* 587–593.

Palmer, J. R., Wise, L. A., Hatch, E. E., Troisi, R., Titus-Ernstoff, L., Strohsnitter, W., Kaufman, R., Herbst, A. L., Noller, K. L., Hyer, M., & Hoover, R. N. (2006). Prenatal diethylstilbestrol exposure and risk of breast cancer. *Cancer Epidemiology, Biomarkers & Prevention: A Publication of the American Association for Cancer Research.*

Pan, B. A., Rowe, M. L., Singer, J. D., & Snow, C. E. (2005). Maternal correlates of growth in toddler vocabulary production in low-income families. *Child Development, 76,* 763–782.

Panigrahy, A., Filiano, J., Sleeper, L. A., Mandell, F., Valdes-Dapena, M., Krous, H. F., Rava, L. A., Foley, E., White, W. F., & Kinney, H. C. (2000). Decreased serotonergic receptor binding in rhombic lip-derived regions of the medulla oblongata in the sudden infant death syndrome. *Journal of Neuropathology and Experimental Neurology, 59,* 377–384.

Papalia, D. (1972). The status of several conservation abilities across the life-span. *Human Development, 15,* 229–243.

Park, S., Belsky, J., Putnam, S., & Crnic, K. (1997). Infant emotionality, parenting, and 3-year inhibition: Exploring stability and lawful discontinuity in a male sample. *Developmental Psychology, 33,* 218–227.

Parke, R. D. (2004). The Society for Research in Child Development at 70: Progress and promise. *Child Development, 75,* 1–24.

Parke, R. D., & Buriel, R. (1998). Socialization in the family: Ethnic and ecological perspectives. In W. Damon (Series Ed.) & N. Eisenberg (Vol. Ed.), *Handbook of child psychology: Vol. 3. Social, emotional, and personality development* (5th ed., pp. 463–552). New York: Wiley.

Parke, R. D., Grossman, K., & Tinsley, R. (1981). Father–mother–infant interaction in the newborn period: A German–American comparison. In T. M. Field, A. M. Sostek, P. Viete, & P. H. Leideman (Eds.), *Culture and early interaction.* Hillsdale, NJ: Erlbaum.

Parke, R. D., Ornstein, P. A., Rieser, J. J., & Zahn-Waxler, C. (1994). The past as prologue: An overview of a century of developmental psychology. In R. D. Parke, P. A. Ornstein, J. J. Rieser, & C. Zahn-Waxler (Eds.), *A century of developmental psychology* (pp. 1–70). Washington, DC: American Psychological Association.

Parker, J. D., Woodruff, T. J., Basu, R., & Schoendorf, K. C. (2005). Air pollution and birth weight among term infants in Califiornia. *Pediatrics, 115,* 121–128.

Parker, L., Pearce, M. S., Dickinson, H. O., Aitkin, M., & Craft, A. W. (1999). Stillbirths among offspring of male radiation workers at Sellafield nuclear reprocessing plant. *Lancet, 354,* 1407–1414.

Parler, B. D. (2001). Raising a child: The traditional way. In *Aboriginal Head Start (Urban and Northern Communities) National Newsletter.* Spring/summer 2001 (p. 6). Ottawa: Health Canada.

Parr, J. (1982). Introduction. In J. Parr (Ed.), *Childhood and family in Canadian history* (pp. 7–16). Toronto: McClelland and Stewart Limited.

Parten, M. B. (1932). Social play among preschool children. *Journal of Abnormal and Social Psychology, 27,* 243–269.

Patenaude, A. F., Guttmacher, A. E., & Collins, F. S. (2002). Genetic testing and psychology: New roles, new responsibilities. *American Psychologist, 57,* 271–282.

Paterson, D. S., Trachtenberg, F. L., Thompson, E. G., Belliveau, R. A., Beggs, A. H., Darnell, R., Chadwick, A. E., Krous, H. F., & Kinney, H. C. (2006). Multiple serotogenic brainstem abnormalities in sudden infant death syndrome. *Journal of the American Medical Association, 296,* 2124–2132.

Patrick, K., Norman, G. J., Calfas, K. J., Sallis, J. F., Zabinski, M. F., Rupp, J., & Cella, J. (2004). Diet, physical activity, and sedentary behaviors as risk factors for overweight in adolescence. *Archives of Pediatric Adolescent Medicine, 158,* 385–390.

Patterson, C. J. (1992). Children of lesbian and gay parents. *Child Development, 63,* 1025–1042.

Patterson, C. J. (1995a). Lesbian mothers, gay fathers, and their children. In A. R. D'Augelli & C. J. Patterson (Eds.), *Lesbian, gay, and bisexual identities over the lifespan: Psychological perspectives* (pp. 293–320). New York: Oxford University Press.

Patterson, C. J. (1995b). Sexual orientation and human development: An overview. *Developmental Psychology, 31,* 3–11.

Patterson, C. J. (1997). Children of gay and lesbian parents. In T. H. Ollendick & R. J. Prinz (Eds.), *Advances in clinical child psychology* (Vol. 19, pp. 235–282). New York: Plenum.

Patterson, G. R. (1984). Siblings: Fellow travelers in coercive family processes. In R. J. Blanchard (Ed.), *Advances in the study of aggression* (pp. 174–213). New York: Academic.

Patterson, G. R. (1995). Coercion: A basis for early age of onset for arrest. In J. McCord (Ed.), *Coercion and punishment in long-term perspective* (pp. 81–105). New York: Cambridge University Press.

Patterson, G. R., DeBaryshe, B. D., & Ramsey, E. (1989). A developmental perspective on antisocial behavior. *American Psychologist, 44*(2), 329–335.

Patton, D., Mackay, T. L. & Broszeit, B. (2005). Alcohol and other drug use by Manitoba student. Retrieved August 22, 2007 from http://www.afm.mb.ca/pdf/Alcohol%20and%20other%20drug%20use%20by%20Manitoba%20students%202005%20report.pdf.

Pauen, S. (2002). Evidence for knowledgebased category discrimination in infancy. *Child Development, 73,* 1016–1033.

Paus, T., Zijdenbos, A., Worsley, K., Collins, D. L., Blumenthal, J., Giedd, J. N., Rapoport, J. L., & Evans, A. C. (1999). Structural maturation of neural pathways in children and adolescents: In vivo study. *Science, 283,* 1908–1911.

Pawelski, J. G., Perrin, E. C., Foy, J. M., Allen, C. E., Crawford, J. E., Del Monte, M., Kaufman, M., Klein, J. D., Smith, K., Springer, S., Tanner, J. L., & Vickers, D. L. (2006). The effects of marriage, civil union, and domestic partnership laws on the health and well-being of children. *Pediatrics, 118,* 349–364.

Pearce, M. J., Jones, S. M., Schwab-Stone, M. E., & Ruchkin, V. (2003). The protective effects of religiousness and parent involvement on the development of conduct problems among youth exposed to violence. *Child Development, 74,* 1682–1696.

Pellegrini, A. D., & Archer, J. (2005). Sex differences in competitive and aggressive behavior: A view from sexual selection theory. In B. J. Ellis & D. F. Bjorklund (Eds.), *Origins of the social mind: Evolutionary psychology and child development* (pp. 219–244). New York: Guilford.

Pellegrini, A. D., & Gufstafson, K. (2005). Boys' and girls' uses of objects for exploration, play, and tools in early childhood. In A. D. Pellegrini & P. K. Smith (Eds.), *The nature of play* (pp. 113–135). New York: Guilford.

Pellegrini, A. D., & Long, J. D. (2002). A longitudinal study of bullying, dominance, and victimization during the transition from primary school through secondary school. *British Journal of Developmental Psychology, 20,* 259–280.

Pellegrini, A. D., Kato, K., Blatchford, P., & Baines E. (2002). A short-term longitudinal study of children's playground games across the first year of school: Implications for social competence and adjustment to school. *American Educational Research Journal, 39,* 991–1015.

Pelleymounter, N. A., Cullen, M. J., Baker, M. B., Hecht, R., Winters, D., Boone, T., & Collins, F. (1995). Effects of the obese gene product on body regulation in ob/ob mice. *Science, 269,* 540–543.

Pennington, B. F., Moon, J., Edgin, J., Stedron, J., & Nadel, L. (2003). The neuropsychology of Down Syndrome: Evidence for hippocampal dysfunction. *Child Development, 74,* 75–93.

Pepler, D. J., & Sedighdeilami, F. (1998). *Aggressive girls in Canada.* Report No. W-98-30E. Ottawa: Applied Research Branch, Strategic Policy, Human Resources Development Canada.

Pepper, S. C. (1942). *World hypotheses.* Berkeley: University of California Press.

Pepper, S. C. (1961). *World hypotheses.* Berkeley: University of California Press.

Perera, F. P., Rauh, V., Whyatt, R. M., Tsai, W.-Y., Bernert, J. T., Tu, Y.-H., et al. (2004). Molecular evidence of an interaction between prenatal environmental exposures and birth outcomes in a multiethnic population. *Environmental Health Perspectives, 112,* 626–630.

Perlman, M., & Ross, H. S. (1997). The benefits of parent intervention in children's disputes: An examination of concurrent changes in children's fighting styles. *Child Development, 64,* 690–700.

Perozynski, L., & Kramer, L. (1999). Parental beliefs about managing sibling conflict. *Developmental Psychology, 35,* 489–499.

Perrin, E. C., and the Committee on Psychosocial Aspects of Child and Family Health. (2002). Technical report: Coparent or second-parent adoption by same-sex parents. *Pediatrics, 109*(2), 341–344.

Persad, V. L., Van den Hof, M., Dube, J. M. & Zimmer, P. (2002). Incidence of open neural tube defects in Nova Scotia after folic acid fortification. *Canadian Medical Association, 167,* 241–245.

Pesonen, A., Raïkkönen, K, Keltikangas-Järvinen, L., Strandberg, T., & Järvenpää, A. (2003). Parental perception of infant temperament: Does parents' joint attachment matter? *Infant Behavior & Development, 26,* 167–182.

Peter, K. A. (1983). The certainty of salvation: Ritualization of religion and economic rationality among Hutterites. *Comparative Studies in Society and History, 25,* 222–240.

Petersen, A. C. (1993). Presidential address: Creating adolescents: The role of context and process in developmental transitions. *Journal of Research on Adolescents, 3*(1), 1–18.

Petersen, A. C., Compas, B. E., Brooks-Gunn, J., Stemmler, M., Ey, S., & Grant, K. E. (1993). Depression in adolescence. *American Psychologist, 48*(2), 155–168.

Peterson, C. C. (1999). Children's memory for medical emergencies: 2 years later. *Developmental Psychology, 35,* 1493–1506.

Peterson, C., & McCabe, A. (1994). A social interactionist account of developing decontextualized narrative skill. *Developmental Psychology, 30,* 937–948.

Peterson, J. M., Neimanis, I. M., Goebel, C. R., & Kraftcheck, D. J. (2004). Informed consent for uninsured services: A primary care perspective on the new childhood vaccines. *Canadian Medical Association Journal, 171,* 877–879.

Peth-Pierce, R. (1998). *The NICHD study of early child care.* Retrieved September 24, 2002, from http://www.nichd.nih.gov/publications/pubs/early_child_care.htm

Petitto, L. A., & Kovelman, I. (2003). The bilingual paradox: How signing-speaking bilingual children help us to resolve it and teach us about the brain's mechanisms underlying all language acquisition. *Learning Languages, 8,* 5–18.

Petitto, L. A., & Marentette, P. F. (1991). Babbling in the manual mode: Evidence for the ontogeny of language. *Science, 251,* 1493–1495.

Petitto, L. A., Holowka, S., Sergio, L., & Ostry, D. (2001). Language rhythms in babies' hand movements. *Nature, 413,* 35–36.

Petitto, L. A., Katerelos, M., Levy, B., Gauna, K., Tetrault, K., & Ferraro, V. (2001). Bilingual signed and spoken language acquisition from birth: Implications for mechanisms underlying bilingual language acquisition. *Journal of Child Language, 28,* 1–44.

Petrill, S. A., Lipton, P. A., Hewitt, J. K., Plomin, R., Cherny, S. S., Corley, R., & DeFries, J. C. (2004). Genetic and environmental contributions to general cognitive ability through the first 16 years of life. *Developmental Psychology, 40,* 805–812.

Pettit, G. S., Bates, J. E., & Dodge, K. A. (1997). Supportive parenting, ecological context, and children's adjustment: A seven-year longitudinal study. *Child Development, 68,* 908–923.

Pharaoh, P. D. P., Antoniou, A., Bobrow, M., Zimmern, R. L., Easton, D. F., & Ponder, B. A. J. (2002). Polygenic susceptibility to breast cancer and implications for prevention. *Nature Genetics, 31,* 33–36.

Phelps, J. A., Davis, J. O., & Schartz, K. M. (1997). Nature, nurture, and twin research strategies. *Current Directions in Psychological Science, 6*(5), 117–121.

Phillips, D. F. (1998). Reproductive medicine experts till an increasingly fertile field. *Journal of the American Medical Association, 280,* 1893–1895.

Phinney, J. S. (1998). Stages of ethnic identity development in minority group adolescents. In R. E. Muuss & H. D. Porton (Eds.), *Adolescent behavior and society: A book of readings* (pp. 271–280). Boston: McGraw-Hill.

Phinney, J. S., & Cobb, N. J. (1996). Reasoning about intergroup relations among Hispanic and Euro-American adolescents. *Journal of Adolescent Research, 11,* 306–324.

Phipps, S. A., Burton P. S., Osberg, L. S. & Lethbridge, L. N. (2006). Poverty and the extent of child obesity in Canada, Norway and the United States. *The International Association for the Study of Obesity, 7,* 5–12.

Piaget, J. (1929). *The child's conception of the world.* New York: Harcourt Brace.

Piaget, J. (1932). *The moral judgment of the child.* New York: Harcourt Brace.

Piaget, J. (1951). *Play, dreams, and imitation* (C. Gattegno & F. M. Hodgson, Trans.). New York: Norton.

Piaget, J. (1952). *The origins of intelligence in children.* New York: International Universities Press. (Original work published 1936)

Piaget, J. (1962). *The language and thought of the child* (M. Gabain, Trans.). Cleveland, OH: Meridian. (Original work published 1923)

Piaget, J. (1969). *The child's conception of time* (A. J. Pomerans, Trans.). London: Routledge & Kegan Paul.

Piaget, J. (1972). Intellectual evolution from adolescence to adulthood. *Human Development, 15,* 1–12.

Piaget, J., & Inhelder, B. (1967). *The child's conception of space.* New York: Norton.

Piaget, J., & Inhelder, B. (1969). *The psychology of the child.* New York: Basic Books.

Picker, J. (2005). The role of genetic and environmental factors in the development of schizophrenia. *Psychiatric Times, 22,* 1–9.

Pickett, W., Craig, W., Harel, Y., Cunningham, J., Simpson, K., Molcho, M., Mazur, J., Dostaler, S., Overpeck, M. D., Currie, C. E. on behalf of the HBSC Violence and Injury Writing Group. (2005). Cross-national study of fighting and weapon carrying as determinants of adolescent injury. *Pediatrics, 116,* 855–863.

Pickett, W., Streight, S., Simpson, K., & Brison, R. J. (2003). Injuries experienced by infant children: A population-based epidemiological analysis. *Pediatrics, 111,* e365–e370.

Pierce, K. M., Hamm, J. V., & Vandell, D. L. (1999). Experiences in after-school programs and children's adjustment in first-grade classrooms. *Child Development, 70*(3), 756–767

Pierroutsakos, S. L., & DeLoache, J. S. (2003). Infants' manual exploration of pictorial objects varying in realism. *Infancy, 4,* 141–156.

Pike, A., Coldwell, J., & Dunn, J. F. (2005). Sibling relationships in early/middle childhood: Links with individual adjustment. *Journal of Family Psychology, 19,* 523–532.

Pillow, B. H., & Henrichon, A. J. (1996). There's more to the picture than meets the eye: Young children's difficulty understanding biased interpretation. *Child Development, 67,* 803–819.

Pines, M. (1981). The civilizing of Genie. *Psychology Today, 15*(9), 28–34.

Plant, L. D., Bowers, P. N., Liu, Q., Morgan, T., Zhang, T., State, M. W., Chen, W., Kittles, R. A., & Goldstein, S. A. (2006). A common cardiac sodium channel variant associated with sudden infant death in African Americans, SCN5A S1103Y. *The Journal of Clinical Investigation, 116*(2), 430–435.

Pleck, J. H. (1997). Paternal involvement: Levels, sources, and consequences. In M. E. Lamb et al. (Eds.), *The role of the father in child development* (3rd ed., pp. 66–103). New York: Wiley.

Plomin, R. (1990). The role of inheritance in behavior. *Science, 248,* 183–188.

Plomin, R. (1996). Nature and nurture. In M. R. Merrens & G. G. Brannigan (Eds.),

The developmental psychologist: Research adventures across the life span (pp. 3–19). New York: McGraw-Hill.

Plomin, R. (2001). Genetic factors contributing to learning and language delays and disabilities. *Child & Adolescent Psychiatric Clinics of North America, 10*(2), 259–277.

Plomin, R., & Daniels, D. (1987). Why are children in the same family so different from one another? *Behavioral and Brain Sciences, 10*, 1–16.

Plomin, R., & DeFries, J. C. (1999). The genetics of cognitive abilities and disabilities. In S. J. Ceci & W. M. Williams (Eds.), *The nature nurture debate: The essential readings* (pp. 178–195). Malden, MA: Blackwell.

Plomin, R., & Kovas, Y. (2005). Generalist genes and learning disabilities. *Psychological Bulletin, 131*, 592–617.

Plomin, R., & Rutter, M. (1998). Child development, molecular genetics, and what to do with genes once they are found. *Child Development, 69*(4), 1223–1242.

Plomin, R., & Spinath, F. M. (2004). Intelligence: Genetics, genes, and genomics. *Journal of Personality and Social Psychology, 86*, 112–129.

Plomin, R., Dale, P., Simonoff, E., Eley, T., Oliver, B., Price, T., Purcell, S., Bishop, D., & Stevenson, J. (1998). Genetic influence on language delay in two-year-old children. *Nature Neuroscience, 1*, 324–328.

Plomin, R., Owen, M. J., & McGuffin, P. (1994). The genetic bases of behavior. *Science, 264*, 1733–1739.

Plotkin, S. A., Katz, M., & Cordero, J. F. (1999). The eradication of rubella. *Journal of the American Medical Association, 281*, 561–562.

Plumert, J. M., Pick, H. L., Jr., Marks, R. A., Kintsch, A. S., & Wegesin, D. (1994). Locating objects and communicating about locations: Organizational differences in children's searching and direction-giving. *Developmental Psychology, 30*, 443–453.

Plumert, J., & Nichols-Whitehead, P. (1996). Parental scaffolding of young children's spatial communication. *Developmental Psychology, 32*, 523–532.

Polit, D. F., & Falbo, T. (1987). Only children and personality development: A quantitative review. *Journal of Marriage and the Family, 49*, 309–325.

Pollock, L. A. (1983). *Forgotten children.* Cambridge, England: Cambridge University Press.

Pomerantz, E. M., & Eaton, M. M. (2001). Maternal intrusive support in the academic context: Transactional socialization processes. *Developmental Psychology, 37*, 174–186.

Pomerantz, E. M., & Saxon, J. L. (2001). Conceptions of ability as stable and selfevaluative processes: A longitudinal examination. *Child Development, 72*, 152–173.

Pomerantz, E. M., Wang, Q., & Ng, F. (2005). Mothers' affect in the homework context: The importance of staying positive. *Developmental Psychology, 41*, 414–427.

Pomery, E. A., Gibbons, F. X., Gerrard, M., Cleveland, M. J., Brody, G. H., & Wills, T. A. (2005). Families and risk: Prospective analyses of familial and social influences on adolescent substance use. *Journal of Family Psychology, 19*, 560–570.

Pong, S. L. (1997). Family structure, school context, and eighth-grade math and reading achievement. *Journal of Marriage and the Family, 59*, 734–746.

Pong, S., Dronkers, J., & Hampden-Thompson, G. (2003). Family policies and children's school achievement in single- versus two-parent families. *Journal of Marriage and the Family, 65*, 681–699.

Pope, A. W., Bierman, K. L., & Mumma, G. H. (1991). Aggression, hyperactivity, and inattention-immaturity: Behavior dimensions associated with peer rejection in elementary school boys. *Developmental Psychology, 27*, 663–671.

Population Reference Bureau. (2005). Human population: Fundamentals of growth; World health Retrieved April 11, 2005, from http://www.prb.org/Content/NavigationMenu/PRB/Educators/Human Population/Health2/World Health1.htm.

Posada, G., Gao, Y., Wu, F., Posada, R., Tascon, M., Schoelmerich, A., Sagi, A., Kondo-Ikemura, K., Haaland, W., & Synnevaag, B. (1995). The secure-base phenomenon across cultures: Children's behavior, mothers' preferences, and experts' concepts. In E. Waters, B. E. Vaughn, G. Posada, & K. Kondo-Ikemura (Eds.), Caregiving, cultural, and cognitive perspectives on secure-base behavior and working models: New growing points of attachment theory and research (pp. 27–48). *Monographs of the Society for Research in Child Development, 60*(2–3, Serial No. 244).

Posner, M. L., & DiGirolamo, G. J. (2000). Cognitive neuroscience: Origins and promise. *Psychological Bulletin, 126*(6), 873–889.

Post, S. G. (1994). Ethical commentary: Genetic testing for Alzheimer's disease. *Alzheimer Disease and Associated Disorders, 8*, 66–67.

Posthuma, D., & de Gues, E. J. C. (2006). Progress in the molecular-genetic study of intelligence. *Current Directions in Psychological Science.*

Povinelli, D. J., & Giambrone, S. (2001). Reasoning about beliefs: A human specialization? *Child Development, 72*, 691–695.

Power, T. G., & Chapieski, M. L. (1986). Childrearing and impulse control in toddlers: A naturalistic investigation. *Developmental Psychology, 22*, 271–275.

Powlishta, K. K., Serbin, L. A., Doyle, A. B., & White, D. R. (1994). Gender, ethnic, and body type biases: The generality of prejudice in childhood. *Developmental Psychology, 30*, 526–536.

Pratt, M. W., & Savoy-Levine, K. M. (1998). Contingent tutoring of long-division skills in fourth and fifth graders: Experimental tests of some hypotheses about scaffolding. *Journal of Applied Developmental Psychology, 19*, 287–304.

Prechtl, H. F. R., & Beintema, D. J. (1964). The neurological examination of the full-term newborn infant. *Clinics in Developmental Medicine, 12.* London: Heinemann.

Pressley, M. (1998). *Reading instruction that works: The case for balanced teaching.* New York: The Guilford Press.

Pressley, M., Wharton-McDonald, R., Mistretta-Hampston, J., & Echevarria, M. (1998). Literacy instruction in 10 fourth- and fifth-grade classrooms in upstate New York. *Scientific Studies of Reading, 2*, 159–194.

Price, J. M. (1996). Friendships of maltreated children and adolescents: Contexts for expressing and modifying relationship history. In W. M. Bukowski, A. F. Newcomb, & W. W. Hartup (Eds.), *The company they keep: Friendship in childhood and adolescence* (pp. 262–285). New York: Cambridge University Press.

Princiotta, D., & Chapman, C. (2006). *Homeschooling in the United States: 2003.* (NCES 2006-042). Washington, DC: National Center for Education Statistics, U.S. Department of Education.

Prochner, L. & Doyon, P. (1997). Researchers and their subjects in the history of child study: William Blatz and the Dionne quintuplets. *Canadian Psychology, 38*, 103–110.

Pruden, S. M., Hirsh-Pasek, K., Golinkoff, R. M., & Hennon, E. A. (2006). The birth of words: Ten-month-olds learn words through perceptual salience. *Child Development, 77*, 266–280.

Pruett, K. D. (1998). Research perspectives: Role of the father. *Pediatrics, 102* (Suppl.), 1253–1261.

Psychosocial Paediatrics Committee, Canadian Paediatric Society. (1997). Effective discipline for children. *Paediatrics & Child Health, 2*(1), 29–33.

Psychosocial Paediatrics Committee, Canadian Paediatric Society. (2003). Impact of media use on children and youth. Retrieved July 25, 2007 from http://www.cps.ca/english/statements/PP/pp03-01.htm.

Public Health Agency of Canada. (2002). Chapter 3: The home experience. Retrieved September 3, 2007 from http://www.phac-aspc.gc.ca/dca-dea/publications/hbsc_03_e.html.

Public Health Agency of Canada. (2002). Improving the health of Canada's Aboriginal people. Retrieved July 25, 2007 from http://www.phac-aspc.gc.ca/ph-sp/phdd/report/toward/back/impro.html.

Public Health Agency of Canada. (2003). Canadian families: What do we look like? Retrieved August 17, 2007 from http://www.canadian-health-network.ca/servlet/ContentServer?cid=1058896870298&pagename=CHN-RCS%2FCHNResource%2FCHNResourcePageTemplate&c=CHNResource&lang=En.

Public Health Agency of Canada. (2003). Canadian incidence study of reported child abuse and neglect-major findings. Retrieved August 22 2007 from http://www.phac-aspc.gc.ca/cm-vee/csca-ecve/index.html.

Public Health Agency of Canada. (2004). HIV/AIDS among aboriginal peoples in Canada: A continuing concern. Retrieved August 22 2007 from http://www.phac-aspc.gc.ca/publicat/epiu-aepi/epi_update_may_04/9_e.html.

Public Health Agency of Canada. (2004). Young people in Canada: Their health and well-being-Chapter 11: Conclusions. Retrieved September 3 2007 from http://www.phac-aspc.gc.ca/dca-dea/publications/hbsc-2004/chapter_11_e.html.

Public Health Agency of Canada. (2005). Make every mother and child count. Retrieved from www.phac-aspc.gc.ca/rhs-ssg/pdf/whd_05epi_e.pdf on July 15, 2007.

Public Health Agency of Canada. (2006). *HIV and AIDS in Canada. Surveillance Report to December 31, 2005.* Ottawa, ON: Surveillance and Risk Assessment Division, Centre for Infectious Disease Prevention and Control, Public Health Agency of Canada.

Public Health Agency of Canada. (2006). Populations at risk. Retrieved August 22, 2007 from http://www.phac-aspc.gc.ca/aids-sida/populations_e.html.

Public Health Agency of Canada. HIV/AIDS epi update. (2004, May). Perinatal transmission of HIV. Retrieved on August 7, 2007 from http://www.phac-aspc.gc.ca/publicat/epiu-aepi/epi_update_may_04/7_e.html.

Putallaz, M., & Bierman, K. L. (Eds.). (2004). *Aggression, antisocial behavior, and violence among girls: A developmental perspective.* New York: Guilford.

Quadrel, M. J., Fischoff, B., & Davis, W. (1993). Adolescent (in)vulnerability. *American Psychologist, 48*, 102–116.

Quasha, S. (1980). *Albert Einstein: An intimate portrait*. Larchmont, NY: Forest.

Quattrin, T., Liu, E., Shaw, N., Shine, B., & Chiang, E. (2005). Obese children who are referred to the pediatric oncologist: Characteristics and outcome. *Pediatrics, 115*, 348–351.

Quinn, P. C., Westerlund, A., & Nelson, C. A. (2006). Neural markers of categorization in 6-month-old infants. *Psychological Science, 17*, 59–66.

Quintero, R. A., Abuhamad, A., Hobbins, J. C., & Mahoney, M. J. (1993). Transabdominal thin-gauge embryofetoscopy: A technique for early prenatal diagnosis and its use in the diagnosis of a case of Meckel-Gruber syndrome. *American Journal of Obstetrics and Gynecology, 168*, 1552–1557.

Rabiner, D., & Coie, J. (1989). Effect of expectancy induction on rejected peers' acceptance by unfamiliar peers. *Developmental Psychology, 25*, 450–457.

Rabson, M. (August 30, 2001). School system fails aboriginals: Lewis. *Winnipeg Free Press*, A9.

Racine, T. P., Carpendale, J. I. M. & Turnbull, W. (2006). Cross-sectional and longitudinal relations between mother-child talk about conflict and children's social understanding. *British Journal of Psychology, 97*, 521–536.

Racine, T. P., Carpendale, J. I. M. & Turnbull, W. (2007). Parent-child talk and children's understanding of beliefs and emotions. *Cognition and Emotion, 21*, 480–494.

Raine, A., Mellingen, K., Liu, J., Venables, P., & Mednick, S. (2003). Effects of environmental enrichment at ages 3–5 years in schizotypal personality and antisocial behavior at ages 17 and 23 years. *American Journal of Psychiatry, 160*, 1627–1635.

Rakison, D. H. (2005). Infant perception and cognition. In B. J. Ellis & D. F. Bjorklund (Eds.), *Origins of the social mind* (pp. 317–353). New York: Guilford.

Rakoczy, H., Tomasello, M. and Striano. T. (2004). Young children know that trying is not pretending: A test of the "behaving-as-if " construal of children's early concept of pretense. *Developmental Psychology, 40*, 388–399.

Rakyan, V. K., & Beck, S. (2006). Epigenetic variation and inheritance in mammals. *Current Opinion in Genetics and Development, 16*, 573–577.

Ram, A., & Ross, H. S. (2001). Problem solving, contention, and struggle: How siblings resolve a conflict of interests. *Child Development, 72*, 1710–1722.

Ramey, C. T., & Campbell, F. A. (1991). Poverty, early childhood education, and academic competence. In A. Huston (Ed.), *Children reared in poverty* (pp. 190–221). Cambridge, England: Cambridge University Press.

Ramey, C. T., & Ramey, S. L. (1998a). Early intervention and early experience. *American Psychologist, 53*, 109–120.

Ramey, C. T., & Ramey, S. L. (1998b). Prevention of intellectual disabilities: Early interventions to improve cognitive development. *Preventive Medicine, 21*, 224–232.

Ramey, C. T., & Ramey, S. L. (2003, May). *Preparing America's children for success in school*. Paper prepared for an invited address at the White House Early Childhood Summit on Ready to Read, Ready to Learn, Denver, CO.

Ramey, C. T., Campbell, F. A., Burchinal, M., Skinner, M. L., Gardner, D. M., & Ramey, S. L. (2000). Persistent effects of early childhood education on high-risk children and their mothers. *Applied Developmental Science, 4*(1), 2–14.

Ramey, S. L. (1999). Head Start and preschool education: Toward continued improvement. *American Psychologist, 54*, 344–346.

Ramey, S. L., & Ramey, C. T. (1992). Early educational intervention with disadvantaged children: To what effect? *Applied and Preventive Psychology, 1*, 131–140.

Ramoz, N., Reichert, J. G., Smith, C. J., Silverman, J. M., Bespalova, I. N., Davis, K. L., et al. (2004). Linkage and association of the mitochondrial aspartate/glutamate carrier SLC25A12 gene with autism. *American Journal of Psychiatry, 161*, 662–669.

Ramsey, P. G., & Lasquade, C. (1996). Preschool children's entry attempts. *Journal of Applied Developmental Psychology, 17*, 135–150.

Randall, D. (2005). *Corporal punishment in school*. FamilyEducation.com. Retrieved April 20, 2005, from http://www.familyeducation.com/article/0,1120,1–3980,00.html.

Rapoport, J. L., Addington, A. M., & Frangou, S., Psych, M. (2005). The neurodevelopmental model of schizophrenia: Update 2005. *Molecular Psychiatry, 10*, 434–449.

Rask-Nissilä, L., Jokinen, E., Terho, P., Tammi, A., Lapinleimu, H., Ronnemaa, T., et al. (2000). Neurological development of 5-year-old children receiving a low-saturated-fat, low-cholesterol diet since infancy. *Journal of the American Medical Association, 284*(8), 993–1000.

Rathbun, A., West, J., & Germino-Hausken, E. (2004). From kindergarten through third grade: Children's beginning school experiences (NCES 2004–007). Washington, DC: National Center for Education Statistics.

Rauh, V. A., Whyatt, R. M., Garfinkel, R., Andrews, H., Hoepner, L., Reyes, A., Diaz, D., Camann, D., & Perera, F. P. (2004). Developmental effects of exposure to environmental tobacco smoke and material hardship among inner-city children. *Neurotoxicology and Teratology, 26*, 373–385

Raver, C. C. (2002). Emotions matter: Making the case for the role of young children's emotional development for early school readiness. *Social Policy Report, 16*(3).

Raymond, J. M. (1991). *The nursery world of Dr. Blatz*. Toronto: University of Toronto Press.

Reaney, P. (2006, June 21). Three million babies born after fertility treatment. *Medscape*. Retrieved January 29, 2007, from http://www.medscape.com/viewarticle/537128

Reese, E. (1995). Predicting children's literacy from mother–child conversations. *Cognitive Development, 10*, 381–405.

Reese, E., & Cox, A. (1999). Quality of adult book reading affects children's emergent literacy. *Developmental Psychology, 35*, 20–28.

Reese, E., & Fivush, R. (1993). Parental styles of talking about the past. *Developmental Psychology, 29*, 596–606.

Reese, E., & Newcombe, R. (in press). Training mothers in elaborative reminiscing enhances children's autobiographical memory and narrative. *Child Development*.

Reese, E., Haden, C., & Fivush, R. (1993). Mother–child conversations about the past: Relationships of style and memory over time. *Cognitive Development, 8*, 403–430.

Reichenberg, A., Gross, R., Weiser, M., Bresnahan, M., Silverman, J., Harlap, S., et al. (2006). Advancing paternal age and autism. *Archives of General Psychiatry, 63*(9), 1026–1032.

Reid, J. R., Patterson, G. R., & Loeber, R. (1982). The abused child: Victim, instigator, or innocent bystander? In D. J. Berstein (Ed.), *Response structure and organization*. Lincoln: University of Nebraska Press.

Reijo, R., Alagappan, R. K., Patrizio, P., & Page, D. C. (1996). Severe oligozoospermia resulting from deletions of azoospermia factor gene on Y chromosome. *Lancet, 347*, 1290–1293.

Reilly, J. J., Jackson, D. M., Montgomery, C., Kelly, L. A., Slater, C., Grant, S., & Paton, J. Y. (2004). Total energy expenditure and physical activity in young Scottish children: Mixed longitudinal study. *Lancet, 363*, 211–212.

Reinisch, J. M., Sanders, S. A., Mortensen, E. L., Psych, C., & Rubin, D. B. (1995). In utero exposure to phenobarbital and intelligence deficits in adult men. *Journal of the American Medical Association, 274*, 1518–1525.

Reis, S. M. (1989). Reflections on policy affecting the education of gifted and talented students: Past and future perspectives. *American Psychologist, 44*, 399–408.

Reiss, A. L., Abrams, M. T., Singer, H. S., Ross, J. L., & Denckla, M. B. (1996). Brain development, gender and IQ in children: A volumetric imaging study. *Brain, 119*, 1763–1774.

Remez, L. (2000). Oral sex among adolescents: Is it sex or is it abstinence? *Family Planning Perspectives, 32*, 298–304.

Rende, R., Slomkowski, C., Lloyd-Richardson, E., & Niaura, R. (2005). Sibling effects on substance use in adolescence: Social contagion and genetic relatedness. *Journal of Family Psychology, 19*, 611–618.

Rescorla, L. (1991). Early academics: Introduction to the debate. In L. Rescorla, M. C. Hyson, & K. Hirsh-Pasek (Eds.), *Academic instruction in early childhood: Challenge or pressure?* (*New Directions for Child Development, 53*, pp. 5–11). San Francisco: Jossey-Bass.

Resnick, L. B. (1989). Developing mathematical knowledge. *American Psychologist, 44*, 162–169.

Resnick, M. D., Bearman, P. S., Blum, R. W., Bauman, K. E., Harris, K. M., Jones, J., Tabor, J., Beuhring, T., Sieving, R. E., Shew, M., Ireland, M., Bearinger, L. H., & Udry, J. R. (1997). Protecting adolescents from harm: Findings from the National Longitudinal Study on Adolescent Health. *Journal of the American Medical Association, 278*, 823–832.

Rest, J. R. (1975). Longitudinal study of the Defining Issues Test of moral judgment: A strategy for analyzing developmental change. *Developmental Psychology, 11*, 738–748.

Rest, J. R., Deemer, D., Barnett, R., Spickelmier, J., & Volker, J. (1986). Life experiences and developmental pathways. In J. R. Rest (Ed.), *Moral development: Advances in theory and research*. New York: Preager.

Rest, J., Narvaez, D., Bebeau, M. J., & Thoma, S. J. (1999). *Postconventional moral thinking*. Mahwah, NJ: Lawrence Erlbaum Associates.

Reuters. (2004a). Canada first country to ban sale of baby walkers.

Revised Regulations of Ontario. (1990). Day Nurseries Act. Regulation 262. Toronto: Printer of Ontario.

Revised Statutes of British Columbia. (1996). Health Professions Act: Midwives Regulation. Victoria, BC: Queen's Printer.

Reynolds. A. J. and Temple, J. A. (1998). Extended early childhood intervention and school achievement: Age thirteen findings from the Chicago Longitudinal Study. *Child Development, 69*, 231–246.

Reynolds, A. J., Temple, J. A., Robertson, D. L., & Mann, E. A. (2001). Long-term effects of an early childhood intervention on educational achievement and juvenile arrest: A 15-year follow-up of low-income children in public schools. *Journal of American Medical Association, 285*(18), 2339–2346.

Reynolds, C. R., Lowe, P. A., & Saenz, A. L. (1999). The problem of bias in psychological assessment. In C. R., Reynolds, & T. B., Gutkin (Eds.), *The handbook of school psychology* (pp. 549–595). New York, NY: John Wiley & Sons, Inc.

Reynolds, G. (1998). Welcoming place: An urban community of Inuit families. *Canadian Children, 23*(1), 5–11.

Rhee, S. H. & Waldman, I. D. (2002). Genetic and environmental influences on antisocial behavior: A meta-analysis of twin and adoption studies. *Psychological Bulletin, 128,* 490–529.

Ricciuti, H. N. (1999). Single parenthood and school readiness in white, black, and Hispanic 6- and 7-year-olds. *Journal of Family Psychology, 13,* 450–465.

Ricciuti, H. N. (2004). Single parenthood, achievement, and problem behavior in white, black, and Hispanic children. *Journal of Educational Research, 97,* 196–206.

Rice, C., Koinis, D., Sullivan, K., Tager-Flusberg, H., & Winner, E. (1997). When 3-year-olds pass the appearance–reality test. *Developmental Psychology, 33,* 54–61.

Rice, M. L. (1982). Child language: What children know and how. In T. M. Field, A. Huston, H. C. Quay, L. Troll, & G. E. Finley (Eds.), *Review of human development research.* New York: Wiley.

Rice, M. L. (1989). Children's language acquisition. *American Psychologist, 44*(2), 149–156.

Rice, M. L., Huston, A. C., Truglio, R., & Wright, J. (1990). Words from "Sesame Street": Learning vocabulary while viewing. *Developmental Psychology, 26,* 421–428.

Rice, M., Oetting, J. B., Marquis, J., Bode, J., & Pae, S. (1994). Frequency of input effects on SLI children's word comprehension. *Journal of Speech and Hearing Research, 37,* 106–122.

Richardson, H. R. L., Beazley, R. P., Delaney, M. E., & Langille, D. B. (1997). Factors influencing condom use among students attending high school in Nova Scotia. *The Canadian Journal of Human Sexuality, 6,* 185–196.

Richardson, J. (1995). *Achieving gender equality in families: The role of males* (Innocenti Global Seminar, Summary Report). Florence, Italy: UNICEF International Child Development Centre, Spedale degli Innocenti.

Richie, D. (1984). *The films of Akira Kurosawa.* Berkeley: University of California Press.

Riddell, R. P. (2007). Review of WISC-IV advanced clinical interpretation. *Canadian Psychology, 48,* 51–53.

Riddle, R. D., Johnson, R. L., Laufer, E., & Tabin, C. (1993). Sonic hedgehog mediates the polarizing activity of the ZPA. *Cell, 75,* 1401–1416.

Rideout, V. J., Vandewater, E. A., & Wartella, E. A. (2003). *Zero to six: Electronic media in the lives of infants, toddlers and preschoolers.* A Kaiser Family Foundation Report.

Rieder, M. J. (2002). Ecstasy. *Paediatrics and Child Health, 7,* 71–72.

Riemann, M. K., & Kanstrup Hansen, I. L. (2000). Effects on the fetus of exercise in pregnancy. *Scandinavian Journal of Medicine & Science in Sports. 10*(1), 12–19.

Rifkin, J. (1998, May 5). Creating the "perfect" human. *Chicago Sun-Times,* p. 29.

Rios-Ellis, B., Bellamy, L., & Shoji, J. (2000). An examination of specific types of *ijime* within risk and promotive factors in families, schools, and communities: A contextual model of positive youth development in adolescence. *Pediatrics, 119,* 47–53.

Ripple, C. H., Gilliam, W. S., Chanana, N., and Zigler, E. (1999). Will fifty cooks spoil the broth? The debate over entrusting Head Start to the states. *American Psychologist, 54,* 327–343. Risk and promotive factors in families, schools, and communities: A contextual model of positive youth development in adolescence. *Pediatrics, 119,* 47–53.

Ristow, M., Muller-Wieland, D., Pfeiffer, A., Krone, W., & Kahn, R. (1998). Obesity associated with a mutation in genetic regulator of adiposity differentiation. *New England Journal of Medicine, 339,* 953–959.

Ritchie, L., Crawford, P., Woodward- Lopez, G., Ivey, S., Masch, M., & Ikeda, J. (2001). *Prevention of childhood overweight: What should be done?* Berkeley, CA: Center for Weight and Health, U.C. Berkeley.

Ritter, J. (1999, November 23). Scientists close in on DNA code. *Chicago Sun-Times,* p. 7.

Rivara, F. P. (1999). Pediatric injury control in 1999: Where do we go from here? *Pediatrics, 103*(4), 883–888.

Rivara, F. P., & Grossman, D. C. (1996). Prevention of traumatic deaths to children in the United States: How far have we come and where do we need to go? *Pediatrics, 97,* 791–798.

Rivera, J. A., Sotres-Alvarez, D., Habicht, J.-P., Shamah, T., & Villalpando, S. (2004). Impact of the Mexican Program for Education, Health and Nutrition (Progresa) on rates of growth and anemia in infants and young children. *Journal of the American Medical Association, 291,* 2563–2570.

Roberts, G. C., Block, J. H., & Block, J. (1984). Continuity and change in parents' child-rearing practices. *Child Development, 55,* 586–597.

Roberts, I., Kramer, M., & Suissa, S. (1996). Does home visiting prevent childhood injury? A systematic review of randomized controlled trials. *British Medical Journal, 312,* 29–33.

Robin, D. J., Berthier, N. E., & Clifton, R. K. (1996). Infants' predictive reaching for moving objects in the dark. *Developmental Psychology, 32,* 824–835.

Robins, R. W., & Trzesniewski, K. H. (2005). Self-esteem development across the lifespan. *Current Directions in Psychological Science, 14*(3), 158–162.

Robinson, T. N., Wilde, M. L., Navacruz, L. C., Haydel, K. F., and Varady, A. (2001). Effects of reducing children's television and video game use on aggressive behavior: A randomized controlled trial. *Archives of Pediatric and Adolescent Medicine, 155,* 17–23.

Rochat, P. Querido, J. G., & Striano, T. (1999). Emerging sensitivity to the timing and structure of proto conversations in early infancy. *Developmental Psychology, 35,* 950–957.

Rochat, P., & Striano, T. (2002). Who's in the mirror? Self-other discrimination in specular images by 4- and 9-month-old infants. *Child Development, 73,* 35–46.

Rock, A. M. L., Trainor, L. J., & Addison, T. L. (1999). Distinctive messages in infant-directed lullabies and play songs. *Developmental Psychology, 35,* 527–534.

Roderick, M., Engel, M., & Nagaoka, J. (2003). *Ending social promotion: Results from Summer Bridge.* Chicago: Consortium on Chicago School Research.

Rogan, W. J, Dietrich, K. N., Ware, J. H., Dockery, D. W., Salganik, M., Radcliffe, J., Jones, R. L., Ragan, N. B., Chisolm Jr., J. J., Rhoads, G. G., for the Treatment of Lead-Exposed Children Trial Group. (2001). The effect of chelation therapy with succimer on neuropsychological development in children exposed to lead. *New England Journal of Medicine, 344,* 1421–1426.

Rogler, L. H. (2002). Historical generations and psychology: The case of the Great Depression and World War II. *American Psychologist, 57*(12), 1013–1023.

Rogoff, B. (1990). *Apprenticeship in thinking: Cognitive development in social context.* New York: Oxford University Press.

Rogoff, B. (1998). Cognition as a collaborative process. In W. Damon (Ed.), D. Kuhn, & R. S. Siegler (Vol. Eds.), *Handbook of child psychology: Vol. 2. Cognition, perception, and language* (5th ed., pp. 679–744). New York: Wiley.

Rogoff, B., & Morelli, G. (1989). Perspectives on children's development from cultural psychology. *American Psychologist, 44,* 343–348.

Rogoff, B., Mistry, J., Göncü, A., & Mosier, C. (1993). Guided participation in cultural activity by toddlers and caregivers. *Monographs of the Society for Research in Child Development, 58*(8, Serial No. 236).

Rokach, A., & Neto, F. (2001). The experience of loneliness in adolescence: A cross cultural comparison. *International Journal of Adolescence and Youth, 9,* 159–173.

Rome-Flanders, T., Cronk, C., & Gourde, C. (1995). Maternal scaffolding in mother–infant games and its relationship to language development: A longitudinal study. *First Language, 15,* 339–355.

Ronca, A. E., & Alberts, J. R. (1995). Maternal contributions to fetal experience and the transition from prenatal to postnatal life. In J. P. Lecanuet, W. P. Fifer, N. A. Krasnegor, & W. P. Smotherman (Eds.), *Fetal development: A psychobiological perspective* (pp. 331–350). Hillsdale, NJ: Erlbaum.

Roopnarine, J., & Honig, A. S. (1985, September). The unpopular child. *Young Children,* pp. 59–64.

Roopnarine, J. L., Hooper, F. H., Ahmeduzzaman, M., & Pollack, B. (1993). Gentle play partners: Mother–child and father–child play in New Delhi, India. In K. MacDonald (Ed.), *Parent–child play* (pp. 287–304). Albany: State University of New York Press.

Roopnarine, J. L., Talokder, E., Jain, D., Josh, P., & Srivastav, P. (1992). Personal well-being, kinship ties, and mother–infant and father–infant interactions in single-wage and dual-wage families in New Delhi, India. *Journal of Marriage and the Family, 54,* 293–301.

Rose, A. J., & Rudolph, K. D. (2006). A review of sex differences in peer relationship processes: Potential trade-offs for the emotional and behavioral development of girls and boys. *Psychological Bulletin, 132,* 98–131.

Rose, S. A. (1994). Relation between physical growth and information processing in infants born in India. *Child Development, 65,* 889–902.

Rose, S. A., & Feldman, J. F. (1997). Memory and speed: Their role in the relation of infant information processing to later IQ. *Child Development, 68,* 630–641.

Rose, S. A., & Feldman, J. F. (2000). The relation of very low birth weight to basic cognitive skills in infancy and childhood. In CA. Nelson (Ed.), *The effects of early adversity on neurobehavioral development. The Minnesota Symposia on Child Psychology* (Vol. 31, pp. 31–59). Mahwah, NJ: Lawrence Erlbaum Associates.

Rose, S. A., Feldman, J. F., & Jankowski, J. J. (2001). Attention and recognition memory in the 1st year of life: A longitudinal study of preterm and full-term infants. *Developmental Psychology, 37,* 135–151.

Rose, S. A., Feldman, J. F., & Jankowski, J. J. (2002). Processing speed in the 1st year of life: A longitudinal study of preterm and full-term infants. *Developmental Psychology, 38*, 895–902.

Rosenblum, G. D., & Lewis, M. (1999). The relations among body image, physical attractiveness, and body mass in adolescence. *Child Development, 70*, 50–64.

Rosengren, K. S., Gelman, S. A., Kalish, C. W., & McCormick, M. (1991). As time goes by: Children's early understanding of growth in animals. *Child Development, 62*, 1302–1320.

Rosenthal, C., & Gladstone, J. (2000). *Grandparenthood in Canada.* Ottawa: The Vanier Institute of the Family.

Rosenthal, E. (2003, July 20). Bias for boys leads to sale of baby girls in China. *New York Times,* sec. 1, p. 6, col. 3.

Rosenthal, R., & Vandell, D. L. (1996). Quality of care at school-aged child-care programs: Regulatable features, observed experiences, child perspectives, and parent perspectives. *Child Development, 67*, 2434–2445.

Ross, D. P., Roberts, P. A., & Scott, K. (1998). *Mediating factors in child development outcomes: Children in lone-parent families.* Catalogue No. W-98-8E. Ottawa: Applied Research Branch, Strategic Policy, Human Resources Development Canada.

Ross, G., Lipper, E. G., & Auld, P. A. M. (1991). Educational status and school-related abilities of very low birth weight premature children. *Pediatrics, 8*, 1125–1134.

Ross, H. S. (1996). Negotiating principles of entitlement in sibling property disputes. *Developmental Psychology, 32*, 90–101.

Ross, J., & Wyatt, W. (2000). Sexual behaviour. *WHO Policy Series: Healthy Policy for Children and Adolescents,* Series No. 1. pp. 115–120.

Rossel, C., & Ross, J. M. (1986). *The social science evidence on bilingual education.* Boston: Boston University Press.

Rossi, R. (1996, August 30). Small schools under microscope. *Chicago Sun-Times,* p. 24.

Rotenberg, K. J., & Cerda, C. (1995). Racially based trust expectancies of Native American and Caucasian children. *The Journal of Social Psychology, 134*, 621–631.

Rotenberg, K. J., & Eisenberg, N. (1997). Developmental differences in the understanding of and reaction to others' inhibition of emotional expression. *Developmental Psychology, 33*, 526–537.

Rotermann, M. (2005). Sex, condoms and STDs among young people. Statistics Canada, Catalogue No. 82-003. *Health Reports, 16*, 39–45.

Rothbart, M. K., & Hwang, J. (2002). Measuring infant temperament. *Infant Behavior & Development, 130*, 1–4.

Rotheram-Borus, M. J., & Futterman, D. (2000). Promoting early detection of human immunodeficiency virus infection among adolescents. *Archives of Pediatric and Adolescent Medicine, 154*, 435–439.

Roudebush, J. R., Kaufman, J. Johnson, B. H., Abraham, M. R. & Clayton, S. P. (2006). Patient- and family-centered perinatal care: Partnerships with childbearing women and families. *Journal of Perinatal and Neonatal Nursing, 20*, 201–209.

Rouse, C., Brooks-Gunn, J., & McLanahan, S. (2005). Introducing the issue. *The Future of Children, 15*(1), 5–14.

Roush, W. (1995). Arguing over why Johnny can't read. *Science, 267*, 1896–1898.

Rovee-Collier, C. (1996). Shifting the focus from what to why. *Infant Behavior and Development, 19*, 385–400.

Rovee-Collier, C. (1999). The development of infant memory. *Current Directions in Psychological Science, 8*, 80–85.

Rowland, A. S., Umbach, D. M., Stallone, L., Naftel, J., Bohlig, E. M., & Sandler, D. P. (2002). Prevalence of medication treatment for attention-deficit hyperactivity disorder among elementary school children in Johnston County, North Carolina. *American Journal of Public Health, 92*, 231–234.

Royal Commission on New Reproductive Technologies. (1993). *Proceed with care: Final report of the Royal Commission on New Reproductive Technologies.* Ottawa: Canadian Government Publishing

Rozen, S., Skaletsky, H., Marszalek, J. D, Minx, P. J., Cordum, H. S., Waterston, R. H., Wilson, R. K., & Page, D. C. (2003). Abundant gene conversion between arms of palindromes in human and ape Y chromosomes. *Nature, 423*, 810–811, 813.

Rubin, D. H., Krasilnikoff, P. A., Leventhal, J. M., Weile, B., & Berget, A. (1986, August 23). Effect of passive smoking on birth-weight. *Lancet,* pp. 415–417.

Rubin, K. (1982). Nonsocial play in preschoolers: Necessary evil? *Child Development, 53*, 651–657.

Rubin, K. H., Bukowski, W., & Parker, J. G. (1998). Peer interactions, relationships, and groups. In W. Damon (Series Ed.) & N. Eisenberg (Vol. Ed.), *Handbook of child psychology: Vol. 3. Social, emotional, and personality development* (5th ed., pp. 619–700). New York: Wiley.

Ruble, D. M., & Brooks-Gunn, J. (1982). The experience of menarche. *Child Development, 53*, 1557–1566.

Ruble, D. N., & Dweck, C. S. (1995). Self-conceptions, person conceptions, and their development. In N. Eisenberg, (Ed.), *Social development: Review of personality and social psychology* (pp. 109–139). Thousand Oaks, CA: Sage.

Ruble, D. N., & Martin, C. L. (1998). Gender development. In W. Damon (Series Ed.) & N. Eisenberg (Vol. Ed.), *Handbook of child psychology: Vol. 3. Social, emotional, and personality development* (5th ed., pp. 933–1016). New York: Wiley.

Rudolph, K. D., Lambert, S. F., Clark, A. G., & Kurlakowsky, K. D. (2001). Negotiating the transition to middle school: The role of self-regulatory processes. *Child Development, 72*(3), 929–946.

Rudy, D., & Grusec, J. (2001). Correlates of authoritarian parenting in individualist and collectivist cultures and implications for understanding the transmission of values. *Journal of Cross Cultural Psychology, 32*, 202–212.

Rueter, M. A., & Conger, R. D. (1995). Antecedents of parent–adolescent disagreements. *Journal of Marriage and the Family, 57*, 435–448.

Ruff, H. A., Bijur, P. E., Markowitz, M., Ma, Y. C., & Rosen, J. F. (1993). Declining blood lead levels and cognitive changes in moderately lead-poisoned children. *Journal of the American Medical Association, 269*, 1641–1646.

Ruffman, T., Slade, L., & Crowe, E. (2002). The relation between children's and mothers' mental state language and theory-of-mind understanding. *Child Development, 73*, 734–751.

Ruiz, F., & Tanaka, K. (2001). The *ijime* phenomenon and Japan: Overarching consideration for cross-cultural studies.

Psychologia: An International Journal of Psychology in the Orient, 44, 128–138.

Rushton, J. P., & Jensen, A. R. (2005). Thirty years of research on race differences in cognitive ability. *Psychology, Public Policy, and Law, 11*, 235-294.

Russen, I. D., Liu, S., Sauve, R., Joseph, K. S. & Kramer, M. S. (2004). Sudden infant death syndrome in Canada: Trends in rates and risk factors, 1985–1998. Retrieved from www.pnac-aspc.gc.ca/publicat/cdic-mcc/25-1/a_e.html on July 15, 2007.

Rutland, A. F., & Campbell, R. N. (1996). The relevance of Vygotsky's theory of the "zone of proximal development" to the assessment of children with intellectual disabilities. *Journal of Intellectual Disability Research, 40*, 151–158.

Rutter, M. (2002). Nature, nurture, and development: From evangelism through science toward policy and practice. *Child Development, 73*, 1–21.

Rutter, M. (2007). Gene-environment interdependence. *Developmental Science, 10*, 12–18.

Rutter, M., & the English and Romanian Adoptees (ERA) Study Team. (1998). Developmental catch-up, and deficit, following adoption after severe global early privation. *Journal of Child Psychology and Psychiatry, 39*, 465–476.

Rutter, M., O'Connor, T. G., and the English and Romanian Adoptees (ERA) Study Team. (2004). Are there biological programming effects for psychological development? Findings from a study of Romanian adoptees. *Developmental Psychology, 40*, 81–94.

Ruttman, D., Field, B., Lundquist, A. Callahan, M. & Jackson, S. (2000). Substance use and pregnancy [computer file]: Conceiving women in the policy-making process. Ottawa, ON: Status of Women Canada. Retrieved July 22, 2007 from http://www.swc-cfc.gc.ca/.

Ryan, A. (2001). The peer group as a context for the development of young adolescent motivation and achievement. *Child Development, 72*(4), 1135–1150.

Ryan, A. S. (2000). *Ross Mothers Survey.* Abbott Park, IL: Ross Products Division, Abbott Laboratories.

Ryan, B. A., & Adams, G. R. (1998). *Family relationships and children's school achievement: Data from the National Longitudinal Survey of Children and Youth.* Catalogue No. W-98-13E. Ottawa: Applied Research Branch, Strategic Policy, Human Resources Development Canada.

Ryan, V., & Needham, C. (2001). Nondirective play therapy with children experiencing psychic trauma. *Clinical Child Psychology and Psychiatry (special issue), 6*, 437–453.

Rymer, R. (1993). *An abused child: Flight from silence.* New York: HarperCollins.

Saarni, C., Mumme, D. L., & Campos, J. J. (1998). Emotional development: Action, communication, and understanding. In W. Damon (Series Ed.) & N. Eisenberg (Vol. Ed.), *Handbook of child psychology: Vol. 3. Social, emotional, and personality development* (5th ed., pp. 237–309). New York: Wiley.

Sabbagh, M. A., & Taylor, M. (2000). Neural correlates of theory-of-mind reasoning: An event-related potential study. *Psychological Science, 11*(1), 46–50.

Sachs, B. P., Kobelin, C., Castro, M. A., & Frigoletto, F. (1999). The risks of lowering the cesarean-delivery rate. *New England Journal of Medicine, 340*, 54–57.

Sack, W. H., Beiser, M., Baker-Brown, G., & Redshirt, R. (1994). Depressive and suicidal symptoms in Indian school children: Findings from the Flower of Two Soils. *American Indian & Alaska Native Mental Health Research, 4,* 81–96.

Sadeh, A., Raviv, A., & Gruber, R. (2000). Sleep patterns and sleep disruptions in school age children. *Developmental Psychology, 36*(3), 291–301.

Saffran, J. R. & Thiessen, E.D. (2003). Pattern induction by infant language learners. *Developmental Psychology, 39,* 484–494.

Saigal, S., Hoult, L. A., Streiner, D. L., Stoskopf, B. L., & Rosenbaum, P. L. (2000). School difficulties at adolescence in a regional cohort of children who were extremely low birth weight. *Pediatrics, 105,* 325–331.

Saigal, S., Stoskopf. B., Streiner, D., Boyle, M., Pinelli, J., Paneth, N., & Goddeeris, J. (2006). Transition of extremely low-birth-weight infants from adolescence to young adulthood: Comparison with normal birth-weight controls. *Journal of the American Medical Association, 295,* 667–675.

Sainte-Marie, B. (1996). *Biography.* Retrieved August 1, 2002, from http://creative-native. com/biograp.htm

Saklofske, D. H., & Schwean, V. L. (1995). Psychological and educational assessment of children. In K. Covell (Ed.), *Readings in child development* (pp. 185–208). Toronto: Nelson.

Saklofske, D.H., Caravan, G., & Schwartz, C. (2000). Concurrent validity of the Wechsler Abbreviated Scale of Intelligence (WASI) with a sample of Canadian children. *Canadian Journal of School Psychology, 22,* 392–399.

Salihu, H. M., Shumpert, M. N., Slay, M., Kirby, R. S., &Alexander, G. R. (2003). Childbearing beyond maternal age 50 and fetal outcomes in the United States. *Obstetrics and Gynecology, 102,* 1006–1014.

Salisbury, A., Law, K., LaGasse, L. and Lester, B. (2003). Maternal-fetal attachment. *Journal of the American Medical Association, 289,* 1701.

Salzinger, S., Feldman, R. S., Hammer, M., & Rosario, M. (1993). Effects of physical abuse on children's social relations. *Child Development, 64,* 169–187.

Sameroff, A. J., Seifer, R., Baldwin, A., & Baldwin, C. (1993). Stability of intelligence from preschool to adolescence: The influence of social and family risk factors. *Child Development, 64,* 80–97.

Sampson, R. J. (1997). The embeddedness of child and adolescent development: A community-level perspective on urban violence. In J. McCord (Ed.), *Violence and childhood in the inner city* (pp. 31–77). Cambridge, England: Cambridge University Press.

Samuelsson, M., Radestad, I., & Segesten, K. (2001). A waste of life: Fathers' experience of losing a child before birth. *Birth, 28,* 124–130.

Sandberg, S., Järvenpää, S., Penttinen, A., Paton, J. Y., & McCann, D. C. (2004). Asthma exacerbations in children immediately following stressful life events: A Cox's hierarchical regression. *Thorax, 59,* 1046–1051.

Sandler, D. P., Everson, R. B., Wilcox, A. J., & Browder, J. P. (1985). Cancer risk in adulthood from early life exposure to parents' smoking. *American Journal of Public Health, 75,* 487–492.

Sandler, W., Meir, I., Padden, C., & Aronoff, M. (2005). The emergence of grammar: Systematic structure in a new language. *Proceedings of the National Academy of Sciences, 102,* 2661–2665.

Sandnabba, H. K., &Ahlberg, C. (1999). Parents' attitudes and expectations about children's cross-gender behavior. *Sex Roles, 40,* 249–263.

Sandstrom, M. J., & Coie, J. D. (1999). A developmental perspective on peer rejection: Mechanisms of stability and change. *Child Development, 70*(4), 955–966.

Sankey, G. R. (1995). Transition to work: A concern for many Canadian youth. *Counseling, 10,* 5–10.

Santer, L. J., & Stocking, C. B. (1991). Safety practices and living conditions of low-income urban families. *Pediatrics, 88,* 111–118.

Santos, F., & Ingrassia, R. (August 18, 2002). The face of homelessness has changed: Family surge at shelters. *New York Daily News.* Retrieved from www.nationalhomeless.org/ housing/ familiesarticle.html.

Santos, I. S., Victora, C. G., Huttly, S., & Carvalhal, J. B. (1998). Caffeine intake and low birthweight: A population-based case-control study. *American Journal of Epidemiology, 147,* 620–627.

Sargent, J. D., & Dalton, M. (2001). Does parental disapproval of smoking prevent adolescents from becoming established smokers? *Pediatrics, 108*(6), 1256–1262.

Satchell, M., & Pati, S. (2005). Insurance gaps among vulnerable children in the United States, 1999–2001. *Pediatrics, 116,* 1155–1161.

Satcher, D. (2001). *Women and smoking: A report of the Surgeon General.* Washington, DC: Department of Health and Human Services.

Saudino, K. J. (2003a). Parent ratings of infant temperament: Lessons from twin studies. *Infant Behavior & Development, 26,* 100–107.

Saudino, K. J. (2003b). The need to consider contrast effects in parent-rated temperament *Infant Behavior & Development, 26,* 118–120.

Saudino, K. J., Wertz, A. E., Gagne, J. R., & Chawla, S. (2004). Night and day: Are siblings as different in temperament as parents say they are? *Journal of Personality and Social Psychology, 87,* 698–706.

Savage, S. L., & Au, T. K. (1996). What word learners do when input contradicts the mutual exclusivity assumption. *Child Development, 67,* 3120–3134.

Savic, I., Berglund, H., & Lindström, P. (2005). Brain response to putative pheromones in homosexual men. *Proceedings of the National Academy of Sciences, 102,* 7356–7361.

Savin-Williams, R. C. (2006). Who's gay? Does it matter? *Current Directions in Psychological Science, 15,* 40–44.

Sax, L. J., Astin, L. W., Korn, W. F., & Mahoney, K. M. (1996). *The American freshman: Norms for fall, 1995.* Los Angeles: UCLA Higher Education Institute.

Saxe, G. B., Guberman, S. R., & Gearhart, M. (1987). Social processes in early number development. *Monographs of the Society for Research in Child Development, 52*(216).

Saxe, R., Tenenbaum, J. B., & Carey, S. (2005). Secret agents: Inferences about hidden causes by 10- and 12-month old infants. *Psychological Science, 16,* 995–1001.

Scaldwell, W., Frame, J., & Cookson, D. (1985). Individual assessment of Chippewa, Muncey and Oneida children using the WISC–R. *Canadian Journal of School Psychology, 1,* 15–21.

Scarr, S. (1992). Developmental theories for the 1990s: Development and individual differences. *Child Development, 63,* 1–19.

Scarr, S. (1993). Biological and cultural diversity: The legacy of Darwin for development. *Child Development, 64,* 1333–1353.

Scarr, S. (1997b). Why child care has little impact on most children's development. *Current Directions in Psychological Science, 6*(5), 143–148.

Scarr, S. (1998). American child care today. *American Psychologist, 53,* 95–108.

Scarr, S., & McCartney, K. (1983). How people make their own environments: A theory of genotype-environment effects. *Child Development, 54,* 424–435.

Schacter, D. L. (1999). The seven sins of memory: Insights from psychology and cognitive neuroscience. *American Psychologist, 54,* 182–203.

Schanberg, S. M., & Field, T. M. (1987). Sensory deprivation illness and supplemental stimulation in the rat pup and preterm human neonate. *Child Development, 58,* 1431–1447.

Scheers, N. J., Rutherford, G. W., & Kemp, J. S. (2003). Where should infants sleep? A comparison of risk for suffocation of infants sleeping in cribs, adult beds, and other sleeping locations. *Pediatrics, 112,* 883–889.

Scheidt, P., Overpeck, M. D., Whatt, W., & Aszmann, A. (2000). In C. Currie, K. Hurrelmann, W. Settertobulte, R. Smith, & J. Todd (Eds.), *Health and health behaviour among young people: A WHO crossnational study (HBSC) international report* (pp. 24–38.). WHO Policy Series: Healthy Policy for Children and Adolescents, Series No. 1. Copenhagen, Denmark: World Health Organization Regional Office for Europe.

Schemo, D. J. (2004, August 19). Charter schools lagging behind, test scores show. *New York Times,* pp. A1, A16.

Scher, M. S., Richardson, G. A., & Day, N. L. (2000). Effects of prenatal crack/cocaine and other drug exposure on electroencephalographic sleep studies at birth and one year. *Pediatrics, 105,* 39–48.

Scherer, M. (1985, January). How many ways is a child intelligent? *Instructor,* pp. 32–35.

Schieve, L. A., Meikle, S. F., Ferre, C., Peterson, H. B., Jeng, G., & Wilcox, L. S. (2002). Low and very low birth weight in infants conceived with use of assisted reproductive technology. *New England Journal of Medicine, 346,* 731–737.

Schieve, L. A., Rice, C., Boyle, C., Visser, M. S., & Blumberg, S. J. (2006). Mental health in the United States: Parental report of diagnosed autism in children aged 4–17 years—United States, 2003–2004. *Morbidity and Mortality Weekly Report, 55*(17), 481–486.

Schilpp, P. A. (1970). *Albert Einstein: Philosopher-scientist* (3rd ed.). La Salle, IL: Open Court. (Original work published 1949)

Schissel, B., & Fedec, K. (1999). The selling of innocence: The gestalt of danger in the lives of youth prostitutes. *Canadian Journal of Criminology, 41,* 33–57.

Schlegel, A., & Barry, H. (1991). *Adolescence: An anthropological inquiry.* New York: Free Press.

Schmitt, B. D. (1997). Nocturnal enuresis. *Pediatrics in Review, 18,* 183–190.

Schmitt, B. D., & Kempe, C. H. (1983). Abused and neglected children. In R. E. Behrman & V. C. Vaughn (Eds.), *Nelson textbook of pediatrics* (12th ed.). Philadelphia: Saunders.

Schmitz, S., Saudino, K. J., Plomin, R., Fulker, D. W., & DeFries, J. C. (1996). Genetic and environmental influences on temperament in middle childhood: Analyses of teacher and tester ratings. *Child Development, 67,* 409–422.

Schnaas, L., Rothenberg, S. J., Flores, M., Martinez, S., Hernandez, C., Osorio, E., Velasco, S.R., & Perroni, E. (2006). Reduced intellectual development in children with prenatal lead exposure. *Environmental Health Perspectives, 114*(5), 791–797.

Schneider, B. H., Atkinson, L., & Tardif, C. 2001). Child-parent attachment and children's peer relations: A quantitative review. *Developmental Psychology, 37*, 86–100.

Schneider, H., & Eisenberg, D. (2006). Who receives a diagnosis of attention-deficit hyperactivity disorder in the United States elementary school population? *Pediatrics, 117*, 601–609.

Schneider, M. (2002). *Do school facilities affect academic outcomes?* Washington, DC: National Clearinghouse for Educational Facilities.

Scholer, S. J., Mitchel, E. F., & Ray, W. A. (1997). Predictors of injury mortality in early childhood. *Pediatrics, 100*, 342–347.

Schore, A. N. (1994). *Affect regulation and the origin of the self: The neurobiology of emotional development.* Hillsdale, NJ: Erlbaum.

Schulenberg, J., O'Malley, P., Backman, J., & Johnston, L. (2005). Early adult transitions and their relation to well-being and substance use. In R. A. Settersten, Jr., F. F. Furstenberg, Jr., & R. G. Rumbaut (Eds.), *On the frontier of adulthood: Theory, research, and public policy* (pp.417–453). (John D. and Catherine T. MacArthur Foundation Series on Mental Health and Development, Research Network on Transitions to Adulthood and Public Policy.) Chicago: University of Chicago Press.

Schultin, A.B., Malone, P. S., & Dodge, K. A. (2005). The effect of school-based kindergarten transition policies and practices on child academic outcomes. *Developmental Psychology, 41*, 860–871.

Schumann, C. M., & Amaral, D. G. (2006). Stereological analysis of amygdala neuron number in autism. *The Journal of Neuroscience, 26(29)*, 7674–7679.

Schumann, J. (1997). The view from elsewhere: Why there can be no best method for teaching a second language. *The Clarion: Magazine of the European Second Language Acquisition, 3(1)*, 23–24.

Schupf, N., Kapell, D., Nightingale, B., Rodriguez, A., Tycko, B., & Mayeux, R. (1998). Earlier onset of Alzheimer's disease in men with Down syndrome. *Neurology, 50*, 991–995.

Schwartz, D., Chang, L., & Farver, J. M. (2001). Correlates of victimization in Chinese children's peer groups. *Developmental Psychology, 37(4)*, 520–532.

Schwartz, D., McFadyen-Ketchum, S. A., Dodge, K. A., Pettit, G. S., & Bates, J. E. (1998). Peer group victimization as a predictor of children's behavior problems at home and in school. *Development and Psychopathology, 10*, 87–99.

Schwartz, J. (2004). Air pollution and children's health. *Pediatrics, 113*, 1037–1043.

Schwebel, D. C., & Plumert, J. M. (1999). Longitudinal and concurrent relations among temperament, ability estimation, and injury proneness. *Child Development, 70*, 700–712.

Schweinhart, L. J., Barnes, H. V., & Weikart, D. P. (1993). Significant benefits: The High/Scope Perry Preschool Study through age 27. *Monographs of the High/Scope Educational Research Foundation, 10*. Ypsilanti, MI: High/Scope.

Schwimmer, J. B., Burwinkle, T. M., Varni, J. W. (2003 April). Health-related quality of life of severely obese children and adolescents. *Journal of the American Medical Association, 289(14)*, 1813–1819.

Scott, G., & Ni, H. (2004). Access to health care among Hispanic/Latino children: United States, 1998–2001. *Advance Data from Vital and Health Statistics,* No. 344. Hyattsville, MD: National Center for Health Statistics.

Scrivener, L. (2000). *Terry Fox: His story.* Toronto: McClelland & Steward Ltd.

Sedlak, A. J., & Broadhurst, D. D. (1996). *Executive summary of the third national incidence study of child abuse and neglect* (NIS-3). Washington, DC: U.S. Department of Health and Human Services.

Segalowitz, S. J. (1995). Brain growth and the child's mental development. In K. Covell (Ed.), *Readings in child development* (pp. 51–71). Toronto: Nelson.

Seifer, R. (2003). Twin studies, biases of parents, and biases of researchers. *Infant Behavior & Development, 26*, 115–117.

Seifer, R., Schiller, M., Sameroff, A. J., Resnick, S., & Riordan, K. (1996). Attachment, maternal sensitivity, and infant temperament during the first year of life. *Developmental Psychology, 32*, 12–25.

Seiner, S. H., & Gelfand, D. M. (1995). Effects of mother's simulated withdrawal and depressed affect on mother–toddler interactions. *Child Development, 60*, 1519–1528.

Seitz, V. (1990). Intervention programs for impoverished children: A comparison of educational and family support models. *Annals of Child Development, 7*, 73–103.

Selman, R. L. (1980). *The growth of interpersonal understanding: Developmental and clinical analyses.* New York: Academic.

Selman, R. L., & Selman, A. P. (1979, April). Children's ideas about friendship: A new theory. *Psychology Today,* pp. 71–80.

Seltzer, J. A. (1998). Father by law: Effects of joint legal custody on nonresident fathers' involvement with children. *Demography, 35*, 135–146.

Seltzer, J. A. (2000). Families formed outside of marriage. *Journal of Marriage and the Family, 62*, 1247–1268.

Seminara, S. B., Messager, S., Chatzidaki, E. E., Thresher, R. R., Acierno Jr., J. S., Shagoury, J. K., Bo-Abbas, Y., Kuohung, W., Schwinof, K. M., Hendrick, A. G., Zahn, D., Dixon, J., Kaiser, U. B., Slaugenhaupt, S. A., Gusella, J. F., O'Rahilly, S., Carlton, M. B. L., Crowley Jr., W. F., Aparicio, S. A. J. R., & Colledge, W. H. (2003). The GPR54 gene as a regulator of puberty. *New England Journal of Medicine, 349*, 1614–1627.

Sen, A., Partelow, L., & Miller, D. C. (2005). *Comparative indicators of education in the United States and other G8 countries: 2004* (NCES 2005-021). Washington, DC: National Center for Education Statistics.

Senghas, A., & Coppola, M. (2001). Children creating language: How Nicaraguan sign language acquired a spatial grammar. *Psychological Science, 12*, 323–328.

Senghas, A., Kita, S., & Ozyürek, A. (2004). Children creating core properties of language: Evidence from an emerging sign language in Nicaragua. *Science, 305*, 1779–1782.

Serbin, L. A., Moller, L. C., Gulko, J., Powlishta, K. K., & Colburne, K. A. (1994). The emergence of gender segregation in toddler playgroups. In C. Leaper (Ed.), *Childhood gender segregation: Causes and consequences* (New Directions for Child Development, 65, pp. 7–17). San Francisco: Jossey-Bass.

Serbin, L., Poulin-Dubois, D., Colburne, K. A., Sen, M., & Eichstedt. J. A. (2001). Gender stereotyping in infancy: Visual preferences for knowledge of gender stereotyped toys in the second year. *International Journal of Behavioral Development, 25*, 7–15.

Serres, L. (2001). Morphological changes of the human hippocampal formation from midgestation to early childhood. In C. A. Nelson & M. Luciana (Eds.), *Handbook of developmental cognitive neuroscience* (pp. 45–58). Cambridge, MA: MIT Press.

Sethi, A., Mischel, W., Aber, J. L., Shoda, Y., & Rodriguez, M. L. (2000). The role of strategic attention deployment in development of self-regulation: Predicting preschoolers' delay of gratification from mother-toddler interactions. *Developmental Psychology, 36*, 767–777.

Shah, T., Sullivan, K., & Carter, J. (2006). Sudden infant death syndrome and reported maternal smoking during pregnancy. *American Journal of Public Health, 96(10)*, 1757–1759.

Shanahan, M. J., & Flaherty, B. P. (2001). Dynamic patterns of time use in adolescence. *Child Development, 72(2)*, 385–401.

Shanahan, M., Porfeli, E., & Mortimer, J. (2005). Subjective age identity and the transition to adulthood: When do adolescents become adults? In R. A. Settersten, Jr., F. F. Furstenberg, Jr., & R. G. Rumbaut (Eds.), *On the frontier of adulthood: Theory, research, and public policy* (pp. 225–255). (John D. and Catherine T. MacArthur Foundation Series on Mental Health and Development, Research Network on Transitions to Adulthood and Public Policy.) Chicago: University of Chicago Press.

Shankaran, S., Das, A., Bauer, C. R., Bada, H. S., Lester, B., Wright, L. L., & Smeriglio, V. (2004). Association between patterns of maternal substance use and infant birth weight, length, and head circumference. *Pediatrics, 114*, e226–e234.

Shanner, L. & Nisker, J. (2001). Bioethics for clinicians: 26. Assisted reproductive technologies. *Canadian Medical Association, 164*, 1589–1594.

Shannon, J. D., Tamis-LeMonda, C. S., London, K., & Cabrera, N. (2002). Beyond rough and tumble: Low income fathers' interactions and children's cognitive development at 24 months. *Parenting: Science and Practice, 2(2)*, 77–104.

Shannon, M. (2000). Ingestion of toxic substances by children. *New England Journal of Medicine, 342*, 186–191.

Sharma, A. R., McGue, M. K., & Benson, P. L. (1996a). The emotional and behavioral adjustment of United States adopted adolescents, Part I: An overview. *Children and Youth Services Review, 18*, 83–100.

Sharma, A. R., McGue, M. K., & Benson, P. L. (1996b). The emotional and behavioral adjustment of United States adopted adolescents, Part II: Age at adoption. *Children and Youth Services Review, 18*, 101–114.

Shatz, M., & Gelman, R. (1973). The development of communication skills: Modifications in the speech of young children as a function of listener. *Monographs of the Society for Research in Child Development, 38(5, Serial No. 152)*.

Shaw, G. M., Velie, E. M., & Schaffer, D. (1996). Risk of neural tube defect–affected pregnancies among obese women. *Journal of the American Medical Association, 275*, 1093–1096.

Shaw, P., Greenstein, D., Lerch, J., Clasen, L., Lenroot, R., Gogtay, N., Evans, A., Rapoport, J., & Gledd, J. (2006). Intellectual ability and cortical development in children and adolescents. *Nature, 440*, 676–679.

Shayer, M., Ginsburg, D., & Coe, R. (2007). Thirty years on—a large anti-Flynn effect? The Piagetian test Volume and Heaviness norms 1975–2003. *British Journal of Educational Psychology, 77*, 25–41.

Shaywitz, B. A., Sullivan, C. M., Anderson, G. M., Gillespie, S. M., Sullivan, B., & Shaywitz, S. E. (1994). Aspartame, behavior, and cognitive function in children with attention deficit disorder. *Pediatrics, 93*, 70–75.

Shaywitz, S. (2003). *Overcoming dyslexia: A new and complete science-based program for overcoming reading problems at any level.* New York: Knopf.

Shaywitz, S. E. (1998). Current concepts: Dyslexia. *New England Journal of Medicine, 338,* 307–312.

Shea, K. M., Little, R. E., & the ALSPAC Study Team (1997). Is there an association between preconceptual paternal x-ray exposure and birth outcome? *American Journal of Epidemiology, 145,* 546–551.

Shea, S., Basch, C. E., Stein, A. D., Contento, I. R., Irigoyen, M., & Zybert, P. (1993). Is there a relationship between dietary fat and stature or growth in children 3 to 5 years of age? *Pediatrics, 92,* 579–586.

Sherman, L. W., & Berk, R. A. (1984, April). The Minneapolis domestic violence experiment. *Police Foundation Reports,* pp. 1–8.

Shevell, T., Malone, F. D., Vidaver, J., Porter, T. F., Luthy, D. A., & Comstock, C. H., Hankins, G. D., Eddleman, K., Dolan, S., Dugoff, L., Craigo, S., Timor, I. E., Carr, S. R., Wolfe, H. M., Bianchi, D. W., D'Alton, M. E. for the FASTER Research Consortium. (2005). Assisted reproductive technology and pregnancy outcome. *Obstetrics and Gynecology, 106,* 1039–1045.

Shields, A. E., Comstock, C., & Weiss, K. B. (2004). Variations in asthma by race/ethnicity among children enrolled in a state Medicaid program. *Pediatrics, 113,* 496–504.

Shields, B. J., & Smith, G. A. (2006). Success in the prevention of infant walker-related injuries: An analysis of national data, 1990–2001. *Pediatrics, 117,* 452–459.

Shields, M. K., & Behrman, R. E. (2004). Children of immigrant families: Analysis and recommendations. *The Future of Children, 14*(2), 4–15. Retrieved October 8, 2004, from http://www.futureofchildren.org.

Shiono, P. H., & Behrman, R. E. (1995). Low birth weight: Analysis and recommendations. *The Future of Children, 5*(1), 4–18.

Shonkoff, J., & Phillips, D. (2000). Growing up in child care. In I. Shonkoff & & D. Phillips (Eds.), *From neurons to neighborhoods* (pp. 297–327). Washington, DC: National Research Council/Institute of Medicine

Shulman, S., Scharf, M., Lumer, D., & Maurer, O. (2001). Parental divorce and young adult children's romantic relationships: Resolution of the divorce experience. *American Journal of Orthopsychiatry, 71,* 473–478.

Shwe, H. I., & Markman, E. M. (1997). Young children's appreciation of the mental impact of their communicative signals. *Developmental Psychology, 33*(4), 630–636.

Sick, W. T., Perfetti, C. A., Jin, Z., & Tan, L. H. (2004). Biological abnormality of impaired reading is constrained by culture. *Nature, 431,* 71–76.

Sieccan [Sex Information and Education Council of Canada]. (2000). Common questions about sexual health education. *Canadian Journal of Human Sexuality, 9,* 129–137.

Siegal, M., & Peterson, C. C. (1998). Preschoolers' understanding of lies and innocent and negligent mistakes. *Developmental Psychology, 34*(2), 332–341.

Siegel, A. C., & Burton, R. V. (1999). Effects of baby walkers on motor and mental development in human infants. *Journal of Developmental and Behavioral Pediatrics, 20,* 355–361.

Siegler, R. S. (1995). How does change occur: A microgenetic study of number conservation. *Cognitive Psychology, 28,* 225–273.

Siegler, R. S. (1998). *Children's thinking* (3rd ed.). Upper Saddle River, NJ: Prentice Hall.

Siegler, R. S., & Booth, J. L. (2004). Development of numerical estimation in young children. *Child Development, 75,* 428–444.

Siegler, R. S., & Opfer, J. E. (2003). The development of numerical estimation: Evidence for multiple representations of numerical quantity. *Psychological Science, 14,* 237–243.

Siegler, R. S., & Richards, D. (1982). The development of intelligence. In R. Sternberg (Ed.), *Handbook of human intelligence.* London: Cambridge University Press.

Sieving, R. E., Oliphant, J. A., & Blum, R. W. (2002). Adolescent sexual behavior and sexual health. *Pediatrics in Review, 23,* 407–416.

Sigman, M., Cohen, S. E., & Beckwith, L. (1997). Why does infant attention predict adolescent intelligence? *Infant Behavior and Development, 20,* 133–140.

Signorello, L. B., Nordmark, A., Granath, F., Blot, W. J., McLaughlin, J. K., Anneren, G., Lundgren, S., Exbom, A., Rane, A., & Cnattingius, S. (2001). Caffeine metabolism and the risk of spontaneous abortion of normal karyotype fetuses. *Obstetrics & Gynecology, 98*(6), 1059–1066.

Silver, R. M., Landon, M. D., Rouse, D. J., Leveno, K. J., Spong, C. Y., Thom, E. A., et al., & National Institute of Child Health and Human Development Maternal-Fetal Medicine Units Network. (2006). Maternal morbidity associated with multiple repeat cesarean deliveries. *Obstetrics and Gynecology, 107*(6), 1226–1232.

Silvern, S. B. (1998). Educational implications of play with computers. In D. P. Fromberg & D. Bergen (Eds.), *Play from birth to twelve and beyond: Contexts, perspectives, and meanings* (pp. 530–536). New York: Garland.

Simmons, R. G., Blyth, D. A., & McKinney, K. L. (1983). The social and psychological effect of puberty on white females. In J. Brooks-Gunn & A. C. Petersen (Eds.), *Girls at puberty: Biological and psychological perspectives.* New York: Plenum.

Simmons, R. G., Blyth, D. A., Van Cleave, E. F., & Bush, D. M. (1979). Entry into early adolescence: The impact of school structure, puberty, and early dating on self-esteem. *American Sociological Review, 44*(6), 948–967.

Simner, M. L. (1993). Beginning reading instruction: A position paper on beginning reading instruction in Canadian schools. *Canadian Journal of School Psychology, 9,* 96–99.

Simner, M. L. (1998). The Canadian Psychological Association's stand on beginning reading instruction. *Canadian Journal of Research in Early Childhood Education, 7,* 157–158.

Simon, G. E. (2006). The antidepressant quandary—Considering suicide risk when treating adolescent depression. *New England Journal of Medicine, 355,* 2722–2723.

Simon, G. E., Savarino, J., Operskalski, B., & Wang, P. S. (2006). Suicide risk during antidepressant treatment. *American Journal of Psychiatry, 163,* 41–47.

Simons, R. L., Chao, W., Conger, R. D., & Elder, G. H. (2001). Quality of parenting as mediator of the effect of childhood defiance on adolescent friendship choices and delinquency: A growth curve analysis. *Journal of Marriage and the Family, 63,* 63–79.

Simons, R. L., Lin, K.-H., & Gordon, L. C. (1998). Socialization in the family of origin and male dating violence: A prospective study. *Journal of Marriage and the Family, 60,* 467–478.

Simonton, D. K. (1990). Creativity and wisdom in aging. In J. E. Birren & K. W. Schaie (Eds.),

Handbook of the psychology of aging (pp. 320–329). New York: Academic Press.

Simpson, G. A., & Fowler, M. G. (1994). Geographic mobility and children's emotional/ behavioral adjustment and school functioning. *Pediatrics, 93,* 303–309.

Simpson, G. B., & Foster, M. R. (1986). Lexical ambiguity and children's word recognition. *Developmental Psychology, 22,* 147–154.

Simpson, G. B., & Lorsbach, T. C. (1983). The development of automatic and conscious components of contextual facilitation. *Child Development, 54,* 760–772.

Simpson, J. E. (2005). Choosing the best prenatal screening protocol. *New England Journal of Medicine, 353,* 2068–2070.

Simpson, K. (2001). The role of testosterone in aggression. *McGill Journal of Medicine, 6,* 32–40.

Sinclair, Judge M., Phillips, D., & Bala, N. (1991). Aboriginal child welfare in Canada. In N. Bala, J. Rornick, & R. Vogl (Eds.), *Canadian child welfare law.* Toronto: Thompson Publishing.

Singer, D. G., & Singer, J. L. (1990). *The house of make-believe: Play and the developing imagination.* Cambridge, MA: Harvard University Press.

Singer, J. L., & Singer, D. G. (1981). *Television, imagination, and aggression: A study of preschoolers.* Hillsdale, NJ: Erlbaum.

Singer, J. L., & Singer, D. G. (1998). Barney & Friends as entertainment and education: Evaluating the quality and effectiveness of a television series for preschool children. In J. K. Asamen & G. L. Berry (Eds.), *Research paradigms, television, and social behavior* (pp. 305–367). Thousand Oaks, CA: Sage.

Singer, L. T., Minnes, S., Short, E., Arendt, K., Farkas, K., Lewis, B., Klein, N., Russ, S., Min, M. O., & Kirchner, H. L. (2004). Cognitive outcomes of preschool children with prenatal cocaine exposure. *Journal of the American Medical Association, 291,* 2448–2456.

Singh, K. K., Barroga, C. F., Hughes, M. D., Chen, J., Raskino, C., McKinney, R. E., & Spector, S. A. (2003, November 15). Genetic influence of CCR5, CCR2, and SDF1 variants on human immunodeficiency virus 1 (HIV-1)- related disease progression and neurological impairment, in children with symptomatic HIV-1 infection. *Journal of Infectious Disease, 188*(10), 1461–1472.

Singhal, A., Cole, T. J., Fewtrell, M., & Lucas, A. (2004). Breastmilk feeding and lipoprotein profile in adolescents born preterm: Follow-up of a prospective randomised study. *Lancet, 363,* 1571–1578.

Sipos, A., Rasmussen, F., Harrison, G., Tynelius, P., Lewis, G., Leon, D. A., et al. (2004). Paternal age and schizophrenia: A population based cohort study. *British Medical Journal, 329,* 1070–1073.

Sit, C., Yeung, D. L., He, M., & Anderson, G. H. (2001). The growth and feeding patterns of 9- to 12-month-old Chinese Canadian infants. *Nutrition Research, 21,* 505–516.

Skadberg, B. T., Morild, I., & Markestad, T. (1998). Abandoning prone sleeping: Effects on the risk of sudden infant death syndrome. *Journal of Pediatrics, 132,* 234–239.

Skinner, B. F. (1957). *Verbal behavior.* New York: Appleton-Century-Crofts.

Skinner, D. (1989). The socialization of gender identity: Observations from Nepal. In J. Valsiner (Ed.), *Child development in cultural context* (pp. 181–192). Toronto: Hogrefe & Huber.

Skinner, J. D., Carruth, B. R., Moran, J., III, Houck, K., & Coletta, F. (1999). Fruit juice intake is not related to children's growth. *Pediatrics, 103,* 58–64.

Skjaerven, R., Wilcox, A. J., & Lie, R. T. (1999). A population-based study of survival and childbearing among female subjects with birth defects and the risk of recurrence in their children. *New England Journal of Medicine, 340,* 1057–1062.

Skoe, E. E., & Diessner, R. E. (1994). Ethics of care, justice, identity, and gender: An extension and replication. *Merrill-Palmer Quarterly, 40,* 272–289.

Skolnick, A. A. (1993). "Female athlete triad" risk for women. *Journal of the American Medical Association, 270,* 921–923.

Slade, A., Belsky, J., Aber, J. L., & Phelps, J. L. (1999). Mothers' representation of their relationships with their toddlers: Links to adult attachment and observed mothering. *Developmental Psychology, 35,* 611–619.

Slobin, D. (1973). Cognitive prerequisites for the acquisition of language. In C. Ferguson & D. Slobin (Eds.), *Studies of child language development.* New York: Holt, Rinehart, & Winston.

Slobin, D. (1983). Universal and particular in the acquisition of grammar. In E. Wanner & L. Gleitman (Eds.), *Language acquisition: The state of the art.* Cambridge, England: Cambridge University Press.

Sly, R. M. (2000). Decreases in asthma mortality in the United States. *Annals of Allergy, Asthma, and Immunology, 85,* 121–127.

Slyper, A. H. (2006). The pubertal timing controversy in the USA, and a review of possible causative factors for the advance in timing of onset of puberty. *Clinical Endocrinology, 65,* 1–8.

Small, M. Y. (1990). *Cognitive development.* New York: Harcourt Brace.

Smedje, J., Broman, J. E., & Hetta, J. (1999). Parents' reports of disturbed sleep in 5–7-year-old Swedish children. *Acta Paediatrica, 88,* 858–865.

Smedley, A., & Smedley, B. D. (2005). Race as biology is fiction, racism as a social problem is real: Anthropological and historical perspectives on the social construction of race. *American Psychologist, 60,* 16–26.

Smetana, J., Crean, H., & Campione-Barr, N. (2005). Adolescents' and parents' changing conceptions of parental authority. In J. Smetana (Ed.), *Changing boundaries of parental authority during adolescence: New directions for child and adolescent development, no. 108* (pp. 31–46). San Francisco: Jossey-Bass.

Smetana, J. G., & Bitz, B. (1996). Adolescents' conception of teachers' authority and their relations to rule violations in school. *Child Development, 67,* 1153–1172.

Smetana, J. G., Metzger, A., Gettman, D. C., & Campione-Barr, N. (2006). Disclosure and secrecy in adolescent-parent relationships. *Child Development, 77,* 201–217.

Smilansky, S. (1968). *The effects of sociodramatic play on disadvantaged preschool children.* New York: Wiley.

Smith, A., & Schneider, B. H. (2000). The inter-ethnic friendships of adolescent students: A Canadian study. *International Journal of Intercultural Relations, 24,* 247–258.

Smith, B. A., & Blass, E. M. (1996). Taste-mediated calming in premature, preterm, and full-term human infants. *Developmental Psychology, 32,* 1084–1089.

Smith, E., & Jackson, A. (2002). *Does a rising tide lift all boats? The labour market experiences and incomes of recent immigrants, 1995 to 1998.* Ottawa: Canadian Council on Social Development.

Smith, G. C. S., Pell, J. P., Cameron, A. D., & Dobbie, R. (2002). Risk of perinatal death associated with labor after previous cesarean delivery in uncomplicated term pregnancies. *Journal of the American Medical Association, 287,* 2684–2690.

Smith, G. C., Wood, A. M., Pell, J. P., & Dobbie, R. (2005). Sudden infant death syndrome and complications in other pregnancies. *Lancet, 366,* 2107–2111.

Smith, K. A., Fairburn, C. G., & Cowen, P. J. (1999). Symptomatic release in bulimia nervosa following acute tryptophan depletion. *Archives of General Psychiatry (72C), 56*(2), 171–176.

Smith, L. B., & Thelen, E. (2003). Development as a dynamic system. *Trends in cognitive sciences, 7,* 343–348.

Smith, L. M., LaGasse, L. L., Derauf, C., Grant, P., Shah, R., Arria, A., Huestis, M., Haning, W., Strauss, A., Grotta, S. D., Liu, J., & Lester, B. M. (2006). The infant development, environment, and lifestyle study: Effects of prenatal methamphetamine exposure, polydrug exposure, and poverty on intrauterine growth. *Pediatrics, 118,* 1149–1156.

Smith, M. M., & Lifshitz, F. (1994). Excess fruit juice consumption as a contributing factor in nonorganic failure to thrive. *Pediatrics, 93,* 438–443.

Smith, P. K. (2005a). Play: Types and functions in human development. In A. D. Pellegrini & P. K. Smith (Eds.), *The nature of play* (pp. 271–291). New York: Guilford.

Smith, P. K. (2005b). Social and pretend play in children. In A. D. Pellegrini & P. K. Smith (Eds.), *The nature of play* (pp. 173–209). New York: Guilford.

Smith, P. K., & Levan, S. (1995). Perceptions and experiences of bullying in younger pupils. *British Journal of Educational Psychology, 65,* 489–500.

Smith, R. (1999, March). The timing of birth. *Scientific American,* pp. 68–75.

Smith, R. (2007). Parturition. *New England Journal of Medicine, 356,* 271–283.

Smith, V. K., & Rousseau, D. M. (2005). *SCHIP enrollment in 50 states.* Washington, DC: Kaiser Commission on Medicaid and the Uninsured.

Smith-Khuri, E., Iachan, R., Scheidt, P. C., Overpeck, M. D., Gabhainn, S. N., Pickett, W., & Harel, Y. (2004). A crossnational study of violence-related behaviors in adolescents. *Archives of Pediatrics and Adolescent Medicine, 158,* 539–544.

Snarey, J. R. (1985). Cross-cultural universality of social-moral development: A critical review of Kohlbergian research. *Psychological Bulletin, 97,* 202–232.

Snow, C. E. (1990). The development of definitional skill. *Journal of Child Language, 17,* 697–710.

Snow, C. E. (1993). Families as social contexts for literacy development. In C. Daiute (Ed.), *The development of literacy through social interaction (New Directions for Child Development, 61,* pp. 11–24). San Francisco: Jossey-Bass.

Snow, M. E., Jacklin, C. N., & Maccoby, E. E. (1983). Sex-of-child differences in father–child interaction at one year of age. *Child Development, 54,* 227–232.

Snyder, J., Bank, L., & Burraston, B. (2005). The consequences of antisocial behavior in older male siblings for younger brothers and sisters. *Journal of Family Psychology, 19,* 643–653.

Snyder, J., Cramer, A., Afrank, J., & Patterson, G. R. (2005). The contributions of ineffective discipline and parental hostile attributions of child misbehavior to the development of conduct problems at home and school. *Developmental Psychology, 41,* 30–41.

Snyder, J., West, L., Stockemer, V., Gibbons, S., & Almquist-Parks, L. (1996). A social learning model of peer choice in the natural environment. *Journal of Applied Developmental Psychology, 17,* 215–237.

Snyder, T. D., & Hoffman, C. M. (2002). *The digest of education statistics: 2001.* Washington, DC: National Center for Education Statistics.

Snyder, T. D., Hoffman, C. M., & Geddes, C. M. (1997). *Digest of education statistics 1997* (NCES 98-015). Washington, DC: U.S. Department of Education, National Center for Education Statistics.

Sobolewski, J. M., & Amato, P. J. (2005). Economic hardship in the family of origin and children's psychological well-being in adulthood. *Journal of Marriage and Family, 67,* 141–156.

Sobolewski, J. M., & King, V. (2005). The importance of the coparental relationship for nonresident fathers' ties to children. *Journal of Marriage and Family, 67,* 1196–1212.

Sobsey, D. (2002). Exceptionality, education, and maltreatment. *Exceptionality, 10,* 29–46.

Society for Adolescent Medicine. *Journal of Adolescent Health, 36,* 92–93.

Society for Assisted Reproductive Technology & the American Fertility Society. (1993). Assisted reproductive technology in the United States and Canada: 1991 results from the Society for Assisted Reproductive Technology generated from The American Fertility Society Registry. *Fertility and Sterility, 59,* 956–962.

Society for Assisted Reproductive Technology & the American Society for Reproductive Medicine. (2002). Assisted reproductive technology in the United States: 1998 results generated from the American Society for Reproductive Medicine/Society for Assisted Reproductive Technology Registry. *Fertility & Sterility, 77*(1), 18–31.

Society for Assisted Reproductive Technology, The American Fertility Society. (1993). Assisted reproductive technology in the United States and Canada: 1991 results from the Society for Assisted Reproductive Technology generated from The American Fertility Society Registry. *Fertility and Sterility, 59,* 956–962.

Society for Neuroscience. (2005). *Brain facts: A primer on the brain and nervous system.* Washington, DC: Author.

Society of Obstetricians and Gynaecologists of Canada. (1993, March). *The use of folic acid for the prevention of neural tube defects.* SOGC Policy Statement no. 19. Ottawa: Health Canada.

Society of Obstetricians and Gynaecologists of Canada. (1996a). *Fetal health surveillance in labour.* Policy Statement No. 45. Ottawa: Author.

Society of Obstetricians and Gynaecologists of Canada. (1998). *Healthy beginnings: Guidelines for care during pregnancy and childbirth.* Policy Statement No. 71. Ottawa: Author

Society of Obstetricians and Gynaecologists of Canada. (2000a). *Be careful what you wish for...* [Press Release, June 27, 2000].

Society of Obstetricians and Gynaecologists of Canada. (2000b). *Healthy beginnings: The complete get-ready-for-baby guide.* Ottawa: Author.

Society of Obstetricians and Gynaecologists of Canada. (2006). Sex Facts in Canada 2006. Retrieved September 2, 2007 from http://www.masexualite.ca/media-room/fact-sheets-1.aspx.

Society of Obstetricians and Gynecologists of Canada. (2007). Women's Health Information: Pregnancy: Multiple Birth. Retrieved November 11, 2007 from http://sogc.medical.org/health/pregnancymultiple_e.asp.

Soenens, B., Vansteenkiste, M., Luyckx, K., & Goossens, L. (2006). Parenting and adolescent problem behavior: An integrated model with adolescent self-disclosure and perceived parental knowledge as intervening variables. *Developmental Psychology, 42*, 305–318.

Sokol, R. J., Delaney-Black, V., & Nordstrom, B. (2003). Fetal alcohol spectrum disorder. *Journal of the American Medical Association, 209*, 2996–2999.

Sokol, R. Z., Kraft, P., Fowler, I. M., Mamet, R., Kim, E., & Berhane, K. T. (2006). Exposure to environmental ozone alters semen quality. *Environmental Health Perspectives, 114*(3), 360–365.

Solowij, N., Stephens, R. S., Roffman, R. A., Babor, T., Kadden, R., Miller, M., et al., for the Marijuana Treatment Research Group. (2002). Cognitive functioning of long-term heavy cannabis users seeking treatment. *Journal of the American Medical Association, 287*, 1123–1131.

Somers, M. & Willms, J. D. (2002). Maternal depression and childhood vulnerablility. In Willms, J. D. *Vulnerable Children* (pp. 211–228). Edmonton, AB:The University of Alberta Press.

Sondergaard, C., Henriksen, T. B., Obel, C., & Wisborg, K. (2001). Smoking during pregnancy and infantile colic. *Pediatrics, 108*(2), 342–346.

Sonenstein, F. L., Pleck, J. H., & Ku, L. C. (1991). Levels of sexual activity among adolescent males in the United States. *Family Planning Perspectives, 23*(4), 162–167.

Sood, B., Delaney-Black, V., Covington, C., Nordstrom-Klee, B., Ager, J., Templin, T., Janisse, J., Martier, S., & Sokol, R. J. (2001). Prenatal alcohol exposure and childhood behavior at age 6 to 7 years: I. Dose-response effect. *Pediatrics, 108*(8), e461–e462.

Sophian, C., & Wood, A. (1997). Proportional reasoning in young children: The parts and the whole of it. *Journal of Educational Psychology, 89*, 309–317.

Sophian, C., Garyantes, D., & Chang, C. (1997). When three is less than two: Early developments in children's understanding of fractional quantities. *Developmental Psychology, 33*, 731–744.

Sophian, C., Wood, A., & Vong, K. I. (1995). Making numbers count: The early development of numerical inferences. *Developmental Psychology, 31*, 263–273.

Sorensen, T., Nielsen, G., Andersen, P., & Teasdale, T. (1988). Genetic and environmental influence of premature death in adult adoptees. *New England Journal of Medicine, 318*, 727–732.

Sorof, J. M., Lai, D., Turner, J., Poffenbarger, T., & Portman, R. J. (2004). Overweight, ethnicity, and the prevalence of hypertension in school-aged children. *Pediatrics, 113*. 475–482.

Soubhi, H., Raina, P., & Kohen, D. (2001). *Effects of neighbourhood, family, and child behaviour on childhood injury in Canada*. Report No. W-01-6E. Ottawa: Applied Research Branch, Strategic Policy, Human Resources Development Canada.

Sowell, E. R., Thompson, P. M., Welcome, S. E., Henkenius, A. L., Toga, A. W., & Peterson, B. S. (2003). Cortical abnormalities in children and adolescents with attention-deficit hyperactivity disorder. *Lancet, 362*, 1699–1701.

Spady, D. W., Saunders. D. L., Schopflocher, D. P., & Svenson, L. W. (2004). Patterns for injury in childhood: A population-based approach. *Pediatrics, 113*, 522–529.

Spelke, E. (1994). Initial knowledge: Six suggestions. *Cognition, 50*, 431–445.

Spelke, E. S. (1998). Nativism, empiricism, and the origins of knowledge. *Infant Behavior and Development, 21*(2), 181–200.

Spelke, E. S. (2005). Sex differences in intrinsic aptitude for mathematics and science? A critical review. *American Psychologist, 60*, 950-958.

Spencer, H. (1898). *The principles of psychology*. New York: Appleton. (Original work published 1878.)

Spencer, J. P., Clearfield, M., Corbetta. D., Ulrich, B., Buchanan, P., & Schöner, G. (2006). Moving toward a grand theory of development: In memory of Esther Thelen. *Child Development, 77*, 1521–1538.

Spencer, J. P., Smith, L. B., & Thelen, E. (2001). Tests of a dynamic systems account of the A-not-B error: The influence of prior experience on the spatial memory abilities of two-year-olds. *Child Development, 72*, 1327-1346.

Spencer, M. B., & Dornbusch, S. M. (1998). Challenges in studying minority youth. In R. E. Muuss & H. D. Porton (Eds.), *Adolescent behavior and society: A book of readings* (pp. 316–330). Boston: McGraw-Hill.

Sperling, M. A. (2004). Prematurity—A window of opportunity? *New England Journal of Medicine, 351*, 2229–2231.

Spieker, S. J., Nelson, D. C., Petras, A., Jolley, S. N., & Barnard, K. E. (2003). Joint influence of child care and infant attachment security for cognitive and language outcomes of low-income toddlers. *Infant Behavior & Development, 26*, 326–344.

Spinath, F. M., Price, T. S., Dale, P. S., & Plomin, R. (2004). The genetic and environmental origins of language disability and ability. *Child Development, 75*, 445–454.

Spinrad, T. L., Eisenberg, N., Harris, E., Hanish, L., Fabes, R. A., Kupanoff, K., Ringwald, S., & Holmes, J. (2004). The relation of children's everyday nonsocial peer play behavior to their emotionality, regulation, and social functioning. *Developmental Psychology, 40*, 67–80.

Spira, E. G., Brachen, S. S., & Fischel, J. E. (2005). Predicting improvement after first-grade reading difficulties: The effects of oral language, emergent literacy, and behavior skills. *Developmental Psychology, 41*, 225–234.

Spitz, R. A. (1945). Hospitalism: An inquiry into the genesis of psychiatric conditioning in early childhood. In D. Fenschel et al. (Eds.), *Psychoanalytic studies of the child* (Vol. 1, pp. 53–74). New York: International Universities Press.

Spitz, R. A. (1946). Hospitalism: A follow-up report. In D. Fenschel et al. (Eds.), *Psychoanalytic studies of the child* (Vol. 1, pp. 113–117). New York: International Universities Press.

Spohr, H. L., Willms, J., & Steinhausen, H.-C. (1993). Prenatal alcohol exposure and long-term developmental consequences. *Lancet, 341*, 907–910.

Squire, L. R. (1992). Memory and the hippocampus: A synthesis of findings with rats, monkeys, and humans. *Psychological Review, 99*, 195–231.

Sroufe, L. A. (1979). Socioemotional development. In J. Osofsky (Ed.), *Handbook of infant development*. New York: Wiley.

Sroufe, L. A. (1997). *Emotional development*. Cambridge, England: Cambridge University Press.

Sroufe, L. A., Bennett, C., Englund, M., Urban, J., & Shulman, S. (1993). The significance of gender boundaries in preadolescence: Contemporary correlates and antecedents of boundary violation and maintenance. *Child Development, 64*, 455–466.

Sroufe, L. A., Carlson, E., & Shulman, S. (1993). Individuals in relationships: Development from infancy through adolescence. In D. C. Funder, R. D. Parke, C. Tomlinson-Keasey, & K. Widaman (Eds.), *Studying lives through time: Personality and development* (pp. 315–342). Washington, DC: American Psychological Association.

St. Clair, D., Xu, M., Wang, P., Yu, Y., Fang, Y., Zhang, F., Zheng, X., Gu, N., Feng, G., Sham, P., & He, L. (2005). Rates of adult schizophrenia following prenatal exposure to the Chinese famine of 1959-1961. *Journal of the American Medical Association, 294*, 557–562.

Staff, J., Mortimer, J. T., & Uggen, C. (2004). Work and leisure in adolescence. In R. M. Lerner & L. Steinberg (Eds.). *Handbook of adolescent development* (2nd ed., pp. 429–450). Hoboken, NJ: Wiley.

Stahl, S. A., & Miller, P. D. (1989). Whole language and language experience approaches for beginning reading: A quantitative research synthesis. *Review of Educational Research, 59*, 87–116.

Stahl, S. A., McKenna, M. C., & Pagnucco, J. R. (1994). The effects of whole-language instruction: An update and a reappraisal. *Educational Psychologist, 29*, 175–185.

Standing Senate Committee on Human Rights. (2007). *Children: The silenced citizens. Effective implementation of Canada's international obligations with respect to the rights of children. Final report of the Standing Senate Committee on Human Rights*. Ottawa, ON: Senate Committees Directorate.

Standley, J. M. (1998). Strategies to improve outcomes in critical care: The effect of music and multimodal stimulation on responses of premature infants in neonatal intensive care. *Pediatric Nursing, 24*, 532–538.

Stapleton, S. (1998, May 11). Asthma rates hit epidemic numbers; experts wonder why. *American Medical News, 41*(18). Retrieved from http://www. amaassn.org/special/asthma/newsline/special/ep idem.htm.

Starfield, B. (1991). Childhood morbidity: Comparisons, clusters, and trends. *Pediatrics, 88*, 519–526.

Starr, J. M., Deary, I. J., Lemmon, H., & Whalley, L. J. (2000). Mental ability age 11 years and health status age 77 years. *Age and Ageing, 29*, 523–528.

States look to detention for pregnant drug users. (1998, May 2). *Minneapolis Star-Tribune*, p. A15.

Statistics Canada (n.d.). *Our Youth*. Retrieved July 7, 2007 from http://www43.statcan.ca/02/02b/02b_004_e.htm.

Statistics Canada. (1994). *Low income cut-offs* (Catalogue No. 13-551-XPB). Ottawa: Author.

Statistics Canada. (1996). *1996 Census Nation tables*. Retrieved September 24, 2002, from http://www.statcan.ca/english/census96/nation.htm.

Statistics Canada. (1998). *National Population Health Survey, 1996–97*. Ottawa: Author.

Statistics Canada. (1999). *Leading causes of death at different ages, 1997*. Ottawa: Author.

Statistics Canada. (1999). National Longitudinal Survey of Children and Youth: transition into adolescence. Retrieved October 18, 2007 from http://www.statcan.ca/Daily/English/990706/d990706a.htm.

Statistics Canada. (2000). *Average hours per week of television viewing, fall 2000*

(Catalogue no. 87F0006XPB). Retrieved September 24, 2002, from http://www.statcan.ca/english/Pgdb/People/Culture/arts23.htm.

Statistics Canada. (2000, October 20). Teenage pregnancy. *The Daily*. Retrieved September 20, 2002, from http://www.statcan.ca/Daily/English/001020/d001020b.htm.

Statistics Canada. (2002). *The Daily: Deaths.* Retrieved on July 8 from http://www.statcan.ca/Daily/English/020507/d020507b.htm.

Statistics Canada. (2002). Youth in Transition Survey. Retrieved August 26, 2007 from http://www.statcan.ca/Daily/English/020123/d020123a.htm.

Statistics Canada. (2002a). *Women in Canada: Work chapter updates.* Catalogue No. 89F0133XIE. Ottawa: Minister of Industry.

Statistics Canada. (2002b). *Changing conjugal life in Canada.* Catalogue No. 89-576-XIE. Ottawa: Minister of Industry.

Statistics Canada. (2002c). *General social survey—Cycle 15: Family history.* Catalogue No. 89-575-X1E. Ottawa: Minister of Industry.

Statistics Canada. (2003). National longitudinal survey of children and youth: Childhood obesity. Retrieved July 22, 2007 from www.statcan.ca/Daily/English/021018/d021018b.htm.

Statistics Canada. (2004). *The Daily: Canadian Community Health Survey.* Retrieved September 2, 2007 from http://www.statcan.ca/Daily/English/040615/d040615b.htm.

Statistics Canada. (2004). The People: Our Youth. Retrieved July 8, 2007 from http://www.43.statcan.ca/02/02b/02b_004_e.htm.

Statistics Canada. (2005). Diabetes: Introduction. Retrieved on August 7, 2007 from http://www.statcan.ca/english/research/82-619-MIE/82-619-MIE2005002.htm.

Statistics Canada. (2005). The People: High School Graduation. Retrieved October 23, 2007 from http://www43.statcan.ca/02/02c/02c_005f_e.htm.

Statistics Canada. (2005a). *The Daily: Early sexual intercourse, condom use and sexually transmitted diseases.* Retrieved September 2, 2007 from http://www.statcan.ca/Daily/English/050503/d050503a.htm.

Statistics Canada. (2005b). *The Daily: Divorce 2003.* Retrieved October 7, 2007 from http://www.statcan.ca/Daily/English/050309/d050309b.htm.

Statistics Canada. (2005b). *The Daily: National Longitudinal Survey of Children and Youth: Home environment, income and child behaviour.* Retrieved October 24, 2007 from http://www.statcan.ca/Daily/English/050221/d050221b.htm.

Statistics Canada. (2006). Back to School Factbook: Working while in school. Retrieved August 28, 2007 from http://www.statcan.ca/english/freepub/81-004-XIE/2006003/backto.htm.

Statistics Canada. (2006). Canadian community health survey: Obesity among children and adults. Retrieved August 21, 2007 from http://www.statcan.ca/Daily/English/050706/d050706a.htm.

Statistics Canada. (2006). *Deaths 2004.* (Catalogue no. 84F0211XIE). Ottawa, ON: Minister of Industry.

Statistics Canada. (2006). Readiness to learn at school and child and family characteristics. Retrieved August 10, 2006 from http://www.statcan.ca/english/research/89-599-MIE/2006004/results.htm.

Statistics Canada. (2006a). Family Portrait: Continuity and Change in Canadian Families and Households in 2006, 2006 Census. Catalogue No. 97-553-XIE. Ottawa, ON: Ministry of Industry.

Statistics Canada. (2006b). Television viewing, by age and sex, by province. Ottawa, ON: Author. Retrieved November 28, 2007 from http://www40.statcan.ca/l01/cst01/arts23.htm.

Statistics Canada. (2007). Census families, number and average size. Retrieved August 17, 2007 from http://www40.statcan.ca/l01/cst01/famil40.htm.

Statistics Canada. (2007). Deaths, by selected grouped causes, age group and sex, Canada, provinces and territories, annual. Ottawa, ON: Author. Retrieved October 12, 2007 from http://cansim2.statcan.ca/cgi-win/CNSMCGI.PGM.

Statistics Canada. (2007). Family portrait: Continuity and change in Canadian families and households in 2006: National portrait: Individuals: More young adults aged 20 to 29 living in the parental home. Retrieved October 18, 2007 from http://www12.statcan.ca/english/census06/analysis/famhouse/ind7.cfm.

Statistics Canada. (2007). Labour Force Survey. Retrieved on August 16, 2007 from http://www.statcan.ca/Daily/English/051213/d051213c.htm.

Statistics Canada. (undated). Canada's ethnocultural portrait: The changing mosaic. Retrieved August 13 2007 from http://www12.statcan.ca/english/census01/products/analytic/companion/etoimm/canada.cfm.

Staub, E. (1996). Cultural-societal roots of violence: The examples of genocidal violence and of contemporary youth violence in the United States. *American Psychologist, 51,* 117–132.

Stauder, J. E. A., Molenaar, P. C. M., & Van der Molen, M. W. (1993). Scalp topography of event-related brain potentials and cognitive transition during childhood. *Child Development, 64,* 769–788.

Stein, M. A., Mendelsohn, J., Obermeyer, W. H., Amromin, J., & Benca, R. (2001). Sleep and behavior problems in school-aged children. *Pediatrics, 107,* 1–9.

Steinberg, L. (1988). Reciprocal relation between parent–child distance and pubertal maturation. *Developmental Psychology, 24,* 122–128.

Steinberg, L. (2000, January 19). Should juvenile offenders be tried as adults? A developmental perspective on changing legal policies. Paper presented as part of a Congressional Research Briefing entitled "Juvenile Crime: Causes and Consequences." Washington, DC.

Steinberg, L. (2005). Psychological control: Style or substance? In J. Smetana (Ed.), *Changing boundaries of parental authority during adolescence: New directions for child and adolescent development, no. 108* (pp. 71–78). San Francisco: Jossey-Bass.

Steinberg, L., & Darling, N. (1994). The broader context of social influence in adolescence. In R. Silberstein & E. Todt (Eds.), *Adolescence in context.* New York: Springer.

Steinberg, L., & Scott, E. S. (2003). Less guilty by reason of adolescence: Developmental immaturity, diminished responsibility, and the juvenile death penalty. *American Psychologist, 58,* 1009–1018.

Steinman, G. (2006). Mechanisms of twinning: VII. Effect of diet and heredity on the human twinning rate. *The Journal of Reproductive Medicine, 51*(5), 405–410.

Stennes, L. M., Burch, M. M., Sen, M. G., & Bauer, P. J. (2005). A longitudinal study of gendered vocabulary and communicative action in young children. *Developmental Psychology, 41,* 75–88.

Stephens, J. C., Schneider, J. A., Tanguay, D.A., Choi, J., Acharya, T., Stanley, S. E., Jiang, R., Messer, C. J., Chew, A., Han, J.-H., Duan, J.,Carr, J. L., Lee, M.S., Koshy, B.,

Madan Kumar, A., Zhang, G., Newell, W. R., Windemuth, A., Xu, C., Kalbfleisch, T. S., Shaner, S. L., Arnold, K., Schulz, V., Drysdale, C. M., Nandabalan, K., Judson, R. S., Ruano, G., & Vovis, G. F. (2001). Haplotype variation and linkage disequilibrium in 313 human genes. *Science, 293,* 489–493.

Sternberg, R. J. (1984, September). How can we teach intelligence? *Educational Leadership,* pp. 38–50.

Sternberg, R. J. (1985a). *Beyond IQ: A triarchic theory of human intelligence.* New York: Cambridge University Press.

Sternberg, R. J. (1985b, November). Teaching critical thinking, Part I: Are we making critical mistakes? *Phi Delta Kappan,* pp. 194–198.

Sternberg, R. J. (1987, September 23). The use and misuse of intelligence testing: Misunderstanding meaning, users over-rely on scores. *Education Week,* pp. 22, 28.

Sternberg, R. J. (1993). *Sternberg Triarchic Abilities Test.* Unpublished manuscript.

Sternberg, R. J. (1997). The concept of intelligence and its role in lifelong learning and success. *American Psychologist, 52,*1030–1037.

Sternberg, R. J. (1999). A triarchic approach to the understanding and assessment of intelligence in multicultural populations. *Journal of School Psychology, 37,* 145–159.

Sternberg, R. J. (2004). Culture and intelligence. *American Psychologist, 59,* 325–338.

Sternberg, R. J. (2005). There are no public policy implications: A reply to Rushton and Jensen (2005). *Psychology, Public Policy, and Law, 11,* 295–301.

Sternberg, R. J., & Clinkenbeard, P. (1995). A triarchic view of identifying, teaching, and assessing gifted children. *Roeper Review, 17,* 255–260.

Sternberg, R. J., Grigorenko, E. L., & Kidd, K. K. (2005). Intelligence, race, and genetics. *American Psychologist, 60,* 46–59.

Sternberg, R. J., Grigorenko, E. L., & Oh, S. (2001). The development of intelligence at midlife. In M. E. Lachman (Ed.), *Handbook of midlife development* (pp. 217–247). New York: Wiley.

Sternberg, R. J., Torff, B., & Grigorenko, E. L. (1998). Teaching triarchically improves school achievement. *Journal of Educational Psychology, 90*(3), 374–384.

Stevens, J. H., & Bakeman, R. (1985). A factor analytic study of the HOME scale for infants. *Developmental Psychology, 21,* 1106–1203.

Stevenson-Hinde, J., & Shouldice, A. (1996). Fearfulness: Developmental consistency. In A. J. Sameroff & M. M. Haith (Eds.), *The five to seven year shift: The age of reason and responsibility* (pp. 237–252). Chicago: University of Chicago Press.

Stewart, M. J., Neufeld, A., Harrison, M. J. Spitzer, D., Hughes, K. and Makwrimba, E. (2006). Immigrant women family caregivers in Canada: Implications for policies and programmes in health and social sectors. *Health and Social Care in the Community, 14,* 329–340.

Stice, E., & Bearman, K. (2001). Body image and eating disturbances prospectively predict increases in depressive symptoms in adolescent girls: A growth curve analysis. *Developmental Psychology, 37*(5), 597–607.

Stice, E., Presnell, K., & Bearman, S. K. (2001). Relation of early menarche to depression, eating disorders, substance abuse, and comorbid psychopathology among adolescent girls. *Developmental Psychology, 37,* 608–619.

Stice, E., Presnell, K., Shaw, H., & Rohde, P. (2005). Psychological and behavioral risk factors for obesity onset in adolescent girls: A prospective study. *Journal of Consulting and Clinical Psychology, 73,* 195–202.

Stick, S. M., Burton, P. R., Gurrin, L., Sly, P. D., & LeSouëf, P. N. (1996). Effects of maternal smoking during pregnancy and a family history of asthma on respiratory function in newborn infants. *Lancet, 348,* 1060–1064.

Stipek, D. (2002). At what age should children enter kindergarten? A question for policy makers and parents. *SRCD Social Policy Report, 16*(2), 1–16.

Stipek, D. J., & Ryan, R. H. (1997). Economically disadvantaged preschoolers: Ready to learn but further to go. *Developmental Psychology, 33,* 711–723.

Stipek, D. J., Gralinski, H., & Kopp, C. B. (1990). Self-concept development in the toddler years. *Developmental Psychology, 26,* 972–977.

Stipek, D., & Byler, P. (2001). Academic achievement and social behaviors associated with age of entry into kindergarten. *Journal of Applied Developmental Psychology, 22,* 175–189.

Stoecker, J. J., Colombo, J., Frick, J. E., & Allen, J. R. (1998). Long- and short-looking infants' recognition of symmetrical and asymmetrical forms. *Journal of Experimental Child Psychology, 71,* 63–78.

Stoelhorst, M. S. J., Rijken, M., Martens, S. E., Brand, R., den Ouden, A. L., Wit, J.-M., & Veen, S., on behalf of the Leiden Follow-up Project on Prematurity. (2005). Changes in neonatology: Comparison of two cohorts of very preterm infants (gestational age <32 weeks): The Project on Preterm and Small for Gestational Age Infants 1983 and the Leiden Follow-up Project on Prematurity 1996–1997. *Pediatrics, 115,* 396–405.

Stoll, B. J., Hansen, N. I., Adams-Chapman, I., Fanaroff, A. A., Hintz, S. R., Vohr, B., & Higgins, R. D., for the National Institute of Child Health and Human Development Neonatal Research Network. (2004). Neurodevelopmental and growth impairment among extremely low-birth-weight infants with neonatal infection. *Journal of the American Medical Association, 292,* 2357–2365.

Strassberg, Z., Dodge, K. A., Pettit, G. S., & Bates, J. E. (1994). Spanking in the home and children's subsequent aggression toward kindergarten peers. *Development and Psychopathology, 6,* 445–461.

Straus, M. A. (1994a). *Beating the devil out of them: Corporal punishment in American families.* San Francisco, CA: Jossey-Bass.

Straus, M. A. (1994b). Should the use of corporal punishment by parents be considered child abuse? In M. A. Mason & E. Gambrill (Eds.), *Debating children's lives: Current controversies on children and adolescents* (pp. 196–222). Newbury Park, CA: Sage.

Straus, M. A. (1999). The benefits of avoiding corporal punishment: New and more definitive evidence. Paper presented at the Changing Family and Child Development Conference, Banff, Alberta, Canada.

Straus, M. A., & Paschall, M. J. (1999, July). *Corporal punishment by mothers and children's cognitive development: A longitudinal study of two age cohorts.* Paper presented at the Sixth International Family Violence Research Conference, University of New Hampshire, Durham, NH.

Straus, M. A., & Stewart, J. H. (1999). Corporal punishment by American parents: National data on prevalence, chronicity, severity, and duration, in relation to child and family characteristics. *Clinical Child and Family Psychology Review, 2*(2), 55–70.

Straus, M. A., Sugarman, D. B., & Giles-Sims, J. (1997). Spanking by parents and subsequent antisocial behavior of children. *Archives of Pediatric and Adolescent Medicine, 151,* 761–767.

Straus, M. A., & Field, C. J. (2003). Psychological aggression by American parents: National data on prevalence, chronicity, and severity. *Journal of Marriage and Family, 65,* 795–808.

Straus, M. A., & Stewart, J. H. (1999). Corporal punishment by American parents: National data on prevalence, chronicity, severity, and duration, in relation to child and family characteristics. *Clinical Child and Family Psychology Review, 2*(21), 55–70.

Streissguth, A. P., Aase, J. M., Clarren, S. K., Randels, S. P., LaDue, R. A., & Smith, D. F. (1991). Fetal alcohol syndrome in adolescents and adults. *Journal of the American Medical Association, 265,* 1961–1967.

Streissguth, A. P., Martin, D. C., Barr, H. M., Sandman, B. M., Kirchner, G. L., & Darby, B. L. (1984). Intrauterine alcohol and nicotine exposure: Attention and reaction time in 4-year-old children. *Developmental Psychology, 20,* 533–541.

Striano, T. (2004). Direction of regard and the still-face effect in the first year: Does intention matter? *Child Development, 75,* 468–479.

Strobel, A., Camoin, T. I. L., Ozata, M., & Strosberg, A. D. (1998). A leptin missense mutation associated with hypogonadism and morbid obesity. *Nature Genetics, 18,* 213–215.

Strohschein, L. (2005). Parental divorce and child mental health trajectories. *Journal of Marriage and Family, 67,* 1286–1300.

Strömland, K., & Hellström, A. (1996). Fetal alcohol syndrome: An ophthalmological and socioeducational prospective study. *Pediatrics, 97,* 845–850.

Stuart, J. (1991). Introduction. In Z. Zhensun & A. Low, *A young painter: The life and paintings of Wang Yani—China's extraordinary young artist* (pp. 6–7). New York: Scholastic.

Stubbs, M. L., Rierdan, J., & Koff, E. (1989). Developmental differences in menstrual attitudes. *Journal of Early Adolescence, 9*(4), 480–498.

Stuebe, A. M., Rich-Edwards, J. W., Willett, W. C., Manson, J. E., & Michels, K. B. (2005). Duration of lactation and incidence of type 2 diabetes. *Journal of the American Medical Association, 294,* 2601–2610.

Sturges, J. W., & Sturges, L. V. (1998). In vivo systematic desensitization in a single-session treatment of an 11-year-old girl's elevator phobia. *Child & Family Behavior Therapy, 20,* 55–62.

Stuttering Foundation. (2006). *Stuttering: Straight talk for teachers* (Pub. No. 0125). Memphis, TN: Author.

Subar, A. F., Krebs-Smith, S. M., Cook, A., & Kahle, L. L. (1998). Dietary sources of nutrients among U.S. children, 1989–1991. *Pediatrics, 102,* 913–923.

Substance Abuse and Mental Health Services Administration (SAMHSA). (2004, October 22). Alcohol dependence or abuse and age at first use. *The NSDUH Report.* Retrieved December 18, 2004, from http://oas.samhsa.gov/2k4/ageDependence/ageDependence.htm.

Sudden Infant Death Syndrome. *New England Journal of Medicine, 351,* 978–986.

Suddendorf, T. (2003). Early representational insight: 24-month-olds can use a photo to find an object in the world. *Child Development, 74,* 896–904.

Suicide: Part I. (1996, November). *The Harvard Mental Health Letter,* pp. 1–5.

Sullivan, P. (1994). Growth in membership of phys-ed lobby group sign of growing concern about children's fitness. *Canadian Medical Association Journal, 151,* 634–635.

Sun, Y. (2001). Family environment and adolescents' well-being before and after parents' marital disruption. *Journal of Marriage and the Family, 63,* 697–713.

Suomi, S., & Harlow, H. (1972). Social rehabilitation of isolate-reared monkeys. *Developmental Psychology, 6,* 487–496.

Surkan, P. J., Stephansson, O., Dickman, P. W., & Cnattingius, S. (2004). Previous preterm and small-for-gestational-age births and the subsequent risk of stillbirth. *New England Journal of Medicine, 350,* 777–785.

Susman, E. J., & Rogol, A. (2004). Puberty and psychological development. In R. M. Lerner & L. Steinberg (Eds.), *Handbook of adolescent psychology* (2 ed.) (pp. 15–44). Hoboken, NJ: Wiley.

Susman-Stillman, A., Kalkoske, M., Egeland, B., & Waldman, I. (1996). Infant temperament and maternal sensitivity as predictors of attachment security. *Infant Behavior and Development, 19,* 33–47.

Susser, E. S., & Lin, S. P. (1992). Schizophrenia after prenatal exposure to the Dutch hunger winter of 1944–1945. *Archives of General Psychiatry, 49,* 983–988.

Sutcliffe, A., Loft, A., Wennerholm, U. B., Tarlatzis, V., & Bonduelle, M. (2003, July). The European study of 1,523 ICSI/IVF versus naturally conceived 5-year-old children and their families: Physical development at five years. Paper presented at conference of European Society of Human Reproduction and Embryology, Madrid.

Sutherland, N. (2000). *Children in English-Canadian society: Framing the twentieth-century consensus.* Waterloo, ON: Wilfrid Laurier University Press.

Suzuki, D. (2000). The nature of things. In H. Newbold (Ed.), *Life stories: World renowned scientists reflect on their lives and the future of life on earth* (pp. 55–73). Berkeley, CA: University of California Press.

Suzuki, L. A., & Valencia, R. R. (1997). Race-ethnicity and measured intelligence: Educational implications. *American Psychologist, 52,* 1103–1114.

Swain, I. U., Zelazo, P. R., & Clifton, R. K. (1993). Newborn infants' memory for speech sounds retained over 24 hours. *Developmental Psychology, 29,* 312–323.

Swain, M., & Lapkin, S. (1991). Additive bilingualism and French immersion education: The roles of language proficiency and literacy. In A. G. Reynolds (Ed.), *Bilingualism, multiculturalism, and second language learning: The McGill conference in honour of Wallace E. Lambert* (pp. 203–216). Hillsdale, NJ: Lawrence Erlbaum Associates.

Swallen, K. C., Reither, E. N., Haas, S. A., & Meier, A. M. (2005). Overweight, obesity, and health-related quality of life among adolescents: The National Longitudinal Study of Adolescent Health. *Pediatrics, 115,* 340–347.

Swan, S. H. (2000). Intrauterine exposure to diethylstilbestrol: Long-term effects in humans. *APMIS, 108,* 793–804.

Swan, S. H., Kruse, R. L., Liu, F., Barr, D. B., Drobnis, E. Z., Redmon, J. B., Wang, C., Brazil, C., Overstreet, J. W., & Study for Future Families Research Group. (2003). Semen quality in relation to biomarkers of pesticide exposure. *Environmental Health Perspectives, 111,* 1478–1484.

Swanston, H. Y., Tebbutt, J. S., O'Toole, B. I., & Oates, R. K. (1997). Sexually abused children

5 years after presentation: A case-control study. *Pediatrics, 100,* 600–608.

Swarr, A. E., & Richards, M. H. (1996). Longitudinal effects of adolescent girls' pubertal development, perceptions of pubertal timing, and parental relations on eating problems. *Developmental Psychology, 32,* 636–646.

Swedo, S., Rettew, D. C., Kuppenheimer, M., Lum, D., Dolan, S., & Goldberger, E. (1991). Can adolescent suicide attemptors be distinguished from at-risk adolescents? *Pediatrics, 88*(3), 620–629.

Swingley, D., & Fernald, A. (2002). Recognition of words referring to present and absent objects by 24-month olds. *Journal of Memory and Language, 46,* 39–56.

Symons, D., & Carr, T. (1995). Maternal employment and early infant social development: Process and policy. In K. Covell (Ed.), *Readings in child development: A Canadian perspective.* Toronto: Nelson Canada.

Symons, D. K. (1998). Post-partum employment patterns, family-based care arrangements, and the mother–infant relationship at age two. *Canadian Journal of Behavioural Science, 30,* 121–131.

Symons, D. K. & Clark, S. E. (2000). A longitudinal study of mother–child relationships and theory of mind in the preschool period. *Social Development, 9,* 3–23.

Szaflarski, J. P., Holland, S. K., Schmithorst, V. J., & Weber-Byars, A. (2004). An fMRI study of cerebral language lateralization in 121 children and adults. Paper presented at the 56th Annual Meeting of the American Academy of Neurology, San Francisco, CA.

Szkrybalo, J., & Ruble, D. N. (1999). "God made me a girl": Sex category constancy judgments and explanations revisited. *Developmental Psychology, 35,* 392–403.

Szkrybalo, J., & Ruble, D. N. (1999). God made me a girl: Sex category constancy judgments and explanations revisited. *Developmental Psychology, 35,* 392–403.

Tackett, J. L., Krueger, R. F., Iacono, W. G. & McGue, M. (2005). Symptom-based subfactors of DSM-defined conduct disorder: Evidence for etiologic distinctions. *Journal of Abnormal Psychology, 114,* 483–487.

Taddio, A., Nulman, L., Goldbach, M., Ipp, M., & Koren, G. (1994). Use of lidocain-prilocain cream for vaccination pain in infants. *Journal of Pediatrics, 124,* 643–648.

Takanishi, R. (1993). The opportunities of adolescence: Research, interventions, and policy. *American Psychologist, 48,* 85–87.

Talwar, V., & Lee, K. (2002). Development of lying to conceal a transgression: Children's control of expressive behavior during verbal deception. *International Journal of Behavioral Development.*

Tamburro, R. F., Gordon, P. L., D'Apolito, J. P., & Howard, S. C. (2004). Unsafe and violent behavior in commercials aired during televised major sporting events. *Pediatrics, 114,* 694–698.

Tamis-LeMonda, C. S., Bornstein, M. H., & Baumwell, L. (2001). Maternal responsiveness and children's achievement of language milestones. *Child Development, 72*(3), 748–767.

Tamis-LeMonda, C. S., Shannon, J. D., Cabrera, N. J., & Lamb, M. E. (2004). Fathers and mothers at play with their 2- and 3-year-olds: Contributions to language and cognitive development. *Child Development, 75,* 1806–1820.

Tan, N. C., Lim, L. H. & Gu, K. (2003). Factors influencing caregiver's use of an infant walker. *Asia Pacific Family Medicine, 2,* 16–22.

Tanda, G., Pontieri, F. E., & DiChiara, G. (1997). Cannabinoid and heroin activation of mesolimbic dopamine transmission by a common N1 opiod receptor mechanism. *Science, 276,* 2048–2050.

Tao, K.-T. (1998). An overview of only child family mental health in China. *Psychiatry and Clinical Neurosciences, 52*(Suppl.), S206–S211.

Tarabulsy, G. M., Provost, M.A., Deslandes, J., St-Laurent, D., Moss, E., Lemelin, E., Bernier, A., & Dassylva, J. (2003). Individual differences in infant stillface response at 6 months. *Infant Behavior & Development, 26,* 421–438.

Tarasuk, V. (2005). Household food insecurity in Canada. *Lippincott Williams & Wilkins, 4,* 299–312.

Task Force on Suicide in Canada. (1994). *Suicide in Canada: Update of the Report of the Task Force on Suicide in Canada.* Ottawa, ON: Minister of National Health and Welfare. Retrieved November 29, 2007 from http://www.phac-aspc.gc.ca/mh-sm/pdf/suicid_e.pdf.

Taylor, J. A., Krieger, J. W., Reay, D. T., Davis, R. L., Harruff, R., & Cheney, L. K. (1996). Prone sleep position and the sudden infant death syndrome in King's County, Washington: A case-control study. *Journal of Pediatrics, 128,* 626–630.

Taylor, M. (1997). The role of creative control and culture in children's fantasy/reality judgments. *Child Development, 68,* 1015–1017.

Taylor, M. G. (1996). The development of children's beliefs about social and biological aspects of gender differences. *Child Development, 67,* 1555–1571.

Taylor, M., & Carlson, S. M. (1997). The relation between individual differences in fantasy and theory of mind. *Child Development, 68,* 436–455.

Taylor, M., Carlson, S. M., Maring, B. L., Gerow, L., & Charley, C. M. (2004). The characteristics and correlates of fantasy in school-age children: Imaginary companions, impersonation, and social understanding. *Developmental Psychology, 40,* 1173–1187.

Taylor, M., Cartwright, B. S., & Carlson, S. M. (1993). A developmental investigation of children's imaginary companions. *Developmental Psychology, 28,* 276–285.

Taylor, R. D., & Roberts, D. (1995). Kinship support in maternal and adolescent well-being in economically disadvantaged African-American families. *Child Development, 66,* 1585–1597.

Taylor, S., Way, B., Welch, W., Hilmert, C., Lehman, B., & Eisenberger, N. (2006). Early family environment, current adversity, the serotonin transporter promoter polymorphism, and depressive symptomatology. *Biological Psychiatry, 60*(7), 671–676.

Teachman, J. D., Paasch, K., & Carver, K. (1996). Social capital and dropping out of school early. *Journal of Marriage and the Family, 58,* 773–783.

Teachman, J. D., Tedrow, L. M., & Crowder, K. D. (2000). The changing demography of America's families. *Journal of Marriage and Family, 62,* 1234–1246.

Teen sex down, new study shows: Secretary Shalala announces new teen pregnancy prevention grant programs [Press release]. (1997, May 1). Washington, DC: National Center for Health Statistics.

Teller, D. Y., & Bornstein, M. H. (1987). Infant color vision and color perception. In P. Salapatek & L. B. Cohen (Eds.), *Handbook of infant perception: Vol. 1. From sensation to perception* (pp. 185–236). Orlando, FL: Academic Press.

Teplin, L. A., McClelland, G. M., Abram, K. M., & Mileusnic, D. (2005). Early violent death among delinquent youth: A prospective study. *Pediatrics, 115,* 1586–1593.

Terman, L. M., & Oden, M. H. (1959). *Genetic studies of genius: Vol. 5. The gifted group at mid-life.* Stanford, CA: Stanford University Press.

Termine, N. T., & Izard, C. E. (1988). Infants' responses to their mothers' expressions of joy and sadness. *Developmental Psychology, 24,* 223–229.

Tesman, J. R., & Hills, A. (1994). Developmental effects of lead exposure in children. *Social Policy Report of the Society for Research in Child Development, 8*(3), 1–16.

Tester, D. J., Carturan, E., Dura, M., Reiken, S., Wronska, A., Marks, A. R., & Ackerman, M. J. (2006, May). *Molecular and functional characterization of novel RyR2-encoded cardiac ryanodine receptor/ calcium release channel mutations in sudden infant death syndrome.* Presentation at Heart Rhythm 2006, the 27th Annual Scientific Sessions of the Heart Rhythm Society, Boston.

Test-tube baby: It's a girl. (1978, August 7). *Time,* p. 68.

Teti, D. M., & Ablard, K. E. (1989). Security of attachment and infant–sibling relationships: A laboratory study. *Child Development, 60,* 1519–1528.

Teti, D. M., Gelfand, D. M., Messinger, D. S., & Isabella, R. (1995). Maternal depression and the quality of early attachment: An examination of infants, preschoolers, and their mothers. *Developmental Psychology, 31,* 364–376.

Teti, D. M., Sakin, J. W., Kucera, E., Corns, K. M., & Eiden, R. D. (1996). And baby makes four: Predictors of attachment security among preschool-age firstborns during the transition to siblinghood. *Child Development, 67,* 579–596.

Thacker, S. B., Addiss, D. G., Goodman, R. A., Holloway, B. R., & Spencer, H. C. (1992). Infectious diseases and injuries in child day care: Opportunities for healthier children. *Journal of the American Medical Association, 268,* 1720–1726.

Thal, D., Tobias, S., & Morrison, D. (1991). Language and gesture in late talkers: A one-year follow-up. *Journal of Speech and Hearing Research, 34,* 604–612.

Thapar, A., Fowler, T., Rice, F., Scourfield, J., van den Bree, M., Thomas, H., Harold, G., & Hay, D. (2003). Maternal smoking during pregnancy and attention deficit hyperactivity disorder symptoms in offspring. *American Journal of Psychiatry, 160,* 1985–1989.

Thapar, A., Langley, K., Fowler, T., Rice, F., Turic, D., Whittinger, N., Aggleton, J., Van den Bree, M., Owen, M., & O'Donovan, M. (2005). Catechol O-methyltransferase gene variant and birth weight predict early-onset antisocial behavior in children with attention-deficit/hyperactivity disorder. *Archives of General Psychiatry, 62,* 1275–1278.

The first test-tube baby. (1978, July 31). *Time,* pp. 58–70.

The Health of Canada's Children: A CICH Profile. (undated). Families in crisis. Retrieved July 25, 2007 from http://www.cich.ca/PDFFiles/ProfileFactSheets/English/FamilyCrisis.pdf.

The John Howard Society of Newfoundland. (1998). *Youth and the criminal justice system: Some highlights of youth crime and the treatment of young offenders in Canada.* St. John's, NF: Author.

Thelen, E. (1995). Motor development: A new synthesis. *American Psychologist, 50*(2), 79–95.

Thelen, E., & Fisher, D. M. (1982). Newborn stepping: An explanation for a "disappearing" reflex. *Developmental Psychology, 18,* 760–775.

Thelen, E., & Fisher, D. M. (1983). The organization of spontaneous leg movements in newborn infants. *Journal of Motor Behavior, 15,* 353–377.

Theodore, A. D., Chang, J. J., Runyan, D. K., Hunter, W. M., Bangdiwala, S. I., & Agans, R. (2005). Epidemiological features of the physical and sexual maltreatment of children in the Carolinas. *Pediatrics, 115,* 331–337.

Thoma, S. J., & Rest, J. R. (1999). The relationship between moral decision making and patterns of consolidation and transition in moral judgment development. *Developmental Psychology, 35,* 323–334.

Thomas, A., & Chess, S. (1977). *Temperament and development.* New York: Brunner/Mazel.

Thomas, A., & Chess, S. (1984). Genesis and evolution of behavioral disorders: From infancy to early adult life. *American Journal of Orthopsychiatry, 141*(1), 1–9.

Thomas, A., Chess, S., & Birch, H. G. (1968). *Temperament and behavior disorders in children.* New York: New York University Press.

Thomas, R. M. (1996). *Comparing theories of child development* (4th ed.). Pacific Grove, CA: Brooks-Cole.

Thomas, W. P., & Collier, V. P. (1997). *School effectiveness for language minority students.* Washington, DC: National Clearinghouse for Bilingual Education.

Thomas, W. P., & Collier, V. P. (1998). Two languages are better than one. *Educational Leadership, 55*(4), 23–28.

Thompson, A. M., Campagna, P. D., Rehman, L. A., Murphy, R. J. L., Rasmussen, R. L. & Ness, G. W. (2005). Physical activity and body mass index in grade 3, 7, and 11 Nova Scotia students. *Official Journal of the American College of Sports Medicine, 37,* 1902–1908.

Thompson, D. C., Rivara, F. P., & Thompson, R. S. (1996). Effectiveness of bicycle safety helmets in preventing head injuries: A case-control study. *Journal of the American Medical Association, 276,* 1968–1973.

Thompson, P. M., Cannon, T. D., Narr, K. L., van Erp, T., Poutanen, V., Huttunen, M., Lonnqvist, J., Standertskjold-Nordenstam, C., Kaprio, J., Khaledy, M., Dail, R., Zoumalan, C.I., & Toga, A. W. (2001). Genetic influences on brain structure. *Nature Neuroscience, 4,* 1253–1258.

Thompson, P. M., Giedd, J. N., Woods, R. P., MacDonald, D., Evans, A. C., & Toga, A. W. (2000). Growth patterns in the developing brain detected by using continuum mechanical tensor maps. *Nature, 404,* 190–193.

Thompson, R. A. (1990). Vulnerability in research: A developmental perspective on research risk. *Child Development, 61,* 1–16.

Thompson, R. A. (1991). Emotional regulation and emotional development. *Educational Psychology Review, 3,* 269–307.

Thompson, R. A. (1998). Early sociopersonality development. In W. Damon (Series Ed.) & N. Eisenberg (Vol. Ed.), *Handbook of child psychology: Vol. 3. Social, emotional, and personality development* (4th ed., pp. 25–104). New York: Wiley.

Thompson, S. L. (2001). The social skills of previously institutionalized children adopted from Romania. *Dissertation Abstracts International: Section B. The Sciences and Engineering, 61(7-B),* 3906.

Thomson, E., Mosley, J., Hanson, T. L., & McLanahan, S. S. (2001). Remarriage, cohabitation, and changes in mothering behavior. *Journal of Marriage and Family, 63,* 370–380.

Thorne, A., & Michaelieu, Q. (1996). Situating adolescent gender and self-esteem with personal memories. *Child Development, 67,* 1374–1390.

Tiedemann, D. (1897). *Beobachtungen über die entwickelung der seelenfähigkeiten bei kindern* [Record of an infant's life]. Altenburg, Germany: Oscar Bonde. (Original work published 1787)

Tilghman, S. M. (1999). The sins of the fathers and mothers: Genomic imprinting in mammalian development. *Cell, 96,* 185–193.

Timiras, P. S. (1972). *Developmental psychology and aging.* New York: Macmillan.

TIMSS International Study Center. (1998). *Mathematics and achievement in the final year of secondary school: IEA's Third International Mathematics and Science Report.* Chestnut Hill, MA: Author.

Tincoff, R., & Jusczyk, P. W. (1999). Some beginnings of word comprehension in 6-month-olds. *Psychological Science, 10,* 172–177.

Tisak, M. S., & Tisak, J. (1996). My sibling's but not my friend's keeper: Reasoning about responses to aggressive acts. *Journal of Early Adolescence, 16,* 324–329.

Tisdale, S. (1988). The mother. *Hippocrates, 2*(3), 64–72.

Tjepkema, M. (2004). Use of cannabis and other illicit drugs. In Statistics Canada Catalogue No. 82-003-XIE, *Health Reports, 15 (4),* 43–47.

Today's Family News. (undated). Stats and facts. Retrieved on August 2, 2007 from http://www.fotf.ca/tfn/family/statsFacts/Stats&Facts.htm.

Toga, A. W., Thompson, P. M., & Sowell, E. R. (2006). Mapping brain maturation. *Trends in Neurosciences, 29(3),* 148–159.

Tolan, P. H., Gorman-Smith, D., & Henry, D. B. (2003). The developmental ecology of urban males' youth violence. *Developmental Psychology, 39,* 274–291.

Tomlinson, M., Cooper, P., & Murray, L. (2005). The mother-infant relationship and infant attachment in a South African peri-urban settlement. *Child Development, 76,* 1044–1054.

Tong, S., Baghurst, P. A., Sawyer, M. G., Burns, J., & McMichael, A. J. (1998). Declining blood lead levels and changes in cognitive function during childhood: The Port Pirie Cohort Study. *Journal of the American Medical Association, 280,* 1915–1919.

Torrance, E. P. (1966). *The Torrance Tests of Creative Thinking: Technical-norms manual* (Research ed.). Princeton, NJ: Personnel Press.

Torrance, E. P. (1974). *The Torrance Tests of Creative Thinking: Technical-norms manual.* Bensonville, IL: Scholastic Testing Service.

Torrance, E. P., & Ball, O. E. (1984). *Torrance Tests of Creative Thinking: Streamlined (revised) manual, Figural A and B.* Bensonville, IL: Scholastic Testing Service.

Totsika, V., & Sylva, K. (2004). The Home Observation for Measurement of the Environment revisited. *Child and Adolescent Mental Health, 9,* 25–35.

Townsend, N. W. (1997). Men, migration, and households in Botswana: An exploration of connections over time and space. *Journal of Southern African Studies, 23,* 405–420.

Townson, M. (2000). A report card on women's poverty. Canadian Centre on Policy Alternatives.

Trainor, C., & Mihorean, K. (Eds.). (2001). *Family violence in Canada: A statistical profile.* Ottawa: Canadian Centre for Justice Statistics and Statistics Canada.

Tramontana, M. G., Hooper, S. R., & Selzer, S. C. (1988). Research on the preschool prediction of later academic achievement: A review. *Developmental Review, 8,* 89–146.

Trautner, H. M., Ruble, D. N., Cyphers, L., Kirsten, B., Behrendt, R., & Hartmann, P. (2005). Rigidity and flexibility of gender stereotypes in childhood: Developmental or differential? *Infant and Child Development, 14,* 365–381.

Treasury Board of Canada Secretariat. (2005). Canada's performance report 2005–annex 3–indicators and additional information. Retrieved from www.tbs-sct.gc.ca/report/govrev/05/ann304_e.asp on July 15, 2007.

Treffers, P. E., Hanselaar, A. G., Helmerhorst, T. J., Koster, M. E., & van Leeuwen, F. E. (2001). [Consequences of diethylstilbestrol during pregnancy; 50 years later still a significant problem.] *Ned Tijdschr Geneeskd, 145,* 675–680.

Tremblay, D. G. (2007). *"More time for daddy." Quebec leads the way with its new parental leave policy.* Canadian Centre for Policy Alternatives. Retrieved July 22, 2007, from http://policyalternatives.ca/MonitorIssues/2007/02/MonitorIssue1593/index.cfm?pa=8E767075.

Tremblay, M. S., & Willms, J. D. (2000). Secular trends in the body mass index of Canadian children. *Canadian Medical Association Journal, 163,* 1429–1433.

Tremblay, R. E., Boulerice, B., Harden, P. W., McDuff, P., Perusse, D., Pihl, R. O., & Zoccolillo, M. (1996). Do children in Canada become more aggressive as they approach adolescence? In Human Resources Development Canada & Statistics Canada, *Growing up in Canada: National Longitudinal Survey of Children and Youth.* Ottawa: Author.

Trimble, J. E., & Dickson, R. (2005). Ethnic gloss. In C. B. Fisher & R. M. Lerner (Eds.), *Encyclopedia of applied developmental science* (Vol. I, pp. 412-415). Thousand Oaks, CA: Sage.

Trocmé, N. et al. (2005). *Canadian Incidence Study of Reported Child Abuse and Neglect, 2003: Major Findings.* Ottawa, ON: Public Health Agency of

Trocmé, N., & Wolfe, D. (2001). *Child maltreatment in Canada: Selected results from the Canadian Incidence Study of Reported Child Abuse and Neglect.* Ottawa: Minister of Public Works and Government Services Canada.

Trocmé, N., MacLaurin, B., Fallon, B., Daciuk, J., Billingsley, D., Tourigny, M., Mayer, M., Wright, J., Barter, K., Burford, G., Hornick, J., Sullivan, R., & McKenzie, B. (2001). *Canadian incidence study of reported child abuse and neglect: Final report.* Ottawa: Health Canada.

Trocmé, N., MacMillan, H, Fallon, B., & De Marco, R. (2003). Nature and severity of physical harm caused by child abuse and neglect: Results from the Canadian Incidence Study. *Canadian Medical Association Journal, 169(9),* 911–915.

Troiano, R. P. (2002). Physical inactivity among young people. *New England Journal of Medicine, 347,* 706–707.

Tronick, E. (1972). Stimulus control and the growth of the infant's visual field. *Perception and Psychophysics, 11,* 373–375.

Tronick, E. Z. (1980). On the primacy of social skills. In D. B. Sawin, L. O. Walker, &

J. H. Penticuff (Eds.), *The exceptional infant: Psychosocial risk in infant environment transactions*. New York: Brunner/Mazel.

Tronick, E. Z. (1989). Emotions and emotional communication in infants. *American Psychologist, 44*(2), 112–119.

Tronick, E. Z., Morelli, G. A., & Ivey, P. (1992). The Efe forager infant and toddler's pattern of social relationships: Multiple and simultaneous. *Developmental Psychology, 28,* 568–577.

Troseth, G. L., Saylor, M. M., & Archer, A. H. (2006). Young children's use of video as a source of socially relevant information. *Child Development, 77,* 786–799.

Tryba, A. K., Peña, F., & Ramirez, J. M. (2006). Gasping activity in vitro: A rhythm dependent on 5-HT2A receptors. *Journal of Neuroscience, 26*(10), 2623–2634.

Tsai, J., & Floyd, R. L. (2004). Alcohol consumption among women who are pregnant or who might become pregnant—United States, 2002. *Morbidity and Mortality Weekly Report, 53*(50), 1178–1181.

Tsao, F. M., Liu, H. M., and Kuhl, P. K. (2004). Speech perception in infancy predicts language development in the second year of life: A longitudinal study. *Child Development, 75,* 1067–1084.

Tucker, P., Irwin, J. D. Bouck, L. M. & Pollett, G. (2006). Preventing paediatric obesity; recommendations from a community-based qualitative investigation. *Obesity Reviews, 7,* 251–260.

Turati, C., Simion, F., Milani, I., & Umilta, C. (2002). Newborns' preference for faces: What is crucial? *Developmental Psychology, 38,* 875–882.

Turkheimer, E., Haley, A., Waldron, J., D'Onofrio, B., & Gottesman, I. I. (2003). Socioeconomic status modifies heritability of IQ in young children. *Psychological Science, 14,* 623–628.

Turnbull, M., Hart, D. & Lapkin, S. (2003). Grade 6 French immersion student's performance on large-scale reading, writing and mathematics tests: Building Explanations. *Alberta Journal of Educational Research, 49,* 6–23.

Turner, C. F., Ku, L., Rogers, S. M., Lindberg, L. D., Pleck, J. H., & Sonenstein, F. L. (1998). Adolescent sexual behavior, drug use, and violence: Increased reporting with computer survey technology. *Science, 280,* 867–873.

Turner, P. J., & Gervai, J. (1995). A multidimensional study of gender typing in preschool children and their parents: Personality, attitudes, preferences, behavior, and cultural differences. *Developmental Psychology, 31,* 759–772.

Turrisi, R., Wiersman, K. A., & Hughes, K. K. (2000). Binge-drinking-related consequences in college students: Role of drinking beliefs and mother-teen communication. *Psychology of Addictive Behaviors, 14*(4), 342–345.

Tuulio-Henriksson, A., Haukka, J., Partonen, T., Varilo, T., Paunio, T., Ekelund, J., Cannon, T. D., Meyer, J. M., & Lonnqvist, J. (2002). Heritability and number of quantitative trait loci of neurocognitive functions in families with schizophrenia. *American Journal of Medical Genetics, 114*(5), 483–490.

Twenge, J. M. (2000). The age of anxiety? Birth cohort change in anxiety and neuroticism, 1952–1993. *Journal of Personality and Social Psychology, 79,*1007–1021.

U.S. Bureau of the Census. (1998). *Household and family characteristics: March 1998* (Update) (Current Population Reports, P20-514). Washington, DC: U.S. Government Printing Office.

U.S. Census Bureau. (2003). *Population in the United States: Population characteristics. June, 2002.* Washington, DC: U.S. Government Printing Office.

U.S. Consumer Product Safety Commission. (1991). *Statistics on shopping cart safety.* Washington, DC: Author.

U.S. Department of Agriculture & U.S. & Department of Health and Human Services. (2000). *Dietary guidelines for Americans* (5th ed.), USDA Home and Garden Bulletin No. 232. Washington, DC: U.S. Department of Agriculture.

U.S. Department of Health and Human Services (USDHHS). (1996). *HHS releases study of relationship between family structure and adolescent substance abuse* [Press release]. Retrieved September 24, 2002, from http://www. hhs.gov/news/press/1996pres/960906b.html

U.S. Department of Health and Human Services (USDHHS). (1999a). *Blending perspectives and building common ground: A report to Congress on substance abuse and child protection.* Washington, DC: U.S. Government Printing Office.

U.S. Department of Health and Human Services (USDHHS). (1999b). *Healthy People 2000 Review* (PHS 99–1256). Washington, DC: Author.

U.S. Department of Health and Human Services (USDHHS). (1999c). *Healthy People 2000 Review* (PHS 99-1256). Washington, DC: Author.

U.S. Department of Health and Human Services (USDHHS). (2004). *Child maltreatment 2002.*

U.S. Department of Health and Human Services Administration on Children, Youth, and Families. (2006). *Child maltreatment 2004.* Washington, DC: U.S. Government Printing Office.

U.S. Department of Health and Human Services (USDHHS), Administration on Children, Youth, and Families. (2006). *Child maltreatment 2006.* Washington, DC: U.S. Government Printing Office.

U. S. Department of Health and Human Services Maternal and Child Health Bureau. (2005). *Newborn screening: Toward a uniform screening panel and system—Report for public comment.* Retrieved September 13, 2005, from www.mchb.hrsa.gov/screening.

U.S. Environmental Protection Agency. (1994). *Setting the record straight: Secondhand smoke is a preventable health risk* (EPA Publication No. 402-F-94-005). Washington, DC: U.S. Government Printing Office.

U. S. Preventive Services Task Force. (2006). Screening for speech and language delay in preschool children: Recommendation statement. *Pediatrics, 117,* 497–501.

Umberger, F. G., & Van Reenen, J. S. (1995). Thumb sucking management: A review. *International Journal of Orofacial Myology, 21,* 41–47.

UNAIDS. (2006). Report on the global AIDS epidemic. Geneva: Author.

UNAIDS/WHO Joint United Nations Programme on HIV/AIDS and World Health Organization (2004). *AIDS epidemic update* (Publication No. UNAIDS/04.45E). Geneva: Author.

UNESCO. (2004). *Education for All Global Monitoring Report 2005—The quality imperative.* Retrieved November 10, 2004 from http://www.unesco.org/ education/ GMR2005/press

UNICEF. (2002). Official summary of *The State of the World's Children 2002.* Retrieved September 19, 2002, from http://www.unicef. org/pubsgen/sowc02summary/index.html.

UNICEF. (2003). *Social monitor 2003.* Florence, Italy: Innocenti Social Monitor, UNICEF Innocenti Research Centre.

United Nations Children's Fund and World Health Organization (WHO). (2004). *Low birthweight: Country, regional and global estimates.* New York: UNICEF.

University of Virginia Health System. (2004). How chromosome abnormalities happen: Meiosis, mitosis, maternal age, environment. Retrieved September 16, 2004, from http:// www.healthsystem.virginia.edu/UVAHealth/ peds_genetics/happen.cfm.

Vainio, S., Heikkiia, M., Kispert, A., Chin, N., & McMahon, A. P. (1999). Female development in mammals is regulated by Wnt-4 signalling. *Nature, 397,* 405–409.

Valadez-Meltzer, A., Silber, T. J., Meltzer, A. A., & D'Angelo, L. J. (2005). Will I be alive in 2005? Adolescent level of involvement in risk behaviors and belief in near-future death. *Pediatrics, 116,* 24–31.

Valeski, T. N., & Stipek, D. J. (2001). Young children's feelings about school. *Child Development, 72*(4), 1198–1213.

Van, P. (2001). Breaking the silence of African American women: Healing after pregnancy loss. *Health Care Women International, 22,* 229–243.

Van de Vijver, F. J. R. (2002). Cross-cultural assessment: Value for money? *Applied Psychology: An International Review, 51,* 545–566.

Van de Vijver, F. J. R. & Phalet, K. (2004). Assessment in multicultural groups: The role of acculturation. *Applied Psychology: An International Review, 53,* 215–236.

Van de Vijver, F. J. R. & Tanzer, N. K. (2004). Bias and equivalence in cross-cultural assessment: An overview. *Revue Europeenne de Psychologie Appliquee, 54,* 119–135.

Van den Boom, D. C. (1989). Neonatal irritability and the development of attachment. In G. A. Kohnstamm, J. E. Bates, & M. K. Rothbart (Eds.), *Temperament in childhood* (pp. 299– 318). Chichester, England: Wiley.

Van den Boom, D. C. (1994). The influence of temperament and mothering on attachment and exploration: An experimental manipulation of sensitive responsiveness among lower-class mothers with irritable infants. *Child Development, 65,* 1457–1477.

Van Dyck, J. (1995). *Manufacturing babies and public consent: Debating the new reproductive technologies.* New York: New York University Press.

van Goozen, S. H. M., Fairchild, G., Snoek, H., & Harold, G. T. (2007). The evidence for a neurobiological model of childhood antisocial behavior. *Psychological Bulletin, 133,* 149–182.

van IJzendoorn, M. H. (1995). Adult attachment representations, parental responsiveness, and infant attachment: A meta-analysis on the predictive validity of the Adult Attachment Interview. *Psychological Bulletin, 117*(3), 387–403.

van IJzendoorn, M. H., & Juffer, F. (2005). Adoption is a successful natural intervention enhancing adopted children's IQ and school performance. *Current Directions in Psychological Science, 14,* 326–330.

van IJzendoorn, M. H., & Kroonenberg, P. M. (1988). Cross-cultural patterns of attachment: A meta-analysis of the strange situation. *Child Development, 59,* 147–156.

van IJzendoorn, M. H., & Sagi, A. (1997). Cross-cultural patterns of attachment: Universal and contextual dimensions. In J. Cassidy & P. Shaver (Eds.), *Handbook on attachment theory and research.* New York: Guilford Press.

van IJzendoorn, M. H., & Sagi, A. (1999). Cross-cultural patterns of attachment: Universal and contextual dimensions. In J. Cassidy & P. R. Shaver (Eds.), *Handbook of attachment: Theory, research, and clinical applications* (pp. 713–734). New York: Guilford.

van IJzendoorn, M. H., Juffer, F., & Poelhuis, C. W. K. (2005). Adoption and cognitive development: A meta-analytic comparison of adopted and nonadopted children's IQ and school performance. *Psychological Bulletin, 131*, 301–316.

van IJzendoorn, M. H., Vereijken, C.M. J. L., Bakermans-Kranenburg, M. J., & Riksen-Walraven, J. M. (2004). Assessing attachment security with the Attachment Q Sort: Meta-analytic evidence for the validity of the observer AQS. *Child Development, 75*, 1188.

van Noord-Zaadstra, B. M., Looman, C. W., Alsbach, H., Habbema, J. D., te Velde, E. R., & Karbaat, J. (1991). Delayed childbearing: Effect of age on fecundity and outcome of pregnancy. *British Medical Journal, 302*, 1361–1365.

Van Voorhis, B. J. (2007). In vitro fertilization. *New England Journal of Medicine, 356*, 379–386.

Van Voorhis, B. J., Greensmith, J. E., Dokras, A., Sparks, A. E., Simmons, S. T., & Syrop, C. H. (2005). Hyperbaric oxygen and ovarian follicular stimulation for in vitro fertilization: A pilot study. *Fertility and Sterility, 83*(1), 226–228.

Vance, M. L., & Mauras, N. (1999). Growth hormone therapy in adults and children. *New England Journal of Medicine, 341*(16), 1206–1216.

Vandell, D. L. (2000). Parents, peer groups, and other socializing influences. *Developmental Psychology, 36*, 699–710.

Vandell, D. L., & Bailey, M. D. (1992). Conflicts between siblings. In C. U. Shantz & W. W. Hartup (Eds.), *Conflict in child and adolescent development* (pp. 242–269). New York: Cambridge University Press.

Vandell, D. L., & Ramanan, J. (1992). Effects of early and recent maternal employment on children from low income families. *Child Development, 63*, 938–949.

Vargha-Khadem, F., Gadian, D. G., Watkins, K. E., Connelly, A., Van Paesschen, W., & Mishkin, M. (1997). Differential effects of early hippocampal pathology on episodic and semantic memory. *Science, 277*, 376–380. variables? *Psychological Science, 16*, 866–870.

Vasilyeva, M., & Huttenlocher, J. (2004). Early development of scaling ability. *Developmental Psychology, 40*, 682–690.

Vasilyeva, M., Huttenlocher, J., & Waterfall, H. (2006). Effects of language intervention on syntactic skill levels in preschoolers. *Developmental Psychology, 42*, 164–174.

Vaswani, M., & Kapur, S. (2001). Genetic basis of schizophrenia: Trinucleotide repeats: An update. *Progress in Neuro-Psychopharmacology & Biological Psychiatry, 25*(6), 1187–1201.

Vaughn, B. E., Stevenson-Hinde, J., Waters, E., Kotsaftis, A., Lefever, G. B., Shouldice, A., Trudel, M., & Belsky, J. (1992). Attachment security and temperament in infancy and early childhood: Some conceptual clarifications. *Developmental Psychology, 28*, 463–473.

Vecchiotti, S. (2003). Kindergarten: An overlooked educational policy priority. *SRCD Social Policy Report, 17*(2), 1–19.

Veenstra, R., Lindenberg, S., Oldehinkel, A. J., De Winter, A. F., Verhulst, F. C., & Ormel, J. (2005). Bullying and victimization in elementary schools: A comparison of bullies, victims, bully/victims, and uninvolved preadolescents. *Developmental Psychology, 41*, 672–682.

Ventura, S. J., Martin, J. A., Curtin, S. C., & Mathews, T. J. (1998). *Report of final natality statistics, 1996* (Monthly Vital Statistics Report, 46[11, Suppl.]). Hyattsville, MD: National Center for Health Statistics.

Ventura, S. J., Martin, J. A., Curtin, S. C., & Mathews, T. J. (1999). *Births: Final data for 1997* (National Vital Statistics Reports, 47[18]). Hyattsville, MD: National Center for Health Statistics.

Ventura, S. J., Matthews, T. J., & Curtin, S. C. (1999). Declines in teenage birth rates 1991–1998: Update of national and state trends. *National Vital Statistics Reports, 47*(6). Hyattsville, MD: National Center for Health Statistics.

Verma, S., & Larson, R. (2003). Editors' notes. In S. Verma and R. Larson (Eds.)., (2002). Chromosomal congenital anomalies and residence near hazardous waste landfill sites. *Lancet, 359*, 320–322.

Verschueren, K., Buyck, P., & Marcoen, A. (2001). Self representations and socioemotional competence in young children: A 3-year longitudinal study. *Developmental Psychology, 37*, 126–134.

Verschueren, K., Marcoen, A., & Schoefs, V. (1996). The internal working model of the self, attachment, and competence in five-year-olds. *Child Development, 67*, 2493–2511.

Vgontzas, A. N., & Kales, A. (1999). Sleep and its disorders. *Annual Review of Medicine, 50*, 387–400.

Viner, R. M., & Cole, T. J. (2005). Television viewing in early childhood predicts adult body mass index. *Journal of Pediatrics, 147*, 429–435.

Vitaro, F., Tremblay, R. E., Kerr, M., Pagani, L., & Bukowski, W. M. (1997). Disruptiveness, friends' characteristics, and delinquency in early adolescence: A test of two competing models of development. *Child Development, 68*, 676–689.

Vohr, B. R., Wright, L. L., Poole, K., & McDonald, S. A. for the NICHD Neonatal Research Network Follow-up Study. (2005). Neurodevelopmental outcomes of extremely low birth weight infants <30 weeks' gestation between 1993 and 1998. *Pediatrics, 116*, 635–643.

Vondra, J. I., & Barnett, D. (1999). A typical attachment in infancy and early childhood among children at developmental risk. *Monographs of the Society for Research in Child Development, Serial No. 258, 64*(3).

Vosniadou, S. (1987). Children and metaphors. *Child Development, 58*, 870–885.

Votruba-Drzal, E., Coley, R. L., & Chase-Lansdale, P. L. (2004). Child care and low-income children's development: Direct and moderated effects. *Child Development, 75*, 296–312.

Vrijheld, M., Dolk, H., Armstrong, B., Abramsky, L., Bianchi, F., Fazarinc, I., Garne, E., Ide, R., Nelen, V., Robert, E., Scott, J. E. S., Stone, D., & Tenconi, R. (2002). Chromosomal congenital anomalies and residence near hazardous waste landfill sites. *The Lancet, 359*, 320-322.

Vuchinich, S., Angelelli, J., & Gatherum, A. (1996). Context and development in family problem solving with preadolescent children. *Child Development, 67*, 1276–1288.

Vuori, L., Christiansen, N., Clement, J., Mora, J., Wagner, M., & Herrera, M. (1979). Nutritional supplementation and the outcome of pregnancy: 2. Visual habitation at 15 days. *Journal of Clinical Nutrition, 32*, 463–469.

Vygotsky, L. S. (1956). *Selected psychological investigations*. Moscow: Izdstel'sto Akademii Pedagogicheskikh Nauk USSR.

Vygotsky, L. S. (1978). *Mind in society: The development of higher psychological processes*. Cambridge, MA: Harvard University Press.

Wade, N. (2001, October 4). Researchers say gene is linked to language. *New York Times*, p. Al.

Wagner, C. L., Katikaneni, L. D., Cox, T. H., & Ryan, R. M. (1998). The impact of prenatal drug exposure on the neonate. *Obstetrics and Gynecology Clinics of North America, 25*, 169–194.

Wahlbeck, K., Forsen, T., Osmond, C., Barker, D. J. P., & Erikkson, J. G. (2001). Association of schizophrenia with low maternal body mass index, small size at birth, and thinness during childhood. *Archives of General Psychiatry, 58*, 48–55.

Wainright, J. L., Russell, S. T., & Patterson, C. J. (2004). Psychosocial adjustment, school outcomes, and romantic relationships of adolescents with same-sex parents. *Child Development, 75*, 1886–1898.

Waisbren, S. E., Albers, S., Amato, S., Ampola, M., Brewster, T. G., Demmer, L., Eaton, R. B., Greenstein, R., Korson, M., Larson, C., Marsden, D., Msall, M., Naylor, E. W., Pueschel, S., Seashore, M., Shih, V. E., & Levy, H. L. (2003). Effect of expanded newborn screening for biochemical disorders on child outcomes and parental stress. *Journal of the American Medical Association, 290*, 2564–2572.

Wakefield, M., Reid, Y., Roberts, L., Mullins, R., & Gillies, P. (1998). Smoking and smoking cessation among men whose partners are pregnant: A qualitative study. *Social Science and Medicine, 47*, 657–664.

Waknine, Y. (2006). Highlights from MMWR: Prevalence of U.S. birth defects and more. *Medscape*. Retrieved January 9, 2006, from http://www.medscape.com/viewarticle/521056.

Wakschlag, L. S., Lahey, B. B., Loeber, R., Green, S. M., Gordon, R. A., & Leventhal, B. L. (1997). Maternal smoking during pregnancy and the risk of conduct disorder in boys. *Archives of General Psychiatry, 54*, 670–676.

Wald, N. J. (2004). Folic acid and the prevention of neural-tube defects. *New England Journal of Medicine, 350*, 101–103.

Waldman, I. D. (1996). Aggressive boys' hostile perceptual and response biases: The role of attention and impulsivity. *Child Development, 67*, 1015–1033.

Walk, R. D., & Gibson, E. J. (1961). A comparative and analytical study of visual depth perception. *Psychological Monographs, 75*(15), 44.

Walker, R. B., Conn, J. A., Davies, M. J. & Moore, V. M. (2005). Mother's views on feeding infants around the time of weaning. *Public Health Nutrition, 9*, 707–713.

Wallach, M. A., & Kogan, M. (1965). *Modes of thinking in young children: A study of the creativity–intelligence distinction*. New York: Holt.

Waller, M. W., Hallfors, D. D., Halpern, C. T., Iritani, B., Ford, C. A., & Guo, G. (2006). Gender differences in associations between depressive symptoms and patterns of substance use and risky sexual behavior among a nationally representative sample of U.S. adolescents. *Archives of Women's Mental Health, 9*, 139–150.

Wallerstein, J. S., Lewis, J. M., & Blakeslee, S. (2000). *The unexpected legacy of divorce: A 25-year landmark study*. New York: Hyperion.

Walma van der Molen, J. (2004). Violence and suffering in television news: Toward a broader conception of harmful television content for children. *Pediatrics, 113,* 1771–1775

Walsh, S., Shulman, S., Bar-On, Z., & Tsur, A. (2006). The role of parentification and family climate in adaptation among immigrant adolescents in Israel. *Journal of Research on Adolescence, 16,* 321–350.

Walston, J.T., & West, J. (2004). *Full-day and half-day kindergarten in the United States: Findings from the early childhood longitudinal study, kindergarten class of 1998–99* (NCES 2004-078). U.S. Department of Education, National Center for Education Statistics. Washington, DC: U.S. Government Printing Office.

Wang, D. W., Desai, R. R., Crotti, L., Arnestad, M., Insolia, R., Pedrazzini, M. Ferrandi, C., Vege, A., Rognum, T., Schwartz, P. J., & George,, A. L. (2007). Cardiac sodium channel dysfunction in sudden infant death syndrome. *Circulation, 115,* 368–376.

Wang, H., Parry, S., Macones, G., Sammel, M. D., Kuivaniemi, H., Tromp, G., Argyropoulous, G., Halder, I., Shriver, M. D., Romero, R., & Strauss, J. F., III. (2006). A functional SNP in the promoter of the SERPINH1 gene increases risk of preterm premature rupture of membranes in African Americans. *Proceedings of the National Academy of Sciences, USA, 103,* 13463–13467.

Wang, Q. (2004). The emergence of cultural self-constructs: Autobiographical memory and self-description in European American and Chinese children. *Developmental Psychology, 40,* 3–15.

Wang, Y., & Lobstein, T. (2006). Worldwide trends in childhood overweight and obesity. *International Journal of Obesity, 1*(1), 11–25.

Ward, M. (1998). *The family dynamic: A Canadian perspective* (2nd ed.). Toronto: ITP Nelson.

Ward, M. G. K. & Bennett, S. (2003). Studying child abuse and neglect in Canada: We are just at the beginning. *Canadian Medical Association, 169,* 911–915.

Wardle, J., Robb, K. A., Johnson, F., Griffith, J., Brunner, E., Power, C., et al. (2004). Socioeconomic variation in attitudes to eating and weight in female adolescents. *Health Psychology, 23,* 275–282.

Watamura, S. E., Donzella, B., Alwin, J., & Gunnar, M. R. (2003). Morning-to-afternoon increases in cortisol concentrations for infants and toddlers at child care: Age differences and behavioral correlates. *Child Development, 74,* 1006–1020.

Waters, E., & Deane, K. E. (1985). Defining and assessing individual differences in attachment relationships: Q-methodology and the organization of behavior in infancy and early childhood. *Monographs of the Society for Research in Child Development, 50,* 41–65.

Waters, E., Wippman, J., & Sroufe, L. A. (1979). Attachment, positive affect, and competence in the peer group: Two studies in construct validation. *Child Development, 50,* 821–829.

Waters, K. A., Gonzalez, A., Jean, C., Morielli, A., & Brouillette, R. T. (1996). Face-straight-down and face-near-straight-down positions in healthy prone-sleeping infants. *Journal of Pediatrics, 128,* 616–625.

Watson, A. C., Nixon, C. L., Wilson, A., & Capage, L. (1999). Social interaction skills and theory of mind in young children. *Developmental Psychology, 35*(2), 386–391.

Watson, J. B., & Rayner, R. (1920). Conditioned emotional reactions. *Journal of Experimental Psychology, 3,* 1–14.

Webb, M. (1991). *David Suzuki: Superstar of science.* Mississauga, ON: Copp Clark Pitman.

Wechsler, D. (1996). *Wechsler Intelligence Scale for Children–III. Canadian manual supplement.* Toronto: The Psychological Corporation.

Wechsler, D. (2003). *Wechsler Intelligence Scale for Children–Fourth Edition: Canadian.* Toronto, ON: Harcourt Assessment.

Weese-Mayer, D. E., Berry-Kravis, E. M., Maher, B. S., Silvestri, J. M., Curran, M. E., & Marazita, M. L. (2003). Sudden infant death syndrome: Association with a promoter polymorphism of the serotonin transporter gene. *American Journal of Medical Genetics, 117A,* 268–274.

Weese-Mayer, D. E., Berry-Kravis, E. M., Zhou, L., Maher, B. S., Curran, M. E., Silvestri, J. M., et al. (2004). Sudden Infant Death Syndrome: Case-control frequency differences at genes pertinent to autonomic nervous system embryological development. *Pediatric Research, 56,* 391–395.

Wegman, M. E. (1992). Annual summary of vital statistics: 1991. *Pediatrics, 90,* 835–845.

Wegman, M. E. (1994). Annual summary of vital statistics: 1993. *Pediatrics, 94,* 792–803.

Wegman, M. E. (1999). Foreign aid, international organizations, and the world's children. *Pediatrics, 103*(3), 646–654.

Weinberg, M. K., & Tronick, E. Z. (1996). Infant affective reactions to the resumption of maternal interaction after still face. *Child Development, 67,* 905–914.

Weinberger, B., Anwar, M., Hegyi, T., Hiatt, M., Koons, A., & Paneth, N. (2000). Antecedents and neonatal consequences of low Apgar scores in preterm newborns. *Archives of Pediatric and Adolescent Medicine, 154,* 294–300.

Weinberger, D. R. (2001, March 10). A brain too young for good judgment. *New York Times.* Retrieved from http://www.nytimes. com/2001/03/10/.

Weinreb, L., Wehler, C., Perloff, J., Scott, R., Hosmer, D., Sagor, L., and Gundersen, C. (2002). Hunger: Its impact on children's health and mental health. *Pediatrics, 110,* 816.

Weinstock, H., Berman, S., & Cates, W., Jr. (2004). Sexually transmitted diseases among American youth: Incidence and prevalence estimates, 2000. *Perspectives on Sexual and Reproductive Health, 36,* 6–10.

Weisner, T. S. (1993). Ethnographic and ecocultural perspectives on sibling relationships. In Z. Stoneman & P. W. Berman (Eds.), *The effects of mental retardation, visibility, and illness on sibling relationships* (pp. 51–83). Baltimore, MD: Brooks.

Weiss, B., Amler, S., & Amler, R. W. (2004). Pesticides. *Pediatrics, 113,* 1030–1036.

Weiss, B., Dodge, K. A., Bates, J. E., & Pettit, G. S. (1992). Some consequences of early harsh discipline: Child aggression and a maladaptive social information processing style. *Child Development, 63,* 1321–1335.

Weiss, L. G., Saklofske, D. H., Prifitera, A., Chen, H.-Y., & Hildebrand, D. (1999). The calculation of the WISC–III general ability index using Canadian norms. *Canadian Journal of School Psychology, 14,* 1–9.

Weissman, M. M., Warner, V., Wickramaratne, P. J., & Kandel, D. B. (1999). Maternal smoking during pregnancy and psychopathology in offspring followed to adulthood. *Journal of the American Academy of Child and Adolescent Psychiatry, 38,* 892–899.

Weisz, J. R., McCarty, C. A., & Valeri, S. M. (2006). Effects of psychotherapy for depression in children and adolescents: A meta-analysis. *Psychological Bulletin, 132,* 132–149.

Weisz, J. R., Weiss, B., Han, S. S., Granger, D. A., & Morton, T. (1995). Effects of psychotherapy with children and adolescents revisited: A meta-analysis of treatment outcome studies. *Psychological Bulletin, 117*(3), 450–468.

Weitzman, M., Gortmaker, S., & Sobol, A. (1992). Maternal smoking and behavior problems of children. *Pediatrics, 90,* 342–349.

Welch-Ross, M. K. (1997). Mother–child participation in conversation about the past: Relationships to preschoolers' theory of mind. *Developmental Psychology, 33*(4), 618–629.

Welch-Ross, M. K., & Schmidt, C. R. (1996). Gender-schema development and children's story memory: Evidence for a developmental model. *Child Development, 67,* 820–835.

Wellman, H. M., & Cross, D. (2001). Theory of mind and conceptual change. *Child Development, 72,* 702–707.

Wellman, H. M., & Gelman, S. A. (1998). Knowledge acquisition in foundational domains. In W. Damon (Series Ed.), D. Kuhn, & R. S. Siegler (Vol. Eds.), *Handbook of child psychology: Vol. 2. Cognition, perception, and language* (5th ed., pp. 523–573). New York: Wiley.

Wellman, H. M., & Woolley, J. D. (1990). From simple desires to ordinary beliefs: The early development of everyday psychology. *Cognition, 35,* 245–275.

Wellman, H. M., Cross, D., & Watson, J. (2001). Meta-analysis of theory-of-mind development: The truth about false belief. *Child Development, 72,* 655–684.

Wells, G. (1985). Preschool literacy-related activities and success in school. In D. R. Olson, N. Torrence, & A. Hilyard (Eds.), *Literacy, language, and learning* (pp. 229–255). New York: Cambridge University Press.

Wen, S. W., Mery, L. S., Kramer, M. S., Jimenez, V., Trouton, K., Herbert, P., & Chalmers, B. (1999). Attitudes of Canadian women toward birthing centres and midwife care for childbirth. *Canadian Medical Association Journal, 161,* 708–709.

Wen, S.W., Goel, V. & Williams, J.I. (1996). Utilization of health care services by immigrants and other ethnic/cultural groups in Ontario. *Ethnicity and Health, 1,* 99–109.

Wender, P. H. (1995). *Attention-deficit hyperactivity disorder in adults.* New York: Oxford University Press.

Wentworth, N., Benson, J. B., & Haith, M. M. (2000). The development of infants' reaches for stationary and moving targets. *Child Development, 71,* 576–601.

Wentzel, K. R. (2002). Are effective teachers like good parents? Teaching styles and student adjustment in early adolescence. *Child Development, 73,* 287–301.

Werker, J. F. (1989). Becoming a native listener. *American Scientist, 77,* 54–59.

Werker, J. F., & Tees, R. C. (1999). Experiential influences on infant speech processing: Towards a new synthesis. In J. T. Spence, J. M. Darley, & D. J. Foss (Associate Eds.), *Annual Review of Psychology, 50* (pp. 509–535). Palo Alto, CA: Annual Reviews.

Werker, J. F., Cohen, L. B., Lloyd, V. L., Casasola, M., & Stager, C. L. (1998). Acquisition of word–object associations by 14-month-old infants. *Developmental Psychology, 34,* 1289–1309.

Werker, J. F., Pegg, J. E., & McLeod, P. J. (1994). A cross-language investigation of infant preference for infant-directed communication. *Infant Behavior and Development, 17,* 323–333.

Werler, M. M., Louik, C., Shapiro, S., & Mitchell, A. A. (1996). Prepregnant weight in relation to risk of neural tube defects. *Journal* *of the American Medical Association, 275,* 1089–1092.

Werner, E. E. (1985). Stress and protective factors in children's lives. In A. R. Nichol (Ed.), *Longitudinal studies in child psychology and psychiatry.* New York: Wiley.

Werner, E. E. (1987, July 15). *Vulnerability and resiliency: A longitudinal study of Asian Americans from birth to age 30.* Invited address at the Ninth Biennial Meeting of the International Society for the Study of Behavioral Development, Tokyo.

Werner, E. E. (1989). Children of the garden island. *Scientific American, 260*(4), 106–111.

Werner, E. E. (1993). Risk and resilience in individuals with learning disabilities: Lessons learned from the Kauai longitudinal study. *Learning Disabilities Research and Practice, 8,* 28–34.

Werner, E. E. (1995). Resilience in development. *Current Directions in Psychological Science, 4*(3), 81–85.

Werner, E., Bierman, L., French, F. E., Simonian, K., Conner, A., Smith, R., & Campbell, M. (1968). Reproductive and environmental casualties: A report on the 10-year follow-up of the children of the Kauai pregnancy study. *Pediatrics, 42,* 112–127.

Westen, D. (1998). The scientific legacy of Sigmund Freud: Toward a psychodynamically informed psychological science. *Psychological Bulletin, 124,* 333–371.

Wexler, I. D., Branski, D., & Kerem, E. (2006). War and children. *Journal of the American Medical Association, 296,* 579–581.

Whalen, C. K., Jamner, L. D., Henker, B., Delfino, R. J., & Lozano, J. M. (2002). The ADHD spectrum and everyday life: Experience sampling of adolescent moods, activities, smoking, and drinking. *Child Development, 73,* 209–228.

Whalley, L. J., & Deary, I. J. (2001). Longitudinal cohort study of childhood IQ and survival up to age 76. *British Medical Journal, 322,* 819.

Whalley, L. J., Starr, J. M., Athawes, R., Hunter, D., Pattie, A., & Deary, I. J. (2000). Childhood mental ability and dementia. *Neurology, 55,* 1455–1459.

Whitaker, R. C., Wright, J. A., Pepe, M. S., Seidel, K. D., & Dietz, W. H. (1997). Predicting obesity in young adulthood from childhood and parental obesity. *New England Journal of Medicine, 337,* 869–873.

White, A. (2001). Alcohol and adolescent brain development. Retrieved from http://www.duke.edu/~amwhite/alc_adik_pf.html.

White, B. L. (1971, October). *Fundamental early environmental influences on the development of competence.* Paper presented at the Third Western Symposium on Learning: Cognitive Learning, Western Washington State College, Bellingham, WA.

White, B. L., Kaban, B., & Attanucci, J. (1979). *The origins of human competence.* Lexington, MA: Heath.

Whitehurst, G. J., & Lonigan, C. J. (1998). Child development and emergent literacy. *Child Development, 69,* 848–872.

Whitehurst, G. J., Falco, F. L., Lonigan, C. J., Fischel, J. E., DeBaryshe, B. D., Valdez-Menchaca, M. D., & Caufield, M. (1988). Accelerating language development through picture book reading. *Developmental Psychology, 24,* 552–559.

Whitehurst, G. J., Zevenbergen, A. A., Crone, D. A., Schultz, M. D., Velting, O. N., and Fischel, J. E. (1999). Outcomes of an emergent literacy intervention from Head Start through second grade. *Journal of Educational Psychology, 91,* 261–272.

Whitrow, G. J. (1967). *Einstein: The man and his achievement.* New York: Dover.

WHO/UNICEF Constitution on HIV Transmission and Breastfeeding. (1992). Consensus statement from the WHO/UNICEF Constitution on HIV Transmission and Breastfeeding, Geneva. *Weekly Epidemiological Record, 67,* 177–184.

Whyatt, R. M., Rauh, V., Barr, D. B., Camann, D. E., Andrews, H. F., Garfinkel, R., Hoepner, L. A., Diaz, D., Dietrich, J., Reyes, A. Tang, D., Kinney, P. L., & Perera, F. P. (2004). Prenatal insecticide exposures and birth weight and length among an urban minority cohort. *Environmental Health Perspectives, 112*(110), 1125–1132.

Wideman, R. (1990). *David Suzuki.* Markham, ON: Fitzhenry & Whiteside.

Widom, C. S. (1989). The cycle of violence. *Science, 244,* 160–166.

Wiggins, S., Whyte, P., Higgins, M., Adams, S., Theilmann, J., Bloch, M., Sheps, S. B., Schechter, M. T., & Hayden, M. R. (1992). The psychological consequences of predictive testing for Huntington's disease. *New England Journal of Medicine, 327,* 1401–1405.

Wilcox, A. J., Baird, D. D., Weinberg, C. R., Hornsby, P. P., & Herbst, A. L. (1995). Fertility in men exposed prenatally to diethylstilbestrol. *New England Journal of Medicine, 332,* 1411–1416.

Wilcox, A. J., Dunson, D., & Baird, D. D. (2000). The timing of the "fertile window" in the menstrual cycle: Day specific estimates from a prospective study. *British Medical Journal, 321,* 1259–1262.

Wilens, T. E., Faraone, S. V., & Biederman, J. (2004). Attention-Deficit Hyperactivity Disorder in adults. *Journal of the American Medical Association, 292,* 619–623.

Wilgosh, L., Meyer, M., & Mueller, H. H. (1996). Longitudinal study of effects on academic achievement for early and late age of school entry. *Canadian Journal of School Psychology, 11,* 43–51.

Wilkins, K. (2005). Deaths involving firearms. Analytical Studies and Report, Statistics Canada. Retrieved August 23, 2007 from http://www.guncontrol.ca/English/Home/Works/KeepingKidsSafe.pdf.

Williams, D. L., Goldstein, G., & Minshew, N. J. (2006). Neuropsychologic functioning in children with autism: Further evidence for disordered complex information-processing. *Child Neuropsychology: A Journal on Normal and Abnormal Development in Childhood and Adolescence, 12*(4–5), 279–298.

Williams, E. R., & Caliendo, M. A. (1984). *Nutrition: Principles, issues, and applications.* New York: McGraw-Hill.

Williams, G. J. (2001). The clinical significance of visual-verbal processing in evaluating children with potential learning related visual problems. *Journal of Optometric Vision Development, 32*(2), 107–110.

Williams, J. E., & Best, D. L. (1982). *Measuring sex stereotypes: A thirty-nation study.* Beverly Hills, CA: Sage.

Williams, J., Wake, M., Hesketh, K., Maher, E., & Waters, E. (2005). Health-related quality of life of overweight and obese children. *Journal of the American Medical Association, 293,* 70–76.

Williams, P. L., Innis, S. M., Vogel, A. M. P., & Stephen, L. J. (1999). Factors influencing infant feeding practices of mothers in Vancouver. *Canadian Journal of Public Health, 90,* 114–119.

Willinger, M., Hoffman, H. T., & Hartford, R. B. (1994). Infant sleep position and risk

for sudden infant death syndrome: Report of meeting held January 13 and 14, 1994. *Pediatrics, 93,* 814–819.

Willms, J. D. (1996). Indicators of mathematics achievement in Canadian elementary schools. In Human Resources Development Canada and Statistics Canada, *Growing up in Canada: National Longitudinal Survey of Children and Youth.* Catalogue No. 89-550-MPE, No. 1 (pp. 69-82). Ottawa: Author.

Willms, J. D. (2002). Research findings bearing on Canadian social policy. In Willms, J. D. *Vulnerable Children.* (pg. 331–358). University of Alberta Press.

Willms, J. D. (2004). Early childhood obesity: a call for early surveillance and preventative measures. *Canadian Medical Association, 171,* 243–245.

Willows, N. D., Johnson, M. S. & Ball, G. D. C. (2007). Prevalence estimates of overweight and obesity in Cree preschool children in northern Quebec according to international and US reference criteria. *American Journal of Public Health, 97,* 312–316.

Wilson, A. (1996). *Heartbeat of the earth: A First Nations artist records injustice and resistance.* Gabriola Island, B.C.: New Society Publishers.

Wilson, B., & Steinman, C. (2000). *Hungercount 2000, a surplus of hunger: Canada's annual survey of emergency food programs.* Toronto: Canadian Association of Food Banks.

Wilson, B., & Tsoa, E. (2001). *Hungercount 2001, food bank lines in insecure times: Canada's annual survey of emergency food programs.* Toronto: Canadian Association of Food Banks.

Wilson, E. O. (1975). *Sociobiology: The new synthesis.* Cambridge, MA: Belknap Press of Harvard University Press.

Wilson, K., & Ryan, V. (2001). Helping parents by working with their children in individual child therapy. *Child and Family Social Work (special issue), 6,* 209–217.

Wilson-Costello, D., Friedman, H., Minich, N., Siner, B., Taylor, G., Schluchter, M., & Hack, M. (2007). Improved neurodevelopmental outcomes for extremely low birth weight infants in 2000–2002. *Pediatrics, 119,* 37–45.

Winerip, M. (1999, January 3). Homework bound. *Education Life supplement to New York Times,* pp. 28–31, 40.

Winner, E. (1997). Exceptionally high intelligence and schooling. *American Psychologist, 52*(10), 1070–1081.

Winner, E. (2000). The origins and ends of giftedness. *American Psychologist, 55,* 159–169.

Winzer, M. A. (1996). *Children with exceptionalities in Canadian classrooms* (4th ed.). Scarborough, ON: Allyn & Bacon.

Winzer, M. A. (1997). *Special education in early childhood: An inclusive approach.* Toronto: Allyn & Bacon.

Wisner, K. L., Chambers, C., & Sit, D. K. Y. (2006). Postpartum depression: A major public health problem. *Journal of the American Medical Association, 296,* 2616–2618.

Wolchik, S. A., Sandler, I. N., Millsap, R. E., Plummer, B. A., Greene, S. M., Anderson, E. R., et al. (2002). Six year follow-up of a randomized, controlled trial of preventive interventions for children of divorce. *Journal of the American Medical Association, 288,* 1874–1881.

Wolfe, D. A. (1985). Child-abusive parents: An empirical review and analysis. *Psychological Bulletin, 97*(3), 462–482.

Wolfe, D. A., Edwards, B., Manion, I., & Koverola, C. (1988). Early intervention for parents at risk of child abuse and neglect:

A preliminary investigation. *Journal of Consulting and Clinical Psychology, 56,* 40–47.

Wolff, P. H. (1963). Observations on the early development of smiling. In B. M. Foss (Ed.), *Determinants of infant behavior* (Vol. 2). London: Methuen.

Wolff, P. H. (1966). The causes, controls, and organizations of behavior in the newborn. *Psychological Issues, 5* (1, Whole No. 17), 1–105.

Wolff, P. H. (1969). The natural history of crying and other vocalizations in early infancy. In B. M. Foss (Ed.), *Determinants of infant behavior* (Vol. 4). London: Methuen.

Wolff, R. (1993). *Good sports: The concerned parent's guide to Little League and other competitive youth sports.* New York: Dell.

Wolraich, M. L., Lindgren, S. D., Stumbo, P. J., Stegink, L. D., Appelbaum, M. I., & Kiritsky, M. C. (1994). Effects of diets high in sucrose or aspartame on the behavior and cognitive performance of children. *New England Journal of Medicine, 330,* 301–307.

Wolraich, M. L., Wibbelsman, C. J., Brown, T. E., Evans, S. W., Gotlieb, E. M., Knight, J. R., Ross, C., Shubiner, H. H., Wender, E H., & Wilens, T. (2005). Attention-deficit/ hyperactivity disorder among adolescents: A review of the diagnosis, treatment, and clinical implications. *Pediatrics, 115,* 1734–1746.

Wolraich, M. L., Wilson, D. B., & White, J. W. (1995). The effect of sugar on behavior or cognition in children: A meta-analysis. *Journal of the American Medical Association, 274*(20), 1617–1621.

Woman delivers a baby boy after refusing a caesarean. (1993, December 30). *New York Times,* p. A12.

Wong, A. H. C., Gottesman, I. I., & Petronia, A. (2005). Phenotypic differences in genetically identical organisms: The epigenetic perspective. *Human Molecular Genetics, 14,* Review Issue 1, 1093–1116.

Wong, C. A., Scavone, B. M., Peaceman, A. M., McCarthy, R. J., Sullivan, J. T., Diaz, N. T., Yaghmour, E., Marcus, R.-J. L., Sherwani,S. S., Sproviero, M. T., Yilmaz, M., Patel, R., Robles, C., & Grouper, S. (2005). The risk of cesarean delivery with neuraxial analgesia given early versus late in labor. *New England Journal of Medicine, 352,* 655–665.

Wong, C. K., Murray, M L., Camilleri-Novak, D., & Stephens, P. (2004). Increased prescribing trends of paediatric psychtropic medications. *Archives of the Diseases of Children, 89,* 1131–1132.

Wong, T., Singh, A., Mann, J., Hansen, L. & McMahon, S. (2004). Gender differences in bacterial STIs in Canada. *BMC Women's Health, 4,* 1–8.

Wood, D. (1980). Teaching the young child: Some relationships between social interaction, language, and thought. In D. Olson (Ed.), *The social foundations of language and thought.* New York: Norton.

Wood, D., Bruner, J., & Ross, G. (1976). The role of tutoring in problem solving. *Journal of Child Psychiatry and Psychology, 17,* 89–100.

Wood, W., & Eagly, A. (2002). A cross-cultural analysis of the behavior of women and men: Implications for the origins of sex differences. *Psychological Bulletin, 128,* 699–727.

Woodruff, T. J., Axelrad, D. A., Kyle, A. D., Nweke, O., Miller, G. G., and Hurley, B. J. (2004). Trends in environmentally related childhood illnesses. *Pediatrics, 113,* 1133–1140.

Woodward, A. L., Markman, E. M., & Fitzsimmons, C. M. (1994). Rapid word learning in 13- and 18-month olds. *Developmental Psychology, 30,* 553–566.

Woodward, S. A., McManis, M. H., Kagan, J., Deldin, P., Snidman, N., Lewis, M., & Kahn, V. (2001). Infant temperament and the brainstem auditory evoked response in later childhood. *Developmental Psychology, 37,* 533–538.

Wooley, J. D., Phelps, K. E., Davis, D. L. and Mandell, D. J. (1999). Where theories of mind meet magic: The development of children's beliefs about wishing. *Child Development, 70,* 571–587.

Woolley, J. D. (1997). Thinking about fantasy: Are children fundamentally different thinkers and believers from adults? *Child Development, 68*(6), 991–1011.

Woolley, J. D., & Boerger, E. A. (2002). Development of beliefs about the origins and controllability of dreams. *Developmental Psychology, 38*(1), 24–41.

World Bank. (2006). *Repositioning nutrition as central to development.* Washington, D.C.: Author.

World Health Organization. (2003). The world health report—shaping the future. Retrieved February 14, 2004, from http://www.who.int/ wrh/2003/chapter1en/index2.html.

Worswick, C. (2001). *School performance of the children of immigrants in Canada, 1994–1998.* Ottawa: Statistics Canada.

Wright, J. C., Huston, A. C., Murphy, K. C., St. Peters, M., Pinon, M., Scantlin, R., & Kotler, J. (2001). The relations of early television viewing to school readiness and vocabulary of children from low-income families: The Early Window Project. *Child Development, 72*(5), 1347–1366.

Wright, J. T., Waterson, E. J., Barrison, I. G., Toplis, P. J., Lewis, I. G., Gordon, M. G., MacRae, K. D., Morris, N. F., & Murray Lyon, I. M. (1983, March 26). Alcohol consumption, pregnancy, and low birth weight. *Lancet,* pp. 663–665.

Wright, M. J. (1999). The history of developmental psychology in Canada. *Canadian Journal of Research in Early Childhood Education, 8,* 31–36.

Wright, M. J. (2002). Flashbacks in the history of psychology in Canada: Some early "headline" makers. *Canadian Psychology, 43,* 21–34.

Wright, S. C., Taylor, D. M., & Ruggiero, K. M. (1996). Examining the potential for academic achievement among Inuit children: Comparisons on the Raven Coloured Progressive Matrices. *Journal of Cross-Cultural Psychology, 27,* 733–753.

Wright, V. C., Chang, J., Jeng, G., & Macaluso, M. (2006). Assisted reproduction technology surveillance—United States, 2003. *Morbidity and Mortality Weekly Report* (Surveillance Summaries), *55*(SS04), 1–22.

Wright, V. C., Schieve, L. A., Reynolds, M.A., & Jeng, G. (2003). Assisted Reproductive Technology Surveillance—United States, 2000. Division of Reproductive Health, National Center for Chronic Disease Prevention and Health Promotion. Retrieved from http://www. cdc.gov/reprod.

Wrigley, J., & Dreby, J. (2005). Fatalities and the organization of child care in the United States; 1985–2003. *American Sociological Review, 70*(5), 729–757.

Wu, T., Mendola, P., & Buck, G. M. (2002). Ethnic differences in the presence of secondary sex characteristics and menarche among U.S. girls: The Third National Health and Nutrition Survey, 1988–1994. *Pediatrics, 11,* 752–757.

Wu, Z., Hou, F. & Schimmele, C. M. (2006). Does cohabitation matter? The effects of non- marital cohabitation disruption on children's behavior. Retrieved August 17 2007 from http://paa2006.princeton.edu/download. aspx?submissionId=60144.

Wulczyn, F. (2004). Family reunification. In David and Lucile Packard Foundation, Children, families, and foster care. *The Future of Children, 14*(1). Retrieved from http://www. futureofchildren.org.

Wynn, K. (1992). Evidence against empiricist accounts of the origins of numerical knowledge. *Mind and Language, 7,* 315–332.

Wyrobek, A. J., Eskenazi, B., Young, S., Arnheim, N., Tiemann-Boege, I., Jabs, E. W., Glaser, R. L., Pearson, F. G., & Evenson, D. (2006). Advancing age has differential effects on DNA damage, chromatin integrity, gene mutations, and aneuploidies in sperm. *Proceedings of the National Academy of Sciences of the United States of America, 103*(25), 9601–9606.

Xu, B., Wratten, N., Charych, E. I., Buyske, S., Firestein, B. L., & Brzustowicz, L. M. (2005). Increased expression in dorsolateral prefrontal cortex of CAPON in schizophrenia and bipolar disorder. *PLoS Medicine, 2*(10), 999–1007.

Yager, J., & Andersen, A. E. (2005). Anorexia nervosa. *New England Journal of Medicine, 353,* 1481–1488.

Yamada, H. (2004). Japanese mothers' views of young children's areas of personal discretion. *Child Development, 75,* 164–179.

Yamazaki, J. N., & Schull, W. J. (1990). Perinatal loss and neurological abnormalities among children of the atomic bomb. *Journal of the American Medical Association, 264,* 605–609.

Yang, B., Ollendick, T. H., Dong, Q., Xia, Y., & Lin, L. (1995). Only children and children with siblings in the People's Republic of China: Levels of fear, anxiety, and depression. *Child Development, 66,* 1301–1311.

Yange, X., Leventhal, T., Brooks-Gunn, J., & Earls, F.J. (2005). Neighborhood residence and mental health problems of 5- to 11-year-olds. *Archives of General Psychiatry, 62,* 554–563.

Yarrow, M. R. (1978, October). *Altruism in children.* Paper presented at program, Advances in Child Development Research, New York Academy of Sciences, New York, NY.

Yazigi, R. A., Odem, R. R., & Polakoski, K. L. (1991). Demonstration of specific binding of cocaine to human spermatozoa. *Journal of the American Medical Association, 266,* 1956–1959.

Yingling, C. D. (2001). Neural mechanisms of unconscious cognitive processing. *Clinical Neurophysiology, 112*(1), 157–158.

Yip, T., Seaton, E. K., & Sellers, R. M. (2006). African American racial identity across the lifespan: Identity status, identity content, and depressive symptoms. *Child Development, 77,* 1504–1517.

Yokota, F., & Thompson, K. M. (2000). Violence in G-rated animated films. *Journal of the American Medical Association, 283,* 2716–2720.

Yoshikawa, H. (1994). Prevention as cumulative protection: Effects of early family support and education on chronic delinquency and its risks. *Psychological Bulletin, 115*(1), 28–54.

Young, K. A., Holcomb, L. A., Bonkale, W. L., Hicks, P. B., Yazdani, U., & German, D. C. (2007). 5HTTLPR polymorphism and enlargement of the pulvinar: Unlocking the backdoor to the limbic system. *Biological Psychiatry.*

Youngblade, L. M., & Belsky, J. (1992). Parent–child antecedents of 5-year-olds' close friendships: A longitudinal analysis. *Developmental Psychology, 28,* 700–713.

Youngblade, L. M., Theokas, C., Schulenberg, J., Curry, L., Huang, I.-C., & Novak, M. (2007). Risk and promotive factors in families, schools, and communities: A contextual model of positive youth development in adolescence. *Pediatrics, 119*, 47–53.

Youth violence: A report of the Surgeon General (2001, January). Retrieved from http://www.surgeongeneral.gov/ library/youthviolence/ default.htm.

Yu, S. M., Huang, Z. J., & Singh, G. K. (2004). Health status and health services utilization among U.S. Chinese, Asian Indian, Filipino, and Other Asian/Pacific Islander children. *Pediatrics, 113*(1), 101–107.

Yuan, W., Holland, S. K., Cecil, K. M., Dietrich, K. N., Wessel, S. D., Altaye, M., et al. (2006). The impact of early childhood lead exposure on brain organization: A functional magnetic resonance imaging study of language function. *Pediatrics, 118*, 971–977.

Yunger, J. L., Carver, P. R., & Perry, D. G.(2004). Does gender identity influence children's psychological well-being? *Developmental Psychology, 40*, 572–582.

Yurgelon-Todd, D. (2002). Inside the Teen Brain. Retrieved from http://www.pbs.org/wgbh/pages/frontline/shows/teenbrain/interviews/todd.html.

Zadoroznyj, M. (2007). Postnatal care in the community: Report of an evaluation of birthing women's assessments of a postnatal home-care programme. *Health & Social Care in the Community, 15*, 35–44.

Zahn-Waxler, C., Friedman, R. J., Cole, P. M., Mizuta, I., & Hiruma, N. (1996). Japanese and U.S. preschool children's responses to conflict and distress. *Child Development, 67*, 2462–2477.

Zahn-Waxler, C., Radke-Yarrow, M., Wagner, E., & Chapman, M. (1992). Development of concern for others. *Developmental Psychology, 28*, 126–136.

Zametkin, A. J. (1995). Attention-deficit disorder: Born to be hyperactive. *Journal of the American Medical Association, 273*(23), 1871–1874.

Zametkin, A. J., & Ernst, M. (1999). Problems in the management of Attention-Deficit-Hyperactivity Disorder. *New England Journal of Medicine, 340*, 40–46.

Zarbatany, L., Hartmann, D. P., & Rankin, D. B. (1990). The psychological functions of preadolescent peer activities. *Child Development, 61*, 1067–1080.

Zeanah, C. H., Smyke, A. T., Koga, S.F., & Carlson, E. (2005). Attachment in institutionalized and community children in Romania. *Child Development, 76*, 1015–1028.

Zeedyk, M. S., Wallace, L., & Spry, L. (2002). Stop, look, listen, and think? What young children really do when crossing the road. *Accident Analysis and Prevention, 34*(1), 43–50.

Zelazo, P. D., & Boseovski, J. J. (2001). Video reminders in a representational change task: Memory for cues but not beliefs or statements. *Journal of Experimental Child Psychology, 78*, 107–129.

Zelazo, P. D., & Müller, U. (2002). Executive function in typical and atypical development. In U. Goswami (Ed.), *Handbook of childhood cognitive development* (pp. 445–469). Oxford: Blackwell.

Zelazo, P. D., Müller, U., Frye, D., & Marcovitch, S. (2003). The development of executive function in early childhood. *Monographs of the Society for Research in Child Development, 68* (3, Serial No. 274).

Zelazo, P. R., Kearsley, R. B., & Stack, D. M. (1995). Mental representations for visual sequences: Increased speed of central processing from 22 to 32 months. *Intelligence, 20*, 41–63.

Zeskind, P. S., & Stephens, L. E. (2004). Maternal selective serotonin reuptake inhibitor use during pregnancy and newborn neurobehavior. *Pediatrics, 11*, 368–375.

Zhang, Y., Proenca, R., Maffei, M., Barone, M., Leopold, L., & Friedman, J. M. (1994). Positional cloning of the mouse obese gene in its human homologue. *Nature, 372*, 425–431.

Zhao, Y. (2002, May 29). Cultural divide over parental discipline. *New York Times*. Retreived from http://www. nytimes.com/2002/05/29/ nyregion/ 29DISC.html?ex.

Zhensun, Z., & Low, A. (1991). *A young painter: The life and paintings of Wang Yani: China's extraordinary young artist*. New York: Scholastic.

Zhu, B.-P., Rolfs, R. T., Nangle, B. E., & Horan, J. M. (1999). Effect of the interval between pregnancies on perinatal outcomes. *New England Journal of Medicine, 340*, 589–594.

Zigler, E. (1998). School should begin at age 3 years for American children. *Journal of Developmental and Behavioral Pediatrics, 19*, 37–38.

Zigler, E. F. (1987). Formal schooling for four-year-olds? *North American Psychologist, 42*(3), 254–260.

Zigler, E., & Styfco, S. J. (1993). Using research and theory to justify and inform Head Start expansion. *Social Policy Report of the Society for Research in Child Development, 7*(2), 1–21.

Zigler, E., & Styfco, S. J. (1994). Head Start: Criticisms in a constructive context. *American Psychologist, 49*(2), 127–132.

Zigler, E., Taussig, C., & Black, K. (1992). Early childhood intervention: A promising preventative for juvenile delinquency. *American Psychologist, 47*, 997–1006.

Zimiles, H., & Lee, V. E. (1991). Adolescent family structure and educational progress. *Developmental Psychology, 27*, 314–320.

Zimmerman, B. J., Bandura, A., & Martinez-Pons, M. (1992). Self-motivation for academic attainment: The role of self-efficacy beliefs and personal goal setting. *American Educational Research Journal, 29*, 663–676.

Zimmerman, F. J., & Christakis, D. A. (2005). Children's television viewing and cognitive outcomes: A longitudinal analysis of national data. *Archives of Pediatrics & Adolescent Medicine, 159*(7), 619–625.

Zimrin, H. (1986). A profile of survival. *Child Abuse and Neglect, 10*, 339–349.

Zinman, B. (2006). Diabetes in Aboriginal Canadians: Lessons from the Sandy Lake health and diabetes project. *Medscape Diabetes & Endocrinology, 8*. Retrieved on August 7, 2007 from http://www.medscape.com/viewarticle/519822.

Zito, J. M., Safer, D. J., dosReis, S., Gardner, J. F., Magder, L., Soeken, K., Boles, M., Lynch, F., & Riddle, M.A. (2003). Psychotropic practice patterns for youth: A 10-year perspective. *Archives of Pediatrics and Adolescent Medicine 57*(1), 17–25.

Zlotkin, S. (2003). Clinical nutrition: 8. The role of nutrition in the prevention of iron deficiency anemia in infants, children and adolescents. *Canadian Medical Association, 168*, 59–63.

Zola, M. (1984). *Terry Fox*. Toronto: Grolier Limited.

Zubenko, G. S., Maher, B., Hughes, H. B., III, Zubenko, W. N., Stiffler, J. S., Kaplan, B. B., & Marazita, M. L. (2003). Genome-wide linkage survey for genetic loci that influence the development of depressive disorders in families with recurrent, early-onset, major depression. *American Journal of Medical Genetics Part B: Neuropsychiatric Genetics, 123*(1), 1–18.

Zucker, K. J., Wilson-Smith, D. N., Kurita, J. A., & Stern, A. (1995). Children's appraisals of sex-typed behavior in their peers. *Sex Roles, 33*, 703–725.

Zuckerman, B. S., & Beardslee, W. R. (1987). Maternal depression: A concern for pediatricians. *Pediatrics, 79*, 110–117.

Zuvekas, S. H., Vitello, B., & Norquist, G. S. (2006). Recent trends in stimulant medication use among U.S. children. *American Journal of Psychiatry, 163*, 574–585.

Credits: Photos, Figures, and Tables

Chapter 1

Opener: © Rob Melnychuk/Digital Vision/ Getty Images; **p. 3:** Contemporary portrait of Victor of Aveyron from DE L'EDUCATION D'UN HOMME. Reproduced by kind permission of the British Library; **p. 11:** National Archives of Canada/PA-185530

Chapter 2

Opener: © John Feingersh/Corbis Stock Market; **p. 21:** Bettmann © Corbis; **p. 25:** National Library of Medicine; **p. 27:** UPI/Corbis-Bettmann; **p. 28:** © Joe McNally; **p. 29:** © Steve Mason; **p. 30:** © Yves De Braine/Black Star; **p. 31:** A.R. Luria/Dr. Michael Cole, Laboratory of Human Cognition, University of California, San Diego; **p. 38:** © Howard J. Radzyner/ Phototake; **p. 43:** © James Wilson/ Woodfin Camp & Associates

Chapter 3

Opener: Antonio Mo/Getty Images; **p. 53:** © Lester Sloan/Woodfin Camp & Associates; **p. 55:** Papalia, D., S.W. Olds, and R.D. Feldman (2001) From *Human Development,* Eighth Edition. Copyright © 2001. Reprinted with the permission of The McGraw-Hill Companies; **p. 58:** © Nancy Richmond/ The Image Works; **p. 60:** Ritter, J. (1999, November 23) From "Scientists close in on DNA code," *Chicago Sun-Times,* p. 7. Reprinted with special permission from the Chicago Sun-Times, Inc. © 1999; **p. 61:** Adapted from AAP Committee on Genetics (1996) Copyright © by the American Academy of Pediatrics. Reprinted with permission; **p. 62:** Milunsky, A. (1992) Adapted from *Heredity and Your Family's Health.* Copyright © 1992. Reprinted with the permission of Little, Brown, and Company, Inc.; **p. 68:** Babu, A. and K. Hirschhorn. (1992) From *A Guide to Human Chromosome Defects,* Third Edition [Birth Defects: Original Article Series, 28 (2)]; **p. 70:** © Thomas K. Wanstall/The Image Works; **p. 70 (tongue curling):** © David Young-Wolff/ PhotoEdit

Chapter 4

Opener: © Jose Luis Pelaez Inc./Blend Images/Getty Images; **p. 84 (1 month):** © Petit Format/Nestle/Science Source/ Photo Researchers; **p. 84 (2 months):** © Petit Format/Nestle/Science Source/ Photo Researchers; **p. 84 (3 months):** © Lennart Nilsson/Albert Bonniers Forlag AB, A CHILD IS BORN, Dell Publishing Company; **p. 84 (4 months):** © Ralph Hutchings/Visuals Unlimited; **p. 84 (5 months):** © James Stevenson/ PhotoResearchers; **p. 85 (6 months):** © Lennart Nilsson/Albert Bonniers Forlag AB, A CHILD IS BORN, Dell Publishing Company; **p. 85 (7 months):** © Petit Format/Nestle/Science Source/ Photo Researchers; **p. 85 (8 months):** © Petit Format/Nestle/Science Source/ Photo Researchers; **p. 85 (9 months–newborn):** © Tom Galliher/Corbis; **p. 86 (Figure 4-2):** From *Human Development,* 10th edition, by Diane E. Papalia, Sally Wendkos Olds, and Ruth Duskin Feldman, p. 88. Copyright © 2007 by The McGraw-Hill Companies, Inc. Reprinted by permission of The McGraw-Hill Companies, Inc.; **p. 87 (Figure 4-3):** From "Preventing birth defects even before pregnancy," by J. E. Brody in *The New York Times,* June 28, 1995. Copyright © 1995 by The New York Times Co. Reprinted with permission; **p. 89:** PhotoDisc/ Getty Images; **p. 94:** © Mugshots/ Corbis Stock Market; **p. 98 (Figure 4-4):** From "Advanced maternal age—How old is too old?" by L. J. Heffner in *New England Journal of Medicine, 351*(19), pp. 1927–1929. November 4, 2004. Copyright © Massachusetts Medical Society. All rights reserved; **p. 101 (Figure 4-5):** Statistics Canada 2006

Chapter 5

Opener: © Bob Daemmrich/Stock Boston; **p. 105:** Bettmann/Corbis; **p. 107 (Box 5-1):** Olds, S.W. (1995) Excerpts [approximately 930 words] from *Having a Baby in the Himalyas.* Copyright © 1995 by Sally Wendkos Olds. Reprinted with permission; **p. 107:** © Erol Gurian/Corbis Images; **p. 109 (Figure 5-1):** Lagercrantz, H., and T.A. Slotkin. (1986) Adapted from "The 'stress' of being born," *Scientific American, 254*(4), 1986, 100–107. Reprinted with the permission of Patricia J. Wynne; **p. 114 (Table 5-2):** Timiras, P.S. (1972) From *Developmental Physiology and Aging* by P.S. Timiras, Macmillan Publishing Co. Reprinted by permission of the author; **p. 115 (Table 5-3):** Apgar, V. (1953) Adapted from "A proposal for a new method of evaluation of the newborn infant," *Current Research in Anesthesia & Analgesia, 32,* 1953, 260–267. Reprinted with the permission of Williams & Wilkins; **p. 117 (Table 5-4):** Prechtl, H.F.R., and J.J. Beintema (1964). Adapted from "The neurological examination of the full-term newborn infant," *Clinics in Developmental Medicine,* No. 12. Reprinted with permission. Wolff, P.H. (1966) Adapted from "The causes, controls, and organizations of behavior in the newborn," *Psychological Issues,* 5 (1, Whole No. 17), 1–105. Copyright © 1966. Reprinted with permission; **p. 118:** © Angela Hampton/Alamy; **p. 123:** © Mike Teruya/Free Spirit Photography; **p. 125:** Harlow Primate Laboratory, University of Wisconsin; **p. 127:** © PhotoDisc/Getty Images

Chapter 6

Opener: © Michael Newman/PhotoEdit; **p. 131:** Library of Congress; **p. 134:** © Richard Lord/The Image Works; **p. 137 (Figure 6-3):** From *Brain Facts: A Primer on the Brain and Nervous System,* p. 10. Copyright © 2005, 2006 The Society for Neuroscience. Reprinted with permission; **p. 138 (Figure 6-4):** From *Human Development,* 10th ed., by Diane E Papalia, Sally Wendkos Olds, and Ruth Duskin Feldman, Fig. 4-6, p. 134. Copyright © 2007 The McGraw-Hill Companies Inc. Reprinted by permission of The McGraw-Hill Companies, Inc.; **p. 139 (Figure 6-5):** Conel, J.L. (1939–1967) From *The Postnatal Development of the Cerebral Cortex.* Copyright © 1939–1967 by the President and Fellows of Harvard College. Reprinted with the permission of the publisher; **p. 142 (Figure 6-6):** Nash, J.M. (1997) From "Fertile lands," *Time,* February 3, 1997, pp. 49–56. Copyright © 1997 by Time, Inc. Reprinted with permission; **p. 143 (Table 6-2):** "Early human reflexes." Adapted in part from Gabbard, C.P. (1996) From *Lifelong Motor Development,* Second Edition. Madison, WI: Brown and Benchmark; **p. 143 (Rooting reflex):** © Astier/ Photo Researchers; **(Darwinian reflex):** © Lew Merrim/Monkmeyer; **(Tonic neck reflex):** © Laura Dwight/ Black Star; **(Moro reflex):** © Mimi Forsyth/Monkmeyer; **(Babinski reflex):** © Elizabeth Crews; **(Walking reflex):** © Elizabeth Crews; **p. 145:** Courtesy

Children's Hospital of Michigan; **p. 146:** © Creatas/PictureQuest; **p. 151:** © Innervisions

Chapter 7

Opener: © Laura Dwight/Corbis Images; **p. 161:** Neg. No. 326799 Courtesy Department of Library Services/ American Museum of Natural History; **p. 164:** Courtesy, Carolyn Rovee-Collier; **p. 164 (Figure 7-2):** From "Current theory and research on infant learning and memory: Application to early interventions," by Carolyn Rovee-Collier and Kimberly Boller in *Infants and Young Children, 7*(3), pp. 1–12, January 1995. Reprinted by permission of Lippincott, Williams and Wilkins. All Rights Reserved; **p. 166 (Table 7-1):** From "The Home Observation for Measurement of the Environment Revisited," by Vasiliki Totsika and Kathy Sylva in *Child and Adolescent Mental Health, 9*(1), pp. 25–35, February 2004, Table 1. Reprinted by permission of Blackwell Publishing; **p. 168 (Figure 7-3):** Adapted from "The Mismatch Between Opportunity and Investment" from *How Nurture Becomes Nature: The Influence of Social Structures on Brain Development* by B. Perry, 2002. http:// www.ChildTrauma.org; **p. 171:** © Enrico Ferorelli; **p. 174:** © DeLoache, J. S., Uttal, D.H., & Rosengren, K. S. (2004). Scale errors offer evidence for a perception-action dissociation early in life. *Science, 304,* 1047–1029. Photo by Jackson Smith; **p. 176:** © James Kilkelly; **p. 180 (Figure 7-5):** Baillargeon, R. and J. DeVos. (1991) From "Object permanence in young infants: Further evidence," *Child Development,* Vol. 62, 1991, pp. 1227–1246. Copyright © by the Society for Research in Child Development, Inc.; **p. 181 (Figure 7-6):** Baillargeon, R. (1994) Adapted from "How do infants learn about the physical world?" *Current Directions in Psychological Science,* Vol. 3, No. 5, 1994, pp. 133–139. Reprinted with the permission of Blackwell; **p. 186:** © PhotoDisc/Getty Images; **p. 190 (Figure 7-7):** Petitto, L.A. and P.F. Marentette. (1991) From "Babbling in the manual mode: Evidence for the ontogeny of language," *Science, 251,* 1991, pp. 1493–1495. Copyright © 1991 by the American Association for the Advancement of Science. Reprinted with permission.

Chapter 8

Opener: Brand X Pictures/PunchStock; **Opener verse:** Hartford, J. (1971) Excerpt from "Life Prayer," *Work Movies.* Copyright © 1968 by Ensign Music Corporation. Reprinted with permission; **p. 195:** © Ken Heyman/ Woodfin Camp; **p. 196 (Table 8-1):** Sroufe, L.A. (1979) Adapted from "Socioemotional development." In J. Osofsky (ed.), *Handbook of Infant Development.* Copyright © 1979 by John Wiley & Sons. Adapted with permission; **p. 199 (Figure 8-1):** Lewis, M. (1997) Adapted from "The self in self-conscious emotions." In S.G. Snodgrass and R.L. Thompson (eds.), "The self across psychology: Self-recognition, self-awareness, and self-concept," *Annals of the New York Academy of Sciences,* Vol. 818. Reprinted with the permission of the New York Academy of Sciences and Professor Michael Lewis; **p. 200:** © Ruth Duskin Feldman; **p. 201 (Table 8-2):** Thomas, A. and S. Chess. (1984). Adapted from "Genesis and evolution of behavioral disorders: From infancy to early adult life," *American Journal of Psychiatry, 141*(1), 1984, pp. 1–9. Copyright © 1984 by the American Psychiatric Association. Adapted with permission; **p. 204:** © Jonathan Finlay; **p. 205 (Table 8-3):** Thompson, R.A. (1998) Based on "Early sociopersonality development." In N. Eisenberg (ed.), *Handbook of Child Psychology, Volume 3,* pp. 37–39. Copyright © 1998. Reprinted with permission; **p. 212:** © Robert Brenner/ PhotoEdit; **p. 218:** © Ellen Senisi; **p. 220:** © Ellen Senisi/The Image Works

Chapter 9

Opener: © Ariel Skelley/Corbis Images; **p. 227:** © Cynthia Jonson/Liaison; **p. 228:** © Michael Newman/PhotoEdit; **p. 229:** © David Young-Wolff/ PhotoEdit; **p. 233 (Figure 9-1):** Reprinted with permission of Simon & Schuster Adult Publishing Group from *Solve Your Child's Sleep Problems* by R. Ferber. Copyright © 1985 by Richard Ferber, M.D.; **p. 235 (Table 9-2):** Corbin, C.B. (1973) Adapted from *A Textbook of Motor Development.* Copyright © 1973. Reprinted with permission of The McGraw-Hill Companies; **p. 236:** © Laura Dwight/PhotoEdit; **p. 237 (Figure 9-2):** Kellog R. (1970) From *Analyzing Children's Art.* Copyright © 1969, 1970 by Rhoda Kellogg.

Reprinted with the permission of the Mayfield Publishing Company; **p. 238 (Figure 9-3):** Bar chart from Ch. 1, "Global Health: Today's Challenges," Fig. 1-4 in *The World Health Report- Shaping the Future,* 2003. Published by the World Health Organization; **p. 238 (Figure 9-4):** From "WHO estimates of the causes of death in children," by J. Bryce, C. Boschi-Pinto, K. Shibuya, and the WHO Child Health Epidemiology Reference Group in *The Lancet, 365,* 2005, pp. 1147–1152. This is reprinted with permission from Elsevier; **p. 239 (Figure 9-5):** Statistics Canada 2007; **p. 244:** © Tony Freeman/PhotoEdit; **p. 248 (Table 9-4):** Kendall-Tackett, K.A., L.M. Williams, and D. Finkelhorn (1993). Adapted from "Impact of sexual abuse on children: A review and synthesis of recent empirical studies," *Psychological Bulletin, 113,* 1993, pp. 164–180. Copyright © 1993 by the American Psychological Association. Reprinted with permission.

Chapter 10

Opener: © Bob Daemmrich/PhotoEdit; **p. 255:** Bettmann/Corbis; **p. 257 (Table 10-3):** From "Number sense growth in kindergarten: A longitudinal investigation of children at risk for mathematics difficulties," by Nancy C. Jordan, David Kaplan, Leslie Nabors Olah, and Maria N. Locuniak in *Child Development, 77*(1), January–February 2006, Table 1, p. 104. Reprinted by permission of Blackwell Publishing; **p. 260:** © Shelia Sheridan/Monkmeyer; **p. 264:** Ryan McVay/© PhotoDisc, Volume 66; **p. 266 (Table 10-5):** Berk, L. and R. Garvin. (1984). Adapted from "Development of private speech among low income Appalachian children," *Developmental Psychology, 202*(2), 1984, 271–284. Copyright © 1984 by the American Psychological Association. Adapted with permission; **p. 272:** © Eriks Stone/Photo Researchers; **p. 274:** CP Picture Archive/Cathie Coward

Chapter 11

Opener: © CLEO Photo/Index Stock Imagery; **Opener quotation:** Excerpt from *The People, Yes* by Carl Sandburg. Copyright © 1936 by Harcourt, Brace & Company and renewed 1964 by Carl Sandburg. Reprinted by permission of the publisher; **p. 281:** CP Picture Archive; **p. 284:** © Laura Dwight/

Index

Name Index

Halterman, J.S., 329
Halverson, C.F., 291
Hamilton, B.E., 90, 94, 95, 99, 108, 110, 111, 118, 119, 121, 122
Hamilton, C.E., 222
Hamilton, L., 375, 376
Hamilton, M., 293
Hamm, J.V., 373
Hammad, T.A., 394
Hammer, M., 248
Hampden-Thompson, G., 441
Hampson, J.G., 288
Hampson, J.L., 288
Hamre, B.K., 351
Han, S.S., 393
Han, W.J., 220
Handmaker, N.S., 94
Hanish, L.D., 298
Hanley, W.B., 117
Hanney, L., 393
Hans, S.L., 302
Hanselaar, A.G., 93
Hansen, D., 97
Hansen, L., 464
Hansen, M., 412, 413
Hanson, T.L., 380
Hara, H., 389
Hardy, R., 122
Hardy-Brown, K., 191
Hareven, T., 10
Hargrove, J., 427
Harland, B.F., 95
Harlow, H.F., 125
Harlow, M.K., 126
Harmer, S., 262
Harmon, A., 69
Harnishfeger, K.K., 340
Harold, G.T., 391, 475
Harrell, J.S., 323
Harris, E., 476
Harris, G., 69
Harris, M.L., 207
Harris, P.L., 262
Harris, S., 123
Harris, S.J., 108
Harrison, A.O., 10
Harriss, S.R., 148
Harrist, A.W., 211
Hart, C., 325
Hart, C.H., 203, 306, 311, 384
Hart, D., 359
Hart, S.N., 249
Harter, S., 212, 282, 283, 370, 371
Hartmann, D.P., 382, 384
Hartup, W.W., 262, 311, 350, 382, 383, 384, 386, 474, 478
Harvard Medical School, 392, 393, 414, 416, 423
Harvey, G., 315
Harvey, W., 54
Harwood, R., 427
Harwood, R.L., 216
Hasebe, Y., 469
Haslett, S.J., 455
Haswell, K., 213
Hatano, G., 256
Hatch, E.E., 93
Hatcher, P.J., 348
Hauck, F.R., 155
Haugaard, J.J., 376
Haugh, S., 287
Hauser, W.A., 96
Hausfather, A., 223

Hawes, A., 294
Hawkins, D.L., 390
Hawkins, J., 112
Hawkins, J.D., 418, 462, 479
Hawkins, M., 97
Hay, D.F., 219
Hay, T.C, 249
Hayes, A., 68
Hayne, H., 172
Haynes, O.M., 206
He, J., 325
He, M., 121
He, Y., 41, 384, 385
Health Canada, 13, 67, 95, 108, 134, 135, 154, 155, 156, 157, 222, 411, 412, 422
Heard, D., 105
Heath, S.B., 344
Hebb, D.O., 6
Hedges, L.V., 257
Heffner, L.J., 98, 123
Helgason, A., 95
Helmerhorst, T.J., 93
Helms, J.E., 14, 43, 344
Helms-Erikson, H., 292
Helwig, C.C., 338, 436
Heming, G., 276
Hennon, E.A., 187
Henrichon, A.J., 261
Henriksen, T.B., 95
Henry, D.B., 478
Herbert, J., 172
Herbst, A.L., 93
Herdt, G., 405
Herman-Giddens, M.E, 246
Hernandez, D., 471
Hernandez, D.J., 10
Hernandez-Reif, M., 121, 210
Heron, J., 97
Heron, M.P., 153, 421
Herrenkohl, T.I., 479
Herrnstein, R.J., 343
Hersich, 146
Hertenstein, M.J., 149, 211
Hertsgaard, L., 207
Hertwig, R., 239
Hertzen, V., 328
Hertzman, C., 12, 222, 223, 242, 247
Hesketh, K., 324
Hesketh, T., 310
Hessl, D., 144
Hesso, N.A., 154
Hetherington, E.M., 71, 375, 378, 379
Hetzel, B.S., 91
Hewlett, B.S., 127, 128
Heywood, C., 217
Hickling, A.K., 256
Hickman, M., 413
Hildebrand, D., 341
Hill, D., 144
Hill, J.L., 68
Hill, J.P., 467
Hill, K.G., 463
Hill, N.E., 352
Hillier, L., 459
Hillman, L.S., 156
Hills, A., 244
Hilton, S., 97
Hinckley, A.F., 98
Hinds, T.S., 95
Hines, A.M., 379

Hines, M., 287, 288
Hippocrates, 54
Hiripi, E., 416
Hirsh-Pasek, K., 187, 264
Hiruma, N., 308
Hitlin, S., 14
Hix, H.R., 261
Hjertholm, E., 265
Ho, W.C., 227
Hoban, T.F., 117, 234, 319, 412, 413
Hobbins, J.C., 100
Hobson, J.A., 234
Hock, E., 213
Hodges, E.V.E., 390
Hodgins, S., 422
Hoek, H.W., 90
Hoff, E., 191
Hoff, T., 460, 462
Hofferth, S.L., 372, 394
Hoffman, C., 287
Hoffman, C.M., 360, 412
Hoffman, H.J., 156
Hoffmann, J.P., 418
Hoffrage, U., 239
Hofman, P.L., 121
Hofmann, V., 208
Hohne, E.A., 185
Holden, G.W., 303
Holland, S.K., 189, 190
Holloway, B.R., 240
Holloway, R.L., 189
Holm, M., 167
Holmbeck, G., 467
Holowka, S., 189, 190
Holsti, L., 122
Holtzman, 69
Honeycutt, H., 34, 72
Honig, A.S., 311, 312
Hooper, F.H., 217
Hopfensperger, J., 446
Hopkins, B., 152, 197
Hopkins, C., 418
Hopkins, L.M., 100
Horan, J.M., 119
Horbar, J.D., 121
Hornsby, P.P., 93
Horwood, L.J., 134, 421
Hospital for Sick Children (Toronto), 93
Hossler, A., 363
Hou, F., 13, 243, 379, 398
Houck, K., 135
Hoult, L.A., 122
Howard, K.I., 467
Howard, S.C., 388
Howe, M.L., 14
Howe, M.L.., 269
Howe, N., 309, 382
Howell, A.J., 480
Howell, R.R., 116
Howes, C., 222, 295, 387
Hoyert, D.L., 94, 95, 153, 421
Huang, C.-W., 349
Huang, G.G., 355, 359
Hubbard, F.O.A., 197
Hudgins, R., 96
Hudnall, C.E., 381
Hudson, J., 269
Hudson, J.I., 416
Huebner, R.R., 198
Huesmann, L.R., 388
Huffman, L.C., 205

Hughes, C., 306
Hughes, D., 457
Hughes, K., 10
Huizink, A.C., 97
Hujoel, P.P., 98
Hulme, C., 267, 348
Hulsey, T.C., 154
Hum, M., 41
Human Resources Development Canada, 94
Humphreys, A.P., 320
Humphreys, G.W., 38
Hunsaker, S.L., 363
Hunt, J.I., 414
Hunt, W., 105
Hurwitz, M.D., 389
Huston, A.C., 221, 268, 388
Huston, H.C., 353
Hutchins, C.L., 356
Hutsman, 134
Huttenlocher, J., 181, 191, 254, 257, 264, 337, 343, 351
Huttly, S., 95
Huttunen, M., 97
Hwang, C.P, 217
Hwang, S.J., 90
Hyde, J.S., 286, 439
Hyde, M.L., 147
Hyle, P., 218
Hyman, I., 13, 243, 398
Hymel, K.P., 249

Iacono, W.G., 476
Iannotti, R.J., 306
Iervolino, A.C., 287
Iglowstein, I., 233, 412
Ikonomidou, C., 94
Impagnatiello, F., 77
Infante-Rivard, C., 95, 96
Ingersoll, E.W., 117, 121
Ingersoll, G.M., 409, 411
Ingham, P.W., 83
Ingoldsby, B.B., 10
Ingram, J.L., 141
Inhelder, B., 259, 335, 337
Innis, S.M., 134
Institute of Medicine, 69
International Human Genome Sequencing Consortium, 69
Ipp, M., 197
Irwin, J.D., 229
Irwin, S.H., 326
Isaacsohn, J.L., 75
Isabella, R., 202
Isabella, R.A., 205
Isley, S., 312
Itard, J.-M.-G., 3
Ito, S., 93
Iverson, J.M., 186
Ivey, P., 127
Iwamoto, K., 93
Izard, C., 375
Izard, C.E., 198, 206, 209

Jaakkola, J.J.K., 242
Jaccard, J., 460, 473
Jackson, A., 243, 355
Jackson, D.W., 434
Jackson, S., 91
Jacob, M.C., 56
Jacobsen, T., 208
Jacobson, J.L., 134, 208
Jacobson, S.W., 134

Index

hostile attribution bias, 387
  influences on, 307–308
  instrumental aggression, 306, 386
  media violence and, 307, 388–389
  in middle childhood, 386–390
  overt aggression, 306
  relational aggression, 306,
    386–387
  and social information processing,
    387–388
  types of, 387–388
air pollution, health risks, 98, 99, 244
alcohol consumption
  and birth defects (*See* fetal alcohol
    syndrome (FAS))
  and breastfeeding, 135
  drinking habits of adolescents, 419
  early initiation, 420
alleles, 62
alpha 1 antitrypsin deficiency, 64
alpha thalassemia, 64
Al-Sayyid Bedouin Sign
  Language, 190
altruism, 304–305
ambivalent (resistant) attachment, 205
amniocentesis, 99, 100
amnion, 83
amniotic sac, 83, 87
amygdala, 202
analgesics, 111
androgens, 93, 288, 404, 405
Anencephaly, 64
angiotensin-converting enzyme
  (ACE) inhibitors, 93
angry cry, 197
animalculists, 54
animism, 256
anoxia, 114
antibiotics, 133
antibiotic tetracycline, 93
antidepressants, 210, 421
anti-social tendencies, neurobiological
  deficits and, 391
Apgar scale, 115–116
applied research, 6
aptitude tests, 341
artificial insemination, 57, 59
artificial insemination by a donor
  (AID), 57
artistic development, 227, 236
art therapy, 393
Asperger disorder, 140
Aspirin, 93
assimilation, and cognitive growth, 30

assimilation (policy), 11
assisted reproduction technology
  (ART), 53, 56–57, 59–60
asthma, 328–329
atherosclerosis, 136
attachment
  Adult Attachment Interview
    (AAI), 207
  ambivalent (resistant) attachment,
    205
  avoidant attachment, 205
  defined, 204
  disorganized attachment, 205
  intergenerational transmission of
    attachment patterns, 207
  patterns of, 204–205
  secure attachment, 205
  separation anxiety, 207
  stranger anxiety, 207
  Stranger Situation, 204–205, 206
  temperament and, 206–207
  Waters and Dean Attachment
    Q-set (AQS), 206
attention-deficit/hyperactivity
  disorder (ADHD), 63, 65, 361–362
authoritarian parents, 302–303, 384,
  442
authoritative parents, 302–303, 384,
  437, 442, 469–470, 478
autism
  advanced paternal age and, 99
  Asperger disorder, 140
  and early intervention, 141
  hereditary influence on, 77, 141
  pervasive developmental disor-
    der–not otherwise specified,
    140
  possible signs of, 140
  thimerosal and, 140
autism spectrum disorders
  (ASDs), 140
autobiographical memory, 269,
  270, 271
autonomy, *vs.* shame and doubt, 26,
  212–213
autonomy-supportive parents, 270
avoidant attachment, 205
axons, 138

Babinski reflex, 143
baby biographers, 4–5
barbiturates, 93
basic research, 6
basic trust *vs.* basic mistrust, 203–204

Bayley Scales of Infant
  Development, 165
bed-sharing, 155, 156
behavioural genetics, and heritability,
  70–71
behavioural measures, 37–38
behaviour inhibition system, 392
behaviourism
  classical conditioning, 27–28, 163
  cognitive development, 162–164
  learning theory, 27–28
  operant conditioning, 28, 163, 189
behaviour modification, 28, 393
behaviour therapy. See behaviour
  modification
beta thalassemia (Cooley's anemia),
  64, 68
bi-directional influences, 17, 23–24,
  29, 32, 74
bilingual children, 191, 263
bilingual education, 358
binocular vision, 147
bioecological theory, 32–33
biological approach, to gender
  development, 287–288, 289
bipolar disorder, 421
birth complications
  birth trauma and, 114
  breech position, of fetus, 110
  low birth weight, 118–121
  postmaturity, 122
  prematurity, 118–119, 121
birth defects, 87. *See also* fetal
  alcohol syndrome (FAS); genetic
  and chromosomal abnormalities
  advanced paternal age and, 77, 99
  air pollution and, 98, 99
  cocaine use and, 96, 99
  diabetes and, 97
  environmental toxins and, 99
  folic acid deficiency and, 92
  incidence of birth defects among
    males, 87
  infections and, 96–99
  insecticides and, 99
  iodine deficiency and, 90
  lead exposure and, 99
  malnutrition and, 90–92, 119
  marijuana use and, 96
  maternal age and, 67, 98, 119
  maternal illnesses and, 96–97
  maternal stress and, 97
  medications and, 93–94
  obesity and, 92

outside environmental hazards and, 98–99
radiation exposure and, 99
smoking and, 94–95, 99
vitamin C deficiency and, 90
vitamin D deficiency and, 90
birthing centres, 108
bisexual identity, 459
blastocyst, 83, 86
blastocyst transfer, 59
blended family. *See* stepfamily
blue colouring, neonatal skin condition, 113
body dissatisfaction, 323, 444
body image, 322, 323, 414–415
body mass index (BMI), 322
bonding, parental, 125–127, 134.
See also attachment
bottle-feeding, 133
Bradley Method, 111
the brain
axons, 138
brain cells, 138–140
brain growth spurts, 136–138
brain stem, 137, 138, 190
cell death, 139–140
cerebellum, 137, 138
cerebral cortex, 200
cerebral hemispheres, 137
cerebrum, 137, 138
corpus callosum, 137
dendrites, 138, 139
development of, 35, 136–145, 410
differentiation, 139
and emotional development, 199–200
frontal cortex, 318, 410
frontal lobe, 137, 138, 200, 410
glial cells, 138, 139
grey matter, 288, 317, 342, 410
hippocampus, 141, 182, 200
hypothalamus, 405
integration, 139
and language development, 183–184, 189, 190
lateralization, 137, 189, 190
left hemisphere of, 137
lobes, 137, 138
major parts of, 137–138
motor cortex, 190
neurons, 138–140
neurotransmitters, 138
occipital lobe, 137, 138
parietal cortex, 318

parietal lobe, 137, 138, 317
planum temporale, 189
plasticity, 15, 16, 35, 144–145
pons, 190
prefrontal cortex, 182, 317, 338, 410
and reflex behaviour, 136–145
right hemisphere of, 137
synapses, 138
temporal lobe, 137, 138, 410
volume, 35
weight of, 136
white matter, 317, 410
Braxton-Hicks contractions, 109
Brazelton Neonatal Behavioural Assessment Scale (NBAS), 115–116
breastfeeding
and alcohol consumption, 135
bed-sharing and, 156
benefits and cautions, 134–135, 136
and HIV/AIDS transmission, 135
and use of medications, 93
breast milk, 133–135
breech position, of fetus, 110
Building Better Babies Pregnancy Outreach Program, 92
bulimia nervosa, 416
bullies, 389–390
bullying, 386–390, 476

caesarean delivery, 110–111, 119, 122
caffeine consumption, during pregnancy, 95–96
Canada
childhood poverty, 374
corporal punishment, 299
diversity, 13
education, 440
FAS affected infants, 94
infant mortality rate, 152–153
infant mortality rates, 100
low-birth weight babies, 118, 119, 120
maltreatment, 245–246
parenting style, 304
prenatal care, 100–101
teenage pregnancy rates, 463
Canadian Assisted Human Reproductive Act, 60
Canadian Charter of Rights and Freedoms, 14
Canadian Immunization Guide, 158

Canadian Incidence Study of Reported Child Abuse and Neglect, 421
Canadian Task Force on Preventative Health Care, 134
canalization, 72–73
cancer, 93, 99, 135
cardiovascular disease. *See* heart disease
career counselling, 444–445
caregiver-infant bond, 125
caseosa, 113
case studies, 39–40
categorization, understanding of, 171, 179, 335
causality, understanding of, 171, 179–180, 256, 335
cell death, 139–140
central executive, 268
central nervous system, 136
cephalocaudal principle, 83
cerebellum, 137, 138
cerebral cortex, 200
cerebrum, 137, 138
cervical cancer, 93
cervix, 55
charter schools, 357
childbirth. *See also* birth complications
birth process, 109–112
and bonding, 125
caesarean delivery, 110–111, 119, 122
contemporary setting for, 108
and culture, 106–108
in earlier times, 106
episiotomy, 109–110
forceps birth, 109, 110
induced delivery, 118, 119
labour, 109
medicated delivery, 111
natural childbirth, 111
parturition, 109
risks of, 106–108
stages of, 109–110
traverse position, of fetus, 110
uterine contractions, 109
vacuum extraction, 109–110
vaginal birth, 109–110, 111
water birth, 111
child care
child-care effects, 222
demand for, 221–222

impact on disadvantaged
children, 224
child custody, 377
child development
bi-directional influences, 17,
23–24, 32, 74
contexts of, 10–15, 17
continuous development *vs.*
qualitative change, 23–24
critical (sensitive) periods of,
15–16
culture and ethnicity and, 12–14
domains of development, 7
environmental factors and, 9–10
family and, 10
heredity and, 9–10
historical context and, 12–14
and human development, 5, 17
individual differences, 9, 17
influences on, 9–10
maturation processes and, 9
non-normative influences, 15
normative influences, 14–15
periods of development, 7–9
socio-economic status (SES)
and, 10–12
timing of influences and, 15
child development (scientific field).
See also developmental theory
as developmental science, 5
early approaches, 4–5
field of, 4
lifespan studies, 5
new frontiers, 5–6
study of, 4–9
child-directed speech, 191–192
childhood
early experience, effects of, 17
periods of, 8
as social construction, 7
childhood depression, 392–393
childhood fears, 308–309
childhood poverty, 241, 243, 374
chlamydia, 464
chlorpyrifos, 99
cholesterol, 136
chorion, 83
chorion control study, 71
chorionic villus sampling, 100
chromosomal abnormalities, 67–68.
See also genetic and chromosomal
abnormalities
chromosome 10, 75
chromosome 19, 405

chromosomes, 60
chronic medical conditions, 326
chronosystem, 33
cilia, 55
circular reactions, 169–170
classical conditioning, 27–28, 163
classic learning theory. *See* behaviourism
class inclusion, 335
cleft lip, 63
cleft palate, 63, 65
climbing stairs, as developmental
milestone, 149
cliques, 474
clone, 63
cocaine use, and birth defects, 96, 99
code mixing, 191
code switching, 191
coenzyme Q10, 56
cognitive development, 190
behaviourist approach, 162–164
cognitive neuroscience approach,
162, 182
defined, 7
information-processing approach,
162, 175–182
Piagetian approach, 162, 168–175
psychometric approach, 162,
165–168
social-contextual approach,
162, 183
cognitive-developmental theory.
See Kohlberg's cognitive-
developmental theory
cognitive neuroscience, 38
cognitive neuroscience approach, to
cognitive development, 162, 182
cognitive perspective
developmental theory, 29–32
gender-schema theory, 291–292
Kohlberg's cognitive-developmental
theory, 290–291
cognitive-stage theory (Piaget),
29–30
cohabiting family, 375, 379
cohort, defined, 15
collaborative research, 47
colour-blindness, 66
comforting, a crying baby, 126
commitment, 453
committed compliance, 215–216
common-law family. *See* cohabiting
family
compensating experiences, 397

compensatory preschool programs,
274–276
componential element, 345
COMPT, 63
computational models, 31
computer literacy, 357
conception, 54–55, 56
conceptual knowledge, 433
concordant, 71
concrete operations, 334–338
categorization, 335
causality, 335
class inclusion, 335
deductive reasoning, 335
horizontal décalage, 336
inductive reasoning, 335
number, 336–337
seriation, 335
spatial thinking, 335
transitive inference, 335
conduct disorder (CD), 391
confidentiality. *See* privacy and
confidentiality, right to
confounds, 43
congenital adrenal hyperplasia
(CAH), 288
congenital hypothyroidism, 116
conscience, 215
conservation, 258, 336
constructive conflict, 216
constructive play, 295
constructivist math, 355
contextual perspective, 32–33
contraception, 461–462
contractions, uterine, 109
control group, 42
controlled experiments, 43–44
conventional morality, 435, 436
convergent thinking, 364
cooperative co-parenting, 377
coordination of secondary schemes,
169, 170
co-regulation, 372–373
corporal punishment, 247, 299,
300–301, 307
corpus callosum, 137
correlational studies, 39, 40–41
corticotropin-releasing homone
(CRC), 110–111
co-twin control study, 71
counselling, in preconception
care, 101
counting, 257
Cradleboard Teaching Project, 281